Saturn's Moons
W. G. Sebald – A Handbook

LEGENDA

LEGENDA, founded in 1995 by the European Humanities Research Centre of the University of Oxford, is now a joint imprint of the Modern Humanities Research Association and Routledge. Titles range from medieval texts to contemporary cinema and form a widely comparative view of the modern humanities, including works on Arabic, Catalan, English, French, German, Greek, Italian, Portuguese, Russian, Spanish, and Yiddish literature. An Editorial Board of distinguished academic specialists works in collaboration with leading scholarly bodies such as the Society for French Studies and the British Comparative Literature Association.

MHRA

The Modern Humanities Research Association (MHRA) encourages and promotes advanced study and research in the field of the modern humanities, especially modern European languages and literature, including English, and also cinema. It also aims to break down the barriers between scholars working in different disciplines and to maintain the unity of humanistic scholarship in the face of increasing specialization. The Association fulfils this purpose primarily through the publication of journals, bibliographies, monographs and other aids to research.

LONDON AND NEW YORK

Routledge is a global publisher of academic books, journals and online resources in the humanities and social sciences. Founded in 1836, it has published many of the greatest thinkers and scholars of the last hundred years, including adorno, einstein, Russell, Popper, Wittgenstein, Jung, Bohm, Hayek, Mcluhan, Marcuse and Sartre. Today Routledge is one of the world's leading academic publishers in the Humanities and Social Sciences. It publishes thousands of books and journals each year, serving scholars, instructors, and professional communities worldwide.

www.routledge.com

Saturn's Moons

W. G. Sebald – A Handbook

EDITED BY JO CATLING AND RICHARD HIBBITT

Routledge
Taylor & Francis Group

LONDON AND NEW YORK

2011

First published 2011 by Modern Humanities Research Association and Routledge

2 Park Square, Milton Park, Abingdon, Oxfordshire OX14 4RN
52 Vanderbilt Avenue, New York, NY 10017

Routledge is an imprint of the Taylor & Francis Group, an informa business

First issued in paperback 2020

ISBN 978-1-906540-02-9 (hbk)
ISBN 978-0-367-60329-8 (pbk)

CONTENTS

Acknowledgements   x

Note on the Text   xii

List of Contributors   xiii

Introduction   1
JO CATLING and RICHARD HIBBITT

PART I: THE WRITER IN CONTEXT

1.   A Childhood in the Allgäu: Wertach, 1944–52   16
MARK M. ANDERSON

2.   The Sternheim Years: W. G. Sebald's *Lehrjahre* and
Theatralische Sendung 1963–75   42
RICHARD SHEPPARD
    App. 1: W. G. Sebald, review of a production of *Minna von Barnhelm* (1970)

3.   At the University: W. G. Sebald in the Classroom   109
GORDON TURNER
    App. 1: Translation exercise set at UEA
    App. 2: Memo to students from Sebald
    App. 3: Summary of courses taught by Sebald at UEA, 1970–2001

4.   A Watch on Each Wrist: Twelve Seminars with W. G. Sebald   143
LUKE WILLIAMS

5.   The Crystal Mountain of Memory: W. G. Sebald as a
University Teacher   154
FLORIAN RADVAN

6.   Against *Germanistik*: W. G. Sebald's Critical Essays   161
UWE SCHÜTTE
    App. 1–3: Colloquia and research symposia organized by Sebald at UEA

7.   Englishing Max   195
MICHAEL HULSE

8.   Translating W. G. Sebald — With and Without the Author   209
ANTHEA BELL

9.   Sebald's Photographic Annotations   217
CLIVE SCOTT

10.   The Disappearance of the Author in the Work: Some Reflections
on W. G. Sebald's *Nachlass* in the Deutsches Literaturarchiv Marbach   247
ULRICH VON BÜLOW

11.   *Bibliotheca abscondita*: On W. G. Sebald's Library   265
      JO CATLING

      AFTERWORD
      Max Sebald: A Reminiscence   299
      STEPHEN WATTS

LYRISCHES INTERMEZZO: FOUR POEMS FOR MAX SEBALD
      For my Friend, Max Sebald   309
      STEPHEN WATTS
      For Max   311
      ANNE BERESFORD
      Redundant Epitaphs   312
      MICHAEL HAMBURGER
      Il ritorno in patria   315
      MICHAEL HULSE

PART II: THE WRITER IN DIALOGUE
1.   'Rediscovered' Pieces by W. G. Sebald   318
      (1) Die hölzernen Engel von East Anglia   319
      (2) Leben Ws   324
      (3) Waterloo   334
      (4) Two Poems by Michael Hulse, translated by W. G. Sebald   336
      (5) Feuer und Rauch   338
      (6) Ausgrabung der Vergangenheit (on Michael Hamburger)   344
      (7) Michael Hamburger: Nomination for the degree of Honorary DLitt   346
2.   Three Conversations with W. G. Sebald   349
      (1) Echoes from the Past: Conversation with Piet de Moor (Brussels, 1992)   350
      (2) Lost in Translation? Conversation with Jon Cook (Norwich, 1999)   356
      (3) In This Distant Place: Conversation with Steve Wasserman
          (Los Angeles, 2001)   364
3.   A Catalogue of W. G. Sebald's Library   377
      JO CATLING

PART III: A BIBLIOGRAPHIC SURVEY

1. Primary Bibliography   446
    RICHARD SHEPPARD

2. Secondary Bibliography   497
    JO CATLING, RICHARD HIBBITT, and LYNN WOLFF

3. Reviews of Works by W. G. Sebald   548
    JO CATLING and RICHARD HIBBITT

4. Audio-Visual Bibliography   581
    GORDON TURNER

5. An Index to Interviews with W. G. Sebald   592
    RICHARD SHEPPARD

6. W. G. Sebald: A Chronology   619
    RICHARD SHEPPARD

    Index   661

ACKNOWLEDGEMENTS

The editors would like to acknowledge the generous support of the British Academy Small Grants Fund in the preparation of this project. Mark Anderson wishes to thank the Alexander von Humboldt-Stiftung for supporting his research.

We would particularly like to thank Clive Scott, Richard Sheppard, Gordon Turner, and the Sebald Estate for all their support.

We are especially grateful to Brigid Purcell for translating Florian Radvan's essay and for helping to prepare the appendices, bibliographies, Index, and Chronology, to Richard Sheppard for translating the essays by Ulrich von Bülow and Uwe Schütte and for transcribing the interview with Steve Wasserman, to Reinier van Straten for translating Piet de Moor's interview with W. G. Sebald, and to Gordon Turner for transcribing the interview with Jon Cook and for editing the transcripts.

The editors and contributors would also like to acknowledge the help of the following: Gertrud Aebischer-Sebald; Hans-Jörg Albrecht; Rhian Atkin; Jennifer Baines; Roger Baines; Ernst Baumeler; Helen Buchanan and Jill Hughes of the Taylor Institution, the University of Oxford; Bojan Bujić; Helmut Bunk; Sarah Burbidge and Rowena Burgess of the HUM Research Office, UEA; the *Mitarbeiter* and *Mitarbeiterinnen* of the Deutsches Literaturarchiv Marbach, especially Jutta Bendt, Nicolai Riedel, Ellen Strittmatter, and Ulrich von Bülow; Jan Ceuppens; Patrick Charbonneau; Maria Consta; Jon Cook; Tony Cross; Adam Czerniawski; Sarah Elsegood and Bridget Gilles, UEA library; Barbara Epler; John Flower; Bob and Mary Franklin; David Frier; Hiroko Furukawa; Iain Galbraith; Carmen Gómez García; John Gordon; Russell Goulbourne; Richard Hamburger; Rodger and Sheila Hayward-Smith; Irène Heidelberger-Leonard; Ria van Hengel; Andrew Hobson; Jürgen Hosemann; Michael Hutchins; Iannis Kalifatidis; Alan Klein; Tali Konas; Jakob Lothe; Nigel Luckhurst; Philip Mann; Caroline Mason; Ioanna Meïtani; Sven Meyer; Piet de Moor; See-young Park; David Pattison; Erminia Passannanti; James Peters of the University of Manchester; Terry Pitts; Simon Prosser; Albert Rasche; Michael Robinson; Gabriella Rovagnati; Nigel Saint; Anita Schiffer-Fuchs; Etta Schwanitz; Louise Steinman; Roger Stoddard; Carol O'Sullivan; Hitoko Suzuki; George Szirtes; Reinbert Tabbert; Jan Peter Tripp; Stefan Tobler; Robert Treffer; Ada Vigliani; Anthony Vivis; Ruth Vogel-Klein; Steve Wasserman; Helen Watanabe-O'Kelly; Richard Weihe; John White; Christine Wilson.

We would like to thank the Estate of W. G. Sebald for permission to quote from and reproduce his works throughout the volume, the Deutsches Literaturarchiv Marbach for permission to reproduce materials in Chapter Ten, and the Houghton Library at Harvard University for permission to reproduce Michael Hulse's draft translations of *The Rings of Saturn* in Chapter Seven.

Our thanks also go to Theo Collier, Luke Ingram, and Scott Moyers from the Wylie Agency, to Graham Nelson at Legenda and to Polly Fallows, and to all the colleagues, friends, readers, scholars and translators who have provided us with information, materials or photographs for the book.

We have made every attempt to acknowledge copyright and permissions throughout and would be pleased to add any missing details where appropriate.

The publication of this book would not have been possible without the generous donations of many of W. G. Sebald's former students and colleagues (see p. 660). We are profoundly grateful for their support.

We gratefully acknowledge permission to publish the following pieces:

Thomas Bader (Buchhandlung zum Wetzstein, Freiburg), letter from W. G. Sebald dated 28 March 2000

Jon Cook, 'Lost in Translation?', transcript of a conversation with W. G. Sebald, Centre for the Creative and Performing Arts, University of East Anglia, Norwich, 9 February 1999

Piet de Moor, 'Echoes from the Past', interview with W. G. Sebald, trans. from the Dutch by Reinier van Straten. (This piece was originally published in *Knack* magazine, Brussels, 6 May 1992)

Steve Wasserman, 'In this Distant Place', transcript of a conversation with W. G. Sebald, Los Angeles Public Library, 17 October 2001

University of East Anglia, various documents appertaining to W. G. Sebald's research and teaching activities

We gratefully acknowledge permission to reprint the following pieces:

Anne Beresford, 'For Max', originally published in *Collected Poems 1967–2006* (London: Katabasis, 2006)

Michael Hamburger, 'Redundant Epitaphs', originally published in *Wild and Wounded: Shorter Poems 2000–2003* (London: Anvil, 2004)

Michael Hulse, 'Il ritorno in patria', originally published in *The Secret History* (Todmorden: Arc, 2009)

Michael Hulse, 'An Botho Strauss in Berlin' and 'Raffles Hotel Singapur' (translated by W. G. Sebald), originally published in *Sprache im technischen Zeitalter* (June 1995)

Stephen Watts, 'For my Friend, Max Sebald', originally published in *Gramsci & Caruso* (Olomouc: Periplum, 2003)

NOTE ON THE TEXT

Contributors to this volume were given the freedom to refer to W. G. Sebald in the way that they considered to be appropriate. Many of those who knew him personally therefore refer to 'Max Sebald'. To avoid excessive repetition, the editors also make use of the abbreviation WGS. The other commonly used abbreviations are DLA, which refers to the Deutsches Literaturarchiv in Marbach am Neckar, near Stuttgart (the national German literary archive, which houses W. G. Sebald's *Nachlass*), UEA (University of East Anglia), and BCLT (British Centre for Literary Translation at UEA, founded by W. G. Sebald).

For similar reasons it was decided not to use abbreviations to denote Sebald's works or to stipulate specific editions, allowing contributors to refer to the editions they use themselves; our editorial policy has been simply to ensure that readers are supplied with the page references to German and English versions of the texts where the latter are available. In most cases the original titles of Sebald's works are obvious to those who do not read German, but where necessary we remind readers that, for instance, *Schwindel. Gefühle.* is translated as *Vertigo*, or *Luftkrieg und Literatur* as *On the Natural History of Destruction*. If a work has been translated into English or an English translation is due to be published, the title of the translation is given in italics; if the work has not been translated, an English translation of the title is given in roman. For example, we refer to two forthcoming English translations of Sebald's works: *Logis in einem Landhaus* (*A Place in the Country*) and *Über das Land und das Wasser* (*Across the Land and the Water*). Works which are yet to be translated are referred to as follows: *Unheimliche Heimat* (Strange Homeland) and *Die Beschreibung des Unglücks* (The Description of Misfortune). Articles, poems and shorter pieces by Sebald which have been published in English translation are given in inverted commas as follows: 'Kafka im Kino' ('Kafka Goes to the Movies').

As a general rule we have used the published English translations of Sebald's works by Anthea Bell, Michael Hamburger and Michael Hulse. Quotations from published translations are indicated in the endnote references. Other translations from German (or other languages) into English are the authors' own, unless otherwise stated. We have aimed, wherever possible, to give readers access both to the original sources and to the English translation, where available.

JMC and RMH

LIST OF CONTRIBUTORS

MARK M. ANDERSON is Professor of German and Comparative Literature at Columbia University in New York. He is the author of *Kafka's Clothes: Ornament and Aestheticism in the Habsburg Fin de Siècle* (1992) as well as numerous essays on Austrian and German literature from the turn of the century to the present. He has edited and translated works by Ingeborg Bachmann and Thomas Bernhard, and was the founder and first director of the Berlin Consortium for German Studies.

ANTHEA BELL, OBE, has worked as a translator from German and French for many years. Her translations from German encompass modern and classic fiction by authors including E. T. A. Hoffmann, Kafka, and Stefan Zweig. Among her translation awards are the 2003 Austrian State Prize for Literary Translation, and in 2002, for the translation of W. G. Sebald's *Austerlitz* (Hamish Hamilton, 2001), the Schlegel-Tieck Prize, the Helen and Kurt Wolff Prize (USA), and, with the author, the Independent Foreign Fiction Prize. She also translated W. G. Sebald's *Luftkrieg und Literatur* (under the author's own choice of English title, *On the Natural History of Destruction*) and his posthumous collection *Campo Santo*.

ULRICH VON BÜLOW was born in 1963 and studied German literature in Leipzig, after which he worked as a reader for the publishing house Hinstorff Verlag in Rostock. In 1992 he joined the Deutsches Literaturarchiv in Marbach, where he has been Director of the Manuscripts Department since 2006. He is the author of books and essays on writers including Franz Fühmann and Arthur Schnitzler, and the editor of works by Rainer Maria Rilke, Erich Kästner, Karl Löwith, and Martin Heidegger. Recent publications include *Wandernde Schatten: W. G. Sebalds Unterwelt*, co-edited with Heike Gfrereis and Ellen Strittmatter (2008), which accompanied the Marbach exhibition on Sebald of the same year.

JO CATLING studied Modern Languages at Wadham College, Oxford, and the Universities of Freiburg im Breisgau and Tübingen. She returned to Norwich from Durham in November 1993 to take up a post in German Literature and Language at UEA, where she taught alongside Max Sebald until 2001. Currently located in the School of Literature and Creative Writing, in addition to her work on Sebald she has published widely on Rilke (particularly Rilke and translation), and is editor of *A History of Women's Writing in Germany, Austria and Switzerland* (2000). Her current project is the translation of Sebald's essay volumes *Logis in einem Landhaus* (*A Place in the Country*), *Die Beschreibung des Unglücks*, and *Unheimliche Heimat* (in one volume as *Silent Catastrophes*), to be published by Hamish Hamilton (UK) and Random House (USA).

RICHARD HIBBITT is Lecturer in French at the University of Leeds and Assistant Editor of the journal *Comparative Critical Studies*. He studied French, German, and comparative literature at Royal Holloway (University of London), the University of Augsburg, and the University of East Anglia. His publications include *Dilettantism and its Values: From Weimar Classicism to the Fin de Siècle* (2006).

MICHAEL HULSE's poetry has won him first prizes in the National Poetry Competition and the Bridport Poetry Prize (twice), and Eric Gregory and Chol-mondeley Awards from the Society of Authors, and has taken him on reading tours throughout the world. He has worked in universities, publishing, and documentary television, has edited literary quarterlies, poetry series and anthologies, and literature classics, and has translated more than sixty books from the German, among them works by W. G. Sebald, the Nobel Prize winners Elfriede Jelinek and Herta Müller, Goethe, and Rilke. He is a permanent judge of the Günter Grass Foundation's biennial international literary award, the Albatross Prize, and co-founder of an international award for poetry on a medical subject, the Hippocrates Prize.

FLORIAN RADVAN studied English, German, and comparative literature at the universities of Bayreuth, Bonn, and East Anglia, where he wrote a doctoral thesis on modern German theatre supervised by W. G. Sebald. He is a qualified schoolteacher currently on secondment to the Germanistisches Institut (Faculty of Philology) at the University of Bochum. His publications include essays on Friedrich Hebbel, Gert Ledig, Conrad Ferdinand Meyer, W. G. Sebald, and Peter Weiss.

UWE SCHÜTTE was born in 1967 and studied English literature, German litera-ture, and history at the universities of Munich and East Anglia, where he wrote a doctoral thesis on Gerhard Roth's *Die Archive des Schweigens*, supervised by W. G. Sebald. He is Reader in German at Aston University, Birmingham, where he has worked since 1999. His publications include *Auf der Spur der Vergessenen: Gerhard Roth und seine 'Archive des Schweigens'* (1997), *Basis-Diskothek Pop und Rock* (2004, updated 2008), *Edmund Mach: Meine abenteuerlichen Schriften* (2009), *Arbeit an der Differenz: Zum Eigensinn von Heiner Müllers Prosa* (2010), *Heiner Müller* (2010), *Thomas Bernhard* (2010) and *W. G. Sebald* (forthcoming 2011), the last three with Vandenhoeck and Ruprecht, Göttingen.

CLIVE SCOTT is Professor Emeritus of European Literature at the University of East Anglia, and a Fellow of the British Academy. His principal research interests lie in comparative poetics (*The Poetics of French Verse: Studies in Reading*, 1998; *Channel Crossings: French and English Poetry in Dialogue 1550–2000*, 2002 (awarded the R. H. Gapper Book Prize, 2004)); in literary translation, and in particular the translation of poetry (*Translating Baudelaire*, 2000; *Translating Rimbaud's 'Illuminations'*, 2006); and in photography's relationship with writing (*The Spoken Image: Photography and Language*, 1999; *Street Photography: From Atget to Cartier-Bresson*, 2007). He is at present engaged in the preparation of books on the translation of Apollinaire's poetry, and on the relationship between translation and reading as the source of a writing practice. A close colleague of Max Sebald throughout Sebald's career at UEA.

RICHARD SHEPPARD was born in 1944 and taught German and European Literature at UEA between 1967 and 1987 and German at Oxford (Magdalen and Christ Church) from 1987 to 2005. He is a Fellow Emeritus of Magdalen College, Oxford, and lives permanently in France. His publications are mainly on twentieth-century European and German literature, especially Dada, Expressionism, and Modernism. He was a close colleague and friend of Max Sebald from 1970 onwards.

GORDON TURNER was a close friend, colleague, and at one time neighbour of Max Sebald, first meeting him when they were both interviewed in May 1970 for three lectureships in the German Sector at UEA. Between 1970 and 2001 his areas of responsibility included German Honours Language, in particular *Landeskunde*, Applied Linguistics, TEFL, and Drama (including eighteen German theatre productions); he was also Director of the James Platt Language Centre as well as of the Translation and Interpreting Programme. He is the curator of the Sebald Sound Archive, which locates and transcribes audio and video recordings either made by or featuring WGS.

STEPHEN WATTS is a poet, editor, and translator, with roots in the Italian Alps and in Whitechapel. He has twice won second prize in the National Poetry Competition, and his most recent books include *Gramsci & Caruso* (2004), *The Blue Bag* (2005), *Mountain Language / Lingua di montagna* (2009), *The Language of it* (DVD 2007), and a video-poem *Journey to my Father* (2009). He edited Amarjit Chandan's *Sonata for Four Hands* (2010) and has co-translated poetry by Ziba Karbassi (2009), Adnan al-Sayegh (2009), and Meta Kusar (2010). He has done much work as a poet in schools and hospitals and in 2006 worked with HI-Arts in Inverness on the social issues of suicide and recovery. In 2007 he was awarded a major Arts Council grant for his writing and research. He met W. G. Sebald in 1990 and they remained close friends until the latter's death in 2001.

LUKE WILLIAMS was born in 1977. He grew up in Scotland and now lives in London. He studied history at Edinburgh University and creative writing at UEA. His first novel, *The Echo Chamber*, will be published in 2011 by Hamish Hamilton in the UK and Penguin Viking in the USA.

LYNN WOLFF completed her PhD at the University of Wisconsin, Madison, in 2010 with a dissertation entitled 'A Hybrid Poetics for a Contentious Past: W. G. Sebald's Literary Historiography'. Her research interests include German and French literature and philosophy from the eighteenth century to the present day, holocaust studies, gender studies, narratology, photography, translation, and world literature. She has written articles on W. G. Sebald, Bernhard Schlink, and the 1780 essay contest of the Prussian Royal Academy. She is currently preparing a research project that focuses on the transdiscursive constitution of knowledge in the eighteenth century.

INTRODUCTION

Jo Catling and Richard Hibbitt

In 1988 W. G. Sebald published his long poem *Nach der Natur* (*After Nature*) in an initial print run of 2000 copies. This publication marks the moment when Sebald the university lecturer, academic researcher, and critic, known to his friends and colleagues as Max, emerged publicly as the writer W. G. Sebald, now acclaimed as one of the most original and significant literary voices of our time. In little more than a decade Sebald followed *Nach der Natur* with the four works of prose that have established his reputation: *Schwindel. Gefühle.* (*Vertigo*), *Die Ausgewanderten* (*The Emigrants*), *Die Ringe des Saturn* (*The Rings of Saturn*) and *Austerlitz*. This period also saw the publication of his Zurich lectures on the aerial bombardment of Germany during World War II as *Luftkrieg und Literatur* (*On the Natural History of Destruction*), as well as the appearance of two collections of essays on Austrian and 'Alemannic' writers and artists, *Unheimliche Heimat* (Strange Homeland) and *Logis in einem Landhaus* (*A Place in the Country*), additions to a body of critical work that stretches back to the late 1960s. It concluded with work on two interlinked collections of poems, one English, one German, in collaboration with visual artists: *For Years Now* with Tess Jaray and, with Jan Peter Tripp, *Unerzählt* (*Unrecounted*). Since his much-lamented untimely death in 2001, two further collections have appeared: the prose pieces on Corsica and critical essays assembled in *Campo Santo*, and the selection of published and early poems *Über das Land und das Wasser* (*Across the Land and the Water*), an English edition of which is in preparation at the time of writing. Hitherto unpublished or rediscovered critical essays, pieces of journalism and interviews are still being published as they gradually come to light, and the process of translation and dissemination into ever-widening circles is an ongoing one. We are fortunate that Sebald's *oeuvre* still holds some surprises for us.

With hindsight, this astonishingly prolific period of creativity can be viewed as the results of a life spent reading, thinking, talking, and writing about the place of literature in our culture and society. Sebald, who had written poetry and prose from an early age, wrote a first, unpublished, novel in his twenties. At the same time he developed his reputation as an idiosyncratic and provocative literary critic, keen to challenge normative or dominant methodologies. By the age of 26 he had embarked on a career as a university lecturer which would exert a profound influence on his work, enabling him to discuss literature with generations of students and colleagues and to publish a number of critical works. For those who know his books on Carl Sternheim and Alfred Döblin, and especially his first collection of essays, *Die Beschreibung des Unglücks* (The Description of Misfortune), his engagement with Stendhal, Ernst Herbeck, and Kafka in *Schwindel. Gefühle.* does not appear such a radical departure; the critic and the 'creative' writer (a designation he viewed at times with some scepticism) coexisted throughout his life. Indeed, as the interview with Piet de Moor, published here in English for the first time, shows, this first book of prose fiction may be said to have its origins in precisely such literary essays and journeyings. The gradual rediscovery of the assorted articles he published in German-language newspapers and literary journals in the 1970s and 1980s, several of which are reprinted in Part II of the present volume, adds further nuances to our understanding of his work.

Sebald's achievements as a writer rest both on the breadth and depth of his thematic concerns and on his formal innovation. In early 2000 he referred to 'the semi-documentary prose fiction for which I have become known',[1] displaying a characteristic tendency to attribute any classification of his work to others. Yet this description provides a succinct appraisal of the genre-defying appeal of his writing, which combines fact with fiction, autobiography with biography, quotation with invention, and text with image. This deliberately hybrid form enabled him to present a multifaceted exploration of the human condition and of the notion of identity, embracing questions of memory, displacement, suffering, travel, history, and natural history. However, as many commentators have observed, Sebald's elegiac tone and preoccupation with loss were allied to a remarkable ability to find interest and value in the minutiae of life; reflections on human failings are balanced by a profound concern with human qualities and possibilities, and beyond that with the natural world as a whole in its threatened or resilient juxtapositions with the ravages of human history.

The international appeal of Sebald's work is evident not only in the enthusiastic critical reception and the growing number of languages into which his works have been translated (at the time of writing, *Austerlitz* has been translated into almost thirty languages).[2] It is also evident in the vast number of responses to his works by academics, artists, performers, and other writers; the bibliographies collected in Part III of this volume testify to the vast array of different ways in which readers have responded to his works, from academic studies to art exhibitions. In the course of the last fifteen years a substantial body of critical literature has been published in English and in German, as well as in a number of other languages.[3] The three distinct parts of the present work are designed to complement these studies by combining critical essays, original work and interviews, and bibliographies, while the title alludes both to the different satellites of its subject and to its aim to provide resources for future use. Part I consists of a consciously heterogeneous collection of essays, embracing the biographical, the bibliographical, and the critical, discussing Sebald as reader, teacher, critic, and writer. The differing lengths of the pieces mirror this heterogeneity, allowing each author to explore his or her subject with a commensurate freedom. However, all the essays share the aim of reflecting on the various qualities of Sebald's work from different but intertwined perspectives, showing how his writing grew out of his studies, teaching, reading, and travels. Following a short 'Lyrisches Intermezzo' with poems written in memory of Sebald, Part II brings together a number of little-known pieces by him, new publications of three different interviews, and a catalogue of his *Nachlassbibliothek* or personal library.

The volume begins with Mark Anderson's essay 'A Childhood in the Allgäu: Wertach, 1944–1952', which argues that Sebald's childhood in rural southern Germany played a crucial role in shaping his identity: in the ways in which he understood himself both as human being and as writer. Anderson shows how these formative experiences of family and surroundings are refracted through the 'intensely personal, semi-autobiographical fictions that we value today', illustrating his thesis by references not only to works such as *Nach der Natur, Die Ausgewanderten*, and *Schwindel. Gefühle.*, but also to various critical essays, interviews, and speeches. He places particular emphasis on the fundamental role which Sebald's maternal grandfather Josef Egelhofer played in his life, demonstrating how the parallels Sebald makes between Egelhofer and the Swiss writer Robert Walser are symptomatic of a desire to explore the 'logic' of coincidences he observed through his life. This connection is part of a wider interest in the 'marginal and powerless', which Anderson links to Sebald's interest in various 'outsider' figures, in writers such as J. P. Hebel and Ernst Herbeck, and in Austrian literature *tout court*. By referring to 'Sebald's imaginary Allgäu', Anderson suggests that the landscape of Sebald's childhood transcends its physical status to play a paradigmatic symbolic role in his writing.

The biographical baton is taken up by Richard Sheppard in his essay 'The Sternheim Years: W. G. Sebald's *Lehrjahre* and *Theatralische Sendung* 1963–1975'. Sheppard traces Sebald's student years in Freiburg, Fribourg, and Manchester, and his early experiences of teaching in both Manchester and St Gallen, culminating in his appointment to a lectureship at the University of East Anglia. These years also saw the genesis of his first published work as a critic: his monograph on Carl Sternheim, which began life as a Swiss 'mémoire de licence' in 1966, became a British master's dissertation in 1968, and was finally published as a German book in 1969. Drawing on extensive research into a wide range of sources ranging from newspaper archives and school reports to personal correspondence and conversations, Sheppard shows how Sebald's view of literature and literary criticism was profoundly influenced by his varied experiences as a student. This literary apprenticeship began at the University of Freiburg im Breisgau, where enforced study of a conservative curriculum was complemented by Sebald's emerging interest in such varied topics as the theories of the Frankfurt School, the legacy of National Socialism in West Germany, and in amateur dramatics. It also saw his early critical and literary publications in the student newspaper, which contain *in nuce* many of the themes and approaches familiar to readers of his later work. Sebald's move after two years to the Université de Fribourg, in French-speaking Switzerland, resulted in the further development of a critical disposition characterized by a desire to read texts in their socio-historical context and to question received opinion. A year later he took up a post as *Lektor* in the Department of German at the University of Manchester, where he spent two years teaching German and writing his master's thesis. Sheppard's close reading of Sebald's thesis shows how he developed his sociological approach to Sternheim's work to produce a nuanced reading which reflected on his own status as thinker and writer. At the same time Sebald directed a particularly successful student production of Büchner's *Leonce und Lena*, which Sheppard links to a subtle interest in theatre and the theatrical that recurs throughout his subsequent career. (Sebald's review of a 1970 production of Lessing's *Minna von Barnhelm* is reprinted at the end of the chapter.)[4] After a year spent teaching in a private school in St Gallen, Switzerland, Sebald returned to Manchester to work again as a *Lektor*. This period saw the completion and publication of his book on Sternheim, which established Sebald's reputation as an idiosyncratic and provocative critic (a theme developed by Uwe Schütte in Chapter 6). Sheppard's essay ends with a postscript considering the liberal academic atmosphere at the University of East Anglia in the early 1970s, where he and Sebald were colleagues. This includes brief consideration of 'Die hölzernen Engel von East Anglia' (The Carved Wooden Angels of East Anglia), a piece Sebald wrote for the travel section of *Die Zeit*, which displays an interest in geography and history — in place and time — that would characterize much of his later work. (This piece is included in Part II of the present volume.)

The next three chapters provide different reflections on W. G. Sebald as a teacher. In 'At the University: W. G. Sebald in the Classroom', his UEA colleague Gordon Turner describes how generations of students were influenced by Sebald's teaching over a period of more than three decades. Turner's commentary draws on the testimonies of over twenty former students who are quoted here verbatim, thus creating a polyphonous collage of first-hand accounts of Sebald's influence in the classroom. These voices create a multifaceted image of a teacher who was inspiring, demanding, humorous and irreverent, encompassing his comments as a marker and his opinions of the internet, the publishing industry, and the general state of post–World War II German literature. The affection and gratitude evinced by these personal recollections demonstrate how Sebald inspired generations of students to think for themselves and to appreciate literature, which he described to them as 'a way of knowing oneself'. Turner also traces the development in Sebald's pedagogic style, showing how he gradually came to see language teaching as a means of encouraging creative personal expression, rather than simply a linguistic exercise. His former students remark on how Sebald's books bring back his voice from the classroom; those of us who were not taught by him will also recognize the combination of eclecticism, digression, polemics, and understated purpose. The description of the courses that he taught and his desire to place literature in socio-historical and philosophical contexts shows how tutorial, seminar, and lecture were opportunities for him to discuss ideas with his students which would eventually find expression in his critical and literary works. Sebald's teaching at UEA embraced literature, language, cinema, and, latterly, creative writing; this unique mosaic of personal testimonies bears witness to the effects of his varied interests. To complete the picture, an overview of his teaching, and a sample of course outlines and reading lists from the 1970s to 2001, are provided in an Appendix.

In 'A Watch on Each Wrist: Twelve Seminars with W. G. Sebald', the writer Luke Williams recalls being taught on the MA in Creative Writing by Sebald in the autumn semester of 2001. He identifies Sebald's ability to combine modernist uncertainty with emotional engagement as the quality which had already appealed to him as a reader and aspiring writer, describing the feeling of strange excitement he experienced on discovering that the writer whom he admired would be one of his teachers at UEA. Williams recounts a trip to London to see Sebald and Anthea Bell read together from *Austerlitz*, followed by a chance encounter in the train back to Norwich and a cautionary tale about the temptations of confusing art and life. Drawing on the notes and diary entries he and other students made after Sebald's classes, he provides a fascinating insight into Sebald's view of literature and of the business of writing: here is a teacher who speaks to his students as fellow writers and engages critically with their work, emphasizing the importance of precision and arguing that 'aesthetics is not a value-free area'. This assemblage of notes, recollections, and quotations gradually becomes an account of Williams's own critical engagement with Sebald and with himself, as he acknowledges the trap of trying to emulate Sebaldian 'authenticity' without thinking about the workings of fiction. What emerges from this personal response to Sebald as writer and teacher also constitutes a detailed personal guide to the ethics of literature.

The final piece on Sebald as teacher is 'The Crystal Mountain of Memory: W. G. Sebald as a University Teacher' by Florian Radvan, Sebald's last PhD student at UEA. Echoing Sebald's own journey as a student, Radvan describes how he came to England as a visiting student in 1994 and ended up staying to complete a doctorate on post-war German theatre. He recounts how Sebald's undergraduate teaching typified a refreshingly liberated approach to the text which focussed particularly on its textuality — an approach shaped by teaching literature in a foreign-language context. Radvan argues that the immediacy of this initial approach by means of close reading correlates with the form of the literary essay, suggesting that Sebald's teaching in the British system influenced his use of the essay as a liberating form of critical disquisition, based on the personal engagement with the text that he encouraged from his students. He reflects not only on Sebald's comments as a supervisor but also on their correspondence during these years, from which it becomes clear that Sebald's conception of supervision was one of intellectual exchange, to the extent that the thesis was confidently encouraged to write itself, as it were. Radvan characterizes Sebald as a *Grenzgänger* [border-crosser], not only with regard to his bi-cultural status as an 'English German', but also in his blurring of literature and literary studies, fiction and reality, and biography and autobiography. His own essay ends with a consideration of the similarities between Sebald and the writer and artist Peter Weiss, who was similarly preoccupied with remembering and creating the untold stories of the dead. In this respect Radvan presents a twofold essay on memory: on his own memories of Sebald, and on Sebald's reference to literature as a form of restitution, which he interprets as giving back lost memories through writing.

These reflections on Sebald's view of literature are followed by Uwe Schütte's chapter 'Against *Germanistik*: W. G. Sebald's Critical Essays', which shows how Sebald's idiosyncratic approach and style as a literary critic was also shaped to some extent by his position as an *Auslandsgermanist* outside mainstream German academia. Schütte, a PhD student of Sebald's at UEA in the 1990s, argues that Sebald's deliberate aim of writing against the grain was partly motivated by a desire not to separate literature and criticism, which necessitated a mode of writing unconstrained by institutionalized critical discourse. He proposes that the implicit starting point for Sebald's critical essays is the conviction not only that twentieth-century history has revealed the negative capacities of humankind, but that an ongoing process of exploitation is constantly apparent. Schütte traces a development in Sebald's criticism from the 1970s, where the influence of Adorno is unmistakeable, to a later mode of critical writing, identified with an Anglo-Saxon tradition of literary criticism or critical essays, where the biographical becomes more and more significant. The authors about whom Sebald chose to write reflect this melancholy conviction in a number of different ways: well-known writers such as Elias Canetti, Peter Handke, Kafka, Roth (Joseph and Gerhard), and Robert Walser (each nevertheless embodying his own 'outsider' position), but also other so-called 'minor' or 'outsider' writers such as Herbert Achternbusch and Ernst Herbeck, who exemplify the ways in which literature can become a means of personal liberation. Schütte suggests a parallel between the disregard for traditional boundaries that Sebald sees as specifically Austrian and the disregard for the traditional boundaries of academic criticism that he displays in his own engagement with his subjects. This unorthodox approach is underpinned by what Schütte describes as 'secular redemption through the word'; the emancipatory power of the written word which offers a form of redemption for the writer, the critic, and the reader.

Chapters 7 and 8 focus on the process of translating Sebald's works, bringing together essays by Sebald's first two English translators (the late Michael Hamburger is represented later in the book by the poem he wrote in memory of Sebald, and by two short pieces by Sebald relating to him in Part II). In 'Englishing Max Sebald', Michael Hulse reflects on his work as Sebald's translator during the 1990s, beginning with the original reader's report he wrote recommending *Die Ausgewanderten* to the Harvill Press; reprinted here, this report constitutes one of the earliest English-language responses to Sebald's work. When he accepted a subsequent invitation to translate it into English, Hulse referred to *Die Ausgewanderten* as 'a beautiful, sustainingly human book'. From the outset the process of translation involved an integral element of collaboration: Hulse would send Sebald draft translations, which he would return with comments and suggestions (facsimiles of some of Sebald's annotations to the draft versions are included here). This element of collaboration was enhanced by the fact that Sebald translated two of Hulse's own poems from English into German at the same time; these are reprinted in Part II.[5] Drawing on their unpublished correspondence, Hulse shows how Sebald's approach to writing raises a particular ethical question for the translator with regard to the use of sources. For example, in the case of the references to Joseph Conrad in Part v of *Die Ringe des Saturn*, the ethical challenge concerns the translation from German into English of material based on original English sources and the extent to which the translator should acknowledge these sources in the return to English. The ensuing discussions cast an interesting light both on Sebald's view of 'fictionalization' and on the role of the translator as reader and critic. Hulse concludes by reflecting on Sebald's response to the demands placed upon him as his reputation grew and on their respective views of the differing attitudes to history in England and Germany.

In 'Translating W. G. Sebald — With and Without the Author', Anthea Bell takes up the story of the relationship between author and translator. For Bell this began with an initial request in 1999 to translate *Luftkrieg und Literatur,* which appeared in English as *On the Natural History of Destruction* in 2003. This request was then superseded by the invitation to translate a new work, *Austerlitz,* which was still in the process of being written. Bell describes their *modus operandi* over the following two years, which similarly consisted in the main of batches of draft translations being posted to Sebald and then returned with handwritten annotations and accompanying letters. In the case of *Austerlitz,* the comments on the first draft translations actually preceded the completion of the original manuscript, raising an interesting question of mutual influence of source and translation. At the same time work was also under way on the various pieces collected in *On the Natural History of Destruction,* to be followed later by the posthumous *Campo Santo* (as many readers will know, the contents of the original German publications are slightly different from the English editions). Reflecting on Sebald's extensive knowledge of English vocabulary, Bell discusses some of the particular words or turns of phrase in *Austerlitz* that exercised them, ranging from the nomenclature of moths in the early chapters, to the accounts of life in Theresienstadt, where Sebald proposed a number of changes in order to produce a similar effect for English readers, and to the repetition of 'said Austerlitz', which she likens to the 'return of a piece of music now and then to its home key'. The essay ends with a reflection on the abrupt curtailment of this collaboration and the process of 'second-guessing' involved in translating the essays and prose pieces subsequently collected in *Campo Santo.* Although the 'Corsican book' was never finished, Bell concludes by suggesting that the four published extracts from it in this eponymous volume are a characteristic example of Sebald's mixture of melancholy lyricism and dry humour.

The final three chapters concern themselves in different ways with Sebald's *Nachlass* or archive. In 'Sebald's Photographic Annotations', Clive Scott considers the annotations Sebald made on his personal copies of four books: Roland Barthes's *Camera Lucida,* John Berger's *About Looking,* Clive Scott's *The Spoken Image: Photography and Language,* and Susan Sontag's *On Photography.* Scott presents his investigation into Sebald's use of photographs as an ongoing dialogue between the four critical texts, Sebald's own texts, and the other theorists and artists they inevitably invoke: Walter Benjamin, Siegfried Kracauer, and Jan Peter Tripp. Beginning by arguing that 'ekphrasis' is a more appropriate term than 'caption' when it comes to analysing how Sebald writes (or may not write) about images, Scott proposes that photography acts as a counter to history by populating the past. He suggests that Sebald's description of photographs as 'unsuspected' refers both to the presentation of the unknown and to the means by which we attach ourselves to history, considering that Sebald's view of the photograph seems perhaps to be more phenomenological than semiological, residing more in the unpredictability of its effect than in its indexical and cultural value. With specific regard to the genesis of *Austerlitz,* he reflects on Sebald's annotation that 'there are no photographs of Aust.[erlitz]', the fact that there *are* three photographs of the fictional protagonist, and the relationship to the Proustian notion of involuntary memory encoded in the text. Scott's discussion also encompasses photographs as a means of potential redemption which necessitates the viewer's collaboration, the significance of *trompe l'œil*, the effect of deliberately low production values, and Sontag's own reading of Sebald. He concludes by proposing four specific ways in which Sebald makes us rethink photography — and in so doing places the Sebaldian use of the photograph into the ongoing theoretical debate on the subject.

In 'The Disappearance of the Author in the Work: Some Reflections on W. G. Sebald's *Nachlass* in the Deutsches Literaturarchiv Marbach', Ulrich von Bülow reflects on the acquisition of Sebald's manuscripts, files, papers, and personal library by the German national literary archive. He suggests that the distinctive character of Sebald's *Nachlass* — literally 'what is left behind' — can be attributed to the particular role that notions such as legacy, remnants, documentation, and posterity play in Sebald's work, which is linked in turn to how he perceived his own literary persona and the creation of identity *per se*. The first part of the essay discusses specific examples from Sebald's works, such as Ambros Adelwarth's diary and Max Aurach/Ferber's preservation of family papers, which typify both the aleatory character of what remains and the author's combination of appropriation, invention, and 'falsification'. In *Die Ringe des Saturn* the concept of what is left behind encompasses both Thomas Browne's skull and the entire contents of Somerleyton Hall. For Jacques Austerlitz, all that remains of his family is a small book and two photographs, which also raises the question of the role of photography; as von Bülow suggests, every photograph can be seen as a kind of *Nachlass*. He then turns his attention to Sebald's *Nachlass* in the archive in Marbach, reflecting on what Sebald preserved for posterity and what he discarded or destroyed: although there is much material for the researcher who wishes to piece together the genesis of the works, there is very little by way of personal material such as correspondence and diaries. Sebald's papers — some of which are shown here as facsimiles — give an indication as to how he planned works and drafted projects, furnishing illuminating insights into his writing methods and into his unfinished projects both on Corsica and on European history between 1870 and 1945, a project designated as W. W. (World War) which was to draw on eyewitness accounts of English, French, and German experiences. Ultimately, von Bülow argues, the disappearance of the author into the work is perhaps the other half of Sebald's *Nachlass*: although the author's persona is largely absent from the physical archive, it is interwoven into the different texts.

In '*Bibliotheca abscondita*: On W. G. Sebald's Library', Jo Catling considers both Sebald's personal library and the roles which specific authors, books, and libraries play in his works. She examines Sebald's particular use of intertextual references, commenting on his borrowings — both overt and covert — of material by writers such as Benjamin, Borges, and Browne, Goethe and Hölderlin, Pessoa and Walser. This entails a wider exploration of literature as both labyrinth and maze, where the reader follows the narrator in the hope of finding either the centre or the way out. In her discussions of the books from Sebald's library in his *Nachlass* in Marbach and of his relationship to books in general, Catling argues that Sebald was not an inveterate collector or bibliophile, but a pragmatist who would regularly give books away or sell them once particular projects had been completed. She examines the representation of personal and public libraries in Sebald's works — for example in

Paris, Prague, Wertach, and Verona — arguing that Sebald's own use of libraries was closely linked to his interest in travel and a deliberately haphazard process of discovery. The final part of the essay is concerned with the materiality of Sebald's relationship to his books: the ways in which his personal library was organized; the annotations he made in his books and how these relate to his own writing; the miscellaneous items such as tickets, leaves, and photographs left between the pages, reminders of books read and journeys made. Catling has also compiled a catalogue of Sebald's personal library which combines the Marbach archive with other sources; this is included at the end of Part II of the present volume.

In the Afterword, 'Max Sebald: A Reminiscence', the poet Stephen Watts reflects on his friendship with W. G. Sebald, which began with his being awarded a bursary by the British Centre for Literary Translation in 1991. It transpired that Sebald was already aware of Watts's poetry, having heard a poem of his broadcast on the radio in 1983. Watts traces a lineage from Hölderlin's poem 'Patmos' (in its translation by Michael Hamburger), through his own poem 'Lord in Dream', to its echo in Sebald's *Nach der Natur* (*After Nature*), reflecting on the workings of creativity. He describes how their friendship was based on a mutual interest in both writing and walking, which led to many of the walks around the East End of London familiar to readers of *Austerlitz*. It gradually becomes clear that the fabric of their friendship is as much a part of the Sebald 'archive' as the annotations he made in his books, or the notes and drafts in the Marbach *Nachlass*; an archive measured in writing and photographs, in fact and fiction, in what is remembered and what is forgotten. Watts ends his reminiscence by considering the significance of the Alps in both his own and Sebald's life, which by 'coincidence' brings the book back to its starting point. A 'Lyrisches Intermezzo' between Parts I and II is provided by four poems in memory of Sebald written by Anne Beresford, Michael Hamburger, Michael Hulse, and Stephen Watts himself.

The voices of poets writing about him form a bridge to Sebald's own voice in Part II, which opens with a group of little-known shorter pieces written by Sebald himself. Presented here in loose chronological order, together with the review of a production of *Minna von Barnhelm* appended to Chapter 2, the sample teaching materials between Chapters 3 and 4, and details of symposia and seminar series convened by Sebald between Chapters 6 and 7, these varied texts reflect the wide range of Sebald's journalistic, translational, academic, and administrative activity, as well as shedding light on the genesis of some of his later projects. The first article, the aforementioned 'Die hölzernen Engel von East Anglia', published in the travel section of *Die Zeit* in 1974,[6] was kindly sent to one of the editors by Reinbert Tabbert following her citation of the poem 'Norfolk' in an earlier article,[7] and may be seen as prefiguring both the penultimate section of *Nach der Natur* and the Suffolk meanderings of *Die Ringe des Saturn*.[8] The next piece, 'Leben Ws: Skizze einer möglichen Szenenreihe für einen nichtrealisierten Film' (Life of W: Sketch for a Possible Scenario for an Unrealized Film) about the life of Wittgenstein, first published in 1989 in the *Frankfurter Rundschau*,[9] offers an insight into Sebald's early engagement with the medium of film as a crossover between biography, fiction, and documentary. Together with 'Waterloo',[10] a precursor of part of the fifth section of *Die Ringe des Saturn* published as an *Erzählung* in the 'Folio' supplement of the *Neue Zürcher Zeitung*, it was 'rediscovered' (along with 'Feuer und Rauch' below) by the present editors in a box of cuttings and photocopies while working on the Secondary Bibliography in Marbach in 2007. Sebald's preoccupation with Wittgenstein is, of course, familiar to many readers from both the 'Paul Bereyter' story in *Die Ausgewanderten*, and from *Austerlitz*, and this 'sketch', with its snapshot-like scenes, prefigures Sebald's preoccupation with the visual in his later works and, indeed, touches on a wide range of what have since become known as characteristic 'Sebaldian' themes around *Heimat* and emigration, survival and isolation, and the outsider as genius (or vice versa). The text 'Feuer und Rauch: Über eine Abwesenheit in der deutschen Nachkriegsliteratur' (Fire and Smoke: On an Absence in German Post-war Literature) was read out in Cologne in late 1997, on the occasion of Sebald's receiving the Heinrich Böll Prize,[11] and is, as this date suggests, closely related to material from his lectures on *Luftkrieg und Literatur* ('Air War and Literature') held that autumn in Zurich and better known in English as *On the Natural History of Destruction*, a title derived from Solly Zuckerman's own abandoned attempts to formulate an appropriate response to the scale of destruction he witnessed on first visiting Cologne in 1945, on which Sebald comments here. However, the text, which with its East Anglian opening seems to echo *Die Ringe des Saturn* and its characteristic blend of fiction and essay, also relates to, or perhaps derives from, the abandoned 'Corsica project', and prefigures the story of Gerald Ashman (here called Aylmer) in *Austerlitz*.

Interpolated between these longer prose texts are Sebald's 1995 translations of two of Michael Hulse's poems, 'To Botho Strauss in Berlin' and 'Raffles Hotel (Singapore)'.[12] Sebald's own activities as a translator (rather than as an active collaborator with translators of his own work, particularly into English) are little known; but in fact some of his earliest publications are translations of poetry: four poems from Roger McGough's *gig*, published alongside some of his own poems in *ZET: Das Zeichenheft für Literatur und Graphik* in 1975.[13] Twenty years later, the translations of Michael Hulse's poems reproduced here appeared in an issue of *Sprache im technischen Zeitalter* devoted to modern British poetry, at a time when the latter was already engaged upon translating *Die Ausgewanderten*. Naturally, as a university teacher of German, Sebald will have taught translation classes in the course of his career (even if this seems sometimes to have been under sufferance: see Chapter 3 and Appendix 3.2), and he was acutely aware, through friends and colleagues — not least the poet and translator Michael Hamburger — of the actualities and hardships of a translator's life; factors which may have contributed to his decision to set up the British Centre for Literary Translation at the University of East Anglia in 1989. It is fitting, then, that the last of the texts by Sebald reproduced here should take up the theme of translation implicitly, with two pieces devoted to Michael Hamburger. The text 'Ausgrabung der Vergangenheit' (Excavating the Past),[14] written in 1998 on the occasion of a reading by Michael Hamburger at the Solothurner Literaturtage in Switzerland, focuses on Hamburger's own poetry and their shared love of trees, as well as the sense of horror at the ongoing destruction of the natural world which forms such a strong theme in *Die Ringe des Saturn* (the seventh section of which of course culminates in a visit to the poet's Suffolk home). However, it also contains its own 'hidden' translation of lines from Hamburger's poem 'Afterlives', reflecting on the destruction wrought by the hurricane of 1987 and, perhaps, the possibilities of redemption and survival thereafter. Finally, as a form of tribute to Michael Hamburger, we have been given the opportunity of reproducing the (anonymous, but attributable) 1987 university memo recommending him for the degree of Honorary DLitt (Doctor of Letters) at UEA, which he was awarded — as the accompanying photograph shows — in 1988.

The next section comprises three interviews or 'conversations' with W. G. Sebald, two of which have been transcribed especially for this volume. While a glance at Section J of the Primary Bibliography included in this volume (and indeed the Index of (published) Interviews compiled by Richard Sheppard in Part III, which supplements Gordon Turner's Audio-Visual Bibliography) shows that Sebald's interviews were not quite as rare as some of his interviewers might have believed, the three pieces here complement those gathered by Lynne Sharon Schwartz in *The Emergence of Memory: Conversations with W. G. Sebald* and other interviews which have already been either reprinted or transcribed.[15] The first of these 'Three Conversations with W. G. Sebald' is a translation from Dutch of a 1992 interview with Piet de Moor, entitled 'Echoes from the Past', for the Belgian journal *Knack*, in connection with the first Dutch translation of *Schwindel. Gefühle.* (the first prose work of Sebald's to be translated into any language). This may thus be said to mark the beginning of Sebald's international career as a writer; as mentioned above, it sheds fascinating light on the origins of his writing in the interface of the 'creative' and the 'critical' and the attempt, through writing — which he also describes as a forensic activity akin to the process of memory — to create 'tiny pools of timelessness'. The second 'conversation', which we have entitled 'Lost in Translation?', represents a transcript of a discussion with Sebald's UEA colleague, Professor Jon Cook, in the context of the annual spring Visiting Writers Festival at the Centre for the Creative and Performing Arts at UEA in February 1999, following the publication of the English translation by Michael Hulse of *Die Ringe des Saturn* (*The Rings of Saturn*). It brackets a reading (from *The Emigrants*) with a detailed discussion, encouraged by not quite naive questions from the audience, of the painstaking process (or 'business', as Sebald might have put it) of translation, and complements Michael Hulse's account of their collaboration in Chapter 7. The final piece, 'In this Distant Place', is the transcript of a 2001 'conversation' with Steve Wasserman in Los Angeles (in the ALOUD at Central Library series), which accompanied a reading from *Austerlitz*. Here the discussion centres on those 'shards of frozen moments', the photographs which are such an integral part of Sebald's texts, and the role which their 'appellative presence', as Sebald terms it, plays in the curious dialectic of remembering and forgetting threaded through his texts.

Part II concludes with the Catalogue of Sebald's Library, compiled by Jo Catling in his office at UEA, at his former home, The Old Rectory, and in the Deutsches Literaturarchiv in Marbach am Neckar, where the largest portion of this *Nachlass-bibliothek* is now housed. While such an enterprise can never hope to present a complete picture — Sebald habitually sold, gave away, or otherwise disposed of books he no longer had a use for — it nonetheless represents a detailed snapshot of his interests and reading, and may serve as a useful source of reference for future students and scholars of Sebald's work.

Part III of the book brings together a wide range of bibliographical and biographical material. The Primary Bibliography, compiled by Richard Sheppard in conjunction with Sebald scholars, publishers, and translators from around the world, aims to present a full list of all the known publications of Sebald's works in German and in translation, including interviews, juvenilia, and pieces written for various newspapers. The Secondary Bibliography, compiled by the editors in conjunction with Lynn Wolff, aims to provide a similarly comprehensive record of the monographs, edited volumes, special journal editions, articles, and book chapters published on Sebald's works, as well as a record of the tributes, poems, and art works inspired by him.[16] For ease of consultation this is followed by a separate bibliography which details the reviews of Sebald's works that we have been able to locate to date, including pieces in Dutch, English, French, and German (for reasons of space, pieces in other languages will appear in an online version of the bibliography). The final bibliography, the Audio-Visual Bibliography compiled by Gordon Turner, aims to detail all the extant audio and visual sources either featuring Sebald or on the subject of his works, encompassing radio and television broadcasts, interviews, adaptations, and readings. It is perhaps a fitting testimony that the final entries refer to broadcasts that were never made, such as a mooted German television piece on the life of Immanuel Kant, or to broadcasts that none of the editors or contributors has seen, such as a Swiss television programme about the Allgäu. An index of the substantial number of published interviews, compiled by Richard Sheppard, rounds off this section and provides a detailed account of the themes and preoccupations to which Sebald continually returns in interviews, as in his works. Lastly, the Chronology, like the photographs interspersed, in an echo of Sebald's own practice, throughout the volume, brings together a vast array of detail concerning the life and movements of a writer and academic, which appears, seen in this light, as more peripatetic than perhaps even he himself realized.

There is always a temptation, in a volume of this kind, to hunt down one further detail or chase up one last review or reading: indeed, as will be seen, many of the areas touched upon here have the potential to become full-length studies in their own right. Remembering, though, that Sebald, unlike Nabokov, preferred his butterflies (and indeed moths) not 'fixed and wriggling on a pin' (as T. S. Eliot has it), but rather un-netted and flying free, on or off the page, it is fitting to step back and say — for the moment at least — 'enough is enough', quoting in conclusion the words from Walter Benjamin highlighted in Sebald's copy of *Angelus Novus*: 'Jede Leidenschaft grenzt ja ans Chaos, die sammlerische aber an die Erinnerungen' [Every passion borders on the chaotic, but the collector's passion borders on the chaos of memories].[17]

Notes to the Introduction

1. This quotation comes from Sebald's application for a Fellowship from NESTA (National Endowment for Science, Technology and the Arts). See pp. 257–59 of this volume for the full source.

2. See the Primary Bibliography for full publication details of Sebald's works, including translations.

3. It is impossible to do justice here to the existing body of Sebald scholarship without resorting to crude simplification and classification. The Secondary Bibliography in this volume aims to show the wide variety of available material and to list the contributions by established Sebald scholars; readers are also recommended to consult here the particular individual pieces by Scott Denham, J. J. Long, Richard Sheppard, and Lynn Wolff that give critical overviews of developments in the field. The editors would also like to acknowledge in particular the pioneering work of Marcel Atze and Franz Loquai, especially with regard to the works collected in their edited volume *Sebald. Lektüren*. (Eggingen: Isele, 2005).

4. See Primary Bibliography D.1.

5. See Primary Bibliography M.A.2.

6. See Primary Bibliography F.C.1.

7. See Primary Bibliography F.A.1(iv).1: cited in Jo Catling, 'Gratwanderungen bis an den Rand der Natur: W. G. Sebald's Landscapes of Memory', in *The Anatomist of Melancholy: Essays in Memory of W. G. Sebald*, ed. by Rüdiger Görner (Munich: iudicium, 2003), pp. 19–50 (p. 32).

8. For a discussion of this topic, see also Jo Catling, 'W. G. Sebald: Ein "England-Deutscher"? Identität–Topographie–Intertextualität', in *W. G. Sebald: Intertextualität und Topographie*, ed. by Irène Heidelberger-Leonard and Mireille Tabah (Berlin: LIT Verlag, 2008), pp. 25–53.

9. See Primary Bibliography F.C.4.

10. See Primary Bibliography F.C.5: 'Europäische Flânerien: W. G. Sebalds intertextuelle Wanderungen zwischen Melancholie und Ironie', in *Gedächtnis und Widerstand: Festschrift für Irène Heidelberger-Leonard*, ed. by Mireille Tabah with Sylvia Weiler and Christian Poetini (Tübingen: Stauffenberg, 2009), pp. 139–54.

11. See Primary Bibliography D.66.

12. The editors would like to take this opportunity to thank Michael Hulse for alerting us to the existence of these translations.

13. W. G. Sebald (trans.), four poems by Roger McGough, *ZET*, 3.12 (December 1975), 6–8. See Primary Bibliography, Section M, for details of these and other translations by Sebald. For his own poems see F.A.2 and also F.A.1.

14. See Primary Bibliography D.67.

15. See *The Emergence of Memory: Conversations with W. G. Sebald*, ed. by Lynne Sharon Schwartz (New York: Seven Stories Press, 2007); see Section J of the Primary Bibliography for other interviews and reprints; see the Audio-Visual Bibliography for radio and television interviews with Sebald.

16. The Bibliographies contain material published up to 2010. However, the year 2011 will see publication of a number of books and projects on, and translations of, Sebald. Where we are aware of these they have been included in 'Postscript' or 'Forthcoming' sections at the end of the relevant Bibliography; see also the Chronology.

17. Walter Benjamin, 'Ich packe meine Bibliothek aus', in *Ausgewählte Schriften*, II: *Angelus Novus* (Frankfurt a.M.: Suhrkamp, 1966), pp. 169–78 (p. 169); 'Unpacking my Library', in *Illuminations*, trans. by Harry Zohn (London: Fontana, 1992), pp. 61–69 (pp. 61–62).

PART I

The Writer in Context

CHAPTER 1

A Childhood in the Allgäu:
Wertach, 1944–52

Mark M. Anderson

> bin ich,
> dem anderwärts furchtbaren Zeitlauf zum Trotz,
> am Nordrand der Alpen, wie mir heut scheint,
> aufgewachsen ohne einen Begriff der Zerstörung.
>
> *Nach der Natur*
>
> [I grew up
> despite the dreadful course
> of events elsewhere, on the northern
> edge of the Alps, so it seems
> to me now, without any
> idea of destruction.]
>
> *After Nature*[1]

'How far [...] must one go back to find the beginning?', asks W. G. Sebald in the third part of his long narrative poem *Nach der Natur* (*After Nature*), and then suggests an answer himself:

> Wie weit überhaupt muß man zurück, um
> den Anfang zu finden? Vielleicht
> bis zu jenem Morgen des 9. Januar 1905,
> an dem der Großvater und die Großmutter
> bei klirrender Kälte in einer offenen
> Kutsche von Kloster Lechfeld nach
> Obermeitingen fuhren, sich trauen zu lassen.
> Die Großmutter im schwarzen taftenen Kleid
> mit einem Papierblumenstrauß, der Großvater
> in der Uniform, den messingverzierten
> Helm auf dem Kopf.
>
> [How far, in any case, must one go back
> to find the beginning? Perhaps
> to that morning of January 9 1905,
> on which Grandfather and Grandmother
> in ringing cold drove in an open
> landau from Kloster Lechfeld
> to Obermeitingen, to be married.

Grandmother in a black taffeta dress
with a bunch of paper flowers, Grandfather
in his uniform, the brass-embellished
helmet on his head.][2]

Sebald is speaking here of his maternal grandparents, Josef Egelhofer and Theresia Harzenetter, who indeed were married on that date and shortly afterwards established themselves in Wertach im Allgäu, a small mountain village where Egelhofer had recently found work as the regional constable. The marriage would produce four children, including the youngest, Rosa Genoveva ('Rosi'), Sebald's mother. It was here that she met Georg Sebald, a young soldier in the *Wehrmacht* on a skiing holiday with his division, and here that they married in 1936. And although she followed her husband when he was stationed in Bamberg during the war, it was to the relative safety of her parents' home in Wertach that she returned in late summer 1943, where she gave birth to a son, Winfried Georg, on 18 May 1944. Sebald spent the first eight years of his life in this remote setting on the northern edge of the Alps in what was, or so it seems, a happy, even blissful childhood.

The importance of a writer's youth can hardly be overestimated. The first impressions of nature, language, and family all weigh decisively if often imperceptibly on what will become an author's characteristic themes and voice. This truism is no less valid for W. G. Sebald who, despite spending most of his adult life

FIG. 1.1
On the balcony of Grüntenseestraße 3,
Wertach, on the occasion of
W. G. Sebald's baptism (May 1944), with
his maternal grandparents, his father, and
his sister Gertrud.
© Gertrud Aebischer-Sebald

in England, remained intensely if ambivalently connected to his regional origins, drawing on these early impressions as the true substance of his writing. His first unpublished novel, written while he was still a student, is set in the Allgäu, as are the autobiographical sections of his first three published works, *Nach der Natur* (*After Nature*), *Schwindel. Gefühle.* (*Vertigo*), and *Die Ausgewanderten* (*The Emigrants*). One project he was working on at the end of his life was to take place in the Allgäu and deal with the 'éducation sentimentale' of his parents' generation during the Third Reich. In short, even when he appears to be describing other places, Sebald's native region invariably works its way into the narrative. The flatlands of England, the lake region of northern Italy, the gorges around Ithaca, New York, even Jerusalem or the muddy streets of a Lithuanian shtetl can remind him of home. For this cosmopolitan, emigrant writer who left Germany when he was 21 and rarely returned except for short visits to his parents, the Allgäu was never very far away.

Where is the Allgäu, and, more importantly, what did it represent to W. G. Sebald? The region (for it is not a state or 'Land') is located in the south-west corner of Bavaria along the Austrian border, close to Switzerland and extending into the south-east corner of Baden-Württemberg. Its identity is inseparable from its breathtaking landscape: the majestic Alps, green fields, sparkling lakes and rivers that have made the Allgäu a prime tourist site throughout the year. In landscape and folklore it is close to the Tyrol, the adjacent mountainous region of Austria and northern Italy that figures so prominently in Sebald's first prose work *Schwindel. Gefühle.* Even today some Allgäuer still dress in *Lederhosen* summer and winter, as did Sebald's father, and yodelling clog dancers may still be found providing the entertainment at local tourist festivals. The population is predominantly Catholic, and even small towns exhibit impressively large baroque churches with ornate marble columns and the characteristic *Zwiebeltürme* (onion-domed spires). Typical of the region as well are the timber-framed farmhouses adorned with colourful frescos and hopeful inscriptions — 'Gott segne dieses Haus!' (God bless this house!) — and with bright-red geraniums at the windows and balconies. It is primarily an agricultural region, with dairy farming and logging traditionally providing its main sources of income.

Most Germans think of the Allgäu as part of Bavaria, which is certainly true: no less a figure than King Ludwig the Second, the 'mad' nineteenth-century monarch whose fairytale-like castle Neuschwanstein lies a short distance to the east of Wertach, authorized the village's coat of arms in 1872. However, the region also shares features with Swabia to the north and west, to which it is linked historically and linguistically. Officially, the Allgäu belongs to the state of Bavaria, but its administrative region is Swabia. Hence the term 'Bayerisch-Schwaben' (Bavarian Swabia), a seemingly contradictory moniker that originated in 1805 with the battle of Austerlitz when Napoleon, to reward Bavaria for its support in his military victory, gave it a portion of Swabian territory and elevated it to the status of a kingdom. (Sebald's use of the name 'Austerlitz' in his novel thus had a personal connection for him, recalling his own Allgäu heritage.) Perhaps for this reason the region resists simple categorization. For if Bavaria famously claims to be different from the rest

FIG. 1.2 (left). The house at Grüntenseestraße 3 (c. 1941). WGS was born on the top floor (right-hand bedroom) on 18 May 1944. The family lived here until early 1947. From left to right: his maternal grandfather Josef Egelhofer; his mother Rosa (1914–2003) and his maternal grandmother Theresia Egelhofer (née Harzenetter) (1880–1949). The baby in the pram is his older sister Gertrud. His maternal grandparents married on 9 January 1905 in Untermeitingen; both were originally from Swabia, and moved to Wertach on 1 September 1912 from Binnroth (Schwaben) where Josef was born. © Gertrud Aebischer-Sebald

FIG. 1.3 (below, left). W. G. Sebald's *Geburtshaus* at Grüntenseestraße 3, Wertach. © Richard Sheppard (April 2005)

FIG. 1.4 (below, right). Close-up of the *Geburtshaus* showing the recent commemorative plaque (cf. Fig. III.4). © Richard Sheppard (April 2005)

FIG. 1.5. Wertach (1935). The remote village had probably changed very little by the time of Sebald's birth in May 1944. The *Geburtshaus* is hidden by the parish church of St Ulrich in the right foreground. © Courtesy of Fotohaus Heimhuber GmbH (Sonthofen)

of Germany, the Allgäu prides itself on being different from the rest of Bavaria, a kind of geographical, linguistic, and cultural borderland that borrows significant parts of its identity from Swabia, Switzerland, and Austria. Sebald's favourite authors tended to come from these same regions, which shared with the Allgäu not only the southern mountainous landscape but a similar dialect and linguistic sensibility. The Swiss writers Gottfried Keller and Robert Walser; Austrians like Adalbert Stifter and Thomas Bernhard; Swabians such as Friedrich Hölderlin and the 'calendar author' Johann Peter Hebel (who wrote poems in Alemannic dialect), constituted his pantheon of literary classics, where Goethe, Schiller, Thomas Mann, and others are noticeably lacking. But the Allgäu is hardly a cultural powerhouse. It has no university, and so students must travel either to Augsburg or Munich, both around two hours north-east by train, or (like Sebald) to Freiburg im Breisgau in the Black Forest. And it has produced remarkably few renowned artists, scientists or politicians; apparently, W. G. Sebald is its first internationally acclaimed writer (see Figure 1.4).

Wertach lies some three thousand feet above sea level on the floor of a gently sloping valley traversed by two rivers, the Starzlach and the Wertach. The Grünten mountain peak, popularly known as the 'guardian of the Allgäu', rises impressively in the distance to almost six thousand feet. The name 'Wertach' is of Celtic origin, dating from before the time of Christ when the first settlers arrived in the valley, and originally designated the river 'Virdo' (pronounced 'verda'). Postcards from the 1930s show a picturesque village of low houses dominated by a white church with a slanted red roof and an elegant bell tower (Figure 1.5). Virtually unchanged

FIG. 1.6 (above). Wertach destroyed by fire (16 April 1893).

FIG. 1.7 (right). The church in Wertach after the fire.

Both © Courtesy of Geiger Verlag. Taken from Otto Hengge, *Wertacher Album: Erinnerungen in Bildern* (Horb am Neckar: Geiger, 1997)

Fig. 1.8 (upper). Farmhouse in the Allgäu.
Fig. 1.9 (lower). Moving timber by sleigh in the Allgäu.
Both © Courtesy of Geiger Verlag. Taken from Otto Hengge,
Wertacher Album: Erinnerungen in Bildern
Fig. 1.10 (opposite). Plaque beneath statue of St George and the dragon
on the wall below St Ulrich's church in Wertach. © Mark Anderson

today, it has great appeal for tourists in search of Bavarian 'Gemütlichkeit' for their hiking and skiing holidays. But this serene exterior belies Wertach's historic struggle for survival. Romans and Germanic tribes battled for control of the region as early as the third century, and in 955 Bishop Ulrich, the 'warrior from Lechfeld', consecrated the first parish church. Plagues, famines, marauding armies, and fires regularly devastated the village. The wall of the local cemetery behind the church bears a long list of dates of the most destructive conflagrations; the last one took place in 1893 and left little more than the smoking embers of a few buildings and the nave of the collapsed church, exposed to the open sky (see Figures 1.6 and 1.7). Pictures of those ruins are remarkably similar to scenes of destruction from World War II — an ironic detail considering Sebald's fascination with the violence of that war, which left Wertach untouched.

The climate is also harsh, with a short summer high in the mountains that makes it impossible to grow most crops. Dairy farming has long constituted the village's main source of income (including its famous Weisslack beer cheese), and each year it holds a celebration honouring the momentous return of its cows from a season of grazing in the uplands. Until tourism improved its financial situation after World War II, the village was poor and could barely sustain its population, which has only recently risen above two thousand inhabitants. Pictures from the early part of the twentieth century, when Sebald's grandparents were raising their family there, show children standing barefoot in the muddy, unpaved streets; nursing mothers taking a break from their farm work; horse-drawn wagons transporting timber down vertiginously steep paths from the mountains (Figures 1.8 and 1.9). Given these difficult circumstances, it is hardly surprising that the region developed such a sombre, fatalistic view of life. Behind the church, near the large monument for Wertach's fallen soldiers in World War I, is an older plaque with a simple rhymed inscription (Figure 1.10 below):

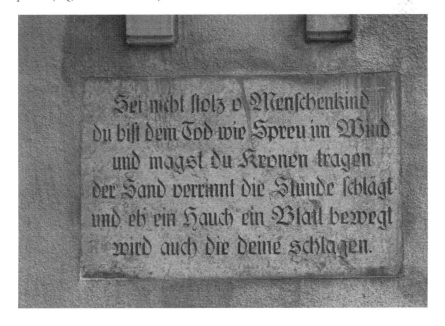

Sei nicht stolz o Menschenkind
du bist dem Tod wie Spreu im Wind
und magst du Kronen tragen
der Sand verrinnt die Stunde schlägt
und eb ein Hauch ein Blatt bewegt
wird auch die deine schlagen.

Sei nicht stolz o Menschenkind
du bist dem Tod wie Spreu im Wind
und magst du Kronen tragen
der Sand verrinnt, die Stunde schlägt
und eh ein Hauch ein Blatt bewegt
wird auch die deine schlagen.

[Don't be proud, O Child of Man
for death sees you as chaff in the wind
and though crowns may adorn your head
the sand will flow, the hour strike
and before a breeze has rustled a leaf
Your hour will strike as well.]

This biblical meditation on last things, typical for the region, is all the more likely to have caught Sebald's attention since it sits beneath an impressive statue of St George — his (and his father's) name saint — conquering the dragon (Figure 1.11). In any case, Sebald's own brooding, melancholic preoccupation with death in his literary writings has much in common with the Catholicism of his native region, though he was not religious in any formal sense, and despised religious hypocrisy. He himself calls attention to the epigraph to his uncle's elementary school class picture from the year 1917 — 'in der Zukunft | liegt der Tod uns zu Füßen' [in the future | death lies at our feet] — calling it 'einer jener dunklen Orakelsprüche, | die man nie mehr vergißt' [one of those obscure oracular sayings | one never again

FIG. 1.11. Statue of St George and the dragon in Wertach. Cf. *Schwindel. Gefühle.* (Eichborn), p. 265; *Vertigo* (Vintage), p. 242. © Mark Anderson

FIG. 1.12. View over Sonthofen (1952).
© Courtesy of Fotohaus Heimhuber GmbH (Sonthofen)

forgets].[3] And in an interview he dwells in characteristically morbid, jocular fashion on his early familiarity with death in Wertach, where, for instance,

> you couldn't bury the dead in the winter because the ground was frozen and there was no way of digging it up. So you had to leave them in the woodshed for a month or two until the thaw came. You grew up with this knowledge that death is around you [...]. Now it's all obliterated, of course. But somehow it got stuck in my mind, and I think it's possibly from that quarter that my preoccupation [with the dead] stems.[4]

Despite or perhaps because of these archaic traits, Sebald experienced Wertach as something of a paradise, far from the desolation afflicting most of post-war Germany. Untouched by the bombing, the village existed in a kind of time warp connecting it to previous centuries. Life moved at a slower, more elemental pace, in rhythm with the seasons, the sun, and the moon. Without a rail link to the outside world, few travellers came here, and few of its residents had reason to leave; a mail bus and the occasional taxi provided the sole means of motorized transport. After the war, Sebald's father briefly commuted to Sonthofen, some twenty kilometres through steep winding roads, by bicycle (Figure 1.12). Machines were not widely introduced until the 1950s, farm animals still a familiar feature of daily life. Looking back at his childhood, Sebald emphasized the village's 'pre-modern' silence, its link to an earlier era in human history even as other parts of the world — indeed, neighbouring towns in the Allgäu — had fully entered the modern period. There were no books, no classical music concerts, no cinemas. He amused himself with odds and ends he found lying around the house — bits of string that he used to

FIG. 1.13. WGS aged six on his first day at school in Wertach (1950).
© Gertrud Aebischer-Sebald

construct spider-like webs where he would lie in wait. An image of this happy period is provided by a photograph of him aged six, on his first day at school: a smiling blond boy dressed in *Lederhosen* and a striped shirt, his thumbs confidently hooked into the straps of his leather backpack (Figure 1.13).

A good deal of Sebald's happiness as a child — and the reason, perhaps, he singles out his maternal grandparents' wedding as the true beginning of his own life — was due to Josef Egelhofer, in whose house he was born and under whose tutelage he spent the first eight years of his life. Because Sebald's father was largely absent during this period, initially because of the war, then because of his employment in the town of Sonthofen, Sebald's grandfather played an unusually large role in his early education. Born in 1872 in Rot an der Rot, a Swabian village near Memmingen in 'Lower' Allgäu (which, in the somewhat confusing terminology of the region, designates its northern district), Egelhofer had little formal education. He trained and worked briefly as a blacksmith, but shortly after the turn of the century he secured a position as village constable in Wertach, in 'Upper' Allgäu, about an hour's drive to the south, that he would hold for the rest of his working life. There is a striking portrait of him in uniform, taken in 1920 when he was 48, which gives a good sense of the elegance and easy authority he projected in his role as 'Gendarme' (as it was called in the region's typically French-inflected Bavarian

Fig. 1.14. Josef Egelhofer (6 July 1872–14 April 1956), Sebald's maternal grandfather, never fought in the First World War, because of a heart defect. Instead he became Wertach's village policeman, and that is the uniform he is wearing here (1920).
© The Estate of W. G. Sebald

German) (Figure 1.14). The job consisted mainly in patrolling the surroundings for poachers and vagrants and, on Saturday nights, keeping drunken farmers from brawling at the local taproom. He spent much of his time outdoors, on foot, in constant interaction with the local residents, for whom he was a familiar and respected figure, if not quite a native son. In this small, isolated world he was part of the elite, which included the mayor, the priest, and the better-off farmers.

Egelhofer and his wife had four children, all of them born and raised in Wertach. Initially, the family led a peaceful life together and was spared during the 'Great War', since Egelhofer suffered from a heart defect that exempted him from military service, and the children were too young to serve. But inflation and unemployment in Germany during the 1920s broke the family apart, forcing the three eldest children to emigrate to the USA to work as domestic servants. 'Unsereiner ist eben damals [...] in Deutschland auf keinen grünen Zweig gekommen' [people like us simply had no chance in Germany],[5] remarks 'Uncle Kasimir' in *Die Ausgewanderten* (*The Emigrants*), and though fictional and perhaps never uttered by Sebald's own uncle, the phrase captures the real siblings' situation. Their emigration, in any case, constitutes Sebald's 'family' connection to a historical and existential phenomenon that would mark his own life as an emigrant and that he repeatedly probed in his writing, both academic and literary. The eldest child was Annie (she appears

FIG. 1.15 (upper). Three of Rosa Egelhofer's siblings had emigrated to America in the 1920s. Her sister Fanny came back to visit Wertach with her two children in 1951. This photo was taken then in front of the left-hand corner of the Weinstube Steinlehner (FIG. 1.16). WGS is the boy on the left standing next to his cousin (his other cousin is the tall girl in the centre of the picture). His aunt Fanny is on the extreme left of the picture standing next to Rosa. Their father, Josef Egelhofer, is on the extreme right of the picture. © Gertrud Aebischer-Sebald

FIG. 1.16 (lower). The Weinstube Steinlehner, Grüntenseestraße 9, Wertach (date unknown). The Sebald family lived here on the first floor from early 1947 until they moved to Sonthofen, Am Alten Bahnhof 3, on 16 December 1952. It remained a *Weinstube* until 1963. © Familie Steinlehner

Fig. 1.17. The kitchen at Grüntenseestraße 3, Wertach, 1942–43.
From left to right: W. G. Sebald's maternal grandparents, his mother Rosa
with his sister Gertrud, his paternal grandparents. © Gertrud Aebischer-Sebald

as the unmarried, tearful 'Aunt Theres' in the 'Ambros Adelwarth' story in *Die Ausgewanderten* (*The Emigrants*), followed by Fanny (the model for 'Aunt Fini' in the same story) and then Josef ('Uncle Kasimir') (Figures 1.15 and 1.16). The fictional character Ambros Adelwarth, incidentally, who is said in the text to be a brother of Sebald's maternal grandmother, and hence his great-uncle, was in fact modelled after the brother of Fanny's husband (the fictional 'Uncle Theo'), a man named Stehmer and therefore not a blood relative of the Egelhofers at all. But the name 'Adelwarth' has a direct family connection for Sebald: the maiden name of his maternal great-grandmother (the mother of Theresia Harzenetter) was Genoveva Adelwarth, whose first name was passed on to Sebald's mother.

Rosa Genoveva or 'Rosi' Egelhofer was born on 20 July 1914, shortly before the outbreak of World War I. She was 13 when her two sisters left home and she herself went away to a Catholic boarding school in Klosterwald. Interestingly, Sebald's mother appears in the story under her own name and the details regarding her early life correspond to her actual biography. She wanted to follow her siblings to America, but her parents insisted that at least one child remain at home. 'Ich habe versucht, sie zu trösten damit, daß sie ja den Kasimir noch habe,' remarks the fictional Aunt Fini of her younger sister in the Allgäu-accented German she still speaks, 'aber dann ist auch der Kasimir, wie die Rosa grad fünfzehn war, nach Amerika gegangen. So kommt eben immer eines zum andern' [I tried to console her [about our departure] by saying she still had Kasimir, but then Kasimir left for America too, when Rosa was just fifteen. That's the way it always is […] one thing after another].[6] And so Rosa stayed in Wertach, and became known as the Egelhofers' 'Fehl' (Allgäu dialect for 'Mädchen' or girl), devoted to her parents and, soon enough, to her own growing family (see Figure 1.18).

FIG. 1.18 (upper). The young WGS and Gertrud with their mother on a bridge over the Wertach, about one kilometre north of Wertach just off the road to the Oberjoch (autumn–winter 1944). The wooden bridge has been replaced by a metal one, but the shape of the hill behind them is just recognizable among the trees. © Gertrud Aebischer-Sebald

FIG. 1.19 (lower). Josef Egelhofer on a walk with his grandchildren Winfried and Gertrud, Wertach (1948). © Gertrud Aebischer-Sebald

Perhaps because of the missed experiences with his own children, perhaps because of the gap left by a son-in-law at war, or perhaps simply because he liked children and was a naturally gifted pedagogue — in any case Egelhofer doted on his two grandchildren, Gertrud (born 31 July 1941) and Winfried. (He had less contact with Sebald's younger sister, Beate, who was born in 1951, shortly before the family left for Sonthofen.) By this time Egelhofer was in his seventies and already retired, which meant he had plenty of time to spend with his young charges. From his blacksmith training he was good with his hands and had a knack for conjuring toys out of nothing. He made skis for the children, for instance, and built a cart out of an old barrel that he used to transport them around the village (Figure 1.19). Though he left school early, Egelhofer was intelligent and intellectually curious, especially about the natural world (Gertrud calls him a 'Naturphilosoph'). He had an extensive knowledge of plants, flowers, and medicinal herbs, which he would put into carefully labelled jars and keep on the kitchen windowsill. Though he had no interest in literature and never read novels or plays, he did read a daily newspaper and used a country almanac printed in nearby Kempten to note the seasons, cycles of the moon, people's birthdays, and dates of other important events; Sebald's own fascination with dates and historical coincidences may have got off to an early start here. One of the reasons he so likes the writings of the Swabian 'calendar author' Johann Peter Hebel, he tells us, is that

> mein Großvater, dessen Sprachgebrauch in vielem an den des Hausfreunds erinnerte, die Gewohnheit hatte, auf jeden Jahreswechsel einen Kempter Calender zu kaufen, in welchem er dann die Namensfeste seiner Anverwandten und Freunde, den ersten Frost, den ersten Schneefall [...], Gewitter, Hagelschlag und ähnliches mehr [...] vermerkte.

> [my grandfather, whose use of German in many respects recalls that of the 'House Friend', had the habit of buying a Kempten calendar (almanac) at the start of each new year in which he noted the name days of his relatives and friends, the first frost, the first snowfall, thunderstorms, hail and similar things.][7]

He also taught his grandson the alphabet, reading stories aloud so often that the boy knew them by heart.

Egelhofer's great passion however was for walking. As village gendarme he didn't use a car or a horse but patrolled on foot, and even in retirement he took daily three- and four-hour walks through the village and the surrounding countryside, taking his grandson everywhere with him. Numerous pictures from the family's photo albums show them together on a country road or in a meadow in the mountains: the tall elderly Egelhofer smartly dressed in a three-piece suit and trilby, his spindly-legged grandson in *Lederhosen* and a striped shirt. He called his grandson 'Mändle', a nickname he invented that meant 'little man' and that gently poked fun at the boy's seriousness as well as his slight build. 'If you get any skinnier, Mändle,' he would remark, 'you'll be able to hide behind a broomstick.' Oddly enough, the name has a Jewish ring to it (variations of the name 'Mendel' occur repeatedly among Ashkenazic Jewry), and one wonders if, in his later study of the history of German Jews, Sebald did not feel a private kinship to them through his grandfather's dialect nickname for him.

FIG. 1.20. Gertrud and the young WGS with their maternal grandparents near Wertach (*c.* 1947–48). © The Estate of W. G. Sebald

Many of Sebald's passions later in life — for long walks, gardening, maps and country almanacs, for the natural world in general — can be traced back to these early lessons with his grandfather. But the intensity of their emotional bond goes beyond simple pedagogy, or Egelhofer's gentle, caring nature. It has something to do with the special way that the war disrupted the normal family structure in Germany for children of Sebald's generation, when their soldier fathers never returned home, or returned home 'late' from prisoner-of-war camps, demoralized and physically diminished. Gertrud concurs with her brother's assessment that he was essentially raised by Egelhofer, not by his father, who spent two years in a French POW camp after the war and lived apart from the family until Sebald was eight, visiting only at weekends. Egelhofer not only filled the space left by an absent father, he also represented an intelligent, forgiving, non-military kind of authority that formed such a marked contrast with Sebald's soldier father, a stickler for order and discipline. When Georg Sebald reproached his son for some failure or other, Egelhofer would stick up for him, even completing house chores in his place. He was his protector, and appears as such in the autobiographical story 'Il ritorno in patria' in *Schwindel. Gefühle. (Vertigo)*, where the narrator's mother and grandfather, not his father, wrap him in wet blankets to protect him from a life-threatening fever.

Egelhofer died in April 1956, one month before Sebald's twelfth birthday, and though it took him many years to recognize it, he never got over the loss. Quite simply, his grandfather represented the security and happiness of what could be called in German the 'heile Welt' — an intact, safe world not yet fissured by the awareness of history in the large sense. In this vein, the adult Sebald could say of just such a trusted and beloved 'guide': 'er habe sich nie in seinem Leben, weder zuvor noch später, derart wohl gefühlt wie damals in der Gesellschaft dieses Mannes' [never in his life, neither before nor later, did he feel as good as he did then, in the company of that man].[8] These are in fact the words he gave to his fictional character Dr Henry Selwyn in *Die Ausgewanderten* (*The Emigrants*), who early in his life befriends a 65-year-old Swiss mountain guide named Johannes Naegeli and goes 'everywhere' with him on his walks. His departure from Naegeli, who dies in a mountain accident, grieves him deeply:

> nichts [ist mir] so schwergefallen wie der Abschied von Johannes Naegeli. Selbst die Trennung [von meiner Frau] hat mir nicht annähernd denselben Schmerz bereitet wie die Trennung von Naegeli, den ich noch immer auf dem Bahnhof von Meiringen stehen und winken sehe.

> [nothing felt as hard, as I realize now looking back, as saying goodbye to Johannes Naegeli. Even the separation [from my wife] [...] did not cause me remotely as much pain as the separation from Naegeli. I can still see him standing at the station at Meiringen, waving.][9]

Naegeli does seem to constitute one of Sebald's fictional tributes to his grandfather, just as he himself shares traits with Selwyn (the choice of the doctor's fictional name, so close to his own, is hardly fortuitous). Indeed, one might ask whether Sebald's narrators, who often find themselves deeply (though non-erotically) attached to much older men, do not in some way reflect his early attachment to Josef Egelhofer, the teacher and companion he loved 'more than anything' in the world.

With this turn to fiction we come to the point where history and what one might call the landscape of Sebald's 'imaginary homeland' begin to merge. This subjective realm is as least as important as the external chronology, and merits some comment. In an interview granted shortly before his death, Sebald noted that he had been raised by his grandfather, 'who was born in 1872 in the "deep South"'.[10] Both the date and the geographical marker are telling, for Sebald is emphasizing his own link through his grandfather to the nineteenth century, as well as to the region of southern Swabia, Switzerland, and Austria. Through his grandfather's German, in other words, he had a more or less direct literary connection to authors like Adalbert Stifter, Gottfried Keller, Eduard Mörike, and Johann Peter Hebel, who wrote their works before the so-called 'Zivilisationsbruch' [rupture in civilization] that Sebald repeatedly identified as beginning with World War I. (The fictional Dr Selwyn develops his friendship with Naegeli, significantly, in 1913.) Often dismissed as conservative or sentimental 'Biedermeier' realists, these writers nonetheless provided Sebald with a model for his own literary voice, which, as critics have noted, has an old-fashioned, nineteenth-century tone in addition to its regional 'southern' accent.

But another way of looking at this question is to say that in his narrations Sebald is speaking with the accent and diction of Josef Egelhofer, who himself learnt to read and write in the 1870s, when Keller and Mörike were still writing (Stifter died in 1868). To be sure, Egelhofer was not a writer, and psychologically it may make more sense to say that the author of *Die Ausgewanderten* (*The Emigrants*) was initially drawn to the writings of Stifter and Keller precisely because they reminded him of his grandfather's use of German. But part of Sebald's imaginary biography consists precisely in establishing links or 'coincidences' that blur such distinctions. In his collection of late essays, *Logis in einem Landhaus* (*A Place in the Country*), for instance, Sebald dwells at some length on the similarities between Egelhofer and the Swiss writer Robert Walser in physical appearance, dress, and daily habits. Walser was born four years after Egelhofer in Biel/Bienne near Bern, in a mountain region similar to the Allgäu; they both died in 1956, Egelhofer on 14 April following a late snowfall ('in der Nacht auf Walsers letzten Geburtstag' [the night before Walser's last birthday], as Sebald points out),[11] Walser during an afternoon walk in the mountains on 25 December.

> Vielleicht sehe ich darum den Großvater heute, wenn ich zurückdenke an seinen von mir nie verwundenen Tod, immer auf dem Hörnerschlitten liegen, auf dem man den Leichnam Walsers, nachdem er im Schnee gefunden und fotografiert worden war, zurückführte in die Anstalt.

> [Perhaps that is the reason why now, when I think back to my grandfather's death, to which I have never been able to reconcile myself, in my mind's eye I always see him lying on the horn sledge on which Walser's body — after he had been found in the snow and photographed — was taken back to the asylum.][12]

In offering this characteristically fanciful association of his own grandfather with a major German writer of the twentieth century, Sebald is also suggesting Egelhofer's link with the marginalized and the dispossessed. Not that there was any direct connection: Walser gave up his promising literary career at an early age to live an impoverished, secluded life for thirty years in a mental asylum. This was certainly not Egelhofer's life trajectory (though it also recalls Hölderlin's life story, which was equally significant for Sebald, or indeed that of Ernst Herbeck, as Uwe Schütte discusses in Chapter 6 of this volume). But in his modest existence as village gendarme, his grandfather came to symbolize for Sebald an idealized, itinerant marginality, a 'wanderer' in the German Romantic sense, isolated and 'homeless'. A consummate Allgäuer on the one hand, Egelhofer did not truly belong to Wertach since he was born in Lower Allgäu (an hour's drive today to the north!). He and his wife were 'Zugereiste', as she said, outsiders to the native villagers even after living there for half a century. He never owned property, living in a comfortable but inexpensively rented apartment, always moving though never quite at home. He wore a uniform ('the brass-embellished | helmet') and commanded respect, but never fought in a war, never had to kill or destroy (unlike Sebald's own father and his father). So taken was he with this Romantic, anti-authoritarian image that Sebald even spent a day amid dusty documents in a Munich archive trying to establish a (dubious) link between his grandfather and Rudolf Egelhofer, the leader of the communist army during Munich's short-lived revolutionary government following World War I, who was assassinated by Freikorps nationalists. And while working on an academic study of Holocaust survivors who later committed suicide, he felt particularly drawn to the Austrian-Jewish philosopher Jean Améry, a member of the resistance who was tortured by the SS and sent to Auschwitz, 'in particular because he originated from an area not far from [where] I grew up' and because Améry's accent recalled his grandfather's.[13]

Supporting this conception of Egelhofer's marginal, itinerant and 'homeless' condition was the family history of emigration to the USA, where Sebald's aunts and uncles had worked in menial jobs and lived out their lives in unremarkable, financially modest circumstances. Annie, or 'Aunt Theres', for instance, worked for a wealthy family named Wallerstein in a large apartment on Fifth Avenue in New York; brother Josef found work in America as a tinsmith (though not on the roofs of New York skyscrapers, as 'Uncle Kasimir' does in *Die Ausgewanderten* (*The Emigrants*)), then as a mechanic and in a brewery. The figure of Ambros Adelwarth, a homosexual and severely depressed man who dies in a mental asylum, represents an extreme but not fundamentally different variation on this 'family' theme, which is probably one of the reasons Sebald made Adelwarth into a (fictional) blood relative.

Although he never lost sight of the very real differences between the Egelhofers' economic emigration and, say, that of Jewish emigrants of Nazi Germany, or the persecution of homosexuals, Sebald nonetheless grouped this maternal side of his origins with the marginal and powerless, not the powerful. Walser, Hölderlin, Hebel belong to this imaginary geography not just because of their regional, linguistic proximity to the Allgäu, but also because of the marginal, estranged circumstances of their biographical existences. In his essay on Hebel, for instance, he notes that the 'calendar' author's highly sophisticated literary style made use of 'dialektaler und demodierter Wendungen'[14] [dialectal and outmoded turns of phrases] that create an effect of 'Verfremdung' [estrangement], rather than regional identity — a description that could easily be applied to Sebald's own writing. Stifter, Hofmannsthal, and Thomas Bernhard also belong to this imaginary homeland because of the typically Austrian literary tradition — as Sebald the professional Germanist knew well — of focussing on the 'small' subjects of human existence, on details of the natural world, rather than 'les grands discours' of world history, in order to understand 'jene Seite des Lebens [...], | die man vorher nicht sah' [that side of life that | one could not see before].[15]

We find ourselves here deep in the heart of Sebald's imaginary Allgäu. Not the actual territory that tourists know, nor even the homeland of native residents, but an invented and fiercely personal space that was built up over several decades of reading, travelling, and meditating on the mysterious 'coincidences' connecting him to the outside world — on small but for him significant signs like Egelhofer's nickname for him as a child, which provided a link to literary personages like Stefan Zweig's 'Book Mendel' and the Viennese-Jewish world he represents; or Kafka's figure for the Wandering Jew, Jäger (Hunter) Gracchus, who dies in a mountain accident in the Black Forest, where Sebald first attended university; or Nabokov's residence in French-speaking Switzerland in the 1960s, when Sebald was living not far away in Fribourg, with his sister: 'I knew the whole territory and I knew these lifts going up into the mountains that he talks about [in his autobiography].'[16] These are the manifold odds and ends, the 'bits of string' that Sebald used to make sense of his own existence — and, of course, to produce the intensely personal, semi-autobiographical fictions that we value today.[17]

To be sure, Sebald's appreciation of the physical beauty of his native homeland as well as his seemingly nostalgic attachment to the modest, almost timeless world of his grandfather did not blind him to the often provincial, hypocritical, politically reactionary aspects of the 'real' Allgäu. In a speech he gave in Munich at the opening of the *Opernfestspiele* in July 2001, he recalls the ambivalence aroused by a postcard he discovered in England depicting a painted panorama of the Allgäu mountains and a group of Tyrolean folk dancers in Oberstdorf, where he went to high school, thinking that the ten costumed men and women had 'hier in ihrem staubigen englischen Exil auf mich gelauert, um mich daran zu erinnern, daß ich meiner vaterländischen Vorgeschichte, in der ja das Trachtlerische keine unbedeutende Rolle gespielt hat, nie würde entkommen können' [been lying in wait for me here in their dusty English exile, just to remind me that I would never be able to escape the early history of my native land, where costumes and tradition played a not insignificant part].[18] Sebald emigrated to England and stayed there, after all, partly because he did not want to live in the Allgäu or indeed in Germany (like both of his sisters, incidentally, who left home early and settled in Switzerland, thereby continuing the Egelhofer tradition). Nonetheless, he did not give up his regional identity in order to 'pass' as an Englishman, as the elderly Dr Selwyn has done in *Die Ausgewanderten* (*The Emigrants*). His German retained the Allgäu accent it always had (quite different from his father's thick Bavarian accent), and he enjoyed speaking and corresponding with school friends in dialect, deploying it with considerable humour and self-irony. A story he told at the end of his life gives a sense of the peculiarly mixed feelings he maintained for his homeland. As a boy he had learnt to play the zither, a typical Allgäu instrument that his father appreciated but that he disliked and resolutely refused to play after three years of study. Nonetheless, when his grandfather lay on his deathbed in Sonthofen, he took the zither out of its case and played for him

> die paar Sachen [...] die mir nicht von Grund auf zuwider gewesen sind, zuletzt, wie ich noch weiß, einen langsamen Ländler in C-Dur, der mir beim Spielen bereits, so will es mir jetzt in der Erinnerung erscheinen, so zeitlupenhaft zerdehnt vorgekommen ist, als dürfte er nie ein Ende nehmen.

> [the few pieces I did not loathe from the bottom of my heart, ending, as I still remember, with a slow *ländler* in C major, which even as I played it, or so it appears to me now, seemed to be very long drawn out and to go on in slow motion as if it would never end.][19]

Acknowledgements

Much of the information contained in this chapter stems from W. G. Sebald's sister, Gertrud Aebischer-Sebald, who has patiently answered my questions about her brother's childhood. Without her invaluable recollections and insights, which I have tried as often as possible to corroborate through other sources, this essay could not have been written. Thanks go also to Professor Richard Sheppard, Sebald's former colleague at the University of East Anglia, who has generously helped me with advice and his own memories at every step.

Notes to Chapter 1

1. W. G. Sebald, *Nach der Natur: Ein Elementargedicht* (Frankfurt a.M.: Fischer, 1995), p. 76; W. G. Sebald, *After Nature*, trans. by Michael Hamburger (London: Hamish Hamilton, 2002), pp. 86–87.
2. *Nach der Natur*, p. 71; *After Nature*, pp. 81–82.
3. *Nach der Natur*, p. 72; *After Nature*, p. 82.
4. Eleanor Wachtel, 'Ghost Hunter', interview with W. G. Sebald, 16 October 1997, in *The Emergence of Memory: Conversations with W. G. Sebald*, ed. by Lynne Sharon Schwartz (New York: Seven Stories Press, 2007), pp. 37–61 (pp. 39–40); see also the interview with Steve Wasserman in the present volume, p. 370.
5. W. G. Sebald, *Die Ausgewanderten* (Frankfurt a.M.: Fischer, 1994), p. 117; W. G. Sebald, *The Emigrants*, trans. by Michael Hulse (London: Harvill, 1996), p. 80.
6. *Die Ausgewanderten*, p. 110; *The Emigrants*, p. 76.
7. W. G. Sebald, 'Es steht ein Komet am Himmel: Kalenderbeitrag zu Ehren des rheinischen Hausfreunds', in *Logis in einem Landhaus* (Munich: Hanser, 1998), pp. 11–41 (pp. 13–16). This essay includes several pictures of just such an almanac.
8. *Die Ausgewanderten*, p. 24; *The Emigrants*, p. 14.
9. *Die Ausgewanderten*, p. 24; *The Emigrants*, p. 14.
10. 'In Conversation with W. G. Sebald', in *Writers in Conversation with Christopher Bigsby*, 2 vols (Norwich: EAS Publishing / Pen&inc., 2001), II, 139–65 (p. 142).
11. W. G. Sebald, 'Le promeneur solitaire: Zur Erinnerung an Robert Walser', in *Logis in einem Landhaus*, pp. 127–68 (p. 137); W. G. Sebald, 'Le promeneur solitaire: A Remembrance of Robert Walser', trans. by Jo Catling, introduction to Robert Walser, *The Tanners*, trans. by Susan Bernofsky (New York: New Directions, 2009), pp. 1–36 (p. 8). Uncannily, but entirely in keeping with the 'logic' of coincidences he observed throughout his life, Sebald's own death on 14 December 2001 combines the date and month of Egelhofer's and Walser's deaths.
12. 'Le promeneur solitaire', p. 137; 'Le promeneur solitaire', trans. by Catling, pp. 8–9.
13. Wachtel, 'Ghost Hunter', p. 38.
14. 'Es steht ein Komet am Himmel', p. 21.
15. *Nach der Natur*, p. 98; *After Nature*, p. 112.
16. Wachtel, 'Ghost Hunter', p. 53.
17. On the subject of 'odds and ends / bits of string', see the interview with Gertrud Aebischer-Sebald by Ruth Vogel-Klein: '"Ein Fleckerlteppich": Interview with Gertrud Th. Aebischer-Sebald (March 2005)', in *W. G. Sebald: Mémoire. Transferts. Images / Erinnerung. Übertragungen. Bilder*, ed. by Ruth Vogel-Klein (= *Recherches Germaniques*, special issue 2 (2005)), pp. 211–20.
18. W. G. Sebald, 'Moments musicaux', in *Campo Santo*, ed. by Sven Meyer (Munich: Hanser, 2003), pp. 223–39 (pp. 225–26); W. G. Sebald, 'Moments musicaux', in *Campo Santo*, trans. by Anthea Bell (London: Penguin, 2005), pp. 188–205 (p. 191).
19. 'Moments musicaux', in *Campo Santo*, p. 228; 'Moments musicaux', in *Campo Santo*, trans. by Bell, p. 193.

Fig. 1.21. WGS transferred to the primary school (*Volksschule*) in Sonthofen in 1952 and spent roughly two years there. He was taught by Armin Mueller (1910–83), an outstanding teacher on whom Paul Bereyter in *Die Ausgewanderten* (*The Emigrants*) would later be loosely based. Mueller, the teacher of the fourth class when this photo was taken (Whitsun, 25 April 1954), is standing on the left. The man wearing a top hat is *Schulleiter* Schneider.
© Adolf Lipp (Sonthofen) (former friend and colleague of Mueller)

FIG. 1.22 (upper). WGS often spoke of his charismatic art teacher, Franz Meier. Meier taught in Oberstdorf 1959–76 and in the new *Gymnasium* in Sonthofen 1976–93. He studied at the *Kunstakademie* and the Ludwig-Maximilians-Universität, Munich. This photo was taken during a school visit to the Munich art galleries (1962–63). Second from the right is Barbette Aenderl, who died not long before WGS and whose family history he was intending to work into a book that he was planning. © Prof. Dr Rainer Galaske; courtesy of Heidi Nowak

FIG. 1.23 (lower). WGS described Franz Meier as someone who 'taught him how to see' and how to appreciate non-representational modern art. In this photograph (summer 1963), WGS (third from the left) is taking part in one of Herr Meier's art classes outside the school in Oberstdorf. © Prof. Dr Rainer Galaske; courtesy of Franz Meier

Fig. 1.24 (left). WGS giving a *Fasching* speech in the *Am Walten*, Sonthofen. © Prof. Dr Ursula Liebsch

Fig. 1.25 (below). *Fasching* in the Nebelhorn Hotel, Oberstdorf (February 1963). Gerhard Eschweiler is standing immediately behind the microphone, WGS to the right of it. His sister Gertrud is sitting third from the left in the front row. © Heidi Nowak

FIG. 1.26. WGS in his room in his parents' flat in Sonthofen (late 1963). According to Rainer Galaske (who got to know WGS in March 1961 when he joined the *Oberrealschule* in Oberstdorf and became one of his best friends), they had been listening to records by Joan Baez and Bob Dylan on the evening when this photo was taken. By this time WGS was already a student at the University of Freiburg im Breisgau. © Prof. Dr Rainer Galaske

CHAPTER 2

The Sternheim Years:
W. G. Sebald's *Lehrjahre* and
Theatralische Sendung 1963–75

Richard Sheppard

Man wird als Schriftsteller die Erfahrung machen, daß, je präziser, gewissen-
hafter, sachlich angemessener man sich ausdrückt, das literarische Resultat für
um so schwerer verständlich gilt, während man, sobald man lax und verant-
wortungslos formuliert, mit einem gewissen Verständnis belohnt wird.

[You will discover as a writer that the more precisely, conscientiously, dispassion-
ately you express yourself, the more incomprehensible the literary result will be
thought to be, whereas, as soon as you formulate your thoughts in a sloppy and
irresponsible way, you will be rewarded with a certain comprehension.]

THEODOR W. ADORNO, *Minima Moralia*[1]

'Well roared, Lion!'

SHAKESPEARE, *A Midsummer Night's Dream*

Freiburg (1963–1965)

On 15 July 1963 Max Sebald received his *Zeugnis der Reife* (equivalent to A-level
certificate) from the Catholic humanist Dr Eduard Beßler (1899–1974), headmaster
of the *Oberrealschule* in Oberstdorf (now the Gertrud-von-le-Fort Gymnasium),
southern Bavaria, after passing the *Abitur* as the third youngest member of his class[2]
(see Figures 2.1, 2.2, 2.3, and 2.4). His highest grades were in German and Music
('sehr gut' [A]).[3] One may feel that the accompanying report, probably written by
his class teacher, Dr (later Studienprofessor) Kurt Eberhard (1926–2005) (Figure
2.5),[4] was prophetically perceptive:

> Die rege Mitarbeit des Schülers im Unterricht, vor allem in Deutsch, wirkte
> vorbildlich auf die Klasse. Er bemühte sich stets, die aufgeworfenen Fragen zu
> durchdenken und in eine persönlich verfügbare Form zu bringen. Lobend zu
> erwähnen ist seine Teilnahme am Schulchor. Anerkennung verdient auch seine
> Mitarbeit bei der Laienspielgruppe der Schule. Seine stilistischen Fähigkeiten
> kamen ihm bei der Ausarbeitung der Schülerzeitung zustatten. Das Betragen
> des Schülers war sehr ordentlich.

> [The student's lively participation in lessons, especially German, had a model
> effect on the class. He invariably put a lot of effort into thinking through
> the questions under discussion and arriving at an answer that was generally

FIG. 2.1 (upper). WGS receiving his *Abitur* certificate from *Oberstudiendirektor* Eduard Beßler (1899–1974), Oberstdorf (15 July 1963). © Prof. Dr Ursula Liebsch

FIG. 2.2 (lower). The *Oberrealschule* in Oberstdorf (since July 1974 the Gertrud-von-le-Fort *Gymnasium*), c. 1960. © Helmut Bunk

FIG. 2.3 (upper). *Abiturfeier* (7 July 1963). WGS is in the centre to the right of the tree; his friend Rainer Galaske, the editor of the school magazine *Der Wecker*, stands (wearing glasses) just to the right of him; Barbette Aenderl (FIG. 1.22) stands third from the left of Dr Eberhard (see FIG. 2.5). © Heidi Nowak

FIG. 2.4 (lower). WGS (third from the right) with his classmates (11th class) at the *Burgsportfest* in Sonthofen (June 1961). His close friends Helmut Bunk, Rainer Galaske, Walter Kalhammer (1944–2006), Jürgen Kaeser, and Gerhard Eschweiler are, from right to left of the photo respectively: just to the left of WGS, second to the left of WGS, sitting at the front of the picture, at the very back of the picture, and fourth from the left of the picture. © Prof. Dr Rainer Galaske; courtesy of Dr Jürgen Kaeser

FIG. 2.5. Dr (later *Studienprofessor*) Kurt
Eberhard (1926–2005), who taught WGS
German and History in the *Oberstufe* at
Oberstdorf. © Prof. Dr Rainer Galaske;
courtesy of Heidi Nowak

comprehensible. His participation in the school choir deserves special mention,
as does his work with the amateur dramatics group. His ability to write stylish
German came into its own when he helped edit the school magazine. His
behaviour has been consistently very good.]

Max then studied German and English for four semesters at the Albert-Ludwigs-
Universität in Freiburg im Breisgau, from autumn 1963 to summer 1965[5] — a
period that would feature briefly in his first, unpublished, autobiographical novel.
He matriculated at Freiburg two months before the death of Walter Rehm (1901–
63), the Professor of Modern German Literature at Freiburg since 1943, at the end of
a period when the number of students studying *Germanistik* there had quadrupled,
from 300 in 1950 to 1200 in 1963, and the subject was attracting more and more
students who, like Max, were not from the traditional *Bildungsbürgertum*. The
Freiburg syllabus was expanding at that time to include such topics as Romanticism,
Naturalism, and early twentieth-century modernists like Brecht and Musil, and
there was some experimentation with new teaching methods.[6] Nonetheless his
time at Freiburg fell within a period when *Germanistik* was still dominated by ways
of thinking established during the classical period that involved sharp distinctions
between 'Kultur und Profanität, hoher Dichtung und niederer Schriftstellerei,
Bildungshierarchie und Pöbelgeschmack' [culture and profanity, elevated letters
and lowbrow wordsmithery, educational hierarchies and mob taste].[7] By 1963,
however, such concepts and polarities were starting to be questioned — a process
that was closely connected with the run-up to '1968' and the theoretical debates
about the nature of literature, literary criticism, and the value of literary studies
which continue today.[8] Max would have had no problem with the doctrine that the

FIG. 2.6. WGS began his studies at Freiburg im Breisgau in autumn 1963. In early 1964 he moved into the *Max-Heim* (Maximilianstraße 15), a student hostel for about thirty men. Here, he probably shared a room with Albrecht Rasche on the second floor that looked out over what was then an extensive back garden with a sequoia tree. The *Max-Heim* ceased to be a student residence in the mid-1960s and now houses a university institute. Its back garden has been drastically shortened to make way for new buildings. © Richard Sheppard (July 2005)

history of modernity was one of cultural decline. But his atypical social background (in his NESTA application (see note 49) Max would describe his family as 'petit-bourgeois') and lively interest in contemporary literature (European and American), literature and politics (Brecht), and popular counter-culture and film would have caused him to be sceptical of the concomitant idea that high art and elevated letters offered a refuge from modernity's encroachment through their participation in 'ein zeitenthobenes Reich des Geistes' [a transcendent realm of the spirit].[9] Although Max already had a developed interest in metaphysics and retained this throughout his life, he would have been uneasy with any critical discourse that sundered 'Geist und Leben' [spirit and life].[10]

Max spent his first semester at Freiburg in lodgings, and was tutored on Shakespeare by a slightly older student, Dietrich Schwanitz (1940–2004), who later became a maverick Professor of English at the University of Hamburg (1978–97) (see Figure 2.8) and a controversial novelist whose best-known work is *Der Campus* (1995). Schwanitz was probably drawn to Max partly because he was not a scion of the *Bildungsbürgertum*, either. He also helped Max obtain a room for his remaining three semesters at Freiburg in the small student hostel known as the *Max-Heim*, at Maximilianstraße 15, about a mile south of the University (Figures 2.6 and 2.7). When, in 1966, the residence was turned into the home of various university institutes, an article in the Freiburg student newspaper, probably by Schwanitz, characterized it as follows: 'Studenten und Studentenzeitung, Avantgardepoeten und

FIG. 2.7. WGS in the garden of the *Max-Heim* at Maximilianstraße 15, Freiburg im Breisgau (summer 1965). © Etta Schwanitz (née Uphoff)

FIG. 2.8. In November 1964, various residents of the *Max-Heim* and friends formed themselves into the 'Gruppe 64'. In this photo (1965) we see the group's four principal members: WGS, Etta Uphoff (later Schwanitz), Albrecht Rasche, and Dietrich Schwanitz (1940–2004). © Etta Schwanitz (née Uphoff) and Dr Albrecht Rasche

53

FIG. 2.9. Bernhard Holeczek (1941–94),
an art historian who later became the
Director of the Wilhelm-Hack Art
Museum in Ludwigshafen, was a fifth
member of the 'Gruppe 64' (though
this photo was taken two years earlier,
in 1962). Like WGS, Holeczek became
centrally interested in the role played
by chance in modern art, and in 1992
co-edited a catalogue entitled *Zufall als
Prinzip: Spielwelt, Methode und System
in der Kunst des 20. Jahrhunderts* (The
Principle of Coincidence: Play, Method,
and System in Twentieth-Century Art).
© Dr Irmtraut Holeczek

Fachschaften haben in manchem zurückliegenden Semester in der Maximilianstraße
ein Zentrum gehabt, in dem die Fäden von Anregung und Kritik, Planung und
Organisation zusammenliefen' [Students and student newspaper, avant-garde poets,
and groups of faculty student reps have, in many a bygone semester, had a centre in
the Maximilianstraße where various strands of inspiration and criticism, planning
and organization, could join together].[11] The intellectual atmosphere in the hostel
was so distinct that, by the start of winter semester (WS) 1964/65, the group around
Schwanitz was calling itself the 'Gruppe 64' (Figures 2.8 and 2.9). While at school,
Max had been one of a group of five sixth-formers who spent much time together
discussing literature, philosophy, music, politics, art, and so on (Figures 2.10, 2.11,
2.12, and 2.13), and the group in the *Max-Heim* must have filled the considerable gap
left in Max's life when that group dispersed after *Abitur*. It was here, in 1964, that
Max got to know the slightly older Albrecht (Albert) Rasche (now a distinguished
psychoanalyst; see Figure 2.8) and the future art historian and art museum director
Bernhard Holeczek (1941–94) (see Figure 2.9). In December 1964 an announcement
in the student newspaper, the *Freiburger Studenten-Zeitung*, proclaimed that Gruppe
64 had formally come into being on 21 November with the aim of discussing its
members' literary productions.[12] Despite this open-sounding invitation, however,
according to Rasche and a Sonthofen friend who visited Max there in summer
semester (SS) 1965, it was extremely difficult to gain entrée to the Group because
of the high-powered, even aggressive nature of its intellectual debates.

FIG. 2.10 (above). WGS, Lotte Küsters (now Prof. Dr Ursula Liebsch) and
Werner Braunmüller skiing on the Hahnsköpfle in the Kleinwalsertal
near Oberstdorf (c. March 1959). © Prof. Dr Ursula Liebsch

FIG. 2.11 (below). Class party (c. 1960). From left to right: Walter Kalhammer,
Helmut Bunk, WGS. © Helmut Bunk and Dr Jürgen Kaeser

FIG. 2.12 (upper). Class excursion, probably spring 1959. Left to right: Jürgen Kaeser, unidentified, K. H. Schmidt, WGS, Klaus Schilling, Friedemann Reich, Holger Börner, unidentified. © Dr Jürgen Kaeser

FIG. 2.13 (lower). In the summer, WGS, with a small group of his closest friends (Werner Braunmüller, Lotte Küsters (see FIG. 2.10), Jürgen Kaeser, Walter Kalhammer), used to go swimming in the Starzlachklamm, Winkel, in the mountains to the east of Sonthofen. (In FIG. 1.12, the Starzlachklamm is in the forest in the centre of the picture.) WGS was an excellent swimmer and in this photo (c. 1960) he and a friend are jumping from a high rock into the pool beneath. But the picture is proleptic in other ways since the image of flying through the air — either by choice as a gesture of freedom or involuntarily, like Walter Benjamin's Angel of History — recurs frequently in his literary work. © Prof. Dr Ursula Liebsch

From 1964, the *Max-Heim* group played an increasingly important part in the production of the *Freiburger Studenten-Zeitung*. Rasche first features as one of its editors in July 1964 and Schwanitz in November 1964; and in January 1965 Max, for the first and only time, is named, together with Rasche and Schwanitz, as responsible for its literary section. Rasche published poems there; Schwanitz published all manner of things (often pseudonymously); and between November 1964 and December 1965 Max published seventeen items there (one review, four prose pieces, and twelve poems, about which more will be said below; see also note 28), making him the second most frequent literary contributor after Schwanitz during that period.

Schwanitz was also an energetic proponent of amateur dramatics and probably encouraged Max, who had played the second guard in a school production of Anouilh's *Antigone* on 10–11 April 1962 (Figures 2.14 and 2.15), in the same direction when they became friends in autumn 1963.[13] While at Freiburg, Max would play the Cockney character Cocky in Eugene O'Neill's one-act drama *In the Zone* (1917) (Figure 2.16) when Schwanitz directed it in Freiburg's Studio-Bühne from 29 January to 5 February 1964. Max then played Snug the joiner / Lion in Shakespeare's *A Midsummer Night's Dream* when, in celebration of the 400th anniversary of its author's birth, it was staged in the Auditorium Maximum in Freiburg on 1 and 2 July 1964, with Etta Uphoff (see note 11) as a fairy, Rasche as Starveling, and Schwanitz as Bottom. Max went on to direct the first performance in Germany of J. P. Donleavy's *Fairy Tales of New York* (1961), in the Studio-Bühne on 9 and 12 July 1965. No reviews appeared in the local or student press, but one may speculate as to why Max was drawn to this at that time little-known work. Although set in modern-day New York, the play is inherently surreal, with three of the actors (of whom Rasche was one) playing several roles across its four acts. The play is an anti-*Pilgrim's Progress*, with Christian, its hero, undergoing various trials to arrive at a self-parodic, fairytale ending. The play's black humour involves a strong fascination with human mortality and folly, and it sharply satirizes the American dream. In Act III, for instance, Christian muses — as Max would do in his later works, particularly *Die Ringe des Saturn* — on the human and environmental damage that is done in the name of progress (in this case that caused by building the huge system needed to supply New York with water).

In comparison with the intellectual vitality of the *Max-Heim*, Max seems to have found the teaching at the university uninspiring — which may or may not help explain why he called his pet hamster 'Hegel'. Although he was able to study some of the modern American literature that had interested him at school (WS 1963/64; WS 1964/65; SS 1965), there seems to have been a fair smattering of routine courses on language and philology (e.g. 'English Pronunciation' (WS 1963/64), 'Translation from German into English' (WS 1963/64), 'English Intonation' (SS 1964), 'An Introduction to Middle-High German' (SS 1964), 'An Introduction to Old English' (SS 1964), 'Nithart von Reuenthal' (WS 1964/65)), and even when the material looks more promising *prima facie*, Max seems to have felt that it was, on the whole, taught in a restrictive and uninspiring way. He later recorded that he had attended a first-year seminar on E. T. A. Hoffmann's *Der goldene Topf* (*The Golden Pot*) and

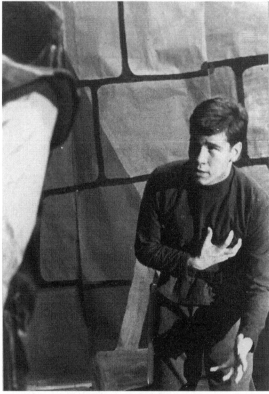

FIG. 2.14 (above). The production of Jean Anouilh's *Antigone* staged by the Oberrealschule Oberstdorf on 10 April 1962 in the Turnhalle, Oberstdorf, and in the Generaloberst-Beck-Kaserne, Sonthofen, on 11 April 1962. WGS, playing First Guard, is seated at the right of the picture. © Sigrid Neumeier

FIG. 2.15 (left). WGS playing First Guard. © Sigrid Neumeier

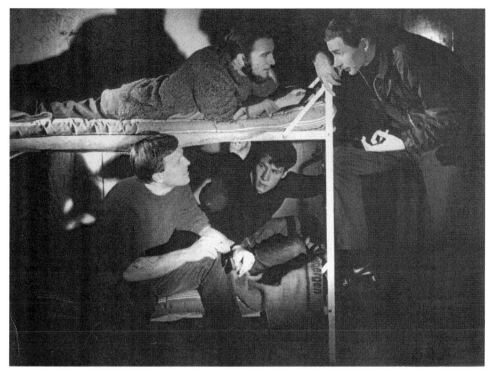

FIG. 2.16. WGS (bottom centre) playing Cocky in Eugene O'Neill's *In the Zone* (January–February 1964). The man on the left is an American called Bob Barcklow.
© Etta Schwanitz (née Uphoff) and Dr Albrecht Rasche

was disturbed to find that this 'strange tale' was being studied without any reference to the 'Realien' (historical events) of the immediately preceding epoch (i.e. the turmoils of the Napoleonic period, which he would come to regard as a major watershed in modern European history).[14]

But like so many other German students of their generation, the *Max-Heim* group began to discover the writings of Benjamin and the Frankfurt School and to use them as a critical corrective both to the classical, *geistesgeschichtlich* (history of ideas) approach to literature, and to the newer school of *werkimmanente Kritik*. Although its theoretical roots were firmly embedded in the aesthetics of German Idealism, *werkimmanente Kritik* was the post-1945 German equivalent of New Criticism and shared its central doctrine of the transcendent autotelicity of art. Thus Max would later write that the Jewish thinkers of the Frankfurt School helped him to understand the works of the neglected Johann Peter Hebel and gave him the means 'zur Erforschung der bürgerlichen Sozial- und Geistesgeschichte' [of exploring bourgeois social and cultural history] in general.[15]

The earliest theoretical works acquired by Max as a student were by Theodor W. Adorno, Walter Benjamin, Ernst Bloch, Max Horkheimer, and Herbert Marcuse: Etta Schwanitz recalls that Adorno's *Minima Moralia* was particularly important for the *Max-Heim* group.[16] The enduring importance of these authors for Max — who habitually disposed of books that he considered worthless — can be inferred from the fact that his library still contained many of their books, often densely annotated, at the time of his death.[17] Their significance for Max's entire work is crucial, with Benjamin probably overtaking the others in importance by the time Max became an established author.[18]

Equally importantly, Max's time at Freiburg coincided with the Auschwitz trials in Frankfurt (23 December 1963–19 August 1965). These made him increasingly aware of the enormity of the atrocities committed during the *NS-Zeit* (Third Reich) and of the extent to which these had been conveniently forgotten during the preceding two decades. In an interview of January 2001 he said:

> [The Auschwitz trials were] the first *public* acknowledgement that there was such a thing as an unresolved German past. There were daily one-page reports about that trial in the *Frankfurter Allgemeine Zeitung* for many months. I read these reports every day and they suddenly shifted my vision. I realized that there were subjects of much greater urgency than the writings of the German Romantics. I understood that I had to find my own way through that maze of the German past and not be guided by those in teaching positions at that time.[19]

The dates of the trials mesh with the dates when Max acquired many of the Frankfurt School texts listed in note 17, and as his reading developed his theoretical and historical consciousness, so the events in Frankfurt caused him increasingly to believe that the post-war German university system had been tacitly colluding in the cover-up which the Auschwitz trials were bringing to an end. Thus, in an interview of 1999 he stated:

> German colleges in those days were unreformed, completely overrun, undersourced. You would sit in lectures with 1,200 other people and never talk to your teachers. Libraries were practically nonexistent. [...] All my teachers had gotten jobs during the Brownshirt years and were therefore compromised, either because they had actually supported the regime or had been fellow travelers or otherwise been silent. But the strictures of academic discourse prevented me from saying what I wanted to say or even investigating the kinds of things that caught my eye. Everyone avoided all the kinds of issue that ought to have been talked about. Things were kept under wraps in the classroom as much as they had been at home. I found that insufficient.[20]

Such a generalization is of course, as Rasche agrees, far too extreme, notwithstanding the fact that, as Herrmann concedes, there was little public discussion at Freiburg University of the *NS-Zeit* or the behaviour then of the older generation of academics.[21] Rehm, for instance, had been an anti-Nazi humanist and occasionally spoke 'mit grimmiger Bitterkeit' [with fierce bitterness] about his colleagues at other universities who had been on the opposite side from him during the Third Reich.[22] Erich Ruprecht (see note 14), whom Etta Schwanitz recalls as 'unworldly' but of 'great integrity', was never a member of the NSDAP (National Socialist Party). Indeed, although he had trained and worked at Freiburg during the *NS-Zeit* and written his first doctoral thesis on the significance of myth in Wagner and Nietzsche (*Der Mythos bei Wagner und Nietzsche: Seine Bedeutung als Lebens- und Gestaltungsproblem* (1938)), the published version is completely untouched by National Socialist ideology and is dedicated to his own father, rather than to a prominent public personality. Finally, Herrmann, who paints a less extreme picture of the political record of Freiburg's Germanists,[23] singles out Joachim W. Storck (b. 1924), an *Assistent* of Rehm's who had left Freiburg just before Max matriculated, as a shining example of someone who felt obliged and able to react passionately 'auf alle NS-Spuren in Universität und Gesellschaft' [to all traces of Nazism in the University and society in general].[24] Nevertheless, in Max's estimation, the contextless study of literature, institutionalized non-communication, the mass rally style of teaching, the impossibility of raising certain questions with teachers who appeared to have a vested interested in silence, and poor research resources increasingly seemed to be ways of perpetuating an all-too-comfortable relationship with the recent past in the 'kleinen, feinen, eng mensurierten, bildungsbürgerlichen Nische' [the well-groomed, small-town refuge for rule-bound duelling students and scions of the classically educated upper middle classes] that was Freiburg.[25]

During Max's final term at Freiburg in summer semester 1965, Professor Ronald Peacock (1907–93), who had been the Henry Simon Professor of German at the University of Manchester until 1962, when he moved to Bedford College (University of London), spent six months at Freiburg standing in for the regular Professor of Modern German Literary History.[26] Max participated in his advanced seminar on European Drama of the 1890s (Hauptmann, Wedekind, Hofmannsthal, Wilde, Chekhov) and gave a paper entitled 'The Conflict of World-Views in Shaw's *Man and Superman*' which attracted a mark of 'sehr gut/ausgezeichnet' (A/A+). According to Etta Schwanitz, Max was particularly impressed by Peacock's 'more personal, less academic way of talking about literature' and evident belief in the free play of ideas. Conversely, Max so impressed Peacock that five years later he agreed to act as one of his three referees when he applied for an Assistant Lectureship in German at UEA:

> [Mr. Sebald] contributed a quite brilliant paper [... which covered] Shaw's attitude to various trends of thought around the turn of the century. It gave evidence of wide reading, complete command of philosophical ideas as expressed in literature, and incisive powers of description, interpretation and criticism.[27]

This first encounter with the arguably more relaxed approach to the study of literature, allowing Max to bring his extra-curricular intellectual activities to bear on his formal studies, can be seen as a major reason for Max's decision to come to England, where he remained for nearly thirty-five years.

Of the fourteen items that Max published in the *Freiburger Studenten-Zeitung*, four are particularly interesting.[28] The first, 'Gottes Rosenöl-Baum' (God's Perfumed Rose-Tree), a review of Georg Lukács's reissued two-part history of modern German Literature (*Skizze einer Geschichte der neueren deutschen Literatur*), shows that although Max was moving to the left in his thinking, he was critical of Stalinism and overtly politicized literature. The second item, 'Jeden Abend...' (Every Evening), a short prose piece whose ending directly recalls that of Kafka's *Der Proceß* (*The Trial*), deals with a protagonist who lives in a country where 'Melancholie und Schwermut' (melancholy and heaviness of soul) attract the severest penalties and so is forced to suppress these sides of himself. But he is denounced by a girl, arrested by executioners, and reaches the melancholic insight on the morning of his execution 'daß dies in seinem Leben wenig Unterschied mache, ob er tot sei oder nicht' [that it made little difference for his life whether he was dead or not]. As the melancholic side of Max's nature was all but unknown to his schoolfriends, this prose piece and his essay on Leonce and Jacques that he wrote in winter semester 1964/65 (see note 14) are noteworthy for being his first texts where it surfaces. The third item, 'Erinnertes Triptychon einer Reise aus Brüssel' (Remembered Triptych of a Journey from Brussels), a long free-verse poem about a train journey from Brussels to Basel, is much stronger than any of the other poems from Max's time at Freiburg and clearly anticipates *Nach der Natur* (*After Nature*) (1988) in its form. Given Max's later strident antipathy to Expressionism, the influence of the early Gottfried Benn is also surprisingly audible and the poem, like the last quatrain of Benn's early poem 'Untergrundbahn' ('Underground Train'), ends in the invocation of idyllic 'Südlichkeit' [sense of the warm south] on the Greek island of Santorini (which Max never visited). The fourth item, 'Erinnern' (Remembering), involves a character called Max and is a faintly surreal prose piece recalling an anxious journey.[29] Here again one can see in embryo a major topos of Max's fictional work of the 1990s: travel as a fearful descent into the unknown.

Fribourg (1965–1966)

In summer 1965, after a brief holiday in Italy with Rasche, Max took his first step away from Germany by moving to the much smaller and newer University of Fribourg in Catholic, French-speaking Switzerland: founded in 1889, by 1965 it comprised about five thousand students (Figure 2.17). Six factors seem to have played a part in this move: Fribourg had better facilities; he could live in the flat of his older married sister Gertrud at 11 rue de Lausanne, five minutes down the hill from the university (Figures 2.18 and 2.19); he could be less close to and less financially dependent on his parents; his teachers were politically untarnished; he could complete his degree course after six semesters (rather than the normal eight); and it is likely that he found the pre-modern town, with its proximity to mountains and unique concentration of undamaged medieval and Renaissance buildings, highly congenial (Figures 2.20 and 2.21). Certainly, Max was much more at home academically at Fribourg than he had been in Freiburg: he learnt to speak French; he responded more positively to his mentors; the seminars and courses look, *prima facie*, a lot more interesting; and he was not distracted by extra-curricular activities. So after one semester, on 3 March 1966, he presented a sixty-page typescript *mémoire de licence* (BA dissertation) entitled 'Zu Carl Sternheim: Kritischer Versuch einer Orientierung über einen umstrittenen Autor' (On Carl Sternheim: A Critical Attempt to Come to Terms with a Controversial Author) to the Philosophy Faculty. This enabled him to gain his *licence ès lettres* (*summa cum laude*) — equivalent to a first-class BA — in July 1966.[30]

During Max's studies in Fribourg (WS 1965/66; SS 1966) his professors were the philologist and medievalist Eduard Studer (1919–92), a Swiss national from Solothurn who taught at Fribourg from 1955 to 1988; James Smith (1904–72), the Professor of English, who taught there from 1947 to 1969; and the Germanist Ernst Alker (1895–1972), an Austrian who taught there from 1947 to 1969.[31] It is difficult

FIG. 2.17. The main entrance of the University of Fribourg (founded 1889).
© Richard Sheppard (April 2005)

FIG. 2.18. During his year in Fribourg,
WGS was able to stay with his sister
Gertrud and brother-in-law Jean-Paul in
their flat at 11, rue de Lausanne, not far
from the University.
© Richard Sheppard (April 2005)

FIG. 2.19. The view over the roofs of old Fribourg from the room WGS occupied at 11, rue de Lausanne (1966). © U. E. Sebald; courtesy of Gertrud Aebischer-Sebald

FIG. 2.20. Fribourg, Switzerland, a town of *c.* 35,000 inhabitants, has one of the biggest concentrations of medieval buildings in Europe. © unknown; courtesy of Richard Sheppard

FIG. 2.21. Photo taken by
WGS in 1965/66 of the
Rue de la Grande Fontaine,
Fribourg, in the old medieval
and Renaissance part of the
city. © U. E. Sebald; courtesy
of Gertrud Aebischer-Sebald

to assess the impact that Studer made on Max, but besides being a competent philologist and medievalist, he was a passionate local historian and antiquarian with an eye for the interestingly obscure and obscurely interesting, such as Max himself would develop in East Anglia.[32] Certainly, Gertrud had the clearest recollection of Studer's name when I talked to her at length in April 2005. Max also probably attended one or more of the following courses given in English by Smith: 'Shakespeare's *Cymbeline*' (WS 1965/66); 'The Poems of John Dryden' (WS 1965/66); 'Some Aspects of Jacobean Tragedy' (SS 1966); and '*Coriolanus*' (SS 1966). Of these, the courses on Shakespeare are the most likely since Smith's reputation as a lecturer on Shakespeare was considerable and Max's knowledge and understanding of Shakespeare are evident throughout his academic publications and, more subtly, in a number of his literary works.[33] By the time Max matriculated, Smith, 'alone responsible for all the literary teaching in an understaffed [English] department', was becoming increasingly overworked, worn down, and unhappy. An old-style Catholic, he was also becoming unhappy with the Roman Church as it existed after the reforms instigated by the Second Vatican Council (11 October 1962–8 December 1965).[34] Smith's increasingly dark frame of mind is perhaps reflected in the subject matter of his lecture courses at the time, and even at this early stage of Max's life it is not impossible that that part of his disposition which was prone to melancholia may have responded to this aspect of Smith.

But Max almost certainly had the greatest affinity with Alker and definitely attended at least two of his following courses: the history of post-Expressionist German literature (WS 1965/66; SS 1966); the beginnings of the German novel (WS 1965/66; SS 1966); Schiller (WS 1965/66); the comedies of Hofmannsthal with special reference to *Der Schwierige* (WS 1965/66) and a seminar on selected chapters from Thomas Mann's *Felix Krull* (SS 1966). According to Bruno Stephan Scherer, Alker had been a vocal anti-Nazi since the 1920s and rejected all forms of nationalism and racism. His essay on *Blut und Boden-Literatur* (blood and soil literature), published in the Catholic journal *Hochland* in 1935, had given currency to the derogatory concept of 'Blubo-Literatur' and provoked violent denunciations in the Nazi press.[35] Scherer also records that Alker, unlike the anti-Nazi Germanists in Freiburg, had experienced political exile from 1934 to 1942 (when he worked as a German *Lektor* at the University of Lund in Sweden), from 1942 to 1946 (when he occupied the same position at the Stockholm Handelshochschule), and in Fribourg from 1947 until his death.[36]

Alker was also a devout, but liberal-minded Catholic, and Scherer's characterization suggests other reasons why Max may well have seen him as a kindred spirit, a role model even. He believed that literature should be studied in its social context, albeit not exclusively so; he was deeply critical of modern materialism and extreme forms of capitalism and Communism alike; and he had no time for narrow, sectarian dogmatism. He treated colleagues, students, and other people in general with a mixture of helpfulness, courteous respect, and old-world Viennese charm. He had an excellent and sophisticated sense of humour: he loved *bons mots*, telling anecdotes, and the witty, hard-hitting turn of phrase, and, realizing that 'wit and irony create distance',[37] he was well known around the University for his ability to deliver the ironic, even sarcastic riposte: Max, too, is remembered by many colleagues, students and friends for just such characteristics. According to Scherer, '[sein] Humor [...] half ihm [Alker], den Zusammenbruch des Donaureiches und andere minder tragische Konflikte zu bestehen' [(his) sense of humour helped him to cope with the collapse of the Austro-Hungarian Empire and other, less tragic conflicts].[38] In similar vein, Max told a Reutlingen audience on 12 December 1990, after a reading of *Schwindel. Gefühle. (Vertigo)*, that in his fiction he sought to intersperse humorous episodes with passages dealing with periods of 'seelische[n] Anfechtungen' (great spiritual trouble).[39]

Nor can it be any coincidence that Alker was a much-published specialist in nineteenth-century German literature with a particular interest in Keller, Stifter, and those writers of the declining Habsburg Empire (Schnitzler, Rilke, Hofmannsthal, Musil, Kraus, Kafka, Werfel, Roth, Broch, Doderer) whose childhood and youth, as Scherer put it, 'und somit die wesentlichen Quellen ihres Werks noch tief im alten Österreich steckten, von den Autoren des 19. Jahrhunderts zu schweigen, deren Werke allerdings den Schatten des Finis Austria warfen' [were still deeply rooted in the older Austria, not to mention those nineteenth-century writers whose works already foreshadowed the end of the Austro-Hungarian Empire].[40] Max's childhood was rooted in an older, disappearing, Catholic Bavaria, geographically close to Austria; he was drawn to precisely those areas of Austrian literature that interested Alker; *Logis in einem Landhaus* resonates with a nostalgia for a lost world of certainties; and his literary imagination, fed *inter alia* by Benjamin's philosophy of history (note 17), is full of the shadows that fall when a *heile Welt* (intact world) collapses in on itself (Figure 2.22).

As mentioned above, a major outcome of Max's year in Fribourg was his *mémoire* on the dramatist Carl Sternheim, 'Zu Carl Sternheim: Kritischer Versuch einer Orientierung über einen umstrittenen Autor'. His school record, his participation

FIG. 2.22. A Sunday afternoon walk (*c.* 1948) on the outskirts of Wertach. The photo
was probably taken from Enthalb der Ach (now built over) since the mountain called the
Reuterwanne can be seen very clearly in the background. The toddler in the foreground
is W. G. Sebald's elder sister, Gertrud. The photo graphically illustrates the idyllic landscape
amidst which he grew up and which, in later years, he would frequently contrast with the
horrors of the *NS-Zeit* and the depredations suffered by so much of the rest of Germany
in the immediate post-war years. © The Estate of W. G. Sebald

in a seminar on modern American drama at Freiburg (WS 1963/64), his taste for
amateur dramatics, and his response to Peacock's teaching indicate that he had a
developed interest in modern drama when he arrived at Fribourg. But his particular
interest in Sternheim probably had three catalysts. First, the multi-volume edition
of Sternheim's work, edited by Wilhelm Emrich, that began appearing in 1963;
second, the wave of interest in expressionist art and literature that followed the
groundbreaking Marbach exhibition of 1960; and third, Alker's survey course
on modern literature. Accordingly, the bibliography of thirty-seven books (pp.
58–60) includes the Emrich edition and fourteen recent publications dealing with
Expressionism and expressionist drama; moreover, Alker's history of German
literature from 1832 to 1914 identifies precisely those flaws in Sternheim's work
on which Max would focus in his *mémoire*.[41] Alker commented on Sternheim's
indecisiveness over matters of class; his 'schablonenhafte Figuren' [stereotyped
characters] with 'ihre krampfhaft zurechtgestutzte Substantiv-Sprache (halb abge-
hackter preußischer Offiziersjargon, halb französiertes Übersetzungsdeutsch)' [their
contorted, artificially constructed noun-based speech (half the staccato jargon of
Prussian officers, half badly translated, frenchified German)]; the tedious 'Inkon-
sequenz' [inconsequentiality] of his allegedly satirical plays; his inability to create
a plot and characters that were believable; the deep ambivalence of Sternheim's

comedy *Die Schule von Uznach oder Neue Sachlichkeit* (*The School in Uznach or New Objectivity*) (1926); and the gulf that separated him in reality from the Expressionists with whom convention had aligned him.

Although Max's *mémoire* developed Alker's critique, its methodology, using the leverage supplied by the Frankfurt School, was less impressionistic and more ideological. Accordingly, the bibliography includes Benjamin's *Illuminationen* (*Illuminations*) and *Ursprung des deutschen Trauerspiels* (*The Origin of German Tragic Drama*; see note 17) together with Lukács's 1909 essay 'Zur Soziologie des modernen Dramas' ('Towards the Sociology of Modern Drama') and book of essays on the sociology of literature that had appeared in 1961.[42] Moreover, Benjamin's *Einbahnstraße* (*One-Way Street*), plus the second volume of Adorno's three-volume *Noten zur Literatur* (*Notes on Literature*; see note 17) and *Jargon der Eigentlichkeit* (*The Jargon of Authenticity*) are mentioned in footnotes on pages 23, 2, and 40 of the *mémoire* respectively.[43] So, although the *mémoire* begins by acknowledging the dangers of vulgar Marxism, it also states that Sternheim's work involves profound contradictions for which *werkimmanente Kritik*, with its stress on formal unity, cannot account and which become comprehensible only through the application of sociological, psychological, and biographical criteria (p. 1).[44]

The *mémoire* puts Sternheim into an ideological perspective by using two aspects of Lukács's assessment of modern drama. On the one hand, Lukács argues that because modern drama lacks 'das Festliche, das Religiöse' [the festal, the religious dimension] and has to make do with 'dem Amüsanten' [the merely amusing], its didactic aims are doomed to flatness and superficiality.[45] But on the other, Lukács hails the best new drama as the 'Drama des Individualismus, und dies mit einer Kraft, einer Intensität und Ausschließlichkeit, wie es ein Drama noch niemals gewesen ist' [drama of individualism, and this with a power, intensity, and focussed exclusivity such as drama has never known before].[46] Within this polarity, Max's critique of Sternheim runs as follows. Wilhelmine Germany was marked by contradictions between 'eine abstrakte, künstlich geschaffene Staatsidee' [an abstract, artificially created idea of the state] and a 'gänzliche ideologische Ratlosigkeit' [total lack of ideological direction] (p. 5), and between 'dem äußerlichen Glanz und Pomp des Reiches und seiner tatsächlichen Substanz' [the superficial glitter and pomp of the Second Reich and its actual reality] (p. 6). Inspired by Nietzsche's philosophy (p. 9), dissident Wilhelmine intellectuals who sought to resolve these contradictions often espoused a radical individualism that in Max's view — and here he goes beyond Lukács — was tantamount to an 'immoralism' (p. 9). But in Sternheim's 'comedies of bourgeois life' this immoralism was perverted into an amoral indifference which seduced the playwright into such a complicity with the morality of the bourgeois who feature in his plays that he ended up by glorifying that very class whose failings he apparently wished to expose (pp. 9–10). So, because they lack the 'ethische Gebundenheit' [real ethical commitment] (p. 14) which, in Lukács's estimation, can derive only from a religious consciousness, Sternheim's comedies cannot be regarded as 'Vehikel eines sozialpolitischen Evangeliums' [vehicles of a socio-political gospel] (p. 10), and fall into the gulf that separates (ethically directed) satire from (amoral/formalistic) art for art's sake (p. 23). Where true satire should use rigid, absolute, and uncompromising criteria to test 'die Realität auf ihre Realität' [the reality of reality] (p. 28), Sternheim's would-be satires are reluctant to judge and naively indifferent to ethics. Thus his aggressiveness becomes a 'ziellose [...] Geste' [pointless gesture], 'schiere[r] Zynismus' [sheer cynicism] (p. 29), and his characters are nothing more than two-dimensional stereotypes (pp. 47–48). Echoes of Alker's case against Sternheim are unmistakeable; further echoes are found in Max's discussion of Sternheim's language. But Max has learnt from Adorno and Benjamin that linguistic inadequacies, particularly the reified jargon that, following Alker, he found in Sternheim's plays, point to a deeper malaise that is related, in an as yet unspecified way, to more complex socio-political problems.

It is not the task of this chapter to examine whether Max's case is tenable, and in any case the validity of the argument is, perhaps, not of great importance when one remembers that one is dealing with an ambitious BA dissertation by a 21-year-old student. Right or wrong, the *mémoire* is impressive for a passionate but controlled sense of moral anger that is absent from Lukács's bloodless theorizing about drama and Alker's cursory dismissal of Sternheim. The same affective charge, once tempered by irony and more judiciously directed, would become a major driving force behind Max's literary and polemical works of the 1990s.[47] For these latter are critiques of a post-Christian world that has come off its hinges, in which megalomaniacs like Napoleon and Hitler are exalted and enabled to do 'untold' damage to the humble and meek.

But it is worth asking why Max expends such anger on so minor a target as Sternheim. Partly, I imagine, because of Emrich's status within the contemporary academic establishment (p. 55), partly because the study of Sternheim in the 1960s did not involve reading and evaluating reams of secondary literature (a task that never appealed to Max), and partly because 'Sternheim' was to some extent a metonym for 'Prussia': that northern, Protestant Germany from which Max was anxious, even then, to dissociate himself.[48] But the *mémoire* also suggests three other, weightier reasons. On page 41 Sternheim is accused of 'eine spielhafte Reduzierung des Wirklichen' [a playful miniaturization of reality] and of trivializing the 'Erschütterung, die der Literatur zu Beginn unseres Jahrhunderts widerfahren ist' [shattering experience that befell literature at the beginning of our century]: Max would spend much of his life as a critic accusing post-1945 German literature of continuing down this road. Then again, it seems to me that the anger of the *mémoire* is directed not just at Sternheim and his class, but also at Max's parents' class — the *petite bourgeoisie* of the 1920s — because of its own 'lack of ideological direction' and 'real ethical commitment' when faced with the rise of Nazism.[49] Finally, on page 33 of the *mémoire*, Max, like Alker, distinguishes between the respective linguistic experimentation of Sternheim and the Expressionists. But he takes Alker's ideas further by associating Expressionism with the 'profunde Sprachverzweiflung, von der Art wie sie Hofmannsthal [...] in seinem Chandos-Brief beschrieben hat' [kind of profound despair over language that Hofmannsthal described in his Chandos letter]. Where, Max argues, Sternheim is simply playing with the nihilism that plagued early modernism, Hofmannsthal is struggling to find a way through it via his *alter ego* Lord Chandos. Allusions to Hofmannsthal's Chandos letter ('Ein Brief') occur throughout his work right up to *Austerlitz*, whose protagonist undergoes a crisis that is a replay of that of Chandos. As I have shown elsewhere, Max had a very developed proleptic sense such that the concerns of his critical work from the 1970s onwards prefigure those of his later literary work.[50] So at this point in the *mémoire* we are touching on a very deep reason for Max's angry rejection of Sternheim: the latter's perceived refusal to confront the 'Leere' [emptiness] and 'Starre' [inner frigidity] that were major symptoms of depersonalized, secularizing modernity as described by Lukács in the essay cited above (pp. 286–88) and are a constant concern in Max's life and work.[51]

Manchester (1966–1968)

As the Senate minutes of the University of Manchester for 23 February and 17 March 1966 record, Max Sebald was appointed as an Assistant (*Lektor*), initially for the academic year 1966–67, at a salary of £824 per annum.[52] Professor Ruedi Keller, who oversaw language teaching in Manchester's German Department at the time, tells me that Manchester never advertised for *Lektoren* or looked for them via the DAAD (German Academic Exchange Service): 'Our usual method of recruitment was by recommendations from German colleagues. We had especially close relations with Erlangen and most of our Assistants came from there.'[53] So it is not obvious what brought Max to England, and when he fictionalized his Manchester experiences in 'Max Aurach' / 'Max Ferber' in *Die Ausgewanderten* (*The Emigrants*) he would merely say that 'verschiedene Erwägungen' (various considerations) had determined his choice.[54] But, as discussed in Chapter 1, *Wanderlust* was part of Max's make-up, and emigration part of his family history: his mother's three older siblings, Annie, Fanny, and Josef (Joe) (see Figure 1.15), had all moved to New York in the mid-1920s to escape the poverty of the rural Allgäu. Moreover, Professor Tabbert (see note 18) told me in a letter of 7 April 2005 that Max wanted to get a paid job for the sake of financial independence and to acquire a higher degree (i.e. a Manchester MA) as rapidly as possible (a full-time *Magisterarbeit* at a German-speaking university would have taken two years). Nevertheless, given the idyllic nature of the Allgäu, the rural locations of small-town Freiburg and Fribourg, and the fact that Max, like the narrator of one of his stories, had hardly ever been much further away from home than a five- or six-hour train journey (cf. *Die Ausgewanderten*)[55] apart from a brief visit to London in 1962 or 1963, his choice of a metropolitan university like Manchester is strange. Thirty-five years later, Max would tell Chris Bigsby that his application to Manchester derived from his positive encounter with (the unnamed) Professor Peacock, and Peacock's reference of 22 April 1970 (see note 27) supports this claim, for it indicates that he had followed Max's post-Freiburg career with interest and even read his Sternheim book. So Max seems to have sought his advice about jobs in England, discovered how Manchester employed German *Lektoren*, and applied on spec.[56] (Whether he knew anything about Manchester when he did so is a question to which still I do not have the answer.)

Max registered with the Manchester police on 13 September 1966, but he did not, as 'Max Aurach' / 'Max Ferber' suggests, spend his first six months living in

FIG. 2.23. The Arosa Hotel, situated at the junction of Wilmslow Road and Mauldeth Road, Withington. Although the narrator of 'Max Aurach' / 'Max Ferber' spends his first six months in Manchester living in the Hotel Arosa, WGS did not in fact live there. However, from January 1967 he would have passed the hotel on his way to the University from Didsbury by bus. The hotel was demolished in *c.* 1998/99 and replaced by a new housing development called Arosa Court which bears the plaque 'Arosa Court 1999'.
© Ken Whittaker (1968)

FIG. 2.24.
12 Ferndene Road, Withington, Manchester. WGS lived here for a few weeks in September 1966.
© Richard Sheppard (July 2005)

FIG. 2.25. 25 Stockton Road, Chorlton-cum-Hardy, Manchester. WGS lived here from October to December 1966.
© Richard Hibbitt (August 2009)

the Arosa Hotel (Figure 2.23). His first lodgings, probably found via the University's Accommodation Office, was a single room in 12 Ferndene Road, Withington, one of a row of semi-detached houses from the 1930s that seems to have been owned by a Jewish refugee called van Perlstein (Figure 2.24). Friends who visited him there shortly after his arrival remember that the landlady was very concerned 'to keep everything bolted and barred', and confirms that his room was at that time as dismal as the fictional Hotel Arosa.[57] So within a couple of weeks Max moved westwards — to 25 Stockton Road, Chorlton-cum-Hardy, three miles south-west of the city centre (Figure 2.25).[58] This house is a tall, narrow, dark three-storey building that was constructed as one of a pair in 1902, and Max's new room seems to have been no great improvement. At that time, it had only one window and so was dark, dingy, and freezing cold; the furniture consisted only of a bed, table, and chair, and at night mice would run along the curtain-rail!

The acute culture shock and sense of isolation that Max suffered during his first term at Manchester could not have been helped by his Baudelairean/Benjaminian *flâneries* through scenes of slum clearance and urban decay (Figures 2.26 and 2.27) or by his reading of Michel Butor's *L'Emploi du temps* (*Passing Time*).[59] Max's low spirits help to explain why he was particularly drawn to what Professor David Blamires (see Figures 2.32 and 2.33), who had taught at Manchester since 1960 ('just

FIG. 2.26. Slum clearance in Manchester (1966/67).
© W. G. Sebald; courtesy of the Estate of W. G. Sebald

FIG. 2.27. Derelict factories in Manchester (1966/67).
The chimneys bear a strange resemblance to the columns of an
ancient temple. © W. G. Sebald; courtesy of the Estate of W. G. Sebald

before the time when smokeless zones started making an extraordinary difference to the quality of the air and public buildings were cleaned'), aptly called the 'idiosyncratic and skewed', 'neo-Dickensian' aspects of the city that would feature in 'Max Aurach' / 'Max Ferber'.[60] Objectively, the ruinous cityscapes described by Max were disappearing thanks to the Manchester Development Plan that had been approved in 1961 by the Ministry of Housing and Local Government. Subjectively, such unwonted scenes became the correlatives of his inner sense of melancholy, alienation, and exile in a strange land. Tabbert, too, speaks of Max's melancholy at that time and even recalls him saying that at times he felt close to madness. Tabbert also confirms that during the same period Max identified strongly with Hölderlin the homeless wanderer,[61] and this explains why, when he came to muse on his melancholic peregrinations through the desolate leftovers of nineteenth-century Manchester in *Nach der Natur* (*After Nature*), the relevant passage (3. IV) would be cast in a metre that recalls Hölderlin:

> Viel bin ich damals
> über die brachen elysäischen
> Felder gegangen und habe das Werk
> der Zerstörung bestaunt[62]

> [Oft[en] at that time
> I rambled over the fallow
> Elysian Fields, wondering
> at the work of destruction...].

Compare the opening lines of Hölderlin's 'Der Main' ('The River Main'):

> Wohl manches Land der lebenden Erde möcht
> Ich sehn, und öfters über die Berg enteilt
> Das Herz mir[63]

> [Oh many a land of the living would
> I see, and often, over the mountains,
> My heart speeds from me].

The relationship between the two poems is, however, a highly ironic one. Hölderlin, the 'heimatloser Sänger' (homeless singer or bard) of the second poem, goes on to yearn for a mythicized Greece and the idealized, hospitable riverscapes of his fatherland. In *Nach der Natur* Max, in chosen exile from a fatherland of which he was becoming increasingly critical, goes on to recall the heaped-up wreckage and forgotten suffering of what Disraeli had called:

> die wundervollste
> Stadt der Neuzeit [...],
> ein himmlisches Jerusalem,
> dessen Bedeutung allein die Philosophie
> zu ermessen vermöge.

> [the most wonderful city of modern times,
> a celestial Jerusalem
> whose significance only philosophy
> could gauge.]

FIG. 2.28 (left). Reinbert Tabbert outside 26 Kingston Road, Didsbury, Manchester (1967).
© W. G. Sebald; courtesy of Prof. Reinbert Tabbert
FIG. 2.29 (right). 26 Kingston Road, Didsbury, in the late 1960s. © U. E. Sebald

It had been built:

> an den Ufern
> des Irk und des Irwell, jener
> jetzt toten mythischen Flüsse,
> die schillernd zu besseren Zeiten
> geleuchtet haben azurblau,
> karminrot und giftig grün[64]

> [on the banks
> of the Irk and the Irwell, those
> mythical rivers now dead,
> which [iridescent] in better times
> shone azure blue,
> carmine red and [poison] green].

On 14 January 1967, Max and another, older *Lektor*, Reinbert Tabbert (Figure 2.28) (see note 18), moved into the more spacious ground-floor flat of 26 Kingston Road in 'leafy Didsbury' (Figures 2.29 and 2.30), a more upmarket suburb where many university staff lived.[65] As Tabbert confirms, Max, who had found their new accommodation, cheered up considerably, and the sombre descriptions of Max that mark Tabbert's letters to his fiancée during the previous term cease.[66] Being the property of two architects called Peter and Dorothy Jordan, the house had

FIG. 2.30 (left). WGS standing in front of 26 Kingston Road, Didsbury (spring 1967).
© Sigrid Neumeier

FIG. 2.31 (right). View over Didsbury Park (1967/68)
from the upper floor of 26 Kingston Road. © The Estate of W. G. Sebald

been modernized and made really habitable; to the back it overlooked Didsbury Park (Figure 2.31); and Max, who liked a well-appointed house, could indulge his enthusiasm for cooking.[67]

Now settled, on 16 March 1967 Max completed the unpublished (and untitled) novel that he had begun during the previous autumn. Tabbert, who read the corrected typescript, heard him read extracts and wrote to his fiancée on 31 October 1966: 'Er wird großartig, hat die Farbigkeit der Blechtrommel, ist aber reicher an geistreichen Reflexionen, und statt durch Derbheit zeichnet er sich durch Anmut und Melancholie aus' [It's going to be great, it's got all the colour of the *Tin Drum*, but it involves much more witty reflection, and it's distinguished not by coarseness but by grace and melancholy].[68] Elsewhere, Tabbert says that the novel deals with two of the final days of a period of study in Freiburg, followed by a journey that takes the protagonist, Josef, to his girlfriend in Switzerland and his parents in the Allgäu. The text is interwoven with recollections of the protagonist's childhood and a short stay in Belgium and includes a short manuscript continuation dealing with Freiburg's old university library. This, claims Tabbert, 'liest sich wie eine Vorstudie zu der Beschreibung der neuen Pariser Nationalbibliothek gegen Ende des Romans *Austerlitz*' [reads like a preliminary study for the depiction of the new Bibliothèque nationale in Paris that occurs towards the end of the novel *Austerlitz*]. Etta Schwanitz, who is familiar with two versions of the text, adds that

FIG. 2.32. A German Department meeting, Manchester (1967). Left to right: WGS,
Professor Ruedi Keller, Dr Stan Kerry, Dr (later Professor) David Blamires,
Professor Idris Parry (1916–2008), Dr (later Professor) Peter Skrine.
© Dr Wolf Dieter Ortmann and John Gibbons

the Freiburg section contains a vivid and instantly recognizable picture of life in
the *Max-Heim*.[69]

The Manchester German Department was clearly very congenial, and by British
standards of the time, lively and progressive (Figures 2.32 and 2.33). Someone who
studied German there from 1965 to 1969 and was taught by Max describes these
years as 'the golden days of German at Manchester',[70] and Professor Eda Sagarra,
who taught German there at the time (Figure 2.34), paints the following picture of
the period just before Max's arrival:

> Among Mancunian Germanists [...] Ronald Peacock must have a particular
> place, and not alone for the brilliance of his research. During his distinguished
> tenure of the Henry Simon Chair [of German] from 1945 to 1962, he had, as
> his colleague and friend, one of the most distinguished of French Scholars,
> the Russian-born Eugène Vinaver. Together they made Manchester a leading
> centre, not just of their own disciplines, but of what was, in effect, Comparative
> Literature. Ronald was a man of many parts. [...] A literary scholar possessing
> the nature of an artist, it was he who ensured German linguistics the place
> it holds in Manchester today. He did so by appointing the Swiss linguist, R.
> E. Keller [see Figure 2.32] to a lectureship in the early 1950s. A decade later
> Ronald was successful in securing a second chair for German, to which in
> due course Ruedi Keller was appointed. Manchester thus became, along with
> Oxford and Glasgow, one of the very few departments in Britain at that time
> where German studies had such a profile.[71]

When Max arrived, the core of the syllabus was, as elsewhere, the canon of German
literature, with the twentieth-century course concentrating on 'Kafka, Thomas
Mann, Brecht, Trakl *et al.*'.[72] But Professor Blamires writes that the late Professor

FIG. 2.33. Party at 8 Clothorn Road, Didsbury, Manchester (1966/67).
Left to right: Dr (later Professor) David Blamires, WGS, Dr (later Professor) Ray Furness.
© Dr Wolf Dieter Ortmann

Idris Parry (1916–2008) (see Figure 2.32), Peacock's successor, 'brought a more imaginative approach to literary texts' and was centrally interested in 'people like Rilke, Hesse, Canetti, Hofmannsthal'.[73] The combination of a liberal atmosphere, wide-ranging syllabus, and congenial flat must have made Max want to stay for a second year and realize his intention, expressed to Tabbert in October 1966, of writing a part-time MA thesis there as quickly as possible. So on 25 May 1967 the Senate minutes record his reappointment for 1967–68.[74]

Professor Tabbert recalls that Max was invited to the homes of four or five permanent members of staff during his first year in Manchester, and Professor Sagarra remembers him being on 'warm and friendly terms with the younger members of staff'.[75] But apart from Tabbert, no one has very clear recollections of Max during that first year. Professor Blamires remembers him as 'a likeable, reliable colleague' and regarded him as a 'fairly private person with a lot going on inside him', but had no knowledge of 'what he did with himself outside the department'.[76] Professor Keller remembers him as 'a very pleasant, interesting, thoughtful young man, newly married and obviously concerned and perhaps uncertain about a future career'.[77] Professor Raymond Furness (see Figure 2.33), a specialist in twentieth-century literature with a self-confessed predilection for the 'off-beat, outré and stuff outside the "canon"', possibly — notwithstanding his enthusiasm for Wagner — had a greater intellectual affinity with Max than anyone else in the German Department.[78] But even he writes:

> I was bogged down in domesticity, paternity, wheeling my infant son through Fog Lane Park in the rain and didn't see a great deal of Max socially. He wasn't one for going to bars, wasn't into lunch-time boozing, I remember. He used to visit junk shops in Manchester and snapped up some interesting things [...]. Max lived in a handsome flat overlooking Didsbury Park but didn't entertain a great deal.[79]

FIG. 2.34. Party at 8 Clothorn Road, Didsbury (1966/67). Left to right:
Dr (later Professor) Eda Sagarra; Professor Albert Sagarra (1917–2008),
petrochemist, polymath, and authority on things maritime; WGS.
© Dr Wolf Dieter Ortmann

In October 1967 (i.e. just after Max, now married, had moved to a more spacious, top-floor flat in the same Didsbury house), Martin Durrell joined the German Department and also set up home in Didsbury. But, he recalls, it was not until Max's second stay in Manchester (see below) that he and his wife used to go out for a drink with him 'fairly regularly', usually at the Old Cock in Didsbury.[80] So overall, one is left with the impression that Tabbert, who, like Schwanitz and Rasche in Freiburg, was some years older than Max and with whom Max used to take all his meals 'except on the one day when both Max and I had to work without a break at the university', had been Max's major source of companionship, at least until Tabbert's return to Germany in July 1967 to complete his doctorate.[81]

According to *Die Ringe des Saturn* (*The Rings of Saturn*), Max soon also got to know Dr Stanley Sephton Kerry, the longest-serving member of the German Department apart from the two professors,[82] and former colleagues confirm that Max's portrait of him in Part VII of that work catches something of the original (Figure 2.35; see also Figure 2.32).[83] Kerry was born on 29 September 1923, served in the Army between 1943 and 1946, studied German (Honours) and Russian (Subsidiary) at Manchester, and graduated with a first in 1947: Professor Keller remembers that Peacock 'regarded him as one of his most brilliant students'. Kerry was an Assistant Lecturer at Manchester from 1948 to 1951, a Lecturer from 1951 to 1961, and a Senior Lecturer from 1961 until his death during the night of 16–17 February 1980. While an Assistant Lecturer, Kerry began a doctoral thesis on Schiller's aesthetics which he submitted in 1957. The external examiner, Professor Elizabeth Wilkinson (1909–2001) of University College London, for many years the doyenne of classical German studies, regarded it very highly and in 1961 it was published by Manchester University Press as *Schiller's Writings on Aesthetics*. But thereafter Kerry's 'brilliance

FIG. 2.35. Dr Stanley Sephton Kerry (1923–80)
(1966/67). A fictionalized description of
Dr Kerry is to be found in *Die Ringe des
Saturn* (Eichborn), pp. 230–33;
The Rings of Saturn (Harvill), pp. 185–87.
© Dr Wolf Dieter Ortmann

of mind never led to publications' even though he also had developed interests in
Goethe and Thomas Mann, and he seems to have devoted an increasing amount of
time to the study of all things Japanese.[84]

Kerry died unexpectedly of an undiagnosed heart condition at almost exactly
the same age as Max (56), and no one who knew the two of them finds it hard to
understand why Max should have remembered him so vividly. First, like Max, he
was a 'loner'. Colleagues describe him as 'nervous', 'taciturn', 'helpful and friendly,
if rather reserved and withdrawn', a 'rather shy, but friendly person [who] did his
teaching very conscientiously, but didn't spend more time in the department than
he had to'. After Kerry's death, Professor Blamires wrote in his diary that he was
'a loyal, conscientious colleague and friend, gentle, considerate, tactful, subtle-
minded, willing to give the benefit of the doubt. I don't think I ever heard him say
a nasty word about anyone'. Professor Blamires also noted that

> everyone who knew him was stunned at the loss [...] since Stan was one of
> those understanding, undemanding people to whom colleagues felt they could
> easily turn for quiet friendship and support. [...] The funeral was very well
> attended, with colleagues and students from Manchester and former colleagues
> from Oxford and London in addition to family, friends and neighbours
> [...]. Donations in Stan's memory resulted in the establishment of a prize
> for excellence in modern literature in the final exams taken in the German
> Department.

Another long-standing colleague, Dr Rosemary Wallbank-Turner, comments:

> Stan [...] was possessed of a subtlety of mind seldom equalled in my experience.

This, combined with a self-deprecation and ironization which interfered with his writing, meant that his quiet humour was only available to equally quiet and perceptive listeners. Doubtless he found one in Max.[85]

Second, Kerry's 'interest in philosophy dominated his approach to literature' — and Max's approach to literature during his Manchester years already had a pronounced philosophical slant.[86] Third, like Max, Kerry was an outstanding linguist and fluent in Russian as well as German. His widow tells me that he was drawn to the 'complexities of Japanese, simply because of the difficulties inherent in the language',[87] and as *Die Ringe des Saturn* suggests, he was so fascinated by Japanese culture that he and his wife laid down a Japanese garden 'behind his bungalow in Wythenshaw[e]' (in fact the Kerrys lived a little further out to the west, in Sale, Cheshire).[88]

But in Max's imagination, Kerry would become more than another unusual Englishman whom Max found so engaging, and *Die Ringe des Saturn* unobtrusively presents him as one of the untold multitude of innocent, gifted, harmless victims who are prematurely and unjustly sacrificed on the altar of history. The clues are to be found when Max describes him as a listener:

> Die Haltung, die er dabei einnahm, erinnerte an die eines Menschen, *der gegen den Wind geht*, oder an einen *Skiflieger, der gerade abgehoben hat* vom Schanzentisch. Tatsächlich hatte man im Gespräch mit Stanley nicht selten den Eindruck, *als segelte er aus der Höhe hernieder.*[89] (my italics)

> [The leaning posture which he adopted recalled that of a man *walking into the wind*, or a ski jumper *who has [just] launched himself into the air [from the ramp]*. Talking to Stanley, one not uncommonly had the feeling *that he came gliding down from on high*.]

This is not simply a person, but one of the many avatars of Benjamin's Angel of History who appear in Max's work (cf. notes 18 and 142): facing into the wind, flying, and all but powerless to control his descent (cf. also Figure 2.13).

During his first eighteen months in England, Max's major extra-curricular preoccupation was the composition of his 226-page MA thesis 'Carl Sternheim und sein Werk im Verhältnis zur Ideologie der spätbürgerlichen Zeit' ('The Relationship of Carl Sternheim and his Work to the Ideology of the Late-Bourgeois Epoch'), with Professor Idris Parry as his 'hands-off' supervisor.[90] Where the bibliography of Max's *mémoire* contained thirty-seven items, that of the thesis contains 118, and its content suggests that by the time Max presented it in March 1968, two months before his twenty-fourth birthday, he was familiar with the canonical German-speaking authors from the eighteenth to the early twentieth century, and also with such less canonical works (at the time) as Robert Musil's *Der Mann ohne Eigenschaften* (*The Man without Qualities*) and Hans Henny Jahnn's *Perrudja*.[91] The extended bibliography contains a markedly more left-wing slant, listing three works by Benjamin, one by Bloch, two by Horkheimer, one by Lukács, one by Karl Mannheim, and one by Marcuse. Moreover, where the *mémoire*'s bibliography included nothing by Adorno and its text mentioned his work only twice, the bibliography of the thesis lists six works by him: *Noten zur Literatur* (*Notes to Literature*), *Minima Moralia*, *Versuch über Wagner* (*In Search of Wagner*), *Jargon der Eigentlichkeit* (*The Jargon of Authenticity*), *Kierkegaard: Konstruktion des Ästhetischen* (*Kierkegaard: Construction of the Aesthetic*), and *The Authoritarian Personality*. Finally, the thesis cites Adorno about twenty times — more than Benjamin (6), Bloch (1), Horkheimer (2), Lukács (2), and Marcuse (2) put together.[92]

Three of the citations come from a letter from Adorno to Max of 28 April 1967 in response to a letter from Max of 24 April, when work on the thesis was well under way. Max had been disturbed to find a mildly approving mention of Sternheim in *Minima Moralia*, aphorism 100, and asked Adorno how, given his other views, he had reached this conclusion. Adorno evaded the question on the grounds that it was 'überaus diffizil' [more than normally difficult] and required 'viel weitergreifender Erwägungen, als ich, unter äußerstem Arbeitsdruck, jetzt anstellen und gar Ihnen kommunizieren kann' [a far more wide-ranging and considered explanation than I, owing to extreme pressure of work, have time to set down and communicate to you]. But he did take the time to say other things that caught Max's eye. For instance, the first passage from Adorno's letter cited speaks of 'jene süchtige, paranoide Verliebtheit, die vom Potential ihres Gegenteils nicht zu trennen ist' [that addictive, paranoid infatuation which cannot be separated from the potential of its opposite];[93] and the third such passage speaks of the 'kritische Kraft' [critical power] of a spiritual/intellectual phenomenon that is peculiar to the late-bourgeois epoch and 'untrennbar [...] von einer eigentümlichen Faszination durch den Gegenstand der Kritik' [inseparable [...] from a peculiar fascination with the object of criticism] (p. 219). Standing like brackets at the beginning and end of the thesis, these quotations testify to Adorno's particular importance for Max and prompt us to enquire into the reason for Max's fascination with his chosen dialectical other.[94]

Despite the greater prominence of the Frankfurt School, the central thrust of the thesis is close to that of the *mémoire* and is defined thus in the thesis abstract (which, unlike the thesis itself, is in English):

> It is the aim of this thesis to explain the way in which the contradictory nature of Carl Sternheim's personality and work is directly conditioned by the antinomies of the late bourgeois era, which find their paradigmatic expression in the coincidence of rationalism and irrationalism. To this end a sociological scheme is introduced, which demonstrates why Sternheim is seen as being hopelessly trapped in the process of assimilation and being pathologically dependent on the late bourgeois society. Thus this thesis sets out to prove that not only was Sternheim unable to create an ethically and aesthetically valuable and independent work, but, further was forced to reproduce the fallacies, idiosyncrasies and prejudices of the Wilhelminian ideology. (p. 225)

Nevertheless, the *mémoire* and the MA dissertation differ in several important respects. To begin with, Max now uses Frankfurt School texts in three interconnected ways. He has searched *Noten zur Literatur* and *Minima Moralia* for proof-texts with which to judge Sternheim's person and work (pp. 16, 22, 52, 113, 130, and 172).[95] His reading of Marcuse's essay on industrialization and capitalism in the work of Max Weber from volume II of *Kultur und Gesellschaft* (*Culture and Society*) enables him to write, in advance of his reading of *Dialektik der Aufklärung* (*The Dialectics of Enlightenment*), of the way that liberal rationalism turns into irrationalism and negates itself

(p. 36). And his critique of Sternheim's reified language and dogmatic attitudes has hardened (pp. 128 and 204), after being reinforced by Benjamin's concepts (from the *Wahlverwandtschaften* (*Elective Affinities*) section of *Illuminationen* (see note 17)) of 'Sachgehalt' [material content] and 'Wahrheitsgehalt' [truth content] (pp. 18 and 144). Where, Max claims, in a great work of art these two elements form a 'nicht mehr lösbare Einheit' [indissoluble unity], in Sternheim's lesser work they are sundered.

At a structural level, Max has, somewhat reluctantly (pp. 8 and 15), added an introduction that includes a perfunctory review of preceding research (pp. 7–23) and a new chapter on Sternheim's prose work where he discusses the latter's novel *Europa* as a failed *Bildungsroman*. The textual basis of the discussion has also broadened, and in the chapter on the historical background of Sternheim's work more empirical considerations replace Lukács's theory. But the most striking difference concerns Max's stated intention (p. 4): to understand and account for (rather than just conduct a moral polemic against) the allegedly paradigmatic contradictions (p. 15) in Sternheim's personality and work. Although the dissertation does not always succeed in this aim, especially in the rather impressionistic chapter on Sternheim's language (pp. 134–69), it does allow Max to take a less denunciatory, more reasoned attitude to Sternheim's individualism, especially as that is encapsulated in what he regarded as Sternheim's central doctrine of the 'eigene Nuance' [individual idiom]. In the *mémoire*, Max had simply referred to Sternheim's *idée fixe* of the 'eigene Nuance', according to which 'jeder, auch der schlimmste Pfahlbürger, seine Persönlichkeit rücksichtslos zu entwickeln hat' [everyone, even the worst kind of *petit bourgeois*, has to develop his personality regardless of others] (p. 10). But in the thesis, for want of a definition by Sternheim himself (p. 76), Max defines the same concept as follows:

> Bei Sternheim ist die 'eigene Nuance' die Verwirklichung der zwar von der Gesellschaft verursachten, von ihr aber gleichwohl unterdrückten Sekundärtriebe, die sich als Brutalität, Geld- und Sexualgier realisieren. [...] Ihre Freisetzung enthüllt die destruktiven Energien, an denen die bürgerliche Gesellschaft schließlich zugrunde ging. (p. 80)

> [In Sternheim's work, the 'eigene Nuance' means the realization of those secondary drives which, although generated by society, are also repressed by it, and manifest themselves as brutality, financial and sexual rapacity. [...] Their free liberation exposes those destructive forces which, in the end, destroyed bourgeois society.]

Max's more dispassionate approach to his material also generates a new chapter entitled 'Ein psychosoziologisches Modell' ('A Psycho-social Model') (pp. 91–133) — the most closely argued and theoretically complex part of the thesis.

Here, Max argues that all Sternheim's failings derive from a double, or rather a triple, bind. Sternheim the half-Jew allowed himself to be assimilated too well into the rich middle class of an authoritarian society. But because, deep down, he sensed that this was both illegitimate and impossible — a 'mißlungene Assimilation' [unsuccessful assimilation], as Max's reading of and correspondence with Adorno had encouraged him to put it[96] — he suffered from profound feelings of anxiety and insecurity which he labelled 'mit dem populären Begriff "Nervenleiden"' [with the popular concept of 'nervous illness']. These feelings then manifested themselves 'in seiner häufig völlig unmotiviert scheinenden Aggressivität und Brutalität gegenüber jener Klasse, in der er so gern triumphiert hätte, und sodann in der übertriebenen Sorge um Bedeutung und Anerkennung der eigenen Person' [in an often completely unmotivated and brutal aggressiveness *vis-à-vis* that very class in which he would have so much liked to be super-successful and, consequently, in an exaggerated concern about the significance of and recognition due to his own person] (pp. 110–11). Because, Max concludes, this ambivalent social position was structurally identical with the Oedipus complex from which Sternheim in any case suffered, it reinforced that complex, and the resultant psychological tangle manifested itself in Sternheim's work in a range of neurotic features.[97]

So bearing in mind Max's first and third citations from Adorno's letter, and leaving aside the question of whether his analysis is credible, what does the thesis do that the *mémoire* had not done already? First, as Kafka had done via Josef K. and K., Max is now confronting (rather than simply denouncing) someone with whom he feared he had common traits, and the spoof dating discussed in note 94 bears obliquely on this assertion. So, when working through those fears via an imaginary other, he censures Sternheim for several things that could, and indeed would, be said by hostile critics about his own literary work.[98] By doing this, Max, like Proust and Kafka in his own estimation (p. 191), was acquiring a greater awareness of and hence distance from his own psycho-social situation. Second, he was also starting to establish a theoretical basis for the negative attitude to all forms of irrationalism that would inform his critical and creative work and, in all probability, was already turning him away from Marcuse (see note 92). On pages 41 and 46 he uses proof-texts from *Noten zur Literatur* and *Jargon der Eigentlichkeit* to criticize the irrationalism of *Lebensphilosophie* (vitalism) and art for art's sake and then goes on to censure Sternheim, whose work is accused of evincing both aberrations, for seeing the major generative force behind art as 'das Irrationale, die Intuition' [the irrational — intuition] (p. 59), as though intuition — a thoroughly positive human faculty that is better described as a-rational or meta-rational — were of the same order as the destructive, amoral irrationalism that he saw in Sternheim's bourgeois characters (p. 80). Yet following Adorno and Horkheimer, Max came to believe that, after Napoleon, reason also took a dialectical turn and lost its emancipatory function.[99]

Third, when Max lists Sternheim's writerly faults, he is identifying those traps into which he would not wish to fall once he became a writer himself — an act of prolepsis that is very clearly implied in the concluding words of the thesis: 'Insofern ließe sich aus dem Werk und der Person Carl Sternheims ein Modell herleiten, das bei der Bewertung der immanenten Fehleinstellungen spätbourgeoiser Literatur von großem Nutzen sein könnte' [To this extent one could extrapolate a model from the work and personality of Carl Sternheim that could be of great use for the evaluation of those false attitudes which are intrinsic to late-bourgeois literature] (p. 218). But he is also identifying two qualities that were, in his view, indispensable to high literature in an age bereft of certainties. To begin with, there is the 'potenzierte Ironie' [potentiated sense of irony] to which he had briefly alluded in the *mémoire* and which he found, above all, in *Felix Krull* (cf. note 95). Max had almost certainly got to know Mann's most untypical novel in summer semester 1966 when studying with Alker in Fribourg, and he quite unexpectedly accords it lavish praise as a literary model just before his thesis reaches its conclusion (pp. 194–99).[100] Then there is the perceived obligation of major prose fiction to create 'das Gefühl vom unwiderruflichen Ablauf der Zeit' [the sense of the irrevocable passing of time] while simultaneously protesting 'gegen die Gewalt des Vergehens' [against the violence of transience] (p. 177). As a disquisition on Sternheim, the thesis may be flawed, but it lays down two of the major foundation stones on which Max's literary *oeuvre* would later be so carefully built.

With the thesis nearly completed, Max could return to a less heavy-duty interest: amateur dramatics. Manchester's German Department had quite a reputation for its annual production, and on 5 and 6 March 1968, with Max directing a play that he had studied in detail at Freiburg (WS 1964/65), the German Society staged Büchner's *Leonce und Lena* in the University Theatre, Devas Street (Figure 2.36). The production is still remembered by Max's former colleagues and was very well received, with the Director of Manchester's Goethe-Institut coming backstage after the performance to congratulate Max in person. And when recommending Max for the UEA post, Professor Keller would say in his reference of 21 April 1970: '[*Leonce und Lena*] was an outstanding and memorable event. Professor Hugh Hunt, the Director of the University Theatre, wrote me a letter afterwards expressing his

FIG. 2.36. A rehearsal for Büchner's *Leonce und Lena* (Manchester, spring 1968). WGS is on the right, Leonce (played by Stephen Swaby) is on the left, Lena (played by Barbara Dean) is in the centre.
© U. E. Sebald

admiration and appreciation for the production.' More importantly, John Prudhoe (who succeeded Hunt as Professor of Drama in the University's Department of Drama) published a long and very insightful review praising Max's 'skill as a director'. It began:

> [Sebald's] choice of play [...] proved to be the first ace he had up his sleeve. The metaphor suggests itself because he seems to have modelled his whole production on Valerio's idea that Leonce is a 'Kartenkönig' [playing-card King], Valerio his knave and Lena his *Lebkuchen* Queen of Hearts. From the moment the lights went up on the first tableau the sense of stylisation was there. It not only suggested the 'unreal reality' of Büchner's play, it enabled the actors to mime the sense of what they were saying to an extent which a less well-chosen play would not have allowed. The result was an evening of genuine theatre.[101]

He then continued:

> The costumes and properties throughout were excellent. They were also in the best traditions of modern German theatre where the problem of uniting the historical with the modern, so that a contemporary significance shines through a classic play, is so often better solved than in our own. [...] Even the semi-Brechtian use of slides paid dividends: the distance between the romanticism of the gardens and palaces in the slides used during the first half and the boredom of Büchner's dialogue was the Alienation Effect well used.[102]

And he concluded:

> This production aimed at 'professionalism' in the only sense that has any real meaning. It was disciplined and sought to find that relationship between life and art which produced true style. It succeeded in achieving this remarkably well.[103]

Stephen Swaby, the third-year student who played Leonce, was equally complimentary from another point of view:

> I cannot recall anyone associated with the production who did not enjoy the process or stand in awe of the freshness of his ideas and approach. And how many of that cast owe their knowledge of Albinoni's Adagio to Max's use of it throughout the production? Melancholic or what?
> Max wielded an enormous talent modestly; it was typical of the man to suggest one day that I write the programme notes and to expend as much effort on the motivation and discipline of the minor parts as of the others. I cannot recall him ever having to raise his voice. He simply commanded respect — as a thinker and a sensitive director who could produce real style. I remember not knowing what to do with my hands during one particularly 'lonesome' stretch. Max lived the thing through with me for nearly an hour and we arrived at a solution.[104]

It is easy to see why Max should have opted for Büchner's play.[105] It is short, more compact even than the Donleavy play staged in Freiburg, and Max prized concision on stage.[106] It deals, albeit parodically, with a bored, melancholic, Hamlet-like figure.[107] And it ironically debates the question of whether the world is governed by 'Vorsehung' (providence) or 'Zufall' (chance) — the philosophical problem behind

Max's literary investigations of the (in)significance of coincidence.[108] Prudhoe also identified aspects of this little production that would characterize Max's literary work of the 1990s: stylization, a concern with 'das Unheimliche' (the uncanny — what Prudhoe refers to as 'unreal reality'), the recollection of the past in such a way that it sheds light on the present,[109] the desire to make people think rather than just to entertain them, and a disciplined professionalism. And Swaby, whose comments on Max's way with students could be echoed by dozens of those whom he taught at UEA (see Chapters 3 to 5 of this volume), recognized in Max's directing style the discipline, originality and painstaking attention to detail that he would later invest in his literary texts.

The production was so successful that Max wrote to Tabbert on 12 March 1968:

> Von allen Seiten werfen sie mir jetzt Freundlichkeiten und ähnliche Schweinereien an den Kopf. Wie mir zu Ohren kommt, ist gar ein Betreiben in Gang, mir einen Sessl [sic] als Ass[istant] Lec[turer] im Drama-Department zu verschaffen.[110]

> [Now, from all sides, they're pelting me with friendly comments and similar bloody nonsense. And I hear on the grapevine that there's even a move afoot to get me a nice little job as assistant lecturer in the Drama Department.]

Nothing came of this and Max was never again involved in amateur dramatics, either in Manchester or in Norwich — though in February 1970 he did publish a sardonic review of a performance of *Minna von Barnhelm* that the ensemble Die Brücke had staged in the Manchester University Theatre (see Appendix 2.1, p. 107).[111] But his flair for and interest in the theatrical did not go to waste (see *A Radical Stage: Theatre in Germany in the 1970s and 1980s*, the proceedings of a 1987 UEA colloquium that Max edited; Primary Bibliography A.4). It simply went underground to re-emerge in his teaching style, the self-image that he studiously cultivated, the innumerable reading-evenings that he gave between 1990–2001, his carefully staged interviews with their attendant photographs (by no means such rare events as some of Max's interviewers were beguiled into believing), and the public controversies, with all their provocative use of alienation effects, which Max seems to have courted and thoroughly relished.

St Gallen (1968–1969)

According to Professor Ursula Liebsch (née Küsters), one of his five closest school-friends (see Figure 2.10), Max realised that his chances of getting a job within the German university system were slim at best, and began in c. autumn 1967 to consider training as a German-language teacher (*Dozent*) with the Munich Goethe-Institut after leaving Manchester. Although Max applied to take such a course in December 1967, he changed his mind (though he was later to return to the idea in 1975) and, after holidaying in Yugoslavia in summer 1968, spent the academic year 1968–69 as a teacher in the (private) Rosenberg-Schule in St Gallen, Switzerland. But having to teach everything at the school, he was soon unhappy with its strict regime and on 2 October 1968 wrote to Tabbert: 'Mir ist die Arbeit in der Schule ein Kreuz & ich werde sie an den Nagl [*sic*] hängen müssen. Ich habe wieder zu kritzeln begonnen' [Work in the school is becoming a pain & I'll have to chuck it in. I've started scribbling again].[112] According to Tabbert, one of Max's 'scribblings' was a theatrical monologue based on the fantastic anecdotes of a trickster-figure called Friedrich Schiel, a veteran of the imperial Austrian Army whom he had got to know in Yugoslavia. Although he sent it to the famous Austrian actor Helmut Qualtinger (1928–86), he never got a reply.[113] Max also used his first six months in St Gallen to turn his MA thesis into a book, for its 'Vorwort' (Foreword) is signed off 'St. Gallen, April 1969'. By late 1968, he had decided that he wanted to return to university to write a doctoral dissertation on Döblin and outlined his thinking in a second letter to Adorno (14 December; see note 94):

> In Cambridge möchte ich an einem Ph.D. über Döblin arbeiten. Soweit ich es absehen kann, sollte dieses Unternehmen hinauslaufen auf eine Analyse der Krise des Romans, des Erzählens überhaupt. Denn wie sehr Döblin auch versuchte, allen hergebrachten Formen des Erzählens über den Schatten zu springen, so konnte ihm sein bestes eben doch nur in den wenigen Fällen gelingen, wo er — wie in der 'Reise nach Polen' — das dokumentarische Material zu seinem wichtigsten Vehikel machte. Ich bin mir noch nicht klar, wie ich es anfassen werde, möchte aber diese notwendige 'Objektivierierung' der Kunst umschreiben als eine ihrer letzten Möglichkeiten.[114]

> [In Cambridge, I would like to work on a PhD on Döblin. As far as I can foresee, this project should issue in an analysis of the crisis of the novel and of narration in general. For try as Döblin might to transcend all conventional forms of narration by radically adapting them, his best work succeeds only in those few instances — as in his 'Journey to Poland' — where he made documentary material his most important vehicle. I am still not clear how I shall go about it, but I would like to describe this 'objectification' of art as one of its last possibilities.]

To this end, he asked Adorno, on the basis of their exchange of letters of 1967 and a sample of his written work, to write in support of his application for a three-year Fellowship in Modern Languages at Sidney Sussex College, Cambridge.[115]

Manchester (1969–1970)

Perhaps unsurprisingly, given the interests of the Cambridge German Department at that time, Max's application was unsuccessful. Nevertheless, in July 1969 he withdrew his application to train as a *Dozent* at the Munich Goethe-Institut and returned to Manchester for the academic year 1969–70 as a *Lektor* on a salary of £960 per annum, taking up residence in his old flat in Kingston Road, where Peter Jonas was living during the final year of his studies (see note 81).[116] During this year, Professor Ray Furness, 'always a great fan', came to know and like Max sufficiently 'to make fun of this lugubrious German with the Zapata moustache, so very German in his rejection of things German, so very much of his time' and 'to get irritated at times by the anti-German stance, the preference for the oddities and eccentricities of English life'.[117] Furness also developed a sharp eye for the enigmas and oddities of Max's personality: 'Was he a lugubrious optimist? A hilarious pessimist? He certainly didn't exude hilarity, but the mournful exterior did conceal an elusive sense of humour'; 'the more I think about Max, the more elusive he becomes somehow. His stance was oblique, quizzical, bemused. Yet intensely moral, whatever that means. We talked a huge amount about death, as you can imagine.'[118]

Max and Furness also shared an enthusiasm for long walks, during which they talked at length about twentieth-century German literature. Furness knew and was enthusiastic about Hans Henny Jahnn's *Perrudja*, and tells me that Max, who had already discovered Borges, introduced him to Wolfgang Hildesheimer's *Tynset* (a work that Max came to see as pivotal for post-1945 German literature and included on UEA reading lists as early as spring 1971; it was still on reading lists as late as 1993) (see Appendix 3.3, p. 135). He also encouraged Furness to plough through Döblin's *Berge, Meere, Giganten* (*Mountains, Seas, Giants*) on the grounds that he would 'enjoy the descriptions of monsters and cataclysms'. It also seems that Max was avidly reading his way into post-1945 German literature, which became one of his two major specialisms at UEA. In short, he was doing a great deal of creative reading outside the canon.

Even Manchester, however, was not immune to processes of urban renewal, and on 7 April 1970, Max wrote to Tabbert in a mixture of English and German, remarking on the modernization of Manchester and the gradual disappearance of the older, decaying city that had fascinated him three years previously: 'The bus fare has doubled. The Times costs eight pence. The precinct is growing. Buildings are getting face-lifts. Stations are being closed. Foreign newspapers are sold. Business is thriving. Continental shops open up.' But he did not see these developments as a change for the better, and the letter continues:

> Aber das nächtliche Gemurmel der urbs sacra mancuniensis ist geblieben, und auch das Gefühl, daß etwas Barbarisches passiert im Bezirk der Conurbation. Man hat die ganze Information zur Hand, aber sie verbindet sich nur dann zu einem Muster, wenn man ihre Trostlosigkeit mit der Hoffnungslosigkeit der Phantasie noch unterbietet. It seems unavoidable.[119]

> [But the nocturnal hubbub of the urbs sacra mancuniensis has remained, and also the sense that something barbaric is happening throughout the conurbation. One has all the facts at one's fingertips but they form a pattern only when one realizes that their desolate bleakness is surpassed only by a hopeless failure of imagination. It seems unavoidable.]

Here, just before Max turned 26, we can see his 'melancholy' side causing him to put a negative sign over a process of urban renewal that conventional wisdom regarded as progress. Such dialectical inversions would come to typify his literary work (see Figure 2.37).

Having by now decided to become a career academic rather than a school- or language-teacher, the most important event of the first part of Max's third year in Manchester was the publication of his book on Sternheim: *Carl Sternheim: Kritiker und Opfer der Wilhelminischen Ära* (Carl Sternheim: Critic and Victim of the Wilhelmine Era) on 3 October 1969 in a print run of 2000. Far from being identical with his MA thesis, it involves major structural revisions. The thesis's original foreword

FIG. 2.37.

'Oft bin ich auf der Wanderung
durch die Straßenzüge eingekehrt
in eine der vielen infernalisch
glitzernden Wirtschaften, mit Vorliebe
freilich in Liston's Music Hall'

[Often on my wanderings
through the streets I resorted
to one of the many infernally
glittering hostelries, for preference
to Liston's Music Hall]

(*Nach der Natur*, 3. IV (Eichborn), p. 91;
After Nature, p. 98); cf. *Die Ausgewanderten*
(Eichborn), p. 351; *The Emigrants* (Harvill),
pp. 234–35.
© Prof. Dr Reinbert Tabbert (1967)

(pp. 4–6) has been completely reworked and its conclusion (pp. 218–19) has been partially merged with its introduction (pp. 7–23) to form the book's introduction (pp. 12–20).[120] Chapter 1 of the thesis (pp. 24–43, i.e. the historical background) has been cut completely; Chapters 2–6 of the thesis have been renumbered as Chapters 1–5 (and in some cases retitled); Chapter 5 of the book is divided into two (not three) sections; and the unused part of the thesis's conclusion has been reworked to form the book's afterword (pp. 126–27). There are minor alterations to the five chapters that form the body of the book and one substantial addition on pp. 118–19 ('Weil die selbstvergessene [...] dem Munde genommen hatte') where the polemic against the self-satisfied Wilhelmine bourgeoisie is intensified. Max's predilection for long paragraphs has also become very evident. Although the book's bibliography is shorter by fourteen items, its theoretical underpinning has been strengthened. Mannheim's *Ideologie und Utopie* (*Ideology and Utopia*) has been omitted, but Benjamin's *Ursprung des deutschen Trauerspiels* and Bloch's *Durch die Wüste: Frühe Aufsätze* (*Through the Desert: Early Essays*) have been added; and the two shorter pieces by Horkheimer have been replaced by his two-volume *Kritische Theorie* (1968), Max's annotated copy of which, acquired soon after its publication, is in the DLA.

Correspondingly, the major changes occur in the book's introduction with the eirenic tone of the thesis being replaced by an aggressive initial statement: 'Da es sich bei dieser Revision vorwiegend um eine Destruktion handelt' [As this revision is predominantly concerned with destruction] (p. 7). Similarly, the paragraph in the thesis's introduction ('Aber auch im Falle [...] Bestätigung erfahren') where Max sought to reassure his examiners that his case against Sternheim was ultimately based on 'werkimmanente Kriterien' [criteria that are derived from Sternheim's work itself] (p. 22) is missing from the book, whose introduction, unlike that of the thesis, ends by openly admitting its 'Vernachlässigung tradierter Methodik' [neglect of traditional methodology] (p. 20).

So here we can see the 24-year-old already jettisoning empirically based history on behalf of his own convictions, and declaring open war on Sternheim, *werk-immanente Kritik*, and the German literary-critical establishment in general.[121] To justify the methodological shift, which is highly significant for his later work, he cited another Max (Horkheimer): 'gegenwärtig [sind] bestimmte Grundeinsichten in das Wesen der Gesellschaft [...] bedeutsamer [...] als der Besitz oder Nichtbesitz ausgedehnter Spezialkenntnisse' [in the present time, certain basic insights into the essential nature of society are more significant than the possession or non-possession of extensive specialist knowledge] (p. 20). When I read this and note that the area bombing of Dresden, given wide publicity by David Irving's controversial book of 1963 (German translation 1964), is mentioned on the book's penultimate page (p. 126), I recall the words that came to Sir Arthur Harris when he was standing on the Air Ministry roof during the Blitz of 1940 and often repeated thereafter: 'They have sown the wind, and now they're going to reap the whirlwind.' For in the Sternheim book we are seeing Max's first major raid in his metaphorical 'Luftkrieg' (air war) against Germany. It was not primarily concerned with accuracy or fairness, and its most violent current, unnamed as yet, is Benjamin's destructive wind of history. Nor can I help wondering how many of Max's anglophone admirers understand that a straight, albeit subterranean line runs from his early saturation in revisionist Marxism to the nostalgia-laden critique of the postmodern, 'hamburgerized world' (Max's phrase) that informs his literary work of the 1990s.[122]

Max's book may have been intended as a bomb, but when it appeared, it did not cause damage of the hoped-for magnitude.[123] Either Sternheim was too new an arrival in the German canon; or established Sternheim specialists like Emrich and Hellmuth Karasek could not be bothered to take issue with a young, unknown language-teacher who was not even living in Germany; or Max's densely written book was simply too difficult for many readers to follow. But after Max had been interviewed for the Assistant Lectureship at UEA in spring 1970, I distinctly remember one of the interviewing panel, Professor (then Dr) Colin Good (1941–2000), telling me that the younger members of the panel had had to argue quite forcibly on Max's behalf because of the book's 'unorthodox' nature.

The first major review of Max's book known to me was written by a Soviet Sternheim-specialist from the Soviet University of Perm who had been sent a copy by Karasek, and it appeared in *Die Zeit* just before Max moved from Manchester to Norfolk.[124] Its author, Valerij Poljudow, bristled with unconcealed rage and, as an orthodox Marxist, took violent exception to Max's ahistorical methodology. He also pointed out the difficulties that Sternheim had experienced in both Wilhelmine and Nazi Germany because of his pacifism. He denied that Sternheim was in any sense a proto-Fascist, wondered whether Max, in his turn, was a neo-Nazi, and criticized him sharply, with some justification, for persistently quoting Sternheim out of context. So having decided that it would take a whole book to refute him, Poljudow concluded:

> Alles, was Sebald schreibt, ist barer Unsinn [...]. Ist das Buch durchgelesen, so hat man das Gefühl, Sternheim sei kein Kritiker und Opfer der Wilhelmin-ischen Ära, sondern Opfer des Kritikers W. G. Sebald, eines angehenden Gymnasiallehrers.
>
> [Everything that Sebald writes is sheer nonsense [...]. Once you have read the book through, you have the feeling that Sternheim is not the critic and sacrificial victim of the Wilhelmine era but the sacrificial victim of the critic W. G. Sebald, a trainee grammar-school teacher.]

Nothing daunted, Max, back in Sonthofen after a three-month holiday in France, published a carefully constructed, sober, and very sarcastic letter in reply.[125] Essentially, he accused Poljudow of an 'erzpositivistische[n] Geradsinnigkeit' [dyed-in-the-wool positivism that is incapable of lateral thinking] and of being so indoctrinated by the (totalitarian Soviet) system that he was blind to the complex fault-lines in Sternheim's work and the historical forces that had generated them. Poljudow's sympathy for Sternheim, Max implied, derived from the fact that he was in a similar situation and so was inevitably blind to the book's central thesis, namely the extent to which Sternheim's work had, despite his better instincts, been warped by his failed assimilation into Wilhelmine society and its ideology. He then concluded with a nice ideological sideswipe:

> Es sollte im übrigen zu denken geben, daß die Immanenz der Kunst nebst den ornamentalen Zugeständnissen an den sogenannten historischen Hintergrund im Ural [i.e. Perm] genauso sakrosankt zu sein scheint wie im Freiburg im Breisgau oder in Zürich.

> [It should give pause for thought to realize that the immanence of art, alongside a few ornamental concessions to so-called historical background, seems to be as sacrosanct in the Urals as it is in Freiburg im Breisgau or Zurich.]

On 10 October 1970, shortly after he began work at UEA, Max published one final essay on Sternheim, in the *Frankfurter Rundschau*, Germany's leading left-liberal newspaper before the appearance of *taz* (*Die Tageszeitung*) in 1979.[126] Although his basic case had not changed, the article is written with lucidity, concision, and a compassion for Sternheim that were less than conspicuous in his thesis and book. Indeed, with the benefit of hindsight one has the clear sense that the writer of this piece has come out of the cold and settled down, that he knows who he is, understands what he is doing and why he is doing it, and has lost the need to fight quite so pugnaciously. Similarly, when Max took part in the radio discussion of the following spring involving Karasek and Peter von Matt (see note 124), he kept his cool admirably and restricted himself to thirteen lucid and pointed responses to questions and charges, often put at length and with some force, by the more experienced Karasek (22 interventions) and von Matt (21 interventions). Even if the debate ends inconclusively, in a draw, his case gained in convincingness by becoming less strident, less denunciatory, and less obscurely theoretical.

Meanwhile, in spring 1970, Max had been applying for other university jobs and was offered a post in the Drama Department of the University of Bangor 'to deal with 19th- and 20th-century German and French drama via English translations exclusively' — an offer that he declined because 'this would have completely exiled me'.[127] At 11.15 a.m. on 26 May 1970, Max was interviewed in Earlham Hall, then UEA's administrative centre, and two days later he was offered a post as Assistant Lecturer in German Language and Literature in the School of European Studies (EUR) at a starting salary of £1480 per annum. He accepted, with alacrity, on 1 June, for by then, as he had stated in his letter of application of 21 March, it was his 'ambition to remain in Britain and, if possible, take up a career as a teacher at a British university'. Unlike the Bangor post, Max's new job allowed him to remain firmly embedded in two areas of German culture and, equally importantly, to develop still further his interest in other European literatures.

In his application, Max had outlined his thinking about Döblin. Instead of focussing on the aesthetic problems posed by Döblin's work (cf. his letter to Adorno of December 1968), he claimed that he now wished 'to examine the theme of rebellion and resignation as the central issue of Döblin's writings' and to collect material for a short biography of that author 'which I hope to publish in Rowohlt's series of literary monographs'.[128] Although this latter plan came to nothing, his new project would issue in his doctorate (1974) and second book (1980).

Max, I was told, performed outstandingly at interview, but his case must have been considerably helped by three glowing references. Professor Parry wrote on 21 April:

> He has given us excellent service as Lektor, being both popular and effective with his students. [... He] is a man of rare literary perception. He is immersed in literature and knows his twentieth-century facts and trends in detail. [...] He's a pleasant, gentle, sincere person, a scholar to the fingertips. There is no doubt that he is a worker: he gets things done. [...] I may say that we've given him a second run as a Lektor only because we have no permanent post to offer.

Professor Keller wrote on the same day:

> We normally keep Assistants for one year only but made an exception in the case of Mr. Sebald. He was really outstanding as a teacher and in his contact with students. His lecture courses were much better attended than voluntary courses normally are. He lectured on various aspects of contemporary literature and life in Germany. His conversation classes, too, appear to have been most stimulating and rewarding. [...] It was with great pleasure that I accepted Mr. Sebald's request to become an assistant a second time. He very much likes the intellectual climate of a British university. He has always been a most conscientious and cooperative colleague.

And Professor Peacock was, if anything, even more enthusiastic in his letter of 22 April:

> I recommend Mr. Sebald to your attention with the greatest pleasure and a very keen sense of his first-rate qualities as a scholar in the field of German Literature and Modern European Literary trends in general.
>   May I say first that, although he is German, he has a very remarkable command of English, extending to a technical command of English critical

vocabulary, which in my view puts him on an equal footing with English candidates.

[... His Sternheim book] is a very striking and masterly contribution to the analysis of the work of this dramatist, and contains points of view which must necessarily lead to a revision of the traditional estimate of Sternheim. Sebald has a genuinely original mind which shows itself in [an] ability to apply from the start generative ideas to his interpretations of literature, as contrasted with the average, more painstaking forms of analysis and classification which are useful but uninspired.

I recommend him to you with great confidence as a first-rate scholar, as an extremely genuine and likeable person, and as one whose interests and talents would enable him to make a notable contribution to the post concerned.

Peacock, as Professor Sagarra confirms, was a man of considerable prescience.[129]

Postscript: UEA (1970–1975)

Founded in 1964, the University of East Anglia occupied an exposed position in the middle of what had been Norwich's municipal golf course whose bunkers, which radical students occasionally decorated with oppressed gnomes that they had liberated from adjacent bourgeois gardens, were still incongruously visible (Figure 2.38). The School of European Studies, always known as EUR, had admitted its first students in 1964 and in late 1967 moved from a log-cabin site just north of Earlham Road to the bizarrely named Arts Block amidst the golf course. EUR was marked by several academic features that Max, like most of us who taught there, valued greatly. It was multidisciplinary, consisting of five 'Sectors' (French, German, Russian, Scandinavian, and History). These were not, however — despite the occasional sign declaring, for example, 'You are now entering the Skandinavian Sektor' — separated by red and white barriers and warning notices in several languages. On the contrary, the interchange between people working across a range of languages and disciplines — unusual in British universities at the time — made for a very creative atmosphere.[130] In this emancipatory environment, interaction with colleagues from other disciplines, for example Dr Robert Short, a French cultural historian and world-renowned expert on Surrealism and the historical avant-gardes, and an enthusiastic proselytizer of their doctrines, or Dr (later Professor) Thomas Elsaesser, then a lecturer in Comparative Literature, with whom Max taught a joint course on German film, must have played their part in encouraging him to cross generic boundaries, both as a critic and as a writer of fiction.[131] Most of the faculty were young by today's standards and several, including Max and myself, were still working on their doctorates — an almost unimaginable situation nowadays.[132] The basic teaching unit was the seminar or class of fifteen students with lectures as optional extras,[133] and one could experiment with new seminar courses without having to go through a long and bureaucratic committee procedure. People put tremendous energy into their teaching with nary a thought of feedback questionnaires, quality assurance, and TQAs. The 'raeification' of research culture had not even begun: UEA's academic staff were trusted to act like professionals and not terrorized into behaving like self-absorbed Chaplinesque workers on demented production lines, and most people honoured that trust. Those

FIG. 2.38. The University of East Anglia in the early 1970s,
situated in the middle of what had been the municipal golf course.
© John Gibbons; courtesy of The University of East Anglia

of us who taught anything connected with German history and culture could draw
on excellent library holdings, mainly thanks to UEA's first Librarian, Dr Willi
Guttsman (1920–93), a German-Jewish refugee and noted historian of German
Social Democracy (Figure 2.39).[134]

EUR was non-hierarchical and, in the best sense, anarchic. While this could be
stimulating, it could also have a disturbing effect on those who preferred or were
used to more stable, conventional structures, something which became all too evident when '1968' finally made it up the A11 and reached UEA, albeit three years late
and in a appropriately toytown way (Figure 2.40).[135] Relations between senior and
junior faculty and faculty and students were friendly and informal: almost everyone
used Christian names, not academic titles. The central administration was relatively
unobtrusive and certainly not heavy-handed. The then Dean of EUR, who had
chaired the committee that appointed Max, was the distinguished German-Jewish
historian Professor Werner Mosse (1918–2001) (see Figure 2.39), but the two senior
faculty members who were of most importance for Max in the 1970s were the
founding Dean of EUR, Professor James Walter McFarlane (1920–99) — 'Big
Mac' as he was popularly known, and, inevitably, 'PVC Mac' once he became Pro-
Vice-Chancellor (see Figure 2.39) — and Professor Brian Rowley (b. 1923) (Figure
2.41). The former was an internationally renowned Scandinavianist and especially
well known for his translations of Ibsen: he supervised Max's PhD on Döblin. The
latter, an expert in German literature of the eighteenth and nineteenth centuries,

FIG. 2.39. UEA's Deans and first Vice-Chancellor Frank Thistlethwaite (1915–2003) (front row, centre), *c.* 1970. Professor Werner Mosse (1918–2001) (the Dean of the School of European Studies) is second from left in the back row. Professor James Walter McFarlane (1920–99) (Pro-Vice-Chancellor and Sebald's doctoral supervisor) is third from left in the back row. The Librarian Dr Willi Guttsman (1920–93) is on the extreme right of the back row. Both Mosse and Guttsman were German-Jewish refugees. © John Gibbons; courtesy of the University of East Anglia

FIG. 2.40. Revolution at the University of East Anglia (early 1970s). The 'adorn(o)ed' building is the hapless chaplaincy. © John Gibbons; courtesy of the University of East Anglia

FIG. 2.41. Professor Brian Rowley, UEA's
first Professor of German. Photo taken at
Congregation (*c.* 1983).
© unknown; courtesy of Richard Sheppard

with a particular love of Goethe, Mörike, and Fontane, was also a passionate and highly knowledgeable collector of old postcards. Both were extremely wise, kindly, and enlightened individuals who were working actively for the liberalization of the British university system. They could spot talent of various kinds; they did not appoint or try to make academic staff in their image; they encouraged their younger colleagues to innovate and develop their strengths; they were undogmatic about approaches to and interpretation of literary texts; they understood what it meant to be the *primus inter pares* and they knew how to temper authority and status with a good-humoured tolerance of youthful iconoclasm. In Max's mind, EUR and UEA must have been the opposite of Freiburg in every respect, and in his later life he often expressed his appreciation of the quality of life at British universities in the 1960s and 1970s and his regret over the 'Stalinist' developments of the mid-1980s.[136]

The *Journal of European Studies*, founded in spring 1971 by three slightly older colleagues in EUR, Dr (later Professor) John Flower, Dr (later Professor) Tony Cross, and Dr (later Professor) Franz Kuna (1933–2010), grew naturally out of the above situation as an interdisciplinary forum — then a rarity in British universities. As such, it provided Max with a platform from which he could express his opinions on literature and criticism via a series of hard-hitting reviews. Uwe Schütte discusses these in detail in Chapter 6 of the present volume, so all I will say here is that they are informed by the conviction that the Idealist aesthetic underpinning *werkimmanente Kritik*, with its central notion of the (transcendent) autotelicity of literature, was hopelessly compromised.

I had been at UEA since 1967 and it took me several years to get to know Max well — not least because most of the writers and theoreticians who exercised this daunting young German were then unknown to me, having spent three very dull years at Cambridge (1962–65) not quite accepting canonical attitudes to canonical texts from 1494 to the end of history in 1930. Nevertheless, we were both, albeit very differently, interested in Modernism, non-canonical texts, the interdisciplinary study of literature, and German metaphysics; we both believed that literature should have some relevance for life; we shared a developed and irreverent sense of humour; we mistrusted *werkimmanente Kritik* and the classical *Bildungsideal*; and we were both in reaction against what went on in conventional German departments. I remember Max in the early 1970s as a far less troubled person than, according to his Manchester friends, he had been there — though two of his earliest articles are already marked by the preoccupation with mortality and the sense of an ending so typical of his literary work.[137]

The intellectual and professional freedom enjoyed by Max at a new, progressive university was, of course, a major reason for his relative contentment during the early 1970s. Another, more backwards-looking, derived from the anomalous, peripheral situation of East Anglia, as described in a forgotten article, 'Die hölzernen Engel von East Anglia' (The Carved Wooden Angels of East Anglia) (see Part II in this volume, pp. 319–23) written with German tourists in mind and published in the travel section of *Die Zeit* on 26 July 1974.[138] Until the M11 was built and the railway line to London was electrified in the early 1980s, Norwich, with its cathedral (which some Saxon freedom fighter of the late 1960s adorned with the slogan 'Normans Out'), over fifty medieval churches, and more than three hundred unmodernized pubs ('a church for every week and a pub for every day of the year', as the local saying goes), was still a secluded idyll which the Industrial Revolution had largely passed by.[139] So forgotten a place was Norwich that UEA, during its early years, was regularly confused with the more left-wing University of Essex at Colchester, fifty miles to the south, on the southern edge of East Anglia, and suffered correspondingly in the media. Rural East Anglia, too, was still the kind of pre-modern environment that appealed to Max, and if you owned a car, then picturesque houses, cottages, parsonages, and even mansions could be acquired very cheaply in the countryside that began where Norwich ended, without much intervening suburban sprawl. So it was no accident that initially Max should have set up home in Wymondham,[140] then a secluded, picturesque village about seven miles south-west of Norwich city centre that is dominated by a fine abbey church dating from the twelfth century. He lived there until he went back to Germany in 1975 to train as a teacher of German language at the Goethe-Institut in Munich: originally intending to stay for a calendar year, he became dissatisfied after six months, and returned to UEA in June 1976, whereupon he and his wife acquired and restored The Old Rectory in Poringland, a village some five miles south of Norwich (Figures 2.42 and 2.43).

In 'Die hölzernen Engel', as in *Nach der Natur* (*After Nature*) 3. vi, the mood and shape of *Die Ringe des Saturn* are already visible, for the piece tells of 'den Geschmack der ostenglischen Melancholie' [the flavour of East Anglian melancholy], 'die Leere

Fɪɢ. 2.42. The Old Rectory, Poringland. Postcard from the early twentieth century.
© unknown; courtesy of U. E. Sebald

Fɪɢ. 2.43. The Old Rectory, Poringland, just before the Sebalds moved in (1976). It had been empty for four years and was in a state of extreme dilapidation that would take several years to put right. This view no longer exists as a house now obstructs it. © U. E. Sebald

der Vergänglichkeit' [the emptiness of transitoriness], ruins galore (albeit beautiful ones), deserted Orford Ness, 'Gerüchte längst vergangener Schlachten' [rumours of battles long past], and the 'spätbürgerliche Monstrosität Sandringham' [late-bourgeois monstrosity that is Sandringham]. It also indicates very strongly that Max was finding plenty of solace in 'olde worlde' East Anglia. He describes the region's eccentricity, its unspoilt pubs serving Adnams (real) ale, comfortable, well-appointed hotels that could still offer 'ein Stück Gastlichkeit aus dem 18. Jahrhundert' [a piece of eighteenth-century hospitality], magnificent cathedrals and churches, relatively few traces of 'die Wucherungen der letzten 150 Jahre' [the depredations of the last 150 years], 'die Präsenz und Zugänglichkeit seiner [Norwich's] Vergangenheit' [the presence and accessibility of Norwich's past], the large empty beaches of Holkham Bay, landscapes by Constable, marzipan villages like Lavenham, antique shops 'deren es in East Anglia ungleich mehr und bessere gibt als sonst irgendwo' [of which there are immeasurably more and better ones in East Anglia than anywhere else], and local auctions where you could pick up antiques for a song. For Max, East Anglia in the early 1970s still contained many tangible, consoling residues of a *temps* that was rapidly becoming *perdu*.[141] But, he concludes, the most important attraction in which visitors might 'sich verschauen' [lose themselves in contemplation] were 'die hölzernen Engel [...], die die *hammerbeam*-Decken in vielen der zahllosen Kirchen mit scheinbarer Leichtigkeit auf dem Rücken tragen' [the (carved) wooden angels [...] that carry on their backs with apparent ease the hammer-beam roofs of many of the countless churches]. For Max in his early years at UEA, such angels, of which there are fine examples in Wymondham Abbey, were still effective guardians, beings who effortlessly prevented a religious and architectural past from collapsing in on itself and becoming rubble. They had not yet become the helpless Benjaminian angel who, as more than a few commentators have perceived, would oversee the increasingly lost, ruined, and alienated landscapes of Max's literary work of the 1990s.[142]

Acknowledgements

I was a colleague of Max's in the School of European Studies (EUR) at the University of East Anglia (UEA) from 1970 to 1987 and remained in touch with him from 1987 until his death in 2001. For this reason, I have referred to him by the first name by which he was generally known from about summer 1966 (see note 29). Many people have helped me to compile this chapter, but my special thanks are due to Ute Sebald; Gertrud Aebischer-Sebald; Etta Schwanitz; Sir Peter Jonas; Professor Reinbert Tabbert; Dr James Peters, the Archivist of the University of Manchester; and Max's former colleagues at that university.

The title of this chapter alludes to Goethe's novel *Wilhelm Meisters Lehrjahre* (*Wilhelm Meister's Apprenticeship*) (1795–96); the original, posthumously published version of the novel was entitled *Wilhelm Meisters theatralische Sendung* (*Wilhelm Meister's Theatrical Mission* [or *Calling*]) (published 1911; written 1777–85?). It also alludes to W. G. Sebald's 1987 essay on Herbert Achternbusch: 'Die Kunst der Verwandlung: Herbert Achternbuschs theatralische Sendung' ('The Art of Transformation: Herbert Achternbusch's Theatrical Mission') (see Primary Bibliography D.38).

Notes to Chapter 2

1. Theodor W. Adorno, *Minima Moralia: Reflexionen aus dem beschädigten Leben* (Frankfurt a.M.: Suhrkamp, 1962), no. 64; extract trans. by RWS.

2. Max's family — together with his widowed maternal grandfather Josef Egelhofer (1872–1956), a retired 'Gendarmerie-Kommissar' — moved from the Alpine village of Wertach, where Max was born in 1944, to a new flat in the larger, but still very rural town of Sonthofen on 16 December 1952 so that his father could start work there as a civilian employee of the local police. Before attending secondary school in Oberstdorf, to the south of Sonthofen amid the mountains by the Austro-Bavarian border, Max spent one and a half years in the *Volksschule* in Sonthofen (1953–54) and two years (1954–56) at the Catholic *Gymnasium* Sankt Maria Stern in Immenstadt, just to the north of Sonthofen. Dr Beßler's guiding educational beliefs during Max's time at the Oberstdorf school are very clearly expressed in the speeches he gave at the school's prize-giving ceremonies in July 1962 and 1963. See -ad-, '"Lebt im Geiste der humanitas christiana!": 47 Abiturienten verließen die Oberrealschule Oberstdorf', *Allgemeines Anzeigeblatt* (Immenstadt), 21–22 July 1962, Aus dem Oberallgäu section, pp. 12–13, and -ad-, 'Sich im Geiste der Humanitas bewähren: 76 Abiturienten nahmen Abschied von der Oberrealschule', *Allgemeines Anzeigeblatt* (Immenstadt), 19 July 1963, Aus dem Oberallgäu section, p. 12.

3. Certificate dated 17 July 1963 in the Deutsches Literaturarchiv Marbach (DLA). He did well in Religious Studies, English, Geography, Biology, Art, and PE ('gut' [B]), less well in Latin, History, and Chemistry ('befriedigend' [C]), and only passably in Maths and Physics ('ausreichend' [D]).

4. Dr Eberhard taught German and history and was also a prominent and active member of the SPD (Social Democratic Party) in Oberstdorf. See: -ad-, 'Rückblick bei der SPD', *Allgäuer Anzeigeblatt* (Immenstadt), 28 February 1963, Aus dem Oberallgäu section, p. 10; cf. Horst Weiß, 'Dr. Kurt Eberhard', *Jahresbericht 2004/5 Gertrud-von-le-Fort Gymnasium Oberstdorf*, pp. 10–11.

5. Although Freiburg University Archive cannot release any information on Max's studies there until the tenth anniversary of his death on 14 December 2011 (letter to RWS from the Freiburg University Archive of 2 February 2005), some of his *Seminar-Scheine* (attendance certificates) have survived among his papers (DLA): cf. note 14 and the Chronology in Part III of this volume.

6. Hans Peter Herrmann, 'Die Widersprüche waren die Hoffnung: Eine Geschichte der Reformen am Institut für Neuere deutsche Literaturgeschichte der Universität Freiburg im Breisgau 1956 bis 1977', in *Innovation und Modernisierung: Germanistik von 1965 bis 1980*, ed. by Klaus-Michael Bogdal and Oliver Müller (Heidelberg: Synchron, 2005), pp. 67–107 (especially pp. 68–79).

7. Herrmann, p. 70. Given the prevailing ethos of the Oberstdorf *Oberrealschule* while Max was there (see note 2), he would have assimilated such values from an early age.

8. Herrmann, p. 70.

9. Herrmann, p. 70. Details of his early publications in the school magazine may be found in the Primary Bibliography, H.A.1–H.A.12. Max's close schoolfriend Rainer Galaske (see Fig. 2.3), now a distinguished Professor of Medicine, who edited the school magazine referred to on Max's *Abitur-Zeugnis* (*Der Wecker* (The Alarm-Clock)), also recalls the two of them listening to protest songs by Bob Dylan and Joan Baez at the end of 1963.

10. Herrmann, p. 74.

11. Conversations with Etta Schwanitz (née Uphoff) of 21 June and 1 October 2005; Leander Vierheilig, 'Das Studentenheim Maximilianstraße ist aufgelöst', *Freiburger Studenten-Zeitung* (hereafter *FS-Z*), 16.3 (May 1966), pp. 7–8 (University Archive, Freiburg, D53/223). Schwanitz's most provocative fictional work was, of course, *Der Campus* (1993; film version 1998), and according to Etta Schwanitz, his widow, he showed a draft version to Max who then helped him to get the work published. Like Max, Schwanitz would become deeply critical of the German university system and something of an exile in his own profession. He played a key role in Max's *Habilitation* in Hamburg on 16 April 1986.

12. *FS-Z*, 14.7 (December 1964), p. 26.

13. See -ad-, '"Antigone" — von Oberrealschülern aufgeführt', *Allgäuer Anzeigeblatt* (Immenstadt), 14–15 April 1962, Aus dem Oberallgäu section, p. 19.

14. 'Vorstellung neuer Mitglieder [autumn]: W. G. Sebald', *Jahrbuch 1997* (Darmstadt: Deutsche Akademie für Sprache und Dichtung, 1998), pp. 189–90; 'Mit einem kleinen Strandspaten Abschied von Deutschland nehmen', interview with Uwe Pralle, *Süddeutsche Zeitung*, 22–23 December 2001, Literatur section, p. 16. The seminar in question was entitled 'Introduction to the Study of Modern German Literary History (Romantic Fairy-Tales, Poetry)' and given in Max's second semester at Freiburg (SS 1964) by Professor Erich Ruprecht (1906–97) with the help of his Assistant, Dr Horst Meixner (b. 1932), who would later become a distinguished Professor of German at the University of Mannheim and a noted authority on German Romanticism. Max contributed a paper on 'Caricature and the Grotesque: The Depiction of Bourgeois Society in Hoffmanns *Der goldene Topf*' for which Meixner gave him a 'gut' [B]. On the whole his grades for literary essays in Freiburg seem to have been surprisingly poor. In WS 1963/64 an essay on *A Streetcar Named Desire* was marked 'mangelhaft/befriedigend' [D+]; in WS 1964/65 essays entitled 'The Idiosyncrasy of Hemingway, Fitzgerald and Faulkner' and 'Leonce in Büchner's *Leonce und Lena* and Jacques in Shakespeare's *As You Like It*: A Comparison' received only a 'gut' [B] and 'befriedigend' [C] respectively; and in SS 1965 an essay on 'The Question of Reality and Ideal in Thoreau with Special Reference to *Walden*' was marked as 'voll befriedigend' [B+]. Indeed, the only indication of future promise before Max's very last term at Freiburg was the 'sehr gut' [A] that he got in SS 1964 for English essay-writing.

15. W. G. Sebald, 'Es steht ein Komet am Himmel: Kalenderbeitrag zu Ehren des rheinischen Hausfreunds', *Logis in einem Landhaus* (Munich: Hanser, 1998), pp. 9–41 (p. 12). Although the connection between Hebel and the Frankfurt School may seem a strange one, Max is almost certainly thinking of Johann Peter Hebel, *Kalendergeschichten*, selected and with an afterword by Ernst Bloch, Sammlung Insel, 7 (Frankfurt a.M.: Insel-Verlag, 1965), since in a letter of 2000 to a Freiburg book-dealer Max would name Hebel's *Kalendergeschichten* as one of his fourteen favourite books (see Figure 11.1, p. 264). The Marxist philosopher Ernst Bloch (1885–1977) was not a member of the Frankfurt School, but he was a friend of Adorno and Lukács.

16. Conversations of 21 June and 1 October 2005. Hans Peter Herrmann, who began to study at Freiburg in 1951 and taught there from 1957 to his retirement in 1994 (Herrmann, p. 67) (see note 6), identifies *Minima Moralia* as the bridge between *werkimmanente Kritik* (his own preferred approach to literature in the 1950s and 60s) and a more ideological critical methodology: 'Erschrocken habe ich später entdeckt, dass andere, Gleichaltrige und Jüngere, an anderen Universitäten ihre Adorno-Lektüre und ihre Kenntnis der Frankfurter Schule genutzt haben zu einer kritischen Auseinandersetzung mit der Stellung der Universität in der Gesellschaft; ich habe in Freiburg Adorno vor allem als Kunsttheoretiker und Literaturinterpreten gelesen und die *Minima Moralia* als ein geistreiches Buch mit klugen Aperçus aus einer aussichtslosen Welt' [I was shocked to discover later that others, coevals as well as people younger than myself at other universities, were using their reading of Adorno and their knowledge of the Frankfurt School to mount a critique of the place of the university in society. When I was at Freiburg, I read Adorno first and foremost as a theoretician of art and an interpreter of literature and his *Minima Moralia* as a wittily intelligent book, the product of a world without prospects that was full of clever *aperçus*] (Herrmann, p. 74).

17. The following texts by the five named authors that Max probably acquired during his time at Freiburg are now housed, along with the greater part of his library, in the DLA. I am most grateful to have been allowed access to them: Theodor W. Adorno, *Noten zur Literatur*, 3 vols (Frankfurt a.M.: Suhrkamp, 1963–65) (vols I and II acquired in December 1963 and vol. III in March 1965); Walter Benjamin, *Ursprung des deutschen Trauerspiels* (Frankfurt a.M.: Suhrkamp, 1963) (acquired in July 1964); Walter Benjamin, *Einbahnstraße* (Frankfurt a.M.: Suhrkamp, 1962) (acquired in August 1964); Walter Benjamin, *Ausgewählte Schriften* [I]: *Illuminationen*, Die Bücher der Neunzehn, 78 (Frankfurt a.M.: Suhrkamp, 1961) (acquired in March 1965); Walter Benjamin, *Ausgewählte Schriften*, II: *Angelus Novus* (Frankfurt a.M.: Suhrkamp, 1966) (probably acquired in 1966); Theodor W. Adorno, *Minima Moralia: Reflexionen aus dem beschädigten Leben* (Frankfurt a.M.: Suhrkamp, 1962) (probably acquired in 1964); Theodor W. Adorno, *Musikalische Schriften*, II: *Quasi una fantasia* (Frankfurt a.M.: Suhrkamp, 1963) (probably acquired *c.* 1965); Ernst Bloch, *Geist der Utopie* (Frankfurt a.M.: Suhrkamp, 1964) (probably acquired *c.* 1965); Ernst Bloch, *Spuren*, neue erweiterte Ausgabe (Frankfurt a.M.: Suhrkamp, 1964) (probably acquired 1964/65 since it contains a bookmark from the Freiburg bookshop where Max presumably bought it).

18. See Reinbert Tabbert, 'Max in Manchester: Außen- und Innenansicht eines jungen Autors', *Akzente*, 50.1 (2003), 21–30 (p. 23). Tabbert, a Professor at the PH Schwäbish-Gmünd, got to know Max well when they were *Lektoren* in Manchester 1966–67 and records that Max's enthusiasm for the Frankfurt School and Benjamin so affected his own attitude to literature and literary criticism that it caused him problems when he was examined on his doctoral thesis on Harold Pinter at the University of Tübingen in May 1968 ('Max in Manchester', p. 22; see also Reinbert Tabbert, 'Tanti saluti cordiali. Max', *Literaturen*, 2004.5 (2004), 46–49 (p. 48)). Cf. W. G. Sebald, 'Laudatio auf Wolfgang Schlüter' (1997), in *Mörike-Preis der Stadt Fellbach 1991–2000*, ed. by Christa Linsenmaier-Wolf (Fellbach: [n. pub.], 2000), pp. 149–54 (p. 150) where Benjamin, whose portrait hung outside Max's office in UEA for more than a decade (see Fig II.5, p. 376), is tacitly used as the touchstone against which to judge the value of other authors. James Atlas interviewed Max in Norwich on 6–7 February 1998, and although he probably knew little about Max's intellectual antecedents, he noticed, as I had, that 'with his thinning mane of white hair, rimless glasses and bushy mustache' Max resembled 'the Frankfurt theorist Walter Benjamin' (James Atlas, 'W. G. Sebald: A Profile', *Paris Review*, 41 (1999), 278–95 (p. 282)). Benjamin's Ninth Thesis on History, involving the *Angelus Novus*, is one of the key passages for understanding Max's literary work of the 1990s since references to and avatars of Benjamin's Angel of History (cf. *Illuminationen*, pp. 272–73) abound there (see note 142).

19. 'In Conversation with W. G. Sebald', in *Writers in Conversation with Christopher Bigsby*, by Christopher Bigsby, 2 vols (Norwich: EAS Publishing / Pen&inc., 2001), II, 139–65 (pp. 146–47). Post-1945 German literature was one of the 'subjects of much greater urgency' referred to by Max (cf. note 14), for Herrmann confirms (p. 70) that during the pre-1968 period, no Freiburg academic was interested in the political literature of the Weimar Republic or post-war literature. Max's contemporaries at Oberstdorf also recall that the history syllabus at their school stopped with the First World War, but insist that outside school hours they were very preoccupied with the question of how the *NS-Zeit* could have happened. Certainly, the *Allgäuer Anzeigeblatt*, the local newspaper for Sonthofen that was published in Immenstadt, carried impressive articles in the early 1960s that dealt with pertinent and painful issues. See, for instance: Yevgeni Yevtuschenko, 'Babi Jar', trans. by Ernst Kux, *Allgäuer Anzeigeblatt*, 26–27 January 1963, Feuilleton, p. 23; Peter Kritzer, 'Heute vor dreißig Jahren: Betrachtungen zu einem schwarzen Tag in Deutschlands Geschichte', *Allgäuer Anzeigeblatt*, 30 January 1963, unpaginated; Heinrich Kaltenegger, 'Der Untergang der "Weißen Rose": Vor zwanzig Jahren: Die Geschwister Scholl starben für die Freiheit', *Allgäuer Anzeigeblatt*, 20 February 1963, p. 3.

20. Atlas, pp. 289–90; see also 'In Conversation with W. G. Sebald', pp. 146–47. That such bigger issues also exercised the Gruppe 64 can be inferred from Dietrich Schwanitz, 'War es gut, daß der 20. Juli ein Mißerfolg war?', *FS-Z*, 14.5 (July 1964), 3–5.

21. Herrmann, pp. 71 and 74.

22. Herrmann, p. 73.

23. Herrmann, pp. 69–75.

24. Herrmann, p. 73.

25. Herrmann, p. 71.

26. Freiburg University Archive, B24/2770.

27. Reference dated 22 April 1970, personal file W. G. Sebald, UEA. I am grateful to Mrs Ilse Peacock for allowing me to reproduce her husband's reference. Max's advanced interest in Shaw was almost certainly fuelled by Schwanitz, who was then becoming a Shaw specialist and would, in 1969, present his first doctoral thesis on this playwright at the University of Freiburg ('Formale Entwicklungstendenzen im Werke George Bernard Shaws' (Formal Developments in the Work of George Bernard Shaw)).

28. Winfried Sebald, 'Gottes Rosenöl-Baum', *FS-Z*, 14.6 (November 1964), 21; 'Jeden Abend...', *FS-Z*, 14.7 (December 1964), 26; 'Erinnertes Triptychon einer Reise aus Brüssel', *FS-Z*, 15.5 (July 1965), 26; 'Erinnern', *FS-Z*, 15.7 (December 1965), 24. 'Erinnertes Triptychon einer Reise aus Brüssel' is reprinted in W. G. Sebald, *Über das Land und das Wasser: Ausgewählte Gedichte 1964–2001*, ed. by Sven Meyer (Munich: Hanser, 2008), pp. 14–18. For the full list of items published in the *FS-Z*, see Primary Bibliography H.B.1–H.B.10.

29. At school, Max had been known as 'Sébé' (or 'Wies[e]' when he published in *Der Wecker* (see note 9)). His family called him Winfried and his part in O'Neill's play earned him the soubriquet

FIG. 2.44. The Ordensburg, Sonthofen (April 2005), one of three built by the Nazis as élite training schools 1934–37. The building, now the Generaloberst-Beck-Kaserne, dominates the hills to the east of Sonthofen and can be clearly seen in the centre/right of FIG. 1.12.
© Richard Sheppard (2005)

'Koki' in Freiburg. From quite an early age he was given to signing letters with imaginatively funny pseudonyms. But in *c*.1966 he decided to drop his first two given names. He disliked 'Winfried' because it was too Germanic (and so, like Wagner, *Sauerkraut*, and *Lederhosen*, ideologically compromised) and 'Georg' because that was the first name of his father, a regular soldier who had served in the *Reichswehr* and the *Wehrmacht*, narrowly escaping capture at Stalingrad, and was now a Major in the logistics branch of the *Bundeswehr* in Sonthofen (Figure 2.44). Instead, Max later claimed, he decided to use the shortened version of his 'third first name, which is one of the traditional names which you find in eightenth- and nineteenth-century German everywhere' ('In Conversation with Chris Bigsby', pp. 163–64; see Primary Bibliography J.34). But Max's sister Gertrud tells me (email of 2 February 2008) that he never had a third given name: 'It is a fairy-tale, most probably his own.' So the name of the street and hostel in Freiburg, Wilhelm Busch's mischievous character, Horkheimer, and the figure who appears in the piece in the *FS-Z* all probably played their part in Max's decision.

30. Letters to RS from Mme Christine Fracheboud of the Administration of the University of Fribourg of 25 January and 18 February 2005. A copy of the *mémoire* exists in the Bibliothèque Cantonale et Universitaire, Fribourg (UM 875) and was made available to me by the kindness of M. Alain Bosson. It will be published in the double (memorial) number of *Journal of European Studies* that will appear on the tenth anniversary of Max's death. The examiners' reports may still exist, but they are not currently available. The more liberal laws governing Swiss archives permit us to know more about Max's studies in Fribourg (WS 1965/66; SS 1966).

31. Letter to RS from Mme Christine Fracheboud of [March] 2005.

32. See Anton Näf, 'Eduard Studer (1919–1992) als Wissenschaftshistoriker', in *Germanistik in Deutschfreiburg oder die Suche nach dem Gral: Eduard Studer zum Gedenken*, Schriftenreihe der Deutschfreiburgischen Arbeitsgemeinschaft, 15 (Freiburg i.Ü.: Deutschfreiburgische Arbeitsgemeinschaft, 1994), pp. 23–38.

33. See Verena Olejniczak Lobsien, 'Herkunft ohne Ankunft: Der Chronotopos der Heimatlosigkeit bei W. G. Sebald', in *Herkünfte: Historisch–Ästhetisch–Kulturell*, ed. by Barbara Thums and

others (Heidelberg: Winter, 2004), pp. 223–48 (pp. 230–33); cf. Jo Catling, 'W. G. Sebald: Ein "England-Deutscher"? Identität–Topographie–Intertextualität', in *W. G. Sebald: Intertextualität und Topographie*, ed. by Irène Heidelberger-Leonard and Mireille Tabah (Berlin: LIT Verlag, 2008), pp. 25–53.

34. See James Smith, *Shakespearian and Other Essays*, ed. by Edward M. Wilson (Cambridge: Cambridge University Press, 1974). For an account of Smith's life, see pp. 343–51 (p. 346).

35. Bruno Stephan Scherer, '"Selbstgespräch des Leides und der Nacht": Ernst Alker 1895–1972', in *Ernst Alker* (Freiburg [Schweiz]: Paulusdruck, 1974), pp. 7–8. See also *Ernte und Aussaat: In memoriam Ernst Alker*, ed. by Egon H. Rakette (Munich: Langen-Müller, 1973).

36. Scherer, p. 8.

37. Scherer, pp. 8–9.

38. Scherer, p. 9.

39. hob, 'Ein morbider Trickspezialist der Literatur', *Reutlinger General-Anzeiger*, 14 December 1990, p. 8; cf. Richard Sheppard, 'Dexter — Sinister: Some Observations on Decrypting the Mors Code in the Work of W. G. Sebald', *Journal of European Studies*, 35 (2005), 419–63 (pp. 422–25 and 452 n. 9).

40. Scherer, p. 9.

41. Ernst Alker, *Die deutsche Literatur im 19. Jahrhundert (1832–1914)* (Stuttgart: Alfred Kröner, 1962), pp. 745–46. Max knew this book, for he misquotes it on pp. 31–32 of the *mémoire*. Alker's book was a reworked, one-volume edition of his *Geschichte der deutschen Literatur von Goethes Tod bis zur Gegenwart*, 2 vols (Stuttgart: Cotta, 1949–50).

42. Georg Lukács, *Schriften zur Literatursoziologie*, ed. by Peter Ludz (Neuwied: Hermann Luchterhand, 1961); Lukács's 1909 essay appears there on pp. 261–96.

43. Theodor W. Adorno, *Jargon der Eigentlichkeit: Zur deutschen Ideologie* (Frankfurt a.M.: Suhrkamp, 1965) (acquired February 1966). During his Fribourg period Max also acquired (March 1966) Theodor W. Adorno, *Versuch über Wagner* (Munich and Zurich: Droemersche Verlagsanstalt Th. Knaur Nachf.: August 1964). Both are extant in the DLA.

44. References to Sebald's University of Fribourg *mémoire de licence* [BA dissertation], entitled 'Zu Carl Sternheim: Kritischer Versuch einer Orientierung über einen umstrittenen Autor' (On Carl Sternheim: A Critical Attempt to Come to Terms with a Controversial Author), are henceforth in the body of the text in parentheses.

45. Lukács, 'Zur Soziologie des modernen Dramas', p. 265.

46. Lukács, 'Zur Soziologie des modernen Dramas', p. 284.

47. Having read Empson's *Seven Types of Ambiguity*, Max already understood the importance of literary irony as a means of distantiation, and on page 41 of the *mémoire* he accuses Sternheim's language of lacking ambiguity, 'die das Vermögen der Sprache zur Ironie begründet' [which forms the basis of linguistic irony]. This ambiguity, Max then states, 'die der "New Criticism" als konstituierendes Element der Kunstsprache nachgewiesen hat' [which 'New Criticism' has shown to be a constituent element of literary language], 'setzt vor allem in ethisch-ästhetischen Dingen ein echt kritisches Bewußtsein voraus, dessen Objektivität durchaus subjektiv sein kann' [presupposes above all a genuinely critical consciousness in matters of ethics and aesthetics whose objectivivity can be thoroughly subjective].

48. When editing his class's *Abiturzeitung* (school-leavers' newspaper) in June–July 1963, Max contributed an anonymous article in dialect entitled 'Die Breissen' which both satirized and re-inscribed the stereotypical Bavarian image of the North German. Cf. also Tabbert's remark: 'Zwar hat ihm das preußische Milieu, dem ich [...] entstammte, nie sehr behagt (wie man seiner Magisterarbeit über Sternheim und seiner Doktorarbeit über Döblin ablesen kann)' [Though it is the case that [Max] was never comfortable with the Prussian milieu from which I [...] hailed (as can be inferred from his MA thesis on Sternheim and his PhD on Döblin)] ('Tanti saluti cordiali', p. 46).

49. At the time of his death, Max held a NESTA (National Endowment for Science, Technology and the Arts) Fellowship. He originally intended to use it to produce a 'semi-documentary' book on 'the "éducation sentimentale", under the fascist regime, of the social class to which my parents belonged' on the grounds that 'little has been written about the way in which ordinary people became imbued with the values of the fascist system' (application for leave of absence

dated 2 August 2000, personal file, UEA). He later modified this never-to-be-realized scheme (see Ulrich von Bülow's discussion in Chapter 10 of this volume).

50. See Sheppard, 'Dexter — Sinister', pp. 437–38.

51. Among Max's books in the DLA is his copy of Hugo von Hofmannsthal, *Ausgewählte Werke*, ed. by Rudolf Hirsch, 2 vols (Frankfurt a.M.: Fischer, 1957). 'Ein Brief' is on pp. 337–48 of vol. II: on page 346 Max has circled the words 'Leere' [emptiness] and 'Starre (meines Innern)' [inner frigidity]. For a groundbreaking account of Max's position within (post)modernity, see J. J. Long, *W. G. Sebald: Image, Archive, Modernity* (Edinburgh: Edinburgh University Press, 2007), especially pp. 168–74. However, Long misses the connection between *Austerlitz* and 'Ein Brief' (cf. pp. 152–55).

52. Letters to RS from Dr James Peters of 27 January and 7 March 2005. According to Dr Peters, Max's personal file no longer exists.

53. Letter to RS of 31 March 2005; Professor Tabbert confirmed this in a letter to RS of 7 April 2005.

54. W. G. Sebald, 'Max Aurach', in *Die Ausgewanderten* (Frankfurt a.M.: Eichborn, 1992), pp. 219–355 (p. 219); 'Max Ferber', in *The Emigrants*, trans. by Michael Hulse (London: Harvill, 1997), pp. 149–237 (p. 149).

55. *Die Ausgewanderten*, p. 219; *The Emigrants*, p. 149.

56. See 'In Conversation with W. G. Sebald', p. 149. Professor Keller agrees with this account (letter to RWS of 25 May 2005).

57. The Arosa Hotel (now demolished) stood on the corner of Wilmslow Road and Mauldeth Road in Withington, and Max would have passed it when travelling between the University and Didsbury (where he later lived).

58. Letter to RWS from Dr Peters of 7 March 2005.

59. Butor had been a French *lecteur* in Manchester 1951–53, and while living in Chorlton in mid-November 1966 Max was reading *L'Emploi du temps*, which deals with Butor's experiences in Manchester. His heavily annotated copy (Paris: Éditions de Minuit, 1957) is among his books in the DLA.

60. Letters to RWS of 22 February and 3 March 2005; see also Phill Bamford, *Manchester: 50 Years of Change* (London: HMSO, 1995).

61. 'Max in Manchester', pp. 23–25.

62. W. G. Sebald, *Nach der Natur: Ein Elementargedicht* (Nördlingen: Greno, 1988), p. 82. The translation is taken from *After Nature*, trans. by Michael Hamburger (London: Penguin, 2002), p. 95; the square brackets in the translated text denote my suggested revisions of Hamburger's version.

63. Friedrich Hölderlin, 'Der Main', in *Werke und Briefe*, ed. by Friedrich Beißner und Jochen Schmidt, 2 vols (Frankfurt a.M.: Insel-Verlag, 1969), I: *Gedichte: Hyperion*, pp. 52–53 (p. 53) (my translation (RWS)).

64. *Nach der Natur*, pp. 83–84; *After Nature*, pp. 95–96.

65. Letter to RWS from Professor Martin Durrell of 14 February 2005; Tabbert, too, describes Didsbury as 'ländlich' [rural] ('Max in Manchester', p. 26), letter to RS of 7 April 2005.

66. Cf. 'Max in Manchester', pp. 23–26.

67. 'Max in Manchester', p. 26. Coincidentally, Peter Jordan (b. Munich, 1923) was a Jewish *émigré* to Britain (May 1939): his wife (b. 1930) was English. Peter was probably the first German Jew whom Max met in England and he would later weave his story into 'Max Aurach' / 'Max Ferber'. See Klaus Gasseleder, 'Erkundungen zum Prätext der Luisa-Lanzberg-Geschichte aus W. G. Sebalds *Die Ausgewanderten*', in *Sebald. Lektüren.*, ed. by Marcel Atze and Franz Loquai (Eggingen: Isele, 2005), pp. 157–75 (especially pp. 160–61, nn. 10, 11, and 12). Peter Jordan also lent Max copies of memoirs written by himself, his aunt (Thea Gebhardt), his uncles, and his grandfather (all from Munich), and Max would later use these, too, especially Thea Gebhardt's (subsequently published by Klaus Gasseleder as *Zwei Gesichter: Aus der Chronik einer jüdischen Familie, eines fränkischen Dorfes und eines Weltbades in der ersten Hälfte des 20. Jahrhunderts* (Geldersheim: Vetter, 2005). The Herr Deutsch (Figure 2.45) whom Max names as his Manchester landlord (*Nach der Natur*, p. 87; *After Nature*, pp. 99–100) lived at 8 Clothorn Road, and was in fact the landlord of two other *Lektoren* during the academic year 1966–67: Wolf Dieter Ortmann and Dietmar

FIG. 2.45. Mr and Mrs Deutsch, the landlords of 8 Clothorn Road, Manchester (fictionalized as the narrator's landlords in *Nach der Natur*, 3. IV (Eichborn), p. 92; *After Nature*, pp. 99–100). © Dr Wolf Dieter Ortmann

Kremser. Apparently, and contrary to what is said in *Nach der Natur*, the Deutschs were in the 'rag trade' and had come to Manchester from Berlin in 1928.

68. 'Max in Manchester', p. 23.

69. Reinbert Tabbert, 'Erinnerung an W. G. Sebald, einen Ausgewanderten aus dem Allgäu', *Literaturblatt für Baden und Württemberg*, 6.9 (2002), 10–11 (p. 11); conversation with Etta Schwanitz of 21 June 2005. A copy of the novel exists in Sebald's *Nachlass* (DLA).

70. Letter to RWS from Stephen Swaby of 28 May 2005.

71. Eda Sagarra, 'The Centenary of the Henry Simon Chair at the University of Manchester (1996): Commemorative Address', *German Life and Letters*, 51 (1998), 511–24.

72. Letter to RWS from Professor Idris Parry of 31 March 2005.

73. Letter to RWS from Professor David Blamires of 8 March 2005. Parry was probably the first native British Germanist to recognize the stature of Elias Canetti (who lived in Manchester 1911–13). He published 'Elias Canetti's Novel *Die Blendung*' in *Essays in German Literature*, I, edited by F. Norman (London: Institute of Germanic Studies, 1965), pp. 145–66, and may well have pointed Max towards Canetti's work. Certainly, *Die Blendung* appeared on one of Max's UEA reading lists as early as 1972.

74. Letter to RWS from Professor Tabbert of 7 April 2005; letter to RWS from Dr Peters of 13 April 2005.

75. Letter to RWS from Professor Tabbert of 7 April 2005; letter to RWS from Professor Eda Sagarra of 28 June 2005.

76. Letters to RWS of 22 February and 3 March 2005.

77. Letter to RWS of 25 February 2005.

78. Cf. Max's approving remarks on non-canonical authors in 'Laudatio auf Wolfgang Schlüter', p. 152.

79. Letters to RWS of 21 and 26 February 2005.

80. Letter to RWS of 14 February 2005; email to RWS of 3 March 2010.

81. Tabbert, 'Tanti saluti cordiali', pp. 46 and 47. After Tabbert left, the very top flat in 26 Kingston Road, right under the eaves, was occupied by Peter Jonas (b. 1946, now Sir Peter Jonas, the

Intendant of the Munich Staatsoper from 1993 to 2006), who had begun to study singing and musicology at the Northern School of Music in autumn 1966. Sir Peter, who spent many evenings with Max and his wife, wonders 'how they stuck the noise' of his singing and told me that he 'learnt a lot from talking to Max' but that it took him a good few years to understand what that was (conversation of 20 June 2005).

82. W. G. Sebald, *Die Ringe des Saturn* (Frankfurt a.M.: Eichborn, 1995), p. 231; cf. *The Rings of Saturn*, trans. by Michael Hulse (London: Harvill, 1998), p. 186.

83. *Die Ringe des Saturn*, pp. 230–33; *The Rings of Saturn*, pp. 185–87.

84. Letters to RWS from Professor Keller of 4 March 2005, Dr Peters of 7 March 2005, and Mrs Stella Cox (Kerry's widow) of 3 and 12 April 2005.

85. Letters to RWS from Professor Keller of 4 March 2005, Professor Parry of 7 March 2005, Professor Blamires of 8 March 2005, and Dr Rosemary Wallbank-Turner of 6 June 2005.

86. Letter to RWS from Professor Keller of 4 March 2005.

87. Letter to RWS from Mrs Stella Cox of 3 April 2005.

88. *Die Ringe des Saturn*, pp. 232; *The Rings of Saturn*, p. 186. For an appreciation of the life and work of Professor Parry which mentions Max, see Eda Sagarra, 'Idris Frederick Parry (1916–2008)', *German Life and Letters*, 61 (2008), 295–96.

89. *Die Ringe des Saturn*, p. 233; *The Rings of Saturn*, pp. 186–87.

90. The only extant copy of this thesis is in the Manchester University Archives. No examiners' reports survive, but the thesis was awarded a distinction (see Max's letter to Tabbert of 1 August 1968 in 'Tanti saluti cordiali', p. 48). Max's MA certificate (DLA) is dated 11 July 1968.

91. Although *Perrudja* was the source of an epigraph for one chapter of the thesis (p. 201), Max replaced it in the book version with a quotation from Jules Verne.

92. The two texts by Lukács that form the theoretical framework of the *mémoire* do not feature in the thesis, where Lukács is represented by *Von Nietzsche bis Hitler*, a densely annotated copy of which is extant in the DLA. The last two named works by Adorno are not extant in the DLA; nor is Herbert Marcuse, *Kultur und Gesellschaft*, 2 vols (Frankfurt a.M.: Suhrkamp, 1965), or anything else by that author. Professor Tabbert tells me that he and Max read and discussed with approval Marcuse's *Triebstruktur und Kultur* (*Eros and Civilization*) but that neither of them thought well of Marcuse's *Der eindimensionale Mensch* (*One-dimensional Man*) (conversation of 25 June 2005). Certainly, Max makes no use of these latter two works in any of his critical essays (cf. Sheppard, 'Dexter — Sinister', pp. 438–39) apart from one very early newspaper piece which Max would never list in any of his bibliographies (W. G. Sebald, ' "Ein Ding, das nicht seinesgleichen hatte": Utopie und Paradies: Phantasie über ein Thema von Döblin', *Frankfurter Rundschau*, 25 September 1971, Feuilleton, p. iv). Here, referring to Marcuse's *Eros and Society* [*sic*], Max cites an uncharacteristic passage that speaks not of the liberating power of Eros but of 'das Nirwanaprinzip nicht als Tod, sondern als Leben' [the Nirvana principle not as death, but as life].

93. W. G. Sebald, 'Carl Sternheim und sein Werk im Verhältnis zur Ideologie der spätbürgerlichen Zeit' (The Relationship of Carl Sternheim and his Work to the Ideology of the Late-Bourgeois Epoch) (unpublished master's dissertation, University of Manchester, 1968), p. 6. Henceforth all references to this work are given in parentheses within the body of the text.

94. For a description of Adorno's pressurized life in spring 1967, see Marcel Atze and Sven Meyer, ' "Unsere Korrespondenz": Zum Briefwechsel zwischen W. G. Sebald and Theodor W. Adorno', in *Sebald. Lektüren.*, ed. by Atze and Loquai, pp. 17–38 (p. 25). On page 6 of the thesis Max implied that he had already received more than one letter from Adorno (cf. 'in Brie*fen*', the dative plural). The originals of Max's letter to Adorno of 24 April 1967 and one that he would write to Adorno on 14 December 1968 (i.e. six months *after* the submission of the MA thesis) exist in Adorno's papers, as does a carbon copy of Adorno's reply to Max's letter of 28 April 1967. All three have been published in Atze and Meyer, 'Unsere Korrespondenz', pp. 10–16. But on page 133 of the thesis Max cites extensively from what he claims is a second letter from Adorno to himself dated 17 May 1967: no carbon copy of this second letter survives, nor is its original in Max's papers. A comparison of the three passages cited by Max in his thesis with the carbon copy of 28 April shows, however, that all three come from this one letter. So what is going on? This is not a case of academic dishonesty: rather, we are dealing at one level with Max the 'Schelm' [trickster] having a straight-faced laugh at his examiners' expense in the private

context of an unpublished thesis. As I have argued elsewhere (Sheppard, 'Dexter — Sinister', pp. 440–41), this side of Max's character is never very far from the surface of his fictions, and sources close to Max tell me that a lot of 'authentic' dates in his literary work actually relate to himself or family members: for instance, Gracie Irlam's birthday ('Max Aurach' / 'Max Ferber', in *Die Ausgewanderten*, p. 152; *The Emigrants*, p. 225) is, like the non-existent letter from Adorno of 1967, dated to 17 May 1944 — the day before Max's own birthday. But at a more serious level, Max's hoax also suggests that what applies to Sternheim is also of relevance to himself: he, like Sternheim, could be regarded as a case of 'failed assimilation' into German — or any other — society.

95. The DLA copy contains six marginalia reading 'St[ernheim]', five reading 'KR', and twenty reading 'KRULL'. Of the latter twenty-five, only five refer with any probability to Mann's *Felix Krull*: the others seem to refer to the protagonist of Sternheim's play *Die Kassette* (1912).

96. On pages 97–98 Max cites an extensive passage from *The Authoritarian Personality* (p. 683) which distinguishes between 'successful and unsuccessful identification'; on page 168 he cites *Noten zur Literatur*, i, p. 149, where Adorno states: 'Die assimilatorische Sprache ist die von mißlungener Identifikation' [assimilatory language is that of unsuccessful identification]; and Adorno's letter to Max of 28 April 1967 observes that they were obviously both concerned with the symptomatology not just of assimilation [Anpassung], but of 'unsuccessful assimilation' (*Sebald. Lektüren.*, ed. by Atze and Loquai, p. 14). Max adapts and uses the latter passage in his thesis (p. 133), but, significantly, footnotes its source as the spoof letter of 17 May 1967 (cf. note 94).

97. Max's use of the term 'Oedipus complex' raises the question of his familiarity, at this time, with the work of Freud. In a long conversation of 1 October 2005, Albrecht Rasche, who studied psychology at Freiburg before becoming a psychoanalyst in the 1970s and subsequently a specialist in dream analysis, tells me of his own reading of Freud's *Traumdeutung* (*The Interpretation of Dreams*) in 1964; Rasche also owned a pocketbook edition of *Totem und Tabu*. So Max may well have picked up a certain amount of Freudian terminology during his time in the *Max-Heim*. The published evidence suggests, however, that he began to read Freud in depth only much later in his life (cf. Sheppard, 'Dexter — Sinister', pp. 431–33, 437–38, and 455 n. 29).

98. E.g. Sternheim's 'Stilisierung des künstlerischen Subjekts zu einer von priesterlichen Sendungsbewußtsein erfüllten Person' [stylization of the artistic subject into a person who is filled with a sacerdotal consciousness of mission] (pp. 60–61); his tragic compulsion 'zur kontinuierlichen Reproduktion der pathologischen Zusammenhänge einer Spätzeit' [continually to reproduce the pathological interconnections of an age that is coming to its end] (p. 114); his judgmentalism (p. 128); his love of 'Exkurse in die Philosophie und Siedlungsgeschichte' [excursions into philosophy and the history of human settlements] and need to display 'seine umfassenden philologischen und fremdsprachlichen Kenntnisse' [his comprehensive knowledge of philology and foreign languages] (p. 132). Cf. for example Joachim Fritz-Vannahme, 'Promeneur im Proseminar', *Die Zeit*, 13 October 1995, Literatur section, p. 2; Adam Thirlwell, 'Kitsch and W. G. Sebald', *Areté*, no. 12 (autumn 2003), 27–54, and Ferdinand Mount, 'A Master Shrouded by Mist', *Spectator*, 26 February 2005, pp. 40–42.

99. Pralle, 'Mit einem kleinen Sandspaten Abschied von Deutschland nehmen', p. 16; cf. Sheppard, 'Dexter — Sinister', pp. 422–23, and Max's rejection of Marcuse's works in which libidinal freedom is championed as the means of combatting social repression (cf. note 92).

100. It is of interest to note that Krull's narrative situation is very close to Max's own in the Wertach section of *Schwindel. Gefühle.* How could the adult Krull recall his childhood in such detail? How could the adult Max, whose family left Wertach for Sonthofen when Max was eight and a half, do likewise? The answer is likely to be that he wove fictions around some salient remembered childhood experiences.

101. John Prudhoe, '*Leonce und Lena* by Georg Büchner', *Staff Comment* (University of Manchester), no. 46 (March 1968), 18–19 (p. 18).

102. Prudhoe, '*Leonce und Lena* by Georg Büchner', pp. 18–19. The backdrop slides (supplied by Tabbert) were of Weikersheim Castle, a baroque palace between Bad Mergentheim and Rothenburg ob der Tauber (conversation with RWS of 25 June 2005).

103. Prudhoe, '*Leonce und Lena* by Georg Büchner', p. 19.

104. Letter to RWS from Swaby of 28 May 2005.

105. Swaby also tells me that 'the cast started with a script that "had been found by chance" on a train

in Germany [i.e. written by Max himself (RWS)]. The idea was binned after a few weeks and we went with *Leonce* [...]. I think most of us realized its true origins.' Tabbert had sight of this script (which was written in 1967) and helped Max correct it (conversation with RWS of 25 June 2005). Professor Sagarra also tells me that while at Manchester, Max wrote her a Viennese-style comedy, 'just a few pages [...]. It was very much *à la* Nestroy, intrigue and *Sprachspiel* [wordplay] with an eye for the stage.' This manuscript is now lost (letter to RWS of 28 June 2005).

106. When Martin Durrell took over the German play from Max for the 1968/69 session, he remembers Max describing the most important aspect of the director's role as 'cutting half the text': 'as I was tackling Brecht's *Schweik* at the time, I found this immensely valuable advice' (letter to RWS of 14 February 2005). I remember Max saying the same thing to me in the early 1980s in connection with Brecht's *Dreigroschenoper*. Both Max's thesis (p. 144) and subsquent book (p. 80) refer to the 'Gesetz ästhetischer Ökonomie' [law of aesthetic economy], and when he took part in the discussion on Sternheim that was broadcast by SRF (Swiss Radio) on 17 February 1971 (reproduced in *Sebald. Lektüren.*, ed. by Atze and Loquai, pp. 39–55), he remarked: 'Man muß als Regisseur eine sehr harte Hand haben, um das Stück in eine Richtung klar herauszustellen' [As a director, you need a very firm hand in order to make sure that the play moves in one clear direction] (p. 45).

107. Max acquired a paperback copy of *Hamlet* (DLA) in March 1966 (William Shakespeare, *Hamlet*, bilingual version, trans. by Schlegel and Tieck, ed. by L. L. Schücking (Reinbek bei Hamburg: Rowohlt, 1965). Quotations and allusions occur throughout his academic work (cf. the title of his first academic article (note 137)). Tabbert, who saw the young Max as a Hamlet-like figure, recalls that they wanted to celebrate their move to Didsbury with a party whose theme was to be 'There are more things in heaven and earth than may be dreamt in your philosophy' [*sic*] ('Max in Manchester', pp. 27 and 25).

108. See Sheppard, 'Dexter — Sinister', pp. 424–25.

109. Cf. 'Recovered Memories', interview with Maya Jaggi [13 September 2001], *Guardian*, 22 September 2001, Saturday Review section, pp. 6–7 (p. 6).

110. Tabbert, 'Tanti saluti cordiali', p. 47.

111. Max Sebald, 'Minna von Barnhelm: Lessing', *Staff Comment* (University of Manchester), no. 54 (February 1970), pp. 29–30.

112. Tabbert, 'Tanti saluti cordiali', p. 46; his address in St Gallen was Metzgergasse 14.

113. Tabbert, 'Tanti saluti cordiali', pp. 46–47.

114. See Winfried Georg Sebald, *Carl Sternheim: Kritiker und Opfer der Wilhelminischen Ära* (Stuttgart: Kohlhammer, 1969), p. 11; Max's second letter to Adorno is reproduced in *Sebald. Lektüren.*, ed. by Atze and Loquai, pp. 15–16.

115. Nicholas Rogers, the Archivist of Sidney Sussex College, tells me that all papers relating to unsuccessful candidates for Research Fellowships in the 1960s have been weeded out (letter to RWS of 1 June 2005).

116. In 'Max Aurach' / 'Max Ferber', Max collapses his narrator's three years in Manchester into a single continuum and dates the start of his year in Switzerland as 1969 (*Die Ausgewanderten*, p. 263; *The Emigrants*, p. 176). See also Sir Peter Jonas, '"Wir alle sind doch Emigranten": Lesung für W. G. Sebald: Sir Peter Jonas erinnert sich an den Freund', *Abendzeitung* (Munich), 28 January 2002, Kultur section, p. 17.

117. Professor Furness, letters to RWS of 21 and 26 February and 11 April 2005; conversation with RWS of 11 April 2005.

118. Ibid. In this latter connection, Furness particularly remembers a strange nursery rhyme that he would recite to Max, for whom it held a special fascination:

> There was a man of double deed
> Who sowed his garden full of seed.
> And when the seed began to grow
> 'Twas like a garden full of snow.
> And when the snow began to melt
> 'Twas like a ship without a belt.
> And when the belt began to crack
> 'Twas like a stick across my back.

And when my back began to smart
'Twas like a pen-knife in my heart.
And when my heart began to bleed
'Twas death, and death, or death indeed.

119. Tabbert, 'Max in Manchester', p. 29.
120. For publication details see note 114. Henceforth all references to this text are given in parentheses within the body of the text.
121. It is important to remember that when Max, the son and son-in-law of professional soldiers, was writing his Sternheim book, the student revolts of the late 1960s, which began in Berlin on 2 June 1967 when the police shot Benno Ohnesorg during a visit of the Shah of Iran, had by no means run their course. The Sternheim book can thus be seen as a long-distance contribution to those revolts — in which Max otherwise took no part. Certainly, Thea Sternheim, Sternheim's second wife, saw the book in this light, for on 4 December 1969 she noted in her diary: 'Zeitweilig geht Sebalds Zorn so hoch[,] daß ich mich frage[,] ob er als Individualempörung oder als Sprachrohr einer Klique anzusehen ist: in letzterem Fall wäre es ein Auftakt, dem weitere folgen werden. In jeder Hinsicht welch erschreckender Mangel an Toleranz und Humor bei dieser zornigen Jugend von heute' [Sebald's anger is sometimes so great that I ask myself whether it should be regarded as the outrage of an individual or whether he is speaking on behalf of a clique: if the latter, then we're dealing with an opening salvo that will be followed by others. In every respect what a frightful lack of tolerance and humour with these angry young people of today] (cited in Atze and Meyer, 'Unsere Korrespondenz', p. 33). For a discussion of the methodological shortcomings of Max's Sternheim monograph, see Manfred Durzak, 'Sebald — der unduldsame Kritiker: Zu seinen literarischen Polemiken gegen Sternheim und Andersch', in *W. G. Sebald: Schreiben ex patria / Expatriate Writing*, ed. by Gerhard Fischer (Amsterdam: Rodopi, 2009), pp. 435–45 (especially pp. 439–42). Professor Durzak is not, however, familiar with the book's two antecedents and underestimates the probable impact of the political context on its aggressive tone.
122. See Long, *W. G. Sebald: Image, Archive, Modernity*, passim.
123. Letters to RWS from Dr Alexander Schweikert (Kohlhammer Verlag) of 3 and 14 March 2005.
124. Valerij Poljudow, 'Eins mit seinen Gegnern? Sebalds Sternheim-Polemik', *Die Zeit*, 14 August 1970, Feuilleton, p. 15; reproduced in *Sebald. Lektüren.*, ed. by Atze and Loquai, pp. 56–58. When Max applied for the UEA post, he said that his book had received 'various positive reviews in German newspapers and journals' and that it had been discussed in the Westdeutscher Rundfunk, Cologne, in January 1970. To date the WDR has not been able to locate this broadcast, and I know of only two reviews that had appeared between October 1969 and late March 1970. One, by Marianne Kesting, must have first appeared in the *Frankfurter Allgemeine Zeitung* and was reprinted in *Auf der Suche nach der Realität: Kritische Schriften zur modernen Literatur* (Munich: Piper, 1972), pp. 197–201; the other, by Gustav Konrad, appeared in *Welt und Wort*, 2.2 (February 1970), 55. Konrad's review is completely dismissive, mainly because of Max's use of 'erborgten Kategorien' [borrowed categories] and lack of familiarity with Sternheim's work as a whole. Kesting's review is more even-handed: even though Max has neglected Sternheim's 'Hauptwerk' [major writings] from his middle period and uses him as an Aunt Sally (p. 197), the book is one of the first serious analyses of the Sternheim problem, and it should be taken seriously because, unlike earlier studies, it breaks the consensus (p. 200). On 17 February 1971, Max's book on Sternheim was discussed on Swiss radio (DRS II) in a programme in which he himself participated; the transcript has been reproduced by Marcel Atze in *Sebald. Lektüren.*, ed. by Atze and Loquai, pp. 39–55.
125. W. G. Sebald, 'Sternheims Narben', *Die Zeit*, 28 August 1970, Modernes Leben section, p. 46; reproduced in *Sebald. Lektüren.*, ed. by Atze and Loquai, pp. 59–60.
126. W. G. Sebald, 'Ein Avantgardist in Reih und Glied: Kritische Überlegungen zum Verständnis des Dramatikers Carl Sternheim und seiner Widersprüche', *Frankfurter Rundschau*, 10 October 1970, Feuilleton, p. v; reproduced in *Sebald. Lektüren.*, ed. by Atze and Loquai, pp. 61–64.
127. Tabbert, 'Tanti saluti cordiali', p. 47.
128. Personal file, UEA. Max's enthusiasm for the 'rororo' volumes, with their grainy black-and-white photographs and unfashionably biographical approach to literature, can be gauged from the fact that his personal library in the DLA contains 43 such volumes (see Figure 11.8, p. 283).

129. Ibid., cf. Sagarra, 'The Centenary of the Henry Simon Chair', pp. 511–12. In her letter to me of 28 June 2005 Professor Sagarra complements the three references, remembering Max best 'for the flair with which he combined his many gifts', for 'his capacity to undermine traditional British images of "the" German', as a 'warm and witty friend', a 'wonderfully engaged and clever teacher', and 'someone who explored areas of German literature and philosophy unknown to the British Germanist'.

130. See Michael Sanderson, *The History of the University of East Anglia* (London: Hambledon and London, 2002), pp. 63–68; also Christopher Smith, *'Max': W. G. Sebald As I Saw Him* (privately printed pamphlet for the author by the Solen Press, Norwich, 2007). The latter publication gives a good insight into the everyday life of EUR.

131. See Richard Sheppard, 'Woods, Trees and the Spaces in between', *Journal of European Studies*, 39 (2009), 79–128 (pp. 105–07).

132. The irreverent young used to say: 'EUR has few middle-aged people on its staff and most of these are under 30.'

133. See Sanderson, pp. 81–84.

134. See Sanderson, pp. 113–15; Barry Taylor, 'Willi Guttsman', *Library Association Records*, 100 (1998), 277; R. J. Evans, 'W. L. Guttsman', *German History*, 16 (1998), 417–22. At least five German-Jewish, German, or Jewish exiles were teaching at UEA during the 1970s and 1980s, all of whom were known to Max.

135. The first big occupation of UEA's Arts Block, which I remember watching with considerable interest together with Max and other colleagues, took place in March 1971. We were allowed back inside briefly to fetch research materials on condition that we did no administration while we were in the building — a condition to which we readily assented in the name of revolution. For an excellent account of UEA's 'time of troubles', see Sanderson, pp. 187–222.

136. See for instance 'Characters, Plot, Dialogue? That's Not Really my Style...', interview with Robert McCrum, *Observer*, 7 June 1998, Review section, Books, p. 17.

137. W. G. Sebald, 'Alles Schöne macht das Mißlungene ärger: Am Fall Günter Eich: Poesie in den Steingärten: Erinnerung als eine Form des Vergessens', *Frankfurter Rundschau*, 6 February 1971, Feuilleton, p. iv; 'The Undiscover'd Country: The Death Motif in Kafka's *Castle*', *Journal of European Studies*, 2 (1972), 22–34.

138. W. G. Sebald, 'Die hölzernen Engel von East Anglia: Eine individuelle Bummeltour durch Norfolk and Suffolk', *Die Zeit*, 26 July 1974, Reise section, p. 38.

139. I once saw a shirtless, sunburnt agricultural labourer wearing a battered trilby and with strings round the knees of his trousers cycling blithely through the virtually traffic-free city centre, for all the world like a survivor from Hardy's Wessex and completely oblivious to modernity. Rural Norfolk existed in even more of a time warp. In the early 1970s we had to stop our car on one occasion to allow a mole to cross the road near a village called Great Snoring and to do likewise on another occasion because two weasels were totally absorbed in a fight in the middle of an empty main road.

140. In 'Dr Henry Selwyn' (*Die Ausgewanderten*, p. 3; *The Emigrants*, p. 8) Wymondham becomes Hingham, a village even further away from, and to the west of, Norwich. Uwe Schütte, one of Max's last PhD students, develops the point about peripheries to cover Max's life, critical work, and professional situation ('Für eine "mindere" Literaturwissenschaft: W. G. Sebald und die "kleine" Literatur aus der österreichischen Peripherie, und von anderswo', *Modern Austrian Literature*, 40 (2007), 93–107 (pp. 93–94 and 106 n. 1)); and Anja K. Johannsen relates the concept of peripheries to Max's tacit concept of the intellectual (see *Kisten, Krypten, Labyrinthe: Raumfigurationen in der Gegenwartsliteratur: W. G. Sebald, Anne Duden, Hertha Müller* (Bielefeld: transcript verlag, 2008), pp. 103–04).

141. The reference is not gratuitous, since Max had been reading Proust since his time at school and university; cf. Franz Loquai, 'Max und Marcel: Eine Betrachtung über die Erinnerungskünstler Sebald und Proust', in *Sebald. Lektüren.*, ed. by Atze and Loquai, pp. 212–17 (p. 213); see also the three essays by Richard Bales in the Secondary Bibliography.

142. See note 18, also, for example, Eberhard Falke, 'Mords-Erinnerung', *Die Zeit*, 27 November 1992, p. 69; Martin Chalmers, 'Angels of History', *New Statesman*, 12 July 1996, p. 45; Michael Rutschky, 'Das geschenkte Vergessen', *Frankfurter Rundschau*, 21 March 2001, p. 1.

Appendix 2.1: Review by W. G. Sebald of a performance of Lessing's *Minna von Barnhelm* by the ensemble 'Die Brücke' at the University Theatre, Manchester, early 1970

It was with scepticism rather than with interest that I awaited the second play which the Brücke ensemble presented in the University Theatre. Lessing's *Minna von Barnhelm* is considered stale, tackled and worn out by generations of provincial producers and bored pupils, a sad example of the famous German comical tradition, which never gives you a chance to laugh. The restrictions of the two main parts are so hard to overcome on stage that most productions leave the impression of Tellheim as a rather imbecile Prussian officer and of Minna as a wistful aunt with some talent for intrigues. Above all the play cannot as readily be brought up to date as some other classics. Its original intention must be saved, if yet another nail is not to be contributed to its coffin.

Considering this, Axel von Ambesser's and Dieter Brammer's production was in fact something of a rescue action. Allowing for the comical[,] it did not allow for boredom, and this bias towards a boulevard style seems to have induced the producers to suppress the darker aspects of the story. The puzzling passage for instance in which Tellheim identifies with the Moor of Venice has been deleted and along with it the possibility of a ruinous end. It was Just — sympathetically acted by Joost Siedhoff — who added a touch of seriousness. When he found himself isolated by the good fortune of his master, his mimic [*sic*] hinted at a set of counterpoints which could stimulate as many reflections as the servants' imitation of their employers' happiness. Thus Lessing's main intention did finally come across as a good ending, not a happy end but the victory of reason, so gracefully personified in Eva Kotthaus's Minna. The most brilliant achievement was perhaps Peter Lieck's, who, in Riccaut, presented a unique and cross-eyed mixture of utter confusion and sheer calculation. Even Dieter Brammer's landlord was far more than the petty bourgeois as which he is usually conceived. When, towards the end of the play, he rushed across the stage, in order to receive Graf von Bruchsal, he carried a little dog in his arms, a gesture nobody would have expected from so egoistic a character. All of a sudden the comical had become human, just as before, with all their earnestness, the human actions had become comical.

This review, signed 'Max Sebald', was originally published in the University of Manchester staff magazine *Staff Comment* in February 1970 (see Primary Bibliography D.1). We gratefully acknowledge permission to reprint it here.

FIG. 3.1. W. G. Sebald, early 1980s.
© John Gibbons; courtesy of the University of East Anglia

CHAPTER 3

❖

At the University:
W. G. Sebald in the Classroom

*Gordon Turner**

When in October 1970, at the age of 26, Max Sebald took up his original appointment at UEA as Assistant Lecturer in German Literature and Language (in which post he would be required to divide his teaching duties between the two disciplines), it was clear that he greatly relished the opportunity to break the mould in terms of teaching. The contrast with the more traditional redbrick university ethos could not have been greater. As part of this newly established university with its clearly stated motto 'Do Different', the then School of European Studies (EUR) combined such disciplines as Literature, History, Modern Languages, and Comparative Literature. With its highly committed and predominantly young faculty it offered new possibilities in multidisciplinary approaches. At the time teaching was conducted in small group seminars, rather than in larger lecture circuses, with the onus on the seminar leader in question to orchestrate discussions and oversee group activities such as presentations.

Max's enthusiasm and desire to innovate had been apparent from the outset at a pre-teaching weekend of the German Sector (the break in tradition was obvious at the time in the avoidance of the word Department) in late June 1970. Fizzing with ideas and radiating considerable energy at all turns, he contributed easily and without inhibition to discussions of the German and European literature programmes and, to a lesser extent, to the German Honours Language programme (see Appendix 3.3 for details of the courses he taught while at UEA). His experience of more traditional approaches to literature and language teaching at the universities of Freiburg, Fribourg, and Manchester would have been very different (see Chapter 2 of the present volume) and it was soon apparent to teaching colleagues and students alike that Max was a force to be reckoned with both inside and outside the classroom.

The comments on his teaching made by former students, a selection of which appears below, closely match my own experience of him in action. I had the privilege of team-teaching with Max on numerous occasions and was thus able to observe him in the classroom at first hand. We collaborated on German language classes at so-called preliminary level (Grammar in Context) and at second-year level (Critique of Translation and Essay Writing), as well as on early attempts at applied language teaching in the final year (Introduction to Interpreting Techniques). What was immediately striking to me, as a language-teaching colleague, was his unusual German, fascinating in its structure and content, with elements of French — no doubt as a result of his time spent living in the Swiss canton of Fribourg — as well as a fair sprinkling of unusual turns of phrase from a number of European languages, as a student notes:

> I loved the way classes were interspersed with little anecdotes or the way that he would even lapse into French in order to express himself better in certain contexts. (1996–2000)

Max's approach to planning language classes was always sure-footed; once the direction of the teaching was established, he would fire off ideas and suggestions on how our teaching aims could be achieved. His easy-going and relaxed attitude in the classroom reflected very much his philosophy in his everyday dealings. As a gifted and totally natural raconteur, Max could easily hold those around him in his thrall. He would often break off from the teaching task in hand to recount a little anecdote or make an amusing observation, often involving the differences between life in Germany and Britain, which were more apparent particularly in the 1970s and the early 1980s. These diversions had the obvious effect of relaxing the atmosphere in the classroom.

An article on this subject makes little sense without the comments and reminiscences of the UEA students who attended his literature seminars and German language classes. In inviting contributions from former students of Max's (some as far back as the early 1970s) there was perhaps always a risk that any responses would reflect rather the profound regret at his untimely death and contain only highly emotional comments, which might in turn impede any insights. Ultimately, however, what many of the respondents have to say transcends the mawkish and the maudlin, helping to build a fascinating and wide-ranging picture of Max both inside and outside the classroom.[1]

First Encounters

What is at once striking from responses across the years is the indelible nature of the memories of that first meeting with Max. In effect, as put so aptly by a friend shortly after his death, to know Max was to be a little in love with him. A respondent from the 1980s neatly encapsulates this feeling:

> You think that by the time you reach university, you have got over schoolyard crushes, but I loved Max Sebald. All my peers did too — his deep, dulcet Bavarian tones, his kindness and 'twinkliness'. And he said amazing things. (1983–87)

Clearly the impact of meeting and being taught by Max was immediate:

> Under an iron grey East Anglian sky, when most of what was in my head was such a mess, so chaotic, there was this person who was so, in every sense, beautiful. I had never met anyone like him. (1972–76)

> He was always a very real presence at UEA, both on a physical and intellectual level. (1973–78)

> My abiding memories of him, going back to my undergraduate days, are of a
> beaming smile and his friendly teasing about the length of my beard. (1969–77)

Interestingly, there is not always complete unanimity in students' recollections of
first meetings with Max, as the following comments indicate:

> He was elegant, enigmatic and unattainable with his horn-rimmed glasses,
> gaucho moustache and long, belted raincoat and he was plain Dr Sebald in those
> days. (1972–76)

> I think I was in awe of Max most of the time actually and didn't relax enough
> to absorb all his pearls of wisdom. (1977–81)

> Our first impressions of Max were, of course, that he was incredibly good-
> looking, but shy and reserved and quite detached, although not aloof. (1977–81)

> I remember him as a kind, warm individual and someone one felt one could talk
> to. Although he was obviously profoundly intelligent, he was not intimidating.
> (1983–87)

At times, the experience of being taught by Max obviously had dramatic, almost
life-changing consequences for his students:

> Max was one of the first lecturers I met at UEA. I knew at once he was special
> and felt inspired to learn. I changed my course from history to literature and
> never looked back. (1985–89)

> Max did not realize just how much of a difference he had made to me as a
> lecturer [...] never spoke to him a great deal [...] but he affected me in the brief
> moments that I did speak with him. (1995–99)

Another frequently occurring image in students' recollections is that of Max's
voice, 'that voice speaking to me still down the years' (1972–76). The memory of
it clearly remains with all who met him, whether journalists, critics, colleagues, or
students:

> There was that rich dark chocolate voice leading us through the mystery of
> German Literature. (1972–76)

> I think what I probably remember most of all, apart from his moustache when
> he was younger, was the richness of his voice when he spoke English in his
> classic southern German accent. (1977–83)

> I remember a great deal of what Max taught and many of his illuminating
> aphorisms, all delivered in those inimitable Bavarian warm tones. (1981–85)

In the Classroom

In the light of the intensity of the above impressions, the vivid nature of respondents'
memories of his teaching — what he taught and how he went about teaching it —
comes as no surprise:

> Max was very entertaining to listen to and he had a great sense of humour
> and irony. With his infectious giggle, he liked nothing more than to mock
> things that he had observed. We remember him talking about how *bürgerlich*
> [bourgeois] people in his home town were, with their *Stammplatz* [regular
> place] at the hairdressers and the things they talked about in there. (1977–83)

FIG. 3.2. Finals party at the home of
Dr Colin Good (1941–2000)
in Norwich (28 June 1983).
© Demelsa Healey and Kathryn Walker

He was a very calm and relaxed teacher, of course, of great intellect — a teacher who extracted great responses from his students and who knew how to stimulate them without putting direct pressure on them. (1977–81)

My memory of Max is as very patient, very understed with an ironic, humorous touch and very mid-European — I must admit I thought he was Austrian (and not German). (1972–76)

Max Sebald talked to you as if he had known you for a very long time as an old spirit. He must have been just nine years older than me then and yet he seemed from a different, more brilliant age. There was absolutely nothing about him of the tarnished mid-70s in England and Germany at that time. He was quite simply extraordinary. (1972–76)

I remember his study where the seminars were held as being quite dark, with not much of an outlook and him sitting in a low chair, almost hiding behind the coats hanging above him (perhaps it was just because it was too small to be used for teaching purposes!). (1977–81)

It was one of his main characteristics to be quietly in the background, preferably invisible, too — a bit like the wiring hidden behind the plaster on the wall, without which no electricity would flow. (1981–85)

The Seminar Leader

For all the excitement and brilliance of his teaching, enrolling for and participating
in one of his seminars was obviously not considered an easy option:

> Max was excellent at presenting us with the material, but he certainly didn't
> spoon-feed us. When you sat down to write an essay, often you were not sure
> exactly what he wanted! (1977–81)

> I remember taking more than one course with him, which concentrated on just
> two or three books, in one case Döblin's *Berlin Alexanderplatz* and Kafka's *Das
> Schloss* (*The Castle*). It seemed almost like a soft option at first, but in retrospect
> I think he knew exactly what he was doing, as it meant that we really had to
> get to grips with the texts in a great deal of detail rather than being able to get
> away with a quick read and spouting generalizations. (1969–77)

> They were rewarding seminars to attend because of the high standards he
> expected. Woe betide you if you hadn't read the books (it would be better not
> to turn up at all) and if you hadn't thought in advance about the work. They
> were also entertaining and fascinating because Max wove in so many other
> aspects to expand the study of the literary texts — politics, philosophy, new
> ideas in theology or psychology. (1975–79)

There is also obvious appreciation of Max's technique in approaching literary topics
and helping to bring them to life as well as of his ability to interweave themes in
his seminars:

> Max made literature accessible and fascinating, drawing parallels with art, film,
> and psychology, etc. (1985–89)

> We would sit in his office on Thursday afternoons, around six of us, thinking
> through our latest text, discussing the complexities of life and the passions that
> make life worthwhile. (1981–85)

> I recall how in quiet, modulated steps we went down the pathways through
> the strange lands of Romanticism. In architect-modelled seminar rooms with
> institutional floor polish and plastic chairs, we were suddenly in the *Märchen*
> [fairy tale], seeing the candlelight through an Austrian window, taking on the
> sense of loss, of wandering, of darkness, of self-discovery. (1972–76)

> What he taught and the way he taught opened our eyes; he made us question
> the world, think about opposites, about parallels, ironies, inequalities, about
> reality and unreality, sanity and insanity, about memory and the historical
> contexts of what we were reading. We had never really done this before. It was
> exciting and different. (1985–89)

> He was so quiet and unassuming that it was easy to forget he was there. I recall
> a deep and moving seminar, in my case mostly about contemporary literature
> which often meant dealing with the Third Reich, extremely upsetting for me
> personally as I was born in the second year of World War II. His unique gift was
> to lead us straight into the subject matter. His calm voice and sure tread seemed
> to facilitate this transfer from now to then, feeling totally the then. (1981–85)

It is clear that, right from the start, Max was determined in his teaching not to
shy away from confronting his students with the realities of growing up in a post-

war Germany which he perceived as being in denial about its immediate National Socialist past. In this respect he was typical of a number of young Germans of his generation: he was not afraid to voice criticism of Germany, the vehemence of which could sometimes shock:

> What made Max interesting was that he was talking to us about the history of his time; he had direct experience as a child of life in post-war Germany. He was sensitive to the silence after the war about what happened and what was left unsaid, and how this was reflected in the literature of the time: there was a cultural vacuum, with everyone floundering around, not knowing how to come to terms with the past or deal with a sense of unreality. (1977–81)

> I took his Post-War German Literature seminar in the spring of 1981 and it was a revelation. He somehow meshed together the (then) previous thirty-odd years of German culture and prepared me for the (then) forthcoming year abroad by making me understand the background of the culture I was about to get dunked in. It was invaluable. It was the first time I was made to understand fully the tragedy of the post-war generation; it made me look at things very differently as I made my way through that year abroad, at a time when the post-war generation was still an important force in German society. (1979–83)

Impact of his Teaching

These exemplary teaching techniques obviously paid off, both motivating his students and bringing tangible results in their self-esteem:

> Max was so graciously full of interest in what we had to say, so questioning, so full of compliments and praise. (1977–81)

> He had a way of making his students feel special. All the time he was bringing out our potential, inspiring us to think for ourselves and encouraging us to have the confidence to speak our minds. (1985–89)

> To be given the confidence to approach these things! To be given the skills and insight somehow to have the tiniest equity in the dialogue that [students] wanted to achieve! 'Yes you can look at these ideas', Max said in so many ways. 'Yes, you can have a valuable response to the work if you think.' (1972–76)

> I had no idea how eminent he was. Perhaps he was less so in the mid-1980s. But my heart raced whenever he spoke to me. I clamoured to speak out in his seminars, and I wanted to say something perceptive. I wanted him to think I was clever. (1983–87)

> He truly was the first person in my life who listened and then looked at the landscape of what I had to say. Somehow he winnowed through the rubbish and the noise and the half-articulated thoughts and found something there that I had barely even known myself. (1972–76)

The Adviser

In its early days UEA was justly proud of its pastoral system, which involved a formalized, although certainly not formal, relationship between an 'Adviser' (faculty) and 'Advisee' (student). Coming from a different academic background

FIG. 3.3. Graduands' party 1988: the man on Max Sebald's right is
Daniel Limon, Lecturer in French; the empty chair has just been vacated
by Professor Clive Scott, FBA. © Petra Leseberg (UEA 1984–88)

and tradition, Max cannot at first have found this aspect of his work as an academic
in the UK easy, particularly when he was dealing with personal issues:

> He was 'Adviser' to us both, but neither of us remembers him being particularly
> comfortable or effective in this role. (1977–81)

On the other hand this appears to have been less of a problem whenever Max
found himself pitched against the university administration, particularly in terms
of academic regulations, which at times greatly frustrated his *laissez-faire* approach
to such matters. In this respect he was not slow to take up a cause on behalf of
students:

> I remember Max sorting out a problem which happened during our year abroad,
> when we received letters to say that we had failed our German coursework!
> This was due to some marks not having been entered correctly and Max dealt
> with it very efficiently. (1977–81)

The Language Teacher

That Max's input to the German Honours language teaching during the early 1970s
was perhaps not as remarkable as his literature teaching is less a reflection on his
ability as a language teacher than of the prevailing ethos in the School of European
Studies, which at the time tended to rate the value of foreign languages less highly
than that of the other disciplines on offer. The following anecdote best sums up his
somewhat eclectic approach to language teaching at the time:

> As a piece of homework, Max once set us the task of writing an essay on
> the subject *Sexualität, Perversion, Gewalt* [Sexuality, Perversion, Violence] (a
> somewhat typical Sebald topic). Imagine my delight, when, in reply to my
> question about how long it should be, he replied: It can be as long or as short as
> you like. You can submit a book or an aphorism. But if you submit an aphorism,
> the work will have to be all the better for being short, and I will assess and
> grade it all the more strictly. (1968–72)

The sea change in his approach to teaching language skills dates from his return
from leave of absence in the mid-1970s. Appearing to have lost his momentum
somewhat and beginning to question his motivation, as well as the wisdom of
committing to a permanent career as a Germanist in the UK, Max had sought leave
of absence to return to Germany and work under the auspices of the Goethe-Institut
in Munich, with a view to exploring the possibility of a career in that organization
with which he had first become acquainted in Manchester in the late 1960s. This
work originally involved some teacher training and subsequent exposure to the
teaching of German as a Foreign Language at all levels and, most difficult of all for
him, what he regarded as the tedium and sterility of dealing with learners with little
or no feeling for German in the *Öde* [soulless place] (his own description!) of, as it
so happens, Schwäbisch Hall.

Despite, or, more likely, because of, this evidently dispiriting and uncomfortable
experience, Max returned to UEA to take up his German-language teaching with
considerable vigour, triggered in part by his awareness of the relevance of language
skills at an advanced level. Comments after 1976 reflect his new commitment to
language teaching:

> The most interesting part (of my file) consisted of a few translations and
> excerpts from the German-language discussion group we had to take part in
> after our year abroad with the aim of reinforcing our language skills. Max
> cajoled and provoked us into expressing our opinions on various topics. I think
> he liked to try out his own ideas by just airing them in a class and seeing what
> reaction they got. You got the impression he valued your opinion when you
> contributed. (1975–79)

> I came very close to completing my time at UEA without having any classes
> with Max, and yet that final-year language class with him probably did as much
> for my German and general language skills as the rest of my degree course.
> (1996–2000)

The extent to which Max took his duties as a German-language teacher seriously
is exemplified by a particular encounter he had with developments in the British
academic system. Over the years the German Honours Language Programme was
overhauled on a number of occasions, not least when the German Sector expanded
to include colleagues who hitherto had worked in the Language Centre. At this
time of unusually high numbers of language students, it was agreed that the heavy
marking load would be shared on a rotating basis between all (including literature-
teaching) colleagues in the Sector and, accordingly, the so-called English–German
'Translation Circus' for final-year German Honours students, known as 3GH, was
instituted. This meant that every week students had to hand in a translation, selected

by a language teacher and distributed in dossier form in advance, which would be marked to be returned and discussed the following week. The Translation Circus was an admittedly blunt teaching instrument and the plenary system of returning marked work undoubtedly generated tensions between colleagues, but matters came to a head when, as per the schedule, Max came to mark a translation into German of a text in English, the obscure and precious nature of which both frustrated and irritated him (see Appendix 3.1). As befitting UEA's aim to 'do different', the text in question was not the usual extract from a novel favoured by most universities, Oxbridge and redbrick alike. Instead it was taken from a somewhat recherché book edited by Jan Morris (whose travel writing Max greatly admired) and consisted of quotations from different press reactions to a stirring debate which took place at the Oxford Union in 1933. Driven to distraction in the midst of the marking process, obviously on the night before the translations were due to be returned, he resorted to the portable typewriter which he was to use for his first literary efforts to hammer out in German a furious and damning deconstruction of the unsuitable and 'impossible' (a favourite Sebald word) nature of the English text, which he felt had been chosen with a blatant disregard for its merit as a piece of writing, let alone as one for translation (see Appendix 3.2). The resulting broadside — an excellent example of Sebald in full flight — conveys very well his feelings: horror and amazement at the choice of text as well as total sympathy for the students who had been asked to translate it. Making the effort to come in early on the day that the translation was due to be returned, Max ensured that the document was photocopied and deposited in students' pigeonholes, cancelling the handing-back session at the same time. Needless to say, Max also personally took severely to task the colleague who had been unwise enough to choose the text in the first place!

The Administrator

By the late 1970s the earlier gloomy predictions concerning the future of the study of German at British universities were being fulfilled. Against a background of swingeing cuts in the education budget, the number of students applying to study German Literature was in steep decline. On his return to UEA Max had involved himself more actively in academic policy-making at degree level, eventually taking on the mantle of EUR Admissions Officer between 1978 and 1982:

> Max was also effective at relaunching the German course package, making it more interdisciplinary, to attract more students. This led to our year being dubbed 'the last of the summer wine'. (1977–81)

The Marker

There seems to be a discernible progression in Max's approach to marking and providing his students with helpful feedback. Whereas to begin with — and perhaps in line with his experience of the German academic tradition — comments at the end of a piece of work were kept to a minimum and often did little more than accentuate the positive, his confidence in his ability as a teacher increased greatly, as did a feeling that he had valid comments to make. This was no doubt also a reflection of his growing reputation as a writer:

> When I tracked down essays which I'd kept, I could find no record of comments written by Max; not even my dissertation on Thomas Mann contained his appraisal. (1981–85)

> When you submitted an essay at the end of the seminar, Max's marking was firm but fair, and his comments minimal, which meant they were valued all the more. Typically, there would be half a dozen ticks in pencil down the margin, and at the end a grumble or two about points you could have made better, then a grudging acknowledgement 'not a bad piece overall'. If he judged it an intelligent, well-constructed essay you were simply overwhelmed. In other words, I think, he let you do the thinking, guided you where he wanted you to go, but then kept his own opinions out of the result — rather like his enigmatic self in his own books. (1975–79)

> I've read his comments on my essays. For '*Gastarbeiter* oder der gewöhnliche Kapitalismus: Gunter Wallraff', Max wrote:

>> 'Im allgemeinen recht gut (B+)' [On the whole rather good].

> In contrast he wrote a whole side in response to 'The Aesthetics of War: Ernst Jünger's ambivalent attitude towards the spectacle of destruction':

>> The essay contains a fair number of useful observations and remarks bearing on the problem. However, the prose given is somewhat haphazard and the structure of the argument therefore is not as clear as it might have been. [....] While it is true that you do attempt this it must be said also that you could have done it more convincingly [here, and on] p. 10 where you talk about 3 or 4 different things in a somewhat disorganized way. Still it is quite a good piece of work. (B+?)

>> 'Kafka, a German Jewish Writer':

>>> Apart from a number of factual errors quite a solid piece of work. Perhaps you could come and see me so that we can discuss one or two things in relation to this essay. (B+)

>> An essay about Heinrich Boll:

>>> A determined attempt to discover some of the patterns underlying the documentary prose style. You make some interesting points but there is a lack of conciseness, concentration which seems largely due to stylistic flaws. (B)

> I really think he was quite gentle and restrained about my weaknesses! (1977–81)

Later students write in similar vein:

> The comments on his Dissertation Report bear testament to what a great teacher he was:

>> Apart from minor mistakes and a fairly steady sprinkling of not quite idiomatic phrases — which I would accept as the hallmark of authenticity — the author shows he is able to sustain an argument in the foreign language.

> Now, there must be a hundred ways of saying 'nice try, but you've got a long way to go'. Max put it his way, and made me feel I had actually achieved something. (1979–83)

FIG. 3.4. Dr Michael Henry Parkinson (1945–94).
See *Die Ringe des Saturn* (Eichborn), pp. 12–14;
The Rings of Saturn (Harvill), pp. 5–7.
Michael never knew his father, Sergeant Henry
Parkinson (Glider Pilot Regiment, Army
Air Corps), for he was killed, aged 28, on 20
September 1944, the fourth day of the Battle of
Arnhem, probably during the fighting in the
Oosterbeek pocket. He is one of the 1680
Allied war dead who are now buried in
Arnhem Oosterbeek Military Cemetery. I don't
think Max knew this. (Richard Sheppard)
© John Gibbons; courtesy of Dr Christopher Smith

My ultimate reward came in my final year when I picked up a marked essay from Max. It was called 'Im Bedenken des Gesehenen: A Study of the Experience of *Glück* as Suggested by Peter Handke in *Die Lehre der Sainte-Victoire*'. Max had given me an A and covered the last page with his scrawl: 'It seems to me that you ought to try to do something where you can use your talent for writing ...' (1983–85)

He asked me to stay behind after a seminar. I felt my heart beating loudly as I presumed that I was about to be asked what has possessed me to write such an awful essay. It really wouldn't have surprised me at the time. Instead I stood in shock as Max told me that my essay was one of the best that he had ever read; that I could write and that I should never let anyone tell me otherwise. On the back page of the essay he had written: 'This is an outstanding piece of work, extraordinarily perceptive, beautifully written, succinct and in several of its turns, quite astonishingly profound. I felt quite privileged to be allowed to read it.' (1995–99)

Supervising Postgraduate Students

Among other roles required of Max was that of MA supervisor. He had himself been on the receiving end as a postgraduate student only recently; while working as a *Lektor* at the University of Manchester in the late 1960s, he had embarked upon an MA on the dramatist Carl Sternheim. The subsequent dissertation formed the basis of his Sternheim monograph in German, published in 1969, which caused controversy in Germany, not only for the content but also for the tone and style in which it was written (see Chapters 2 and 6 of this volume).

On his appointment at UEA Max had immediately plunged himself into a PhD thesis on Alfred Döblin, although writing it in acceptable academic English and in line with British academic conventions proved a challenge. His initial approach at the time was one that he would adopt for the process of English translations of his writing. He would write a draft chapter in German and then consult English-speaking colleagues on ways of conveying the sense of the original, undoubtedly elegant but also complicated, image-laden German. However, at this point in his career it is clear that he had not yet understood, let alone become versed in, the tradition of academic writing in Britain. Even then Max had begun to push against traditional or accepted notions of writing. This latter point about academic writing appears to be further underlined in this recollection from a postgraduate student:

> I ended up proofreading and English-checking Max's PhD on Döblin; I also wrongly assumed that his PhD thesis was what a PhD should be like (I'd already read quite a few boring ones, German, English and American). (1972–75)[2]

This unorthodox approach is apparent in the recollections of one of his first supervised postgraduate students:

> My strongest memory of Max was during my MA year when he oversaw my attempts to find connections between, if I remember correctly, Kafka and Nietzsche. Being Max, he of course wanted something very creative and slightly to the left of centre. So I was encouraged to take my research into esoteric areas such as the impact of illness on their writings, in turn taking me firmly out of my comfort zone, which essentially was putting together very lengthy essays stating the obvious. The whole exercise therefore stretched me considerably. The dissertation ended up far fuller of original thought and as such was considerably shorter than my other offerings at the time. Digging out my MA stuff after many years I found the offending piece. I thought he might have written all manner of comments on it (much as other academic colleagues used to) but the grade was the sole addition. He gave me an A− and told me that he was interested in trying to get it published. I remember a combination of relief and pride ensued, although he did nothing about it. (1973–78)

By contrast another postgraduate student from around the same period writes:

> Max was also the internal examiner of my postgraduate thesis, of course. He was a hard taskmaster but did eventually pass it although not without making me rewrite large sections of it first! (1969–77)

The following postgraduate student remembers Max's teaching favourably after encountering him in intellectually combative mode:

> Early on in my research student career, I sat in on Max's modern drama seminar, which I found very stimulating intellectually, and quite fascinating pedagogically, as I had never been to a seminar before (having studied at Cambridge). As a result of this, I had quite a few chats with Max about modern European drama, which was my main research area, read his Sternheim book, and asked him why he had written a book about an author whom he clearly detested. The reply was along the lines of 'because these people are so awful' followed by a belly laugh (which seemed to me at the time like Beckett's authentic laugh at despair). (1972–75)

The Academic and Writer

It is a common perception among colleagues and friends that where his writing was concerned Max played his cards very close to his chest, revealing, if anything, very little, and, if ever, very often after the event. Even though we knew that Max would occasionally submit pieces for publication in German periodicals and literary magazines, successes such as the publication of *Nach der Natur* (*After Nature*) in 1988, as well as his being shortlisted for the Ingeborg-Bachmann-Preis in Klagenfurt, Austria, in 1990, were communicated to us casually in typical throwaway lines. A case in point is the story which he recounted on his return to UEA shortly after receiving the Johannes-Bobrowski-Medaille in Berlin in June 1994. At one of our regular convivial gatherings in the German Sector office, Max described how, early in the morning after the award ceremony in Berlin, he had made his way down to the shores of the Wannsee. He had with him what he dubbed the 'indescribably hideous' plaque which he had received at the ceremony. Unable to contemplate ever being able to find houseroom for it, Max, an aesthete through and through, had hurled it into the water, where, he assured his incredulous colleagues and to his evident glee, it had sunk without trace.

Needless to say, his increasing fame as a writer was registered by his students, as indicated in these comments from those who had known him before his success as well as those whom he was teaching at the time:

> I was *wie vom Himmel gefallen* with surprise when I heard that Max had written books and was hailed the new hero of German literature; the phrase *stille Wasser gründen tief* immediately sprang to mind. Max *never* let on! Not even with one single hint when he invited me out to tea in the Suffolk countryside one afternoon; just walking and talking, having a cup of tea in one of those hidden private gardens with a few tables and picnic benches. (1981–85)

> It was in the discussions as part of the Handke seminar that Max might well have given a clue about his intention to write, when he talked about literature as being 'a way of knowing oneself'. (1974–78)

> Discovering Max's novels, I remember being taken aback by the melancholy side of his writings. It just wasn't how I remembered him. (1969–77)

> I always saw him as extremely introvert and private, not in the least encouraging me to talk to him and disturb him. No wonder really, if his own literary work was growing silently during those years within him. (1981–85)

> Max was critical of writers who dealt badly with the subject, by being over-sentimental and not dealing with guilt and responsibility for the war. He talked about his own feelings of guilt as a survivor, as many of the children in his own school died of malnutrition. He may have also discussed his own guilt as a deserter, or someone living in exile, which certainly comes out in his book *Die Ausgewanderten*. (1977–81)

> Reading *The Rings of Saturn* was like being back in a Max Sebald seminar, as his thoughts jumped from one theme to another and deftly brought all the strands together to make sense and a sudden new insight. (1975–79)

> If you can't hear his ironic/melancholic/amused voice, then you can't get the tone of his writing. (1972–75)

> I took European Autobiographical Writing, taught by Max in 1997 during my second year of undergraduate studies at UEA. I knew at the time that he had written literary works but, to my shame, I hadn't read any of them when I took the module. So I was largely unaware of Max's particular connections with the themes of exile and memory as well as loss, which pervade his writing. (1995–99)

> My essay was on Nabokov's *Speak, Memory*, where themes close to Max's heart are clearly evident. While my essay appeared to say something in a big way to him, his response, in fact, validated my own sense of exile felt at the time and allowed me to see something positive in myself again. (1995–99)

In 1999 there followed the somewhat surprising decision to transfer five colleagues from the School of Modern Languages and European Studies (EUR) to the School of English and American Studies (EAS): three Professors of European Literature, including Max, and two more junior colleagues.[3] With his reputation as a writer established, Max made waves in a first-year (English) lecture series with hitherto less forcefully expressed but typically idiosyncratic views, exemplified by the following contribution:

> Sebald, as a writer and polemicist, was fully engaged in a literary renovation of throwing out the old, and heralding in the new. His extensive, but productive, dissatisfaction with things as they were was first made apparent to me in a lecture he gave to my year in the winter of 1999. The lecture began by attacking the state of publishing — the number of published writers had increased tenfold in the last decade, but with little impact upon quality — then proceeded to critique the pointless prose of the weekend broadsheets, before finishing by condemning the stagnancy of the novel genre, in particular its inability to meet the demands of representing the atrocities committed by both sides during the Second World War.
>
> The uniqueness of this lecture centred on the fact that the deliverer had, to a large extent, responded to the last criticism by renovating the novel in his creative work, which I cannot classify according to any existing generic scheme owing to its constant narrative oscillations — between travelogue, detective story, autobiography. He was asking future producers of literature, as represented by our class in that lecture theatre, to rethink, perhaps even reject, the dominance of the verbal narrative conventions that have been handed down to us. As for rantings about terrible translations of German literary works — well, some people's ears must have felt that they were on fire! (1999–2002)

What these recollections seem to confirm is the sense that, as Max's reputation grew as a writer, so he felt able to express his opinions about literature and other subjects considerably more vehemently in seminars and lectures, particularly so, perhaps, once he had joined the School of English and American Studies and began to teach on the Creative Writing programmes.

Anecdotes

The deep affection for Max as a teacher is clearly seen in the responses from former students, many of them touching on his great sense of humour, which was always apparent to anyone who spent any time in his company and which manifested itself in some wonderfully told stories. As a raconteur Max was second to none. However, the following anecdotes serve to give an insight into the different facets of Max both in and outside the classroom:

> We were a group of four studying Post-Second World War West German Literature with Max in the late 70s / early 80s. We distinctly remember that Max introduced the subject by stating that most of the literature written after the war was complete rubbish. There followed a long pause, after which somebody asked 'Why are we studying it then?'! (1977–81)

> In the particular year that I was taking my finals, I had a revision session with him in which he dropped pretty heavy hints about what was on the exam paper! I think he told me in no uncertain terms to re-read two particular texts. I was rather surprised and very grateful, and I think this reflects his kindness and desire for his students to succeed. (1983–87)

> In the spring of 1983, during revision for Finals, I had wanted a session with him — as he had offered everybody — about his Post-War German Literature seminar. I remember we both had a series of mishaps, which prevented us meeting on campus; so he suggested I visit him at his home on a Saturday. I duly drove out one Saturday, where he cheerfully gave me a couple of hours of undivided attention, tea and biscuits, and a great deal of help for my revision, without once making me feel guilty about cutting into his weekend. (1979–83)

> Max often brought his dog into the university and walked him around the Broad. I remember the dog particularly well because we once all went to his house in Poringland for a seminar and I was wearing deep-red shoes, which I had recently polished. During the course of my deep concentration on the subject we were discussing I was obviously rubbing the dog with my foot as he lay at my feet, until his fur turned a lovely shade of bright pink! Max was highly amused and accused me of turning his dog into a punk! (1977–81)

It is well known that Max did not extend either his usual sense of humour or his forbearance to any form of technology, as the following two recollections from language students illustrate:

> One of our assignments was to select a topic to present to the seminar group and then lead a discussion for the rest of the class time. It sounded like a bit of a nightmare and I was even more put off by the idea of disappointing Max with the horrors of inaccurate German that such a task was likely to produce in me. Unbeknown to me, when I selected my topic, 'Die Schattenseite des Internet' [The Dark Side of the Internet], I hit on one of Max's bugbears.
> I had, therefore, barely started before Max launched into a tirade about the evils of the Internet and modern technology. I remember him getting more and more worked up about it, with the rest of us sitting there and letting him have the discussion time to himself. The look of disappointment when he

realized that the seminar was over and that he would have to stop and let us go was unforgettable, and it was undoubtedly the most memorable class of my university career. (1996–2000)

I remember him teaching an Interpreting class in the final year with a colleague and struggling to get to grips with the technology in the language laboratory. The subsequent curses in German came straight through the headphones. (1979–83)

By comparison it is good to be reminded of Max's sense of fun and his love of dressing up:

He was a great actor and brilliant master of disguise — cf. his incredible costumes at the annual *Fasching* party.[4] He was compelled to attend incognito because, at the time, by my reckoning, 95% of the female students fancied him something rotten. (1972–75)

No further proof of the feelings that Max generated in his female students is needed than the one in this contribution:

In with my box of memories from UEA I came across a Christmas card from a fellow student containing a particularly telling comment as we approached our first Christmas break away from UEA in Year One. 'A month without Max!' she lamented, these words being displayed as prominently as the seasonal greeting the card was intended to convey. Clearly the prospect of a whole month without Max's weekly seminar was too much to bear for a first-year student who, like the rest of us, had been captivated by his charismatic teaching style and had so quickly developed great affection for him as a person. (1981–85)

Final Thoughts

The Max we knew would have hated what he would have regarded as all the fuss and 'bother' about him and his memory since his death in December 2001,[5] yet it seems fitting to conclude with a series of comments which best put into context and at the same time pay fitting tribute to the thirty-one years that he spent working as a teacher and academic:

Max was an inspiration to me as to so many other people. I remember his seminars with great fondness. He was certainly one of the people who inspired me to try to pursue a career using my German, and I have been lucky to be able to stick with it. (1977–81)

As I look back to the time when I was taught by Max, what floods back to me are feelings of warmth and strength. (1972–76)

I associate [with Max] very positive feelings and, like many others, I would characterize him as warm, approachable, understanding, modest, and, it goes without saying, very knowledgeable and intellectual. One was always very conscious of the German seriousness beneath his easy manner and that dry, ironic sense of humour. (1977–85)

My mind is still infinitely better for his teaching. My life is so much richer. (1972–76)

FIG. 3.5. Dr Janine Rosalyn Dakyns (1939–94), on the left.
See *Die Ringe des Saturn* (Eichborn) pp. 13–17; *The Rings of Saturn* (Harvill), pp. 7–10.
© John Gibbons; courtesy of the University of East Anglia

FIG. 3.6. The wall of Janine Dakyns's office at UEA, *c.* late August 1994. © Mary Fox

He opened up a particular way of seeing, almost a methodology, so that there are signs of him everywhere in my life. I remember him talking about the solace gained from walking on one's own; of how we all like to secure our territory — and how important it is to step out of it; of how the sight of a pylon coming into view is a comfort, something familiar. (1985–89)

I will always be grateful to Max that he helped to develop my lifelong passion for great literature. (1981–85)

It is a great privilege to have had such a truly inspirational teacher. Not only was he an original thinker, he was erudite, extraordinarily modest, kind, caring, and gentle, with a great sense of humour. I shall always have an image in my mind of his lovely smile and sad eyes. (1985–89)

In 2001, some ten months after coming across my old files again, I was travelling on a train when my newspaper fell open at the obituary page. His face was still Max in the photo, the moustache still the same shape with eyes still creased in the same smiling lines. Finally it was clear, it really was all far too late to try and express my gratitude. (1972–76)

In conclusion, what finer epitaphs than these to sum up the legacy of Max the teacher as well as Sebald the writer?

It was clear that in his teaching Max also had very high standards of what constituted valid, enduring culture. Occasionally, when I have come across an outstanding piece of work that surpasses its medium, I think, 'This would have got Max's approval'. I've read all his books and in my view he passes his own test, because they are transcendental and will have longevity. (1975–79)

And when I read your books now, I am aware of so much more to you than my small, post-school, pre-real-world mind ever conceived. (1983–87)

With thanks to the former students whose recollections
form the bulk of this essay:

Stephen Bardle	Catherine Lewis (née Ross)
Natalie Batcock	Dominic O'Sullivan
Theresa Bateman (née McCabe)	Alison Ravnkilde
Barbara Beckett	Belinda Rhodes
Cecilia Carr	Clare Savory
Mike (Mick) Clark	Ruth Terry
Anne Fitzpatrick (née Friswell)	Fiona Traynor (née Bowman)
Steve Giles	Kathryn Walker
John Goldthorpe	Andy Webb
Christian Goodden	Sineadh Wheeler
Gerlinde King	Wendy Widmer

Caroline Winter-Jones

Notes to Chapter 3

* In March 1970 the University of East Anglia advertised three posts for Lecturers in German: one for German Literature only, one 50% German Literature and 50% German Honours Language, and one for German Honours Language only. In the following May, Sebald was appointed to the post combining the teaching of literature and language, while the writer of this chapter was appointed to the language-teaching post. Cedric Williams was appointed to the third post. Our close friendship and collaboration date from our first encounter in the pre-interview waiting room that May and were cemented by the realization in October 1970 that we had both chosen to live in the Norfolk market town of Wymondham.

1. The contributions in this chapter come from the twenty-three former students listed above, who graduated between 1972 and 2002. Some responded to a written request for recollections from my former colleague Richard Sheppard via the UEA alumni magazine *Ziggurat*, while others with whom we were already in regular contact were approached directly and invited to send in their thoughts and comments. They are designated here by the dates when they were students at UEA.

2. This is one of a number of claims by colleagues and postgraduate students to have proofread and checked Max's doctoral thesis which, to his dismay, he had been required to submit in English! The person he acknowledges in the preface as having been of (perhaps greatest) assistance in this respect is our former colleague, Cedric Williams.

3. The other colleagues transferred were Professor Clive Scott (European Literature), Professor Michael Robinson (Scandinavian), Dr Jo Catling (German Literature and Language), and Dr Glen Creeber (Media Studies).

4. During the 1970s and up to the mid-1980s there was an active and vibrant German Society in the School, offering a wide and varied programme with annual events such as *Fasching* and a German drama production. Yet despite the obvious success of *Leonce und Lena* in Manchester (see Fig. 2.36, p. 79), Max never to my knowledge offered to direct a play in German at UEA or involved himself actively in the eighteen German drama productions that I oversaw, though he did agree to coach the two principal male actors in my production of *Leonce und Lena* when we were having problems with a particular scene. He was, however, a great help with a German Drama Video Workshop which I set up for and with second-year students, and took on the task of overseeing a reworking of Schiller's *Die Verschwörung des Fiescos zu Genua* into a *Bugsy Malone*-type Chicago-based gangster drama, *Fiasko*. The resultant script was an excellent pastiche. Sadly, because of the difficulties of recording quickly and efficiently in UEA's television studio in the 1970s, the opus was never completed and the original recording — on reel-to-reel videotape — is probably no longer extant.

5. As he is alleged to have said after the memorial service in Norwich Cathedral for Sir Malcolm Bradbury on 10 February 2001, 'Don't ever let anyone do anything like that for me.'

Appendix 3.1: Translation exercise at UEA

3GH: TEXT 5

SOME REACTIONS TO THE OXFORD UNION 'KING AND COUNTRY' DEBATE

(9 February 1933)

Question for Debate

'That this House will in no circumstances fight for its King and Country'

This was the most celebrated debate in the history of the Oxford Union, for
the passing of the motion by 275 votes to 153 was widely taken to demonstrate
the degeneracy of Oxford, and so of Young England. The national press gave
the debate enormous publicity, but varied in its responses ...

> Daily Express: There is no question but that the woozy-minded Communists,
> the practical jokers, and the sexual indeterminates of Oxford have scored
> a great success in the publicity that has followed this victory ... Even
> the plea of immaturity, or the irresistible passion of the undergraduate
> for posing, cannot excuse such a contemptible and indecent action as the
> passing of that resolution.

> Manchester Guardian: The obvious meaning of this resolution (is) youth's
> deep disgust with the way in which past wars 'for King and Country' have
> been made, and in which, they suspect, future wars may be made ...

While this is how one private citizen reacted, in a letter to Isis:

> Dear Sir
>   I don't know much about the Oxford Union, but I judge from the report
> that the majority of its members have declared that they will not endanger
> their precious skins in fighting for their country, that the Union consists
> chiefly of aliens and perverts. It is a pity that the sweet creatures' names
> are not published. The police would find them useful.
>
>   Joseph Banister

Source: Jan Morris (ed.), The Oxford Book of Oxford, OUP, Oxford 1978,
         pp.374-75 (with minor omissions)

Appendix 3.2: Memo to students from WGS

ALL 3GH

Entschuldigt zunächst bitte, dass ich Euch diese Fehlerkorrektur nicht persön-
lich !! zum Vortrag bringe. Ich erstens - wie heisst es doch so schön - dienstlich
verhindert. Ausserdem fürchte ich mich ein wenig, vor Euch aufzutreten, weil das
nun ja ein wirklich ein ziemlich unmöglicher Text gewesen ist. Zuletzt denkt Ihr,
ich hätte ihn herausgesucht und bewerft mich mit diversen Viktualien. Ich habe den
Text aber nicht herausgesucht; vielmehr hab ich mich beim Korrigieren mindestens
genauso gegiftet wie Ihr beim Übersetzen. Die Schwierigkeit bei der Sache lag vor
allem darin, dass der Text sehr viele idiomatische, halbidiomatische, idiotische und
halbidiotische Wendungen enthält, die man in 'richtiges' Deutsch nur übertragen
kann, wenn man sich wirklich genauestens in der Sprache auskennt. Ich werd's jetzt
einmal probieren, muss dabei, der Sache entsprechend, allerdings hie und da etwas
frei verfahren.

Einige Reaktionen auf die vom dem Studentenverband der
Universität Oxford veranstaltete Debatte zum Thema
'König und Vaterland'.

Entschliessungsantrag:

"Dieses Haus (die hier Versammelten) werden unter keinen Umständen für König
und Vaterland kämpfen".

Diese Debatte war wohl die aufsehenerregendste (berühmt geht hier nicht so gut)
in der Geschichte des Studentenverbandes der Universität Oxford; denn die Tat-
sache nämlich, dass der Antrag mit x zu y Stimmen angenommen wurde, sahen weite
Kreise als Beweis für die Degeneriertheit (as distinct from Degeneration) Oxfords
und damit der der englischen Jugend überhaupt. Die nationale Presse sorgte dafür,
dass die Debatte in der Öffentlichkeit eine enorme Resonanz hervorrief, obschon
die Reaktionen der einzelnen Blätter (Zeitungen) auseinandergingen.

Daily Express: Zweifellos konnten die wirrköpfigen Kommunisten xxxxxxxxxxx sowie
die Witzbolde und die sexuell indefiniten Kreaturen an der Universität Oxford
das öffentliche xxxxxx Aufsehen, das diese Debatte erregte, als einen beträcht-
lichen Erfolg verbuchen...Doch selbst der Hinweis auf xxxxxxx die Unreife der
Studenten und auf den für sie charakteristischen Hang, sich theatralisch in
Szene zu setzen, kann nicht als Entschuldigung für eine derartig verachtenswerte
und unanständige Aktion, wie die Annahme dieser Resolution sie vorstellte, zi-
tiert werden.

Manchester Guardian: Der offensichtliche Sinn dieser Resolution liegt darin, dass
xixx in ihr der tiefe Abscheu der Jugend vor der Art zum Ausdruck kommt, in der
in der Vergangenheit die Kriege 'Für König und Vaterland' angezettelt wurden, und
in der, wie sie xxxxt vermuten, Kriege auch in Zukunft gemacht werden, ein Abscheu
vor der Scheinheiligkeit der Nation, die über die Ängstlichkeit und Narrheit der
Politiker, über niedrigste Gier, interne Eifersucht (I couldn't figure out what
'communal' means in this context) und Korruption den Mantel eines emotionalen
Symbols deckt, den sie (Nor could I figure out xxx what 'they' refers to at
this point) nicht verdient haben.

Die folgende Passage exemplifiziert noch die Reaktion eines Privatmanns:

Sehr geehrte Redaktion,

Ich bin über den Studentenverband der Universität Oxford nur unzulänglich in-
formiert (weiss nicht viel über ist hier schon etwas zu primitiv), schliesse jedoch aus dem Bericht, in dem es heisst, die Mehrheit seiner Mitglieder hätten
erklärt, sie würden ihre feine Haut nicht für ihr Land zu Markte tragen, dass
der Verband zum Grossteil aus Ausländern und Perversen besteht. Schade, dass
die Namen dieser Süssen nicht veröffentlicht wurden. Es wäre dies für die
Polizei gewiss sehr nützlich gewesen.

Joseph Banister
Carpenter
xxxxxxxxxx
Bethlehem

einem Brief an die Zeitschrift ISIS entnommene

PS: Entschuldigt auch den unordentlichen Zuschnitt dieses Blatts. Die Mitternacht
rückt näher schon. - Die Session am Donnerstag fällt natürlich aus.

Appendix 3.3: Summary of courses taught by WGS at UEA, 1970–2001

This list does not aim to provide a comprehensive term-by-term and (latterly) semester-by-semester account of W. G. Sebald's teaching, but to give an overview of the subjects he taught, the courses he devised, and the way in which this both reflected his research (and later, perhaps, his own writing) interests and evolved in dialogue with the changing priorities of the academic environment. The interdisciplinary nature of UEA and its traditional strengths in comparative literature meant that, then as now, an unusually high proportion of courses were open to students without a knowledge of German, running alongside the more traditional pattern of 'national literature' courses. In many cases there is a slight change of title, but the basic content remains largely the same (cf. the Kafka reading lists at the beginning and end of the sample lists which follow).

EUR: School of European Studies (1970–78)

Honours seminars: Language

Honours German language teaching (50% of teaching duties)
Advanced Language (LANG 2): Interpreting

Honours seminars: Literature

1970–74	Twentieth-Century European Novel
1971–75	European Drama 1870–1918
1971–	West German Literature I (1945–63)
1972–73, 1975–82	Literature and Politics in Twentieth-Century Germany (co-taught)
1973–74	German Literature in the Wilhelmine Period
1973–76	Austrian Literature
1976–79	Examples of Nineteenth- and Twentieth-Century Austrian Drama
1976–	The Radical Stage: New Concepts of Theatre in Post-war European Drama★
1977–	Franz Kafka★
1977–	West German Literature II (1963 to the present day)
1978–	European Drama 1880–1918

EUR: School of Modern Languages and European History (1979–93)

1979–	Examples of Nineteenth- and Twentieth-Century Austrian Drama
	Post-war German Literature (also known as West German Literature)
	New Theatrical Concepts in Twentieth-Century European Drama
	Franz Kafka
1980–	German Cinema in the Twenties★
1981–82	German Cinema / Weimar Culture (with Dr Thomas Elsaesser, English and American Studies)
1984–	Examples of Short Prose Fiction in Nineteenth- and Twentieth-Century German Literature

★An asterisk indicates that a copy of the course description is appended (pp. 132–42).

With the introduction of the modular Common Course Structure and semester pattern, the courses were as follows:

EUR: School of Modern Languages and European Studies

Language: contributions to:

> First-Year German Language Option: Literary Texts
> Second-Year German Language Option: *Literarische Texte*
> Final-Year Honours German

Literature

1993–	Introduction to German Literature (later known as Introduction to German Studies I)
	Post-war German Writing 1945–70★
1994–	Nature and Society: Nineteenth-Century German Short Prose Fiction★
	German Prose Fiction from Thomas Mann to Peter Handke
	Contemporary German Writing★
	MA in Literary Translation / MA in Comparative Literature: 'Case Studies' module (three seminars on the translation into English of *Die Ausgewanderten / Die Ringe des Saturn*)
1995–	Franz Kafka
	German Cinema in the Twenties
1996–97	MA in European Writing: Major Trends in European Fiction (1950–90)★ (co-taught)
1997–	Images of Nature: European Cultural Studies II
1998–	Introduction to German Studies I

EAS: School of English and American Studies

1999–2000	European Autobiographical Writing★
2000–01	Examples of Nineteenth-Century European Prose Fiction★
2001–02	Kafka's Shorter Fiction
	Reading Kafka's Novels★
	Contribution (lecture) to co-taught first-year English 'Literature in History' (Contemporary/ Creative Writing section)
	MA in Creative Writing: Prose Fiction

In some cases the course was designed by WGS and was co-taught (as with the MA unit 'Major Trends in European Fiction', for the successful but short-lived MA in European Writing); in other cases, owing to patterns of leave and suchlike, it either did not run or was taught by others. Thus the 'unit' (to use the technical term then current) 'Post-war German Writing 1945–1970' was in fact taught, in the Autumn Semester of 1993/94, first by Anthony Vivis and then, following her appointment, by Jo Catling, with guidelines and materials provided by WGS; and it appears that 'Examples of Nineteenth-Century European Prose Fiction', included in the English and American Studies course catalogue for Spring 2001 and represented here by a handwritten course outline, did not actually run at all. It will, though, come as little or no surprise to the reader that the courses taught most consistently throughout W. G. Sebald's teaching career should have been, on the one hand, Kafka and, on the other, post-war and contemporary German literature.

Courses taught by W. G. Sebald: A selection of reading lists

UNIVERSITY OF EAST ANGLIA

School of European Studies

Term 4/7

Dr. Sebald

FRANZ KAFKA

(Restricted to twenty takers; a
reading knowledge of German is not
required.)

In this course we will try to look at "the life and works" of Franz Kafka
avoiding, as far as possible, the digests and trappings of what is by now
a hypertrophic body of secondary literature. I should like to advise
those who decide to sign up for this seminar to read KAFKA during the
vacation with as much patience and persistence as they can afford.
Our discussions in the seminar will be based mainly on the following
texts.

Forschungen eines Hundes (Investigations of a Dog)

Bericht an eine Akademie (Report to a Academy)

Der Prozess (The Trial)

Das Schloß (The Castle)

Apart from these photocopied excerpts from Kafka's diaries, notebooks
etc. will be made available at the beginning of term. One of the
early sessions will be devoted to a selection of visual material.

MS/edeS
May 1977

UNIVERSITY OF EAST ANGLIA

School of Modern Languages
and European History

Summer Term

Dr. Sebald

The Radical Stage - New theatrical Concepts
in C20th European Drama

This seminar examines theatrical models which were developed in conscious
opposition to the more established forms of drama. We shall attempt to
sort out the different implications of drama and theatre and to define
the notion of "radicality" as an aesthetic (and political) category.

1. Essential reading by all students:

Jarry	Ubu Plays	Methuen
Artaud	The theatre and its double	Calder & Boyars
Grotowski	Towards a poor theatre	Methuen
Genet	The Blacks	Faber
De Ghelderode	Chronicles of Hell and/or La Balade) du Grand Macabre (not available in) Photocopy translation))	
Gombrowicz	The Marriage	Calder bks.
Beckett	Endgame	Faber
Pinter	The Caretaker	Methuen
Weiss	Marat/Sade	Calder bks.
Handke	Kaspar	Methuen
Bond	The Fool	Methuen
Brook	The empty space	Penguin

2. Recommended reading:

Abel	Metatheatre
Bently	The Theatre of Commitment
Brustein	The Theatre of Revolt
Gouhier	L'essence du Théâtre
Kott	Theatre Notebook
Lumley	New Trends in C20th Drama
Moore	The Stanislawski System
Selden	Theatre Double Game

UNIVERSITY OF EAST ANGLIA
School of Modern Languages
and European History

Dr Max Sebald

GERMAN CINEMA IN THE TWENTIES

This seminar will examine an important chapter of film history: Expressionist
and Realist film-making in Germany in the 1920s.   We will look at the work
of Fritz Lang, F. W. Murnau and other prominent film makers of the Weimar period,
notably Stellan Rye, R. Wiere, P. Jutzi, Brecht/Dudow.

The course is designed, in the first instance, for those students who intend
to take Film Studies as their Minor Subject but should also be of considerable
interest to students reading German History, German Literature or German Studies.

Films (subject to booking confirmation)

1.	Der Student von Prag	(dir. Stellan Rye/P. Wegener)
2.	The Cabinet of Dr Caligari	(dir. R. Wiene)
3.	Nosferatu	(dir. F. W. Murnau)
4.	Dr Marbuse	(dir. Fritz Lang)
5.	Metropolis	(dir. Fritz Lang)
6.	The Last Laugh	(dir. F. W. Murneau)
7.	M	(dir. Fritz Lang)
8.	Mutter Krauses Fahrt ins Glück	(dir. P. Jutzi)
9.	Kuhle Wampe	(dir. Brecht/Dudow)

Essential Reading:

S. Kracauer	From Caligari to Hitler (University of California Press)
L. Eisner	The Haunted Screen (Thames and Hudson)
P. Gay	Weimar Culture (Penguin)
J. Willett	The New Sobriety (Thames and Hudson)
J. Petley	Capital and Culture: German Cinema (BFI Publications)
A. Kaes (ed.)	Kino-Debatte (dtv Wissenschaft)
H. Korte (ed.)	Film und Realität in der Weimarer Republik (Fischer)

Apart from these secondary texts, E. T. A. Hoffmann's story Der Sandmann, which
is available in English translation, might prove a useful point of reference.

W. G. S.
May 1984

UNIVERSITY OF EAST ANGLIA
School of Modern Languages
and European History

Professor W. G. Sebald

Post-War German Literature - From 1945 to 1968
Autumn Semester 1993

Essential Reading:

Hans Erich Nossack	Der Untergang	(1948)	
Arno Schmidt	Leviathan	(1948)	Fischer
Heinrich Böll	Der Zug war pünktlich	(1949)	dtv
Alfred Andersch	Die Kirschen der Freiheit	(1952)	Diogenes
Günter Grass	Katz und Maus	(1961)	Luchterhand
Peter Weiss	Die Ermittlung	(1965)	Suhrkamp
Wolfgang Hildesheimer	Tynset	(1965)	Suhrkamp
Jean Améry	Jenseits von Schuld und Sühne	(1968)	dtv

Recommended Reading:

Hermann Kasack	Die Stadt hinter dem Strom	(1947)	
Hans Werner Richter	Die Geschlagenen	(1949)	dtv
Wolfgang Borchert	An diesem Dienstag	(1949)	Rowohlt
Wolfgang Koeppen	Das Treibhaus	(1953)	Suhrkamp
Alfred Andersch	Sansibar oder der letzte Grund	(1957)	Diogenes
Marlen Haushofer	Die Tapetentür	(1957)	Fischer
	Die Mansarde	(1966)	Fischer
Heinrich Böll	Wo warst Du Adam?	(1951)	dtv
	Hierzulande - Aufsätze zur Zeit	('63)	dtv
	Frankfurter Vorlesungen	(1966)	dtv
Martin Walser	Ehen in Philippsburg	(1957)	Suhrkamp
Günter Grass	Die Blechtrommel	(1958)	Luchterhand
Peter Weiss	Abschied von den Eltern	(1961)	Suhrkamp
	Fluchtpunkt	(1962)	"
	Rapporte I	(1966)	"
Heinar Kipphardt	Joel Brand	(1965)	"

NB: Try and read at least some of the prescribed texts during
the vacation.

ACADEMIC YEAR 1996-97

SEMESTER: Spring

CODE NO: EURG2A86

UCU: 20

ORGANISER: Professor W. G. Sebald

UNIT TITLE: **CONTEMPORARY GERMAN WRITING**

TIMETABLE SLOT:

TEACHING MODE: Seminars

METHOD OF ASSESSMENT: Coursework: 50%
Examination: 50%

PREREQUISITES: Good reading knowledge of German

RESTRICTIONS: Maximum enrolment: 20

UNIT AIMS / DESCRIPTION:

This unit will look at a range of works by German writers from 1970 to the present day.   The question of political commitment, documentary and operative writing, the so-called new sensitivity and post-modern experimentation will be discussed.   Not all texts are currently readily available in affordable editions.   Photocopied excerpts will be provided from those texts which are difficult to obtain (marked ph'copy exc. on the reading list below).

Essential reading:

P. Weiss	Vietnam-Diskurs, in Stücke II (2 vols.), Suhrkamp ph'copy exc.
G. Grass	Aus dem Tagebuch einer Schnecke, dtv
H. Böll	Die verlorene Ehre der Katharina Blum, dtv
G. Walraff	Der Aufmacher, Kiepenheuer und Witsch
F. S. Kroetz	Stallerhof/Geisterbahn, ph'copy exc.
H. M. Enzensberger	Der Untergang der Titanic, Suhrkamp taschenbuch
A. Kluge	Neue Geschichten 1 - 18, ph'copy exc.
T. Bernhard	Prosa, ph'copy exc.
P. Handke	Die Angst des Tormanns, Suhrkamp taschenbuch

EURG2A81

UNIVERSITY OF EAST ANGLIA

School of Modern Languages &
European History

Professor W. G. Sebald

Nature and Society:

Nineteenth-Century German Short Prose Fiction

Essential Reading:

J. W. von Goethe	Novelle, Reclam
Ludwig Tieck	Der blonde Eckbert, Reclam
H. von Kleist	Die Marquise von O., Reclam
E. T. A. Hoffmann	Der Sandmann, Reclam
Johann Peter Hebel	Aus dem Schatz Kästlein, Reclam
Georg Büchner	Lenz, Reclam
Adalbert Stifter	Der Hochwald, Reclam
Theodor Storm	Aquis Submersus, Reclam
Gottfried Keller	Kleider machen Leute, Reclam
Theodor Fontane	L'adultera, Reclam

ACADEMIC YEAR 1996-97

SEMESTER: Spring

UCU: 20   **ORGANISER:** Professor W. G. Sebald

UNIT TITLE: MAJOR TRENDS IN EUROPEAN FICTION

TIMETABLE SLOT:

TEACHING MODE: Seminars

METHOD OF ASSESSMENT: Coursework: 100%

PREREQUISITES: None

RESTRICTIONS: None

UNIT AIMS / DESCRIPTION:

Despite the declaration, frequently made in the 1960s, that the death of literature was imminent, the postmodernist era has proved immensely fruitful. In particular, a host of new models and hybrids of narrative fiction, many of them works of outstanding quality, have appeared on the scene. Arguably, the most interesting attempts to transcend the received limitations of fiction were made in the literatures of continental Europe. It is the purpose of this module to examine a set of texts representative of the various ways in which fiction re-invented itself in the years from 1950 to 1990.

Principal Texts:

Beckett:	Molloy	John Fletcher
Robbe Grillet:	Jealousy	Ralph Yarrow
Sarraute:	Tropismes; Between Life & Death	Ralph Yarrow
Simon:	The Flanders Road	John Fletcher
Bernhard:	Gargoyles	Max Sebald
Ransmayer:	The Last World	Max Sebald
Grass:	Diary of a Snail	Max Sebald
Jelinek:	The Piano Teacher	Max Sebald
Borgen:	The Scapegoat	Janet Garton
Dineson:	Babette's Feast	Kerstin Petersson
Hansen:	The Liar	Michael Robinson

ACADEMIC YEAR 1999/2000

SEMESTER: Spring   **CODE NO:** EURE2A48

UCU: 20   **ORGANISER:** Professor W G Sebald

UNIT TITLE: EUROPEAN AUTOBIOGRAPHICAL WRITING

TIMETABLE SLOT: E (E2*3)   **SUBJECT:** Lit

TEACHING MODE: Seminars

METHOD OF ASSESSMENT: WW (50% Coursework, 50% Examination)

PREREQUISITES: None

RESTRICTIONS: Maximum enrolment: 20

UNIT AIMS/DESCRIPTION:

This unit will look at a range of autobiographical works by 20ᵗʰ-century European writers. As several of the texts which we will discuss in the seminars are available only in relatively costly editions or out or print, students will be expected to play a very active role in presenting these less accessible texts to the group.

Essential texts:

V. Nabokov	Speak Memory, Penguin/Library
G. Perec	W or the Memory of Childhood, Harvill
E. Canetti	The Tongue Set Free, A. Deutsch/Library
J.P. Sartre	Words, Penguin/Library
P. Weiss	Leavetaking, Boyars/Library
G. Grass	From the Diary of a Snail, Out of print/Library
P. Levi	If that is a Man, Vintage/Library
B. Wilkomirski	Fragments, Picador

Examples of
19th c. European Prose Fiction

week 1. Background, socio-historical:
        socio-psychological etc

week 2. Kleist Marquise v. O.

week 3. Hoffmann, The Sandman

week 4. Pushkin. The Queen of Spades

week 5. Flaubert, A Simple Heart

week 6   "

week 7   Reading week

week 8   Stifter.

week 9   Turgenev. Spring Torrents

week 10 Fontane. Effie Briest

week 11   "

week 12 Chekhov. Lady with the Lapdog.
         Incl

Stifter / Recluse / Lake
Lime = / Water,
Stone / marble

READING KAFKA'S NOVELS

WORK PLAN

Week 1:   Introduction: Biographica

Week 2:   *The Trial*: Arrest - Conversation with Frau Grubach -
Fräulein Bürstner - First Examination

Week 3:   *The Trial*: In the Empty Assembly Hall - The Student - The Offices -
B's Friend - The Whipper

Week 4:   Reading Week

Week 5:   Presentations

Week 6:   *The Trial*: The Uncle Leni - The Advocate - The Manufacturer - The
Painter

Week 7:   *The Trial*: Merchant Block - Dismissal of the Advocate - In the
Cathedral - The End

Week 8:   *The Castle*: Chapters 1-6

Week 9:   *The Castle*: Chapters 7-14

Week 10:   *The Castle*: Chapters 15-20

Week 11:   *The Castle*: Chapters 21-25

Week 12:   Summary

ESSENTIAL READING
The Trial and *The Castle* in the Penguin edition

Students will have to submit one essay of 3000-4000 words. The deadline for
submission is Wednesday of week 12.

As this is a level 3 unit the essays must show evidence of a good deal of secondary
reading.

Please note also that work presented in seriously flawed English will be marked
down.

KAFKA - SELECT BIBLIOGRAPHY

Brod M.	*Franz Kafka - A Biography*
Hayman, R.	*K-A Biography*
Pawel, E.	*The Nightmare of Reason*
Zischler, H.	*Kafka geht ins Kino*
Hackermüller, R.	*Das Leben, das mich stört - Kafkas Letzte Jahre*
Janouch, G.	*Conversations with Kafka*
Northey, A.	*Kafka's Relatives*
Anderson, M.	*Kafka's Clothes*
Beck, E.	*Kafka & the Yiddish Theatre*
Boa, E.	*Kafka - Gender, Class and Race*
Canetti, E.	*Kafka's Other Trial*
Robertson, R.	*Kafka - Judaism, Politics & Literature*
Gilman, S.	*Franz Kafka, The Jewish Patient*
Müller-Seidel, W.	*Die Deportation des Menschen*
Robert, M.	*As Lonely as Franz Kafka*
Deleuze-Guattari	*Kafka*
Citati, P.	*Kafka*
Heller, E.	*Kafka*
Kuna, F.	*Kafka*
Kuna, F.	*On Kafka*
Politzer, H.	*Franz Kafka*
Spears, R.	*Franz Kafka*
Stern, J.P.	*The Dear Purchase*
Stern, J.P.	*The World of Franz Kafka*
Pascal, R.	*Kafka's Narrators*
Koelb, C.	*Kafka's Rhetoric*
Dowden, S.	*Kafka & the Critical Imagination*
Gray, R.	*Kafka's Castle*
Neumeyer, P.	*The Castle*
Mathews, A.	*Rhetoric and Evolution in the Published Interpretations of >Der Prozess< (UEA PhD)*
Binder, H.	*Kafka Kommentar* 4 volumes
Binder, H	*Kafka Handbuch*

CHAPTER 4

A Watch on Each Wrist:
Twelve Seminars with W. G. Sebald

Luke Williams

I

I want to write about the two incarnations in which I knew W. G. Sebald: first through his writing, and then through his being my tutor at UEA. When I first encountered his work, in the winter of 1999, I had recently moved to Paris, a city new to me. I discovered my French was worse than I thought. Having arrived there with no plan, for no clear reason, I was experiencing a sense of mounting frustration and bewilderment. What was frustrating was not the fact of my bewilderment — I had become used to the sensation — but that I wished to articulate it, and yet had found no way to do so. I did not want simply to forget or overcome my confusion, but, through writing, to examine its complicated paths. And yet the very confusion about which I wanted to write was preventing me from writing anything much at all. Whenever I tried to set something down, my prose seemed bleak and tedious. Reading Sebald offered me a brilliant example: here was writing which spoke honestly about loss and confusion, about a world on the verge of destruction, in a voice that was itself clear and precise. What is more, Sebald's voice seemed to recognize the difficulty, even the impossibility, of expressing that sense of loss and confusion, even as he set out do so.

At the time I was trying to write my way into a novel. I had come to a standstill. I suspect now this was related to the books I had been reading. In my early twenties I had felt drawn to a cadre of writers who had opposed themselves to what has come to be known as literary realism: Fernando Pessoa, for instance, and Nathalie Sarraute, Alain Robbe-Grillet, Georges Perec, Salman Rushdie. I had no desire to write the kind of novel which tried to imitate reality, at least the 'realism' of clock time and easy human empathy and knowing narrators, the kind that flourished in the nineteenth century and which, despite the insights of literary modernism, was — and remains — the predominant form. What I especially resisted was the characterization in realist novels: it was true that the heroes of those tales were sometimes confused or destabilized, but, it seemed to me, only superficially; because their confusion was not really confusion, not the kind of bafflement I was experiencing, which tended to unsettle all things, all feelings, and which pointed toward silence. No, these writers created a kind of teasing befuddlement, I felt.

They toyed with confusion, tamed character, and made internal disorder seem ultimately quite knowable.

Books such as Robbe-Grillet's *Jealousy* or Rushdie's *Midnight's Children* were not so articulate. If they wrote about character at all they wrote of an empty vessel, into which many elements might be poured. They spoke of the world and its people not as repositories of meaning but as things impossible for the imagination to grasp. It was a notion to which my sense of bewilderment bore witness. So I wanted my own novel to exist in their company. But — and this is where my problem lay — I also felt tired of the empty play of character or absence of story in these books, which were at times too coolly intellectual, concerned only with abstract structural problems. They rarely gave me pleasure, and less often left me feeling emotionally engaged. What is more, I could not understand how the radical insights these novels offered up — the dissolution of character, the breakdown of language and perspective — could lead to such confident, endlessly playful books.

It was with these thoughts in my mind, coupled with my feeling of isolation in a foreign city, that I discovered *The Rings of Saturn*. I read: 'Lost in the thoughts that went round in my head incessantly, and numbed by this crazed flowering, I stuck to the sandy path until to my astonishment, not to say horror, I found myself back again at the same tangled thicket from which I had emerged about an hour before.' I read: 'he was convinced that everything he had written hitherto consisted solely in a string of the most abysmal errors and lies.' And this: 'It is difficult to imagine the depths of despair into which those can be driven who, even after the end of the working day, are engrossed in their designs and who are pursued, into their dreams, by the feeling that they have got hold of the wrong thread.'[1] This sentence appears in the end-section of *The Rings of Saturn*. After nearly three hundred pages of speaking about loss and confusion in the most compelling way, Sebald admits the possibility, even the probability, of being mistaken. James Wood recognizes this: 'Sebald and his characters are haunted by the incomprehensible, the indecipherable, the wrong turn. And Sebald includes his own thread, his own course, in this category.'[2] *The Rings of Saturn*, together with Sebald's other books then published in English, which I read one after another, offered an example of the kind of book I wanted to write, the kind that accommodated the radical insights of literary modernism, were haunted by those insights, and still left the reader emotionally engaged.

Some time later I returned to the UK. I got a job. I rewrote the first chapter of my novel. I was still unhappy with the result, but my efforts seemed a little less false. Though I still felt confused, writing had given me relief. I sent my first chapter to the UEA Creative Writing MA. I did not then know Sebald was teaching on it. When I heard I was accepted onto the course, I gave up my job and prepared to move to Norwich. How strange and exciting to learn, some four months later, shortly before arriving at UEA, that I was to be taught by Sebald.

Before the first seminar I had an (as it turned out) illusory encounter with my future tutor. Around that time *Austerlitz* was being published in the UK, and Sebald was to appear in London to read from and talk about his latest work. So I caught the train from Norwich on the evening of his reading, bought the book at the venue (it was not yet out in the shops), and took my place in the audience. I remember little about the event, only that Sebald, who spoke flawless English, read first from the German edition of *Austerlitz*, then had his translator (Anthea Bell) read the same passage from the UK edition. Later he told the interviewer (Maya Jaggi) that he wrote and read in German because he feared he had a 'funny accent'.[3] Immediately after the talk I left. I was new to London and took the wrong bus to Liverpool Street Station, so I missed my train. The next and final departure was not for another hour. So I sat on one of the station's moulded plastic chairs and opened *Austerlitz*. I read: 'When I entered the great hall of the Centraal Station with its dome arching sixty metres high above it...'. I read: 'the railway passengers seemed to me somehow miniaturized, whether by the unusual height of the ceiling or because of the gathering dusk, and it was this, I suppose, which prompted the passing thought, nonsensical in itself, that they were the last members of a diminutive race.' I looked at the late passengers in their crumpled suits, many of them eating burgers from colourful boxes. Then I saw Sebald. He was standing by the ticket desk. He too was waiting for the Norwich train. I hid *Austerlitz* in my bag. Sebald was smoking a cigarette, which struck me somehow as odd. I took *Austerlitz* from my bag, thought about removing the dust jacket. Conscious that its author might spot me reading his book, and in truth half-willing him to do so, I continued from where I had left off. 'One of the people waiting in the *Salle des pas perdus* was Austerlitz', I read. 'When I finally went over to Austerlitz with a question about his obvious interest in the waiting-room, he was not at all surprised by my direct approach but answered me at once.'[4] I tried to force myself not to look at Sebald, who had moved to the turnstile. My dilemma was this: should I board the train as soon as the turnstile opened, before Sebald, leaving to chance our plainly fated meeting; or should I allow him to go first, stepping afterwards into his carriage, thus nudging fate in the right direction?

It is important to mention at this point that, informed by his books, I had the idea that Sebald could hardly step onto a bus or train without some fortuitous meeting. (I recalled the episode in *Vertigo* when the narrator, travelling on a bus during his quest to retrace 'Dr. K.'s' 1913 Italian journey, meets twin boys who bear an uncanny resemblance to Kafka himself.[5]) I had been snared by the strange logic of these books, where coincidence, in the form of a finely patterned series of meetings and discoveries, takes the place of the conventional plot-device of cause and effect. So it seemed perfectly natural, even likely, that I was to meet Sebald that evening (just as his other odd notions, notions which, if taken to their logical conclusion, would put in jeopardy the common understanding of the world — that, for instance, we have 'appointments to keep in the past'[6] — can seem plausible, even inevitable, under the spell of his imagination). But I was confused; had in fact succumbed to the very mistake that Sebald's books, like those others which challenged literary realism, counselled against: I was ascribing to lived experience a clarity or inevitability which existed only in the falsifying narratives of the realists. For if in Sebald's prose coincidence takes the place of conventional plot, coincidence also works against itself. Events in his books are so artfully arranged that only in the non-place of fiction could such a finely patterned set of coincidences occur. I did not recognize this at the time, however; standing there in Liverpool Street Station, some two metres behind Sebald, waiting for the signal to proceed onto the platform and board the train, I continued to blend fiction (Sebald's) with reality (my own).

I didn't meet him that evening on the train, although we sat in the same carriage. Instead I intermittently read *Austerlitz* and watched its author as he talked to a woman in a parallel seat. The two conversed animatedly for almost the entire journey, and if I felt disappointed I was not in her place, I also felt privileged to be witnessing the live process of Sebald's research (although I later discovered that this woman was one of his colleagues at UEA and had perhaps accompanied him to the talk).[7]

II

The most economical way, I think, of conveying my experience of Sebald as a creative writing teacher is to transcribe an edited version of the diary entries I made during that winter term of 2001.[8]

26 September

First seminar. Each of us students — fourteen in total — introduced ourselves. We spoke a little about our writing projects and our hopes for the course. Some, the more reticent, were prompted by questions from Sebald. He was friendly and curious, as I had expected, but also witty, which somehow I had not imagined him to be. When my turn came I talked for far too long. After the last student had finished speaking, Sebald said something like, 'I suppose I'd better tell you something about myself.' He went on to say that he was more surprised than anyone to find himself here, in front of a bunch of creative-writing students, since the university had until now regarded him as nothing more than an obscure scholar of German-language literature. But his 'prose works' had recently become known to UEA, and so here he was. The upshot of these prose works having come to light, he told us, had had a second fortunate effect, which was that he was now given greater leeway at the university. The staff were happier to indulge what he called his 'eccentricities' (which he didn't go into). Best of all, he said, he no longer had to deal with the tedious administrative duties that academics are nowadays everywhere forced to carry out. He then proceeded to tell us that despite the privileges being an author can convey, at least in the university environment, there is very little else to say in favour of the profession. You must be already slightly disturbed if your goal is to spend your lifetime staring at a blank piece of paper, he told us. What is more, the process of writing itself is often quite different from how you might imagine. Being always on your own, for instance, with your own thoughts, trying to make sense of them, being forced to constantly invent things — is this not a recipe for mental ruin? Think hard about whether you really want to be a writer, he told us, and if you decide that you do, make sure you take another job as well. Teaching is not a bad option, he said. Neither is it a bad idea to become a barrister. Best of all, he told us, is to get involved in the medical profession, because you will hear many strange stories, which later at your desk you can make use of.

3 October

In our first meeting we had been told to bring a passage of writing we admired. The passages were photocopied and distributed at the end of class. I had not been able to decide between two of my favourite writers: a section from Georges Perec's *Life A User's Manual* — a novel set almost entirely at one minute to eight — and a short story by Ingo Schulze. In the end I had chosen Schulze, a German writer, probably, stupidly, because I wanted to impress Sebald. We spent the whole of this second seminar looking at the passages. Mine was in fact the first Sebald picked out. For a moment I was thrilled. I thought that he had chosen it for its merits. It was not the case. In fact he seemed to hate it. He tore it apart (and by extension my taste). The story was clumsy, artless, imprecise. Worse, he said, you just couldn't *see* what the author was talking about. He disliked one line in particular that went something like this (I'm too ashamed to go and look it up): 'Only when the dimpled sewer covers started to spit ice cubes up onto the road, like smoothly licked sweets, were we able to walk normally again.'[9] I can't *see* it, Sebald kept on saying. Perhaps it's my bad English, he said, but I can't imagine a spitting sewer cover. What on earth does such a sewer cover look like? No one, myself least of all, had an answer. And why, he went on, if the road was presumably covered with ice cubes, had the author highlighted this fact as the moment when 'we' (and note that he never in fact tells us who this 'we' are) were able to walk normally again? Wouldn't the pedestrians be slipping about all over the place? I certainly wouldn't go out on such a day, he said. I myself made a pathetic attempt to defend the story, but I could hardly speak. And I stayed mute for the rest of the class. Sebald treated every piece to this scrupulous criticism. He tore into Don DeLillo's *Underworld* for its inconsistencies of perspective. How on earth can the narrator be so sure about all the things he seems to know? How can he be in so many places at the same time? One minute, Sebald said, he's describing the Arizona desert from the ground-level view, from the perspective of an iguana, and the next from high above. In the space of a few lines he has become a bird of prey spying on the iguana, probably so he can gobble it up. Discussing a Raymond Carver story Sebald got us all to stand up and try to act out some motion the narrator's wife carried out. We had to stick strictly to the description in the text. She was doing something like taking a chicken out of the oven while turning to her husband and saying something about the chicken. Sebald was right. It was impossible, the way Carver described it, for the human body to move in precisely this way. He went on to say that it's very difficult, not to say impossible, to get physical movement right when writing. The important thing is that it should work for the reader, even if it's not meticulous. You can use ellipses, he said, abbreviate a sequence of actions, you needn't laboriously describe each one. Out of all the passages the only one Sebald liked unreservedly was from Jim Crace's *Being Dead*.

I'm still shocked. Sebald's point, it seems to me, was simple. That precision in writing fiction — especially in writing fiction — is an absolutely fundamental value. He summed up by saying that if you look carefully you can find problems in all writers, or almost all (Kafka being an exception; especially, he told us, if you look at the reports he wrote for the Workers' Accident Insurance Institute!). He told us that even those writers who have talent and scrupulousness must be on their guard against sloppiness and indulgence. He gave, as an example of sloppiness, Günter Grass, who, he said, had started off writing quite well but had lately let his writing slip. He thought it had happened since Grass had won the Nobel Prize. Probably, he said, Grass's publisher has been too scared to edit his latest manuscripts.

I'm going to stop writing now and take a look at my chapters. I won't go to sleep until I've tightened them up.

17 October

It was uncomfortable in class today. For the first time we saw Sebald riled, not angry exactly, but agitated, even perplexed. It was clear that one of the hand-ins, H.'s, had affected him quite strongly. The story was set in an unnamed city under curfew. Food was becoming harder and harder to come by. Citizens were being shot. There was some kind of confused relationship between a man and a woman. In the end the two turned to cannibalism. Most of us liked the story. I did too, although I think it is heavily indebted to the Peter Carey story 'Room No. 5 (Escribo)', which I read last summer. This time Sebald didn't make his usual criticisms about superfluous sentences or too many characters being introduced all at once or lack of concrete detail, but went straight to his point. There is something wrong with the way the story is told, he said. It's the voice. You are writing about horrendous things. Horrific events. Are you sure you know what you are writing about? Have you actually been to such a place? Have you yourself witnessed such horror? H. replied that she had lived in Jerusalem for nine years. That surprised him. We talked about the story some more. There really wasn't a lot to say (it is always the case that the better, tighter hand-ins get shorter crits). But Sebald wasn't willing to let it go. He said again that he had a problem with the voice, with the way the narrator approaches the horror she is describing. He told us that horror is everywhere now, there is so much of it, in all walks of life, everywhere we look. I went into my local video shop, he said. It's filled with nasty videos. A generation who have never known war is being raised on horror. Then he asked a few questions. How do you surpass horror once you've reached a certain level? How do you stop it appearing gratuitous? He answered himself. Let me get this right. You (he was addressing the whole class) might think that because you are writing fiction you needn't be overly concerned to get the facts straight. But aesthetics is not a value-free area. And you must be particularly careful if your subject concerns horrific events. You must stick absolutely to the facts. The most plausible, perhaps even the only, approach is the documentary one. I would say that writing about an appalling state of affairs is incommensurable with traditional aesthetics.

I can't quite understand Sebald's point, though I'm not willing to dismiss it. I thought at first he was reiterating Adorno's dictum, that writing poetry after Auschwitz is barbaric. It can't be, though, because all Sebald's work picks over the barbarism of the twentieth century, often focussing on the Holocaust, if obliquely. And he implied that you can write about such things, if only you stick to the facts. But facts are slippery, especially in times of emergency, as Sebald surely knows. So his problem with H.'s story cannot be related to her writing fiction about horrid events *per se*. It must lie with the way she chose to write about them. And, in fact, thinking about the story now, there is something gratuitous about it. That absolutely flat tone. The horror never seems to touch the narrator. H.'s point is that those who experience dreadful events every single day become numbed to them. As a comment on human behaviour this may be true, and on that I don't think Sebald could argue with her. But I think Sebald's problem lay elsewhere. I think it lay deeper than his argument over aesthetics. He had had an unpleasant reaction to the story, you could hear it in his voice. For him the story had crossed some kind of line. I'm thinking of Coetzee's *Disgrace*, when David Lurie chooses to cremate dead dogs himself rather than witness workers breaking the dogs' legs so as to fit the corpses better into the cremation fire. And he chooses to do this for no clear or logical reason, but because of a private instinct: 'For his idea of the world, a world in which men do not use shovels to beat corpses into a more convenient shape for processing.'[10] I think Sebald's reaction had something similarly private about it. I think it had something to do with the fact that he has chosen as his subject unspeakable events, and it's my guess it took him a lot of thinking and self-searching to decide in fact to voice them. That's perhaps why he published fiction only relatively late in his life. It had probably taken years for him to feel confident enough about his form, to trust himself to approach his subject in writing. And it is now hard for him to countenance another, weaker, more common-sense method. He's too involved in his own vision.

31 October

It strikes me that Sebald is not your usual UEA-type creative-writing tutor. I always knew that. What I didn't expect was how opposed, even hostile, is his attitude to the kind of writing that usually comes out of UEA. He rarely states his hostility explicitly. And in fact if you were to analyse any one of his seminars you would not necessarily deduce what I am sure is a deeply felt antipathy to the flat realist style (those confident, quirky male protagonists, the breathy girl-child narrators who are always somehow damaged, the sentiment masked as irony, the smooth metonymy, the easy generalizations) most of the class produce. Taken together, his comments and digressions, such as the one today on time ('Physicists now say there is no such thing as time: everything coexists; the artificial thing is actually chronology'), add up to a fairly sustained attack on the UEA/realist aesthetic. This afternoon he even took a swipe at that dinosaur Ian McEwan! We were looking at S.'s story which follows the misadventures of an English family in a campsite in south-west France. It was a pretty good story, most of us agreed. Sebald was enthusiastic about it too. He said what he liked best was the detail. The focus on camping equipment: the different types of tent poles, mattresses, stoves, the names of certain kinds of knots specific to the camping world, and so on. It was for him a whole new vernacular, he said. I could translate a page of Ian McEwan in half an hour, he said, but a camping manual! That is another matter entirely. And two Sainsbury's managers talking to each other are a different species altogether.

Here's a (necessarily incomplete) list of his polemic comments so far:

- I can only encourage you to steal as much as you can. No one will ever notice. You should keep a notebook of tidbits, but don't write down the attributions, and then after a couple of years you can come back to the notebook and treat the stuff as your own without guilt.
- It's very good that you write through another text, a foil, so that you write out of it and make your work a palimpsest.
- In the twentieth century we know that the observer always affects what is being said. So you have to talk about where you got your sources, how it was talking to that woman in Beverly Hills, the trouble you had at the airport, etc. Writing that does not acknowledge the uncertainty of the narrator is an imposture, jaded, even dangerous.
- In the nineteenth century the omniscient narrator *was* God. Totalitarian and monolithic. The twentieth century with all its horrors was more demotic. We have to acknowledge our own sense of ignorance and of insufficiency and try and write with this always in mind.
- I find it hard to countenance writing in the third person.
- There is a certain merit in leaving some parts of your writing obscure.
- Writing should not create the impression that the writer is trying to be 'poetic'.
- *On time*: Chronology is entirely artificial and essentially determined by emotion. Contiguity suggests layers of things, the past and present somehow coalescing or coexisting.

I think quite a few class members find his perspective hard to follow, or are hostile to it. For example P. said he did not worry about these kinds of things (I think he meant first- vs. third-person narration) and disliked 'experimental' writing generally (as if his own social realist style is the right way and any diversion from this 'experimental'!). I think what is new in Sebald can be seen in the way he himself dealt with the issue of realism. His writing mostly eschews realism, not just in its structural radicalism but in that he seeks a kind of verisimilitude of the nether world. Isaac Babel once said of Tolstoy that if the world could write itself, it would write like him. It strikes me that if the dead were to write themselves, they would write like Sebald.

21 November

By all means be experimental, Sebald said today in class, but let the reader be part of the experiment. Write about obscure things but don't write obscurely. This advice brought me up short. I think my own writing suffers on this account. I am too ready to pack my writing with obscure facts, oblique references, and I want everything to be tricksy. Plus, I'm always having to mask the essayist in me. This is exactly the trap that Sebald, in his writing, (mostly) circumvents. What marks him out is his ability to blend the essay form with the purely fictional. His books leap (and it is a leap, since so often the fiction takes over in a passage of flight, often in a dream sequence when the narrator flies above both the landscape and his own rational thoughts) into the fictional. He rarely makes the mistake, as I do (and others in the class whom his writing has influenced), of believing that obscure information or antique objects have charm in themselves. He never transposes raw facts into his texts. If he did they would read as stillborn. I must keep this in mind. Information is not appealing merely because it's authentic.

5 December

This afternoon in class I had a bizarre momentary vision of Sebald. It was one of those seminars when everyone seemed tired and distracted. The story we were discussing was poor. It concerned an autistic child and his mother's attempt to come to terms with the affliction. It was clunky and depressing. You could hear the 'grinding noises' (Sebald's phrase) of the plot. And the discussion was rambling too, going nowhere really. At one point, as he sometimes does, Sebald started talking at length. He told us about his boyhood hatred for the 'old Nazi' who gave him zither lessons. He told us about his Austrian friend who had graphomania. He told us that Princess Diana regarded Charles and the Windsors as nothing other than a bunch of German upstarts. At one point I started looking at my classmates. I thought about how we had been thrust together in this class. I thought about how raw the crits could be, how I had read about some very private things, how some of the criticisms had bordered on personal attacks. I thought about the very different personalities in the class and how most of us were in some way nutty. Some with ambition. Some with neuroses. Some with jealousy or past hurt. And some were just odd-looking. Sebald was still talking. He was telling us about a writer called Ödön von Horváth, who had escaped Germany when the Nazis came to power. I looked over at the window. It was raining outside. I could hear the drops tapping against the glass. Horváth, Sebald told us, was exiled in Paris, where he consulted a clairvoyant, who warned him to steer clear of the city of Amsterdam, never to ride on trams, on no account to go in a lift, and to avoid lightning at all costs. Horváth took this advice very seriously. At one point I stopped looking at the faces of my classmates and instead watched Sebald. He was leaning back in his chair. His legs were stretched out in front of him, his body a long diagonal. His eyes looked up at the ceiling and the round glass of his spectacles reflected the strip light. Both his hands were placed on the back of his head; together his arms made a coathanger shape, of a pair of 'V's. Horváth, Sebald was saying, despite all his precautions, was one day walking on the Champs Elysées when a branch fell and killed him. Sebald continued to talk, perhaps he was telling us more about the writer Horváth, perhaps he had moved on to something else. But I was no longer following him, because I'd noticed something strange. He was wearing a watch on each wrist. On his left wrist he wore a cheap digital watch, face up. On his right an analogue watch, its face turned round to the underside of his wrist. The rain continued. Sebald talked on. But I wasn't following him. I kept looking at the watches on his wrists. Why two watches? Why one digital and one analogue? Why was the analogue watch turned face down? I didn't know.

III

Less than two weeks after this last diary entry Sebald was killed. Someone read about it in the local paper and the news travelled quickly around the class. Shocked, we tried to give his death a meaning. Someone suggested (ridiculously) that it was appropriate that Sebald, who was happiest while travelling, had died on the move. We all vowed to keep our essays with his handwritten comments on them. I wanted to find a reason for his early, incomprehensible death. I wanted, hopelessly, to read his next book, which he had mentioned once or twice in class. I thought about the few times I had spoken to him personally. It was tempting to think that he had singled me out among the students. But it wasn't true.

These last years I have thought about his death quite a bit. I have read, and thought about, his writing even more. I recently found a passage from Kierkegaard. It said something about it being one thing for a life to be over, and quite another for a life to be finished by reaching a conclusion. Though of course it is over, there can be no conclusion to Sebald's life. It is too easy to think in terms of conclusions. To do so is to give his life false meaning. It would be to ascribe to muddled existence a clarity it can never have. Like my mistake that evening at Liverpool Street Station, it would be to confuse fiction (Sebald's) with reality (his own).

Notes to Chapter 4

1. W. G. Sebald, *The Rings of Saturn*, trans. by Michael Hulse (London: Harvill, 1999), pp. 171, 7, and 283.
2. James Wood, 'W. G. Sebald's Uncertainty', in *The Broken Estate: Essays on Literature and Belief* (London: Pimlico, 2000), p. 284.
3. See 'The Last Word', edited conversation with Maya Jaggi in the Queen Elizabeth Hall, London, on the occasion of the St Jerome Lecture 2001 (24 September 2001), *Guardian*, 21 December 2001, section G2, pp. 4–5; see Primary Bibliography J.46. The unabridged version of this event is published as 'St Jerome Lecture 2001: W. G. Sebald in Conversation with Maya Jaggi and Anthea Bell', *In Other Words*, no. 21 (Summer 2003), 5–18. This contains additional material, as well as contributions by Anthea Bell and questions by members of the audience; see Primary Bibliography J.46(a).
4. W. G. Sebald, *Austerlitz*, trans. by Anthea Bell (London: Hamish Hamilton, 2001), pp. 5, 6, and 7.
5. W. G. Sebald, *Vertigo*, trans. by Michael Hulse (London: Harvill, 1999), p. 88.
6. *Austerlitz*, trans. by Bell, p. 360.
7. The 'woman on the train' was one of the editors of this volume: she had indeed travelled to London for the reading, but the meeting on the train was — how could it be otherwise? — coincidental. (Eds)
8. I have edited the diary entries to make them clearer and so that the focus is on Sebald. I have also integrated some notes that two fellow students, David Lambert and Robert McGill, wrote during the seminars and handed to our class after Sebald's death. I am grateful to them both. On this subject see also David Lambert and Robert McGill, 'Writing Tips: The Collected "Maxims" of W. G. Sebald', *Five Dials*, 5 (2009), 8–9 <http://fivedials.com/fivedials> [accessed 3 April 2009].
9. The passage is from Ingo Schulze, *33 Moments of Happiness: St Petersburg Stories*, trans. by John E. Woods (London: Picador, 1999), p. 255. It in fact reads: 'Not until the dented sewer covers began spitting ice cubes up on to the sidewalks like well-licked pieces of candy was our normal gait restored to us.'
10. J. M. Coetzee, *Disgrace* (London: Vintage, 2000), p. 146.

Fig. 5.1. WGS in his office at UEA, late 1990s.
© Roger Baines

CHAPTER 5

The Crystal Mountain of Memory:
W. G. Sebald as a University Teacher

Florian Radvan

I first got to know W. G. Sebald, who has since come to be regarded as a literary voice *sui generis*, not as an author but as a university teacher and mentor. When I arrived at the University of East Anglia in autumn 1994 to study English and Comparative Literature, and later to write a doctoral thesis under his supervision, he did not yet exist on my map of contemporary literature. Thus I did not, in the beginning, see him as the mournful, melancholy traveller who roams through many of his prose texts and who is so familiar a figure from the critical reception of his works (particularly in the German press). It was only later that I noticed the discrepancy between the two images of Sebald and the roles that were assigned to each of them: the pragmatic and (in the best sense) inscrutably humorous university teacher Max, and the author Sebald, who became identified professionally by the initials W. G. and was soon to be internationally renowned.

It was primarily through him that I became acquainted with *Auslandsgermanistik* (the study of German literature abroad) in England, with its delightfully down-to-earth approach, seemingly liberated from the constraints of theory. It was here that I learnt to appreciate working with the material of language, something that takes place more intensively by virtue of the foreign-language context. In introductory courses at UEA, which I myself taught later on as a postgraduate student, it was by no means taboo to work closely with the primary texts, beginning with the reconstruction of content and moving on, through the examination of literary motifs, to the formation of one's own initial hypotheses regarding interpretation. One was almost forced to discuss the elementary questions about choice of words and syntax and to learn to think the text through from the perspectives of a foreign language and a foreign culture. Not least for this reason the seminars and tutorials of my years in England have remained in my memory much more clearly and vividly than the lectures in Germany that I attended both before and since. But not only was the English way of teaching and imparting knowledge new and fascinating; how different did W. G. Sebald himself seem to me, epitomizing as he did the very opposite of the traditional German professor, lacking the usual aura of self-importance and inapproachability and encouraging instead an intellectual 'open door policy'.

Like the southern German idiom which had been preserved beneath the surface after thirty years in England, his helpfulness, his pragmatism, and his sense of the inscrutable depths of life are for me inseparably linked with his personality. But it was equally characteristic of him that he would mention his own publications only in passing, the literary prizes and his great success with both critics and the reading public (for example in America), usually when cover for his teaching timetable had to be organized. The defining qualities of his attitude to work as an author were, it seems to me now, modesty and discretion.

Each educational system gives rise to specific kinds of texts. That became clear to me in England as regards the genre of the essay. The essay is based on a strategy of writing which I recognized again later in W. G. Sebald's literary criticism: an equally elegant and critical positioning towards the subject of enquiry, an impartiality towards any current intellectual fashions, a foregrounded and often pointed scepticism, a mode of argument accompanied by occasional digressions and in general — as one might say, with reference to Adorno's essay on The Essay — by the shimmering interplay between scholarship and art.

That said, this was something I had first to learn, for at the end of one of my early essay assignments, an analysis of Kafka's 'Ein Bericht für eine Akademie' ('A Report to an Academy'), I read the following comment (in English):

> You do have a tendency (in this piece at any rate) to restrict yourself to reporting the work of other scholars and to refrain from direct engagement with the text. Perhaps you should have tried to identify (against and across existing interpretations) the story's case which is, as one can say with hindsight, a lament about the foundering of the hopes which four or so generations had invested in the idea and practice of integration.

While W. G. Sebald's criticism was doubtless to be understood as a comment on my essay and its line of argument, it also exposed my conditioning in the German school and university system, in other words the reluctance to pit one's own opinion against the wealth of secondary literature, and a methodical approach ultimately lacking in inspiration.

One of the things that characterized Sebald as a mentor was the way he valued individuality. If I asked him for one of the references that are regularly required for applications, he would usually send a handwritten document. On one occasion he remarked that he could no longer bring himself to work with a typewriter or a computer: 'Das handgekritzelte Format hat immerhin den Vorteil, dass es von dem üblichen PC-Perfektionismus sich abhebt' [The version scrawled in one's own hand at least has the advantage of distinguishing itself from the usual PC perfect-ionism].[1]

I am looking through the letters that W. G. Sebald wrote to me from The Old Rectory (the former vicarage near Norwich that he had moved into in the mid-1970s), and which he always signed in English, 'Best wishes, as ever, Max'. As well as comment on my work, they always contained news from the department. With hindsight, it is noticeable that he often mentioned the death of colleagues, as here in July 1999: 'Von hier gibt es nichts Gutes zu berichten. Ich bin in der letzten Zeit viel auf Begräbnissen gewesen, u.a. auf dem von Roger Fowler, der bei der End-of-term-party in seinem Haus an einem schweren Herzschlag gestorben ist' [There's no good news from this end. I've been to a lot of funerals lately, among others Roger Fowler's. He died of a massive heart attack during an end-of-term party at his home].[2] And just over a year later, in December 2000: 'Sie werden gehört haben, daß Malcolm Bradbury gestorben ist. Auch Colin Good, der früher im German Sector war und den Sie wohl nicht mehr gekannt haben. Die Einschläge kommen immer näher!' [You'll have heard that Malcolm Bradbury has died. Colin Good too — he used to be in the German Sector, but you won't have known him. The blows are getting closer all the time!][3] Is it an exaggeration to see this as a premonition of his own death, which at the time was not far off?

In one of his letters W. G. Sebald enclosed a postcard with a photograph of Surabaya, captioned in Dutch and English. It was taken on 12 January 1933 and came from the collection of the Deutsches Auslands-Institut (German Overseas Institute) in Stuttgart. It shows workers in a large factory shed standing beside a machine that resembles a cannon, filling sacks with sugar and taking them away on wooden carts. Like all illustrations in his prose texts, from *Schwindel. Gefühle. (Vertigo)* to *Austerlitz*, this photograph derives its vitality from the magic of black and white. Since it had no obvious relevance to the letter, it triggered a process of *Semantisierung*, or finding meaning. Like the narrator in Sebald's texts, I tried to combine things which did not seem to belong together, which — whether by chance, intuition, or association — must bear some relation to each other. Today, this photograph, which was taken exactly forty years before I was born, seems to me a good example of Sebald's narrative games with coincidence and of the way in which he sought to uncover the hidden connections which bind together not only the lives of people but also the existence(s) of texts.

Sebald's prose, whether fiction or non-fiction, has always aroused my curiosity about the world and about literature. I am constantly amazed by how expressive and witty his language is, with its inherent subtle irony, and also of course by the way in which history's great misfortunes and the *Schmerzensspuren* (traces of pain) are contained in his words. The fact that the texts reveal as much of his personality as they conceal shows how skilfully the narration carries the play of text and intertext, and how successfully it oscillates between documentary and 'fake'.

Shortly after I had finished my thesis in May 2001, we met in a Norwich church that had been converted into a pub. He presented me with Siegfried Melchinger's *Geschichte des politischen Theaters* [History of Political Theatre]. For twenty or more years the two-volume edition had stood in his office — almost untouched, he said — so that the afternoon sun had bleached the spines into illegibility. But for a long time the books contained the aroma of that room, which emerged if you riffled through the pages with your finger. Years later too, like the aroma trapped in the books, the strongest impression of W. G. Sebald remained that of a *Grenzgänger* — of one who not only continually crosses frontiers, but also blurs them and allows them to dissolve into one another. In his case it was the frontiers between literary studies and literature, between fiction and reality, and between biography and autobiography. These memories of Sebald as a *Grenzgänger* have been the guiding light of my own path ever since.

Both at the time and subsequently I considered it a stroke of great good fortune to have met W. G. Sebald during a phase of disillusionment with the English university system, when academics and educational administrators alike seemed increasingly interested in 'corporate identity' and 'streamlining'. In consequence, for him the focus of work shifted towards the writing of literary texts. And life beyond the university circus will have exercised a decisive influence on his activity as a teacher of literature: ranging from poetological reflections and questions of reception and critical review to the absurdities of the business of literature, something he would describe anecdotally and not without a trace of sarcasm. From time to time we would also talk about the translations of his prose texts into English, which he did not produce himself, but rigorously checked and, he related, then read aloud. As a university professor who was also an author, he would have been regarded with suspicion, if not mockery, within the German academic establishment, and his creative texts would probably have been dismissed as *Professorenprosa* — fiction written by academics.

One subject which often came up between us was the work and life of Peter Weiss, who in the end was one of the focal points of our discussions. On 22–23 December 2001, a few days after his death, the *Süddeutsche Zeitung* published a long interview with W. G. Sebald, in which he spoke again about his home in the Allgäu, about the implications the silence on the subject of National Socialism had in the 1950s, and about his involvement with the study of literature.[4] In this context too he mentioned the name of Peter Weiss, another emigrant, who in 1938, three decades before Sebald's move to England, had left with his parents for western Sweden. The two certainly have more in common than the feeling of having been an outsider looking in at Germany and its literature, an outsider who — according to Sebald — famously sees more than those taking part on the inside. They both made a late debut as authors, when in their forties. 'Für mich', said Sebald, 'begann die reflektierte Auseinandersetzung mit der deutschen Vergangenheit mit der Lektüre von Peter Weiss' [For me the reflective engagement with the German past began with my reading of Peter Weiss].[5] And he mentioned some of Weiss's works, including the autobiographical writings *Abschied von den Eltern* (*Leavetaking*) and *Fluchtpunkt* (*Vanishing Point*), but also the Auschwitz documentary play *Die Ermittlung* (*The Investigation*), as being the texts which had influenced him most. W. G. Sebald wrote elsewhere that Weiss's entire work had been intended

> als ein Besuch bei den Toten, den eigenen zunächst, der viel zu jung verun-
> glückten Schwester, die er nicht aus dem Gedächtnis bringt, dem Jugendfreund
> Uli, dessen Leiche 1940 an den dänischen Strand gespült wird, bei den Eltern,
> von denen er nie ganz Abschied nimmt, und schließlich auch bei all den
> anderen zu Staub und Asche gewordenen Opfern der Geschichte

> [as a visit to the dead: first his own dead, his sister who died so sadly young
> and who haunted his mind; Uli, the friend of his youth, whose corpse was
> washed up on the Danish shore in 1940; his parents, to whom he never entirely
> said goodbye; and then all the other victims of history who are now dust and
> ashes].[6]

As well as Weiss the author, he was interested in Weiss the artist. A collage from the series that accompanies *Abschied von den Eltern* seems to me to illustrate Sebald's strategy of (literary) remembrance: it shows a boy of eight or ten, dressed up in a sailor suit, deep in thought whilst he lifts a spadeful of earth. Behind the boy the elements of a bourgeois world can be seen: a domed building, a theatre, a few houses, factories and chimneys with smoke emerging from them, a couple of children playing, and adults strolling around. It is the Campo Santo in Pisa, blended in a metamorphic manner with the industrial architecture of the nineteenth century. Turning away from this world but also unnoticed by it, the boy digs. He is digging in the opposite direction from the many horizontal or semi-horizontal lines in the collage, into the depths. He is digging away into an underworld that is almost entirely paved over, sealed up with stones or buildings. The boy is left to his own devices, an outsider. Beside him lie blank white sheets of paper and pages of books. Is he digging them up or burying them?

Closer inspection reveals that, as with many of Weiss's collages, the proportions and perspectives are not accurate, so that the compact grouping of the buildings merely gives the appearance of order. It would better be described as a stage set. Does the boy want, quite literally, to get to the bottom of the representational world that surrounds him? Does he want to lay it bare or undermine its apparent magnificence? At both an actual and a metaphorical level I have found connections here with W. G. Sebald and his texts, in which, persistently and unobtrusively, he uncovers a subterranean source of the past which was at first invisible. The stories represent archaeological research into memory, in the course of which layers of (family) biographies previously buried in the unconscious are revealed. And these are often the hitherto untold stories of those who have been lost to history.

It was the same with the conversations we used to have in his office or in one of the cafés on campus. From time to time he would draw on a long black cigarette-holder, giving (as it says somewhere in *Austerlitz*) an uncommonly elegant impression. The view that biographies and people's lives were among the most fascinating subjects was something that W. G. Sebald often emphasized. Generally speaking, the progress of my thesis played only a minimal role in our discussions. I had the impression that he placed unquestioning faith in it. What interested us both particularly was the role and the self-perception of authors, especially between the 1920s and the 1960s, in other words from the Weimar Republic to the year 1968, with its explicit politicization of literature and society. Turning attention from the texts to the biographical connections could also lead to fascinating case studies such as Walter Erich Schäfer, one of the most influential and undoubtedly also the best artistic directors of the post-war period, who among other things initiated what came to be known as the 'Stuttgarter Ballettwunder' (Stuttgart Ballet Miracle). Moreover, Schäfer had also been one of the most performed dramatists between 1930 and 1945, a fact that had been completely ignored in literary and theatre studies. So W. G. Sebald asked me whether, in addition to an analysis of the texts, one should not

> einige grundsätzliche Überlegungen zu der sog. 'trahison des clercs' anstellen [...], über Leute also, die (wie der Fall Schäfer es in Reinkultur demonstriert) aus beruflichem Ehrgeiz und blankem Opportunismus (viel mehr als aus ideologischer Überzeugung) mit dem Regime sich arrangierten[7]

[address a few fundamental considerations to the so-called 'trahison des clercs', in other words about people who, as Schäfer's case demonstrates to perfection, came to an accommodation with the regime for reasons of professional ambition and naked opportunism, rather than from ideological conviction].

This characteristic example of his intellectual curiosity led me to a project on Schäfer.[8]

On 17 November 2001, barely a month before W. G. Sebald's death, the opening ceremony of the first Literaturhaus Baden-Württemberg took place in Stuttgart. He had been invited to give the opening lecture, in which, taking personal reminiscence as his starting point, he reflected on literary authorship (see Figure 5.2). 'Wozu also Literatur?' [What is the purpose of literature?] Sebald posed this question to bring his speech to a close. 'Es gibt viele Formen des Schreibens; einzig aber in der literarischen geht es, über die Registrierung der Tatsachen und über die Wissenschaft hinaus, um einen Versuch der Restitution' [There are many forms of writing; only in literature, however, can there be an attempt at restitution over and above the mere recital of facts, and over and above scholarship].[9] By this attempt at restitution I think he meant giving back a lost memory through writing, thereby creating a memorial to those 'denen das größte Unrecht widerfuhr' [to whom the greatest injustice was done].[10] For the author and university teacher W. G. Sebald this was a duty, perhaps even the primary duty, of literature.

Translated from the German by Brigid Purcell

Notes to Chapter 5

1. Letter from WGS to FR of 1 August 2001.
2. Letter from WGS to FR of 3 July 1999.
3. Letter from WGS to FR of 1 December 2000.
4. W. G. Sebald, 'Mit einem kleinen Strandspaten Abschied von Deutschland nehmen' [Taking Leave of Germany with a Bucket and Spade], interview with Uwe Pralle, *Süddeutsche Zeitung*, 22–23 December 2001, Literatur section, p. 16. See Primary Bibliography J.42.
5. Ibid.
6. W. G. Sebald, 'Die Zerknirschung des Herzens: Über Erinnerung und Grausamkeit im Werk von Peter Weiss', in *Campo Santo*, ed. by Sven Meyer (Munich: Hanser, 2003), pp. 128–48 (p. 129); 'The Remorse of the Heart: On Memory and Cruelty in the Work of Peter Weiss', in *On The Natural History of Destruction*, trans. by Anthea Bell (London: Hamish Hamilton, 2003), pp. 173–95 (p. 176).
7. Letter from WGS to FR of 10 May 1998.
8. See Florian Radvan, *Eine deutsche Theaterkarriere: Der Dramatiker und Generalintendant Walter Erich Schäfer* (Trier: Wissenschaftlicher Verlag Trier, 1999).
9. W. G. Sebald, 'Ein Versuch der Restitution', in *Campo Santo*, ed. by Sven Meyer (Munich: Hanser, 2003), pp. 240–48 (p. 248); W. G. Sebald, 'An Attempt at Restitution', in *Campo Santo*, trans. by Anthea Bell (London: Hamish Hamilton, 2005), pp. 206–15 (p. 215).
10. 'Ein Versuch der Restitution', p. 248; 'An Attempt at Restitution', p. 215.

FIG. 5.2. WGS reading at the opening of the *Literaturhaus* in Stuttgart
on 17/18 November 2001. © Dr Heiner Wittmann

CHAPTER 6

Against *Germanistik*:
W. G. Sebald's Critical Essays

Uwe Schütte

As a literary scholar, W. G. Sebald was primarily interested in literature from the fringes of German-speaking Europe and the remoter edges of the established canon, though as a professor of German literature he was, of course, thoroughly conversant with the canonical German writers. Nonetheless, the names of such writers from the German *Bildungsbürgertum* (educated middle classes) as Lessing, Goethe, and Thomas Mann are conspicuously absent from the bibliographies of his critical writings. By contrast, there is a striking preponderance of Austrian and Alemannic names over German ones, for while Sebald published only about ten essays on German writers, he wrote almost thirty articles on Austrian literature of the nineteenth and twentieth centuries. Moreover, nineteen essays on Austrian writers and topoi connected with Austrian literature are collected in the two volumes of essays *Die Beschreibung des Unglücks* (The Description of Misfortune) (1985) and *Unheimliche Heimat* (Strange Homeland) (1991), which made his name as an Austrianist in both Germany and Austria. It is true that among the Austrian writers discussed by Sebald one can find more than a few who in the meantime have found their way into the canon and occupy places next to established authors like Adalbert Stifter, Hugo von Hofmannsthal, and Franz Kafka: one thinks of contemporary writers like Elias Canetti, Thomas Bernhard, Peter Handke, and Gerhard Roth. However, one looks in vain in his critical work for the likes of Franz Grillparzer, Robert Musil, and Heimito von Doderer, finding in their place Charles Sealsfield, Peter Altenberg, and Jean Améry.

At the beginning of his academic career, Sebald mainly concerned himself with German writers, Carl Sternheim and Alfred Döblin in particular. He wrote his *licence* dissertation and master's thesis on the former and his doctoral thesis on the latter. He subjected both writers to a searching critique and, in so doing, called into question the overwhelmingly positive reputations which they had acquired at the hands of established *Germanistik*. Accordingly, his book on Sternheim (the published version of his master's thesis) begins as follows: 'Es ist der Zweck der vorliegenden Arbeit, das von der germanistischen Forschung in Zirkulation gebrachte Sternheim-Bild zu revidieren' [The aim of this book is to revise the current image of Sternheim as propounded by scholars of German literature].[1] Sebald's master's dissertation and doctoral thesis, those academic rites of passage, also served as a means of setting himself apart from institutionally established *Germanistik*. His career as a scholar and critic was thus formed by defining himself in opposition to an academic discipline that was, in his eyes, conservative and compromised.

In this context, the academic reviews that Sebald published during the 1970s in the innovative and forward-looking *Journal of European Studies*, founded in 1971 by three slightly older colleagues in UEA's School of European Studies, are particularly informative.[2] Though still working on his own doctorate, Sebald is very critical of the studies by established academics he is reviewing, on the grounds that they do not measure up to what, in his view, constitutes an appropriate mode of literary criticism. Thus, while less than halfway through his own thesis on Döblin, Sebald begins his discussion of Leo Kreutzer's monograph on that author as follows: 'Döblin scholarship was until recently almost non-existent. Since coming into being, however, it has taken an uninspiring course.' Sebald considers it particularly significant that

> Kreutzer's account of the development of Döblin's *oeuvre* does not go beyond 1933. Granted that the novels written in exile do not attain the standard of the earlier works, it is precisely through such ideologically problematic novels as the three volumes on the revolution of 1918 that Leo Kreutzer and other German critics might have found a way out of their impasse.[3]

Here, Kreutzer's alleged strategy of bracketing out problematic material is singled out as being typical of much *Germanistik*. Such attempts to bring literary *oeuvres* into line suggest an institutionalized level of suppression and attempts at covering up in a discipline compromised, in Sebald's view, by National Socialism. Thus, in a review of a history of Yiddish literature in German-speaking lands, Sebald levels the following charge:

> From its early beginnings *Germanistik* as a discipline was fatefully wed [*sic*] to the growth of German ideology and it is therefore quite consistent that Yiddish literature from the early middle-ages to the nineteenth century should fail to figure in the clerks' account of the unadulterated tradition which extends from the *Hildebrandslied* to the novels of Gustav Freytag. And it strikes one as the supreme quirk in all this that the efforts of the one established academic in present-day Germany who is actively engaged in researching Yiddish texts are somewhat marred by his own past record of antisemitic activities.[4]

That Sebald felt that this taint marked not only German but also Austrian *Germanistik* is apparent from the following remark — flying in the face of all the niceties of academic reviewing — made a decade and a half later when discussing Joseph McVeigh's *Kontinuität und Vergangenheitsbewältigung in der österreichischen Literatur nach 1945* [Continuity and Coming to Terms with the Past in post-1945 Austrian Literature]. Referring to Austria's line-up of leading Germanists of that era he writes:

> Literary historians such as Nadler, Kindermann, Langer, and Adalbert Schmidt remained influential into the early 1960s and did their best to obfuscate the moral and aesthetic issues which should have been brought onto the agenda in those years. Indeed I remember vividly a lecture delivered by Adalbert Schmidt in this country in the early 1970s which made my hair stand on end.[5]

For Sebald, as his very first review makes clear, his decision to occupy a 'progressive position against the ideology of the established elders of literary studies'[6] meant, above all, the deployment of the ideas of Walter Benjamin and the critical theory of the Frankfurt School. Thus, discussing the allegedly new critical direction taken by Jochen Schulte-Sasse's handbook *Literarische Wertung* (Literary Evaluation), Sebald complained that

> any truly progressive German criticism is pushed under the mat. As though Benjamin had never put pen to paper and shown how it might be done, [Schulte-Sasse] concerns himself exclusively with the hoary casuistry of those who still chase after the essence of literature.[7]

Conversely, when reviewing a collection of essays that sought to explore possible links between literary scholarship and critical theory, Sebald also complained, on the one hand, that the texts under discussion were drowning under the weight of theory and, on the other, that the all-important ideas of the Frankfurt School had been watered down by over-zealous proselytes:

> It appears that what we are currently witnessing, at least as far as Germany is concerned, is the gradual transformation of a form of literary criticism neglectful of criticism to one neglectful of literature. This is not to say that 'critical theory' has nothing to offer; it is only to suggest that Horkheimer, Adorno and Benjamin are still a far better choice than some of their proselytizing adepts.[8]

It was, then, entirely logical that Sebald should have decided to write to Adorno himself, saying, in his second letter (14 December 1968), that he would not have made the original contact 'wenn ich nicht auf dem Umweg über Ihre Bücher ein so großes Zutrauen zu Ihnen gefaßt hätte' [if I had not developed so great a trust in you via your books].[9] In his first letter (24 April 1967), Sebald asks Adorno to explain a remark about Sternheim in *Minima Moralia* which he claimed not fully to understand, adding that 'meine Kritik an Sternheim [stützt sich allein auf dem] was ich aus Ihren, Horkheimers und Marcuses Büchern und Aufsätzen gelernt habe' [my critique of Sternheim [rests solely] on what I have learnt from your, Horkheimer's and Marcuse's books and essays].[10] It is certainly the case that, in both his master's thesis on Sternheim and the book version, Sebald quotes extensively from the publications of the Frankfurt School — particularly those by Adorno — in order to give weight to his critical argument against Sternheim. (See also Chapter 2 of the present volume.)

Sebald, who as a young scholar did not belong to any institutionalized circle of Germanists and hence did not benefit either from the patronage of an established professor or from the support of an academic foundation, may thus be regarded as a self-proclaimed disciple of the Frankfurt School. His dissenting stance towards *Germanistik* in German universities can be seen as a kind of student revolt undertaken on the battlefield of literary criticism which, in keeping with the provocative tone of the times, expressed itself in 'his direct attack on literary critics, his arrogant, aggressive tone, his many doubtful generalizations, and his doctrinaire, jargonistic style', as one reviewer of his Sternheim book put it.[11]

Ulrich Simon has correctly argued that the 'self-styled role of provocateur' is a consistent hallmark of Sebald's critical writings,[12] and this is particularly true of two controversial interventions from the 1990s. First, there was his 1993 essay on Alfred Andersch in *Lettre international*,[13] in which Sebald argued that the author, who was widely regarded as the quintessential politically committed intellectual, was in need of re-evaluation because of the dubious relationship between the literary quality and moral integrity of his work, especially in view of his opportunistic behaviour during the Third Reich. Second, Sebald caused a stir among both professional colleagues and the German literary establishment when, in late 1997, he gave a series of public lectures in Zurich on air war and literature, published as *Luftkrieg und Literatur* ('Air War and Literature: Zurich Lectures', in *On the Natural History of Destruction*). Here, he accused post-war German literature of ignoring the area bombing of German cities by the Allies during World War II and suggested reasons for this strange omission that did not redound to Germany's credit.

Another provocative essay is that on the Jewish author Jurek Becker, which was originally intended for a collection of essays in his honour in 1992.[14] However, owing to the extremely critical stance Sebald took against both Becker's work and its admirers, it was rejected by the editor and did not appear in the volume. The essay, which remained unpublished in Sebald's lifetime,[15] argues that Becker's novels suffer from a lack of authenticity on account of the missing emotional involvement on the part of the author. This was, in Sebald's view, attributable to a psychological mechanism designed to repress painful memories, which he refers to as an 'Erinnerungsembargo' [embargo on remembering].[16] While, as Sebald concedes, this is completely understandable as a psychological defence against traumatic experience, at the same time, he argues, it serves to prevent the reader from grasping the true reality of the author's autobiographical experiences, such as his incarceration in the Łódź ghetto.

Seen in the light of Sebald's persistent campaign against the academic establishment, his critical writings of the 1970s cannot be dismissed simply as youthful 'Imponiergehabe' [braggadocio],[17] even if one cannot entirely disregard this aspect; it is, rather, symptomatic of a lifelong aversion to the phenomenon of institutionalized *Germanistik*. The counter-attacks were never long in coming,[18] and so it is somewhat ironic that this critical *enfant terrible* and self-styled outsider should come to be one of the most internationally renowned German authors of the post-war period, his literary work encountering almost unreserved acclaim. This incorporation of W. G. Sebald's work into the canon of contemporary literature has led to its author becoming the object of a posthumous process of assimilation from various sides and with differing motives by parties who, in part at least, proceed in exactly the same way as the Germanists he criticized so harshly in the post-war period, omitting or ignoring any aspect of a given work which appears problematic. In order to make Sebald into a paradigmatic proponent of such topoi as exile, mass deportation, memory and the Shoah from the perspective of a non-Jewish German, controversial essays like the Andersch essay or the air-war lectures had to be relegated to the status of regrettable aberrations on the margins of his *oeuvre*, even though they are central to our understanding of the development of an author who was not only a creative writer, but also a literary critic and essayist.

After publishing his controversial books on Sternheim and Döblin, it was logical that Sebald should go on to concern himself primarily with writers with whose work he could identify. Even though he continued, during the following years, to produce major essays on German writers like Peter Weiss, Alexander Kluge, and Herbert Achternbusch, and paid tribute to such older Alemannic, Swabian, and Swiss writers as Johann Peter Hebel, Gottfried Keller, Eduard Mörike, and Robert Walser in his 1998 essay collection *Logis in einem Landhaus* (*A Place in the Country*), from the mid-1970s onwards, Sebald's research interests were clearly focussed on Austrian literature. This affinity is readily explained in terms of his own biography. Since he had grown up in a village in the Allgäu Alps, close to the border with the Austrian province of Tyrol, in a literal sense, too, Austria was much closer to home than, say, the Bavarian capital Munich. The picture of life in rural Austria, as presented in novels he would later read, inevitably reminded him of his own experiences on the periphery of southern Germany. Like those provincial authors emerging in Austria from the 1960s onwards, Sebald was someone who, coming from a relatively modest background, freed himself from its provincial restrictiveness through the bourgeois institution of literature. And like them, too, Sebald discovered that this process of emancipation was tantamount to an expulsion. His realization that 'möglicherweise das Winkelwesen der Heimat die Auswanderung in die entferntesten Länder [provoziert]' [it is possibly the obscurity of one's home[land] which causes one to emigrate to the most distant lands][19] had a marked effect on his own life, taking him via Freiburg and Switzerland to Manchester, and finally to Norwich.

Sebald's essays on Austrian literature reached a non-professional readership by way of two well-received collections of critical essays, the first of which appeared in September 1985 with the evocative title *Die Beschreibung des Unglücks* (The Description of Misfortune). Gerhard Melzer comments in a review:

> Sebald richtet seinen ganzen Scharfsinn darauf, jenen komplexen Prozeß zu rekonstruieren, in dessen Verlauf das schreibende Subjekt sein *Unglück* ins Werk setzt. Dabei gilt es dreierlei: zum einen, das System der Symbolisierungen zu entschlüsseln, hinter dem das schreibende Subjekt sein Unglück *verbirgt*, zum anderen, überhaupt erst den *lebensgeschichtlichen* Schlüssel für diese Symbolisierungen zu finden, und schließlich, eins aufs andere sinnvoll zu beziehen.[20]

> [Sebald applies his subtle and penetrating mind to the reconstruction of that complex process during which the writing subject inscribes his unhappiness or misfortune into the literary work. This process has three aspects: first, the decoding of the symbolic system behind which the writing subject *conceals* his misfortune or unhappiness, second, the discovery of the *biographical* key to this symbolic system, and third, the fruitful application of the one to the other.]

In concentrating on this hidden subtext, Melzer concludes, Sebald succeeds in tracking down 'Zusammenhänge[n] zwischen Leben und Schreiben [...], die zwar prinzipiell längst bekannt sind, aber im Einzelfall doch verblüffen' [connections between literature and life which have, in principle, been well known for a long time but which never fail to amaze when they come to light in a particular case].

In 1986 Sebald gained his *Habilitation* at the University of Hamburg on the strength of *Die Beschreibung des Unglücks*, and two years later he was awarded a Chair in European Literature at UEA. Although Sebald had been 'scribbling', as he used to put it, since his student years, the publication of his 'elemental poem' *Nach der Natur* (*After Nature*) in summer 1988 marked the official beginning of his second career as a writer, and the publication of *Schwindel. Gefühle.* (*Vertigo*) in March 1990 secured him a reputation among the German-speaking cognoscenti. Scarcely had this appeared than his second volume of critical essays, *Unheimliche Heimat* (Strange Homeland), was published in March 1991. Here, Sebald explored the concept of *Heimat* (homeland), one of the central categories of Austrian literature, but he did so from a much broader perspective than that of the usual 'Heimat-/Anti-Heimat-literatur' dichotomy. As he explained in his introduction:

> [Der Heimatbegriff] ist verhältnismäßig neuen Datums. Er prägte sich in eben dem Grad aus, in dem in der Heimat kein Verweilen mehr war, in dem einzelne und ganze gesellschaftliche Gruppen sich gezwungen sahen, ihr den Rücken zu kehren und auszuwandern. Der Begriff steht somit, wie das ja nicht selten der Fall ist, in reziprokem Verhältnis zu dem, worauf er sich bezieht. Je mehr von der Heimat die Rede ist, desto weniger gibt es sie.[21]

> [The concept of *Heimat* [home, homeland] is a relatively recent one. As it became increasingly difficult to remain in the home country, and as individuals and entire social groups found themselves forced to turn their backs on their country of origin and emigrate, so the term *Heimat* gained ever greater currency. The concept thus stands, as is often the case, in an inverse relationship to that to which it refers. The more people talk about *Heimat*, the less real it becomes.]

Hans Christian Kosler commented in his review as follows:

> Diesem Autor sind Haarspaltereien fremd. Sebald geht es weniger um penible Begriffsbestimmungen als vielmehr darum zu zeigen, wie jene vage Sehnsucht nach einer festen topographischen Größe, jener Strohhalm der Illusion, an dem man sich klammerte, zum poetischen Gelingen kleinerer wie größerer Werke beitrug.[22]

> [Hair-splitting is alien to Sebald, for this writer is less concerned with the niggling definition of concepts and more concerned to show how that vague yearning for a fixed topographical area, that wisp of an illusion to which one was wont to cling desperately, contributed to the successful realization of both lesser and greater works.]

In essence, the positive reception of Sebald's collections of critical essays on Austrian and Alemannic literature may in large measure be attributed to the fact that his elegant style of writing and critical approach had little in common with the usual kind of academic criticism. For Sebald, literary criticism meant interrogating texts and then listening carefully for answers which went beyond the confines of the purely aesthetic and touched upon social, political, and even metaphysical issues, as Martin Swales notes:

> Common to all his essays is the need to define the world portrayed in any particular fiction and to extrapolate from this some sense of the universe of discourse and signification which the writer in question inhabits and to which he gives expression.[23]

For this reason, Sebald always considered it important to investigate the way in which literary texts are grounded in their various contexts, and in a 1979 review of a book on GDR literature that failed to contextualize the works under discussion, he goes so far as to invoke the supreme arbiter of *Geistesgeschichte* in order to make his case: 'Hegel argued that the poorer a work of art the more important become the circumstances — political, social, psychological, biographical — that surround it. Hutchinson's study almost completely disregards this basic principle.'[24] In another review, Sebald criticizes an interpretation of Peter Weiss's *Marat/Sade* which, with its superficial description of that play as an 'outstanding achievement', in his view fails to do justice to its complexities:

> Too obediently Professor Durzak follows in the footsteps of literature demonstrating the methods of academic processing rather than an independent analysis. The 'clerks', it seems, have once again renounced their duties. Or does criticism really have no more than an ancillary function as the dogsbody of literature?[25]

So one might say that, in Sebald's view, in order to be relevant, criticism has to keep faith with literature by breaking faith with the rules and norms of established literary studies; literary criticism can lead to genuinely original insights only if it is able to free itself from institutionalized critical discourse. Thus, in a 1988 review of Elizabeth Boa's book on Frank Wedekind, Sebald passed the following judgement: 'She is at her best where she leaves the prescribed patterns of academic discourse and trusts her own critical sense to lead her into the less discovered territories.'[26]

The same kind of accolade could be awarded to Sebald's first essay on the schizophrenic poet Ernst Herbeck, also known as 'Alexander', who occupies a pivotal place in his critical work. Sebald was one of the first critics to acknowledge the unique literary quality of Herbeck's poetry.[27] His first essay on Herbeck, 'Kleine Traverse: Über das poetische Werk des Alexander Herbrich' (*En travers*: The Poetical Works of Alexander Herbrich [aka Ernst Herbeck]), first published in late 1981,[28] simply ignored the usual scholarly claim to objectivity which stipulates a clear division between the critic and the subject. Rather, every paragraph testified to the author's unmistakeable sympathy for and championing of the Gugging psychiatric patient, something which is also evident in the second section of *Schwindel. Gefühle.* (*Vertigo*) where, in a moving literary monument to Herbeck, the narrator recounts an excursion along the Danube which he undertook with the poet.[29] One cannot emphasize too strongly the unusual process by which, for Sebald, critical essays form the starting point for literary creation — not just in the case of Herbeck, but also in that of Kafka, who also plays an important intertextual role in *Schwindel. Gefühle.* (*Vertigo*). In this sense Sebald's critical essays prepare the ground for his literary works, as Hugo Dittberner suggests: 'Sebald ist ein Autor der Lektüren, in stärkerem Maße noch als die meisten anderen Gegenwartsautoren' [Sebald is an author who reads — to a much greater extent even than most other contemporary writers].[30]

Sebald's emancipated form of literary criticism is necessarily subjective, but by no means anti-theoretical on that account. Indeed, the essay on Herbeck evinces a deeper understanding of the enigmatic beauty of psychopathological poetry, not least because it involves interdisciplinary points of reference ranging from Freudian psychoanalysis to the anthropological ideas of Rudolf Bilz and the ethnological studies of Konrad Lorenz and to Gilles Deleuze and Félix Guattari's concept of *littérature mineure*. This methodological eclecticism is reflected in Sebald's stated intention in the introduction to *Die Beschreibung des Unglücks*:

> Das fallweise Verfahren, das je nach den vor ihm auftauchenden Schwierigkeiten ohne viel Skrupel seine analytische Methode wechselt, stimmt selbst zu der vorbedachten Rücksichtslosigkeit, mit der in der österreichischen Literatur traditionelle Grenzlinien etwa zwischen ihrem eigenen Bereich und dem der Wissenschaft übergangen werden.[31]

> [This approach, taking each case on its merits and altering, without too much ado, its analytical method according to the difficulties arising in any given text, also corresponds to the deliberate disregard with which, in Austrian literature, traditional boundaries between categories are overlooked, for example between its own sphere and that of science or philosophy.]

As far as Herbeck's pithy texts are concerned, originating as they did during writing therapy sessions in the Gugging psychiatric hospital near Klosterneuburg, Sebald sets out from the epistemological assumption that, out of regard for their own system of logic, scientific and scholarly explanations like to leave out of account those things which do not fit their conceptual principles ('Aus Respekt vor der eigenen Logik unterschlägt die "wissenschaftliche Explikation" gern das, was ihr Konzept stört').[32] For this reason, he explains, 'Die Einsicht in die eigene Unzulänglichkeit [...] wäre wohl der adäquateste Ausgangspunkt für eine Studie zu der zustandsgebundenen Kunst Alexanders' [insight into one's own inadequacy is probably the most appropriate starting point for a study of Herbeck's art, contingent as it is upon his mental state] (132). In choosing to write about Herbeck, Sebald sends a clear signal that German literary scholarship was guilty of a serious omission; whereas art history had, in the wake of the pioneering work of people like the Heidelberg psychiatrist Hans Prinzhorn (1886–1933), found a place for the visual work of psychiatric patients via the concept of *art brut* ('outsider art'), the literary texts of talented patients like Herbeck were ignored as aesthetically worthless.[33]

What so fascinated Sebald about Herbeck's writing was his knack of coming close to valid insights by travelling along 'wrong' roads ('auf "falschen" Wegen in die Nähe richtiger Einsicht gelang[en]') (135). Believing that 'in der Schizophrenie menschheitsgeschichtlich ältere Formen der Äußerung wieder zutage treten' [schizophrenia allowed more archaic modes of expression to come to light] (138), Sebald sums things up very aptly by relating the poetological principle underpinning Herbeck's poems to Lévi-Strauss's concept of *bricolage*, suggesting that Herbeck's playful use of language had an astonishing affinity with the way in which so-called 'primitive' people go about their mythopoetic work, synthesizing randomly accumulated 'odds and ends' to create something which is both improvised and surprisingly novel. In this way, Herbeck's schizophrenic texts turn out to be a literary expression of what Lévi-Strauss called *pensée sauvage*.

Another author who excited Sebald's interest because he, like Herbeck, was far removed from what is normally considered to be literature, was the anarchic filmmaker, actor, painter, dramatist, and prose writer Herbert Achternbusch. Although

Achternbusch's case is less extreme than that of Herbeck, Sebald saw him, too, as a paradigmatic representative of 'minor' literature which was, however, all the more important on that account. As he writes in the context of Herbeck's poems, such literature defines 'den Ort unserer Hoffnung' [the location of our hopes] more exactly than does 'der geordnete Diskurs' [orderly discourse]: 'In dem Maße, in dem die Kultur, wie die Wissenschaft vor ihr, in den Bann der Verwaltung gerät, wächst die potentielle Bedeutung der kleinen Literatur, als deren Botschafter man Herbeck verstehen sollte' [The more culture, like science before it, falls prey to the world of *administration* [i.e. bureaucracy], the greater the potential significance of 'minor' literature, as whose ambassador one should regard Herbeck, becomes] (140–41).

Of Achternbusch's texts, Sebald comments (needless to say in a positive sense): 'Näher sind noch nicht viele an die Sprache der Schizophrenie herangekommen, ohne selber den Verstand zu verlieren' [Not many have yet got as close to the language of schizophrenia without losing their own minds], and this is why, for him, Achternbusch's writings read like 'der Tribut eines davongekommenen an seine leider in der Reservation lebenden Brüder' [the tribute of one who has escaped the reservation to his brothers who, sadly, are still living there].[34] A comparison of such writings with established literature is inevitably to the detriment of the latter: 'Vergleicht man die Texte Achternbuschs mit den kunstfertig gedrechselten Sequenzen der akkreditierten Großschriftsteller, so wird unmittelbar deutlich, daß sie die schon längst nicht mehr geheure Wirklichkeit unserer Zeit mit stupender Genauigkeit erfassen' [If one compares Achternbusch's texts with the artfully turned periods of our accredited writers, it is immediately apparent that the former grasp with stupendous accuracy the ever more disquieting reality of our age].[35]

Sebald also sees in Achternbusch, as in Herbeck, an example of the literary *bricoleur* or *Bastler*, using his texts as an example in order to differentiate between two contrasting literary types: 'engineer' versus *bricoleur* (*Bastler*). Whereas, according to Sebald, the established author stands for 'den Typus des Ingenieurs [...], der "in Bezug auf jene Zwänge, die einen Zivilisationsstand zum Ausdruck bringen, immer einen Durchgang zu öffnen versuchen wird, um sich *darüber* zu stellen [...]"' [will always attempt to open up a way through those restrictive pressures which express a state of civilization, in order to find a way of overcoming them], the *bricoleur* or *Bastler* (i.e. Achternbusch) remains 'freiwillig oder gezwungen *darunter*' [voluntarily or involuntarily subjected to them]. Achternbusch nonetheless contrives to create 'Wortfügungen und Bilder [...], die einem professionellen Literaten nicht einmal im Traum einfallen würden' [verbal constellations and images that would not occur to a professional man of letters even in his wildest dreams].[36]

In connection with a surreal scene from one of Achternbusch's plays, in which the dying inmates of the Munich municipal old people's home on the Luise Kiessel-bach-Platz are shoved out through an attic window onto the roof to be left as food for the gulls, Sebald remarks that in such scenes we are dealing with images that teach us the meaning of fear ('die einen schon das Fürchten lernen'), adding:

> Freilich haben die Opfer dieses sinistren Entsorgungssystems nichts mehr von
> der Einsicht, die uns beim Lesen solcher Passagen aufgeht. Andererseits aber
> läßt sich das für eine Veränderung der von uns arrangierten und tolerierten

gesellschaftlichen Zustände notwendige emotionale Potential nur über die Evokation der Leiden unserer eingesperrten Genossen akkumulieren.[37]

[Of course, the victims of this sinister disposal system cannot benefit from the insights which dawn on us as we read such passages. But on the other hand, the emotional charge needed to change the social situation we have set up and accept as normal can be built up only by evoking the sufferings of our imprisoned comrades.]

Such marginal or outsider literature thus not only represents a bastion of empathy and solidarity, but is also the locus of what Peter Weiss called an 'aesthetic of resistance', retaining the utopian hope of societal change.

Sebald was, of course, not unaware that a fundamental restructuring of the social order is conceivable only as a result of individual emancipation. This explains why a central preoccupation of his critical essays is concerned with the limitations and possibilities of emancipation through the writing of literature. Austrian literature, particularly of the post-war period, provided him with a rich range of raw material. Thus Sebald notes, for example:

In der Tat ist Josef Winklers ganzes monomanisches Werk, und ist ein Großteil der von Graz inspirierten zeitgenössischen österreichischen Literatur ein Versuch, die Erfahrung der Erniedrigung und der moralischen Vergewaltigung auszugleichen durch einen auf die eigene Herkunft gerichteten bösen Blick.[38]

[Josef Winkler's entire, monomanic *oeuvre*, together with a large portion of the contemporary Austrian literature inspired by Graz, is actually an attempt to compensate for the experience of humiliation and moral violation by casting a malevolent eye on one's own origins.]

And the same applies to authors like Franz Innerhofer,[39] the early Peter Handke, and others: 'Bevormundung, Unterdrückung, Knechtschaft, Gefangenschaft, Leibeigenschaft — in diese Reihe mußten fast zwangsläufig alle neueren österreichischen Autoren die von ihnen in der Heimat gemachten gesellschaftlichen Erfahrungen einordnen' [Oppressive upbringing, repression, servitude, imprisonment, serfdom — these are the categories into which almost all modern Austrian writers had to fit the experience of socialization which they underwent in their homeland].[40] For Sebald, then, writing as a means of escaping from social disadvantage — literature as self-emancipation — constituted a process of empowerment which 'in vielem wie die Assimilationsbewegung der Juden im ausgehenden 19. und zu Beginn des 20. Jahrhunderts [verlief] und [...] darum auch wie diese eine Literatur von großer Breitenwirkung und hoher Qualität hervorgebracht [hat]' [in many respects followed the same course as the Jewish movement towards assimilation in the late nineteenth and early twentieth centuries and so, like its antecedent, produced works of great resonance and high quality].[41] At the same time, however, with reference to selected ghetto-stories by Jewish nineteenth-century writers, Sebald also indicates the dead ends into which such a project of emancipation could issue.[42]

For literature to serve as an escape route from lowly and oppressive circumstances, it is necessary to take the basic but radical step of claiming the right to speak by forging a language of one's own. This is why Sebald continually returns to the paradigmatic early work of Peter Handke, where 'der Zusammenhang von Sprachlosigkeit, Sprachfindung und Sprachverlust von zentraler Bedeutung [ist]. Überall gibt es Stumme, Wortlose, für die der Erzähler berichtet von der Schädigung und Zerstörung ihrer Person' [the interconnection of speechlessness, loss, and discovery of a language are of central importance. Everywhere you look you find people who have no voice or words and on whose behalf the narrator relates the events which have damaged and destroyed them as persons].[43] In Sebald's estimation, truly 'minor' writers like Herbeck and Achternbusch exemplify, in an even more extreme way, the process through which literary language and writing can become the means of liberation from highly disadvantaged circumstances:

> Wenn der junge Mönch sagt, ihm schmerze die Zunge, und er finde keinen Sinn in der deutschen Sprache, so redet er damit dem Herbert Achternbusch aus dem Herzen. Wer wie dieser Autor aus der Aphasie sich herausgewerkelt hat, weiß vielleicht, was es heißt, wenn man das Maul nicht mehr aufbringt.[44]

> [When the young monk says that his tongue hurts and he can find no meaning in the German language, he is acting as the mouthpiece for Herbert Achternbusch's own, heartfelt words. Whoever, like this writer, has, as it were, worked his way out of a state of aphasia by his own efforts knows what it means when you can't get your mouth open.]

The implicit starting point for Sebald's literary essays is the melancholy conviction that, during the course of the twentieth century, the history of mankind finally showed itself to be on a downward path and that, therefore, the two disastrous world wars were simply preludes to a total and imminent catastrophe, and that, additionally, a creeping process of exploitation is perpetually destroying the natural basis of our lives. He cites Franz Kafka as someone who shared this dark sense of history, reading those of his stories which deal centrally with evolution as a way of acquiring a better understanding of the destabilizing factors in human history:

> Die Konjekturen, die Kafka in seinen Verwandlungsgeschichten verfolgt, sind in einer Zeit wie der gegenwärtigen, in der eine tiefgreifende Mutation der Menschheit sich anzubahnen scheint, von unabweisbarem Interesse. Es ist bemerkenswert, wie wenig der Kritik bislang dazu eingefallen ist, obschon doch gerade die erkenntnistheoretische Dimension des Problems einer Vorausschau in eine artgeschichtlich andere Verfassung Kafka nachhaltig beschäftigt hat.[45]

> [The hypotheses which Kafka explores in his stories of transformation are of crucial concern at a time like the present, when humankind seems poised on the verge of a far-reaching mutation. It is strange how little critical attention has thus far been paid to this, despite the fact that it is precisely the epistemological dimension of anticipating a radically altered human species which most persistently preoccupied Kafka.]

Only on a superficial level does Sebald read 'Ein Bericht für eine Akademie' ('A Report to an Academy') as a text about the evolutionary leap from animal to human: the symbolic structure of Kafka's parables, he claims, allows the reader to draw much more far-reaching conclusions, though one needs to 'take a ruler and extend the author's tentative vectors of suggestion out to infinity' ('Kafkas Parabeln erlauben aufgrund ihrer referentiellen Struktur sehr viel weiterreichendere Schlüsse. Man muß allerdings das Hauslineal anlegen und die vom Autor angedeuteten Vektoren ins Weiße hinaus ausziehen').[46] Accordingly, the report about the transformation of the ape Rotpeter into a human being, or rather, about his forced assimilation into the human race, becomes a paradigmatic example of the evolutionary step which still awaits humankind:

> Aus dieser Konstellation ergibt sich eine Interlinearversion des Textes, die davon erzählt, daß nach uns die Maschinen kommen werden, ein Märchen also, das jetzt, da die Maschinen dabei sind, uns die Last des Wissens abzunehmen, in die Wirklichkeit übersetzt wird. Wenn uns, vermittels unserer Kommunikation mit den Maschinen, die Anverwandlung der elektronisch gesteuerten Intelligenz, die Ausschaltung redundanter moralischer Skrupel und damit die Vervollkommnung der instrumentellen Vernunft gelungen sein wird, dann wird uns unsere menschliche *vie antérieure* wohl ebensowenig erinnerlich sein wie dem Affen sein animalisches Vorleben.[47]

> [If one reads between the lines of Kafka's story, it tells us that we shall be succeeded by machines — a fable which, now that the machines are actually in the process of relieving us of the burden of knowledge, is fast becoming a reality. Once we have succeeded, by means of our communication with machines and the assimilation of electronically controlled intelligence, in eliminating redundant moral scruples and thus in perfecting instrumental reason, our previous existence as human beings will no doubt mean as little to us as his earlier life as an animal does to Kafka's ape.]

As Sebald points out, Kafka's text makes it clear 'daß der Übergang von einem Aggregatzustand zum andern, vom Tier zum Menschen und vom Menschen zur Maschine durchaus fließend ist' [that the transition between one state and the next — from animal to human and human to machine — is a thoroughly fluid one],[48] and for a long time now we have been making significant progress in this process of voluntary disenfranchisement, which Sebald illustrates with reference to the medium of television:

> War der Hund das Inbild des treuen Hausgenossen, so ist jetzt ein sprachfähiges Gerät unser beständigster Kompagnon. Eine Zeitlang gaben wir in einer seltsamen Charade noch vor, es sei der Hund der Stimme seines Herrn aus dem Apparat hörig, obschon der Hund, wie wir wissen, so dumm gar nicht ist. Wir sind es ja, die stumm vor dem Kasten sitzen, dem wir unsere Stimme geliehen haben. In dieser gehorsamen Stellung probieren wir schon, wie es sein wird, wenn die des Worts mächtigen Maschinen uns nicht mehr zu Wort kommen lassen [...].[49]

> [If the dog was once the very image of the faithful companion, now it is an appliance capable of speech which is our constant companion. For a while, in a kind of strange charade, we pretended that the dog was in thrall to his master's voice emanating from the instrument, although dogs, as we well know, are really not that stupid. Now we are the ones who sit mutely in front of the box to which we have lent our voice. In this obedient attitude we rehearse how it will be when the mighty machines of the word no longer allow us to have any say [...].]

One point of reference Sebald continually returns to is Elias Canetti, to whom he devoted one of his earliest essays.[50] A remark he made about Canetti in one of his later essays can be equally well applied to himself: '"Die Strenge der

Fachdisziplinen", von der Canetti wenig hält, ahndet Grenzverletzungen und zwingt die Wirklichkeit ins System ihrer Kategorien. Was nicht paßt, wird abgeschnitten' ['The rigidity of academic disciplines', which Canetti holds in low regard, punishes territorial infringements and forces reality to conform to their categories. Anything which does not fit is cut off].[51] It is, though, precisely the things that get cut off that persistently attract Sebald's attention. For him, as his essays make clear — despite his pessimism about mankind's heedless business of destruction — literature represents the last refuge against the colonizing tendencies of the discourse of reason: the realm of metaphysics.[52] And in his important essay on Gerhard Roth's 1984 novel *Landläufiger Tod* (Common Death),[53] he identifies the presence of the transcendent in, for example, the narrator Franz Lindner's visit to the graveyard with his aunt, during which she tells her nephew of an ascent, many years previously, of the Schneeberg mountain and of the profoundly moving panoramic view from the top of mountain peaks and valleys. The metaphysical experience, as Sebald comments on this passage, 'is mostly one which comes about in a state of contemplation when the self is completely and utterly forgotten' ('Die metaphysische Erfahrung ist zumeist eine, die sich über ein ganz und gar selbstvergessenes Schauen ergibt'). Moreover,

> Der metaphysische Augen- und Überblick entspringt einer profunden Faszination, in welcher sich eine Zeitlang unser Verhältnis zur Welt verkehrt. Im Schauen spüren wir, wie die Dinge uns ansehen, verstehen, daß wir nicht da sind, um das Universum zu durchdringen, sondern um von ihm durchdrungen zu sein.
>
> [The metaphysical vision and overview derive from a profound fascination in which our relation to the world is temporarily turned upside-down. While looking we sense how things are looking at us, and we understand that we are not here in order to pervade the universe, but to be pervaded by it.][54]

The author who, in Sebald's view, best embodies the literary ability to see what lies behind the world of things is Peter Handke. His 1986 narrative *Die Wiederholung* (*Repetition*) represents for Sebald in many ways a model example of the transcendent purpose of true literature, namely '[die] Sichtbarmachung einer schöneren Welt kraft allein des Wortes' [the making visible of a more beautiful world by virtue of the word alone].[55] The reception of Handke's writing since the publication of *Langsame Heimkehr* (*A Long Way Around*) in 1979 provides ample evidence that such an ambitious programme would, almost inevitably, be dismissed as a piece of esoteric extravagance by the 'parasitäre[n] Spezies [...] die an der Literatur ihr Wirtshaus hat' [the parasitical species which lives off literature][56] — in other words, mainstream *Germanistik*. Sebald mounts an impassioned defence of his writer colleague against the critics, praising

> die in den neueren Büchern Handkes entwickelte Metaphysik, die das Gesehene und Wahrgenommene übertragen will in die Schrift. Es gibt offensichtlich heute kein Diskursverfahren mehr, in dem die Metaphysik noch einen Platz beanspruchen dürfte. Und doch hat Kunst, wo und wann immer sie sich wirklich ereignet, zum Bereich der Metaphysik den engsten Bezug. Um diese Proximität zu erkunden, bedarf der Schriftsteller einer

nicht zu unterschätzenden Tapferkeit, während es natürlich für die Kritik und Wissenschaft, die die Metaphysik nur mehr als eine Art Rumpelkammer ansehen, ein leichtes ist, mit dem allgemeinen Verweis sich zu begnügen, daß in den höheren Regionen die Luft dünn und die Absturzgefahr groß ist.[57]

[the metaphysical ideas that Handke develops in his recent work which seek to translate what has been seen and perceived into the written word. Nowadays there is evidently no longer any discursive context in which metaphysics can claim a place as of right. And yet art, wherever and whenever it comes into being, is most intimately connected to the realm of metaphysics. In order to explore this relationship, the writer must have recourse to an unprecedented degree of courage, whereas for criticism and science, which now only regard metaphysics as a kind of lumber room, it is easy to get away with the general remark that the air is thin in the higher regions and the risk of falling great.]

The rest of Sebald's remarkable essay centres on the concept of redemption. In Sebald's reading, Filip Kobal, the narrator and protagonist of *Die Wiederholung*, is a messianic redeemer figure whose biography 'manche Züge [aufweist], die aus Handkes eigener Familiengeschichte, so wie sie etwa in *Wunschloses Unglück* berichtet wird, bekannt sind' [evinces many features familiar from Handke's own family history, as told, for example, in *Wunschloses Unglück* (*A Sorrow Beyond Dreams*)].[58] So what Handke, who grew up amid rural poverty, relates is the story of a young man from peasant stock who, by means of the written word, 'die Wandlung vollziehen soll von einem niedergedrückten Dasein in eine Haltung stolzer Unbeugsamkeit' [has to achieve the transformation from an oppressed existence to an attitude of proud indomitability].[59]

But the author of these words, a provincial from the Allgäu brooding on Austrian literature at the easternmost edge of England, doubtless discerns in the emancipatory power of the written word his own means to redemption. The oppressive burden of our increasingly alienated modern reality is set against an ideal state of weightlessness: in *Die Wiederholung*, Sebald suggests, the fact that there are passages which 'fast ein Gefühl der Levitation vermitteln' [almost communicate a feeling of levitation][60]

ist ein Maß für die außergewöhnliche Qualität dieser Erzählung, deren insgeheimes Ideal [...] eines der Leichtigkeit ist. Nicht daß der Erzähler sorglos wäre oder unbeschwert; er wendet nur, statt von dem zu reden, was auf ihm lastet, seinen Sinn darauf, etwas herzustellen, was ihm und dem vielleicht gleichfalls trostbedürftigen Leser hilft, den Verlockungen der Schwermut standzuhalten.[61]

[is a measure of the exceptional quality of this story, whose secret aim is one of lightness. Not that the narrator is lighthearted or free from care; but instead of talking about what burdens him, he turns his attentions to producing something which helps both him and the reader — who is perhaps equally in need of solace — to withstand the temptations of melancholy.]

As this and similar passages cited above indicate, from the 1980s onwards Sebald was no longer primarily concerned with polemical essays aimed at setting himself apart from the institutionalized discourse of *Germanistik*; rather, in terms of both style and content, he moved ever closer to a mode of writing about literature that has, on the surface at least, scarcely anything in common with his academic writings of the 1970s, where the stylistic influence of Adornian jargon all too often makes itself apparent.

A constant feature, however, of Sebald's idiosyncratic approach to literature throughout his career was his biographical standpoint. Ruth Klüger summarizes the importance of 'biographism' (an approach viewed as naively heretical by most contemporary academics)[62] for an understanding of Sebald's *oeuvre* as follows:

> In seinen literaturwissenschaftlichen Essays [...] durchbricht Sebald das Tabu gegen den Biografismus, den wir Germanisten als naiv zu verachten gelernt haben. Sebald verbindet unbekümmert Leben und Werk, denn das eine ist ihm Ausdruck des anderen. [...] Genau dieses Prinzip überträgt er auf sein eigenes literarisches Werk: Da erzählt er Biografien, die teils authentisch, teils erfunden sind, und bringt sich selber mit ein. Das Werk ist ein sozusagen holistisches Unternehmen, in dem die Entwicklung Europas eingefangen wird in die Geschichte seiner verschiedenen Epochen und diese in die Biografie des Einzelnen, die sich wiederum ausweitet in die Geschichte Europas.[63]

> [In his academic essays, Sebald flouts the taboo against 'biographism' which we Germanists have learnt to scorn as a naive approach. Sebald blithely connects life and work, for as far as he is concerned, the one is the expression of the other. [...] It is precisely this principle that he carries over into his own literary work, where he narrates biographies which are partly authentic, partly invented, and brings himself into the stories as he does so. His work is, so to speak, a holistic undertaking in which the development of Europe is bound up with the histories of its individual epochs and in which, conversely, these are bound up with individual life histories which then spread out into the broader history of Europe.]

Sebald's writings about Alfred Andersch and Robert Walser are perfect examples of the biographical approach so typical of his later essays. It is often forgotten that his piece on Andersch, which triggered a veritable scandal, was intended as an implicit rejoinder to Stephan Reinhardt's 1990 biography. In this sense, the essay could be seen alongside the academic reviews Sebald published early in his career, and also provides a link back to his books on Sternheim and Döblin. The polemical nature of the essay, and the biographical arguments underpinning the attack on Andersch were, to a certain extent, occasioned by Reinhardt's biographical apologia for Andersch. By contrast, Sebald's essay on Walser is evidently a labour of love and its biographical approach the result of a deeply-felt psychological affinity. As Kurt Flasch remarks, with particular reference to the Walser text, the generic label of 'essay' 'klingt zu glatt und distanziert für Sebalds Notate seiner Wanderungen zu verstörten Brüdern. Hier wird niemand "charakterisiert" oder eingeordnet. Ein Autor legt dem anderen die Hand auf den Arm' [seems too bland and objective to describe Sebald's writings about his wanderings in search of his psychologically disturbed brethren. Here no one is being 'characterized' or pigeonholed. Rather, one author is taking another by the arm].[64]

In contrast to the detailed biographical documentation in the essay about Andersch, Sebald notes that, in the case of the Swiss author Walser: 'Dermaßen weit sind die uns aus Walsers Leben überlieferten Szenen auseinander, daß man von einer Geschichte oder von einer Biografie eigentlich nicht sprechen kann: eher, will mir scheinen, von einer Legende' [So far apart are the scenes of Walser's life which have come down to us that one cannot really speak of a story or of a biography at all, but rather, or so it seems to me, of a legend].[65] Consequently, he finds himself obliged to fill out the biographical gaps with conjectures and suppositions and to proceed in a way that is not so much empirical and scientific as empathetic and imaginative. As in his works of fiction, Sebald inserts photographs into his essay as visual points of reference, placing every known portrait photo of Walser next to one another in order to hint at 'die lautlose Katastrophe [...], die zwischen ihnen sich abgespielt hat' [the silent catastrophe which has taken place between each].[66] As early as *Schwindel. Gefühle.*, when recounting his excursion with Ernst Herbeck along the Danube, Sebald had used a cropped photograph of Walser, allegedly a picture of Herbeck, in order to link the two authors.[67] As Mark Anderson discusses in Chapter 1 of this volume, in the essay on Walser, Sebald goes on to construct an associative bridge to his own family history, highlighting various similarities between Walser's appearance and that of his grandfather Josef Egelhofer, noting that they not only had in common general bearing and individual characteristics but also that they died in the same year, 1956:

> Vielleicht sehe ich darum den Großvater heute, wenn ich zurückdenke an seinen von mir nie verwundenen Tod, immer auf dem Hörnerschlitten liegen, auf dem man den Leichnam Walsers, nachdem er im Schnee gefunden und fotografiert worden war, zurückführte in die Anstalt. Was bedeuten solche Ähnlichkeiten, Überschneidungen und Korrespondenzen? Handelt es sich nur um Vexierbilder der Erinnerung, um Selbst- oder Sinnestäuschungen oder um die in das Chaos der menschlichen Beziehungen einprogrammierten, über Lebendige und Tote gleichermaßen sich erstreckenden Schemata einer uns unbegreiflichen Ordnung?
>
> [Perhaps that is the reason why now, when I think back to my grandfather's death, to which I have never been able to reconcile myself, in my mind's eye I always see him lying on the horn sledge on which Walser's body — after he had been found in the snow and photographed — was taken back to the asylum. What is the significance of these similarities, overlaps, and coincidences? Are they rebuses of memory, delusions of the self and of the senses, or rather the schemes and symptoms of an order underlying the chaos of human relationships and applying equally to the living and the dead, which lies beyond our comprehension?][68]

One may be inclined to reject such questions as irrational; certainly they are not a prime concern of the discipline of *Germanistik*, with its roots in the Enlightenment tradition. Sebald, though, is concerned with the recuperation of a transcendent moment in an otherwise unrelievedly immanent present, a form of magical thinking expressed in terms of superstition, traces of which he tracked down in the texts of both so-called 'insane' and 'normal' authors in order to transpose them into his critical writings. Accordingly, his essay on Roth's *Landläufiger Tod* concludes with the observation that the art of writing ('die Kunst des Schreibens') is possessed of a dignity 'die damit zu tun hat, daß man standhaft an verlorenen Positionen festhält und sich seinen Aberglauben nicht nehmen läßt, ist doch in diesem nicht weniger

Wissen als Glaubwürdigkeit an der Wissenschaft' [which is connected with the fact that one steadfastly keeps on defending hopeless positions and keeps hold of one's superstition, for, after all, there is no less truth in irrational beliefs than credibility in the natural sciences].[69]

Sebald's uncanny affinity with Walser, however, extends not only to biographical associations but also into the area of literature. On reading Walser's novel *Der Räuber* (*The Robber*), Sebald discovers a narrative constellation staggeringly similar to a story from *Die Ausgewanderten* (*The Emigrants*). And as if that were not enough, in the same passage of Walser's novel Sebald comes across the highly unusual compound *Trauerlaufbahn* ('career in mourning') which he himself had used in the above story and which he had until then believed to be an invention entirely his own.[70] Commenting on this experience, Sebald writes:

> Ich habe immer versucht, in meiner eigenen Arbeit denjenigen meine Achtung zu erweisen, von denen ich mich angezogen fühlte, gewissermaßen den Hut zu lüften vor ihnen, indem ich ein schönes Bild oder ein paar besondere Worte von ihnen entlehnte, doch ist es eine Sache, wenn man einem dahingegangenen Kollegen zum Andenken ein Zeichen setzt, und eine andere, wenn man das Gefühl nicht loswird, daß einem zugewinkt wird von der anderen Seite.

> [I have always tried, in my own works, to mark my respect for those writers with whom I felt an affinity, to raise my hat to them, so to speak, by borrowing an attractive image or a few expressions, but it is one thing to set a marker in memory of a departed colleague, and quite another when one has the persistent feeling of being beckoned to from the other side.][71]

To reach across to that 'other side', to grasp it imaginatively as the hidden complement of our increasingly materialistic world in blind thrall to the mindless pursuit of profit, was an aim which, towards the end of his life, Sebald came to pursue in both his literary and his essayistic writings, seeking doubtless to give people the courage necessary to withstand the gravitational pull of everyday circumstances: to open up the possibilities of reading literary texts — as he himself did — without heeding the strictures of academic criticism, of deciphering the meaning which may lie hidden behind the coincidences between our lives and those of others.

Coincidences such as, for instance, the discovery Sebald makes in the context of Walser's story *Kleist in Thun*: in the second half of the 1960s, so he claims, he found, in a biography of Gottfried Keller he had bought second-hand in Manchester, a sepia photograph of the very house on the island in the Aare in which Kleist had worked on his first drama:

> Langsam habe ich seither begreifen gelernt, wie über den Raum und die Zeiten hinweg alles miteinander verbunden ist, das Leben des preußischen Schriftstellers Kleist mit dem eines Schweizer Prosadichters, der behauptet, Aktienbrauereiangestellter gewesen zu sein in Thun, das Echo eines Pistolenschusses über dem Wannsee mit dem Blick aus einem Fenster der Heilanstalt Herisau, die Spaziergänge Walsers mit meinen eigenen Ausflügen, die Geburtsdaten mit denen des Todes, das Glück mit dem Unglück, die Geschichte der Natur mit der unserer Industrie, die der Heimat mit der des Exils.

[Since then I have slowly learnt to grasp how everything is connected across space and time, the life of the Prussian writer Kleist with that of a Swiss author who claims to have worked as a clerk in a brewery in Thun, the echo of a pistol shot across the Wannsee with the view from a window of the Herisau asylum, Walser's long walks with my own travels, dates of birth with dates of death, happiness with misfortune, natural history and the history of our industries, that of *Heimat* with that of exile.][72]

It requires real humility to be as self-effacing as this, conscious of one's status as just a minuscule part of a greater whole which can at best be grasped intuitively, if at all. At any rate Sebald leaves one in no doubt that he understood the finely spun, ephemeral tissue of the literary text as a central component of that all-encompassing order; which is why the close study of literature can help us — possibly — to conceive of the inconceivable. Such study demands complete immersion in the text, which in turn presupposes a respectful attitude towards literature (in contrast to what tends to happen in literature departments, where texts are often reduced to nothing more than springboards for the airing of current theory or hermeneutic methodologies). Such respect, however, has nothing to do with the pseudo-religious worship of art and literature: it is, as it were, simply a form of higher seriousness. If texts are subjected to such 'serious' reading, they may in turn trigger in the reader that emancipatory impulse which spurred on authors like Walser to continue writing in the face of the adversities of personal circumstances, society and history:

> Walser muß [...] gehofft haben, daß er sich den Schatten, die von Anfang an über seinem Leben lagen und deren unaufhaltsames Längerwerden er früh voraussieht, schreibend, durch die Verwandlung von etwas sehr Schwerem in etwas beinahe Gewichtsloses, würde entziehen können. Sein Ideal war die Überwindung der Gravitation.

> [Walser must [...] have hoped, through writing, to be able to escape the shadows which lay over his life from the beginning, and whose lengthening he anticipates at an early age, transforming them on the page from something very dense to something almost weightless. His ideal was to overcome the force of gravity.][73]

Such a transformation of the oppressive into the liberating, which is tantamount to the lifting of the burden of reality, becomes the utopian aim of great literature like that of Robert Walser. As early as his master's thesis on Sternheim, Sebald had stated that 'die Qualität der Erlösung' [the quality of redemption] is the mark of all true art ('Kennzeichen aller wahren Kunst').[74] The desire to achieve such secular redemption through the word and by means of literature was, without doubt, one of the central motives behind W. G. Sebald's writings.

Translated from the German by Richard Sheppard/Jo Catling

Notes to Chapter 6

1. Winfried Georg Sebald, *Carl Sternheim: Kritiker und Opfer der Wilhelminischen Ära* (Stuttgart: Kohlhammer, 1969), p. 7. For the evolution of Sebald's work on Sternheim, see Richard Sheppard's essay in Chapter 2 of this book, especially pp. 60–64, 75–79, 83–86.

2. These would probably never have been published if the atmosphere at the newly founded UEA (1964) and the editorial policy of the new interdisciplinary *Journal of European Studies* (*JES*) (1971) had not been so liberal in those heady, post-1968 years. *JES*, it must be realized, grew naturally out of the founding ideal of a School of Studies, then a rarity at departmentalized British universities, in which the study of European Literature was positively encouraged and the boundaries between disciplines, notably those between literature and history and those between the various national literatures, had been made more porous. A *European Studies Review* was founded at about the same time at the equally new University of Lancaster, but its focus was socio-political. Sebald was completely at home in such an institution and so probably felt encouraged by the very nature of *JES* to make more daring utterances and judgements. Amazingly, no one ever complained about his reviews (letter from Professor John Flower (one of the founding editors of *JES*) to Richard Sheppard of 18 December 2007). Two decades later, such an atmosphere may well have helped Sebald to develop modes of writing within a conservative literary culture that spanned institutionalized generic boundaries (cf. Juliane Römhild, ' "Back in Sebaldland": Zur Rezeption von W. G. Sebald in der britischen Tagespresse', *Zeitschrift für Germanistik*, 15 (2005), 393–99 (p. 394). (RWS)

3. W.G.S., review in English of Leo Kreutzer, *Alfred Döblin: Sein Werk bis 1933, Journal of European Studies*, 1 (1971), 276. See Primary Bibliography, G.4. Hereafter numbers for entries in the Primary Bibliography are given in brackets at the end of the note where relevant.

4. W.G.S., review in English of Helmut Dinse, *Die Entwicklung des jiddischen Schrifttums im deutschen Sprachgebiet, Journal of European Studies*, 4 (1974), 304. (G.14)

5. W. G. Sebald, review in English of Joseph McVeigh, *Kontinuität und Vergangenheitsbewältigung in der österreichischen Literatur nach 1945, Modern Language Review*, 85 (1990), 531. The talk by Schmidt, on Adalbert Stifter, took place at UEA in the early 1970s. (G.30).

6. W.G.S., review in English of J[ochen] Schulte-Sasse, *Literarische Wertung, Journal of European Studies*, 1 (1971), 273. (G.1).

7. Ibid.

8. M.G.S., review in English of Horst Albert Glaser and others, *Literaturwissenschaft und Sozialwissenschaften: Grundlagen und Modellanalysen* (Stuttgart: Metzler, 1971), *Journal of European Studies*, 2 (1972), 76. (G.5).

9. *Sebald. Lektüren.*, ed. by Marcel Atze and Franz Loquai (Eggingen: Isele, 2005), p. 16.

10. *Sebald. Lektüren.*, ed. by Atze and Loquai, p. 12.

11. Donald G. Daviau, review of Winfried Georg Sebald, *Carl Sternheim: Kritiker und Opfer der Wilhelminischen Ära*, *Germanic Review*, 47 (1972), 234–36 (p. 236).

12. Ulrich Simon, 'Der Provokateur als Literaturhistoriker: Anmerkungen zum Literaturbegriff und Argumentationsverfahren in W. G. Sebalds essayistischen Schriften', in *Sebald. Lektüren.*, ed. by Atze and Loquai, pp. 78–104 (p. 80).

13. W. G. Sebald, 'Between the Devil and the Deep Blue Sea: Alfred Andersch: Das Verschwinden in der Vorsehung', *Lettre international*, no. 20 (Spring 1993), 80–84. (D.57).

14. *Jurek Becker*, ed. by Irène Heidelberger-Leonard (Frankfurt a.M.: Suhrkamp, 1992).

15. W. G. Sebald: 'Ich möchte zu ihnen hinabsteigen und finde den Weg nicht: Zu den Romanen Jurek Beckers', Nachlass W. G. Sebald, Deutsches Literaturarchiv Marbach (DLA). This essay has recently been published by the author of this chapter: W. G. Sebald, 'Ich möchte zu ihnen hinabsteigen und finde den Weg nicht: Zu den Romanen Jurek Beckers', *Sinn und Form*, 62.2 (2010), 226–34, followed by a commentary: Uwe Schütte, 'Weil nicht sein kann, was nicht sein darf. Anmerkungen zu W. G. Sebalds Essay über Jurek Beckers Romane', *Sinn und Form*, 62.2 (2010), 235–42. (D.53).

16. Sebald 'Ich möchte zu ihnen hinabsteigen und finde den Weg nicht', p. 234.

17. Klaus Müller-Salget, 'Neuere Tendenzen in der Döblin-Forschung', *Zeitschrift für Deutsche*

Philologie, 103 (1984), 263–77 (p. 270); see further Richard Sheppard, 'W. G. Sebald's Reception of Alfred Döblin', in *Alfred Döblin: Beyond the Alexanderplatz*, ed. by Steffan Davies and Ernest Schonfield (Berlin: de Gruyter, 2008), pp. 350–76.

18. Cf. Müller-Salget and, *vis-à-vis* the Andersch controversy, Volker Wehdeking, 'Das Nachleben von Andersch in Texten anderer Autoren', in *Alfred Andersch: Perspektiven zu Leben und Werk aus der Sicht der neunziger Jahre*, ed. by Irène Heidelberger-Leonard and Volker Wehdeking (Bad Homburg: Opladen, 1994), pp. 213–20.

19. W. G. Sebald, *Die Beschreibung des Unglücks: Zur österreichischen Literatur von Stifter bis Handke* (first published Salzburg: Residenz, 1985; subsequently Franfurt a. M.: Fischer, 1994), p. 10. All further references are to this edition. Sebald's interest in Austrian literature may be traced back at least to his encounter with Prof. Ernst Alker at the Université de Fribourg (see Chapter 2, pp. 56–64 above) and, at the University of Manchester, with his colleagues in the German Department, Prof. Idris Parry, Dr Ray Furness, and Dr Eda Sagarra (see pp. 71–75 and 82–83 above). At UEA, which used to offer a final-year, two-term Special Subject on Austrian Literature, Sebald became one of a small group of colleagues centrally interested in Austrian Literature as a literary culture in its own right — in effect, a mini Austrian department within the German Sector, consisting of Dr Franz Kuna (1933–2010), an Austrian national and Anglist who had a particular interest in Kafka (see Primary Bibliography D.8); Keith Pollard, a Stifter specialist; and Dr Cedric Wiliams, who in 1974 published *The Broken Eagle: The Politics of Austrian Literature from Empire to Anschluss*. Dr Kuna had a very good relationship with the Austrian Institute in London, and was instrumental in securing funding for an Austrian *LektorIn* from the mid-1960s to 2001. This constellation was very probably unique in Britain at the time and certainly provided a fruitful environment for Sebald's *Auseinandersetzung* with the problematic of Austrian Literature. (RWS)

20. Gerhard Melzer, 'Österreichische Literatur in Einzelansichten: W. G. Sebalds Essaysammlung *Die Beschreibung des Unglücks*', *Neue Zürcher Zeitung*, 28–29 June 1986, Literatur und Kunst section, p. 68; repr. in *W. G. Sebald*, ed. by Franz Loquai (Eggingen: Isele, 1997), pp. 55–57.

21. W. G. Sebald, *Unheimliche Heimat: Essays zur österreichischen Literatur* (first published Salzburg: Residenz, 1991; subsequently Frankfurt a. M.: Fischer, 1995), pp. 11–12. All further references are to this edition.

22. Hans Christian Kosler, 'Der Strohhalm der Illusion: W. G. Sebalds Essays zur österreichischen Literatur', *Süddeutsche Zeitung*, 19–20 October 1991, SZ am Wochenende section, p. iv; repr. in *W. G. Sebald*, ed. by Loquai, pp. 75–76. Cf. Gisela Ecker, '"Heimat" oder Die Grenzen der Bastelei', in *W. G. Sebald: Politische Archäologie und melancholische Bastelei*, ed. by Michael Niehaus and Claudia Öhlschläger (Berlin: Schmidt, 2006), pp. 77–88.

23. Martin Swales, 'Theoretical Reflections on the Work of W. G. Sebald', in *W. G. Sebald: A Critical Companion*, ed. by J. J. Long and Anne Whitehead (Edinburgh: Edinburgh University Press, 2004), pp. 23–28 (p. 26).

24. M. Sebald, review in English of Peter Hutchinson, *Literary Presentations of Divided Germany: The Development of a Central Theme in East German Fiction 1945–1970*, *Journal of European Studies*, 9 (1979), 287–88. (G.19).

25. W. G. Sebald, review in English of Manfred Durzak, *Dürrenmatt, Frisch, Weiss: Deutsches Drama der Gegenwart zwischen Kritik und Utopie*, *Journal of European Studies*, 3 (1973), 97–98. (G.9).

26. W. G. Sebald, review of Elizabeth Boa, *The Sexual Circus: Wedekind's Theatre of Subversion*, *British Journal of Aesthetics*, 28 (1988), 400. (G.25).

27. Ernst Herbeck / Alexander Herbrich (1920–91), a long-stay schizophrenic patient whose cleft palate made verbal communication doubly difficult, lived in the so-called 'Haus der Künstler' (founded in 1981 by Leo Navratil (1921–2006) as the Zentrum für Kunst und Therapie) in the Niederösterreichische Landesanstalt für Psychiatrie und Neurologie at Gugging, near Klosterneuburg. (Coincidentally, Ludwig Wittgenstein had worked as an under-gardener in Klosterneuburg in August 1920, and Kafka had died in the nearby Sanatorium Hoffmann in June 1924.) Judging by Sebald's annotated books in the DLA, he got to know Herbeck's poetry in the late 1970s via *Alexanders poetische Texte*, ed. by Leo Navratil (Munich: DTV, 1977), and Leo Navratil, *Gespräche mit Schizophrenen* (Munich: DTV, 1978). For Christmas 1980, Navratil sent Sebald an (inscribed) copy of his *Schizophrenie und Sprache, Schizophrenie und Kunst: Zur*

Psychologie der Dichtung und des Gestaltens (Munich: DTV, 1976). Sebald visited Klosterneuburg while on research leave in October 1980 and spent a week researching at the institute in Gugging (cf. *Schwindel. Gefühle. (Vertigo)*; see note 29). (RWS)

28. W. G. Sebald, 'Kleine Traverse: Über das poetische Werk des Alexander Herbrich', *Manuskripte*, no. 74 (1981) 35–41, repr. as 'Eine kleine Traverse: Das poetische Werk Ernst Herbecks', in *Die Beschreibung des Unglücks*, pp. 131–48. (D.17/D.17(a)).

29. See W. G. Sebald, *Schwindel. Gefühle.* (Frankfurt a.M.: Eichborn, 2001), pp. 46–56; W. G. Sebald, *Vertigo*, trans. by Michael Hulse (London: Vintage, 2002), pp. 38–49.

30. Hugo Dittberner, 'Das Ausführlichste oder: ein starker Hauch Patina: W. G. Sebalds Schreiben', *Text + Kritik*, no. 158 (April 2003), 6–14 (p. 7).

31. W. G. Sebald, 'Vorwort', in *Die Beschreibung des Unglücks*, pp. 9–13 (p. 9).

32. Sebald, 'Eine kleine Traverse: Das poetische Werk Ernst Herbecks', p. 131. Henceforth all references to this essay are taken from the edition cited in full in note 19 and are given in parentheses within the body of the text.

33. Sebald is known to have had in his UEA office a box of slides labelled 'Art Brut', possibly for teaching purposes, including a number of slides of the work of Swiss 'outsider artist' and psychiatric patient Adolf Wölfli. (Eds)

34. W. G. Sebald, 'Die weiße Adlerfeder am Kopf: Versuch über den Indianer Herbert Achternbusch', *Manuskripte*, no. 79 (1983), 75–79 (p. 77). (D.20(a)).

35. 'Die weiße Adlerfeder am Kopf', p. 78.

36. 'Die weiße Adlerfeder am Kopf', p. 77.

37. 'Die weiße Adlerfeder am Kopf', p. 78.

38. W. G. Sebald, 'Damals vor Graz: Randbemerkungen zum Thema Literatur & Heimat', in *TRANS-GARDE: Die Literatur der 'Grazer Gruppe'*, ed. by Kurt Bartsch and Gerhard Melzer (Graz: Droschl, 1990), pp. 141–53 (p. 147). (D.51). Josef Winkler (b. 1953) is a member of the progressive Austrian writers' union, Grazer Autorenversammlung.

39. Franz Innerhofer (1944–2002 [suicide]) was an illegitimate child from a Catholic peasant background. His novels deal with the hardships and abuse that he suffered as a child, the rawness of peasant life, and his own situation as an outsider in Austrian society.

40. Sebald, 'Damals vor Graz', p. 148.

41. 'Damals vor Graz', p. 149.

42. Cf. W. G. Sebald, 'Westwärts–Ostwärts: Aporien deutschsprachiger Ghettogeschichten', *Literatur und Kritik*, 23 (1989), 159–77; repr. in *Unheimliche Heimat*, pp. 40–64. (D.46).

43. Sebald, 'Damals vor Graz', p. 148.

44. Sebald, 'Die weiße Adlerfeder am Kopf', p. 77.

45. W. G. Sebald, 'Tiere, Menschen, Maschinen: Zu Kafkas Evolutionsgeschichten', *Literatur und Kritik*, 21 (1986), 194–201 (p. 195). (D.36).

46. 'Tiere, Menschen, Maschinen', p. 196.

47. 'Tiere, Menschen, Maschinen', p. 197.

48. Ibid.

49. 'Tiere, Menschen, Maschinen', p. 198.

50. W. G. Sebald, 'Gedanken zu Elias Canetti', *Literatur und Kritik*, 8 (1972), 280–85. (D.7).

51. W. G. Sebald, 'Summa Scientiae: System und Systemkritik bei Elias Canetti', in *Die Beschreibung des Unglücks*, pp. 93–102 (p. 95). (D.15(b)).

52. When interviewed by Professor Christopher Bigsby, a UEA colleague, in January 2001, Sebald said that one of the things that had always interested him most was the 'much-despised discipline of metaphysics, which was relegated from philosophy proper generations ago'. See 'In Conversation with W. G. Sebald', in *Writers in Conversation with Christopher Bigsby*, ed. by Christopher Bigsby, 2 vols (Norwich: EAS Publishing / Pen&inc., 2001), II, 139–65 (p. 159). See Primary Bibliography J.34. (RWS)

53. W. G. Sebald, 'In einer wildfremden Gegend: Zu Gerhard Roths Roman *Landläufiger Tod*', in *Unheimliche Heimat*, pp. 145–61 (p. 158). (D.35).

54. 'In einer wildfremden Gegend', p. 158; 'In a Completely Unknown Region: On Gerhard Roth's Novel *Landläufiger Tod*', trans. by Markus Zisselsberger, *Modern Austrian Literature*, 40.4 (2007), pp. 29–39 (p. 37). See also Richard Sheppard, 'Dexter — Sinister: Some Observations on

Decrypting the Mors Code in the Work of W. G. Sebald', *Journal of European Studies*, 35 (2005), 419–63 (p. 425).

55. W. G. Sebald, 'Jenseits der Grenze: Peter Handkes Erzählung *Die Wiederholung*', in *Unheimliche Heimat*, pp. 162–78 (p. 163). (D.54).

56. 'Jenseits der Grenze', p. 164.

57. 'Jenseits der Grenze', pp. 163–64.

58. 'Jenseits der Grenze', p. 169.

59. 'Jenseits der Grenze', p. 173.

60. 'Jenseits der Grenze', p. 176. Cf. Ben Hutchinson, 'Die Leichtigkeit der Schwermut: W. G. Sebalds "Kunst der Levitation"', *Jahrbuch der Deutschen Schillergesellschaft*, 50 (2006), 457–77, and Helen Finch, '"Die irdische Erfüllung": Peter Handke's Poetic Landscapes and W. G. Sebald's Metaphysics of History', in *W. G. Sebald and the Writing of History*, ed. by Anne Fuchs and J. J. Long (Würzburg: Königshausen & Neumann, 2007), pp. 179–97.

61. 'Jenseits der Grenze', pp. 176–77.

62. See Simon, 'Der Provokateur als Literaturhistoriker', pp. 82–87.

63. Ruth Klüger, 'Wanderer zwischen falschen Leben: Über W. G. Sebald', *Text + Kritik*, no. 158 (April 2003), 95–102 (p. 99).

64. Kurt Flasch, 'Landhaus mit Wasseradern: W. G. Sebalds Wanderungen zu verstörten Brüdern', *Neue Zürcher Zeitung*, 6 October 1998, Neue Literatur section, p. B.5.

65. W. G. Sebald, 'Le promeneur solitaire: Zur Erinnerung an Robert Walser', in *Logis in einem Landhaus* (Munich: Hanser, 1998), pp. 127–68 (p. 132); W. G. Sebald, 'Le promeneur solitaire: A Remembrance of Robert Walser', trans. by Jo Catling, introduction to Robert Walser, *The Tanners*, trans. by Susan Bernofsky (New York: New Directions, 2009), pp. 1–36 (p. 4). (D.68(a)).

66. 'Le promeneur solitaire', p. 134; 'Le promeneur solitaire', trans. by Catling, p. 5.

67. Sebald, *Schwindel. Gefühle.*, p. 46; *Vertigo*, p. 39.

68. Sebald, 'Le promeneur solitaire', pp. 137–38; 'Le promeneur solitaire', trans. by Catling, pp. 8–9.

69. Sebald, 'In einer wildfremden Gegend', p. 161.

70. Sebald, 'Le promeneur solitaire', p. 139; 'Le promeneur solitaire', trans. by Catling, p. 10.

71. Ibid.

72. 'Le promeneur solitaire', p. 162–63; 'Le promeneur solitaire', trans. by Catling, pp. 31–32.

73. 'Le promeneur solitaire', p. 141; 'Le promeneur solitaire', trans. by Catling, p. 12.

74. Sebald, *Carl Sternheim*, p. 23.

Appendix to Chapter 6:
Colloquia and research symposia organized by W. G. Sebald at UEA

The first of the three documents that follow is the programme for a Colloquium on Contemporary German Drama held at UEA in 1987, to which Sebald contributed a paper on Herbert Achternbusch's 'theatralische Sendung' (theatrical mission) and which gave rise to his only edited book, *A Radical Stage: Theatre in Germany in the 1970s and 1980s* (see Primary Bibliography A.4 and D.38). The second, the outline of a research project entitled 'Writing in the Shadow of the Shoah' details a series of research seminars with visiting writers and scholars from home and abroad planned for 1990–92. This was probably designed to culminate in the European Writers' Forum, organized under the auspices of the British Centre for Literary Translation and funded by the Arts Council, which brought together internationally acclaimed writers and their translators and which was held at UEA on 4 and 5 December 1992. The flyer for this event forms the third document here; this was also the occasion on which the photograph at Figure 7.1 was taken.

The editors would like to thank Dr Richard Weihe, Professor John White, the Estate of Michael Hamburger, and Anthony Vivis for their trouble in locating these documents and for kindly sharing them with us.

Appendix 6.1

C O N T E M P O R A R Y   G E R M A N   T H E A T R E   C O L L O Q U I U M

UNIVERSITY OF EAST ANGLIA - NORWICH

30 March - 1 April 1987

Monday 30 March

19.00 - 19.15   Introductory Session

                  Conference Room - Library

19.15 - 20.00   SIBYLLE WIRSING (Berlin)
                  Theatertrauer - Die Bühnen zwischen Verwaltung und Kunst

                  Conference Room - Library

20.15 - 21.00   University Reception

                  Upper Dining Room - Refectory Building

Tuesday 31 March

10.00 - 10-45   DAVID BRADBY (Canterbury)
                  Blacking Up - Two Productions by Peter Stein

                  Committee Room I - Senate House

10.45 - 11-15   Coffee

11.15 - 12.00   PETER IDEN (Frankfurt)
                  Erinnerung und Widerspruch - Funktionen des deutschen Theaters

                  Committee Room I - Senate House

12.00 - 12.45   Discussion

12.45 - 14.00   Lunch

14.15 - 15.00   GÜNTHER RÜHLE (Frankfurt) *Intendant*
                  Woher und Wohin - Bewegungen im derzeitigen deutschen Theater

                  Committee Room I - Senate House

/Cont...

Tuesday Continued

15.00 - 15.45   HOLGER SANDIG (Erlangen)
                 Theater zwischen Neoverismus und Neuer Sensibilität

15.45 - 16.00   Tea

16.00 - 16.45   Discussion

16.45 - 17.30   a) LUCINDA RENNISON (Berlin)
                    Dramatisches Talent hat sie nicht, doch viele schöne
                    Worte - Friederike Roth's Language for the Stage

                    Committee Room I - Senate House

                 b) STEPHEN GILES (Nottingham)
                    Tankred Dorst's 'Deutsche Stücke'

                    Committee Room II - Senate House

18.00 - 19.00   Dinner

20.00 - 22.00   Workshop/Open Forum:
                 Translation and Transposition - Contemporary German Plays
                 in and into English

                 Drama Studio - University Village

Wednesday 1 April

10.00 - 10.45   THOMAS SCHMITT (Erlangen)
                 Theater der Bilder

                 Committee Room I - Senate House

10.45 - 11.15   Coffee

11.15 - 12.00   a) IRMELA SCHNEIDER (Berlin)
                    Mythos und Mythosparodie in einigen Stücken von Botho Strauss

                    Committee Room I Senate House

                 b) MORAY MCGOWAN (Strathclyde)
                    Subject, Politics, Theatre - Reflections on Kroetz

                    Committee Room II - Senate House

12.00 - 12.45   Discussion

/Cont...

Wednesday Continued

12.45 - 14.00   Lunch

14.15 - 15.00   a) TONY MEECH (Hull)
                    Theatre in the GDR - A New Definition of 'eingreifendes
                       Theater'

                    Committee Room I - Senate House

                 b) HORST CLAUS (Bristol)
                    Die schönste Zeit im Leben, die kommt nicht von allein -
                       The West Berlin 'Grips'-Theatre

                    Committee Room II - Senate House

15.00 - 15.45   a) HAMISH REID (Nottingham)
                    Homburg-Machine - Heiner Müller and the Shadow of Nuclear War

                    Committee Room I - Senate House

                 b) JULIAN HILTON (Norwich)
                    Back to the Future - Volker Braun and the German Theatrical
                       Tradition

                    Committee Room II - Senate House

15.45 - 16.00   Tea

16.00 - 16.45   Discussion

16.45 - 17.30   a) RÜDIGER GÖRNER (London)
                    Die Spannung der Langeweile - Über Thomas Bernhard

                    Committee Room I - Senate House

                 b) W.G. SEBALD
                    Verwandlungskunst - Achternbuschs theatralische Sendung

                    Committee Room II - Senate House

17.30 - 18.00   Concluding Session

                 Committee Room I - Senate House

19.00 - 23.00   BUFFET followed by BAR

                 Sainsbury Centre Restaurant

                              *****

Appendix 6.2

School of Modern Languages and European History

University of East Anglia
Norwich   NR4 7TJ   England
Telephone Norwich (0603) 56161
FAX (0603) 58553 Telex 975197

'Writing in the Shadow of the Shoah'

Topics and Authors

8 November 1990	Georges Perec (FR)	David Bellos, Manchester
28 February 1991	Tadeusz Kantor (POL)	George Hyde, UEA
23 May 1991	Ladislav Fuks (CSFR)	
	Jiri Weil	Frantisek Fröhlich, Prague
	Arnost Lustig	
20 June 1991	Jurek Becker (G)	Irene Heidelberger-Leonard,
		Brussels
29 October 1991	Anne Duden (G)	Sigrid Weigel, Essen
31 October 1991	George Steiner (UK)	Klaus Briegleb, Hamburg
November 1991	David Grossman (IS)	Clive Sinclair, Herts.
November 1991	Danilo Kis (YUG)	Gabi Gleichman, Stockholm
March 1992	Aharon Appelfeld (IS)	Bryan Cheyette, Leeds
Spring 1992	Grete Weill (G)	Moray McGowan, Sheffield
Spring 1992	Else Lasker Schüler (IS)	Elinor Shaffer, UEA
Summer 1992	Jean Cayrol (FR)	John Fletcher, UEA
Autumn 1992	Piotr Rawicz (FR)	Anthony Rudolf, London
Autumn 1992	Tadeusz Borowski (POL)	George Hyde, UEA

Dates still to be confirmed:

The Survivor Syndrome	William Niederland, New York
H. G. Adler (GB)	John White, London
Primo Levi (IT)	David Robey, Manchester
Paul Celan (G)	

2

Jean Améry (AUST./BEL.)

Robert Antelme (FR)

Pierre Gascar (FR)

Peter Weiss (SW/FRG)   Max Sebald, UEA

Charlotte Delbo (FR)

Norman Manea (RUM)   Rosalind Belben, London

Adolf Rudnicki (POL)

Julian Stryjkowski (POL)

Appendix 6.3

Programme

Friday 4th December 1992

19.30 University Library Conference Room

Opening Address
PROFESSOR JAMES McFARLANE

followed by a reading by
HANS MAGNUS ENZENSBERGER

Saturday 5 December 1992
University Library Conference Room

Readings in the original language and English translation:

11.00 JULIAN RIOS
12.00 RYSZARD KAPUŚCIŃSKI
13.00 CEES NOOTEBOOM
14.00 LARS GUSTAFSSON
15.00 MARIE CARDINAL
16.00 JAAN KAPLINSKI
17.00 GIANNI CELATI

19.30 – 21.30 Lecture Theatre 1

Forum Discussion

Chair: JON COOK

Tickets
£2.00 Concessions £1.00
from Waterstone's Norwich
UEA (telephone 53625)
and London Street (telephone 632426)
or from Beryl Ranwell
University of East Anglia
Norwich NR4 7TJ
Telephone: 0603 56161 extension 2737

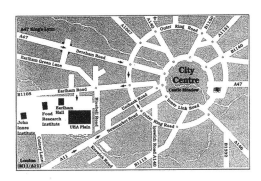

the british centre for literary translation · university of east anglia · norwich

National Writers' Meeting 1842

EUROPEAN ARTS FESTIVAL

EUROPEAN WRITERS' FORUM

4th & 5th December 1992

NORWICH

School of Modern Languages and European History · University of East Anglia
Norwich NR4 7TJ · Telephone: 0603 56161 Ext 2737

Arts Council Funded

Participants

MARIE CARDINAL
Born in 1929 in Algeria, **Marie Cardinal** took a degree in philosophy in 1948. From 1953 to 1960 she taught philosophy in Salonica, Lisbon, Vienna and Montreal and began working as a freelance journalist for "Elle" and "L'Express". Described as the "French Fay Weldon", Marie Cardinal won the Prix International du Premier Roman with her first novel: **Ecoutez la Mer** (1962). **Les Mots pour le Dire**, published in English as **The Words to Say It**, won the Prix Lettere in 1975. **Les Grands Désordres** (1987) charts the author's own confrontation with her daughter's drug addiction. The book was published in English translation in 1991 as **Devotion and Disorder**.

GIANNI CELATI
Gianni Celati, who lives in Bologna, is one of Italy's most important writers. He started writing on the recommendation of Italo Calvino who wrote the introduction to his first book. His fictions **Comiche**, **Le Avventure di Guizzardi** and **La Banda dei Sospiri** were published to critical acclaim in the 1970s. In 1985 **Voices From the Plains** was published in English, and immediately recognised as one of the outstanding books of the year. In 1990 he was awarded the Mondello Prize, the foremost Italian literary award, for his entire oeuvre.

HANS MAGNUS ENZENSBERGER
Hans Magnus Enzensberger, born in 1929, published his first collection of poems in 1957. This has been followed by a panoramic range of more than seventy other titles. They include literary monographs, dramatic texts, essays, volumes of poetry, prose works, anthologies and translations. From 1985 onwards, he has also edited over one hundred volumes in the series: "Andere Bibliothek". This unique collection of books, a readers' paradise, brings together all literary genres in works from more than twenty different countries. Among his recent works in English translation are: **Mediocrity and Delusion**, **Political Crumbs**, **The Sinking of the Titanic**, and **Europe, Europe**.

LARS GUSTAFSSON
Lars Gustafsson is a prolific writer of novels, poems and polemic articles, and a well-known figure in contemporary Swedish cultural debate. Trained as a philosopher, he is interested in existential and epistemological questions. In his view the world is incapable of rational explanation, and his writings convey a sense of the mysterious and the uncanny, the uncertainty of identity and the unknowableness of reality. Among his works translated into English are **Sigismund** (1976), **Forays into Swedish Poetry** (1976), **The Tennis Players** (1977) and **The Death of a Beekeeper** (1978). He was editor of the prestigious **Bonniers Litterära Magasin** 1962–72.

JAAN KAPLINSKI
Jaan Kaplinski is an Estonian poet, whose Polish father was a victim of the Soviet Holocaust. He is perhaps the most remarkable poet to emerge out of Eastern Europe at the end of the Cold War. **The Wandering Border** and **The Same Sea in Us All** are the two collections which have established his name in the West. His most recent volume **I am the Spring in Tartu** is written in English by this multi-lingual poet who has himself translated from the Chinese, English, French, Polish and Spanish. Gary Snyder said of him: "Kaplinski is re-thinking Europe, revisioning history, in these poems of our times. Elegant, musing, relentless, inward, fresh. Poems of gentle politics and love that sometimes scare you."

RYSZARD KAPUŚCIŃSKI
Ryszard Kapuściński is the Polish Graham Greene. He has witnessed and written about some twenty wars in the developing countries and achieved international fame with **The Emperor**, an account of the downfall of Haile Salassie, which was adapted for the Royal Court Theatre in London by Jonathan Miller. Kapuściński's other publications include **The Shah**, which describes the revolt in Iran, and **The Football War** on conflicts in Angola and Central America. Kapuściński is now completing a book on the disintegration of the Soviet Empire and working on a documentary for BBC-TV on Stalin's Labour Camps.

CEES NOOTEBOOM
Cees Nooteboom, born in 1933, published his first novel **Philip and the Others** in 1955, to great critical acclaim. He is a novelist, poet and playwright. In 1962 he became a columnist for "De Volkskrant", then started to travel and publish his first travel books: **An Afternoon in Bruay** (1963), **A Night in Tunisia** (1965), **A Morning in Bahia** (1968) and **An Evening in Isphahan** (1978). In 1969 Nooteboom received the Dutch Daily Press Prize for his columns on the 1968 May revolution in Paris. His novel **Rituals** (1980) has already been called a classic. Nooteboom's poetry is almost obsessively concerned with the difficulty, the near-impossibility, of communication.

JULIAN RIOS
Julian Rios, who lives in Madrid, is best known as the author of **Larva: Midsummer Night's Babel**, a novel set in London which has led to Rios being described as a "Spanish James Joyce". It was published in Britain in 1991 in a translation by R.A. Allen, S.J. Levine and the author. Rios is also active as an art critic. As well as a book on Eduardo Arroyo, he has published a long conversation with Kitaj on his life and work. This book: **Impressions of Kitaj** is due for publication in English in 1992.

Translators

William R. Brand, Peter Bush, Martin Chalmers, Adam Czerniawski, Adrienne Dixon, Hans Magnus Enzensberger, Richard Alan Francis, Michael Hamburger, Sam Hamill, Jaan Kaplinski, Suzanne Jill Levine, Antonia Lloyd-Jones, Robert Lumley, Christopher Middleton, Karin Montin, Katarzyna Mroczkowska-Brand, Julian Rios, Yvonne L. Sandstrom, J.K. Swaffar, Riina Tamm, G.H. Weber, John Weinstock.

the british centre for literary translation

FIG. 7.1. Hotel Nelson, Norwich, December 1992, in connection with the European Writers'
Forum organized by the British Centre for Literary Translation (BCLT) at UEA
on 4 and 5 December (see Appendix 6.3, pp.189–90). Left to right: Hans-Magnus
Enzensberger, Adam Czerniawski (Translator in Residence, later Associate Director, BCLT),
Max Sebald (Director, BCLT), Emeritus Professor James Walter McFarlane, Antonia Byatt
(Arts Council). © John Gibbons; courtesy of the University of East Anglia

FIG. 7.2. UEA, 1991. Left to right: WGS, Beryl Ranwell (BCLT Secretary),
Erminia Passannanti (Visiting Translator and BCLT Bursary Holder),
Ralf Jeutter (PhD student).
© Valentina Ippolito; courtesy of Dr Erminia Passannanti

FIG. 7.3 (upper). Fellbach, near Stuttgart, *c.* 22 or 23 April 1997, when WGS received the *Mörike-Preis*, at the Fellbacher Literaturtage. Left to right: Wolfgang Schlüter, WGS, the Mayor of Fellbach (Friedrich-Wilhelm Kiel), the journalist and critic Sigrid Löffler. © Thomas Schlegel

FIG. 7.4 (lower). WGS awarding the *Förderpreis des Mörike-Preises* to Wolfgang Schlüter in Fellbach on 22 April 1997. The Mayor, Friedrich-Wilhelm Kiel, is on the left. Wolfgang Schlüter was a guest translator at BCLT on several occasions during the 1990s. © Thomas Schlegel

FIG. 7.5. A British Council seminar entitled 'Translation' held at a Dominican monastery in Walberberg near Cologne, 24–25 January 1998. The seminar was chaired by A. S. Byatt (pictured here standing in front of WGS), and the participating writers and translators pictured here include Jonathan Barker, Tibor Fischer, John Fuller, Philip Hensher, A. L. Kennedy, and Lawrence Norfolk. WGS was invited as a special guest; translators Michael Hulse and Iain Galbraith were also present (not pictured).
© Anita Schiffer-Fuchs

CHAPTER 7

Englishing Max

Michael Hulse

Before there was any thought of my translating Max Sebald's writings into English, I knew him slightly, because in the academic year 1990–91 I had been one of a number of translators invited to give a talk in the inaugural series of guest lectures at the University of East Anglia's British Centre for Literary Translation, then a young institution. I no longer remember whether I talked on Schiller or Rilke in English on that occasion (in 1992, invited back to conduct a workshop, I took the other of the two as my subject); nor do I remember, if I ever knew, whether it was Max himself or Adam Czerniawski or George Hyde or some other colleague from whom the original idea to invite me came. On that first occasion, and on the second in 1992, I recall having only a very few minutes of conversation with Max, in some dismal space lined with office doors, and it is the warmth of our rapport, and his doleful humour, and the sense of being in the presence of someone who knew and savoured and valued his words, that stay in my mind, rather than any particulars of what was said. Although the house published very little poetry (and that mainly eastern European writing in translation), the publisher of my poetry at that time was Harvill; and every now and then mine was one opinion editor Bill Swainson would solicit of a foreign title Harvill was thinking of acquiring. The last book I'd read for him before Max's, if memory serves, was by an Estonian writer, Viivi Luik, whose book *The Seventh Spring of Peace* I had warmed to but with a nagging misgiving; its strength I had described to Bill as 'beauty, but pedestrian beauty'. Max's *Die Ausgewanderten* was sent to me by Bill on 17 March 1993, and at that date, though naturally aware that the book had been acclaimed throughout the serious German press, I had read neither that nor any other publication by him. To the hindsight of today, gifted with the understanding that Max was a significant writer, this may seem extraordinary; to me too, once I settled to *Die Ausgewanderten*, it seemed that I was reading something I had known all my life, and that it could not really be possible that I had ever been unacquainted with a text so self-evidently of the highest order.

In my report to Harvill, which I am no longer able to date exactly, I devoted two pages to an account of the content of *Die Ausgewanderten* before making this judgement and recommendation:

> From the narrative outlines it is almost certainly impossible to guess at the moving and quietly beautiful impact that very nearly every syllable of this book

makes. It is difficult to speak of it without reaching for the kind of superlatives that, by seeming overstated, would themselves violate the dignity of what is a very attractively understated book. In its utterly unpretentious, unsentimental, firm, patient, loving way, this is an important, a great book.

Any one of the reasons for claiming this might seem in itself almost perverse, but together they evidence a book that is quite unlike anything else I have read.

Fundamentally the tone is elegiac, but there are many moments of the whimsical, grotesque or strange. Sebald is meticulously observant, and his prose style has a kind of ampleness that seems designed to have big pockets in its folds, places where an observer can turn about and produce something that seems incidental, unexpected.

Behind this stance and style is always the ethical awareness that the act of remembering, of naming and detailing, is the one sure way to show respect to the past. Sebald's elegy, never shrill, is for the lost Jews of central Europe, for the loss of their way of life and culture but also for quite specific individual losses. It is like a kaddish spoken softly by a very civilized man weighted with sadness and alive with love of what is and what was.

The narrative technique draws no attention to its own skill, but its mature command is arresting. Personal recollections of driving on freeways or travelling to Manchester or Deauville are followed by remembrances voiced for old people Sebald talked to or for those whose writings he had access to. The emphasis on authenticity has profound implications.

It is impossible not to want to read on. The tone of Sebald's book is deeply human, his narratives always intrinsically interesting. I find this an essential and unbearably moving book, and could only see it as a real acquisition for Harvill.

That was what I wrote then; some points I would phrase differently now, but the essential respect for the moral as well as writerly greatness of *Die Ausgewanderten* would remain. Harvill acted on the recommendation and bought the rights. At no other time has a publisher's response to my judgement given me greater satisfaction.

It hadn't occurred to me that Harvill might ask me to translate the book. Other things were on my mind. Privately, the twelve months from April 1993 to April 1994, when he died, were marked by my father's declining health. Professionally, this was a period when my commitments to television documentary work for Deutsche Welle in Cologne were increasing, and it was also in 1994 that I was invited by Ludwig Könemann to be general editor of a literature classics series (in English) for the new publishing house he had established eighteen months earlier. Nonetheless, when Harvill's approach came I immediately agreed, partly because I was profoundly convinced of the importance of the book and partly because Max declared he'd be willing to look at draft translation material and offer suggestions. This was something I welcomed, because his English had already struck me as rich and nuanced and because an author can take liberties a translator cannot and should not take. My journal for 28 September 1993 noted a 'Sebald sample for Bill' as something requiring immediate attention, and on 15 November I wrote, 'Bill tells me I'm getting the Sebald book to do. A beautiful, sustainingly human book — the kind I want to translate.'

There are many things I might say about the work on *Die Ausgewanderten*, which extended over more than a year at draft stage, from early 1994 to mid-1995, and wasn't finally concluded till November 1995. Each of the four narrative drafts was sent to Max, who wrote his suggestions and changes onto a copy which he sent to Harvill, where again it was read for house style and additional editorial suggestions were made. From my sending Max the final narrative in early June 1995 to my returning the entire typescript to Harvill on 19 November that year, with almost all Max's and Bill Swainson's suggestions incorporated, there was still an interval of almost six months. The process was time-consuming. But it was felt by all involved to be worthwhile. Many enigmas surfaced (was it possible to see Mount Olympus from Constantinople? — what was meant by serving under the chimney?) but here I shall merely draw attention to one exchange between Max and myself in mid-1995.

On 7 June 1995 I sent Max my draft of the last of the four narratives in *Die Ausgewanderten*. My pocket diary for 1995 noted 'Sebald deadline' under 10 April, but that spring I had had reading tours of my own in India, Belgium, and Turkey, and a heavy television and publishing schedule, as well as other commissioned work such as an essay for *Text + Kritik* on the British reception of German literature, so I privately felt I had not done at all badly to turn the work in by June. In a lengthy letter which touched, among other things, on Max's translations of two of my poems for *Sprache im technischen Zeitalter* (see Part II of this volume, pp. 336–37), I put to Max a matter which had been much on my mind throughout my work on *Die Ausgewanderten*:

> There is something I very much want to ask, which derives really from some of the reviews of the book, where the butterfly man is identified with Nabokov and there is much talk of the 'intertextuelles Spiel' [intertextual play] in your 'Erzählungen' [narratives], and so forth. Now, the impression conveyed — that your narratives are fictions — troubles me, since my own reading of them depends to a substantial extent, I think, on my feeling that what matters in them is true. I'm not trying to be simple-minded about the word 'true': I realise that in reconstructing past lives and circumstances to which one wasn't privy, one is going to use a generous licence, and furthermore (as we are tirelessly reminded) the past may always be a kind of fiction anyway. What I mean, in a very elementary way, is that it matters to me that these people and the shapes of their lives are genuine. One reviewer writes of the 'Grenzbereich zwischen dokumentarischer Aufzeichnung und phantastischer Fiktion' [border area between documentary record and fantastical fiction], a fashionable way of putting it if ever there was one; and, while I don't think he is wrong, in any final sense, it seems to me faintly ... I don't know if this is what I mean ... offensive to put it like that. That fiction and imagination are in some manner involved I do not question, but it matters to me to locate them within the documentary aspect of your texts, as a token of your dedication to your quest for these lives, rather than without it, where it would be something different — no less arresting, but somehow embroidery rather than substance. How I should formulate the question I might ask, I don't know, but, as you see, it has something to do with where the literal truth stops and your imaginative re-creations or additions begin.[1]

On 19 June 1995 Max wrote thanking me for the final draft (sometimes he wrote to me in German, at other times in English, as on this occasion):

About the degree of fictionality in *Die Ausgewanderten*: I quite understand your concern & can assure you that all four stories are, almost entirely, grounded in fact, except that, in the Bereyter story I have added (a very few) touches of Wittgenstein's life as a primary teacher & that the fourth story is a sort of collation of two lives. Aurach's Lebens- & Vorgeschichte [life story] is that of my landlord in Manchester & the details about the painter are based on Frank Auerbach who came to England from Berlin much at the same time as my landlord. There is, thus, practically nothing in the stories that could be said to [be] invented, apart, that is, from the appearances Nabokov makes in all four stories. And I hope that this too is not unjustified. The passage about the butterfly boy in Kissingen is based on 'Speak, Memory' & whilst I do not know whether Aurach's mother ever happened to see the young Russian boy in Kissingen, what is certain is that they were both there at the same time. The same goes for Nabokov & my great uncle Adelwarth in Ithaca. So what I did was no more than extending the vectors a little. Fictionalization, as I see it, is, in this text, not a matter of substance, that is to say it is nothing to do with making up characters, events that befall them & complicated plots. Rather, the sense of fiction, the feeling that one is at a level removed, by a notch or so, from reality is meant to come out of adjusting the 'Sehschärfe' [focus] of the telescope one looks through, so that some things seem very distant & others (especially those which are in the past) quite close & immediate. That is why negotiating the tenses, as you probably found when translating, was so difficult. There are many more modes of the past than those allowed by Imperfect, Perfect & Pluperfect![2]

This answer, I felt, though canny and perhaps even wily, marked a genuine attempt by Max to address what he realized was, for me, potentially a moral rather than an aesthetic dilemma raised by his writing; his answer nonetheless foregrounded aesthetic criteria.

Even before publication of *The Emigrants* in mid-1996 I'd enlisted my old friend Greg Gatenby, founder of the Harbourfront International Literature Festival in Toronto and its director for a quarter of a century, to invite Max to read. Harbourfront under Greg was agreed by writers throughout the world to be the venue they most enjoyed and valued appearing at. Max, however, was his own man: 'Your Canadian friend did write', he wrote to me on 11 April 1996, '& I was flattered to receive the invitation to read at the Harbourfront. But I had to decline as I already have two "engagements" in the last week of October. And the semester will be in full swing.' The truth was that, though he did his share of public engagements, he was not drawn to the public role of the writer, or to larger gatherings. Even the party given in his honour by his publisher, Christopher MacLehose, on 18 June 1996, shortly after *The Emigrants* appeared, produced something resembling a long sigh of weariness from Max, in a letter of 30 June:

Bei der Party bei Christopher beispielsweise war es, vor knapp zwei Wochen, so, daß ich, nach einem ganzen Tag voller Examiners meetings um fünf Uhr von Norwich mit der Bahn losfuhr, um sieben in London dann nur nach ewigem Hin- und Herrennen in Liverpool Street ein Taxi bekam (die Fahrer schauten sich alle das Spiel gegen Holland an), die Konversation mit den Eingeladenen (wie immer) anstrengend fand, & dann, als ich mit dem letzten Zug, ziemlich gerädert schon, heimfahren wollte, um 11.30 herausfand, daß irgendwo zwischen Colchester & Chelmsford ein Lokalzug entgleist war, weshalb wir dann, in dem mit Fußballfans rappelvollen Zug, ewig auf der Strecke standen & schließlich von Chelmsford bis Ipswich mit Doppeldeckerbussen befördert wurden & von Ipswich nach Norwich in einem Triebwagen. Es war schon hell, als wir hier ankamen.[3]

[Take the party at Christopher's, for instance, just under a fortnight ago. I took the train from Norwich at five after a long day of examiners' meetings, then at seven o'clock in London found a taxi at Liverpool Street only after an eternity of chasing to and fro (the cabbies were all watching the Holland match), found conversation with the invited guests a strain (as always), & then, pretty exhausted already and hoping to take the last train home, learnt at 11.30 that a local train had derailed somewhere between Colchester & Chelmsford, which meant that our train crammed with football fans didn't move for ages & at length we were transferred from Chelmsford to Ipswich on double-decker buses & from Ipswich to Norwich in a diesel carriage. It was already light when we arrived here.]

The Emigrants made Max's name familiar to everyone in the English-speaking world who took an interest in serious writing; the unanimity of praise is a matter of historical record. Though he sometimes expressed reservations about Harvill in his letters to me, the house was unequivocal in its commitment to Max's work, and indeed the letter commissioning me to translate *Die Ringe des Saturn* was dated 11 June 1996, a full week before the party that involved Max in his wearisome night out. Harvill were anxious to see a draft completed by the end of the year. Private troubles, however, threw out my schedule in the second half of the year, and it wasn't till the early months of 1997 that I was delivering the chapters in quick succession. Thanking me on 2 February 1997 for the second instalment, Max hoped that I had 'recovered a bit from the trauma of separation' (and, expressing pleasure at the good reception *The Emigrants* had enjoyed in the UK and USA, remarked, 'It could so easily have sunk without a trace'). In another letter of 7 May that year he announced that he had 'just sent chapter IV back to Bill & hope[d] to be able to complete V shortly'. *The Rings of Saturn* continually raised complex issues for a translator, particularly in Max's use of source material, and I had written, in a letter I can't now date exactly:

> I've found material [...] in the biographies of Conrad by Frederick Karl, Jocelyn Baines and Jeffrey Meyers [...] Also, of course, the text of *Heart of Darkness*. I feel sure, especially in the return to Kazimierówka, that there must be a terribly obvious source I have missed consulting. Spellings etc. that differ from spellings in your original: Zhitomir [Žitomir], Józef Teodor (for Teodor Josef), Teofila [Theophila], Déléstang [Delestang], Somogyi [Somoggy], Kazimierówka [Kazimierowska], Société Anonyme Belge, and others transliterated from Russian.[4]

In response to these and other comments from myself, Max wrote in that letter of 7 May:

> I am taking on board the various questions you have raised as I go along. Most of them are easily resolved. Over the troublesome business of the quotations (Browne, Conrad etc.) you must have cursed me more than once because of the

'unreliable' way in which I deploy them. I often change them quite deliberately. The long quote, for instance, in which Apollo describes Vologda was substantially rewritten by me. I did not have another source. I therefore now changed your version, which goes back to the proper source, so that it follows more closely my own (partly fabricated) rendering of this passage. There is a great deal in the text that is simply made up. The statement, for example, that the boy Conrad K. does his homework 'in einem fensterlosen Kabinett' cannot claim to rely on a verifiable account. This is just how I saw it. But I am grateful to you for pointing out what are clearly involuntary lapses like the reference, in connection with Swinburne, to the k. & k. monarchy.[5]

The translation issues posed by *Die Ringe des Saturn* are of interest because they throw significant light on Max's method of assembling telling narratives from sources he felt free to take liberties with. Here, as a first example, is an excerpt from the fifth section, which opens with the narrator's claim to have fallen asleep over a BBC documentary about Roger Casement, and to have remembered verbatim passages cited in the film commentary, such as the following:

> Ich habe ihn einmal, so ein mir seltsamerweise wortwörtlich gegenwärtig gebliebenes Zitat aus dem Kongo-Tagebuch Conrads, nur mit einem Stecken bewaffnet und nur in Begleitung eines Loanda-Jungen und seiner englischen Bulldoggen Biddy und Paddy in die gewaltige Wildnis aufbrechen sehen, die im Kongo jede Niederlassung umgibt. Und einige Monate darauf sah ich ihn dann, seinen Stecken schwingend, mit dem Jungen, der das Bündel trug, und den Hunden aus der Wildnis wieder hervorkommen, etwas magerer vielleicht, aber sonst so unbeschadet, als kehrte er gerade von einem Nachmittagsspaziergang im Hyde Park zurück.[6]

The German text's pointer to Conrad's Congo diary was as little help to me for purposes of translation as, say, the Thomas Browne textual pointers in the first section had been. It was quickly established that the passage didn't occur in the diary. Its actual provenance I located with the help of Frederick Karl's indispensable biography of Conrad, where it is quoted in a footnote;[7] the source was a letter to Conrad's long-standing friend and correspondent Cunninghame Graham. In translating it into German, Max had made a number of changes. He added the comment that, in the Congo, the wilderness surrounds every settlement; he added the adjective 'englisch' to the bulldogs, but removed their colours, as he also removed the word 'crookhandled' to characterize the stick; the phrases 'for all weapons' and 'for all company', which gave an Edwardian air of the casual to Conrad's letter, were stripped out, reduced in the German text to a repeated 'nur'; the 'leaner' quality of Casement was retained but not his 'browner' appearance on emerging from the 'wilderness' (a word repeated in Max's German text but not in Conrad's letter); Conrad's 'quietly serene' had become 'unbeschadet', which contrived to make Conrad seem to place an eyebrow-raising emphasis on Casement's emerging unscathed; and the park had become not just any park but one iconically recognizable to every German reader, Hyde Park. My policy at such points was to restore the original (i.e. in this case Conradian) text, on the one hand because re-translating a translation intrinsically made no sense, on the other because it was a way of silently prompting Max to consider whether his adaptation of texts for German readers remained appropriate when re-conceived for an anglophone readership far more conversant with the work of Conrad (see Figure 7.6). The text we ended up with, following minor interventions,[8] was in essence that of Conrad's letter:

> I've seen him start off into an unspeakable wilderness (thus the exact words of a quotation from Conrad, which has remained in my head) swinging a crookhandled stick, with two bulldogs: Paddy (white) and Biddy (brindle) at his heels and a Loanda boy carrying a bundle. A few months afterwards it so happened that I saw him come out again, leaner, a little browner, with his stick, dogs, and Loanda boy, and quietly serene as though he had been for a stroll in the park.[9]

A second example of these difficulties was the description of Vologda discussed by Max in the letter of 7 May. His German text reads:

> Vologda, so schreibt Apollo Korzeniowski im Sommer 1863 an seinen Vetter, ist ein einziges Sumpfloch, dessen Strassen und Wege aus umgelegten Baumstämmen bestehen. Die Häuser, auch die aus Brettern zusammengezimmerten buntbemalten Paläste des Provinzadels, stehen auf Pfählen mitten im Morast. Alles ringsum versinkt, verfault und verrottet. Es gibt nur zwei Jahreszeiten, einen weißen und einen grünen Winter. Neun Monate lang fährt die Eisluft vom Nordmeer herunter. Das Thermometer sinkt auf unvorstellbare Tiefen. Man ist umgeben von einer endlosen Finsternis. Während des grünen Winters regnet es ohne Unterlaß. Der Schlamm dringt bei den Türen herein. Die Leichenstarre geht über in einen grauenhaften Marasmus. Im weißen Winter ist alles tot, im grünen Winter alles am Sterben.[10]

In this case I located an original text, namely an English rendering of Apollo Korzeniowski's letter, in Jocelyn Baines's biography of Conrad,[11] and with that help constructed a draft translation thus:

> Vologda, Apollo Korzeniowski wrote in summer 1863 to his Zagórski cousins, is a great three-verst marsh on which logs and trees are placed parallel to each other in crooked lines; everything rotting and shifting under one's feet; this is the only means of communication available to the natives. Alongside these logs, piles have been driven in at intervals and on these Italian villas have been erected by the nobility of the province, all of whom live here. The climate consists of two seasons of the year: a white winter and a green winter. The white winter lasts nine-and-a-half months and the green one two-and-a-half. We are now at the onset of the green winter: it has already been raining ceaselessly for twenty-one days and that's how it will be to the end. During the whole winter the frost remains at minus twenty-five or thirty degrees. The population is a nightmare: disease-ridden corpses.

This return to the authentic utterance of his sources was not, of course, what Max wanted. It reintroduced elements of anecdotal material that were too much involved with Apollo's own life; it partly weakened his own emphasis (apparent also in his interpolation that wilderness surrounded every Congo settlement) that the wretchedness of the primordial is forever menacing the frail purchase of 'civilization'; and it edited out his own 'ownership' of the text. The version we ended up with (Figure 7.7) was his own, and restored the contours of his German rewriting of Apollo's letter:

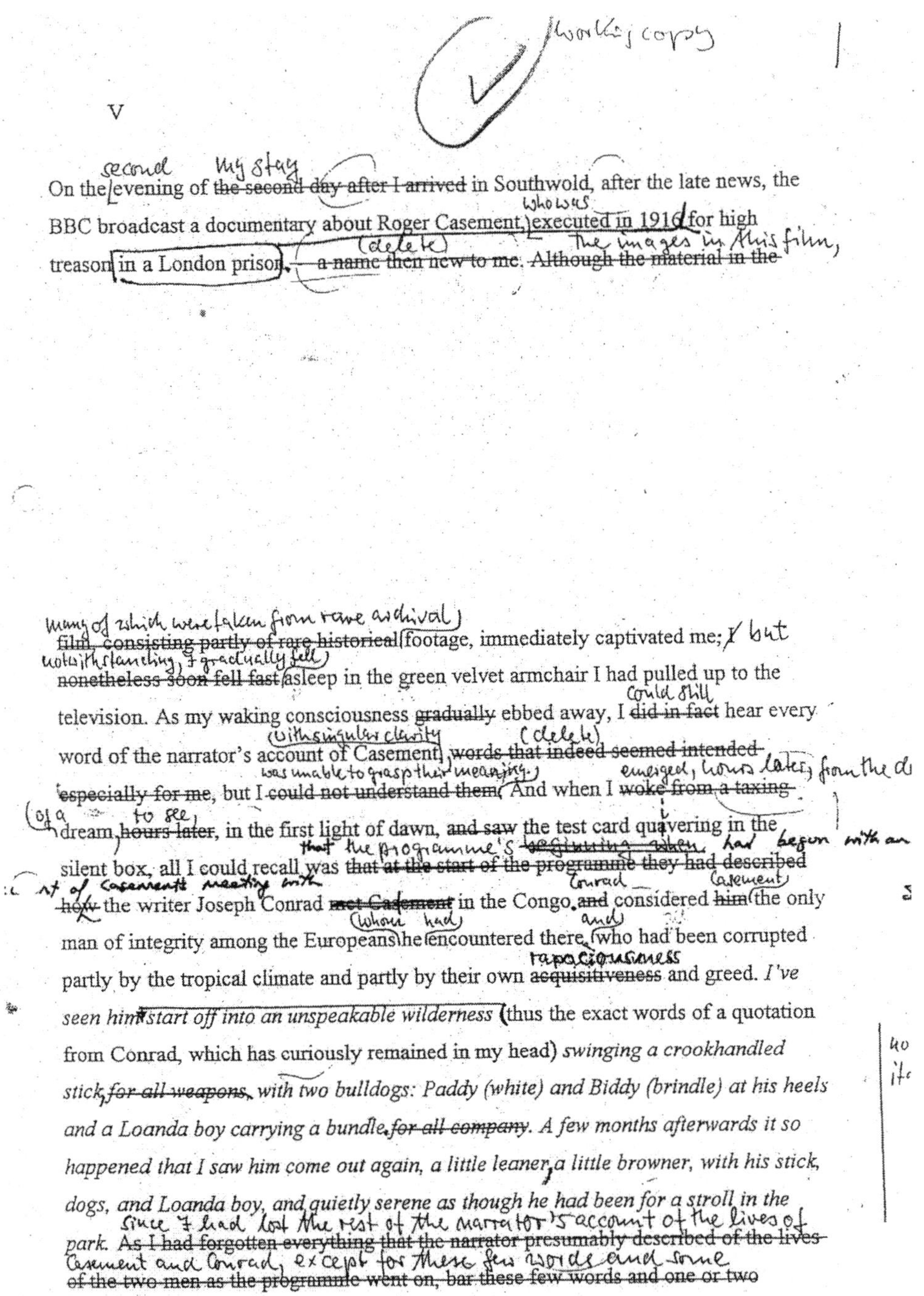

[working copy] ✓

V

On the *second* / *my stay* ~~evening of the second day after I arrived~~ in Southwold, after the late news, the BBC broadcast a documentary about Roger Casement, *who was* executed in 1916 for high treason ~~in a London prison,~~ *(delete)* ~~— a name then new to me. Although the material in the~~ *The images in this film,*

many of which were taken from rare archival) ~~film,~~ consisting partly of ~~rare~~ historical footage, immediately captivated me; ✗ *but* *notwithstanding, I gradually fell* ~~nonetheless soon fell fast~~ asleep in the green velvet armchair I had pulled up to the *could still* television. As my waking consciousness ~~gradually~~ ebbed away, I ~~did in fact~~ hear every *(with singular clarity)* *(delete)* word of the narrator's account of Casement, ~~words that indeed seemed intended~~ *was unable to grasp their meaning.* *emerged, hours later, from the* ~~especially for me, but I could not understand them.~~ And when I ~~woke~~ *from a taxing* *(of a* *to see)* ~~dream, hours later,~~ in the first light of dawn, ~~and saw~~ the test card quavering in the *that the programme's* ~~beginning when, had begun with an~~ silent box, all I could recall was ~~that at the start of the programme they had described~~ *nt of Casement's meeting with* *Conrad* *Casement)* ~~how~~ the writer Joseph Conrad ~~met Casement~~ in the Congo, ~~and~~ considered him *(whom had)* *and* the only man of integrity among the Europeans he encountered there, ~~who had been corrupted~~ *rapaciousness* partly by the tropical climate and partly by their own ~~acquisitiveness~~ and greed. *I've seen him ✗ start off into an unspeakable wilderness* (thus the exact words of a quotation from Conrad, which has curiously remained in my head) *swinging a crookhandled stick,* ~~for all weapons,~~ *with two bulldogs: Paddy (white) and Biddy (brindle) at his heels and a Loanda boy carrying a bundle,* ~~for all company.~~ *A few months afterwards it so happened that I saw him come out again, a little leaner, a little browner, with his stick, dogs, and Loanda boy, and quietly serene as though he had been for a stroll in the* *Since I had lost the rest of the narrator's account of the lives of* park. ~~As I had forgotten everything that the narrator presumably described of the lives~~ *Casement and Conrad, except for these few words and some* ~~of the two men as the programme went on, bar these few words and one or two~~

FIG. 7.6. W. G. Sebald's annotations to Michael Hulse's draft translation of the 'Conrad chapter' (Part v) of *Die Ringe des Saturn* (page 1 of the draft).
© The Estate of W. G. Sebald
Translation © Michael Hulse; courtesy of the Houghton Library, Harvard

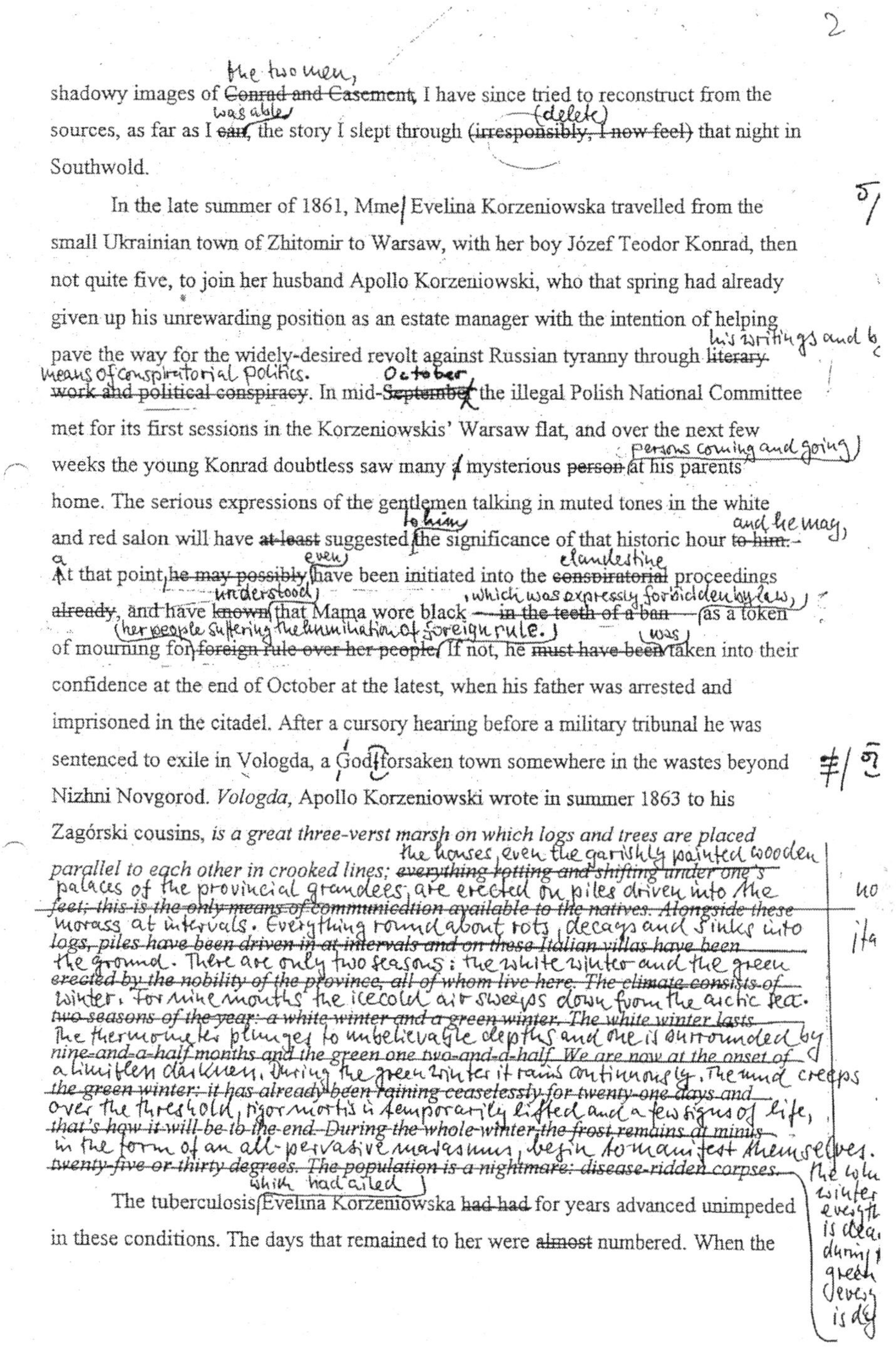

2

shadowy images of ~~Conrad and Casement~~ [the two men,] I have since tried to reconstruct from the sources, as far as I ~~can~~ [was able], the story I slept through ~~(irresponsibly, I now feel)~~ [(delete)] that night in Southwold.

5/

In the late summer of 1861, Mme Evelina Korzeniowska travelled from the small Ukrainian town of Zhitomir to Warsaw, with her boy Józef Teodor Konrad, then not quite five, to join her husband Apollo Korzeniowski, who that spring had already given up his unrewarding position as an estate manager with the intention of helping pave the way for the widely-desired revolt against Russian tyranny through ~~literary~~ [his writings and by] [means of conspiratorial politics.] ~~work and political conspiracy~~. In mid-~~September~~ [October] the illegal Polish National Committee met for its first sessions in the Korzeniowskis' Warsaw flat, and over the next few weeks the young Konrad doubtless saw many [a] mysterious ~~person~~ [persons coming and going] at his parents' home. The serious expressions of the gentlemen talking in muted tones in the white and red salon will have ~~at least~~ suggested [to him] the significance of that historic hour ~~to him~~ [and he may,]. At that point ~~he may possibly~~ [even] have been initiated into the ~~conspiratorial~~ [clandestine] proceedings [understood] already, and have ~~known~~ that Mama wore black [, which was expressly forbidden by law,] ~~—in the teeth of a ban—~~ as a token of mourning for ~~foreign rule over her people~~ [her people suffering the humiliation of foreign rule.] If not, he ~~must have been~~ [was] taken into their confidence at the end of October at the latest, when his father was arrested and imprisoned in the citadel. After a cursory hearing before a military tribunal he was sentenced to exile in Vologda, a Godforsaken town somewhere in the wastes beyond Nizhni Novgorod. *Vologda*, Apollo Korzeniowski wrote in summer 1863 to his

#/

Zagórski cousins, *is a great three-verst marsh on which logs and trees are placed parallel to each other in crooked lines;* [the houses, even the garishly painted wooden palaces of the provincial grandees, are erected on piles driven into the morass at intervals. Everything round about rots, decays and sinks into the ground. There are only two seasons: the white winter and the green winter. For nine months the icecold air sweeps down from the arctic sea. The thermometer plunges to unbelievable depths and one is surrounded by a limitless darkness. During the green winter it rains continuously. The mud creeps over the threshold, rigor mortis is temporarily lifted and a few signs of life, in the form of an all-pervasive marasmus, begin to manifest themselves.] ~~everything rotting and shifting under one's feet; this is the only means of communication available to the natives. Alongside these logs, piles have been driven in at intervals and on these Italian villas have been erected by the nobility of the province, all of whom live here. The climate consists of two seasons of the year: a white winter and a green winter. The white winter lasts nine-and-a-half months and the green two-and-a-half. We are now at the onset of the green winter: it has already been raining ceaselessly for twenty-one days and that's how it will be to the end. During the whole winter the frost remains at minus twenty-five or thirty degrees. The population is a nightmare: disease-ridden corpses.~~

no

i/a

the whole winter everything is dead during green [...] is dy[...]

The tuberculosis [which had ailed] Evelina Korzeniowska ~~had had~~ for years advanced unimpeded in these conditions. The days that remained to her were ~~almost~~ numbered. When the

FIG. 7.7. W. G. Sebald's annotations to Michael Hulse's draft translation of the 'Conrad chapter' (Part v) of *Die Ringe des Saturn* (page 2 of the draft). © The Estate of W. G. Sebald Translation © Michael Hulse; courtesy of the Houghton Library, Harvard

Vologda, Apollo Korzeniowski wrote in summer 1863 to his Zagórski cousins, is a great three-verst marsh on which logs and trees are placed parallel to each other in crooked lines; the houses, even the garishly painted wooden palaces of the provincial grandees, are erected on piles driven into the morass at intervals. Everything round about rots, decays and sinks into the ground. There are only two seasons: the white winter and the green winter. For nine months the ice-cold air sweeps down from the Arctic sea. The thermometer plunges to unbelievable depths and one is surrounded by a limitless darkness. During the green winter it rains week in week out. The mud creeps over the threshold, rigor mortis is temporarily lifted and a few signs of life, in the form of an all-pervasive marasmus, begin to manifest themselves. In the white winter everything is dead, during the green winter everything is dying.[12]

Two sets of ethics meet at a moment like this. One is the author's: the author makes a decision which balances concerns about aesthetic impact and concerns about answerability to the verifiable facts of historical record. The other is the translator's: the translator makes a decision which balances concerns about fidelity to what his author has written and concerns about answerability to the verifiable facts of historical record. My own instinct is always that whatever exists as a historical document should not be falsified; at the same time, as a translator I believe that in cases of doubt the author has the final say, and it was that principle that I followed here. In general, I probably adopted ninety per cent of Max's suggestions.

A third and final example from this fifth section of *The Rings of Saturn* strikingly highlights Max's approach to the material he reworked. It is the description of Conrad's passage to the Congo:

> Tag für Tag ist das Meeresufer unverändert, als bewege man sich nicht von der Stelle. Und doch, so schreibt Korzeniowski, sind wir an verschiedenen Landungsplätzen und Faktoreien vorbeigekommen mit Namen wie Gran' Bassam oder Little Popo, die allesamt irgendeiner grotesken Farce zu entstammen scheinen. Einmal passierten wir ein Kriegsschiff, das vor einem trostlosen Küstenstrich lag, auf dem nicht das geringste Anzeichen einer Ansiedlung zu sehen war. So weit das Auge reichte, nur der Ozean und der Himmel und der hauchdünne grüne Streifen der Buschvegetation. Schlapp hing die Fahne vom Mast herunter, träge hob und senkte sich der schwere eiserne Kahn auf der schmierigen Dünung, und in regelmäßigen Abständen feuerten die langen Sechs-Zoll-Kanonen offenbar ziel- und zwecklos hinein in den fremden afrikanischen Kontinent.[13]

Though Conrad has of course been vigorously received in Germany, his work does not have the position and importance in the German reader's overall picture of the course of modern literature that it possesses for anglophone readers; *Heart of Darkness* does not have the same exalted status, nor are key passages as familiar. It is difficult to imagine the English writer who would have had the temerity to appropriate so much of Marlow's narrative in that famous passage from *Heart of Darkness*:

> Every day the coast looked the same, as though we had not moved; but we passed various places — trading places — with names like Gran' Bassam, Little Popo, names that seemed to belong to some sordid farce acted in front of a sinister backcloth. [...] Once, I remember, we came upon a man-of-war anchored off the coast. There wasn't even a shed there, and she was shelling the

bush. [...] Her ensign dropped limp like a rag; the muzzles of the long eight-inch guns stuck out all over the low hull; the greasy, slimy swell swung her up lazily and let her down [...] In the empty immensity of earth, sky, and water, there she was, incomprehensible, firing into a continent.[14]

In producing the draft translation (see Figure 7.8) of this part of Max's text, I did my best to reconcile his re-casting with Marlow's account. After one or two minor changes, we arrived at this final version:

> Day after day the coastline was unchanging, as if the vessel were making no progress. And yet, wrote Korzeniowski, we passed a number of landing places and trading posts with names like Gran' Bassam or Little Popo, all of them seeming to belong in some sordid farce. Once we passed a warship anchored off a dreary beach where not the smallest sign of any settlement was to be seen. As far as the eye could reach there was nothing but ocean, sky, and the hair-thin green strip of bush vegetation. The ensign hung limp from the mast, the ponderous iron vessel rose and fell on the slimy swell, and at regular intervals the long six-inch guns fired off shells into the unknown African continent, with neither purpose nor aim.[15]

There are a number of points that could be discussed here; the change from eight-inch to six-inch guns always struck me as particularly pointless, but I was pleased that Max allowed the restored 'sordid' to stand, which, as Conrad had known, was an apter word than 'grotesk' for the imperial farce. But what is arguably of greater significance than these questions of detail is the blurring of narrative voice. Max's text has just quoted from a letter Conrad wrote to his aunt Marguerite Poradowska; only three sentences later, the words 'wrote Korzeniowski' could easily be taken by the unwary reader as a suggestion that the description of the voyage similarly occurred in that letter to his aunt, and there is no indication in Max's text that the source has shifted to a fictionalized account, indeed to a particular narrator within that fiction. This conflation of sources and blurring of distinctions naturally has implications for critical interpretation; for the translator — who gives a text its closest of all readings, for it is impossible to translate what has not been fully understood — the experience can be like walking across a minefield.

Max always took the critical responses implicit in my translations in a positive spirit, and professed himself grateful for every aspect of my work on his texts; of the translations themselves he was invariably complimentary when speaking or writing to me. The relationship between Max and myself was warm and strong, and marked by mutual respect and a sense of shared ground in our intellectual temperaments. We easily found a tone and register when we talked together, and I found his sense of humour as dark as my own. On one occasion, when I visited Max privately in Poringland and we spent an evening over a passable pub dinner, we talked a great deal of the historical sense expressed by German and English contemporary society, of poetry (he was generous in his admiration of mine, and self-deprecating about his own), of the literature of walking (I remember his interest not only in Rousseau and Robert Walser but also in Seume, whose *Spaziergang nach Syrakus* (*A Stroll to Syracuse*) I asked him about), and of much else that I unfortunately made no notes of. Max had been in no doubt from the outset of the high regard in which I held

dark, into the infinite white wastes that ~~touched~~ met (at the horizon and) the starry skies, where villages amidst

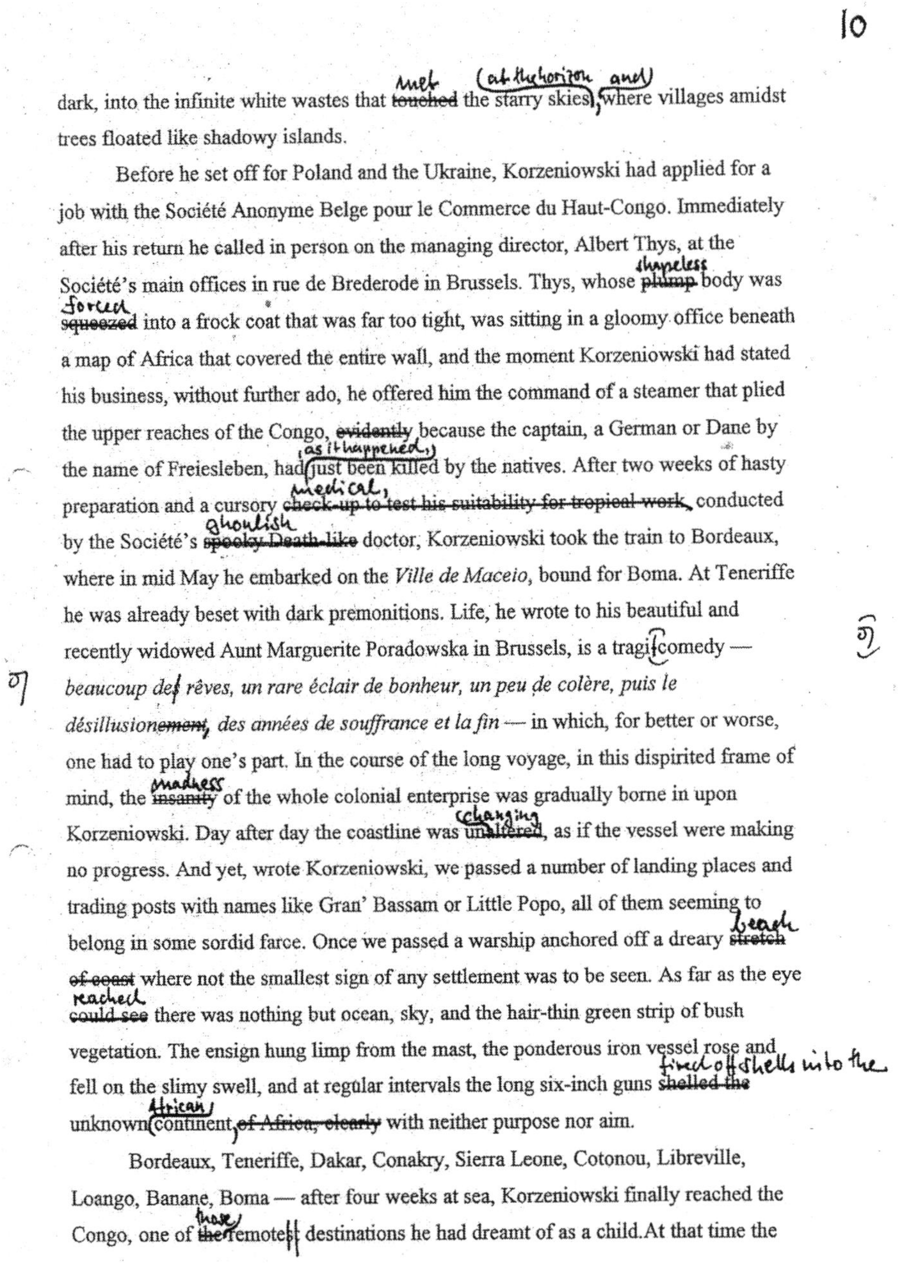

trees floated like shadowy islands.

Before he set off for Poland and the Ukraine, Korzeniowski had applied for a

job with the Société Anonyme Belge pour le Commerce du Haut-Congo. Immediately

after his return he called in person on the managing director, Albert Thys, at the

Société's main offices in rue de Brederode in Brussels. Thys, whose ~~plump~~ shapeless body was

~~squeezed~~ forced into a frock coat that was far too tight, was sitting in a gloomy office beneath

a map of Africa that covered the entire wall, and the moment Korzeniowski had stated

his business, without further ado, he offered him the command of a steamer that plied

the upper reaches of the Congo, ~~evidently~~ because the captain, a German or Dane by

the name of Freiesleben, had (as it happened,) ~~just been killed~~ by the natives. After two weeks of hasty

preparation and a cursory ~~check-up to test his suitability for tropical work~~ medical, conducted

by the Société's ~~spooky Death-like~~ ghoulish doctor, Korzeniowski took the train to Bordeaux,

where in mid May he embarked on the *Ville de Maceio*, bound for Boma. At Teneriffe

he was already beset with dark premonitions. Life, he wrote to his beautiful and

recently widowed Aunt Marguerite Poradowska in Brussels, is a tragi comedy —

beaucoup des rêves, un rare éclair de bonheur, un peu de colère, puis le

désillusionement, des années de souffrance et la fin — in which, for better or worse,

one had to play one's part. In the course of the long voyage, in this dispirited frame of

mind, the ~~insanity~~ madness of the whole colonial enterprise was gradually borne in upon

Korzeniowski. Day after day the coastline was ~~unaltered~~ changing, as if the vessel were making

no progress. And yet, wrote Korzeniowski, we passed a number of landing places and

trading posts with names like Gran' Bassam or Little Popo, all of them seeming to

belong in some sordid farce. Once we passed a warship anchored off a dreary ~~stretch~~ beach

~~of coast~~ where not the smallest sign of any settlement was to be seen. As far as the eye

~~could see~~ reached there was nothing but ocean, sky, and the hair-thin green strip of bush

vegetation. The ensign hung limp from the mast, the ponderous iron vessel rose and fired off shells into the

fell on the slimy swell, and at regular intervals the long six-inch guns ~~shelled the~~

unknown (continent, ~~of Africa, clearly~~ African with neither purpose nor aim.

Bordeaux, Teneriffe, Dakar, Conakry, Sierra Leone, Cotonou, Libreville,

Loango, Banane, Boma — after four weeks at sea, Korzeniowski finally reached the

Congo, one of ~~the~~ those remotest destinations he had dreamt of as a child. At that time the

FIG. 7.8. W. G. Sebald's annotations to Michael Hulse's draft translation of the
'Conrad chapter' (Part V) of *Die Ringe des Saturn* (page 10 of the draft).
© The Estate of W. G. Sebald
Translation © Michael Hulse; courtesy of the Houghton Library, Harvard

his work, and he was aware too that, like others, I was happy to do whatever was in my power to confirm his presence. With the British Council in Cologne I discussed having Max to the annual Walberberg seminar, which brings British writers and one or two bridgehead figures together with German academics, translators, and critics. In his letter of 30 June 1996, Max wrote to me: 'Ein Brief vom B. Council mit der von Dir erwähnten Einladung zu dem Walberberg Seminar war auch bereits da. Es wäre sicher eine gute Sache, doch werde ich wohl nicht zusagen können' [A letter from the British Council had already arrived, with the invitation to the Walberberg seminar that you mentioned. It would doubtless be a good thing, but it's unlikely that I shall be able to accept]. As he explained, he was already receiving more invitations than he could possibly accept. (Two years later, however, he did agree to come to the Walberberg retreat, in January 1998; see Figure 7.5, p. 194.) In October 1997 I happened to be in Boston when Max read there, and, at their request, introduced him to Keith Botsford and Saul Bellow. My journal for Wednesday, 15 October noted:

> Last night to the Goethe Institut at 170 Beacon Street to hear Max Sebald. The usual story: because the GI insists on holding events at its own premises, the audience was practically non-existent. However, a fine reading. Max has declined the Hamburg offer to chair a school of creative writing.

A month later, when Max was in Cologne to receive the city's Heinrich Böll Prize, I heard him read about the bombing of the city to the invited award ceremony guests;[16] the next day I took him to lunch in the *Stapelhäuschen* (a fifteenth-century building left almost untouched when every other on that stretch of the left bank was levelled in the Second World War) with Greg Gatenby, who happened to be visiting at the same time. Greg's views on literature were generally better informed and more clear-sighted than those of most others I knew, and, uneasy at his scepticism about Max's writing, I was glad of the opportunity to bring the two men together; they liked each other, but remained at arm's length. I think it was on that day that Max made a remark that came naturally out of many things we had talked of in those years but which he had never put quite so baldly: 'The Germans have no sense of history.' Insofar as he seemed to want to contrast the Germans with the English, who in my own view tend to substitute heritage culture and costume drama for historical understanding and have done much less work on grasping the nature of Empire than the Germans have done on grappling with the legacies of the Third Reich, I was inclined to argue; but, standing in a place where so many of the new buildings had been conceived as replicas or imitations of destroyed old buildings, and to that degree perpetuated the annihilation of historical process that can be seen in many physical and conceptual forms in Germany, it was impossible not to agree, at least in part.

In the end, Max and I went our separate ways. I agreed against my better judgement to translate *Schwindel. Gefühle.* (*Vertigo*), a book that is of interest, as anything from such a writer must be, but is weaker than the three major achievements and gives only hints of what was to come. In the spring of 1999 I heard that Max had been complaining in a public meeting of the work he had to do to 'correct' my translations. Since his own wish had been to have input into my work at draft stage,

I was naturally angry at this breach of what I had taken to be our code of conduct, and phoned him for clarification; he assured me that he had been misreported. But the incident left an unpleasant aftertaste in my mouth, and when I next talked to Harvill (that May, I believe) I said that it was unlikely that I would want to translate another of Max's books. In August of that year, on a reading tour in Australia, I was startled by a question from the audience at the Melbourne Literature Festival which raised the same issue of Max's weariness at his task. That made my mind up. For his part, Max understandably found my pace too slow — in my freelance years I was invariably over-committed — and, perhaps with the encouragement of his new agent, Andrew Wylie, began to look for another translator. In reply to a note at Christmas 1999, Max wrote to me on 22 January 2000 that he had decided on Anthea Bell as his new translator: 'Perhaps you would agree that, from your point of view also, our partnership has now reached its limits.' In a further letter of 4 February he added: 'Andrew Wylie & Harvill had nothing to do with it.' That was the last I heard from him, and we never met again.

Notes to Chapter 7

1. Letter from MH to WGS, 7 June 1995.
2. Letter from WGS to MH, 19 June 1995.
3. Letter from WGS to MH, 30 June 1996.
4. Letter from MH to WGS, n.d. [early 1997?].
5. Letter from WGS to MH, 7 May 1997.
6. W. G. Sebald, *Die Ringe des Saturn* (Frankfurt a.M.: Eichborn, 1995), p. 132; cf. note 9.
7. Frederick Karl, *Joseph Conrad: The Three Lives* (New York: Farrar, Straus & Giroux, 1979), p. 554.
8. There are other minor changes. Conrad's 'a park' became 'the park', perhaps through an error in my own transcription; 'a little leaner' became simply 'leaner', I think at the subsequent suggestion of Bill Swainson.
9. W. G. Sebald, *The Rings of Saturn*, trans. by Michael Hulse (London: Harvill, 1998), p. 104.
10. *Die Ringe des Saturn*, p. 134; cf. note 12.
11. Jocelyn Baines, *Joseph Conrad* (London: Weidenfeld & Nicolson, 1960), pp. 13–14.
12. *The Rings of Saturn*, p. 105.
13. *Die Ringe des Saturn*, pp. 10–11.
14. Joseph Conrad, *Heart of Darkness*, ed. by Robert Hampson (London: Penguin, 1995), p. 30.
15. *The Rings of Saturn*, p. 117.
16. See Primary Bibliography D.66 and Part II, p. 338–42 ('Feuer und Rauch').

CHAPTER 8

Translating W. G. Sebald —
With and Without the Author

Anthea Bell

One of the attractions of a freelance translator's life is the sheer variety it offers. When the Preacher in Ecclesiastes said that time and chance happeneth to us all, he meant it in his usual mood of profound pessimism, but some chances are pleasant, and for me it was a happy if also rather alarming one to be asked to translate W. G. Sebald's *Austerlitz*. I have often been asked just how it came about, and I think I should explain. At first I had no idea that Max Sebald's forthcoming new 'novel' would be involved, or as some would say his new narrative, since from *Schwindel. Gefühle. (Vertigo)* to *Austerlitz* they had tended to be some way from conventional fiction. *Austerlitz* itself, while never officially labelled a novel by Max Sebald, in fact appears to me more of a novel, as the term is usually understood, than its predecessors. It may even be regarded as a novel within a novel: first there are the framework chapters in which the unnamed but typically Sebaldian narrator, Max Sebald's own *alter ego*, describes his acquaintanceship with the eponymous Jacques Austerlitz, then there is the inner core of the book, Austerlitz's own account of his life, with the two narratives alternating and interlocking.

However, it was about a different book that I was approached. In the summer of 1999 Max Sebald's then publishers, Harvill, were — or so I was given to understand — thinking of forging ahead in some haste with the English publication of his lectures delivered in Zurich in 1997, published in German as *Luftkrieg und Literatur* ('Air War and Literature'), together with his reflections on the reactions to those lectures in the correspondence that he received. To make the material up to book length in the German original, he had added his essay on Alfred Andersch. The rationale at the time for the sudden wish to bring this project forward, again so I understood, was its topical relevance; the publishers felt that the Allied fire bombing of German cities in the Second World War, so graphically described by Max Sebald and the eyewitnesses of the time whom he invokes, could be regarded as parallel to the NATO bombing campaign in Kosovo in the first half of 1999. Topicality, of course, comes and goes, and can die down as quickly as it appeared to surface, but that was the general idea, and I was also told that, because of the urgency, Max's regular translator was too busy to do it. Michael Hulse was the translator of his other prose works, including the beautiful English version of *Die Ringe des Saturn*, which I knew well. It had particularly attracted me because I grew up in its East

Anglian setting, and it was fascinating to see Max's melancholy, cultivated, Central European mind bent on the scenes of my childhood.

I was thus one of three translators invited by Harvill to submit sample translations from *Luftkrieg und Literatur*; I learnt afterwards, from Max himself, that three more samples had been commissioned by the editor of an architectural magazine planning to publish an extract from the work. After that no more was heard for months, and presumably the topical factor evaporated anyway with the end of the NATO action in Kosovo in midsummer that year. I was therefore taken by surprise when in December Max's new agent got in touch to ask me to translate not just *Luftkrieg und Literatur* but also the next novel, *Austerlitz*, not yet completed. I was in fact placed in what I felt then, and indeed still feel, was a rather awkward situation, but you do not say no to translating an author of Max's stature. The idea was that initially I should translate some thirty pages of *Austerlitz*, to be offered around by the agent. Max was in touch with me — we had already met now and then at translation seminars held by the BCLT, his own brainchild — and we went ahead. I greatly valued our correspondence over nearly two years about the translation of his books; like so much else, it was cut short by his tragic death in late 2001. His letters were beautifully handwritten; notoriously, he was not a man for modern electronics, and when a computer was delivered to his room at the University he refused to have anything to do with it. I cheerfully embrace as much electronic assistance as I can get, so mine were typewritten, for in any case it is unkind to expect anyone to read my handwriting.

It was with the *Austerlitz* sample that we began work, and the method as then established continued when the book was complete. I would send my draft translation, in batches, to Max by post (again, no email attachments for him), he wrote his comments on it and sent it back. We might continue to discuss some points over several exchanges of letters, but while he looked through what I had just sent, I would be drafting the next batch of chapters.

At first, however, I saw only the *Austerlitz* sample for publishers, which I remember translating over Christmas and the New Year at the turn of the millennium. Would the magic date cause all computers to crash? That particular alarm turned out to be misplaced, but I had carefully made a disk copy of the sample in English just in case. It was what I have always thought of as the Welsh idyll: the young Austerlitz's visits to his schoolfriend Gerald's home, with its beautiful natural scenery, its quirky oddities (those cockatoos) and equally quirky human characters, in particular Great-Uncle Alphonso. The agency quickly found publishers, in the shape of Hamish Hamilton in the UK and Random House in the USA. Max was still working on the novel, and sometimes said, with great modesty, that he wasn't sure if it was any good. When at last I received the entire manuscript I was in no doubt about that. It arrived, by another happy chance, on a beautiful summer's day, and I sat in the garden reading, spellbound by everything about it: the concept, the two narratives, perhaps above all the inimitable Sebaldian style, in which one rediscovers the pleasures of classical German and the joys of many winding subordinate clauses. I remember that after the translation of *Austerlitz* was finished, next on my schedule was a novel by an author in a more usual modern German style: a good novel of its own kind, but the contrast was disconcerting, almost comical.

Before I received the full manuscript of the novel, however, I had also been going ahead with the draft of *Luftkrieg und Literatur*. Although for a long time Max still referred to it in English as 'Air War and Literature', I think — though I am not sure — that the change of title for the English-language version was at least in part his own idea. Nothing was ever going to reflect the alliteration of the German title. And a good alternative was provided by the mention at the end of the first lecture of Solly Zuckerman's plan, never realized, to write for the journal *Horizon* on what he had seen in the ruined city of Cologne after the Allied bombing raids of the Second World War: Lord Zuckerman had intended to call his account 'On the Natural History of Destruction', but shelved the project because, he said in his autobiography, 'My first view of Cologne called for a more eloquent piece than I could ever have written.' The unused title was pressed into service for the English version of *Luftkrieg und Literatur*. Its choice was further justified by the subtitle of the essay first published in 1982 in *Orbis Litterarum*, 'Zwischen Geschichte und Naturgeschichte: Über die literarische Beschreibung totaler Zerstörung' ('Between History and Natural History: On the Literary Description of Total Destruction'),[1] which covers some of the same material, and was included in the final, posthumous volume of Max Sebald's essays and his sketches for a Corsican book, *Campo Santo* (like *Austerlitz*, that presented no title problems).

For the English edition of *Luftkrieg und Literatur*, Max had also chosen to add his essays on Jean Améry and Peter Weiss. That could have made for complications in *Campo Santo*, for the German edition of the posthumous volume also contained the Améry and Weiss essays. Fortunately, it is quite an extensive book, comprising much that Max had written for publication in various journals and periodicals but which had not before found its way into a book. Many of the original sources were academic works, but he had also contributed to some other periodicals, for instance 'Kafka Goes to the Movies', published as 'Kafka im Kino' in the *Frankfurter Rundschau* in January 1997, which began as a review of a book entitled *Kafka geht ins Kino* by Hanns Zischler.[2] Even without the Weiss and Améry essays, then, we still had quite enough left for a book-length English edition.

So I had the pleasure and privilege of working closely with Max Sebald until just over halfway through those three last prose works of his. Our work on *Austerlitz* in particular remains vivid in my mind, and always will. Famously, although he preferred to stay with his mother tongue, Max's English would easily have enabled him to write in it in the first place, or indeed translate himself. Perhaps because of his own excellent command of English, he was prepared to believe me if I was absolutely sure that a certain phrase was right: for instance, a 'fancy waistcoat', which he queried, wondering if it should not be 'a fanciful waistcoat'. In another passage, I am not now sure that I was right: it is the page where young Austerlitz in Prague, during the childhood that he blotted out of his mind on coming to England, tells us how he described to his nursemaid Vera the tailor in the building over the road eating his supper. In the English version he tells her, 'Now he's taking a long drink from his glass.' Max suggested 'draught'; I argued that in the mouth of a child, the word would appear too literary. The fact is, I said, that children do pick up unexpected literary terms and use them, but I felt at the time that the reader's

FIG. 8.1. Solly Zuckerman, OM (1904–93), the distinguished biologist, was one of the founding fathers of the University of East Anglia. During World War II, he supported Sir Arthur Tedder and Henry Tizard against Sir Arthur Harris's policy — which was backed by Churchill — of the saturation bombing of German cities. In 1960 he became chief scientific adviser to the Ministry of Defence and argued against the development of a nuclear arsenal. WGS interviewed Zuckerman about the area bombing of Germany on 28 September 1981, during one of Zuckerman's annual visits to UEA. © John Gibbons; courtesy of the University of East Anglia

reaction would depend on the perception that such a word was not childlike. I'm still not certain that I ought not to have gone along with Max's 'draught'.

Again because of Max's excellent English, I was disproportionately pleased when I could introduce him to anything he didn't already know, such as the vernacular name for the *Waldrebe*, the wild clematis, *Clematis vitalba*, or 'traveller's joy' — 'What a lovely name!' he wrote in on my draft translation. I could also, of course, have offered him 'old man's beard', which might in retrospect have been better suited to the mood of the framework narrator in *Austerlitz* seeing its grey seed heads from the train on his way to London for an eye examination, but he liked the idea of traveller's joy anyway.

His interest in natural history is evident in his books; there are Gerald's homing pigeons in *Austerlitz* (and indeed Max himself was fond of pigeons, which feature in most of his works). And of course there was his fascination with moths. They come into *The Rings of Saturn* and again into *Austerlitz*, when Gerald's Great-Uncle Alphonso, a keen naturalist, sets a moth trap so that the boys, on holiday at Andromeda Lodge, can observe those nocturnal insects. Max was considerably amused when I confessed, in the course of our correspondence, to having suffered all my life from a moth phobia (it is not quite as widespread as classic arachnophobia, but is fairly common all the same), and he told me in turn something I did not know, that Graham Greene had had a bird phobia. In fact my moth phobia came in quite useful; I knew a great many vernacular English names of moths from the time when I tried to cure myself of the phobia by the 'cognitive' method of slow familiarization, at first using pictures of the object of the phobic's fears. I had to give it up after a while; it was perhaps making me a little more comfortable with moths, but oddly enough less comfortable with butterflies (which fly in what, to the phobic, is a less sinister way). But in the course of staring at moth pictures, I had collected up a great many of the beautiful English vernacular names of the creatures. When it came to translating the moth passage of *Austerlitz*, not quite all the names had precise English vernacular equivalents for the German moth names, and I sent Max my own list of the prettiest names. It is a tribute to the power of his writing that, although I would have fled the scene in panic in real life, I rather enjoyed translating this moth passage. Max, incidentally, decided to leave out the death's-head hawk moth altogether because, he said, it seemed to sound much nastier in English than the German *Totenkopf*. Had I inadvertently conveyed to him something of the horror the mere name of it conjures up in me?

In fact he did some rewriting in general for the English edition, especially in the account of life at Theresienstadt, where in the original he made effective use of the appalling jargon typically employed by the Nazi bureaucracy. It was going to be very tricky to get just the same effect in English, and he made a few alterations and small cuts, although the nine-page sentence still occupies its nine pages. In my very first draft I put a full stop about two pages into this passage, and then immediately took it out again; I knew without being told that it must remain one long, continuous sentence in English, to convey the mindless, busy haste of the regime in the camp as it prepares to present the appearance of a happy holiday camp for Jews, for the benefit of a visiting Red Cross delegation. The sentence is sufficiently punctuated by the occasional 'said Austerlitz', a recurrent phrase throughout the book. Max, I remember, was a little worried about this repeated 'said Austerlitz', but to me it felt both right and satisfyingly rhythmical, like the return of a piece of music now and then to its home key.

I think that this passage, and indeed others, must have given the designers at Hamish Hamilton some problems in the placing of the odd little illustrations and photographs for which Max was well known in his fictions. That, fortunately, was not my problem; I simply indicated the place where a picture should come as closely as possible to a certain passage of text. It must have been something of a jigsaw puzzle. Similarly, some of these little pictures — which cannot be called illustrations, but are more like an occasional gloss on the text — occur in the earlier part of *On the Natural History of Destruction*. That book also included, in the German text, a photograph of Andersch. If Max had lived, I think the publishers might have asked if he wished to include pictures of Améry and Weiss in the essays on them, or even, if it was available, a reproduction of the picture by Weiss himself described in some detail.

Austerlitz appeared in English in the early autumn of 2001. By that time I had already drafted most of the translation of *On the Natural History of Destruction*. Max had been through these parts of the book, and a little later I sent him my draft of the three essays on Andersch, Améry, and Weiss. And then, on 14 December that year, came the car crash that so tragically killed him.

The shock to everyone who knew and worked with Max was great. Since I had quite recently sent him back my version of that first part, now revised in line with his own wishes, I wondered whether I would be crossing in the post with his revisions of the second part, and hardly knew what to feel about the prospect. Nothing arrived until just after Christmas; then his revisions of the Andersch essay, which he had just finished making, were found on his desk and sent on to me. I spent a long wintry Sunday going through the essay, adding them. As usual, Max had been thoughtful of the English reader, and had, for instance, changed and slightly cut some of his remarks on Andersch's style. Quotations from one of his novels, *Efraim* (*Efraim's Book*), had to be given in English from the published translation by Ralph Manheim, whose English could not easily be reconciled with Max's strictures on the original German. It was an extraordinary feeling to be in mental communication with Max, so to speak, for the last time, and I felt I must finish the work in a single day, because it would be so hard to return to it next morning. After that I was on my own. It will be appreciated that I approached my own revision of the Améry and Weiss essays with the utmost trepidation, wondering the whole time what Max would say to this or that phrase. When the book came out, I was extraordinarily grateful to Irène Heidelberger-Leonard, the outstanding authority on Jean Améry, for saying that she had liked my version of the essay on him.

In these two essays, as in the whole of *Campo Santo*, I could only do my best to second-guess what Max Sebald himself would have said of a certain passage. The critical essays included in *Campo Santo* are fascinating in themselves, although of course they presented some problems both to me and to the editors on both sides of the Atlantic. For instance, the quotations from Günter Grass's *Aus dem Tagebuch einer Schnecke* (*From the Diary of a Snail*) in the essay on him and Wolfgang Hildesheimer, 'Konstruktionen der Trauer: Günter Grass und Wolfgang Hildesheimer' ('Constructs of Mourning: Günter Grass and Wolfgang Hildesheimer'),[3] were taken from the published English version, again translated by Ralph Manheim. One quotation, hard as I might search the early pages of the novel, where the German page numbering told me it ought to come, still proved elusive. Only when I read the publisher's note to the English edition did I discover that some passages had been omitted for legal reasons, not further explained. Fair enough; that meant I should translate the quotation myself, but copy-editors and proofreaders of course kept asking me for a page reference to the English version, for addition to the Notes on that essay in line with the other Grass quotations. I had to keep explaining why I couldn't provide one. And while 'that' rather than 'which' is the relative of choice today in the copy-editing manuals, Max had a definite preference for 'which', so I had used it more than I normally would. When I explained to the editors, they too respected what I felt would have been his wishes.

I particularly enjoyed the shorter pieces towards the end of the collection: on Max's friend the artist Jan Peter Tripp, on Bruce Chatwin, on Kafka, on Nabokov. But most of all I regretted that the Corsican book was never completed, although I understand that it was set aside so that he could concentrate on *Austerlitz*. We were not to have both. However, the four passages from the book on Corsica are Max in his characteristic melancholy and lyrical mood, and with those touches of dry humour that, although it is not a quality of his so often remarked upon, is also typical of his writing.

Translating *Campo Santo* was, again, a farewell to a part of my professional life that I had especially appreciated. I would have liked to be able to talk or write to Max himself about it, as I kept doing in my mind; the literary translator is always, as it were, playing a part like an actor, trying his or her hardest to *become* the author of the original. That, of course, is impossible; in my view no perfect translation can ever be achieved, but we have at least to try to make the pretence convincing, and to walk what I think of as the tightrope of illusion.

Notes to Chapter 8

1. See Primary Bibliography D.18.
2. Hanns Zischler, *Kafka geht ins Kino* (Reinbek bei Hamburg: Rowohlt, 1996); cf. *Kafka Goes to the Movies*, trans. by Susan H. Gillespie (Chicago: University of Chicago Press, 2002). See Primary Bibliography G.31.
3. See Primary Bibliography D.24.

Fig. 8.2. Self-portrait of W. G. Sebald, Manchester 1967.
© The Estate of W. G. Sebald; by kind permission of Prof. Dr Reinbert Tabbert

CHAPTER 9

❖

Sebald's Photographic Annotations

Clive Scott

As Dominique Baqué points out, the theorization of photography is only a relatively recent phenomenon, owing its inauguration, more or less, to Walter Benjamin and his 'Little History of Photography' of 1931, followed by 'The Work of Art in the Age of Mechanical Reproduction' of 1936.[1] Despite the rapid expansion of writing on photography and photography's assimilation into academe, a short sequence of canonical texts and commentators has attracted to itself what looks to many like a disproportionate authority — Gisèle Freund, Susan Sontag, Roland Barthes, John Berger, Philippe Dubois, Rosalind Krauss — and kept the critical monopoly clearly in the Gallo-Anglo-American triangle. By and large, Max Sebald's reading in photography seems to keep to this critical highway. I have been perusing his annotations of Susan Sontag's *On Photography* (UK publication 1978), John Berger's *About Looking* (1980), Roland Barthes's *La Chambre claire: Note sur la photographie* (1980) in its English translation by Richard Howard (*Camera Lucida: Reflections on Photography*, 1984), and Clive Scott's *The Spoken Image: Photography and Language* (1999).[2] My immediate regret is that I cannot do comprehensive justice to these annotations: they are simply too numerous; much important material has to be relegated to footnotes, without discussion. But it is perhaps possible, even from a partial investigation, to construct a view of Sebald's abiding photographic preoccupations. I had intended to restrict myself to a systematic itemization of, and commentary on, Sebald's annotations in these four texts, but quickly realized that the need to cross-refer would scotch that plan and that I could not avoid opening my discussion onto the work of Siegfried Kracauer and Jan Peter Tripp, among others. Out of the resulting, barely controllable flow, I have carved a sequence of five roughly circumscribed sections.

Preliminary Considerations: Ekphrasis, Contingency, Memory

There is, for example, a group portrait from 1860 of the Russian Ambassador to Berlin, Baron von Budberg and his family. The Ambassador, in a dandy's white summer outfit, has his back turned on the camera, whilst his wife, an exhausted *femme de trente ans*, has a melancholic eye on the children. A very serious, very dark girl of perhaps twelve gazes straight into the lense [*sic*] from underneath a wide-brimmed florentine hat as do two twin-like young boys of precisely that hermaphroditic beauty which Thomas Mann so desperately attempted to evoke in *Death in Venice*. Thus the casual *raffinement* of this scene reminds

FIG. 9.1. Group portrait of the Russian Ambassador to Berlin, Baron von Budberg,
and his family (1860). © Märkisches Museum, Berlin

one of the insufficiency of literary and, to be sure, historical descriptions. Old
photographs have much to commend them.[3]

One might wonder from which volume of Sebald's central tetralogy this is an
extract. The theme of twinning and *dédoublement* is a recurrent motif in Sebald's
work. The beauty of the young boys reminds us of the young dervish photographed
already as a memory in the third story of *Die Ausgewanderten*. But in fact these are
the closing lines of a review of Franz Hubmann's *Dream of Empire: The World of
Germany in Original Photographs 1840–1914* (1973), by someone who signs himself,
as on other occasions, M.[ax] S.[ebald] rather than W.G.S. Sebald's ekphrastic
paragraph still cannot quite tell the photograph, and casts itself as an (unwilling) act
of interference and mediation necessitated only by the photograph's own absence.

Criticism has been inclined to describe the references to the (photographic)
images within the Sebaldian text as captions, and it is true that Sebald sidelines
passages in Sontag's *On Photography* on captions,[4] in particular Benjamin's belief in
their 'revolutionary use value' and Sontag's contrary assertion that 'no caption can
permanently restrict or secure a picture's meaning'. Even though there are images
within Sebald's text apparently without textual reference, or whose relationship
with a textual reference is uncertain, I want to suggest that 'caption' is not as
appropriate for textual reference as 'ekphrasis', however brief that reference is. What

FIG. 9.2. View from the Flamingo Hotel in Antwerp
(*Austerlitz*, p. 412 (Hanser) / p. 410 (Hamish Hamilton)). © The Estate of W. G. Sebald

I understand by caption is this:

(1) a tendentious intervention by a third party designed to influence the reading of an image (the caption oversteps the neutrality of the title);
(2) an attempt to distil or interpret the meaning of an image;
(3) something which cannot exist in the same time as the image, a reaction to the image as image which endows it with a justification.

If I take a simple example: Sebald returns to Antwerp at the end of *Austerlitz* and stays at the Flamingo Hotel on the Astridsplein

> in einem braun tapezierten häßlichen Zimmer, das nach rückwärts hinausging auf Brandmauern, Abluftkamine und flache, mit Stacheldraht voneinander getrennte Dächer. Ich glaube, es war gerade irgendein Volksfest in der Stadt. Jedenfalls heulten bis in den frühen Morgen hinein die Martinshörner und Polizeisirenen.

> [in an ugly room with brown wallpaper looking out on fire-walls, ventilation chimneys and flat roofs separated from each other by barbed wire at the back of the building. I think there was some kind of popular festival going on in the city at the time; in any case, the wailing of ambulance and police sirens went on until early in the morning].[5] (Figure 9.2)

We do not need a photograph to release Holocaust overtones. In fact we do not need a photograph at all. In fact, we might say that while the caption necessitates the presence of an image, ekphrasis assumes its absence. So I would want to say the following about ekphrasis:

(1) Ekphrasis makes text coincident with the perception of the image (not pre or post), intensifying the assimilability of the photograph's past (that is to say, the photograph is not illustrative or exemplary or typical or representative as it might be with a caption: it is *prima materia*, raw, originary);

(2) Captions express a point of view; ekphrasis establishes a point of view, a perceptual subjectivity. Consequently, we look at images from a position of perceptual involvement, however neutral the description;

(3) Ekphrasis is more interested in narrativizing than in interpreting. It is natural, therefore, that its ambitions should be metonymic rather than metaphorical. Sebald's photographs are unframed and let us easily into their blind fields. Indeed, peculiarly, the ekphrasis of the Sebaldian photo is an ekphrasis of the blind field, spatial (the hotel room) and temporal (the city at the time);

(4) If ekphrasis presupposes the visual absence of its subject, why, when they coexist in the text, is neither the text nor the picture afflicted with redundancy? Because their mutual function is not to provide or endorse information, but to dramatize the unstable relationship between the shown and its telling. Because the text does not respond to an absence but generates it: the photographs are like spectral versions of themselves, fragile, emerging or fading, never quite at their point, never quite fixed. And they are spectral, too, in the sense of being doubles of the text.

In his preface to O'Grady and Pyke's *I Could Read the Sky* (1997), John Berger suggests that the advantage of black-and-white photographs is 'that they remind you of this search for what can't be seen, for what's missing' and concludes: 'And so they work together, the written lines and the pictures and they never say the same thing. They don't know the same things, and this is the secret of living together.'[6]

Martin Swales singles out melancholy and contingency as the identifying features of Sebald's narratives,[7] features which are equally the presiding spirits of photography. About photography's necrophilia enough has already been said, and Sebald's sidelinings compulsively return whenever this theme is touched on in Barthes's *Camera Lucida*.[8] About contingency one might say that only through chance can coincidence be attained, that only in the recalcitrance of the unordered and unorderable can those webs of similarity, repetition, correspondence spin themselves into an unbidden and thus revelatory existence. In the essay 'Ein Versuch der Restitution' ('An Attempt at Restitution') Sebald describes his method of procedure thus: 'im Einhalten einer genauen historischen Perspektive, im geduldigen Gravieren und in der Vernetzung, in der Manier der *nature morte*, anscheinend weit auseinander liegender Dinge' [in adhering to an exact historical perspective, in patiently engraving and linking together apparently disparate things in the manner of a still life]; and he adds: 'Immerfort frage ich mich seither, was sind das für unsichtbare Beziehungen, die unser Leben bestimmen, wie verlaufen die Fäden' [I have kept asking myself since then what the invisible connections that determine our lives are, and how the threads run].[9] In what does the photograph's contingency reside? In the instantaneousness of its taking: the camera does not depict an instant so much as generate it, construct it as a gravitational point for memory and meaning, prevent it from wasting itself as a split second of undifferentiated becoming. But by this very process, it puts the viewer under strange obligations. Photographs populate the past. History itself seems to evacuate the past, leaving behind only famous figures, events, places, statistics. Photography has acted against this tendency: it puts in front of us figures we can no longer discount, coming as if to reclaim their memory, to reach forward from the past and interfere with our perception of things. Benjamin's description of Hill's photograph of a Newhaven fishwife (Elizabeth Johnstone) eloquently acknowledges this moving demand to remain in consciousness:

> With photography, however, we encounter something new and strange: in Hill's Newhaven fishwife, her eyes cast down in such indolent, seductive modesty, there remains [...] something that cannot be silenced, that fills you with an unruly desire to know what her name was, the woman who was alive there, who even now is still real and will never consent to be wholly absorbed in 'art'.[10]

But it is not just the photographed figure who demands to be identified; it is also the photographed moment: in the same, just-quoted review, Sebald observes:

> But for all that, the volume contains a great many of those intriguing pictures which open up vistas into an unsuspected and yet strangely immediate past, pictures which seem to demand the identification of that moment, long since eroded, when life was arrested.[11]

But, at the same time as the camera fixes the image, it sends it out of control, in the sense that the photograph is infinitely available to scrutiny and exploitation, to the gossip it might beget, to the contexts it might so easily be appropriated for.

The very immediacy of the photographic makes it peculiarly pressing, peculiarly urgent, peculiarly inexhaustible and persistent.[12] And this is partly what allows photographs to pass from memory into post-memory,[13] to persuade us that images which we were not contemporary with are still crying out for justice, still demanding entry to the viewer's memory. And when Sebald remarks that photographs present this 'strangely immediate past' as 'unsuspected', there are perhaps two senses in which we should interpret this 'unsuspected'. First, photographs are unsuspected simply because they bring to us scenes from lives that take place predominantly outside our consciousness. Few of us stop to ask what else is going on in the world as we take a sip of tea or read another paragraph; if we did, the experience would recurrently paralyse us. Sebald's patient quest, patient opening up of parallel worlds, not just across space, but across time, too — in Bergsonian manner, the past merely accumulates as a self-enlarging present — creates the process whereby individual memories become the collective memory of the next generation, a generation still able to act in response to that past. Photographs dramatize the processes of the raising of memory or of its abandonment on the floor of the ocean. But he who raises the wreck runs risks: 'Das Risiko besteht darin, daß [...] derjenige, in dem die Erinnerung fortlebt, den Zorn der andern auf sich zieht, die nur in Vergessenheit weiterleben können' [It is a risk because [...] those in whom memory lives on bring down upon themselves the wrath of others who can continue to live only by forgetting].[14]

The second sense relates to the camera's capacity to turn 'any-moments-what-ever' into photographs. The space we live in, the temporal continuity we live through, are full of potential photographs, freeze-frames; space and time are constantly carried away from themselves, from the meanings they would make available as a set of photographic stills. But from time to time the shutter is released, the camera compels time and space to declare themselves as particular configurations, transforms passage into destiny, teleology, history. The camera is

FIG. 9.3. Max Aurach's / Ferber's father on the Brauneck
(*Die Ausgewanderten* (Eichborn), p. 278 / *The Emigrants* (Harvill), p. 186).
© The Estate of W. G. Sebald

the conduit whereby we attach ourselves to history. And, naturally, the camera brings with it its own relentless logic: the single, so-called synthetic portrait (Kracauer's 'Gedächtnisbild' [memory image]; see below) gives way to the tirelessly amassed 'file of photographs' of the chosen subject.[15] But Sebald's photographs are remarkably thrifty with themselves, are unsuspected because they are exceptional: for example, there is one photograph of Max Aurach (Ferber),[16] in the second form at school, one photograph of his father on the Brauneck ('Es gehört zu den wenigen, sagte Aurach, die aus diesen Jahren erhalten geblieben sind' [one of the few that have survived from those years, said Ferber]) (Figure 9.3),[17] one of Cosmo Solomon ('Es ist die einzige in meinem Besitz befindliche Aufnahme von Cosmo Solomon' [It is the only photograph of Cosmo Solomon that I possess] (Figure 9.4).[18] But this does not make them more synthetic or privileged. Sebald's 'unsuspected' is the 'unsuspected' of the beachcomber who comes across a message in a bottle, or, rather, a bottle without a message, or a bottle which might have had a message. These images have no claims to significance other than their own arbitrary survival, frame-frozen out of time's impenetrable narrativity.

FIG. 9.4. Cosmo Solomon (*Die Ausgewanderten* (Eichborn), p. 134 /
The Emigrants (Harvill), p. 92). © The Estate of W. G. Sebald

Clive Scott and Roland Barthes

This section is principally concerned with Sebald's annotations of Scott's *The Spoken Image: Photography and Language* (1999), which cast particular light perhaps on the only book that succeeded it, *Austerlitz*. But reference to Barthes's work becomes almost immediately necessary, as throughout this chapter.

Sebald gravitates towards a phenomenological view of the photograph rather than a semiological one. Rather than images shareable by virtue of a shared code, images mediated by another language, images reduced to a cultural average, Sebald plays by the gamble of triggered viscerality, of that unpredictable moment of psychic or emotional laceration. His pencil is at work on the pages of *The Spoken Image* devoted to Barthes's 'The Photographic Message' and *Camera Lucida*,[19] picking out in particular the relationship between the photograph and traumatic experience ('The trauma is a suspension of language, a blocking of meaning' (double-sidelined))[20] — enacted in *punctum* — and the way in which that optical trauma may 'turn out to trigger an involuntary memory, or some other deeply embedded association' (double-sidelined);[21] picking out, too, and relatedly, the photograph's pure evidential force, of time's being in an object (Barthes: 'its testimony bears not on the object but on time' (single-sidelined)).[22] *Punctum*, 'the pre-linguistic and language-denying moment of visual contact with the photographed subject' (double-sidelined),[23] may signal a new visual trauma, or the repetition of a past trauma, or the route to the resolution of a trauma (our own or someone else's), or the surfacing of other kinds of unconscious material, or the eruption of involuntary memory. What is important perhaps is *punctum*'s ability to liquidate *studium*, to divert the meaning of apparently documentary photographs into completely new channels of significance:

> c'est que la présence du punctum change le sens de la photo. Sa seule présence change la lecture. Un détail emporte le sens, fait prédominer un sens sur les autres. Mais c'est une des techniques principales d'interprétation de la psychanalyse.[24]

FIG. 9.5. Lewis Hine, 'Idiot Children in an Institution. New Jersey, 1924'.
© Courtesy of George Eastman House, International Museum of Photography and Film

[it is that the presence of *punctum* changes the meaning of the photo. Its
presence alone changes the reading. A detail hijacks meaning, makes one
meaning predominate over others. But this is one of the principal techniques
of psychoanalytical interpretation.]

Barthes, then, can say, as if large numbers of photographs, and not particularly our
own, were for us potentially screen-memories: 'Very often the *Punctum* is a "detail",
i.e. a partial object. Hence, to give examples of *punctum* is, in a certain fashion, to
give myself up.'[25] For Sebald, reading photographs seems seriously to have been a
way of provoking this kind of self-surrender. Barthes identifies as *punctum*, in Lewis
Hine's photograph 'Idiot Children in an Institution. New Jersey, 1924' (Figure 9.5),
the boy's huge Danton collar and the girl's bandaged finger;[26] Sebald's alternative,
pencilled in the blank space between sections, is 'and how the little boy seems to
stand in a kind of shallow hole & the girl almost appears to levitate'.

If photographs are unpredictable repositories of the *unheimlich*, we need to
emphasize that other people's photographs are likely to plunge us, uncannily, into
our own *heimlich*: others, we discover, have lived our lives in anticipation, just as
we live the lives of others — this is nowhere more vividly expressed, perhaps,
than in the pages devoted to Michael Hamburger in *Die Ringe des Saturn*.[27] And
Barthes devotes a short section of *Camera Lucida* to those photos which, at a deep,
fantasmatic level we wish not to visit but to inhabit, photos which generate 'a kind
of second sight which seems to bear me forward to a utopian time, or to carry me
back to somewhere in myself'. Then follows the passage quadruple-sidelined by
Sebald: 'a double movement which Baudelaire celebrated in *Invitation au voyage* and
La Vie antérieure. Looking at these landscapes of predilection, it is as if *I were certain*
of having been there or of going there.'[28]

But these observations can only trigger a dialectical movement; for however much we feel chronology and spatial separation being undone, and the cards of existence being constantly shuffled and re-shuffled, things must, as a counter-impulse, be firmly and exactly put in their place. We should recall the view expressed in the review with which we opened, that photographs must have the chance to recover their poignant specificity, the moment of their sudden 'death', that singularity and inimitability of being there which interpretation will come to erode: 'pictures which seem to demand the identification of that moment, long since eroded, when their life was arrested.'[29] Additionally, and with reference to Sebald's annotations of Barthes, we should note that all photographs, as if by a *choc en retour*, nail the viewer, too, to his or her specific time and place: photographs remind us that we are victims of the ruthless mystery of temporality just as they are; the there-and-then of the photograph is what it is only because my here-and-now is what *it* is. Barthes puts it thus: 'I am the reference of every photograph, and this is what generates my astonishment in addressing myself to the fundamental question: why is it that I am alive *here and now*?' (question double-sidelined).[30] The testimony of the photograph bears not on the object but on time, both past and present.

Two quotations in *The Spoken Image* from Michel Tournier's *The Erl-King* attract single-sidelining, the first being Abel Tiffauges's declaration that photography is 'instantaneous and occult' (where 'occult' is also ringed),[31] the second his view that 'Photography promotes reality to the plane of dream'.[32] This passage leads into Scott's fuller analysis of the photograph's inevitable transformation from the indexical to the iconic, part of which is the suggestion that the instant becomes the moment: 'The instant is transformed into the moment. The sense of duration within the image increases. The image loses instanta-[neity even though it may present the instantaneous].'[33] Not only does Sebald double-sideline the first two printed lines (as indicated), but he circles the word 'duration' and writes in the margin 'nichts ist vorbei // überdauern' [nothing is over // to outlast]. At the foot of the page, Sebald has noted: 'dachte ich mir // so wie dies Kind noch im Vater war so ist der Vater nicht verschwunden & ist auf eine gewisse Weise gegenwärtig mit mir' [I thought to myself // just as this child was still in his father, so my father has not disappeared and is in a sense co-present with me], a thought which does not seem to relate directly to the text, but which keeps in mind this interchange between the generations so important to Sebald's de-sedimentation of time and his urge to reverse chronology, or to wed the achronological, as much as to reconstitute the past.

Sebald's final annotations for Chapter 1 of *The Spoken Image* relate to a paragraph which elaborates on the distinction between the instant and the moment: the moment derives an expandability from its metonymic and metaphoric capacities which the instant does not share and by virtue of which 'we feel able to inhabit it and be inhabited by it' (double-sidelined).[34] Within the experience of the moment, we are 'susceptible to the beckonings [glossed by Sebald as 'Verlockungen'] of memory and feel a power to persist' (double-sidelined;[35] back to the theme of 'überdauern', see below).[36]

Sebald's annotating pencil then disappears for six chapters and returns in Chapter 8 ('The Narrative Resources of the Photograph'), as questions connected with the

FIG. 9.6. Austerlitz in the Stower Grange rugby team
(*Austerlitz* (Hanser), p. 114 / (Hamish Hamilton) p. 106). © The Estate of W. G. Sebald

family album are broached. The album bibliographizes images, narrativizes them, gives them cohesion and momentum. 'Ironically, however, the family album carries within it the mechanisms of its own deconstruction. Photographs fall out or are replaced; the narrative threatens to ramify or begs questions' (single-sidelined).[37] The precariousness of the photograph's life as a material object — and the poor quality of the photographs in Sebald's work seems designedly to encode a sense of threat, a fadingness, a recuperability supplied on sufferance and for a limited period — is partly determined by methods of storage and presentation.[38] And of methods of storage, the most conducive to the vagaries of memory, and the most vulnerable to misadventure, is the shoebox: 'surrendering to chance encounters with prints which [the viewer] must shape into narratives — not narratives of external time, but narratives of inner duration, memory, resurrected illusion; in short, narratives of the narrator (*temps du récit*)' (double-sidelined).[39] It should be added that, for all the photograph's reproducibility, the family photographer is peculiarly forgetful of negatives and comes to treat the one print as unique, the only one, the one with the obligation to survive. This may be a defence mechanism: the single album is the only access route, and the non-proliferation of prints a sign of the family's desire to keep it in the family, to prevent the promiscuous and unguarded existence of images appropriated by others for purposes impossible to predict or control. And this singleness of the image is perhaps what makes it peculiarly the meeting point of the first and the last, an encounter in its absolute novelty shot through with farewell. Sebald's date of birth (18.5.1944) is similarly both a date of birth[40] and a date of death.[41]

'There is plenty of evidence to suppose that people look upon their photographs as evidence of their living, as the sources of their narrative (photobiography)'

Fig. 9.7 (above). Austerlitz behind the camera in front of the Antikos Bazar (Terezín) (*Austerlitz*, (Hanser) p. 282 / (Hamish Hamilton) p. 276). © The Estate of W. G. Sebald

Fig. 9.8 (right). Austerlitz as the Rose Queen's pageboy (*Austerlitz*, (Hanser) p. 266 / (Hamish Hamilton) p. 258). © The Estate of W. G. Sebald

(underlined and double-sidelined).[42] 'Others spoke of the loss of photographs as a taking away of their history, a loss of the richness of identity; even the damaging of photographs was regarded as an emotional or psychological wounding' (double-sidelined).[43] Against the first of these two passages, Sebald writes: 'Aber von Aust. [erlitz] gibt es keine Bilder' [But there are no photographs of Aust.(erlitz)]. We have already had something to say about the necessary scarcity of photographs in Sebald's work but, in fact, there are three photographs of Austerlitz: in the Stower Grange rugby team (Figure 9.6), behind the camera in front of the Antikos Bazar in Terezín (Figure 9.7), and as the Rose Queen's pageboy (Figure 9.8), another self challenging the viewer with his look across the years:

> Und immer fühlte ich mich dabei durchdrungen von dem forschenden Blick des Pagen, der gekommen war, sein Teil zurückzufordern und der nun im Morgengrauen auf dem leeren Feld darauf wartete, daß ich den Handschuh aufheben und das ihm bevorstehende Unglück abwenden würde.

> [I always felt the piercing, inquiring gaze of the page boy who had come to demand his dues, who was waiting in the grey light of dawn on the empty field for me to accept the challenge and avert the misfortune lying ahead of him.][44]

We shall have more to say about the photographic look. But to imagine the absence of photographs of Austerlitz is to imagine the facilitation of the transfer of subjectivity and narratorial position, just as it is to imagine preventing anyone laying hands on Austerlitz in the belief that they can take a quick route to knowledge, to transform the proper difficulties of memory into easy visual appropriation. Photographs may be testimonies of and to the sitter; but they may also be betrayals, a handing over of the sitter to those without warrants to view him.

About photography's relationship with memory nobody can really decide: memory or *aide-mémoire*, something remembered or something commemorated, voluntary or involuntary memory? Proust's Marcel observes that his memory's supposed snapshots of Venice are powerless to restore Venice to him in the way that treading on the uneven paving stones in the Guermantes's courtyard can: 'die besondere Unebenheit der Pflastersteine unter den Sohlen meiner Schuhe' [the peculiar unevenness of the paving stones under the soles of my shoes], Sebald notes in the margin.[45] This phrase recurs, in modified form, in the account of Austerlitz's trip to Prague in search of his mother:

> und vollends wie ich, Schritt für Schritt bergan steigend, die unebenen Pflastersteine der Šporkova unter meinen Füßen spürte, war es mir, als sei ich auf diesen Weg schon einmal gegangen, als eröffnete sich mir, nicht durch die Anstrengung des Nachdenkens, sondern durch meine so lange betäubt gewesenen und jetzt wiedererwachenden Sinne, die Erinnerung.

> [and still more so when I felt the uneven paving of the Šporkova underfoot as step by step I climbed uphill, it was as if I had already been this way before and memories were revealing themselves to me not by means of any mental effort but through my senses, so long numbed and now coming back to life.][46]

If voluntary memory is the archival memory, then it 'preserves the past for us by dispossessing us of it, by taking away our indispensability in its recovery' (double-sidelined).[47] Sebald seems to concur in the view that, if we are to re-inhabit memory, we must outwit the lure of likeness or documentary fidelity: photographs need to have about them something incongruent, ill-fitting, something which deflects the viewer from likeness, because likeness lifts being to the surface and is too short-term an objective. To achieve penetrative intimacy, we must pursue the 'unlike like'. And so we come back to Barthes, to the photograph in which he could retrieve his mother ('The Winter Garden'), the photograph which was a bad likeness, the photograph of his mother as Barthes never knew her, long before he was ever thought of: '[whereas the only one which has] given me the splendour of her truth is precisely a lost photograph, one which does not look "like" her, the photograph of a child I never knew' (triple-sidelined).[48] In this sense, likeness is the fulcrum between voluntary and involuntary memory: without likeness, the voluntary tips towards the involuntary. This is why other people's photographs, and not our own, are the surest route back to ourselves:

> [While our own photographs tend to limit us to externalized and archival memory, to what we recognize, other people's] photographs, whatever their date or location, may act as the trigger to a memory whose eruption we cannot control, a memory which we may not, indeed, at first recognize, but can only inarticulately experience. Real memories are those we are shaken by before we can properly identify them.[49]

(This passage is double-sidelined, the text underlined from 'a memory whose eruption' to the end.)

In Scott's chapter on texts by John Berger and Jean Mohr (Chapter 9), Sebald double-sidelines an extract from the introductory dream-narrative for *A Seventh Man: The Story of a Migrant Worker in Europe* (1975), in which Berger asks a visiting friend: 'Did you come by photograph or train?' and adds by way of explanation: 'All photographs are a form of transport and an expression of absence.'[50] But this journey across space and time that a photograph is, bringing us our loved ones and their absence, distils its poignancy more in the materiality of the photograph than in its image content. We do not need, perhaps do not wish, to scrutinize the images of the ones we love, 'because we do not require knowledge of them', as Scott's text continues, and, single-sidelined by Sebald, 'because the photograph is only a temporary substitute, a pledge with only fiduciary value; to look too closely might be to break a spell'.[51] In some circumstances, photographs have this talismanic value, keeping relationships intact, representing a gift of the self that only the loss or destruction of the photograph can reverse. In these circumstances, the other life, the life of the photograph, is put on hold, subjected to cryogenesis, allowed to fossilize;[52] the photograph, we say, 'arrests time', which, for its part, does not stop running; it would be more accurate to say that the photograph makes contact with time in an instant of its passing. But this is the tense — future in the past, or past in the future — of photographic mirage; even as the shutter is released, it is too late. Unfortunately, the photograph does not allow us to travel in time. In Bergsonian fashion, the past is always an integral part of a cumulative present which, like the Heracleitian river, one can never re-enter in the same place. The final passage marked by Sebald in this chapter is Berger's disabused account of the world of the migrant worker: 'Increasingly he may begin to live by way of

memory and anticipation, until the two of them become indistinguishable, until he
anticipates his release in the future as the moment when he will rejoin all that was
left in the past.'[53] In this account, the present cannot really be inhabited; or, rather,
the only present that can be inhabited is that of a set of photographs whose hoped-
for resuscitation will surely fail. Sebald, one might argue, wilfully falls prey to the
same 'illusion': the time of the photograph can be returned to, the photograph
can re-originate itself, the threads be picked up and the past's unfinished business
fruitfully resumed. But he well knows the Heracleitian edict: photographs do keep
the future open, but only on condition that we re-narrate the photograph in our
own voice, and that we create a new space of reception for it to enter.

The final marginal marks, in *The Spoken Image*'s tenth and last chapter ('In
Conclusion: Modern Narrative in Photograph and Film'), occur sporadically
against its concluding paragraph, a summary of the relationship between text and
photograph. One of the purposes of the book is to provide an account of the various
generical ways in which photographs are subject to language, and to suggest that
photographs have strategies at their disposal for outwitting language and recovering
a real degree of expressive autonomy. The final paragraph reiterates the case for a
photography which has learnt how to break free from language's stranglehold:

> But however powerful language is in determining the power-play of the photo-
> graph, the photograph is artful in its evasions and slippages. (p. 327, double-
> sidelined)

> [Faced with photography's weak intentionality, we assume] that without the
> support of language, photographs would become souls lost in the limbo of their
> own gratuitousness. (p. 327, double-sidelined)

> [When this is so [i.e. when language has a bad memory and cannot repeat
> itself reliably]], the photograph escapes the plottings and mappings of history
> and re-enters the carnival (in the Bakhtinian sense), recovering [its intrinsic
> unreliability.] (p. 327, double-sidelined)

> [the photographic image is 'fixed' and] 'fixing', an indelible trace from the
> world of its taking; and yet its effects are unpredictable. (p. 328, double-
> sidelined)

> Apparently one hundred per cent evidence, the photograph never, finally, gives
> itself away. (p. 328, double-sidelined)

Siegfried Kracauer and Jan Peter Tripp

When Sebald uses the word 'überdauern' [to survive] about the photograph, he
seems to intend two things. First, the photograph quite literally survives, while
those it pictures pass away. In his essay on the work of Jan Peter Tripp, 'Wie Tag
und Nacht: Über die Bilder Jan Peter Tripps' (1993), reprinted in *Logis in einem
Landhaus* (1998) and translated by Michael Hamburger by way of an added afterword
to his translation of *Unerzählt* (2003) in *Unrecounted* (2004), Sebald remarks: 'Da die
Dinge uns (im Prinzip) überdauern, wissen sie mehr von uns als wir über sie'[54]
[Because (in principle) things outlast us, they know more about us than we know
about them][55] and relates Tripp's still-life painting to Merleau-Ponty's 'regard

préhumain' [pre-human gaze]: 'denn umgekehrt sind in solcher Malerei die Rollen des Betrachters und des betrachteten Gegenstands' [for in such paintings the roles of the observer and the observed objects are reversed].[56] Elinor Shaffer adds the further gloss: 'Photographs as deployed by Sebald in his fictions have this ominous quality of ruling over and containing the experience of our dead selves to which we have no more access.'[57]

   But this predicament is complicated by the paradoxical condition of the photograph that lies behind it: the photograph is 'das vor uns aufgeschlagene Buch unserer Geschichte' [the book of our history opened before us],[58] perhaps, but these images of the past are also images 'vom Rätselhaftesten an einem Menschenleben' [of what is most enigmatic about a human life].[59] Photography both reveals and conceals, while, it might be argued, painting only reveals, however ambiguously: paintings have no blind field and do not so much actively collapse three dimensions into two as begin with the conventions of two-dimensional representation. In the photograph, all is evident that can be evident. As the photograph traverses time, becomes detached from its moorings, loses its context — despite 'überdauern', Sebald too admits that the moment of the photograph is 'long since eroded'[60] — so it understands itself less well, loses its power to bear unequivocal testimony. And yet its power remains evidential; without that exerted pressure, many (family) photographs would be chaff in the wind. And so, equally and oppositely, the photograph continues to know, to be the witness now struck dumb, the witness which mutely calls us to account, to provide the collapsed third dimension. And yet, for each viewer, that third dimension is different, and each viewer, too, unless released into the blind field by a latency in the image, unless helped to an unfolding, an unpacking, a voice restored, will experience that 'narrative claustrophobia, which allows only unavoidable choices' (double-sidelined).[61] While such a condition would in no wise trouble a semiologist — the knowledge that the photograph holds as *studium* can be read off in what is visible to anyone, indifferently, as the average knowledge contained in the image and circumscribed by the frame: the 'dandy's white summer outfit', the 'wide-brimmed florentine hat', the 'hermaphroditic beauty', and the 'casual *raffinement*' — the phenomenologist feels that some justice has not been done, that memory has been betrayed, that immediacy has only produced trauma, embarrassment, vertigo, perplexity. And yet the phenomenologist may also be haunted by the suspicion that the photographic image has, as it were, drawn into itself, vampirically, all the reality of that of which it is a copy; it absents its subject in more ways than one, usurping identity, authenticity:

> Und weil das Abbild noch fortdauerte, wenn das Abgebildete längst vergangen war, so lag auch die ungute Ahnung nicht fern, daß dem Abgebildeten, den Menschen und der Natur, ein geringerer Grad von Authentizität eigne als der Kopie, daß die Kopie das Original aushöhle, wie es auch heißt, daß einer, der seinem Doppelgänger begegnet, sich selber vernichtet fühlt.

> [And because the copy lasted long after what it had copied was gone, there was an uneasy suspicion that the original, whether it was human or a natural scene, was less authentic than the copy, that the copy was eroding the original, in the same way as a man meeting his doppelganger is said to feel his real self destroyed.][62]

Stefanie Harris has already pointed to the pertinence of Siegfried Kracauer's essay 'Die Photographie' (1927) (collected in *Das Ornament der Masse*, 1977) for Sebald's work, as has, at greater length, George Kouvaros.[63] The similarities and differences between them are instructive. Kracauer's is a negative view of photography that does not square well with Sebald's. Where Sebald can use 'überdauern' of the photograph, Kracauer uses it only of the memory image, the 'Gedächtnisbild': 'Das letzte Gedächtnisbild überdauert seiner Unvergeßlichkeit wegen die Zeit; die Photographie, die es nicht meint und faßt, muß wesentlich dem Zeitpunkt ihrer Entstehung zugeordnet sein' [The last memory image outlasts time because it is unforgettable; the photograph, which neither refers to nor encompasses such a memory image, must be essentially associated with the moment in time at which it came into existence].[64] Kracauer, like Sebald, insists that a photographic record must be supplemented by an oral tradition, that the generations following thus have peculiar obligations; but for Kracauer, the photograph is fighting a losing battle, taking its subjects towards a limbo, an anonymity, a *studium* value. As the photographic image increasingly disengages itself from a present knowledge, so its referentiality becomes increasingly gratuitous, and likeness increasingly helpless to make its claim. Compared with the spirit of the photograph — incision in a specific space–time continuum — the 'Gedächtnisbild' is highly selective and deformative, since significance to the remitember is its guiding criterion; it is a process of distillation which works towards the last image, the monogram, the subject's history condensed. While Sebald may believe that photographs should be replaced in their moment — 'pictures which seem to demand the identification of that moment, long since eroded, when their life was arrested'[65] — he also finds it easy to equate them, in many respects, with a 'Gedächtnisbild'. This is partly because photographs, for Sebald, are not passive, they do not 'get smaller' as they age, do not increasingly surrender life-value to sign-value; on the contrary, one might say, their power grows, they cast longer shadows,[66] they are more and more endowed with a cognitive power (they look back at us); in short, their pre-remembering us, even though they never knew us, is an integral part of the way we remember them. Sebald's 'Gedächtnisbild' is, therefore, no process of distillation or manipulation or compression, but an ongoing negotiation in which the remembering self must undergo a series of enlargements instigated by the expansion of the remembered subject; remembering is not recall but revitalization, and it is sobering for us to acknowledge that our own (self-)importance is proportional to what we are happy to forget, is dependent on the 'schwache[s] Gedächtnis der Menschheit' [short memory of mankind].[67]

For Kracauer, then, only the present-day photographic image gives access to the life of the original, achieves a certain transparency; otherwise it enters a ghostly state in which the non-coincidence of image and original generates both comedy and a shudder. This dissociative mechanism, this lost unity, leaves the person as a sum of his or her photographable accessories, a gathering of fragments around a nothing: 'Diese gespenstische Realität ist *unerlöst*' [this ghost-like reality is *unredeemed*].[68] 'Unerfüllt & unerlöst' are the words Sebald writes beside the double-sidelined sentences in *The Spoken Image*: 'All photographs are taken in the past, a necessary condition of their existing at all. But equally intrinsic to them is their discontinuity, or their having only momentarily touched a continuity; they are unfulfilled.'[69] Where Kracauer attributes the absence of 'Erlösung' [redemption, liberation] to an irretrievable disintegration of unity brought about by the camera — the camera is an instrument of the Fall — for Sebald photographs are both the subject and instrument of a potential redemption which we, the viewers, have to work hard to bring about. In a passage in Scott which precedes a brief consideration of phototherapy, Sebald underlines and double-sidelines the words 'our emotional and psychological drives, anxieties, etc. are locked in our own photographs', circling the phrase 'locked in', and then, against the clause 'that the curse must be lifted' in the sentence 'But if it is through photographs that we have been condemned to neurosis, alienation, insecurity, then it is through photographs that the curse must be lifted, that the psychic and the social can be re-engineered, and that we can find our way back to a representable self, or a self properly represented', Sebald puts a quadruple sideline and writes: 'daß der Bann gebrochen werden kann // heraustreten & weiterleben' [that the spell can be broken // to step out of it and continue living].[70] Photographs, in this reading, far from being confined to a fast-receding, diminishing, and disintegrative past, are future-orientated; it is as if they swap their identity as still photographs for that of film stills (photograms), waiting to rejoin a continuity from which they have been temporarily evicted, waiting to participate in a narrative whose unfolding and outcome no one can guess at. For in truth, there is no outcome; Austerlitz has still to find the traces of his father. But, to do Kracauer justice, one might claim that, in his 'other' essay on photography, which acts as the first chapter of *Theory of Film* (1960), he withdraws from the rather bleak view of photography we have just described. In this latter account, Kracauer lists, as the fourth of photography's 'affinities', indeterminateness, and as its third, endlessness:

> A photograph, whether portrait or action picture, is in character only if it precludes the notion of completeness. Its frame marks a provisional limit; its content refers to other contents outside that frame; and its structure denotes something that cannot be encompassed — physical existence.[71]

It is peculiarly important to remind ourselves that Sebald's essay on Tripp first appeared in 1993 and to remember that Tripp, whom Sebald 'rediscovered' in Stuttgart in May 1976, had been to school with him in Oberstdorf.[72] Sebald's meditations on Tripp grow from and into the thick of his writing, precisely because Tripp's business is with *trompe l'œil*: 'Tatsächlich gelingt Tripp nicht nur die Interpolierung der dritten Dimension in die Fläche, so, daß man schauend manchmal meint, über die Bildschwelle treten zu können' [In fact Tripp manages not only to interpolate the third dimension into his surfaces, so that, looking, one sometimes thinks one can cross the pictorial threshold];[73] but he succeeds, too, in transmitting the tactility of materials. But the bad name of *trompe l'œil* — a meaningless and meretricious attempt at a visual confidence trick — was confirmed by the arrival of photography. What really matters are the differences and divergences introduced by Tripp between the source-photographs and his paintings: the mechanical relation between the focussed and the unfocussed is suspended, additions are made, as are subtractions, tones are changed, some elements are emphasized, others reduced, and so on. And this to release a metaphysicality: 'Je länger ich die Bilder Jan Peter Tripps betrachte, desto mehr begreife ich, daß sich hinter dem Illusionismus der Oberfläche eine furchterregende Tiefe verbirgt. Sie ist sozusagen das metaphysische Unterfutter der Realität' [The longer I look at the pictures of Jan Peter Tripp, the better I understand that behind the illusions of the surface a dread-inspiring depth is concealed. It is the metaphysical lining of reality, so to speak].[74] Perhaps the refusal of high production values in the reproduction of photographs in the Sebaldian text is a way of keeping open a path to the metaphysical.

And yet one might say that the Trippian *trompe l'œil* has a significant role to play as a model for Sebald's mode of narration. One might say that Sebald transposes to the dimension of time what *trompe l'œil* acts out in space. If *trompe l'œil* undermines the protective safety of the Albertian window by allowing a space behind the window to open out into the space of the viewer, by allowing two dimensions momentarily to become three dimensions again, then Sebald presents us with stories and photographs which, far from falling back, regressing, into the past in which their origins and making lie, reach forward and invade the space of the contemporary narrator–spectator. And yet we will discover that the apparent projection into our space is in fact a flat surface, a limit, as likely to be experienced as irretrievable loss as pressing presence (again one thinks of the 'resurrection' of Johannes Naegeli; see note 52).

But there is a more literal sense in which *trompe l'œil* operates. We might remember that in nineteenth-century American *trompe l'œil* paintings, photographs were often the bait. Sebald, it seems, wishes us to view the distinction between the different arts, and between what is imagined and what is imagined as real, between what is depicted and what is recorded or transcribed, as fragile, precarious. There is no point in *trompe l'œil* unless our deception is proportional to our undeception. As Sybille Ebert-Schifferer puts it: 'This implies that the goal of *trompe l'œil* is not the continuous deception of the viewer [...], but rather the feeling of astonishment at one's own perception.'[75] *Trompe l'œil* dramatizes the delusions of perceptual expectation, of two-dimensional evidentiality, of spatial–temporal continuities. So we think these are photographs? Just as reported direct speech passes itself off as direct speech, so photographs pass themselves off as passports, or train tickets, or miniatures, or postcards or engravings or catalogues. Different degrees of clarity or graininess in the photographs change the intensity and direction of the *trompe l'œil*.

And there is a further reason which might have drawn Sebald to the photograph as a *trompe-l'œil*, as the image whose very absence of pretension should be a cause for suspicion.[76] In the final section of *Camera Lucida*, Barthes identifies two ways in which society tames the madness that photography is: by turning it into art (hardly a solution in the Sebaldian case) and by universalizing and banalizing it, so that it loses its specificity as a medium, so that it becomes the type of all modern images, filters all experience, mediates all emotion (double-sidelined in Sebald's copy is 'pleasure passes through the image').[77] Images take the place of beliefs; the ousting of fanaticism is paid for by the surrender of authenticity; we build a world without difference (indifferent) at the price of 'nauseated boredom' (this whole passage is double-sidelined).[78] For Sebald, language maintains a crucial inequality: ekphrasis is sometimes inadequate, but sometimes, conversely, the image impoverishes. But the *trompe-l'œil* of photography perhaps restores photography to itself by alerting us to its dangerous gregariousness and promiscuities.

In the final pages of his essay on Tripp, Sebald comes to consider Tripp's depiction of a pair of women's shoes in sunlight on a tiled floor, 'Déclaration de guerre' (1988) (Figure 9.9), and the incorporation of this image into the later, smaller image 'Déjà vu oder der Zwischenfall' (1992) (Figure 9.10). It would be easy to think of Sebaldian memory as a process of sedimentation, or *mise en abyme*, whereby consciousnesses are (infinitely) reflected in each other and deepen the enigma, the founding event (*Zwischenfall*), at the end of a corridor in time, and whereby, too, these reflections are all instances of *déjà vu*. This model has much to commend it, but it may suggest, rather too much, a stratification of clearly separated layers, whereas the flexibility and expandability of Sebald's prose seems expressly designed to capture a permeability which allows layers to run or leak into each other. Sebald's *mise en abyme* is no post-structural act of deferral or constantly self-undermining play of consciousness, but rather the channel through which he can both remember himself into other people's existences and remember them into his. This is, after all, what the intertext for Sebald is: the 'quotation' from existence which compels us to explore our own knowledge of the world — for every shoe intimates someone else's shoe and every dog summons someone else's dog — as patiently as need be, as patiently as a particular kind of prose style allows us. But as Sebald points out, only by giving ourselves this time 'treten wir ein in die erzählte Zeit und in die Zeit der Kultur' [[do] we enter into time recounted and into the time of culture].[79]

In the end, we must suppose, I think, that the dog of *Déjà vu* is, in a peculiar sense, Sebald's camera/photographing device: it is 'der Geheimnisträger, der mit Leichtigkeit läuft über die Abgründe der Zeit' [bearer of the secret, who runs with ease over the abysses of time],[80] who 'weiß manches genauer als wir' [knows many things more accurately than we do],[81] and whose vision is a peculiar mixture of the domesticated eye and the wild, alien eye which has the power to see through us.[82]

Susan Sontag and John Berger

Much of what Sebald sidelines in Sontag's *On Photography* relates to family and tourist snaps; to the use of photography to confer significance, shape experience, live voyeuristically; to photography's connection with death and decay; to its beautification of reality. This cursory summary is not intended to minimize the importance of Sontag's work to Sebald's photographic thinking; far from it, her presence is ubiquitous. Sebald's own first published reference to Sontag dates back to 1984.[83] But in this section, I would like to write about the relationship a little more speculatively.

We have some indication, again from annotations, of the issues that preoccupied Sebald as he read Sontag's Introduction to Benjamin's *One-Way Street and Other Writings* (1979) — the proportionality of meaning to deadness; melancholy, will and

FIG. 9.9 (upper)
Jan Peter Tripp, 'Déclaration de guerre' (1988) (Jan Peter Tripp, *Die Aufzählung der Schwierig-keiten: Arbeiten von 1985–92* (Offenburg: Reiff Schwarzwaldverlag, 1993), pp. 52–53, #155; W. G. Sebald and Jan Peter Tripp, *Unrecounted*, trans. by Michael Hamburger (London: Hamish Hamilton, 2004), p. 91). © Jan Peter Tripp

FIG. 9.10 (lower)
Jan Peter Tripp, 'Déjà vu oder der Zwischenfall' (1992)
(Jan Peter Tripp, *Die Aufzählung der Schwierigkeiten: Arbeiten von 1985–92*, pp. 54–55, #162; W. G. Sebald and Jan Peter Tripp, *Unrecounted*, trans. by Michael Hamburger, p. 92).
© Jan Peter Tripp

work; the melancholic's intensity and exhaustiveness of attention — and her *Under the Sign of Saturn* (1980): the victories and defeats of the will (Benjamin), exiles and teachers (Canetti), the German duty to confront Nazism in the first person, the will to say more, melancholy (Syberberg); but, of course, we lack his response to Sontag's *Regarding the Pain of Others* (2003), a meditation on the visual depiction of suffering and more particularly on war photographs. One can only suppose that Sebald would have reacted with mixed feelings to the suggestion that 'photographs lay down routes of reference, and serve as totems of causes: sentiment is more likely to crystallize around a photograph than around a verbal slogan'.[84] It is perhaps easy enough to accept the crystallizing power of photographs, the purchase they suddenly provide on a situation which threatens to be too large and fluid for the mind to encompass; but we must believe, perhaps, that the objective of memory — to get the picture straight — will always be thwarted, that, as Sontag herself mentions, hitherto unknown photographs will continually emerge to 'revolutionize' our view of history and continue to rail against any creeping fossilization of view. But beneath this proposal, Sontag *does* want to suggest that photographs are filter-processes by which we identify and limit what we are prepared to take into account. Sebald's writing, on the other hand, is an apologia for the oral tradition, for verbal accounts of verbal accounts, often activated by photographs it is true. Photographs are not so much memories, as shorthands or repositories of memory, points at which the biography of the viewed is able to become the autobiography of the viewer, or vice versa, and public evidence to become the private imaginary, a chain reaction which is passed on from generation to generation, from memory to post-memory. Sontag denies the concept of collective memory in favour of collective instruction: photographs make public rather than make private.[85] But Sebald's oral lines are the process whereby collective instruction becomes collective memory, in a process of endless sharing, endless modulations of private association and appropriation. And Sontag, uncharacteristically, is led to a formulation which seems to make possible a contradictoriness in her own feelings about this process: 'The problem is not that people remember through photographs, but that they remember only the photographs. This remembering through photographs eclipses other forms of understanding and remembering.'[86] Is that 'remembering through photographs' of the second sentence a tacit disagreement with her own assertion?

Sontag devotes a short paragraph to Sebald, in which, it seems, she wishes to imply that Sebald, too, is happy to let narratives resolve themselves into pictures.[87] The relevant paragraph begins with the sentence: 'To remember is, more and more, not to recall a story but to be able to call up a picture' and continues:

> Even a writer as steeped in nineteenth-century and early modern literary solemnities as W. G. Sebald was moved to seed his lamentation-narratives of lost lives, lost nature, lost cityscapes with photographs. Sebald was not just an elegist, he was a militant elegist. Remembering, he wanted the reader to remember, too.[88]

But for Sebald, photographs are points of departure rather than points of arrival, or enjoy oblique or problematic relations with the text. They are not points of convergence in the author–narrator–reader triangle, but points of radiation, visual coincidences which are as much visual accidents, capricious in what they let loose. It is no surprise that, in his annotations at least, Sebald should have envisaged that there should be no pictures of Austerlitz. Austerlitz is perhaps designed as a consciousness not fully in possession of itself, drifting, changing, as easy to enter as to leave, an available first person, an available machine of, and pretext for, narrative — he always picks up the story without further ado — never ready to be transfixed in a photograph.

We are mistaken if we tar Sebald too exclusively with the phenomenological brush. For, after all, what catches his eye in the photograph of the Russian Ambassador and his family is the dandy's white summer outfit, the wide-brimmed Florentine hat, and so on. In John Berger's account of August Sander's *Young Farmers* (1914), it is the opening paragraph on the meanings of the suit which attracts Sebald's double sideline.[89] And it is Berger's observation about the behaviour of newspapers — 'A paper like the *Sunday Times* continues to publish shocking photographs about Vietnam or about Northern Ireland whilst politically supporting the policies responsible for the violence' (p. 38) — which he double-sidelines in the essay on Don McCullin's war photography, 'Photographs of Agony'. Berger's own approaches to photography cross back and forth between the semiological and phenomenological, but many of the essays in *About Looking* gravitate towards the position described in the piece on Paul Strand (unmarked by Sebald): 'Such photographs enter so deeply into the particular that they reveal to us the stream of a culture or a history which is flowing through that particular subject like blood' (p. 43).

In his response to Susan Sontag's *On Photography*, 'Uses of Photography', through the suggestion that the culture of capitalism has telescoped the eye of God into the camera (Nadar in his balloon above Paris, passage double-sidelined by Sebald, p. 53), Berger returns to phenomenological thinking:

> The faculty of memory led men everywhere to ask whether, just as they themselves could preserve certain events from oblivion, there might not be other eyes noting and recording otherwise unwitnessed events. [...] What was seen by this supernatural eye was inseparably linked with the principle of justice. It was possible to escape the justice of men, but not this higher justice from which nothing or little could be hidden. (pp. 53–54)

It is not this paragraph that Sebald marks, but passages which immediately follow and which (a) imagine this supernatural eye (God or history) passing its judgements in processes of remembering (redemption) or forgetting (condemnation to outer darkness) (double-sidelined, p. 54), and (b) observe the replacement, in the latter half of the twentieth century, of the principle of judgement in photography by the opportunism of spectacle (double-sidelined, pp. 54–55). Berger does not let the historical dimension of these uses and abuses of the image entirely out of his sight, and it invests his temporary conclusion, also marked by Sebald:

> [Cameras define reality in the two ways essential to the workings of an advanced industrial society:] as a spectacle (for masses) and as an object of surveillance (for rulers). The production of images also furnishes a ruling ideology. Social change is replaced by a change in images. (pp. 55–56, double-sidelined)

Berger's solution to this parlous state of affairs lies in the migration of the principles of the private use of photography to the public sphere: the photographer acts on behalf of those involved in the event rather than for the rest of the world. Russian war photographs

> were not taken to please generals, to boost the morale of a civilian public, to glorify heroic soldiers or to shock the world press: they were images addressed to those suffering what they depict. And given this integrity towards and with their subject matter, such photographs later became a memorial, to the

20 million Russians killed in the war, for those who mourn them. (p. 60, last
sentence double-sidelined by Sebald)

Conclusion: Sebald and Thinking about Photography

My final section is devoted to a short sequence of general observations on photography, about which Sebald's work makes us think again.

(*a*) In the naive belief that photographs belong, and bear witness, to the time
and place of their taking, we take them to commemorate a memory, because a
photograph cannot be that memory. And then two things: this conventionalized,
superficial version of memory, this *aide-mémoire*, detaches itself from indexicality,
from time and place, and begins to float free. But this kind of image, the snapshot,
with no aspirations to become an 'image' and with no possibility of returning,
wholeheartedly as it were, to its place of origin — those who might speak
confidently about that origin gradually lose that confidence or realize that the truth
they can tell might as well be untrue, for all the good that it can do — must come
to occupy an uncertain place, a place of suspended animation in which it can neither
bear witness to something else nor escape into a meaning of its own.

(*b*) Before marking Barthes's equation of the theatre, death, and photography,
Sebald double-sidelines Barthes's general observation: 'Yet it is not (it seems to
me) by Painting that Photography touches art, but by Theater.'[90] This might recall
François Soulages's correction of Barthes's definition of the *noeme* of photography as
'ça-a-été' to 'ça-a-été-joué'.[91] We perform ourselves before the camera, just as the
world performs, just as the viewfinder creates a stage. If the camera spectacularizes
reality, ludifies it, theatricalizes it, then the camera, against its nature one might
say, provides a licence for the imaginary. And, as Clément Rosset warns, we
should distinguish strenuously between the imaginary, which is one of the modes
of prehension of the real, and the illusory, which is the mode, par excellence, of
denying the real.[92]

(*c*) Photography acts as a thematic matrix, or complex, multidimensional
Ur-experience in Sebald's work. In his 1989 article 'Westwärts–Ostwärts: Aporien
deutschsprachiger Ghettogeschichten',[93] Sebald refers to Sontag's analogy between
photography and the artificial ruin, deepening the historical character of a
landscape, a passage sidelined and accompanied by an illegible comment in his copy
of *On Photography* (p. 80). This takes us suggestively forward to Simon Ward's far-
reaching chapter on ruins (not of an artificial kind) and poetics in Sebald's work.[94]
Although Sebald does not mark in his copy of *Camera Lucida* the passage where
Barthes writes of photo-portraits of himself as 'a subject who feels he is becoming
an object: I then experience a micro-version of death (of parenthesis): I am truly
becoming a specter',[95] he does put in the margin, against Barthes's reference to St
Veronica's napkin, 'Ge = sp. bilder', which I take to be 'Gespensterbilder' [images
or photographs of ghosts].[96] Photography is, of course, intimately linked with the
presence of the double, and Sebald double-sidelines the passage in which Barthes
notes that 'the Photograph is the advent of myself as other: a cunning dissociation of

consciousness from identity',[97] and goes on to remark how odd it is that men had the most to say about the vision of the double before photography; in this respect, we actively repress photography's profound madness. And, as part of this meditation on photography and the double, Barthes expresses the wish for a History of Looking. Much has been written about looking in Sebald, not least apropos of the pairs of eyes which gaze out of *Unerzählt* and their earlier manifestation in the Nocturama in Antwerp,[98] or, earlier still, in the eyes of Henri Beyle and Angela Pietragrua.[99] Section 46 of *Camera Lucida* is an investigation of the photographic look, picking up its connection with the 'air', the subject of the previous section. The power of the photographic look lies in its withheldness, its being held back by its unreleased intensity; the sitter or subject looks at nothing with eyes nonetheless full of what is retained. Sebald triple-sidelines the sentences '[Now the Look, if it insists (all the more, if it lasts, if it] traverses, with the photograph, Time) — the Look is always potentially crazy: it is at once the effect of truth and [the effect of madness]' and '[But since all those patients still] look at me, nearly a hundred years later, I have the converse notion: that whoever looks you straight in the eye is mad'.[100]

(*d*) In *Camera Lucida* Barthes writes little, systematically, about the relationship between language and the photograph. But one thing he does say is that, while language is powerless to authenticate itself, is by nature fictional (an observation double-sidelined by Sebald),[101] the photograph 'is authentication itself' (underlined by Sebald). I am not sure that this is the most useful of oppositions, (i) because the camera itself generates its own kinds of inauthenticity, as Barthes himself admits, particularly in the posed portrait (Sebald double-sidelines Barthes's comment '[I do not stop imitating myself, and because of this, each time I] am (or let myself be) photographed, I invariably suffer from a sensation of inauthenticity, sometimes of impos-[ture (comparable to certain nightmares)]';[102] and (ii) because, even though text displaces the documentary towards the imaginary, the imaginary is, as we have said, as much authentic reality as the factual.

Notes to Chapter 9

1. Dominique Baqué, *La Photographie plasticienne: Un art paradoxal* (Paris: Éditions du Regard, 1998), p. 91.
2. Susan Sontag, *On Photography* (Harmondsworth: Penguin, 1982); John Berger, *About Looking*, (London: Writers and Readers, 1980); Roland Barthes, *Camera Lucida: Reflections on Photography*, trans. by Richard Howard (London: Fontana, 1984); Clive Scott, *The Spoken Image: Photography and Language* (London: Reaktion Books, 1999). Sebald's personal copies of the first three of these books are now in the Deutsches Literaturarchiv Marbach. I wish to thank Richard Sheppard and Jo Catling most warmly for making these annotations available to me and for alerting me to other, related lines of enquiry.
3. W. G. Sebald, review of Franz Hubmann, *Dream of Empire: The World of Germany in Original Photographs 1840–1914*, ed. by J. M. Wheatcroft, *Journal of European Studies*, 3 (1973), 286. See Primary Bibliography G.11.
4. Susan Sontag, *On Photography* (Harmondsworth: Penguin, 1982), pp. 107–08.
5. W. G. Sebald, *Austerlitz* (Munich: Hanser, 2001), p. 412; W. G. Sebald, *Austerlitz*, trans. by Anthea Bell (London: Hamish Hamilton, 2001), p. 410.
6. John Berger, preface to Timothy O'Grady and Steve Pyke, *I Could Read the Sky* (London: Harvill, 1997), unpaginated.

7. Martin Swales, 'Intertextuality, Authenticity, Metonymy? On Reading W. G. Sebald', in *The Anatomist of Melancholy: Essays in Memory of W. G. Sebald*, ed. by Rüdiger Görner (Munich: iudicium, 2003), pp. 81–87 (p. 83).

8. For the record, one might note Sebald's underlining of Barthes's choice of the word *Spectrum* to indicate the photographic subject and his explanatory reference to 'the return of the dead' (p. 9). He also underlines: 'I feel that the Photograph creates my body or mortifies it, according to its caprice' (p. 11), and double-sidelines the passage on the relationship between photography, the theatre, and death (pp. 31–32), which concludes: 'however "lifelike" we strive to make it [...], Photography is a kind of primitive theatre, a kind of *Tableau Vivant*, a figuration of the motionless and made-up face beneath which we see the dead.' He further double-sidelines Barthes's declaration that the photograph certifies 'that the corpse is alive, as corpse: it is the living image of a dead thing' (p. 79) and, further down the same page, the passage about the films of actors now dead: 'I can never see or see again in a film certain actors whom I know to be dead without a kind of melancholy: the melancholy of Photography itself (I experience this same emotion listening to the recorded voices of dead singers).' On page 84, where Barthes observes that photographic presence is as much of a metaphysical as of a political order, Sebald quotes Balzac in the margin: 'Je suis le colonel Chabert — celui qui est mort à Eylau', a reference which takes us forward to *Austerlitz*, where Vera finds in the pages of *Le Colonel Chabert* two photographs, one of the stage of a provincial theatre, the other of Austerlitz as pageboy; later Austerlitz turns to Vera's Balzac volumes, and to *Le Colonel Chabert* in particular, as a remedy against his frustrations with the new Bibliothèque nationale (*Austerlitz*, pp. 259–64 and 395–97; *Austerlitz*, trans. by Bell, pp. 256–60 and 393–95). Again, double-sidelining occurs where Barthes speaks of young photographers as the unwitting agents of Death, and of photography as the new social locus of Death: 'perhaps in this image which produces Death while trying to preserve life' (p. 92). And with Barthes's own disappearance, a second death will occur: the death of this mortifying photograph of his parents, the only photograph of them he has — 'for once I am gone, no one will any longer be able to testify to this [his parents' love for each other]: nothing will remain but an indifferent Nature' (p. 94), to which Sebald sardonically adds 'et même pas ça'. Every photograph brings an experience of the vertigo of time defeated (p. 97, double-sidelined) and, in doing so, imperiously predicts the death of the spectator (here Barthes himself) (p. 97, double-sidelined). And within this melancholy of Photography, in the love stirred by Photography, Barthes finds another core, another music, 'its name oddly old-fashioned: Pity' (p. 116, double-sidelined); in the action of *punctum* is the urge to enter the image and embrace what is dead, what is going to die, 'as Nietzsche did when, as Podach tells us, on January 3, 1889, he threw himself in tears on the neck of [double-sidelined] a beaten horse: gone mad for Pity's sake' (p. 117).

9. W. G. Sebald, 'Ein Versuch der Restitution', in *Campo Santo*, ed. by Sven Meyer (Munich: Hanser, 2003), pp. 240–48 (pp. 243–44); W. G. Sebald, 'An Attempt at Restitution', in *Campo Santo*, trans. by Anthea Bell (London: Hamish Hamilton, 2005), pp. 206–16 (p. 210).

10. Walter Benjamin, 'Little History of Photography', in *Selected Writings, II: 1927–1934*, ed. by Michael W. Jennings, Howard Eiland, and Gary Smith, trans. by Rodney Livingstone and others (Cambridge, MA: Belknap Press, 1999), pp. 507–30 (p. 510).

11. Sebald, review of Hubmann, *Dream of Empire*, p. 286.

12. Sontag is wrong, it seems to me, to suggest that images anaesthetize, that the photograph takes you from the more real to the less real (*On Photography*, p. 20). Sebald single-sidelines this passage, but his eye may have been more on Sontag's concomitant proposal that photographs corrupt conscience and the ability to be compassionate.

13. See Marianne Hirsch, *Family Frames: Photography, Narrative, and Postmemory* (Cambridge, MA: Harvard University Press, 1997), pp. 1–15.

14. W. G. Sebald, 'Zwischen Geschichte und Naturgeschichte: Über die literarische Beschreibung totaler Zerstörung', in *Campo Santo*, pp. 69–100 (p. 87); W. G. Sebald, 'Between History and Natural History: On the Literary Description of Total Destruction', in *Campo Santo*, trans. by Bell, pp. 68–101 (p. 87).

15. Alexander Rodchenko, 'Against the Synthetic Portrait, For the Snapshot, 1928', in *Russian Art of the Avant-Garde: Theory and Criticism 1902–1934*, ed. and trans. by John E. Bowlt (London: Thames and Hudson, 1988), pp. 250–54.

16. If we leave out of account the close-up of his right eye, which appears in the original German edition but neither in the English nor in the French translation.

17. W. G. Sebald, *Die Ausgewanderten* (Frankfurt a.M.: Eichborn, 1992), p. 278; W. G. Sebald, *The Emigrants*, trans. by Michael Hulse (London: Vintage, 2002), p. 186.

18. *Die Ausgewanderten*, p. 134; *The Emigrants*, p. 92.

19. Of the five words ringed in Sebald's copy of *Camera Lucida*, two relate to the drama of visual encounter: 'fulguration' (p. 49) and 'intensity' (p. 77). The other three, not surprisingly perhaps, are 'heimlich' (p. 40), 'metaphysical' (p. 84), and 'Jerusalem' (p. 97). Handwritten marginal comments in *Camera Lucida*, not discussed elsewhere, are: top margin, p. 51: 'Der doppelte Boden' [false floor]; p. 77, bottom margin: 'Die Zugbilder/Sehnsucht des Fortfahrenkönnens' (n and s run together) [images of trains/longing to be able to get away]; p. 79, bottom margin: 'Foto des Vaters beim Rechnen' [photo of father at his accounts]; p. 83, beneath Kertész's photograph of Ernest: 'Hemdbluse' [smock].

20. Scott, *The Spoken Image*, p. 24. Trauma has inevitably been a recurrent preoccupation in Sebaldian criticism. It is not the business of this piece to review that criticism. But, as a start, one might consult the essays collected in Part V ('Haunting, Trauma, Memory') of *W. G. Sebald: A Critical Companion*, ed. by J. J. Long and Anne Whitehead (Edinburgh: Edinburgh University Press, 2004), and Section 3 ('History and Trauma') of *W. G. Sebald: History — Memory — Trauma*, ed. by Scott Denham and Mark McCulloh (Berlin: de Gruyter, 2006). On the specific relationship between photography and trauma, see Ulrich Baer, *Spectral Evidence: The Photography of Trauma* (Cambridge, MA: MIT Press, 2002); and on the ways in which this relationship bears on Sebald, and on other aspects of photography and memory in Sebald's work, see, among others, Stefanie Harris, 'The Return of the Dead: Memory and Photography in W. G. Sebald's *Die Ausgewanderten*', *German Quarterly*, 74 (2001), 379–91; J. J. Long, 'History, Narrative, and Photography in W. G. Sebald's *Die Ausgewanderten*', *Modern Language Review*, 98 (2003), 117–37; Heiner Boehncke, 'Clair obscur: W. G. Sebalds Bilder', *Text + Kritik*, no. 158 (April 2003), 43–62; Markus R. Weber, 'Die fantastische befragt die pedantische Genauigkeit: Zu den Abbildungen in W. G. Sebalds Werken', *Text + Kritik*, no. 158 (April 2003), 63–74; Carolin Duttlinger, 'Traumatic Photographs: Remembrance and the Technical Media in W. G. Sebald's *Austerlitz*', in *W. G. Sebald*, ed. by Long and Whitehead, pp. 155–71; Richard Crownshaw, 'Reconsidering Postmemory: Photography, the Archive, and Post-Holocaust Memory in W. G. Sebald's *Austerlitz*', *Mosaic*, 37 (2004), 215–36; George Kouvaros, 'Images that Remember Us: Photography and Memory in *Austerlitz*', *Textual Practice*, 19 (2005), 173–93; Samuel Pane, 'Trauma Obscura: Photographic Media in W. G. Sebald's *Austerlitz*', *Mosaic*, 38 (2005), 37–54; Silke Horstkotte, 'Fantastic Gaps: Photography Inserted into Narrative in W. G. Sebald's *Austerlitz*', in *Science, Technology and the German Cultural Imagination*, ed. by Christian Emden and David Midgley (Berlin: Lang, 2005), pp. 269–86; Elizabeth Chaplin, 'The Convention of Captioning: W. G. Sebald and the Release of the Captive Image', *Visual Studies*, 21 (2006), 42–53; Maya Barzilai, 'On Exposure: Photography and Uncanny Memory in W. G. Sebald's *Die Ausgewanderten* and *Austerlitz*', in *W. G. Sebald*, ed. by Denham and McCulloh, pp. 205–18; and Lilian R. Furst, 'Realism, Photography, and Degrees of Uncertainty', in *W. G. Sebald*, ed. by Denham and McCulloh, pp. 219–29.

21. Scott, *The Spoken Image*, p. 25.

22. *The Spoken Image*, p. 24.

23. *The Spoken Image*, p. 24. There are two further definitions of *punctum* that are double-sidelined: '(the unpredictable penetration of the spectator by a particular visual detail)' (p. 24) and prescient lines from Larkin's 'Lines on a Young Lady's Photograph Album' (*The Less Deceived*, 1955): 'Or is it just *the past*? Those flowers, that gate, | These misty parks and motors, lacerate | Simply by being over' (p. 27). Sebald quadruple-sidelines the gloss that follows: 'These words take us straight to Barthes's *punctum*, the laceration of the spectator by a detail, or by the very pastness, the "that-has-been" of the photo' (p. 27).

24. Emmanuel Garrigues, *L'Écriture photographique: Essai de sociologie visuelle* (Paris: L'Harmattan, 2000), p. 67.

25. Barthes, *Camera Lucida*, p. 43.

26. *Camera Lucida*, p. 51.

27. 'Wie kommt es, daß man in einem anderen Menschen sich selber und wenn nicht sich selber, so doch seinen Vorgänger sieht? Daß ich dreiunddreißig Jahre nach Michael zum erstenmal durch den englischen Zoll gegangen bin, daß ich jetzt daran denke, meinen Lehrberuf aufzugeben, wie er es getan hat, daß er sich in Suffolk und ich mich in Norfolk mit dem Schreiben plage, daß wir beide den Sinn unserer Arbeit bezweifeln und daß wir beide an einer Alkoholallergie leiden, das ist nicht weiter verwunderlich. Aber warum ich gleich bei meinem ersten Besuch bei Michael den Eindruck gewann, als lebte ich oder als hätte ich einmal gelebt in seinem Haus, und zwar in allem geradeso wie er, das kann ich mir nicht erklären' [How is it one perceives oneself in another human being, or, if not oneself, then one's own precursor? The fact that I first passed through British customs thirty-three years after Michael, that I am now thinking of giving up teaching as he did, that I am bent over my writing in Norfolk and he in Suffolk, that we both are distrustful of our work and both suffer from an allergy to alcohol — none of these things are particularly strange. But why it was that on my first visit to Michael's house I instantly felt as if I lived or had once lived there, in every respect precisely as he does, I cannot explain] (*Die Ringe des Saturn: Eine englische Wallfahrt* (Frankfurt a.M.: Eichborn, 1995), pp. 227–28; *The Rings of Saturn*, trans. by Michael Hulse (London: Vintage, 1998), pp. 182–83).
28. Barthes, *Camera Lucida*, p. 40.
29. Sebald, review of Hubmann, *Dream of Empire*, p. 286.
30. Barthes, *Camera Lucida*, p. 84.
31. Scott, *The Spoken Image*, p. 32.
32. *The Spoken Image*, p. 33.
33. *The Spoken Image*, p. 34. Here, as elsewhere, square brackets within a quotation indicate text not sidelined.
34. *The Spoken Image*, p. 37.
35. Ibid.
36. Other, apparently less significant annotations in Chapter 1 are: (i) the single sidelining of the sentence 'Barthes pirouettes out of a tight spot' (p. 24); (ii) the double sidelining of one of the explanations for Barthes's choice of the photograph of his mother as he never knew her, namely the absence of the need 'to understand it as a *shared* experience' (p. 25); (iii) the double sidelining of '[the photograph endows the subject with] a peculiar sovereignty, as well as vulnerability' (p. 26); (iv) the double sidelining of 'The inevitable pastness of the photo, is, to Barthes, the source of its innate melancholy; photographs seem to give us what, in fact, they dispossess us of' (p. 27); (v) the encircling of the phrase 'turning aside' (p. 31); (vi) the single sidelining of 'The important thing is that the photograph as image has pretensions to style because of the painterly techniques it uses' (p. 36).
37. Scott, *The Spoken Image*, p. 231.
38. Sebald also single-sidelines comments about the flip album as an alternative to the book: 'Already the flip album destroys the narrative of the page, by removing the need to order and edit to the same degree, and by allowing greater variation in viewing speed. The photographs are no longer consecrated by "mounting"' (p. 232).
39. Scott, *The Spoken Image*, p. 235.
40. Sebald, *Die Ausgewanderten*, p. 60; *The Emigrants*, p. 40.
41. Sebald, *Austerlitz*, p. 417; *Austerlitz*, trans. by Bell, p. 415.
42. Scott, *The Spoken Image*, p. 235.
43. Ibid.
44. Sebald, *Austerlitz*, p. 264; *Austerlitz*, trans. by Bell, p. 260.
45. Scott, *The Spoken Image*, p. 236.
46. Sebald, *Austerlitz*, p. 216; *Austerlitz*, trans. by Bell, pp. 212–13.
47. Scott, *The Spoken Image*, p. 236.
48. Barthes, *Camera Lucida*, p. 103, quoted in Scott, *The Spoken Image*, p. 236.
49. Scott, *The Spoken Image*, p. 237.
50. *The Spoken Image*, p. 261.
51. Ibid.
52. This process is acted out by the body of Johannes Naegeli, held frozen in the Oberaar glacier for seventy-two years, but finally delivered up, not intact but as 'ein Häufchen geschliffener

Knochen und ein Paar genagelter Schuhe' [a few polished bones and a pair of hobnailed boots] (*Die Ausgewanderten*, p. 37; *The Emigrants*, p. 23).

53. Scott, *The Spoken Image*, p. 262.

54. W. G. Sebald, 'Wie Tag und Nacht: Über die Bilder Jan Peter Tripps', in Jan Peter Tripp, *Die Aufzählung der Schwierigkeiten: Arbeiten von 1985–92* (Offenburg: Reiff Schwarzwaldverlag, 1993), p. 57; repr. in W. G. Sebald, *Logis in einem Landhaus* (Munich: Hanser, 1998), pp. 169–88 (p. 173) (page references are to this edition).

55. W. G. Sebald, 'As Day and Night, Chalk and Cheese: On the Pictures of Jan Peter Tripp', in W. G. Sebald and Jan Peter Tripp, *Unrecounted*, trans. by Michael Hamburger (London: Hamish Hamilton, 2004), pp. 78–94 (p. 79).

56. 'Wie Tag und Nacht', p. 174; 'As Day and Night', p. 80.

57. Elinor Shaffer, 'W. G. Sebald's Photographic Narrative', in *The Anatomist of Melancholy*, ed. by Görner, pp. 51–62 (p. 51).

58. Sebald, 'Wie Tag und Nacht', p. 173; 'As Day and Night', pp. 79–80.

59. 'Wie Tag und Nacht', p. 174; 'As Day and Night', p. 80.

60. Sebald, review of Hubmann, *Dream of Empire*, p. 286.

61. Scott, *The Spoken Image*, p. 247.

62. Sebald, 'Kafka im Kino', in *Campo Santo*, pp. 193–209 (pp. 200–01); Sebald, 'Kafka Goes to the Movies', in *Campo Santo*, trans. by Bell, pp. 156–73 (p. 164).

63. Harris, 'The Return of the Dead', p. 383; Kouvaros, 'Images that Remember Us', pp. 184–89.

64. Siegfried Kracauer, *Das Ornament der Masse: Essays* (Frankfurt a.M.: Suhrkamp, 1977), pp. 28–29; Siegfried Kracauer, *The Mass Ornament: Weimar Essays*, ed. and trans. by Thomas Y. Levin (Cambridge, MA: Harvard University Press, 1995), pp. 53–54.

65. Sebald, review of Hubmann, *Dream of Empire*, p. 286.

66. 'Dennoch ist es mir bis heute, wenn ich Photographien oder dokumentarische Filme aus dem Krieg sehe, als stammte ich, sozusagen, von ihm ab und als fiele von dorther, von diesen von mir gar nicht erlebten Schrecknissen, ein Schatten auf mich, unter dem ich nie ganz herauskommen werde' [Yet to this day, when I see photographs or documentary films dating from the war I feel as I were its child, so to speak, as if those horrors I did not experience had cast a shadow over me, and one from which I shall never entirely emerge] (*Luftkrieg und Literatur: Mit einem Essay zu Alfred Andersch* (Frankfurt a.M.: Fischer, 2001), pp. 77–78; *On the Natural History of Destruction: With Essays on Alfred Andersch, Jean Améry and Peter Weiss*, trans. by Anthea Bell (London: Hamish Hamilton, 2003), p. 71).

67. W. G. Sebald, 'Das Geheimnis des rotbraunen Fells: Annäherung an Bruce Chatwin', in *Campo Santo*, pp. 215–22 (p. 222); W. G. Sebald, 'The Mystery of the Red-Brown Skin: An Approach to Bruce Chatwin', in *Campo Santo*, trans. by Bell, pp. 179–87 (p. 187).

68. Kracauer, *Das Ornament der Masse*, p. 32; Kracauer, *The Mass Ornament*, p. 56.

69. Scott, *The Spoken Image*, p. 243.

70. *The Spoken Image*, pp. 237–38.

71. Siegfried Kracauer, *Theory of Film: The Redemption of Physical Reality* (New York: Oxford University Press, 1960), pp. 19–20.

72. See Sebald, 'Ein Versuch der Restitution', in *Campo Santo*, pp. 240–48 (p. 243); 'An Attempt at Restitution', in *Campo Santo*, trans. by Bell, pp. 206–15 (p. 209).

73. Sebald, 'Wie Tag und Nacht', pp. 174–75; 'As Day and Night', p. 81.

74. 'Wie Tag und Nacht', p. 181; 'As Day and Night', pp. 86–88.

75. Sybille Ebert-Schifferer, 'Trompe l'Œil: The Underestimated Trick', in *Deceptions and Illusions: Five Centuries of Trompe-l'Œil Painting*, ed. by Sybille Ebert-Schifferer (Washington: National Gallery of Art, in association with Lund Humphries, 2002), p. 24.

76. We will remember the passage in Barthes (*Camera Lucida*, p. 99), double-sidelined by Sebald, which puts the amateur closer than the professional to the *noeme* of photography.

77. Barthes, *Camera Lucida*, p. 118.

78. *Camera Lucida*, p. 119.

79. Sebald, 'Wie Tag und Nacht', p. 184; 'As Day and Night', pp. 90–91.

80. 'Wie Tag und Nacht', p. 188; 'As Day and Night', p. 94.

81. Ibid.

82. In this connection, and remembering Tripp's etching of the eyes of Sebald's dog Maurice/ Moritz in *Unerzählt*, one might quote those lines from John Berger's essay 'Why Look at Animals?' (*About Looking* (London: Writers and Readers, 1980), pp. 1–26), underlined by Sebald: 'The animal scrutinises [man] across a narrow abyss of non-comprehension. [...] The man too is looking across a similar, but not identical, abyss of non-comprehension. And this is so wherever he looks. He is always looking across ignorance and fear' (p. 3). The non-comprehending reciprocal scrutiny of animal and human reappears in *Austerlitz*, in the observation of Marie de Verneuil: 'Sie sagte damals, was mir unvergeßlich geblieben ist, sagte Austerlitz, daß die eingesperrten Tiere und wir, ihr menschliches Publikum, einander anblickten à travers une brèche d'incomprehension' (*sic*) [said Austerlitz, she said something which I have never forgotten, she said that captive animals and we ourselves, their human counterparts, view one another *à travers une brèche d'incompréhension*] (p. 372; trans. by Bell, pp. 368–69)].

83. See W. G. Sebald, 'Helle Bilder und dunkle: Zur Dialektik der Eschatologie bei Stifter und Handke', *Manuskripte*, no. 84 (1984), 58–64; repr. in W. G. Sebald, *Die Beschreibung des Unglücks* (Frankfurt a.M.: Fischer, 1994), pp. 165–86 (p. 178).

84. Susan Sontag, *Regarding the Pain of Others* (London: Penguin, 2004), p. 76.

85. *Regarding the Pain of Others*, pp. 76–77.

86. *Regarding the Pain of Others*, p. 79.

87. Sontag expresses the view, in her essay on Sebald entitled 'A Mind in Mourning' (2000) (*Where the Stress Falls: Essays* (London: Jonathan Cape, 2002), pp. 41–48), that the photographs in *Vertigo* have 'the charm and, in many instances, the imperfections of relics'; that, in *The Emigrants*, they 'seem talismanic'; that, in *The Rings of Saturn*, 'they seem, less interestingly, merely illustrative' (p. 47).

88. Sontag, *Regarding the Pain of Others*, p. 80.

89. Berger, *About Looking*, p. 34. Further references to the essays in this collection are given in the text.

90. Barthes, *Camera Lucida*, p. 31.

91. François Soulages, *Esthétique de la photographie: La Perte et le reste* (Paris: Nathan, 1998), pp. 63–66.

92. Clément Rosset, *Fantasmagories suivi de Le Réel, l'imaginaire et l'illusoire* (Paris: Éditions de Minuit, 2006), p. 85.

93. W. G. Sebald, 'Westwärts–Ostwärts: Aporien deutschsprachiger Ghettogeschichten', *Literatur und Kritik*, 23, 233–34 (1989), 159–77; repr. in *Unheimliche Heimat* (Salzburg: Residenz, 1991), pp. 40–64 (Primary Bibliography D.46).

94. Simon Ward, 'Ruins and Poetics in the Works of W. G. Sebald', in *W. G. Sebald*, ed. by Long and Whitehead, pp. 58–71.

95. Barthes, *Camera Lucida*, p. 14.

96. *Camera Lucida*, p. 82.

97. *Camera Lucida*, p. 12.

98. Sebald, *Austerlitz*, p. 7; *Austerlitz*, trans. by Bell, p. 3.

99. W. G. Sebald, *Schwindel. Gefühle.* (Frankfurt a.M.: Eichborn, 1990), pp. 15–16; *Vertigo*, trans. by Michael Hulse (London: Harvill, 1999), pp. 11–12.

100. Barthes, *Camera Lucida*, p. 113.

101. *Camera Lucida*, p. 87.

102. *Camera Lucida*, p. 13.

FIG. 9.11. Jan Peter Tripp, 'W. G. Sebald' (1988), Kohle/Leinwand (charcoal on canvas).
© Jan Peter Tripp

CHAPTER 10

The Disappearance of the
Author in the Work

Some Reflections on W. G. Sebald's *Nachlass*
in the Deutsches Literaturarchiv Marbach

Ulrich von Bülow

Every literary *Nachlass* — the books and papers an author leaves behind — has its own distinct character. The form this takes is largely a matter of chance, since writers rarely think of organizing their papers for the benefit of posterity, and only a few try to influence the reception of their works by ordering their *Nachlass* in advance. Those who do, tend more or less naively to indicate those papers which they think are important, while work they do not like or which they consider a failure is designated accordingly — always assuming it is not simply destroyed out of hand.

W. G. Sebald's *Nachlass* is a special case; as this chapter will argue, it owes its unique character to the fact that Sebald's own fictional works are centrally concerned with the phenomenon of the *Nachlass* and what is left to posterity. It may be argued that even during his lifetime, Sebald considered his papers in terms of his future *Nachlass*: just as he consciously stylized himself in his works, so too he consciously selected what he would leave to the reading public. His twofold attitude to his *Nachlass* may be seen as an expression of his ambivalent attitude to his own literary persona.

In order to demonstrate this, this chapter will begin by examining the contexts in which *Nachlässe* and remains, whether literary or non-literary, feature in Sebald's work. It will then describe the way he preserved his own papers for posterity, examining what kinds of questions he encouraged and what kind of information he declined to provide.

I

From the outset, the topos of the *Nachlass* has an important and varied function throughout Sebald's fictional works. This goes beyond the classic narrative ploy whereby a narrator tells his readers how he came into the possession of another's papers, before reproducing them *in extenso* as though he were a mere disinterested editor: for Sebald's narrator(s), the topos of what is left behind (the *Nachlass*) is always bound up with questions of identity.

In the 'Elementargedicht' [elemental poem] *Nach der Natur* (*After Nature*), the ambitious explorer G. W. Steller attempts to learn something about the scientific researches of his predecessor, the 'Academy member' Daniel Messerschmidt. However:

> aus dem schwer
> melancholischen Menschen
> [hat er] nichts mehr herausbringen können.
> Dafür studiert er jetzt seinen Nachlaß.
> Einen ganzen Sommer verbringt er
> über die Zettelwirtschaft gebeugt [...].
>
> [[he] came too late
> to get anything out of
> the deeply melancholic man.
> Instead, he now studies his papers.
> He spends the whole summer
> bent over the jumble of cards.][1]

Steller's study of the *Nachlass* is, however, not merely research for its own sake; it also leads him to identify with the personality of the dead man — a process that finally leads him to propose marriage to Messerschmidt's widow and ask her to accompany him on his expedition.

In Sebald's prose works, too, the narrators have a pronounced interest in literary and non-literary remains alike. For instance, in 'Il ritorno in patria', the fourth part of *Schwindel. Gefühle.* (*Vertigo*), the first-person narrator spends time rummaging around in the attic of an old house in W[ertach] and pondering 'die mögliche Herkunft und Geschichte' [the possible provenance and history] of the things he finds there.[2] More deliberate and systematic by nature than Steller, he wishes to establish their possible 'provenance and history' because he is looking for tangible evidence of people particularly close to him during his childhood, who are thus connected with his own biography.

In *Die Ausgewanderten* (*The Emigrants*) the situation is even more complicated. In the third story, Sebald's researcher-narrator is entrusted by Tante Fini with the diary of his late relative, Great-Uncle Ambros Adelwarth, containing the entries from his journey to Jerusalem.[3] To his astonishment, the narrator is easily able to read the crabbed script, with which the reader has already become familiar via three illustrations:

> Die Entzifferung der winzigen, nicht selten zwischen mehreren Sprachen wechselnden Schrift [...] wäre wahrscheinlich nie von mir zuwege gebracht worden, hätten sich nicht die vor beinahe achtzig Jahren zu Papier gebrachten Zeilen sozusagen von selber aufgetan.
>
> [Deciphering his tiny handwriting, which not infrequently moved to and fro between several languages, was a [...] task [...] I should probably never had accomplished if those words committed to paper almost eighty years before had not, as it were, opened up of their own accord.][4]

We are dealing here not with a typically Sebaldian case of appropriation by assimilation, but with a knowing nod directed at those in the know: anyone familiar with

Sebald's handwriting will immediately recognize the writing shown in the journal illustrations as his own.[5]

The falsified document points to the paradoxical relationship between author and narrator. On the one hand, Sebald suggests they are one and the same by means of numerous 'authentic' citations and so enters into an 'autobiographical pact' with the reader.[6] On the other hand, however, this pact is consciously broken by an act of falsification of which only the author — but not his narrator — is aware. This ambivalent play on identity and difference is perfectly encapsulated in the narrator's remark that the handwriting in the journal appears to him at once strange and familiar.

One can also understand this falsification as an indicator of the contingent nature of any *Nachlass*. As the survival of what is passed down depends on chance, and as, in Aristotle's view, it is not the task of the narrator to communicate what actually happened but only what could have happened, it may have seemed natural to the author to lend chance a helping hand by fabricating a missing document whose erstwhile existence seemed to him at least plausible.

Similarly, Max Aurach / Max Ferber, the protagonist of the longest story in *Die Ausgewanderten*, carefully preserves the papers of those members of his family who are no more. So he does not simply hand over the 'nachgelassene[n] Blätter seiner Mutter' [pages of handwritten memoirs penned by his mother][7] to the narrator, he 'entrusts' them to his responsibility ('überantwortet'),[8] thereby stressing the ethical dimension that is involved in any dealings with another's *Nachlass*. The narrator then extensively cites the life story, reaching far back into the past, of a woman he had never met but whose story gripped him immediately and preoccupied him greatly ('auf das nachhaltigste').[9] The source or pre-text of the Luisa Lanzberg story is an unpublished text by a real person, Thea Frank-G[ebhardt]. Having tracked down the original manuscript, Klaus Gasseleder has recently shown that Sebald significantly reworked it to suit his own narrative purposes.[10] The reader, of course, knows nothing of this, and cannot therefore question whether such use of texts by others is legitimate.

The narrator of *Die Ringe des Saturn* (*The Rings of Saturn*) encounters many and various legacies and remains during the course of his travels, sometimes in unexpected form. In the first section, for instance, he pursues the wanderings of the skull of the Norwich physician and writer Sir Thomas Browne along a bewildering number of tortuous byways, citing as he does so, and not without irony, Browne's treatise on pre-Christian cremation and burial customs. For Browne, the funerary objects found in graves, rather than the human body itself, were the symbols of the 'Unzerstörbarkeit der menschlichen Seele' [indestructibility of the human soul][11] — 'remains' in a very real sense, which nevertheless held out the promise of immortality.

In Part II of *Die Ringe des Saturn*, the narrator considers the interior decoration and furnishings of Somerleyton Hall as the *Nachlass* of an entire family and is fascinated by its chance and unexpected aspects:

> Als ich an jenem Augustnachmittag [...] durch Somerleyton Hall gewandert
> bin, habe ich verschiedentlich an eine Pfandleihanstalt denken müssen oder

ein Brockenhaus. Aber gerade das Überzählige, gewissermaßen schon auf den Versteigerungstag Harrende der durch die Generationen angesammelten Dinge ist es gewesen, das mich eingenommen hat für diesen letzten Endes aus lauter Absurditäten bestehenden Besitz.

[As I strolled through Somerleyton Hall that August afternoon [...], I was variously reminded of a pawnbroker's or an auction hall. And yet it was the sheer number of things, possessions accumulated by generations and now waiting, as it were, for the day when they would be sold off, that won me over to what was, ultimately, a collection of oddities.][12]

This last sentence is characteristic of the relationship of the itinerant narrator to his objects (and subjects), for he regards the entire cultural landscape of East Anglia as the *Nachlass* or remains of a society and as an inheritance that, even as he tries to make it his own, fills him with increasingly ambivalent feelings.

In Sebald's last prose work, *Austerlitz*, legacies and things left behind have a particular significance, inasmuch as Jacques Austerlitz's doubts regarding his own identity clearly go hand in hand with his almost complete lack of familial inheritance. From his adoptive father he has inherited not much more than a little book of sermons,[13] while everything once owned by his real parents in Prague ('die gesamte Hinterlassenschaft') was confiscated by the Germans after the annexation of Czechoslovakia.[14] During his strenuous and time-consuming researches into his past, Austerlitz acquires, thanks to a fortunate coincidence, two more photographs which probably belonged to his parents, one of which shows him as a five-year-old child.[15] Featured both in the book and on its dust jacket, this visual relic reveals to Austerlitz his true identity, up to then buried beneath the rubble of history — even though the picture, ironically enough, shows a boy in disguise for a fancy-dress ball.

The close connection between *Nachlass* and photography in Sebald's work can be explained both in terms of Sebald's particular affinity with the latter medium and by the nature of photography itself (see Chapter 9 of the present volume). Photographs are both authentic traces of human beings at one particular moment in time and snapshots in which time stands still, and these features are also characteristic of any given *Nachlass*. The totality of things owned by any given individual is in a constant state of flux throughout his or her life; new papers and objects are constantly acquired, while others are lost, sold, or thrown away. This process of flux ceases only at death, hence the term *Nachlass*: literally something left behind. As with photographs, such remains suddenly become a static constellation of unrelated elements. Like the details of a photographic image, these things have their own origins and history and so possess considerable narrative potential. These parallels serve to explain the aesthetic significance of both photographs and *Nachlässe* in Sebald's works.

Those who concern themselves frequently with photographs will, from time to time, conceive of themselves as photographic objects; and anyone thinking about phenomena connected with literary remains may well, by analogy, be inclined to think of their own papers in terms of a potential *Nachlass*. This kind of thinking exactly corresponds to the way in which Sebald the writer achieves aesthetic distance. This takes the form not only of spatial distancing by such means as 'levitation'; more particularly, a temporal distance is also achieved by looking back on the present from a standpoint of '*outre-tombe*'.[16] Seen from this perspective, the things one owns may appear as a *Nachlass* even during one's own lifetime.

For all their interest in the *Nachlässe* of others, none of Sebald's protagonists, all of whom are characterized by a will to self-extinction ('Selbstauslöschung'), evinces any desire to leave anything to posterity:

> Eines Abends, sagte Austerlitz, habe ich meine sämtlichen gebündelten und losen Papiere, die Notizbücher und Notizhefte, die Aktenordner und Vorlesungsfaszikel, alles, was bedeckt war mit meiner Schrift, aus dem Haus getragen, am unteren Ende des Gartens auf den Komposthaufen geworfen und schichtweise mit verrottetem Laub und ein paar Schaufeln Erde bedeckt.

> [One evening, said Austerlitz, I gathered up all my papers, bundled or loose, my notepads and exercise books, my files and lecture notes, anything with my writing on it, and carried the entire collection out of the house to the far end of the garden, where I threw it on the compost heap and buried it under layers of rotted leaves and spadefuls of earth.][17]

But Austerlitz's hoped-for release from the 'burden weighing down on my life' ('Last meines Lebens')[18] does not come about, a conclusion that points to a fundamental contradiction in Sebald's work. Where, on the one hand, Sebald's characters aspire to a state of self-extinction, on the other hand they want to tell the story of their lives; in other words, to leave something behind. As a result, the narrator is implicitly faced with an ethical problem, for whoever narrates the story of a person who quite explicitly desires erasure of his or her own being is not, it would seem, acting in that person's interests.

This ambivalence, the paradoxical desire to hand on yet not to hand on, can also express itself in the way one views one's own papers. The most celebrated case is probably that of Franz Kafka, who left his friend Max Brod with the instruction to burn all his manuscripts. But had Kafka really wanted this to happen, he would have destroyed the papers himself. Brod recognized this ambivalence and preserved the manuscripts in order to publish them himself. Oddly enough, Sebald, though frequently referring to Kafka in his academic and fictional work, nowhere commented on this apparent paradox.[19]

II

Sebald's literary *Nachlass*, which has been housed in the DLA since 2004, consists in the main of the contents of sixty-eight box files, labelled and thus to some extent authorized by Sebald himself: these, we can assume, are the papers he wanted to leave to posterity (Figure 10.1). In addition, the *Nachlass* contains a few assorted papers from his study on which he had been working just before his death, some pictures, a series of appointments diaries, and his working library, which has also been acquired by the Marbach archive.[20]

The papers preserved by Sebald for posterity relate almost exclusively to his work as a writer. There is surprisingly little in the way of correspondence, and those letters which are extant are almost entirely devoid of personal information. Apart from correspondence with publishers, editors, archivists, and other people who could provide him with source material, Sebald mainly kept letters from critics

FIG. 10.1. Sebald's box files. © DLA Marbach (Chris Korner)

and readers seeking to set him straight on factual matters or attempting to enlarge on the subject matter of his books by telling him their own life stories. Sebald's readership, it seems, was rarely inclined to separate fact from fiction.

While Sebald's *Nachlass* tells us little about his private life, his papers do document in detail the origins and reception of his works. He made a particular point of archiving material relating to his four major works of prose fiction. In many cases he also preserved the sources he drew on: newspaper cuttings, photocopies of passages from books, photographs and correspondence relating to his research — and this allows us to reconstruct their archival origins and intertextual relationships to a considerable, not to say unusual degree. Whereas some authors write down their texts in a connected, linear fashion, correct what they have written, and then produce a fresh draft, Sebald began his work less by planning his text as a whole and more by chiselling away at individual sentences.

Clearly he was a 'Papierarbeiter' who liked working with paper, trying out sentences on paper — and sometimes, even, in books — in pencil, felt-tip pen, or biro until they had taken on a provisional shape with which he was happy. Thereafter he would type them out, frequently making further amendments before copying them out again. Often he would use a fresh sheet of paper for each sentence. This non-linear, concentrated way of working means that there exist many drafts and variants of some passages — for example the opening pages of *Die Ringe des Saturn* (Figure 10.2) — but only one of others. Only once he had constructed all

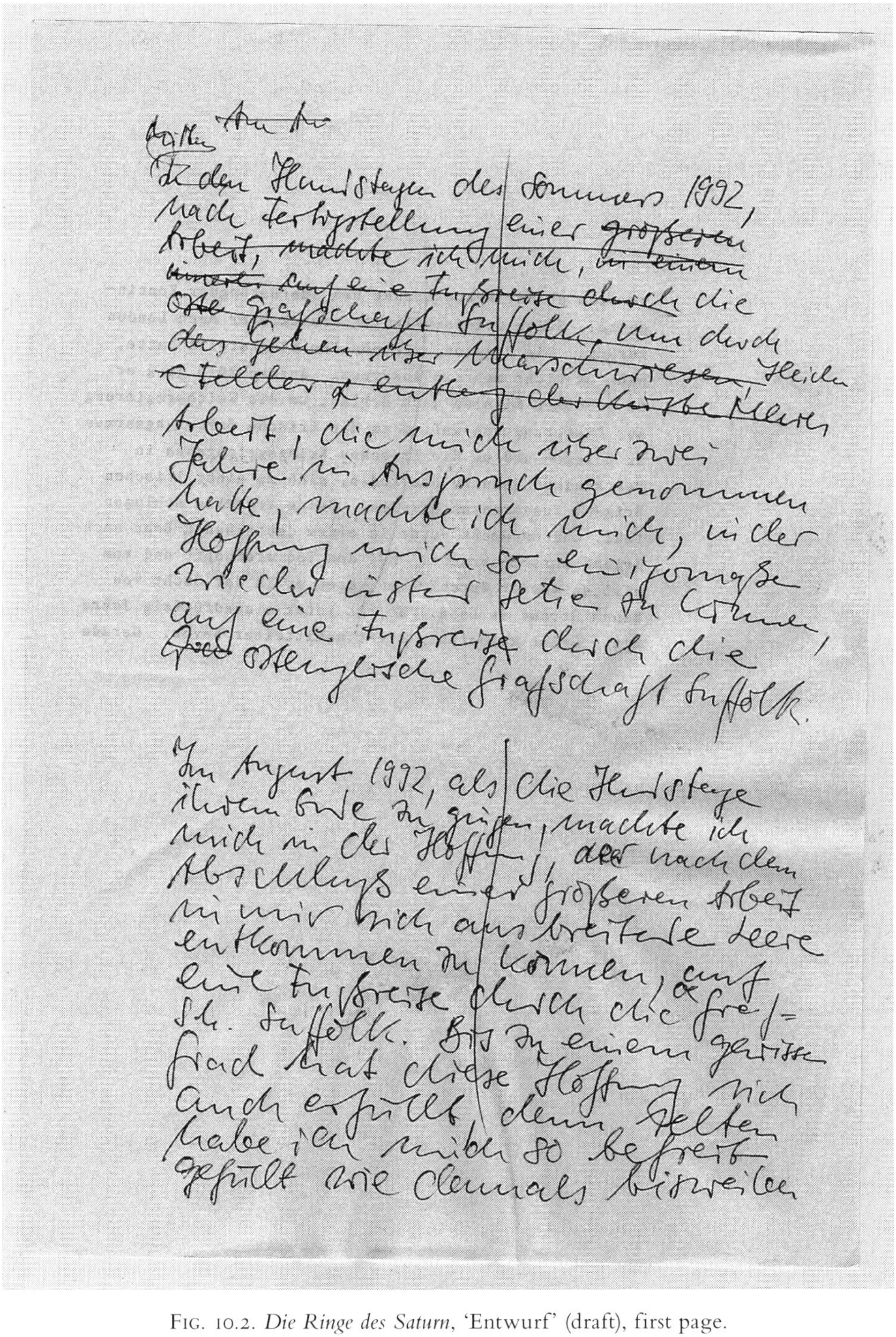

FIG. 10.2. *Die Ringe des Saturn*, 'Entwurf' (draft), first page.
© The Estate of W. G. Sebald; courtesy of DLA Marbach

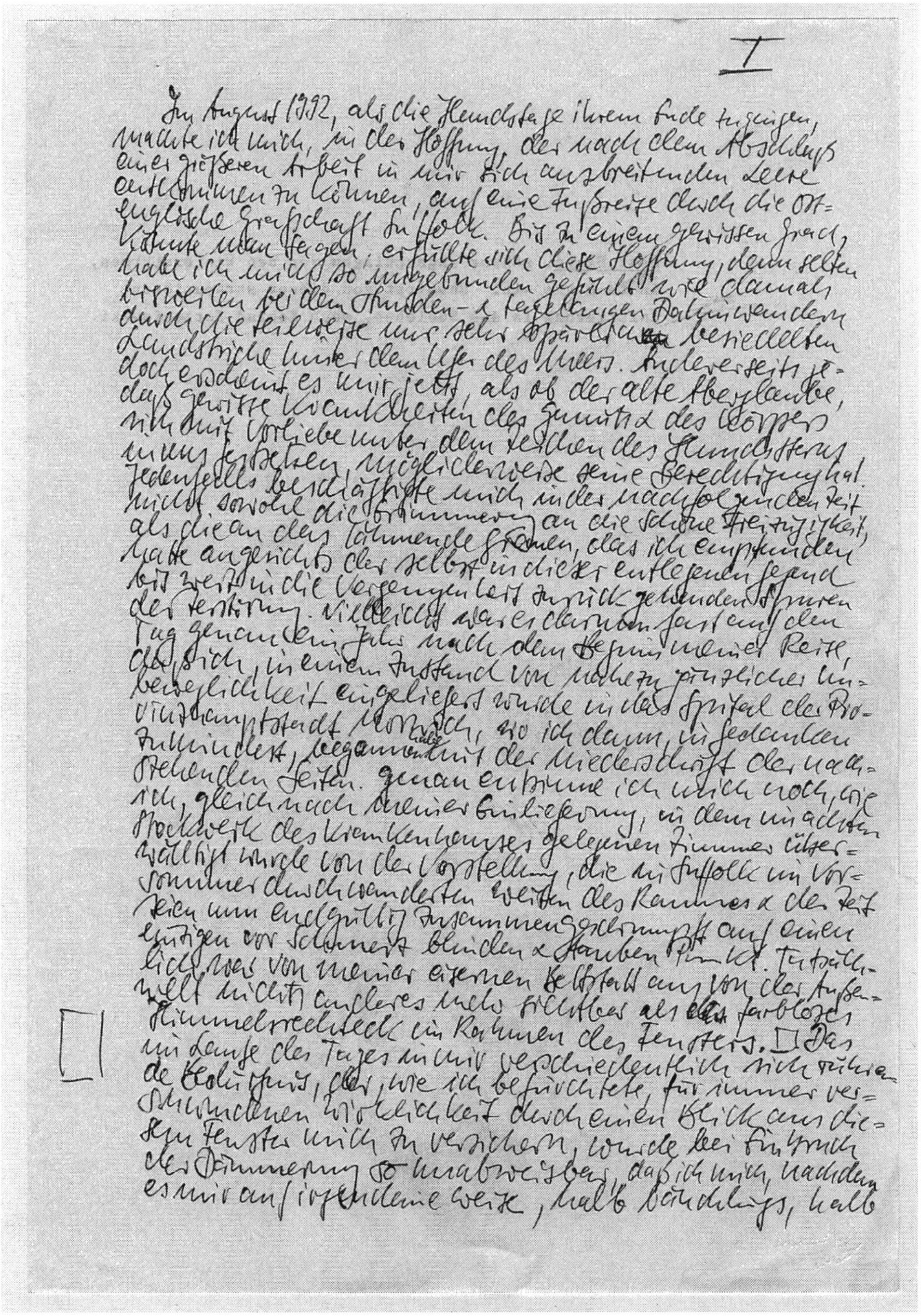

FIG. 10.3. *Die Ringe des Saturn*, 'Handschrift' (manuscript), first page.
© The Estate of W. G. Sebald; courtesy of DLA Marbach

his sentences did Sebald assemble them into a continuous longhand draft, usually on lined paper, amending and correcting as he went along. This first consecutive version of the text — designated by the author, in a laconically ironic gesture, as the 'Handschrift' (manuscript) — scarcely differs from the printed text, with places where images are to be inserted already indicated by symbols (Figure 10.3).

Sebald rarely bothered to preserve the subsequent typescript versions, which usually involve only minor corrections of detail. However, some typescript pages do survive, as he was wont to recycle them as scrap paper, drafting new works on the back. Accordingly, there are also only a few sets of proofs in the DLA, except in the case of *Austerlitz*, where he retained two sets of proofs for purposes of documentation. Sebald had calculated very precisely where the illustrations were to go in relation to the text, but the typesetter omitted to ensure that the printed pages conformed to those of the typescript. Consequently the first set of proofs was unusable, and the book had to be reset.[21]

The folders of material relating to Sebald's prose works often contain several identical series of illustrations for use in subsequent editions of his books with his various publishers. In many cases he gave them the choice of alternative photographs, differing somewhat in size and shape, and this helps explain why the illustrations in the various editions — and translations — are not always identical.[22]

The manuscript versions of the various translations — which Sebald always stored with particular care — are especially informative. Although Sebald's command of English was well-nigh perfect, and although he had founded the British Centre for Literary Translation at UEA in 1989 and, indeed, directed it for five years, he did not, as is well known, translate his books himself. Nonetheless, he worked over his translators' manuscripts so extensively — in part with the help of the then secretary to the UEA German Sector, Beryl Ranwell (see Figure 7.2, p. 192) — as to be considered a co-translator at the very least (Figure 10.4). So it seems probable that the unmistakeable 'Sebald-sound' was recreated in the ears of his anglophone readers by means of the interaction of the native English translator, preoccupied with accuracy and 'correct' English, and a German-speaking author trying, by means of his interventions, to do justice to the idiosyncrasies of his particular brand of German. It is noticeable that the French typescripts attracted far fewer interventions, and that he suggested fewer still in the Italian translations. For each of his major works in the Marbach *Nachlass* he also kept box files containing reviews of his work sent in by his literary agent and publishers from all over the world. There is very often no sign of his having read them; many are still in the envelopes in which they arrived.

Sebald, though, was far less punctilious when it came to preserving materials relating to his other books. The manuscripts of his poetry, even including *Nach der Natur* (*After Nature*), were housed in only three box files, consisting in the main of typescripts and carbon copies. The same applies to his critical essays, speeches, and interviews. Drafts of plays and an early (unpublished) novel exist mainly as typescripts. There is, however, a large amount of material relating to *Luftkrieg und Literatur* (*On the Natural History of Destruction*): photocopied pages from books, and numerous letters from mainly critical readers pointing out sources he has overlooked, and which, indeed, they sometimes enclose.

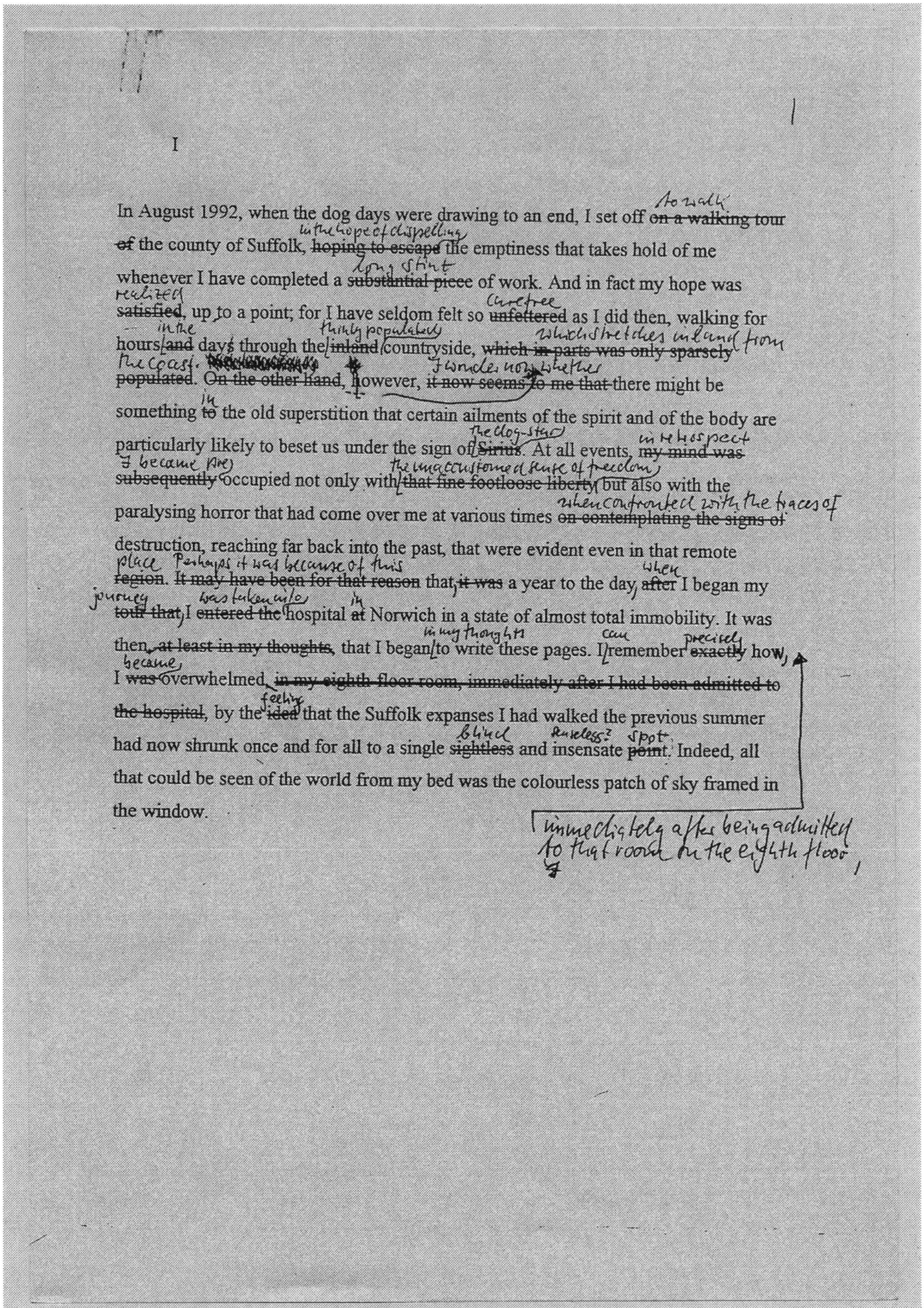

I

In August 1992, when the dog days were drawing to an end, I set off on a walking tour of the county of Suffolk, hoping to escape the emptiness that takes hold of me whenever I have completed a substantial piece of work. And in fact my hope was satisfied, up to a point; for I have seldom felt so unfettered as I did then, walking for hours and days through the inland countryside, which in parts was only sparsely populated. On the other hand, however, it now seems to me that there might be something to the old superstition that certain ailments of the spirit and of the body are particularly likely to beset us under the sign of Sirius. At all events, my mind was subsequently occupied not only with that fine footloose liberty but also with the paralysing horror that had come over me at various times on contemplating the signs of destruction, reaching far back into the past, that were evident even in that remote region. It may have been for that reason that it was a year to the day after I began my tour that I entered the hospital at Norwich in a state of almost total immobility. It was then, at least in my thoughts, that I began to write these pages. I remember exactly how, I was overwhelmed, in my eighth floor room, immediately after I had been admitted to the hospital, by the idea that the Suffolk expanses I had walked the previous summer had now shrunk once and for all to a single sightless and insensate point. Indeed, all that could be seen of the world from my bed was the colourless patch of sky framed in the window.

FIG. 10.4. *Die Ringe des Saturn*, 'English translation Michael Hulse, amendments Beryl Ranwell, Max Sebald, Nov. 96–Sep. 97', first page.
© The Estate of W. G. Sebald; courtesy of DLA Marbach

A further few boxes, labelled, like the others, by Sebald himself, contained materials relating to other unfinished or abandoned book projects. As these materials seem to be particularly extensive, this probably indicates that the author still intended to make use of them. After ceasing work on his Corsica project, Sebald published several extracts in books and periodicals during his lifetime and these, together with a hitherto unpublished extract, were published posthumously in *Campo Santo* in 2003.[23] Besides much documentary material, the *Nachlass* also contains two longish prose pieces relating to Corsica: a diary version of his narrator's journey and a prose version which grew out of the diary version. Taken together, these show how Sebald interwove factual and fictional material at every stage (see Figure 10.5).[24] While Sebald's diarist-narrator arrives in Corsica on a scheduled flight, the narrator of the prose version flies there in a private aircraft belonging to a friend called Gerald Ashman: during the journey Ashman recounts the story of his life in considerable detail.[25] Various elements of this story would make their way into *Austerlitz*, albeit in a different form and with times and places changed to suit the new context. Whereas in the Corsica fragment the pilot refers to his property Andromeda Lodge, in the vicinity of Norwich,[26] in *Austerlitz* a country house of the same name, where the protagonist had stayed in his youth, is situated near the Welsh coast;[27] moreover, the interior decoration of the Lodge described in the Corsica fragment is transposed, in *Austerlitz*, to a mansion called Iver Grove near Oxford, whose owner is one James Mallord Ashman.[28] Similarly, a travelling circus in Corsica which had made an impression on Sebald's diarist on 4 September 1995 turns up again in *Austerlitz* — this time in an industrial area of Paris located between the Gare d'Austerlitz and the Quai d'Austerlitz.[29]

Such transpositions of motifs and episodes are characteristic of Sebald's way of working. The patchy, incomplete biographies that he narrates derive from many heterogeneous sources and combine semi-authentic fragments of reality in a way that has more to do with aesthetic than with historic criteria. Sebald referred in an interview to Claude Lévi-Strauss's concept of 'bricolage' to describe his way of working,[30] and his sister recalls him comparing it to the patchwork method involved in making a 'Fleckerlteppich' or rag-rug.[31]

Two of the box files contained materials relating to Sebald's last project, which he usually designated with the letters W[orld] W[ar]; most of the papers found on his desk after his death also relate to this project. Although there is little in the way of actual drafts, there exist a considerable number of preliminary studies, extracts from historical accounts and copies of archival documents. In his application to NESTA (the National Endowment for Science, Technology and the Arts) of early 2000 Sebald described this project as follows:

> My intention is to research for and begin with the drawing of an extensive narrative which will encompass the period 1900–1950. Several of my forebears will pass review, among them Rudolf Egelhofer, commander of the Red Army at the time of the Munich Soviet, who was murdered in 1919 by the right-wing free corps. The 'éducation sentimentale', under the fascist regime, of the social class to which my parents belonged will be another prominent topic, as will be my father's progress during the war and the post-war years which were the years of my childhood. I should point out that the form this will take is *not* that

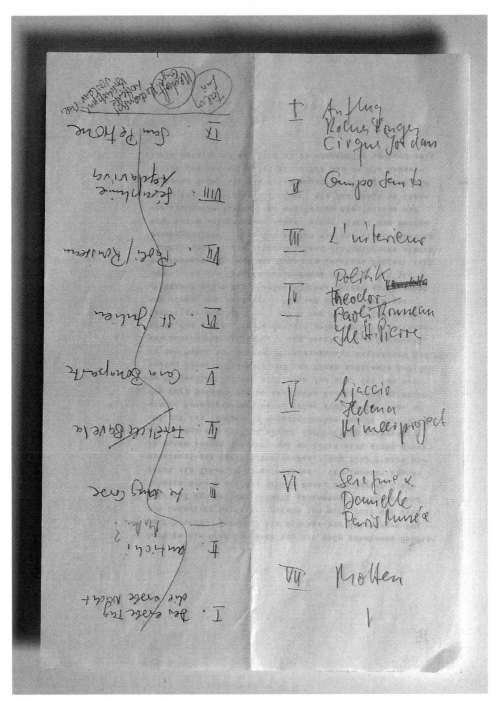

FIG. 10.5. From the dossier 'Aufzeichnungen aus Korsika: Zur Natur- und Menschenkunde'
(Notes from Corsica: On its Anthropology and Ecology). Plans for chapter outline.
© The Estate of W. G. Sebald; courtesy of DLA Marbach

of (auto)biography; it will be more like the semi-documentary prose fiction for which I have become known. Accounts of the process of research will also be included as integral parts of the narrative.

Part of his research plans involved field trips to Sonthofen,

where I grew up and where the Nazis, soon after seizing power, built the *Ordensburg*, a school designated to promote the formation of a new fascist elite. Further I intend to visit places through which my father passed between the so-called Polish campaign and his time as a prisoner of war in France.

The collected material, notes, and excerpts seem, however, to suggest that the focus of Sebald's project shifted in the course of his research, with the Franco-German conflicts between 1870 and 1945, and especially the military operations in the Saint-Quentin area, moving centre stage. In one of the two short drafts relating to the project, the narrator visits a long-standing French friend called Sophie in the mill at Berthenicourt, just to the south-east of Saint-Quentin, where he is given access to her grandfather's diary to read about his experiences during the Great War. The narrator's research into his own ancestors, which takes him, among other places, to the *Kriegsarchiv* in Munich, suggests that Sebald was probably planning a parallel account, using the experiences of German (as well as French) soldiers; no doubt, as always in Sebald's *oeuvre*, chance events and coincidences would have played an important part in the narrative.

It is scarcely possible to reconstruct what the overall structure of the work was intended to have been. Most of the excerpted material is drawn from French, German, and English eyewitness accounts from World War I; possibly it was also conceived as a kind of alternative to Ernst Jünger's heroic war diary, *In Stahlgewittern* (*Storm of Steel*), published in 1920. As well as family trees and papers relating to real-life ancestors of his, the *Nachlass* contains a loose sheet of paper juxtaposing real people with projected fictional characters — a clear example of the way in which, in this project too, Sebald intended to adapt factual, documentary material to suit his compositional and aesthetic purpose (see Figure 10.6). Because the author was still evidently engaged in collecting source material, the outlines of the plot and the main characters had not been finalized. Other than a few books and photocopies dealing with the *Ordensburg* in Sonthofen, there are almost no documents relating to World War II preserved among this material. Nevertheless, notwithstanding the early stage of the project, the assembled source material is far more extensive than the preliminary materials for his published works preserved in the *Nachlass*. From this one may deduce that, on completion of a given work, Sebald normally preserved only a fraction of his source material for archival purposes.

Nearly everything in Sebald's *Nachlass*, then, relates to specific books and projects, with the exception of a card index (probably relating to his early academic work) and some photographs and pictures from his study (e.g. Figures 10.7 and 11.1, p. 343).

III

If one assumes that Sebald made a conscious choice about what he wanted to preserve for posterity, it is very striking how little in the way of private and personal

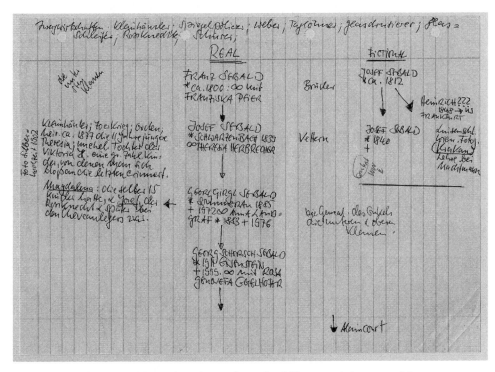

FIG. 10.6. Unnumbered page from the folder containing material
for the 'WW' project showing 'real' and 'fictional' family trees.
© The Estate of W. G. Sebald; courtesy of DLA Marbach

material is to be found in the *Nachlass*. Why is it that his papers relate almost
exclusively to his work, especially to the genesis of his four major works of prose
fiction? As a literary scholar, Sebald was well aware of the use to which editors and
researchers are apt to put a writer's *Nachlass*. Indeed, in his own essays on other
writers he himself used posthumously published letters and diaries to shed light
on his subjects' hidden psychology and so to interpret their works. So perhaps he
exscinded all personal information to prevent others from applying this method to
his own work.

Modesty scarcely seems to have been the motivation, if one considers how
frequently and consciously Sebald endowed his narrators and characters with his own
features and character traits. Yet the very fact that he was continually transforming
himself into literature could be the reason underlying his extraordinary discretion.
The figure of the author is inextricably entwined into his texts by means of narrative
devices, documentary material, and quotations and allusions interwoven in the
text by means of projections and analogies. He reinvented himself anew in each
book; the aesthetic configurations were always also a means of self-representation.
This was, ultimately, the only way in which he wanted to be remembered by
posterity. Seen in this light, W. G. Sebald's *Nachlass* is an expression of his aesthetic
existence.

Translated from the German by Richard Sheppard/Jo Catling

FIG. 10.7. Photograph framed and captioned by Sebald:
'Cave canem or Which of these twelve is the odd one out?'
© The Estate of W. G. Sebald; courtesy of DLA Marbach

Notes on Chapter 10

1. W. G. Sebald, *Nach der Natur* (Nördlingen: Greno, 1988), p. 44; *After Nature*, trans. by Michael Hamburger (London: Hamish Hamilton, 2003), p. 51.

2. W. G. Sebald, *Schwindel. Gefühle.* (Frankfurt a.M.: Fischer, 2005), p. 247; *Vertigo*, trans. by Michael Hulse (London: Harvill, 1999), p. 226.

3. W. G. Sebald, *Die Ausgewanderten* (Frankfurt a.M.: Eichborn, 1992), p. 186 (cf. the illustrations on pp. 187, 194–95, and 200–01); *The Emigrants*, trans. by Michael Hulse (London: Harvill, 1997), p. 126 (cf. the illustrations on pp. 127, 132, and 135).

4. *Die Ausgewanderten*, p. 188; *The Emigrants*, pp. 126–28.

5. The description of the fictional journey consists partly of paraphrase or quotations from François-René de Chateaubriand, *Itinéraire de Paris à Jérusalem*. Sebald's copy (Paris: Garnier-Flammarion, 1968) is preserved in the Deutsches Literaturarchiv Marbach (DLA).

6. Cf. Philippe Lejeune, *Le Pacte autobiographique* (Paris: Éditions du Seuil, 1975).

7. *Die Ausgewanderten*, p. 289; *The Emigrants*, p. 192.

8. *Die Ausgewanderten*, p. 327; the published English translation reads 'handed them over to me' (*The Emigrants*, p. 218).

9. *Die Ausgewanderten*, p. 327; *The Emigrants*, p. 218.

10. See Klaus Gasseleder, 'Erkundungen zum Prätext der Luisa-Lanzberg-Geschichte aus W. G. Sebalds *Die Ausgewanderten*: Ein Bericht', in *Sebald. Lektüren.*, ed. by Marcel Atze and Franz Loquai (Eggingen: Isele, 2005), pp. 157–75 (especially p. 173).

11. W. G. Sebald, *Die Ringe des Saturn* (Frankfurt a.M.: Eichborn, 1995), p. 38; *The Rings of Saturn*, trans. by Michael Hulse (London: Harvill, 1998), p. 26.

12. *Die Ringe des Saturn*, p. 49–50; *The Rings of Saturn*, p. 36.

13. Cf. W. G. Sebald, *Austerlitz* (Munich: Hanser, 2001), pp. 69–71 and 76–77; *Austerlitz*, trans. by Anthea Bell (London: Penguin, 2001), pp. 65–66 and 72–73.

14. Cf. *Austerlitz*, p. 259; *Austerlitz*, trans. by Bell, pp. 254–55.

15. *Austerlitz*, pp. 262–64; *Austerlitz*, trans. by Bell, pp. 258–60.

16. In *Die Ringe des Saturn*, Sebald quotes extensively from Chateaubriand's *Mémoires d'outre-tombe*. His copy (Paris: Librairie Générale Française, 1973) is preserved in the DLA.

17. *Austerlitz*, p. 180; *Austerlitz*, trans. by Bell, p. 176.

18. Ibid.

19. The exception to this being a remark in an interview with Toby Green for Amazon in 1999: Green: '[Kafka]'s a rarity because he didn't want to be published.' Sebald: 'But he couldn't bring himself to burn the stuff' ('The Questionable Business of Writing', interview with Toby Green, recorded late 1999). See Primary Bibliography J.31. (Eds)

20. See Chapter 11 of this volume, where Jo Catling discusses Sebald's *Bibliotheca abscondita*, and the Catalogue of Sebald's library (Part II, pp. 377–441).

21. I am grateful to Sebald's *Lektor*, Wolfgang Matz of the Hanser Verlag, for providing me with this information.

22. See Lise Patt, 'Introduction: Searching for Sebald: What I Know for Sure', in *Searching for Sebald: Photography after W. G. Sebald*, ed. by Lise Patt and Christel Dillbohner (Los Angeles: Institute of Cultural Inquiry, 2007), pp. 16–97 (especially pp. 39–41), and Carsten Strathausen, 'Going Nowhere: Sebald's Rhizomatic Travels', in *Searching for Sebald*, ed. by Patt, pp. 472–91 (especially pp. 485–86); see also Chapter 9 of this volume, where Clive Scott discusses Sebald's use of photography.

23. See W. G. Sebald, *Campo Santo*, ed. by Sven Meyer (Munich: Hanser, 2003); W. G. Sebald, *Campo Santo*, trans. by Anthea Bell (London: Penguin, 2006). The 'Corsican' pieces are 'Kleine Exkursion nach Ajaccio' ('A Little Excursion to Ajaccio'); 'Die Alpen im Meer' ('The Alps in the Sea'); '*La cour de l'ancienne école*'; and the hitherto unpublished eponymous piece 'Campo Santo'; to which one might add 'Moments musicaux'; cf. Primary Bibliography E.B.30–E.B.32 and D.75 (Eds).

24. W. G. Sebald, 'Aufzeichnungen aus Korsika: Zur Natur- & Menschenkunde', edited on the basis of the manuscript by Ulrich von Bülow, in *Wandernde Schatten: W. G. Sebalds Unterwelt*, ed. by

Ulrich von Bülow, Heike Gefrereis, and Ellen Strittmatter (Marbach am Neckar: Deutsche Schillergesellschaft, 2008), pp. 129–209 (1st draft, pp. 129–58; 2nd draft, pp. 159–209).

25. W. G. Sebald, 'Aufzeichnungen aus Korsika', p. 129; pp. 166–75. Sebald also makes use of some of these details in the text he wrote for the Heinrich Böll Prize in 1997, where Andromeda Lodge and Seething airfield recur; in this text the pilot's name is Gerald Aylmer. See W. G. Sebald, 'Feuer und Rauch: Über eine Abwesenheit in der deutschen Nachkriegsliteratur', *Frankfurter Rundschau*, 29 November 1997; see also Primary Bibliography D.66. The piece is reprinted in Part II of the present volume, pp. 338–42.

26. 'Aufzeichnungen aus Korsika', pp. 159–63.

27. *Austerlitz*, pp. 117–19; *Austerlitz*, trans. by Bell, pp. 113–15.

28. *Austerlitz*, pp. 150–57; *Austerlitz*, trans. by Bell, pp. 146–53.

29. 'Aufzeichnungen aus Korsika', pp. 183–88; *Austerlitz*, pp. 383–85; *Austerlitz*, trans. by Bell, pp. 380–84.

30. See W. G. Sebald, 'Wildes Denken', interview with Sigrid Löffler, *Profil*, 19 April 1993, p. 106. Sebald's books in the DLA include the Suhrkamp paperback translation of Lévi-Strauss's *La Pensée sauvage* (*Das wilde Denken*) (1973): on p. 29 'bricolage' ('Bastelei') is heavily underlined. See also Chapter 6 of this volume, where Uwe Schütte discusses Sebald's critical use of this concept.

31. '"Ein Fleckerlteppich": Interview von Ruth Vogel-Klein mit Gertrud Th. Aebischer-Sebald', in *W. G. Sebald: Mémoire. Transferts. Images / Erinnerung. Übertragungen. Bilder*, ed. by Ruth Vogel-Klein (= *Recherches Germaniques*, special issue 2 (2005)), pp. 211–20 (p. 217).

The Old Rectory, Upgate, Poringland, Norfolk NR14 7SH

28 ᵗᵘ 2000

[handwritten letter in German cursive]

FIG. 11.1. W. G. Sebald, 'Favourite books', in response to a request from the Buchhandlung zum Wetzstein, Salzstrasse 31, Freiburg, for their window display. The books named here are as follows: John Berger, *Ways of Seeing*; Robert Walser, *Aus dem Bleistiftgebiet*; Vladimir Nabokov, *Sprich Erinnerung (Speak, Memory)*; Ernst Herbeck, *Alexander*; Giorgio Bassani, *Brille mit Goldrand*; John Aubrey, *Lebensentwürfe (Brief Lives)*; Thomas Bernhard, *Wittgensteins Neffe*; Adalbert Stifter, *Aus der Mappe meines Urgroßvaters*; Bohumil Hrabal, *Schöntrauer-Trilogie*; Heinrich von Kleist, *Die Marquise von O.*; Gustave Flaubert, *Drei Erzählungen (Trois Contes)*; Georges Perec, *W oder Erinnerung einer Kindheit (W ou le souvenir d'enfance)*; Johann Peter Hebel, *Kalendergeschichten*; Claude Simon, *[Le] Jardin des Plantes*. © The Estate of W. G. Sebald; courtesy of Thomas Bader (Freiburg im Breisgau).

CHAPTER 11

Bibliotheca abscondita:
On W. G. Sebald's Library

Jo Catling

> To travel, at least in a certain manner, is to write (first of all because
> to travel is to read), and to write is to travel [...].
> Through the skylight of the page I find myself elsewhere.
> MICHEL BUTOR, 'Travel and Writing'[1]

Into the Labyrinth

'Ob, was und wieviel ein Dichter gelesen hat, braucht an sich keineswegs aufschluß-
reich zu sein' [Whether, what, and how much a poet has read need not of itself
be illuminating at all]: thus Michael Hamburger in 1961 at the beginning of his
description of Hugo von Hofmannsthal's library.[2] Nevertheless, there is a certain
expectation, as Arno Schmidt suggests, that 'ein *Verzeichnis seiner Bibliothek*' [a
catalogue of his library] is the most telling legacy an author can leave with regard
to his works,[3] and the expectations of W. G. Sebald's library, variously referred to as
his *Nachlassbibliothek*, *Personalbibliothek*, or *Arbeitsbibliothek*, as a source of information
about the author's literary preferences and intertextual practice are no exception:
the avid scrutiny of his annotations and underlinings, which the presence of the
major part of the library in the Deutsches Literaturarchiv Marbach (DLA) has
facilitated, will no doubt provide scholars with a rich seam of material for a long
while to come.

Moreover, not only is Sebald, as Hugo Dittberner suggests, 'ein Autor der
Lektüren, in stärkerem Maße noch als die meisten anderen Gegenwartsautoren'
[an author who reads — to a greater extent even than most other contemporary
authors],[4] but, as both Marcel Atze and Ulrich von Bülow point out in different
contexts, his works contain numerous references to libraries, archives, and
Nachlässe, whether imagined or actual,[5] encountered during his own researches
or his narrators' travels (the two often overlapping) — a fictional world which at
every turn covertly acknowledges its own debt to such intertextual antecedents as
Browne, Borges, and Benjamin.

Despite what the title of this chapter may suggest, though, its purpose is not
primarily to explore the relation of Sir Thomas Browne's imaginary library, the
'MUSÆUM CLAUSUM | or | Bibliotheca Abscondita' in Part X of *Die Ringe des*

Saturn (The Rings of Saturn),[6] to Borges's even more fanciful Library of Babel, still less to equate Sebald's own library with either. Nonetheless, the seventeenth-century Norwich physician and philosopher Sir Thomas Browne represents a kind of leitmotif in Sebald's work, mainly though not exclusively in *Die Ringe des Saturn;*[7] he also shares with Browne what Umberto Eco calls *la vertigine della lista,*[8] and his description of Browne's 'labyrinthine' prose style, his 'gefahrvolle[r] Höhenflug der Sprache' (translated by Michael Hulse as 'parlous loftiness in his language') amounting almost to a self-portrait, is well known:

> Wie die anderen Schriftsteller des englischen 17. Jahrhunderts führt auch Browne ständig seine ganze Gelehrsamkeit mit sich, einen ungeheuren Zitaten-schatz und die Namen aller ihm voraufgegangenen Autoritäten, arbeitet mit weit ausufernden Metaphern und Analogien und baut labyrinthische, bisweilen über ein, zwei Seiten sich hinziehende Satzgebilde, die Prozessionen oder Trauerzügen gleichen in ihrer schieren Aufwendigkeit. Zwar gelingt es ihm, unter anderem wegen dieser enormen Belastung, nicht immer, von der Erde abzuheben, aber wenn er, mitsamt seiner Fracht, auf den Kreisen seiner Prosa höher und höher getragen wird wie ein Segler auf den warmen Strömungen der Luft, dann ergreift selbst den heutigen Leser noch ein Gefühl der Levitation.

> [In common with other English writers of the seventeenth century, Browne wrote out of the fullness of his erudition, deploying a vast repertoire of quotations and the names of authorities who had gone before, creating complex metaphors and analogies, and constructing labyrinthine sentences that sometimes extend over one or two pages, sentences that resemble processions or a funeral cortège in their ceremonial lavishness. It is true that, because of the immense weight of the impediments he is carrying, Browne's writing can be held back by the force of gravitation, but when he does succeed in rising higher and higher through the circles of his spiralling prose, borne aloft like a glider on warm currents of air, even today the reader is overcome by a sense of levitation.][9]

Thus in Sebald's later evocation of Browne's 'Bibliotheca abscondita or Musæum Clausum',[10] as well as of Borges's *Tlön,* it is hard to resist the temptation to discern not only an intertextual relationship but also a knowing, or knowingly ironic, self-referentiality, an ironic metaphor for the work in question, or indeed the whole business of writing, researching, and collating in Browne's

> Katalog merkwürdiger Bücher, Bildnisse, Antiquitäten und sonstiger absonder-licher Dinge, von denen dies oder jenes tatsächlich Teil einer von Browne selber zusammengetragenen Raritätensammlung gewesen sein mag, das allermeiste aber offenbar zum Bestand eines rein imaginären, einzig im Inneren seines Kopfes existierenden und nur über die Buchstaben auf dem Papier zugänglichen Schatzhauses gehörte.

> [catalogue of remarkable books [...] listing pictures, antiquities and sundry singular items that may have formed part of a collection put together by Browne but were more likely products of his imagination, the inventory of a treasure house that existed purely in his head and to which there is no access except through the letters on the page.][11]

Moreover, Borges cites Browne at the end of 'Tlön, Uqbar, Orbis Tertius',[12] and, in a deliberate kind of *mise en abyme,* this passage is cited in turn at the end of the third section of *Die Ringe des Saturn*, taking the reader within the space of a few lines deep into a self-referential Borgesian labyrinth in which art or literature, as a translation of the world into itself, will soon have displaced the world altogether:[13]

> Es bleibt somit ungeklärt, ob es Uqbar je gegeben hat oder ob es bei der Beschreibung dieses unbekannten Landes nicht ähnlich wie bei dem Enzyklopädistenprojekt Tlön [...] darum geht, über das rein Irreale im Laufe der Zeit zu einer neuen Wirklichkeit zu gelangen. Die labyrinthische Konstruktion Tlöns, so merkt ein Nachtrag aus dem Jahr 1947 an, steht im Begriff, die bekannte Welt auszulöschen. [...] Die Welt wird Tlön sein. Mich aber, so schließt der Erzähler, kümmert das nicht, ich feile in der stillen Muße meines Landhauses weiter an einer tastenden, an Quevedo geschulten Übertragung des *Urn Burial* von Thomas Browne (die ich nicht drucken zu lassen gedenke).

> [It thus remains unclear whether Uqbar ever existed or whether the description of this unknown country might not be a case similar to that of Tlön, the encyclopedist's project [...] which aimed at creating a new reality, in the course of time, by way of the unreal. The labyrinthine construction of Tlön, reads a note added to the text in 1947, is on the point of blotting out the whole world. [...] The world will be Tlön. But, the narrator concludes, what is that to me? In the peace and quiet of my country villa I continue to hone my tentative translation, schooled on Quevedo, of Thomas Browne's *Urn Burial* (which I do not mean to publish).][14]

The disappearance of the world into the library and into literature, 'die Erfindung von Welten zweiten oder dritten Grades' [our attempts to invent secondary or tertiary worlds]:[15] this can be taken as one more instance of that theme so beloved of Sebald, the insidious, at times destructive effect of writing and literature.[16] This *mise en abyme* effect of receding mirrors is typical of Sebald's multilayered texts and is explicitly referenced in the narrators' respective wanderings in both *Schwindel. Gefühle.* (*Vertigo*) and *Die Ringe des Saturn*, mirroring his readings, and is suggestive of the paths along which the author leads his narrators and readers alike into, or rather through, 'die labyrinthische Konstruktion' of the text.

This is emblematized in the repeated evocation, in both texts, of the concept of the maze or labyrinth, and here a practical distinction between maze and labyrinth, as applied to their contemporary installation in, say, cloisters or the gardens of country houses may be of interest:

> The labyrinth is not a maze. In a maze there are many paths and crossroads. [...] The visitor [...] must choose the right path and make a decision. The path may turn out to be wrong. For whoever enters upon the chosen path may 'go astray', get 'on the wrong track', become 'lost to the world'. [...] On his way, he cannot see the centre. It may suddenly appear. Or he may unexpectedly find himself back at the entrance. In the labyrinth, there is only one path, and that always leads to the centre. [...] The walker in the labyrinth always has the centre in view. As he moves forward, he walks along the complete path of the labyrinth; he is constantly aware that he is approaching the centre and moving away from it again. After many detours, and after walking the entire length of the labyrinth, he inevitably reaches the centre.[17]

In *Die Ringe des Saturn*, the 'in der Mitte des geheimnisvollen Geländes gelegene Eibenlabyrinth von Somerleyton' [Somerleyton yew maze, in the heart of the mysterious estate][18] evoked in Part II — referred to in the text as a labyrinth even though, on the above criteria, it is technically (and functionally) a maze — is, in Part VII, 'revisited' as the narrator contrives to get lost on Dunwich Heath; the labyrinthine image is then echoed in a dreamscape, culminating in one of those narratorial overviews so typical of this work and underlined by a cutout aerial view of the Somerleyton maze 'von dem ich im Traum mit absoluter Sicherheit wußte, daß es einen Querschnitt darstellte durch mein Gehirn' [which I knew in my dream, with absolute certainty, represented a cross-section through my brain].[19]

The narrator, then, loses himself in the maze;[20] for the reader, however, one assumes the pattern is designed to be that of a labyrinth, with the 'roter Faden' or Ariadne's thread of the narrative and its interlocking allusions to guide one safely to the centre of the concentric rings of the narrative (which, like those of Saturn as described in the book's epitaph from the Brockhaus Encyclopedia, consist of fragments and particles, 'Staubteilchen, die den Planeten in dessen Äquatorebene in kreisförmigen Bahnen umlaufen' [describing circular orbits around the planet's equator]) and, crucially, back out again.[21] Within the reprise of the maze in the dream sequence in Part VII it is literature, textual references which seem to be what the narrator holds on to as he emerges from this giddying experience: the quotation from Hölderlin in Michael Hamburger's English translation, standing out in the German of the original, may perhaps function also as a symbol of dislocation and disorientation, as, arguably, are the subsequent quotations (in German) from, and allusions to, the final scenes of King Lear, interwoven into the apocalyptic vision on the heath and cliffs of dream-Dunwich in both Die Ringe des Saturn and Nach der Natur (After Nature): 'raunender Wahnsinn auf der Heide von Suffolk' [Whispering madness on the heathland of Suffolk].[22] In this context one might also be struck by the far from coincidental echoes of Hugo von Hofmannsthal's 'Chandos letter' at the end of the narrator's visit to Michael Hamburger in Die Ringe des Saturn, with its allusion to a crisis of language, as the water beetle in the 'Hölderlinpumpe' crosses 'von einem dunklen Ufer zum anderen' — a metaphor of both translated words and translated lives:[23]

> mit einem mir bis in die Haarwurzeln gehenden Erschauern sah ich, in dem schwachen Schein, der von einem der Wohnzimmerfenster auf das ummauerte Brunnenloch fiel, wie ein Schwimmkäfer auf dem Spiegel des Wassers ruderte von einem dunklen Ufer zum andern.

> [by the faint light that fell from the living-room window into the well I saw, with a shudder that went to the roots of my hair, a beetle rowing across the surface of the water, from one dark shore to the other.][24]

It will, then, come as no surprise to the reader that, in Sebald's copy of Hofmannsthal's Erzählungen und Aufsätze,[25] the text of 'Ein Brief' (as the 'Chandos letter' is more properly known) contains a high proportion of annotations, particularly sidelinings and pencil circlings around the words 'Leere' (emptiness, vacuity) and 'Starre' (stasis, stagnation): both terms which recur frequently in Die Ringe des Saturn. Indeed, much of what Michael Hamburger, in the article cited at the beginning of this piece (see note 2), writes of Hofmannsthal's library can also be said to apply to W. G. Sebald's Nachlassbibliothek, although one might initially be inclined to feel that the two writers have little in common. However, Sebald published widely on the Austrian author, and, as several commentators have noted, echoes of the latter's works — in particular the 'Chandos letter' — recur frequently in his *oeuvre*. Like Hofmannsthal, Sebald may be classed as a 'lesende[r] Dichter', a reading writer, as Hamburger notes of the former:

> schon früh erhob man gegen ihn den Vorwurf der Abhängigkeit, oft ohne die ganze Frage gründlich zu erwägen, auf welche Weise und zu welchem Zweck sich ein Künstler der Werke eines anderen bedient.[26]

> [the accusation of dependence [or: influence] was one levelled at him at an early stage, often without a thorough consideration of the ways and purposes for which an artist makes use of another's work.]

Sebald, too, is a prodigious borrower of others' words, mostly — although not always — with a nod in their direction, as he admits in his essay on Robert Walser, 'Le promeneur solitaire', in *Logis in einem Landhaus*:

> Ich habe immer versucht, in meiner eigenen Arbeit denjenigen meine Achtung zu erweisen, von denen ich mich angezogen fühlte, gewissermaßen den Hut zu lüften vor ihnen, indem ich ein schönes Bild oder ein paar besondere Worte von ihnen entlehnte.

> [I have always tried, in my own works, to mark my respect for those writers with whom I felt an affinity, to raise my hat to them, so to speak, by borrowing an attractive image or a few expressions.][27]

One may indeed often find that these 'besondere Worte' (particular expressions) are indicated in Sebald's own copies of the relevant texts (or indeed — for example in the case of Walser — in the holdings of the UEA library). Fascinating though a study of such literary sources or *Quellen* undoubtedly is, however, the discovery of such sources does not necessarily indicate either 'Abhängigkeit' (dependence, influence) or a lack of originality. As Michael Hamburger notes on Hofmannsthal:

> doch ist ein Urteil über die Originalität [...] erst berechtigt, nachdem man die Anwendung und Verarbeitung jeder einzigen Quelle untersucht hat. [...] Nur über die Art der Originalität, über die Stellung des Dichters zum eigenen Ich und zur Außenwelt, ist manches daraus zu schließen. Der *Ulysses* von James Joyce, Eliots *Waste Land* und Valérys *Mon Faust*, um nur drei Werke zu nennen, deren Originalität wohl kaum in Frage steht, sind noch vergleichbar reichere Gebiete für den Quellenforscher.[28]

> [yet a judgement as to originality [...] is only justified when one has investigated the use and adaptation of every single source. [...] All one may conclude is that it shows us something about the kind of originality, the poet's position with regard to himself and the outside world. James Joyce's *Ulysses*, Eliot's *Waste Land*, and Valéry's *Mon Faust* — to name but three works whose originality is scarcely in question — are, relatively speaking, far more fruitful fields of enquiry for the researcher into sources.]

On Sebald's Library

> Wäre es nicht anmaßend, hier auf eine scheinbare Objektivität und Sachlichkeit pochend die Hauptstücke oder Hauptabteilungen einer Bücherei Ihnen aufzuzählen, oder deren Entstehungsgeschichte, oder selbst deren Nutzen für den Schriftsteller Ihnen darzulegen?
>
> [Would it not be presumptuous of me if, in order to appear convincingly objective and down-to-earth, I enumerated for you the main sections or prize pieces of a library, if I presented you with their history or even their usefulness to a writer?]
>
> WALTER BENJAMIN, 'Ich packe meine Bibliothek aus'
> ('Unpacking my Library')[29]

Despite such reservations as those expressed by Walter Benjamin above, this chapter will explore some of the paths down which a consideration of the author, W. G. Sebald, his library (but also his narrators and their libraries), and his texts entices the reader: the Ariadne's thread is the *Nachlassbibliothek* in the DLA and the catalogue of that library, in Marbach and in *Privatbesitz* elsewhere, published in this volume, to which this chapter may also serve as a preliminary introduction and guide.[30] As Ulrich von Bülow notes in Chapter 10, a *Nachlass* is only ever a *Bestandsaufnahme*, a snapshot of a moment frozen in time: it can never aspire to be the complete picture, although some ways of widening the perspective will be explored in what follows.

The first tranche of W. G. Sebald's library — 445 volumes (since augmented to some 1255 volumes) — arrived in Marbach, along with the manuscripts and papers constituting his literary *Nachlass*, in January 2004, and comprised the volumes most heavily annotated or felt to be of most relevance to his literary *oeuvre*, including for example his copies of Adorno (and other members of the Frankfurt School), Benjamin, Proust, Joseph Roth, and Wittgenstein, to name but a few. Following the sale of The Old Rectory in Poringland (Sebald's family home near Norwich for twenty-five years; see Figures 2.42–43, p. 93, and Figure III.3, p. 591) in August 2006, a further 800-odd volumes were incorporated into the DLA holdings, with a final few boxes, consisting largely of maps, travel and nature guides, and art books, arriving in December 2007 and June 2008 in the context of preparations for the major exhibition *Wandernde Schatten: W. G. Sebalds Unterwelt* (*Wandering Shadows: W. G. Sebald's Underworld*) (September 2008–January 2009) in the award-winning Literaturmuseum der Moderne in Marbach, with the exhibition itself constructed almost as a hall of mirrors (Figures 11.2a–11.2b).

This brings us, then, to a consideration of the contents of W. G. Sebald's library. Marcel Atze entitles his speculative 1997 article 'Bibliotheca Sebaldiana'[31] — positing this, by way of conclusion, as a title for an eventual 'Verzeichnis seiner Bibliothek'. Such a title might, though, have a number of connotations: first, the actual library in the sense of the *Nachlassbibliothek*, the books in W. G. Sebald's possession at the time of his death; and second, the kinds of libraries present in his fiction, some of them idealized (or at any rate fictionalized), some decidedly dystopian. To this one might add a third, virtual and only partially verifiable, dimension: a true 'Bibliotheca Sebaldiana', which would be different again from an imaginary library (were it

Figs. 11.2a and 11.2b. Entrance to the W. G. Sebald exhibition 'Wandernde Schatten'
in the Literaturmuseum der Moderne, Marbach am Neckar, September 2008.
© DLA Marbach (11.2a); © Lynn Wolff (11.2b)

possible to reconstruct such a thing) comprised of the books and quotations which go to make up his own works.[32] Rather, it might encompass not only all the author's books (including those no longer in his possession, as well as those whose ownership is only virtual) but also the libraries of others, whether institutional or the libraries of, perhaps, friends and relations — Mathild's library in W., for example, and also the 'wohlfeile Ausgaben des Volksbühnenbunds' [inexpensive editions published by the Volksbühnenbund] from the parental 'Wohnzimmerschrank' [armoire] outlined in 'Il ritorno in patria', to name but a few.[33]

This virtual complete library would also have to encompass the other libraries which Max Sebald had at his disposal during his time at UEA: the erstwhile 'German Sector' library, to a large extent supplied by the Goethe-Institut, the Austrian Institute, and Inter-Nationes, and with multiple copies of the course books current at the time; and, more importantly, the University Library at UEA, the German section of which at least (as suggested in the context of Walser, above) he tended to regard as a kind of extension of his personal library, and whose holdings in turn to some extent reflect his personal and professional teaching interests.[34] As Marcel Atze notes:

> Es ist keine zwingende Voraussetzung, daß ein Autor, auch wenn er sich als manischer Leser bezeichnen mag, eine große Bibliothek sein eigen nennen muß. Dafür gibt es ja öffentliche und wissenschaftliche Einrichtungen, die durch teilweise jahrhundertlanges Sammeln viele Wünsche erfüllen können.[35]

> [There is no absolute prerequisite for an author, even one who describes himself as an obsessive reader, to own an extensive library. There are public and academic institutions which can, on the basis of centuries' worth of collecting, fulfil many a need and desire.]

Accordingly, a number of books in the library's German Literature section — and indeed elsewhere — bear witness to the discreet but distinctive Sebaldian *Lesespuren*, in the form of pencil sidelinings in the margins, along with the occasional note or initial; but to compile a list of such volumes (particularly in the absence of borrowing records) would necessitate a study in its own right.

Any attempt at inclusivity in recreating a virtual 'Bibliotheca Sebaldiana' is, moreover, somewhat undermined by Sebald's habit of disposing of books he no longer had use for, whether because a project was completed, the books were no longer relevant, or in order to create shelf space; or a combination of the above. Set against the list of favourite books spontaneously produced at the request of the Buchhandlung zum Wetzstein in Freiburg im Breisgau which prefaces this chapter (see Figure 11.1), then, is the much longer ten-page handwritten book list found on the desk in his office at UEA, later identified as being identical with that addressed to Herbert Blank's Wissenschaftliches Antiquariat in Stuttgart in October 2001, with the following accompanying note on University of East Anglia headed paper:[36]

School of English and American Studies
W. G. Sebald
11 X 01

Sehr geehrter Blank,
    anbei eine (leider nicht sehr ordentliche) handschriftliche Liste von Büchern, die ich entbehren könnte. Falls Sie (oder Kollegen) sich prinzipiell

für diese Ladung interessieren sollten, wäre ich Ihnen dankbar für eine vage Einschätzung des Gesamterlöses, mit dem ich rechnen könnte, damit ich weiß, ob sich die Spedition lohnt.

    Mit freundlichen Grüßen

       W. Sebald

PS: Wo nicht anders vermerket, sind die Bücher alle geb. Exemplare & ohne Randnotizen & Unterstreichungen.[37]

[Dear [Herr] Blank,

    Enclosed is an unfortunately not very neat handwritten list of books which I could do without. If you (or your colleagues) were interested in principle in such a shipment, I should be grateful for a rough estimation of the total amount I might reckon with, in order to decide whether it is worth the cost of sending them.

    With best wishes

       W. Sebald

PS: Unless otherwise indicated, the books are all hardback editions & without marginal notes & underlinings.]

It may be that Sebald was streamlining his books with a view to retirement (it seems clear that, in planning to use the NESTA award (see Chapter 2, note 49) to buy himself out of teaching for four consecutive spring semesters from 2000–01, his intention was to retire at the age of 60) or there may have been other motives; moreover, it is consistent with a pattern, also identified in the preceding chapter by Ulrich von Bülow in considering the manuscript *Nachlass*, of clearing the decks once a project was completed. Thus the books remaining in his library also include a substantial number of hardbacks which, one may surmise from the above, he was intending to dispose of, or had at least earmarked for potential sale.

    Contrary to Marcel Atze's wishful identification of the author with the fictive narrator of his texts as a *Sammler* or collector (with all the Benjaminian resonances that entails), even as a *Bibliophile*,[38] with some possible exceptions, the author W. G. Sebald does not, then, seem to have been particularly acquisitive where his library was concerned. Not for him the 'Papierlandschaft' [paper universe][39] of the overflowing shelves (tables, floors, even walls) of his colleagues (cf. the description of Janine Dakyns's office in *Die Ringe des Saturn* (see Figures 3.5 and 3.6, p. 125), and also his comments on the present author's own disordered office next door to his own); his office at UEA (cf. Figure 5.1, p. 153), and perhaps to an even greater degree his study in The Old Rectory in Poringland, were models of calm and order. Any superfluous paper would be immediately relegated to the waste-paper bin, and indeed even books may sometimes have met with this fate. The author of the present chapter more than once happened upon a book in one of the few second-hand bookshops in Norwich to retain a small foreign-language section (Ellis & Ellis, St Giles) only to discover the telltale scrawled signature (or more rarely the discreet embossed stamp) within; and when, on a later occasion, a consignment of books destined for recycling was intercepted, she was informed that the bookshop in question was no longer interested in foreign (or at least German) books, as there was no market for them. Suggestions that such books, if surplus to requirements,

FIG. 11.3. W. G. Sebald's desk in the downstairs study in
The Old Rectory, Poringland. © Jo Catling (summer 2006)

be placed in the corridor for students to help themselves to would be met with a
characteristic 'liest doch sowieso keiner' [nobody will read this stuff anyway].[40]

To get a complete picture of the Sebaldian library, then, one would need to trace
all the books he sold, gave away, or otherwise disposed of;[41] but the hypothetical
catalogue would also, as Atze suggests, need to encompass a kind of virtual library,
including those instances where the reader has the sense that Sebald 'must' have
known this book but it cannot (or can no longer) be traced to his possession. Some
of the adventurously acquired books referred to in the texts are, admittedly, indeed
extant; for example,

> [die] in Manchester von mir antiquarisch erstandene[n] dreibändige[n] Keller-
> Biografie von Bächthold, die mit einiger Gewißheit aus dem Nachlaß eines aus
> Deutschland vertriebenen Juden stammte

> [in an antiquarian bookshop in Manchester [I had acquired] a copy of Bächt-
> hold's three-volume biography of Gottfried Keller which had almost certainly
> belonged to a German-Jewish refugee].[42]

This edition, for example, in its green covers, may now be consulted in the
Nachlassbibliothek in Marbach, and the picture which is the reason for invoking it
in 'Le promeneur solitaire' — the 'schöne Sepia-Fotographie von dem ganz von
Buschen und Bäumen umstandenen [Kleist-]Haus auf der Aare-Insel' [attractive
sepia photograph depicting [Kleist's] house on the island in the Aare, completely
surrounded by shrubs and trees] in Thun — is also extant. While there is no reason
to doubt the circumstances of acquisition related in the text (which in this case after

all is a literary essay rather than a work of fiction), there is also no way of proving whether this is one of those coincidences which have meanwhile come to acquire the adjective 'Sebaldian', or whether it is not rather a device for linking together the disparate yet interlocking essays in *Logis in einem Landhaus* to form a coherent volume, as in the use of a Rousseau title, 'Le promeneur solitaire', for the essay on Robert Walser, and the evocation within that essay of both the Île Saint-Pierre in the Bielersee / Lac de Bienne and the Rousseau monument on an island in Lake Geneva.[43]

Finally, too, there will always remain, tantalizingly and one assumes deliberately, books such as those referred to in the texts that the reader, like the narrator, searches for in vain in bookshops and library catalogues. Atze gives the example of the book *Das Böhmische Meer* (The Seas of Bohemia) (which, notwithstanding the Shakespearian and Rhenish resonances, has also always struck the present author as a Bachmann reference) being read on the train by the 'Winter Queen' in 'Il ritorno in patria';[44] a book which, the narrator says, 'is, alas, not listed in any bibliography, in any catalogue, or indeed anywhere at all' ('in keiner Bibliographie, in keinem Katalog, es ist nirgends verzeichnet') and whose existence therefore cannot — as with Borges's Uqbar — be verified, but neither can it be conclusively denied.

The Library in the Text and the Author in the Library

> Für mich ist es sehr wichtig, wenn ich irgendwo hinfahre, zu begreifen, was für eine Geschichte das Land hat, was für Zusammenhänge es gibt zwischen dem walischen, extremen Puritanismus und dem Anblick der walischen Berge.
>
> [For me it is very important, whenever I go somewhere, to understand what kind of history the country(side) has, what the connections are between the extreme form of Welsh puritanism and the sight of the Welsh mountains.]
>
> W. G. Sebald, interview with Jean-Pierre Rondas, 22 May 2001[45]

Marcel Atze refers to Sebald as an 'unermüdlicher Bücherdurchwanderer' (literally a 'tireless wanderer through (or among) books'), thus bringing neatly together the motifs of libraries and travelling adumbrated in the quotation from Michel Butor prefacing this chapter. As Atze also notes, Sebald's narrators and protagonists encounter in their respective travels a perhaps unusual number of personal and public libraries, archives and *Nachlässe* (see note 3). Sometimes, of course, these travels have been undertaken with the aim of consulting a particular archive, whether for academic or for creative purposes; indeed, the two often overlap, most noticeably perhaps in *Schwindel. Gefühle.*, where journeys described by the narrator often double as research trips — or were undertaken as such — for the author's academic writing. These libraries and archives evoked in the texts include not just the minuscule Sailors' Reading Room in Southwold in *Die Ringe des Saturn*, or the Biblioteca Civica in Verona in 'All'estero' (*Schwindel. Gefühle.*) — not to mention the monumental and disturbing 'Très Grande Bibliothèque' in *Austerlitz* or the cloistered claustrophobia of the state archives and libraries in Prague[46] — but also a number of private and personal archives of, as we have seen, varying degrees of fictionality (as in the examples above of Borges and Browne).

The contents of these more personal libraries, recollected from childhood and revisited by the narrator in 'Il ritorno in patria', have a strange way of bridging fact and fiction. The books in Mathild Seelos's library, for example, the origins of which are tellingly obscure, have a familiar ring to them:

> In einem Regal, zu dem es mich gleich hinzog, lehnte, in sich zusammengesunken, wie es den Anschein hatte, die bald an die hundert Bände umfassende, inzwischen in meinem Besitz befindliche und mir in zunehmenden Maße wichtig werdende Bibliothek der Mathild. Neben Literarischem aus dem letzten Jahrhundert, neben Reiseberichten aus dem hohen Norden, neben Lehrbüchern der Geometrie und der Baustatik und einem türkischen Lexikon samt kleinem Briefsteller, die wohl einmal dem Baptist gehört hatten, gab es da zahlreiche Werke spekulativen Charakters, Gebetbücher aus dem 17. und frühen 18. Jahrhundert mit zum Teil drastischen Abschilderungen der uns alle erwartenden Pein. [...] Zum anderem fanden sich zu meinem Erstaunen mit den geistigen Schriften vermischt mehrere Traktate von Bakunin, Fourier, Bebel, Eisner, Landauer sowie der autobiographische Roman der Lily von Braun. Auf meine, die Herkunft dieser Bibliothek betreffende Frage wußte der Lukas nur zu berichten, daß die Mathild immer irgend etwas studiert und darum, wie mir vielleicht noch erinnerlich sei, im Dorf als eine überspannte Person gegolten habe.

FIG. 11.4. Part of W. G. Sebald's library while still at The Old Rectory, showing Lily Braun's *Memoiren einer Sozialistin*. © The Estate of W. G. Sebald

[On a shelf that immediately attracted my attention was Mathild's library, comprising almost a hundred volumes, which have since come into my possession and are proving ever more important to me. Besides various literary works from the last century, accounts of expeditions to the polar regions, textbooks on geometry and structural engineering, and a Turkish dictionary complete with a manual for the writing of letters, which had probably once belonged to Baptist, there were numerous religious works of a speculative character, and prayer-books dating back two or three hundred years, with illustrations, some of them perfectly gruesome, showing the torments and travails that await us all. In among the devotional works, to my amazement, there were several treatises by Bakunin, Fourier, Bebel, Eisner, and Landauer, and an autobiographical novel by the socialist Lily von Braun. [...] When I enquired about the origins of the books, Lukas was able to tell me only that Mathild had always been a great reader, and because of this, as I might perhaps remember, was thought of by the villagers as peculiar, if not deranged.][47]

This passage is, of course, a good example of the typical Sebaldian blend of fact and fiction, designed, no doubt, to tantalize the reader. Although there is no real means of establishing which of the books in Sebald's *Nachlassbibliothek* may actually have their origins in Mathild's library, some of the works mentioned do have at least an echo in Sebald's actual library, such as Alex Bein's 1934 biography of Theodor Herzl, or Lily Braun's *Memoiren einer Sozialistin* (see Figure 11.4). Nonetheless, a fictionalizing element may perhaps be detected in the attribution of an aristocratic 'von' — perhaps dictated by the rhythm of the sentence, perhaps by Sebald's love of contradiction — to the feminist author Lily Braun (née Amalie von Kretschmann), who despite her aristocratic background never used the 'von' in print, publishing instead under the surname of her second husband. Meanwhile the 'Gebetbücher' (prayer books) do seem to be of family provenance, albeit not necessarily from the 'W.' branch of the family; and the 'Literarische[s] aus dem letzten Jahrhundert, [...] Reiseberichte[n] aus dem hohen Norden' and even the 'Lehrbücher[n] der Geometrie und der Baustatik' cited above could equally well be a part of an imagined 'Bibliotheca Sebaldiana', a kind of reflected library self-portrait. Only the Turkish dictionary and letter-writing manual strike an unusual, exotic note — which, one may argue, is precisely their function in the text.

In 'Il ritorno in patria', too, we encounter the disparaging reference to the parental 'library' bought from a travelling salesman, part of the standard sitting-room furniture, and locked safely away, one assumes unread, with the best china 'hinter den Glastüren des Aufsatzes' [behind the glass doors] of the 'massive[r] Wohnzimmerschrank' [ponderously ornate armoire]:

Vermerkt werden muß außerdem noch, daß auf dem Wohnzimmerschrank die Wohnzimmeruhr auf ihre lieblose Art die Stunden zählte und daß im Aufsatz des Schranks nebst dem chinesischen Teeservice eine Reihe in Leinen gebundener dramatischer Schriften ihren Platz hatten, und zwar diejenigen Shakespeares, Schillers, Hebbels und Sudermanns. Es waren dies wohlfeile Ausgaben des Volksbühnenverbands, die der Vater, der gar nie auf den Gedanken gekommen wäre, ins Theater zu gehen, und noch viel weniger auf den, ein Theaterstück zu lesen, in einer Anwandlung von Kulturbewußtsein eines Tages einem Reisevertreter abgekauft hatte.

[It should also be mentioned that on the top of the armoire stood the living room clock which counted out the hours with its cold and loveless chimes, and that in the upper half of the armoire, next to the bone china tea service, was a row of clothbound dramatic works by Shakespeare, Schiller, Hebbel and Sudermann. These were inexpensive editions published by the Volksbühnenverband, which my father, who would probably never have taken it into his head to go to the theatre, and less still to read a play, had bought one day, in a passing moment of aspiration to higher ideals, from a travelling salesman.][48]

While identifying the narrator (or indeed author) with such a 'Reisevertreter' might in this case be a step too far — he checks in to the Engelwirt in W. as a '"foreign correspondent"' ('"Auslandskorrespondent"') — there does seem to be a sense in which, for the author and his narrators, as for Kafka (and his protagonists) with whom this designation in *Schwindel. Gefühle.* is presumably intended to resonate, the whole 'anstrengendes Geschäft' [strenuous business] of writing, and the travels and travails of research it entails, is seen as a wearisome burden, as the author points out in an interview with Jean-Pierre Rondas in May 2001:

> es ist erstaunlich [...] wo man überall hin muss, wie schwierig es ist, bestimmte Dinge herauszufinden, welche Umwege man machen muss, wie schwierig es ist, bestimmte Personen zum Reden zu bringen, in gewisse Archive oder Bibliotheken vorzudringen.[49]

> [it is extraordinary all the places one has to go to, how hard it is to find out certain things, the detours one has to make, how difficult it is to get some people to talk, to get into certain archives or libraries.]

It is perhaps worth noting, *entre parenthèses*, that, for all his academic credentials, Sebald did not consider himself a natural researcher. Not only did he profess to be baffled by the electronic age increasingly encroaching upon the libraries he frequented, and in his view putting an end to the old-fashioned pleasures of browsing or riffling through a card catalogue, with its possibilities of unexpected discoveries and coincidences; he also seemingly did not hold with the single-minded pursuit of only one strand of enquiry. However, his dissatisfaction with institutional libraries — 'Die Bibliotheken wollen ja heute die Leser draußen halten, und wenn man dann drinnen ist, findet man nicht was man braucht, und man hat nur fünf Tage: das ist extrem schwierig' [libraries today want to keep the readers out, and once you do get in you can't find what you need, and you only have five days: it's extremely difficult] — is paralleled by a need to go to the sources as 'die Voraussetzung fürs Schreiben' [the prerequisites for writing]: 'Ich brauche das Material und das Material findet man nur, indem man sucht und lange und geduldig bestimmten Wegen nachgeht' [I need the material, and you only find the material by looking and following, slowly and patiently, certain paths].[50] Increasingly, he seems to have used libraries and archives not so much for research in the academic sense — though he was rightly adamant about the amount of research involved in so-called 'creative writing' — but as a stimulus to the imagination, 'eine Provokation des Zufalls' [a provoking of coincidence], a seemingly much more haphazard or, as he puts it, 'diffuse' process which he describes in the Rondas interview as one not of seeking but of finding, like a dog, perhaps Kafka's dog, zigzagging across a field:

Man muss den Zufall auch provozieren. Auf diese Weise findet man immer sehr eigenartige Dinge, mit denen man nie gerechnet hat, ja, die man auf eine rationale Weise nie vorfinden kann und sicher nicht, wenn man recherchiert, wie es einem an der Universität beigebracht wurde, immer geradeaus, rechts, links, rechter Winkel und so weiter. Man muss auf eine diffuse Weise recherchieren. Es soll ein Fund sein, also genau wie ein Hund sucht, hin und her, rauf und runter, manchmal langsam und manchmal schnell. Das hat jeder von uns schon gesehen, wie die Hunde das machen beim Feldlaufen, und wenn ich sie betrachte, habe ich das Gefühl, dass sie meine Brüder sind.[51]

[Coincidence also has to be provoked. That way you always find very unusual things, things which you never expected to find, which indeed you can never find by rational means and certainly not if you research as one is taught to at university, straight ahead, right, left, at right angles, and so on. You have to research in a diffuse way. It has to be a find, just as a dog searches, back and forth, up and down, sometimes slow and sometimes fast. We have all seen how dogs run around like that in a field, and when I observe them I have the feeling that they are my brothers.]

Travelling to Read, Reading to Travel

> Man muss sich dem Weg überlassen, der sich vor einem aufrollt.
> [You have to follow the path which opens up in front of you.]
> W. G. Sebald, interview with Jean-Pierre Rondas[52]

For Sebald, then, research, and writing, are inextricably bound up with travelling — and it is no surprise, given his self-confessed 'Erdkundemanie' [passion for geography][53] that his library should have contained large numbers of maps, brochures, and guidebooks as well as *Naturführer*, field guides to the natural world (as well as to English stately homes, gardens, and gardening). We have a situation, then, where the narrator is travelling to research the very books which in turn detail these travels. To take one example: in *Schwindel. Gefühle.* research in (one conjectures) Vienna and Klosterneuburg for articles in *Die Beschreibung des Unglücks* (e.g. 'Eine kleine Traverse', the essay on Ernst Herbeck) then also provides material for the narrator's excursion with Herbeck in 'All'estero'; and the Viennese section of that narrative also seems to pre-echo, in a way, the *flâneries* of Peter Altenberg, 'Le Paysan de Vienne' in *Unheimliche Heimat*.[54] Indeed, some of Sebald's earliest publications, in the Graz journal *Manuskripte* in the 1980s, suggest that the essays collected in the two volumes of Austrian essays were not, in fact, composed sequentially and separately. The same can be said for the two books *Schwindel. Gefühle.* and *Die Ausgewanderten* (*Vertigo* and *The Emigrants*), stories from which (like the separate sections of *Nach der Natur*) appear in successive issues of *Manuskripte* in 1988, blurring the boundaries between literary essay and creative writing (the Stendhal section of *Schwindel. Gefühle.* being a case in point).[55] Similarly, if we believe the account in the interview with Susan Salter Reynolds (although even where interviews are concerned one can never of course be quite sure whether the web of fiction does not continue to be spun even in front of an audience's eyes),[56] the journey recounted 'All'estero' may have coincided with a Kafka conference in Riva. One might conjecture that such a putative research visit may in turn have fed into 'Dr Ks Badereise nach Riva' ('Dr K. Takes the Waters in Riva'), though this would fail to take account of such possible sources as a 1983 issue of Klaus Wagenbach's journal *Freibeuter* entitled *Franz Kafka, nachgestellt* — with annotations in pinkish-purple felt pen to match its cover design — containing articles on Kafka in the cinema, Kafka and Casanova, and 'Drei Sanatorien Kafkas' (Three Kafka Sanatoriums), or Anthony Northey's article 'Kafka in Riva, 1913', photocopies of which were filed with Sebald's teaching materials.[57]

As John Zilcosky notes, while agreeing with Susan Sontag's identification of him as a travel writer, 'Sebald is also a textual traveller within the European travel writing tradition; his journeys follow in the footsteps of others (Stendhal, Kafka, Casanova), or take place only in his head, when he reads travel stories (Conrad's, Diderot's, Grillparzer's)'.[58] What is more, the books he is researching and/or writing are themselves palimpsests. If, despite Sebald's apparent lack of affinity for all Goethe stands for in terms of a canonical national German literature, the title of *The Emigrants* — *Die Ausgewanderten* — can be read as evoking, or invoking, echoes of Goethe's *Unterhaltungen deutscher Ausgewanderten* (*Conversations of German Refugees*), then it should perhaps come as no surprise that the paths of 'All'estero' not only follow in the footsteps of Kafka's *Badereise* skirting the southern borders of the Austro-Hungarian Empire, to Desenzano and on to Riva, or of Stendhal's amorous

FIGS. 11.6 and 11.7. Bookshelves to left and right of fireplace in the downstairs study of The Old Rectory (January 2004). © U. E. Sebald

literary adventurings along the same lakeshore, but also on occasion cross the path of Goethe on his own *Italienische Reise* 'Vom Brenner bis Verona'. Thus in Verona, the narrator of 'All'estero' 'ging dann sogleich, einer alten Gewohnheit gemäß, in den Giardino Giusti' [went immediately to the Giardino Giusti, [according to] a long-standing habit], commenting on the ancient cypresses, which remind him of the yews in English churchyards, 'von denen die eine oder die andere vielleicht an die zweihundert Jahre schon gestanden hatte an ihren Platz' [some of which had been growing there for as long as two hundred years].[59] This reference to 'eine[r] alte[n] Gewohnheit' [a long-standing habit] seems to be a nod in the direction of Goethe's paradigmatic *Italienische Reise*, where Goethe not only admires the venerable 'ungeheuere Zypressen' [enormous cypresses] in the same Giardino Giusti, plucking a twig from one of them, but also, not quite coincidentally, suggests that they may have been the inspiration for the yew topiary found in gardens in more northerly climes.[60] Accordingly, Sebald's personal copy of the *Italienische Reise* turns out to bear discreet pencil markings around these mid-September entries, for example against the passage relating to Limone's lemon groves and the alternating nocturnal breezes on Lake Garda.[61]

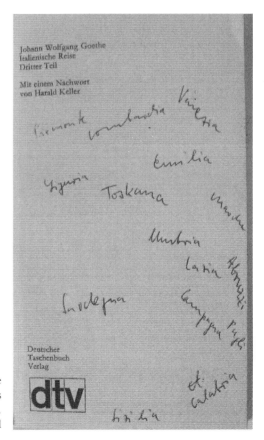

FIG. 11.5. 'Map' of Italy from the flyleaf of Sebald's copy of Goethe's *Italienische Reise* (Munich: dtv, 1962). © The Estate of W. G. Sebald

The Author and his Books: Bibliotheca Sebaldiana?

The Platypus and the Mermaid and Other Figments of the Classifying Imagination[62]

> Die Dinge haben eine stumme Geschichte. Die Realien, die sind für mich von Bedeutung. [...] Unglücklich bin ich nicht beim Sammeln, aber ich habe nicht diese Freude. Ein Sammler muss ja nachher klassifizieren, einordnen, die Schmetterlinge und die Käfer aufspießen, sie beschriften.
>
> [Objects have a mute history. Real things, that is what has significance for me. [...] I'm not unhappy when I am collecting, but I don't relish it. A collector has to classify everything afterwards, put it in order, stick the butterflies and the beetles on pins and write labels for them.]

W. G. SEBALD, interview with Jean-Pierre Rondas[63]

As is the case with most academics, Max Sebald's library was divided into home and office, though one also imagines a fairly fluid transfer between the two. Roughly speaking, the books located in his office at UEA mainly related to teaching and to current or recent projects; as well as reference works (the ten red binders of the *Kritisches Lexikon zur deutschsprachigen Gegenwartsliteratur* (KLG), for example), and textbooks which had strayed in from the erstwhile German Sector library formerly housed in secretary Beryl Ranwell's office,[64] this collection mostly contained works by contemporary and post-war German authors and volumes on twentieth-century German history, as well as classics of early-twentieth-century prose fiction: Kafka and Döblin, of course, but also, for example, a well-thumbed copy of Thomas Mann's *Doktor Faustus*. There were also a number of books relating to the history of German cinema (again a teaching interest), as well as a small collection of Penguin classics of European literature in translation, most likely relating to the course 'Examples of Nineteenth-Century European Prose Fiction' (see Appendix 3.3, p. 140).

The books in this snapshot may thus be seen to correspond by and large to Max Sebald's teaching interests, but of course no clear line can be drawn between teaching and research, and research and creative writing — though it would probably be fair to say that most of the latter was done away from the campus. Some books on higher shelves (a six-volume edition of Gotthelf, for instance) seem of less obvious relevance to either; and indeed, as mentioned earlier, it seems likely that a substantial number of the lesser-used books in his possession had been earmarked for possible sale to the Wissenschaftliches Antiquariat of Herbert Blank.

In Sebald's home at The Old Rectory, there was ample space for a more extensive library, though this too was perfectly ordered and uncluttered, with Austrian literature on the left and German on the right of the fireplace in the main downstairs study (where, on a shelf below the Austrian volumes, an increasing amount of space was taken up with editions of his own works: see Figures 11.6 and 11.7). In the adjacent 'living room', where the aesthetic aspect to the arrangement of the books was even more noticeable, the wall of bookshelves was more evidently devoted to the classics, to other literatures (particularly French), to books with dedications from friends and colleagues, and to such 'collections' as he had: for example, a number of the attractive volumes of the Eichborn series 'Die andere

Fig. 11.8. Sebald's collection of Rowohlt *Bildmonographien*. © The Estate of W. G. Sebald

Bibliothek' (in which of course his own first three prose works were first published); the 'decorative' Everyman editions on a shelf above the door (see Figure 11.9), and some other editions acquired at such places as the Aylsham book auction (apparently as much for their attractive bindings as for their contents, for example the editions of Dickens and Stevenson); and also, more pertinently perhaps, the paperback 'Rowohlt Klassiker' bilingual Shakespeare edition from student days (Figure 11.10), and the shelf of Rowohlt *Bildmonographien* (Figure 11.8). He was especially fond of this series, and the way an author's life and circumstances were brought to bear on the works; the 'Realien' displayed in the accompanying photographs were a source of inspiration (often quite literally, in that a number of the photographs contained therein find their way into his own works),[65] and on at least one occasion he mooted the idea of setting up a similar series in English.

The pages at the back of these volumes, where other works in the series are listed, often show circles or ticks denoting further copies of interest, or possibly volumes already acquired; similar annotations occur in volumes of the series 'edition suhrkamp', and to a lesser extent the hardback 'Bibliothek Suhrkamp', as well as in the 1960s 'dtv Goethe-Gesamtausgabe' which he acquired as a student (see Figure 11.5 and Figures 11.11–11.14). Hidden away in other parts of the house were collections of maps and guidebooks and further books acquired at auction, as well as the aforementioned 1960s Goethe, in addition to the reference works, and copies of the periodicals in which his own essays were published, located in a smaller upstairs study.[66]

W. G. Sebald's *Arbeitsbibliothek*, then, contains much of what one would expect from a professional Germanist, however iconoclastic.[67] The amount of 'Austrian'

FIG. 11.9. Bookshelves in living room, The Old Rectory, showing the collection of Everyman editions above the door and collection of Rowohlt Shakespeare at top left (January 2004). © U. E. Sebald

literature is perhaps noteworthy (though unsurprising given his two books of essays on Austrian literature, *Die Beschreibung des Unglücks* (1986) and *Unheimliche Heimat* (1991)); the more usual 'classics' of German and other literatures are present but in, one might say, much less prominent positions. It is also a strikingly European, cosmopolitan, and polyglot library; nonetheless, although Sebald lived in England for over thirty years, some commentators have been struck by how little in the way of English literature — or at any rate contemporary English literature — the library contains; this is arguably all the more striking in that UEA is noted for its MA programme in Creative Writing (on which, indeed, he taught from 2000).[68] The exception which proves the rule is the work of the poets Stephen Watts, Anne Beresford, and Michael Hamburger,[69] and indeed the translations of Hölderlin by the last-named; attentive readers of *Die Ringe des Saturn* will have noticed not only the *King Lear* allusions mentioned above, but also the fact that, as mentioned above, the italicized quotations in English in Part VII (on Dunwich Heath) are taken from Michael Hamburger's translations of, respectively, 'Brod und Wein' and 'Patmos'.[70] Indeed Hölderlin, though named explicitly on only a few occasions in Sebald's *oeuvre*, turns out to have been a considerable source of inspiration on many fronts. In *Nach der Natur* (*After Nature*), lines from, for example, 'Stutgard' and 'Griechenland' echo through Part v of 'Die dunckle Nacht fahrt aus' ('Dark Night Sallies Forth'), in which Hölderlin, along with Haller, is indeed mentioned by name, while the epigraph to 'Dr Henry Selwyn' in *Die Ausgewanderten* is adapted from Hölderlin's 'Elegie':[71] 'Zerstöret das Letzte | die Erinnerung nicht' (translated by Michael Hulse as 'And the last remnants | memory destroys'). These lines are underlined in Sebald's copy of Hölderlin,[72] where the original couplet reads 'Danken möcht ich, aber wofür? verzehret das Letzte | Selbst die Erinnerung nicht?', an interrogative, with 'consume' instead of the 'destroy' of the epigraph.[73] Space prevents a discussion here of the resonances and different possible readings of this line; however, it may be of interest to note that the elusive epigraph from 'Max Aurach' / 'Max Ferber' in *Die Ausgewanderten*: 'Im Abenddämmer kommen sie | und suchen nach dem Leben' [They come when night falls | to search for life] can also be discovered by means of the annotations in Sebald's library. Notwithstanding the fact that, in a recently published letter of February 2001, in reply to an enquiry by Torleiv Andersson, Sebald claims — 'if memory does not deceive me' — to have made up this last epigraph himself,[74] it appears to have its origins not in, say, an obscure corner of Heine, but to derive, surprisingly enough, from a free adaptation of the German translation of lines from one of the 'Odes of Ricardo Reis' by Fernando Pessoa:

> Os deuses desterrados,
> Os irmãos de Saturno,
> Às vezes, no crepúsculo
> Vêm espreitar a vida.
>
> Die Götter, die verbannten
> Geschwister des Saturn;
> kommen im Abenddämmern
> und spähen nach dem Leben.[75]

This little-known *trouvaille* should not, however, be used to create the impression that Sebald's library contained a wide collection of Portuguese and Latin American literature, though he did, of course, own a number of books by Borges (likewise in German translation). Where Italian literature is concerned, it too is mostly present in German translation or (in the case of Dante) in a bilingual edition, the exception being Leonardo Sciascia's *1912 + 1* (Milan: Adelphi, 1986), the eponymous date of which will resonate with readers of *Schwindel. Gefühle. (Vertigo)*.[76] Mention should also be made of the works not just of Primo Levi (in English) and Italo Calvino (in German) but of the five volumes, heavily annotated and underlined, of the Ferrarese stories by Giorgio Bassani (also in German translation), whose *Brille mit Goldrand* (*Gli occhiali d'oro*) features as one of the 'favourite books' on the Freiburg bookshop's list, along with Georges Perec's *W ou le souvenir d'enfance* (see Figure 11.1). Strangely enough, Sebald's own copy of this last is in English (possibly for teaching purposes), but on the whole the works in his French library — including, *inter alia*, works by Rousseau, Chateaubriand, Stendhal, Balzac, Flaubert, and, in the twentieth century, Michel Butor (*L'Emploi du temps*), Saint-Exupéry (*Vol de nuit*), Claude Simon (whose *Jardin des Plantes* is another 'favourite book'), and Natalie Sarraute (*Enfance*) — tend to be in the original language (with the notable exception of the Suhrkamp edition of Proust, in German translation, acquired on its appearance in the 1960s), while he owned editions of Casanova (cf. the Venice passages in *Schwindel. Gefühle.*) in both German and French.

FIG.. 11.10. Sebald's student Shakespeare in the bilingual 'rainbow' Rowohlt editions.
© The Estate of W. G. Sebald

The relative lack of contemporary English writers in the *Nachlassbibliothek* is made up for by an emphasis on earlier epochs (many of them acquired in the Everyman series, which Sebald seems to have collected piecemeal in local second-hand bookshops), and on the seventeenth century in particular: the works of Sir Thomas Browne, of course, and Shakespeare, but also Donne, Pepys, Aubrey's *Lives*, Bacon. There is, as well, secondary literature on that epoch: Barker's *Tremulous Private Body*, for example, the cover of which features Rembrandt's *Dr Tulp's Anatomy Lesson*, has some close echoes, albeit in German, in the Rembrandt passage of the opening section of *Die Ringe des Saturn*; while at an earlier stage of Sebald's academic career, Kermode's *The Sense of an Ending* has been heavily annotated,[77] as has (to return to the German poetic tradition) the two-volume Rowohlt paperback *Lyrik des Barock*.

Clearly it is not possible to embark here upon a detailed enumeration of the *Nachlassbibliothek* in its entirety; the importance of Adorno, Benjamin, and their like, and of contemporary criticism, such as that by (for example) John Berger, Barthes, Lévi-Strauss, Theweleit, Navratil, or Starobinski, has been noted elsewhere, and the accompanying Catalogue must suffice to give an overview in particular of the wide range of German literature, *Germanistik*, and other more 'topographical' holdings. Instead, a few comments on the putative stages of acquisition and annotation may give a snapshot, in what follows, of the speculative *Entstehungsgeschichte* (story of its genesis) of the library.

Acquisition

> Von allen Arten, sich Bücher zu verschaffen, wird als die rühmlichste betrachtet, sie selbst zu schreiben. [...] Schriftsteller sind eigentlich Leute, die Bücher nicht aus Armut sondern aus Unzufriedenheit mit den Büchern schreiben, welche sie kaufen könnten, und die ihnen nicht gefallen.

> [Of all the ways of acquiring books, writing them oneself is regarded as the most praiseworthy method. [...] Writers are really people who write books not because they are poor, but because they are dissatisfied with the books which they could buy but do not like.]

WALTER BENJAMIN,
'Ich packe meine Bibliothek aus' ('Unpacking my Library')[78]

Contemplating Sebald's library and the inscriptions, dedications, and annotations, it is possible to conjecture a rough order of acquisition, which may be divided into a number of phases, tentatively sketched in what follows.

The earliest books whose acquisition is recorded date from the 1960s. Like many of us, one suspects, in student days Sebald was prone to writing his full name and the date and place the book was acquired on the flyleaf, often horizontally, still at the time using the name Winfried. Thus Benjamin's *Ursprung des deutschen Trauerspiels* is signed in blue ink 'e.l. Winfried Sebald Juli 1964', and *Illuminationen* (in black ink) 'Winfried Sebald März 1965'; given the crucial importance of Benjamin to all of Sebald's work, it goes without saying that these volumes are heavily annotated, as are those of Adorno and other proponents of the Frankfurt School (notably the *Dialektik der Aufklärung*).[79] One of the earliest dated acquisitions (it should be noted that such volumes are a tiny minority; with a single exception — from 1968[80] — the dating ceases around 1966) is Shakespeare's *The Tempest / Der Sturm*, in the parallel-text series (using the Schlegel–Tieck translation) 'Rowohlts Klassiker der Literatur und der Wissenschaft: Englische Literatur', signed in pencil 'exlibris Winfr. Sebald Okt 62'. The book had appeared only that year (the series was launched in the late 1950s) and he seems to have acquired — or retained — eighteen further volumes from this rainbow-spined series published between 1958 and 1969 (Figure 11.10), including *Richard III* (April 1963), *A Midsummer Night's Dream* (February 1964), *As You Like It* (November 1964), *Troilus and Cressida* ('J 66'), and, of course, *Hamlet* (March 1966). It is worth noting that the earliest 'Winfried' gives way, in 1966, to 'W. Sebald' and then, in the copy of *Hamlet*, to plain 'Sebald'. On the other, undated, volumes the signature moves from the bottom right of the flyleaf to the top left endpaper inside the front cover: most of the books, acquired presumably through the 1970s and into the 1980s, are signed in this way, sometimes in black ink, sometimes in felt-tip pen of a colour matching the book's cover: this is often carried over, too, into the underlinings. A study of the signatures in the Suhrkamp Proust *Werkausgabe* and the dtv *Goethe-Gesamtausgabe* may, like the Shakespeare, be taken as examples of this evolving style (see Figs 11.11–14 overleaf).

Such timescales of acquisition must of course remain largely speculative, but two further marks of ownership should be noted here. The first is a brown *ex libris* affixed in the top left-hand corner inside the front cover of the books in question; its form

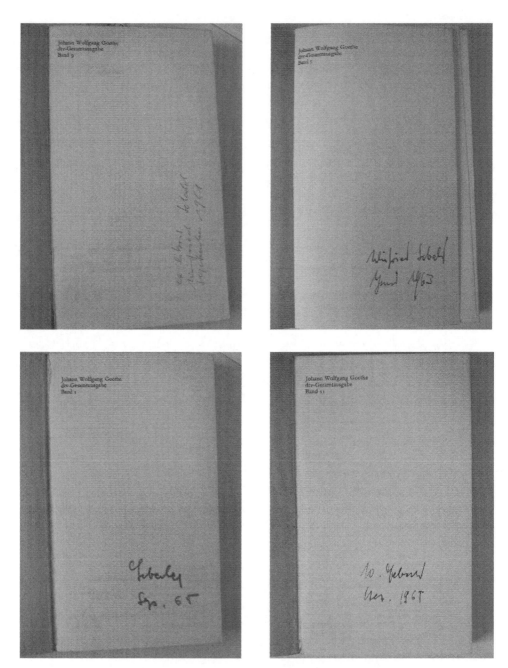

FIGS. 11.11, 11.12, 11.13, 11.14. 'Ex libris W. G. Sebald':
Four early examples of signatures in the dtv paperback edition of Goethe
he collected as a student. Could Goethe's *Faust* (FIG. 11.11) really be one of the
first books acquired by WGS? © The Estate of W. G. Sebald

is shown on the cover of Atze and Loquai's *Sebald. Lektüren*. Roughly speaking, this might be said to apply to books acquired in the later 1970s and the 1980s, though as there is no date of acquisition noted this is difficult to establish with any certainty. In the late 1980s and early 1990s (again, the same caveat must apply) one finds a discreet embossed stamp, bearing the words 'Library of W. G. Sebald' encircling the initials 'WGS', on the lower right-hand corner of the flyleaf of a substantial number of books, but this too seems to have been discarded, and the most recent books bear no trace of ownership save the occasional, and one may speculate increasingly discreet, *Lesespuren* or marginal notes next to passages of interest.

Annotation

> Auch die literarischen Quellen und Einflüsse gehören nämlich zu den Mitteln, deren sich die Dichtung zu ihren Metamorphosen bedient. [...] Gerade die mit Anstreichungen, Kreuzen und Randbemerkungen versehenen Stellen in den Büchern bestätigen, auf wie viele verschiedene Weisen [er] gelesen hat, auf wie viele verschiedene Weisen er das Gelesene in seine eigenen Werke aufgenommen hat.

> [Literary sources and influences are also part of the means literature uses to effect its metamorphoses. [...] It is precisely the passages marked with annotations, crosses, and marginal notes in the books which confirm in how many different ways [he] read, in how many different ways he incorporated what he read into his own works.]

MICHAEL HAMBURGER, 'Hofmannsthals Bibliothek'[81]

W. G. Sebald's habit of reading with pencil in hand (or indeed biro, or even, on some occasions, felt-tip pen) makes his library, like Hofmannsthal's in the description by Michael Hamburger above, a treasure trove for researchers and *Quellenforscher*, although here a note of caution should be sounded; just as the presence or absence of a book in Sebald's library is not conclusive proof of his having read, or not read, it, so too the presence or absence of *Lesespuren* (literally 'reading traces') in the guise of annotations, underlining, circling, or sidelining is not always a reliable guide to the significance of a particular passage for its reader, other than at the moment of underlining. As Michael Hamburger points out in the case of Hofmannsthal, such sources need not necessarily imply influence; nor need the absence of explicit or covert references mean that a given author or work is not significant.[82] Likewise, while many of the direct and indirect quotations to be found in both Sebald's academic and fictional works are helpfully (for the researcher) underlined or 'sidelined' in the editions he used, the fact that a potential source is not mentioned directly does not, as suggested above, rule out its significance. Again, Michael Hamburger's discussion of Hofmannsthal's annotations and notes on books read sums up the matter neatly:

> [Es] wird [...] nicht immer möglich sein, [...] festzustellen, ob [er] ein erwähntes Buch als Leser, als Kritiker oder als Dichter verwertet hat; ob es zu jenen gehörte, in denen er Aufklärung oder Belehrung suchte; ob zu jenen, mit denen er die eigene Phantasie anregte, oder die ihm halfen, irgendeine Lücke in der eigenen Erfahrung zu füllen, einen historischen Hintergrund auszumalen, eine dramatische Motivierung mit Einzelheiten aus dem Leben anderer Menschen zu verstärken.[83]

[It will not always be possible to establish whether [he] made use of a particular book as a reader, a critic, or a writer; whether it was one of those he read for enlightenment or instruction, or used as a stimulus to his own creative imagination, or which helped him to fill in a gap in his own experience, to elaborate historical background details, or to intensify a dramatic motive with details from the life of another person.]

The evolving styles of annotation in Sebald's library, one may conjecture, correspond roughly to the phases outlined in the discussion of signatures and *ex libris* above. No exhaustive study can be undertaken here, but one may summarize, tentatively, that the earliest books tend to be the most heavily annotated, partly because of what some would see as a natural tendency to find a great deal worthy of underlining at the early stages of an academic *Laufbahn*; and partly as a result of repeated re-readings for academic, and indeed creative, purposes, at first in ink or ballpoint, then, as with the Rowohlt Shakespeare mentioned above, in a variety of coloured felt pens. This phase, possibly to be identified with the 1970s and early 1980s, gives way to the use of pencil and the occasional black or blue biro, and the underlinings are on the whole replaced by the characteristic 'double sidelinings' (see Clive Scott's comments in Chapter 9 of this volume), although the two may exist, as it were, side by side. In some works, particularly review copies or translations, a number of terms are circled, sometimes accompanied by question marks in the margin: these seem to denote an uncertainty about, or disagreement with, the terms employed. In general, though there are always exceptions, these *Lesespuren* become fainter and less definite in more recently read books. Of course, there may also be the palimpsest effect of repeated readings for different purposes (again, early copies of works of Benjamin, or indeed of Kafka, would be an example here). In library copies, annotations are inevitably limited to discreet pencil sidelinings, with the occasional comment or cryptic initial in the margin; there is, in these cases, the additional difficulty of attributing such marks to Sebald, rather than to other users with whose marginalia they may (albeit rarely, many books in the German section of the UEA library being somewhat underused) be intermixed.

'Einlagen' and notes: the travelling book

Was die Aufzeichnungen betrifft, die sich meistens auf den Vorsatzblättern der Bücher befinden, ist es in vielen Fällen nicht selbstverständlich, daß sie sich auf das gelesene Buch beziehen, da Hofmannsthal dieses oft — ebenso wie lose Zettel oder Briefumschläge — zu Notizen für eigenen Werke benutzte; ganz besonders, wenn er unterwegs war, wie die in manchen Büchern noch jetzt enthaltenen Straßenbahnfahrscheine für die Strecke Rodaun-Wien bezeugen.

[As far as the notes are concerned, mostly on the flyleaf or endpapers of the books, in many cases it is by no means evident that they refer to the book in question, since Hofmannsthal often used the book he was reading — as well as loose scraps of paper and the backs of envelopes — to make notes for works of his own; particularly when travelling, as the tram tickets for the journey from Rodaun to Vienna still to be found in some of his books demonstrate.]

MICHAEL HAMBURGER, 'Hofmannsthals Bibliothek'[84]

Sebald, too, reads while travelling, perhaps travels while reading (Butor):[85] instead of the tram ticket (though these occur too, from Munich, for example, as well as Vienna) we find the boarding card, or sometimes a receipt from the station buffet or bookshop where, one may conjecture, the book in question was acquired during one of his research trips or, latterly, reading tours. For example, on his last, exhausting whistle-stop reading tour of the USA after the publication of Anthea Bell's translation of *Austerlitz*, his in-flight reading was, it seems, a book on homing pigeons: Scott Moyers, then Sebald's editor at Random House, who accompanied him on the tour, relates his wonderment at the ability of such a bird, released from a ship, to return to that same ship even though its location was then different[86] (a resonant metaphor for the layers of dislocation and 'unheimliche Heimat' in Sebald's works). His fascination with doves and pigeons (*Tauben* in German covers both of the English terms) is well documented, inasmuch as they recur in almost all his works (much like Nabokov and his butterflies, who find their 'Schattenseite' [dark side] in the moths of *Austerlitz*, though with arguably a less clearly defined or overt literary purpose) — and, importantly, they tie in with, or tie together, the similarly recurring motifs of 'levitation', flight (in the literal sense), and migration. One may speculate that this — peculiarly apposite — reading material was in connection with Sebald's next project, still in the planning stages, relating to the First World War, when carrier pigeons were extensively used to convey messages from the front. Fittingly, perhaps, there is no trace of such a book in his library; however, a cutting from the *New York Times* about racing pigeons was inserted in the American edition of *Austerlitz* from which, one assumes, he will have been reading on the tour,[87] as is suggested by the additional presence in that copy of fan letters and faxes relating to various reading dates, as well as the trademark leaf bookmarks — one of them, at least, from a *ginkgo biloba*.

Indeed leaves, and occasionally grasses and flowers, often occur in the guise of bookmarks; and a child's drawings, sometimes designated 'bookmark' in a youthful hand, are another frequent, and poignant, occurrence. It would take an article of a different scope to attempt to attribute a system to such inserts, and would likely prove a sterile undertaking quite contrary to the spirit of their insertion. More systematic, and perhaps of more interest to the scholar, are the book reviews or related articles (often from German broadsheets such as *Die Zeit*) inserted in the relevant book, while letters and postcards may sometimes relate to the book in question (particularly if a gift) and at other times be, again, merely convenient place markers, along with occasional theatre or museum tickets, tram tickets, and their modern-day equivalent, the boarding card.[88]

The books in the library, then, are themselves implicated in the journeys of their owner, and — again like Hofmannsthal's books (in the quotation above) — often bear the traces of spontaneous ideas, or else momentary distraction. A case in point is the apparent trying out of phrases or sentences which later find their home in the works, particularly *Austerlitz*, frequently noted in pencil in the margins or endpapers of books with no immediately obvious connection to that work (see also Chapter 9 of the present volume), although one also finds embryonic reading lists, course outlines, phone numbers and other apparently random jottings. The most notable example, however, is the chronology of *Austerlitz* sketched out in the back of one of Sebald's 'favourite books', Claude Simon's *Le Jardin des Plantes*.[89] It is in the back of another volume of Claude Simon's, *Le Tramway*, published by Les Éditions de Minuit in April 2001, that we find a fully formed verbal sketch or snapshot evoking a summer morning in a (presumably) French café (Figure 11.15); in this way the book — in this case, fittingly, named after a means of transport — becomes also a travelling notebook or sketchbook, a further springboard for the creative process.

One may conclude this brief glimpse into Sebald's library as it began, with Michael Hamburger's closing remarks on the library of that other 'lesende[r] Dichter', or 'reading writer', Hugo von Hofmannsthal:

> Abschließend soll noch einmal betont werden, daß die Anzahl und Verschiedenartigkeit der mitgeteilten Bezüge keineswegs für die Abhängigkeit Hofmannsthals sprechen. Wenn einige davon bis jetzt der Forschung entgangen sind, so beweist gerade dies die außerordentliche Fähigkeit Hofmannsthals, das von anderen Geborgte mit Eigenem zu verschmelzen — eine durchaus dichterische Fähigkeit.[90]

> [In conclusion we should emphasize once more that the number and diversity of the available references by no means testify to dependence on the part of Hofmannsthal. If some of them have thus far escaped the notice of researchers, this just goes to demonstrate his extraordinary ability to blend what was borrowed from others with words of his own; an ability which is the hallmark of a true poet.]

Like Hugo von Hofmannsthal in Hamburger's description, then, one may see W. G. Sebald, too, as one of those writers who 'return to themselves via long detours':

> Zu den Umwegen gehörten die Werke anderer Menschen, die [er] lesend erlebte, darum auch wie alles Erlebte in das eigene Werk aufnahm. [...]
>   Außerdem ist es ein Gesetz, daß der wahre Dichter nur das von anderen übernehmen kann, was er schon selber besitzt; das Fremde verhilft zur Katalyse des Eigenen.[91]

> [These detours included the works of others, experienced through reading and therefore incorporated, like everything [he] experienced, into his own work. [...]
>   What is more, it is axiomatic that the true poet can only take (over) from others that which he already possesses: the other becomes a catalyst for the self.]

Notes to Chapter 11

1. Michel Butor, 'Travel and Writing', trans. by John Powers and K. Lisker, *Mosaic*, 8.1 (Fall 1974), 2–3.
2. Michael Hamburger, 'Hofmannsthals Bibliothek', *Euphorion*, 55 (1961), 15–76 (p. 16).
3. Cited in Marcel Atze, 'Bibliotheca Sebaldiana: W. G. Sebald — ein Bibliophile? Eine Spekulation', in *W. G. Sebald*, ed. by Franz Loquai (Eggingen: Isele, 1997), pp. 228–43 (p. 243). See also: Axel Gellhaus, 'Marginalien: Paul Celan als Leser', in *Der glühende Leertext: Annäherungen an Paul Celans Dichtung*, ed. by Christoph Jamme und Otto Pöggeler (Munich: Fink, 1993), pp. 41–65; '*Wann ordnest Du Deine Bücher?*': Die Bibliothek H. C. Artmann, ed. by Marcel Atze and Hermann Böhm (Vienna: Sonderzahl, 2006); Dietmar Rieger, *Imaginierte Bibliotheken: Bücherwelten in der Literatur* (Munich: Fink, 2002).
4. Hugo Dittberner, 'Das Ausführlichste oder: ein starker Hauch Patina: W. G. Sebalds Schreiben', *Text + Kritik*, no. 158 (April 2003), 6–14 (p. 7).
5. Atze, 'Bibliotheca Sebaldiana'; cf. Ulrich von Bülow, Chapter 10 of the present volume.

6. W. G. Sebald, *Die Ringe des Saturn* (Frankfurt a.M.: Eichborn, 1995), p. 337; W. G. Sebald, *The Rings of Saturn*, trans. by Michael Hulse (London: Harvill, 1998), p. 271.

7. Sebald's own library contained the following works by or relating to Sir Thomas Browne (the peregrinations of whose own library would be a study in its own right): *The Works of Sir Thomas Browne*, ed. by Charles Sayle, 3 vols (Edinburgh: John Grant, 1927); *Religio Medici* (London: Dent (Everyman), 1928); Sir Thomas Browne, *Religio Medici 1643*, trans. by Werner von Koppenfels (Mainz: Dieterich'sche Verlagsbuchhandlung, 1998); Cha[rle]s Williams, *Souvenir of Sir Thomas Browne* (Norwich: Jarrolds, 1905). See also Anne Fuchs, *Schmerzensspuren der Geschichte: Zur Poetik der Erinnerung in W. G. Sebalds Prosa* (Cologne: Böhlau, 2004), pp. 99–107 ('The Labyrinth of Truth'); Ben Hutchinson, *W. G. Sebald: Die dialektische Imagination* (Berlin: de Gruyter, 2009), pp. 124–27; Susanne Schedel, *Wer weiß, wie es vor Zeiten wirklich gewesen ist? Textbeziehungen als Mittel der Geschichtsdarstellung bei W. G. Sebald* (Würzburg: Königshausen & Neumann, 2004), pp. 134–44 and p. 151.

8. Umberto Eco, *The Infinity of Lists* [*La vertigine della lista*], trans. by Alastair McEwen (London: MacLehose, 2009).

9. *Die Ringe des Saturn*, p. 28; *The Rings of Saturn*, p. 19. See Jo Catling, 'Gratwanderungen bis an den Rand der Natur: W. G. Sebald's Landscapes of Memory', in *The Anatomist of Melancholy: Essays in Memory of W. G. Sebald*, ed. by Rüdiger Görner (Munich: iudicium, 2003), pp. 19–50 (pp. 25–28); Ben Hutchinson also refers to this 'art of levitation' in 'Die Leichtigkeit der Schwermut: W. G. Sebalds "Kunst der Levitation"', *Jahrbuch der Deutschen Schillergesellschaft*, 50 (2006), 457–77.

10. Cf. also Sir Thomas Browne, 'Musæum Clausum, or Bibliotheca Abscondita', in *The Works of Sir Thomas Browne*, ed. by Geoffrey Keynes, 6 vols (London: Faber, 1931), v: *Miscellaneous Writings*, pp. 131–42 (p. 131).

11. *Die Ringe des Saturn*, pp. 337–38; *The Rings of Saturn*, p. 271.

12. Jorge Luis Borges, 'Tlön, Uqbar, Orbis Tertius', in *Fictions*, trans. by Andrew Hurley (London: Penguin, 2000), pp. 7–25 (p. 25).

13. On Borges, see Schedel, *Wer weiß, wie es vor Zeiten wirklich gewesen ist?*, pp. 144–54; Gabriele Eckart, 'Against "Cartesian Rigidity": W. G. Sebald's Reception of Borges', in *W. G. Sebald: Schreiben ex patria / Expatriate Writing*, ed. by Gerhard Fischer (Amsterdam: Rodopi, 2009), pp. 509–21; on Browne and Borges in *Die Ringe des Saturn*, see also Mandana Covindassamy, 'Trois anneaux de Saturne: Chateaubriand, Borges et Thomas Browne: Itération des références littéraires et production du sens', in *W. G. Sebald: Mémoire. Transferts. Images / Erinnerung. Übertragungen. Bilder*, ed. by Ruth Vogel-Klein (= *Recherches Germaniques*, special issue 2 (2005)), pp. 157–72, especially pp. 163–72.

14. *Die Ringe des Saturn*, pp. 92–93; *The Rings of Saturn*, pp. 70–71.

15. *Die Ringe des Saturn*, p. 91; *The Rings of Saturn*, p. 69.

16. A similar critique of mechanical, and non-mechanical, reproduction is offered by Henri Beyle's (Stendhal's) account of the displacement of experience and memory by representation: see W. G. Sebald, *Schwindel. Gefühle.* (Frankfurt a.M.: Fischer, 2000), p. 11; *Vertigo*, trans. by Michael Hulse (London: Harvill, 1999), p. 8 (*Prospetto d'Ivrea*). The *reductio ad absurdum* comes in *Austerlitz*, with the erection of 'La Très Grande Bibliothèque' on the site of memory (the 'Lager Austerlitz', a repository of looted Jewish effects, on the eponymous Quai in Paris), thus literally burying that memory beneath an edifice dedicated to the preservation of the written word. See also James L. Cowan, 'Sebald's *Austerlitz* and the Great Library: A Documentary Study', in *W. G. Sebald: Schreiben ex patria / Expatriate Writing*, ed. by Fischer, pp. 193–212.

17. Uwe Wolff, 'On the Way to the Centre: The Labyrinth Is Not a Maze', in Jürgen Hohmuth and others, *Labyrinths and Mazes* (Munich: Prestel, 2003), pp. 8–13 (p. 8). In the same volume, Adrian Fisher points out that 'Labyrinths are built on a flat surface, so that everyone can see each other, whereas mazes are created with vertical barriers of hedges or fences, so that everyone remains hidden' (Adrian Fisher, 'The Maze Maker', in *Labyrinths and Mazes*, pp. 98–103 (pp. 99–100)). See also Nigel Pennick, *Mazes and Labyrinths* (London: Robert Hale, 1994). In Sebald's text, though, the term 'Labyrinth' stands for both.

18. *Die Ringe des Saturn*, p. 51; *The Rings of Saturn*, p. 58.

19. *Die Ringe des Saturn*, p. 216; *The Rings of Saturn*, p. 173.

20. In the actual yew maze in Somerleyton, however, this is quite hard to do (although it may well depend on one's personal sense of direction, whether the day is bright or overcast, and whether, perhaps, one is carrying a copy of *Die Ringe des Saturn* open at the relevant page, with an aerial view of the maze neatly presented). The source of the image is in all probability a tourist brochure advertising Somerleyton Hall.

21. Cf. also, in *Schwindel. Gefühle.*, the image of the 'labyrinth' map of Milan (p. 122; *Vertigo*, p. 107). Interestingly, no mention is made in that work of the box maze to be found in the Giardino Giusti in Verona.

22. W. G. Sebald, *Nach der Natur: Ein Elementargedicht* (Frankfurt a.M: Fischer, 1995), p. 98; *After Nature*, trans. by Michael Hamburger (London: Hamish Hamilton, 2002), p. 108. For a detailed analysis of these intertextual allusions see Jo Catling, 'W. G. Sebald: Ein "England-Deutscher"? Identität–Topographie–Intertextualität', in *W. G. Sebald: Intertextualität und Topographie*, ed. by Irène Heidelberger-Leonard and Mireille Tabah (Berlin: LIT Verlag, 2008), pp. 25–53.

23. See Catling, 'W. G. Sebald: Ein "England-Deutscher"?'; cf. Iain Galbraith, 'Michael Hamburger's "Chandos Moment"? Reflections on the "Niemandsland-Variationen"', in *From Charlottenburg to Middleton: Michael Hamburger (1924–2007): Poet, Translator, Critic*, ed. by Joyce Crick, Martin Liebscher, and Martin Swales (Munich: iudicium, 2010), pp. 70–88.

24. *Die Ringe des Saturn*, p. 238; *The Rings of Saturn*, p. 173.

25. Hugo von Hofmannsthal, *Ausgewählte Werke*, ed. by Rudolf Hirsch, 2 vols (Frankfurt a.M.: Fischer, 1957), II: *Erzählungen und Aufsätze*.

26. Hamburger, 'Hofmannsthals Bibliothek', p. 16.

27. W. G. Sebald, 'Le promeneur solitaire: Zur Erinnerung an Robert Walser', in *Logis in einem Landhaus* (Munich: Hanser, 1998), pp. 127–68 (p. 139); 'Le promeneur solitaire: A Remembrance of Robert Walser', trans. by Jo Catling, introduction to Robert Walser, *The Tanners*, trans. by Susan Bernofsky (New York: New Directions, 2009), pp. 1–36 (p. 10).

28. Hamburger, 'Hofmannsthals Bibliothek', p. 16.

29. Walter Benjamin, 'Ich packe meine Bibliothek aus', in *Ausgewählte Schriften*, II: *Angelus Novus* (Frankfurt a.M.: Suhrkamp, 1966), pp. 169–78 (p. 169) [the edition in Sebald's library]; 'Unpacking my Library', in *Illuminations*, trans. by Harry Zohn (London: Fontana, 1992), pp. 61–69 (p. 61).

30. See 'A Catalogue of W. G. Sebald's Library' in Part II of this volume, pp. 377–441.

31. Atze, 'Bibliotheca Sebaldiana' (see note 3 above).

32. Christian Wirth has begun to put together such a list, under the heading 'Bibliotheca Sebaldiana', on his website <http://www.wgsebald.de/bibl/biblioteca.html> [accessed 30 April 2010], and notes: 'Ob es sich um reale oder virtuelle Buchquellen handelt, das herauszufinden bleibt der immer größer werdenden Schar von bibliophilen Sebaldianern vorbehalten' [Whether we are dealing with real or virtual books is something which may be left to the ever-increasing host of bibliophile Sebald readers to discover].

33. *Schwindel. Gefühle.*, pp. 244–46, pp. 210–11; *Vertigo*, pp. 224–25, p. 194.

34. One should perhaps also include in this virtual catalogue the *Handbibliothek* of the British Centre for Literary Translation, mainly containing reference works and works translated by visiting translators on residencies (known as 'bursaries'). Some few library books also unaccountably found their way into Sebald's own library, for example, a UEA Library copy of Thomas Bernhard's *Der Untergeher* (admittedly the library owned more than one copy of the text), and a 1974 copy of *Die Jagdgesellschaft*, by the same author, which bears the stamp 'Goethe-Institut e.V. Bibliothek', perhaps dating from his time at the Goethe-Institut in Munich.

35. Atze, 'Bibliotheca Sebaldiana', pp. 228–29.

36. The volumes to which this list relates have been designated [★] in the Catalogue.

37. © The Estate of W. G. Sebald. With thanks for the kind permission to reproduce this note.

38. Atze, 'Bibliotheca Sebaldiana', p. 232 (where he also provides the caveat that this would involve identifying the author with his narrator or protagonist).

39. See *Die Ringe des Saturn*, pp. 15–16; *The Rings of Saturn*, pp. 8–9.

40. This did, even at the time, give me pause for thought as to its implications for the future UEA German syllabus. Alas, I can no longer recall which particular book or books were the subject of this exchange; but after that Max Sebald would from time to time pass on to me books he no

longer had use for (an edition of Wedekind springs to mind, a book on Berlin); and occasionally I would come into my office to find a pile of books on the chair, sometimes with a note 'Can you use these?', sometimes left anonymously.

41. Such books, including those alluded to above, are listed (where known), in the section 'Books disposed of by the author' in the Catalogue.

42. 'Le promeneur solitaire', p. 162; 'Le promeneur solitaire', trans. by Catling, p. 31.

43. The 1998 collection *Logis in einem Landhaus*, to be published by Hamish Hamilton in an English translation by Jo Catling as *A Place in the Country* in 2011, contains, in addition to the Walser essay, pieces on both Gottfried Keller and Jean-Jacques Rousseau. (Primary Bibliography D.68(a), D.72, D.69(a).)

44. Atze, 'Bibliotheca Sebaldiana', p. 228; cf. *Schwindel. Gefühle.*, pp. 278–80; *Vertigo*, pp. 255–56. See also Ingeborg Bachmann, 'Böhmen liegt am Meer', in *Werke*, I (Munich: Piper, 1993), pp. 167–68; William Shakespeare, *The Winter's Tale*, Act III, Scene 3. On the Shakespearian resonances and connections to events of 1612/13(!), see Verena Olejniczak Lobsien, 'Herkunft ohne Ankunft: Der Chronotopos der Heimatlosigkeit in W. G. Sebald', in *Herkünfte: historisch-ästhetisch-kulturell*, ed. by Barbara Thums et al (Heidelberg: Winter, 2004), pp. 221–48 (pp. 229–32).

45. Jean-Pierre Rondas, '"So wie ein Hund, der den Löffel vergißt": Ein Gespräch mit W. G. Sebald über *Austerlitz*', interview on *Austerlitz* [22 May 2001], in *Literatur im Krebsgang: Totenbeschwörung und memoria in der deutschsprachigen Literatur nach 1989*, ed. by Arne De Winde and Anke Gilleir, Amsterdamer Beiträge zur neueren Germanistik, 64 (Amsterdam: Rodopi, 2008), pp. 351–63 (p. 360). (Primary Bibliography J.41.1.)

46. W. G. Sebald, *Austerlitz* (Munich: Hanser, 2001), p. 207; W. G. Sebald, *Austerlitz*, trans. by Anthea Bell (London: Hamish Hamilton, 2001), p. 203; see also Cowan, 'Sebald's *Austerlitz* and the Great Library: A Documentary Study'.

47. *Schwindel. Gefühle.*, pp. 244–46; *Vertigo*, pp. 224–25.

48. *Schwindel. Gefühle.*, pp. 211–12; *Vertigo*, p. 194. Some of these books, along with a few others left in the parental apartment in Sonthofen, are still extant, notably *Friedrich Schiller: Sein Leben und seine Dichtungen*, 4 vols (Berlin: Volksbühnen-Verlags und Vertriebs G.m.b.h, 1924); William Shakespeare, *Dramatische Werke*, trans. by Schlegel and Tieck, 6 vols (Berlin: Volksbühnen-Verlags und Vertriebs G.m.b.h, 1924). With thanks to Gertrud Aebischer-Sebald for volunteering this information.

49. Rondas, '"So wie ein Hund, der den Löffel vergißt"', p. 356.

50. Ibid.

51. Rondas, '"So wie ein Hund, der den Löffel vergißt"', p. 357.

52. Rondas, '"So wie ein Hund, der den Löffel vergißt"', p. 356.

53. W. G. Sebald, 'Ein Versuch der Restitution', in *Campo Santo*, ed. by Sven Meyer (Munich: Hanser, 2003), pp. 240–48 (p. 241); 'An Attempt at Restitution', in *Campo Santo*, trans. by Anthea Bell (London: Penguin, 2005), pp. 206–15 (p. 208).

54. See W. G. Sebald, 'Eine kleine Traverse: Das poetische Werk Ernst Herbecks', in *Die Beschreibung des Unglücks* (Frankfurt a.M.: Fischer, 2005), pp. 131–48; 'Peter Altenberg — Le Paysan de Vienne', in *Unheimliche Heimat* (Frankfurt a. M.: Fischer, 1995), pp. 65–86.

55. See W. G. Sebald, 'Berge oder das ...', *Manuskripte* 28, 99 (March 1988), 71–78; W. G. Sebald, 'Verzehret das letzte selbst die Erinnerung nicht?', *Manuskripte*, 28, 100 (June 1988), 150–58. See also Sebald's comments on the genesis of *Schwindel. Gefühle.* in the interview with Piet de Moor in Part II of the present volume ('Three Conversations with W. G. Sebald'), p. 350.

56. 'A Writer Who Challenges Traditional Storytelling', edited interview with Susan Salter Reynolds [c. 17/18 October 2001], *Los Angeles Times*, Home Edition, 24 October 2001, Southern California Living section, p. E.1. (Primary Bibliography J.51.1.)

57. *Franz Kafka, nachgestellt*, ed. by Barbara Sichtermann (= *Freibeuter*, no. 16 (1983)); Anthony Northey, 'Kafka in Riva, 1913', *Neue Zürcher Zeitung* (Fernausgabe), 24 April 1987, Literatur und Kunst section, p. 37.

58. John Zilcosky, 'Uncanny Travels: The Impossibility of Getting Lost', in *W. G. Sebald: A Critical Companion*, ed. by J. J. Long and Anne Whitehead (Edinburgh: Edinburgh University Press, 2004), pp. 102–20 (p. 102).

59. *Schwindel. Gefühle.*, pp. 80–81; *Vertigo*, pp. 69–70.

60. To this day the largest cypress in the Giardino Giusti, purporting to be the tree in question, bears a plaque with the appropriate Goethe quotation. Cf. Johann Wolfgang von Goethe, *Italienische Reise, Goethes Werke*, xi: *Autobiographische Schriften*, iii, ed. by Erich Trunz (Hamburg: Wegner, 1967), p. 51.

61. Johann Wolfgang von Goethe, *Italienische Reise Erster und Zweiter Teil* (Munich: dtv, 1962), pp. 24–25, p. 23. Cf. *Schwindel. Gefühle.*, p. 106, p. 29; *Vertigo*, p. 93, p. 24. With thanks to Ellen Strittmatter (DLA) for the interest in Sebald's copy of Goethe which led to this intertextual discovery.

62. Title of a work by Harriet Ritvo in Sebald's library (Cambridge, MA: Harvard University Press, 1997).

63. Rondas, '"So wie ein Hund, der den Löffel vergißt"', p. 356. It is perhaps worth noting that Max Sebald's 'own' butterfly (by contrast to those, for example, mounted in collectors' cases in Andromeda Lodge in *Austerlitz*), immortalized both in *Austerlitz* and in the poster and catalogue of the Marbach exhibition, was not evidently one captured or collected but one that strayed into the house or garage, rather in the manner, perhaps, of the lost moths in *Austerlitz* (pp. 136–37 (Hanser); pp. 132–83 (Harvill)). See the cover of *Wandernde Schatten: W. G. Sebalds Unterwelt*, ed. by Ulrich von Bülow, Heike Gfrereis, and Ellen Strittmatter (Marbach am Neckar: Deutsche Schillergesellschaft, 2008).

64. The eight turquoise volumes of the bulky *Verzeichnis lieferbarer Bücher*, for example, were always our 'bible' when devising new courses or setting up reading lists.

65. The same claim may be made for the Pléiade 'Album' series — notably the *Album Stendhal* as a (re)source for *Schwindel. Gefühle.* — although in this case the source copies tend to be those in the UEA library.

66. The following books were noted by the DLA as having been found on the study desk: Philip Hoare, *Spike Island: The Memory of a Military Hospital* (London: 4th Estate, 2001); John Horne and Alan Kramer, *German Atrocities 1914: A History of Denial* (New Haven and London: Yale University Press, 2001); *1914–1918: La Grande Guerre vécue, racontée, illustrée par les combattants*, ed. by [René] Christian-Frogé, Preface by Maréchal Foch, 2 vols (Paris: Aristide Quillet, 1922), ii: *1917–*; Peter Oldham, *Battleground Europe: The Hindenburg Line* (London: Leo Cooper, 1997, repr. 2000); William Howard Russell, *Meine sieben Kriege: Die ersten Reportagen von den Schlachtfeldern des 19. Jahrhunderts*, trans. by Matthias Fienbork (Frankfurt a.M: Eichborn, 2000). All are now in the DLA.

67. See Chapter 6 of the present volume.

68. See Chapter 4 of the present volume.

69. These books are among a number of dedicated copies in Sebald's library, from friends, colleagues, and admirers (see also 'Lyrisches Intermezzo: Four Poems for Max Sebald' in Part II of the present volume, p. 308–15): such works are designated in the Catalogue in Part II with a [W] (= *Widmungsexemplar*) and include works by the aforementioned, as well as, among others, Adam Czerniawski, Günter Herburger, Wolfgang Schlüter, and Xavier Marías. See also W. G. Sebald, 'Ausgrabung der Vergangenheit', in Part II of the present volume, p. 344: 'die Zahl der Schriftsteller, die ich nicht missen möchte, [wird] immer geringer. Viel mehr als ein Fähnlein von sieben bringe ich kaum noch zusammen. Michael Hamburger ist aber, nebst Robert Walser, stets mit dabei' [the number of writers I could not live without grows ever smaller. I can scarcely now muster more than a small troop of seven or so. Michael Hamburger, though, along with Robert Walser, is always one of them].

70. *Die Ringe des Saturn*, p. 216, p. 227; *The Rings of Saturn*, pp. 173–74; p. 182. See Catling, 'W. G. Sebald: Ein "England-Deutscher"?', for a more detailed discussion of this intertextuality.

71. See Mark M. Anderson, 'Tristes Tropes: W. G. Sebald und die Melancholie der deutsch-jüdischen Vergangenheit', in *Gedächtnis und Identität: Die deutsche Literatur nach der Vereinigung*, ed. by Fabrizio Cambi (Würzburg: Königshausen & Neumann, 2008), pp. 231–42.

72. Friedrich Hölderlin, *Werke und Briefe*, ed. by Friedrich Beißner and Jochen Schmidt, 2 vols (Frankfurt a.M.: Insel, 1969), ii: *Gedichte: Hyperion*, p. 100.

73. 'Dr Henry Selwyn' was originally published as 'Verzehret das letzte selbst die Erinnerung nicht?', *Manuskripte*, 28, 100 (June 1988), 150–58 (cf. Primary Bibliography E.B.12).

74. See Torleiv Andersson, '"Det siste har jeg funnet på selv": Noen betraktinger løst forbundet med et brev fra W. G. Sebald', *Vinduet*, 64.1 (2010), 76–79. A facsimile of the letter, dated 21 February 2001, is reproduced there on p. 79. It seems not quite clear to what extent Sebald is being deliberately vague about the attribution of all four epigraphs. With thanks to Theo Collier (Wylie Agency, London) for drawing this volume to my attention.

75. Fernando Pessoa, *Alberto Caeiro, Dichtungen; Ricardo Reis, Oden*, bilingual Portuguese–German edn, trans. by Georg Rudolf Lind (Frankfurt a.M.: Fischer, 1989), pp. 178–79. The German verse is sidelined in Sebald's copy. An approximate English translation might read as follows: 'The gods, the banished ones / those siblings of Saturn / sometimes in the dusk they come / and search for life.'

76. Cf. also Schedel, *Wer weiß, wie es vor Zeiten wirklich gewesen ist?*, pp. 154–65.

77. Publication details of all books mentioned may be found in the Catalogue in Part II of this volume, p. 377–441.

78. Benjamin, 'Ich packe meine Bibliothek aus', p. 171; 'Unpacking my Library', p. 63.

79. See also Chapter 2 in this volume, pp. 53–54 and p. 96 n. 17.

80. Alfred de Vigny, *Servitude et grandeur militaires* (Paris: Gallimard, 1965).

81. Hamburger, 'Hofmannsthals Bibliothek', p. 17.

82. Ibid.

83. Ibid.

84. Ibid.

85. See the quotation which prefaces this chapter. Michel Butor had, of course, been a *lecteur* in Manchester not long before Sebald arrived there as *Lektor*, and the latter's heavily annotated copy of *L'Emploi du temps* bears the following inscription in black ink on the first page: 'Sunday night 12th/13th November 1966 Chorlton/Bleston' (Bleston being the fictional name Butor gives to Manchester, and Chorlton the suburb of that city in which Sebald had at that time recently found lodgings; see also Chapter 2).

86. Conversation with JMC in Norwich, 29 December 2009. On the subject of homing pigeons, see also 'Feuer und Rauch', Part II, p. 339, and Anthea Bell's comments in Chapter 8 (p. 212).

87. W. G. Sebald, *Austerlitz*, trans. by Anthea Bell, 1st edn (New York: Random House, 2001) (DLA).

88. See also the section 'Einlagen' (inserts) in the Marbach exhibition catalogue *Wandernde Schatten*.

89. This volume is one often exhibited in the permanent exhibition in the Literaturmuseum der Moderne, along with the manuscript of *Austerlitz*.

90. Hamburger, 'Hofmannsthals Bibliothek', p. 75.

91. 'Hofmannsthals Bibliothek', p. 76.

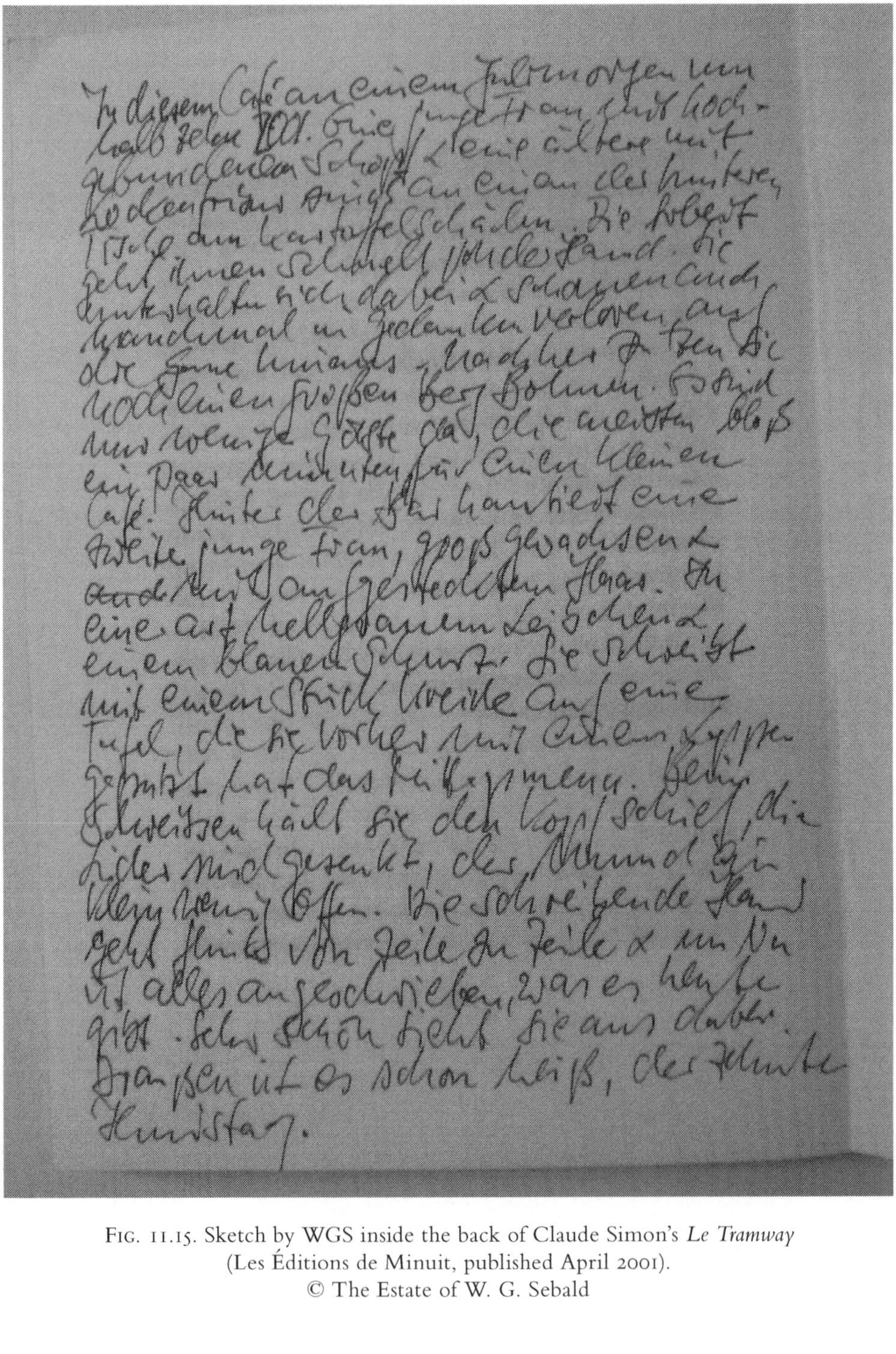

FIG. 11.15. Sketch by WGS inside the back of Claude Simon's *Le Tramway* (Les Éditions de Minuit, published April 2001).
© The Estate of W. G. Sebald

AFTERWORD

Max Sebald: A Reminiscence

Stephen Watts

I first got to know Max in 1990.

I had replied, rather hesitantly, to a notice, perhaps in the *TLS*, announcing some 'fellowships' and bursaries at the recently established British Centre for Literary Translation (BCLT) at UEA. I had not replied immediately, and I did so without a great deal of hope, because I was quite used to negative responses from academic sources. And after all I was applying for a bursary without being a translator — at the time I wasn't — but rather because I was compiling a bibliography of twentieth-century poetry in English translation. I was expecting a curt reply pointing out that since I wasn't a translator I wasn't eligible for a bursary. Instead I received a warm letter — I still have it somewhere — saying how valuable my project sounded and encouraging me to apply. It was, in my experience, typical of Max Sebald: warm, open, encouraging. I applied for a bursary and received one. That entailed living on campus for a month, which I did in March 1991. And during that month I got to know Max better, more closely.

But there is a sense in which he'd come to know me before I knew him, and since this sort of layered experience and time shift is close to the heart of his work — at least as I sense his work — it is perhaps worth explaining what I mean. This one example was repeated in various ways throughout the time that I knew him. It turned out that he had heard me reading a poem of mine on Radio 3, sometime in December 1983. The poem had been awarded a prize in that year's National Poetry Competition and there was a programme about the awards on the radio. Max — as he related to me after we had actually met — had been driving home from his work at UEA with the music channel on in his car, and he said that my poem had 'arrested' him so that momentarily he had forgotten he was driving and the car had started slipping across the road before he had righted its direction. He told me on a number of occasions how taken he had been by my poem and by the fact that its tone and language struck a chord inside him in ways most British poetry that he knew at that time didn't. It is difficult for me to say these things, because the sense in which I write and intend them may, of course, be much changed or slanted by the facts of his later death and high reputation. In writing all this now, I am far from trying to identify myself with his reputation. I do not feel the need to in any way, because I had his friendship and intellectual and moral sympathy: these are what mattered to me, and the loss of these is what I most lamented after his death.

There are, though, two other things I ought to say, even concerning this slippage, relating to when we first met. First, that the momentary loss of control at the wheel of his car when he heard my poem became an echo, for me at least, of the loss of control in the car accident that killed him and nearly killed his daughter. It seems almost certain that the head-on collision with an oncoming lorry in December 2001 was not what killed him, but rather that a sudden and intense heart attack had already ended his life instantaneously and itself caused the loss of control that led to his car crossing into the path of the lorry. But for me it was sobering, at the very least, to feel the echo of his car beginning to veer across the road back in December 1983. Such is the thin difference between lives and fictions.

The second thing I need to say is that whatever it was in my poem that struck deep chords in Max loosened something in his work. Those years of the mid-1980s were crucial both to his writing and to his creative development. He had already established an academic reputation with essays on Kafka, in particular, but also on modern German theatre and Austrian writers, and he had quietly been writing, and occasionally publishing, some poetry. He had also been at the very least 'storing up' various senses of prose and had perhaps written early versions of a novel; but he was not at that juncture able to burst the limits that really had to break before he could write his work of the late 1980s and on through the 1990s until his death. He had in a sense to break down language before this could happen, and happen it did, in some crisis of the mid-1980s and in particular at the time of his journey across the Alps in 1985, where he seems to have lost some sense of himself only to discover himself anew, in prose and poetic prose. This process, which in him was allowed to be controlled at the same time as it was loose and open — something difficult to achieve and something key to creativity — was of course composed of very many elements. If this were a longer study of Max Sebald's life and work I could look in more detail at some of them. But as it's a personal reminiscence I will keep to the personal, at least inasmuch as it may have relevance to his work. The poem Max heard me read on the radio in 1983 opens with the line: 'Lord in dream I was lifted out of London' (though this was a dream flight and not a plane's take-off).

This of course in itself is a 'reading after' Hölderlin, of his great poem 'Patmos' and its invocation of flight, of flight more as passage than of leaving. I might add, for its additional poignancy, that my reading of Hölderlin's poem came 'after' the English of Michael Hamburger, of Michael Hamburger's Hölderlin, with all the later-to-be-intensified echoes of that in Sebald's work. But when Max Sebald heard me read my poem 'Lord in Dream' in December 1983, it loosened something within him, and it veered not only his car, but also — as he told me after we had met, near on eight years later — a layer of his language. The long poem *Nach der Natur* (*After Nature*) that he was contemplating and also composing through the mid-1980s begins its final section — again in Michael Hamburger's English translation:

> Lord, I dreamed
> that to see Alexander's battle
> I flew all the way to
> Munich.[1]

Max told me on not a few occasions that as he heard my words 'Lord in dream' on the radio they sank into him and emerged later as a 'door' into the poem he was trying to write. I want to stress that I am saying this not to include myself by association in Max Sebald's poem, but rather to cast some light on the seemingly hidden processes of creativity, and creativity, if you want it, 'out of breakdown and the opening out of language'. It was not for nothing that he was drawn to such writers as Ernst Herbeck and Robert Walser.

I knew Max best in the early and mid-1990s. Later in that decade various things meant that we were less able either to meet or to meet with the same unfettered fluidity as before. Both his academic burdens and the effects of his literary life meant that he simply had less time. And for my part I also found that research and other demands of writing and living restricted my 'open' time.

But I did see him: during the 1990s I had two further research bursaries at UEA and also attended various conferences and such events. From 1996 I was, in addition, on the 'advisory panel' for BCLT and would cross paths with Max (who by then, though no longer director, was a lifetime panel member) at meetings in London and Norwich. From time to time we were able to take long or short walks in the grounds of UEA and he would talk about his worries and sometimes his hopes, whether among the kitchen gardens of the Hall that he loved or out among the oaks and other trees that he also loved, out toward the perimeter of the grounds in the wind and rains of those days. I have to say again that the openness of his friendship and his generosity of spirit were what, at the time and now looking back, struck me the most. I was immediately drawn to his warmth and open spirit, his humour, and I want to say this, not against talk of the melancholy in his writing, but alongside it. He was, quite simply, a very warm person whom it was both a delight and a support to know.

I have lived in the Whitechapel area of London since 1977. I talked about Tower Hamlets and this part of the inner East End quite a lot with Max and we met, from time to time, at Liverpool Street Station, a couple of times at least at McDonald's (and thus, for what it's worth, I can verify the ordinary 'truth' of such meetings over cups of tea that Sebald mentions in *Austerlitz*. He was, lest it be forgotten, very much the ordinary man, a son and grandson of the lower-middle class, even if he pulled at all that meant throughout his adult life. He would meet at McDonald's certainly for convenience's sake, and also I think because he knew many people had little other option). In 2000 we met at Liverpool Street and we walked through the old Spitalfields Market, across Commercial Street, up Puma Court and then down through the ward of St Mary's, across Brick Lane and Greatorex Street to Whitechapel High Street, and from there along to Stepney Green, turning left up Globe Road, then into Alderney Road (Alderney Street, as he names it in *Austerlitz*). I remember well the door in the wall, the old woman who looks after the graveyard, her dog, and the time Max and I walked in that suddenly open zone of grass and graves, which was hidden from most of the intense city that surrounds it.

Max used his camera quite a lot in the cemetery, one of the images making its way into the last pages of *Austerlitz*. On the way back we stopped for a biryani at the Dhaka Biryani House across on the opposite side of Mile End Road, not perhaps something Max relished as much as I did, and then walked through Whitechapel down to the western end of Cable Street. To Wilton's Music Hall where we heard Fiona Shaw perform — as I recall — Eliot's *The Waste Land* — or am I wrong? The dates of her performance would I suppose date our walk that day. It's accurate to say that I know parts of the inner East End inside out and that Max much enjoyed both walking and talking with me there. I should also point out that I am sure he walked there on his own and with other friends. Clearly for instance he walked through Tower Hamlets cemetery in Mile End behind Saint Clement's Hospital and I did not walk there with him, to the best of my memory.

But memory is a strange animal, and particularly in the writings of Max Sebald. It is surely one of the loveliest and yet most disquieting aspects of his world. A very small episode or example here: when I first moved to London I used to walk voraciously and everywhere. Especially in the East End (and especially to the top floors of tower blocks, though that isn't relevant to what I want to say now). From the late 1970s through to about the late 1980s I would often walk from Shadwell — where I live — to the Isle of Dogs, then still a zone of dereliction about to undergo transformation. Not infrequently I would walk along the Highway, past Ratcliff to Limehouse, along either Commercial Road or the then still quiet Narrow Street, onto West Ferry and right the way down, either by foot along the road and in and out of the cut-off estates or mazing through the dead docks, right down to Island Gardens and then through the foot tunnel under the Thames to Greenwich.

Now I know that I described this walk to Max and for sure there on page 139 of the English edition of *Austerlitz* is the brief sentence: 'Then we walked the rest of the way in silence, going on downstream from Wapping and Shadwell to the quiet basins which reflect the towering office blocks of the Docklands area, and so to the foot tunnel running under the bend in the river.'[2] In terms of Sebald's writings, this is curt and trimmed. A mere sentence of forty-four words. Did Max walk this himself? Did he? Did I walk there with him? Or did he simply 'lift' the outline of my memory into his text, as a writer of fiction, or non-fiction, reasonably might? Is it possible I can have forgotten whether we walked there on one occasion together? Yet it is a function, almost, not only of the slippage of memory, but also of the very style and attributes (the layering and accretions) of Sebald's work that I, as now one of his readers, should not be able accurately to recall this detail of our friendship, this detail of his creative work. Other things I can remember clearly and in detail, and I can be balanced and 'objective' about them. This detail, not. It hardly matters: maybe it only matters to mention it as an example of the distressings of memory that characterize Max Sebald's work. Maybe only for that reason do I not delete these last lines, seemingly pointless, from my page or mind or machine.

My last memories of Max are clearer, more reliable, if not always exact.

The last time we met in Spitalfields was — and I must try to pinpoint the date — sometime early in 2001. He was still working on the manuscript of *Austerlitz* (though close to finishing it) and had for many months intended to photograph my rucksack so as to use its image in his text. So he came to where I worked — Toynbee Studios, close to Aldgate East and a five-minute walk from Liverpool Street Station — and photographed the rucksack where it hung on an old (and now discarded) wooden shelf. It served his purpose. It isn't his rucksack — not, at least, the rucksack he owned and walked with. And I say this because some references to the photograph and rucksack in Sebald scholarship say that it is. Does it matter? Should I bother to 'correct' an error of information, rather than perpetuate what after all would be a typically 'Sebaldian' (horrible word he must hate!) illusion of truth? But, even so, it was and still is my rucksack, taken over of course by Max in his 'fictions'. To that extent it went over into his 'ownership' and that of whoever cares to read *Austerlitz*. But it was mine, it was an ex-Swedish Army rucksack that I had bought in Charing Cross Road, though not for ten shillings thirty years before (as Max has it) but rather for ten pounds perhaps six years before we met in 2001. It served me well. I am an inveterate walker in the city and elsewhere. And it has carried not only my provisions, my keep, but also many of my thoughts, both in the sense that I would put half-poems and lines written on odd scraps into the rucksack for 'safe' keeping, but also in the wider sense that it was a haven for me on my back. I said to Max that it was 'the one thing I could rely on' and in this I must have been echoing Ludwig Wittgenstein. Just as Max echoes many people and sources, without always saying so, in his work. But we did also, Max and I at this last meeting, talk of Wittgenstein at some length. He whose *Tractatus* I had read when I was 15 and 16 and myself embarking on something of a creative breakdown. He whose photograph — together with those of Walter Benjamin and others — Max had put in the corridor outside his office at UEA (see Figs. II.5–II.6, p. 376). And at this juncture in *Austerlitz* Max does write of Wittgenstein, of the 'outlandish' but 'uncanny' physical resemblance that the narrator remarks between Austerlitz and the philosopher.

Again, does any of this matter? These details, in a sense personal, in a sense not. What I do not want to do is to seem to be overemphasizing what matters little, or even more so to seem to be aggrandizing my self in someone else's text, especially when that person was a close friend and a very highly thought-of writer. It is, I want to say, enough for me that I had Max Sebald's close friendship, that I retain the friendship of others of his close friends and family, and that I, we, all have had to lament his death and abbreviated life, and to cope with such loss. And yet, just maybe some of what I am saying does matter a little and should be heard. If so, it would be precisely in these zones of mimesis and memory, so-called 'fact' and of fiction, the method of writing memory and history into what is neither fiction, nor essay, nor prose reverie or epic poem, but rather all of them at once. I think that as time passes and as scholarship unravels Sebald's work it will become apparent to what extent he leant into other people's lives and writings. For some this may detract from him; others may see it, as I do, as one of his greatest achievements.

In those same pages of *Austerlitz* Max quotes two lines from an early poem of mine: 'And so I long for snow to sweep across the low heights of London | London a lichen mapped on mild clays and its rough circle without purpose.'[3] It's from a poem titled 'Fragment ...' which I wrote sometime in the late 1970s and which first appeared in a slim book *The Lava's Curl* in 1990. (In fact I gave Max a copy of this book in 1991 when I went to UEA on my first bursary.) This poem, and these lines in particular with their link line 'the lonely railyards and trackhuts', describe, if a poem does describe, the zone between Bow, Hackney Wick, and Stratford that the line in from Norwich passes through as it draws its way toward inner London. I wasn't writing of that mainline journey so much as of the wastelands of railway and canal (and of the whole hinterland of Stratford with its then poverties and migration — and what might Max have made of its current regeneration?) that anyone living in London E15 at that time had to pass through. But it must have echoed with Max as the landscape he saw from the train window on all the journeys from Norwich into London and out again that he had to make in his professional life. Anyone who knew him will immediately recall the mix of dismay, exhaustion, horror, and abysmally comic acceptance with which he referred to those atrophying train journeys.

In *Austerlitz* these lines come to him as he stands in the Harley Street waiting room of a Czech ophthalmologist, having just travelled to Liverpool Street from Norwich through the zones of London that 'remain alien and incomprehensible in spite of all the years that have passed since my arrival in England' (zones, bear in mind, very close to where Dr Selwyn grew up on his arrival here). As he (and, of course, here we readers are called on to occupy this zone of narrator-author) waits and ponders in the Harley Street room he/I 'thought of the onset of winter in the mountains, the complete absence of sound, and my childhood wish for everything to be snowed over, the whole village and the valley all the way to the mountain peaks, and how I used to imagine what it would be like when we thawed out again and emerged from the ice in spring'.[4] And as he stood in the waiting room remembering the snow of the Alps, he imagined out there in the gathering dusk the city districts of London being covered and buried in snow. Overwhelmed in white just as his sight is being examined, just as journeying becomes more and more incomprehensible.

I want to say one other thing, something that I alluded to earlier.

And that is to do with Max Sebald's sense of the Alps. For me he is very much a writer 'from the Alps'. This might seem a strange, and misleading, thing to say of someone who lived much of his adult life in Manchester and then Norfolk, and who ostensibly wrote little of mountains. But I want to say it for various reasons. Not just that he was born and spent his childhood in the foothills of the Alps and within their sight. Not just because his first move away from the edge of Germany was into Switzerland, to Fribourg, or that he taught for a short while in St Gallen. Not that he held in high esteem the poetry of Ernst Herbeck, the writings of Robert Walser and of other Swiss and Austrian writers. Nor that I'd want at all to 'define' Herbeck, Walser, and others as 'writers of the Alps'. Not just for his evocation of those mountains in his first published work, the long poem *Nach der Natur* — those beautiful, painful words (painful aesthetically but also as moral history):

> So, when the optic nerve
> tears, in the still space of the air
> all turns as white as
> the snow on the Alps.[5]

Not simply for the once again beautiful references in *The Emigrants*:

> And so they are ever returning to us, the dead. At times they come back from
> the ice more than seven decades later and are found at the edge of the moraine,
> a few polished bones and a pair of hobnailed boots.[6]

Not only because his journey across the Alps in 1985 was part of a crucial, painful
movement in his creative trajectory that was close to the heart of a crisis, even
though this does seem to hold objective significance that goes beyond any personal
sense of his work I or anyone else may have. And not only because I think that
Schwindel. Gefühle. is for sure a key work in his *oeuvre* and also one of the great
texts of late-twentieth-century writing. Though I think this is true and that it is
significant as such. Not because he used to say, half-jokingly and half in mimesis
of Nabokov and others, that to live out his life in a Swiss hotel was one possibility
in an increasingly difficult range (rather rage!) of choices. No, there is something
else, something to do with the human spirit in the written word, that I may find
difficult to express, and that I am trying to allude to. In an interview with Eleanor
Wachtel, Sebald says:

> I grew up in a very small village, very high up in the Alps, about three thousand
> feet above sea level. And in the immediate post-war years, it was in many ways
> quite an archaic place. For instance, you couldn't bury the dead in the winter
> because the ground was frozen and there was no way of digging it up. So you
> had to leave them in the woodshed for a month or two until the thaw came.
> You grew up with this knowledge that death is around you [...]. So I was
> from a very early point on very familiar, much more familiar than people are
> nowadays, with the dead and the dying.[7]

Then, between talking briefly about how photographs 'hover somewhere at the
perimeter of our lives' and how the dead in Corsican culture, as in other pockets
of Europe until very recently, had an unquestioned place in the lives of the living,
he says of all this, but also perhaps of himself: 'it is just a remnant of a much more
archaic way of looking at things.'[8]

In the spring before he died I lent him a slim volume by Mario Rigoni Stern,
a writer I was surprised to learn he hadn't come across before. A writer from the
north Italian Altipiano, Rigoni Stern was born in 1921 and died in 2008. He
fought on the front line at the Battle of Stalingrad and is perhaps best known for
his 1953 novel *Il sergente nella neve* (*The Sergeant in the Snow*), in which he writes
of this and of the wayward return from there to Italy. (This latter has echoes of
Primo Levi's 'nomadic' return to Turin, and the two writers became close from the
mid-1950s.) Rigoni Stern's life, like Sebald's and like most of those Sebald wrote
about, was forced by war and the bad politics of Europe. But Rigoni Stern also
wrote in compassionate detail of the Italian mountains he lived in and the people
he lived among, as one of them. And about 'community': communities not only of
people, but of animals and trees and plants. The book I lent Max was *Inverni lontani*
(roughly 'far-off winters') (1999), a forty-page prose work whose Einaudi cover
had a reproduction of Brueghel's painting of two peasants walking through an icy
village. It wasn't a best choice of Rigoni — as a book, it veers at times toward the
sentimental — but it was the one I had to hand. Max posted it back to me during
the late summer with a brief note. The book had touched him even so: and I still
wonder about this and other 'lost' closenesses.

The last time I talked to Max was at the 'reception' following the St Jerome Lecture (as it was still then known) he gave in mid–September 2001. I am not much at ease at such occasions and we talked only briefly. But I gave him a copy of a longish poem I had recently finished, simply called 'Praha Poem'.[9] The last note I had from him was a postcard the following day saying that he'd read it on the last train back from Liverpool Street and that he'd liked it a great deal. I'm glad that I'd overcome my unease and had gone to the reception. I mention this because, once more, there's more to what happened than was apparent, more layers to it all than I had realized at the time. I had written the poem in Prague and Moravia, where I had gone 'seemingly to break down or else to avoid doing so' (as the 'Praha Poem' says), in May 2001, and some of the most intense sensations of that visit were precisely in the Mala Strana, Kampa, and even Šporkova, where Jacques Austerlitz finally meets Vera Ryšanová and his own forgotten childhood. So what! How many people other than me have walked those streets with such feelings, many of them citizens of the city, not mere visitors as I was. (Or in the poems of Vítězslav Nezval where Prague takes on a real quotidian magic.) And yet there is something uncanny about it: I don't think I'd known Max was writing *Austerlitz*, other than in a general way. I had not really talked to him about it, had forgotten that he'd been to Prague (though where else would he go, except maybe to Vilnius), but was drawn exactly to those parts of Mala Strana, Seminar Park, Strassova. (Places the great photographer Josef Sudek lived in, haunted and was haunted by, though I am not at all sure how well Max knew his work.[10]) This is clearly a personal reflection, and many other things could be said: but as a reader of *Austerlitz* just a few months later, it was hard for me to leave it at that. I am sure that my own personal tastes or sense of the self biases me in this.

My family came from the high Italian Alps. My grandfather (on my mother's side, my father's seemingly being solid English) left his village in the Alta Val Camonica almost twenty years before the First World War and died young in London in 1924. I know that this sense of the Alps — Max's childhood being spent in its German foothills, my mother's roots being in the high Italian valleys — provided a link between us. That last time we met in Spitalfields, we talked of walking together one day across the Alps from Precasaglio to Wertach, time and everything else allowing. Of course we might never have managed to. It would be a long walk, with no doubt many side-tracks and excursuses, going in space well above the snow line, in time back at least to the slip of a man into the Similaun glacier five thousand years ago, let alone the span of geological time and the insane bludgeonings of 'yellow' histories that have surrounded the Alps almost for ever. But I take it as a signifier of his concerns, and not merely of a wish to walk with me across a patch of land, that motivated Max to think of doing this. After all he was not one to walk in company (though he did say to me that he thought I was one of the few people he could imagine walking with), so the idea of walking across the Alps must have held some very strong sense for him. For me it would be like carving a section through the brain of a glacier — as I wrote later in my poem — but quite what it might have meant for Max I can only guess. I haven't done that walk yet. It remains to be done. I hope that I will.

Notes to the Afterword

1. W. G. Sebald, *After Nature*, trans. by Michael Hamburger, 3. VII (London: Penguin, 2003), p. 109; *Nach der Natur*, 3. VII (Frankfurt a. M.: Fischer, 1995), p. 96. Cf. Stephen Watts, 'Lord in Dream', in *The Lava's Curl* (Walsden, West Yorkshire: Grimaldi, 1990), p. 14.

2. W. G. Sebald, *Austerlitz*, trans. by Anthea Bell (London: Penguin, 2002), pp. 139–40.

3. Sebald, *Austerlitz*, trans. by Bell, p. 51; Watts, *The Lava's Curl*, p. 17.

4. Sebald, *Austerlitz*, trans. by Bell, p. 50.

5. Sebald, *After Nature*, p. 37; *Nach der Natur*, p. 33.

6. W. G. Sebald, *The Emigrants*, trans. by Michael Hulse (London: Harvill, 1997), p. 23.

7. Eleanor Wachtel, 'Ghost Hunter', interview with W. G. Sebald, 16 October 1997, in *The Emergence of Memory: Conversations with W. G. Sebald*, ed. by Lynne Sharon Schwartz (New York: Seven Stories Press, 2007), pp. 37–61 (p. 39); cf. Chapter 1, p. 25.

8. Wachtel, 'Ghost Hunter', p. 40.

9. Stephen Watts, 'Praha Poem', in *Gramsci & Caruso* (Olomouc: Periplum, 2003), p. 130.

10. The cover photograph of the Harvill edition of *Vertigo* (see Primary Bibliography B.B.1.5) features *Untitled* (1930) by Josef Sudek. It is not known whether this choice was made by the author or by the publishers. (Eds)

LYRISCHES INTERMEZZO

Four Poems for Max Sebald

Stephen Watts

Anne Beresford

Michael Hamburger

Michael Hulse

For my Friend, Max Sebald

Stephen Watts

('Tell them I had a wonderful life'
Ludwig Wittgenstein)

Two months ago I was
talking to you in the Lithuanian forests : telling you
how old women from out of Druskininkai were walking
the blue floors of those stretched oceans with buckets
of mushrooms and moss

There space is old, trees are tall, memory is pain,
history is full of partisans and a sufi music conjures all
of us to whirl where the stalks of the forest barely sway.
I sensed you there because of the rotting of the music
and I knew you'd care.

Your room still is full of photographs
your realm looked after by trees. You who eschewed all
computer trails have been taken away by a skidding wheel
by black ice or a seizure of the heart, lifelong discourse
and your daughter's hurt

All I can do now is stagger
round my rooms mewling out your name Max, Max :
what will happen to language now, now you are not here
and who is left and how many remain of the anarchists
on the ice-floes of speech

These last weeks I had been
writing you postcards in my head : Max come to Whitechapel.
Come soon. Come and talk. Come and walk. Where are you?
Why did you? : but this has become an explosion of words
on the scarp of my pain

We'd talked about walking
from my village to yours : cutting a section across the Alps
or a section through a glacier's brain. From Precasaglio
in the Alta Valcamonica to Wertach in the Allgäu.
Now I will do that without you.

Before we met and surely ever since
we've been talking to each other. And even when the other
was not there we'd carry on in monologues to hear. I shall
go on talking to you for as long as my mouth can speak :
or what is the point of language

From where did I come
to this scarred field : you first heard my voice in your car,
you last lost your own voice there : what silence in the water,
what bird-smoke, what rough circle in our language has
brought us back to here?

Dear friend, what is the use of speech :
I now asking of you questions you can no longer reach —
yet as you drift off to the snow-hole of your hills I hear
you say 'they are ever returning to us, the dead' —
Max, I am listening ...

17–19 December 2001 (and early January 2002)

Trees silhouetted against a winter sky, from Framingham Earl churchyard, Norfolk

For Max

Anne Beresford

January 3rd 2002

Four o'clock, the light almost gone,
trees black against a fiery sun,
a pheasant disturbs the silence
as he stalks across the lawn.

In my hand one of your cigarettes
from a packet you'll not be needing now.
My heart has been heavy ever since
that summer afternoon when you said goodbye
and somehow I knew we'd not meet again.

It was miraculous
how snow and ice melted last night,
enabling us to sit in the Norman church
and wonder at your violent passing.

And as we stood shivering round your grave,
a robin suddenly lit by the flowers
eyed us cheerfully,
left us with his crumbs of comfort.

St Andrew's Church, Framingham Earl. Both © Jo Catling (mid-January 2002)

Redundant Epitaphs

Michael Hamburger

(for friends not named)

1

Night now,
Returned from Egypt, Thrace,
Mexico, Scythia, Tibet,
Wherever by tenants of stellar space-time
Tombs with the things of day
Were furnished, for the dark,
Night crops were eaten, night sculptures carved
By those who deferred to darkness,
Like swallows homed to it, diving,
Built the best homes, the surest
To distract the vicarious few
From the leisure not long but limitless
Of their souls' before and after;
Theirs too, the countless unnamed
Who on daybeds of rock lay down
To rest wrenched limbs from labour.

Yes, light they loved, darkly,
When with gold and jewels they decked
The illustrious, illumined,
Light's play on surfaces,
Facets, fibres, flesh,
Colours invisible
But for light's breaking, rejection
Of the waves not received.
From the more durable dark
Gold, jewels had issued
And for darkness again
Were walled up, in unknowing.

2

Night now,
Advent of frozen rebirth,
The blue-green, the blood-red radiance
Wiped off the western sky
And by morning moonshine no more
Than negatives, black on white, greyish,
Spectral the spectrum's whole range.

Blinded, maimed, spent,
He who'd fought and suffered it
Waited, longed for night
To absolve, absorb him,
Take back the contours, colours
Retained in memory's darkroom,
Mend him once and for all.

Night cased in metal struck
This other who slowly had gathered
Fractions, refractions of light
From the things of day, darkened,
Lovingly had composed them,
He the quick taker of snapshots

Against the sundown dazzle,
The murk that blots it below.
Then white,
The days' air hazed, opaque,
White on black, equalized,
Skeletal twigs, residual stalks
Stark on the snowsheet's blankness.

3

Night now.
A dog whines for his lost companion,
Mentor and keeper who lately, recalled by pity
Broke off secluded work,
For the sick dog's healing crossed land and sea.
Without nightlight of stars or candle the dog lives on,
In absence beyond recall.

While eyes hunger, hands move,
Human love defies it,
With tinsel decks the tree,
With birdfeed the garden table,
Exchanges tokens, gifts,
Brightnesses even after the funeral service,
Against loss, abeyance;
To the habit of selfhood, business always unfinished,
Emptier years makes its way.
To more light again, to more making?
A dog's love denies it.

4

Night, then,
Capacious enough to contain
The quirks and quiddities
Alive in sunset, ever,
Reflecting the light or hidden,
Known or unknown,
Knowing, unknowing,
Traceable yet or bare
As gravestones the weathers washed.
To the open new grave a robin came down,
An icy wind blew
On the bird safe there among the living
And those more truly levelled
Than sunlight lets creatures be —
All reduced, irreducible there,
In one darkness stood and lay.

The robin that appeared in the churchyard after
W. G. Sebald's funeral (3 January 2002).
© Gertrud Aebischer-Sebald

Il ritorno in patria

Michael Hulse

i.m. Max Sebald

Returning to the Ionian town of his birth,
Seferis found the windows of his childhood home were broken;
the iron door was rusted; the shutters of the upper storey rotted.
He was unable to find his initials
which he had carved on a wall when he was ten.
The wheel–well still drew water —
a tiny donkey turned it, and a mulberry gave shade —
but the old plane tree had died
that bustled with sparrows in the afternoons.
Of the ten windmills that bristled on the hills behind the harbour,
all that remained were a handful of ruins.

Smyrna, he wrote in his journal, had lost its shadow.
At Ephesus the cyclamen wore tones of the Ionian sky.
What was the harbour was sunken now, dry ground,
the mouth of the tomb of a once great city
and its dead surrounding plain —
this was the conductor of the souls
of the vanished harbours of Asia Minor.

For the moment, he wrote, there is consolation
in twilight on the slopes of Ionia,
the cyclamen, in which one may sense the tremors
of the great soul of Heraclitus.

PART II

The Writer in Dialogue

1
'Rediscovered' Pieces by W. G. Sebald

(1)   *Die hölzernen Engel von East Anglia*
      Originally published in *Die Zeit*, 26 July 1974

(2)   *Leben Ws*
      Originally published in *Frankfurter Rundschau*, 22 April 1989

(3)   *Waterloo*
      Originally published in *Neue Zürcher Zeitung Folio*, October 1991

(4)   *'An Botho Strauss in Berlin' and 'Raffles Hotel Singapur'*
      Two Poems by Michael Hulse, translated by W. G. Sebald
      Originally published in *Sprache im technischen Zeitalter*, June 1995

(5)   *Feuer und Rauch: Über eine Abwesenheit in der deutschen Nachkriegsliteratur*
      Originally published in *Frankfurter Rundschau*, 29 November 1997

(6)   *Ausgrabung der Vergangenheit* (on Michael Hamburger)
      Originally published in *Tages-Anzeiger* (Zurich), 22 May 1998

(7)   *Michael Hamburger: Nomination for the degree of Honorary DLitt*
      UEA Memo written 1987 (first publication)

(1) Die hölzernen Engel von East Anglia:
Eine individuelle Bummeltour
durch Norfolk und Suffolk

Wer die graue Nordsee überquert hat, dem öffnet sich, wenn er am Morgen in Harwich wieder Land gewinnt, die weite ostenglische Provinz, von der aus man einst leichter nach Amsterdam als nach London gelangte und die auch, nachdem sie von der Bahn erschlossen war, in ihrem exzentrischen Dasein verharrte.

Folgen Sie zunächst einem verwinkelten Sträßchen nach Manningtree, East Bergholt und Ipswich, das Sie am besten, ohne sich umzusehen Richtung Woodbridge durchqueren. Mit etwas Glück kommen Sie hier noch zum Frühstück zurecht, etwa im Crown Hotel oder im Bull, in dem Lord Tennyson und Edward Fitzgerald mit Vorliebe einkehrten, letzterer der famose Übersetzer Omar Kayyams, welcher stets mit festgebundenem Zylinder segeln ging. In einem der beiden Häuser findet sich gewiß ein Platz für die Nacht, sofern Sie nicht vorziehen, etwas außerhalb in Seckford Hall zu logieren, um dem angeblich noch umgehenden Thomas Seckford Ihre Aufwartung zu machen.

Es ist nun an der Zeit, die erste Exkursion zu unternehmen, etwa in die Sandlings, eine von Fasanen bevölkerte Gegend, die zum Meer hin liegt. In Sutton Hoo, wo vor dreizehnhundert Jahren ein grandioses Schiffsbegräbnis zelebriert wurde, können Sie die Leere der Vergänglichkeit studieren, eh' Sie durch den Wald von Rendlesham zum Dörfchen Butley fahren. Hier soll es eine noch nicht verhunzte Wirtschaft geben; leisten Sie sich also ein Glas, denn am Nachmittag ist ja wieder alles dicht.

Von Butley sind es kaum vier Kilometer nach Orford. Besteigen Sie zunächst den Turm der Kirche, um einen Begriff zu bekommen von der sehr eigenartigen Umgebung. Parallel zur Küste fließt da der Fluß Ore, vom Meer nur durch eine ganz schmale, aber 15 km lange Kiesbank getrennt, auf die man mit einem kleinen Fährschiffchen übersetzen kann. Orford selbst hat ein Castle aus dem 12. Jahrhundert und ein Restaurant für geräucherte Viktualien, inklusive Aal, in dem Sie einiges einkaufen sollten, denn gleich nordwärts liegt Iken, ein Platz, der eine einmalige Aussicht über das weite Bett der Alde gewährt und sich geradezu offeriert für ein *piquenique en campagne*. Es ist von hier nicht weit nach Aldeburgh, wo allsommerlich von Benjamin Britten protegierte Festwochen stattfinden.

In einer halben Stunde können Sie schon wieder in Woodbridge retour sein, eben günstig zum Abendessen, wonach Sie, die späte Dämmerung ausnützend, noch eine kleine Tour ans Meer hinab machen sollten, nach Shingle Street, einer winzigen Häuserzeile an desolater Küste, wo Sie auf den Geschmack der ostenglischen Melancholie und das Bedürfnis nach einer hochprozentigen *nightcap* kommen können.

Der nächste Morgen sieht Sie auf dem Weg nach Framlingham zu einem enormen, dreizehntürmigen Castle, das heimkehrende Kreuzfahrer nach sarazenischem Muster errichtet haben. Vom Wehrgang der eindrucksvollen Anlage sehen Sie über die hübsche Stadt bis weit ins Land hinaus. Dennington, einen Sprung nördlich, weist eine Kirche auf, die in ihrer großen Einfachheit ein hervorragendes Exempel ist in dem an Kirchen mehr als nur reichhaltigen East Anglia. Wenn Sie abends in Southwold sein möchten, das ich Ihnen zum zweiten Aufenthalt empfehle, stehen Ihnen jetzt zwei Wege offen. Entweder fahren Sie über Heveningham, wo sich ein der Inspektion wohl wertes Landschloß aus dem 18. Jahrhundert findet, oder zunächst nordwestwärts über den ausgesprochen schönen Ort Eye und von dort über Fressingfield, das sinnigerweise ein renommiertes Restaurant beherbergt, wieder östlich zur Küste hinunter.

In jedem Fall sind Sie abends bequem in Southwold, wo Sie getrost ein paar Tage bleiben können, wenn Sie sich den Luxus im besten Hotel am Ort gönnen wollen. Sie identifizieren es am leichtesten an der Theke, an der fünfzigerlei Whisky zu haben sind und an einem Kellner, der mit einem kleinen Xylophon im Haus herumgehend zu den Mahlzeiten bittet. Außerdem gibt es in Southwold Adnams, das beste englische Bier, und nicht zuletzt den schönen, von kleinen Parks durchsetzten Ort selbst, die See, Gerüchte längst vergangener Schlachten und mitten unter den Häusern einen großen weißen Leuchtturm.

Von Southwold sind es allenfalls zwei Stunden nach Norwich, dem Zentrum East Anglias. Im Mittelalter eine der bedeutendsten englischen Städte, hat Norwich später etwas den Anschluß verpaßt, und die Wucherungen der letzten 150 Jahre haben ihr also relativ wenig zugesetzt. Es gibt hier fünfzig mittelalterliche Kirchen und eine Kathedrale, die, 1096 begonnen, zu den großen Beispielen sakraler Architektur überhaupt zählt. Was an Norwich vorab beeindruckt, ist die Präsenz und Zugänglichkeit seiner Vergangenheit. Die Geschäftshäuser um den täglichen Markt im Zentrum bieten ein vollkommenes Panorama. Verabsäumen Sie nicht, das Viertel hinter der Kathedrale zu durchwandern. Es führt da eine Straße zum Fluß hinab, bis zu einem Fährtor, durch das die Bischöfe einst geräuschlos ihre Residenz verließen. Sie werden dort unten mit einiger Verwunderung entdecken, daß Norwich nicht zuletzt auch eine Hafenstadt ist.

Die 30 km Land, die es vom Meer trennen, sind durchzogen von einem Netz von Wasserstraßen und lagunenartigen Seen, und nur zu Schiff kann man diesen vielleicht faszinierendsten Teil Norfolks wirklich kennenlernen. Im Sommer allerdings tummelt sich halb England auf diesem Freizeitparadies, und ich rate Ihnen für diesmal zu einem Ausflug mit dem Auto. Folgen Sie dem Yare-Fluß über Surlingham, Rockland St Mary und Loddon nach Fritton zu einem waldumwachsenen See. Von hier nordwestlich nach Reedham, wo Sie auf einer Fähre übersetzen können. Dann nach Acle und zum Castle bei Caister-on-Sea, hinauf nach Winterton und zurück Richtung Norwich über Ludham und Ranworth. Ranworth hat eine sehr schöne kleine Kirche, von deren Turm man einen memorablen Ausblick über die Landschaft der *Broads*, Seen, Flußarme und Marschwiesen, hat.

Die nächste Etappe führt in den Norden. Verlassen Sie Norwich Richtung Fakenham, um bald schon rechts nach Reepham abzuzweigen ins 18. Jahrhundert. Am weiteren Weg nach Aylsham liegt die Kirche von Sall[e] gottverlassen in den Feldern und wartet in staubiger Geduld auf verschlagene Besucher. Über

Aylsham kommen Sie nach Blickling, zu einem der großen Häuser East Anglias. Es präsentiert sich mit denkwürdigem Effekt unvermittelt nach einer Wegbiegung, von zwei riesenhaften und schier endlosen Eibenhecken in die schönste Perspektive gesetzt.

Weiter nordwärts sodann nach Aldborough und über Baconsthorpe und Holt nach Blakeney, einem exquisiten Dorf an der Küste. Etwas westlich liegen Wells und Holkham, wo Sie ein weiterer Landsitz samt unabsehbarem Park erwartet. Das Haus ist bester Palladian Bombast und sollte nicht ausgelassen werden. Außerhalb des Parks liegt das Victoria Hotel, wo sich eine gute Nacht verbringen läßt, und von hier können Sie in ein paar Minuten zur Holkham Bay, einem Sandstrand von ungeheurer Weite und Schönheit, hinabspazieren.

Anderntags führt die Route über Overy, North Creake und Walsingham, das sogenannte englische Nazareth, südwärts nach Fakenham. Von hier folgen Sie der direkten Straße nach King's Lynn, einer Hafenstadt mit ausgesprochen prägnantem Charakter. Zwei Tage zahlen sich hier schon aus und vielleicht ein Abstecher nach Norden zum Castle Rising und zur königlichen Domäne Sandringham. Freilich nur für insgeheime Royalisten, denn Sandringham ist eine spätbürgerliche Monstrosität. Westwärts der Straße zieht sich die Küste des Wash, einer Wattenbucht, in der ein beträchtlicher Teil der Seehunde des nördlichen Meeres das Licht der Welt erblickt.

Haben Sie King's Lynn, seine hanseatische Atmosphäre, die Reminiszenzen weltweiten Handels und grönländischer Walfischerei ausgekostet, so begeben Sie sich am günstigsten Richtung Swaffham auf einem kleinen Umweg über Castle Acre zur schönsten Ruine East Anglias. Zum Lunch können Sie ohne weiteres in der Regency Stadt Swaffham sein und am Nachmittag in der südwestlich gelegenen Oxborough [sic] Hall. Das befestigte Haus geht aufs 15. Jahrhundert zurück und ist eine wirklich obligatorische Sehenswürdigkeit.

Am Abend erwartet Sie Ely, das Sie über Southery und Brandon Creek erreichen. Über Ely und seine Kathedrale wäre ein eigener Führer zu schreiben. Ich möchte Ihnen hier wieder eine Turmbesteigung ans Herz legen, eine recht anstrengende allerdings. Aber Ely aus der Vogelperspektive wird Sie die *tour de force* nicht vergelten lassen.

Eigentlich läge nunmehr Cambridge am Weg, aber vielleicht verschiebt man das besser auf ein anderes Mal, denn es fällt ein wenig aus dem Rahmen dieser Reise. Verzichten Sie großherzig auf die gelehrsame Welt, in deren Reservat im Sommer die Touristen einander auf die Füße steigen, und wechseln Sie herüber nach Bury St Edmunds, das Sie um vieles zugänglicher und weniger frequentiert finden werden. Das Angel Hotel ist hier das ideale Quartier, ein Gebäude, das ein Stück Gastlichkeit aus dem 18. Jahrhundert vermittelt. In einem Park gegenüber liegen die Ruinen einer Abtei, die bis zur Reformation zu den bedeutendsten geistlichen Einrichtungen im Lande gehörte. Abgesehen aber von historischen Reliquien zeichnet Bury die Atmosphäre einer behäbigen Provinzstadt aus. Versäumen Sie nicht die Kirche St Mary und ihren Friedhof und nicht das Uhrenmuseum im Angel Corner House, in dem eine stattliche Versammlung wundersamer Chronometer einem aufs beste die Zeit vertreibt.

Wer Richtung Haverhill aus Bury herausfährt, kommt bald nach Horringer und damit nach Ickworth Hall, dem Stein gewordenen Spleen des vierten Earl of Bristol. Das Gebäude datiert von 1796 und besteht aus einer riesigen Rotunda, in welcher der Earl — im bürgerlichen Beruf Bischof — zu leben gedachte, und zwei ausladenden Flügeln, die als Museum für seine auf endlosen europäischen Streifzügen ergatterten Kunstschätze dienen sollten.

Südwärts kommen Sie nach Clare, einem Dorf voller schöner alter Häuser, und dann den Stour-Fluß entlang nach Long Melford, dessen lange Hauptstraße eine ausgiebige Promenade rechtfertigt. Zu Long Melford gehört Melford Hall, eines der besten elisabethanischen Häuser Englands. Ickworth ist eher ein monumentales Kuriosum, Melford Hall aber, das Gebäude und die Anlage, ist von ebenso ausgewogener wie unaufdringlicher Schönheit und darf auf keinen Fall ausgelassen werden.

Tags darauf sollten Sie vielleicht noch die Kirche von Melford sich ansehen und dann die kleine Strecke nach Norden zu dem fast allzu pittoresken Städtchen Lavenham fahren. Die Historizität dieses Orts scheint so vollkommen, als wäre sie von Walt Disney erfunden. Wie dem auch sei, von hier aus begeben Sie sich nun endgültig Richtung Harwich, und zwar über Kersey, einer weiteren Illustration aus dem Bilderbuch der Geschichte, über Boxford, Polstead und Stoke-by-Nayland, dessen Kirchturm aus Constables Landschaften immer wieder mal auftaucht. Und dann geradewegs herüber nach Harwich.

Wieviele Tage Sie für eine solche ostenglische Reise veranschlagen müssen, hängt davon ab, wie sehr Sie sich in die hölzernen Engel verschauen, die die *hammerbeam*-Decken in vielen der zahllosen Kirchen mit scheinbarer Leichtigkeit auf dem Rücken tragen, und wie lange Sie in den Antiquitätenläden hängenbleiben, deren es in East Anglia ungleich mehr und bessere gibt als sonst irgendwo. Sollte es gar einmal regnen, kaufen Sie sich eine Lokalzeitung und suchen im Inseratenteil nach der nächsten Möbelauktion. Sofern es Ihnen nicht an Mut fehlt, zum rechten Zeitpunkt die Hand zu heben, sollte es mich wundernehmen, wenn Sie auf dem Dach Ihres Autos nicht ein Stück nach Hause brächten, das Ihnen auf lange Zeit hinaus eine gute Erinnerung an East Anglia sichert.

This piece was first published in the 'Reise' (travel) section of *Die Zeit* on 26 July 1974, illustrated by photographs of the cathedrals in Ely and Norwich and accompanied by a map of the itinerary and information on ferry crossings, hotels, car hire, and exchange rates (it is not clear whether this information was supplied by Sebald or the editors of the travel section; many of the hotels listed are mentioned in the text). An English translation by Richard Sheppard, 'The Carved Wooden Angels of East Anglia: A Leisurely Tour through Norfolk and Suffolk', is forthcoming in the *Journal of European Studies* (see Primary Bibliography F.C.1). I am grateful to Professor Reinbert Tabbert (Reutlingen) for sending me a copy of this piece in connection with the poem 'Norfolk' cited in the article 'Gratwanderungen bis an den Rand der Natur: W. G. Sebald's Landscapes of Memory', in *The Anatomist of Melancholy: Essays in Memory of W. G. Sebald*, ed. by Rüdiger Görner (Munich: iudicium, 2003), pp. 19–50. As explored in a further article ('W. G. Sebald: Ein "England-Deutscher?"

Identität–Topographie–Intertextualität', in *W. G. Sebald: Intertextualität und Topographie*, ed. by Irène Heidelberger-Leonard and Mireille Tabah (Berlin: LIT Verlag, 2008), pp. 25–53), the piece, describing a recommended route from Harwich through Suffolk to Southwold, and via Norwich to Wells and King's Lynn, returning via Ely and Bury St Edmunds, not only echoes some of Sebald's early poems collected in *Über das Land und das Wasser* (*Across the Land and the Water*), but also prefigures the penultimate section of *Nach der Natur* (*After Nature*) and, of course, *Die Ringe des Saturn* (*The Rings of Saturn*). The 'wooden angels' of the title refer to the carved angels on the hammerbeam roofs of many medieval East Anglian churches, such as Blythburgh (near Aldeburgh) or Wymondham Abbey. (JMC)

(2) Leben Ws:
Skizze einer möglichen Szenenreihe
für einen nichtrealisierten Film

Der Film LEBEN Ws soll die Geschichte einer solitären Figur, diejenige des Philosophen Ludwig Wittgenstein erzählen und zwar nicht in der Form einer Dokumentation oder bebilderten Biographie, sondern in der reinen Form von Bildern, aus denen sich das Leben Ws zusammengesetzt hat. Der Natur reiner Bilder entsprechend, geht es also um die Konstruktion eines achronologischen, asyntaktischen 'Satzes', in welchem 'ausgesprochen' werden soll, worüber W. zeit seines Lebens sich weitgehend ausgeschwiegen hat. Der Kontrapunkt, nach dem verfahren werden könnte, ist der Todesbegriff, wie ihn Wittgenstein andeutungsweise hier und da entwickelt hat.

Freilich werden einige — wenn auch diskontinuierliche — Ebenen der Kohärenz eingebracht werden müssen. Zum einen etwa die Jahre in Cambridge 1929–51, insbesondere wohl die der Kriegs- und Nachkriegszeit, zum anderen die in einem späten Leben in zunehmendem Maß gewichtige Ebene der Erinnerung bzw. Vorerinnerung oder Antizipation des Endes. Wie diese Ebenen miteinander zu vermitteln sind, wird sich erst im jeweils einzelnen Fall herausarbeiten lassen. Mit einer konventionellen Erzählstruktur wird sich diese Geschichte gewiß nicht bewältigen lassen; es soll jedoch auch der Anschein des 'Avantgardistischen' geflissentlich vermieden werden. Der Erfassung des 'Zeitstils' des jeweiligen Jahrzehnts unseres Jahrhunderts und des ausgehenden letzten soll besondere Aufmerksamkeit zukommen. Schon dadurch wird sich eine ins Visuelle transportierte Struktur ergeben.

Zu den Themenbereichen gehören in erster Linie 'widersprüchliche Paarungen' wie Kindheit/ Alter, Lehren/Lernen, Natur/Technik, Isolation/Gesellschaft, Juden/Deutsche, Heimat/Exil, Männerfreundschaft/Frauenliebe und umgekehrt, Reichtum/Armut. Was das Bildmaterial betrifft, so ist die hauptsächliche Schwierigkeit die eines embarras de richesse, denn das Leben Ws spielte sich ja immer an Orten und in Umgebungen und Milieus ab, die an Bildern weit mehr hergeben würden, als sich ohne weiteres bewältigen ließe. Es wird nicht leicht sein, die dem Subjekt angemessene Disziplin bei der Auswahl der richtigen Bilder zu wahren.

Als unmittelbarer Anlaß für das Projekt: Ws hundertster Geburtstag 1989, am 26. April, den er bestimmt nicht hätte feiern wollen. Er kam sich immer zu alt vor.

W.G.S.

W. im Zug nach Cambridge — 1929. Die ostenglische Landschaft. Weit. Dunkel. Grün. Ws Hinausschauen. Stimme (off): 'W. ist auf dem Weg nach Cambridge, wo er bereits unmittelbar vor dem Krieg einige Jahre gewesen war, nachdem er sein Ingenieurstudium in Manchester abgebrochen hatte. 1913 starb sein Vater und hinterließ ihm, wie den Geschwistern, ein gewaltiges Vermögen. In der ersten Hälfte des Jahres 1914 entwickelte W. während eines längeren Aufenthalts in Norwegen einen neuen Symbolismus für die sogenannten 'Wahrheitsfunktionen'. Im August 1914 rückt er als Freiwilliger in ein österreichisches Festungsartillerieregiment ein und beginnt das erste Notizbuch zu seiner logisch-philosophischen Abhandlung, eine Arbeit, die ihn durch die Kriegsjahre an der russischen und italienischen Front begleitet. Nach der Rückkehr aus dem campo concentramento im Sommer 1919 entledigt sich W. durch Schenkung seines Vermögens und beginnt im September eine Ausbildung zum Volksschullehrer. Das ist nun bald zehn Jahre her. Sechs Jahre lang ist er in den entlegensten Dörfern von Niederösterreich als Lehrer tätig gewesen. Im April 1926 gab er nach 'einem unguten Zwischenfall' den Lehrerberuf auf und arbeitete eine Zeitlang als Hilfsgärtner bei den barmherzigen Brüdern im Kloster Hütteldorf. 1927 und 28 baute er für seine Schwester Margarete ein Haus in der Wiener Kundmanngasse. Kurz vor der Fertigstellung des Hauses ließ er den Plafond eines saalartigen Raumes um 3 Zentimeter heben, um die Proportionen zu berichtigen. Jetzt ist W. wieder auf dem Weg nach Cambridge.

★

W's Ankunft in Cambridge. Januar 1929. Es liegt ein wenig Schnee. Keynes, wie stets sehr vornehm, holt W. vom Bahnhof ab. Fahrt ins College. W's (für K) 'ungeheure' Intensität, an der Grenze des Erträglichen. Bereits auf dem Bahnsteig. Dann beim Tee im College. Dazwischen das *absolute* Schweigen im Auto.

★

Unmittelbar anschließend unterhalten sich Keynes und Russell in Russells Studierzimmer über W., der im College-Hof fotografiert. Sie stehen am Fenster und sehn auf W. hinunter. W. fotografiert die Fassade, hinter der sie sich befinden; hinter der 'über' ihn geredet wird.

———————

W. nach einer Vorlesung Russells 1912. Er ist hier noch in seinem spätbürgerlichen Anzug — comme il faut. Redet heftig auf R. ein. Seine philosophische Begeisterung. Weist auf eine Unstimmigkeit in R's Vortrag hin. Virtuos in seinem noch unebenen Englisch. Russell dann schwer angeschlagen.

★

Im Garten von Ramseys Haus. Mai 1929. Gäste, nachmittags. Lettice Ramsey, die Fotografin, die sehr den Wschen Schwestern gleicht, mit W. über 'Bilder', das Machen von Bildern. W. diesmal zurückgelehnt, sagt nur wenig, ist aber offensichtlich in Übereinstimmung mit L. R. — W. hat Frauen gegenüber, im Gegensatz zu den anderen Männern (wie die Kamera zeigt), keinen Redezwang. L. R. zeigt einige winzige Zeichen der Zuneigung zu W. Er jedesmal irgendwie erschüttert.

★

W. am Bodensee mit Marguerite, der Schweizerin. Herbst 1928. W. sagt, er habe immer das Gefühl, gleich etwas zu tun oder zu sagen, was für ihn furchtbar wäre. Die Nähe der beiden. Der Schatten, über den W. nicht hinwegkann.

★

Spaziergang mit Piero Sraffa. Coton Footpath Cambridge. Herbst 32. Sraffa schildert die italienischen Verhältnisse. Die praktische Inszenierung des faschistischen

Mythus. W. zumeist schweigsam. Sein Ausbruch über die Grenzenlosigkeit der Dummheit der Menschen.

————————

Seminar im Clare College. Winternachmittag. Failing light. Ws perforierter Vortragsstil. Manchmal schier endlose Pausen.

W. in der Volksschule in Trattenbach. Gesangsunterricht. Als Stummfilm. Er bläst auf der Klarinette und dirigiert bisweilen. Als das Lied zu Ende ist, räumen die Kinder ihre Sachen auf, geh'n hinaus, wo sie noch im Schnee herumrennen. W. gibt seine Klarinette in den Strumpf, in dem er sie aufhebt. Tritt ans Fenster. Eines der Kinder ist in der Klasse zurückgeblieben. Schaut mit ihm hinaus. Das Licht ganz ähnlich wie in der vorhergehenden Szene im Clare College.

★

Wieder das Seminar im Clare College. Die Studenten brechen auf. — W. ans Fenster. Schaut hinaus. Hat einen Anfall von Skrupulantismus, ihn und die Philosophie betreffend. Wendet sich abrupt um und macht diesbezüglichen Anmerkungen zu Francis Skinner, der zurückgeblieben ist und noch schreibt. 'What *are* you writing?? Not any of this nonsense of mine, I hope.' 'Oh yes.' 'I *have* to go to the cinema now. And I need a shower. Will you come along??'

★

Im Kino in der ersten Reihe. W. völlig fasziniert. Essend. Englischer oder amerikanischer Spielfilm aus dem Jahre 1933.

★

Weihnachten 1933/34. Wien, im Haus in der Kundmanngasse. Die Familie. W. bei Gelegenheit allein im Garten, das Haus im Dunkelwerden. Seine unbewegliche Masse. An- und ausgehend Lichter. Wie Signale.

★

1927. W. am Zeichenbrett mit Bauplänen für das Haus. Marguerite im etwas im Hintergrund, auch sie an etwas zeichnend. W. pfeift auf seine virtuose Art leis vor sich hin. Etwas von Brahms.

★

1935. In der Wohnung über dem Gemüseladen in Cambridge, die W. jetzt mit Francis Skinner teilt. F. richtet das Frühstück. Man hört W. (im off) Brahms pfeifen. Dann beim Frühstück. F. liest aus der Times vor. Betreffend die Nürnberger Gesetze. W. reagiert nicht. Aber Zeichen der Verstimmung gegenüber F.

★

Bild des Vaters zu Pferd, das Gewehr im Anschlag. In einer Schneelandschaft. W. und F. S. russisch lernend bei Fanja Pascal. Auf dem Rückweg der beiden durch Cambridge macht ein Straßenphotograph unaufgefordert eine Aufnahme von ihnen. W. gibt ihm Anschrift und Geld.

———————————

Beim russischen Botschafter Maisky in London. W. ausnahmsweise mit Krawatte.
Im Vorzimmer wartend, betrachtet W. eine Zeitlang die Fotographie, die ihn und
F. S. auf der Straße in C. zeigt.

★

W. in der Sowjetunion. Eine Reihe sehr kurzer Sequenzen. Alles aus großer Dist-
anz. Leningrad, Moskau, Kasan. Im Gespräch mit diversen Kontaktpersonen. Ohne
Ton. Nur einmal, als die Mathematikprofessorin Yanovska ausruft: 'Was, der große
Wittgenstein' und dann eilends das Zimmer betritt, in dem W. auf sie wa[r]tet.

———————————

W. und F. S. in einem Gewächs- und Palmenhaus. Event.[uell] Kew Gardens.
Er hat den Plan, in die S. U. auszuwandern, aufgegeben. Die Weitläufigkeit des
Landes habe ihm Schwindel erregt. Er könne nur in der äußersten Beschränkung
existieren. Habe den Mut nicht, das wenige aufzugeben, das ihm am Leben
erhalte. Reine Logik in Kasachstan. Das sei der Gipfel der Abstraktion. In die
Praxis übertragen. Er habe den Mut nicht, von hier abzuspringen, obschon er sich
völlig überflüssig erachte. Er sei der mutloseste Mensch überhaupt. Hingegen seine
Brüder. Er sehe immer wieder das Ende, das sie genommen hätten. Rudi 1904 in
Berlin in einer Gastwirtschaft in der Brandenburgstraße. Zyankali. Hans 1902 in
Havanna. Immer sehe er das Boot noch auf hoher See. Kurt bei Kriegsende an der
italienischen Front. Er sei ein Übrigbleiber. De trop. Auch Paul hätte sich sicher das
Leben genommen, wenn er nicht seinen Arm eingebüßt hätte. Und er selber habe
fortwährend daran gedacht. Als ganz junger Mensch schon. Wer den Mut nicht
habe, die anderen zu verlassen, würde von den anderen verlassen werden. — Wenn
nur die Schwestern nicht solche Engel gewesen wären.

★

Photo der drei Schwestern mit den beiden jüngsten Brüdern.

★

Gewächshaus. Die Vegetation. Immer tiefer ins Grün hinein.

★

Waldweg auf der Hochreith. Paul und W. als Sechs- und Vierjährige, Hand in
Hand.

★

Konklave in Cambridge, bei dem W. die Professur für Philosophie zugesprochen
wird. Hinweise auf seine Genialität.

★

Waldweg in Norwegen. W. mit F. S. Dann Ausblick auf den Fjord. Schimmerndes
Herbstlicht.

★

Das Boot des Bruders Hans. Anscheinend steuerlos.

★

Norwegen, wie in der vorhergehenden Szene. W.: 'I shall have to see my people in Austria as soon as possible.' Continues about this beastly business of having to become British. But the alternative would be to hold a German passport.

Hochreith Anfang Juli 1939. Terrasse. Ausblick und Licht ähnlich schimmernd wie zuvor in Norwegen. W. bespricht mit den Geschwistern die äußerst gefährliche Lage, in der sie sich nun befinden. Pauls engagierter Bericht über die Verhältnisse in Wien, den Wiener Antisemitismus, von dem die Deutschen noch etwas lernen könnten. Erörterung der Implikationen der Rassengesetze für die Familie. Die Erpressung der Juden, die das Land verlassen wollen. W. erklärt sich bereit, nach Berlin zu fahren, um mit der Reichsbankdevisenstelle zu verhandeln.

★

W. im D-Zug nach Berlin mit Direktor Groller, dem Vermögensverwalter der Familie. Grenzbhf. Gmünd. Uniformierte. Kontrollen. Einige die aussteigen müssen. Darunter ein etwa zehnjähriger Junge. Blickwechsel mit W., der dadurch zum Zeugen wird. Dampflokomotiven.

★

W. als Zehnjähriger. Seine Dampfmaschinen.

★

W. repariert die Dampfmaschine in der Textilfabrik von Trottenbach [sic].

★

W. zu Groller über die Dampfwalze, die sein Vater einmal entworfen hatte; mit dem Zylinder im Innenraum der Walze. Daß er nicht habe begreifen wollen, daß dies keine Maschine sei, sondern ein starres System. Daß es nur aussähe 'wie' eine Maschine.

Reichsbankdevisenstelle in Berlin. Leiter erklärt W. auf das Sachlichste die Mechanismen der Erpressung.

★

W. in New York mit Groller. Weitere Devisenverhandlungen.

★

Leiter der Reichsstelle für Sippenforschung diktiert einen Brief an das Gauamt für Sippenforschung des NSDAP in Wien, durch den die 'Abstammungssache' Wittgenstein 'geregelt' wird.

*

W. in Cambridge. Er legt bei Fanja das 'Bekenntnis' ab, daß er zu Dreiviertel jüdischer Abstammung sei und nicht bloß zu einem Viertel, wie offensichtlich alle Welt geglaubt habe. Und er, W., sei ein Schweinehund, weil er diese Sache nicht klargestellt habe. Weitere 'Bekenntnis' aus der Schullehrerzeit. Seine immer wieder ausbrechende Gewalttätigkeit. Er habe oft gefühlt, daß er diejenigen umbringen müsse, die ihn nicht verstünden. Dazu habe er oft selbst gehört — Daß Francis jetzt krank sei. Daß er hätte Arzt werden sollen.

*

W. im Kino. Allein. Ein Wildwestfilm.

*

Begräbnis von Francis. W. looking more desperate than usual. Die Eltern von Francis, die Schwester, Fanja, eine Gruppe anderer Leute. W., the odd one out.

*

W. auf einem Spaziergang. Quite wild. Mit Dr. Burnaby. Er könne nicht mehr in C. bleiben. And damn the chair in philosophy. Werde sich für die Dauer des Krieges einer nützlichen Arbeit widmen. In London. Es sei alles schon beschlossen.

*

W. Kartoffelschälend. — Seine Hände. W. Kartoffelschälend auf dem Wachtschiff Gorplana [sic] während des I. Weltkriegs. Die Explosion in der Reparaturwerkstatt. Dann die tiefe Stille. Stumme Kriegsbilder. Ein Stück Text aus dem *Tractatus.*

*

Guys Hospital London. Der Laborant W. in der Dermatologie. Salben mixend. Im Hintergrund ein weiterer Laborant. BBC-Radio-News aus einem kleinen Bagellitempfänger, an deren Ende der zweite Laborant nach Hause geht. W. dann allein. Mikroskop. Bilder. Farbige Blüten der Hautkrankheiten.

*

W. als Hilfsgärnter in Klosterneuburg.

*

Wie vorletzte Szene. W. am Mikroskop. Dr. Reginals. Gespräch über seine Forschungsarbeiten zu Shock und Trauma, die nun in Newcastle fortgesetzt werden sollen. W. will sich dem Projekt anschließen.

*

W. als Labortechniker in Newcastle. Die würdevolle Handarbeit, die er verrichtet. Pulsmessungen. Pulsus paradoxus. Heartbeat. Heart.

*

Unterwegs mit Dr. Reginals. Thema Shock und Trauma. Blick auf Newcastle.

★

1946. W. gibt ein Tutorial in Cambridge. Auffallend die mit schwarzen Papierstreifen 'eingerahmten' Scheiben seiner Fenster. Natur, mit Trauerrand. W. über die Krankheiten des Kopfes, die der Philosoph in sich heilen muß, will er je zu einem klaren Denken kommen. Nur die seltenste Zeit aber sind wir ohne eine Krankheit des Kopfes. Unter den drei Studenten, die an dem Tutorial teilnehmen, ist Ben Richards, der im Gegensatz zu den anderen keine einzige Notiz macht.

★

W., Fotos für sein Album auf das *richtige* Format zuschneidend, indem er winzige Streifen von ihnen abschneidet. B. Richards sitzt seitlich bei ihm am Tisch. W. über seine Unfähigkeit, weiter lehren zu können. Seinen Ekel vor der englischen Zivilisation, vor seiner eigenen Eitelkeit. Daß es ihm unmöglich sei, am High Tabel [*sic*] zu essen. — W. betrachtet das Porträt, das Ben von ihm gemacht hat. Ob er denn nun so aussähe? Spiegelprüfung. Ben tritt hinter ihn. Die beiden Gesichter im Spiegel, das schon alte und das noch junge. 'Schau Dich an und Du wirst Dich nicht verstehen.'

———————

W. u. B. R. im Londoner East End. Die vielen jüdischen Ladenschilder. Waiselfisch, Spiegeltheater Solomon etc. W. sehr anonym mit Schirmmütze und MacIntosh. B. in schwarzglänzender Regenjacke. Ein Straßenfotograf macht eine Aufnahme der beiden zusammengehörenden Passanten. Film steht einen Augenblick still. W. zahlt wieder und gibt dem Fotografen, wie in der früheren Szene, Anschrift und Geld.

★

W. und B. in einem koscheren Restaurant. W. erzählt, daß jüdische Auswanderer oft in Amerika zu sein glaubten, wenn sie in London an Land gesetzt wurden. Sie hatten ja bis New York ihre Passage bezahlt. Manche, die ärmeren, hätten es oft jahrelang nicht gemerkt.

★

College High Table. W. abseits an einem Katzentisch. Der Philosoph als 'Erniedrigter'. Er ist so, wie er ißt.

★

W. in Ottertal. Einbruch der Nacht. Er schmiert sein Butterbrot und trinkt die Milch. Dann geht er hinaus, wo er an einem verabredeten Platz eine Gruppe Schulkinder trifft. Sternkunde. W.s Erklärungen und Vergleiche.

———————

W. 1919 im Gespräch mit Mining, einer der Schwestern, über den Entschluß, den Lehrberuf zu ergreifen. M.s Einwände. Man brauche kein Präzisionsinstrument, um Kisten zu machen. W. hofft, etwas abtragen zu können als Kinderlehrer. Eine Schuld. M.s Unverständnis. W.s Vergleich mit dem Passanten, der draußen gegen den Wind angeht und dessen seltsame Haltung man sich von drinnen nicht erklären kann.

★

W. in Wicklow, Irland 1949. Das Cottage ähnlich armselig ausgestattet wie das Zimmer in Ottertal. W. schreibt eines seiner großen Kontokorrentbücher. Zur Natur. Zum arktischen Wasserhimmel. Über die Farben. Er tritt dann vor das Cottage. Die Farben.

★

Mit einer Gruppe von Bauern an einem Torfstich, in dem ein gut erhaltenes Gerippe eines großen Tieres gefunden wurde. Die Mutmaßungen der Häusler concerning the nature of that animal.

★

Naturhistorisches Museum Wien. Die Schulkinder mit W. in der Abteilung der Dinosauriergerippe. W.s Theorie, daß die Systeme von einer bestimmten Größe zur Katastrophe tendierten. Alle Erfindungen, die wahren, seien zu Anfang sehr klein. Alle Wahnideen hingegen groß. Aber auch die wahren Erfindungen wüchsen sich letztlich zu Wahnideen aus. Das Gemurmel der Kinder untereinander, als W. mit seinen Ausführungen zu Ende ist.

★

Die Kinder auf dem Donauschiff.

Ein anderes Gemurmel. Hörsaal der Cornell University 1949. Das Podium noch leer. Malcolm führt W. hinein. Er macht einen äußerst gebrechlichen Eindruck. Auch abgerissen. Alte Windjacke und army trousers. Much like a tramp. Das Geraune in den Reihen. 'Wittgenstein'. 'That's Wittgenstein', etc.

★

Abends Fahrt auf einen Hügel. Ausblick auf die Stadt Ithaka. Mond. W.s Kommentar, daß er eine Welt ohne Sonne gemacht hätte, wenn es in seiner Macht gestanden hätte. Es würde dann weniger gelesen und geschrieben.

★

Frühjahr 1950. Cambridge im Garten von v. Wright. W. und v. W. in Directors' Chairs. Einige andere Gäste. Der Begriff 'Heimat' taucht auf. W.: dieses sei überhaupt das Fremdeste.

★

W. auf dem Schneeberg. Mit den Schulkindern. Über dem Schauen kann man alles vergessen.

★

W. im Garten v. Ws. wie zuvor. Über die Suche nach der Heimat im Ausland. Die Geschichte der Entdeckung des Franz-Joseph-Lands durch die 'Admiral Tegetthoff'. Die Terra nuova ist aus Eis und Basalt. Die Heimat sei der Ort, an dem man bei einer bestimmten Geisteshaltung nicht bleiben könne. Einer der anwesenden Gäste will einige Aufnahmen machen. W. zeigt sich einverstanden. Geht aber zuerst sein Leintuch holen und hängt es als Paravent auf, vor dem er sich dann zum Porträt setzt. Die letzten Bilder vom lebenden W. werden gemacht.

★

Das Gewitter auf der Hochreith. Eine Photographie davon hat W. überall hin begleitet und war also im Film schon verschiedentlich zu sehn.

★

Der Wind bewegt das Leintuch. Veränderungen der weißen Farbe.

★

Auf den Pennines. 1910. W. und der Freund Eccles. Das Drachenflugexperiment. W. schaut dem Drachen nach, der immer mehr an Höhe gewinnt.

★

Die Stadt Manchester von oben, aus der Vogelperspektive.

[*Die Illustration wurde dem Band* Wittgenstein, *aus dem Suhrkamp Verlag, entnommen.*]

This piece was originally published in the *Frankfurter Rundschau* on 22 April 1989, Feuilleton, p. ZB3 (see Primary Bibliography F.C.4). The title translates as 'The Life of W: Sketch for a Possible Scenario for an Unrealized Film'. In the italicized introductory section, WGS refers to Wittgenstein's hundredth birthday (26 April 1989) as the impetus for the project, despite suggesting that this was not an occasion Wittgenstein would have wanted to celebrate; the sketch itself, a proposal for a film project which did not receive funding, dates from *c.* 1986. (Coincidentally, Derek Jarman's 1993 film *Wittgenstein* also presents the philosopher's life as a series of tableaux, although these are all filmed in the studio with a plain backdrop.)

  The original publication occupies a single broadsheet page, with the text superimposed in blocks of different lengths on an enlarged photograph of Wittgenstein's face, both anticipating the emphasis on eyes and the gaze in *Austerlitz* and *Unerzählt* (*Unrecounted*) and reflecting the preoccupation with photography, and photographs, in the scenario itself. The text contains *in nuce* a number of preoccupations and locales (Klosterneuburg, Vienna, Cambridge, Manchester, etc.) taken up in Sebald's later work: emigration and exile, childhood and teaching, isolation and friendship, suicide and survival; a number of such 'contrasting pairs' are, indeed, indicated in the introductory section. In common with Sebald's later prose works, the text also contains a number of (unmarked) phrases in English. The 62 individual scenes set out here are not numbered but are separated by asterisks (in the version reprinted here a single line indicates where the text is broken up into sections).

We have retained the original orthography, including inconsistencies of punctuation and abbreviations such as 'Wschen', but have corrected a few obvious typographical errors. An English translation by Jo Catling is in preparation.

For the background to the text see also Richard Weihe, 'Wittgensteins Augen: W. G. Sebalds Film-Szenario "Leben Ws"', *fair*, 7.4 (2009), 11–12, based on the original typescript in the DLA *Nachlass,* which is accompanied by 12 photographs of Wittgenstein photocopied from *Ludwig Wittgenstein: Sein Leben in Bildern und Texten*, ed. by Michael Nedo and Michele Ranchetti (Frankfurt a.M.: Suhrkamp, 1983); this is (presumably) also the volume referred to in the note in square brackets at the end of the piece. While there is no record of this volume in Sebald's personal library, the UEA library copy bears discreet sidelinings which seem to point to WGS, and one may conjecture that this volume provided some inspiration for the 'Szenenreihe' (sequence of scenes) in this sketch. The editors would like to thank Dr Weihe, who is preparing a more detailed interpretation of Sebald's 'take' on Wittgenstein, for generously sharing his interim findings. (Eds)

(3) Waterloo

In der Vorweihnachtszeit des vergangenen Jahres habe ich mich einige Tage lang in Brüssel aufgehalten. Ich wohnte in einem kleinen Hotel am Bois de la Cambre, dessen sämtliche Räume und Zimmer mit schweren Mahagonimöbeln aus der Kolonialzeit und mit zahllosen, teilweise ganz enormen Topfpflanzen, Aspidistren, Monsteras und bis unter die vier Meter hohe Decke hinaufgewachsenen Gummibäumen, derart angefüllt war, dass man selbst mitten am Tag den Eindruck einer seltsamen schokoladefarbenen Verfinsterung hatte. Mein Zimmer in dem von mir so genannten Hotel Kongo befand sich im obersten Stock, und dort bin ich, nach meinen ausgedehnten Exkursionen, zumeist schlaflos in der Nacht gelegen auf den mehreren übereinandergetürmten Matratzen einer altertümlichen Bettstatt, halb wie der Froschkönig und halb wie die Prinzessin auf der Erbse.

Draussen standen schwarz die Buchen im Park, rauschten die Automobile über die nasse Fahrbahn so unablässig wie bisher bloss der Sambesi, während ich zurückdachte an die Zeit damals vor fünfundzwanzig Jahren, als ich die Clara in Brüssel besucht hatte. Meine Erinnerung setzte sich zusammen aus lauter versprengten Einzelheiten, Teilansichten, Andenkensplittern und Episoden — also beispielsweise wie die Suppe im Maison du Cygne in einer bauchigen Terrine aufgetragen wurde von einem weissbehandschuhten Ober, oder dass ich Mitleid empfand mit dem bleichen Marat in der Wanne; dass wir in der Domäne Huizingen lange vor einer Vogelvolière, in der es sehr bunt zuging, gestanden haben, dass wir an einem Sonntag nachmittag immer wieder demselben Radrennen begegneten, dass bei auffallend vielen Häusern Bucklige und Irre zu den Fenstern herausschauten und dass wir einmal mit dem Autobus Nr. 83 auf das Schlachtfeld von Waterloo hinausgefahren sind.

Was nun aber dieses Schlachtfeld betraf, so gelang es mir auf keinerlei Weise, mir den Anblick zu vergegenwärtigen, den es geboten hatte —, nur die zu dem Löwenmonument emporführenden Stufen sah ich vor mir — und darum entschloss ich mich, Waterloo noch einmal in Augenschein zu nehmen. Von der Bushaltestelle geht eine gerade Strasse an einem kahlen Acker entlang zu einer Ansammlung hässlicher Gebäude hinauf, in denen teils Devotionalienläden, teils billige Restaurationen untergebracht sind. Von irgendwelchen Besuchern zeigte sich an diesem bleigrauen Dezembertag begreiflicherweise keine Spur. Nicht einmal eine Schulklasse war zu sehen. Der völligen Verlassenheit wie zum Trotz aber marschierte ein unordentlich in historische Kostüme gezwängtes Trüppchen unter Trommel- und Pfeifenlärm in einer Tour durch die paar wenigen Gassen, zuhinterst eine schlampige und ihrem Metier entsprechend grossherzige Marketenderin, die ein kurioses Käfigwägelchen zog, in welches eine Gans eingesperrt war.

Solchermassen animiert zur Revokation der Vergangenheit, kaufte ich mir ein Eintrittsbillett für das Panorama, in dessen Zentrum, wie in jedem Panorama, eine Aussichtsplattform aufgebaut ist, von der aus die Schlacht — bekanntlich ein Lieblingssujet der Panoramakunst — in alle Himmelsrichtungen überblickt werden kann. In einer Art Bühnenlandschaft unmittelbar unterhalb der hölzernen Balustrade liegen lebensgrosse Pferde ausgestreckt im Sand, niedergemachte

Infanteristen, Husaren und Cheveaux-Légers [sic] mit brechendem Blick, die Leiber aus Papiermaché, aber die Versatzstücke, das Lederzeug, die Kürasse, die farbenprächtigen Uniformen allem Anschein nach authentisch. Über die drei-dimensionale, vom kalten Staub der verflossenen Zeit überzogene Horrorszene hinweg schweift der Blick in die Ferne auf das Riesenrundgemälde, das der französische Marinemaler Louis Dumontin im Jahre 1912 auf der 110 × 12 Meter messenden Innenwand der Rotonde ausgeführt hat. Das also, denkt man, langsam im Kreis gehend, ist unsere Geschichte — de holle weg van Ohain, de Hertog van Wellington, de rook van de pruisische batterijen, tegenaanval van de nederlandse cavalerie —, so ungefähr muss es wohl gewesen sein.

Später stehe ich droben auf dem Denkmalskegel. Ringsumher dehnt sich das Feld, worauf einmal 50 000 Soldaten und vielleicht 10 000 Pferde zu liegen gekommen sind. Jetzt ist da nichts als braune Erde. Was haben sie seinerzeit nur mit all den Gebeinen getan? Sind sie unter dem Kegel begraben? Stehn wir auf einem Totenberg? Ist das am Ende unsere Warte? — Ich werfe ein paar Blechmünzen in einen Apparat und höre mir die Schlachtbeschreibung auf Flämisch an. Es ist ein schöner Sommertag gewesen. Gewitterregen. Von den verschiedenen Vorgängen verstehe ich nur die Hälfte. Die Kämpfe wogen, wie es zumeist der Fall ist, hin und her. Ein richtiges Bild ergibt sich nicht.

Erst als ich die Augen schliesse, sehe ich eine Kanonenkugel, die auf schräger Bahn eine Reihe von Pappeln durchquert, dass die grünen Zweige durch die Luft fliegen. Dann sehe ich noch den Fabrizio, blass und mit glühenden Augen, in der Schlacht herumirren und den alten Obersten, wie er nach seinem Sturz vom Pferde sich wieder aufrafft und zu seinem Sergeanten sagt: Ich spüre nichts als nur die alte Wunde in meiner rechten Hand. Vor der Rückfahrt wärme ich mich in einer der Gaststätten ein wenig auf. Am anderen Ende der Stube sitzt eine vielleicht zum Zeitpunkt des Panoramabaus geborene Rentnerin in dem trüben, durch die belgischen Butzenscheiben einfallenden Licht allein an einem Tisch. Sie trägt Hut, Schal, Wintermantel und fingerlose Handschuhe. Die Bedienerin bringt ihr einen Teller mit einem grossen Stück Fleisch. Die Alte schaut es eine Zeitlang an, dann holt sie aus ihrer Handtasche ein scharfes Messerchen mit Holzgriff und Wellenschliff und beginnt es aufzuschneiden.

In der Nähe von Brighton, unweit der englischen Südküste, gibt es zwei Wäldchen, die nach der Schlacht von Waterloo gepflanzt wurden. Das eine hat die Form eines napoleonischen Dreispitzes, das andere diejenige des Stiefels von Wellington. Die Umrisse sind natürlich von der Erde aus nicht wahrzunehmen. Sie waren für Ballonreisende gedacht.

First published under the rubric 'Postkarte' as 'Waterloo' in *Neue Zürcher Zeitung Folio*, no. 91 (October 1991), pp. 71–73: repr. in Jo Catling, 'Europäische Flânerien: W. G. Sebalds intertextuelle Wanderungen zwischen Melancholie und Ironie', in *Gedächtnis und Widerstand: Festschrift für Irène Heidelberger-Leonard*, ed. by Mireille Tabah with Sylvia Weiler and Christian Poetini (Tübingen: Stauffenberg, 2009), pp. 139–54 (pp. 145–46). See that article for a discussion of the piece and how it relates to the 'Waterloo' episode in Part V of *Die Ringe des Saturn* (Eichborn, 1995), pp. 155–60; *The Rings of Saturn* (Harvill, 1998), pp. 122–27. In the original printing the text is prefaced by a sketch (as 'Postcard') of the monument at Waterloo, a cropped version of which appears in *Die Ringe des Saturn*, p. 156; *The Rings of Saturn*, p. 123.

(4) Two Poems by Michael Hulse
translated by W. G. Sebald

An Botho Strauss in Berlin

Dein Leben ist wie eine nackte Szene
kühl unter hohem Plafond

als hättest Du Dich eingemietet wo
der Bühnenbildner Deiner Träume

gerade ausgezogen ist.
Ein Saal am Ende der Premiere

der leere Raum applausgefüllt.
Ich sehe Gott den Schöpfer nach dem Fest

wie Du ihn Dir gedacht, so sitzt er schlafend
in Pantoffeln und Zylinder auf der Treppe des Palasts.

Es werde (murmelt er in seinem Schlummer
traumbewegt vor stiller Furcht) Licht.

Raffles Hotel Singapur

Sagen wir, es segelte einer die Meerenge hinauf und sah
ein Fischerdorf und betrat eine Stadt.
      Sagen wir, die Zukunft hieß Opium
    im Tausch gegen Tee, Paraden auf dem Padang,

Geheimgesellschaften, Rikschas am Collyer Quay
und Aufstände in den Straßen. Sagen wir, die Villa,
    in der ein verkrachter Oberst ein billiges Lokal
  aufgemacht hat, wurde von einem Armenier gekauft

und in ein weißes Hotel verwandelt, Kolonnaden und
Mandelduft, Palmen, Pilaster, Jalousien aus Bambus,
      Pianowalzer drunten in Hof:
    die Braut reicht dem Roué ihre Hand.

Und während sie starben an der Somme und in Passchendaele
mixte der Barmann (sehr sorgsam) den ersten Gin Sling.
    Während sich General Percival auf das köstlichste
    amüsierte und wortstark sich weigerte, Singapur

auf der Landseite zu befestigen, radelten schon
die Japaner über die Halbinsel herunter.
  Denn Geschichte ist die Kunst der Verführung,
   Cocktails auf der Veranda, dann das Diner

um acht und die elegante Verachtung der Ober.
Nach dem Regen wieder ein klarer Himmel. Sterne
   gestanzt in die Indigonacht.
 Ein britischer Lord und seine Gemahlin geleiten

die Gäste zu einem Bankett, Dudelsackbläser spielen
Scotland the Brave, und ein Australier schwört auf sein
  Leben, man habe dem letzten Tiger der Insel unter
   einem Billardtisch den Garaus gemacht.

Ein Empire für Idioten. Den Pool umkreisend in der Stunde
nach Mitternacht denke ich an meinen Vater und an die Klänge
   der Jazz-Band in der Bar. Nach dem Ende des
   Kriegs handelte er in Textilien in Raffles Place

und eines Tages kam zeitig, um ihn zu warnen, sein Fahrer
und fuhr ihn geschwind zu einer Villa hinaus, wo bewaffnete
  Engländer hinter geschlossenen Läden hockten
 einen fanatischen Nachmittag lang und weit in die Nacht

witzelnd und zugleich voller Angst wispernd und spähend
ob nicht vielleicht eine Palme schwankte so wie
   diese jetzt hier in der unschuldigen Luft
  zittert mit dem dunkleren Atem des Saxophons.

[Aus dem Englischen von W. G. Sebald]

These translations were first published in the literary journal *Sprache im technischen Zeitalter* in June 1995 (see Primary Bibliography M.A.2). The original poems, 'To Botho Strauss in Berlin' and 'Raffles Hotel (Singapore)', appeared in Michael Hulse's collection *Eating Strawberries in the Necropolis* (London: Harvill, 1991).

(5) Feuer und Rauch:
Über eine Abwesenheit in der deutschen Literatur

Ein paar Meilen südostwärts von meinem Haus erstreckt sich über ein weites, baumloses Stück Land das Flugfeld von Seething, ein gott- und weltverlassenes Terrain, auf dem nur selten etwas sich regt. Hie und da sieht man vielleicht einen Hasen davonspringen oder, wenn es Nacht wird, eine Eule, die ihre Schleifen zieht mit langsamen Flügelschlag. Im Frühjahr sprießen aus dem Feld Myriaden von mageren hellgrünen Gräsern, die schnell in der Sommerdürre verblassen und im Winter zusammensinken zu einem bleichen, unendlich komplizierten Netzwerk, in dem nicht ein Halm liegt wie der andere. Azurblau wölbt sich über Seething der Himmel, hängt an anderen Tagen grau bis auf die Erde herunter, oder es fahren an ihm die Wolken dahin in großen weißen Geschwadern.

Stundenlang gehe ich oft mit meinem Hund auf diesem leeren Gelände herum, und unweigerlich kommt es mir dabei in den Sinn, daß etwa um die Zeit meiner Geburt von hier aus Abend für Abend schwerbeladene Maschinen aufgestiegen sind, in langer Linie hintereinander, um sich draußen über der Nordsee mit anderen Bomberströmen zu vereinen und Kurs zu nehmen auf Deutschland. Heute wird auf dem Flugfeld von Seething nur noch eine einzige holprige Rollbahn in Betrieb gehalten von einem Amateurfliegerverein.

An einem Tag der offenen Tür, den diese Leute veranstaltet hatten im Sommer des vorvergangenen Jahres, lernte ich Gerald Aylmer kennen, der bei Kriegsende fünfzehn Jahre alt gewesen und auf dem neben dem Flugfeld gelegenen Gutshof Andromeda Lodge aufgewachsen ist, wo er auch heute noch lebt. Aylmer erzählte mir, daß er lange Jahre hindurch in einem Genfer Forschungsinstitut tätig gewesen und daß er von seinem Schweizer Arbeitsplatz jede zweite Woche zumindest in seiner Cessna nach Hause geflogen sei. Die Flugleidenschaft, sagte mir Aylmer, habe von frühester Jugend an sein ganzes Leben bestimmt, und auch heute noch mache er, obschon er sich sonst kaum mehr von seinem Hof begebe, von Seething aus die längsten Ausflüge durch die Luft, nach wie vor voller Verwunderung über die den Menschenverstand (auch den eines Physikers) übersteigende Möglichkeit, das Antlitz der Erde aus der Höhe sehen zu können. Tagelang, so sagte Aylmer schon bei unserer ersten Begegnung, fliege er oft die Küsten entlang, über Städte und Ebenen dahin, von einem Ende der Alpen zum anderen, über die böhmischen und bayerischen Wälder, von Bordeaux aus die schöne Garonne hinauf bis zu ihrem Ursprung und die Donau hinunter bis an das Schwarze Meer.

Ich habe Gerald Aylmer während der seit jenem Tag der offenen Tür vergangenen Monate mehrmals besucht, und es ist noch nicht lange her, daß er mir eines Abends, als wir im Billardzimmer von Andromeda Lodge eine Partie Pool miteinander spielten, erzählte von den, wie er sich ausdrückte, mutmaßlichen Anfängen seiner Flieger- und Flugzeugmanie.

Er glaube nicht, so begann er, daß sie auf ein bestimmtes Erlebnis zurückzuführen sei, doch entsinne er sich, daß ihn bereits als Kind von allen Tieren eigentlich nur die geflügelten interessiert hätten. Obwohl die Vögel uns im Grunde so fremd sind wie die Fische, habe ich immer, sagte Aylmer, die Empfindung gehabt, sie seien meine engsten Verwandten. Nichts hat mich je so geschmerzt wie der Abschied von meinen beiden Brieftauben an dem Tag, an dem ich von hier weg auf eine Schule in Northamptonshire gehen mußte. Der Großvater hatte sie mir zwei Jahre zuvor geschenkt gehabt, und der Vater, der damals als landwirtschaftlicher Berater der Regierung viel im ganzen Land unterwegs war, hat sie, so oft wie möglich, für mich ausgesetzt, Hunderte von Meilen manchmal von Seething entfernt, und immer sind sie wieder zu mir zurückgekehrt. Ich spüre noch heute, sagte Aylmer, die erwartungsvolle Spannung, mit der ich beim Ablauf der von mir errechneten Flugzeit im Taubenhaus saß, und auch das mit nichts in meinem späteren Leben zu vergleichende Glücksgefühl, wenn ich sie einfliegen hörte und gleich darauf sicher in meinen Händen hielt.

In der Schule habe ich dann während der endlosen Studierstunden ein ornithologisches System ausgearbeitet, dessen wichtigstes Einteilungskriterium der Grad der Flugtüchtigkeit war, und wie ich dieses System auch modifizierte, die Tauben rangierten in ihm immer obenan, nicht nur aufgrund der Geschwindigkeit, mit der sie die längsten Strecken zurücklegten, sondern auch aufgrund ihrer vor allen anderen Lebewesen sie auszeichnenden Kunst der Navigation.

Man kann ja, sagte Aylmer, so eine Taube abfliegen lassen von einem Schiff mitten in einem Schneesturm auf der Nordsee, und solange nur ihre Kräfte reichen, wird sie unfehlbar den Weg zurückfinden nach Hause. Bis heute weiß niemand, wie die in einer solch wüsten Leere auf die Reise geschickten Tiere, denen gewiß in Vorahnung der ungeheuren Entfernungen, die sie überwinden müssen, beinah das Herz vor Angst zerspringt, den Ort ihrer Herkunft anpeilen. Jedenfalls sind die mir bekannten wissenschaftlichen Erklärungen, denen zufolge die Tauben sich an den Gestirnen, an den Strömungen der Luft oder an Magnetfeldern orientieren, kaum stichhaltiger als die verschiedenen Theorien, die ich mir als neunjähriger Schüler ausgedacht habe in der Hoffnung, daß ich nach der Lösung dieser Frage in der Lage sein würde, die Tauben auch in umgekehrter Richtung, also beispielsweise von Seething an den Platz meiner Verbannung in Rugby, fliegen zu lassen.

Im übrigen, fuhr Aylmer fort, wurde meine Taubenbegeisterung, wie es zu dieser Zeit gar nicht anders denkbar gewesen ist, bald schon abgelenkt auf den in den Jahren 1941/42 über England und dem Ärmelkanal ausgefochtenen, jeden Knaben selbstverständlich andauernd beschäftigenden Luftkrieg, und wenn ich im Verlauf der nächsten Jahre in den Ferien nach Seething zurückkam, wo seit Anfang 1943 auf der zu unserem Gut gehörenden Grasheide für die US Air Force ein riesiges Flugfeld angelegt wurde, so nahm mich natürlich die damals in meinem Kopf mit allerhand edlen Vorstellungen verbundene, in erster Linie von den ostenglischen Grafschaften ausgehende Zerstörungskampagne völlig in Anspruch.

Ich sah die schweren Liberator-Bomber einen nach dem anderen von der Rollbahn sich in die Luft erheben, und ich sah mich selber schon, im vollen Bewußtsein der Bedeutung meiner Mission, in einer der gläsernen Kabinen sitzen, was, so setzte Aylmer hinzu, weit weniger fantastisch war, als man meinen möchte, denn von den 1944 und 1945 hier stationierten Besatzungen waren nicht wenige nur um drei oder vier Jahre älter, als ich es selber damals gewesen bin.

Auch einer meiner Vettern, Hamish Arbuthnot, war gerade erst neunzehn, als er seinen ersten Angriff flog als Bordkanonier. Ich weiß noch, daß er uns bald darauf einmal besuchte und der am Teetisch vor Staunen wie versteinerten Familie erzählte, wie er auf dem Heimflug bis weit über die holländische Küste hinaus das brennende Köln habe sehen können als einen roten Feuerfleck in der Finsternis. Wäre ich zwei Jahre früher auf die Welt gekommen, sagte Aylmer, so wäre wahrscheinlich auch ich in der Nacht nach Deutschland geflogen und vielleicht verschwunden, gerade wie Hamish, der kurz vor Weihnachten 1944 über dem Ardennerwald, wie man vermutet, abgesprungen und niemals aufgefunden worden ist.

Das brennende Köln — es hat lange gedauert, bis ich mir auch nur eine ungefähre Vorstellung davon zu machen begann, wie es hier und anderwärts in Deutschland aussah, als der Krieg zu Ende war. Zu Beginn der Achtziger erzählte mir Solly Zuckerman, der als wissenschaftler Berater der englischen Regierung nach dem ersten Großangriff auf Köln gegen die Strategie des *area bombing* argumentierte, daß er, als er im Frühjahr 1945 nach Köln kam, beim Herumgehen zwischen den Schutthalden von einer Art geistiger Lähmung befallen worden sei.

Obgleich er durch Luftaufnahmen schon vorbereitet gewesen sei auf das Ausmaß der Zerstörung, habe er doch nicht fassen können, was er nun mit eigenen Augen sah. Er habe damals, sagte Zuckerman, den Plan gefaßt zu einer weitausgreifenden Naturgeschichte der Zerstörung, doch sei ihm dessen Ausführung in der Folge nicht gelungen, in erster Linie, wie er annehme, weil die Ruinenlandschaft, über der eine große Stille lag, als etwas Transreales vor einem sich ausgedehnt habe, das sich sowohl dem wissenschaftlichen Verständnis als auch der Artikulationsfähigkeit entzog. 'My first view of Cologne', schrieb Zuckerman in seiner Autobiographie, 'cried out for a more eloquent piece than I could ever have written.'

Fast scheint es, als habe Zuckerman hier den Auftrag, zu berichten von einem Besuch in der Unterwelt, an die Schriftsteller und Poeten weitergeben wollen. Doch auch diese blieben offenbar nicht verschont von der Paralyse der Wahrnehmungskraft, der affektiven Reaktionen und des Sprachvermögens. Es gibt kaum Beschreibungen der riesigen Feuerbrände und der Steinwüsten, die aus ihnen hervorgingen, nahezu gar nicht von deutscher Seite.

Einiges von dem, was ausländische Journalisten damals in Deutschland sahen, hat Hans Magnus Enzensberger zusammengestellt für den 1990 erschienenen Sammelband *Europa in Trümmern*, in dem sich auch eine von Janet Flanner im März 1945 geschriebene Reportage findet, die beginnt mit den Worten: 'Köln am Rhein ist nun ein Paradigma der Zerstörung. Das nahe gelegene Aachen ging anders zugrunde: sein schönes, melancholisches Gerippe steht noch, aber hinter den eleganten, verzierten Fassaden ist es ausgebrannt. Köln dagegen mit seiner schweren mittelalterlichen Pracht ist in die Luft gesprengt worden. Im Schutt und in der Einsamkeit völliger physischer Zerstörung lehnt Köln, bar jeder Gestalt und schmucklos, an seinem Flußufer. Was von seinem Leben übriggeblieben ist, das kämpft sich mühsam einen Weg durch die zugeschütteten Seitenstraßen: eine geschrumpfte Bevölkerung, schwarz gekleidet und mit Bündeln beladen — stumm wie die Stadt.'

Auf immer, sollte man meinen, hätten diese Bilder den Überlebenden sich einge-
prägt; immer wieder, denkt man, hätten sie erzählen müssen, wie es war, als Köln
und all die anderen deutschen Städte verbrannten. Doch die Betroffenen gaben,
wie Enzensberger bemerkte, die schlechtesten Zeugen ab. Daß das Kapitel der
Zerstörung gewissenhaft verzeichnet ist in den Annalen fast jeder größeren Stadt,
ändert daran nur wenig, denn in der besonderern Form solcher Chroniken erscheint
diese Zerstörung nicht als das grauenvolle Ende einer kollektiven Aberration,
sondern, sozusagen, schon als die erste Stufe des erfolgreichen Wiederaufbaus.

Auch aus der sogenannten Trümmerliteratur erfährt ein Nachgeborener nicht
sehr viel über die realen Lebensverhältnisse in den deutschen Städten in dem halben
Jahrzehnt zwischen 1943 und 1945 [sic]. Als ich 1960, im Alter von sechzehn Jahren,
nachdem ich mit dem Karl-May-Lesen fertig geworden war, zum erstenmal Ullsteins
Taschenbuchausgaben der frühen Romane Bölls in die Hand bekam — *Das Brot der
frühen Jahre* und *Haus ohne Hüter* — da fand ich in diesen Erzählungen kaum etwas,
das mich verwiesen hätte auf die eineinhalb Jahrzehnte erst zurückliegende totale
Zerstörung. Eineinhalb Jahrzehnte, ist das nicht nur ein Augenblick, denke ich
mir heute, wo die Zeit an mir immer schneller vorüberrauscht, und ich frage mich
darum, wie die Schuttberge und die Ruinen in solch kurzer Frist verschwanden aus
dem Gedächtnis der aus ihnen erstandenen neuen Nation.

Der wahre Zustand der materiellen und moralischen Vernichtung, in welchem
das Land sich befand, durfte, so muß man annehmen, aufgrund einer stillschweigend
eingegangenen und für alle gleichermaßen gültigen Vereinbarung nicht beschrieben
werden. Die schreckensvollsten Aspekte des von der überwiegenden Mehrheit der
deutschen Bevölkerung miterlebten Schlußaktes der Zerstörung blieben so ein
schandbares, mit einer Art Tabu behaftetes Familiengeheimnis, das man vielleicht
nicht einmal sich selber eingestehen konnte. Von sämtlichen Ende der vierziger
Jahre entstandenen literarischen Werken ist es eigentlich nur Bölls Roman *Der
Engel schwieg*, der eine annähernde Vorstellung vermittelt von dem Entsetzen, das
damals jeden zu erfassen drohte, der wirklich sich umsah in den Vorhöfen des
Todes. Es leuchtet einem bei der Lektüre sogleich ein, daß gerade diese, von einer
unheilbaren Schwermut geprägte Erzählung der zeitgenössischen Leserschaft, wie
der Verlag und wohl auch Böll selber glaubte, nicht zugemutet werden konnte,
und daß sie darum erst 1992, mit beinahe fünfzigjähriger Verspätung erschienen
ist. Tatsächlich ist, um nur ein Beispiel zu geben, das siebzehnte, den Todeskampf
der Frau Gompertz schildernde Kapitel, in dem von wildem, zerdrücktem Schmerz
und der letzten Peinigung des Leibes und der Seele die Rede ist, von einem
derart radikalen Agnostizismus, daß man darüber auch heute nicht ohne weiteres
hinwegkommt.

Bölls posthumer Roman bezeichnet so eine weiße Stelle in unserem historischen
Atlas. Nie ist, was damals geschah, wirklich in das öffentliche Bewußtsein einge-
drungen oder gar Lehrstoff geworden in der Schule. Und doch zieht sich von dort
her eine schwarze Ader durch unser Leben und durch das Werk Heinrich Bölls bis
hin zu der endzeitlichen, bleiernen Flußlandschaft, in der er die von ihrem Unglück
beinahe schon ausgelöschten Frauen auftreten läßt.

Blicken wir heute, im Bewußtsein dessen, was uns in den letzten zwei Jahrzehnten allmählich aufgegangen ist, zurück auf die in den Nachthimmel hinauflodernden deutschen Städte, so können wir erkennen — vorausgesetzt wir sind fähig zu solch ungeheurem Detachment —, daß dieses Aufflackern nur eine besonders intensive Phase dessen war, was fortwährend und in immer zunehmenden Maße geschieht. Vielleicht müssen wir endlich wirklich begreifen lernen, daß der Stoff unserer Zivilisation selber gewoben ist aus Feuer und Rauch.

[*Gestern hat der Schriftsteller W. G. Sebald (u.a. 'Die Ausgewanderten' und 'Die Ringe des Saturn') den Heinrich-Böll-Preis der Stadt Köln erhalten. Für diesen Anlaß hat der in England lebende Autor den hier publizierten Prosatext geschrieben.*]

This piece was first published in the Feuilleton of the *Frankfurter Rundschau* on 29 November 1997 (see Primary Bibliography D.66), and is the text of the speech WGS read out on the occasion of receiving the Heinrich Böll Prize in Cologne the preceding day. The text is, unsurprisingly, closely related to the lectures on Air War and Literature given in Zurich in November and December 1997, but also to the story of Gerald Ashman (here called Aylmer) in *Austerlitz*, with his fondness for birds, especially pigeons (see Chapters 8 and 11), and to the 'Zweite Fassung' (second draft) of the abandoned 'Corsica project' (see Chapter 10, and Primary Bibliography F.D.2).

Fig. II.1. 'Michael under his mulberry tree': framed photograph of
Michael Hamburger in his garden, inscribed thus on back by WGS.
© The Estate of W. G. Sebald; courtesy of DLA Marbach

(6) Ausgrabung der Vergangenheit

*Den Bäumen und Pflanzen hat der Dichter Michael Hamburger
einige seiner schönsten Gedichte gewidmet.*

Jetzt, wo ich nach und nach ins fortgeschrittenere Alter einrücke, graust es mir
manchmal vor der Menge der Bücher, die ich seit meiner Schulentlassung gelesen
habe. Dementsprechend wird die Zahl der Schriftsteller, die ich nicht missen
möchte, immer geringer. Viel mehr als ein Fähnlein von sieben bringe ich kaum
noch zusammen. Michael Hamburger ist aber, nebst Robert Walser, stets mit dabei.
In einem längeren Kapitel habe ich einmal zu beschreiben versucht, was es mit einer
solchen Wahlverwandtschaft auf sich hat. Von sonderbaren Überschneidungen
zweier Lebensläufe war da die Rede, von den Traumfluchten, durch die Michael
mich führte, von der Ausgrabung einer verschütteten Vergangenheit und von der,
wie wir beide fürchten, endgültig der Zerstörung überantworteten Welt der höheren
Pflanzenarten: der grünen Bäume, denen Michael, nicht nur als Repräsentanten
ihrer jeweiligen Spezies, sondern sozusagen als beseelten Individuen einige seiner
schönsten Gedichte gewidmet hat. Es gibt eine Fotografie, auf der Michael zu
sehen ist vor einem mächtigen Maulbeerbaum in seinem Garten.[1] Bald nachdem
diese Aufnahme gemacht worden war, wurde der Baum in einer Sturmnacht zu
Boden gedrückt, hielt aber jahrelang noch aus gegen den Tod. 'Besser sehen wir
jetzt', schreibt Michael, 'was bleibt. Weniger als der gewesene Baum und mehr
doch durch die Verminderung, an die Erde gelegt, gebettet ins Gras, bei Mohn
und bei saftdunklem Balsam, dort, wo der Schatten war, den grösseres Gedeihen
einst warf.'[2] An der vollkommen unsentimentalen Präzision solcher Zeilen ist mir
aufgegangen, dass Zuneigung und Sachverstand einander nicht ausschliessen, dass
eine gewisse Befähigung zum richtigen Schreiben nicht reicht, dass es so etwas
gibt wie eine Moralität des Ästhetischen, die, letztlich, auf der wahren Anschauung
der Dinge beruht. Für die falsche Anschauung weiss ich kein besseres Beispiel als
das Unwesen, das die Hüter und Heger des deutschen Geistes, allen voran der
Freiburger Rektor mit dem Hitlerbärtchen, mit dem armen Hölderlin trieben.
Damals, in den dreissiger und vierziger Jahren, ist der wahre Platz Hölderlins
nicht, wie es hiess, 'im Erlebnis des deutschen Volkes' gewesen, sondern einzig in
den englischen Übersetzungen, die der junge Exilant Michael Hamburger von den
Elegien, Oden und Hymnen anzufertigen begann in einer dann über lange Jahre
noch fortgesetzten Arbeit, neben der für mich vieles von dem, was sonst Literatur
heisst, verblasst.

[Lesung: Heute, 17.00–17.45 Uhr]

This piece was first published in the *Tages-Anzeiger* (Zurich) on 22 May 1998 (see Primary Bibliography
D.67) to coincide with a reading by Michael Hamburger at the Solothurner Literaturtage (the annual
literary festival in Solothurn, Switzerland) later that day. An English translation by Jo Catling is
currently in preparation.

Notes on 'Ausgrabung der Vergangenheit'

1. See Figure II.1. The photograph also appears on the cover of *Flugasche*, no. 49 (Spring 1994), an issue devoted to Michael Hamburger on the occasion of his seventieth birthday.

2. This is a free translation by Sebald of the closing lines of Michael Hamburger's poem 'Afterlives' (1990), from the collection 'Tree Poems', in *Collected Poems* (London: Anvil Press, 1995), p. 363:

> ...for us
> Who now, more singly seeing, meet what remains,
> Less than the tree it was and more than a tree
> By the diminishment, the lying low,
> Bedded on grass, with poppies and balsam lush,
> Where the shade was its greater prospering cast.

FIG. II.2. The garden of The Old Rectory, Poringland,
after the hurricane of the night of 16–17 October 1987.
Cf. *Die Ringe des Saturn* (Eichborn, 1995), pp. 284–85; *The Rings of Saturn*, pp. 265–68.
© W. G. Sebald; courtesy of U. E. Sebald

(7) Michael Hamburger:
Nomination for the Degree of Honorary DLitt

Michael Peter Leopold Hamburger was born in Berlin in 1924 but was educated at Westminster School and Oxford University. He served in the Army during the Second World War and then became a freelance writer and poet. He was appointed as an Assistant Lecturer in German at University College London in 1952 and in 1955 moved to the University of Reading, where he became a Lecturer and later a Reader. He has also held appointments as a Visiting Professor at numerous universities in the USA. Michael Hamburger now lives in Suffolk and for many years has actively contributed to the literary and academic life of the University of East Anglia. His main work is that of a translator and mediator between cultures. Starting four decades ago, he has clearly become this century's leading translator of German literature, with particular emphasis on German poetry. Himself a refugee from inhumanity, he has sought to make accessible to the English-speaking world what is best and most humane in German culture. His immense contribution in this field ranges from courtly lyrics to the contemporary 'low-brow' political minstrelsy of a Wolf Biermann, but concentrates on major figures in the nineteenth and twentieth centuries. His most remarkable achievement to date is his translation of Holderlin's [*sic*] works (1966). This may, however, shortly be overshadowed by the substantial share he takes in the new English Goethe edition currently appearing in Germany. Michael Hamburger is also a renowned literary critic. He has published several weighty volumes on German literature, among which *Reason and Energy* (1957, revised 1970) proved particularly influential. His main contribution to criticism is, however, *The Truth of Poetry* (1969, revised 1982), a broadly-based exploration and powerfully perceptive analysis of modern poetry in European Languages from Baudelaire to the nineteen-sixties. This is a work from which several generations of students at universities in Britain and abroad, many of them by now university teachers, have substantially benefited. Michael Hamburger has also established himself as a distinguished modern English poet, [with] many volumes appearing from *Flowering Cactus: Poems 1942–1949* (1950) to his *Collected Poems* (1984). Some collections of his poetry have in their turn been translated (by Erich Fried and others) and been published in Germany.

Editors' note on Michael Hamburger

W. G. Sebald particularly prized the work of Michael Hamburger (22 March 1924– 7 June 2007) as a poet and translator[*] and, as the above piece 'Ausgrabung der Vergangenheit' (Excavation of the Past) shows, shared with him an apocalyptic sense of history, particularly in respect of the natural world. Their affinity is evident from Part VII of *Die Ringe des Saturn* with the narrator's visit to Michael Hamburger's

FIG. II.3. Michael Hamburger at Congregation, 30 June 1988, after receiving an Honorary DLitt. The photo shows him standing next to Professor Christine Brooke-Rose.
© John Gibbons, courtesy of the University of East Anglia

home at Marsh Acres and the number of similarities, parallels, and coincidences he comments on. It arises logically from this meeting of minds, and their friendship, that Michael Hamburger should have been asked to translate Sebald's own poetry, including his first book *Nach der Natur* (*After Nature*) and the minimalist final work, *Unerzählt* (*Unrecounted*).

On 17 March 1999, at an event organized in association with BCLT at the university bookshop, Max Sebald gave a most moving address in honour of Michael Hamburger's seventy-fifth birthday (on 22 March). Some ten years earlier, in the late 1980s, he had also been instrumental in persuading UEA to award Michael Hamburger an Honorary DLitt (see Figure II.3). The evidence indicates that the above text, a recommendation submitted to the UEA Honorary Degrees and Appointments Committee on 2 December 1987, was in fact written by Sebald. Richard Sheppard notes: 'On 13 January 1988, UEA's Senate (Minute 29) invited Michael Hamburger to receive the honorary degree of Doctor of Letters at the Congregation that would take place on 30 June and 1 July 1988. Although the supporting recommendation that had gone to the meeting of UEA's Honorary Degrees and Appointments Committee on 2 December 1987 was anonymized, the style and sentiments are definitely Sebald's and the typeface is that of the electric typewriter used by Mrs Beryl Ranwell, the Secretary of the German Sector at the time, which had no *Umlaut* — hence the misspelling of Hölderlin.'

---

* For a longer tribute to Michael Hamburger's life and work, see Elinor Shaffer, 'Michael Hamburger: Voice of Lost Poetry', *Comparative Critical Studies*, 7.2–3 (2010), 285–96. See also the papers of the IGRS memorial symposium, *From Charlottenburg to Middleton: Michael Hamburger (1924–2007): Poet, Translator, Critic*, ed. by Joyce Crick, Martin Liebscher, and Martin Swales (Munich: iudicium, 2010); and Michael Hamburger, *Pro Domo: Selbstauskünfte, Rückblicke und andere Prosa*, ed. by Iain Galbraith (Vienna: Folio, 2007).

2
Three Conversations with W. G. Sebald

The first piece below was initially published in Dutch in 1992 and has been translated into English especially for this volume. The second and third pieces are the transcripts of two conversations around book readings in 1999 and 2001 from 'The Emigrants' and 'Austerlitz' respectively. They are published here for the first time.

(1) Echoes from the Past: A Conversation with Piet de Moor
Published in *Knack* magazine, Brussels, 6 May 1992

(2) Lost in Translation? A Conversation with Jon Cook
(including a reading by WGS)
Centre for the Creative and Performing Arts,
University of East Anglia, Norwich, 9 February 1999

(3) In This Distant Place
A Conversation with Steve Wasserman (including a reading by WGS)
ALOUD at Central Library, Los Angeles Public Library
Los Angeles, 17 October 2001

(1) Echoes from the Past
A Conversation with Piet de Moor

Progress is loss: the Austrian writer Sebald listens to the echoes that momentarily suspend time

'Sebald has written a book of truly remarkable beauty and given visual form to what Stendhal would have called the "travail de l'âme"', wrote the *Neue Zürcher Zeitung* when *Schwindel. Gefühle. (Vertigo)* came out in 1990. The novel, by the Austrian writer W. G. Sebald, who teaches at a university in Britain, is the account of a melancholy traveller who wanders around in a time-worn, almost burnt-out world. He does so in the company of the writers Stendhal and Kafka, who visited northern Italy separated by a gap of exactly one hundred years (1813 and 1913). But in the meantime, the Italian cities have degenerated into infernos, and only in their names does something of the grandeur for which they once stood, still resonate. What is being lamented is the sense of irretrievable loss that wells up in the individual who comprehends how the whole universe becomes burdened with guilt. Dizzy spells (*duizelingen*), emotions, paranoia, states of anxiety: this is the condition of those sensitive souls who are lost at the end of the twentieth century.

W. G. Sebald (WGS): I am not a *littérateur* in the true sense of the word. As a 21-year-old I wrote a novel. When I read it out to my girlfriend, she fell asleep. So I thought I'd better just give it up. For decades after that I stuck to academic work. But I've always kept small notebooks in which I used to make very chaotic notes. *Vertigo* came about by chance. I bought Stendhal's *De l'amour* in a bookshop in Lausanne. It resonated with a great many things that were on my mind because it contained many Italian place names which were familiar to me from the trips I'd made to Italy as a child [cf. Fig. 11.5, p. 281 (Eds)]. I knew Kafka's works well, but not Stendhal's, and yet I was immediately struck by a remarkable convergence. Stendhal was born in 1783, Kafka in 1883. Stendhal stayed in northern Italy in 1813, Kafka in 1913. So then I wrote two literary-biographical essays on the two authors whom I wanted to bring closer together.

While I was doing that writing, I remembered that I, too, had travelled through northern Italy in 1980. I wrote an account of that trip in the long story *All'estero*, which ended up as a part of a triptych in between the stories about Stendhal and Kafka. That is how the book structured itself. In the fourth and final part, *Il ritorno in patria*, I recalled my childhood in the little village of Wertach. It is an attempt on my part to shed light on an emotional propensity of which I became extremely conscious for the first time when I experienced it in the late 1970s: the crisis that besets you in midlife. I wanted to know where it came from. I wrote the final part as a search for my own 'I'.

Knack: Does that end with the apocalypse that you have taking place in 2013?[1]

WGS: Of course, I don't know what 2013 will bring, but whether we shall carry on for that long, either individually or collectively, is uncertain. Even so, it is amazing that we still learnt at school that the world is eternal and that we are all very secure within the balance of Nature. Less than half a century later, this comforting certainty has simply vanished; one day we shall be presented with the bill. Since reaching that insight, we have been under enormous psychic pressure. I believe that because of this the last foundation stone of our secure existence in this world has been removed. The theocratic supports fell away much earlier. After that, we could find solace in the notion that we, as mortal individuals, depend on a greater process that ends in a comforting form. But now, even transcendence can no longer be taken for granted either.

Knack: The travelling narrator has an obsessive tendency to name things. Since all supports have been removed, is that the only way to maintain your individuality in the world?

WGS: It is a kind of conjuration. You almost no longer believe that things, the cities and the villages, really exist. Naples is no longer the Naples where Chateaubriand stayed at the end of the nineteenth century. It is one enormous catastrophe. But the names still retain echoes of the past, an enormous and permanent sense of loss. Nothing remains as it was. And that is why we are also no longer what we once were: we must, in the meantime, have become something completely different, but we aren't quite sure what. Most cities have become a slaughterhouse.[2] The most terrible things happen, mainly hidden from our eyes. I believe that the feeling of a continually increasing and unstoppable loss is possibly the foremost cause of melancholy in my text.

Knack: Does Kafka reappear in every individual?

WGS: I believe so. Kafka experienced his own existence as illegitimate. That would have to be a collective experience. Our existence as a species is not legitimate. We have organized our society in such a way that we threaten to burn ourselves. The topos of fire in the novel fits in with the way in which people use fire and what they have in common with the devices that they use. Fire is the most terrifying thing. Usually you don't see the process of combustion. If you have a refrigerator in a room, you don't, of course, consider that even the refrigerator is ceaselessly burning something.

Knack: Nevertheless, the narrator wants to look after the animals and becomes agitated when he sees the chickens pottering about in the yard. Is this where he confirms the observation that seeing means everything for him?

WGS: From a rational point of view I do not see why another being that wanders this planet should have less right to exist than ourselves. It is the relationships of power that decide who gets locked up and who gets eaten, and who does the eating and the locking up. We stand right at the top, the supreme parasites. I have a thing about chickens. They are a curious mixture of the free-range and the domesticated. That is what is peculiar about chickens. In the past the chickens used to potter about in the yard. Now they don't any more. They're locked up. Yes, the eyes are the most vulnerable part of a person or of an animal. I have a terrible fear of any sort of surgery. I cannot even think about having a cataract operation. That feeling of *Blendung* [blinding],[3] the fear of no longer being able to see, probably has something to do with the fear of castration. There is a very fine short story by E. T. A. Hoffmann called *The Sandman*, in which children are told that if they don't go to sleep, the sandman will come and take away their eyes and put them in a large sack to give to the owl who lives in the moon. Many children are plagued by such nightmares. People who are frightened will try to make themselves as small as possible in order to escape detection. In fairytales, too, metamorphosis into what is very small, shrinkage until you become invisible to the naked eye, is a perspective that offers a chance of salvation. Conversely, everything that is big, colossal, and triumphalist is associated with the demonstration of power, such as fascist architecture. The bigger, the more paranoid.

Knack: Why is your novel full of coincidences that acquire meaning as mysterious signals to the narrator's discourse?

WGS: When striking coincidences occur, you always have the feeling that they have to mean something. But you do not know what. They are probably phenomena that occur on the fringe of life, where the so-called real world is touched by the metaphysical. Metaphysics is something about which nobody talks any more. It is considered ridiculous, devoid of substance, meaningless. In spite of everything I am interested by metaphysical themes in the broadest sense of the word — and when I say that, I am not talking in a religious sense, for that would be alien to me. Highly improbable coincidences, overlaps with other people's lives, elements that cannot be explained in words happen in the course of everyone's life. I believe we have a tendency to overlook and forget that. Our endeavours to reconstruct the historiography of an individual life story are arbitrary attempts to bring order into this chaos.

Knack: Writing is an attempt to bring order into chaos. The writer is the boss. If he or she so wishes, he or she may do as Kafka did seventy years ago. This happens in your book.

WGS: You are marked by experiences that can also be literary in origin. The passages in the text that deal with Kafka and Stendhal find their vindication in just such a way. Our lives are also shaped by our own imagination, by the imaginations of others. What is comforting about art is that within the work of art, provided that it is successful, you can achieve a momentary, self-regulating equilibrium. That, for instance, is what makes the plastic arts, whence time has disappeared, beautiful. I share Peter Handke's view that time plays a central role in narrative literature. For fifteen years now Handke has tried relatively systematically to eliminate time from his texts and to give his prose the plasticity of a three-dimensional pictorial language. That is what grabs us when we visit a museum and see a painting from the seventeenth century. That is a snapshot for all eternity. To put it in somewhat grandiose terms: it is a reflection on eternity made with very few resources. To me, that still seems to be the difficulty.

I myself work like a painter who has to consider how big to make the frame. The painter's craft has always fascinated me. I envy painters because of the craftsmanship that is involved in their art. With writing this is the case to a far lesser extent. Many people ask me, 'Why do you still write when you have such a pessimistic world-view?' It is an attempt to create tiny pools of timelessness.

Knack: The narrator travels erratically, he flees from real and imaginary persecutors and dangers from one city to the next, he has little in common with the average tourist.

WGS: I find all forms of tourism strange. If you travel alone for weeks on end, saying only what is essential because you are staying in a hotel, you end up in a spiritual state of mind that makes you experience reality differently. That state of mind sometimes leaves behind clear traces, which can be activated later. The act of remembering can reawaken things of which you were not even aware on the journey. When the narrator is in northern Italy, a series of social misfits are murdered. The narrator has the premonition that he will be the next victim, a conviction that comes to a head when he goes to eat in a pizzeria in Verona which is owned by a gentleman with the terrifying name of Cadavero. A panicky fear of death takes hold of the narrator. That is a very clear premonition of death. You have the feeling of being marked out for the next murder. Many people are familiar with this phenomenon, although virtually no one will admit to it. Thus, every so often you are confronted with images that are echoes from another world. That becomes very apparent when, after eating your lunch, you are presented with a bill by a restaurateur who appears to be called Cadavero. When the narrator returns to the same spot in Verona years later, the pizzeria appears to be shut. So he asks a passer-by to photograph it for him, because the photographer over the road has refused and simply started to curse when the narrator asked him to take the photo. Something terrible must have happened in the restaurant, but we never find out what.

As is always the case when you are telling stories, there are exaggerations here and there, pictures are painted in colours that are more vivid than they actually were: nevertheless, things happened in as strange a way as I narrated them. Even the crime story has a genuine background. It is the account of two young male murderers who, for many years, committed the most terrible crimes in northern Italy. I felt as if I really had been caught up in their immediate environment. It wasn't an ordinary crime story in which everything falls into place retrospectively, but a chaotic and annihilating run of events just as such things occur in reality.

As a matter of fact there is an interesting parallel between the solving of a crime and the way in which memory works. You try to shed light on something in your mind. Somewhere, pieces of evidence must be lying around under the carpet or in the loft or in other hidden places that offer explanations for the course of your own life. That is why writing is also a forensic activity.

Knack: In your novel you are not sparing with citations from other authors that have been imperceptibly woven into the text. Are these tributes?

WGS: The text is one big homage to Kafka, an author whom I read ceaselessly. But the novel involves a large number of much smaller tributes to other authors. These tributes take the form of citations that have casually crept into the text. I cite Robert Walser and Peter Weiss, authors who mean a great deal to me. By citing them, I pay them tribute beyond the grave.

The literature industry is so immense that you have to make a decision about which author is worth the effort and which is not, otherwise you drown in the sea of publications. I, for instance, have a major problem with post-war German novels, I find them tasteless and deceitful, and this reinforces my sense that aesthetics and ethics condition one another reciprocally. In my work there is an unproblematic transition between the living and the dead. I can say with even greater conviction — and this is bound up with the narrator's melancholy disposition — that the dead interest me more than the living.

Knack: Does your fear of the barber also have something to do with the fear of death?

WGS: Yes, that has to do with fascism. Anyone who grew up in post-war Germany and had a father who was involved with fascism knows what a close-shaven cranium looks like. Your haircut looked like those of the German fascists. Not a single hair that did not run parallel to the others. We as children of the post-war era were extremely terrorized by that haircut. It was a terrible experience to be forcibly sent to such a barber every fortnight. Every winter I still feel the icy wind on my shaven cranium. Down to my very name I want to wipe out fascism. I use only the initials of my forenames: W. G. Sebald stands for Winfried Georg Sebald.

I hate archaic German names and I find it shocking that Jews deliberately began to give their children such names at the beginning of the [twentieth] century. In this way they wanted to show how loyal they were as Germans.

Translated from the Dutch by Reinier van Straten

This interview was initially published in the magazine *Knack* (Brussels) on 6 May 1992 under the title 'Echo's van vroeger: Voortgang is verlies: De Oostenrijkse schrijver Sebald luistert naar de echo's die de tijd even opheffen'; see Primary Bibliography J.4. The Dutch original erroneously gives Sebald's nationality as Austrian. At a time when Sebald was still a relatively unknown author, such confusions about his nationality and ethnicity were very common: after the publication of *Die Ausgewanderten*, for example, many people believed him to be Jewish. This interview probably coincided with the second edition of the first Dutch translation of *Schwindel. Gefühle.* (later translated into English as *Vertigo*). This was the first complete translation of any of Sebald's works (cf. Primary Bibliography B.B.1.1(a)) and had the title *Melancholische dwaalwegen* (Melancholy Meanderings). The more recent translation of the same work has the title *Duizelingen*, or 'dizzy spells', which approximates more closely to one of the more literal German meanings of the title. (Eds)

Notes

1. In the German original, and Dutch (and most other) translations, *Schwindel. Gefühle.* ends with the lines '— 2013 — | Ende'. This is omitted in the English translation.
2. The slaughterhouse chapters of Alfred Döblin's city novel *Berlin Alexanderplatz* form the core of the novel and provide its central image of the city as slaughterhouse. Although Sebald was deeply, not to say violently, critical of Döblin's prose work, he excepted *Berlin Alexanderplatz* for a range of reasons. (RWS)
3. Also the title of Elias Canetti's best-known novel, translated into English as *Auto-da-fé*. Sebald's copy of this, acquired as soon as it appeared in 1965, is heavily annotated. (RWS)

Fig. II.4. Statue of Sir Thomas Browne outside St Peter Mancroft Church, Norwich;
cf. Sebald's comment in an interview for *The Observer* of 7 June 1998: 'In the context of
working on *The Rings of Saturn*, I came across Thomas Browne. I had had the odd glimpse of
Thomas Browne's prose before, and I knew of his existence because he sits outside C&A in
Norwich on a little monument.' (See Primary Bibliography J.25, p. 17.) © Clare Savory

(2) Lost in Translation?
A Conversation with Jon Cook

Max Sebald at the Spring 1999 Visiting Writers' Festival,
Centre for the Creative and Performing Arts,
University of East Anglia
Reading at UEA Drama Studio, Norwich, 9 February 1999

Jon Cook (JC): A very warm welcome to this reading. [...] On a Siberian evening like this it's an indication of the power of the writer who has come to read to us tonight that so many people have come here to hear him read. In England and in the United States [Max Sebald's] work is best known through two books; the first of those is *The Emigrants*, published in German in 1993 and published in England in 1996, and then, most recently, *The Rings of Saturn*, which, again, was published in German in 1995 and in England in 1998. I make that point because, of course, although Max will be shortly reading to us in English, English is not the language that he writes in first; he writes in German first.

The Emigrants was a book that had a considerable impact upon German literary culture when it was first published. It won a number of prizes: the Berlin Literature Prize, the Johannes Bobrowski Medal, and other prizes that I can't quite pronounce. I remember at the time that, whenever I saw Max, he was always *en route* to win yet another prize in Germany and I don't know if there's a prize left in Germany that he hasn't won!

I think it's not hard to see why his work has had the impact that it's had. It reminds me of a statement by another German writer, Walter Benjamin, about the impact of significant new work, namely that it at once abolishes existing literary genres and creates a new one of its own. Max's work is biographical, it's autobiographical, it's fictional, it takes the form of essays, and it's even, in a strange way, a kind of photograph album. So there's this extraordinary mixing and in-mixing of genres of writing in what he does. It's also a work which is profoundly textured. What I mean by that is that it alludes to the work of many other writers; some of those allusions are explicit, as in the case of *The Rings of Saturn* where the work of Sir Thomas Browne, another local writer, is brought to fresh life by the way in which Max reanimates his work within his own writing.

In addition to that extraordinary formal power and that texturedness of language, it's not hard to see why Max Sebald's work reaches home to its readers. He writes, I think, about human beings in a peculiarly direct way, peculiarly direct — it's something very hard to do. That is to say, that he writes about them both in their tenacity, their capacity to survive horrific circumstances, and also in their intense vulnerability at the rapidity with which a life and an existence can be lost. What do I mean by that? I mean that the work he has written and which is available to us in English has an address to a major historical experience, and that's the experience of exile, of emigration, of that strange state where you are either remembering or not remembering — which is as important — the country you can no longer return to; and that seems to me profoundly inscribed in his work. It also has to do with the way in which his work has acknowledged anxieties about traumatic pasts, about complicated histories.

The only thing that I want to add to that is, of course, that in an important sense he is a local writer. *The Rings of Saturn* is a book about East Anglia, a book about walking around East Anglia, a book about finding pasts in East Anglia which most people who live in East Anglia don't know about, and I think that's another part of the book's imaginative power (*The Rings of Saturn*, that is).

I think there's another way in which it has just become a great pleasure, a delight and privilege to be a colleague of Max Sebald's during this period of his literary success. There are remarkable writers who have been in this university and it's good to know that there are still remarkable writers here now. It's something very special about this university, I think, that it has this significant relationship to the writing of literature.

Max will read to us for about half an hour, then there'll be an opportunity for questions and discussion [...]. Thank you again for coming, and it's my privilege and pleasure to introduce to you Max Sebald. [*applause*]

WGS: It wasn't quite easy to find [an extract] of roughly the right length, i.e. of twenty-five to thirty minutes, because most of the building blocks in these books are just a little bit too large for that purpose. So in the end I decided to take a passage from *The Emigrants*. As Jon has already said, this book deals with the calamitous history of the century, which is just now running out, from its inception pretty much to the present day. It tells the stories of four men who, for one reason or another, were exiled and dispossessed. These four men are all people the narrator knew very well at various earlier stages of his life, came into contact with either by accident or coincidence or, as in one case, because he was taught by them at school. They all end their lives in a disastrous way. I think all of them in one way or another commit suicide or are very close to it. This is a phenomenon which is, of course, well known. It's connected with the syndrome that is generally described as the survivor syndrome, and one of the reasons why I started writing this particular book was that at the time in my academic work I was concerned quite a lot with two major figures who were touched by that syndrome: Jean Améry, the Austrian writer, and Primo Levi. Doing work on these two particular writers it somehow occurred to me that I had myself run into, at various points, people who had gone through this career but whose lives were not nearly as public as those of these two writers, whose lives were largely obscure but perhaps for that reason needed to be written about.

One of the four figures in this book is a man called Ambrose Adelwarth, who is the great-uncle of the narrator. He grew up, like the narrator himself, in provincial southern Bavaria, just before the turn of the last century, in a public house in the country — seven girls, he the youngest one, a boy — left home at the age of 14 and entered the hotel trade in a place called Lindau on Lake Constance; from there on through the great hotels in Switzerland and

London, across to Japan and eventually to New York where, even in the time before the First World War, he became a butler in a very wealthy house on Long Island which belonged to a family called the Solomons. This family had a rather wayward son, called Cosmo, and old Solomon decided, having taken a great deal of confidence in his new employee, Ambrose, that he would be the man to, as it were, take his son in hand a little bit, look after him. And this was the start of a, in a sense, rather complex friendship where the two were — it's not quite clear in the text, it's never made, I think, explicitly clear in the text what the relationship precisely is. Are they employer and employee? Are they brothers? Are they a wayward young man and his guardian angel? It's very difficult to determine exactly. At any rate in the period at the end of the *belle époque*, 1912–13, they travel [around] Europe and go as far as the Holy Land, busting casinos on the way, because Cosmo is something of a mathematical genius. The whole story comes, very quickly in the period before the First World War, to a rather gruesome end with Cosmo losing his mind and being interned in a private mental home in Ithaca. Ambrose continues in his work as butler and majordomo in this great house, fulfilling his duties until his retirement and then, in his turn, during his retirement, gets overtaken by a severe depression and decides at one point to intern himself voluntarily in the same place where Cosmo had perished.

This is then in the years after the Second [World] War, and another twenty to thirty years later the narrator picks up the traces of his great-uncle, goes to the States, talks to one [of] his aunts, who still lives there and is a kind of *confidante* of Ambrose, finds out what he can and eventually goes up to Ithaca himself to see whether this place still exists, i.e. this mental home. I think it's round about that passage that I want to pick up the story. First of all a very short section, where the narrator still talks to his aunt:

[WGS reads from *The Emigrants*, trans. by Michael Hulse: 'Needless to say [...] looking very frail and unsteady.' See Primary Bibliography B.B.2.4, pp. 103–04]

After this the narrator leaves his aunt and sometime later drives up to Ithaca himself, has certain difficulties in finding out whether this sanatorium still exists and eventually gets the right information from the porter in the guest house where he stays. And there I pick it up again:

[WGS reads from *The Emigrants*, pp. 108–16: 'The old porter's information [...] in the darkening air.']

JC: I'd like to start by asking what is initially a technical question, in a sense an obvious one, and that has to do with your experience of your work in German and your experience of your work in English and what, for you, is entailed in the question of translation, because I know you involve yourself quite strongly in the translation of your work, although Michael Hulse is your translator. There seem to be a number of questions embedded in that question, about your audiences in Germany and your audiences elsewhere. But I'd like to start really by asking you what you think is lost in translation?

WGS: I think some of the finer grain vanishes in translation, inevitably. I mean you can make small gains in the process of translation also, but, on the whole, I think you tend to lose some of the finer grain, particularly as regards shadings of earlier forms of German. I mean some of the passages in these texts are using forms of German that are no longer current but which were about in the 1920s, say, or '30s and that is, of course, very, very difficult to move across. There are also certain regionalisms because most of this is set in southern Germany and there are quite a number of words that keep coming up, a whole range of them, which you won't find in any dictionary, for which it is then very difficult to find English equivalents. So I think some of the fine grain vanishes and possibly the whole thing is slightly flattened as regards amplitudes of the thing. But the process of translation itself, I think, is something, with a fairly complicated text, that simply needs a lot of patience; and I discovered this only gradually, because I was, as it were, pitched in at the deep end and, like the publishers, I thought that once a translator is found, then the whole thing unravels as one expects it and you get a decent translation at the end. As it turned out, it had to go through a complicated pattern and what generally happens is that the translator produces a draft, which I then work through in great detail, and then I take what I have been able to add to Beryl Ranwell, [...] and together we comb through the whole thing again because I need somebody with a good English ear, which I have not got. It's the tiny details that often make a lot of difference accumulatively. When that is done, it goes off to the Harvill editor, who then has a look at it and then it goes back to the translator. He then fits this all in and sometimes writes back and says, well, I agree with most of your suggestions but not with this one. When the text is then extant, it gets read again two or three times, so it goes through a lot of phases and is very time-consuming. But I think the lesson of that is that it is not important for a book to be instantly translated, as so often happens now, especially the other way round. I mean, anything that a reasonably well-known English and American writer produces almost simultaneously appears on the Continental market and I think that it isn't always in the best interests of the writers that these things should happen so rapidly. For instance, the French translation of *The Emigrants* has only just come out in Paris with a delay of some seven years now or something, and the book still had a very good reception, so it doesn't matter whether it takes seven or eight or fifteen years, but the translation has to be as good as it can be. That I think is probably in this kind of trade the same as everywhere else, that our lives are now determined constantly by pace and increasing pace and what's gone out of them is patience. The more that one could put back of this into our lives, the better I'm sure it would be and, of course, in the university we suffer the same fates, don't we?

JC: That in a sense connects to the next question that I want to ask, which is to do with the tone that I find in both your books published in English, and that is this almost phantasmagoric capacity to maintain a levelness of tone while describing situations of increasing and often unbearable emotional intensity. This seemed to me to be evidenced in the reading that you gave us tonight. Is that something that you are conscious of doing and is it the case, for example, that you have a conception of the work like *The Emigrants* before you start it? Or is it something that you discover as you go along?

WGS: No, I just start somewhere and then ... rewrite like most writers do, I rewrite these things endlessly. I think what makes the difference in this respect is the constant presence of the narrator and, as far as I can see, there's a paradox in it because on the one hand this particular narrator doesn't reveal himself, he doesn't say a great deal about himself but his presence is there in his voice. It's this which I imagine gives the text the kind of thing that you describe, i.e. the way in which the narrator is affected by what he finds, what he is describing is probably what causes this. It's much more difficult to do if you have an authorial narrator who is outside the chamber, as it were, and yet above it all the time. It's this kind of pattern, with narrator presence, which probably helps to achieve that but I'm not entirely sure.

Questions from the Audience

Malcolm Bradbury: What is your relationship with your translator, Michael Hulse?

WGS: It's curiously inverted, the whole thing, because Michael is English but lives in Germany and I am German and live in England! He is a poet and I am a prose writer and so on and so forth. It is a very complicated relationship and much of it is subdued because we daren't talk about the complexities too openly. You can imagine that when you do a draft of something, even if you consider it to be only a preliminary draft, you still — and I know how upset I got when I got essays back from profs when I was a student, which had marks all over them, and even later on when, as a young academic, I tried to get an article published in a journal edited by a German professor, who then went through my manuscript with a red felt tip and I got absolutely furious about it. I can imagine that for Michael Hulse it is not a very uplifting experience to get this stuff back from me with all these suggestions. Of course, some of the suggestions that I might make might be foolish, and that then colours the whole thing because he sees then only this and so on. So it's fraught with all kinds of problems and one must be very careful. I have talked to him several times about it and he says, well I just consider it, and I hope you do as well, as some kind of working partnership and we work this out in tandem. And it can only be done in this way because what one cannot do, I think, is, if you find six problems on a page, then sit down and write a letter in which, paragraph by paragraph, you explain what you think about this particular problem, because you would absolutely never finish. You can only do it by presenting the translator with a *fait accompli* of what you thought might be a better version and then he has to react to it. Luckily, of course, in a sense, Michael Hulse accepts most of the suggestions without raising a fuss about it.

It was a complicated situation, because you probably remember that in the sixties, seventies, most of the German writers like Böll, Grass, and Handke were translated by Ralph Manheim, who always did a very solid job on all the books he dealt with and then, of course, about, I can't remember when it was, but it might be ten years ago, he died and, as a great deal does not get translated from German into English, that also means that there aren't actually very many translators who have a deal of experience. So what we decided to do, and Harvill did agree to that, reluctantly to begin with, was to commission four trial translations of a short passage. [...] But I don't know how it's going to develop from here onwards. We've just started now doing the first prose work, which is *Schwindel. Gefühle.*, and we've got, I think, the first six or seven pages, so it's going to be ... I don't know how much. Combing through *The Rings of Saturn* took — we kept a logbook on that — it took 350 hours, approximately. I suppose it's the only profession where you don't get paid; if you laid concrete slab for 350 hours, you would get a tidy cheque at the end!

Malcolm Bradbury: How do you feel about the relationship between the two texts, the German text and the translated text? Is one the original?

WGS: I think the German is certainly the original. I don't know, it's very odd for me because, of course, in one sense, German ... I use English every day, so it's in a sense closer to me now, but I still feel it to be a very unfamiliar language, nevertheless, and with German it's the other way round: it's very familiar but very distant but, definitely, German is the original thing for me. There are too many things. As it happens, we have just had an MA seminar on some of these translation problems and, of course, if I look at any page now, I find other things that I can't bear to look at, that need changing and so on. It's an endless business.

Q2: Does the sense of loss, regret, and decay discernible in your books correspond to your view of life? Does your view of life get into your books?

WGS: Well. That's one of the questions that one gets asked periodically. It's quite difficult because you write ... certainly, when these books were first published in Germany, the sales label that was attached to them was melancholy, to the degree that I got quite sick of it. What happens then, if you go to literary readings, which are even more widespread in Germany than in this country, because even provincial bookshops do them and then there are the literary institutions in the bigger cities so there are these readings constantly and so I had to trudge round there several times. Of course, the audience has a certain expectation of the author because they identify him very closely with the narrator, or the other way round and they expect you to be on the verge of suicide! If you are not so, then they are quite inclined to sue you under the Trades Descriptions Act. I know this from my own experience as well, but from a German writer who lives in London. She's called Anne Duden (like the orthographic dictionary) and she's a very sophisticated writer, writing experimental prose, which has a lot to do with analysing the most gruesome pictures, of the Italian tradition, scenes of martyrdom, that sort of thing, St George slaying the dragon, descriptions of entrails and so on, which are then all related to a complex psychological state in which the narrator finds herself. When she goes and does a reading, people really want to see somebody who is almost completely self-mutilated, and in fact Anne Duden is a very elegant and most presentable lady, and so when she comes and reads from these texts people think that she's a fraud and impostor so it's quite difficult. That does, of course, not mean that I am constantly given to outbursts of hilarity! I have been called a rather boring and gloomy person by some people.

Q3: How much control do you have over the number of different voices that come into the two texts?

WGS: What you have there is a sort of pattern of primary, secondary, tertiary, and sometimes even longer series of narrators. What that indicates is that the narrator is somebody who only knows very little when he begins to embark on these tales and who has to find out what is involved in the stories that he intends to write about. So he needs these witnesses and I think that it's a natural thing that these witnesses should speak, as it were, for themselves and should be called, as it were, into the witness stand, which is the story. That said, the odd thing about this is that there is also an inversion of this because in one sense, of course, they all speak also with the voice of the narrator. There is not a great deal of difference between all of these voices; they do tend to have the same outlook, a similar tone of voice, and so the moving in and out from secondary to tertiary narrator and back again is something that one scarcely notices, I suppose, as one reads along. But I am simply unable, I think, to write in another way; I think it would be quite difficult for me to write a proper novel which has a plot and, as it were, free-moving independent characters who are directed by an authorial narrator, because I think I would be incapable of doing this. It's something constitutional, I haven't quite fathomed what it is but I do admire people who can work out a plot and a scheme that then kind of rolls of its own accord almost, but I have to sort of move along the banister, as it were, and prop myself up in this way. It['s] also a question, I think, of establishing an emotional relationship with the main figures and the minor witnesses and so on. It's got to do with that also.

Q4: I am struck by the sense of rhythm in your writing. Do you think that poets have a greater sense of rhythm when it comes to translation?

WGS: I don't think that poets have a better ear necessarily than prose writers. I think that there are poets who have better ears or sense of rhythm than prose writers but it is also the other way round. This is an area where I often have to make considerable changes: the rhythm in the German text is very carefully maintained and I always try to see to it that the sentences, which are often very long, are properly scanned because otherwise they cannot be sustained. You need the syntactical structure but you also need, as it were, the organic rhythm around the structure. This is something that can be achieved; this is really the level of craft in translation. There are other areas in translation where you do need competence more, or ingenuity even, but the question of getting the rhythm right is just a question of fiddling and changing and adding and shaving things off and it's very much a craft-type of work. There I'm often astonished how careless translators are — when it's clear in the source text that there is a distinct rhythm, which drives towards a certain point — that they somehow don't see that or hear it. I can only conclude that perhaps they never read it out aloud; I think it's quite important, even as you write, to mutter under your breath quite a lot of the time.

Q5: Given your excellent command of the language, would you ever consider writing a book straight into English?

WGS: I'm not very confident about my ability to write English, and certainly I think it's not something that one can either plan or say that one might want to try in two years' time or so. I think that either it happens or it doesn't. I think if you look at cases where a transition happened from one language into another, it was usually forced by circumstance like in the case of Nabokov, for instance, simply because he knew that his primary audience was no longer the exiles in Berlin and Paris but they were in America. He had to make that effort which was for him, by all accounts, traumatic and a very, very difficult phase. People don't do this lightly and the other thing is, I think, that if you do make a change, it's usually for ever, i.e. you move across and then you stay ... there are very few writers that I can think of who work at the same time in two languages. The only exception that comes to my mind is Beckett, and he really is an exception because he was a fine-tuning micro-engineer, and at that level it is probably possible to work in two, even three languages, but if you do more extensive writing I think it is almost impossible to handle two at the same time. The interference problem is a very difficult one, anyhow.

JC: In a moment we can go through to the foyer where there's a book signing and a glass of wine. Before we do that, [we have] to say thank you very much to Max Sebald for coming here and reading and discussing his work with us here tonight. Thank you very much.

Transcribed by Gordon Turner

Jon Cook is Professor of Literature and Director of the Centre for Creative and Performing Arts at UEA. He joined UEA in 1972, served as Dean of the School of English and American Studies from 1999 to 2003, and Founding Dean of the Faculty of Arts and Humanities from 2004 to 2010. As Founder and Director of the Centre for Creative and Performing Arts, he has over many years brought many highly acclaimed authors to the annual Literary Festival.

(3) In This Distant Place
A Conversation with Steve Wasserman

ALOUD at Central Library: Mark Taper Auditorium,
Los Angeles Public Library, 17 October 2001

Steve Wasserman (SW): Thank you for coming out on this Friday evening, braving all the traffic. It's a huge honour to introduce W. G. Sebald. I suppose the first question in many people's minds is: What does the W. G. stand for? The answer: Winfried Georg Sebald. A few years ago, the *Los Angeles Times* gave him its fiction award for the best fiction of the year. Improbably, we had asked Judith Krantz, the glitzy author of *Princess Daisy*, to present the award. I took a perverse and delicious pleasure in compelling Judith Krantz to read *The Rings of Saturn*, which she afterwards claimed was a very important event in her life. I have no reason to doubt her. The work of W. G. Sebald is, of course, about as un-Californian an exercise in literary achievement as one could imagine. After all, to be a Californian is to be living in a place that is, as Susan Sontag once said, 'America's America', the place where reinvention is the central project of many people who move here, a place given to jettisoning the very idea of history weighing upon the brain of the living like a nightmare. It's the place that privileges forgetfulness over remembrance and where amnesia reigns supreme. Resistance to these ideas is at the heart of much of Sebald's work, since he carries in his work a notion of history as catastrophe. The recognition of the existence of evil and the degradations of time suffuse all of his work — which overall could be said to be an exercise in grieving, in — to use a German word — *Trauerarbeit*, a work of mourning. One is reminded of the great essay that Freud wrote in the midst of the First World War called *Mourning and Melancholia*, which connects melancholy with the inability to work through grief. To understand the past and thereby to exorcise it is Sebald's largest moral and literary ambition. Or at least I take it to be his largest ambition. He will, of course, have an opportunity this evening to correct that impression. His books are ardent, ravishing, and, singly and taken together, the creation — or, perhaps more precisely, the recreation — of a world from which one feels that its creator has the greatest difficulty in actually extricating himself — a predicament shared by the admiring reader. This exercise in the art of empathy, this joint attempt on the part of the author as well as the complicit reader to recover memory, produces a voluptuous and exquisite anxiety. Walter Benjamin once wrote that melancholy is the origin of true historical understanding. The temperament that produces that degree of obsession is one that prompts such a writer to become an artist of endless speaking, and Sebald's voice, from book to book, is one that simply seems to go on and on. One feels one has embarked, in reading Sebald's work, upon a series of explorations. The result is a literary triumph, altogether exceptional in its emotional expressiveness, its beauty, its sincerity, its moral passion, its concern with contemplative virtues.

It's a great honour to present to you W. G. Sebald. [*applause*]

WGS: Thank you very much. Good evening ladies and gentlemen. It's a pleasure to be here in this distant place, totally unfamiliar to me. My first impressions are that it would take me probably fifty years to find my bearings, but as I'm being shepherded about I managed to come to this place on time. I shall read you a short passage from this recently published book *Austerlitz*. It's set in Wales, this particular passage. As some of you may know, 'Austerlitz' is the name of the main character in this text, one Jacques Austerlitz, who was born in Prague in the 1930s, and this four-year-old boy was taken from there in one of the *Kindertransports* which left various German cities but also the Czechoslovak capital at the time just before the outbreak of the Second World War. He was put on the train by his mother, an actress, and ends up in England where he arrives at Liverpool Street in London with his rucksack and little suitcase. He [is] subsequently brought up in Wales by a Welsh Calvinist couple who seek to erase his identity, and he himself later on never looks into the question of his identity until he gets to be near enough 60 years old, at which time he is overtaken by the semi-mute troubles that clouded his mind for most of his life and begins to investigate his own — to him so far covert — past, i.e. he breaks through the barriers which he himself has erected against memory. He is sent to a public school when he is about 14 years old, when his foster mother becomes gravely ill and later on dies and his foster father disappears in a mental asylum in Denbigh, in Wales. At that public school he befriends a younger pupil called Gerald and from then on he spends his summer vacations and many other times at the home of this friend. The passage that I will read to you is about a revisitation of this place at the point where he, having completed his studies at Oxford, is about to go to Paris to begin his research work. The occasion for returning is a funeral, the funeral of the two eccentric uncles, or great-uncles, who lived in that family, one Alphonso and one Evelyn Fitzpatrick. The boy is called — I think I said that — Gerald and the boy's mother is Adela. The father, who was in the Royal Air Force, was shot down over the Ardennes Forest and so this is a short list of the personages that you will encounter in this brief passage.

[WGS reads from *Austerlitz*, trans. by Anthea Bell: 'I think it was in early October 1957, he [Austerlitz] continued abruptly after some time [...] which became increasingly morbid and intractable with the passage of time.' See Primary Bibliography B.B.4.3, pp. 154–65; B.B.4.2, pp. 109–17.] [*applause*]

SW: The format for this conversation will be to chat for a bit and then we'll open it up to questions from the audience. Do speak your question in a reasonably firm and loud voice. I will repeat the question so that everybody actually hears it. Let me begin by saying that one of the most striking aspects of your work is the use of photography and so let's begin by asking you about these photographs and by asking you something about the enigma of photography. Photography, of course, has a way of seeming to be truthful but we all know that very often photographs lie. And yet you litter your work — perhaps 'litter' is a pejorative word [*some laughter from the audience*] — I don't mean it that way

— but you sprinkle these shards of frozen moments as if to suggest that there is a moment of truth and absence that exists at one and the same time, as a device to snare the reader and as a means of transporting the reader. How have you thought yourself about the arrangement of such photographs and how do you, did you stumble upon this arrangement?

WGS: Well I didn't do so deliberately. Photographs are something I've always collected in a random sort of way that began much earlier than my attempts at writing prose fiction. And when I began to write, somehow it became clear to me that they, these images, were part of the material that I had stored up. And so I, right from the beginning, somehow saw no reason for excluding them from the actual process of writing. It seemed to me unquestionable right from the beginning that they had a right to be there, as very frequently they provided the starting points or they came from the photo albums of the people I had talked to — sometimes over long periods of time — and summed up experiences and parts of these people's lives which would have been very, very difficult to convey in words only. So they seemed to me to have, to have a legitimate place [not only] in the process of production but in the finished product also. And then, subsequently, of course, people have started asking me questions like you have just done, and I had to think a little harder about the reasons for [the] presence of these images in a text. And what you are pointing to is certainly one of the main concerns — namely that the reader of fiction wants to, in a sense, be assured in the illusion, which he knows to be an illusion, that what he is reading is not just an invented tale but somehow grounded in fact. And what better way of demonstrating this than including a photograph — which we tend to all believe, certainly at first sight. That said, the photograph, as you yourself have just indicated, also, of course, opens wide the door to forgery. And, indeed, some images of these books are instances of forgery, deliberate forgery. But they are in the minority — they are perhaps five or four per cent of the entire number of images — and the rest are usually from the sources which they suggest they come from, so that it is, in fact, true to say that the relationship between the historic reality behind these fictional stories and the images which are inserted in them is a very close one. The other reason that seems to me increasingly important is the mysterious quality of older photographs. I mean the pictures which we take nowadays on coloured [sic] films and which get developed in an hour in a Kodak shop hold no secrets at all, so it seems to me. But these old black-and-white pictures which one finds in family albums — not all of them, but you always find one or two amongst the bunch — have a mysterious quality where the subject seems to come out of the image and seems to demand an answer about one thing or another. And this kind of appellative presence that these departed persons still have in these pictures was something that struck me as almost uncanny and that I felt that I had to attend to — and this hasn't gone away. I happened yesterday in Philadelphia to look at three photo albums which an elderly couple who [were] exiled from Germany in the 1930s brought along, and indeed, you know, in those albums, as in so many others, there were some images which one found it very hard to look away from and which have this captivating quality that says to the observer: 'Well — what about this? You know I'm no longer here but I still want an answer.'

SW: Yes, one has the feeling, flipping through these photographs, of a kind of detective story, almost as if you're looking at photographs taken at the scene of rather mysterious and unacknowledged crimes similar to the way in which Antonioni in *Blow Up* used the photograph that you thought was taken of one thing, but upon enlargement revealed quite another thing going on. And one turns the pages of your book with both mounting fascination and a kind of growing horror at what might be discovered in these photographs.

WGS: Well yes, they do, if you learn how to read them and if you place them in the right context. The picture which at first sight might be or might seem to be innocent reveals things that perhaps sometimes one would be better off not to know. And this was certainly the case with, say, the photo albums in my own family because my parents, like all people of that generation, had furnished themselves with small portable cameras. These cameras were then in 1939 taken to war and albums were made, for instance, of the Polish Campaign, as it was called. And as a small boy I looked through these albums and I thought there was nothing particularly either exciting or remarkable in them and turned the pages without being disturbed. But when I revisited these albums many years later the images revealed a different quality because I had comprehended by then the historical context. I asked myself why there were pages on which some of the pictures were missing and only the glue was left behind and [where] perhaps a kind of jocular caption had been written underneath but which made no sense without the image. And nowadays, of course, you know what the context was and that pictures can tell different stories depending on when one observes or looks at them and who looks at them.

SW: And when you asked your father about the missing pictures or the pictures that remained, did you ever trust his answer?

WGS: Well my father generally didn't talk about these kinds of things and I knew it would be pointless because whenever you raised the topic of that particular past it would end in family drama and shouting matches, and so after a while, you learnt to leave it. There was a zone of silence around that part of our pre-history which was meticulously maintained by practically everyone in Germany in the post-war years, and this is true until this day. The generation of my parents who were involved in that part of our history is now dying out, and so it falls to the next generation to rescue all of the historical evidence that can still be retrieved. But you cannot retrieve it by talking to these people — not on the whole. The odd one will give you an answer but this is very rare.

SW: It's a curious thing in *Austerlitz* — which, arguably, might be thought of as an exercise in recovered-memory syndrome — that the main character seeks to fill in the absences and hollowed-out portions of his personality, attempts to recreate an identity which is actually tethered to history. The curious thing is that the more he learns, the more overwhelmed he seems to become until finally, right toward the end of the book, at the very moment when he arguably ought to feel the most liberated for having most accumulated what shards of memory could be gathered together, he suffers a breakdown, and has to be hospitalized. I wonder if you've ever thought about considering the necessity of forgetting without which no one can actually move on?

WGS: Yes. Quite. Therefore as a writer interested in these kinds of things and in the habit of talking to people who have been through series of experiences which are highly disturbing, one has to be extremely careful because the psychoanalytic wisdom that it does people good if they talk about their traumas, or try to retrieve the source of their anxieties, is not always true. And so I think one has to step extremely carefully, and certainly it's an almost biological fact that forgetting is what keeps us going and that is also exemplified very clearly in the fact that nobody in Germany in the 1950s and 1960s, not even the writers whose job it would have been to do so, has ever written a line or anything worth mentioning about the collective experience of destruction suffered by the Germans, i.e. the bombing of German cities which was wholesale and which practically everybody experienced. And the only way in which they could rebuild and carry on was to forget, almost by force of will. So naturally, there is a curious dialectic between forgetting and remembering, and they're not just two opposed moral categories, one positive and the other negative, but they're interlaced in an extremely complicated way and in a different fashion in each individual. What is noticeable, though, is that if you do talk to people who have survived political persecution — of whom there are, of course, many in this country and many in England but hardly any in Germany — if you talk to them, you very frequently can find that they manage quite well as long as they hold down a job, as long as they're surgeons in a hospital or ... I don't know ... teachers at a university, or whatever it may be. And then, with the arrival of the retirement age, where many people have difficulties in readjusting in any case, they experience a return of repressed memories and find [it] very hard to fight against them. It's also a general phenomenon of growing older that those memories which refer to events that happened last week or last month are often less clear and less sharply delineated than the memories that refer to one's childhood — which become increasingly obtrusive and acquire a clarity which is highly disturbing often. And in the case of those who have escaped political persecution, who have survived these difficulties, specific psychological difficulties accentuate generally and very frequently lead to periods of severe disturbance, of anxiety attacks, and of a general inability to cope.

SW: One of the things that I most admire in your works is the way you have of opening up from the very specific and then leaping to a very large question. Memorably in *Austerlitz*, for me, the passage that has Austerlitz re-encountering his old Prague nanny, Vera. She tells him about the time when he was a small boy, four years old, more or less, maybe a bit older, that she used to read to him a picture book, which had the seasons, and it revealed the animals throughout the seasons. And one of the pictures showed the squirrels gathering the nuts to bury for the winter months, and she says to him that whenever they turned the page and the same scene showed the snow which had covered everything, that Jacques Austerlitz would always ask: 'But how do the squirrels *know* where to find the nuts?' And then you ask almost right away, or rather the narrator asks — I perhaps should not confuse the narrator of the story with you yourself [**WGS**: No]; that would be a category error although you seem to invite such perverse confusion on the part of your readers — 'How indeed do the squirrels know?' 'What do we know ourselves?' 'How do we remember?' and 'What is it we find in the end?'.

WGS: We hide things also but we don't always know how to recover them, and in that respect we are different from squirrels [*audience laughter*] and, er, either they're superior to us in many ways ... And that squirrel incidentally is, of course, also a reverential gesture toward Nabokov, where squirrels in *Pnin* play a very significant role. As Nabokov is quite important to me, such references turn up occasionally.

SW: What other writers have been important to you?

WGS: Of contemporary writers relatively few, and Nabokov is an exception and he, of course, is as much a nineteenth-century Russian writer as a twentieth-century American writer.

SW: Maybe he was the last nineteenth-century Russian writer?

WGS: Yes. And in Nabokov's work particularly, of course, the autobiography, concerned as it is with questions of memory and remembrance. And what I learnt from him is precisely that attention to detail — that it's not enough to say that his mother was exiled in Prague but it's important to remember that her dachshund was also still there and that he wore a muzzle of wire and that it was a sad *emigré* dog. Because Nabokov's father was assassinated in Berlin, his mother kept his wedding ring, but she had grown rather frail in exile in Prague when [he] visited her, and Nabokov remembers that she had the wedding ring of her husband tied to hers with a bit of string because otherwise it would have fallen off her finger. I think memory resides in details of this almost weightless kind. If it wants to come across to the reader as a token of something that is legitimate, then it has to be attached to this kind of weightless ... weightless ... I'm lacking the word now ... but that's how I think it has to be. The other writers that were important for me were nineteenth-century German prose writers. The prose fiction written in Germany in the nineteenth century didn't quite fit the model of the novel which had evolved in other countries like France and England in the eighteenth and nineteenth centuries. It was not interested to the same extent in social or even political concerns. It was somewhat backward. That nineteenth-century German prose writing was very much attached to the observation of nature, very frequently could be described almost as natural historical writing rather than fiction writing. It was underdeveloped in terms of character construction and its main concern was the production of flawless prose, so that page by page the prose, as it were, stood in its own right like we expect language to stand in its own right in poetry. And it was quite a useful school to go through. I was attached to these writers, the most prominent of whom are Adalbert Stifter and Gottfried

Keller, also because they came from regional backwaters as I myself do and I always felt a particular closeness to them.

SW: You came from a very small rural community, a hamlet ...

WGS: Yes, a tiny village in the Alps, three thousand feet above sea level, cut off from pretty much everything in the post-war years. Nowadays of course [a] skiing resort — and tennis courts, swimming pools, and everything else. But in those days it was almost as if you lived in the seventeenth century. I mean, even anthropologically it would have been a hunting ground, because, say, our burial rites in the post-war years were still those of the seventeenth century. I mean they were archaic. There is a story by Hemingway where he describes, I think, a scene in the Alps, possibly in the Vorarlberg, where the figure, the narrative figure, I can't remember who he is, but [he] tells how the bodies couldn't be buried, because the ground was frozen throughout the winter and they had to keep them in the woodshed and then you bury them in the spring. And that was indeed the case where I grew up, you know: there were always bodies in the woodshed [*audience laughter*] and so it means that my early years were, were shaped by societal mores which from, certainly from the present point of view in LA, seem very, very far removed to say the least!

SW: One has a bit of the feeling that there is a kind of thread throughout your work of a certain kind of requiem for a lost agrarian world that's been pulverized by an industrial behemoth that has won out almost everywhere. Is that ...

WGS [*interrupting*]: Yes. One can regret it although one knows it's unavoidable because it is just a fact of societal and natural evolution that things should have come to this pass. Well, if you know landscapes intimately, say the landscape of the Upper Rhine where it comes out of Lake Constance and then turns the corner at Basle and moves northward, or the Danube before it gets to Vienna and after, between Vienna and Budapest, and if you have a recollection, at least a mental one, of what these landscapes looked like fifty, [a] hundred, two hundred years ago and see how they have been sanitized now, straightened out, controlled, hemmed in, then you do realize that much has been lost and what's been lost is some kind of freedom and some form of beauty which we no longer have access to. For instance, I remember very clearly, and I think I make reference to it in one of these books, the Danube, just before it gets to Vienna, in the 1960s, was unregulated — that is to say, in the spring, when the waters were high, the Danube would leave its bed and flood vast areas to either side — the so-called *Donau-Auen* — and it was a singular spectacle and you could survey it from various vantage points along [the] river. And these spectacular views don't exist any more, because in the 1970s the river was put into a concrete bed, that is to say, weirs and dams were built across it and the whole thing is now something that nobody really wants to look at. And so, of course, things do get changed all the time and built and concreted over — and much is lost, perhaps inevitably. But that doesn't mean that one should not regret that this kind of development goes on all the time.

SW: Let's take some questions from the audience. Or, if there are no questions, I'll continue to ask a couple more — but I suspect there are. Let's take one here.

Q1: I was just wondering if it was getting close to the time — as it happened to Nabokov — that you might start writing in English.

WGS: Oh, I don't think so [*audience laughter*]. But Nabokov had no choice, having moved here and the Russian exile community shrinking further and further. He knew that the time had come to make that move, but he also left testimony of what a traumatic experience it was and how he despaired about ever being able to write a decent page of English prose. It was a very hard time for him and he was not always the best judge of it because, as you probably know, he nearly burnt the manuscript — was it — of *Lolita* — I think it was Vera who rescued it for him.

SW: That's because Roger Straus turned it down at Farrar, Straus.

WGS: Yes, well, one can very easily be mistaken in that way. I have thrown one or two things on the compost heap, and there is reference to that in *Austerlitz*. In the book Austerlitz throws all his papers on the compost heap. I have done the same. It's very difficult to judge; on a good day, if you have two languages, you can manage well in both of them and on a bad day you can't manage in either of them. And so, you know, it doesn't make things easier. Writing is, on the whole, a difficult and painstaking business and one has enough trouble with it in one language, and it also means, of course, moving — as Nabokov did — from one language to another. You usually desert the one that you are leaving because you can't do both at the same time. You can't move to and fro; you must be quite single-minded about it, and I think Nabokov, after moving across, never wrote in Russian again. He still translated, but he never wrote in Russian again.

SW: The English translation seemed to me to be superb. You've been very well served by your translators. What, if anything, has been lost in the translation, or, to put it another way: in German is there some resonance or some echo of some quality for your German readers that in English there isn't?

WGS: Well, something gets lost inevitably, and the texts are often a pastiche of various levels of time. That is to say you may have the first narrator who is in the present and who writes the text referring to a narrator who tells [*sic*] him instead, who speaks from a point of view which is in 1939, and then the language used in 1939 clearly is somewhat different from the language used in the present day. And I *can* manage to do that in German by the judicious use of certain bits of vocabulary, which make it clear to certainly a sensitive reader that this is in the 1930s and couldn't possibly [be] in the 1950s. That's very difficult for a translator to, to get across. So there are elements of fine grain that get lost. And you do occasionally gain something, but that is the exception rather than the rule. There may be the odd passage where English manages to render things more felicitously than German, but, on the whole, you lose a little bit. Well, it's very easy to lose everything, it doesn't take much: if the prosodic rhythm is not maintained, if the text has two or three blunders or half-blunders on every page, readers very soon get irritated and they don't quite know where it comes from, the problem. But they find that they're not inclined to read on, if it's 'bumpy' in any sense. I remember, for instance, how someone once told me I ought to read Herbert's book *The Still Life with Bridle*, I think it's called in the English translation. The person who recommended it to me was Polish and had read it in the original, and so I read the book in English translation and I thought it was an abject failure. But I did realize that it had to do almost exclusively with the clumsiness of the translation, which disfigured the whole text, and I then read [the] French translation of the same book which was superb[1] ... And so you can see from that one instance that translation really is a very, very crucial part of getting a book across. It's not even into another culture, but into some kind of sister culture. So it needs a great deal of care and patience, and in principle it's always possible: if you find the right person to do it, it's possible. But even the right person has to be watched very closely. [*audience laughter*]

Q2: In preparation for your latest book — given the experiences of your protagonist — did you read any memoirs or other accounts by adults whose childhood had been spent away from their homes in France or in England? And if you did, what did you learn from these accounts and which accounts in particular did you learn from?

WGS: Well, the fictional figure of Jacques Austerlitz is based on two real-life stories, one which was written up and the other which I know only from listening to that person. That one was a colleague of mine, a London colleague of mine, who[m] I have known for many years and who over the years has released, as it were, bit by bit, the tale of his life. His life was by no means as tragic as that of Austerlitz, but there [are] many elements in Austerlitz's biography which correspond to his experiences. And the other one was the life of a woman who[m] I didn't know personally ... but with whom I'm corresponding now. She had a television documentary made of her life sometime around 1992 or '93 which I saw by pure chance as I was switching on the television one evening. And I was immediately struck by it simply, perhaps, because she had come, together with her twin sister at the age of two and a half, from a Jewish orphanage in Munich — which was, of course, for me the nearest bigger town — to England. And the, the Welsh background — not in detail but in general outline — is the background of her story. She was indeed taken with her twin sister by a Calvinist fundamentalist Welsh couple and brought up and had her identity erased. [She] never asked any questions about it, but, having passed the age of 50, all of a sudden found herself so troubled, so depressed, and so anxious about everything without knowing really why, that she began to ask the kinds of questions which eventually lead to answers. *Her* story was written up, but I only read the written-up version afterwards by some other person whose name I forget.[2] It's [a] fairly straightforward biographical account full of quite horrific details. But I also read others, needless to say. Once you have a project like this in mind, you read everything that *might* have anything to do with it. I read the autobiographical account [by] Saul Friedländer, who grew up as a small boy in Prague. I think it's called — I read it in German [SW interjects: *When Memory Comes*] — *When Memory Comes*.[3] Yes. And he indeed recounts how he met, I think, his nanny again in Prague and how she had, seemingly, not changed at all. So there are a number of others. There are, of course, also collections of personal accounts and memories from many of the children who came to Britain on these *Kindertransports*. Because in the 1980s, I think, not before, one of their number took it upon herself to bring [the children] together again and from that grew various collections of these memories, i.e. she, the organizer of these reunions, a woman called Bertha Levinsohn [*sic*],[4] I think — encouraged them to write accounts of where they came from and what their lives had been like. What is startling about these accounts is how brief they are. Scarcely one is longer than a page and many of them are no more than two sentences, and from that alone you can judge how hard it is to live with this kind of memory because telling the tale, of course, does help you to get over the worst implications. So you can also see, of course, how far flung they are become. There are these short, very short, potted almost biographies from New Zealand, from Australia, from practically all states of the United States, from all counties in England, I mean, there were very many of them ...

SW: Yes?

Q3: I was wondering ... from reading your books, I get the feeling that you are looking for a home in the world in some way.

WGS: For what?

Q3: From reading your books, I get the feeling that you are looking for a home in the world.

WGS: A home?

Q3: A home. I was wondering. It makes me curious about what took you from Germany to England. Well, you've already spoken about why you continue to write in German, but I was wondering: do you feel at home anywhere or do you feel as a displaced person in the world?

WGS: Well ... You know, if I said I felt like a displaced person — on a bad day I do, but on the whole, it's not the same, you know. Being vilified in your own country, being driven out, having no possibility to return to it for many years and, when you [do] have the possibility, you don't want to return to it because what you experienced there is a different kind of problem from the one that I have encountered. I left Germany of my own accord, perhaps for quite complicated reasons which only became clear to me later on. But at any rate I was always able to return there whenever I wanted — it's not very far away from where I live. And so it would be dramatizing things if I said that I felt displaced. Nevertheless, it is true that if I now return to my native country — which I frequently do almost every month for a day or two for one reason or another — I do feel out of sorts because, after all, I left this place when I was 21 and since then have always lived in what for me are foreign-language environments, either French or German, or rather English. And so coming back there seems to me a mismatch because my compatriots still take me for a German aborigine [*audience laughter*] and, whereas I know that I am not, I have a great distance to [*sic*] them; there are many things in that country that irritate me a great deal. That is not to say that there aren't things in England that irritate me a great deal [*audience laughter*]. So, it just makes life more difficult, and inevitably, of course, it is much simpler, you know, or it would have been much simpler for me if I had stayed at home and had opened a bicycle shop somewhere [*audience laughter*]. Then I might have an emotionally more stable life than I have now!

SW: We'll take two more questions and then I'm afraid our time has run out.

Q4: One of my favourite books is your last book, *The Rings of Saturn*, and that book seems so miraculous and so prospective [?] in every single paragraph [that] I suppose you can somehow anticipate what its argument is going to be. If you don't mind, would you tell us how you created the book in that particular, miraculous way?

WGS: You mean *The Rings of Saturn* now rather than the other one?

Q4: Right, right and how ... [*rest of the question inaudible*]

WGS: Well, this is ... all in the end comes down to serendipity. *The Rings of Saturn* had a very peculiar genesis. I had finished one book before and I wanted to have some time off. So I thought I, as it is told in this text, I wanted to go for a walk — which was my primary concern and which indeed I did, and I had to stay overnight here and there, in hotels. I was quite hard up at that time and I thought: well, I somehow must earn my keep also, so I'm going to write maybe ten very short pieces for the *Frankfurter Allgemeine Zeitung*. They pay quite well and that would pay for the fortnight being on the loose. And when I returned home I sat down — I had somehow roughly worked out what I would write about — I sat down and the short pieces didn't work. I rewrote them again and again, and they wouldn't go into the format and I gradually realized that they wanted to grow sideways and upwards and in all directions and that's how that came about. They were supposed to be ten discrete short pieces and that's why the material there is very heterogeneous: it was never conceived as a work of fiction although, of course, if you look very closely, it certainly is that.

SW: Then one more.

Q5: I was wondering about the narrative device in that there's a narrator but most of the story is told by Austerlitz. And yet there's a narrator so that the result is that we're constantly reminded that Austerlitz is speaking — 'he said'; the narrative, the story is constantly punctuated by 'Austerlitz said'. I was wondering why you chose that structure? I thought it was kind of interesting.

WGS: Well ... Because we only know what we get told by others, and what you have here is ... I find it very hard ... I think I have to turn this round somehow ... I find it very hard to read the standard novel where you have an omniscient narrator, but you never know who he or she is. They never present their credentials and they don't show you their cards.

SW: That's why we have book tours.

WGS: Mmm? [*audience laughter*]

SW [*louder*]: That's why we have book tours.

WGS: Yeah. But I want to know who I'm dealing with and I want to have the moral measure of the person who is telling me something, And you do get that when you talk to real persons because you can always derive from a person's demeanour an idea of what they are like inside. Whereas if you have a narrator who you see running around in a novel arranging everything but whose face you never see, whose inner thoughts you never hear anything about, then I for one find that problematic. And for that reason I tend to have a narrator who has some sort of presence in the text. We don't know exactly who he is but we get a reasonably good idea of what this person's emotional life might be like, and from there you can also then calculate the distance to the story that he tells, and it generally allows you to orientate yourself *vis-à-vis* the figures in the book. So that is the reason for that. And I think if you wanted to sum it up, say it's my dislike of the standard novel format which I find very constricting and artificial.

SW: I want to thank W. G. Sebald for coming tonight and for giving us works which do that magical and miraculous thing of turning us inside out and permitting us to see the world with new eyes. Thanks so much. [*prolonged applause*]

Transcribed by Richard and Carolyn Sheppard and Steve Wasserman. Edited by Steve Wasserman and Gordon Turner. Notes by Richard Sheppard and Steve Wasserman.

Steve Wasserman, a former journalist, is a literary agent in New York. In 2001 he was editor of the *Los Angeles Times Book Review*. This reading and interview was part of the ALOUD literary series, a presentation of the Library Foundation of Los Angeles, curated by Louise Steinman.

Notes

1. Zbigniew Herbert, *Still Life with a Bridle*; translated into French as *Nature morte avec bride et mors*.
2. See Jeremy Josephs with Susi Bechhöfer, *Rosa's Child* (London: I. B. Tauris, 1996).
3. In 2001 Saul Friedländer was a professor at the University of California at Los Angeles, but he and Sebald never met. Sebald owned a copy of the German edition: Saul Friedländer, *Wenn die Erinnerung kommt*, trans. by Helgard Oestreich (Munich: Beck, 1998).
4. See *I Came Alone: The Stories of the Kindertransports*, compiled by Bertha Leverton with Shmuel [Samuel] Lowensohn (Brighton: The Book Guild, 1991). It seems likely that Bertha Leverton, with whom Sebald corresponded regarding this book, also lent him a tape of the TV programme about Susi Bechhöfer; a copy of Leverton's book is extant in Sebald's library. A film, *Into the Arms of Strangers: Stories of the Kindertransport*, based on these recollections, came out in 2000, but Sebald said elsewhere that he had not seen it ('"Ich fürchte das Melodramatische"', interview with Martin Doerry and Volker Hage [27 February 2001], *Der Spiegel*, 12 March 2001, p. 233); Primary Bibliography J.36.

FIGS. II.5 and II.6. Corridor in the Arts Building at UEA, showing W. G. Sebald's former office, with (above) his poster of Walter Benjamin to the right of the door; and (below) his poster of Wittgenstein and other Suhrkamp authors. © Jo Catling (Summer 2006)

3
A Catalogue of
W. G. Sebald's Library

Jo Catling

I am so bold to present you with the List of a Collection, which I may justly
say you have not seen before.

SIR THOMAS BROWNE, 'Musæum Clausum, or Bibliotheca Abscondita'[1]

Denn was ist dieser Besitz anderes als eine Unordnung, in der Gewohnheit
sich so heimisch machte, daß sie als Ordnung erscheinen kann? [...] Jede
Ordnung ist gerade in diesen Bereichen nichts als ein Schwebezustand überm
Abgrund.

[For what else is this collection but a disorder to which habit has accommodated
itself to the extent that it can appear as order? [...] These are the very areas in
which any order is a balancing act of extreme precariousness.]

WALTER BENJAMIN, 'Ich packe meine Bibliothek aus' ('Unpacking my Library')[2]

This catalogue has been compiled on the basis of books remaining in W. G. Sebald's
former office at UEA, at The Old Rectory, Poringland, prior to the sale of that
property in August 2006, and in the Deutsches Literaturarchiv Marbach (DLA),
where the large majority of the items in this catalogue are housed. It also includes
other items known to have been in Sebald's possession which have come to light
since (see Chapter 11 for further details).

For ease of reference, the catalogue has been divided into categories roughly
corresponding to those used for the *Nachlassbibliothek* in the DLA, but also to
Sebald's own tendency to group works by subject. However, these subdivisions are
intended only as a guide, and do not represent a systematic attempt at classification.
In some cases full publication details are not available, but the items have still been
included for the sake of information.

[1] SIR THOMAS BROWNE, 'Musæum Clausum, or Bibliotheca Abscondita', in *The Works of Sir
Thomas Browne*, ed. by Geoffrey Keynes, 6 vols (London: Faber, 1931), V: *Miscellaneous Writings*, pp.
131–42 (p. 131).
[2] WALTER BENJAMIN, 'Ich packe meine Bibliothek aus', in *Ausgewählte Schriften*, II: *Angelus Novus*
(Frankfurt a.M.: Suhrkamp, 1966), pp. 169–78 (pp. 169–70); 'Unpacking my Library', in *Illuminations*,
trans. by Harry Zohn (London: Fontana, 1992), pp. 61–69 (p. 62).

The following abbreviations are used:

[DLA]   Volume held in Sebald's *Nachlassbibliothek* in the Deutsches Literaturarchiv
            Marbach

[W]   *Widmungsexemplar*: volume with signed dedication from author or translator,
            occasionally from editor or relation of author

[*]   Item on list of books earmarked for possible sale to Herbert Blank, Wissen-
            schaftliches Antiquariat, Stuttgart (see Chapter 11 of this volume, pp. 272–
            73)

[D.67 (etc.)] Volume contains essay or extract from a work by WGS; the number refers
            to the corresponding entry in the Primary Bibliography, where full details
            are given. [G.1 (etc.)] indicates a volume reviewed by WGS; see Primary
            Bibliography for details of reviews.

The catalogue is ordered as follows:

(1) Sebaldiana (books by or on Sebald, and journals containing articles by Sebald; see
     also Secondary Literature for other volumes containing examples of his work)

    (a) Books   (d) Contributions to periodicals
    (b) Translations   (e) Secondary works and reviews
    (c) Contributions to other volumes   (f) Varia

(2) Literature

    (a) German and Austrian   (f) Russian
    (b) English   (g) Polish
    (c) French   (h) Czech
    (d) Italian   (i) Classical
    (e) Hispanic and Iberian   (j) Other

(3) Literary Criticism and Secondary Literature

    (a) General   (b) Books on literature by UEA colleagues

(4) Philosophy, Psychology, Anthropology, Religion

(5) History, Culture, Geography

(6) Art and Art History

    (a) Art and photography   (d) Music
    (b) Architecture   (e) Stage and screen
    (c) Gardens

(7) Topography, Travel, Natural History

    (a) Bavaria, Austria, Switzerland,   (e) France, Corsica, Italy
          the Alps   (f) Poland, Czech Republic
    (b) UK (general)   (g) Other guides and atlases
    (c) East Anglia   (h) Maps and road atlases
    (d) Wales   (i) Natural history, gardening

(8) Dictionaries, Phrase Books, Works of Reference

(9) Periodicals

(10) 'Books disposed of by WGS'

1: Sebaldiana

1(a): Books (in chronological order of first German publication)

W. G. Sebald, *Schwindel. Gefühle.* (Frankfurt a.M.: Eichborn, 1990) [DLA]
——*Vertigo*, trans. by Michael Hulse (London: Harvill, 1999) (2 copies) [DLA]
——*Vertigo*, trans. by Michael Hulse (New York: New Directions, 2000) [DLA]
——*Vertigo*, trans. by Michael Hulse (London: Harvill, 2000) [DLA]
——*Vertiges*, French trans. by Patrick Charbonneau (Arles: Actes Sud, 2001) [DLA]
——*Die Ausgewanderten* (Frankfurt a.M.: Eichborn, 1992) [DLA]
——*The Emigrants*, trans. by Michael Hulse (London: Harvill, 1996) [DLA]
——*The Emigrants*, trans. by Michael Hulse (New York: New Directions, 1996) [DLA]
——*The Emigrants*, trans. by Michael Hulse (New York: New Directions, 1997) [DLA]
——*The Emigrants*, trans. by Michael Hulse (London: Harvill, 1997) [DLA]
——*Los emigrados*, Spanish trans. by Teresa Ruiz Rosas, 2nd, rev. edn by Sergio Pawlowsky Glahn (Madrid: Debate, 2000) [DLA]
——*Els emigrats*, Catalan trans. by Anna Soler Horta (Barcelona: Edicions 62, 2001) [DLA]
——*De utvandrede: Fire lange fortellinger*, Norwegian trans. by Geir Pollen (Oslo: Gyldendal, 2001) [DLA]
——*Izseljeni*, Slovenian trans. by Štefan Vevar (Ljubljana: Beletrina, 2001) [DLA]
——*Die Ringe des Saturn: Eine englische Wallfahrt* (Frankfurt a.M.: Eichborn, 1995) [DLA]
——*The Rings of Saturn*, trans. by Michael Hulse (New York: New Directions, 1998) [DLA]
——*The Rings of Saturn*, uncorrected proof copy (London: Harvill, 1998) [DLA]
——*Les Anneaux de Saturne*, French trans. by Bernard Kreiss (Arles: Actes Sud, 1999) [DLA]
——*Gli anelli di Saturno: Un pellegrinaggio in Inghilterra*, Italian trans. by Gabriella Rovagnati (Milan: Bompiani, 1998) [DLA]
——*Los anillos de Saturno: Una peregrinación inglesa*, Castilian trans. by Carmen Gómez and Georg Pichler (Madrid: Debate, 2000) [DLA]
——*Logis in einem Landhaus: Über Gottfried Keller, Johann Peter Hebel, Robert Walser und andere* (Munich, Vienna: Carl Hanser, 1998) [DLA]
——*Luftkrieg und Literatur: Mit einem Essay zu Alfred Andersch* (Munich, Vienna: Carl Hanser, 1999) [DLA]
——*Austerlitz* (Munich, Vienna: Carl Hanser, 2001)
——*Austerlitz*, trans. by Anthea Bell (first edition) (New York: Random House, 2001) [DLA] (2 copies, one with annotations)
——*Austerlitz*, trans. by Anthea Bell, uncorrected proof copy (hardback) (London: Hamish Hamilton, 2001) [DLA]
——*Austerlitz*, trans. by Anthea Bell, advance readers' edition (New York: Random House, 2001) [DLA]
——*Austerlitz*, trans. by Anthea Bell (London: Penguin, 2001) [DLA]

1(b): Translations

Evans, Richard J., *Sozialdemokratie und Frauenemanzipation im deutschen Kaiserreich*, trans. from the English by W. G. Sebald in collaboration with the author (Bonn: Dietz, 1979)

1(c): Contributions to other volumes (full details given in Primary Bibliography)

Assmann, Michael, ed., *Deutsche Akademie für Sprache und Dichtung: Jahrbuch 1997* (Darmstadt: Wallstein, 1998) [D.64]

Braese, Stephan and Werner Irro, eds, *Konterbande und Camouflage: Szenen aus der Vor- und Nachgeschichte von Heinrich Heines marranischer Schreibweise* (Berlin: Vorwerk 8, 2002) [F.A.10]

Jung, Jochen, ed., *Träume: Literaturalmanach 1987* (Salzburg and Vienna: Residenz, 1987) [F.C.3] (2 copies)

Der Komet: Almanach der Anderen Bibliothek auf das Jahr 1991 (Munich: Eichborn, 1990) [F.A.3]

1(d): *Contributions to periodicals (full details given in Primary Bibliography)*

Akzente, 2001.2 B 5384 [F.A.9]

Austriaca, no. 16 (May 1983) [D.23]

Der Deutschunterricht, 35.5 (October 1983) [D.24]

Der Deutschunterricht, 36.4 ([August] 1984) [D.28]

Études Germaniques, 39.3 (July–September 1984) [D.15(a)]

Jewish Quarterly, 43.4 (Winter 1996–97) [J.14]

Journal of European Studies, 2.1 (March 1972) [D.6]

Literary Review (London), no. 280 (October 2001) [J.47]; also contains review of *Austerlitz* by John Murray, 'Looking for his Parents', p. 51

Literatur und Kritik, 8, 65 (June 1972) [D.7]

Literatur und Kritik, 8, 66–67 (July–August 1972) [D.6.1]

Literatur und Kritik, 11, 93 (April 1975) [D.9]

Literatur und Kritik, 14, 125 (June 1978) [D.14]

Literatur und Kritik, 16, 155 (June 1981) [D.16]

Literatur und Kritik, 18, 177–78 (September–October 1983) [D.15]

Literatur und Kritik, 21, 205–06 (July–August 1986) [D.36]

Literatur und Kritik, 23, 233–34 (April–May 1989) [D.46]

Litterae, 2.2 (April 1992) [D.55]

Manuskripte, 21, 74 ([no month] 1981) [D.17]

Manuskripte, 23, 79 ([no month] 1983) [D.20(a)]

Manuskripte, 24, 84 (June 1984) [D.26]

Manuskripte, 24, 85 (October 1984) [E.A.1]

Manuskripte, 25, 89–90 (September 1985) [D.8.1]

Manuskripte, 26, 92 (June 1986) [E.A.2] and [D.35]

Manuskripte, 27, 95 (March 1987) [E.A.3]

Manuskripte, 28, 99 (March 1988) [E.B.1]

Manuskripte, 28, 100 (June 1988) [E.B.12]

Merkur, 38.2 (March 1984) [D.25]

Merkur, 39.2 (February 1985) [D.29]

Het Moment, no. 3 (Winter 1986) [E.A.2.1]

Het Moment, no. 6 (Autumn 1987) [E.A.3.1]

Neue Rundschau, 100.1 (1989) [D.44]

Neue Zürcher Zeitung, 193, 21–22 August 1994, Feuilleton [D.59]

Die Rampe, 1985.1 [D.27]

Die Rampe, 1988.1 [D.40]

Offprints

Neophilologus, 59.3 (1975), 421–34 [D.10]

Neophilologus, 60.2 (1976), 432–41 [D.13]

Neophilologus, 67.1 (1983), 109–17 [D.22]

Orbis Litterarum, 30.4 (1975), 241–50 [D.11]

Orbis Litterarum, 37 (1982), 345–66 [D.18]

Orbis Litterarum, 41 (1986), 265–78 [D.34] (2 copies, one [DLA])

1(e): Secondary works and reviews

Literaturen, 2001.3–4; contains review of *Austerlitz* by Heinrich Detering, pp. 50–51

LOQUAI, FRANZ, ed., *Far from Home: W. G. Sebald* (Bamberg: Fußnoten zur Literatur, 1995) [DLA]

LUCHSINGER, MARTIN, *Mythos Italien: Denkbilder des Fremden in der deutschsprachigen Gegenwartsliteratur* (Cologne: Böhlau, 1996) [DLA] (contains section on *Schwindel. Gefühle.*; see Secondary Bibliography)

W. G. Sebald: Gespräch mit Lebenden und Toten (Munich: Hanser [Autoren, Texte, Bücher, Bogen 48], 2000) [DLA] [B.C.2]

SILL, OLIVER, *Der Kreis des Lebens: Eine Wanderung durch die europäische Moderne* (Bielefeld: Aisthesis, 2001) [DLA] (contains section on Sebald; see Secondary Bibliography)

Spectator, 6 October 2001, containing review of *Austerlitz* by Anita Brookner, 'A Journey without Maps', p. 64

TLS [*Times Literary Supplement*], no. 5056, 25 February 2000, containing review of *Vertigo* by Susan Sontag, 'A Mind in Mourning', pp. 3–4

1(f): Varia

JARAY, TESS, *From the Rings of Saturn and Vertigo, W. G. Sebald*. Eighteen screen printed images each with texts from W. G. Sebald's *The Rings of Saturn* and *Vertigo* (London: Purdy Hicks Gallery, 2001) (brochure accompanying exhibition) [DLA]

2: Literature

2(a): German and Austrian literature

ACHTERNBUSCH, HERBERT, *Die Alexanderschlacht* (Frankfurt a.M.: suhrkamp taschenbuch, 1972)

——*Die Alexanderschlacht: Schriften 1963–71* (Frankfurt a.M.: suhrkamp taschenbuch, 1986)

——*Die Atlantikschwimmer: Schriften 1973–79* (Frankfurt a.M.: suhrkamp taschenbuch, 1986)

——*Die Föhnforscher: Schriften 1984* (Frankfurt a.M.: suhrkamp taschenbuch, 1991)

——*Happy oder Der Tag wird kommen* (Frankfurt a.M.: suhrkamp taschenbuch, 1975)

——*Das Haus am Nil: Schriften 1980–81* (Frankfurt a.M.: suhrkamp taschenbuch, 1987)

——*Das letzte Loch: Filmbuch* (Frankfurt a.M.: suhrkamp taschenbuch, 1982)

——*Die Olympiasiegerin: Filmbuch* (Frankfurt a.M.: suhrkamp taschenbuch, 1984)

——*Die Stunde des Todes* (Frankfurt a.M.: suhrkamp taschenbuch, 1977)

ADLER, H. G., *Eine Reise* (Vienna: Zsolnay, 1999) [★]

'Ortlose Botschaft': Der Freundeskreis H. G. Adler, Elias Canetti und Franz Baermann Steiner im englischen Exil, Schiller-Nationalmuseum Marbach, September–November 1998, ed. by Marcel Atze, Marbacher Magazin, 8 (Marbach am Neckar: Deutsche Schillergesellschaft, 1998) (exhibition catalogue)

ALBUS, ANITA, *Der Garten der Lieder: Ein Buch für Kinder und Andere* (Frankfurt a.M.: Insel, 1975)

——*Der Himmel ist mein Hut. Die Erde ist mein Schuh: Ein Bilderbuch für große und kleine Leute mit Bildern von Anita Albus und Geschichten von Kindern* (Frankfurt a.M.: Insel-Bilderbuch, 1973)

ALTENBERG, PETER, *Semmering 1912* (Berlin: Fischer, 1913) [DLA]

——*Wie ich es sehe* (Berlin: Fischer, 1914) [DLA]

——*Peter Altenberg: Leben und Werk in Texten und Bildern*, ed. by Hans Christian Kosler (Frankfurt a.M.: Fischer Taschenbuch, 1984) [DLA]

    WYSOCKI, GISELA VON, *Peter Altenberg: Bilder und Geschichten des befreiten Lebens* (Frankfurt a.M.: Fischer Taschenbuch, 1986) [DLA]

AMÉRY, JEAN, *Hand an sich legen: Diskurs über den Freitod* (Stuttgart: Klett-Cotta, 1983)

——*Jenseits von Schuld und Sühne: Bewältigungsversuche eines Überwältigten* (Stuttgart: Klett-Cotta, 1980) [DLA]

——*Über das Altern: Revolte und Resignation* (Stuttgart: Klett-Cotta, 1979)

    Jean Améry, ed. by Heinz Ludwig Arnold (= *Text + Kritik*, no. 99 (July 1988)) [D.42]

    Jean Améry (Hans Maier), ed. by Stephan Steiner (Frankfurt a.M.: Stroemfeld/Nexus, 1996)

ANDERSCH, ALFRED, *Efraim* (Zurich: Diogenes, 1967) [★]

——*Die Kirschen der Freiheit* (Zurich: Diogenes Taschenbuch, 1971)

——*Die Rote* (Zurich: Diogenes, 1972) [★]

——*Sansibar oder der letzte Grund* (Zurich: Diogenes, 1970) [★]

——*Sansibar oder der letzte Grund* (Zurich: Diogenes Taschenbuch, 1970)

——*Der Vater eines Mörders* (Zurich: Diogenes Taschenbuch, 1982)

——*Winterspelt* (Zurich: Diogenes, 1974) [★]

    REINHARDT, STEPHAN, *Alfred Andersch: Eine Biographie* (Zurich: Diogenes, 1990) [★]

ARNIM, L. ACHIM VON and CLEMENS BRENTANO, eds, *Des Knaben Wunderhorn: Alte deutsche Lieder*, 3 vols (Munich: dtv, 1963) [DLA]

ARTMANN, H. C., *Der aeronautische Sindtbart* (Salzburg: Residenz, 1972)

——*Aus meiner Botanisiertrommel* (Salzburg: Residenz, 1975)

——*Grünverschlossene Botschaft: 90 Träume* (Frankfurt a.M.: suhrkamp taschenbuch, 1972)

——*How much, schatzi?* (Frankfurt a.M.: suhrkamp taschenbuch, 1973)

——*med ana schwoazzn dintn: gedichta r aus bradnsee* (Salzburg: Otto Müller, 1958)

——*Mein Erbteil von Vater und Mutter* (Hamburg: Merlin, 1969)

——*Das suchen nach dem gestrigen tag* (Neuwied and Berlin: Sammlung Luchterhand, 1971)

——*Überall wo Hamlet hinkam* (Stuttgart: Collispress, 1969) [★]

——*Von denen Husaren* (Frankfurt a.M.: Bibliothek Suhrkamp, 1971)

——*Der zerbrochene Krug (nach Heinrich von Kleist)* (Salzburg and Vienna: Residenz, 1992)

BACHMANN, INGEBORG, *Das dreißigste Jahr* (Munich: dtv, 1966)

——*Bilder aus ihrem Leben* (Munich: Piper, 1983) [DLA]

——*Der Fall Franza; Requiem für Fanny Goldmann* (Munich: Piper, 1979) [DLA] [★]

——*Simultan* (Munich: dtv, 1988)

    HAPKEMEYER, ANDREAS, ed., *Ingeborg Bachmann: Bilder aus ihrem Leben* (Munich: Piper, 1983) [DLA]

    JELINEK, ELFRIEDE, *Isabelle Huppert in* Malina: *Ein Filmbuch, Nach dem Roman von Ingeborg Bachmann, mit Matthieu Carrière als Malina in einem Film von Werner Schroeter* (Frankfurt a.M.: Suhrkamp, 1991; Salzburg and Vienna: Residenz, 1992) [DLA]

BAERMANN STEINER, FRANZ, *Unruhe ohne Uhr: Ausgewählte Gedichte aus dem Nachlass* (Heidelberg: Deutsche Akademie für Sprache und Dichtung, 1954)

BAYER, KONRAD, *Der Kopf des Vitus Bering* (Frankfurt a.M.: Bibliothek Suhrkamp, 1970)

BEER, JOHANN, *Der neu ausgefertigte Jungfer-Hobel*, ed. by Eberhard Haufe (Frankfurt a.M.: Insel-Bücherei, 1968) [DLA]

BENJAMIN, WALTER:

    Walter Benjamin: Gesammelte Schriften, ed. by Rolf Tiedemann and Hermann Schweppenhäuser in collaboration with Theodor W. Adorno and Gershom Scholem, 4 vols (Frankfurt a.M.: Suhrkamp, 1972) (vols III, IV.1 and IV.2), III: *Kritiken und*

Rezensionen, ed. by Hella Tiedemann-Bartels; IV.1–2: *Kleine Prosa: Baudelaire-Über-tragungen*, ed. by Tilman Rexroth (1972) [DLA]

——*Ausgewählte Schriften*, II: *Angelus Novus* (Frankfurt a.M.: Suhrkamp, 1966) [DLA]

——*Der Begriff der Kunstkritik in der deutschen Romantik*, ed. by Hermann Schweppen-häuser (Frankfurt a.M.: suhrkamp taschenbuch wissenschaft, 1973 [DLA]

——*Briefe*, ed. by Gershom Scholem and Theodor W. Adorno, 2 vols (Frankfurt a.M.: Suhrkamp, 1966) [DLA]

——*Einbahnstraße* (Frankfurt a.M.: Bibliothek Suhrkamp, 1962) [DLA]

——*Illuminationen: Ausgewählte Schriften*, ed. by Siegfried Unseld (Frankfurt a.M.: Suhrkamp, 1961) [DLA]

——*Über Kinder, Jugend und Erziehung* (Frankfurt a.M.: edition suhrkamp, 1969) [DLA]

——*Ursprung des deutschen Trauerspiels*, rev. edn by Rolf Tiedemann (Frankfurt a.M.: Suhrkamp, 1963) [DLA]

——*Zur Kritik der Gewalt und andere Aufsätze*, with an afterword by Herbert Marcuse (Frankfurt a.M.: edition suhrkamp, 1965) [DLA]

FULD, WERNER, *Walter Benjamin: Zwischen den Stühlen: Eine Biographie* (Frankfurt a.M.: Fischer Taschenbuch, 1981) [DLA]

PUTTNIES, HANS, and GARY SMITH, *Benjaminiana: Eine biographische Recherche*, Bucklicht Männlein und Engel der Geschichte: Walter Benjamin, Theoretiker der Moderne; Martin Gropius Bau, Berlin, 28 December 1990–28 April 1991 (Giessen: Anabas, 1991) (exhibition catalogue) [DLA]

SCHLÜTER, WOLFGANG, *Walter Benjamin: Der Sammler und das geschlossene Kästchen* (Darmstadt: Jürgen Häusser, 1993) [DLA]

BERNHARD, THOMAS, *Alte Meister: Komödie* (Frankfurt a.M.: Suhrkamp, 1985) [DLA]

——*Amras* (Frankfurt a.M.: Bibliothek Suhrkamp, 1976) [DLA]

——*Der Atem: Eine Entscheidung* (Salzburg and Vienna: Residenz, 1978) [DLA]

——*Auslöschung: Ein Zerfall* (Frankfurt a.M.: Suhrkamp, 1986) [DLA]

——*Der deutsche Mittagstisch: Dramolette* (Frankfurt a.M.: edition suhrkamp, 1988) [DLA]

——*Extinction*, trans. by David McLintock (Harmondsworth: Penguin 20th Century Classics, 1996) [DLA]

——*Frost* (Frankfurt a.M.: suhrkamp taschenbuch, 1972) [DLA]

——*Ja* (Frankfurt a.M.: Bibiliothek Suhrkamp, 1978) [DLA]

——*Die Jagdgesellschaft* (Frankfurt a.M.: Bibiliothek Suhrkamp, 1974) [DLA]

——*Das Kalkwerk* (Frankfurt a.M.: suhrkamp taschenbuch, 1976) [DLA]

——*Die Kälte: Eine Isolation* (Salzburg and Vienna: Residenz, 1981) [DLA]

——*Der Keller: Eine Entziehung* (Salzburg and Vienna: Residenz, 1981) [DLA]

——*Ein Kind* (Salzburg and Vienna: Residenz, 1981) [DLA]

——*Midland in Stilfs: Drei Erzählungen* (Frankfurt a.M.: Bibiliothek Suhrkamp, 1973) [DLA]

——*Prosa* (Frankfurt a.M.: edition suhrkamp, 1975)

——*Ritter, Dene, Voss*, Akademietheater programme 1986/87.2 (Vienna: Burgtheater, 1986) (= Programmbuch Nr. 2, 4 September 1986) [DLA]

——*Die Salzburger Stücke* (Frankfurt a.M.: suhrkamp taschenbuch, 1975) [DLA]

——*Der Schein trügt* (Frankfurt a.M.: Bibliothek Suhrkamp, 1983) [DLA]

——*Der Stimmenimitator* (Frankfurt a.M.: Bibiliothek Suhrkamp, 1982) [DLA]

——*Der Theatermacher*, Burgtheater programme 1986/87.1 (Vienna: Burgtheater, 1986) (= Programmbuch Nr. 1, 1 September 1986) [DLA]

——*Die Ursache: Eine Andeutung* (Salzburg and Vienna: Residenz, 1981) [DLA]

——*Verstörung* (Frankfurt a.M.: Bibiliothek Suhrkamp, 1976) [DLA]

——*Wittgensteins Neffe: Eine Freundschaft* (Frankfurt a.M.: Bibiliothek Suhrkamp, 1983) [DLA]

——*Ungenach* (Frankfurt a.M.: edition suhrkamp, 1975) [DLA]

Thomas Bernhard: Werkgeschichte, ed. by Jens Dittmar (Frankfurt a.M.: suhrkamp taschenbuch materialien, 1981) [DLA]

Thomas Bernhards Welt: Schauplätze seiner Jugend, with photographs by Erika Schmied and an essay by Wieland Schmied (Salzburg and Vienna: Residenz, 1981) [DLA]

BICHSEL, PETER, *Eigentlich möchte Frau Blum den Milchmann kennenlernen* (Olten and Freiburg in Brisgau: Walter, 1972)

——*Kindergeschichten* (Neuwied and Berlin: Luchterhand, 1969)

——*Zur Stadt Paris* (Frankfurt a.M.: Suhrkamp, 1993)

BIENEK, HORST, *Erde und Feuer* (Munich: Hanser, 1984) [*]

BILLER, MAXIM, *Die Tochter* (Cologne: Kiepenheuer & Witsch, 2000) [*]

BLUMENFELD, ERWIN, *Einbildungsroman* (Frankfurt a.M.: Eichborn, 1998) [DLA] [*]

BOBROWSKI, JOHANNES, *Das Land Sarmatien: Gedichte* (Munich: dtv, 1966)

BÖHME, JAKOB:

WEHR, GERHARD, *Jakob Böhme in Selbstzeugnissen und Bilddokumenten* (Reinbek bei Hamburg: rowohlts monographien, 1971) [DLA]

BÖLL, HEINRICH, *Bild, Bonn, Boenisch* (Göttingen: Lamuv, 1985)

——*Der Engel schweig* (Cologne: Kiepenheuer & Witsch, 1992)

——*Frankfurter Vorlesungen* (Munich: dtv, 1968)

——*Gruppenbild mit Dame* (Munich: dtv, 1981)

——*Haus ohne Hüter* (Frankfurt a.M. and Berlin: Ullstein, 1969)

——*Rom auf den ersten Blick: Reisen, Städte, Landschaften* (Göttingen: Lamuv, 1987) [*]

——*Die verlorene Ehre der Katharina Blum* (Munich: dtv, 1980)

——and CHRISTIAN LINDER, *Drei Tage im März: Ein Gespräch* (Cologne: Kiepenheuer & Witsch pocket, 1975)

LINDER, CHRISTIAN, *Böll* (Reinbek bei Hamburg: Rowohlt, das neue Buch [1978])

BÖNI, FRANZ, *Ein Wanderer im Alpenregen* (Frankfurt a.M.: suhrkamp taschenbuch, 1981)

BORCHARDT, RUDOLF, *Der leidenschaftliche Gärtner*, with twelve watercolours by Anita Albus (Nördlingen: Greno, 1987) [*]

——, ed., *Ewiger Vorrat deutscher Poesie* (Munich: Bremer Presse, 1926) [DLA] [*]

BORCHERT, WOLFGANG, *Die traurigen Geranien und andere Geschichten aus dem Nachlaß* (Reinbek bei Hamburg: rororo, 1988)

RÜHMKORF, PETER, *Wolfgang Borchert in Selbstzeugnissen und Bilddokumenten* (Reinbek bei Hamburg: rowohlts monographien, 1987) [DLA]

——*Wolfgang Borchert in Selbstzeugnissen und Bilddokumenten* (Reinbek bei Hamburg: rowohlts monographien, 1996) [DLA]

BRÄKER, ULRICH, *Lebensgeschichte und natürliche Abenteuer des armen Mannes im Tockenburg* (Stuttgart: Reclams Universalbibliothek, 1969) [DLA]

BRANDSTÄTTER, HORST, *Badenwyler Marsch; Theodor Lessing: Der Lärm* (Stuttgart-Berlin: Johannes M. Mayer & Co., 1999) [DLA]

——*Mayer: Eine tatsächliche Komödie* (Weingarten: Drumlin, 1987) [DLA]

——ed., *Asperg: Ein deutsches Gefängnis* (Berlin: Wagenbach, 1978) [DLA]

BRAUN, LILY, *Memoiren einer Sozialistin* (Munich: Albert Langen, 1920) [DLA] [*]

BRECHT, BERTOLT, *Arbeitsjournal*, ed. by Werner Hecht, 2 vols: I, *1938 bis 1942*; II, *1942 bis 1953* (Frankfurt a.M.: suhrkamp taschenbuch, 1993)

——*Arbeitsjournal 1942 bis 1955* (Frankfurt a.M.: suhrkamp taschenbuch, 1993)

——*Schriften zum Theater* (Frankfurt a.M.: Bibliothek Suhrkamp, 1962)

KESTING, MARIANNE, *Bertolt Brecht in Selbstzeugnissen und Bilddokumenten* (Reinbek bei Hamburg: rowohlts monographien, 1960) [DLA]

Steinweg, Reiner, ed., *Auf Anregung Bertolt Brechts: Lehrstücke mit Schülern, Arbeitern, Theaterleuten* (Frankfurt a.M.: edition suhrkamp, 1978)

Brecht, Walter, *Unser Leben in Augsburg, damals: Erinnerungen* (Frankfurt a.M.: Insel, 1985) [DLA] [★]

Brinkmann, Rolf Dieter, *Erkundungen für die Präzisierung des Gefühls für einen Aufstand: Reise, Zeit, Magazin (Tagebuch)* (Reinbek bei Hamburg: Rowohlt, 1987) [★]

——*Rom, Blicke* (Reinbek bei Hamburg: Rowohlt, 1986) [★]

Broch, Hermann, *Hermann Broch: Gesammelte Werke*, 10 vols (Zurich: Rhein-Verlag, 1952–61), I: *Gedichte* (1953); II: *Die Schlafwandler: Eine Romantrilogie* (1951–52); III: *Der Tod des Vergil* (1958); IV: *Die Schuldlosen* (1954); V: *Der Versucher* (1953); VI: *Essays 1: Dichten und Erkennen* (1955); VII: *Essays 2: Erkennen und Handeln* (1955); VIII: *Briefe von 1929 bis 1951* (1957); IX: *Massenpsychologie: Schriften aus dem Nachlaß* (1959); X: *Die unbekannte Größe: Mit den Briefen an Willa Muir* [DLA] [★]

Buber, Martin, *Des Baal-Schem-Tow Unterweisung im Umgang mit Gott* (Berlin: Schocken, [n.d.]) [DLA] [★]

——*Die Erzählungen: Der Chassidim* (Zurich: Manesse Conzett & Huber, 1949) [DLA]

——*Der utopische Sozialismus* (Cologne: Jakob Hegner, 1967) [DLA]

——*Zwischen Gesellschaft und Staat* (Heidelberg: Lambert Schneider, 1952) [DLA]

Büchner, Georg, *Georg Büchner: Werke und Briefe* (Munich: dtv, 1965) [DLA]

——*Lenz* (Stuttgart: Reclams UB, 1990)

    Georg Büchner: Der Katalog, Georg Büchner 1813–1837: Revolutionär, Dichter, Wissenschaftler; Mathildenhöhe, Darmstadt, 2 August–27 September 1987, ed. and curated by the Georg-Büchner-Ausstellungsgesellschaft (Basle and Frankfurt: Stroemfeld / Roter Stern, 1987) (exhibition catalogue)

    Erläuterungen und Dokumente: Georg Büchner, 'Lenz', ed. by Gerhard Schaub (Stuttgart: Reclams UB, 1987)

    Johann, Ernst, *Georg Büchner in Selbstzeugnissen und Bilddokumenten* (Reinbek bei Hamburg: Rowohlt Bildmonographie, 1965) [DLA]

Bürger, Gottfried August, *Des Freiherrn von Münchhausen wunderbare Reisen zu Wasser und zu Lande* (Frankfurt a.M.: Insel-Bücherei, 1968) [DLA]

Burger, Hermann, *Blankenburg: Erzählungen* (Frankfurt a.M.: S. Fischer, 1986)

——*Brenner* (Frankfurt a.M.: suhrkamp taschenbuch, 1992)

Campe, Joachim Heinrich, *Bilder-Abeze*, ed. by Dietrich Leube (Frankfurt a.M.: insel taschenbuch, 1975) [DLA]

Canetti, Elias, *Alle vergeudete Verehrung: Aufzeichnungen 1949–1960* (Munich: Reihe Hanser, 1970) [DLA]

——*Der andere Prozeß: Kafkas Briefe an Felice* (Munich: Reihe Hanser, 1970) [DLA]

——*Das Augenspiel: Lebensgeschichte 1931–1937* (Frankfurt a.M.: Fischer Taschenbuch, 1982) [DLA]

——*Die Blendung* (Frankfurt a.M.: Fischer Bücherei, 1965) [DLA]

——*Die Fackel im Ohr: Lebensgeschichte 1921–1931* (Frankfurt a.M.: Fischer Taschenbuch, 1982) [DLA]

——*Die gerettete Zunge: Geschichte einer Jugend* (Frankfurt a.M.: Fischer Taschenbuch, 1982) [DLA]

——*Die gespaltene Zukunft: Aufsätze und Gespräche* (Munich: Reihe Hanser, 1972) [DLA]

——*Masse und Macht* (Hamburg: Claassen, 1960) [DLA]

Carossa, Hans, *Führung und Geleit: Ein Lebensgedenkbuch* (Leipzig: Insel, 1933) [DLA] [★]

——*Ungleiche Welten: Lebensbericht* (Frankfurt a.M.: suhrkamp taschenbuch, 1978)

Celan, Paul, *Mohn und Gedächtnis* (Frankfurt a.M.: suhrkamp taschenbuch, 1976)

——*Sprachgitter* (Frankfurt a.M.: Fischer, 1974)

Böttiger, Helmut, *Orte Paul Celans* (Vienna: Paul Zsolnay, 1996) [DLA] [★]

Felsteiner, John, *Paul Celan: Poet, Survivor, Jew* (New Haven and London: Yale University Press, 1995) [DLA] [W]

Chamisso, Adalbert von, [*Adalbert von*] *Chamissos gesammelte Werke*, ed. with intro. by Max Koch, 4 vols bound in 2 (Stuttgart: Cotta, [n.d.])

Claudius, Matthias, *Der Wandsbecker Bote* (Zurich: Manesse, 1947) [DLA]

Berglar, Peter, *Matthias Claudius in Selbstzeugnissen und Bilddokumenten* (Reinbek bei Hamburg: rowohlts monographien, 1992) [DLA]

Cohn, Hans W., *With All Five Senses: Poems*, trans. by Frederick G. Cohn, introduction by Michael Hamburger (London: Menard Press, 1999)

Conrady, Karl Otto, ed., *Deutsche Volksbücher* (Reinbek bei Hamburg: rororo klassiker, 1968) [DLA]

Corleis, Gisela, *Unverwandt: Reisen in eine fremde Gegend* (Salzburg and Vienna: Residenz, 1986) [DLA]

David, Jakob Julius, *Novellen* (Salzburg and Vienna: Residenz, 1995) [DLA] [★]

Döblin, Alfred, *Berlin Alexanderplatz* (Munich: dtv, 1965)

——*Die Ermordung einer Butterblume und andere Erzählungen* (Munich: dtv, 1980)

——*Flucht und Sammlung des Judenvolks* (Amsterdam: Querido, 1935) [★]

Schröter, Klaus, *Alfred Döblin in Selbstzeugnissen und Bilddokumenten* (Reinbek bei Hamburg: rowohlts monographien, 1978) [DLA]

Internationale Alfred Döblin-Kolloquien 1980–1983, ed. by Werner Stauffacher, Jahrbuch für Internationale Germanistik, series A: Kongressberichte, 14 (Berne: Peter Lang, 1986) [D.21]

Doderer, Heimito von, *Die Strudelhofstiege* (Munich: dtv, 1966)

Dohse, Christoph, *koma* ([n.p.]: [n. pub.], 1988) [DLA]

Dorst, Tankred, *Toller* (Frankfurt a.M.: edition suhrkamp, 1968)

——, ed., *Die Münchner Räterepublik: Zeugnisse und Kommentar* (Frankfurt a.M.: edition suhrkamp, 1977) [DLA]

Egger, Oswald, ed., *Weltei, gepellt* (= *Der Prokurist*, 11 (1992)) [DLA]

Eich, Günter, *Abgelegene Gehöfte: Gedichte* (Frankfurt a.M.: edition suhrkamp, 1968)

——*Botschaften des Regens* (Frankfurt a.M.: edition suhrkamp, 1963)

——*Träume: Vier Spiele* (Frankfurt a.M.: Suhrkamp, 1962)

——*Unter Wasser; Böhmische Schneider: Marionettenspiele* (Frankfurt a.M.: Suhrkamp, 1964)

——*Zu den Akten: Gedichte* (Frankfurt a.M.: Suhrkamp, 1964)

Eichendorff, Joseph von, *Joseph von Eichendorff: Werke in einem Band*, ed. by Wolfdietrich Rasch (Munich: Hanser, 1977) [DLA]

Eisendle, Helmut, *Die Umstimmer* (Vienna: Thomas Sessler Verlag (Der Souffleurkasten), [n.d.])

Enzensberger, Christian, *Größerer Versuch über den Schmutz* (Munich: dtv sonderreihe, 1971) [DLA]

——*Was ist was* (Nördlingen: Greno, 1987) [★]

Enzensberger, Hans Magnus, *Allerleirauh: Viele schöne Kinderreime versammelt von Hans Magnus Enzensberger* (Frankfurt a.M.: suhrkamp taschenbuch, 1971) [DLA]

——*Aussichten auf den Bürgerkrieg* (Frankfurt a.M.: Suhrkamp, 1993)

——*blindenschrift* (Frankfurt a.M.: Suhrkamp, 1964)

——*Europa in Trümmern: Augenzeugenberichte* (Frankfurt a.M.: Eichborn, 1990) [DLA]

——*Gedichte 1950–1985* (Frankfurt a.M.: suhrkamp taschenbuch, 1986)

——*Die Große Wanderung: 33 Markierungen* (Frankfurt a.M.: Suhrkamp, 1992)

——*Mittelmaß und Wahn: Gesammelte Zerstreuungen* (Frankfurt a.M.: suhrkamp taschenbuch, 1991)

——*Der Untergang der Titanic* (Frankfurt a.M.: suhrkamp taschenbuch, 1981)

——*Kiosk: Neue Gedichte* (Frankfurt a.M.: Suhrkamp, 1995) [DLA]

FELDER, FRANZ MICHAEL, *Aus meinem Leben* (Frankfurt a.M.: suhrkamp taschenbuch, 1987) [DLA]

FEUERBACH, ANSELM VON, *Merkwürdige Verbrechen: Sechzehn Kriminalgeschichten* (Frankfurt a.M.: Eichborn, 1993)

——, and GEORG FRIEDRICH DAUMER, *Kaspar Hauser. Mit einem Bericht von Johannes Mayer und einem Essay von Jeffrey M. Masson* (Frankfurt a.M.: Eichborn, 1995)

FICHTE, HUBERT, *Detlevs Imitationen 'Grünspan'* (Frankfurt a.M.: Fischer Taschenbuch, 1982)

FISCHART, JOHANN, *Affentheuerlich Naupengeheuerliche Geschichtklitterung* (Frankfurt a.M.: Eichborn, 1997) [DLA]

FLEISSER, MARIELUISE, *Abenteuer aus dem Englischen Garten* (Frankfurt a.M.: suhrkamp taschenbuch, 1983)

——*Ein Pfund Orangen* (Frankfurt a.M.: suhrkamp taschenbuch, 1984)

McGOWAN, MORAY, *Marieluise Fleißer* (Munich: C. H. Beck, 1987) [W]

FONTANE, THEODOR, *Theodor Fontane: Gesammelte Werke: Eine Auswahl*, 5 vols (Berlin: Fischer, 1920) [DLA]

——*Effi Briest*, trans. by Douglas Parmée (London: Penguin Classics, 1967)

——*Two Novellas*, trans. by Gabriele Annan (London: Penguin Classics, 1979)

NÜRNBERGER, HELMUTH, *Theodor Fontane mit Selbstzeugnissen und Bilddokumenten* (Reinbek bei Hamburg: rowohlts monographien, 1997) [DLA]

FORSTER, GEORG:

ENZENSBERGER, ULRICH, *Georg Forster: Ein Leben in Scherben* (Frankfurt a.M.: Eichborn, 1996) [DLA]

FORTE, DIETER, *Der Junge mit den blutigen Schuhen* (Frankfurt a.M.: Fischer, 1995) [★]

FRANZOS, KARL EMIL, *Der Pojaz* (Stuttgart and Berlin: Cotta, 1906) [DLA] [★]

FREYTAG, GUSTAV, *Soll und Haben*, 2 vols (Leipzig: Hirzel, 1916)

FRISCH, MAX, *Gesammelte Werke*, ed. by Hans Mayer with Walter Schnitz, 7 vols (Frankfurt a.M.: suhrkamp taschenbuch, 1986) [★]

FROMM, ERICH, *Die Kunst des Liebens* (Frankfurt a.M. and Berlin: Ullstein, 1992)

GAIDA, KLAUS G., ed., *Zeitvertreib*, 2 vols (Cologne: Salon, 1998), I: *Alles suchen und NICHTS finden*; II: *Wo sind WIR stehengeblieben* [DLA]

——, ed., *Zeitvertreib*, supplement: *Es geht GESICHERT weiter* (Cologne: Korridor, 1998) [DLA]

GERHARDIE, WILHELM ALEXANDER, *Vergeblichkeit* (Frankfurt a.M.: Eichborn, 1999) [★]

GEROK, KARL, *Blumen und Sterne: Vermischte Gedichte*, 16th edn (Stuttgart: Greiner & Pfeiffer, [n.d.]) [DLA]

GOETHE, JOHANN WOLFGANG VON:

[*Johann Wolfgang von*] *Goethes Werke*, 36 vols bound in 18 (Stuttgart: Cotta, 1867) [★]

Johann Wolfgang von Goethe: Werke (Basle: Birkhäuser, 1944) (vols I, III, VI), I: *Gedichte*; III: *Faust*; VI: *Die Wahlverwandtschaften*

Johann Wolfgang von Goethe: [Gesamtausgabe], 45 vols (Munich: dtv, 1961–63) (vols I–XLIV), I: *Sämtliche Gedichte: Erster Teil* [DLA]; II: *Sämtliche Gedichte: Zweiter Teil* (October 1961) [DLA]; III: *Sämtliche Gedichte: Dritter Teil* (December 1961) [DLA]; IV: *Sämtliche Gedichte: Vierter Teil* (December 1961) [DLA]; V: *Der West-östliche Divan* (November 1961) [DLA]; VI: *Reineke Fuchs; Hermann und Dorothea; Achilleis* (November 1961) [DLA]; VII: *Frühe dramatische Dichtungen* (January 1962) [DLA]; VIII: *Götz von Berlichingen; Clavigo; Urfaust* (January 1962) [DLA]; IX: *Faust: Der Tragödie erster und zweiter Teil* (February 1962) [DLA]; X: *Weimarer Dramen I: Egmont; Iphigenie auf Tauris; Torquato Tasso* (January 1963; 3rd edn 1967) [DLA];

XI: *Weimarer Dramen II: Die natürliche Tochter; Pandora; Epimenides* (January 1963) [DLA]; XII: *Weimarer Dramen III: Die Geschwister; Elpenor; Nausikaa: Maskenzüge* (May 1962) [DLA]; XIII: *Die Leiden des jungen Werthers: Frühe Prosa* (May 1962) [DLA]; XIV: *Wilhelm Meisters theatralische Sendung* (May 1962) [DLA]; XV: *Wilhelm Meisters Lehrjahre: Erster Teil* (March 1962) [DLA]; XVI: *Wilhelm Meisters Lehrjahre: Zweiter Teil* (March 1962) [DLA]; XVII: *Wilhelm Meisters Wanderjahre: Erster Teil* (April 1962) [DLA]; XVIII: *Wilhelm Meisters Wanderjahre: Zweiter Teil* (April 1962) [DLA]; XIX: *Die Wahlverwandtschaften* (February 1963) [DLA]; XX: *Novellen* (June 1962); XXI: *Maximen und Reflexionen* (February 1963) [DLA]; XXII: *Dichtung und Wahrheit: Erster Teil* (June 1962) [DLA]; XXIII: *Dichtung und Wahrheit: Zweiter Teil* (July 1962) [DLA]; XXIV: *Dichtung und Wahrheit Dritter und Vierter Teil* (July 1962) [DLA]; XXV: *Italienische Reise: Erster und Zweiter Teil* (August 1962) [DLA]; XXVI: *Italienische Reise Dritter Teil* (August 1962) [DLA]; XXVII: *Kampagne in Frankreich; Belagerung von Mainz* (September 1962) [DLA]; XXVIII: *Schweizer Reisen* (September 1962) [DLA]; XXIX: *Aus einer Reise am Rhein, Main, und Neckar* (April 1963) [DLA]; XXX: *Tag- und Jahreshefte* (October 1962) [DLA]; XXXI: *Schriften zur Literatur: Erster Teil* (November 1962) [DLA]; XXXII: *Schriften zur Literatur: Zweiter Teil* (November 1962) [DLA]; XXXIII: *Schriften zur Kunst: Erster Teil* (December 1962) [DLA]; XXXIV: *Schriften zur Kunst: Zweiter Teil* (December 1962) [DLA]; XXXV: *Benvenuto Cellini: Erster Teil* (June 1963) [DLA]; XXXVI: *Benvenuto Cellini: Zweiter Teil* (June 1963) [DLA]; XXXVII: *Schriften zur Anatomie; Zoologie; Physiognomik* (October 1962) [DLA]; XXXVIII: *Schriften zur Geologie; Mineralogie; Meteorologie* (March 1963) [DLA]; XXXXIX: *Schriften zur Botanik und Wissenschaftslehre* (March 1963) [DLA]; XL: *Zur Farbenlehre: Didaktischer Teil* (2nd edn January 1970) [DLA]; XLI: *Geschichte der Farbenlehre: Erster Teil* (May 1963) [DLA]; XLII: *Geschichte der Farbenlehre: Zweiter Teil* (2nd edn March 1970) [DLA]; XLIII: *Tagebücher 1775–1809* (July 1963) [DLA]; XLIV: *Tagebücher 1810–1832* (July 1963) [DLA]

——*Faust: Erster Teil*, Feldpostausgabe (Berlin: Hyperion, [n.d.]) [DLA]

ECKERMANN, JOHANN PETER, *Gespräche mit Goethe* (Munich: dtv, 1976) [DLA]

EISSLER, K. R., *Goethe: Eine psychoanalytische Studie*, 2 vols (Munich: dtv, 1987) [DLA] [*]

SCHLECHTA, KARL, *Goethes Wilhelm Meister* (Frankfurt a.M.: suhrkamp taschenbuch, 1985) [DLA]

WAGENKNECHT, CHRISTIAN, *Erläuterungen und Dokumente: Johann Wolfgang Goethe: Novelle* (Leipzig and Stuttgart: Reclam UB, 1982)

GOETTLE, GABRIELE, *Die Ärmsten! Wahre Geschichten aus dem arbeitslosen Leben*, with photographs by Elisabeth Kmölniger (Frankfurt a.M.: Eichborn, 2000) [DLA]

——*Deutsche Bräuche: Ermittlungen in Ost und West*, with photographs by Elisabeth Kmölniger (Frankfurt a.M.: Eichborn, 1994) [DLA]

——*Deutsche Sitten: Erkundungen in Ost und West*, with photographs by Elisabeth Kmölniger (Frankfurt a.M.: Eichborn, 1991) [DLA]

GOTTHELF, JEREMIAS:
  Der Volks-Gotthelf [Jeremias Gotthelf]: *Die Hauptwerke in 18 Bänden*, 6 vols (Zurich: Rentsch, 1962–66): *Anne Bäbi Jowäger*, I (1963); *Anne Bäbi Jowäger*, II (1963); *Der Geltstag* (1966); *Die Käserei in der Vehfreude* (1965); *Geld und Geist* (1964); *Uli der Knecht* (1962) [*]
  JUKER, BEE, *Wörterbuch zu den Werken von Jeremias Gotthelf* (Zurich: Rentsch, 1972) [*]

GRASS, GÜNTER, *Aus dem Tagebuch einer Schnecke* (Reinbek bei Hamburg: rororo, 1972)

——*Die Blechtrommel* (Darmstadt: Luchterhand, 1960) [DLA]

——*Hundejahre* (Darmstadt: Luchterhand, 1963) [DLA]

——*Katz und Maus* (Reinbek bei Hamburg: rororo, 1963)

GRILLPARZER, FRANZ, *Sämtliche Werke*, 16 vols bound in 4 (Leipzig: Max Hesse, [n.d.]) [DLA] [*]

——*Selbstbiographie*, ed. and with an afterword by Arno Dusini (Salzburg and Vienna: Residenz, 1994) [DLA]

GRIMM, JAKOB and WILHELM, *Kinder- und Hausmärchen*, 3 vols (Stuttgart: Reclam Jubiläumsausgabe, 1984)

GRIMMELSHAUSEN, J. CHR. VON, *Der abenteuerliche Simplicissimus*, 3 vols (Leipzig: Insel, 1908) [DLA]

GRÜNBEIN, DURS, *Grauzone morgens: Gedichte* (Frankfurt a.M.: edition suhrkamp, 1988)

HANDKE, PETER, *Als das Wünschen noch geholfen hat* (Frankfurt a.M.: suhrkamp taschenbuch, 1974)

——*Die Angst des Tormanns beim Elfmeter* (Frankfurt a.M.: suhrkamp taschenbuch, 1979)

——*Falsche Bewegung* (Frankfurt a.M.: suhrkamp taschenbuch, 1978)

——*Die Geschichte des Bleistifts* (Salzburg and Vienna: Residenz, 1982) [DLA]

——*Das Gewicht der Welt* (Frankfurt a.M.: suhrkamp taschenbuch, 1979)

——*Kindergeschichte* (Frankfurt a.M.: Suhrkamp, 1981) [DLA]

——*Der kurze Brief zum langen Abschied* (Frankfurt a.M.: suhrkamp taschenbuch, 1974)

——*Die Lehre der Sainte-Victoire* (Frankfurt a.M.: Suhrkamp, 1980) [DLA]

——*Die linkshändige Frau* (Frankfurt a.M.: suhrkamp taschenbuch, 1981)

——*Mein Jahr in der Niemandsbucht: Ein Märchen aus neuen Zeiten* (Frankfurt a.M.: Suhrkamp, 1994) [DLA] [★]

——*Nachmittag eines Schriftstellers* (Salzburg and Vienna: Residenz, 1987) [DLA]

——*Phantasien der Wiederholung* (Frankfurt a.M.: edition suhrkamp, 1983)

——*Stücke 2* (Frankfurt a.M.: suhrkamp taschenbuch, 1980)

——*Versuch über den geglückten Tag: Ein Wintertagtraum* (Frankfurt a.M.: Suhrkamp, 1992) [DLA]

——*Versuch über die Jukebox* (Frankfurt a.M.: Suhrkamp, 1990) [DLA]

——*Versuch über die Müdigkeit* (Frankfurt a.M.: Suhrkamp, 1990) [DLA]

——*Die Wiederholung* (Frankfurt a.M.: Suhrkamp, 1986) [DLA]

——*Wunschloses Unglück* (Frankfurt a.M.: suhrkamp taschenbuch, 1979)

HASLINGER, ADOLF, *Peter Handke: Jugend eines Schriftstellers* (Salzburg and Vienna: Residenz, 1992) [DLA]

HARLAN, THOMAS, *Rosa* (Frankfurt a.M.: Eichborn, 2000) [★]

HARPPRECHT, KLAUS, *Am Ende der Gemütlichkeit: Ein österreichisches Tagebuch* (Munich: dtv, 1989) [DLA]

HÄRTLING, PETER, *Nachgetragene Liebe* (Darmstadt and Neuwied: Sammlung Luchterhand, 1984)

HARTUNG, HARALD, ed., *Luftfracht. Internationale Poesie 1900 bis 1990* (Frankfurt a.M.: Eichborn, 1991) [★]

HAUFF, WILHELM, *Wilhelm Hauff's sämmtliche Werke mit des Dichters Leben von Gustav Schwab: Siebenzehnte stereotypirte Gesammt-Ausgabe*, 5 vols (Stuttgart: Riegersche Buchhandlung, 1879)

HAUPTMANN, GERHARD:
    TANK, KURT LOTHAR, *Gerhard Hauptmann mit Bildnissen und Selbstzeugnissen* (Reinbek bei Hamburg: rowohlts monographien, 1959) [DLA]

HEBEL, JOHANN PETER, *Werke*, ed. by Eberhard Meckel with an introduction by Robert Minder, 2 vols (Frankfurt a.M.: Insel, 1968) [DLA]

——*Biblische Geschichten* (Zurich: Manesse, 1992) [DLA]

HEINE, HEINRICH, *Sämtliche Werke*, ed. by Oskar Walzel and others, 10 vols (Leipzig: Insel, 1911–15)
    BRIEGLEB, KLAUS, *Bei den Wassern Babels: Heinrich Heine, jüdischer Schriftsteller in der Moderne* (Munich: dtv, 1997) [DLA] [★]
    MARCUSE, LUDWIG, *Heinrich Heine mit Bildnissen und Selbstzeugnissen* (Reinbek bei Hamburg: rowohlts monographien, 1966) [DLA]

STERNBERGER, DOLF, *Heinrich Heine und die Abschaffung der Sünde* (Frankfurt a.M.: Suhrkamp, 1977) [DLA]

HENSEL, SEBASTIAN, *Die Familie Mendelssohn 1729–1847* (Berlin: B. Behr, 1900) [DLA]

HERBECK, ERNST, *Alexanders poetische Texte*, ed. by Leo Navratil, with contributions by Otto Breicha, Roger Cardinal, André Heller, Ernst Jandl, Friederike Mayröcker, Reinhard Priessnitz and Gerhard Roth (Munich: dtv, 1977) [DLA]

——*Alexander* [Alexander Herbrich, i.e. Ernst Herbeck]*: Ausgewählte Texte 1961–1981* (Salzburg and Vienna: Residenz, 1982) [DLA]

——*Im Herbst da reiht der Feenwind: Gesammelte Texte 1960–1991* (Salzburg and Vienna: Residenz, 1992) [DLA]

——, and OSWALD TSCHIRTNER, *Bebende Herzen im Leibe der Hunde*, ed. by Leo Navratil (Munich: Rogner & Bernhard, 1979) [DLA] [W]

    STEINLECHNER, GISELA, *Über die Ver-rückung der Sprache: Analytische Studien zu den Texten Alexanders* (Vienna: Wilhelm Braumüller, 1989) [DLA]

HERBURGER, GÜNTER, *Birne kehrt zurück* (Munich: Luchterhand, 1996) [W]

——*Elsa* (Munich: Luchterhand, 1999) [W]

——*Das Glück: Eine Reise in Nähe und Ferne* (Munich: A1, 1994) [W]

——*Hauptlehrer Hofer: Erzählung* (Frankfurt a.M.: Sammlung Luchterhand, 1990) [W]

——*Humboldt: Reise-Novellen* (Munich: A1, 2001) [W]

——*Im Gebirge: Gedichte* (Darmstadt and Neuwied: Luchterhand, 1998) [W]

——*Kreuzwege* (Ravensburg: Oberschwäbische Verlagsanstalt, 1988) [DLA]

——*Lauf und Wahn: Mit Bildern von der Strecke* (Frankfurt a.M.: Sammlung Luchterhand, 1990) [W]

——*Die Liebe: Eine Reise durch Wohl und Wehe* (Munich: A1, 1996) [W]

——*Der Schrecken Süße* (Munich: A1, 1999) [DLA] [W]

——*Traum und Bahn* (Munich: Luchterhand, 1994) [W]

HERMANN, FRANZ, *Auf Wanderfahrt ins Wunderland: Eine abenteuerliche Reise von Passau nach Indien quer durch die Lande des Islam* (Coburg: A. Rosteutscher, 1937) [DLA]

HERZL, THEODOR, *Vision und Politik: Die Tagebücher Theodor Herzls* (Frankfurt a.M.: suhrkamp taschenbuch, 1976) [DLA]

    BEIN, ALEX, *Theodor Herzl: Biographie* (Vienna: Fiba, 1934) [DLA]

    Theodor Herzl and the Origins of Zionism, ed. by Edward Timms and Ritchie Robertson (Edinburgh: Edinburgh University Press, 1997) (= *Austrian Studies* 8) [DLA]

HERZMANOVSKY-ORLANDO, FRITZ VON, *Der Gaulschreck im Rosennetz: Lustspiel und Ballette* (Vienna and Munich: Albert Langen, 1971) [DLA]

——*Maskenspiel der Genien: Romane und Erzählungen* (Vienna and Munich: Albert Langen, 1971) [DLA]

HESSE, HERMANN:

    ZELLER, BERNHARD, *Hermann Hesse in Selbstzeugnissen und Bilddokumenten* (Reinbek bei Hamburg: rowohlts monographien, 1977) [DLA]

HILBIG, WOLFGANG, *Alte Abdeckerei* (Frankfurt a.M.: Fischer Taschenbuch, 1993)

HILDESHEIMER, WOLFGANG, *Lieblose Legenden* (Frankfurt a.M.: Bibliothek Suhrkamp, 1970)

——*Marbot: Eine Biographie* (Frankfurt a.M.: Suhrkamp, 1981)

——*Masante* (Frankfurt a.M.: suhrkamp taschenbuch, 1988)

——*Mitteilungen an Max über den Stand der Dinge und anderes* (Frankfurt a.M.: Suhrkamp, 1984)

——*Mozart* (Frankfurt a.M.: suhrkamp taschenbuch, 1980)

——*Tynset* (Frankfurt a.M.: Suhrkamp, 1965)

HOCHHUTH, ROLF, *Der Stellvertreter* (Reinbek bei Hamburg: Rowohlt, 1963)

HÖFELE, ANDREAS, *Das Tal* (Frankfurt a.M.: Fischer Taschenbuch, 1979)

HOFFMANN, E. T. A., *Der Sandmann; Das öde Haus* (Stuttgart: Reclam, 1980)

——*Tales of Hoffmann*, trans. by R. J. Hollingdale (London: Penguin Classics, 1982)

——*Der Automaten-Mensch: E. T. A. Hoffmanns Erzählung vom Sandmann*, ed. by Lienhard Wawrzyn (Berlin: Klaus Wagenbach, 1980)

Hoffmann, Heinrich, *Der Struwwelpeter* (Munich: Lucas Cranach, [n.d.])

Hohl, Ludwig, *Nächtlicher Weg* (Frankfurt a.M.: Bibliothek Suhrkamp, 1971)

Hölderlin, Friedrich, *Sämtliche Werke*, ed. by Paul Stapf (Berlin and Darmstadt: Tempel, 1936)

——*Werke und Briefe*, ed. by Friedrich Beißner and Jochen Schmidt, 2 vols (Frankfurt a.M.: Insel, 1969), I: *Gedichte: Hyperion*; II: *Der Tod des Empedokles; Aufsätze; Übersetzungen, Briefe* [DLA]

——*Gesammelte Briefe*, with an introduction by Ernst Bertram (Leipzig: Insel, [n.d.]) [DLA]

——*Poems and Fragments*, trans. and with an introduction and notes by Michael Hamburger; bilingual edition (London: Routledge and Kegan Paul, 1966) [DLA]

Hölderlin: Eine Chronik in Text und Bild, ed. by Adolf Beck and Paul Raabe (Frankfurt a.M.: Insel, 1970) [DLA]

Peters, Uwe Henrik, *Hölderlin: Wider die These vom edlen Simulanten* (Reinbek bei Hamburg: Rowohlt, 1982) [DLA]

Hofmannsthal, Hugo von, *Ausgewählte Werke*, ed. by Rudolf Hirsch, 2 vols (Frankfurt a.M.: Fischer, 1957), I: *Gedichte und Dramen*; II: *Erzählungen und Aufsätze* [DLA]

——*Das gerettete Venedig: Eine Reise nach Venedig unternommen in der Literatur zweier Jahrhunderte zum Zwecke der Besichtigung einiger venezianischer Motive...* (theatre programme, Schaubühne am Halleschen Ufer, Berlin: Spielzeit 1971–72) [DLA]

——*Der Turm* (theatre programme, Deutsches Theater, Berlin) (Berlin: Deutsches Theater, [September] 1992) [E.C.2]

Hamburger, Michael, *Hofmannsthal: Three Essays* (Princeton, NJ: Princeton University Press, 1972) [DLA]

Robertson, Ritchie, *The Dual Structure of Hofmannsthal's 'Reitergeschichte'* (offprint from *Forum for Modern Language Studies*, 14 (1978), 316–31) [DLA] [W]

——*'Ich habe ihm das Beil nicht geben können': The Heroine's Failure in Hofmannsthal's 'Elektra'* (offprint from *Orbis Litterarum*, 41 (1986), 312–31) [DLA] [W]

Volke, Werner, *Hugo von Hofmannsthal in Selbstzeugnissen und Bilddokumenten* (Reinbek bei Hamburg: rowohlts monographien, 1967) [DLA]

Holbein, Ulrich, *Samthase und Odradek* (Frankfurt a.M.: edition suhrkamp, 1990) [DLA]

Horváth, Ödön von, *Gesammelte Werke*, 8 vols (Frankfurt a.M.: edition suhrkamp, 1972) [DLA]

Krischke, Trautgott, and Hans F. Prokop, eds, *Leben und Werk in Dokumenten und Bildern* (Frankfurt a.M.: suhrkamp taschenbuch, 1972) [DLA]

Huchel, Peter, *Chausseen, Chaussen* (Frankfurt a.M: Fischer, 1963)

Innerhofer, Franz, *Schöne Tage* (Frankfurt a.M.: suhrkamp taschenbuch, 1977)

Jahnn, Hans Henny, *Das Holzschiff: Roman* [*Fluß ohne Ufer I.1*] (Frankfurt a.M.: Europäische Verlagsanstalt, 1959) [DLA] [★]

——*Die Niederschrift des Gustav Anias Horn: Roman in drei Teilen, I* [*Fluß ohne Ufer I.2*] (Frankfurt a.M.: Europäische Verlagsanstalt, 1959) [DLA] [★]

——*Die Niederschrift des Gustav Anias Horn, II* [*Fluß ohne Ufer II*] (Frankfurt a.M.: Europäische Verlagsanstalt, 1959) [DLA] [★]

——*Epilog* [*Fluß ohne Ufer III*] (Frankfurt a.M.: Europäische Verlagsanstalt, 1961) [DLA] [★]

Jandl, Ernst, *Der künstliche Baum* (Neuwied and Berlin: Sammlung Luchterhand, 1970)

——*Laut und Luise* (Neuwied and Berlin: Sammlung Luchterhand, 1971)

——*serienfuss* (Darmstadt and Neuwied: Sammlung Luchterhand, 1974)

Jean Paul, *Werke*, ed. by Norbert Miller with afterword by Walter Höllerer, 12 vols (Munich and Vienna: Reihe Hanser, 1975) [DLA]

——*Ideen-Gewimmel* (Frankfurt a.M.: Eichborn, 1996) [DLA]

——*Über das Immergrün unserer Gefühle* (Oxford: D. J. MacColl, 1819) [DLA]

Jelinek, Elfriede, *Die Klavierspielerin* (Reinbek bei Hamburg: rororo, 1990)

Johnson, Uwe, *Jahrestage: Aus dem Leben von Gesine Cresspahl. 1–4* (Frankfurt a.M.: edition suhrkamp, 1988)

——*Mutmassungen über Jakob* (Frankfurt a.M.: Fischer Bücherei, 1962)

Jonke, Gerd, *Der Kopf des Georg Friedrich Händel* (Salzburg and Vienna: Residenz, 1988) [DLA]

Jordan, Wilhelm, *Die Sebalds: Roman aus der Gegenwart*, 2 vols (Stuttgart and Leipzig: Deutsche Verlagsanstalt, 1886), i: *Das alte Haus*; ii: *Exodus*

Jung, Franz, *Der Weg nach unten: Aufzeichnungen aus einer großen Zeit* (Neuwied and Berlin: Luchterhand, 1961) [DLA]

Jung, Jochen, ed., *Österreichische Porträts: Leben und Werk bedeutender Persönlichkeiten von Maria Theresia bis Ingeborg Bachmann*, 2 vols (Salzburg and Vienna: Residenz, 1985) [D.27(a)] [DLA] [★]

Jünger, Ernst:

    Meyer, Martin, *Ernst Jünger* (Munich: dtv wissenschaft, 1993) [DLA] [★]

    Schwilk, Heimo, ed., *Ernst Jünger: Leben und Werk in Bildern und Texten* (Stuttgart: Klett-Cotta, 1988) [DLA]

Kafka, Franz, *Die Aeroplane in Brescia u. andere Texte* (Frankfurt a.M.: Fischer Bibliothek, 1977) [DLA]

——*The Castle*, trans. by J. A. Underwood (London: Penguin, 2000)

——*Die Erzählungen* (Frankfurt a.M.: S. Fischer, 1961)

——*Hochzeitsvorbereitungen auf dem Lande* (Frankfurt a.M.: Fischer Taschenbuch, 1980)

——*Metamorphosis and Other Stories*, trans. and ed. by Malcolm Pasley (London: Penguin, 1992)

——*Die Romane* (Frankfurt a.M.: S. Fischer, 1965)

——*The Trial*, trans. by Idris Parry (London: Penguin, 1994)

    Franz Kafka: Briefe 1900–1912, ed. by Hans-Gerd Koch (Kommentierte Ausgabe) (Frankfurt a.M.: Fischer, 1999) [DLA]

    Franz Kafka: Briefe 1913–März 1914, ed. by Hans-Gerd Koch (Kommentierte Ausgabe) (Frankfurt a.M.: Fischer, 1999) [DLA]

    Franz Kafka: Briefe an die Eltern aus den Jahren 1922–1924, ed. by Josef Čermäk and Martin Svatoš (Frankfurt a.M.: Fischer, 1990) [DLA]

    Franz Kafka: Briefe an Felice und andere Korrespondenz aus der Verlobungszeit, ed. by Erich Heller and Jürgen Born (Frankfurt a.M.: Fischer Taschenbuch, 1982) [DLA]

    Franz Kafka: Briefe an Milena, ed. with an afterword by Willy Haas (Frankfurt a.M.: Fischer Bücherei, 1967) [DLA]

    Franz Kafka: Briefe an Ottla und die Familie, ed. by Hartmut Binder and Klaus Wagenbach (Frankfurt a.M.: Fischer Taschenbuch, 1981) [DLA]

    Franz Kafka: Drucke zu Lebzeiten, ed. by Hans-Gerd Koch, Wolf Kittler, and Gerhard Neumann (Kommentierte Ausgabe) (Frankfurt a.M.: Fischer, 1994) [DLA]

    Franz Kafka: 'Hochlöblicher Verwaltungsausschuß!': Amtliche Schriften, ed. by Klaus Hermsdorf (Frankfurt a.M.: Sammlung Luchterhand, 1991) [DLA]

    Franz Kafka: Nachgelassene Schriften und Fragmente in der Fassung der Handschriften, i, ed. by Malcolm Pasley (Kommentierte Ausgabe) (Frankfurt a.M.: Fischer, 1993) [DLA]

    Franz Kafka: Nachgelassene Schriften und Fragmente in der Fassung der Handschriften, ii, ed. by Jost Schillemeit (Kommentierte Ausgabe) (Frankfurt a.M.: Fischer, 1992) [DLA]

    Franz Kafka: Der Prozeß: Roman in der Fassung der Handschrift, ed. by Malcolm Pasley (Kommentierte Ausgabe) (Frankfurt a.M.: Fischer, 1990) [DLA]

Franz Kafka: Der Proceß: Die Handschrift redet, ed. by Malcolm Pasley (= Marbacher Magazin, no. 52) (Marbach am Neckar: Deutsche Schillergesellschaft, 1990)) [DLA]

Franz Kafka: Der Proceß: Die Handschrift redet, ed. by Malcolm Pasley, rev. 2nd edn (= Marbacher Magazin, no. 52) (Marbach am Neckar: Deutsche Schillergesellschaft, 1991) [DLA]

Franz Kafka: Das Schloß: Roman in der Fassung der Handschrift, ed. by Malcolm Pasley (Kommentierte Ausgabe) (Frankfurt a.M.: Fischer, 1982) [DLA]

Franz Kafka: Tagebücher 1910–1923, ed. by Max Brod (Frankfurt a.M.: S. Fischer, 1967)

Franz Kafka: Tagebücher in der Fassung der Handschrift, ed. by Hans-Gerd Koch, Michael Müller, and Malcolm Pasley (Kommentierte Ausgabe) (Frankfurt a.M.: Fischer, 1990) [DLA]

Franz Kafka: Tagebücher in der Fassung der Handschrift: Kommentarband, ed. by Hans-Gerd Koch, Michael Müller, and Malcolm Pasley (Kommentierte Ausgabe) (Frankfurt a.M.: Fischer, 1990) [DLA]

Franz Kafka: Über das Schreiben, ed. by Erich Heller and Joachim Beug (Frankfurt a.M.: Fischer Taschenbuch, 1983) [DLA]

Franz Kafka: Der Verschollene: Roman in der Fassung der Handschrift, ed. by Jost Schillemeit (Kommentierte Ausgabe) (Frankfurt a.M.: Fischer, 1983) [DLA]

BAUER, JOHANN, and ISIDOR POLLAK, *Kafka und Prag* (photographs) (Stuttgart: Belser, 1971) [G.6] [DLA]

BUBER-NEUMANN, MARGARETE, *Mistress to Kafka: The Life and Death of Milena* (London: Secker and Warburg, 1966) [DLA]

DELEUZE, GILLES, and FÉLIX GUATTARI, *Kafka: Für eine kleine Literatur*, trans. by Burkhart Kroeber (Frankfurt a.M.: edition suhrkamp, 1976) [DLA]

GRÖZINGER, KARL ERICH, *Kafka und die Kabbala: Das Jüdische im Werk und Denken von Franz Kafka* (Frankfurt a.M.: Eichborn, 2002) [DLA]

HACKERMÜLLER, ROTRAUT, *Das Leben, das mich stört: Eine Dokumentation zu Kafkas letzten Jahren, 1917–1924* (Vienna-Berlin: Medusa, 1974) [DLA]

KOCH, HANS-GERD, ed., *'Als Kafka mir entgegenkam...': Erinnerungen an Franz Kafka* (Berlin: Wagenbach, 1995) [DLA]

KRAFT, WERNER, *Franz Kafka: Durchdringung und Geheimnis* (Frankfurt a.M.: Bibliothek Suhrkamp, 1968) [DLA]

KUNA, FRANZ, *Kafka: Literature as Corrective Punishment* (London: Elek, 1974) [DLA]

——*On Kafka: Semi-centenary Perspectives* (London: Paul Elek, 1976) [DLA]

MAIROWITZ, DAVID ZANE, and ROBERT CRUMB, *Kafka for Beginners* (Cambridge: Icon Books, 1993) [DLA]

MÜLLER-SEIDEL, WALTER, *Die Deportation des Menschen: Kafkas Erzählung 'In der Strafkolonie' im europäischen Kontext* (Frankfurt a.M.: Fischer Taschenbuch, 1989) [DLA]

NORTHEY, ANTHONY, *Kafkas Mischpoche* (Berlin: Wagenbach, 1988) [DLA]

ROBERT, MARTHE, *Einsam wie Franz Kafka*, trans. by Eva Michel-Moldenhauer (Frankfurt a.M.: Fischer Taschenbuch, 1987) [DLA]

SCHIRRMACHER, FRANK, ed., *Verteidigung der Schrift: Kafkas 'Prozeß'* (Frankfurt a.M.: edition suhrkamp, 1987) [DLA]

SPEIRS, RONALD, and BEATRICE SANDBERG, *Franz Kafka* (London: Macmillan Modern Novelists, 1997)

WAGENBACH, KLAUS, *Franz Kafka in Selbstzeugnissen und Bilddokumenten* (Reinbek bei Hamburg: Rowohlt Bildmonographien, 1970) [DLA]

——*Franz Kafka: Bilder aus seinem Leben* (Berlin: Wagenbach, 1983) [DLA]

WAGNEROVÁ, ALENA, *Die Famile Kafka aus Prag* (Frankfurt a.M.: Fischer Taschenbuch, 2001) [DLA]

WALSER, MARTIN, *Beschreibung einer Form. Versuch über Franz Kafka* (Frankfurt a.M.: Ullstein Buch, 1972) [DLA]

ZISCHLER, HANNS, *Kafka geht ins Kino* (Reinbek bei Hamburg: Rowohlt, 1996) [G.31]
[DLA]

Franz Kafka 1883–1924. Goethe-Institut exhibition catalogue in English (Berlin: Akademie der Künste, [n.d., 1969?]) [DLA]

Franz Kafka, nachgestellt (= *Freibeuter*, no. 16 (1983)) [DLA]

KAIN, FRANZ, *In Grodek kam der Abendstern: Roman* (Weitra [Austria]: Bibliothek der Provinz, [n.d.]) [DLA]

KEIN, ERNST, *Weana Schbrüch* (Salzburg and Vienna: Residenz, 1990) [*]

KELLER, GOTTFRIED, *Werke*, 4 vols (Leipzig: Insel, 1921), I: *Gedichte; Das Sinngedicht*; II: *Der grüne Heinrich*; III: *Die Leute von Seldwyla; Sieben Legenden; Erzählungen*; IV: *Zürcher Novellen; Martin Salander; Therese*

——*Der grüne Heinrich*, 4 vols (Stuttgart and Berlin: Cotta, 1919)

BAECHTOLD, JAKOB, *Gottfried Keller's Leben*, 3 vols (Stuttgart and Berlin: Cotta, 1895–1903) [DLA]

BREITENBRUCH, BERND, *Gottfried Keller mit Selbstdarstellungen und Bilddokumenten* (Reinbek bei Hamburg: rowohlts monographien, 1994) [DLA]

MUSCHG, ADOLF, *Gottfried Keller* (Frankfurt a.M.: suhrkamp taschenbuch, 1980) [DLA]

WYSLING, HANS, ed., *Gottfried Keller 1819–1890* (Zurich and Munich: Artemis, 1990) [DLA]

KEMPOWSKI, WALTER, *Das Echolot: Ein kollektives Tagebuch*, 4 vols (Munich: Albrecht Knaus, 1993) [DLA] [*]

KIPPHARDT, HEINAR, *Joel Brand: Die Geschichte eines Geschäfts* (Frankfurt a.M.: edition suhrkamp, 1965)

KLEIST, HEINRICH VON, *Gesamtausgabe*, 8 vols (Munich: dtv, 1964–69), I: *Gedichte; Dramen: Erster Teil*; II: *Dramen: Zweiter Teil*, 2nd edn (1968); III: *Dramen: Dritter Teil*, 2nd edn (1969); IV: *Erzählungen*, 5th edn (1972); V: *Andenken; Kleine Schriften* (1964); VI: *Briefe 1793–1804* (1964); VII: *Briefe 1805–1811; Lebensdaten* (1964); VIII: *Lebensspuren* [DLA]

—— *Werke* [including *Gedichte; Die Familie Schroffenstein; Der zerbrochene Krug*], bound in one vol. with an essay 'Ein Bild seines Lebens und Wirkens' by Rudolf Gen ([n.p. [?]: n. pub., n.d.])

——, ed., *Vollständige Ausgabe der Berliner Abendblätter, 1 October 1810–30 March 1811*, with an afterword and index by Helmut Sembdner (Wiesbaden: VMA, [n.d.]) (facsimile of 1925 edn) [DLA]

——*Die Marquise von O...; Die Verlobung in St. Domingo* (Stuttgart: Reclam UB, 1980)

——*The Marquise of O — and Other Stories*, trans. by David Luke (London: Penguin Classics, 1978)

GRATHOFF, DIRK, *Kleists Geheimnisse: Unbekannte Seiten einer Biographie* (Opladen and Wiesbaden: Westdeutscher Verlag, 1993) [DLA]

——*Kleist: Geschichte, Politik, Sprache* (Opladen and Wiesbaden: Westdeutscher Verlag, 1999) [DLA]

SIEBERT, EBERHARD, *Heinrich von Kleist: Leben und Werk im Bild* (Frankfurt a.M.: insel taschenbuch, 1980) [DLA]

ZIMMERMANN, HANS DIETER, *Kleist, die Liebe und der Tod* (Frankfurt a.M.: Athäneum, 1989) [DLA]

KLEMPERER, VICTOR, *Ich will Zeugnis ablegen bis zum letzten*, 2 vols (Berlin: Aufbau, 1995), I: *Tagebücher 1933–1941*; II: *Tagebücher 1942–1945* [DLA] [*]

KLINGEMANN, AUGUST, *Nachtwachen von Bonaventura*, with illustrations by Lovis Corinth, ed. and with an afterword by Jost Schillemeit (Frankfurt a.M.: insel taschenbuch, 1974) [DLA]

KLUGE, ALEXANDER, *Chronik der Gefühle*, 2 vols (Frankfurt a.M.: Suhrkamp, 2000), I: *Basisgeschichten*; II: *Lebensläufe* [DLA]

——*Lebensläufe: Anwesenheitsliste für eine Beerdigung* (Frankfurt a.M.: suhrkamp taschenbuch, 1977)

——*Lernprozesse mit tödlichem Ausgang* (Frankfurt a.M.: edition suhrkamp, 1984)

——*Neue Geschichten, Hefte 1–18: 'Unheimlichkeit der Zeit'* (Frankfurt a.M.: edition suhrkamp, 1978)

—— *Schlachtbeschreibung: Der organisatorische Aufbau eines Unglücks* (Munich: Goldmann, 1978)

——*Theodor Fontane, Heinrich von Kleist, Anna Wilde* (Berlin: Klaus Wagenbach, 1987)

KOEPPEN, WOLFGANG, *Wolfgang Koeppen: Gesammelte Werke*, 6 vols (boxed set) (Frankfurt a.M.: suhrkamp taschenbuch, 1990) [★]

——*Jakob Littners Aufzeichnungen aus einem Erdloch* (Frankfurt a.M.: Suhrkamp Jüdischer Verlag, 1992)

KOGON, EUGEN and WALTER DIRKS, eds, *Frankfurter Hefte: Zeitschrift für Kultur und Politik*, facsimile edn, 7 vols [1946–52] (Frankfurt a.M.: Fischer Taschenbuch, 1978) [★]

KOLLERITSCH, ALFRED, *Allemann* (Salzburg and Vienna: Residenz, 1989) [W]

KOLMAR, GERTRUD, *Das lyrische Werk* (Munich: Kösel, 1960) [DLA] [★]

KÖPF, GERHARD, *Borges gibt es nicht* (Munich: Luchterhand, 1991) [★]

——*Eulensehen* (Munich and Vienna: Hanser, 1989) [★]

——*Ezra & Luis oder die Erstbesteigung des Ulmer Münsters: Ein Spiel* (Innsbruck: Edition Löwenzahn and Eggingen; Edition Isele, 1994)

——*Innerfern* (Frankfurt a.M.: Collection S. Fischer, 1983) [W]

——*Der Kühlmonarch: Eine Selberlebensbeschreibung* (Austin, TX: Dimension Press, 1995) [★]

——*Nurmi oder die Reise zu den Forellen* (Munich: Luchterhand, 1996) [★]

——*Papas Koffer* (Hamburg: Luchterhand, 1993) [★]

——*Piranesis Traum* (Hamburg and Zurich: Luchterhand, 1992) [★]

——*Die Strecke* (Hamburg: Sammlung Luchterhand, 1991)

—— *Vom Schmutz und vom Nest: Aufsätze* (Frankfurt a. M.: Sammlung Luchterhand, 1991) [W]

——*Der Weg nach Eden* (Munich and Zurich: Piper, 1994) [★]

KORTUM, DR KARL ARNOLD, *Die Jobsiade: Ein komisches Heldengedicht in drei Teilen* (Berlin: Deutsche Bibliothek, [n.d.] [pre-1915]) [DLA]

KRACAUER, SIEGFRIED, *Schriften*, 5 vols (Frankfurt a.M.: Suhrkamp, 1971–79) (vols I, II, IV extant), I: *Soziologie als Wissenschaft; Der Detektiv-Roman; Die Angestellten*; II: *Von Caligari zu Hitler*, trans. by Ruth Baumgarten and Karsten Witte (1979); IV: *Geschichte: Vor den letzten Dingen*, trans. by Karsten Witte (1971) [DLA]

KRAUS, KARL, *Die chinesische Mauer* (Frankfurt a.M.: Fischer Bücherei, 1966) [DLA]

——*Die letzten Tage der Menschheit*, 2 vols (Munich: dtv sonderreihe, 1966)

——*Literatur und Lüge* (Munich: dtv, 1962) [DLA]

——*Nachts: Aphorismen* (Munich: dtv, 1968) [DLA]

——*Nestroy und die Nachwelt*, with an afterword by Hans Mayer (Frankfurt a.M.: Bibliothek Suhrkamp, 1975) [DLA]

——*Shakespeares Sonette*, trans. by Karl Kraus (Munich: Kösel 1964)

——*Sittlichkeit und Kriminalität* (Frankfurt a.M.: Fischer Bücherei, 1966) [DLA]

——*Die Sprache* (Munich: dtv, 1969) [DLA]

——*Weltgericht* (Frankfurt a.M.: Fischer Bücherei, 1968) [DLA]

Karl Kraus, ed. by Ulrich Ott and Friedrich Pfäfflin (Marbacher Katalog, 52) (Marbach am Neckar: Deutsche Schillergesellschaft, 1999) (exhibition catalogue) [DLA] [★]

SCHICK, PAUL, *Karl Kraus in Selbstzeugnissen und Bilddokumenten* (Reinbek bei Hamburg: Rowohlt Bildmonographien, 1965) [DLA]

WEIGEL, HANS, *Karl Kraus oder die Macht der Ohnmacht* (Munich: dtv, 1978) [DLA]

KRETZEN, FRIEDERIKE, *Ich bin ein Hügel* (Zurich: Nagel & Kimche, 1998) [W]

——*Indianer* (Basle: Bruckner & Thünker, 1996) [W]

——*Die Probe* (Zurich: Nagel & Kimche, 1991) [W]

——*Die Souffleuse* (Zurich: Nagel & Kimche, 1989)

KROETZ, FRANZ XAVER, *Heimarbeit; Hartnäckig; Männersache: Drei Stücke* (Frankfurt a.M.: edition suhrkamp, 1973)

——*Mensch Meier; Der stramme Max; Wer durchs Laub geht...: Drei neue Stücke* (Frankfurt a.M.: edition suhrkamp, 1979)

——*Oberösterreich; Dolomitenstadt Lienz; Maria Magdalena; Münchner Kindl* (Frankfurt a.M.: edition suhrkamp, 1977)

——*Stallerhof; Geisterbahn; Lieber Fritz; Wunschkonzert: Vier Stücke* (Frankfurt a.M.: edition suhrkamp, 1973)

KÜRNBERGER, FERDINAND, *Der Amerikamüde: Amerikanisches Kulturbild* (Frankfurt a.M.: insel taschenbuch, 1986) [DLA]

LÄNGLE, ULRIKE, *Il Prete Rosso: Zwei Erzählungen* (Salzburg and Vienna: Residenz, 1996) [DLA]

LANDAUER, GUSTAV, *Erkenntnis und Befreiung: Ausgewählte Reden und Aufsätze* (Frankfurt a.M.: edition suhrkamp, 1976) [DLA]

LEDIG, GERT, *Die Stalinorgel*, afterword by Florian Radvan (Frankfurt a.M.: Bibliothek Suhrkamp, 2000) [★]

——*Die Vergeltung* (Frankfurt a.M.: Suhrkamp Verlag, 1999) [★]

LEISEGANG, DIETER, *Lauter letzte Worte: Gedichte und Miniaturen*, ed. by Karl Corino (Frankfurt a.M.: edition suhrkamp, 1980)

LEISEWITZ, JOHANN ANTON, *Schriften* (Vienna: Kaulfuß and Armbruster, 1816) [DLA]

LENZ, HERMANN, *Der Kutscher und der Wappenmaler* (Frankfurt a.M.: Bibliothek Suhrkamp, 1975)

——*Neue Zeit* (Frankfurt a.M.: suhrkamp taschenbuch, 1969)

LENZ, JAKOB MICHAEL REINHOLD, *Werke und Briefe*, ed. by Sigrid Damm, 3 vols (Frankfurt a.M.: insel taschenbuch, 1992) [DLA] [★]

——*Anmerkungen übers Theater: Shakespeare-Arbeiten und Shakespeare-Übersetzungen*, ed.by Hans-Günther Schwarz (Stuttgart: Reclam, 1989)

——*Der Hofmeister* (Stuttgart: Reclam UB, 1991)

——*Der Hofmeister* (Stuttgart: Reclam UB, 1994) (2 copies)

——*Der Hofmeister* (Stuttgart: Reclam UB, 1996)

——*Die Soldaten* (Stuttgart: Reclam UB, 1991)

DAMM, SIGRID, *Vögel, die verkünden Land: Das Leben des Jakob Michael Reinhold Lenz* (Frankfurt a.M.: insel taschenbuch, 1992) [DLA]

HOHOFF, CURT, *Jakob Michael Reinhold Lenz mit Selbstzeugnissen und Bilddokumenten* (Reinbek bei Hamburg: rowohlts monographien, 1988) [DLA]

KRÄMER, HERBERT, ed., *Erläuterungen und Dokumente: J. M. R. Lenz, 'Die Soldaten'* (Stuttgart: Reclam UB, 1990)

LESSING, GOTTHOLD EPHRAIM, *Werke*, ed. by Kurt Wölfel, 3 vols (Frankfurt a.M.: Insel, 1967) [DLA]

LESSING-AKADEMIE-WOLFENBÜTTEL, *Lessings 'Nathan' und jüdische Emanzipation im Lande Braunschweig* (Wolfenbüttel: Lessing-Akademie, 1990) [DLA]

HEIN, JÜRGEN, ed., *Erläuterungen und Dokumente: G. E. Lessing: 'Minna von Barnhelm'* (Leipzig and Stuttgart: Reclam UB, 1970)

LESSING, THEODOR, *Einmal und nie wieder* (Gütersloh: Bertelsmann Sachbuchverlag, 1969) [DLA] [★]

LICHTENBERG, GEORG CHRISTOPH, *Die Heirat nach der Mode* (Frankfurt a.M.: Insel-Bücherei, 1966) [DLA]

——*Der Weg der Buhlerin* (Frankfurt a.M.: Insel-Bücherei, 1969) [DLA]

——*Der Weg des Liederlichen* (Frankfurt a.M.: Insel-Bücherei, 1968) [DLA]

Liliencron, Detlev von, *Kriegsnovellen* (Leipzig: Schuster & Loeffler, [n.d.]) [DLA]

Loquai, Franz, ed., *Die Alpen: Eine Landschaft und ihre Menschen in Texten deutschsprachiger Autoren des 18. und 19. Jahrhunderts* ([Munich]: Goldmann, 1996) [DLA]

Mann, Heinrich, *Politische Essays* (Frankfurt a.M.: Bibliothek Suhrkamp, 1968)

Mann, Thomas, *Buddenbrooks* (Frankfurt a.M.: Fischer Taschenbuch, 1974)

——*Buddenbrooks: Verfall einer Familie* (Berlin: Fischer, 1930) [DLA]

——*Doktor Faustus* (Frankfurt a.M.: Fischer Taschenbuch, 1974)

——*Der Tod in Venedig* (Frankfurt a.M.: Fischer Taschenbuch, 1974)

——*Tonio Kröger; Mario und der Zauberer* (Frankfurt a.M.: Fischer Taschenbuch, 1974)

——*Tristan* (Stuttgart: Reclam UB, 1979)

——*Der Zauberberg*, 2 vols (Berlin: Fischer, 1925) [DLA]

    Thomas Mann: Das essayistische Werk, ed. by Hans Bürgin, 8 vols (Frankfurt a.M. and Hamburg: Fischer Bücherei Moderne Klassiker, 1968) [DLA]

    Baumgart, Reinhard, Joachim Kaiser, Kurt Sontheimer, Peter Wapnewski, and Hans Wysling, *Thomas Mann und München: Fünf Vorträge* (Frankfurt a.M.: Fischer Taschenbuch, 1989) [DLA]

    Harprecht, Klaus, *Thomas Mann: Eine Biographie* (Reinbek bei Hamburg: Rowohlt, 1995) [DLA]

    Schröter, Klaus, *Thomas Mann in Selbstzeugnissen und Bilddokumenten* (Reinbek bei Hamburg: rowohlts monographien, 1968) [DLA]

Marchi, Otto, *Schweizer Geschichte für Ketzer* (Zurich: rotpunktverlag, 1985)

Marloh, Bernd, 'Abendrot: Erzählung' (unpublished typescript, December 2001) [W]

Maron, Monika, *Stille Zeile Sechs* (Frankfurt a.M.: Fischer, 1993)

Marti, Kurt, *Rosa Loui: vierzig gedicht ir bärner umgangsschprach* (Neuwied and Berlin: Luchterhand, 1967)

May, Karl:

    Schmiedt, Helmut, ed., *Karl May* (Frankfurt a.M.: suhrkamp taschenbuch, 1983) [DLA]

Meier, Albert, and others, eds, *Meistererzählungen der deutschen Romantik* (Munich: dtv klassik, 1985)

Menasse, Robert, *Das Land ohne Eigenschaften: Essay zum österreichischen Geist* (Vienna: Sonderzahl, 1992) [DLA] [W]

——*Selige Zeiten, brüchige Welt* (Salzburg and Vienna: Residenz, 1991) [★]

——*Die sozialpartnerschaftliche Ästhetik: Essays zum österreichischen Geist* (Vienna: Sonderzahl, 1990) [DLA] [W]

Merz, Klaus, *Tremolo Trümmer* (Zurich: Ammann, 1988) [W]

Meyer, Conrand Ferdinand, *Novellen* (Munich and Zurich: Droemersche Verlagsanstalt, [n.d.] [pre-1960])

Meyer, E. Y., *Eine entfernte Ähnlichkeit* (Frankfurt a.M.: suhrkamp taschenbuch, 1982)

——*Ein Reisender in Sachen Umsturz* (Frankfurt a.M.: suhrkamp taschenbuch, 1983)

——*Die Rückfahrt* (Frankfurt a.M.: suhrkamp taschenbuch, 1980)

——*In Trubschachen* (Frankfurt a.M.: suhrkamp taschenbuch, 1979)

Mitgutsch, Waltraud Anna, *Die Züchtigung* (Munich: dtv, 1987)

Mörike, Eduard:

    Linsenmaier-Wolf, Christa, *'zu Dreien in Ruhe und Frieden geborgen': Eduard Mörike in Fellbach*, Spuren, 37 (Marbach: Deutsche Schillergesellschaft, 1997) [DLA]

    Holthusen, Hans Egon, *Eduard Mörike mit Selbstzeugnissen und Bilddokumenten*, 9th edn (Reinbek bei Hamburg: rowohlts monographien, 1995) [DLA]

Morsbach, Petra, *Opernroman* (Frankfurt a.M.: Eichborn, 1998) [DLA] [★]

Müller, Wilhelm, *Die Winterreise und andere Gedichte*, ed. by Hans-Rüdiger Schwab (Frankfurt a.M.: insel taschenbuch, 1986) [DLA]

Musäus, J. K. A., *Volksmärchen der Deutschen* (Munich: dtv, 1977) [DLA]

MUSIL, ROBERT, *Der Mann ohne Eigenschaften* (Hamburg: Rowohlt, 1956) [DLA]
    WILLEMSEN, ROGER, *Robert Musil: Vom intellektuellen Eros* (Munich: Serie Piper, 1985) [DLA]
NADOLNY, STEN, *Die Entdeckung der Langsamkeit* (Munich: Serie Piper, 1989)
NESTROY, JOHANN NEPOMUK, *Nestroy: Sämtliche Werke: Historisch-kritische Gesamtausgabe*, 12 vols bound in 15 (Vienna: Kunstverlag Anton Schroll and Co, 1924–30) [DLA] [★]
    BASIL, OTTO, *Johann Nestroy in Selbstzeugnissen und Bilddokumenten* (Reinbek bei Hamburg: rowohlts monographien, 1967) [DLA]
NÖBEL, MANFRED, ed., *Stücke für Puppentheater 1900–1945* (Berlin: Henschelverlag, 1974) [DLA]
NONNENMANN, KLAUS, *Teddy Flesh* (Frankfurt a.M.: Frankfurter Verlagsanstalt, 1988) [★]
NOSSACK, HANS ERICH, *Interview mit dem Tode* (Frankfurt a.M.: Bibliothek Suhrkamp, 1972)
—— *Pseudoautobiographische Glossen* (Frankfurt a.M.: edition suhrkamp, 1971)
NOVALIS [= FRIEDRICH VON HARDENBERG], *Schriften*, ed. by J. Minor, 4 vols (Jena: Diedrichs, 1923) [DLA]
    Novalis, Arabic trans. by Fuad Rifka (Beirut: Dar SADER, 1997) [DLA]
NOWAK, ERNST, *Addio, Kafka* (Salzburg and Vienna: Residenz, 1987) [★]
OCHS, GERHARD, *Der deutsche Krieg: Zwei Erzählungen* (Salzburg and Vienna: Residenz, 1990) [DLA]
PANIZZA, OSKAR, *Aus dem Tagebuch eines Hundes: Mit einem Vorspann für Leser von Martin Langbehn...* (Munich: Matthes and Seitz, 1997) [DLA]
—— *Die kriminelle Psychose, genannt Psicopathia criminalis: Hilfsbuch für Ärzte, Laien, Juristen, Vormünder, Verwaltungsbeamte, Minister etc.* (Munich: Matthes & Seitz, 1978) [DLA]
PEINTNER, MAX, *Krieg nach dem Sieg* (Salzburg and Vienna: Residenz, 1995) [★]
PERUTZ, LEO, *Herr, erbarme dich meiner* (Reinbek bei Hamburg: rororo, 1989) [DLA]
—— *Wohin rollst du, Äpfelchen* (Reinbek bei Hamburg: rororo, 1989) [DLA]
PETZOLDT, LEANDER, ed., *Grause Thaten sind geschehen: 31 Moritaten aus dem verflossenen Jahrhundert*, facsimile edn (Munich: Heimeran, 1968) [DLA]
PICARD, JACOB, *Werke*, ed. by Manfred Bosch, 2 vols (Konstanz: Faude, 1991), I: *Erzählungen aus dem Judentum; Literarische Essays*; II: *Gedichte; Autobiographische Erzählungen* [DLA]
    Jacob Picard 1883–1967. Dichter des deutschen Landjudentums, ed. by Manfred Bosch and Jost Grosspietschs, Literarische Topographie, 3 (Freiburg i.Br.: Kulturamt, 1992) (exhibition catalogue) [DLA]
QUALTINGER, HELMUT, and CARL MERZ, *Der Herr Karl und weiteres Heiteres* (Reinbek bei Hamburg: rororo, 1966)
RAIMUND, FERDINAND, *Gesammelte Werke*, ed. with an introduction by Otto Rommel (Gütersloh: Sigbert Mohn, 1962) [DLA]
    URBACH, REINHARD, ed., *'... den 13. war ich bey ihm': Das Raimund-Tagebuch der Antonie Wagner* (Salzburg and Vienna: Residenz, 1992) [DLA]
RANSMAYR, CHRISTOPH, *Das Labyrinth: Drei Prosastücke* (Frankfurt a.M.: Fischer, 1997) [DLA]
—— *Die letzte Welt: Roman, mit einem Ovidischen Repertoire* (Nördlingen: Franz Greno, 1988) [DLA]
—— *Morbus Kithara: Roman* (Frankfurt a.M.: Fischer, 1995) [DLA] [★]
—— *Die Schrecken des Eises und der Finsternis: Roman*, with 11 illustrations (Frankfurt a.M.: Fischer Taschenbuch, 1987) [DLA]
    KIESEL. HELMUTH, and GEORG WÖHRLES, *'Keinem bleibt seine Gestalt': Ovids 'Metamorphoses' und Christoph Ransmayrs 'Letzte Welt': Essays zu einem interdisziplinären Kolloquium* (Bamberg: Fußnoten zur neueren deutschen Literatur, 1990) [DLA]
RATHENAU, WALTHER:
    WILDE, HARRY, *Walther Rathenau in Selbstzeugnissen und Bilddokumenten* (Reinbek bei Hamburg: rowohlts monographien, 1971) [DLA]

Reck, Friedrich, *Tagebuch eines Verzweifelten* (Frankfurt a.M.: Eichborn, 1994) [DLA]

Reuter, Fritz, *Ausgewählte Werke in sechs Bänden*, 6 vols bound in 2 (Leipzig: Reclam, [n.d.]) [DLA] [*]

Rezzori, Gregor von, *Ein Fremder in Lolitaland: Ein Essay / A Stranger in Lolitaland: An Essay*, bilingual edn, trans. from the American and with an afterword by Uwe Friesel (Hildesheim: Claassen, 1993) [DLA]

——*Ein Hermelin in Tschernopol* (Reinbek bei Hamburg: rororo, 1966)

——*Kain* (Munich: Bertelsmann, 2001) [DLA]

——*Maghrebinische Geschichten* (Reinbek bei Hamburg: rororo, 1964)

——*Memoiren eines Antisemiten* (Frankfurt a.M.: Fischer Taschenbuch, 1981)

Richter, Hans Werner, *Im Etablissement der Schmetterlinge: Einundzwanzig Porträts aus der Gruppe 47* (Munich: dtv, 1988)

Richter, Ludwig, *Bechsteins Märchenbuch* (Leipzig: Georg Wigand, 1857)

Riedl, Joachim, *Das Geniale; Das Gemeine; Versuch über Wien*, with 7 pen and wash drawings by Walter Schmögner (Munich: Piper, 1992) [DLA] [*]

Rilke, Rainer Maria, *Werke*, with an introduction by Beda Allemann, 6 vols (Frankfurt a.M.: Insel, 1984) [*]

——*Gesammelte Gedichte* (Frankfurt a.M: Insel, 1962)

——*Geschichten vom lieben Gott* (Leipzig: Insel, 1928)

   Holthusen, Hans Egon, *Rainer Maria Rilke in Selbstzeugnissen und Bilddokumenten* (Reinbek bei Hamburg: rowohlts monographien, 1962) [DLA]

Rosegger, Peter, *Lebens-Beschreibung: Die Schriften des Waldschulmeisters* (Salzburg and Vienna: Residenz Verlag, 1993) [DLA] [*]

Rosenberg, Otto, *Das Brennglas: aufgezeichnet von Ulrich Enzensberger* (Frankfurt a.M.: Eichborn, 1998) [*]

Roth, Gerhard, *Am Abgrund*, with cover and illustrations by Günter Brus (Frankfurt a.M.: Fischer, 1986) [DLA]

——*Das doppelköpfige Österreich: Essays, Polemiken, Interviews* (Frankfurt a.M.: Fischer Taschenbuch, 1995) [DLA]

——*Im tiefsten Österreich* (Frankfurt a.M.: Fischer, 1990) [DLA]

——*Landläufiger Tod* (Frankfurt a.M.: Fischer, 1984) [DLA]

——*Lichtenberg* (Vienna and Munich: Thomas Sessler (Der Souffleurkasten), 1993)

——*Eine Reise in das Innere von Wien: Essays* (Frankfurt a.M.: Fischer, 1991) [DLA]

——*Die schönen Bilder beim Trabrennen* (Frankfurt a.M.: Fischer Taschenbuch, 1982)

——*Der Stille Ozean* (Frankfurt a.M.: Fischer, 1980) [DLA]

——*Der Stille Ozean* (Frankfurt a.M.: Fischer Taschenbuch, 1985)

——*Winterreise* (Frankfurt a.M.: Fischer Taschenbuch, 1980)

   Schütte, Uwe, *Auf der Spur der Vergessenen: Gerhard Roth und seine Archive des Schweigens* (Vienna: Böhlau, 1997) [DLA] [W]

   Wittstock, Uwe, ed., *Gerhard Roth: Materialien zu 'Die Archive des Schweigens'* (Frankfurt a.M.: Fischer Taschenbuch, 1994) [DLA]

Roth, Joseph, *Werke*, ed. by Klaus Westermann and Fritz Hackert, 6 vols (Cologne: Kiepenheuer & Witsch, 1989–91), i: *Das journalistische Werk 1915–1923*, ed. by Klaus Westermann; ii: *Das journalistische Werk 1924–1928*, ed. by Klaus Westermann (1990); iii: *Das journalistische Werk 1929–1939*, ed. by Klaus Westermann (1991); iv: *Romane und Erzählungen 1916–1929*, ed. by Fritz Hackert (1989); v: *Romane und Erzählungen 1930–1936*, ed. by Fritz Hackert (1990); vi: *Romane und Erzählungen 1936–1940*, ed. by Fritz Hackert (1991) [DLA]

——*Das falsche Gewicht* (Reinbek bei Hamburg: rororo, 1981)

   Nürnberger, Helmuth, *Joseph Roth in Selbstzeugnissen und Bilddokumenten* (Reinbek bei Hamburg: rowohlts monographien, 1981) [DLA]

ROTH, PATRICK, *Die Christustrilogie: Riverside; Johnny Shines; Corpus Christi* (3 vols in slipcase with a CD) (Frankfurt a.M.: Suhrkamp, 1993–98) [W] [★]

——*Meine Reise zu Chaplin* (Frankfurt a.M.: Suhrkamp, 1998) [★]

RÜCKERT, FRIEDRICH, *Werke*, critical edition with commentary by Georg Ellinger, 2 vols (Leipzig and Vienna: Bibliographisches Institut, [1897]), I: *Gedichte*; II: *Lehrgedichte; Erzählungen* [DLA]

——*Kindertodtenlieder*, ed. by Hans Wollschläger (Nördlingen: Greno, 1988) [★]

SAAR, FERDINAND VON, *Ginevra und andere Novellen*, selected and with an afterword by Karlheinz Rosbacher (Frankfurt a.M.: Ullstein Taschenbuch, 1983) [DLA]

SACHS, NELLY, *Ausgewählte Gedichte*, with an afterword by Hans Magnus Enzensberger (Frankfurt a.M.: edition suhrkamp, 1963)

——*Das Leiden Israels: Eli; In den Wohnungen des Todes; Sternverdunkelung* (Frankfurt a.M.: edition suhrkamp, 1964)

DINESEN, RUTH, *Nelly Sachs: Eine Biographie* (Frankfurt a.M.: Suhrkamp, 1992) [★]

SCHÄFER, HANS DIETER, *Auf der Flucht: Meine Kindheit in Bildern* (Neumarkt: Verlag Thomas Reche, 1999) [W]

——*Spät am Leben: Zwanzig Gedichte* (Warmbronn: Keicher, 2001) [DLA]

SCHILLER, FRIEDRICH, *Sämmtliche Werke*, 12 vols bound in 5 (Stuttgart and Tübingen: Cotta, 1838) [DLA]

——*Friedrich Schiller: Sein Leben und seine Dichtungen*, 4 vols (Berlin: Volksbühnen-Verlags und Vertriebs G.m.b.h, 1924)

——*Der Verbrecher aus verlorener Ehre* (Berlin: Wagenbachs Taschenbücher, 1984) [DLA]

SCHITTEK, CLAUDIA, *Der IrrGarten: Ein Buch voller Rätsel* (Frankfurt a.M.: Eichborn, 1992) [DLA] [★]

SCHLEGEL-SCHELLING, CAROLINE, *Die Kunst zu Leben*, ed. and with an essay by Sigrid Damm (Frankfurt a.M.: insel taschenbuch, 1997) [DLA] [W]

SCHLÜTER, WOLFGANG, *Dufays Requiem: Roman* (Frankfurt a.M.: Eichborn.Berlin, 2001) [DLA] [W]

——*Eines Fensters Schatten oder Mercurius' Hochzeit mit der Philologie* (Berlin: KULTuhr, 1984) [DLA]

——*John Field und die Himmels-Electricität: Skizzen* (Frankfurt a.M.: Eichborn.Berlin, 1998) [DLA]

SCHMIDT, ARNO, *Aus dem Leben eines Fauns* (Frankfurt a.M.: Fischer Taschenbuch, 1988)

——*Brand's Haide* (Frankfurt a.M.: Fischer Taschenbuch, 1987)

——*Massenbach: Historische Revue* (Frankfurt a.M.: Fischer Taschenbuch, 1997)

——*Nachrichten von Büchern und Menschen*, 2 vols (Frankfurt a.M.: Fischer Taschenbuch, 1980–81), I: *Zur Literatur des 18. Jahrhunderts*; II: *Zur Literatur des 19. Jahrhunderts*

SCHMIDT, EVA, *Ein Vergleich mit dem Leben* (Salzburg and Vienna: Residenz, 1985) [★]

——*Reigen: Eine Erzählung* (Salzburg and Vienna: Residenz, 1988) [DLA]

SCHNITZLER, ARTHUR, *Die erzählenden Schriften*, 2 vols (Frankfurt a.M.: Fischer, 1961) [DLA]

——*Theaterstücke*, 4 vols (Berlin: Fischer, 1912) [DLA] [★]

——*Die Braut; Traumnovelle* (Stuttgart: Reclam UB, 1976)

——*Jugend in Wien: Eine Autobiographie* (Frankfurt a.M.: Fischer Taschenbuch, 1981) [DLA]

SCHRÖDER, JÜRGEN, and others, eds, *Die Stunde Null in der deutschen Literatur. Ausgewählte Texte* (Stuttgart: Reclam UB, 1995)

SCHROTT, RAOUL, *Le désert de Lop Nor*, trans. from the German by Nicole Casanova (Arles: Actes Sud, 2001) [DLA]

——*Finis Terrae: Ein Nachlass: Roman* (Innsbruck: Haymon, 1995) [DLA] [W]

——*Tropen: Über das Erhabene* (Munich: Hanser, 1998) [DLA]

Schulze, Ingo, *Simple Storys* (Berlin: Berlin Verlag, 1998) [W]

Schwaiger, Brigitte and Eva Deutsch, *Die Galizianerin* (Vienna: Zsolnay, 1982)

Sealsfield, Charles, *Die Farbigen; Nathan, der Squatterregulator* (Berlin: Robert Bein Kommanditgesellschaft, [n.d.]) [DLA] [★]

——*Das Kajütenbuch* (Berlin: Robert Bein Kommanditgesellschaft, [n.d.]) [DLA]

——*Morton oder die große Tour* (Berlin: Robert Bein Kommanditgesellschaft, [n.d.]) [DLA] [★]

——*Österreich wie es ist oder Skizzen von Fürstenhöfen des Kontinents*, trans. from the English and ed. by Viktor Klarwill (Vienna: Kunstverlag Anton Schroll & Co., 1919) [DLA] [★]

——*Der Virey und die Aristokraten oder Mexiko im Jahre 1812*, 2 vols (Berlin: Robert Bein Kommanditgesellschaft, [n.d.]) [DLA] [★]

Spitzer, Daniel, *Wiener Spaziergänge*, ed. by Walter Obermaier, 2 vols (Vienna: Edition Wien, [n.d.]) [DLA] [★]

Stadler, Ernst:

    Sheppard, Richard, *Ernst Stadler (1883–1914): A German Expressionist Poet at Oxford* (Oxford: Magdalen College, 1994) [DLA] [W]

Sternheim, Carl:

    Linke, Manfred, *Carl Sternheim in Selbstzeugnissen und Bilddokumenten* (Reinbek bei Hamburg: rowohlts monographien, 1979) [DLA]

Stifter, Adalbert, *Die fürchterliche Wendung der Dinge: Erzählungen*, ed. by Hans Joachim Piechotta (Darmstadt: Sammlung Luchterhand, 1981) [DLA]

——*Der Hochwald* (Stuttgart: Reclam UB, 1988)

    [*Adalbert Stifter: Collected Works*], 6 vols (Leipzig: Insel, [n.d.]), [i]: *Aus dem alten Wien*; [ii]: *Studien I*; [iii]: *Studien II*; [iv]: *Der Nachsommer*; [v]: *Witiko*; [vi]: *Bunte Steine; Nachlese*

    Briefe (Zurich: Manesse, 1947) [DLA]

    Kosch, Wilhelm, *Adalbert Stifter als Mensch, Künstler, Dichter und Erzieher* (Regensburg: Josef Habbel, [n.d.]) [DLA]

Storm, Theodor, *Gesammelte Werke*, ed. by Albert Köster, 8 vols (Leipzig: Insel, 1923) [DLA]

——*Aquis Submersus* (Stuttgart: Reclam UB, 1973)

Szyrocki, Marian, ed., *Lyrik des Barock*, 2 vols (Reinbek bei Hamburg: rororo klassiker, 1971) [DLA]

Tabori, George, *Mein Kampf: Farce*, trans. by Ursula Tabori-Grützmacher (theatre programme), Akademietheater 1986/87 (Heft 17)

——*Unterammergau oder Die guten Deutschen* (Frankfurt a.M.: edition suhrkamp, 1981)

Tannheimer, Stefanie, *Grüebe a wink: Gedichte und Geschichten in Hintersteiner Mundart* (Hinterstein im Allgäu: Self-publication, [n.d.]) [DLA] [W]

Tepl, Johannes von, *Der Ackermann aus Böhmen*, modern German translation, afterword, and notes by Felix Genzmer, bilingual edn (Stuttgart: Reclam UB, 1973) [DLA]

Thoma, Ludwig, *Neue Grobheiten: Simplicissimus-Gedichte von Peter Schlemihl* (Munich: Albert Langen, 1906) [DLA]

Tieck, Ludwig, *Sämmtliche Werke*, 2 vols (Paris: Tétot Frères, 1857)

    Castein, Hanne, ed., *Erläuterungen und Dokumente: Ludwig Tieck: 'Der blonde Eckbert', 'Der Runenberg'* (Stuttgart: Reclam UB, 1987)

Trakl, Georg, *Das dichterische Werk* (Munich: dtv text-bibliothek, 1972) [DLA]

Trenker, Luis, *Kampf in den Bergen: Das unvergängliche Denkmal an der Alpenfront* (Berlin: Neufeld and Henius, 1931) [DLA]

Tucholsky, Kurt, *Deutschland, Deutschland über alles* (Reinbek bei Hamburg: Rowohlt, 1980)

——*Politische Justiz* (Reinbek bei Hamburg: rororo, 1980)

Turrini, Peter, *Mein Österreich: Reden, Polemiken, Aufsätze* (Darmstadt: Sammlung Luchterhand, 1988) [DLA]

Vesper, Guntram, *Die Inseln im Landmeer und neue Gedichte* (Frankfurt a.M.: Fischer Taschenbuch, 1984)

——*Nördlich der Liebe und südlich des Hasses* (Frankfurt a.M.: Fischer Taschenbuch, 1981)

Vollmann, Rolf, *Die wunderbaren Falschmünzer: Ein Roman-Verführer*, 2 vols (Frankfurt a.M.: Eichborn, 1997) [DLA] [★]

Wackenroder, Wilhelm Heinrich, *Sämtliche Schriften* (Reinbek bei Hamburg: rororo klassiker, 1968) [DLA]

Wallfraff, Günter, *13 unerwünschte Reportagen* (Reinbek bei Hamburg: rororo, 1975)

——, and Jens Hagen, *Was wollt ihr denn, ihr lebt ja noch: Chronik einer Industrieansiedlung* (Reinbek bei Hamburg: rowohlt, 1973)

Walser, Martin, *Gesammelte Geschichten* (Frankfurt a.M.: Suhrkamp, 1983) [★]

——*Jenseits der Liebe* (Frankfurt a.M.: Suhrkamp, 1976) [★]

Walser, Robert, *Romane und Erzählungen*, 6 vols (Frankfurt a.M.: Suhrkamp, 1984), I: *Geschwister Tanner*; II: *Der Gehülfe*; III: *Jakob von Gunten*; IV: *Der Räuber*; V: *Erzählungen 1907-1916*; VI: *Erzählungen 1917-1932*

——*Saite und Sehnsucht*, ed. and with an afterword by Elio Fröhlich, facsimile edn (Zurich: Suhrkamp, 1979) [DLA]

Amann, Jürg, *Robert Walser: Eine literarische Biographie in Texten und Bildern* (Zurich and Hamburg: Arche, 1995) [DLA]

Fröhlich, Elio, and Peter Hamm, eds, *Robert Walser: Leben und Werk in Daten und Bildern. Mit einem Essay von Peter Hamm* (Frankfurt a.M.: insel taschenbuch, 1980) [DLA]

Greven, Jochen, *Robert Walser: Figur am Rande, im wechselnden Licht* (Frankfurt a.M.: Fischer Taschenbuch, 1992) [DLA]

Hinz, Klaus-Michael, and Thomas Horst, *Robert Walser* (Frankfurt a.M.: suhrkamp taschenbuch materialien, 1991) [DLA]

Mitteilungen der Robert-Walser-Gesellschaft, no. 3 (October 1998) (Zurich: Robert-Walser-Gesellschaft, 1998) [DLA]

Mitteilungen der Robert-Walser-Gesellschaft, no. 7 (June 2001) (Zurich: Robert-Walser-Gesellschaft, 2001) [DLA]

Waterhouse, Peter, *Die Geheimnislosigkeit: Ein Spazier- und Lesebuch* (Salzburg and Vienna: Residenz, 1996) [DLA]

Weber, Peter, *Der Wettermacher* (Frankfurt a.M.: Suhrkamp, 1993) [★]

Wedekind, Frank: [see also section 10 below]

Seehaus, Günter, *Frank Wedekind in Selbstzeugnissen und Bilddokumenten* (Reinbek bei Hamburg: rowohlts monographien, 1974) [DLA]

Weil, Grete, *Meine Schwester Antigone* (Frankfurt a.M.: Fischer, 1989)

——*Tramhalte Beethovenstraat* (Frankfurt a.M.: Fischer, 1986)

Weiss, Peter, *Die Ästhetik des Widerstands* (Frankfurt a.M.: Suhrkamp, 1983)

——*Diskurs (Viet Nam Diskurs)* (Frankfurt a.M.: Suhrkamp, 1968)

——*Die Ermittlung* (Frankfurt a.M.: Suhrkamp, 1965)

——*Fluchtpunkt* (Frankfurt a.M.: edition suhrkamp, 1965)

——*Das Gespräch der drei Gehenden* (Frankfurt a.M.: edition suhrkamp, 1963)

——*Nacht mit Gästen; Wie dem Herrn Mockinpott das Leiden ausgetrieben wird*, two plays (Frankfurt a.M.: edition suhrkamp, 1970)

——*Notizbücher 1960–1971*, 2 vols (Frankfurt a.M.: edition suhrkamp, 1982)

——*Rapporte* (Frankfurt a.M.: edition suhrkamp, 1968)

——*Der Schatten des Körpers des Kutschers* (Frankfurt a.M.: edition suhrkamp, 1964)

——*Stücke II*, 2 vols (Frankfurt a.M.: edition suhrkamp, 1977)

——*Die Verfolgung und Ermordung Jean Paul Marats* [...] (Frankfurt a.M.: edition suhrkamp, 1964)

    BRAUN, KARLHEINZ, ed, *Materialien zu Peter Weiss's 'Marat/Sade'* (Frankfurt a.M.: edition suhrkamp, 1971)

WEISSENSTEINER, INGE, *Dur's Ruckarle: Oberstdorfer Mundart* (Kempten: Verlag für Heimatpflege, 1986) [DLA]

——*Isa Huimat: Gedichte und Gedanken aus Oberstdorf* (Kempten: Verlag für Heimatpflege, 1983) [DLA]

WEITLING, WILHELM, *Das Evangelium des armen Sünders* (Leipzig: Reclam UB, 1967) [DLA]

WIELAND, CHRISTOPH MARTIN, *Sämtliche Werke*, 14 vols (Hamburg: Hamburger Reprintausgabe, 1984) [DLA] [★]

——*Comische Erzählungen; Comabus; Der verklagte Amor* (Hamburg: Hamburger Reprintausgabe, 1984) [DLA]

    GRUBER, J. G., *C. M. Wielands Leben* (Hamburg: Hamburger Reprintausgabe, 1984) [DLA]

WILHELM II, KAISER:

    Reden des Kaisers: Ansprachen, Predigten und Trinksprüche Wilhelms II, ed. by Ernst Johann (Munich: dtv, 1966) [DLA]

WILKOMIRSKI, BINJAMIN, *Fragments*, trans. from the German by Carol Brown Janeway (London: Picador, 1996)

WOLF, CHRISTA, *Kindheitsmuster* (Darmstadt and Neuwied: Sammlung Luchterhand, 1983)

——*Sommerstück* (Frankfurt a.M.: Luchterhand, 1989) [★]

——*Was bleibt* (Munich: dtv, 1994)

WÜNSCHE, KONRAD, *Jerusalem Jerusalem* (Frankfurt a.M.: edition suhrkamp, 1966)

ZACHARIA, FRIEDRICH WILHELM, *Poetische Schriften*, III (Vienna: Joh. Tom. Edlen von Trattnern, 1765) [DLA]

ZOBELITZ, HANNS V., *Arbeit: Roman aus dem Leben eines deutschen Großindustriellen* (Jena: Hermann Costenoble, 1905) [DLA]

2(b): English

American Short Stories of the 19th Century (London: J. M. Dent [Everyman], 1930) [DLA]

ARNOLD, MATTHEW, *Essays Literary and Critical* (London: J. M. Dent [Everyman], [n.d.]) [DLA]

AUBREY, JOHN, *Lebens-Entwürfe*, trans. from the English by Wolfgang Schlüter (Frankfurt a.M.: Eichborn, 1994)

    DICK, OLIVER LAWSON, ed., *Aubrey's Brief Lives* (London: Mandarin, 1992) [DLA]

BACON, FRANCIS:

    The Essays of Francis Bacon, Lord Verulam (London: J. M. Dent [Everyman], 1907) [DLA]

BANVILLE, JOHN, *The Newton Letter* (London: Minerva, 1982) [DLA]

BECKETT, SAMUEL:

    BIRKENHAUER, KLAUS, *Samuel Beckett in Selbstzeugnissen und Bilddokumenten* (Reinbek bei Hamburg: rowohlts monographien, 1971) [DLA]

BERESFORD, ANNE, *No Place for Cowards* (London: Katabasis, 1998) [DLA] [W]

BERLIN, ISAIAH, *Tolstoy and History*, taken from 'The Hedgehog and the Fox' (London: Phoenix Paperback, 1996) [DLA]

BLAKE, WILLIAM, *Poems and Prophecies* (London: J. M. Dent [Everyman], 1934) [DLA]

BLOM, PHILIPP, *P: Die Simmons Papiere*, trans. from the English and revised by Philipp Blom (Berlin: Berlin Verlag, 1997) [W]

BOSWELL, JAMES, *The Life of Samuel Johnson*, 2 vols (London: J. M. Dent [Everyman], 1925) [DLA]

BRODSKY, JOSEPH, *Erinnerungen an Petersburg*, trans. from the American by Sylvia List and Marianne Frisch (Munich: Hanser, 1993) [DLA]
——*Ufer der Verlorenen*, trans. from the American by Jörg Trobitius (Munich: Hanser 1991) [DLA]
BROWNE, SIR THOMAS:
   The Works of Sir Thomas Browne, ed. by Charles Sayle, 3 vols (Edinburgh: John Grant, 1927) [DLA]
   ——*Religio Medici* (London: J. M. Dent [Everyman], 1928) [DLA]
   ——*Religio Medici 1643*, trans. by Werner von Koppenfels (Mainz: Dietrich's, 1998) [DLA] [W]
   WILLIAMS, CHAS., *Souvenir of Sir Thomas Browne* (Norwich: Jarrolds, 1905) [DLA]
BROWNING, ROBERT, *Poems and Plays, I: 1833–1844* (London: J. M. Dent [Everyman], 1919) [DLA]
BURNS, ROBERT, *Poems and Songs* (London: J. M. Dent [Everyman], [n.d.]) [DLA]
BUTLER, SAMUEL, *Erewhon Revisited*, 2 vols (London: Jonathan Cape, repr. 1927) [DLA]
BYRON:
   The Works of Lord Byron, 6 vols (London: John Murray, 1829), vols I–V [DLA]
CARLYLE, THOMAS, *The French Revolution*, 2 vols (London: J. M. Dent [Everyman], 1909–11) [DLA]
CARROLL, LEWIS, *Through the Looking Glass and What Alice Found There*, with illustrations by John Tenniel (London: Macmillan, 1921)
CHATWIN, BRUCE, *Utz* (London: Picador, 1989) [DLA]
CHESTERTON, KEITH GILBERT, *Ketzer*, trans. by Monika Noll and Ulrich Enderwitz (Frankfurt a.M.: Eichborn, 1998) [DLA] [*]
COLERIDGE, SAMUEL TAYLOR, *Anima Poetae: From the Unpublished Notebooks of Samuel Taylor Coleridge*, ed. by Ernest Hartley Coleridge (London: Heinemann, 1905) [DLA]
CONRAD, JOSEPH, *The Nigger of the 'Narcissus'*, ed. with an introduction and notes by Cedric Watts (Harmondsworth: Penguin, 1989) [DLA]
COWPER, WILLIAM:
   The Poetical Works of William Cowper, with illustrations by Hugh Cameron (London and Edinburgh: W. P. Nimmo, 1878) [DLA]
   Private Correspondence of William Cowper, Esq. With several of his most intimate friends, now first published from the originals in the possession of his kinsman, John Johnson, LL.D., Rector of Yaxham with Welborne in Norfolk, 2 vols (London: Henry Colburn, 1824) [DLA]
   William Cowper's Esq. Die Aufgabe: The Task, in six volumes, translated into German, ed. with afterword and commentary by Wolfgang Schlüter (Berlin: Edition Qwert zui opü, 1998) [W]
DICKENS, CHARLES, 19 vols (London: Chapman & Hall, [n.d.]), *Christmas Books; Martin Chuzzlewit; Christmas Stories; Little Dorrit; A Child's History of England; Nicholas Nickleby; Sketches by Boz; A Tale of Two Cities; Oliver Twist; Bleak House; The Uncommercial Traveller; Edwin Drood Etc; The Old Curiosity Shop; Barnaby Rudge; Hard Times, Pictures from Italy; American Notes, Reprinted Pieces; Our Mutual Friend; Great Expectations; Pickwick Papers*
DONNE, JOHN, *Poetical Works*, ed. by H. J. C. Grierson, 2 vols (Oxford: Clarendon Press and OUP, 1912–29), I: *Text and Appendices*; II: *Introduction and Commentary* [DLA]
ENRIGHT, D. J., ed., *The Oxford Book of Death* (Oxford and New York: Oxford University Press, 1992) [DLA]
FIELDING, HENRY, *The History of Tom Jones*, 2 vols (London: J. M. Dent [Everyman], 1912) [DLA]

FITZGERALD, EDWARD, trans., *Rubáiyát of Omar Khayyám*, ed. with an introduction by Dick Davis (Harmondsworth: Penguin, 1989) [DLA]

    JACKSON, HOLBROOK, *Edward Fitzgerald and Omar Khayyám: An Essay and a Bibliography* (London and Liverpool: [n. pub.], 1899) [DLA]

    POLNAY, PETER DE, *Into an Old Room: The Paradox of E. Fitzgerald* (London: Secker & Warburg, 1950) [DLA]

GAY, JOHN, *Poetical Works*, ed. by Thomas Park, 3 vols bound in 1 (London: Stanhope, 1812)

GOSSE, EDMUND, *Father and Son: A Study of Two Temperaments*, ed. by Peter Abbs (Harmondsworth: Penguin Twentieth-Century Classics, 1989) [DLA]

GREENE, GRAHAM, *A Sort of Life* (Harmondsworth: Penguin Twentieth-Century Classics, 1972) [DLA]

HAMBURGER, MICHAEL, *Collected Poems 1941–1994* (London: Anvil, 1995) [DLA] [W]

——*Die Erde in ihrem langsamen Traum: Gedicht*, trans. from the English by Peter Waterhouse (Vienna and Bolzano: folio, 1994) [DLA]

——*Late* (London: Anvil, 1997) [DLA] [W]

——*Mr Littlejoy's Rattlebag for the New Millennium* (London: Katabasis, 1999) [DLA] [W]

——*Regionalism, Nationalism, Internationalism*. Offprint from: *Regionalität, Nationalität und Internationalität in der zeitgenössischen Lyrik: Erträge des Siebten Blaubeurer Symposions*, ed. by Lothar Fietz, Paul Hoffmann, and Hans-Werner Ludwig (Tübingen: Attempto [n.d.]) [DLA]

——*String of Beginnings* (London: Skoob Books, 1991) [DLA]

——*The Take-Over* (London: Enitharmon, 2000) [DLA] [W]

——*Traumgedichte*, trans. from the English by Peter Waterhouse (bilingual edn) (Vienna and Bolzano: folio, 1996) [DLA]

——Tübinger Friedrich Hölderlin Preis. *Reden zur Preisverleihung an Michael Hamburger am 21. Oktober 1991* (Tübingen: Eberhard-Karls-Universität [Tübinger Universitätsreden], 1992) [DLA]

    DALE, PETER, *Michael Hamburger in Conversation with Peter Dale* (London: Between the Lines, 1998) [DLA] [W]

HOFFMANN, EVA, *Lost in Translation* (London: Minerva, 1996) [DLA]

HOPKINS, GERARD MANLEY, *Journal (1886–1875) und Frühe Tagebücher (1863–1866)*, trans. from the English by Peter Waterhouse (Salzburg and Vienna: Residenz, 1994) [DLA]

JACOBSON, DAN, *Heshel's Kingdom* (London: Hamish Hamilton, 1998) [DLA]

JONSON, BEN, *The Complete Plays*, 2 vols (London: J. M. Dent [Everyman], 1910), I: (repr. 1934); II: (repr. 1926) [DLA]

KEATS, JOHN, *Poems* (London: J. M. Dent [Everyman], 1916) [DLA]

KINSELLA, THOMAS, *The Familiar* (Manchester: Carcanet Press, 1999) [DLA]

KOSINSKI, JAY, *L'Oiseau bariolé*, trans. from the English by Maurice Pons (Paris: j'ai lu, 1998)

MABEY, RICHARD, *The Book of Nightingales* [first published as *Whistling in the Dark*] (London: Sinclair Stevenson, 1997) [DLA]

MARLOWE, CHRISTOPHER, *The Plays* (London: J. M. Dent [Everyman], 1931) [DLA]

——*Sämtliche Dramen*, trans. from the English and ed. by Wolfgang Schlüter (Frankfurt a.M.: Eichborn.Berlin, 1999) [DLA] [W]

MARTIN, NIKOLAUS, *Prager Winter: Ein ganz normales Leben*, trans. from the English by Peter Hochsieder (Munich: Hanser, 1991) [DLA] [★]

MILTON, JOHN, *Poetical Works* (London: J. M. Dent [Everyman], 1910) [DLA]

Minor Elizabethan Drama: Pre-Shakespearean Comedies (London: J. M. Dent [Everyman], [n.d.]) [DLA]

Minor Elizabethan Drama: Pre-Shakespearean Tragedies (London: J. M. Dent [Everyman], 1929) [DLA]

MORE, THOMAS, *Utopia* (London: J. M. Dent [Everyman], [n.d.]) [DLA]

NABOKOV, VLADIMIR, *Gesammelte Werke*, ed. by Dieter E. Zimmer, 24 vols (Reinbek bei Hamburg: Rowohlt, 1990–96) (vols VI, IX, XVI, XX, XXII, XXIII), VI: *Das wahre Leben des Sebastian Knight*, trans. from the English by Dieter E. Zimmer (1996); IX: *Pnin*, trans. from the English by Dieter E. Zimmer (1995); XVI: *Nikolaj Gogol*, trans. from the English by Jochen Neuburger (1990); XX: *Deutliche Worte*, trans. from the English by Dieter E. Zimmer and others (1993); XXII: *Erinnerung, sprich*, trans. from the English by Dieter E. Zimmer and others (1991); XXIII: *Briefwechsel mit Edmund Wilson 1940–1971*, trans. from the English by Elke Schönfeld (1991) [DLA]

——*Lectures on Literature*, ed. by Fredson Bowers with introduction by John Updike (London: Picador, 1983) [DLA]

——*Speak, Memory: An Autobiography Revisited* (Harmondsworth: Penguin, 1987) [DLA]

——*Nabokov's Butterflies*, ed. by Brian Boyd and Robert Michael Pyles. Unpublished and uncollected writings, new translations from the Russian by Dmitri Nabokov (London: Allen Lane, The Penguin Press, 2000) [DLA]

MORTON, DONALD E., *Vladimir Nabokov mit Selbstzeugnissen und Bilddokumenten* (Reinbek bei Hamburg: rowohlts monographien, 1984) [DLA]

NAIPAUL, V. S., *Dunkle Gegenden: Sechs große Reportagen*, collected and trans. from the English by Karin Graf (Frankfurt a.M.: Eichborn, 1995) [DLA] [★]

NICOLSON, NIGEL, *Portrait of a Marriage* (London: Phoenix, 1996) [DLA]

PEPYS, SAMUEL, *Diary*, 2 vols (London: J. M. Dent [Everyman], 1914–17), I (1917), II (1914) [DLA]

The Illustrated Pepys: From the Diary, selected and edited by Robert Latham (London: Book Club Associates, 1978) [DLA]

POE, EDGAR ALLEN:

Edgar Allen Poe's Tales of Mystery and the Imagination (London: J. M. Dent [Everyman], 1912) [DLA]

PRIESTLEY, J. B., *English Journey* (Harmondsworth: Penguin, repr. 1979) [DLA]

QUINCEY, THOMAS DE, *Confessions of an English Opium-Eater*, introduction by John E. Jordan (London: Dent [Everyman], 1960) [DLA]

——*The English Mail Coach and other Essays* (London, etc: Dent [Everyman], [n.d.]) [DLA]

RUSKIN, JOHN, *The Crown of Wild Olives etc.* (London: J. M. Dent [Everyman], [n.d.]) [DLA]

——*The Ethics of the Dust* (London: J. M. Dent [Everyman], [n.d.]) [DLA]

——*The Seven Lamps of Architecture* (London: J. M. Dent [Everyman], 1910) [DLA]

SASSOON, SIEGFRIED, *The Complete Memoirs of George Sherston* (London: Faber & Faber, 1984) [DLA]

SCHLÜTER, WOLFGANG, ed. and trans., *My Second Self When I Am Gone: Englische Gedichte* (Hamburg: Hamburger Stiftung zur Förderung von Wissenschaft und Kultur, 1991) [DLA] [W]

SHAKESPEARE, WILLIAM, *Shakespeare: Dramatische Werke*, trans. by Schlegel and Tieck, 6 vols (Berlin: Volksbühnen-Verlags und Vertriebs G.m.b.H, 1924)

——*Antonius und Cleopatra / Antony and Cleopatra*, bilingual edn, trans. by Schlegel and Tieck, ed. by L. L. Schücking (Reinbek bei Hamburg: Rowohlts Klassiker, 1962) [DLA]

——*Coriolanus / Coriolanus*, bilingual edn, trans. by Schlegel and Tieck, ed. by L .L. Schücking † (Reinbek bei Hamburg: Rowohlts Klassiker, 1967) [DLA]

——*Hamlet / Hamlet*, bilingual edn, trans. by Schlegel and Tieck, ed. by L. L. Schücking (Reinbek bei Hamburg: Rowohlts Klassiker, 1965) [DLA]

——*Julius Caesar / Julius Caesar*, bilingual edn, trans. by Schlegel and Tieck, ed. by L. L. Schücking (Reinbek bei Hamburg: Rowohlts Klassiker, 1963) [DLA]

——*Die Komödie der Irrungen / The Comedy of Errors*, bilingual edn, trans. by Schlegel and Tieck, ed. by L. L. Schücking † (Reinbek bei Hamburg: Rowohlts Klassiker, 1969) [DLA]

——*König Heinrich IV / Henry IV*, bilingual edn, trans. by Schlegel and Tieck, ed. by L. L. Schücking † (Reinbek bei Hamburg: Rowohlts Klassiker, 1966) [DLA]

——*König Lear / King Lear*, bilingual edn, trans. by Schlegel and Tieck, ed. by L. L. Schücking (Reinbek bei Hamburg: Rowohlts Klassiker, 1960) [DLA]

——*Macbeth / Macbeth*, bilingual edn, trans. by Schlegel and Tieck, ed. by L. L. Schücking (Reinbek bei Hamburg: Rowohlts Klassiker, 1962) [DLA]

——*Mass für Mass / Measure for Measure*, bilingual edn, trans. by Schlegel and Tieck, ed. by L. L. Schücking (Reinbek bei Hamburg: Rowohlts Klassiker, 1964) [DLA]

——*Richard III / Richard III*, bilingual edn, trans. by Schlegel and Tieck, ed. by L .L. Schücking † (Reinbek bei Hamburg: Rowohlts Klassiker, 1958) [DLA]

——*Romeo und Julia / Romeo and Juliet*, bilingual edn, trans. by Schlegel and Tieck, ed. by L. L. Schücking (Reinbek bei Hamburg: Rowohlts Klassiker, 1964) [DLA]

——*Ein Sommernachtstraum / A Midsummer Night's Dream*, bilingual edn, trans. by Schlegel and Tieck, ed. by L. L. Schücking (Reinbek bei Hamburg: Rowohlts Klassiker, 1959) [DLA]

——*Der Sturm / The Tempest*, bilingual edn, trans. by Schlegel and Tieck, ed. by L. L. Schücking (Reinbek bei Hamburg: Rowohlts Klassiker, 1962) [DLA]

——*Troilus und Cressida / Troilus and Cressida*, bilingual edn, trans. by Schlegel and Tieck, ed. by L. L. Schücking † (Reinbek bei Hamburg: Rowohlts Klassiker, 1966) [DLA]

——*Viel Lärmen um Nichts / Much Ado About Nothing*, bilingual edn, trans. by Schlegel and Tieck, ed. by L. L. Schücking † (Reinbek bei Hamburg: Rowohlts Klassiker, 1968) [DLA]

——*Was ihr wollt / Twelfth Night, or What You Will*, bilingual edn, trans. by Schlegel and Tieck, ed. by L. L. Schücking † (Reinbek bei Hamburg: Rowohlts Klassiker, 1967) [DLA]

——*Der Widerspenstigen Zähmung / The Taming of the Shrew*, bilingual edn, trans. by Schlegel and Tieck, ed. by L. L. Schücking (Reinbek bei Hamburg: Rowohlts Klassiker, 1963) [DLA]

——*Wie es euch gefällt / As You Like It*, bilingual edn, trans. by Schlegel and Tieck, ed. by L. L. Schücking (Reinbek bei Hamburg: Rowohlts Klassiker, 1963) [DLA]

——*Das Wintermärchen / The Winter's Tale*, bilingual edn, trans. by Schlegel and Tieck, ed. by L. L. Schücking (Reinbek bei Hamburg: Rowohlts Klassiker, 1965) [DLA]

Holinshed's Chronicles used in Shakespeare's Plays (London: J. M. Dent [Everyman], 1927) [DLA]

SHELLEY, PERCY BYSSHE, *The Plays, Translations and Longer Poems* (London: J. M. Dent [Everyman], 1916) [DLA]

SHERIDAN, RICHARD BRINSLEY, *The Plays* (London: J. M. Dent [Everyman], 1911) [DLA]

SINGER, ISAAC BAHEVIS, *Love and Exile: The Early Years: A Memoir* (Harmondsworth: Penguin, 1984) [DLA]

SNYDER, GARY, *The Real Work: Interviews & Talks 1964–1979*, ed. with an introduction by Wm. Scott McLean (New York: New Directions Paperbacks, 1980) [DLA]

SONTAG, SUSAN, *On Photography* (Harmondsworth: Penguin Books, repr. 1982) [DLA]

——*Under the Sign of Saturn* (London: Writers and Readers Publishing Cooperative, 1983) [DLA]

SPENSER, EDMUND, *Mr Edmund Spensers Epithalamion (1594)*, trans. from the English by Wolfgang Schlüter (Berlin: Marwede, 1992–93) [DLA]

STERNE, LAURENCE, *A Sentimental Journey; Journal to Eliza* (London: J. M. Dent [Everyman], 1930) [DLA]

STEVENS, WALLACE, *Adagia*, trans. from the American by Karin Graf und Joachim Sartorius (Salzburg and Vienna: Residenz, 1992) [DLA]

STEVENSON, ROBERT LOUIS:

The Works of Robert Louis Stevenson, 29 vols (London: Heinemann, *c.* 1924–27) (vols I, III, IV, V, IX, X, XI, XV, XVIII, XX, XXII, XXIII, XXV, XXIX), I: *New Arabian Nights* (1927); III: *The Dynamiter* (*c.* 1927); IV: *Prince Otto* ([n.d.]); V: *Dr Jekyll & Mr Hyde* (1927); IX: *The Black Arrow* ([n.d.]); X: *The Master of Ballantrae* (1924); XI: *The Wrong Box; The Body Snatcher* (1924); XV: *St Ives* (1924); XVIII: *The Amateur Emigrant; The Silverado Squatters* (1924); XX: *In the South Seas* (1924); XXII: *Poems, vol. I* ([n.d.]); XXIII: *Poems, vol. II* (1924); XV: *Virginibus Puerisque & Other Essays in Belles Lettres* (1924); XXIX: *Memories and Portraits and Other Fragments* (1924) [DLA]

STRACHEY, LYTTON, *Books and Characters French & English* (London: Chatto and Windus, 1928) [DLA]

SWIFT, JONATHAN, *Journal to Stella*, introduction by Walter Scott (London: J. M. Dent [Everyman], [n.d.]) [DLA]

SWINBURNE, ALGERNON CHARLES, *Atalanta in Calydon and Erechtheus* (London: Heinemann, 1919) [DLA]

WATTS, STEPHEN, *The Lava's Curl* (Walsden, West Yorkshire: The Grimaldi Press, 1990) [DLA] [W]

WILDE, OSCAR:

HOARE, PHILIP, *Oscar Wilde's Last Stand: Decadence, Conspiracy and the Most Outrageous Trial of the Century* (New York: Arcade, 1997) [DLA] [W]

WOOLF, VIRGINIA, *A Room of One's Own* (Harmondsworth: Penguin Twentieth-Century Classics, [n.d.]) [DLA]

WALDMANN, WERNER, *Virginia Woolf in Selbstzeugnissen und Bilddokumenten* (Reinbek bei Hamburg: rowohlts monographien, 1996) [DLA]

2(c): French

ANTELME, ROBERT, *Das Menschengeschlecht: Als Deportierter in Deutschland*, trans. by Eugen Helmlé (Munich: dtv, 1990)

ARAGON, *Le Paysan de Paris* (Paris: Livre de Poche, 1966) [DLA]

BALZAC, HONORÉ DE, *Le Cousin Pons* (Paris: Calmann-Lévy, [n.d.]) [DLA]

——*L'Israélite* (Paris: Calmann-Lévy, [n.d.]) [DLA]

——*La Maison Nucingen* (Paris: Calmann-Lévy, [n.d.]) [DLA]

——*La Peau de Chagrin* (Paris: Bibliothèque Larousse, [n.d.]) [DLA]

——*La Rabouilleuse* (Paris: Livre de Poche, 1999) [DLA]

BARTHES, ROLAND, *Camera Lucida: Reflections on Photography*, trans. from the French by Richard Howard (London: Flamingo, 1984) [DLA]

——*Mythologies*, selected and trans. from the French by Annette Lavers (Frogmore, St Albans: Paladin, repr. 1976) [DLA]

BLOY, LÉON, *Auslegung der Gemeinplätze*, trans. from the French with a commentary by Hans-Horst Henschen (Frankfurt a.M.: Eichborn, 1995) [DLA]

BOBER, ROBERT, *Berg et Beck* (Paris: P.O.L., 1999) [DLA]

——*Quoi de neuf sur la guerre?* (Paris: Folio, 1999) [DLA]

BRUYCKER, DANIEL DE, *Silex; La Tombe du chasseur* (Arles: Actes Sud, 1999) [DLA]

BUTOR, MICHEL, *L'Emploi du temps suivi de L'Exemple par Georges Raillard* (Paris: 10/18, 1966) [DLA]

CASANOVA, GIACOMO (CHEVALIER DE SEINGALT):

[CASANOVA, JACQUES], *Mémoires de Jacques Casanova de Seingalt/ écrits par lui-même/ suivis de/ Fragments des Mémoires du Prince de Ligne*, 8 vols (Paris: Garnier, [n.d.]) [DLA]

—— *Geschichte meines Lebens*, ed. by Erich Loos, trans. by Heinz von Sauter, 6 vols (Berlin: Propyläen, 1985) [★]

Childs, J. Rives, *Giacomo Casanova de Seingalt mit Selbstzeugnissen und Bilddokumenten*, trans. from the English by Hans-Heinrich Wellmann (Reinbek bei Hamburg: rowohlts monographien, 1996) [DLA]

Chamfort, Nicolas, *Maximes et pensées* (Paris: Livre de Poche, 1970) [DLA]

Chateaubriand, François René de, *Itinéraire de Paris à Jérusalem* (Paris: Garnier Flammarion, 1968) [DLA]

——*Mémoires d'outre-tombe*, 6 vols (Brussels: Meline, Cans et Companie, 1848)

——*Mémoires d'outre-tombe*, 2 vols (Paris: Livre de Poche, 1973) [DLA]

Corday, Charlotte:

Esquiros, Alphonse, *Charlotte Corday*, 2 vols (Paris: Desessart, Éditeur, 1840) [DLA]

Corneille, Pierre, *Chefs d'œuvre*, 3 vols (Paris: Didot, 1800) [DLA]

Coster, Charles de, *Tyll Ulenspiegel und Lamm Goedzak* [...], trans. by Friedrich Oppeln-Bronikowski (Jena: Eugen Diederichs, 1927) [DLA]

Delbo, Charlotte, *Trilogie: Auschwitz und danach*, trans. by Eva Groepler and Elisabeth Thielicke (Basle and Frankfurt a.M.: Stroemfeld; Roter Stern, 1990) (2 copies)

Delpuech, Rosie, *Insomnia: Une traduction nocturne* (Arles: Actes Sud, 1998) [DLA]

Duras, Marguerite, *L'Amant de la Chine du Nord* (Paris: Gallimard, 1991) [DLA]

Finkielkraut, Alain, *Der eingebildete Jude*, trans. by Hainer Kober (Frankfurt a.M.: Fischer Taschenbuch, 1984)

Flaubert, Gustave, *Three Tales*, trans. by Robert Baldick (London: Penguin Classics, 1961)

——*Madame Bovary: Mœurs de Province*, 2 vols (Geneva: Pierre Cailler, 1946) [DLA]

——*Briefe*, ed. and trans. by Helmut Scheffel (Zurich: Diogenes [detebe-Klassiker], 1977) [DLA]

——*Drei Erzählungen / Trois Contes*, bilingual edn, ed. and trans. by Cora van Kleffens and André Stoll (Frankfurt a.M.: Insel, 1983) [DLA]

——*Madame Bovary*, ed. and trans. by Eleanor Marx-Aveling (London and Toronto: J. M. Dent [Everyman], [n.d.]) [DLA]

——*Salammbo*, trans. by J. S. Chartres (London and Toronto: J. M. Dent [Everyman], 1931) [DLA]

——*Salammbô* (Paris: Flammarion, 1964) [DLA]

La Varende, Jean de, *Gustave Flaubert mit Selbstzeugnissen und Bilddokumenten*, trans. from the French by Hans Magnus Enzensberger (Reinbek bei Hamburg: rowohlts monographien, 1996) [DLA]

Fontenelle, Bernard de, *Totengespräche*, trans. by Hans-Horst Henschen (Frankfurt a.M.: Eichborn, 1991) [DLA] [★]

Gaboriau, Émile, *L'Affaire Lerouge* (Paris: Dentu, 1871) [DLA]

Gide, André, *Schwurgericht: Drei Bücher vom Verbrechen* [*La Cour d'assises* (1914), *L'Affaire Redureau* (1930), *La Séquestrée de Poitiers* (1930)], trans. by Ralph Schmidberger and Johanna Borek (Frankfurt a.M.: Eichborn, 1997) [★]

Goldschmidt, Georges-Arthur, *Der bestrafte Narziß*, trans. by Mariette Müller (Zurich: Ammann, 1994) [W]

——*Ein Garten in Deutschland*, trans. by Eugen Helmlé (Frankfurt a.M.: suhrkamp taschenbuch, 1991)

——*Der Spiegeltag*, trans. by Peter Handke (Frankfurt a.M.: suhrkamp taschenbuch, 1989)

Jacottet, Philippe, *Nach so vielen Jahren*, trans. by Elisabeth Edl and Wolfgang Matz (Munich: Hanser, 1998) [DLA]

La Bruyère, *Les Caractères* (Paris: Ernst Flammarion, 1926) [DLA]

Laclos, Pierre Choderlos de, *Liaisons dangereuses* (Paris: Garnier Flammarion, 1964) [DLA]

LA FONTAINE, JEAN DE, *Fables* (Paris: Garnier Flammarion, 1966) [DLA]

MALLARMÉ, STÉPHANE, *Sämtliche Gedichte*, bilingual edn., trans. by Carl Fischer (Heidelberg: Schneider, 1957) [DLA]

MAUPASSANT, GUY DE, *Une vie*, with a preface and commentary by Anne Rey (Paris: Pocket, 1998) [DLA]

MOLIÈRE [JEAN-BAPTISTE POQUELIN], *Molière: Théâtre*, 6 vols (Paris: Plon [1930])

MONTAIGNE, MICHEL DE, *Essais*, selected and trans. by Herbert Lüthy (Zurich: Manesse, 1953) [DLA]

> SCHULTZ, UWE, *Michel de Montaigne mit Selbstzeugnissen und Bilddokumenten* (Reinbek bei Hamburg: rowohlts monographien, 1996) [DLA]

PEREC, GEORGES, *W or the Memory of Childhood*, trans. by David Bellos (London: Collins Harvill, 1989) [DLA]

> BELLOS, DAVID, *Georges Perec: A Life in Words* (London: Harvill, 1995) [DLA]

PROUST, MARCEL, *Auf der Suche nach der verlorenen Zeit*, trans. from the French by Eva Rechel-Mertens, 13 vols (Frankfurt a.M.: edition suhrkamp [werkausgabe], 1964), I: *In Swanns Welt 1*; II: *In Swanns Welt 2*: III: *Im Schatten junger Mädchenblüte 1*; IV: *Im Schatten junger Mädchenblüte 2*, V: *Die Welt der Guermantes 1*; VI: *Die Welt der Guermantes 2*; VII: *Sodom und Gomorra 1*; VIII: *Sodom und Gomorra 2*; IX: *Die Gefangene 1*; X: *Die Gefangene 2*; XI: *Die Entflohene*; XII: *Die wiedergefundene Zeit 1*; XIII: *Die wiedergefundene Zeit 2* [DLA]

> MAURIAC, CLAUDE, *Marcel Proust mit Selbstzeugnissen und Bilddokumenten*, trans. from the French by Eva Rechel-Mertens (Reinbek bei Hamburg: rowohlts monographien, 1997) [DLA]

> STERN, SHEILA, *Proust: Swann's Way* (Cambridge: Cambridge University Press, 1989) [DLA] [W]

RACINE, JEAN:
> *Théâtre complet de J. Racine précedé d'une notice par M. Auger* (Paris: Librairie de Firmin Didot Frères, 1861) [DLA]

RADIGUET, RAYMOND, *Le Diable au corps*, preface etc. by Bruno Vercier (Paris: Flammarion, 1986) [DLA]

RIMBAUD, ARTHUR:
> BONNEFOY, YVES, *Arthur Rimbaud in Selbstzeugnissen und Bilddokumenten* (Reinbek bei Hamburg: rowohlts monographien, 1962)

ROBBE-GRILLET, ALAIN, *La Maison de rendez-vous* (Paris: Éditions de Minuit, 1970) [DLA]

ROUSSEAU, JEAN-JACQUES, *Les Confessions*, 2 vols (Paris: Gallimard, folio, 1979–80), I (1980); II: (1979) [DLA]

——*Meditations of a Solitary Walker*, trans. from the French by Peter France (Harmondsworth: Penguin 60s Classics, 1995) [DLA]

——*La Nouvelle Héloïse*, with a preface by J. Grand-Carteret, 6 vols (Paris: Librairie des Bibliophiles, 1889) [DLA]

——*Träumereien eines einsamen Spaziergängers: Der fünfte Spaziergang*, trans. from the French by Franz Bäschlin (Verkehrsverein Biel und Umgebung (Switzerland), [n.d.]) (brochure) [DLA]

> HOWLETT, MARC-VINCENT, *Jean-Jacques Rousseau: L'Homme qui croyait en l'homme* (Paris: Gallimard, 1994) [DLA]

> HOLMSTEN, GEORG, *Jean-Jacques Rousseau mit Selbstzeugnissen und Bilddokumenten*, (Reinbek bei Hamburg: Rowohlt Bildmonographien, 1994) [DLA]

> STAROBINSKI, JEAN, *Rousseau: Eine Welt von Widerständen*, trans. from the French by Ulrich Raulff (Frankfurt a.M.: Fischer Taschenbuch, 1993) [DLA]

SADE, MARQUIS DE:
> LEVER, MAURICE, *Marquis de Sade: Die Biographie*, trans. from the French by Wolfram Bayer, Dieter Hornig, Günter Seib and Josef Winiger (Munich: dtv, 1991) [DLA]

SAINT-EXUPÉRY, ANTOINE DE, *Œuvres complètes* (Paris: Pléaide, 1996) [DLA]

——*Écrits de guerre 1939–1944*, with a preface by Raymond Aron (Paris: Folio, 1994) [DLA]

—— *Vol de nuit* (Paris: Gallimard, 1995) [DLA]

BERNARDIN DE SAINT-PIERRE, J.-H., *Paul et Virginie et la Chaumière indienne* (Paris: L. Curmer, 1858) [DLA]

SARTRE, JEAN-PAUL, *Words*, trans. from the French by Irene Clephane (Harmondsworth: Penguin Twentieth-Century Classics, 1967) [DLA]

SIMON, CLAUDE, *Le Jardin des Plantes* (Paris: Les Éditions de Minuit, 1997) [DLA]

——*La Route des Flandres* (Paris: Les Éditions de Minuit, 1960) [DLA]

——*Le Tramway* (Paris: Les Éditions de Minuit, 2001) [DLA]

——*Le Vent: Tentative de restitution d'un retable baroque* (Paris: Les Éditions de Minuit, 1975) [DLA]

MADAME DE STAËL, *Über Deutschland*, trans. by Friedrich Buchholz, Samuel Heinrich Catel and Julius Eduard Hitzig, ed. by Monika Bosse (Frankfurt a.M.: insel taschenbuch, 1985) [DLA]

STENDHAL, *De l'Amour* (Paris: Garnier Flammarion, 1965) [DLA]

—— *The Life of Henry Brulard*, trans. from the French and with an introduction by John Sturrock (Harmondsworth: Penguin Classics, 1995) [DLA]

——*Lucien Leuwen*, 2 vols (Paris: Garnier Flammarion, 1982) [DLA]

  NERLICH, MICHAEL, *Stendhal mit Selbstzeugnissen und Bilddokumenten* (Reinbek bei Hamburg: rowohlts monographien, 1993) [DLA]

SULLY, DUC DE:

  BÉTHUNE, MAXIMILIAN DE (Duc de Sully), *Mémoires de Maximilien de Béthune, Duc de Sully*, 10 vols (Liège: F. J. Desoer, 1788) (vols I, II, III, IV, V, VI, VIII, IX, X), I–VI, VIII: *Mémoires de Sully*; IX: *Supplément*; X: *Supplément aux Mémoires de Sully* (London, 1787) [DLA]

VERNE, JULES, *Les 500 millions de la Bégum* (Paris: Livre de Poche, 1966) [DLA]

——*Le Rayon vert* (Paris: Livre de Poche, 1968) [DLA]

  DEHS, VOLKER, *Jules Verne mit Selbstzeugnissen und Bilddokumenten* (Reinbek bei Hamburg: rowohlts monographien, 1993) [DLA]

VIAN, BORIS, *Conte de fées à l'usage des moyennes personnes* (Paris: Pauvert, 1997) [DLA]

VIGNY, ALFRED DE, *Servitude et grandeur militaires* (Paris: Livre de Poche, 1965) [DLA]

VOLTAIRE, *Lettres philosophiques* (Paris: Garnier Flammarion, 1964) [DLA]

2(d): Italian

BASSANI, GIORGIO, *Die Brille mit dem Goldrand*, trans. by Herbert Schlüter (Munich: Serie Piper, [June] 1997) [DLA]

——*Erinnerungen des Herzens: Mit Texten von Giulio Cattaneo, Paolo Ravenna und Eberhard Schmidt*, ed. by Eberhard Schmidt (Munich: Serie Piper, 1991) [DLA]

——*Ferrareser Geschichten*, trans. by Herbert Schlüter (Munich: Serie Piper, [February] 1996) [DLA]

——*Die Gärten der Finzi-Contini*, trans. by Herbert Schlüter (Munich: Serie Piper, [March] 1997) [DLA]

——*Hinter der Tür*, trans. by Herbert Schlüter (Munich: Serie Piper, [June] 1997) [DLA]

——*Der Reiher*, trans. by Herbert Schlüter (Munich: Serie Piper, [February] 1999) [DLA]

BOCCACCIO, GIOVANNI, *The Decameron, or, Ten Days Entertainment*, 4 vols (London: William Sharp, 1822)

——*Das Dekameron* (Berlin: Verlag Neues Leben (Wilhelm Borngräber), [n.d.] [1914?]) [DLA]

CALASSO, ROBERTO, *Die geheime Geschichte des Senatspräsidenten Dr. Daniel Paul Schreber* [*L'impuro folle*], trans. by Reimar Klein (Frankfurt a.M.: edition suhrkamp, 1980) [DLA]

Calvino, Italo, *Eremit in Paris: Autobiographische Blätter*, trans. by Burkhart Kroeber und Ina Martens (Munich: dtv, 2000) [DLA]

——*Sechs Vorschläge für das nächste Jahrtausend: Harvard-Vorlesungen*, trans. by Burkhart Kroeber (Munich: Hanser, 1991) [DLA]

Dante, *Werke: Vita nuova / Neues Leben; Divina commedia / Die göttliche Komödie*. Italian–German bilingual edn, ed. with notes by Dr Erwin Laaths ([n.p.]: Tempel Klassiker, [n.d.]) [DLA]

Jappe, Anselm, ed., *Schade um Italien! Zweihundert Jahre Selbstkritik*, selected, introduced, and trans. by Anselm Jappe (Frankfurt a.M.: Eichborn, 1997) [DLA] [★]

Levi, Primo, *The Drowned and the Saved*, trans. from the Italian by Raymond Rosenthal, with an introduction by Paul Bailey (London: Michael Joseph, 1988) [DLA]

——*If This is a Man / The Truce*, trans. by Stuart Woolf, with an introduction by Paul Bailey (Harmondsworth: Penguin, 1979) [DLA]

——*Moments of Reprieve*, trans. by Ruth Feldman (London: Abacus, 1987) [DLA]

——*Other People's Trades*, trans. by Raymond Rosenthal (London: Michael Joseph, 1989) [DLA]

——*The Periodic Table*, trans. by Raymond Rosenthal (London: Abacus 1990) [DLA]

——*The Sixth Day and Other Tales*, trans. by Raymond Rosenthal (London: Abacus 1990) [DLA]

Magris, Claudio, *Donau: Biographie eines Flusses*, trans. by Heinz-Georg Held (Munich: Hanser, 1988) [G.29] [DLA] [★]

——*Die Welt en gros und en détail*, trans. by Ragni Maria Gschwend (Munich: Hanser, 1999) [DLA]

Ortese, Anna Maria, *Stazione Centrale und andere Mailänder Geschichten*, trans. from the Italian by Barbara Kleiner and Viktoria von Schirach (Munich: Hanser, 1993) [DLA]

Sciascia, Leonardo, *1912 + 1* (Milan: Adelphi, 1986) [DLA]

Segre, Vittorio, *Ein Glücksrabe: Die Geschichte eines italienischen Juden*, trans. from the Italian by Sylvia Höfer and from the English by Hanni Ehlers (Frankfurt a.M.: Eichborn, 1993) [DLA]

Sofri, Adriano, *Der Knoten und der Nagel: Ein Buch zur linken Hand*, with a biographical essay by Carlo Ginzburg, trans. from the Italian by Walter Kögler (Frankfurt a.M.: Eichborn, 1998) [DLA]

Stuparich, Giani, *Ein Sommer in Isola: Geschichten von der Liebe*, trans. from the Italian and with an afterword by Renate Lunzer (Salzburg and Vienna: Residenz, 1991) [DLA]

Svevo, Italo, *Autobiographisches Profil: Tagebuchaufzeichnungen und Notizen–Fabeln–Briefe*, trans. by Ragni Maria Gschwend and Anna Leube (Reinbek bei Hamburg: Rowohlt, 1986) [DLA]

——*Die Novelle vom guten alten Herrn und vom schönen Mädchen*, trans. by Piero Rismondo (Reinbek bei Hamburg: rororo, 1995) [DLA]

——*Zeno Cosini*, trans. by Piero Rismondo (Reinbek bei Hamburg: Rowohlt, 1988) [DLA]

   Bondy, François, and Ragni Maria Gschwend, *Italo Svevo* (Reinbek bei Hamburg: rowohlts monographien, 1995) [DLA]

Tabucchi, Antonio, *Indisches Nachtstück und Ein Briefwechsel*, trans. by Karin Fleischanderl (Munich: Hanser, 1994) [DLA]

——*Lissabonner Requiem: Eine Halluzination*, trans. by Karin Fleischanderl (Munich: Hanser, 1991) [DLA]

Triestino, Anonimo, *Das Geheimnis*, trans. by Christa Pock and Peter Rosei (Salzburg and Vienna: Residenz, 1988) [DLA] [★]

Voghera, Giorgio, *Nostra Signora Morte: Der Tod*, trans. by Renate Lunzer (Salzburg and Vienna: Residenz, 1990) [DLA]

2(e): Hispanic and Iberian literature

ASSIS, MACHADO DE, *Der geheime Grund: Erzählungen*, trans. from the Brazilian Portuguese and with an afterword by Curt Meyer-Clason (Frankfurt a.M.: Eichborn, 1998) [★]

BORGES, JORGE LUIS, *Werke*, ed. by Gisbert Haefs and Fritz Arnold, 20 vols (Frankfurt a.M.: Fischer Taschenbuch, 1991–94) (vols II, V, VII, VIII, XV), II: *Kabbala und Tango: Essays 1930–1932*, trans. by Karl August Horst, Curt Meyer-Clason, Melanie Walz, and Gisbert Haefs (1991); V: *Fiktionen, Erzählungen: 1939–1944*, trans. by Karl August Horst, Wolfgang Luchting, and Gisbert Haefs (1992); VII: *Inquisitionen: Essays 1941–1952*, trans. by Karl August Horst and Gisbert Haefs (1992); VIII: *Einhorn, Sphinx und Salamander: Das Buch der imaginären Wesen*, trans. by Ulla de Herrera, Edith Aron, and Gisbert Haefs (1993); XV: *Buch der Träume*, trans. by Gisbert Haefs (1994) [DLA]

——and OSVALDO FERRARI, *Lesen ist denken mit fremdem Gehirn: Gespräche über Bücher und Borges*, trans. from Spanish by Gisbert Haefs (Zurich: Arche, 1990) [DLA]

CASARES, ADOLFO BIOY, *Abenteuer eines Fotografen in La Plata*, trans. from the Spanish by Peter Schwaar (Frankfurt a.M.: Bibliothek Suhrkamp, 1995) [DLA]

CERVANTES, MIGUEL DE, *The History of the Renowned Don Quixote de la Mancha, Written in Spanish and Translated by Several Hands*, 4 vols (Edinburgh: Donaldson, 1766)

COZARINSKY, EDGARDO, 'Borges: Un texto que es todo para todos', *Cuadernos de Recien-venido* 11, 1999, 5-15 [W]

——*El pase del testigo* (Buenos Aires: Editorial Sudamericana, 2001) [DLA]

MARÍAS, JAVIER, *Als ich sterblich war: Erzählungen,* trans. from the Spanish by Elke Wehr (Stuttgart: Klett Cotta, 1999) [W]

——*Schwarzer Rücken der Zeit*, trans. from the Spanish by Elke Wehr (Stuttgart: Klett Cotta, 2000) [W]

PAZ, OCTAVIO, *Das Vorrecht des Auges: Über Kunst und Künstler*, trans. from the Spanish by Susanne Lange, Michael Nungesser, and Rudolf Wittkopf (Frankfurt a.M.: Suhrkamp, 2001) [DLA]

PESSOA, FERNANDO, *Alberto Caeiro, Dichtungen; Ricardo Reis, Oden*, bilingual Portuguese–German edn, trans. from Portuguese and with an afterword by Georg Rudolf Lind (Frankfurt a.M.: Fischer Taschenbuch, 1989) [DLA]

——*Das Buch der Unruhe des Hilfsbuchhalters Bernando Soares*, trans. from Portuguese and with an afterword by Georg Rudolf Lind (Frankfurt a.M.: Fischer Taschenbuch, 1988) [DLA]

RUIZ ROSAS, TERESA, *Der Kopist*, trans. from the Peruvian Spanish by Alicia Padrós (Zurich: Ammann, 1996) [DLA]

SARAMAGO, JOSÉ, *All the Names*, trans. from the Portuguese by Margaret Jull Costa (London: Harvill Panther, 2000) [DLA]

2(f): Russian

ANDREJEW, LEONID:

DAVIES, RICHARD, *Ein russischer Dichter und seine Welt: Die unbekannten Fotos des Leonid Andrejew*, trans. from the English by Brigitte Weitbrecht (Stuttgart and Zurich: Belser Verlag, 1989)

BABEL, ISAAK, *Erste Hilfe* (Nördlingen: Greno, 1987) [DLA]

——*Tagebuch 1920*, trans. from the Russian, ed. and with a commentary by Peter Urban (Berlin: Friedenauer Presse, 1990) [DLA]

BELYJ, ANDREJ, *Petersburg*, trans. by Gisela Drohla (Frankfurt a.M.: Bibliothek Suhrkamp, 1976) [DLA]

BLOK, ALEXANDER, *Der Sturz des Zarenreichs*, ed. and trans. by Anne Bock (Frankfurt a.M.: Bibliothek Suhrkamp, 1971) [DLA]

CHEKHOV, ANTON, *The Duel and Other Stories*, trans. from the Russian and with an introduction by Ronald Wilks (Harmondsworth: Penguin Classics, 1984) [DLA]

——*The Fiancée and Other Stories*, trans. from the Russian and with an introduction by Ronald Wilks (Harmondsworth: Penguin Classics, 1986) [DLA]

——*The Party*, trans. and with an introduction by Ronald Wilks (Harmondsworth: Penguin Classics, 1985) [DLA]

——*Lady with Lapdog*, trans. and with an introduction by David Magarshak (Harmondsworth: Penguin Classics, 1964, repr. [n.d.]) [DLA]

Anton Tschechow: Meisternovellen (Zurich: Manesse, 1946) [DLA]

GINZBURG, NATALIA, *Anton Čechov: Ein Leben* (Berlin: Wagenbach, 1996) [DLA]

WOLFFHEIM, ELSBETH, *Anton Čechov mit Selbstzeugnissen und Bilddokumenten* (Reinbek bei Hamburg: rowohlts monographien, 1992) [DLA]

DOSTOEVSKY, FYODOR, *The Possessed*, 2 vols, trans. by Constance Garnett with an introduction by J. Middleton Murry (London: Dent [Everyman], 1931) [DLA]

GOGOL, NIKOLAI, *Meistererzählungen*, trans. by Bruno Goetz (Zurich: Manesse, 1993)

——*Tote Seelen oder Tschischikoffs Abenteuer*, trans. by Sigismund von Radecki (Munich: Kösel, 1954)

GONTSCHAROW, IWAN, *Für die Zaren um die halbe Welt* (Frankfurt a.M.: Eichborn, 1998) [DLA] [*]

GORKI, MAXIM, *Erinnerungen an Tolstoy* (Zurich: Verlag Gute Schriften, 1988) [DLA]

HERZEN, ALEXANDER, *Briefe aus dem Westen*, trans. by Friedrich Kapp and Alfred Kurella, with an essay by Isaiah Berlin (Nördlingen: Greno, 1989) [DLA] [*]

IWANOW, WSEWOLOD, *Die Rückkehr des Buddha*, trans. by Günter Dalitz, Erwin Honig, Wilhelm Plackmeyer, and Dieter Pommerenke (Nördlingen: Greno, 1989) [DLA] [*]

MANDELSTAM, OSIP, *Die ägyptische Briefmarke* (Frankfurt a.M.: Bibliothek Suhrkamp, 1965) [DLA]

OSTROWSKIJ, ALEXANDER NIKOLAJEWITSCH, *Aufzeichnungen eines Bewohners von Samoskworetschje*, trans. by Ulrike Zenne (Salzburg and Vienna: Residenz, 1991) [DLA]

PILNJAK, BORIS, *Mahagoni*, trans. by Mascha Schillskaja, Valerian P. Lebedew, Larissa Robiné, and Wolfram Schroeder (Nördlingen: Greno, 1988) [DLA] [*]

PUSHKIN, ALEXANDER, *The Captain's Daughter and Other Tales* (London: Dent [Everyman], 1933) [DLA]

——*Eugene Onegin*. A prose version of Chapter One by Christopher Cahill based on the literal translation of Vladimir Nabokov (New York, 26.V.1999, Pushkin's 200th birthday) (private edn, numbered) [DLA]

PUSHKIN, ALEXANDER, *The Queen of Spades and Other Stories*, trans. by Rosemary Edmonds (London: Penguin Classics, 1978)

ROSANOW, WASSILI, *Abgefallene Blätter*, trans. by Eveline Passet (Frankfurt a.M.: Eichborn, 1996) [DLA] [*]

SAVINKOV, BORIS, *Erinnerungen eines Terroristen*, trans. by Arkadi Maslow, rev. and amended by Barbara Conrad, with fore- and afterwords by Hans Magnus Enzensberger (Nördlingen: Greno, 1985) [DLA] [*]

TOLSTOI, LEO, *Krieg und Frieden*, trans. by Marianne Kegel, 7th edn (Munich: Artemis und Winkler, 1996) [DLA] [*]

——*Childhood, Boyhood, Youth*, trans. and with an introduction by Rosemary Edmonds (Harmondsworth: Penguin Classics, 1981) [DLA]

2(g): Polish

CZERNIAWSKI, ADAM, *Knowledge by Description*, trans. by Iain Higgins (Hull: Carnivorous Arpeggio Press, 1992) [DLA] [W]

——*Strip-Tease*, folder with engraving, no. 151/200 (Łódź: Bibliotheka, 1991, with the cooperation of the BCLT) [DLA]

HERLING, GUSTAW, *Die Insel*, trans. by Maryla Reifenberg (Munich and Vienna: Hanser, 1994) [DLA]

KAPUŚIŃSKI, RYSZARD, *Imperium: Sowjetische Streifzüge*, trans. from the Polish by Martin Pollack (Frankfurt a.M.: Eichborn, 1993) [DLA]

KOCHANOWSKI, JAN, *Treny*, Polish–English bilingual edn, English trans. by Adam Czerniawski (Katowice: Wydawnictwo Uniwersyetu Śląskiego, 1996) [DLA] [W]

LEM, STANISŁAW, *Imaginäre Größe*, trans. by Caesar Rymanarowicz and Jens Reuter (Frankfurt a.M.: suhrkamp taschenbuch [Phantastische Bibliothek], 1981) [DLA]

——*Das hohe Schloß*, trans. by Caesar Rymanarowicz (Frankfurt a.M.: suhrkamp taschenbuch, 1990) [DLA]

——*Philosophie des Zufalls: Zu einer empirischen Theorie der Literatur*, I, trans. by Friedrich Griese (Frankfurt a.M.: Insel, 1983) [DLA]

——*Sade und die Spieltheorie: Essays*, trans. by Friedrich Griese (Frankfurt a.M.: suhrkamp taschenbuch, 1986) [DLA]

——*Über außersinnliche Wahrnehmung: Essays*, II, trans. by Friedrich Griese (Frankfurt a.M.: suhrkamp taschenbuch, 1987) [DLA]

——*Science fiction: Ein hoffnungsloser Fall mit Ausnahmen: Essays*, III (Frankfurt a.M.: suhrkamp taschenbuch, 1987) [DLA]

——*Summa technologiae*, trans. by Friedrich Griese (Frankfurt a.M.: suhrkamp taschenbuch, 1981) [DLA]

LIPSKA, EVA, *Confessions of a Courtesan*. Folder with engraving, no. 132/200 (Łódź: Bibliotheka, 1991 with the cooperation of the BCLT) [DLA]

MICKIEWICZ, ADAM, *Pan Tadeusz*, trans. by George Rapall Noyes (London: Dent [Everyman], 1930) [DLA]

ROSEWICZ, TADEUSZ, *The Door*. Folder with engraving, no. 150/200 (Łódź: Bibliotheka, 1991, with the cooperation of the BCLT) [DLA]

SCHULZ, BRUNO, *Die Republik der Träume: Fragmente, Aufsätze, Briefe, Grafiken I*, ed. by Mikolaj Dutsch, trans. by Josef Hahn and Mikolaj Dutsch (Munich: Hanser, 1967) [DLA]

WITTLIN, JÓZEF, *Mein Lemberg*, trans. by Klaus Staemmler, with photographs by Guido Baselgia (Frankfurt a.M.: Bibliothek Suhrkamp, 1994) [DLA]

2(h): Czech

HRABAL, BOHUMIL, *Harlekins Millionen: Ein Märchen*, trans. by Petr Šimon und Max Rohr (Frankfurt a.M.: suhrkamp taschenbuch, 1989) [DLA]

——*Ich habe den englischen König bedient*, trans. by Karl-Heinz Jahn (Frankfurt a.M.: suhrkamp taschenbuch, 1990) [DLA]

——*Leben ohne Smoking*, trans. by Karl-Heinz Jahn (Frankfurt a.M.: Bibliothek Suhrkamp, 1993) [DLA]

——*Reise nach Sondervorschrift, Zuglauf überwacht*, trans. by Franz Peter Künzel (Frankfurt a.M.: edition suhrkamp, 1969) [DLA]

——*Reise nach Sondervorschrift, Zuglauf überwacht*, trans. by Franz Peter Künzel (Frankfurt a.M.: Bibliothek Suhrkamp, 1994) [DLA]

——*Die Schnur*, trans. by Franz Peter Künzel (Frankfurt a.M.: suhrkamp taschenbuch, 1989) [DLA]

——*Schöntrauer*, trans. by Franz Peter Künzel (Frankfurt a.M.: suhrkamp taschenbuch, 1989) [DLA]

——*Tanzstunden für Erwachsene und Fortgeschrittene*, trans. by Franz Peter Künzel (Frankfurt a.M.: Bibliothek Suhrkamp, 1977) [DLA]

2(i): Classics

> *Griechische Atomisten: Texte und Kommentare zum materialistischen Denken der Antike*, trans. and ed. by Fritz Jürß, Reinmar Müller, and Ernst Günther Schmidt (Leipzig: Reclam UB, 1988) [DLA]
>
> Homer, *Ilias; Odyssee*, trans. by Johann Heinrich Voß (Munich: Winkler, 1957) [DLA]
>
> Horaz (= Quintus Horatius Flaccus), *Sämtliche Gedichte*, bilingual Latin–German edn, with an afterword by Bernhard Kytzler (Stuttgart: Reclam UB, 1992) [DLA]
>
> Lucretius, *The Nature of Things: A Metrical Translation*, trans. by William Ellery Leonhard (London: Dent [Everyman], 1921) [DLA]
>
> Plato:
>> *The Republic of Plato*, trans. from the Greek by H. Spens (London: J. M. Dent [Everyman], 1932) [DLA]
>>
>> Platon, *Gastmahl oder Von der Liebe*, trans. by Friedrich Schleiermacher, ed. by Dr Curt Woyte (Leipzig: Reclam, [n.d.] [1925]) [DLA]
>
> Pliny the Younger, *Briefe*, selected and trans. with an afterword by Mauriz Schuster (Stuttgart: Reclam UB, 1997) [DLA]
>
> Plutarch:
>> *Plutarch's Lives: The Dryden Plutarch*, rev. by Arthur Hugh Clough, 3 vols (London: Dent [Everyman], 1932–33) [DLA]
>
> *Die Erzählungen aus den Tausendundein Nächten*, trans. by Enno Littman, 6 vols (Wiesbaden: Insel 1953) [★]
>
> Virgil:
>> *The Works of Virgil, translated into English verse by Mr Dryden*, 4 vols (Perth: R. Morrison, 1791) [DLA]

2(j) Other

> Andersen, Hans Christian, *Schräge Märchen*, selected and trans. from the Danish by Heinrich Detering and with an essay by Michael Maar (Frankfurt a.M.: Eichborn, 1996)
>
> *Brendans Inseln: Navigatio Sancti Brendani Abbatis*, trans. and ed. by Wolfgang Schlüter (Vienna-Lana: edition per procura, 1997) [DLA]
>
> Christensen, Inger, *Das gemalte Zimmer: Eine Erzählung aus Mantua*, trans. from the Danish by Hanns Grössel, with etchings by Per Kirkeby (Münster: Kleinheinrich, 1993) [DLA]
>
> Dunning, A. J., *Extreme: Betrachtungen zum menschlichen Verhalten*, trans. from the Dutch by Helga van Beuningen (Frankfurt a.M.: Eichborn, 1992) [DLA]
>
> Esterházy, Péter, *Donau abwärts*, trans. from the Hungarian by Hans Skirecki (Salzburg and Vienna: Residenz, 1992) [DLA] [★]
>
> Gustafsson, Lars, *Utopien: Essays*, trans. from the Swedish by Hanns Grössel and others (Munich: Hanser, 1970) [DLA]
>
> ——*Eine Insel in der Nähe von Magora: Gesammelte Erzählungen und Gedichte* (Frankfurt a.M.: Fischer Taschenbuch, 1973) [DLA]
>
> Hernádi, Miklós, *Weiningers Ende*, trans. from the Hungarian by Erika Bollweg (Frankfurt a.M.: Eichborn, 1993) [DLA] [★]
>
> Hiromi, Itō, *Mutter töten: Gedichte und Prosa*, selected and trans. from the Japanese by Irmela Hijiya-Kirschnereit (Salzburg and Vienna: Residenz, 1993) [DLA]
>
> Josephus, Flavius, *Works. The works of Flavius Josephus, the learned and authentic Jewish historian and celebrated warrior, in which are added Three Dissertations concerning Jesus Christ, John the Baptist, James the Just, God's command to Abraham, &c. &c., translated by William*

Whiston A.M., Professor of Mathematics in the University of Cambridge (Halifax: printed and published by William Milner, Cheapside, 1890) [DLA]

KAVAFIS, KONSTANTINOS, *Am hellichten Tag*, trans. from the Greek by Maro Mariolea (Salzburg and Vienna: Residenz, 1989) [DLA]

KIŠ, DANILO, *Garten, Asche*, trans. from the Serbian by Anton Hamm, with an afterword by Ilma Rakusa (Frankfurt a.M.: Bibliothek Suhrkamp, 1997) [DLA]

KRLEŽA, MIROSLAV, *Beisetzung in Theresienburg*, trans. from the Serbo-Croat by Klaus Winkler (Frankfurt a.M.: Bibliothek Suhrkamp, 1964) [DLA]

LEHNING, ARTHUR, *Unterhaltungen mit Bakunin*, trans. by Rolf Binner and Gerd Müller (Nördlingen: Greno, 1987) [DLA] [★]

SUTZKEVER, ABRAHAM, *Griner Akwarium / Grünes Aquarium: Prosastücke*, bilingual Yiddish–German edn, trans. by Jost G. Blum, Michael von Killisch-Horn, and Mirjam Pressler, transcription and afterword by Jost G. Blum (Frankfurt a.M.: Jüdischer Verlag, 1992) [DLA]

TIŠMA, ALEKSANDER, *Das Buch Blam*, trans. from the Serbo-Croat by Barbara Antkowiak (Munich: Hanser, 1995) [★]

3: Literary Criticism and Secondary Literature

3(a): General

ARNOLD, HEINZ LUDWIG, ed., *KLG (Kritisches Lexikon zur deutschsprachigen Gegenwartsliteratur)*, 10 vols in looseleaf binders (Munich: Text + Kritik, 1978, updated to 2000) [★]

ASPETSBERGER, FRIEDBERT, *Literarisches Leben im Austrofaschismus: Der Staatspreis* (Königstein i.Ts.: Hain, 1980) [G.20] [DLA]

BARTSCH, KURT, and GERHARD MELZER, eds, *Trans-Garde: Die Literatur der 'Grazer Gruppe', Forum Stadtpark und manuskripte* (Graz: Droschl, 1990) [D.51]

BENSE, MAX, *Ptolomäer und Mauretanier oder Die theologische Emigration der deutschen Literatur* (Zurich: Haffmans, 1984) [DLA]

BERG, JAN, and others, *Sozialgeschichte der deutschen Literatur von 1918 bis zur Gegenwart* (Frankfurt a.M.: Fischer Taschenbuch, 1981)

BLINN, HANSJÜRGEN, *Informationshandbuch deutsche Literaturwissenschaft* (Frankfurt a.M.: Fischer Taschenbuch, 1990)

BOHN, VOLKER, *Deutsche Literatur seit 1945* (Frankfurt a.M.: Suhrkamp, 1993) [★]

BOYLE, NICOLAS, and MARTIN SWALES, eds, *Realism in European Literature: Essays in Honour of J. P. Stern* (Cambridge: Cambridge University Press, 1986) [DLA] [W]

BRIEGLEB, KLAUS, *Unmittelbar zur Epoche des NS-Faschismus: Arbeiten zur politischen Philologie 1978–1988* (Frankfurt a.M.: suhrkamp taschenbuch wissenschaft, 1989)

——, and SIGRID, WEIGEL, *Gegenwartsliteratur seit 1968* (Munich: dtv, 1992) [★]

BRINKER-GABLER, GISELA, KAROLA LUDWIG, and ANGELA WÖFFEN, eds, *Lexikon deutschsprachiger Schriftstellerinnen 1800–1945* (Munich: dtv, 1986) [DLA]

CARR, G. J., and EDA SAGARRA, eds, *Fin de Siècle Vienna*. Proceedings of the Second Irish Symposium of Austrian Studies held at Trinity College, Dublin, 28. February–2 March 1985 (Dublin: Trinity College, 1985) [D.30]

COUSIN, JOHN W., *A Short Biographical Dictionary of English Literature* (London: Dent [Everyman], 1912) (= [DLA]

Deutsche Literatur 1981: Ein Jahresüberblick, ed. by Volker Hage (Stuttgart: Reclam UB, 1982) [★]

Deutsche Literatur 1982: Ein Jahresüberblick, ed. by Volker Hage (Stuttgart: Reclam UB, 1983) [★]

Deutsche Literatur 1983: Ein Jahresüberblick, ed. by Volker Hage (Stuttgart: Reclam UB, 1984) [★]

Deutsche Literatur 1984: Ein Jahresüberblick, ed. by Volker Hage (Stuttgart: Reclam UB, 1985) [★]

Deutsche Literatur 1985: Jahresüberblick, ed. by Volker Hage (Stuttgart: Reclam UB, 1986) [★]

Deutsche Literatur 1986: Jahresüberblick, ed. by Volker Hage (Stuttgart: Reclam UB, 1987) [★]

Deutsche Literatur 1987: Jahresüberblick, ed. by Franz Josef Görtz, Volker Hage, and Uwe Wittstock (Stuttgart: Reclam UB, 1988) [★]

Deutsche Literatur 1988: Jahresüberblick, ed. by Franz Josef Görtz, Volker Hage, and Uwe Wittstock (Stuttgart: Reclam UB, 1989) [★]

Deutsche Literatur 1990: Jahresüberblick, ed. by Franz Josef Görtz, Volker Hage, and Uwe Wittstock (Stuttgart: Reclam UB, 1991) [★]

Deutsche Literatur 1991: Jahresüberblick, ed. by Franz Josef Görtz, Volker Hage, and Uwe Wittstock (Stuttgart: Reclam UB, 1992) [★]

Deutsche Literatur 1992: Jahresüberblick, ed. by Franz Josef Görtz, Volker Hage, and Uwe Wittstock (Stuttgart: Reclam UB, 1993) [★]

Deutsche Literatur 1993: Jahresüberblick, ed. by Franz Josef Görtz, Volker Hage, and Uwe Wittstock (Stuttgart: Reclam UB, 1994) [★]

Deutsche Literatur 1994: Jahresüberblick, ed. by Franz Josef Görtz, Volker Hage, and Uwe Wittstock (Stuttgart: Reclam UB, 1995) [★]

Deutsche Literatur 1998: Jahresüberblick, ed. by Volker Hage, Rainer Moritz, and Hubert Winkels (Stuttgart: Reclam UB, 1999)

Interpretationen: Erzählungen und Novellen des 19. Jahrhunderts, I (Stuttgart: Reclam, 1988)

FÄHNDERS, WALTER, and MARTIN RECTOR, eds, *Linksradikalismus und Literatur: Untersuchungen zur Geschichte der sozialistischen Literatur in der Weimarer Republik*, 2 vols (Reinbek bei Hamburg: rowohlt, 1974) [DLA]

FISCHER, ERNST, *Von Grillparzer zu Kafka: Sechs Essays* (Frankfurt a.M.: suhrkamp taschenbuch, 1975) [DLA]

FRENZEL, H. A. and E., *Daten deutscher Dichtung: Chronologischer Abriß der deutschen Literaturgeschichte*, 2 vols (Munich: dtv, 1962), I: *Von den Anfängen bis zur Romantik*; II: *Vom Biedermeier bis zur Gegenwart* [DLA]

GRIMM, GÜNTHER E., and HANS-PETER BAYERDÖRFER, eds, *Im Zeichen Hiobs: Jüdische Schriftsteller und deutsche Literatur im 20. Jahrhundert* (Frankfurt a.M.: Athenäum, 1986) [DLA] [★]

HÖRISCH, JOCHEN, *Gott, Geld und Glück: Zur Logik der Liebe in den Bildungsromanen Goethes, Kellers und Thomas Manns* (Frankfurt a.M.: edition suhrkamp, 1983) [DLA]

JENNY-EBERLING, CHARITAS, ed., *Schmetterlinge in der Weltliteratur* (Zurich: Manesse, 2000) [DLA]

KERMODE, FRANK, *The Genesis of Secrecy: On the Interpretation of Narrative* (Cambridge, MA and London: Harvard University Press, 1980) [DLA]

—— *The Sense of an Ending: Studies in the Theory of Fiction* (Cambridge, MA, and London: Oxford University Press, 1970) [DLA]

Klassiker in finsteren Zeiten 1933–1945, ed. by Bernhard Zelber, Schiller-Nationalmuseum, Marbach, 14 May–31 October 1983, Marbacher Katalog, 38, 2 vols (Marbach: Deutsche Schillergesellschaft, 1983) (exhibition catalogue) [DLA] [★]

KLÜGER, RUTH, *Katastrophen: Über deutsche Literatur* (Munich: dtv, 1997)

KRISTEVA, JULIA, *Geschichten von der Liebe*, trans. from the French by Dieter Hornig and Wolfram Bayer (Frankfurt a.M.: edition suhrkamp, 1989) [DLA]

KUDSZUS, WINFRIED, ed., *Literatur und Schizophrenie: Theorie und Interpretation eines Grenzgebiets* (Tübingen: Max Niemeyer; Munich: dtv Wissenschaftliche Reihe, 1977) [DLA]

LOEWY, ERNST, *Literatur unterm Hakenkreuz: Das Dritte Reich und seine Dichtung: Eine Dokumentation* (Frankfurt a.M.: Fischer Bücherei, 1969) [DLA]

LÖWENTHAL, LEO, *Das Bild des Menschen in der Literatur* (Neuwied and Berlin: Luchterhand, 1966) [DLA]

MAAR, MICHAEL, *Die Feuer- und die Wasserprobe: Essays zur Literatur* (Frankfurt a.M.: Suhrkamp, 1997) [DLA]

MACHEINER, JUDITH, *Übersetzen: Ein Vademecum* (Frankfurt a.M.: Eichborn, 1995) [*]

MARTINI, FRITZ, *Deutsche Literaturgeschichte von den Anfängen bis zur Gegenwart* (Stuttgart: Alfred Kröner, 1961) [DLA]

MATT, PETER VON, *Liebesverrat: Die Treulosen in der Literatur* (Munich: dtv, 1991) [DLA] [*]

——*Die verdächtige Pracht: Über Dichter und Gedichte* (Munich: Hanser, 1998) [DLA] [*]

——*Verkommene Söhne, mißratene Töchter: Familiendesaster in der Literatur* (Munich: Hanser, 1995) [DLA] [*]

MINDER, ROBERT, *Dichter in der Gesellschaft* (Frankfurt a.M.: suhrkamp taschenbuch, 1972) [G.8] [DLA]

MOSER, DIETZ-RÜDIGER and others, eds, *Neues Handbuch der deutschsprachigen Gegenwarts-literatur seit 1945* (Munich: dtv, 1993) [*]

MÜLLER, ANDRÉ, *... über die Fragen hinaus: Gespräche mit Schriftstellern* (Munich: dtv, 1988)

NAVRATIL, LEO, *Schizophrene Dichter* (Frankfurt a.M.: Fischer Taschenbuch, 1994) [DLA]

OBERHAUSER, FRED and GABRIELE, *Literarischer Führer durch Deutschland: Ein Insel-Reise-lexikon für die Bundesrepublik Deutschland und Berlin* (Frankfurt a.M.: insel taschenbuch, 1983)

ROBERTSON, RITCHIE, and JUDITH BENISTON, eds, *Catholicism and Austrian Culture* (= *Austrian Studies*, 10 (1999)) [DLA]

ROBERTSON, RITCHIE, and EDWARD TIMMS, eds, *The Habsburg Legacy: National Identity in Historical Perspective* (= *Austrian Studies*, 5 (1994)) [DLA]

Der Ruf (Munich: Nymphenburger Verlagshandlung, 1976)

SCHÄFER, HANS DIETER, *Herr Oelze aus Bremen: Gottfried Benn und Friedrich Wilhelm Oelze* (Göttingen: Wallstein [Göttinger Sudelblätter], 2001) [DLA]

SCHLAFFER, HEINZ, *Der Bürger als Held: Sozialgeschichtliche Auflösungen literarischer Wider-sprüche* (Frankfurt a.M.: edition suhrkamp, 1976) [DLA]

SCHLOSSER, HORST DIETER, ed., *dtv-Atlas zur deutschen Literatur* (Munich: dtv, 1987) [*]

SCHMITT, HANS-JÜRGEN, *Hansers Sozialgeschichte der deutschen Literatur*, XI: *Die Literatur der DDR* (Munich: dtv, 1983) [*]

SCHRÖDER, JÜRGEN, and OTHERS, eds, *Die Stunde Null in der deutschen Literatur: Ausgewählte Texte* (Stuttgart: Reclam, 1995)

SCHWANITZ, DIETRICH, *Englische Kulturgeschichte*, 2 vols (Berne and Stuttgart: UTB, Franke 1995) [W], I: *Die frühe Neuzeit 1500–1760* [*]

——*Englische Kulturgeschichte*, II: *Die Moderne 1760–1914* [*]

SEGEBRECHT, WULF, ed., *Der Bamberger Dichterkreis 1936–1943* (Frankfurt a.M.: Peter Lang, 1987) [DLA]

STAROBINSKI, JEAN, *Psychoanalyse und Literatur*, trans. from the French by Eckhart Rohloff (Frankfurt a.M.: suhrkamp taschenbuch, 1990) [DLA]

STERN, J. P., *The Heart of Europe: Essays on Literature and Ideology* (Oxford: Blackwell, 1992) [DLA] [W]

SZONDI, PETER, *Das lyrische Drama des 'fin de siècle'*, ed. by Henriette Beese (Frankfurt a.M.: suhrkamp taschenbuch wissenschaft, 1975) [DLA]

——*Satz und Gegensatz: Sechs Essays* (Frankfurt a.M.: Insel, 1964) [DLA]

——*Die Theorie des bürgerlichen Trauerspiels im 18. Jahrhundert: Der Kaufmann, der Hausvater und der Hofmeister*, ed. by Gert Mattenklott (Frankfurt a.M.: suhrkamp taschenbuch wissenschaft, 1977) [DLA]

TIMMS, EDWARD, and RITCHIE ROBERTSON, eds, *Austrian Exodus: The Creative Achievements of Refugees from National Socialism* (= *Austrian Studies*, 6 (1995)) [DLA]

——, and RITCHIE ROBERTSON, eds, *Psychoanalysis in its Cultural Context* (= *Austrian Studies*, 3 (1992)) [DLA]

——, and RITCHIE ROBERTSON, eds, *Theatre and Performance in Austria: From Mozart to Jelinek* (= *Austrian Studies*, 4 (1993)) [DLA]

——, and RITCHIE ROBERTSON, eds, *Vienna 1900 from Altenberg to Wittgenstein* (= *Austrian Studies*, 1 (1990)) [DLA] **[D.48]**

WALD LASOWSKI, PATRICK, *Syphilis: Essai sur la littérature française du xix siècle* (Paris: nrf–Gallimard, 1982) [DLA]

WALTER, HANS-ALBERT, *Deutsche Exilliteratur 1933–1950*, 2 vols (Darmstadt and Neuwied: Sammlung Luchterhand, 1972), I: *Bedrohung und Verfolgung bis 1933*; II: *Asylpraxis und Lebensbedingungen in Europa: Deutsche Exilliteratur 1933–1950* [G.13] [DLA]

WALTHER, JOACHIM, *Sicherungsbereich Literatur: Schriftsteller und Staatssicherheit in der Deutschen Demokratischen Republik* (Berlin: Ch. Links, 1996) [DLA] [*]

WOOD, JAMES, *The Broken Estate: Essays on Literature and Belief* (London: Jonathan Cape, 1999) [DLA]

ZONDERGELD, REIN A., *Lexikon der phantastischen Literatur* (Frankfurt a.M.: suhrkamp taschenbuch Phantastische Bibliothek) [DLA]

3(b) Books on literature by UEA colleagues

SCOTT, CLIVE, *The Poetics of French Verse: Studies in Reading* (Oxford: Clarendon Press, 1998)

——*Reading the Rhythm: The Poetics of French Free Verse 1910–1930* (Oxford: Clarendon Press, 1993)

—— *The Spoken Image: Photography and Language* (London: Reaktion, 1999) [W]

—— *Translating Baudelaire* (Exeter: University of Exeter Press, 2000) [W]

—— *Vers Libre: The Emergence of Free Verse in France 1886–1914* (Oxford: Clarendon Press, 1990)

SHEPPARD, RICHARD, *Modernism–Dada–Postmodernism* (Evanston, IL: Northwestern University Press, 2000) [W]

——, ed., *New Ways in Germanistik* (New York: Berg, 1990) [W]

SMITH, CHRISTOPHER, ed., *Norwich Papers IV: Essays in Memory of Michael Parkinson and Janine Dakyns* (Norwich: UEA, 1996) [E.B.15]

WILLIAMS, C[EDRIC] E[LLIS], *The Broken Eagle: The Politics of Austrian Literature from Empire to Anschluss* (London: Paul Elek, 1974) [DLA] [W]

4: Philosophy, Psychology, Anthropology, Religion

ADORNO, THEODOR W., *Impromptus: Zweite Folge neu gedruckter musikalischer Aufsätze* (Frankfurt a.M.: edition suhrkamp, 1968) [DLA]

——*Jargon der Eigentlichkeit: Zur deutschen Ideologie* (Frankfurt a.M.: edition suhrkamp, 1965) [DLA]

——*Mahler: Eine musikalische Physiognomik* (Frankfurt a.M.: Bibliothek Suhrkamp, 1969) [DLA]

——*Minima Moralia: Reflexionen aus dem beschädigten Leben* (Frankfurt a.M.: Bibliothek Suhrkamp, 1962) [DLA]

——*Moments musicaux: Neu gedruckte Aufsätze 1928–1962* (Frankfurt a.M.: edition suhrkamp, 1964) [DLA]

——*Noten zur Literatur*, I (Frankfurt a.M.: Suhrkamp, 1963) [DLA]

——*Noten zur Literatur*, II (Frankfurt a.M.: Suhrkamp, 1963) [DLA]

——*Noten zur Literatur*, III (Frankfurt a.M.: Suhrkamp, 1965) [DLA]

——*Quasi una fantasia: Musikalische Schriften II* (Frankfurt a.M.: Suhrkamp, 1963) [DLA]

——*Versuch über Wagner* (Munich: Knaur Taschenbuch, 1964) [DLA]

SCHEIBLE, HARTMUT, *Theodor W. Adorno in Selbstzeugnissen und Bilddokumenten* (Reinbek bei Hamburg: rowohlts monographien, 1993) [DLA]

ARENDT, HANNAH, *Elemente und Ursprünge totaler Herrschaft*, 2 vols (Frankfurt a.M: Ullstein-Buch, 1975); I: *Antisemitismus*; II: *Imperialismus* [DLA]

The Confessions of St Augustine, trans. from the Latin by E. B. Pusey (London: Dent [Everyman], 1924) [DLA]

BAADER, FRANZ VON, *Gesellschaftslehre*, selected with an introduction and textual notes by Hans Grassl (Munich: Kösel, 1957) [DLA]

——*Über Liebe, Ehe und Kunst: Aus den Schriften, Briefen und Tagebüchern* (Munich: Kösel, 1953) [DLA]

BACHTIN, MICHAIL M., *Die Ästhetik des Wortes*, ed. by Rainer Grübel, trans. from the Russian by Rainer Grübel and Sabine Reese (Frankfurt a.M.: edition suhrkamp, 1979) [DLA]

BARKER, FRANCIS, *The Tremulous Private Body: Essays on Subjection* (London and New York: Methuen, 1984) [DLA]

BASAGLIA, FRANCO, ed., *Die negierte Institution oder Die Gemeinschaft der Ausgeschlossenen: Ein Experiment in der psychiatrischen Klinik in Görz* (Frankfurt a.M.: edition suhrkamp, 1973) [DLA]

BERTAUX, PIERRE, *Mutation der Menschheit: Zukunft und Lebenssinn* (Frankfurt a.M.: suhrkamp taschenbuch, 1979) [DLA]

BILZ, RUDOLF, *Wie frei ist der Mensch? Paläoanthropologie*, 1 (Frankfurt a.M.: suhrkamp taschenbuch wissenschaft, 1973) [DLA]

——*Studien über Angst und Schmerz. Paläoanthropologie*, 2 vols (Frankfurt a.M.: suhrkamp taschenbuch wissenschaft, 1974) [DLA]

BLOCH, ERNST, *Geist der Utopie* (Frankfurt a.M.: Suhrkamp, 1964) [DLA]

——*Das Prinzip Hoffnung*, 3 vols (Frankfurt a.M.: Suhrkamp, 1968) [DLA]

——*Spuren* (Frankfurt a.M.: Bibliothek Suhrkamp, 1964) [DLA]

——*Thomas Münzer als Theologe der Revolution*, III (Frankfurt a.M.: Suhrkamp, 1969) [DLA]

——*Verfremdungen*. 1 (Frankfurt a.M.: Bibliothek Suhrkamp, 1968) [DLA]

——*Vom Hasard zur Katastrophe: Politische Aufsätze aus den Jahren 1934–1939* (Frankfurt a.M.: edition suhrkamp, 1972) [DLA]

BLUMENBERG, HANS, *Die Vollzähligkeit der Sterne* (Frankfurt a.M.: Suhrkamp, 1997) [DLA] [★]

BOHN, VOLKER, *Deutsche Literatur seit 1945* (Frankfurt a.M.: Suhrkamp, 1993) [★]

COCHEM, P. MARTIN VON, CAPUC. ORD., *Güldener Himmels-Schlüssel oder ein Sehr kräfftiges, nutzliches und trostreiches Gebett-Buch* (Einsiedeln, Im Fürstlichen Gotthaus: Johann Eberhard Kälin, 1756)

ELIAS, NORBERT, *über sich selbst* (Frankfurt a.M.: edition suhrkamp, 1990) [DLA]

——*Studien über die Deutschen: Machtkämpfe und Habitusentwicklung im 19. und 20. Jahrhundert*, ed. by Michael Schröter (Frankfurt a.M.: suhrkamp taschenbuch wissenschaft, 1992) [DLA]

——*Humana conditio: Beobachtungen zur Entwicklung der Menschheit* (Frankfurt a.M.: edition suhrkamp, 1990) [DLA]

FOUCAULT, MICHEL, *Wahnsinn und Gesellschaft: Eine Geschichte des Wahns im Zeitalter der Vernunft*, trans. from the French by Ulrich Köppen (Frankfurt a.M.: suhrkamp taschenbuch wissenschaft, 1983) [DLA]

[ANON. / FRANCIS OF ASSISI, ST], *The 'Little Flowers' and the Life of St Francis with the 'Mirror of Perfection'*, with an introduction by Thomas Okey (London: Dent [Everyman], 1931) [DLA]

Freud, Sigmund, *Studienausgabe* (Frankfurt a.M.: Fischer, 1969–74) (vols i, ii, iv, vi–x),
 i: *Vorlesungen zur Einführung in die Psychoanalyse, und Neue Folge*; ii: *Die Traumdeutung*
 (1972); iv: *Psychologische Schriften* (1970); vi: *Hysterie und Angst* (1971); vii: *Zwang,
 Paranoia und Perversion* (1973); viii: *Zwei Kindneurosen* (1969); ix: *Fragen der Gesellschaft:
 Ursprünge der Religion* (1974); x: *Bildende Kunst und Literatur* (1969) [DLA]
——*Sigmund Freud 1956–1939*, ed. by Harald Leupold-Löwenthal (Munich: Goethe-Institut,
 1972) (exhibition catalogue) [DLA]
Freud, Ernst, Lucie Freud, and Ilse Grubrich-Simitis, eds, *Sigmund Freud: Sein
 Leben in Bildern und Texten* (Frankfurt a.M.: Suhrkamp, 1985)
——*Der Wolfsmann vom Wolfsmann: Mit der Krankengeschichte des Wolfsmanns von Sigmund
 Freud, dem Nachtrag von Ruch Mack Brunswick und einem Vorwort von Anna Freud*, ed.
 by Muriel Gardiner (Frankfurt a.M.: Fischer, 1972) [DLA] [★]
Geistliche Seelen-Speis, oder Erhebung des Gemüths zu Gott ([n.p.]: [n. pub.], [pre-1863])
Hamilton, Christopher, *Living Philosophy: Reflections on Life, Meaning and Morality*
 (Edinburgh: Edinburgh University Press, 2001)
Heidegger, Martin, *Einführung in die Metaphysik* (Tübingen: Niemeyer, 1958) [DLA]
Horkheimer, Max, *Zur Kritik der instrumentellen Vernunft: Aus den Vorträgen und
 Aufzeichnungen seit Kriegsende*, ed. by Alfred Schmidt (Frankfurt a.M.: Fischer, 1967)
 [DLA]
——*Kritische Theorie: Eine Dokumentation*, ed. by Alfred Schmidt, 2 vols (Frankfurt a.M.:
 Fischer, 1968) [DLA]
——, and Theodor W. Adorno, *Dialektik der Aufklärung: Philosophische Fragmente*
 (Frankfurt a.M.: Fischer, 1969) [DLA]
Lévi-Strauss, Claude, *Die eifersüchtige Töpferin*, trans. from the French by Hans-Horst
 Herschen, with 5 coloured plates by Anita Albus (Nördlingen: Greno, 1987) [DLA] [★]
——*Mythologien*, iii: *Der Ursprung der Tischsitten*, trans. from the French by Eva
 Moldenhauer (Frankfurt a.M.: suhrkamp taschenbuch wissenschaft, 1976) [DLA]
——*Mythologien*, iv: *Der nackte Mensch*, trans. from the French by Eva Moldenhauer, 2
 vols (Frankfurt a.M.: suhrkamp taschenbuch wissenschaft, 1976) [DLA]
——*Traurige Tropen*, trans. from the French by Eva Moldenhauer (Frankfurt a.M.:
 suhrkamp taschenbuch wissenschaft, 1978) [DLA]
——*Das wilde Denken*, trans. from the French by Hans Naumann (Frankfurt a.M.:
 suhrkamp taschenbuch wissenschaft, 1973) [DLA]
Lorenz, Konrad, *Die Rückseite des Spiegels: Versuch einer Naturgeschichte menschlichen
 Erkennens* (Munich: dtv, 1979) [DLA]
——*Das sogenannte Böse: Zur Naturgeschichte der Aggression* (Vienna: Borotha-Schoeler,
 1968)
Luhmann, Niklas, *Liebe als Passion: Zur Kodierung von Intimität* (Frankfurt a.M.: Suhr-
 kamp, 1982) [DLA]
Lukács, Georg, *Von Nietzsche bis Hitler oder Der Irrationalismus und die deutsche Politik*
 (Frankfurt a.M.: Fischer Bücher des Wissens, 1966) [DLA]
Mackay, Charles, *Zeichen und Wunder: Aus den Annalen des Wahns*, trans. from the
 English by Kurt J. Huch (Frankfurt a.M.: Eichborn, 1992) [DLA] [★]
Marx, Karl, and Friedrich Engels, *Manifest van de Communistische Partij* [Dutch
 translation] (Berlin: Dietz, 1975) [DLA]
Mattenklott, Gert, *Der übersinnliche Leib. Beiträge zur Metaphysik des Körpers* (Reinbek
 bei Hamburg: Rowohlt, 1983) [DLA]
Mill, J. S., *Utilitarianism, Liberty and Representative Government* (London: J. M. Dent
 [Everyman], 1929) [DLA]
Miller, Alice, *Du sollst nicht merken: Variationen über das Paradies-Thema* (Frankfurt a.M.:
 suhrkamp taschenbuch, 1983) [DLA]

MITSCHERLICH, ALEXANDER, ed., *Psychopathographien des Alltags: Schriftsteller und Psycho-analyse* (Frankfurt a.M.: suhrkamp taschenbuch, 1982) [DLA]

——, and MARGARETE, *Die Unfähigkeit zu trauern* (Munich: Serie Piper, 1979)

MITSCHERLICH, MARGARETE, *Erinnerungsarbeit: Zur Psychoanalyse der Unfähigkeit zu trauern* (Frankfurt a.M.: S. Fischer, 1987) [*]

NIETZSCHE, FRIEDRICH, *Jenseits von Gut und Böse: Zur Genealogie der Moral* (Stuttgart: Alfred Kröner, 1964) [DLA]

——*Unzeitgemässe Betrachtungen* (Stuttgart: Alfred Kröner, 1964) [DLA]

    FRENZEL, IVO, *Friedrich Nietzsche in Selbstzeugnissen und Bilddokumenten* (Reinbek bei Hamburg: rowohlts monographien, 1967) [DLA]

PARACELSUS, *Das Licht der Natur: Philosophische Schriften* (Leipzig: Reclam UB, 1973) [DLA]

PASCAL, BLAISE, *Pensées* (Paris: Charpentier, 1847) [DLA]

Johann Michael Sailers vollständiges Gebetbuch für katholische Christen. Neunte mit besonderem Fleiße durchgesehene Ausgabe (Munich: Lentner, 1816)

SCHOLEM, GERSHOM, *Judaica* (Frankfurt a.M.: Bibliothek Suhrkamp, 1963) [DLA]

——*Judaica*, II (Frankfurt a.M.: Bibliothek Suhrkamp, 1970) [DLA]

——*Judaica*, III: *Studien zur jüdischen Mystik* (Frankfurt a.M.: Bibliothek Suhrkamp, 1973) [DLA]

——*Judaica*, IV, ed. by Rolf Tiedemann (Frankfurt a.M.: Bibliothek Suhrkamp, 1984) [DLA]

——*Über einige Grundbegriffe des Judentums* (Frankfurt a.M.: edition suhrkamp, 1970) [DLA]

——*Von Berlin nach Jerusalem: Jugenderinnerungen* (Frankfurt a.M.: Bibliothek Suhrkamp, 1977) [DLA]

——*Walter Benjamin: die Geschichte einer Freundschaft* (Frankfurt a.M.: Bibliothek Suhrkamp, 1975) [DLA]

——*Zur Kabbala und ihrer Symbolik* (Frankfurt a.M.: suhrkamp taschenbuch wissenschaft, 1973) [DLA]

SCHOPENHAUER, ARTHUR:

    Arthur Schopenhauers Briefwechsel und andere Dokumente, selected and ed. by Max Brahn (Leipzig: Insel, 1911) [DLA]

SCHREBER, DANIEL PAUL, *Denkwürdigkeiten eines Nervenkranken*, ed. with an introduction by Samuel L. Weber (Frankfurt a.M.: Ullstein Buch, 1973) [DLA]

SLOTERDIJK, PETER, *Kritik der zynischen Vernunft*, 2 vols (Frankfurt a.M.: edition suhrkamp, 1983) [DLA]

SOMBART, WERNER, *Liebe, Luxus und Kapitalismus: Über die Entstehung der modernen Welt aus dem Geist der Verschwendung* (Berlin: Wagenbachs Taschenbücher, [n.d.]) [DLA]

SWEDENBORG, EMMANUEL, *The Divine Providence* (London: J. M. Dent [Everyman], [n.d.]) [DLA]

TEGLA DAVIES, PARCH. E[DWARD], *Moses: yr Arweinydd Mawr* [in Welsh: *Moses the Great Leader*] (Wrexham: Hughes & Son, Cyoeddwyr, 1922) [DLA]

WITTGENSTEIN, LUDWIG, *Das Blaue Buch: Eine philosophische Betrachtung (Das braune Buch)*, ed. by Rush Rhees (Frankfurt a.M.: suhrkamp taschenbuch wissenschaft, 1980) [DLA]

——*Ludwig Wittgenstein: Briefe: Briefwechsel mit B. Russell, G. E. Moore, J. M. Keynes, F. P. Ramsey, W. Eccles, P. Engelmann und L. von Ficker*, ed. by B. F. McGuinness and G. H. von Wright (Frankfurt a.M.: Suhrkamp, 1980) [DLA]

——*Ludwig Wittgenstein: Familienbriefe*, ed. by Brian McGuinness, Maria Concedtta Ascher, and Otto Pfersmann (Vienna: Verlag Hölder-Pichler-Tempsky, 1996) [DLA]

——*Ludwig Wittgenstein: Geheime Tagebücher 1914–1916*, ed. by Wilhelm Baum, foreword by Hans Albert (Vienna: Turia & Kant, 1991) [DLA]

——*Tractatus logico-philosophicus, Tagebücher 1914–1916, Philosophische Untersuchungen* (Frankfurt a.M.: Suhrkamp, 1963) [DLA]

——*Tractatus logico-philosophicus, Logisch-philosophische Abhandlung* (Frankfurt a.M.: edition suhrkamp, 1963) [DLA]

HEATON, JOHN, and JUDY GROVES, *Wittgenstein for Beginners* (London: Icon Books, 1994)

MCGUINNESS, BRIAN, *Wittgenstein: A Life: Young Ludwig 1889–1921* (Harmondsworth: Penguin Philosophy, 1990) [DLA]

NOLL, JUSTUS, *Ludwig Wittgenstein und David Pinsent: Die andere Liebe der Philosophen* (Berlin: Rowohlt Berlin, 1998) [DLA]

NORMAN, MALCOLM, *Über Ludwig Wittgenstein* (Frankfurt a.M.: edition suhrkamp, 1968) [DLA]

SCHAEFER, CAMILLO, *Wittgensteins Grössenwahn: Begegnungen mit Paul Wittgenstein* (Vienna and Munich: Jugend und Volk, 1986) [DLA]

WUCHTERL, KURT, and ADOLF HÜBNER, *Ludwig Wittgenstein mit Selbstzeugnissen und Bilddokumenten* (Reinbek bei Hamburg: Rowohlts Bildmonographien, 1984) [DLA]

WÜNSCHE, KONRAD, *Der Volksschullehrer Ludwig Wittgenstein: Mit neuen Dokumenten und Briefen aus den Jahren 1919 bis 1926* (Frankfurt a.M.: edition suhrkamp, 1985) [DLA]

5: History, Culture, Geography

Aberle's Wilderer-Album (Rosenheim: Alfred Förg [Rosenheimer Raritäten], 1985) [DLA]

ADENAUER, KONRAD:
   UEXKÜLL, GÖSTA VON, *Konrad Adenauer mit Selbstzeugnissen und Bilddokumenten* (Reinbek bei Hamburg: rowohlts monographien, 1993) [DLA]

ARA, ANGELO, and CLAUDIO MAGRIS, *Triest: Eine literarische Hauptstadt in Mitteleuropa*, trans. from the Italian by Ragni Maria Gschwend (Munich: Hanser, 1987) [DLA] [*]

AVÉ-LALLEMANT, FRIEDRICH CHRISTIAN BENEDICT, *Das deutsche Gaunertum*, facsimile, 2 vols in 1 (Wiesbaden: Ralph Suchier, [n.d.]) [DLA] [*]

BAKER, DAVID, *The Hamlyn Guide to Astronomy*, illustrated by David A. Hardy (London: Hamlyn, 1981) [DLA]

BALFOUR, MICHAEL, *The Kaiser and his Times* (Harmondsworth: Pelican Books, 1972) [DLA]

BAUER, FRITZ and others, eds, *Justiz und NS-Verbrechen: Sammlung deutscher Strafurteile wegen nationalsozialistischer Tötungsverbrechen 1945–1966* (Amsterdam: University Press Amsterdam, 1981)

BAUER, WOLFGANG, *China und die Hoffnung auf Glück: Paradies, Utopien, Idealvorstellungen in der Geistesgeschichte Chinas* (Munich: dtv Wissenschaftliche Reihe, 1974) [DLA]

BEDE, THE VENERABLE, *Bede's Ecclesiastical History of the English Nation* (London: J. M. Dent [Everyman], 1922) [DLA]

BEEVOR, ANTONY, *Stalingrad* (London: Viking, 1998) [DLA]

BENZ, WOLFGANG, ed., *Die Geschichte der Bundesrepublik Deutschland*, vol. IV: Kultur (Frankfurt a.M.: Fischer Geschichte, 1989)

BINDER, CORNELIA, and MICHAEL MENCE, *Last Traces / Letzte Spuren von Deutschen jüdischen Glaubens im Landkreis Bad Kissingen* (Wartmannsroth: C. Binder + M. Mence, 1992) [DLA]

BLACKBURN, JULIA, *Des Kaisers letzte Insel: Napoleon auf Sankt Helena*, trans. from the English by Isabella König [*The Emperor's Last Island*] (Berlin: Berlin Verlag, 1996) [DLA]

BOEHLICH, WALTER, ed., *Der Berliner Antisemitismusstreit* (Frankfurt a.M.: sammlung insel, 1965) [DLA]

BOHRER, KARL HEINZ, ed., *Mythos und Moderne: Begriff und Bild einer Rekonstruktion* (Frankfurt a.M.: edition suhrkamp, 1983) [DLA]

BOVERI, MARGRET, *Tage des Überlebens: Berlin 1945* (Frankfurt a.M.: Eichborn, 1996) [DLA] [*]

British Historical and Political Orations XII to XX Century (London: J. M. Dent [Everyman], 1924) [DLA]

BURCKHARDT, JAKOB, *Weltgeschichtliche Betrachtungen*, ed. by Jakob Oeri (Stuttgart: W. Spemann, 1918) [DLA] [★]

Bürgerliches Gesetzbuch für das deutsche Reich nebst Einführungsgesetz (Leipzig and Vienna: Bibliographisches Institut, [n.d.])

BURTON, ROBERT, *Burton's Anatomy of Melancholy*, 2 vols (London: [n. pub.], 1804) [DLA]

BUSH, SARAH, *The Silk Industry* (Norwich: Shire Publications Ltd, 1993) [DLA]

CARRINGTON, DOROTHY, *The Dream-Hunters of Corsica* (London: Phoenix, 1996) [DLA]

CHRISTIAN-FROGÉ, [RENÉ], ed., *1914–1918: La Grande Guerre vécue, racontée, illustrée par les combattants*, with a preface by M. le Maréchal Foch and a tribute to the French soldier by M. le Maréchal Pétain, II (Paris: Aristide Quillet, 1922) [DLA]

COOK, JAMES:
    Captain Cook's Voyages of Discovery (London: J. M. Dent [Everyman], 1929) [DLA]
    EMERSLEBEN, OTTO, *James Cook* (Reinbek bei Hamburg: rowohlts monographien, 1998) [DLA]

CORBIN, ALAIN, *Meereslust: Das Abendland und die Entdeckung der Küste 1750–1840*, trans. from the French by Grete Osterwald (Berlin: Wagenbach 1990) [DLA] [★]

DARNTON, ROBERT, *Denkende Wollust oder die sexuelle Aufklärung*, trans. from the English by Jens Hagestedt; Jean-Charles Gervaise de Latouche, *Die Geschichte des Dom Bougre, Pförtner der Kartäuser*, trans. from the French by Eva Moldenhauer; Jean-Baptiste d'Argens, *Thérèse philosophe oder Memoiren zu Ehren der Geschichte von Pater Dirrag und Mademoiselle Eradice*, trans. from the French by Eva Moldenhauer (Frankfurt a.M.: Eichborn, 1996)

——*Der Ausdruck der Gemütsbewegungen bei dem Menschen und den Tieren*, ed. by Paul Ekman, trans. by Julius Victor Carus and Ulrich Enderwitz (Frankfurt a.M.: Eichborn, 2000)

DARWIN, CHARLES, *On the Origin of Species* (London: Cassell, 1909) [DLA]

DAWKINS, RICHARD, *The Blind Watchmaker* (Harmondsworth: Penguin, 1991) [DLA]

DENNIS, GEORGE, *Cities and Cemeteries of Etruria*, 2 vols (London: Dent [Everyman], [n.d.]) [DLA]

DINSE, HELMUT, *Die Entwicklung des jiddischen Schrifttums im deutschen Sprachgebiet* (Stuttgart: Metzler, 1974) [G.14] [DLA] [★]

DIRKS, CARL, and KARL-HEINZ JANSSEN, *Der Krieg der Generäle: Hitler als Werkzeug der Wehrmacht* (Berlin: Propyläen, 1999) [DLA]

DUTOURD, JEAN, *Le Feld-maréchal von Bonaparte* (Paris: Flammarion, 1996) [DLA]

ELBOGEN, ISMAR, *Ein Jahrhundert jüdischen Lebens: Die Geschichte des neuzeitlichen Judentums*, ed. by Ellen Littmann (Frankfurt a.M.: Europäische Verlagsanstalt Bibliotheca Judaica, 1967) [DLA]

ELIADE, MIRCEA, *Schamanismus und archaische Ekstasetechnik* (Zurich and Stuttgart: Rascher, [n.d.]) [DLA]

ELSER, JOHANN GEORG, *Un attentat contre Hitler: Procès-verbaux des interrogatoires de Johann Georg Elser*, trans. from the German with an introduction by Bénédicte Savoy (Solin: Actes-Sud, 1998) [DLA]

EMBACHER, HELLA, ALBERT LICHTBLAU, and GÜNTHER SANDER, eds, *Umkämpfte Erinnerung: Die Wehrmachtausstellung in Salzburg* (Salzburg and Vienna: Residenz, 1999) [DLA]

ERICHSON, DR ROLF, *Hochseefischerei*, Beihefte der Reichsstelle für den Unterrichtsfilm F14/1935 (Stuttgart: Kohlhammer, 1935) [DLA]

——*Heringfischerei*, Beihefte der Reichsstelle für den Unterrichtsfilm F184/1938 (Stuttgart: Kohlhammer, 1938) [DLA]

Fermat's Last Theorem (text adapted from TV *Horizon* programme transmitted 15 January 1996) (brochure) [DLA]

FEYERABEND, PAUL, *Wissenschaft als Kunst* (Frankfurt a.M.: edition suhrkamp 1231, 1984) [DLA]

FLEMING, PETER, *Die Belagerung zu Peking: Zur Geschichte des Boxer-Aufstandes*, trans. from the English by Alfred Günther and Till Grupp (Frankfurt a.M.: Eichborn, 1997) [DLA]

FRIEDLÄNDER, SAUL, *Das dritte Reich und die Juden*, I: *Die Jahre der Verfolgung 1933–1939*, trans. from the English by Martin Pfeiffer (Munich: C. H. Beck, 1998) [DLA] [★]

——*Kitsch und Tod: Der Widerschein des Nazismus*, trans. from the French by Michael Grendacher (Munich: dtv, 1986) [DLA]

——*Wenn die Erinnerung kommt*, trans. from the French by Helgard Oestreich (Munich: Beck, 1998) [DLA]

FRIEDRICH, Heinz, ed., *Mein Kopfgeld: Die Währungsreform: Rückblicke nach vier Jahrzehnten* (Munich: dtv Zeitgeschichte, 1988)

FROISSART, JEAN, *The Chronicles of England, France and Spain* (London: J. M. Dent [Everyman], 1930) [DLA]

FUCHS, WERNER, *Todesbilder in der modernen Gesellschaft* (Frankfurt a.M.: Suhrkamp, 1969) [DLA]

GABEL, JOSEPH, *Formen der Entfremdung: Aufsätze zum falschen Bewußtsein*, trans. from the French by Juliane Stiege and Gernot Gather (Frankfurt a.M.: Fischer doppelpunkt, [n.d.]) [DLA]

GAIDA, K. G., and SABINE PROKOT, *Microchiroptera* (Vienna: Falter, 1992) [DLA]

GANTNER, JOSEF, *Die Schweizer Stadt* (Munich: Piper, 1925) [DLA]

GILBERT, MARTIN, *The Holocaust* (London: Fontana, 1987)

GLASER, HERMANN, ed., *1945: Ein Lesebuch* (Frankfurt a.M.: Fischer Geschichte, 1995)

GLOREZ VON MÄHRN, ANDREAS, *Von der Gestalt Natur: Krafft und Würkung der vierfüssigen Thiere Vögel und in Wasser lebenden Fische und Gewürme*, facsimile (Frankfurt a.M.: Insel Bücherei, 1971) (Insel 948) [DLA]

GMELIN, JOHANN GEORG, and GEORG WILHELM STELLER, *Die Große Nordische Expedition von 1733 bis 1743: Aus Berichten der Forschungsreisenden Johann Georg Gmelin und Georg Wilhelm Steller* (Munich: Beck Bibliothek des 18. Jahrhunderts, 1990) [DLA]

GOFFMAN, ERVING, *Asyle: Über die soziale Situation psychiatrischer Patienten und anderer Insassen* (Frankfurt a.M.: edition suhrkamp, 1991) [DLA]

GOLLANCZ, VICTOR, *In Darkest Germany* (London: Victor Gollancz, 1947)

GUMBEL, EMIL JULIUS, *Verschwörer: Zur Geschichte und Soziologie der deutschen nationalistischen Geheimbünde 1918–1924* (Frankfurt a.M.: Fischer, 1984) (Fischer Taschenbuch 4338) [DLA]

HAFFNER, SEBASTIAN, *Failure of a Revolution: Germany 1918–1919*, trans. from the German by Georg Rapp (London: André Deutsch, 1973) [DLA]

HALBWACHS, MAURICE, *Das Gedächtnis und seine sozialen Bedingungen*, trans. from the French by Lutz Geldsetzer (Frankfurt a.M.: suhrkamp taschenbuch wissenschaft, 1985) [DLA]

HALLER, REINHARD, *Prophezeihungen aus Bayern und Böhmen* (Grafenau: Morsak, 1990) [DLA]

HAMANN, BRIGITTE, *Hitlers Wien: Lehrjahre eines Diktators* (Munich: Serie Piper, 2000) [DLA]

HANNOVER-DRÜCK, ELISABETH, and HEINRICH HANNOVER, *Der Mord an Rosa Luxemburg und Karl Liebknecht: Dokumentation eines politischen Verbrechens*, 3rd edn (Frankfurt a.M.: edition suhrkamp, 1972) [DLA]

HARRIS, JOHN, *No Voice from the Hall: Early Memories of a Country-House Snooper* (London: John Murray, 1998) [DLA]

HAWKS, ELLISON, *Stars Shown to the Children* (London: T. C. & E. C. Jack, [1910?]) [DLA]

HEER, HANNES, and KLAUS NAUMANN, eds, *Vernichtungskrieg: Verbrechen der Wehrmacht 1941 bis 1944* (Hamburg: Zweitausendeins, 1997) [DLA]

HERMAND, JOST, and FRANK TROMMLER, *Die Kultur der Weimarer Republik* (Frankfurt a.M.: Fischer Taschenbuch, 1988) [★]

HERMAND, JOST, *Kultur im Wiederaufbau: Die Bundesrepublik Deutschland 1945–1965* (Frankfurt a.M. and Berlin: Ullstein Sachbuch, 1989) [★]

HEYDECKER, JOE J., *Das Warschauer Getto: Foto-Dokumente eines deutschen Soldaten aus dem Jahr 1941*, with a foreword by Heinrich Böll (Munich: dtv Zeitgeschichte, 1984)

JULIUS HIRSCHBERG GESELLSCHAFT / SOCIÉTÉ FRANCOPHONE DE L'HISTOIRE DE L'OPTHA-MOLOGIE, *33. Beiträge zur / Contributions à Geschichte der Augenheilkunde, 33* (Vienna: Facultas, 1991) [DLA]

HITLER, ADOLF, *Mein Kampf* (Munich: Zentralverlag der NSDAP, 1939) [DLA]

HOARE, PHILIP, *Spike Island: The Memory of a Military Hospital* (London: 4th Estate, 2001) [DLA]

HOBBES, THOMAS, *Leviathan* (London: J. M. Dent [Everyman], [n.d.]) [DLA]

HOLMYARD, E. J., *Alchemy* (Harmondsworth: Penguin (Pelican), 1968) [DLA]

HORNE, JOHN and ALAN KRAMER, *German Atrocities 1914: A History of Denial* (New Haven and London: Yale University Press, 2001) [DLA]

HÖSS, RUDOLF:
    BROSZAT, MARTIN, ed., *Kommandant in Auschwitz: Autobiographische Aufzeichnungen des Rudolf Höss* (Munich: dtv Dokumente, 1965)

HUMBOLDT, ALEXANDER VON, *Ansichten der Natur mit wissenschaftlichen Erläuterungen* (Nördlingen: Greno, 1986)

[AUTORENKOLLEKTIV] HUSTER, ERNST-ULRICH, and others, *Determinanten der westdeutschen Restauration 1945–1949* (Frankfurt a.M.: edition suhrkamp, 1979)

HUXLEY, THOMAS HENRY, *Man's Place in Nature and other Essays* (London: J. M. Dent [Everyman], 1908) [DLA]

IGGERS, WILMA, ed., *Die Juden in Böhmen und Mähren: Ein historisches Lesebuch* (Munich: C. H. Beck, 1986) [DLA] [★]

KISS, ENDRE, *Der Tod der k.u.k. Weltordnung in Wien: Ideengeschichte Österreichs um die Jahrhundertwende* (Vienna: Böhlau, 1986) [G.24] [★]

KITTEL, GERHARD, *Die Judenfrage* (Stuttgart: Kohlhammer, 1933) [DLA]

KLEE, ERNST, *'Die SA Jesus Christi': Die Kirche im Banne Hitlers* (Frankfurt a.M.: Fischer Taschenbuch, 1990) [DLA]

—— *'Euthanasie' im NS-Staat: Die 'Vernichtung lebensunwerten Lebens'* (Frankfurt a.M.: Fischer Taschenbuch, 1997) [DLA]

——ed., *Dokumente zur 'Euthanasie'* (Frankfurt a.M.: Fischer Taschenbuch, 1997) [DLA]

—— *Was sie taten — Was sie wurden: Ärzte, Juristen und andere Beteiligte am Kranken- oder Judenmord* (Frankfurt a.M.: Fischer Taschenbuch, 1995) [DLA]

KOENIG, OTTO, *Kultur und Verhaltensforschung: Einführung in die Kulturtheologie*, with a foreword by Konrad Lorenz (Munich: dtv, 1970) [DLA]

KÖNIGSEDER, ANGELIKA, and JULIANE WETZEL, *Lebensmut im Wartesaal: Die jüdischen DPs (Displaced Persons) im Nachkriegsdeutschland* (Frankfurt a.M.: Fischer Geschichte Verlag, 1994) [DLA]

KRAUSS, JOHANN ULRICH, and HELMUT EISENDLE, *Der Irrgarten von Versailles oder Führung durch Äsops Labyrinth der Psyche* (Berlin and Erlangen: Rainer, 1975) [DLA]

KUHNE, LOUIS, *Gesichtsausdruckskunde: Lehrbuch einer neuen Untersuchungs-Art* (Leipzig: [n. pub.], [after 1904]) [DLA]

KUNZE, KONRAD, *dtv-Atlas Namenkunde: Vor- und Familiennamen im deutschen Sprachgebiet* (Munich: dtv, 1998) [DLA] [★]

Landsberg, Paul Ludwig, *Die Erfahrung des Todes*, with an afterword by Arnold Metzger (Frankfurt a.M.: Bibliothek Suhrkamp, 1973) [DLA]

Lange, Friedrich, *Deutscher Seidenbau II. Aufzucht der Raupen: Verarbeitung des Trocken-kokons*, Beihefte der Reichsstelle für den Unterrichtsfilm F213/1939 (Stuttgart and Berlin: Kohlhammer, 1939) [DLA]

Lanzmann, Claude, *Shoah*, with a foreword by Simone de Beauvoir, trans. from the French by Nina Börnsen and Anna Kamp (Munich: dtv Zeitgeschichte, 1988)

Large, David Clay, *Hitlers München: Aufstieg und Fall der Hauptstadt der Bewegung*, trans. from the English by Karl Heinz Siber (Munich: C. H. Beck, 1998) [DLA]

Lautenschlager, Ottmar, ed., *Geschichte der christlichen Religion und Kirche für das Volk*, I (Munich: Verlag des katholischen Büchervereins, 1848) [DLA]

Leitner, Leo, ed., *Kronprinz Rudolf von Österreich: Eine Orientreise vom Jahre 1881* (Salzburg and Vienna: Residenz, 1994) [DLA] [*]

Lepenies, Wolf, *Melancholie und Gesellschaft* (Frankfurt a.M.: Suhrkamp, 1969) [DLA]

Leventhal, Zdenko, *Auf glühendem Boden: Ein jüdisches Überlebensschicksal in Jugoslawien 1941–1947*, ed. by Erhard Roy Wiehn and Jacques Picard (Constance: Hartung-Gorre, 1994) [DLA]

——'Medizinisches in den Schriften Edward Brownes (1642–1708)', (offprint from *Gesnerus*, 39 (1982)) [DLA]

Leverton, Berta, and Shmuel Lowensohn, *I Came Alone: The Story of the Kindertransports*, compiled by Bertha Leverton (Sussex: The Book Guild, 1991) [DLA]

Lichtenstein, Rachel, *Rodinsky's Whitechapel* (London: Artangel, 1999) [DLA]

Lindqvist, Sven, *A History of Bombing*, trans. from the Swedish by Linda Haverty Rugg (London: Granta, 2001) [DLA]

Lockhart, John Gibson, *Life of Napoleon Buonaparte* (Edinburgh: Nimmo, Hay, & Mitchell, 1895) [DLA]

Ludwig, Emil, *Wilhelm der Zweite* (Frankfurt a.M.: Fischer Bücherei, Juli 1968) [DLA]

Mandosio, Jean-Marc, *L'Effondrement de la très grande bibliothèque nationale de France: Ses causes, ses conséquences* (Paris: Éditions de l'Encyclopédie des Nuisances, 1999) [DLA]

Manthey, Jürgen, *In Deutschland und um Deutschland herum: Ein Glossar* (Frankfurt a.M.: Eichborn, 1995) [DLA] [*]

Mayhew, Henry, *Die Armen von London*, trans. from the English by Doris Feldman and others (Frankfurt a.M.: Eichborn, 1996) [DLA] [*]

Mehle, Ferdinand, *Der Kriminalfall Kaspar Hauser* (Kehl: Morstadt, 1995) [DLA]

Meyer-Leviné, Rosa, *Leviné: Leben und Tod eines Revolutionärs* (Frankfurt a.M.: Fischer Taschenbuch, 1974) [DLA]

Michel, Karl Markus, *Gesichter: Physiognomische Streifzüge* (Frankfurt a.M.: Hain, 1990) [DLA]

Milman, Henry Hart, *History of the Jews*, 2 vols (London: J. M. Dent [Everyman], [n.d.]) [DLA]

Mitterrand, François, *Über Deutschland*, trans. from the French by Bernd Schwibs (Frankfurt a.M. and Leipzig: Insel, 1996) [DLA] [*]

Nachama, Andreas, and Gereon Sieverich, eds, *Jüdische Lebenswelten*, Martin Gropius-Bau, Berlin, 12 January–26 April 1992 (Frankfurt a.M.: Jüdischer Verlag; Suhrkamp, 1991) (exhibition catalogue) [DLA] [*]

Nachama, Andreas, Julius H. Schoeps, and Edward van Voolen, eds, *Jüdische Lebenswelten: Essays* (Frankfurt a.M.: Jüdischer Verlag, Suhrkamp, 1991) (in connection with exhibition Jüdische Lebenswelten, Martin Gropius-Bau, Berlin, 12 January–26 April 1992) [DLA]

Napoleon:
   Napoleon Bonaparte and his Times: An Historical Sketch of the French Revolution and the Wars Subsequent on That Event (Glasgow: Blackie & Son, 1844) [DLA]

MAUROIS, ANDRÉ, *Napoleon mit Selbstzeugnissen und Bilddokumenten*, trans. from the French by Ingeborg Esterer (Reinbek bei Hamburg: rowohlts monographien, 1995) [DLA]

NAUMANN, BERND, *Auschwitz: Bericht über die Strafsache gegen Mulka u.a. vor dem Schwurgericht Frankfurt* (Frankfurt a.M.: Fischer Bücherei, 1968)

NIEDERLAND, WILLIAM G., *Folgen der Verfolgung: Das Überlebenden-Syndrom Seelenmord* (Frankfurt a.M.: edition suhrkamp, 1980)

NOSSITER, ADAM, *The Algeria Hotel: France, Memory, and the Second World War* (Boston and New York: Houghton Mifflin, 2001) [DLA]

OHEIM, DR GERTRUD, *Einmaleins des guten Tons: Praktischer Ratgeber* (Gütersloh: Bertelsmann, 1955) [DLA]

OLDHAM, PETER, *Battleground Europe: The Hindenburg Line* (London: Leo Cooper, 2000) [DLA]

PADOVER, SAUL K., *Lügendetektor: Vernehmungen im besiegten Deutschland 1944/45*, trans. from the American by Matthias Fienbork (Frankfurt a.M.: Eichborn, 1999) [DLA]

PALLA, RUDI, *Die Kunst, Kinder zu kneten: Ein Rezeptbuch der Pädagogik* (Frankfurt a.M.: Eichborn, 1997)

—— *Verschwundene Arbeit: Ein Thesaurus untergegangener Berufe* (Frankfurt a.M.: Eichborn, 1994)

PAULUS, MARTIN, EDITH RAIM, and GERHARD ZELGER, eds, *Ein Ort wie jeder andere: Bilder aus einer deutschen Kleinstadt: Landsberg 1923–1958* (Reinbek bei Hamburg: Rowohlt, 1995) [DLA]

PEHLE, MAX, and HANS SILBERBORTH, with MARTIN ISKRAUT, *F. W. Putzgers Historischer Schul-Atlas* (Bielefeld and Leipzig: Velhagen & Klasing, 1935) [DLA]

PEUKERT, DETLEV J. K., *Die Weimarer Republik: Krisenjahre der klassischen Moderne* (Frankfurt a.M.: edition suhrkamp, 1987) [DLA]

PORTER, ROY, ed., *Myths of the English* (Cambridge: Polity Press, 1993) [DLA]

Preussen, Gropius-Bau (former Kunstgewerbemuseum) Berlin, 15. August–15. November 1981; exhibition catalogue, 5 vols (Reinbek bei Hamburg: Rowohlt, 1981), I: *Preußen: Versuch einer Bilanz*, Ausstellungsführer (exhibition guide), ed. by Gottfried Korff, text by Winfried Ranke; II: *Preußen: Beiträge zu einer politischen Kultur*, ed. by Manfred Schlenke; III: *Preußen: Zur Sozialgeschichte eines Staates: Eine Darstelllung in Quellen*, ed. by Peter Brandt with Thomas Hofmann and Reiner Zilkenat; IV: *Preußen: Dein Spree-Athen: Beiträge zu Literatur, Theater und Musik in Berlin*, ed. by Hellmut Kühn; V: *Preußen im Film*, ed. by Axel Marquadt and Heinz Rathsack [DLA]

PRINZ, FRIEDRICH, and MARITA KRAUSS, eds, *Trümmerleben: Texte, Dokumente, Bilder aus Münchner Nachkriegsjahren* (Munich: dtv Zeitgeschichte, 1985)

PROSS, STEFFEN, *'In London treffen wir uns wieder': Vier Spaziergänge durch ein vergessenes Kapitel deutscher Kulturgeschichte nach 1933* (Berlin: Eichborn, 2000) [DLA]

REGELE, HERBERT, ed., *Chronik der Stadt Landsberg a. Lech* (Stadt Landsberg a. Lech, [n.d.]) [DLA]

RITVO, HARRIET, *The Platypus and the Mermaid and other Figments of the Classifying Imagination* (Cambridge, MA and London: Harvard University Press, 1997) [DLA]

ROHRBACH, PAUL, *Unsere koloniale Zukunftsarbeit* (Stuttgart: Die Lese, [n.d.] [pre- 1926]) [DLA]

RÖMER, GERNOT, *Schwäbische Juden: Leben und Leistungen aus zwei Jahrhunderten in Selbstzeugnissen, Berichten und Bildern* (Augsburg: Presse-Druck- und Verlags-GmbH, 1990) [DLA]

ROSENBERG, ALFRED, *Der Mythus des 20. Jahrhunderts: Eine Betrachtung der seelisch-geistigen Gestaltenkämpfe unserer Zeit* (Munich: Hoheneichen, 1933) [DLA]

RÜHL, HANS-JÖRG, ed, *Neubeginn und Restauration: Dokumente zur Vorgeschichte der Bundesrepublik Deutschland 1945–1949* (Munich: dtv dokumente, 1982)

Russell, William Howard, *Meine sieben Kriege: Die ersten Reportagen von den Schlacht-feldern des 19. Jahrhunderts*, trans. from the English by Matthias Fienbork (Frankfurt a.M.: Eichborn, 2000) [DLA]

Schäfer, Bernhard, ed., *Unsere Jüdischen Mitarbeiter in Karlshafen: Austreibung und Leidensweg unter dem Naziregime* (Bad Karlshafen: Verlag des Antiquariats Bernhard Schäfer, 1993) [DLA]

Schäfer, Hans Dieter, *Berlin im zweiten Weltkrieg: Der Untergang der Reichshauptstadt in Augenzeugenberichten* (Munich: Piper, 1991)

Schivelbusch, Wolfgang, *Lichtblicke: Zur Geschichte der künstlichen Helligkeit im 19. Jahrhundert* (Frankfurt a.M.: Fischer Taschenbuch, 1986) [DLA]

——*Eine Ruine im Krieg der Geister: Die Bibliothek von Löwen August 1914 bis Mai 1940* (Frankfurt a.M.: Fischer Taschenbuch Geschichte, 1993) [DLA]

Schlaffer, Hannelore and Heinz, *Studien zum ästhetischen Historismus* (Frankfurt a.M.: edition suhrkamp, 1975) [DLA]

Schmidt, Hermann, *Landsberg am Lech*, with 27 plates (Augsburg: Benno Filser [Deutsche Künstführer], 1929) [DLA]

Schmidt, Siegfried J., ed., *Gedächtnis: Probleme und Perspektiven der interdisziplinären Gedächtnisforschung* (Frankfurt a.M.: suhrkamp taschenbuch wissenschaft, 1991) [DLA]

Schoenberner, Gerhard, *Der gelbe Stern: Die Judenverfolgung in Europa 1933–1945* (Frankfurt a.M.: Fischer Taschenbuch, 1982)

Schorske, Carl E., *Wien: Geist und Gesellschaft im Fin de Siècle*, trans. from the American by Horst Günther (Frankfurt a.M.: Fischer, 1982) [DLA]

Sellner, Albert Christian, *Immerwährender Heiligenkalender* (Frankfurt a.M.: Eichborn, 1993) [DLA] [W]

Šklovskij, Viktor, *Kindheit und Jugend*, trans. from the Russian by Alexander Kaempfe (Frankfurt a.M.: Bibliothek Suhrkamp, 1968) [DLA]

Sonthofen:

    Sonthofen wie's früher war: Bild-Dokumentation Heimatdienst Sonthofen (Sonthofen: [n. pub.], 1987) [DLA]

    Sonthofen: Festbuch zur Stadterhebung (Sonthofen: [n. pub.], 1963) [DLA]

    Happel, Hartmut, *Die Allgäuer Ordensburg in Sonthofen* (Immenstadt: Verlag J. Eberl, 1996) (Verlagsnummer 3–920269) [DLA]

    N.S. Ordensburg Sonthofen, *Erstmalig fand eine Arbeitstagung aller Gauamtsleiter und Kreisleiter der NSDAP auf der Ordensburg Sonthofen vom 16.–23.11.1937 statt* ([n.p.: n. pub., n.d.]) [DLA]

Speer, Albert, *Erinnerungen* (Frankfurt a.M.: Ullstein Taschenbuch, 1969) [DLA]

Speke, John Hanning, *Journal of Discovery to the Source of the Nile* (London: Dent [Everyman], [n.d.]) [DLA]

Spengler, Oswald, *Der Untergang des Abendlandes*, 2 vols (Munich: dtv, 1972) [DLA]

Starke, Günter K. P., *Das Inferno von Braunschweig: Und die Zeit danach* (Cremlingen: Elm, 1994) [DLA]

Stauffenberg, Claus Schenk, Graf von:

    Steffahn, Harald, ed., *Claus Schenk Graf von Stauffenberg* (Reinbek bei Hamburg: rowohlts monographien, 1994) [DLA]

Steinlechner, Gisela, *Fallgeschichten: Krafft-Ebbing, Panizza, Freud, Tausk* (Vienna: WUV-Universitätsverlag, 1995) [DLA]

Steller, Georg Wilhelm (see also Gmelin above):

    Die Grosse Nordische Expedition: Georg Wilhelm Steller (1709–1746): Ein Lutheraner erforscht Siberien und Alaska, Francke Foundation, Halle, 12 May 1996–31 January 1997; exhibition catalogue ed. by Wieland Hintzsche and Thomas Nickol (Gotha: Justus Pethes, 1996) [DLA]

STERN, J. P., *Hitler: The Führer and the People* (Berkeley and Los Angeles: University of California Press, 1992) [DLA]

STERNBERGER, DOLF, *Panorama oder Ansichten vom 19. Jahrhundert* (Frankfurt a.M.: suhrkamp taschenbuch, 1974) [DLA]

——, and others, *Aus dem Wörterbuch des Unmenschen* (Munich: dtv, 1962)

STERNHEIM-PETERS, EVA, *Die Zeit der großen Täuschungen: Eine Jugend im Nationalsozialismus* (Cologne: Verlag Wissenschaft und Politik, 1997) [DLA]

STRACHEY, LYTTON, *Queen Victoria* (London: Chatto and Windus, 1929) [DLA]

THEWELEIT, KLAUS, *Männerphantasien 1: frauen, fluten, körper, geschichte* (Reinbek bei Hamburg: rowohlt taschenbuch, April 1981) [DLA]

——*Männerphantasien 2: männerkörper: zur psychoanalyse des weißen terrors* (Reinbek bei Hamburg: rowohlt taschenbuch, März 1980) [DLA]

——*Buch der Könige 1: Orpheus und Eurydike* (Basle and Frankfurt a.M.: Stroemfeld / Roter Stern, 1988) [DLA] [*]

——*Buch der Könige 2x: Orpheus am Machtpol* (Basle and Frankfurt a.M.: Stroemfeld / Roter Stern, 1994) [DLA] [*]

——*Buch der Könige 2y: Recording Angels' Mysteries* (Basle and Frankfurt a.M.: Stroemfeld / Roter Stern, 1994) [DLA]

UEDING, GERD, *Glanzvolles Elend: Versuch über Kitsch und Kolportage* (Frankfurt a.M.: edition suhrkamp, 1973) [DLA]

VISHNIAC, ROMAN, *A Vanished World*, with a foreword by Elie Wiesel (London: Penguin, 1996)

VONDUNG, KLAUS, *Die Apokalypse in Deutschland* (Munich: dtv, 1988) [DLA] [*]

VOSSLER, KARL, *Die romanischen Kulturen und der deutsche Geist* (Munich: Bremer Presse, 1926) [DLA] [*]

WEIGEL, HANS, *Das Wiener Kaffeehaus* ([n.p.]: Wilhelm Goldmann, 1981) [DLA]

WERTACH:

  ZELLER, JOSEF, *Wertacher Geschichtsbuch: Eine Heimatchronik* (Heimat-Beilage des *Wertacher Landbote*), 3 issues (Wertach: Josef Specht), no. 1: (1937); no. 2: (1938); no. 3: (1939) [DLA]

FICHTER, PATER HEINRICH, *Wertach's wunderbare Rettung* (Chronik: 28.–29. April 1945) (typescript, bound, [n.p.], [n.d.] [DLA]

WESEL, UWE, *Fast Alles, was recht ist: Jura für Nicht-Juristen* (Frankfurt a.M.: Eichborn, 1991) [*]

WIENER KREIS:

  GEIER, MANFRED (ed.), *Der Wiener Kreis mit Selbstzeugnissen und Bilddokumenten* (Reinbek bei Hamburg: rowohlts monographien, 1992) [DLA]

WIESE, HEIDI, *Unter den Straßen von Paris: Geschichte und Micro-Geschichte von Pariser Metro-Stationen* (Bielefeld: Neues Literaturkontor, 1995) [DLA]

WIESEMANN, FALK, *Genizah: Hidden Legacies of the German Village Jews / Genisa: Verborgenes Erbe der deutschen Landjuden* (Vienna: Wiener Verlag, 1992) [DLA]

WILSON, STEPHEN, *The Magical Universe: Everyday Ritual and Magic in Pre-Modern Europe* (London: Hambledon, 2000) [DLA] [W]

WODAK, RUTH, and OTHERS, *'Wir sind alle unschuldige Täter': Diskurshistorische Studien zum Nachkriegsantisemitismus* (Frankfurt a.M.: suhrkamp taschenbuch wissenschaft, 1990) [DLA]

ZIEGLER, ERNST, *Jüdische Flüchtlinge in St. Gallen: Zwei Beispiele* (Rohrschach: Verlag E. Köpfe-Benz AG, 1998) [DLA]

6: Art and Art History

6(a): Art (including photography)

ALBUS, ANITA, *Die Kunst der Künste: Erinnerungen an die Malerei* (Frankfurt a.M.: Eichborn, 1997) [DLA]

Anita Albus, Salzburg, 2 August–30 September 1990, and Zagreb 11 October–11 November 1990; exhibition catalogue ed. by Tugomir Lukšić (Salzburg: Galerie Schloss Neuhaus, 1990) [D.53]

ANON., Untitled photograph album, containing photographs from the Baltic, St Petersburg, Moscow, and Copenhagen with English captions [DLA]

BERGER, JOHN, *About Looking* (London: Writers and Readers Publishing Cooperative, 1980) [DLA]

BERGER, JOHN, *Road Directions: Zeichnungen und Texte*, ed. by Beat Wismer (Zurich: Edition Unikate, 1999) [DLA]

——*Ways of Seeing*. Based on the BBC television series (London: British Broadcasting Corporation and Penguin Books (Pelican), 1981) [DLA]

BOSE, GÜNTHER, and ERICH BRINKMANN, *Circus: Geschichte und Ästhetik einer niederen Kunst* (Berlin: Wagenbach, 1978) [DLA]

America through the Eyes of German Immigrant Painters (Boston: Goethe-Institut, 1975–1976) (exhibition catalogue) [DLA]

DI STEFANO, ARTURO:

    Arturo Di Stefano, Warwick Arts Centre, 27 May–1 July 1995; Preston; Leicester; Purdy Hicks Gallery, London, November–December 1995 (London: Purdy Hicks Gallery, 1995) (exhibition catalogue) [DLA]

    Arturo Di Stefano: Paintings and Woodcuts, 8–30 September 1989 (London: Pomeroy Purdy Gallery, [n.d.]) (exhibition catalogue) [DLA]

    Arturo Di Stefano, 17 May–15 June 1991 (London: Pomeroy Purdy Gallery, 1991) (exhibition catalogue) [DLA]

FRÄNKEL, HUGO, and WINFRIED WOLF, *Lebens Lauf: Menschenbilder aus einer verschütteten Zeit* (Stuttgart: Silberburg, 1991) [DLA]

FRIEDRICH, CASPAR DAVID:

    FIEGE, GERTRUD, *Caspar David Friedrich mit Selbstzeugnissen und Bilddokumenten* (Reinbek bei Hamburg: rowohlts monographien, 1995) [DLA]

Isny i. Allgäu: 15 [5] echte Photographien (Isny: J. Buemann, n.d.])

GRÜNEWALD, MATHIS:

    LÜCKING, WOLF, *Mathis: Nachforschungen über Grünewald* (Berlin: Frölich & Kaufmann, 1983) [DLA]

HUBMANN, FRITZ, *Die gute alte Zeit: Alte Photographien aus Wien* (Salzburg: Verlag St. Peter, 1967) [DLA]

KELLER, HILTGART L., *Reclams Lexikon der Heiligen und der biblischen Gestalten: Legende und Darstellung in der bildenden Kunst* (Stuttgart: Reclam UB, 1987) (= UB 10154) [DLA]

GIEDION-WELCKER, CAROLA, *Paul Klee in Selbstzeugnissen und Bilddokumenten* (Reinbek bei Hamburg: rowohlts monographien, 1961) [DLA]

LEONARDO DA VINCI:

    Leonardo da Vinci (New Haven and London: Yale University Press in association with the South Bank Centre, 1989) (exhibition catalogue, Hayward Gallery)

    CLARK, KENNETH, *Leonardo da Vinci mit Selbstzeugnissen und Bilddokumenten*, trans. from the English by Thomas Puttkarden (Reinbek bei Hamburg: rowohlts monographien, 1995) [DLA]

LLEWELLYN, NIGEL, *The Art of Death: Visual Culture in the English Death Ritual, c. 1500–c. 1800* (London: Reaktion, 1992) [DLA]

Navratil, Leo, *August Walla: Sein Leben und seine Kunst* (Nördlingen: Greno (Delphi) 1988) [DLA]

——*Bilder nach Bildern* (Salzburg and Vienna: Residenz, 1993) [DLA]

——*Gespräche mit Schizophrenen* (Munich: dtv, 1978) [DLA]

——*Die Künstler aus Gugging* (Vienna and Berlin: Medua, 1983) [DLA]

——*Die Künstler und ihre Werke*, 2 vols (Vienna: Brandstätter, 1997), i: *Art Brut und Psychiatrie: Gugging 1946–1986*; ii: *Gugging 1946–1986* [DLA] [*]

——*Schizophrenie und Sprache: Schizophrenie und Kunst: Zur Psychologie der Dichtung und des Gestaltens* (Munich: dtv Wissenschaftliche Reihe, 1976) [DLA] [W]

——*Die Überlegenheit des Bären: Theorie der Kreativität* (Munich: Arcis, 1995) [DLA] [W]

Sammlung Leo Navratil: Arbeiten aus dem Niederösterreichischen Landeskrankenhaus für Psychiatrie und Neurologie Klosterneuburg (Linz: Wolfgang Gurlit Museum, 1980) [DLA]

Peintner, Max, *Bilderschrift: Essay* (Salzburg and Vienna: Residenz, 1984) [DLA]

Max Peintner: Austria, Biennale di Venezia 1986 (Salzburg and Vienna: Residenz, 1986) (exhibition catalogue) [DLA]

Pisanello:

    Hill, George F., *Drawings by Pisanello: A Selection with Introduction and Notes* (New York: Dover Publications, 1965) [DLA]

Poussin, Nicolas:

    Bätschmann, Oskar, *Nicolas Poussin, Landschaft mit Pyramus und Thisbe: Das Liebesglück und die Grenzen der Malerei* (Frankfurt a.M.: Fischer künststück, 1987) [DLA]

Rainer, Arnulf, *Die blühende Steiermark: 36 Überarbeitungen* (Graz: Akademische Druck- und Verlagsanstalt, [n.d.]) [DLA]

——*Totenmasken*, with contributions by Werner Hofmann and Arnulf Rainer (Salzburg and Vienna: Residenz, 1985) [DLA]

Raphael, Max, *Bild-Beschreibung: Natur, Raum und Geschichte in der Kunst: Leonardo, Raffael, Tintoretto et al* (Frankfurt a.M. and New York: Edition Qumran im Campus-Verlag, 1987) [DLA] [*]

Roters, Eberhard, *Kunst ist ein Spiel das ernst macht: Briefe und Texte 1949–1994*, ed. by Eva Züchner in collaboration with Hanna Roters (Cologne: DuMont, 1999) [DLA]

Sander, August, *Antlitz der Zeit*, with an introduction by Alfred Döblin (Munich: Schirmer / Mosel, 1976) [DLA]

Schröppel, Annemarie and Adolf, and Manfred Einsiedler, *Alt-Pfrontner Photoalbum: Bilder von den Anfängen der Photographie bis 1930* (Pfronten: Eberle, [n.d.] [1984]) [DLA]

Seemann, Helfried, and Christian Lunzer, eds, *Klosterneuburg: Die Stadt 1860-1930* (Vienna: Album, 1996)

Shearman, John, *Mannerism* (Harmondsworth: Pelican, 1967) [DLA]

Sprigg, June, and David Larkin, *Shaker: Life, Work and Art* (London: Cassell, 1994)

Stoddard, Roger Eliot, *The Loose Connection: A Build Up of Static in Art* (Newlyn, Cornwall: Andrew Lanyon, 1992) [DLA]

——'François Hemsterhuis: Some Uncollected Authors lviii', offprint from *The Book Collector*, 50.2 (Summer 2001) (enclosed in *The Loose Connection*: see above) [W]

Strasser, René, *Landschaften der Seele* (Rohrschach: Löpfer-Benz AG, 1994) [DLA]

——*Die Stadt als Landschaft* (Rohrschach: Löpfer-Benz AG, 1997) [DLA]

Tripp, Jan Peter, *'Ein 17. Januar': 30 Aquarelle von Landschaften aus dem Elsaß gesehen am Nachmittag des 17. Januars 1985 gemalt im darauffolgenden Herbst & Winter* (Offenbach a.M.: Die Galerie, 1986) [W]

——*Die Aufzählung der Schwierigkeiten: Arbeiten von 1985–92* (Offenburg: Reiff Schwarzwaldverlag, 1993) [W] [D.58]

——*Die Kehrseite der Dinge: Bilder aus zwölf Jahren* (Weingarten: Drumlin Verlag, 1984)

——*Kunstkatalog: 19 Bilder und 16 Texte*, ed. by Wendelin Niedlich (Stuttgart: Verlag Wendelin Niedlich, 1972)

——*MännerBilder* (Stuttgart: Künstlerhaus, 1982)

Turner, J. M. W.:

> Bower, Peter, *Turner's Papers: A Study of the Manufacture, Selection and Use of his Drawing Papers 1787–1820*, 10 October 1990–13 January 1991 ([London]: Tate Gallery, 1990) (exhibition catalogue) [DLA]
>
> Hamilton, James, *Turner: A Life* (London: Hodder and Stoughton, 1997) [DLA]
>
> Powell, Cecilia, *Turner in Germany*, 23 May–10 September 1995 (London: Tate Gallery Publications, 1995) (exhibition catalogue)

Once upon a Time: Visions of Old Japan from the Photos of Beato and Stillfried and the Words of Pierre Loti, English translation by Linda Coverdale (New York: Friendly Press Inc., 1986)

Der vorbehaltlose Blick. Fotografien, Bilder und Handschriften aus einer privaten Sammlung [Volker Kahmen], Westfälischer Kunstverein, Münster, 13 April–25 May 1997; Kunstverein für die Rheinlande und Westfalen, Düsseldorf, Spring 1998 (Westfälischer Kunstverein, Münster / Kunstverein für die Rheinlande und Westfalen, Düsseldorf 1997–98) (exhibition catalogue) [DLA]

Photographs of Waterloo, Brussels and Ostend:

> *Panorama de la Bataille de Waterloo* (Postkartenheft) (Brussels, [n.d.]) [DLA]
>
> *Bruxelles-Brussels: 10 Snapshots (Série 1)* (Brussels, Vereenigde Gravuur Postkaartfabriek, [n.d.]
>
> *Ostende-Oostende: Snapshots (Série 2)* ([n.p.]: NELS, [n.d.])
>
> *Waterloo: 10 Snapshots* (Brussels: D'Hondt et De Grave, n.d.])

Wittwer, Uwe, *Relative Stille / Relatively Still* (Zurich: Edition Ideal, 1999) [DLA]

6(b): Architecture

Antwerpen-Centraal: Een verhaal van tijd und ruimte (Brussels: Willy van Gestel, 1993) [brochure with colour plates of Antwerp Station] [DLA]

Broadgate and Liverpool Street Station (London: Rosehaugh Stanhope Developments plc, 1991) [DLA]

De Somer, Patricia, and De Smet, Gaston, *Het Centraal Station van Antwerpen, een levend monument*, Jordaenshuis, Antwerp, 4–26 October 1986 (City of Antwerp, 1986) (exhibition catalogue) [DLA]

Jaskot, Paul B., *The Architecture of Oppression: The SS, Forced Labor and the Nazi Monumental Building Economy* (London and New York: Routledge, 2000) [DLA]

Kleines Wörterbuch der Architektur (Stuttgart: Reclam UB, 1995) [DLA]

Muthesius, Stefan, *The English Terraced House* (New Haven and London: Yale University Press, 1982) [DLA]

——*The Postwar University: Utopianist Campus and College* (New Haven and London: Yale University Press, 2000) [DLA] [W]

Schlögel, Karl, *Promenade in Jalta und andere Städtebilder* (Munich: Carl Hanser, 2001) [DLA] [★]

——*Das Wunder von Nishnij oder Die Rückkehr der Städte: Berichte und Essays* (Frankfurt a.M.: Eichborn, 1991) [DLA] [★]

Wagner, Otto:

> Geretsegger, Heinz, Max Peintner and Walter Pichler, *Otto Wagner (1841–1918): Unbegrenzte Groszstadt: Beginn der modernen Architektur* (Salzburg and Vienna: Residenz, 1983) [DLA]

6(c): Gardens

Clarke, Ethne, and George Wright, *English Topiary Gardens* (London: Weidenfeld and Nicolson, 1988) [DLA]

Headley, Gwyn, and Wim Meulenkamp, *Follies, Grottoes & Garden Buildings* (London: Aurum Press, 1999) [DLA]

Derek Jarman's Garden, with photographs by Howard Sooley (London: Thames and Hudson, 1996)

Kaut, Hubert, *Wiener Gärten: Vier Jahrhunderte Wiener Gartenkunst* (Vienna: Bergland, 1964) [DLA]

Lambton, Lucinda, *Lucinda Lambton's A to Z of Britain* (London: HarperCollins, 1996) [DLA]

Trotha, Hans von, *Der englische Garten: Eine Reise durch seine Geschichte* (Berlin: Wagenbach, 1999) [DLA]

Williamson, Tom, and Anthea Taigel, *Gardens in Norfolk* (UEA Norwich: Centre for East Anglian Studies, 1990) [DLA]

6(d): Music

Bach, Johann Sebastian:
Johann Sebastian Bach: Leben und Schaffen (Zurich: Manesse, 1957)

Beethoven, Ludwig von:
Ludwig von Beethoven: Briefe und Aufzeichnungen, selected and with an afterword by Rüdiger Görner (Frankfurt a.M. and Leipzig: Insel Bücherei, 1993) [DLA]

Brahms, Johannes:
Neunzig, Hans A., *Johannes Brahms* (Reinbek bei Hamburg: rowohlts monographien, 1988) [DLA]

Clément, Catherine, *Die Frau in der Oper: Besiegt, verraten und verkauft*, trans. from the French by Annette Holoch (Stuttgart: Metzler, 1992) [DLA]

Mahler, Gustav:
Schreiber, Wolfgang, *Gustav Mahler in Selbstzeugnissen und Bilddokumenten* (Reinbek bei Hamburg: rowohlts monographien, 1971) [DLA]
Metzger, Heinz-Klaus, and Rainer Riehn, eds, *Musik-Konzepte: Sonderband Gustav Mahler* (Munich: Edition text + kritik, July 1989) [DLA]

Mozart, Wolfgang Amadeus, *Die Zauberflöte* (Stuttgart: Reclam UB, 1995) [DLA]

Verdi, Giuseppe:
Kühne, Hans, *Giuseppe Verdi mit Selbstzeugnissen und Bilddokumenten* (Reinbek bei Hamburg: rowohlts monographien, 1998) [DLA]

Wagner, Richard:
Richard Wagners Gesammelte Briefe, ed. by Julius Kapp and Emrich Kastner: *Jugend-Briefe*, 2 vols (Leipzig: Hesse & Becker, 1914), I: *Lehr- und Wanderjahre 1830–1843*; II: *1843–1850* [DLA]
Neunzer, Bernd, and Horst Brandstätter, *Wagner: Lehrer, Dichter, Massenmörder. Samt Hermann Hesses Novelle 'Klein und Wagner'* (Frankfurt a.M.: Eichborn, 1996) [DLA]

6(e): Stage and screen

Eisner, Lotte H., *The Haunted Screen* (London: Secker & Warburg, 1983)

Faulstich, Werner, and Helmut Korte, eds, *Fischer Filmgeschichte* [1895–1995], 5 vols (Frankfurt a.M.: Fischer, 1995) [★]

Jordan, Günther, *Erprobung eines Genres: DEFA-Dokumentarfilme für Kinder 1975–1990: Ein Nachlesebuch* (Remscheid: Kinder- und Jugendfilmzentrum, 1991)

Jung, Uli, ed., *Der deutsche Film: Aspekte seiner Geschichte von den Anfängen bis zur Gegenwart* (Trier: Wissenschaftlicher Verlag, 1993)

Korte, Helmut, ed., *Film und Realität in der Weimarer Republik* (Frankfurt a.M.: Fischer Taschenbuch, 1980)

Lang, Fritz:

Elsaesser, Thomas, *Metropolis* (London: BFI, 2000) [W]

Töteberg, Michael, *Fritz Lang mit Selbstzeugnissen und Bilddokumenten* (Reinbek bei Hamburg: rowohlts monographien, 1985) [DLA]

Sinclair, Andrew, *Metropolis: A Film by Fritz Lang* (Godalming, Surrey: Lorrimer (Classic film scripts), 1981)

Leiser, Erwin, *'Deutschland, erwache!': Propaganda im Film des Dritten Reichs* (Reinbek bei Hamburg: rororo aktuell, 1989)

Lubitsch, Ernst:

Renk, Herta-Elisabeth, *Ernst Lubitsch mit Selbstzeugnissen und Bilddokumenten* (Reinbek bei Hamburg: rowohlts monographien, 1992) [DLA]

Piscator, Erwin:

Goertz, Heinrich, *Erwin Piscator in Selbstzeugnissen und Bilddokumenten* (Reinbek bei Hamburg: rowohlts monographien, 1974) (=221) [DLA]

Rapp, Christian, *Höhenrausch: Der deutsche Bergfilm* (Vienna: Sonderzahl, 1997) [DLA]

Stadelmaier, Gerhard, *Letzte Vorstellung: Eine Führung durchs deutsche Theater* (Frankfurt a.M.: Eichborn, 1993) [DLA] [*]

Wiene, Robert:

Sinclair, Andrew, *The Cabinet of Dr. Caligari: A Film by Robert Wiene, Carl Mayer and Hans Janowitz* (Godalming, Surrey: Lorrimer (Classic film scripts), 1984)

7: Topography, Travel, Natural History

7(a): Bavaria, Austria, Switzerland, the Alps

Austria, Grieben's Guide Books, 234 (Vienna and Heidelberg: Carl Ueberreuter, 1951) (with inset maps) [DLA]

Buck, Josef, *Handbuch für Reisende im Allgäu, Lechtal und Bregenzerwald*, facsimile of 1856 edn (Kempten: Tobias Dannheimer, 1983) [DLA]

Deutschland: Michelin Guide 1995 (Clermont-Ferrand: Michelin, 1995) [DLA]

Die kleine Eiszeit: Gletschergeschichte im Spiegel der Kunst, Schweizerisches Alpines Museum Bern, 24 August–16 October 1983; Gletschergarten Museum Luzern, 9 June–14 August 1983 (Berne and Lucerne, 1983) (exhibition catalogue) [DLA]

Großer LBS-Wander-Atlas: Die 150 schönsten Wanderziele unserer bayerischen Heimat, ed. by Landesfremdenverkehrsverband Bayern (Ostfildern: Fink-Kümmerly+Frey, 1982) [DLA]

Henzi, Werner, *St Petersinsel und J.-J. Rousseau's Aufenthalt 1765* (Biel: Heimatkunde-Kommission Seeland, 1956) [DLA]

Das Naturschutzgebiet St. Petersinsel und Heidenweg / Réserve naturelle de l'île Saint-Pierre et du Chemin des Païens (brochure: AONL, Biel) (Berne: [n.p.], 1990)

Hess, Heinrich, ed., *Zeitschrift des deutschen und österreichischen Alpenvereins*, 39 (Munich: [n. pub.], 1908) [DLA]

Prospekt Kloster Irsee (brochure, Schwäbisches Tagungs- und Bildungszentrum, [n.d.]) [DLA]

Seitz, Gabriele, *Wo Europa den Himmel berührt: Die Entdeckung der Alpen* (Munich: Artemis, 1987) [DLA]

Orientierungskarte der Umgebung von Sonthofen und Hindelang im Allgäu [DLA]

Tyndall, John, *The Glaciers of the Alps and Mountaineering in 1861* (London: Dent [Everyman], 1906) [DLA]

7(b): UK (general)

Baedeker's London (Leipzig: Baedeker, 1905) [DLA]

Great Britain and Ireland: Michelin Guide 1988 (Clermont-Ferrand: Michelin, 1988) [DLA]

ANON., *Guidebook to Haddon Hall* (Duke of Rutland) (Derby: English Life Publications, 1990) [DLA]

NICOLSON, ADAM, *The National Trust Book of Long Walks*. Photographs by Charlie Waite (London: Pan Books, 1984) [DLA]

7(c): East Anglia

Framlingham Castle, Suffolk. Department of the Environment Official Handbook. (London: HMSO, 1977) [DLA]

Gardens to Visit in East Anglia 1989 (East Anglia Tourist Board [1989]) [DLA]

Ickworth, Suffolk ([?]: The National Trust, 1990) [DLA]

The Mannington & Wolterton Estate (brochure) [n.d.] [DLA]

Rainthorpe Hall, Norfolk (brochure) [n.d.] [DLA]

BACON, JEAN and STUART, *Dunwich, Suffolk* (Marks Tey: Segment Publications, 1988) [DLA]

—— *Orford and Orford Ness* (Marks Tey: Segment Publications, 1992) [DLA]

GAGE, ERNEST G., *Costessey Hall: A Retrospect of the Jernegans, Jerninghams and Stafford Jerninghams of Costessey Hall, Norfolk* (Old Costessey, Norfolk: Colin L. House, 1991) [DLA]

HAYWARD, JAMES, *Shingle Street: Flame, Chemical and Psychological Warfare in 1940, and the Nazi Invasion that Never Was* (Colchester: Les Temps Modernes, 1994) [DLA]

KINSEY, GORDON, *Orfordness: Secret Site: A History of the Establishment 1915–1980* (Lavenham: Terence Dalton, 1981) [DLA]

SCARFE, NORMAN, *Suffolk: A Shell Guide* (London: Faber & Faber, 1976) [DLA]

SEYMOUR, JOHN, *The Companion Guide to East Anglia*, rev. and with a new chapter by John Burke (London: Collins, 1990) [DLA]

SIMPER, ROBERT, *The Suffolk Sandlings: Alde, Deben and Orwell Country* (Ipswich: East Anglian Magazine Publishing Ltd, 1986) [DLA]

7(d): Wales

Llanwddyn & Lake Vrynwy, centenary edn [1988?], unpaginated pamphlet [DLA]

North Wales (Northern Section), 15th edn (London: Ward Lock & Co. (Illustrated Guide Books) [n.d.]) [DLA]

North Wales (Southern Section), 9th edn (London: Ward Lock & Co. (Illustrated Guide Books) [n.d.]) [DLA]

7(e): France, Corsica, Italy

Compiègne (photocopied extract from Guide Michelin, pp. 138–49) [DLA]

La France au Fil de l'Eau (Paris: Guides Gallimard, 1998) [DLA]

France: Michelin Guide 1991 (Clermont-Ferrand: Michelin, 1991) [DLA]

Paris (Paris: Hachette [Les Guides bleus], 1956) [DLA]

BAEDECKER, KARL, *Sud-Est de la France: Du Jura à la Méditerranée y compris la Corse* (Leipzig and Paris, 1910) [DLA]

CAPELLO, CESARE, *32 Vedute: Ricordi di Napoli* [Milan, 1930] [DLA]

MAYER, HANNES, *Die Wälder Korsikas* (Stuttgart and New York: Gustav Fischer, 1990) [DLA]

MERK, CHARLES, *The Normandy Coast* (London: Unwin, 1911) [DLA]

WARD, PHILIP, *The Aeolian Islands* (New York and Harrow: Oleander Press, 1984) [DLA]

7(f): Poland, Czech Republic

BECHER, PETER and HUBERT ETTL, eds, *Böhmen: Blick über die Grenze: Reise-Lesebuch* (Viechttach: edition lichtung, 1991) [DLA]

Hermanowicza, Henryka, *Kraków cztery pory roku w fotografii* (Cracow: Wydawnictwo Literackie, 1982) [DLA]

Krizek, Vladimir, and Richard Svandrlik, *Marienbad: Eine Plauderei über eine Stadt, die es im Laufe von knappe hundert Jahren schaffte, weltberühmt zu werden*, trans. by Dora Müller (Marienbad: Art Valery, 1996) [DLA]

Rybar, Ctibor, *Prag: Reiseführer* (Prague: CTK–Pressefoto, 1991) [DLA]

Ward, Philip, *Polish Cities: Travels in Cracow and the South, Gdańsk, Malbork and Warsaw* (Cambridge: Oleander Press, [n.d.]) [DLA]

7(g): Other guides and atlases

Atlas ([n.p.: n. pub., n.d.]) [cf. *Schwindel. Gefühle.*] [DLA]

A Literary and Historical Atlas of Europe (London: Dent [Everyman], 1914) [DLA]

A Literary and Historical Atlas of Africa and Australia (London: Dent [Everyman], [pre-1913]) [DLA]

Moyen-Orient: Liban–Syrie–Jordanie–Irak–Iran (Paris: Hachette [Les Guides bleus], 1956) [DLA]

Museum Plantin-Moretus Antwerpen, 20 picture postcards [DLA]

7(h): Maps and road atlases

Aberystwyth [map], Bartholomew's Reduced Survey Sheet 16. Scale 2 miles to an inch. [n.d.] [DLA]

Anglesey Ordnance Survey One-Inch Map, Sheet 106 [DLA]

Bacon's Motoring and Cycling Road Map England and Wales [DLA]

Bacon's New Large Print Map of London and Suburbs (London: G. W. Bacon & Co. Ltd) [DLA]

Barnett's Cambridge [map] [DLA]

George, Wilfrid, *6 Footpath Maps: Footpath map of Bungay and District; Footpath map of Dunwich with Westleton and Minsmere; Footpath map of Lowestoft Central; Footpath map of Norwich Central with Mousehold Heath; Footpath map of The Saints; Footpath map of Southwold with Walberswick and Blythburgh* [DLA]

Gross, Alexander, *The Daily Chronicle War Map of the Balkans* (London, [n.d.]) [DLA]

Lac Léman: Carte topographique de la Suisse, 1:100000 (Berne: Service topographique) [DLA]

Map of Central Africa [DLA]

Michelin Atlas Routier France (Paris: Michelin Éditions du Voyage, 2000) [DLA]

Michelin Motoring Atlas Great Britain and Ireland (Watford: Michelin, 2000) [DLA]

Philips Europe Road Atlas [DLA]

Pwllheli (map) [n.d.]

Touristenkarte der Lüneburger Heide (Bremen: Adolf Sosna jr.) [DLA]

7(i): Natural history, gardening

Common Objects of the Country, Part II (The 'Look about you' Nature Study Books, book VII) (London: T. C. & E. C. Jack Ltd, [pre-1926]) [DLA]

Ground Cover Plants (Wisley Handbook 26) (London: Royal Horticultural Society, 1980)

Bilz, F. E., *Das neue Natur-Heilverfahren* (Leipzig: F. E. Bilz, 1898)

Blackburne-Maze, Peter, *Pruning* (London: Collins Aura Garden Handbooks, 1998)

Bourdu, Robert, *le hêtre* (Arles: Actes Sud, 1996) [DLA]

Brend, William A., *The Story of Ice in the Present and Past* (London: George Newnes, 1902) [DLA]

Chambers, George F., *The Story of the Weather Simply Told for General Readers* (London: George Newnes, 1897) [DLA]

Dähnckes PilzKompaß: Die besten Speisepilze und alle gefährlichen Pilze sicher bestimmen (Munich: Gräfe und Unzer, [n.d.])

DANNEYROLLES, JEAN-LUC, *la tomate* (Arles: Actes Sud, 1999) [DLA]

DUNCAN, JAMES, *British Moths, Sphinxes etc.*, with engravings by Maria Sibilla Merian (Edinburgh etc.: W. H. Lizars [The Naturalist's Library], 1836) [DLA]

FLEGG, JIM, *Green Guide: Birds of Britain and Europe* (London: New Holland, 1992)

FRITZSCHE, HELGA, *Feines Gemüse selbst gezogen* (Munich: Gräfe und Unzer, [n.d.] [DLA]

GORER, RICHARD, *Illustrated Guide to Trees* (Leicester: Galley Press, 1984)

GOUST, JÉRÔME, *thym et sarriette* (Arles: Actes Sud, 1999) [DLA]

HARWERTH, WILLI, *Das kleine Kräuterbuch: Einheimische Heils-, Würz- und Duftpflanzen nach der Natur gezeichnet* (Leipzig: Insel-Bücherei, [n.d.])

JÜNGLING, HEINZ, and PAUL HAGER, *Bestimmungsbuch für Pflanzen*, with illustrations by Angela Paysan and Änne Roth (Stuttgart: Klett, 1970) [DLA]

KNIGHT, F. P., *Plants for Shade* (Wisley Handbook 25) (London: Royal Horticultural Society, 1979)

KREDEL, FRITZ, *Das kleine Buch der Vögel und Nester,* with colour illustrations by Fritz Kredel (Leipzig: Insel Bücherei, [n.d.])

KÜNZLE, JOH., *Chrut und Uchrut: Praktisches Heilkräuterbüchlein von Kräuterpfarrer Joh. Künzle* (Locarno-Minusio: Verlag Kräuterpfarrer Künzle AG, 1961) [DLA]

LANKESTER, SIR RAY, *Essays of a Naturalist* (London: Methuen's Modern Classics, 1927) [DLA]

LICHTENSTERN, HERMANN, *Heilpflanzen: Botanik-Standort-Sammelgut-Sammelzeit-Arzneiliche Verwendung-Zubereitung* (Munich: Goldmann, 1972) [DLA]

LOUDON, J. C., *The Magazine of Natural History and Journal of Zoology, Botany, Mineralogy, Geology and Meteorology*, 3 vols (London: Longman, Rees, Orme, Brown, and Green, 1829–30)

MABEY, RICHARD, *Flora Britannica* (London: Chatto and Windus, 1997)

MARKTANNER, THOMAS, *Welcher Nachtfalter ist das? Spinner, Spanner, Schwärmer und andere häufige Nachtschmetterlinge* (Stuttgart: Kosmos Naturführer, 1992) [DLA]

Monksilver Nursery's Tenth Catalogue, 1 October 1999 [DLA]

NEBELTHAU, OTTO, *Mein Gemüsegarten: Eine nützliche Unterweisung* (Leipzig: Insel Bücherei, [n.d.]) [DLA]

Nicolais SingvogelKompaß: Singvögel in Feld, Wald und Garten sicher bestimmen (Munich: Gräfe und Unzer, [n.d.])

Pahlows BeerenKompaß: Eßbeeren und Giftbeeren sicher bestimmen (Munich: Gräfe und Unzer, [n.d.])

Pahlows HeilpflanzenKompaß: Heilpflanzen sicher bestimmen und gezielt anwenden (Munich: Gräfe und Unzer, [n.d.])

Heinrich Rebau's Naturgeschichte für Schule und Haus: Eine gemeinfassliche und ausführliche Beschreibung aller drei Reiche der Natur, ed. by Traugott Bromme (Stuttgart: H. Thienemann's Verlag (Jul. Hoffmann), 1866)

Royal Horticultural Society Encyclopedia of Gardening (London: Dorling Kindersley, 1992)

SAUER, FRIEDER, *Heimische Nachtfalter nach Farbfotos erkannt: 570 Arten auf 576 Farbfotos* (Karlsfeld: Fauna [Sauers Naturführer], 1993) [DLA]

Simpson's Seeds: The Tomato Book, with recipes contributed by the Tomato Growers' Club (Old Oxted, Surrey: Simpson's Seeds, 1999) [DLA]

Woottens Herbaceous Plants 1999 [Michael Loftus] (Suffolk: Woottens of Wenhaston, 1999) [DLA]

8: Dictionaries, Phrase Books, Works of Reference

Der beredte Italiener: Eine Anleitung, in sehr kurzer Zeit, ohne Hülfe eines Lehreres, leicht und richtig italienisch sprechen zu lernen: Praktisches Hülfsbuch (Berne: J. Heuburger's Verlag, 1878)

Collins German–English English–German Dictionary, by Peter Terrell and others, 2nd edn, rev. 1991 (London: HarperCollins / Ernst Klett, 1991) [DLA]

Collins Robert Concise French–English English–French Dictionary, by Beryl T. Atkins and others (London: Collins, 1983) [DLA]

CRUDEN, ALEXANDER, *Cruden's Complete Concordance to the Old and New Testaments*, ed. by C. H. Irwin, A. D. Adams, and S. A. Waters (London and Redhill: Lutterworth Press, 1945) [DLA]

TRNKA, NINA, *Czech* (New York: Hippocrene Books, 1994, 2nd printing 1998) (Hippocrene Handy *Extra* Dictionaries) [DLA]

Dictionnaire des mots rares et précieux (Paris: Éditions 10/18, 1996, repr. 1998) [DLA]

Encyclopedia Britannica, twelfth edn, 32 vols (London and New York: Encyclopedia Britannica, 1922)

Langenscheidts Taschenwörterbuch der lateinischen und deutschen Sprache, Part I: *Latin–German*, by Prof. Hermann Menge, 22nd edn, rev. by Prof. Heinrich Müller (Berlin-Schöneberg: Langenscheidt KG Verlagsbuchhandlung, 1959) [DLA]

Nouveau Petit Larousse Illustré: Dictionnaire encyclopédique, ed. by Claude Augé, 19th edn (Paris: Librairie Larousse, 1925) [DLA]

Odham's Dictionary of the English Language, Illustrated, ed. by A. H. Smith and J. L. N. O'Loughlin (Watford: Odham's, 1946) [DLA]

The Concise Oxford Dictionary of Current English, ed. by H. W. Fowler and F. G. Fowler, 5th edn rev. by E. McIntosh (Oxford: Clarendon Press, 1967) [DLA]

Oxford Concise English Dictionary, ed. by Judy Pearshall, 10th edn, rev. (Oxford: OUP, 2001) (thumb-indexed) [DLA]

The Oxford Concise English Dictionary (Oxford: OUP, 2001)

The Oxford–Duden German Dictionary (Oxford: Clarendon Press, 1990)

Collins Roget's International Thesaurus, ed. by Robert L. Chapman, British edn (Glasgow: HarperCollins, 1996) [DLA]

SADLER, PERCY, *Exercices anglais ou Cours de thèmes gradués*, 4th edn (Brussels: Société Typographique Belge, 1837) (handwritten exercises bound in) [DLA]

TEXTOR, A. M., *Auf deutsch: Das Fremdwörterlexikon* (Reinbek bei Hamburg: rororo, 1969) [DLA]

Trübners Deutsches Wörterbuch: Im Auftrag der Arbeitsgemeinschaft für deutsche Wortforschung, ed. by Alfred Götze and others, 8 vols (Berlin: De Gruyter, 1939–57) [DLA] [★]

Collins Gem Welsh Dictionary Welsh–English Saesneg–Cymraeg (London: Harper Collins 1992, repr. 1998) [DLA]

Verzeichnis Lieferbarer Bücher/German Books in Print 1996/97: Autoren – Titel – Stichwörter, 8 vols (Frankfurt a.M.: Verlag der Buchhändler-Vereinigung, 1996)

WITHYCOMBE, E. G., *The Oxford Dictionary of English Christian Names*, 2nd edn (Oxford: Clarendon Press, 1959)

9: Periodicals

Camera, 55.2 (February 1976) [DLA]

Camera, 55.5 (May 1976) [DLA]

Der Deutschunterricht, 37.3 (1985)

du, 247,9 (September 1961): *Le Palais Idéal*

du, 463,9 (September 1979): *Kunst der Geisteskranken* [DLA]

du, 586,12 (December 1989): *weiss* [DLA]

du, 618,9 (September 1992): *Balthus* [DLA]

du, 631,10 (October 1993): *Citoyen der Weltliteratur: Der Erzähler V. S. Naipaul* [DLA]

du, 635,2 (February 1994): *Trotzdem: Kultur und Katastrophe* [DLA]

du, 641,9 (September 1994): *Ingeborg Bachmann: Das Lächeln der Sphinx* [DLA]

du, 642,10 (October 1994): *Triest: Am äußersten Ufer* [DLA]

du, 677,11 (November 1997): *Tango: Eine Art Sehnsucht* [DLA]

du, 691,1 (January 1999): *Claude Simon: Bilder des Erzählens* [DLA]

Harvard Design Magazine, no. 9 (Fall 1999): *Constructions of Memory: On Monuments Old and New* [DLA]

Harvard Design Magazine, no. 13 (Winter–Spring 2001): *East of Berlin: Postcommunist Cities Now* [DLA]

Illustrirte Zeitung: Wöchentliche Nachrichten über alle Ereignisse, Zustände und Persönlichkeiten der Gegenwart, no. 28 (January–June 1857) (Leipzig: J. J. Weber)

Illustrirte Zeitung: Wöchentliche Nachrichten über alle Ereignisse, Zustände und Persönlichkeiten der Gegenwart, no. 29 (July–December 1857) (Leipzig: J. J. Weber)

The New Yorker, 14 June 1999 (containing article by Philip Gourevitch, 'The Memory Thief' (on Wilkomirski), pp. 48–68, followed by Adam Gopnik, 'Proust at the Movies', with photographs by François-Marie Banier, pp. 69–70)

10: 'Books disposed of by WGS' (see also Chapter 11 of the present volume)

BACHMANN, INGEBORG:
> PICHL, ROBERT, ed, *Kritische Wege der Landnahme: Ingeborg Bachmann im Blickfeld der neunziger Jahre*. Londoner Symposium 1993 zum 20. Todestag der Dichterin (17.10. 1973) (Vienna: Hora, 1994)

BARICCO, ALESSANDRO, *Silk*, trans. from the Italian by Guido Waldman (London: Harvill, 1997)

DUDEN, ANNE, *Das Judasschaf* (Berlin: Rotbuch, 1985)

FRITZ, MARIANNE, *Was soll man da machen?* (Frankfurt a.M.: Suhrkamp, 1985)

KERSCHBÄUMER, MARIE-THÉRÈSE, *Für mich hat Lesen etwas mit Fließen zu tun...: Gedanken zum Lesen und Schreiben von Literatur* (Vienna: Wiener Frauenverlag, 1989)

MELCHINGER, SIEGFRIED, *Geschichte des politischen Theaters* (Velber: Friedrich, 1971) (see Chapter 5 of the present volume)

MONÍKOVÁ, LIBUŠE, *Pavane für eine verstorbene Infantin* (Munich: dtv, 1988)

ROTERS, EBERHARD, and OTHERS, *Berlin 1910–1933*, trans. by Marguerite Mounier (New Jersey: Wellfleet Press, 1982)

SCHLAG, EVELYN, *Unsichtbare Frauen: drei Erzählungen* (Salzburg and Vienna: Residenz, 1995)

VALÉRY, PAUL, *Über Kunst*, trans. by Carlo Schmid (Frankfurt a.M.: Bibliothek Suhrkamp, 1959) [DLA]

WALSER, ROBERT:
> SEELIG, CARL, *Promenades avec Robert Walser*, trans. by Bernard Kreiss (Zurich: Rivages, 1989) [ownership not definite]

WEDEKIND, FRANK:
> *Frank Wedekind: Gesammelte Werke*, 6 vols (Munich and Leipzig: Müller, 1912–14)
> BOA, ELIZABETH, *The Sexual Circus: Wedekind's Theatre of Subversion* (Oxford: Blackwell, 1987) [G.25]

PART III

❖

A Bibliographic Survey

Fig. III.1. WGS riding near Sonthofen, *c.* 1963–64. © U. E. Sebald

Fɪɢ. III.2. WGS cycling near the flat in Wymondham (1971).

This photo was first published in *Manuskripte* in June 1988 to accompany a pre-publication extract from *Die Ausgewanderten* (later 'Dr Henry Selwyn'); see Primary Bibliography E.B.12. The original caption read: 'Fotografiert von O. im Frühjahr 1971 vor der Mauer von Prior's Gate' [Photographed by O. in Spring 1971 in front of the wall of Prior's Gate]. 'Prior's Gate' is the fictional name of the street where the narrator of 'Dr Henry Selwyn' and his wife live in Hingham, to the west of Wymondham; 'O.', the narrator's partner, becomes 'Clara' in the book version. © U. E. Sebald; courtesy of DLA Marbach

1

Primary Bibliography

An Analytical Bibliography of the Works of W. G. Sebald,
compiled by Richard Sheppard

Do you know what a wasp's nest is like? It's made of something much much
thinner than airmail paper: gray and as thin as possible. [...] It weighs nothing.
For me the wasp's nest is a kind of ideal vision: an object that is extremely
complicated and intricate, made out of something that hardly exists.

W. G. SEBALD, Interview with Sarah Kafatou (1998) (see J.24 below)

ACKNOWLEDGEMENTS

This bibliography was compiled using the following sources as starting points:
Marcel Atze, 'Personalbibliographie W. G. Sebald', in *W. G. Sebald* (*Porträt* 7), ed.
by Franz Loquai (Eggingen: Isele, 1997), pp. 269–83; *Germanistik an Hochschulen
in Großbritannien und Irland: Verzeichnis der Hochschullehrerinnen und Hochschullehrer
1997/98* (London: DAAD, 1998), pp. 174–75; Markus R. Weber, 'Bibliografie W. G.
Sebald', *Text + Kritik*, no. 158 (W. G. Sebald) (April 2003), 112–17; the catalogues
and newspaper cuttings collection of the Deutsches Literaturarchiv, Marbach am
Neckar; the *Autorendokumentation* of the Stadt- und Landesbibliothek, Dortmund;
and the library of Ute Sebald.

While compiling this bibliography, I asked a range of publishing houses to send
me data concerning the printings and print runs of Sebald's works. Some publishers
keep detailed records and responded with great generosity, and I would like to
thank them for their kind co-operation.

Particular thanks are also due to Helen Buchanan and Jill Hughes of the Taylor
Institution, University of Oxford, whose help in the preparation of this bibliography
was indispensable, Professor Mark Anderson (Columbia University) who drew my
attention to the existence of *Der Wecker* (Section H.A) and the source of the title of
E.B.12, Dr Jan Ceuppens (Leuven) who did the same for the title of E.B.13, Ernst
Baumeler (Zürich), Carmen Gómez García (Barcelona), Alan Klein (New York),
Professor Jakob Lothe (University of Oslo), Dr James Peters, the Archivist of the
University of Manchester who unearthed D.1, Terry Pitts (Cedar Rapids, Iowa),
Sven Meyer (Hamburg), Ada Vigliani (Turin), Dr Roger Stoddard (Harvard),
Hansjörg Albrecht (Neuruppin) and Robert Treffer (Augsburg), all of whom
kindly answered detailed bibliographical questions and provided me with much
new material, Simon Prosser (Penguin Books), Professor Clive Scott, FBA (UEA),
who undertook the comparison of B.B.1 and B.B.1(e), Jürgen Hosemann (Fischer

Verlag), who drew my attention to the differences between B.B.1(d) and B.B.1(e), Professor Reinbert Tabbert (Reutlingen) who made many helpful suggestions, Dr Bojan Bujić, Dr David Pattison, Dr Jennifer Baines, and Andrew Hobson (all of Magdalen College, Oxford), who helped me greatly with titles in the Slavonic and Iberian languages, Russian, and Greek respectively, Hitoko Suzuki and Hiroko Furukawa, without whose help we could not have discovered or transliterated the Japanese translations, and Caroline Mason and Dr See-young Park, to whom the same applies in respect of the Chinese and Korean translations respectively.

In order to keep this primary bibliography up to date, the compiler and editors would very much like to hear details of these (or any other items) via the following email address: <richardetcarolyn.sheppard@orange.fr>.

Contents

A   Books: Critical Works
    A.1   Carl Sternheim: Kritiker und Opfer der Wilhelminischen Ära
    A.2   Der Mythus der Zerstörung im Werk Döblins
    A.3   Die Beschreibung des Unglücks: Zur österreichischen Literatur von
                   Stifter bis Handke
    A.4   A Radical Stage: Theatre in Germany in the 1970s and 1980s
    A.5   Unheimliche Heimat: Essays zur österreichischen Literatur
    A.6   Logis in einem Landhaus
    A.7   Luftkrieg und Literatur (On the Natural History of Destruction)
B   Books: Literary Works
B.A   Books: Poetry (see also B.D.3)
    B.A.1   Nach der Natur (After Nature)
    B.A.2   For Years Now
    B.A.3   Unerzählt (Unrecounted)
B.B   Books: Prose Fiction
    B.B.1   Schwindel. Gefühle. (Vertigo)
    B.B.2   Die Ausgewanderten (The Emigrants)
    B.B.3   Die Ringe des Saturn (The Rings of Saturn)
    B.B.4   Austerlitz
B.C   Other Independent Publications (Literary and Critical Works)
B.D   Collected Works and Posthumously Published Anthologies
    B.D.1   Außer Land: Drei Romane und ein Elementargedicht
    B.D.2   Campo Santo
    B.D.3   Über das Land und das Wasser
C   Radio Adaptations of Prose Texts
D   Critical Articles and Essays
    D.1–D.11 (1970–1975)
    D.12–D.17 (1976–1980)
    D.18–D.34 (1981–1985)
    D.35–D.52 (1986–1990)
    D.53–D.60 (1991–1995)
    D.61–D.76 (1996–2001)
E   Extracts from Individual Works
E.A   Extracts from Books of Poetry (B.A.1–B.A.3)
    Nach der Natur (B.A.1)

E.A.1–E.A.6 (1984–2001)
E.A.7–E.A.12 (2002–2010)
For Years Now (B.A.2)
E.A.13–E.A.14 (2001–2010)
Unerzählt (B.A.3)
E.A.15–E.A.16 (2001–2010)

E.B   Extracts from Works of Prose Fiction
Schwindel. Gefühle. (B.B.1)
E.B.1–E.B.8 (1988–2001)
E.B.9–E.B.11 (2002–2010)
Die Ausgewanderten (B.B.2)
E.B.12–E.B.17 (1988–2001)
E.B.18 (2002–2010)
Die Ringe des Saturn (B.B.3)
E.B.19–E.B.24 (1994–2001)
E.B.25–E.B.29 (2002–2010)
The Four Prose Pieces from *Campo Santo* (B.D.2, pp. 7–52)
E.B.30–E.B.32 (1996–2001)
E.B.33–E.B.35 (2002–2010)
Austerlitz (B.B.4)
E.B.36 (2001)
E.B.37–E.B.41 (2002–2010)

E.C.   Extracts from Critical Works (A.1–A.7)
E.C.1–E.C.3 (1982–2001)
E.C.4–E.C.6 (2002–2010)

F   Other Literary Work
F.A   Poetry Written and First Published 1965–2001
F.B   Poetry Written 1965–2001 and Posthumously Published
F.C   Prose Pieces Written and First Published 1965–2001
F.D   Prose Pieces Written 1965–2001 and Posthumously Published
G   Book Reviews (1971–2001)
G.1–G.19 (1971–1980)
G.20–G.30 (1981–1990)
G.31 (1991–1996)

H   Juvenilia (Prose and Poetry) (1961–1965)
H.A   School (1961–1963)
H.B   University of Freiburg (1963–1965)
I   Letters
J   Interviews
J.1–J.12 (1971–1995)
J.13–J.33 (1996–2000)
J.34–J.54 (2001)

K   Collected *obiter dicta*
L   Recorded Texts
M   Translations by W. G. Sebald
M.A   Poetry
M.B   Prose
N   Parodies of Sebald's Work

A. Books: Critical Works

A.1 Winfried Georg Sebald, *Carl Sternheim: Kritiker und Opfer der Wilhelminischen Ära* (Stuttgart, Berlin, Cologne, and Mainz: W. Kohlhammer, [3 October] 1969), 2000 copies. Published version (revised) of an MA thesis written in German at the University of Manchester (1966–68); **A.1X** W. G. Sebald, 'Zu Carl Sternheim: Kritischer Versuch einer Orientierung über einen umstrittenen Autor' [unpublished *licence* (BA) dissertation in German, University of Fribourg (Switzerland), 1965–66], ed. by Richard Sheppard, *Journal of European Studies*, 41.3–4 (forthcoming December 2011) [see also Chapter 2 of the present volume]

A.2 Winfried Georg Sebald, *Der Mythus der Zerstörung im Werk Döblins* (*Literatur-Gesellschaftswissenschaft*, no. 45) (Stuttgart: Ernst Klett, [21 March] 1980), 2500 copies. Published version (extensively revised) of a PhD thesis written in English at the University of East Anglia, Norwich (1970–73)

A.3 W. G. Sebald, *Die Beschreibung des Unglücks: Zur österreichischen Literatur von Stifter bis Handke* (Salzburg and Vienna: Residenz, [1 September] 1985), *c.* 2000 copies; **A.3(a)** (Frankfurt a.M.: Fischer Taschenbuch 12151, [August] 1994); 4000–5000 copies [September] 1994; 3rd printing [January] 2003

A.3.1 W. G. Sebald, *Pútrida patria: Ensayos sobre literatura* [Castilian edition containing translations of the Foreword and five of the ten essays originally published in A.3], trans. by Miguel Sáenz (*Colección Argumentos* A326) (Barcelona: Editorial Anagrama, [April] 2005), pp. 9–104, 5000 copies [c.f. A.5.1]

A.4 W. G. Sebald, ed., *A Radical Stage: Theatre in Germany in the 1970s and 1980s* [selected papers given at a colloquium held at the University of East Anglia, Norwich, 30 March–1 April 1987] (Oxford and New York: Berg, 1988) **A.4(a)** 2nd edition (Providence [RI], Oxford, and Munich: Berg, 1990) [A paperback edition was planned but never appeared; see also Appendix 6.1, pp. 184–86.]

A.5 W. G. Sebald, *Unheimliche Heimat: Essays zur österreichischen Literatur* (Salzburg and Vienna: Residenz, [1 March] 1991), *c.* 2500 copies; **A.5(a)** (Frankfurt a.M.: Fischer Taschenbuch 12150, [January] 1995); 2nd printing [January] 2003; 3rd printing [April] 2004

A.5.1 W. G. Sebald, *Pútrida patria: Ensayos sobre literatura* [Castilian edition containing translations of the Foreword, the Introduction and six of the nine essays originally published in A.5], trans. by Miguel Sáenz (*Colección Argumentos* A326) (Barcelona: Editorial Anagrama, [April] 2005), pp. 107–228, 5000 copies [c.f. A.3.1]

A.5.2 W. G. Sebald, *Pátria Apátrida (Ensaiõs sobre literatura austríaca)* [Portuguese edition], trans. by Telma Costa (Lisbon: Editorial Teorema, [December] 2010)

A.6 W. G. Sebald, *Logis in einem Landhaus: Über Gottfried Keller, Johann Peter Hebel, Robert Walser und andere* (Munich and Vienna: Carl Hanser, [14 September] 1998), 8000 copies; **A.6(a)** (Frankfurt a.M.: Fischer Taschenbuch 14862, [November] 2000); 2nd printing [May] 2001; 4th printing [August] 2003

A.6.1 W. G. Sebald, *Séjours à la campagne. Suivi de Au Royaume des ombres par Jan Peter Tripp* [French edition], trans. by Patrick Charbonneau (Arles: Actes Sud, [10 October] 2005), 5000 copies

A.6.2 W. G. Sebald, *O caminhante solitário: Sobre Gottfried Keller, Johann Peter Hebel, Robert Walser e otros* [Portuguese edition], trans. by Telma Costa (Lisbon: Editorial Teorema [September] 2009)

A.6.3 W. G. Sebald, *A Place in the Country* [British edition], trans. by Jo Catling (London: Hamish Hamilton, forthcoming 2011)

A.6.4 W. G. Sebald, *A Place in the Country* [American edition] (New York: Random House, forthcoming 2011)

A.6.5 W. G. Sebald, *Logies in een landhuis* [Dutch edition], trans. by Ria van Hengel (Amsterdam: De Bezige Bij, forthcoming 2011)

Luftkrieg und Literatur

A.7   W. G. Sebald, *Luftkrieg und Literatur. Mit einem Essay zu Alfred Andersch* [based on three lectures given at the University of Zurich on 30 October, 13 November and 4 December 1997] (Munich and Vienna: Carl Hanser, [11 March] 1999), 5000 copies; 2nd printing [21 July] 2009; **A.7(a)** (Frankfurt a.M.: Fischer Taschenbuch 14,863, [August] 2001); 2nd printing [February] 2002; 3rd printing [August] 2002; 4th printing [July] 2003; 5th printing [January] 2005

A.7.1   W. G. Sebald, *On the Natural History of Destruction. With essays on Alfred Andersch, Jean Améry and Peter Weiss* [American edition], trans. by Anthea Bell (New York: Random House, [11 February] 2003); **A.7.1(a)** (New York: The Modern Library, [February] 2004)

A.7.2   W. G. Sebald, *On the Natural History of Destruction. With essays on Alfred Andersch, Jean Améry and Peter Weiss* [British edition], trans. by Anthea Bell (London: Hamish Hamilton, [February] 2003), 6500 copies; 2nd printing 1500 copies; 3rd printing 1500 copies; 4th printing 1500 copies; 5th printing 1500 copies; **A.7.2(a)** (London: Penguin, 2004), 8500 copies; 2nd printing 3000 copies; 3rd printing 1500 copies

A.7.3   W. G. Sebald, *On the Natural History of Destruction. With essays on Alfred Andersch, Jean Améry and Peter Weiss* [Canadian edition], trans. by Anthea Bell, hardback (Toronto: Alfred A. Knopf Canada [a division of Random House Canada], 2003); **A.7.3(a)** paperback (Toronto: Vintage Canada [Random House Canada], [17 February] 2004)

A.7.4   W. G. Sebald, *Sobre la historia natural de la destrucción* [Castilian edition], trans. by Miguel Sáenz (*Panorama de narrativas* A556) (Barcelona: Editorial Anagrama, [November] 2003), 6000 copies; 2nd printing [December] 2003, 3000 copies; 3rd printing [July] 2005, 3000 copies; **A.7.4(a)** (*Quinteto* 336) (Barcelona: Editorial Anagrama, [January] 2010), 4000 copies

A.7.5   W. G. Sebald, *De natuurlijke historie van de verwoesting* (hardback) [Dutch edition], trans. by Ria van Hengel (Amsterdam: De Bezige Bij, 2004); 2nd printing [July] 2008, 1250 copies

A.7.6   W. G. Sebald, *Storia naturale della distruzione* [Italian edition], trans. by Ada Vigliani (*Biblioteca Adelphi* 463) (Milan: Adelphi [31 October] 2004), 6350 copies; 2nd printing [31 January] 2005), 1836 copies

A.7.7   W. G. Sebald, *De la déstruction comme élément de l'histoire naturelle* [French edition], trans. by Patrick Charbonneau (Arles: Actes Sud, [2 January] 2004), 5000 copies; 2nd printing, 4000 copies

A.7.8   W. G. Sebald, *História Natural da Destruição: Guerra Aérea e Literatura* [Portuguese edition], trans. by Telma Costa (*Outras estórias* [no series number]) (Lisbon: Editorial Teorema, [February] 2006), 2000 copies

A.7.9   W. G. Sebald, *Luftkrig og litteratur* [Norwegian edition], trans. by Geir Pollen (Oslo: Gyldendal Norsk, [8 November] 2007), 600 copies

A.7.10   W. G. Sebald, *Η φυσική ιστορία της καταστροφής* [Greek edition], trans. by Iannis Kalifatidis (Athens: Εκδόσεις Άγρα [Ekdoseis Agra], [late October] 2008), 2000 copies

A.7.11   W. G. Sebald, *Kushu to Bungaku*, [Japanese edition], trans. by Hitoko Suzuki (*Ze-baruto korekushon* 5) (Tokyo: Hakusuisha [September] 2008), 2500 copies

A.7.12   W. G. Sebald, *Sobre a história natural da destruição* [Brazilian edition], trans. by José Marcos Macedo (São Paulo: Companhia das Letras [Editora Schwarcz], 2010)

B. Books (Literary Works)

B.A. Books (Poetry and Short Poetic Prose; see also B.D.3)

Nach der Natur

B.A.1   W. G. Sebald, *Nach der Natur: Ein Elementargedicht. Photographien von Thomas Becker* (Nördlingen: Franz Greno, [late summer] 1988), 2000 copies; **B.A.1(a)** [*Vorzugsausgabe*], 1988 (leather-bound in a cardboard slipcase), unsigned and unnumbered edition, *c.* 100 copies; **B.A.1(b)** *ad libitum* (*Sammlung Zerstreuung* 20) (Berlin: Volk und Welt, [*c.* October] 1990), pp. 310–66; **B.A.1(c)** (Frankfurt a.M.: Fischer Taschenbuch 12055, [March] 1995). B.A.1(c) differs from the three earlier editions in minor ways — mainly over matters of punctuation and typographic errors. B.A.1(b) and B.A.1(c) omit the six double-spread photographs by Thomas Becker which form the endpapers of B.A.1. See also B.D.1.

B.A.1.1   W. G. Sebald, *After Nature* [American edition], trans. by Michael Hamburger (New York: Random House, [September] 2002); **B.A.1.1(a)** (New York: The Modern Library, [July] 2003)

B.A.1.2   W. G. Sebald, *After Nature* [British edition], trans. by Michael Hamburger (London: Hamish Hamilton, [August] 2002); **B.A.1.2(a)** (London: Penguin, 2002), 10,000 copies; 2nd printing 1000 copies

B.A.1.3   W. G. Sebald, *After Nature* [Canadian edition], trans. by Michael Hamburger (Toronto: Vintage Canada [Random House Canada], 2003)

B.A.1.4   W. G. Sebald, *Del natural: Poema rudimentario* [Castilian edition], trans. by Miguel Sáenz (*Panorama de narrativas* PN591) (Barcelona: Editorial Anagrama, [November] 2004), 3000 copies

B.A.1.5   W. G. Sebald, *Naar de natuur* [Dutch edition], trans. by Ria van Hengel (Amsterdam: De Bezige Bij, [20 March] 2006), 2105 copies

B.A.1.6   W. G. Sebald, *D'après nature: Poème élémentaire* [French edition], trans. by Sibylle Muller and Patrick Charbonneau (Arles: Actes Sud, [17 October] 2007), 3000 copies

B.A.1.7   W. G. Sebald, *Εκ του φυσικού* [Greek edition], trans. by Iannis Kalifatidis (Athens: Εκδόσεις Άγρα [Ekdoseis Agra] A.E., [February] 2009), 2000 copies

B.A.1.8   W. G. Sebald, *Secondo natura: Un poema degli elementi* [Italian edition], trans. by Ada Vigliani (*Biblioteca Adelphi* 545) (Adelphi: Milan, [July] 2009), 4580 copies

For Years Now

B.A.2   W. G. Sebald and Tess Jaray, *For Years Now: Poems. Images by Tess Jaray* (London: Short Books, [3 December] 2001); **B.A.2(a)** (Santander: Limite, 2003). B.A.2 and B.A.2(a) contain the following 11 poems, German versions of and variations upon(⋆) which are also to be found in B.A.3, B.A.3.1, B.A.3.1(a), B.A.3.2, B.A.3.2(a), and B.A.3.3: 'It is said' (p. 9); 'Please'⋆ (p. 12); 'Blue' (p. 15); 'Apparently'⋆ (p. 18); 'The smell'⋆ (p. 42); 'Elephants'⋆ (p. 45); 'Feelings'⋆ (p. 48); 'Awful' (p. 51); 'Do you still'⋆ (p. 54); 'It was as if'⋆ (p. 57); 'Seven years'⋆ (p. 66).

Unerzählt

B.A.3   W. G. Sebald and Jan Peter Tripp, *Unerzählt: 33 Texte und 33 Radierungen* (Munich and Vienna: Carl Hanser, [10 March] 2003), 5000 copies; bound in grey cloth with a reproduction of Tripp's portrait of Sebald pasted to the front cover; black-stamped spine; plastic dust jacket imprinted with the authors' names, the book title, and the publisher's name; **B.A.3(a)** *Limitierte Ausgabe* [1], 2003: quarto; bound in grey cloth with a reproduction of Tripp's portrait of Sebald pasted to the front cover; black-stamped spine; plastic dust jacket imprinted with the authors' names, the book title, and the publisher's name, 333 copies, each containing a loose etching entitled 'Max' that is signed and numbered in pencil by Jan Peter Tripp; **B.A.3(b)** *Limitierte Vorzugsausgabe* [2], 2003: half-leather; hand-bound in a slipcase; 33 copies, each containing all 33 of Tripp's hand-signed etchings plus a hand-signed poem by Hans Magnus Enzensberger and a barite print of a photograph of Sebald by Jan Peter Tripp; a further 7 copies of this edition are designated *Künstlerexemplare* (Galerie Brandstätter); **B.A.3(c)** *Limitierte Vorzugsausgabe* [3], 2003: 33 copies, each containing all 33 of Tripp's hand-signed etchings as a boxed set, plus a hand-signed poem by Hans Magnus Enzensberger, a barite print of a photograph of Sebald by Jan Peter Tripp, an original copper-plate engraving and an autograph by Sebald; a further 7 copies of this edition are designated *Künstlerexemplare* (Galerie Brandstätter)

B.A.3.1   W. G. Sebald and Jan Peter Tripp, *Unrecounted: 33 Poems* [American edition], trans. by Michael Hamburger (New York: New Directions, [30 November] 2004) [includes the texts of the 33 original German poems pp. 103–08], one printing, 1206 copies sold by August 2009; **B.A.3.1(a)** (New York: New Directions Paperbook 1087 [1 October] 2007) [includes the texts of the 33 original German poems pp. 103–08], one printing, 695 copies sold by August 2009

B.A.3.2   W. G. Sebald and Jan Peter Tripp, *Unrecounted: 33 Poems* [British edition], trans. by Michael Hamburger (London: Hamish Hamilton, 2004), 5000 copies; **B.A.3.2(a)** (London: Penguin Books, [25 August] 2005), 5000 copies

B.A.3.3   W. G. Sebald and Jan Peter Tripp, *Sin contar: 33 poemas* [Castilian edition], trans. by María Teresa Ruiz and Katja Wirth (*Colección ilustrados* 3) (Madrid: Nórdica Libros [19 March] 2007), 2500 copies

B.B. Books (Prose Fiction)

Schwindel. Gefühle.

B.B.1   W. G. Sebald, *Schwindel. Gefühle.* (*Die Andere Bibliothek* 63) (Frankfurt a.M.: Eichborn, [March] 1990), *Limitierte Bleisatzausgabe*, 10,000 copies; **B.B.1(a)** *Limitierte Bleisatzausgabe* (*Vorzugsausgabe*) (Frankfurt a.M.: Eichborn, [March] 1990), 999 copies: bound in green goatskin leather with a cardboard slipcase and individually numbered; **B.B.1(b)** *Erfolgsausgabe* (2nd printing [offset reprint of B.B.1] 1998); **B.B.1(c)** (Frankfurt a.M.: Fischer Taschenbuch 12054, [October] 1994), 4000 copies; 2nd printing [June] 1996, 2000 copies; 3rd printing [June] 2000; **B.B.1(d)** (Frankfurt a.M.: Fischer Taschenbuch 12054, [February] 2002), 4th printing; 5th printing [March] 2003; 6th printing [July] 2005; **B.B.1(e)** (Frankfurt a.M.: Eichborn, [May/June] 2001). Clive Scott notes that the images in B.B.1(c) are not only distributed differently, they are less successful than those in the three earlier editions. They tend to be smaller and, despite heightened tonal contrasts, less cleanly focussed and legible, and they have an unwelcome rawness. Where the first printing of B.B.1(c) is identical linguistically with B.B.1 and the two subsequent printings, B.B.1(d) has been completely reset and involves 9 linguistic differences, 8 of which are, however, minor and relate to orthography, punctuation, and grammar (cf. pp. 11/11, 102/98, 124/120, 133/127, 144/138, 157/150, 164/158, and 252/242). But where p. 123 of B.B.1 reads: 'bestellte mir einen Express und nahm meinen Schreibblock heraus. In dem schräg [...]', p. 118 of B.B.1(d) reads: 'bestellte mir einen Express, nahm meinen Schreibblock heraus und geriet über die Aufzeichnungen, die ich machte, bald in eine so tiefe Abwesenheit, daß weder das stundenlange Warten, noch die Busfahrt nach Desenzano die geringste Erinnerungsspur hinterließen in mir. Erst in der Bahn, unterwegs nach Mailand, sehe ich mich wieder. Draußen in dem schräg [...]'. [See also B.D.1.]

B.B.1.1   W. G. Sebald, *Melancholische dwaalwegen: roman* [Dutch edition], trans. by Jos Valkengoed (Amsterdam: Van Gennep, 1990); 2nd printing 1991; **B.B.1.1(a)** 2nd (revised) edition 1992

B.B.1.2   W. G. Sebald, *Duizelingen* [new Dutch translation], trans. by Ria van Hengel (hardback) (Amsterdam: De Bezige Bij: [July] 2008), 2500 copies

B.B.1.3   W. G. Sebald, *Czuję. Zawrót głowy* [Polish edition], trans. by Małgorzata Łukasiewicz (*Pisarze Języka Niemieckiego* [no series number]) (Cracow: Wydawnictwo Literackie, 1998); **B.B.1.3(a)** 2nd (slightly revised) edition [that takes account of the Polish spelling reform of 1999] (Warsaw: Wydawnictwo W.A.B., [6 January] 2010)

B.B.1.4   W. G. Sebald, *Vertigo* [American edition], trans. by Michael Hulse (New York: New Directions, [December] 1999); 2nd printing 2000, 6584 copies sold by August 2009; **B.B.1.4(a)** (New York: New Directions Paperbook 925, [29 October] 2001); 7 printings, 21,080 copies sold by August 2009. According to Scott Denham, *c.* 25,000 copies of B.B.1.4/4(a) had been sold by mid-2002; see 'Die englischsprachige Sebald-Rezeption', in *W. G. Sebald: Politische Archäologie und melancholische Bastelei*, ed. by Michael Niehaus and Claudia Öhlschläger (Berlin: Erich Schmidt, 2006), pp. 259–68 (p. 259)

B.B.1.5   W. G. Sebald, *Vertigo* [British edition], trans. by Michael Hulse (London: Harvill Press, [9 December] 1999); **B.B.1.5(a)** (London: The Harvill Press [Panther Books], [21 September] 2000); **B.B.1.5(b)** (London: Vintage Books, [7 November] 2002)

B.B.1.6   W. G. Sebald, *Vertiges* [French edition], trans. by Patrick Charbonneau (Arles: Actes Sud, [3 January] 2001), 5000 copies; **B.B.1.6(a)** (*Collection Folio* 3842) (Paris: Gallimard, [April] 2003)

B.B.1.7   W. G. Sebald, *Vértigo* [Castilian edition], trans. by Carmen Gómez (Madrid: Editorial Debate, [November] 2001); 2nd printing [November] 2003; **B.B.1.7(a)** (*Panorama de narrativas* PN742) (Barcelona: Editorial Anagrama, [November] 2004); 2nd printing [January] 2010, 4000 copies

B.B.1.8   W. G. Sebald, *Vertigini* [Italian edition], trans. by Ada Vigliani (*Fabula* 153) (Milan: Adelphi, [31 October] 2003), 10,210 copies

B.B.1.9   W. G. Sebald, *Vertigo* [Norwegian edition], trans. by Geir Pollen (Oslo: Gyldendal Norsk, [14 March] 2005), 2000 copies; **B.B.1.10(a)** (Oslo: I Gyldendal Pocket, [30 March] 2006), 3100 copies

B.B.1.10   W. G. Sebald, *Mekuramashi* (A Conjuring Trick) [Japanese edition], trans. by Hitoko Suzuki (*Ze-baruto korekushon* 2) (Tokyo: Hakusuisha, [25 November] 2005), 3500 copies

B.B.1.11   W. G. Sebald, *Vertigens. Impressões* [Portugese edition], trans. by Telma Costa (*Outras estórias* [no series number]) (Lisbon: Editorial Teorema, [February] 2007), 2000 copies

B.B.1.12   W. G. Sebald, *Vertigem: Sensações* [Brazilian edition], trans. by José Marcos Macedo (São Paulo: Companhia das Letras [Editora Schwarcz], [October] 2008), 3000 copies

B.B.1.13   W. G. Sebald, *Svindel. känslor* [Swedish edition], trans. by Ulrika Wallenström (*Panache*) (Stockholm: Albert Bonniers, [April] 2009), 2500 copies

B.B.1.14   W. G. Sebald, *Szédület. Érzés.* [Hungarian edition], trans. by Éva Blaschtik (Budapest: Európa, [20 April] 2010), 1300 copies

B.B.1.15   W. G. Sebald, *Αίσθηση ιλίγγου* [Greek edition], trans. by Ioanna Meïtani (Athens: Εκδόσεις Άγρα [Ekdoseis Agra]: [May] 2010), 2000 copies

B.B.1.16   W. G. Sebald, *Peapööritus. Tunded.* [Estonian edition], trans. by Mati Sirkel (Tartu: AS Atlex, [early] 2011)

B.B.1.17   W. G. Sebald, *Huimaus* [Finnish edition], trans. by Oili Suominen (Helsinki: Tammi, forthcoming, 2011)

Die Ausgewanderten

B.B.2   W. G. Sebald, *Die Ausgewanderten: Vier lange Erzählungen* (*Die Andere Bibliothek* 93) (Frankfurt a.M.: Eichborn, [September] 1992), *Limitierte Bleisatzausgabe*, 7000 copies; **B.B.2(a)** *Limitierte Bleisatzausgabe* (*Vorzugsausgabe*) ([September] 1992), 999 copies, bound in red goatskin leather with a cardboard slipcase and individually numbered; **B.B.2(b)** *Erfolgsausgabe* (2nd printing [offset reprint of B.B.2] 1993; 3rd printing [offset reprint of B.B.2] 1997); **B.B.2(c)** (Frankfurt a.M.: Fischer Taschenbuch 12056, [November] 1994), 10,000 copies; 2nd printing 1996; 3rd printing [October] 1997; 4th printing 1998; 5th printing 2000; 6th printing [March] 2001; 7th printing 2002; 8th printing [March] 2002; 9th printing 2002; 10th printing 2003; 11th printing 2006. When overseeing the production of B.B.2(c), Sebald made small but significant changes to the form and deployment of the visual material; **B.B.2(d)** (Frankfurt a.M.: Eichborn, [May–June] 2001). See also B.D.1.

B.B.2.1   W. G. Sebald, *De emigrés. Vier geïllustreerde verhalen* [Dutch edition], trans. by Ria van Hengel (Amsterdam: Van Gennep, 1992); 2nd printing 1993; **B.B.2.1(a)** *De emigrés* [revised Dutch edition], trans. by Ria van Hengel (Amsterdam: De Bezige Bij, [April] 2005), 2500 copies; 2nd printing [July] 2008, 1250 copies

B.B.2.2   W. G. Sebald, *De udvandrede: Fire lange fortællinger* [Danish edition], trans. by Niels Brunse (Copenhagen: Munksgaard-Rosinante, [30 May] 1995)

B.B.2.3   W. G. Sebald, *The Emigrants* [American edition], trans. by Michael Hulse (New York: New Directions, [August] 1996), 4756 copies sold by August 2009; **B.B.2.3(a)** (New York: New Directions Paperbook 853, 1997); 2nd printing 1997, 13 printings, 58,277 copies sold by August 2009. According to Scott Denham (see B.B.1.4), *c.* 50,000 copies of B.B.2.3/3(a) had been sold by mid-2002. In May 2001, Sebald gave the same figure for all English-language sales of *The Emigrants* (see J.37).

B.B.2.4   W. G. Sebald, *The Emigrants* [British edition], trans. by Michael Hulse (London: The Harvill Press, [April–May] 1996); **B.B.2.4(a)** (London: The Harvill Press [Panther Books], [3 July] 1997); **B.B.2.4(b)** (London: Vintage Books, [7 November] 2002)

B.B.2.5   W. G. Sebald, *Los emigrados* [first Castilian edition], trans. by Teresa Ruiz Rosas (Madrid: Editorial Debate, [October] 1996); **B.B.2.5(a)** 2nd printing of the first Castilian edition (Barcelona: Círculo de Lectores, 1998); **B.B.2.5(b)** 2nd (revised) Castilian edition, rev. by Sergio Pawlowsky Glahn (Madrid: Editorial Debate, [January] 2000); **B.B.2.5(c)** 3rd printing of the first Castilian edition (*Panorama de narrativas* PN631) (Barcelona: Editorial Anagrama, [March] 2006), 6000 copies

B.B.2.6   W. G. Sebald, *Göçmenler* [Turkish edition], trans. by Natali Medina (Istanbul: İletişim, 1999)

B.B.2.7   W. G. Sebald, *Les Émigrants: quatre récits illustrés* [French edition], trans. by Patrick Charbonneau (Arles: Actes Sud, [4 January] 1999), 13,800 copies; 2nd printing 2000; **B.B.2.7(a)** (Arles: Collection de poche Babel 259 [January] 2001), 10,000 copies; 2nd printing 2000 copies; **B.B.2.7(b)** (*Collection Folio* 3832) (Paris: Gallimard, [*c.* 25 March] 2003)

B.B.2.8   W. G. Sebald, *Les Émigrants: quatre récits illustrés* [French-Canadian edition], trans. by Patrick Charbonneau (Montreal: Leméac, 1999); **B.B.2.8(a)** (Quebec: Leméac, 2000)

B.B.2.9   W. G. Sebald, *Gli emigrati* [Italian edition], trans. by Gabriella Rovagnati (Milan: Bompiani, [January] 2000)

B.B.2.10   W. G. Sebald, *Gli emigrati* [new Italian translation], trans. by Ada Vigliani (*Fabula* 185) (Milan: Adelphi, [30 April] 2007), 7555 copies

B.B.2.11   W. G. Sebald, *Els emigrats* (*Les millors obres de la literatura universal* [*segle XX*] 136) [Catalan edition], trans. by Anna Soler Horta (Barcelona: edicions 62, [11 June] 2001), 2608 copies

B.B.2.12   W. G. Sebald, *De utvandrede: Fire lange fortellinger* [Norwegian edition], trans. by Geir Pollen (Oslo: Gyldendal Norsk, [2 July] 2001), 1200 copies; **B.B.2.12(a)** (Oslo: I Gyldendal Pocket, [18 March] 2005), 1300 copies

B.B.2.13   W. G. Sebald, *Izseljeni* [Slovenian edition], trans. by Štefan Vevar, with a Slovenian translation by Vesna Velkovrh Bukilica of Susan Sontag, 'A Mind in Mourning' (*Times Literary Supplement*, no. 5056 [13 February 2000], pp. 3–4), as 'Žalovanje duha:

Sebaldova popotovanja po sledeh preteklosti' (A Mind in Mourning: Sebald's Journeys in Search of Some Remnant of the Past), pp. 237–48 (*Knjižna zbirka Beletrina* 65) (Ljubljana: Študentska založba, 2001), 600 copies

B.B.2.14   W. G. Sebald, *Utvandrade: Fyra berättelser* [Swedish edition], trans. by Ulrika Wallenström (Stockholm: Wahlström & Widstrand, [12 April] 2002), 2222 copies

B.B.2.15   W. G. Sebald, *Os emigrantes: quatro contos longos* [Brazilian edition], trans. by Lya Luft (Rio de Janeiro and São Paulo: Editora Record, [April] 2002), 3074 copies

B.B.2.16   W. G. Sebald, *Os emigrantes: quatro narrativas longas* [new Brazilian translation], trans. by José Marcos Macedo (São Paulo: Companhia das Letras [Editora Schwarcz], [June] 2009), 3000 copies

B.B.2.17   W. G. Sebald [זבאלד .ג. ו], המהגרים [Hebrew edition], trans. by Michal Halevi (Jerusalem: Keter-books, [c. November] 2002), afterword by Susan Sontag, trans. by Ada Paldov, pp. 223–29

B.B.2.18   W. G. Sebald, *Väljarändajad* [Estonian edition], trans. by Tiiu Kokla (Tallinn: Varrak, [28 January] 2003), 800 copies

B.B.2.19   W. G. Sebald, *Os Emigrantes: quatro contos longos* [Portuguese edition], trans. by Telma Costa (*Outras estórias* [no series number]) (Lisbon: Editorial Teorema, [September] 2003), 2000 copies

B.B.2.20   W. G. Sebald, *Vieraalla maalla: Neljä kertomusta* [Finnish edition], trans. by Oili Suominen (Helsinki: Kustannusosakeyhtiö Tammi, 2004)

B.B.2.21   W. G. Sebald, *Wyjechali* [Polish edition], trans. by Małgorzata Łukasiewicz (Warsaw: Wydawnictwo W.A.B., [April] 2005), 3780 copies; 2nd (hardback) edn (Warsaw: Wydawnictwo W.A.B., 2010)

B.B.2.22   W. G. Sebald, *Imintachi* [Japanese edition], trans. by Hitoko Suzuki (*Ze-baruto korekushon* 1) (Tokyo: Hakusuisha, [30 September] 2005), 4000 copies

B.B.2.23   W. G. Sebald, *Vystěhovalci* [Czech edition], trans. by Radovan Charvát (Prague and Litomyšl: Paseka, [9 May] 2006), 800 copies

B.B.2.24   W. G. Sebald, *Οι Ξεριζωμένοι: τέσσερα εικονογραφημένα αφηγήματα* [Greek edition], trans. by Iannis Kalifatidis (Athens: Εκδόσεις Άγρα [Ekdoseis Agra], [November] 2006), 2000 copies

B.B.2.25   W. G. Sebald, *Kivándoroltak* [Hungarian edition], trans. by Szijj Ferenc (Budapest: Európa Könyvkiadó, 2006)

B.B.2.26   W. G. Sebald, *Emigranti* [Croatian edition], trans. by Sead Muhamedagić (Zagreb: Vuković & Runjić, [28 August] 2008), 1000 copies

B.B.2.27   W. G. Sebalt, *E-min-ja-dul* [Korean edition], trans. by Jae-Young Lee (Paju-si: Changbi [25 October] 2008), 3000 copies

Die Ringe des Saturn

B.B.3   W. G. Sebald, *Die Ringe des Saturn: Eine englische Wallfahrt* (*Die Andere Bibliothek* 130) (Frankfurt a.M.: Eichborn, [October] 1995), *Limitierte Bleisatzausgabe*, 10,000 copies; **B.B.3(a)** *Limitierte Bleisatzausgabe* (*Vorzugsausgabe*) ([October] 1995), 999 copies; bound in blue goatskin leather with a cardboard slipcase and individually numbered; **B.B.3(b)** *Erfolgsausgabe* (2nd printing [offset reprint of B.B.3] 1995); **B.B.3(c)** Frankfurt a.M.: Büchergilde Gutenberg, [1 October] 1996), 4000 copies [no further printings]; **B.B.3(d)** (Frankfurt a.M.: Fischer Taschenbuch 13655, [December] 1997), 7000 copies; 2nd printing [March] 1998, 2000 copies; 4th printing [July] 2001; 5th printing [January] 2002; 6th printing 2002; 7th printing 2003; 8th printing 2004; 9th printing [August] 2007; **B.B.3(e)** (Frankfurt a.M.: Eichborn, [May–June] 2001]); 3rd printing 2006. [See also B.D.1.]

B.B.3.1   W. G. Sebald, *De ringen van Saturnus. Een Engelse pelgrimage* [Dutch edition], trans. by Ria van Hengel (Amsterdam: Van Gennep, 1996), 2500 copies; **B.B.3.1(a)** [revised Dutch edition] (Amsterdam: De Bezige Bij, [28 October] 2007), 2500 copies

B.B.3.2   W. G. Sebald, *The Rings of Saturn* [American edition], trans. by Michael Hulse (New York: New Directions, [29 May] 1998); 2nd printing 1999, 7564 copies sold by August 2009; **B.B.3.2(a)** (New York: New Directions Paperbook 881), [29 May] 1998; 2nd printing 1999, 10 printings, 38,052 copies sold by August 2009. According to Scott Denham (see B.B.1.4), *c.* 50,000 copies of B.B.3.2/2(a) had been sold by mid-2002

B.B.3.3   W. G. Sebald, *The Rings of Saturn* [British edition], trans. by Michael Hulse (London: The Harvill Press, [4 June] 1998); **B.B.3.3(a)** (London: The Harvill Press [Panther Books], [4 June] 1998); **B.B.3.3(b)** (London: Vintage Books, [7 November] 2002)

B.B.3.4   W. G. Sebald, *Gli anelli di Saturno: Un pellegrinaggio in Inghilterra* [Italian edition], trans. by Gabriella Rovagnati (Milan: Bompiani, [October] 1998). [Federico Fellini's *Roma* (1972) was one of Sebald's favourite films: about 25 minutes into the film, the new ring road around Rome is likened to 'gli anelli di Saturno'.]

B.B.3.5   W. G. Sebald, *Gli anelli di Saturno: Un pellegrinaggio in Inghilterra* [new Italian translation], trans. by Ada Vigliani (*Fabula* 225) (Milan: Adelphi, [October] 2010), 8000 copies

B.B.3.6   W. G. Sebald, *Les Anneaux de Saturne* [French edition], trans. by Bernard Kreiss (Arles: Actes Sud, [1 September] 1999), 11,000 copies; **B.B.3.6(a)** (*Collection Folio* 3833) (Paris: Gallimard, [27 March] 2003)

B.B.3.7   W. G. Sebald, *Los anillos de Saturno: Una peregrinación inglesa* [Castilian edition], trans. by Carmen Gómez García and Georg Pichler (Madrid: Editorial Debate, [January] 2000); 2nd printing [November] 2000; **B.B.3.7(a)** revised edition, trans. by Carmen Gómez García and Georg Pichler (*Panorama de narrativas* PN711) (Barcelona: Editorial Anagrama, [November] 2008), 6000 copies

B.B.3.8   W. G. Sebald, *Os anéis de Saturno* [Brazilian edition], trans. by Lya Luft (Rio de Janeiro and São Paulo: Editora Record, [December] 2002), 3100 copies

B.B.3.9   W. G. Sebald, *Os anéis de Saturno* [new Brazilian translation], trans. by José Marcos Macedo (São Paulo: Companhia das Letras [Editora Schwarcz], [June] 2010), 3000 copies

B.B.3.10   W. G. Sebald, *Saturns ringer: en engelsk valfart* [Norwegian edition], trans. by Geir Pollen (Oslo: Gyldendal Norsk, [27 August] 2002); **B.B.3.10(a)** (Oslo: I Gyldendal Pocket, 2008)

B.B.3.11   V. G. Zebald [В. Г. Зебалд], *Saturnovi prstenovi* [Serbian edition], trans. by Hana Ćopić (*Biblioteka Posle Orfeja.* 13) (Belgrade: Plato, 2006), 1000 copies

B.B.3.12   W. G. Sebald, *Satürn'ün Halkalari: İngiltere'de Bir Hac Yolculuğu* [Turkish edition], trans. by Yeşim Tükel Kiliç (Istanbul: Can Sanat Yayinlari, [August] 2006)

B.B.3.13   W. G. Sebald, *Os anéis de Saturno: uma romagen inglesa* [Portuguese edition], trans. by Telma Costa (*Outras estórias* [no series number]) (Lisbon: Editorial Teorema, [October] 2006), 2000 copies

B.B.3.14   W. G. Sebald, *Saturnus ringar: en engelsk vallfart* [Swedish edition], trans. by Ulrika Wallenström (*Panache*) (Stockholm: Albert Bonniers, [8 May] 2007), 1238 copies; **B.B.3.14(a)** second printing (Falun, Bonniers) (*Panache*) 2008

B.B.3.15   W. G. Sebald, *Dosei no wa* [Japanese edition], trans. by Hitoko Suzuki (*Ze-baruto korekushon* 3) (Tokyo: Hakusuisha, [1 August] 2007), 2800 copies

B.B.3.16   W. G. Sebald, *Pierścienie Saturna: Angielska pielgrzymka* [Polish edition], trans. by Małgorzata Łukasiewicz (Warsaw: Wydawnictwo W.A.B., [February] 2009), 3500 copies

B.B.3.17   W. G. Sebald [זבאלד. ג. ו], שבתאי טבעות [Hebrew edition], trans. by Tali Konas (Jerusalem: Keter-books, [10 May] 2009), 2,700 copies

B.B.3.18   W. G. Sebald, *Οι δακτύλιοι του Κρόνου* [Greek edition], trans. by Iannis Kalifatidis (Athens: Εκδόσεις Άγρα [Ekdoseis Agra]: [16 December] 2009 [not January 2009 as it says in the book]), 2000 copies

B.B.3.19   W. G. Sebald, *Saturnuksen renkaat. Pyhiinvaellus Englannissa* [Finnish edition], trans. by Oili Suominen (Helsinki: Kustannusosakeyhtiö Tammi, [March] 2010)

B.B.3.20   W. G. Sebald, *Saturnovi prsteni: Hodočašće po engleskoj* [Croatian edition], trans. by Andy Jelčić (Zagreb: Vuković & Runjić, [15 June] 2010), 800 copies

B.B.3.21   W. G. Sebald, *Saturni rõngad* [Estonian edition], trans. by Mati Sirkel (Tartu: AS Atlex, [early] 2011)

B.B.3.22   W. G. Sebald, *A Szaturnusz gyűrűi* [Hungarian edition], trans. by Éva Blaschtik (Budapest: Európa Könyvkiadó, forthcoming 2011)

Austerlitz

B.B.4   W. G. Sebald, *Austerlitz* (Munich and Vienna: Carl Hanser, [5 February] 2001), 6000 copies; 2nd printing [28 February] 2001, 5000 copies; 3rd printing [15 March] 2001, 6000 copies; 4th printing [18 April] 2001, 3000 copies; 5th printing [23 January] 2002, 3000 copies; 6th printing [16 April] 2002, 2000 copies; 7th printing [25 November] 2002, 1500 copies; 8th printing [17 November] 2006, 1000 copies; **B.B.4(a)** (Frankfurt a.M., Vienna, and Zurich: Büchergilde Gutenberg, [1 October] 2001), 3000 copies; **B.B.4(b)** (Frankfurt a.M.: Fischer Taschenbuch 14864, [January] 2003); 2nd printing [October] 2003; 3rd printing [November] 2006; **B.B.4(c)** (*Süddeutsche Zeitung Bibliothek* 93), [cheap hardback edition for distribution with the *SZ*] (Munich: Impressum München–Süddeutsche Zeitung, [2 February] 2008), 29,000 copies. The title page of B.B.4(a) and the cover of the first printing of B.B.4(b) describes the book as a 'Roman' (novel); this is corrected in subsequent printings of B.B.4(b).

B.B.4.1   W. G. Sebald, *Austerlitz* [Canadian edition], trans. by Anthea Bell (Toronto: Alfred A. Knopf Canada [a division of Random House Canada], [October] 2001), 4000 copies; **B.B.4.1(a)** (Toronto: Vintage Canada [Random House Canada], [3 September] 2002), 12,000 copies

B.B.4.2   W. G. Sebald, *Austerlitz* [American edition], trans. by Anthea Bell (New York: Random House, [6 November] 2001); **B.B.4.2(a)** (New York: The Modern Library, [September] 2002)

B.B.4.3   W. G. Sebald, *Austerlitz* [British edition], trans. by Anthea Bell (London: Hamish Hamilton, [October] 2001); **B.B.4.3(a)** 'Uncorrected Proof Copy', limited edition of 100 signed and numbered copies of the proof (London: Hamish Hamilton, 2001); **B.B.4.3(b)** (London: Penguin, [4 July] 2002), 32,470 copies in the first 26 printings

B.B.4.4   W. G. Sebald, *Austerlitz* [Finnish edition], trans. by Oili Suominen (Helsinki: Kustannusosakeyhtiö Tammi, 2002); second printing 2003

B.B.4.5   W. G. Sebald, *Austerlitz* [Italian edition], trans. by Ada Vigliani (*Fabula* 143) (Milan: Adelphi, [31 May] 2002), 15,540 copies; 2nd printing [30 September] 2002, 3303 copies; **B.B.4.5(a)** (Milan: Edizione Gli Adelphi 281, [31 March] 2006), 6424 copies; 2nd printing [31 March] 2008, 2745 copies

B.B.4.6   W. G. Sebald, *Austerlitz* [Castilian edition], trans. by Miguel Sáenz (*Panorama de narrativas* PN521) (Barcelona: Editorial Anagrama, [November] 2002), 16,000 copies; **B.B.4.6(a)** paperback edition (*Compactos Anagrama* CM350), [October] 2004, 3000 copies; 2nd printing of paperback edition (*Compactos Anagrama* CM350), [April] 2005, 3000 copies; 3rd printing of paperback edition (*Compactos Anagrama* CM350), [May] 2007, 4000 copies; 4th printing of paperback edition (*Compactos Anagrama* CM350), [December] 2009, 2000 copies; 5th printing of paperback edition (*Colección Compactos* 350), [October] 2010; **B.B.4.6(b)** hardback edition (*Biblioteca Anagrama* 68) (Barcelona: Editorial Anagrama, 2010)

B.B.4.7   W. G. Sebald, *Austerlitz* [French edition], trans. by Patrick Charbonneau (Arles: Actes Sud, [11 October] 2002), 8000 copies; second printing 1000 copies; **B.B.4.7(a)** (*Collection Folio* 4380) (Paris: Gallimard, [20 April] 2006)

B.B.4.8   W. G. Sebald, *Austerlitz* [Dutch edition], trans. by Ria van Hengel (hardback) (Amsterdam: De Bezige Bij, [January] 2003), 6000 copies; 3rd printing [July] 2008, 2500 copies; **B.B.4.8(a)** (2nd printing as a mid-price paperback edition) (Amsterdam: Ulysses-De Bezige Bij, [April] 2006), 2000 copies

B.B.4.9   W. G. Sebald, *Austerlitz* [Catalan edition], trans. by Anna Soler Horta (*Colecció El Balancí* 471) (Barcelona: Edicions 62, [1 May] 2003), 3185 copies

B.B.4.10   W. G. Sebald, *Ausuterurittsu* [Japanese edition], trans. by Hitoko Suzuki (Tokyo: Hakusuisha, [10 August] 2003), 7600 copies [awarded the Lessing Prize for translators by the Federal German Government (2003)]. A revised translation is due to appear at an unspecified date as part of the *Ze-baruto korekushon*.

B.B.4.11   W. G. Sebald, *Austerlitz* [Swedish edition], trans. by Ulrika Wallenström (Stockholm: Wahlström & Widstrand, [14 August] 2003), 2028 copies

B.B.4.12   W. G. Sebald, *Austerlitz* [Danish edition], trans. by Niels Brunse (paperback) (Copenhagen: Tiderne Skifter, [11 November] 2003), 852 copies

B.B.4.13   W. G. Sebald, *Austerlitz* [Portuguese edition], trans. by Telma Costa (*Outras estórias* [no series number]) (Lisbon: Editorial Teorema, [October] 2004), 2000 copies; 2nd printing 1000 copies

B.B.4.14   W. G. Sebald, *Austerlitz* [Norwegian edition], trans. by Geir Pollen (Oslo: Gyldendal Norsk, [15 April] 2004), 2500 copies; 2nd printing [24 August] 2004, 3100 copies; **B.B.4.13(a)** (Oslo: I Gyldendal Pocket, [18 March] 2005), 1900 copies; 2nd printing [19 May] 2005, 3100 copies

B.B.4.15   W. G. Sebald, *Austerlitz* [Slovenian edition], trans. by Štefan Vevar (*Knjižna zbirka Beletrina* 126) (Ljubljana: Študentska založba, [9 August] 2005), 600 copies

B.B.4.16   V. G. Zebald [В. Г. Зебальд], *Аустерлиц* [Russian edition], trans. by Marina Koreneva (Saint Petersburg: Издательство 'Азбука-классика' [Izdatel'stvo 'Azbuka-klassika'], 2006)

B.B.4.17   W. G. Sebald, *Austerlitz* [Croatian edition], trans. by Andy Jelčić (Zagreb: Vuković & Runjić, [7 July] 2006), 1200 copies

B.B.4.18   W. G. Sebald, *Άουστερλιτς* [Greek edition], trans. by Ioanna Meïtani (Athens: Εκδόσεις Άγρα [Ekdoseis Agra], [November] 2006), 2000 copies

B.B.4.19   W. G. Sebald [זבאלד. ג. ו], אוסטרליץ [Hebrew edition], trans. by Yonatan Nirad (Jerusalem: Keter-books, [c. November] 2006)

B.B.4.20   W. G. Sebald, *Austerlitz* [Hungarian edition], trans. by Éva Blaschtik (Budapest: Európa Könyvkiadó, 2007)

B.B.4.21   W. G. Sebald, *Austerlitz* [Polish edition], trans. by Małgorzata Łukasiewicz (Warsaw: Wydawnictwo W.A.B., [October] 2007)

B.B.4.22   V. G. Zēbalds, *Austerlics* [Latvian edition], trans. by Silvija Ģibiete (Riga: Dienas Gramata, [3 January] 2008), 1000 copies

B.B.4.23   W. G. Sebald, *Austerlitz* [Turkish edition], trans. by Gülfer Tunali (Istanbul: Can Yayinlari, [1 April] 2008)

B.B.4.24   W. G. Sebald, *Austerlitz* [Brazilian edition], trans. by José Marcos Macedo (São Paulo: Companhia das Letras [Editora Schwarcz], [May] 2008), 4000 copies

B.B.4.25   W. G. Sebald, *Austerlitz* [Romanian edition], trans. by Irina Nisipeanu (Bucharest: Curtea Veche Publishing, [November] 2008), 1500 copies

B.B.4.26   W. G. Sebald, *Austerlitz* [Czech edition], trans. by Radovan Charvát (Prague and Litomyšl: Paseka, [February] 2009), 1000 copies

B.B.4.27   W. G. Sebald, *Austerlitz* [Estonian edition], trans. by Mati Sirkel (Tallinn: Varrak, [March] 2009), 600 copies

B.B.4.28   W. G. Sebalt, *A-u-s-ter-ritz* [Korean edition], trans. by Mi-Hyun Ahn (Seoul: Eul-Yu-Mun-Hwa-Sa, [March] 2009), 2000 copies

B.B.4.29   W. G. Sebald, *Aositelici* [Chinese edition], trans. by Diao Chengjun (Nanjing: Yilin Press, [August] 2010), 5000 copies

B.C. Other Independent Publications (Literary and Critical Works)

B.C.1   W. G. Sebald, '*Am deutschen Ozean*' (Frankfurt a.M.: [n. pub.], [*c.* September] 1995); contains **pre-publication** Part IV of B.B.3 (pp. 17–41); issued by the Deutsche Genossenschaftsbank to commemorate Sebald winning the Preis der LiteraTour Nord in 1994, with a *laudatio* by Sigrid Löffler (pp. 9–15)

B.C.2   W. G. Sebald, *Bogen 48: Gespräch mit Lebenden und Toten* (Munich and Vienna: Carl Hanser, [December] 2000), 8000 copies; contains two **pre-publication extracts** from B.B.4 (pp. 47 and 168–69), also Andrea Köhler, 'Gespräch mit Toten', *Neue Zürcher Zeitung* (Internationale Ausgabe) (Literatur und Kunst), 222, 23–24 September 2000, pp. 49–50) and Susan Sontag, 'Ein trauernder Geist' ('A Mind in Mourning', see B.B.2.13 for details)

B.C.3   W. G. Sebald, *Young Austerlitz*, trans. by Anthea Bell [one of 70 miniature pocket books published to celebrate the 70th anniversary of the founding of Penguin Books] (London: Pocket Penguins 28, 2005), 45,000 copies; **post-publication extract** from B.B.4.3(b), pp. 61–137 [B.B.4.2(a), pp. 44–96] ('I grew up, began Austerlitz that evening ... came back down to us at break of day')

B.C.4   W. G. Sebald, *Il passeggiatore solitario: In ricordo di Robert Walser* [Italian edition of A.6, pp. 127–68 and D.68(a)], trans. by Ada Vigliani (*Biblioteca minima* 4) (Milan: Adelphi, [30 April] 2006), 11,290 copies

B.C.5   W. G. Sebald, *El paseante solitario: En Recuerdo de Robert Walser* [Castilian edition of A.6, pp. 127–68 and D.68(a)], trans. by Miguel Sáenz (*Biblioteca de Ensayo* 40 [*serie menor*]) (Madrid: Ediciones Siruela, 2007); 2nd printing (March 2008), 1558 copies

B.C.6   W. G. Sebald, *Zerstreute Reminiszenzen: Gedanken zur Eröffnung eines Stuttgarter Hauses*, ed. by Florian Höllerer (Warmbronn: Ulrich Keicher, [September] 2008), 800 copies. Booklet version of D.76, including a facsimile of *Der Wecker*, 1.4 [*c.* June 1962] (H.A.6[a]–H.A.8[a]), published to accompany the exhibition in the Literaturhaus, Stuttgart [Breitscheidstrasse 4] (23 September–17 December 2008)

B.D. Collected Works and Posthumously Published Anthologies

B.D.1   W. G. Sebald, *Außer Land: Drei Romane und ein Elementargedicht* (*Jubiläumsausgabe*) (boxed set comprising B.A.1, B.B.1, B.B.2, and B.B.3) (Frankfurt a.M.: Eichborn, [May/June] 2001). These were also sold as separate, out-of-box copies and are distinct from the editions of B.B.1(e), B.B.2(d), and B.B.3(e) published by Eichborn at exactly the same time.

B.D.2   W. G. Sebald, *Campo Santo*, ed. by Sven Meyer (Munich and Vienna: Carl Hanser, [8 September] 2003), 6000 copies; 2nd printing [3 November] 2003, 2000 copies; 3rd printing [9 December] 2003, 1500 copies; **B.D.2(a)** (Frankfurt a.M.: Fischer Taschenbuch 16527, [January] 2006)

B.D.2.1   W. G. Sebald, *Campo Santo* [American edition], trans. by Anthea Bell (New York: Random House, [8 March] 2005); **B.D.2.1(a)** (New York: The Modern Library, [23 February] 2006)

B.D.2.2   W. G. Sebald, *Campo Santo* [British edition], trans. by Anthea Bell (London: Hamish Hamilton, 2005), 5700 copies; **B.D.2.2(a)** (London: Penguin Books, [23 February] 2006), 5000 copies; 2nd printing 1000 copies

B.D.2.3   W. G. Sebald, *Campo Santo* [Castilian edition], trans. by Miguel Sáenz (*Panorama de narrativas* PN675) (Barcelona: Editorial Anagrama, [October] 2007), 8000 copies; **B.D.2.3(a)** (*Compactos Anagrama* CM520) (Barcelona: Editorial Anagrama, [March] 2010), 2010 copies

B.D.2.4   W. G. Sebald, *Camposanto* [Galician edition], trans. by Catuxa López Pato (*literaria* 248) (Vigo: Editorial Galaxia, [29 October] 2007), 1500 copies

B.D.2.5   W. G. Sebald, *Campo Santo* [Portuguese edition], trans. by Telma Costa (Lisbon: Editorial Teorema, [1 March] 2008), 2000 copies

B.D.2.6   W. G. Sebald, *Campo Santo* [French edition], trans. by Patrick Charbonneau and Sibylle Muller (Arles: Actes Sud, [4 February] 2009), 3000 copies

B.D.2.7   W. G. Sebald, *Campo Santo* [Dutch edition], trans. by Ria van Hengel (Amsterdam: De Bezige Bij, [15 November] 2010)

B.D.3   W. G. Sebald, *Über das Land und das Wasser: Ausgewählte Gedichte 1964–2001*, ed. by Sven Meyer (Munich and Vienna: Carl Hanser, [10 September] 2008), 3000 copies; 2nd printing [December] 2008, 1500 copies; poems listed individually under F.A, F.B, and H.B

B.D.3.1   W. G. Sebald, *Utvalgte Dikt* [selected poems in Norwegian translation], trans. by Geir Pollen, in *Vinduet: Gyldendals Tidsskrift for Litteratur*, 64.1 ([29 March] 2010), [pp. 87–90]. This little anthology is published within *Vinduet* in the form of an uncut 'cut out and keep' octavo pamphlet [*Vinduet i lommeformat!* no. 9] and consists of 10 poems from B.D.3 (listed individually under F.A, F.B and H.B.).

B.D.3.2   W. G. Sebald, *Across the Land and the Water: Selected Poems, 1964–2001* [British edition], trans. by Iain Galbraith (London: Penguin, forthcoming 2011)

C. Radio Adaptations of Prose Texts (cf. Audio-Visual Bibliography)

C.1   W. G. Sebald, *Max Aurach: Hörspiel*; adapted from B.B.2 by Ulrich Gerhardt, first broadcast on Bayern 2 on 20 May 1994; repeated on 29 November 1999

C.2   W. G. Sebald, *Aurachs Mutter: Hörspiel;* adapted from B.B.2 by Ulrich Gerhardt, first broadcast on Bayern 2 on 10 February 1995; **C.2(a)** repeated as *Färbers* [*sic*] *Mutter* on 25 October 2004

C.3   W. G. Sebald, Sunday Play: *The Emigrants: Ambrose Adelwarth*, adapted from B.B.2.4 by Edward Kemp, featuring John Wood, Henry Goodman, Eleanor Bron, Ed Bishop, Margaret Robertson, Andrew Sachs, John Schwab and others, first broadcast on BBC Radio 3 from 7.30 to 8.50 p.m. on 3 March 2001; **C.3(a)** repeated as *The Emigrants: Ambrose Adelwarth* in Drama on 3 on BBC Radio 3 from 9.30 to 11.00 p.m. on 14 July 2002

D. Critical Articles and Essays (listed in loose order of composition)

*Unless detailed information is given to the contrary,
the various versions are identical or all but identical.*

1970–1975 (D.1–D.11)

D.1   W. G. Sebald, 'Minna von Barnhelm: Lessing' [review of a performance by *Die Brücke* in the University Theatre, Manchester], *Staff Comment* [University of Manchester], no. 54 (February 1970), 29–30; **D.1(a)**; repr. as Appendix 2.1 in the present volume, p. 107

D.2   W. G. Sebald, 'Sternheims Narben', *Die Zeit* (Modernes Leben), 35, 28 August 1970, p. 46; **D.2(a)** in *Sebald. Lektüren.*, ed. by Marcel Atze and Franz Loquai (Eggingen: Isele, 2005), pp. 59–60

D.3   W. G. Sebald, 'Ein Avantgardist in Reih und Glied: Kritische Überlegungen zum Verständnis des Dramatikers Carl Sternheim und seiner Widersprüche', *Frankfurter Rundschau* (Feuilleton), 235, 10 October 1970, p. v; **D.3(a)** in *Sebald. Lektüren.*, ed by Atze and Loquai, pp. 61–64

D.4   W. G. Sebald, 'Alles Schöne macht das Mißlungene ärger: Am Fall Günter Eich: Poesie in den Steingärten, Erinnerung als eine Form des Vergessens', *Frankfurter Rundschau* (Feuilleton), 31, 6 February 1971, p. iv

D.5   W. G. Sebald, '"Ein Ding, das nicht seinesgleichen hatte": Utopie und Paradies: Phantasie über ein Thema von Döblin', *Frankfurter Rundschau* (Feuilleton), 222, 25 September 1971, p. iv

D.6   W. G. Sebald, 'The Undiscover'd Country: The Death Motif in Kafka's *Castle*', *Journal of European Studies*, 2.1 (March 1972), 22–34; **D.6(a)** in *Franz Kafka's The Castle:* ed. by Harold Bloom (*Modern Critical Interpretations*) (New York: Chelsea House, 1988), pp. 35–49

D.6.1   W. G. Sebald, 'Thanatos: Zur Motivstruktur in Kafkas *Schloss*', *Literatur und Kritik*, 8, 66–67 (July–August 1972), 399–411; **D.6.1(a)** as 'Das unentdeckte Land: Zur Motivstruktur in Kafkas *Schloß*', in A.3, pp. 78–92 and 191–92 [The text of D.6.1 is largely the same as that of D.6, but the footnotes differ significantly. D.6.1(a) is a significantly altered and shortened version of D.6.1: the central thesis of the English and German originals has been more sharply focussed.]

D.6.1(a).1 As 'El país por descubrir (Sobre la estructura de motivos de *El castillo* de Kafka)', in A.3.1, pp. 42–60

D.7   W. G. Sebald, 'Gedanken zu Elias Canetti', *Literatur und Kritik*, 8, 65 (June 1972), 280–85

D.8   W. G. Sebald, 'The Law of Ignominy: Authority, Messianism and Exile in *The Castle*' [first given as a paper at the conference to mark the 50th anniversary of Kafka's death that took place at UEA, 7–10 July 1974], in *On Kafka: Semi-Centenary Perspectives*, ed. by Franz Kuna (London: Paul Elek, [22 July] 1976), pp. 42–58 and 186; **D.8(a)** (New York: Barnes & Noble [at that time a division of Harper & Row], 1976), pp. 42–58 and 186

D.8.1   W. G. Sebald, 'Das Gesetz der Schande: Macht, Messianismus und Exil in Kafkas *Schloß*', *Manuskripte*, 25, 89–90 (September 1985), 117–21; **D.8.1(a)** in A.5, pp. 87–103 and 186–87. D.8.1 is not identical with D.8: although the thrust of the argument is the same, D.8.1 is much more clearly written and omits the final passage in which Samuel Beckett's *Molloy* is quoted at length; D.8.1(a) is largely identical with D.8.1 (it, too, omits the final passage), but differs from the earlier version in two respects: 'daß es ihm ... durch die Hoffnung' (p. 118) is compressed to 'daß der messianischen ... zukommt' (p. 92); 'und eben diese ... Leben zutrug' (p. 118) is reworked into 'ganz als sei ... ausmacht' (pp. 92–93)

D.8.1(a).1   As 'La ley de la vergüenza (Poder, mesianismo y exilio en *El Castillo* de Kafka)', in A.5.1, pp. 142–61

D.8.1(a).2   As 'A lei da vergonha: Poder, messianismo e exílio em *O Castelo*, de Kafka', in A.5.2, pp. 77–92 and 173–75

D.9   W. G. Sebald, 'Fremdheit, Integration und Krise: Über Peter Handkes Stück *Kaspar*' [written autumn 1974], *Literatur und Kritik*, 11, 93 (April 1975), 152–58; **D.9(a)** in B.D.2, pp. 57–68 and 251–52; **D.9(b)** in B.D.2(a), pp. 57–68 and 251–52

D.9(a).1   As 'Strangeness, Integration and Crisis: On Peter Handke's Play *Kaspar*', in B.D.2.1, pp. 53–64 and 209–10; **D.9(a).1(a)** in B.D.2.1(a), pp. 53–64 and 209–10.

D.9(a).2   As 'Strangeness, Integration and Crisis: On Peter Handke's Play *Kaspar*', in B.D.2.2, pp. 55–67 and 218–19; **D.9(a).2(a)** in B.D.2.2(a), pp. 55–67 and 218–19.

D.9(a).3   As 'Extrañeza, integración y crisis: Sobre la pieza "Kaspar" de Peter Handke', in B.D.2.3, pp. 53–63 and 229–31; **D.9(a).3(a)** in B.D.2.3(a), pp. 53–63 and 229–31

D.9(a).4   As 'O alleo, integración e crise: Sobre o *Kaspar* de Peter Handke', in B.D.2.4, pp. 61–72 and 253–54

D.9(a).5   As 'Estranheza, integração e crise: Sobre a peça *Kaspar*, de Peter Handke', in B.D.2.5, pp. 51–60 and 214–15

D.9(a).6   As 'L'Étranger, intégration et crise: A propos de la pièce de Peter Handke, *Gaspard*', in B.D.2.6, pp. 57–68 and 243–44

D.9(a).7   As 'Vreemdheid, integratie en crisis: Over Peter Handkes toneelstuk Kaspar', in B.D.2.7, pp. 61–72 and 255–56

D.10   W. G. Sebald, 'Zum Thema Messianismus im Werk Döblins', *Neophilologus*, 59.3 (July 1975), 421–34; anticipates and overlaps significantly with A.2, pp. 59–73

D.11   W. G. Sebald, 'Schock und Ästhetik: Zu den Romanen Döblins', *Orbis Litterarum*, 30.4 ([late] 1975), 241–50; anticipates and overlaps significantly with A.2, pp. 154–60

1976–1980 (D.12–D.17)

D.12   W. G. Sebald, 'Humanitaranism and Law: Arnold Zweig, *Der Streit um den Sergeanten Grischa*', in *The First World War in Fiction: A Collection of Critical Essays*, ed. by Holger Klein (London and Basingstoke: The Macmillan Press, 1976), pp. 126–35 and 225–27; **D.12(a)** 2nd (revised) edition (1978), pp. 126–35 and 225–27

D.13   W. G. Sebald, 'Mord an den Vätern: Bemerkungen zu einigen Dramen der spätbürgerlichen Zeit', *Neophilologus*, 60.2 (April 1976), 432–41

D.14   W. G. Sebald, 'Das Wort unter der Zunge: Zu Hugo von Hofmannsthals Trauerspiel *Der Turm*', *Literatur und Kritik*, 14, 125 (June 1978), 294–303 (cf. E.C.2)

D.15   W. G. Sebald, 'Summa Scientiae: System und Systemkritik bei Elias Canetti' [first delivered at a symposium on Canetti organized in Vienna (1979) by the Wiener Kunstverein and the Burgtheater], *Literatur und Kritik*, 18, 177–78 (September–October 1983), 398–404; **D.15(a)** as 'Kurzer Versuch über System und Systemkritik bei Elias Canetti', *Études Germaniques*, 39.3 (July–September 1984), 268–75; **D.15(b)** in A.3, pp. 93–102 and 193. All three are largely identical, but D.15(b) omits a passage from D.15, p. 401 and D.15(a), p. 272 ('Dem vom System ... gar nicht mehr').

D.15(b).1   As '"Summa Scientiae" (Sistema y crítica del sistema en Elias Canetti)', in A.3.1, pp. 61–71

D.16   W. G. Sebald, 'Wo die Dunkelheit den Strick zuzieht: Einige Bemerkungen zum Werk Thomas Bernhards' [probably based on a paper given to the CUTG (Conference of University Teachers of German in Great Britain) at the University of Sussex 22–24 September 1980], *Literatur und Kritik*, 16, 155 (June 1981), 294–302; **D.16(a)** in A.3, pp. 103–14 and 194. D.16(a) omits most of D.16, p. 294 ('Einzig ein gewisser ... dieses Autors')

D.16(a).1   As 'Cuando la oscuridad pone punto final (Sobre Thomas Bernhard)', in A.3.1, pp. 72–85

D.17   W. G. Sebald, 'Kleine Traverse: Über das poetische Werk des Alexander Herbrich [= Ernst Herbeck]' [written November–December 1980], *Manuskripte*, 21, 74 ([no month], 1981), 35–41; **D.17(a)** as 'Eine kleine Traverse: Das poetische Werk Ernst Herbecks' in A.3, pp. 131–48 and 196–97. The two versions have different epigraphs; in D.17 Sebald calls the poet 'Alexander', and in D17(a) 'Herbeck'. Not included in A.3.1; **D.17(b)** in *Ernst Herbeck: die Vergangenheit ist klar vorbei*, ed. by Leo Navratil und Carl Aigner (Vienna and Krems: Chr. Brandstätter Verlag and Kunsthalle Krems, 2002), pp. 154–67. This volume also contains D.56(a).

1981–1985 (D.18–D.34)

D.18   W. G. Sebald, 'Zwischen Geschichte und Naturgeschichte: Versuch über die literarische Beschreibung totaler Zerstörung mit Anmerkungen zu Kasack, Nossack und Kluge' [written autumn–winter 1981–82], *Orbis Litterarum*, 37.4 ([late] 1982), 345–66; **D.18(a)** as 'Zwischen Geschichte und Naturgeschichte: Über die literarische Beschreibung totaler Zerstörung', in B.D.2, pp. 69–100 and 252–56; **D.18(b)** in B.D.2(a), pp. 69–100 and 252–56

D.18(a).1   As 'Between History and Natural History: On the Literary Description of Total

Destruction', in B.D.2.1, pp. 65–95 and 210–14; **D.18(a).1(a)** in B.D.2.1(a), pp. 65–95 and 210–14

D.18(a).2   As 'Between History and Natural History: On the Literary Description of Total Destruction', in B.D.2.2, pp. 68–101 and 219–24; **D.18(a).2(a)** in B.D.2.2(a), pp. 68–101 and 219–24

D.18(a).3   As 'Entre historia e historia natural: Sobre la descripción literaria de la destrucción total', in B.D.2.3, pp. 64–91 and 231–36; **D.18(a).3(a)** in B.D.2.3(a), pp. 64–91 and 231–36

D.18(a).4   As 'Entre a historia e a historia natural: Sobre a descrición literaria da destrucción', in B.D.2.4, pp. 73–103 and 254–59

D.18(a).5   As 'Entre história e história natural: Sobre a descrição literária da destruição total', in B.D.2.5, pp. 61–87 and 215–19

D.18(a).6   As 'Entre histoire et histoire naturelle: Sur la description littéraire de la destruction totale', in B.D.2.6, pp. 69–98 and 244–49

D.18(a).7   As 'Tussen geschiedenis en natuurlijke historie: Over de literaire beschrijving van de totale verwoesting', in B.D.2.7, pp. 73–104 and 256-60

D.19   Winfried G. Sebald, 'Alfred Döblin oder die politische Unzuverlässigkeit des bürgerlichen Literaten' [paper given at the International (MLA) Alfred Döblin-Colloquium in New York, (end December) 1981], in *Internationale Alfred Döblin-Kolloquien: Basel 1980, New York 1981, Freiburg im Breisgau 1983* (*Jahrbuch für Internationale Germanistik, Reihe A, Kongressberichte*, 14), ed. by Werner Stauffacher (Berne: Peter Lang, 1986), pp. 133–39

D.20   W. G. Sebald, 'Die weisse Adlerfeder am Kopf: Versuch über Herbert Achternbusch' [paper given at the Britisch-Deutsches Germanistentreffen in Berlin, 12–18 April 1982], in *Subjektivität, Innerlichkeit, Abkehr vom Politischen? Tendenzen der deutschsprachigen Literatur der 70er Jahre*, ed. by Keith Bullivant and Hans Joachim Althof (Bonn: DAAD, 1986), pp. 175–88; **D.20(a)** as 'Die weiße Adlerfeder am Kopf: Versuch über den Indianer Herbert Achternbusch', *Manuskripte*, 23, 79 ([no month], 1983), 75–79

D.21   Winfried G. Sebald, 'Preussische Perversionen: Anmerkungen zum Thema Literatur und Gewalt, ausgehend vom Frühwerk Alfred Döblins' [paper given at the International Alfred Döblin-Colloquium in Freiburg im Breisgau, *c.* 8–10 June 1983], in Stauffacher, op. cit. [D.19], pp. 231–38

D.22   W. G. Sebald, 'Die Mädchen aus der Feenwelt: Bemerkungen zu Liebe und Prostitution mit Bezügen zu Raimund, Schnitzler und Horváth' [originally conceived in early 1978], *Neophilologus*, 67.1 (January 1983), 109–17. [The content overlaps significantly with that of D.29]

D.23   W. G. Sebald, 'Unterm Spiegel des Wassers: Peter Handkes Erzählung von der Angst des Tormanns', *Austriaca: Cahiers universitaires d'information sur Autriche*, 9, 16 (May 1983), 43–56; **D.23(a)** in A.3, pp. 115–30 and 195–96. [D.23(a) adds a final clause: 'die auf verschiedene Weise an das erinnern, was in den Kindern zugrunde gerichtet wird.']

D.23(a).1   As 'Bajo el espejo del agua (El relato de Peter Handke sobre el miedo del portero)', in A.3.1, pp. 86–104

D.24   Winfried Georg Sebald, 'Konstruktionen der Trauer: Zu Günter Grass *Tagebuch einer Schnecke* und Wolfgang Hildesheimer *Tynset*' [written in the first quarter of 1983], *Der Deutschunterricht*, 35.5 (October 1983), 32–46; **D.24(a)** as 'Konstruktionen der Trauer: Günter Grass und Wolfgang Hildesheimer', in B.D.2, pp. 101–27 and 256–59; **D.24(b)** in B.D.2(a), pp. 101–27 and 256–59

D.24(a).1   As 'Constructs of Mourning: Günter Grass and Wolfgang Hildesheimer', in B.D.2.1, pp. 97–123 and 215–17; **D.24(a).1(a)** in B.D.2.1(a), pp. 97–123 and 215–17

D.24(a).2   As 'Constructs of Mourning: Günter Grass and Wolfgang Hildesheimer', in B.D.2.2, pp. 102–29 and 224–26; **D.24(a).2(a)** in B.D.2.2(a), pp. 102–29 and 224–26

D.24(a).3   As 'Construcciones del duelo: Günter Grass y Wolfgang Hildesheimer', in B.D.2.3, pp. 92–115 and 236–39; **D.24(a).3(a)** in B.D.2.3(a), pp. 92–115 and 236–39

D.24(a).4   As 'Constructos do dó: Sobre Günter Grass e Wolfgang Hildesheimer', in B.D.2.4, pp. 105–30 and 259–61

D.24(a).5   As 'A construção do luto: Günter Grass e Wolfgang Hildesheimer', in B.D.2.5, pp. 88–110 and 219–21

D.24(a).6   As 'Constructions du deuil: Günter Grass et Wolfgang Hildesheimer', in B.D.2.6, pp. 99–122 and 249–52

D.24(a).7   As 'Vormen van rouw: Günter Grass en Wolfgang Hildesheimer', in B.D.2.7, pp. 105-31 and 261-63

D.25   W. G. Sebald, 'Literarische Pornographie? Zur *Winterreise* Gerhard Roths' [drafted summer 1983], *Merkur*, 38.2 (March 1984), 171–80; **D.25(a)** as 'Der Mann mit dem Mantel: Gerhard Roths *Winterreise*', in A.3, pp. 149–64 and 197–98. D.25(a) differs significantly from D.25 on pp. 150–51 (where new material is added and the original developed), also on pp. 152, 153 and 154–55 (additions) and 161–62 (additions); D.25 has no epigraph, but D.25(a) is prefaced by a citation from Wilhelm Müller's *Die Winterreise*: 'Mein Herz ist wie erstorben | kalt starrt ihr Bild darin.' Not included in A.3.1

D.26   W. G. Sebald, 'Helle Bilder und dunkle: Zur Dialektik der Eschatologie bei Stifter und Handke' [first delivered as a paper at the Aachen TU in June 1983], *Manuskripte*, 24, 84 (June 1984), 58–64; **D.26(a)** in A.3, pp. 165–86 and 198–200. D.26(a) omits 'und daß ... sich zuträgt' (D.26, p. 60); 'herausströmt' on D.26, p. 63 becomes 'heraustönt' on D.26(a), p. 184. Not included in A.3.1

D.27   W. G. Sebald, 'Bis an den Rand der Natur: Versuch über Adalbert Stifter' [written between 3 January and 3 May 1984], *Die Rampe*, 1985.1 (1985), 7–35; **D.27(a)** as 'Adalbert Stifter', in *Österreichische Porträts*, ed. by Jochen Jung, 2 vols (Salzburg: Residenz, [autumn] 1985), I, 232–55; **D.27(b)** as 'Versuch über Stifter', in A.3, pp. 15–37 and 187–88. D.27(a) has no footnotes but is otherwise identical with D.27; D.27(b) omits two passages from D.27: p. 15 ('Freilich schweigt ... recht verunstaltet') and p. 23 ('Stifter führte ... seine Erlösung'). Not included in A.3.1

D.27(b).1   As 'To the Edge of Nature: An Essay on Stifter', trans. by Anthea Bell, *Southern Humanities Review*, 39.4 (Fall 2005), 305–24

D.28   W. G. Sebald, 'Die Zweideutigkeit der Toleranz: Anmerkungen zum Interesse der Aufklärung an der Emanzipation der Juden' [originally conceived in autumn 1974], *Der Deutschunterricht*, 36.4 ([August] 1984), 27–47

D.29   W. G. Sebald, 'Das Schrecknis der Liebe: Überlegungen zu Schnitzlers *Traumnovelle*', *Merkur*, 39.2 (February 1985), 120–31; **D.29(a)** in A.3, pp. 38–60 and 188–89. D.29 has no footnotes and the phrase 'Travestie des gesenkten weiblichen Blicks' does not appear there on p. 130; D.29(a) contains the following additions: p. 38 ('In einem durch ... acht'); pp. 38–39 ('Die Idee der ... die Rede ist'); pp. 39–40 ('Der These vom ... der Explizität'); pp. 41–43 ('Das in gegenseitiger ... nachgerechnet werden muß'); pp. 46–47 ('In der Episode ... in sich tragen'); pp. 50–52 ('Die im vorigen ... Arbeiterinnen'). [The content of both versions overlaps significantly with that of D.22]

D.29(a).1   As 'El espanto del amor (Sobre *Relato soñado* de Schnitzler)', in A.3.1, pp. 15–41

D.30   W. G. Sebald, 'Venezianisches Kryptogramm: Hofmannsthals *Andreas*' [early 1985], in *Fin-de-siècle Vienna*, ed. by G. J. Carr and Eda Sagarra [proceedings of the Second Irish Symposium in Austrian Studies, Trinity College, Dublin, 28 February–2 March 1985], (Dublin: Trinity College, [late] 1985), pp. 143–60; **D.30(a)** in A.3, pp. 61–77 and 190–91. Not included in A.3.1

D.30.1   As 'Ο Ανδρέας του Χόφμανσταλ: Βενετσιάνικο κρυπτόγραμμα', trans. by Iannis Kalifatidis, in Hugo von Hofmannsthal, *Ανδρέας* [*Andreas*], trans. by Iannis Kalifatidis (Athens: Εκδόσεις Κίχλη [Ekdoseis Kichli], forthcoming 2011)

D.31   W. G. Sebald, 'Vorwort' (spring 1985), in A.3, pp. 9–13

D.31.1   As 'Prólogo', in A.3.1, pp. 9–14

D.32   W. G. Sebald, 'Heimat und Exil: Bemerkungen zu Jean Améry' [probably written autumn 1985], *Die Presse* (Vienna) (Literaricum), 11,540, 30–31 August 1986, p. iv [early and very differently worded version of D.42]

D.33   W. G. Sebald, 'Mit den Augen des Nachtvogels' [probably written autumn 1985], *Zeit im Bild: Frankfurter Rundschau am Wochenende*, 2, 3 January 1987, p. ZB3; **D.33(a)** as 'Mit den Augen des Nachtvogels: Über Jean Améry', *Études Germaniques*, 42.3 (July–September 1988), 313–27; **D.33(b)** in B.D.2, pp. 149–70 and 260–61; **D.33(c)** in B.D.2(a), pp. 149–70 and 260–61; **D.33(d)** in *Jean Améry: Werke*, ed. by Irène Heidelberger-Leonard, 9 vols (Stuttgart: Klett-Cotta, 2002–09), IX: *Materialien* (2008), pp. 505–26; D.33(a) adds: p. 315 ('dem sie sich stellte'); p. 317 ('daß die Haltung ... brechen müßte'); p. 318 ('ce mélange indécent de banalité et d'apocalypse'); p. 320 ('allenfalls theologisch ... nicht relevante'); p. 322 ('wie Cioran vermerkte' and 'Toute nostalgie ... l'irréversible'); p. 323 ('la conscience ... l'Incurable' and 'und zogen ... cesse de mourir'); p. 324 ('Zweifellos hätte ... mémoire'). The three subsequent versions are identical with D.33(a). D.33(a) is not included in the English-language versions of *Campo Santo* (B.D.2.1/1(a) and B.D.2.2/(a)) having been published in the English-language versions of *Luftkrieg und Literatur* (*On the Natural History of Destruction*), A.7.1/1(a), A.7.2/2(a), A.7.3/3(a) (see D.33(a).1/1(a), D.33(a).2/2(a), and D.33(a).3/3(a)).

D.33(a).1   As 'Against the Irreversible: On Jean Améry', in A.7.1, pp. 145–67 and 200–02; **D.33(a).1(a)** in A.7.1(a), pp. 145–67 and 200–02

D.33(a).2   As 'Against the Irreversible: On Jean Améry', in A.7.2, pp. 149–71 and 203–04; **D.33(a).2(a)** in A.7.2(a), pp. 149–71 and 203–04

D.33(a).3   As 'Against the Irreversible: On Jean Améry', in A.7.3, pp. 145–67 and 200–02; **D.33(a).3(a)** in A.7.3(a), pp. 145–67 and 200–01

D.33(a).4   As 'Con los ojos del ave nocturna: Sobre Jean Améry', in B.D.2.3, pp. 134–51 and 241–42

D.33(a).5   As 'Cos ollos dunha ave nocturna: Sobre Jean Améry', in B.D.2.4, pp. 151–70 and 263–64

D.33(a).6   As 'Contra o irreversíel: sobre Jean Améry', in A.7.8, pp. 125–44 and 167–68; **D.33(a).6(a)** As 'Com os olhos da ave nocturna: Sobre Jean Améry', in B.D.2.5, pp. 128–45 and 222–23

D.33(a).7   As 'Με τα μάτια της γλαυκός: Σκέψεις πάνω στον Jean Améry', in A.7.10, pp. 173–200 and 234–36 (translator's notes pp. 269–78)

D.33(a).8   As 'Yakousei no tori no me de: Jean Améry ni tsuite', in A.7.11, pp. 131–51 and 7–8

D.33(a).9   As 'Avec les yeux de l'oiseau de nuit: Sur Jean Améry', in B.D.2.6, pp. 143–62 and 253–54

D.33(a).10   As 'Met de ogen van de nachtvogel: Over Jean Améry, in B.D.2.7, pp. 153-74 and 264-65

D.34   W. G. Sebald, 'Die Zerknirschung des Herzens: Über Erinnerung und Grausamkeit im Werk von Peter Weiss' [written autumn 1985–early 1986], *Orbis Litterarum*, 41.3 ([autumn] 1986), 265–78; **D.34(a)** in *Zeit und Bild: Frankfurter Rundschau am Wochenende*, 292, 15 December 1990, p. ZB3; **D.34(b)** in B.D.2, pp. 128–48 and 259–60; **D.34(c)** in B.D.2(a), pp. 128–48 and 259–60. D.34(a) has no epigraph; the following extracts from D.34 are not included in D.34(a): pp. 265–66 ('Das Bild ... garantieren'); pp. 267–68 ('Die damit ... charakterisieren sollte'); p. 275 ('Der Massenmord ... sollte'). D.34, D.34(b) and D.34(c) are identical. D.34 is not included in the English-language versions of *Campo Santo* (B.D.2 and B.D.2.1) having been published in the English-language versions of *Luftkrieg und Literatur* (*On the Natural History of Destruction*), A.7.1/1(a), A.7.2/2(a), A.7.3/3(a) (see D.34(b).1, D.34(b).2 and D.34(b).3).

D.34(b).1   'The Remorse of the Heart: On Memory and Cruelty in the Work of Peter Weiss', in A.7.1, pp. 171–91 and 202; **D.34(b).1(a)** in A.7.1(a), pp. 171–91 and 202

D.34(b).2   As 'The Remorse of the Heart: On Memory and Cruelty in the Work of Peter Weiss', in A.7.2, pp. 175–95 and 204–05; **D.34(b).2(a)** in A.7.2(a), pp. 175–95 and 203–05

D.34(b).3   As 'The Remorse of the Heart: On Memory and Cruelty in the Work of Peter Weiss', in A.7.3, pp. 171–91 and 202; **D.34(b).3(a)** in A.7.3(a), pp. 171–91 and 202

D.34(b).4   As 'El remordimiento del corazón: Sobre memoria y crueldad en la obra de Peter Weiss', in B.D.2.3, pp. 116–33 and 239–40; **D.34(b).4(a)** in B.D.2.3(a), pp. 116–33 and 239–40

D.34(b).5   As 'O remorse do corazón: Sobre a memoria e a crueldade na obra de Peter Weiss', in B.D.2.4, pp. 131–49 and 262

D.34(b).6   As 'Sinceros remorsos: Sobre memória e crueldade na obra de Peter Weiss', in: A.7.8, pp. 145–62 and 168–69; **D.34(b).6(a)** as 'O coração contrito: Sobre memória e crueldade na obra de Peter Weiss', in B.D.2.5, pp. 111–27 and 221–22

D.34(b).7   As 'Η συντριβή της καρδιάς: Μνήμη και αγριότητα στο έργο του Peter Weiss', in A.7.10, pp. 201–26 and 236–37 (translator's notes pp. 279–85)

D.34(b).8   As 'Sainamareta kokoro: Peter Weiss no sakuhin ni okeru souki to zankoku', in A.7.11, pp. 153–71 and 8–9

D.34(b).9   As 'Le Cœur mortifié: Souvenir et cruauté dans l'œuvre de Peter Weiss', in A.7.7, pp. 123–41 and 252–43

D.34(b).10   As 'De wroeging van het hart: Over herinnering en wreedheid in het werk van Peter Weiss', in B.D.2.7, pp. 132–52 and 263–64

1986–1990 (D.35–D.52)

D.35   W. G. Sebald, 'In einer wildfremden Gegend: Zu Gerhard Roths Roman *Landläufiger Tod*', *Manuskripte*, 26, 92 (June 1986), 52–56; **D.35(a)** in A.5, pp. 145–61 and 191–92; **D.35(b)** in *Gerhard Roth: Materialien zu 'Die Archive des Schweigens'*, ed. by Uwe Wittstock (Frankfurt a.M.: Fischer Taschenbuch 11274, 1992), pp. 164–65. Not included in A.5.1

D.35(a).1   As 'In a Completely Unknown Region: On Gerhard Roth's Novel *Landläufiger Tod*', trans. by Markus Zisselsberger, *Modern Austrian Literature*, 40.4 ([December] 2007), 29–39

D.35(a).2   As 'Estranhas paragens: Sobre o romance de Gerhard Roth, *Landläufiger Tod* (A Morte Corrente)', in A.5.2, pp. 133-47-92 and 179–80

D.36   W. G. Sebald, 'Tiere, Menschen, Maschinen: Zu Kafkas Evolutionsgeschichten' [its origins go back to January 1983], *Literatur und Kritik*, 21, 205–06 (July–August 1986), 194–201

D.37   W. G. Sebald, 'Es schweigt der Berg, und manchmal spricht er: Vom Unsagbaren zum Unsäglichen: Zu Hermann Brochs berühmtem "Bergroman"', *Zeit und Bild: Frankfurter Rundschau am Wochenende*, 254, 1 November 1986, p. ZB3; **D.37(a)** as 'Una montagna bruna: Zum Bergroman Hermann Brochs', in A.5, pp. 118–30 and 188–89. D.37 omits D.37(a), p. 118 ('Von seinem ersten ... zweibändigen'), and p. 119 ('I Pasenow ... "Pasenow" '). In D.37(a), D.37, col.6 ('Vor allem ... mehr sieht') is transposed to p. 189, n. 24.

D.37(a).1   As ' "Una montagna bruna" (Sobre la novela de montaña de Hermann Broch)', in A.5.1, pp. 178–92

D.37(a).2   As '*Una montagna bruna*: Sobre o romance de montanha, de Hermann Broch', in A.5.2, pp. 107-18 and 176–77

D.38   W. G. Sebald, 'Die Kunst der Verwandlung: Herbert Achternbuschs theatralische Sendung' [paper given at the Colloquium on Contemporary German Theatre, University of East Anglia, Norwich, on 1 April 1987; see Appendix 6.1, p. 186], *Zeit und Bild: Frankfurter Rundschau am Wochenende*, 86, 11 April 1987, p. ZB3; **D.38(a)** in *Patterns of Change: German Drama and the European Tradition*, ed. by Dorothy James and Silvia Ranawake (*Studies in European Thought* 1) (New York: Peter Lang, 1990), pp. 297–306. In D.38(a) 'Kein Wunder ... weiß' has been added on p. 297.

D.38.1   As 'The Art of Transformation: Herbert Achternbusch's Theatrical Mission', in A.4, pp. 174–84; **D.38.1(a)** in A.4(a), pp. 174–84

D.39   W. G. Sebald, 'Surveying the Scene: Some Introductory Remarks' [spring–summer 1987], in A.4, pp. 1–8; **D.39.1(a)** in A.4(a), pp. 1–8

D.40   W. G. Sebald, 'Ansichten aus der Neuen Welt: Versuch über Charles Sealsfield [pseud. Karl Postl (1793–1864)]' [written late spring 1988], *Die Rampe*, 1988.1 ([mid] 1988), pp. 7–36; **D.40(a)** as 'Ansichten aus der Neuen Welt: Über Charles Sealsfield', in A.5, pp. 17–39 and 179–81; **D40(b)** as 'Ansichten aus der Neuen Welt: Über Charles Sealsfield', in Charles Sealsfield, *Ralph Doughby's Esq. Brautfahrt* (1835), ed. by Rolf Vollmann (*Die Andere Bibliothek* 259) (Frankfurt a.M.: Eichborn, [1 July] 2006), pp. 287–303, 7000 copies. D.40 is not included in A.5.1.

D.40(a).1   As 'Vistas do Novo Mundo: Sobre Charles Sealsfield', in A.5.2, pp. 13–34 and 165–68

D.41   W. G. Sebald, 'Preface' (June 1988), in A.4, unpaginated; **D.41(a)** in A.4(a), unpaginated

D.42   W. G. Sebald, 'Verlorenes Land: Jean Améry und Österreich' [first given as a lecture at the University of Passau in January 1988], *Text + Kritik*, no. 99 (July 1988), 20–29; **D.42(a)** in A.5, pp. 131–44 and 189–91. D.42, p. 24 includes 'erwies sich nicht ... Defätismus' and 'unter dem frenetischen ... Art.' D.42 is a second, very differently worded version of D.32.

D.42(a).1   As 'País perdido (Jean Améry y Austria)', in A.5.1, pp. 193–208

D.42(a).2   As 'Η απώλεια της πατρίδας: Ο Jean Améry και η Αυστρία' trans. by Iannis Kalifatidis, in Jean Améry, *Πέρα από την ενοχή και την εξιλέωση* [*Jenseits von Schuld und Sühne*], trans. by Iannis Kalifatidis (Athens: Εκδόσεις Άγρα [Ekdoseis Agra], [December] 2010), pp. 187–203

D.42(a).3   As 'País perdido: Jean Améry e a Áustria', in A.5.2, pp. 119–31 and 177–79

D.43   W. G. Sebald, 'Jean Améry und Primo Levi' [paper given at conference on Jean Améry, Université libre de Bruxelles, early December 1988], in *Über Jean Améry*, ed. by Irène Heidelberger-Leonard (Heidelberg: Carl Winter Universitäts-Verlag, 1990), pp. 115–23. D.43 differs significantly from D.45.

D.43.1   As 'Jean Améry και Primo Levi', trans. by Iannis Kalifatidis, in Jean Améry, *Πέρα από την ενοχή και την εξιλέωση* [*Jenseits von Schuld und Sühne*], trans. by Iannis Kalifatidis (Athens: Εκδόσεις Άγρα [Ekdoseis Agra], [December] 2010), pp. 205–16

D.44   W. G. Sebald, 'Le Paysan de Vienne: Über Peter Altenberg', *Neue Rundschau*, 100.1 ([early] 1989), pp. 75–95; **D.44(a)** as 'Peter Altenberg: Le Paysan de Vienne', in A.5, pp. 65–86 and 183–86. D.44 contains no footnotes and is not included in A.5.1.

D.44(a).1   As 'Peter Altenberg: Le paysan de Vienne', in A.5.2, pp. 57-76 and 170-73

D.45   W. G. Sebald, 'Überlebende als schreibende Subjekte: Jean Améry und Primo Levi: Ein Gedenken', *Zeit und Bild: Frankfurter Rundschau am Wochenende*, 24, 28 January 1989, p. ZB3. D.45 differs significantly from D.43.

D.46   W. G. Sebald, 'Westwärts–Ostwärts: Aporien deutschsprachiger Ghettogeschichten', *Literatur und Kritik*, 23, 233–34 (April–May 1989), 159–77; **D.46(a)** in A.5, pp. 40–64 and 181–83. D.46(a) involves minor variants.

D.46(a).1   As 'Hacia el este, hacia el oeste (Aporías de las historias del gueto alemanas)', in A.5.1, pp. 115–41

D.46(a).2   As 'Para leste, para oeste: Aporias das histórias do gueto em lingual alemã', in A.5.2, pp. 35-56 and 168-70

D.47   W. G. Sebald, 'Ein Kaddisch für Österreich: Über Joseph Roth: Zu seinem 50. Todestag', *Zeit und Bild: Frankfurter Rundschau am Wochenende*, 120, 27 May 1989, p. ZB2; **D.47(a)** as 'Ein Kaddisch für Österreich: Über Joseph Roth', in A.5, pp. 187–88. D.47(a) contains an epigraph from Joseph Roth, *Die Büste des Kaisers*, and on p. 106 adds 'durchaus als ... hat, der'; on p. 113 '1939' replaces '1931'.

D.47(a).1   As 'Un "kaddisch" para Austria (Sobre Joseph Roth)', in A.5.1, pp. 162–77

D.47(a).2   As 'Um *Kadish* pela Áustria: Sobre Joseph Roth', in A.5.2, pp. 93–105 and 175–76

D.48   W. G. Sebald, 'Thomas Bernhard (1931–1989)' [obituary, probably written in spring–summer 1989], *Austrian Studies*, 1 (1990), 215–16

D.49   W. G. Sebald, 'Vorwort' (January 1990), in A.5, p. 9

D.49.1   As 'Prólogo', in A.5.1, p. 107

D.49.2   As 'Prólogo', in A.5.2, p. 5

D.50   W. G. Sebald, 'Einleitung', in A.5, pp. 11–16

D.50.1   As 'Introducción', in A.5.1, pp. 109–14

D.50.2   As 'Introdução', in A.5.2, pp. 7-12 and 165

D.51   W. G. Sebald, 'Damals vor Graz: Randbemerkungen zum Thema Literatur & Heimat' [probably written in spring 1990], in *TRANS-GARDE: Die Literatur der 'Grazer Gruppe'*, ed. by Kurt Bartsch and Gerhard Melzer (Graz: Literaturverlag Droschl, 1990), pp. 141–53; **D.51(a)** in *Heimat im Wort: Die Problematik eines Begriffs im 19. und 20. Jahrhundert*, ed. by Rüdiger Görner (Publications of the Institute of Germanic Studies [University of London] 51) (Munich: iudicium, 1992), pp. 131–39 [given as a paper entitled 'Die Errettung der Heimat durch den bösen Blick: ein Kapitel aus der neuesten österreichischen Literatur' on 19 October 1990, the second day of the symposium 'Heimat – zu einem kulturideologischen Begriff des 19. und 20. Jahrhunderts' in honour of Irina Frowen at the Institute of Germanic Studies, 29 Russell Square]; **D.51(b)** in *Neue Zürcher Zeitung*, 122, 31 May 1991, p. 42. D.51(b) is shorter than D.51 and D.51(a) and omits D.51, pp. 143–44 ('Wenn Gerhard Roth ... mußten'); p. 144 ('Bemerkenswert ... genannt hat'); p. 145 ('Es gäbe folglich ... ausgedehnt werden'); pp. 145–47 ('Das heißt ... aufgebürdet wurde'); p. 147 ('Vielleicht ist das ... so oder so ist das'); and p. 150 ('die damit beginnt ... kurzen Biographie').

D.52   W. G. Sebald, 'Kleine Vorrede zur Salzburger Ausstellung', in *Anita Albus*, ed. by Tugomir Lukšić [catalogue of an exhibition in Salzburg (2 August–30 September 1990) and Zagreb (11 October–11 November 1990)] (Salzburg: Galerie Schloss Neuhaus, 1990), pp. 6, 8, and 10

D.52.1   As 'Mali predgovor za izložbu u Salzburgu' [Croatian version], parallel text in D.52, pp. 7, 9, and 11

D.52.2   As 'Petite Introduction à L'Exposition de Salzbourg' [French version], parallel text in D.52, pp. 7, 9, and 11

1991–1995 (D.53–D.60)

D.53   W. G. Sebald, 'Ich möchte zu ihnen hinabsteigen und finde den Weg nicht: Zu den Romanen Jurek Beckers' [written January–February 1991 and sent to Irène Heidelberger-Leonard for the book that she was editing on Becker (Frankfurt a.M.: Suhrkamp, 1992): she declined to include it on the grounds that the views it expressed were too extreme], *Sinn und Form*, 62.2 (March 2010), 226–34; followed by Uwe Schütte, 'Weil nicht sein kann, was nicht sein darf: Anmerkungen zu W. G. Sebalds Essay über Jurek Beckers Romane', pp. 235–42

D.54   W. G. Sebald, 'Jenseits der Grenze: Peter Handkes Erzählung *Die Wiederholung*', in A.5, pp. 162–78 and 192–94

D.54.1   As 'Más allá de la frontera (El relato de Peter Handke *La Repetición*)', in A.5.1, pp. 209–28

D.54.2   As 'Para lá da fronteira: O conto A Repetitção, de Peter Handke', in A.5.2, pp. 149-64 and 180-82

D.55   'Europäische Peripherien' (Tübinger Literaturforum) [written 15 January 1992], *Litterae: Academiae Scientiarum et Artium Europaeae* (official organ of the European Academy of Sciences and the Arts), 2.2 (April 1992), 32–34, followed by 'Bemerkungen zum Beitrag von W. G. Sebald', 34–36; **D.55(a)** in *Suchbild Europa: Künstlerische Konzepte der Moderne*, ed. by Jürgen Wertheimer (Amsterdam and Atlanta: Rodopi, 1995), pp. 65–67

D.56 W. G. Sebald, 'Des Häschens Kind, der kleine Has: Über das Totemtier des Lyrikers Ernst Herbeck', *Frankfurter Allgemeine Zeitung* (Literatur), 285, 8 December 1992, p. L10; **D.56(a)** in *Ernst Herbeck: die Vergangenheit ist klar vorbei*, ed. by Leo Navratil and Carl Aigner (Vienna and Krems: Chr. Brandstätter Verlag and Kunsthalle Krems, 2002), pp. 184–89 [this volume also contains D.17]; **D.56(b)** in B.D.2, pp. 171–78; **D.56(c)** in B.D.2(a), pp. 171–78.

D.56(a).1 As '*Des Häschens Kind, der kleine Has* [The Little Hare, Child of the Hare]: On the Poet Ernst Herbeck's Totem Animal'; in B.D.2.1, pp. 125–33; **D.56(a).1(a)** in B.D.2.1(a), pp. 125–33

D.56(a).2 As '*Des Häschens Kind, der kleine Has* [The Little Hare, Child of the Hare]: On the Poet Ernst Herbeck's Totem Animal'; in B.D.2.2, pp. 130–39; **D.56(a).2(a)** in B.D.2.2(a), pp. 130–39

D.56(a).3 As 'El lebrato, la liebrecilla: Sobre el animal totémico del poeta Ernst Herbeck', in B.D.2.3, pp. 152–59; **D.56(a).3(a)** in B.D.2.3(a), pp. 152–59

D.56(a).4 As 'O neno da lebre, a pequena lebre: Sobre o animal totémico do poeta Ernst Herbeck', in B.D.2.4, pp. 171–78

D.56(a).5 As '*Des Häschens Kind. Der kleine Has* [cria de lebre, pequena lebre]: Sobre o animal totem do poeta Ernst Herbeck', in B.D.2.5, pp. 146–52

D.56(a).6 As 'L'enfant de la hase, le petit lièvre: A propos de l'animal totémique du poète Ernst Herbeck', in B.D.2.6, pp. 163–69 and 254–55

D.56(a).7 As 'Haasjes kind, de kleine haas: Over het totemdier van de dichter Ernst Herbeck', in B.D.2.7, pp. 175–82

D.57 W. G. Sebald, 'Between the Devil and the Deep Blue Sea: Alfred Andersch: Das Verschwinden in der Vorsehung', *Lettre international: Europas Kulturzeitung*, no. 20 (Spring 1993), 80–84; **D.57(a)** as 'Der Schriftsteller Alfred Andersch', in A.7, pp. 121–60 and 164–66. D.57(a) is a foreshortened version of D.57 and the two versions begin to overlap at 'erfolgssüchtiger'/'erfolgsbedürftiger' (p. 80, col. 2, and p. 123 respectively); there are minor variants on D.57, p. 83, between 'Das also ist Anderschs' and 'Hervorhebung'; D.57(a) omits D.56, p. 83 ('versehentlich ... eines Jeffrey Archer'); **D.57(b)** as 'Der Schriftsteller Alfred Andersch', in A.7(a), pp. 111–47 and 154

D.57(a).1 As 'Between the Devil and the Deep Blue Sea: Alfred Andersch', in A.7.1, pp. 107–42 and 197–200; **D.57(a).1(a)** in A.7.1(a), pp. 107–42 and 197–200

D.57(a).2 As 'Between the Devil and the Deep Blue Sea: Alfred Andersch', in A.7.2, pp. 109–45 and 201–03; **D.57(a).2(a)** in A.7.2(a), pp. 109–45 and 201–03

D.57(a).3 As 'Between the Devil and the Deep Blue Sea: Alfred Andersch', in A.7.3, pp. 107–42 and 197–200; **D.57(a).3(a)** A.7.3(a), pp. 107–42 and 197–200

D.57(a).4 As 'El escritor Alfred Andersch', in A.7.4, pp. 113–47 and 155–58

D.57(a).5 As 'De schrijver Alfred Andersch', in A.7.5, pp. 115–51 and 157–59

D.57(a).6 As 'Lo scrittore Alfred Andersch', in A.7.6, pp. 103–35 and 146–49

D.57(a).7 As 'L'Écrivain Alfred Andersch', in A.7.7, pp. 111–44 and 151–54

D.57(a).8 As 'O escritor Alfred Andersch', in A.7.8, pp. 95–124 and 166–67

D.57(a).9 As 'Forfatteren Alfred Andersch', in A.7.9, pp. 139–83 and 189–91

D.57(a).10 As 'Μεταξύ Σκύλλας και Χάρυβδης: Ο συγγραφέας Alfred Andersch', in A.7.10, pp. 131–72 and 231–34 (translator's notes pp. 262–69)

D.57(a).11 As 'Akuma to konpeki no shinkai no aida: Sakka Alfred Andersch', in A.7.11, pp. 97–129 and 5–7

D.58 W. G. Sebald, 'Wie Tag und Nacht: Über die Bilder Jan Peter Tripps', in Jan Peter Tripp, *Die Aufzählung von Schwierigkeiten: Arbeiten von 1985–92* (Offenburg: Reiff Schwarzwaldverlag, [mid-]1993), pp. 57–62; **D.58(a)** in A.6, pp. 169–88

D.58(a).1   As 'As Day and Night, Chalk and Cheese: On the Pictures of Jan Peter Tripp', trans. by Michael Hamburger, in B.A.3.1, pp. 85–95; **D.58(a).1(a)** in B.A.3.1(a), pp. 85–95

D.58(a).2   As 'As Day and Night, Chalk and Cheese: On the Pictures of Jan Peter Tripp', trans. by Michael Hamburger, in B.A.3.2, pp. 78–94; **D.58(a).2(a)** in B.A.3.2(a), pp. 78–94

D.58(a).3   As 'Le jour et la nuit ...: Les tableaux de Jan Peter Tripp', in A.6.1, pp. 163–81 and 201

D.58(a).4   As 'Como a noite e o dia: sobre os quadros de Jan Peter Tripp', in A.6.2, pp. 143–59

D.59   W. G. Sebald, 'Ich bin Elias Canetti ...', in '"Du darfst keinen Satz vergessen": Stimmen zum Tod von Elias Canetti', *Neue Zürcher Zeitung* (Schweizer Ausgabe) (Feuilleton), 193, 20–21 August 1994, p. 43; **(D.59a)** also in *Neue Zürcher Zeitung* (Fernausgabe) (Feuilleton), 193, 20–21 August 1994, p. 29; **D.59(b)** in *Wortmasken: Texte zu Leben und Werk von Elias Canetti*, ed. by Ortrun Huber (Munich and Vienna: Carl Hanser Verlag, 1995), p. 145

D.60   W. G. Sebald, 'Via Schweiz ins Bordell: Der Schriftsteller W. G. (Max) Sebald erinnert sich an Kafkas Sommerreise 1911', *Die Weltwoche* (Zurich), 40, 5 October 1995, p. 66; **D.60(a)** as 'Kafkas fahrende Gesellen', *metamorphosen* (Heidelberg), 8, 23 (April–June 1998), 36–37; **D.60(b)** as 'Via Schweiz ins Bordell: Zu den Reisetagebüchern Kafkas', in B.D.2, pp. 179–83; **D.60(c)** in B.D.2(a), pp. 179–83

D.60(b).1   As 'To the Brothel by Way of Switzerland', in B.D.2.1, pp. 135–39; **D.60(b).1(a)** in B.D.2.1(a), pp. 135–39

D.60(b).2   As 'To the Brothel by Way of Switzerland', in B.D.2.2, pp. 140–45; **D.60(b).2(a)** in B.D.2.2(a), pp. 140–45

D.60(b).3   As 'Al burdel, pasando por Suiza: Sobre los "Diarios de viaje" de Kafka', in B.D.2.3, pp. 160–64; **D.60(b).3(a)** in B.D.2.3(a), pp. 160–64

D.60(b).4   As 'Cara ao bordel vía Suíza: Sobre os diarios de viaxes de Kafka', in B.D.2.4, pp. 179–83

D.60(b).5   As 'Via Suíça para o bordel: Sobre os cadernos de viagem de Kafka', in B.D.2.5, pp. 153–57

D.60(b).6   As 'Au bordel *via* la Suisse: A propos des *Journaux de voyage* de Kafka', in B.D.2.6, pp. 171–75 and 255–56

D.60(b).7   As 'Via Zwitserland naar het bordeel: Over de reisdagboeken van Kafka, in B.D.2.7, pp. 183–87

1996–2001 (D.61–D.76)

D.61   W. G. Sebald, 'Traumtexturen' [on Vladimir Nabokov], *du: Zeitschrift der Kultur*, 661, 6 (June 1996), 22–25; **D.61(a)** as 'Traumtexturen: Kleine Anmerkung zu Nabokov', in B.D.2, pp. 184–92; **D.61(b)** in B.D.2(a), pp. 184–92

D.61(a).1   As 'Dream Textures: A Brief Note on Nabokov', in B.D.2.1, pp. 141–49; **D.61(a).1(a)** in B.D.2.1(a), pp. 141–49

D.61(a).2   As 'Dream Textures: A Brief Note on Nabokov', in B.D.2.2, pp. 146–55; **D.61(a).2(a)** in B.D.2.2(a), pp. 146–55

D.61(a).3   As 'Texturas oníricas: Breve observación sobre Nabokov', in B.D.2.3, pp. 165–72; **D.61(a).3(a)** in B.D.2.3(a), pp. 165–72

D.61(a).4   As 'Texturas dos soños: Breve apuntamento sobre Nabokov', in B.D.2.4, pp. 185–93

D.61(a).5   As 'Texturas oníricas: Pequena observação sobre Nabokov', in B.D.2.5, pp. 158–65

D.61(a).6   As 'Textures de rêve: Note sur Nabokov', in B.D.2.6, pp. 177–85 and 256

D.61(a).7   As 'Droomtexturen: Kleine notitie over Nabokov', in B.D.2.7, pp. 188–97

D.62   W. G. Sebald, '"Was ich traure weiss ich nicht": Kleines Andenken an Mörike' [speech given on 22 April 1997 when Sebald was awarded the Mörike-Prize at Fellbach], in *Mörike-Preis der Stadt Fellbach an W. G. Sebald: Förderpreis an Wolfgang Schlüter mit Literaturtagen vom 17. bis 24. April 1997: Dokumentation*, ed. by Christa Linsenmaier-Wolf (Fellbach: Stadt Fellbach-Kulturamt, [1997]), pp. 53–62; **D.62(a)** in *Mörike-Preis der Stadt Fellbach 1991–2000: Ein Lesebuch* (*Fellbacher Hefte*, 7), ed. by Christa Linsenmaier-Wolf (Fellbach: [n. pub.], 2000), pp. 137–47; **D.62(b)** in A.6, pp. 75–94

D.62(b).1   As 'Je ne sais ce que je pleure: Pour Mörike, en bref hommage', in A.6.1, pp. 73–91 and 199–200

D.62(b).2   As 'O que choro não sei: pequena evocação de Mörike', in A.6.2, pp. 63–80

D.63   W. G. Sebald, 'Laudatio auf Wolfgang Schlüter' [speech given on 22 April 1997 when Schlüter was awarded the Förderpreis zum Mörike-Preis at Fellbach], in Linsenmaier-Wolf, *Dokumentation* [D.62], pp. 37–42; **D.63(a)** in Linsenmaier-Wolf, *Ein Lesebuch* [D.62(a)], pp. 149–54

D.64   W. G. Sebald, 'Geboren 1944 im Allgäu ...' [speech of acceptance to mark his election to the Deutsche Akademie für Sprache und Dichtung in Darmstadt on 24 October 1997], in *Deutsche Akademie für Sprache und Dichtung: Jahrbuch 1997*, ed. by Michael Assmann (Darmstadt: Wallstein, 1998), pp. 189–90; **D.64(a)** as 'W. G. Sebald', in *'Wie sie sich selber sehen': Antrittsreden der Mitglieder vor dem Kollegium der Deutschen Akademie*, ed. by Michael Assmann [anthology to celebrate the 50th anniversary of the Academy] (Göttingen: Wallstein, 1999), pp. 445–46; **D.64(b)** as 'Antrittsrede vor dem Kollegium der Deutschen Akademie', in B.D.2, pp. 249–50; **D.64(c)** in B.D.2(a), pp. 249–50

D.64(a).1   As 'Acceptance Speech to the Collegium of the German Academy', in B.D.2.1, pp. 207–08; **D.64(a).1(a)** in B.D.2.1(a), pp. 207–08

D.64(a).2   As 'Acceptance Speech to the Collegium of the German Academy', in B.D.2.2, pp. 216–17; **D.64(a).2(a)** in B.D.2.2(a), pp. 216–17

D.64(a).3   As 'Discurso de ingreso ante el Colegio de la Academia Alemana', in B.D.2.3, pp. 222–23; **D.64(a).3(a)** in B.D.2.3(a), pp. 222–23

D.64(a).4   As 'Discurso de entrada na Academia Alemã', in B.D.2.4, pp. 251–52

D.64(a).5   As 'Discurso de entrada para membro da Academia Alemã', in B.D.2.5, pp. 212–13

D.64(a).6   As 'Discours de reception à l'Académie allemande', in B.D.2.6, pp. 239–40

D.64(a).7   As 'Inaugurele rede voor het college van de Deutsche Akademie', in B.D.2.7, pp. 253–54

D.65   W. G. Sebald, 'Operation Gomorrah: Der Luftkrieg und das Schweigen der deutschen Literatur' [based on three lectures given at the University of Zurich, on 30 October, 13 November, and 4 December 1997], *Neue Zürcher Zeitung* (Schweizer Ausgabe) (Literatur und Kunst), 272, 22–23 November 1997, p. 67; **D.65(a)** *Neue Zürcher Zeitung* (Internationale Ausgabe) (Literatur und Kunst), 272, 22–23 November 1997, p. 5; **D.65(b)** in A.7, pp. 35–47 (up to '... eingerichtet hatten'). The last section of D.65/65(a), entitled 'Nekropole', is not included in D.65(b) [see also E.C.3]

D.65bis 'Luftkrieg', *Neue Zürcher Zeitung* (Internationale Ausgabe) (Feuilleton), 250, p. 33, 28 October 1997 ('Die ersten tatsächlichen Bombenschäden ... Abendbrottisch gehörte'). N. B. This is not part of D.65 but probably an extract from one of the lectures; later published in an amended version in A.7, pp. 86–89, with a significantly different opening, quoting from 'Paul Bereyter' (B.B.2, pp. 45–46).

D.65.1   As 'Obliteration', *Guardian* (London) (Saturday Review Section), 48,655, 15 February 2003, pp. 4–6 (edited, post-publication extracts from A.7.2 plus some new material; minor variants)

D.66   W. G. Sebald, 'Feuer und Rauch: Über eine Abwesenheit in der deutschen Nachkriegsliteratur' [read out on the occasion of receiving the Heinrich-Böll-Prize in Cologne on 28 November 1997], *Frankfurter Rundschau am Wochenende* (Feuilleton) (Zeit und Bild), 278, 29 November 1997, p. ZB3; **D.66(a)** in *Köln, Blicke: Ein Lesebuch*, ed. by Jochen

Schimmang (Cologne: DuMont, 1998), pp. 354–60. The content of D.66 overlaps with that of A.7, B.B.4, pp. 52–55 and D.65; **D.66(b)**; in Part II of the present volume, pp. 338–42.

D.67   W. G. Sebald, 'Ausgrabung der Vergangenheit' [brief piece on Michael Hamburger in anticipation of a reading at the Solothurner Literaturtage], *Tages-Anzeiger* (Zurich) (Kulturteil: Sonderteil Literaturtage), 116, 22 May 1998, p. 65; **D.67(a)**; in Part II of the present volume, pp. 344–45

D.68   W. G. Sebald, 'Le promeneur solitaire: Zur Erinnerung an Robert Walser', *Neue Zürcher Zeitung*, 117, 23 May 1998, p. 49; **D.68(a)** in A.6, pp. 127–68. D.68 is a much shorter version of D.68(a) and consists of D.68(a), pp. 131–41 ('Walser ist nach ... inneres Leben steht'). See also B.C.4 and B.C.5.

D.68(a).1   As 'Le promeneur solitaire: En souvenir de Robert Walser', in A.6.1, pp. 123–62 and 200–01

D.68(a).2   As 'Le promeneur solitaire: A Remembrance of Robert Walser' [English version], trans. by Jo Catling, introduction to Robert Walser, *The Tanners* [*Geschwister Tanner*] trans. by Susan Bernofsky (New York: New Directions Paperbook 1140, [August], 2009), pp. 1–36. See also A.6.3.

D.68(a).3   As 'Le promeneur solitaire: em memória de Robert Walser', in A.6.2, pp. 109–42

D.69   W. G. Sebald, 'Rousseau auf der Île de Saint-Pierre', *Sinn und Form*, 50.4 (July–August 1998), 499–513; **D.69(a)** as 'J'aurais voulu que ce lac eût été l'Océan: Anläßlich eines Besuchs auf der Peterinsel', in A.6, pp. 43–74. D.69(a), p. 49 contains minor variants.

D.69(a).1   As 'J'aurais voulu que ce lac eût été l'Océan: A l'occasion d'une visite à l'Île de Saint-Pierre', in A.6.1, pp. 43–71 and 199

D.69(a).2   As 'J'aurais voulu que ce lac eût été l'Océan: a propósito de uma visita à ilha de Saint-Pierre', in A.6.2, pp. 37–62

D.70   W. G. Sebald, 'Vorbemerkung', in A.6, pp. 5–7

D.70.1   As 'Avant-propos', in A.6.1, pp. 9–11

D.70.2   As 'Introdução', in A.6.2, pp. 5–7

D.71   W. G. Sebald, 'Es steht ein Komet am Himmel: Kalenderbeitrag zu Ehren des rheinischen Hausfreunds' [essay on Johann Peter Hebel], in A.6, pp. 9–41

D.71.1   As 'Une comète dans le ciel: Note d'almanach en l'honneur de l'ami rhénan', in A.6.1, pp. 13–41 and 197–98

D.71.2   As 'Há um cometa no céu: nota de almanaque em honra do amigo da casa', in A.6.2, pp. 9–36

D.72   W. G. Sebald, 'Her kommt der Tod, die Zeit geht hin: Anmerkungen zu Gottfried Keller', in A.6, pp. 95–126

D.72.1   As 'La mort s'en vient, le temps s'en va: A propos de Gottfried Keller', in A.6.1, pp. 93–122 and 200

D.72.1   As 'Vem a morte, vai-se o tempo: notas sobre Gottfried Keller', in A.6.2, pp. 81–107

D.73   W. G. Sebald, 'Scomber scombrus oder die gemeine Makrele: Zu Bildern von Jan Peter Tripp' (on an exhibition in the Galerie Brandstätter, Öhningen am Bodensee, ?September–8 October), *Neue Zürcher Zeitung* (Schweizer Ausgabe) (Literatur und Kunst), 222, 23–24 September 2000, p. 86; **D.73(a)** *Neue Zürcher Zeitung* (Internationale Ausgabe) (Literatur und Kunst), 222, 23–24 September 2000, p. 50; **D.73(b)** in Jan Peter Tripp, *Centrales et Occasionelles* (Offenburg: Schwarzwaldverlag, 2001), p. 40; **D.73(c)** in B.D.2, pp. 210–14; **D.73(d)** in B.D.2(a), pp. 210–14

D.73(c).1   As '*Scomber scombrus*, or the Common Mackerel: On Pictures by Jan Peter Tripp', in B.D.2.1, pp. 169–72; **D.73(c).1(a)** in B.D.2.1(a), pp. 169–72

D.73(c).2   As '*Scomber scombrus*, or the Common Mackerel: On Pictures by Jan Peter Tripp', in B.D.2.2, pp. 174–78; **D.73(c).2(a)** in B.D.2.2(a), pp. 174–78

D.73(c).3   As '"*Scomber scombrus*" o caballa común: Sobre cuadros de Jan Peter Tripp', in B.D.2.3, pp. 188–91; **D.73(c).3(a)** in B.D.2.3(a), pp. 188–91

D.73(c).4   As '*Scomber scombrus*, ou a xarda común: Sobre imaxes de Jan Peter Tripp', in B.D.2.4, pp. 211–15

D.73(c).5   As 'Scombra Scombrus ou Cavala Comum: Sobre fotografias de Jan Peter Tripp', in B.D.2.5, pp. 180–83

D.73(c).6   As '*Scomber scombrus* ou le maquereau commun: A propos de deux tableaux de Jan Peter Tripp', in B.D.2.6, pp. 203–06 and 256

D.73(c).7   As 'Scomber scombrus of de gewone makreel: Over schilderijen van Jan Peter Tripp', in B.D.2.7, pp. 215-19

D.74   W. G. Sebald, 'Das Geheimnis des rotbraunen Fells: Annäherung an Bruce Chatwin aus Anlass von Nicholas Shakespeares Biographie', *Literaturen*, 2000.11 (November 2000), 72–75; **D.74(a)** as 'Das Geheimnis des rotbraunen Fells', in *Chatwins Rucksack: Porträts, Gespräche, Skizzen*, ed. by Hans Jürgen Balmes (Frankfurt a.M.: Fischer Taschenbuch 15,508, [June] 2002), pp. 133–46; **D.74(b)** as 'Das Geheimnis des rotbraunen Fells: Annäherung an Bruce Chatwin', in B.D.2, pp. 215–22; **D.74(c)** in B.D.2(a), pp. 215–22

D.74(b).1   As 'The Mystery of the Red-Brown Skin: An Approach to Bruce Chatwin', in B.D.2.1, pp. 173–80; **D.74(b).1(a)** in B.D.2.1(a), pp. 173–80

D.74(b).2   As 'The Mystery of the Red-Brown Skin: An Approach to Bruce Chatwin', in B.D.2.2, pp. 179–87; **D.74(b).2(a)** in B.D.2.2(a), pp. 179–87

D.74(b).3   As 'El misterio de la piel caoba: Aproximación a Bruce Chatwin', in B.D.2.3, pp. 192–98; **D.74(b).3(a)** in B.D.2.3(a), pp. 192–98

D.74(b).4   As 'O segredo do pelello pardo: Unha aproximación a Bruce Chatwin', in B.D.2.4, pp. 217–24

D.74(b).5   As 'O mistério da pele castanho-rubra: Abordagem a Bruce Chatwin', in B.D.2.5, pp. 184–90

D.74(b).6   As 'Le secret du pelage rouge: Approche de Bruce Chatwin', in B.D.2.6, pp. 207–14 and 256

D.74(b).7   As 'Het geheim van de roodbruine huid: Een benadering van Bruce Chatwin', in B.D.2.7, pp. 220-27

D.75   W. G. Sebald, 'Da steigen sie schon an Bord und heben zu spielen an und zu singen', *Frankfurter Allgemeine Zeitung* (Feuilleton), 155, 7 July 2001, p. 45; **D.75(a)** as 'Moments musicaux', in B.D.2, pp. 223–39; **D.75(b)** in B.D.2(a), pp. 223–39

D.75(a).1   As '*Moments musicaux*', in B.D.2.1, pp. 181–96; **D.75(a).1(a)** in B.D.2.1(a), pp. 181–96

D.75(a).2   As '*Moments musicaux*', in B.D.2.2, pp. 188–205; **D.75(a).2(a)** in B.D.2.2(a), pp. 188–205

D.75(a).3   As '"Moments musicaux"', in B.D.2.3, pp. 199–213; **D.75(a).3(a)** in B.D.2.3(a), pp. 199–213

D.75(a).4   As '*Moments musicaux*', in B.D.2.4, pp. 225–40

D.75(a).5   As '*Moments musicaux*', in B.D.2.5, pp. 191–203

D.75(a).6   As '*Moments musicaux*', in B.D.2.6, pp. 215–30

D.75(a).7   As '*Moments musicaux*', in B.D.2.7, pp. 228-43

D.76   W. G. Sebald, 'Zerstreute Reminiszenzen: Gedanken zur Eröffnung eines Stuttgarter Hauses' [first read out at the opening of the Literaturhaus Stuttgart on 17 November 2001], *Stuttgarter Zeitung* (Kultur), 267, 19 November 2001, p. 12; **D.76(a)** as 'Ein Versuch der Restitution', in B.D.2, pp. 240–48; **D.76(b)** as 'Zerstreute Reminiszenzen: Gedanken zur Eröffnung eines Stuttgarter Hauses', in *Betrifft: Chotjewitz, Dorst, Ortheil, Oswald, Rakusa, Sebald, Walser, Zeh*, ed. by Florian Höllerer and Tim Schleider (*edition suhrkamp* 2379) (Frankfurt a.M.: Suhrkamp, 2004), pp. 11–16; **D.76(c)** in B.D.2(a), pp. 240–48; **D.76(d)** as 'Sebalds letzte Rede: Zerstreute Reminiszenzen: Gedanken zur Eröffnung eines Stuttgarter Hauses', *Der Schwabenspiegel: Jahrbuch für Literatur, Sprache und Spiel*, ed. by the Archiv für Literatur aus Schwaben, nos. 6–7 (23 March 2007), pp. 157–62. See also B.C.6.

D.76(a).1   As 'An Attempt at Restitution: A Memory of a German City' [American version], trans. by Anthea Bell, *The New Yorker* [no issue no.], 20 and 27 December 2004, pp. 110, 112, and 114; **D.76(a).1(a)** as 'An Attempt at Restitution', in B.D.2.1, pp. 197–205; **D.76(a).1(b)** in B.D.2.1(a), pp. 197–205

D.76(a).2   As 'An Attempt at Restitution', in B.D.2.2, pp. 206–15; **D.76(a).2(a)** in B.D.2.2(a), pp. 206–15

D.76(a).3   As 'Un intento de restitución', in B.D.2.3, pp. 214–21; **D.76(a).3(a)** in B.D.2.3(a), pp. 214–21

D.76(a).4   As 'Un intento de restitución', in B.D.2.4, pp. 241–49

D.76(a).5   As 'Uma tentativa de restituição', in B.D.2.5, pp. 204–11

D.76(a).6   As 'Une tentative de restitution', in B.D.2.6, pp. 231–38 and 256

D.76(a).7   As 'Et forsøk på restitusjon' [Norwegian version], trans. by Geir Pollen, *Vinduet: Gyldendals Tidsskrift for Litteratur*, 64.1 (March 2010), 68–71

D.76(a).8   As 'Een poging tot restitutie', in B.D.2.7, pp. 244-52

E. Extracts from Individual Works (including Translations)

E.A. Extracts from Books of Poetry (B.A.1–B.A.3)

Nach der Natur (B.A.1)

1984–2001

E.A.1   W. G. Sebald, 'Und blieb ich am äußersten Meer', *Manuskripte*, 24, 85 (October 1984), 23–27; **pre-publication extract** from B.A.1, pp. 36–68. [The title refers to Psalm 139: 9–10.]

E.A.2   W. G. Sebald, 'Wie der Schnee auf den Alpen' [first read out at the Literarisches Colloquium, Berlin, in September 1985], *Manuskripte*, 26, 92 (June 1986), 26–31; **pre-publication extract** from B.A.1, pp. 6–33

E.A.2.1   W. G. Sebald, 'Als de sneeuw op de Alpen' [Dutch version of B.A.1, pp. 6–33/ E.A.2], trans. by Huub Beurskens, *Het moment: Kwartaalboek voor nieuwe literatuur en kunst*, [no vol. no.], 3 (Winter 1986), 120–43

E.A.3   W. G. Sebald, 'Die dunckle Nacht fahrt [*sic*] aus', *Manuskripte*, 27, 95 (March 1987), 12–18; **pre-publication extract** from B.A.1, pp. 70–99. [The title comes from line 9 of 'An den Abend-Stern: Daß Er Ihn balde zu Ihr bringen wolle' by the seventeenth-century German poet Paul Fleming.]

E.A.3.1   W. G. Sebald, 'De donkere nacht zet in' [Dutch version of B.A.1, pp. 70–99/ E.A.3], trans. by Huub Beurskens, *Het moment: Kwartaalboek voor nieuwe literatuur en kunst* [no vol. no.], 6 (Autumn 1987), 129–48

E.A.4   W. G. Sebald, 'Die dunckle Nacht fahrt [*sic*] aus', in *Die Vergangenheit der Zukunft*, ed. by Ludwig Krapf and others (*Forum Allmende: 7. Freiburger Literaturgespräch, 11.–13. November 1993*) (Freiburg i.Br.: Kulturamt, [November] 1993), pp. 43–47; **post-publication** extract from B.A.1, pp. 70–79 (sections I and II), and 88–91 (section V)

E.A.5   W. G. Sebald, 'After Nature', 1999 programme for the Aldeburgh Festival of Music and the Arts; **E.A.5(a)** in *Modern Poetry in Translation*, 16 (2000), 102–04; **pre-publication** extract from B.A.1.2, pp. 105–08

E.A.6   W. G. Sebald, 'from part III of *After Nature*', *Modern Poetry in Translation*, 17 (2001), 248–50; **pre-publication extract** from B.A.1.2, pp. 101–04; **E.A.6(a)** as '*After Nature*, Section 6, Part III' in *Irish Pages*, 1.1 (Spring 2002) (Inaugural Issue: Belfast in Europe), 105-07 [followed by Michael Hamburger, 'Translator's Note on *After Nature* (1999)' and a reprint of Hamburger's obituary of WGS (see Secondary Bibliography)]

E.A.7   W. G. Sebald, 'Dark Night Sallies Forth', *The New Yorker* [no issue no.], 17 and 24 June 2002, p. 126; **pre-publication extract** from B.A.1.1, pp. 81–85. E.A.5 lacks 'For it is hard ... But' (p. 81)

E.A.8   W. G. Sebald, 'After Nature', *Index on Censorship*, 31.3 (July 2002), pp. 183–94; **pre-publication extract** from B.A.1.2, pp. 12–16, 95–100, and 109–13

E.A.9   W. G. Sebald, 'After Nature: Dark Night Sallies Forth', *Guardian* (London) (Saturday Review Section), 48,465, 6 July 2002, p. 35; **pre-publication extract** from B.A.1.2, pp. 95–100 ('In his excitement ... change his whole life')

E.A.10   W. G. Sebald, 'And if I Remained by the Outermost Sea', *The Threepenny Review*, 23.3 (Fall 2002), 10–14; **pre-publication extract** from B.A.1.1, pp. 42–78 [the title refers to Psalm 139: 9–10].

E.A.11   W. G. Sebald, '... Kind, sag mir', in *Das Buch vom Stein: Texte aus fünf Jahrtausenden*, ed. by Matthias Bärmann (Salzburg and Vienna: Jung + Jung, 2005), p. 156; **post-publication extract** from B.A.1. p. 94 ('Kind, sag mir ... noch nirgends gesehn')

E.A.12   W. G. Sebald [extracts from *Nach der Natur* translated into Dutch by Ton Naaijkens], in Ton Naaijkens, 'Naar de natuur: Het begin van een oeuvre', *Armada*, 11, 40 (October 2005), 58–73

For Years Now (B.A.2)

E.A.13   W. G. Sebald, 'Elephants', *The Observer*, 2 December 2001, **pre-publication extract** from B.A.2, p. 45

E.A.14   W. G. Sebald, 'Please', *Brick: A Literary Journal*, 69 (Spring 2002), [no. 7]; **post-publication extract** from B.A.2, p. 12

Unerzählt (B.A.3)

E.A.15   W. G. Sebald / Jan Peter Tripp, 'Unser Blickwechsel in die Tiefe der Erinnerung', *Frankfurter Allgemeine Zeitung* (Feuilleton), 290, 13 December 2002, p. 44; **pre-publication extracts** (with introductory column by 'fvl') from B.A.3, pp. 6-7, 12-13, 16-21, 24-25, 28-29, 34-35, 38-39, 47, 50-51, 55-56, 66-67 ([William Burroughs] 'Plinius sagt'; [Maurice] 'Sende mir bitte'; [Harry Saemann] 'Gefühle'; [Julie Seltz] 'In der Dunkelheit'; [Francis Bacon] 'Am 8. Mai 1927'; [Stéphane Spach] 'Der Fruchtkorb'; [Jérémy Seltz] 'Mitten im Schlaf'; [La comtesse d'Haussonville (Ingres)] 'Beim Erwachen'; [André Masson] 'Schrecklich'; [Barnett Newman] 'In der Sammlung'; [Michael Hamburger] 'Venezianisches'; [Jorge Luis Borges] 'My eye'; [Rembrandt] 'Gleich einem Hund'; [Felix Näger] 'Aus dem Vorderschiff'; [Daniela Näger] 'Blaues'; [Richard Hamilton] 'Ich sehe'; [Samuel Beckett] 'Er wird Dich')

E.A.16   W. G. Sebald, 'Six Poems', *World Literature Today*, 79.1 (January–April 2005), pp. 38–39; **post-publication extracts** from B.A.3, pp. 42–45, 54–55, 58–59, 64–67, and B.A.3.2, pp. 48–51, 60–61, 64–65, 70–71 ([Borges] 'My eye' / 'My eye'; [Rembrandt] 'Gleich einem Hund' / 'Like a dog'; [Brandstätter] 'Im Speisewagen' / 'In the dining-car'; [Onnetti] [*sic*] 'Das Haus' / 'The house'; [Proust] 'Aber die Zeit' / 'But the time'; [Beckett] 'Er wird dich' / 'He will cover')

E.B. Extracts from Works of Prose Fiction
(B.B.1–B.B.4 and B.D.2, pp. 7–52)

Schwindel. Gefühle. (B.B.1)

1988–2001

E.B.1   W. G. Sebald, 'Berge oder das ...', *Manuskripte*, 28, 99 (March 1988), 71–78; **pre-publication extract** from B.B.1, pp. 7–37 (with minor variants)

E.B.2   W. G. Sebald, 'Dr. K.s. Badereise', *proposition: zeitschrift für literatur*, no. 3 (June 1989), 42–51; **pre-publication extract** from B.B.1, pp. 163–91. E.B.2 varies significantly from the later B.B.1: several of the illustrations are different; E.B.2, p. 45 ('Unter dem Portal ... von der Stelle'), becomes 'Daß er das ... weiter und weiter aufspaltete' (p. 171); E.B.2, p. 48 ('und senkte dann ... des Buchs'), becomes 'während diese ... untereinander' (p. 179); E.B.2, p. 49 ('Im Verlauf der Septembertage'), is expanded to 'Am Tag nach ... Herbsttage in Riva' (pp. 183–86).

E.B.3   as '"Wertach": Il Ritorno in Patria, Tagesroman in 21 Teilen', *Augsburger Allgemeine Zeitung*, serialized in 21 parts from no. 140 (21 June 1990), p. 22, to no. 161 (16 July 1990), p. 12; **post-publication extract** from B.B.1, pp. 195–291 ('Im November 1987 ... ganz für sich allein in die folgenden Zeilen sagte:'); **E.B.3(a)** as 'Wertach: Il Ritorno in Patria', *Allgäuer Anzeigeblatt* (Immenstadt), serialized in 22 parts from no. 140 (21 June 1990), *Fernsehprogramm*, p. 13, to no. 161 (16 July 1990), *Fernsehprogramm*, p. 21; **post-publication extract** from B.B.1, pp. 195–291 ('Im November 1987, ... es ist nirgends verzeichnet.'). E.B.3 is three-quarters of a page shorter than E.B.3(a) and omits, for no apparent reason, the four-line poem and from 'Daß ich darauf damals' to 'es ist nirgends verzeichnet.'

E.B.4   W. G. Sebald, 'Beyle, or Love is a Madness Most Discreet', *The Republic of Letters*, 7 (1999), 6–11; **post-publication extract** from B.B.1.4, pp. 3–30 ('In mid-May ... consciousness he died.')

E.B.5   W. G. Sebald, 'Going Abroad', *Granta*, no. 68 (Winter 1999), 175–203; **post-publication extract** from B.B.1.4, pp. 33–72 and 76–81 ('In October 1980 I travelled ... penetrate my heart' and 'On the third day ... transported onward[s]')

E.B.6   W. G. Sebald, 'Vertiges', *Les Inrockuptibles* (Paris) (Supplément), 272, 9 January 2001, p. vi; **post-publication extract** from B.B.1.6, pp. 9–16 and B.B.1.6(a), pp. 11–19 ('A la mi-mai de l'année 1800 ... le vilain petit dragon')

E.B.7   W. G. Sebald, 'Memory's Defeat', *Pen America* (New York), 1.2 (Fall 2001), 77–79; **post-publication extract** from B.B.1.4(a), pp. 3–8 ('In mid-May of the year 1800 ... indeed, one might say they destroy them')

E.B.8   W. G. Sebald, 'A Study of Pisanello', *Modern Painters*, 14.1 (Winter 2001), pp. 50–51; **post-publication extract** from B.B.1.4, pp. 72–76 ('Over the days that ... pizzeria in the Via Roma ...'). [The piece is published with illustrations not included in B.B.1.4 since these are tied in with the exhibition entitled 'Pisanello: Painter to the Renaissance Court' (National Gallery, London, 24 October 2001–13 January 2002)].

2002–2010

E.B.9   [W. G. Sebald], 'Il ritorno in patria: Reiseliteratur von W. G. Sebald, Fotorecherche von Paul Albert Leitner', *Quart Heft für Kultur Tirol*, ed. by the Kultur-Abteilung des Landes Tirol (Innsbruck), 3 ([c. June] 2004), 20–29; **post-publication extract** from B.B.1, pp. 195–204 ('Im November 1987 ... Schiffsreise aus dem überschwemmten Gebirge hinaus'.)

E.B.10   W. G. Sebald, 'Ausflug mit Ernst Herbeck zur Burg Greifenstein', in *die Vergangenheit ist klar vorbei*, ed. by Leo Navratil and Carl Aigner (Vienna and Krems: Chr.

Brandstätter Verlag and Kunsthalle Krems, 2002), pp. 168–73; **post-publication extract** from B.B.1, pp. 46–59 ('[...] faßte ich den Entschluß ... beim Zirkus gewesen war.')

E.B.11   W. G. Sebald, 'Limone sul Garda: Hotel Sole', in *Hotels: Ein literarischer Führer*, ed. by Lis Künzli (Berlin: Eichborn, 2007), pp. 51–53; **post-publication extracts** from B.B.1, pp. 108–09, 112–14 and 122–23 ('Es wird gegen ... weit auf den See hinaus'; 'Der 2. August ... ihn gebeten hatte' and 'Als ich, diese ... eine andere Welt.')

Die Ausgewanderten (B.B.2)

1988–2001

E.B.12   W. G. Sebald, 'Verzehret das letzte selbst die Erinnerung nicht?', *Manuskripte*, 28, 100 (June 1988), 150–58; **pre-publication extract** from B.B.2, pp. 5–37. The epigraph to B.B.2 has intensified 'verzehret' to 'zerstöret' ('verzehret' follows the wording of the quotation from the fourth stanza of Hölderlin's 'Elegie': Sebald's annotated copy is depicted in B.C.6, p. 24); four of the pictures in the two versions differ significantly (see Fig. III.2, p. 497); the text of E.B.12 is largely the same as that of the later B.B.2 with minor variants, but E.B.12, p. 155 ('glänzender Staub, ein ganzes Sternengefild aus der Streusandbüchse Gottes, zitterte im Kegel des Lichts als Vorspiel vor dem Erscheinen der Bilder'), becomes 'und der sonst unsichtbare Zimmerstaub erglänzte zitternd im Kegel des Lichts als Vorspiel vor dem Erscheinen der Bilder' (p. 26); E.B.12, p. 156 ('Montreux'), becomes 'Gstaad' (p. 26); and the final sentence of E.B.12 on p. 158 ('Denn was Genügen gibt, endet dort, wo es genügt, und wo es endet, genügt es nicht mehr') is omitted from B.B.2, p. 37.

E.B.13   W. G. Sebald, 'Und manche Nebelflecken löset kein Auge auf', in *Klagenfurter Texte*, ed. by Heinz Felsbach and Siegbert Metelko (*Serie Piper*, 1284) (Zurich and Munich: Piper, 1990), pp. 111–37 (the quotation used for the title comes from Jean Paul's *Vorschule der Ästhetik*, *Sämtliche Werke*, Part I, v (Darmstadt: Wissenschaftliche Buchgesellschaft, 2000), pp. 7–514 (p. 64), where the writer, commenting on J. G. Hamann, discusses the difference between two unacceptable kinds of poetry); **pre-publication extract** from B.B.2, pp. 39–91; **E.B.13(a)** *Neue Zürcher Zeitung* (Fernausgabe), 116, 24 May 1991, p. 42; **E.B.13(b)** *Neue Zürcher Zeitung* (Schweizer Ausgabe) (Literatur und Kunst), 118 (25–26 May 1991), p. 68; **pre-publication extract** from B.B.2, pp. 39–46, 58–63, 70–73, and 88–93; no illustrations; the epigraph to B.B.2 omits the 'Und' that begins the titles of E.B.13 and E.B.13(a). E.B.13 contains none of the pictures published in the later B.B.2, but does contain two photographs (between pp. 128 and 129) that are unrelated to the text.

E.B.14   W. G. Sebald, 'Die Ausgewanderten. Dr. Henry Selwyn', in *Hereinbrechende Ränder. Zersplittertes Europa. Deuten und Übersetzen*, ed. by Brigitte Labs-Ehlert (II. Literaturbegegnung Schwalenberg [Lippe]) (Detmold: II. Druck des Literaturbüros Ost-westfalen-Lippe, 1993), pp. 7–11; **post-publication extract** from B.B.2, pp. 29–37 ('Mitte Mai 1971 ... ein Paar genagelter Schuhe')

E.B.15   Max Sebald, 'From *Die Ausgewanderten*', in *Essays in Memory of Michael Parkinson and Janine Dakyns*, ed. by Christopher Smith (*Norwich Papers* iv) (Norwich: The School of Modern Languages and European Studies, University of East Anglia, [late] 1996), pp. 325–29; **post-publication extract** from B.B.2.4, pp. 18–23 ('Dr Selwyn did ... a pair of hob-nailed boots')

E.B.16   'Mörike-Preis an W. G. Sebald: Preisverleihung am 22. April 1997: Der Stadtan-zeiger bringt Kostproben aus seinem Werk' [i.e. 'Paul Bereydter' [*sic*]], *Fellbacher Stadtanzeiger*, serialized in five parts in no. 11 (13 March 1997), p. 7; no. 13 (26 March 1997), p. 7; no. 15 (10 April 1997), p. 7; no. 16 (17 April 1997), p. 4; no. 18 (30 April 1997), p. 6; **post-publication extract** from B.B.2, pp. 39–93 ('Im Januar 1984 ... eines Vogels im

Flug.'); **E.B.16(a)** W. G. Sebald, 'Paul Berey[d]ter', in Linsenmaier-Wolf, *Dokumentation*, pp. 133–39 (see D.62)

E.B.17   W. G. Sebald, 'Aus *Die Ausgewanderten*', in Linsenmaier-Wolf, *Ein Lesebuch*, pp. 161–62 (see D.62(a)); **post-publication extract** from B.B.2, pp. 270–72 ('Rein zeitlich gesehen ... Anlaß gegeben hat')

2002–2010

E.B.18   W. G. Sebald, 'Extract from "Max Ferber"', in *Urban Visions: Experiencing and Envisioning the City*, ed. by Stephen Spier (*Critical Forum*, 5) (Liverpool: Liverpool University Press and Tate Liverpool, 2003), pp. 229–51; **post-publication extracts** from B.B.2.4, pp. 149–76 ('Until my twenty-second year ... true work of art looks like'), with the order of several of the photographs rearranged.

Die Ringe des Saturn (B.B.3)

1994–2001

E.B.19   W. G. Sebald, 'Die Heide von Dunwich', *Neue Zürcher Zeitung* (Schweizer Ausgabe) (Literatur und Kunst), 181, 6–7 August 1994, p. 54; **E.B.19(a)** *Neue Zürcher Zeitung* (Fernausgabe) (Literatur und Kunst), 179, 5 August 1994, p. 30; **pre-publication extracts** from B.B.3, pp. 211–18 ('Es war ungewöhnlich ... Schwemmsand grüne Auen wuchsen'); E.B.19/19(a) contain a photograph of the ruined Franciscan abbey mentioned in all three pieces; in the later B.B.3 this is replaced by a more enigmatic aerial view of the labyrinth at Somerleyton (p. 216).

E.B.20   W. G. Sebald, 'Grenzgänge', *Die Weltwoche* (Zurich), Supplement, 8, August 1995, pp. 8–11; **pre-publication extract** from B.B.3, pp. 276–90 and 290–95. E.B.20 omits 'Ich hatte zuvor ... entlangfließt' (p. 290).

E.B.21   W. G. Sebald, 'Die Ringe des Saturn', in *Der Die Das Fremde. Mit einem Komma aufhören*, ed. by Brigitte Labs-Ehlert (IV. Literaturbegegnung Schwalenberg [Lippe]) (Detmold: IV. Druck des Literaturbüros Ostwestfalen-Lippe, 1995), pp. 39–51; **post-publication extract** from B.B.3, pp. 101–18 ('Wie ich an jenem Abend ... Gunhill von Southwold saß')

E.B.22   W. G. Sebald, 'Dunwich & Middleton', in *Der Berliner Literaturpreis 1994*, ed. by Katharina Giebel, Ute Bredemeyer, and Christa Müller (on behalf of the Stiftung Preußische Seehandlung) (Berlin: Volk & Welt, 1996), pp. 75–95; **post-publication extract** from B.B.3, pp. 211–38

E.B.23   W. G. Sebald, 'From Saturn's Rings', *The Republic of Letters* (Boston), no. 3 (January 1998), pp. 14-22; **post-publication extract** from B.B.3.2, pp. 103–34 ('On the eve of my second stay ... into which his body had been thrown.')

E.B.24   [W. G. Sebald], 'Dosei no wa' ['The Rings of Saturn'] [Japanese version], trans. by Motoyuki Shibata, *Shincho* [*New Wave/Tide*], 98.1 (January 2001), 255–67 and 268–69; translation of Part I of B.B.3.2 ('In August 1992 ... does it mean?'); cf. B.B.3.14

2002–2010

E.B.25   W. G. Sebald, 'From *The Rings of Saturn*', in *The Gift: New Writing for the NHS*, ed. by David Morley (Exeter: Stride Publications, 2002), pp. 162–66; **post-publication extract** from B.B.3.3, pp. 3–17 ('In August 1992 ... and over the dead mans's eyes')

E.B.26   W. G. Sebald, 'Heringsernten', in *Geschichten aus der Welt*, ed. by Stefanie Janssen and Reinhard Goltz (Rostock: Hinstorff, 2005), pp. 208–14; **post-publication extract** from B.B.3, pp. 69–79 ('Drei bis vier Meilen ... sonst unaufhaltsamen Verdrängung der Finsternis')

E.B.27   W. G. Sebald, 'Chapter 6 of *The Rings of Saturn*', in *Terrestrial Intelligence: International Science Fiction Now from New Directions*, ed. by Barbara Epler (New York: New Directions, 2006), pp. 53–76; **post-publication extract** from B.B.3.2, pp. 137–66

E.B.28   W. G. Sebald, 'Memoiren von jenseits des Grabs', in *Christian Boltanski. Zeit*, ed. by Ralf Beil [catalogue of an exhibition in the Ausstellungsgebäude Mathildenhöhe, Darmstadt (12 November 2006–11 February 2007)] (Ostfilden-Ruit: Hatje Cantz, 2006), p. 105; **post-publication extract** from B.B.3(d), pp. 302–03 (B.B.3, pp. 316–17) ('Monate und jahrelang ... die von mir fast schon verlassene Welt')

E.B.29   W. G. Sebald, 'Preface', in Thomas Browne, *Urn Burial* (New York: New Directions, [October] 2010), pp. 1-19; **post-publication extract** from B.B.3.2, pp. 9-26 ('... After my discharge from hospital ... urn of Patroclus: what does it mean?')

The Four Prose Pieces from *Campo Santo* (B.D.2, pp. 7–52)
1996–2001

E.B.30   W. G. Sebald, 'Kleine Exkursion nach Ajaccio', *Frankfurter Allgemeine Zeitung* (Bilder und Zeiten), 185, 10 August 1996, unpaginated; **pre-publication extract** from B.D.2, pp. 7–18; **E.B.30(a)** in B.D.2, pp. 7–18; **E.B.30(b)** in B.D.2(a), pp. 7–18

E.B.30.1   As 'A Little Excursion to Ajaccio', in B.D.2.1, pp. 3–14; **E.B.30.1(a)** in B.D.2.1(a), pp. 3–14

E.B.30.2   As 'A Little Excursion to Ajaccio', in B.D.2.2, pp. 3–15; **E.B.30.2(a)** in B.D.2.2(a), pp. 3–15

E.B.30.3   As 'Pequeña excursión a Ajaccio', in B.D.2.3, pp. 9–18; **E.B.30.3(a)** in B.D.2.3(a), pp. 9–18

E.B.30.4   As 'Pequena excursión a Ajaccio', in B.D.2.4, pp. 13–23

E.B.30.5   As 'Pequena Excursão a Ajaccio', in B.D.2.5, pp. 11–20

E.B.30.6   As 'Petite excursion à Ajaccio', in B.D.2.6, pp. 11–21

E.B.30.7   As 'Kleine excursie naar Ajaccio'', in B.D.2.7, pp. 13-24

E.B.31   W. G. Sebald, '"La cour de l'ancienne école"', in *BuchBilderBuch: Geschichten zu Bildern*, ed. by Quint Buchholz (Zurich: Sanssouci, 1997), pp. 15–16; **pre-publication extract** from B.D.2, pp. 51–52; **E.B.31(a)** in B.D.2, pp. 51–52; **E.B.31(b)** in B.D.2(a), pp. 51–52

E.B.31.1   W. G. Sebald, '"La cour de l'ancienne école"' [Dutch version], trans. by Tinke Davids, in *BoekPrentenBoek: Boeken. tekenaar. schrijvers*, ed. by Quint Buchholz (Amsterdam: Van Gennep, 1997), pp. 15–16; **E.B.31.1(a)** in *D[ietsche] W[arande] & B[elfort]: Kaddisj voor een literair archeoloog*, ed. by Jan Ceuppens and Bart Philipsen [special W. G. Sebald number], 150.1 (February 2005), 19–20 (cf. Secondary Bibliography, Section 3)

E.B.31.2   W. G. Sebald, '"Η αυλή του παλιοῦ σχολείου"' ['I avlí tou palioú scholíou'] [Greek version], trans. by Mayóu Tricherióti, Danielle Lagós, and Menélaos Mavros, in *Δυο λόγια σχετικά με τον ποδηλάτη ... [Dio lógia schetiká me ton podiláti ...]*, ed. by Quint Buchholz (Athens and Thessalonika: Γράμματα [Grammata], 1998), pp. 15–16

E.B.31.3   W. G. Sebald, '"La cour de l'ancienne école"' [Castilian version], trans. by María Angeles Grau, in *El Libro de los Libros: Historias sobre imágenes*, ed. by Quint Buchholz (Barcelona: Editorial Lumen, February 1998), pp. 15–16; **E.B.31.3(a)** as '"La cour de l'ancienne école"', trans. by Miguel Sáenz, in B.D.2.3, pp. 47–48; **E.B.31.3(b)** in B.D.2.3(a), pp. 47–48

E.B.31.4   W. G. Sebald, '"Xue Xiao Qian Yuan"' [Chinese version], trans. by Lily Zhang, in *Lin Hun De Chu Ko [Exit of the Soul]*, ed. by Quint Buchholz (*Dreamers Series* 1) (Taiwan: Grimm Press, 1998), pp. 15–16

E.B.31.5   W. G. Sebald, '"Oredoen Hackyoue Anddul"' [Korean version], trans. by Heechang Jang, in *chaek grim chaek*, ed. by Quint Buchholz (Seoul: Minumsa, 2001), pp. 15–16

E.B.31.6   As '*La cour de l'ancienne école*', in B.D.2.1, pp. 47–49; **E.B.31.6(a)** in B.D.2.1(a), pp. 47–49.

E.B.31.7   As '*La cour de l'ancienne école*', in B.D.2.2, pp. 49–51; **E.B.31.7(a)** in B.D.2.2(a), pp. 49–51.

E.B.31.8   As ' "La cour de l'ancienne école" ', in B.D.2.4, pp. 55–56

E.B.31.9   As ' "La cour de l'ancienne école" ', in B.D.2.5, pp. 46–47

E.B.31.10   As ' "La cour de l'ancienne école" ' [Czech version], trans. by Radovan Charvát, in 'W. G. Sebald a Inge Müllerová: Letecká válka a pamět' literatury' ['Air War and the Memory of Literature'], *Revolver Revue* (Prague), 72 (4 September 2008), 209–44 (p. 216); translation of B.D.2/B.D.2(a), pp. 51–52

E.B.31.11   As '*La cour de l'ancienne école*', in B.D.2.6, pp. 53–54

E.B.31.12   As 'La cour de l'ancienne école', in B.D.2.7, pp. 56–57

E.B.32   W. G. Sebald, 'Die Alpen im Meer', in *Terry Winters*, ed. by Peter Pakesch [catalogue of an exhibition in the Kunsthalle, Basle (8 April–4 June 2000)] (Basle: Schwabe, [April] 2000), unpaginated; **E.B.32(a)** W. G. Sebald, 'Die Alpen im Meer. Ein Reisebild' [read out in lieu of a speech at award of the Heine-Prize 2000], in *Heine-Preises 2000 der Landeshauptstadt Düsseldorf an W. G. Sebald* (Düsseldorf: Kulturamt der Landeshauptstadt Düsseldorf, [late December] 2000), pp. 18–26; **E.B.32(b)** as 'Heine-Preis 2000 für W. G. Max Sebald: Die Alpen im Meer: W. G. Sebald mit einem "Reisebild" über Korsika', in *Düsseldorfer Amtsblatt: Die Wochenzeitung aus dem Rathaus*, 51, 51 (23 December 2000), pp. 5–6; **E.B.32(c)** in *Literaturen*, 2001.1 (January 2001), pp. 30–33; **E.B.32(d)** in *Heine-Jahrbuch*, 40 (2001), pp. 174–80; **pre-publication extracts** from B.D.2, pp. 39–50 ('Es war einmal eine Zeit ... wie es gekommen war, wieder davon'); **E.B.32(e)** in B.D.2(a), pp. 39–50

E.B.32(a).1   As 'Kaijo no Alpen' [Japanese version], trans. by Hitoko Suzuki, *De[utsche] Li[teratur]* (Tokyo), 3 (1 November 2004), pp. 131–38

E.B.32(a).2   As 'The Alps in the Sea', in B.D.2.1, pp. 35–46; **E.B.32(a).2(a)** in B.D.2.1(a), pp. 35–46

E.B.32(a).3   As 'The Alps in the Sea', in B.D.2.2, pp. 36–48; **E.B.32(a).3(a)** in B.D.2.2(a), pp. 36–48

E.B.32(a).4   As 'Los Alpes en el mar', in B.D.2.3, pp. 36–46; **E.B.32(a).4** in B.D.2.3(a), pp. 36–46

E.B.32(a).5   As 'Os Alpes no mar', in B.D.2.4, pp. 43–53

E.B.32(a).6   As 'Os Alpes no mar', in B.D.2.5, pp. 36–45

E.B.32(a).7   As 'Nouvelle Parution: Campo Santo: Extrait', in *W. G. Sebald 2009*, ed. by Martina Wachendorff [publisher's catalogue] (Arles: Actes Sud, [February] 2009), pp. 4–5; **pre-publication extract** from E.B.31(a).7(a), pp. 50–51; **E.B.32(a).7(a)** as 'Les Alpes dans la mer', B.D.2.6, pp. 41–51 ('Pas une fois ... qu'il était arrivé') <www.actes-sud.fr/site/default/files/brochure_sebald_0.pdf>

E.B.32(a).8   As 'De Alpen in de zee', in B.D.2.7, pp. 44–55

2002–2010

E.B.33   W. G. Sebald, 'Campo Santo', *Akzente*, 50.1 (February 2003), 3–14; **pre-publication extract** from B.D.2, pp. 19–38; **E.B.33(a)** in B.D.2, pp. 19–38; **E.B.33(b)** in B.D.2(a), pp. 19–38

E.B.33.1   As 'Campo Santo', in B.D.2.1, pp. 15–33; **E.B.33.1(a)** in B.D.2.1(a), pp. 15–33

E.B.33.2   As 'Campo Santo', in B.D.2.2, pp. 16–35; **E.B.33.2(a)** in B.D.2.2(a), pp. 16–35

E.B.33.3   As 'Campo Santo', in B.D.2.3, pp. 19–35; **E.B.33.3(a)** in B.D.2.3(a), pp. 19–35

E.B.33.4   As 'Camposanto' [*sic*], in B.D.2.4, pp. 25–42

E.B.33.5   As 'Campo Santo', in B.D.2.5, pp. 21–35

E.B.33.6   As 'Campo Santo' [Czech version], trans. by Radovan Charvát, in 'W. G. Sebald a Inge Müllerová: "Letecká válka a pamět' literatury" ' ['Air War and the Memory of Literature'], *Revolver Revue* (Prague), 72 (4 September 2008), 209–44 (pp. 217–25)

E.B.33.7   As 'Campo Santo', in B.D.2.6, pp. 23–40

E.B.33.8   As 'Campo Santo' [Norwegian version], trans. by Geir Pollen, *Vinduet: Gyldendals Tidsskrift for Litteratur*, 64.1 ([March] 2010), 108–13

E.B.33.9   As 'Campo Santo', in B.D.2.7, pp. 25–43

E.B.34   W. G. Sebald, 'Campo Santo', in *Hamish Hamilton Almanac (2005)*, ed. by Simon [Prosser], [a one-off version of Hamish Hamilton's catalogue in 'a thousand specially printed copies' that included extracts, commentary, photographs, and drawings by their authors of that season] (London: Hamish Hamilton, [January] 2005), pp. 52–53, 1000 copies; **pre-publication extract** from B.D.2.2, pp. 29–31 ('Remembrance of the dead ... Reaper with sickle in hand')

E.B.35   W. G. Sebald, 'Paradise Lost', *Guardian* (Saturday Review Section), 49,258, 22 January 2005, pp. 4–5; **pre-publication extract** from B.D.2.2, pp. 36–46 ('Once upon a time ... let me look up again')

Austerlitz (B.B.4)

2001

E.B.36   W. G. Sebald, 'Austerlitz', *The New Yorker* [no issue no.], 3 September 2001, pp. 50–71; **pre-publication extracts** from B.B.4.2, pp. 34–72 and 117–43. E.B.36 varies considerably from the other English editions; the central column on p. 63 ('Austerlitz had been ... that evening') and the last three columns on p. 71 ('Austerlitz concluded ... in their company') are omitted from B.B.4.2; unlike the book version E.B.36 is divided into paragraphs.

2002–2010

E.B.37   W. G. Sebald, 'An Extract from *Austerlitz* by W. G. Sebald, trans. by Anthea Bell', *Independent* (Weekend Review: Books), 4832, 13 April 2002, p. 11; **post-publication extract** from B.B.4.3, pp. 320–23 ('Imperceptibly the day ... veiled by a black mist')

E.B.38   W. G. Sebald, 'Austerlitz (Auszug)' [Japanese version], in 'Kioku no meikyu' ['A Labyrinth of Memory'], trans. by Hitoko Suzuki, De[utsche] Li[teratur] (Tokyo), 1 (1 August 2003), 82–104 (pp. 82–101); **post-publication extracts** from B.B.4.10, pp. 3–31 (in B.B.4, pp. 5–46: 'In der zweiten Hälfte ... Haut seiner Knöchel')

E.B.39   W. G. Sebald, 'From *Austerlitz*', *The Republic of Letters* (Boston), 10 (September 2004), 9–12; **post-publication extract** from B.B.4.2, pp. 100–17 ('Time said Austerlitz ... passage of time')

E.B.40   W. G. Sebald, 'Austerlitz', in *Apokalypse: Schreckensbilder in der deutschen Literatur von Jean Paul bis heute: Ein Lesebuch*, ed. by Jürgen Engler (Berlin: Schwartzkopff Buchwerke, [September] 2005), pp. 198–201; **post-publication extract** from B.B.4, pp. 71–76 ('Natürlich sind die ... offenen Augen')

E.B.41   W. G. Sebald, [untitled extracts from *Austerlitz* (German/English)], in *Sabine Hornig: Der zweite Raum / The Second Room*, ed. by Centro Cultural de Belém, Lisbon (catalogue of an exhibition in the Berlinische Galerie, Berlin (23 February–28 May 2006) and the Galerie Barbara Thumm, Berlin (25 February–15 April 2006)) (Ostfildern-Ruit: Hatje Cantz, 2006), p. 4 [English] and p. 5 [German]; **post-publication extracts** from B.B.4, pp. 43–45 ('Der Bau dieser ... Friseurladen umgewandelt worden sein'), and B.B.4.3, pp. 38–40 ('The building of this ... a barber's shop for a while')

E.C. Extracts from Critical Works (A.1–A.7)

1982–2001

E.C.1   Winfried Georg Sebald, '[Sternheims Doktrin von der "eigenen Nuance"]', in *Zu Carl Sternheim (Literaturwissenschaft–Gesellschaftswissenschaft*, 58), ed. by Manfred Durzak (Stuttgart: Ernst Klett, 1982), pp. 41–48; **post-publication extract** from A.1, pp. 38–47

E.C.2   W. G. Sebald, 'Das Wort unter der Zunge', in *Hugo von Hofmannsthal: Der Turm*, Programmheft des Deutschen Theaters, Berlin (Berlin: Deutsches Theater, [September]

1992) [pp. 13–24]; **post–publication extracts** from D.14, pp. 294–96, 297, 298–99 and 299–303 ('Unter den Werken ... Natürlichkeit'; 'An all dem ... zugrunde'; 'Eingelegt ... in ein anderes'; 'Das Panorama ... vorangebracht hat')

E.C.3   W. G. Sebald, 'Operation Gomorra[h]: 28. Juli 1943', in *Der Weltuntergang: Mit einem Lesebuch*, ed. by Ernst Halter and Martin Müller (Zürich: Offizin Zürich Verlags-AG, 1999), p. 232; **post–publication extract** from A.7, pp. 35–39 ('Im Hochsommer 1943 ... zugrunde gingen'); E.C.3(a) as 'Operation Gomorra[h]', in *Hamburg 1943: Literarische Zeugnisse zum Feuersturm*, ed. by Volker Hage (Frankfurt a.M.: Fischer Taschenbuch 16,036, [June] 2003), pp. 253–55; **post–publication extract** from A.7, pp. 35–58 ('Im Hochsommer 1943 ... davontragen konnte') [see also D.65 and D.65bis]

2002–2010

E.C.4   W. G. Sebald, 'Walser im Urwald: Wege durch Zeit und Raum', *du: Zeitschrift der Kultur*, 730, 10 (October 2002), 53; **post–publication extract** from A.6, pp. 162–64 ('Das erste Prosastück, das ich ... einer schneeigen Pelzboa gleicht')

E.C.5   W. G. Sebald, 'Reflections. A Natural History of Destruction', *The New Yorker*, [no issue no.], 4 November 2002, pp. 66–77; **pre–publication extract** from A.7.1, pp. 78–101 ('I grew up with the feeling that ... forty thousand people lost their lives')

E.C.6   As 'Letecká válka a literature (úryvek z eseja)' [Czech version], trans. by Radovan Charvát, in 'W. G. Sebald a Inge Müllerová: Letecká válka a pamět' literatury' ['Air War and the Memory of Literature'], *Revolver Revue* (Prague), 72 (4 September 2008), 209–44 (pp. 232–39); translation of A.7/A.7(a), pp. 35–42 ('Im Hochsommer 1943 ... Schutthalde gefunden hatte')

F. Other Literary Work (in German unless otherwise stated)

F.A. Poetry Written and First Published 1965–2001

F.A.1   Winfried Georg Sebald, ['Five Poems'], *ZET: Das Zeichenheft für Literatur und Graphik*, 2.6 (July 1974), p. 13; F.A.1(a) *Vorzugsausgabe*; identical with F.A.1 except for the inclusion of a loose print

F.A.1(i)   'Panazee'; F.A.1(i)(a) in B.D.3, p. 40

F.A.1(ii)   'Analytische Sommerfrische'; F.A.1(ii)(a) in B.D.3, p. 35

F.A.1(iii)   'Mithräisch'; F.A.1(iii)(a) in B.D.3, p. 41

F.A.1(iv)   'Norfolk'; F.A.1(iv)(a) in B.D.3, p. 48

F.A.1(iv).(a).1   As 'Norfolk' [Norwegian version], trans. by Geir Pollen, *Vinduet: Gyldendals Tidsskrift for Litteratur*, 64.1 ([29 March] 2010), [89]

F.A.1(v)   'Stundenplan'; F.A.1(v)(a) in B.D.3, p. 31

F.A.2   Winfried Georg Sebald, ['Four Poems'], *ZET: Das Zeichenheft für Literatur und Graphik*, 3, 10 (June 1975), pp. 18–19; F.A.2(a) *Vorzugsausgabe*; identical with F.A.2 except for the inclusion of a loose print

F.A.2(i)   'K.'s Auswanderung', p. 18; F.A.2(i)(a) in B.D.3, p. 44

F.A.2(ii)   'Mölkerbastei', p. 18; F.A.2(ii)(a) in B.D.3, p. 46

F.A.2(iii)   'Elisabethanisch', p. 19; F.A.2(iii)(a) in B.D.3, p. 49

F.A.2(iii).(a).1   As 'Elisabetansk' [Norwegian version], trans. by Geir Pollen, *Vinduet: Gyldendals Tidsskrift for Litteratur*, 64.1 ([29 March] 2010), [89]

F.A.2(iv)   'Unerschlossen', p. 19; F.A.2(iv)(a) in B.D.3, p. 32

F.A.2(iv).(a).1   As 'Uutforsket' [Norwegian version], trans. by Geir Pollen, *Vinduet: Gyldendals Tidsskrift for Litteratur*, 64.1 ([29 March] 2010), [89]

F.A.3   W. G. Sebald, 'Das vorvergangene Jahr', *Der Komet: Almanach der Anderen Bibliothek auf das Jahr 1991* (Frankfurt a.M.: Eichborn, 1990), pp. 138–42; F.A.3(a) in B.D.3, pp. 65–68

F.A.4   W. G. Sebald, 'Ein Walzertraum', in Jan Peter Tripp, *Die Aufzählung der Schwierigkeiten: Arbeiten von 1985–92* (Offenburg: Reiff Schwarzwaldverlag, 1993), p. 119; **F.A.4(a)** in *Neue Zürcher Zeitung Folio* [monthly supplement] 3/93 (March 1993), 67 (together with a picture by Jan Peter Tripp, *Das Land des Lächelns* [1990]); **F.A.4(b)** in Loquai (1997), p. 20 (follows on from F.A.7(ii).(a); *Das Land des Lächelns* is on the facing page); **F.A.4(c)** in B.D.3, p. 75

F.A.5   W. G. Sebald, ['The rhino is a heavy beast ...',] (February 1995) (untitled poem in English), *Das Nashorn* (Klassenzeitung der 'Nashornklasse' der Bremer Grollandschule), 11, 36 (July 1995), unpaginated, 99 copies; **F.A.5(a)** in *Das große Nashornbuch (mit einem Vornashorn von Michael Krüger und einem Nachnashorn von Roger Willemsen)*, ed. by Werner Vaudlet and the *Nashornschüler*, (*Reihe Hanser* [no series number]) (Munich: dtv 62024, [May] 2001), p. 89. [In the Grollandschule, children with special educational needs are educated in the same classes as those without learning difficulties. When, in 1995, the Bremen authorities tried to close the school, teachers and pupils sought support from artists and influential members of the cultural world by asking them to send them four-line pieces of doggerel on the subject of the 'Nashorn' (rhinoceros): over the years, 280 were sent in and collected in F.A.5(a).]

F.A.5.1   W. G. Sebald, ['Das Rhino ist ein schweres Tier ...'] (April 1995) (two German versions), both trans. by Hans Wollschläger, in F.A.5, unpaginated; **F.A.5.1(a)** (three German versions), trans. by Dieter H. Stündel [2] and Hans Wollschläger [1], in F.A.5(a), pp. 89 and 90

F.A.6   W. G. Sebald, 'In Bamberg' (May 1996–May 1997) [facsimile of a manuscript], in Loquai (1997), pp. 13–15; **F.A.6(a)** in B.D.3, p. 76

F.A.7   W. G. Sebald, ['Two Poems'], *Die Weltwoche* (Zurich), *Supplement*, 6 (June 1996), pp. 30–31; **F.A.7(a)** in B.D.3, pp. 69–73

F.A.7(i)   'Am 9. Juni 1904'; **F.A.7(i)(a)** in Loquai (1997), pp. 16–18; **F.A.7(i)(b)** in B.D.3, pp. 69–71

F.A.7(ii)   'Neunzig Jahre später'; **F.A.7 (ii)(a)** in Loquai (1997), pp. 18–19 (followed by F.A.4[a]); **F.A.7(ii)(b)** in B.D.3, pp. 72–73

F.A.8   W. G. Sebald, 'Marienbader Elegie' (Marienbad, 14 August 1999), *Neue Zürcher Zeitung* (Schweizer Ausgabe) (Literatur und Kunst), 265, 13 November 1999, p. 84; **F.A.8(a)** *Neue Zürcher Zeitung* (Internationale Ausgabe) (Literatur und Kunst), 265, 13 November 1999, p. 50; **F.A.8(b)** in Michael Hamburger, *Pro Domo: Selbstauskünfte, Rückblicke und andere Prosa*, ed. by Iain Galbraith, (*Reihe Transfer* 72) (Vienna and Bolzano: folio, [early] 2007), pp. 111–13; **F.A.8(c)** in B.D.3, pp. 79–83

F.A.8.1   W. G. Sebald, 'Marienbad Elegy', trans. by Michael Hamburger, *Irish Pages: A Journal of Contemporary Writing*, 1.2 (Autumn–Winter 2002–03), 125–29; followed by Michael Hamburger, 'Translator's Note', and Tess Jaray, 'A Mystery and a Confession' (see Secondary Bibliography)

F.A.9   W. G. Sebald, '[Sechs] Gedichte', *Akzente*, 48.2 (April 2001), pp. 112–21; **F.A.9(a)** in B.D.3, pp. 84–95

F.A.9(i)   'In der schlaflos ...'; **F.A.9(i)(a)** in B.D.3, pp. 84–85

F.A.9(ii)   'Zimmer 645'; **F.A.9(ii)(a)** in B.D.3, pp. 86–77

F.A.9(iii)   'Mein Fahr-Planer im ICE'; **F.A.9(iii)(a)** in B.D.3, pp. 88–89

F.A.9(iv)   'An einem Herbstsonntag 94'; **F.A.9(iv)(a)** in B.D.3, pp. 90–91

F.A.9(v)   'Ruhiges Novemberwetter'; **F.A.9(v)(a)** in B.D.3, pp. 92–94

F.A.9(vi)   'Seit Jahr & Tag'; **F.A.9(vi)(a)** in B.D.3, p. 95

F.A.10   W. G. Sebald, 'Drei Novembergedichte', in *Konterbande und Camouflage: Szenen aus der Vor- und Nachgeschichte von Heinrich Heines marranischer Schreibweise*, ed. by Stephan Braese and Werner Irro (Berlin: Vorwerk 8, 2002), pp. 11–15; **F.A.10(a)** in B.D.3., pp. 96–101

F.A.10(i)   'Im Sommer 1836'; F.A.10(i)(a) in B.D.3, pp. 96–97
F.A.10(ii)   'In Alfermée'; F.A.10(ii)(a) in B.D.3, pp. 98–99
F.A.10(iii)   'In der Nacht auf'; F.A.10(iii)(a) in B.D.3, pp. 100–01
F.A.11   W. G. Sebald, '[Two] Poems' [in English], *Pretext*, 2 (Autumn 2000), 22–25
F.A.11(i)   'October Heat Wave', pp. 22–23
F.A.11(ii)   'I remember', pp. 24–25

F.B. Poetry Written 1965–2001 and Posthumously Published

F.B.1   W. G. Sebald, 'Kinderlied' (*c.* 1967), in Reinbert Tabbert, 'Erinnerung an W. G. Sebald, einen Ausgewanderten aus dem Allgäu', *Literaturblatt für Baden und Württemberg*, 6 (November–December 2002), 10–11; F.B.1(a) in Reinbert Tabbert, 'Max in Manchester: Außen- und Innenansicht eines jungen Autors', *Akzente*, 50.1 (February 2003), 21–30 (pp. 23–24); F.B.1(b) in Reinbert Tabbert, 'Früher Schulweg im Allgäu: Zwei Kindheitserinnerungen des Schriftstellers W. G. Sebald', in *Literatur in Bayern*, 26, 97 (September 2009), 28–30 (p. 30)

F.B.2   W. G. Sebald, 'Albumverse' (November 1966), in 'Max in Manchester', pp. 21–30 (p. 24)

F.B.3   W. G. Sebald, 'Zeitstreichen um Zwölf' (summer 1967), in 'Max in Manchester', pp. 21–30 (p. 30)

F.B.4   'Bleston. A Mancunian Canticle' (poem in five parts), in B.D.3, pp. 22–26
F.B.4(i)   'I. Fête Nocturne', in B.D.3, p. 22
F.B.4(ii)   'II. Consensus Omnium', in B.D.3, p. 23
F.B.4(iii)   'III. The Sound of Music', in B.D.3, p. 24
F.B.4(iv)   'IV. Lingua Mortua', in B.D.3, p. 25
F.B.4(v)   'V. Perdu dans ces Filaments', in B.D.3, p. 26
F.B.5   'Didsbury', in B.D.3, p. 27
F.B.6   'Giuliettas Geburtstag', in B.D.3, p. 28
F.B.7   'Unglücklicher Weise', in B.D.3, p. 29
F.B.8   'L'instruction du roy', in B.D.3, p. 30
F.B.9   'Physikalisches Wunder', in B.D.3, p. 36
F.B.10   'Kalter Zug', in B.D.3, p. 37
F.B.11   'Ausreise aus Bayern', in B.D.3, p. 38
F.B.12   'Etwas im Ohr', in B.D.3, p. 39
F.B.13   'Merkzettel', in B.D.3, p. 42
F.B.14   'Barometerstand', in B.D.3, p. 43
F.B.15   'Durch Holland im Finstern', in B.D.3, p. 45
F.B.15.1   As 'Gjennom Holland i mørket' [Norwegian version], trans. by Geir Pollen, *Vinduet: Gyldendals Tidsskrift for Litteratur*, 64.1 ([29 March] 2010), [126]
F.B.16   'Holkham Gap', in B.D.3, p. 47
F.B.17   'Ballade', in B.D.3, p. 50
F.B.17.1   As 'Ballade' [Norwegian version], trans. by Geir Pollen, *Vinduet: Gyldendals Tidsskrift for Litteratur*, 64.1 ([29 March] 2010), [90]
F.B.18   'Dunkle Stelle', in B.D.3, p. 51
F.B.18.1   As 'Dunkel flekk' [Norwegian version], trans. by Geir Pollen, *Vinduet: Gyldendals Tidsskrift for Litteratur*, 64.1 ([29 March] 2010), [88]
F.B.19   'Poesie für das Album', in B.D.3, pp. 52–53
F.B.20   'Schaurige Wirkung des Höllentälers auf meine Nerven', in B.D.3, pp. 54–55
F.B.21   'Trigonometrie der Sphären', in B.D.3, p. 56
F.B.22   'Day Return', in B.D.3, pp. 57–59
F.B.23   'New Jersey Journey', in B.D.3, pp. 60–62

F.B.24   'Im Abseits', in B.D.3, p. 102

F.B.24.1   As 'Fra sidelinjen' [Norwegian version], trans. by Geir Pollen, *Vinduet: Gyldendals Tidsskrift for Litteratur*, 64.1 ([29 March] 2010), [87]

F.C. Prose Pieces Written and First Published 1965–2001

F.C.1   W. G. Sebald, 'Die hölzernen Engel von East Anglia: Eine individuelle Bummeltour durch Norfolk und Suffolk', *Die Zeit* (Reise), 31, 26 July 1974, p. 38; F.C.1(a) see Part II of the present volume, pp. 319–23

F.C.1.1   W. G. Sebald, 'The Carved Wooden Angels of East Anglia: A Leisurely Tour through Norfolk and Suffolk', ed. and trans. by Richard Sheppard, *Journal of European Studies*, 41.3–4 (forthcoming December 2011)

F.C.2   W. G. Sebald, 'Statement zur österreichischen Literatur', *Manuskripte*, 25, 89–90 (September 1985), 229

F.C.3   W. G. Sebald, 'Die Kunst des Fliegens' [written in the first half of 1986] in *Träume: Literaturalmanach 1987*, ed. by Jochen Jung (Salzburg and Vienna: Residenz, 1987), pp. 134–38; F.C.3(a) in *The Undiscover'd Country: W. G. Sebald and the Poetics of Travel*, ed. by Markus Zisselsberger (Rochester, NY: Camden House, [c. October] 2010), pp. 31–34

F.C.4   W. G. Sebald, 'Leben Ws. Skizze einer möglichen Szenenreihe für einen nichtrealisierten Film' [Wittgenstein's 100th birthday fell on 26 April 1989], *Zeit und Bild: Frankfurter Rundschau am Wochenende*, 94, 22 April 1989, p. ZB3; F.C.4(a); see Part II of the present volume, pp. 324–33

F.C.5   W. G. Sebald, 'Postkarte: Waterloo', *Neue Zürcher Zeitung Folio* (monthly supplement), 10/91 (October 1991), 71–73 [an early version of B.B.3, pp. 155–60 and prefaced by the sketch of the monument at Waterloo, a cropped version of which appears in B.B.3, p. 156]; F.C.5(a) as 'Waterloo', in Jo Catling, 'Europäische Flânerien: W. G. Sebalds intertextuelle Wanderungen zwischen Melancholie und Ironie', in *Gedächtnis und Widerstand: Festschrift für Irène Heidelberger-Leonard*, ed. by Mireille Tabah with Sylvia Weiler and Christian Poetini (Tübingen: Stauffenberg, [November] 2009), pp. 139–54 (pp. 145–46); F.C.5(b); see Part II of the present volume, pp. 334–35

F.D. Prose Pieces Written 1965–2001 and Posthumously Published

F.D.1   W. G. Sebald, [Two excerpts from an unpublished novel of 1965–early 1967], in Reinbert Tabbert, 'Erinnerung an W. G. Sebald, einen Ausgewanderten aus dem Allgäu', *Literaturblatt für Baden und Württemberg*, 9.6 (November–December 2002), 10–11

F.D.2   W. G. Sebald, 'Aufzeichnungen aus Korsika. Zur Natur- & Menschenkunde', Aus dem Nachlass herausgegeben von Ulrich von Bülow, in *Wandernde Schatten: W. G. Sebalds Unterwelt* (*marbacherkatalog 62*) (catalogue of the exhibition at the Literaturmuseum der Moderne, Marbach, 26 September 2008–1 February 2009), ed. by Ulrich von Bülow, Heike Gefreeis, and Ellen Strittmatter (Marbach am Neckar: Deutsche Schiller-gesellschaft, 2008), pp. 129–209. [Two draft versions of the abandoned 'Corsica project', parts of which appeared as E.B.30, E.B.31, E.B.32 and E.B.33.]

F.D.2(i)   [Erste Fassung], pp. 129-58

F.D.2(i).1   As 'Ombres errantes. Aux limbes de la création' [French version of first [diary] version of Corsican project], trans. by Patrick Charbonneau, *fario: Revue de littérature et d'art*, no. 9 ([December] 2010), 9–53

F.D.2(ii)   [Zweite Fassung], pp. 159-209

G. Book Reviews (1971–1996)

The following abbreviations are used in this section:
JES = *Journal of European Studies*
MLR = *Modern Language Review*

1971–1980

G.1   W.G.S., Review in English of J[ochen] Schulte-Sasse, *Literarische Wertung* (*Realienbücher für Germanisten*) (Stuttgart: J. B. Metzlersche Verlagsbuchhandlung, 1971), *JES*, 1.3 (September 1971), 273

G.2   W.G.S., Review in English of Marianne Kesting, *Entdeckung und Destruktion: Zur Strukturwandlung der Künste* (Munich: Wilhelm Fink, 1970), *JES*, 1.3 (September 1971), 274

G.3   W.G.S., Review in English of Ludwig Giesz, *Phänomenologie des Kitsches: Ein Beitrag zur anthropologischen Ästhetik* (*Theorie und Geschichte der Literatur und der schönen Künste* 17) (Munich: Wilhelm Fink, 1971), *JES*, 1.3 (September 1971), 274

G.4   W.G.S., Review in English of Leo Kreutzer, *Alfred Döblin: Sein Werk bis 1933* (*Sprache und Literatur* 66) (Stuttgart: Kohlhammer, 1970), *JES*, 1.3 (September 1971), 276

G.5   M.G.S., Review in English of Horst Albert Glaser, Peter Hahn, and others, *Literaturwissenschaft und Sozialwissenschaften: Grundlagen und Modellanalysen* (Stuttgart: J. B. Metzlersche Verlagsbuchhandlung, 1971), *JES*, 2.1 (March 1972), 76

G.6   W. G. Sebald, Review in German of Johann Bauer and Isidor Pollak (photographs), *Kafka und Prag*, trans. by Vera Cerny (Stuttgart: Belser, 1971), *Literatur und Kritik*, 7, 66–67 (July–August 1972), 421–22

G.7   M.S., Review in English of Heinz Politzer, *Franz Grillparzer oder das abgründige Biedermeier* (Vienna: Molden, 1972), *JES*, 2.3 (September 1972), 305

G.8   M.S., Review in English of Robert Minder, *Dichter in der Gesellschaft: Erfahrungen mit deutscher und französischer Literatur* (*Suhrkamp Taschenbuch* 33) (Frankfurt a.M.: Suhrkamp, 1972), *JES*, 2.3 (September 1972), 310–11

G.9   W.G.S., Review in English of Manfred Durzak, *Dürrenmatt, Frisch, Weiss: Deutsches Drama der Gegenwart zwischen Kritik und Utopie* (Stuttgart: Reclam, 1972), *JES*, 3.1 (March 1973), 97–98

G.10   W.G.S., Review in English of W. Edgar Yates, *Nestroy: Satire and Parody in Viennese Popular Comedy* (Cambridge: Cambridge University Press, 1972), *JES*, 3.2 (June 1973), 182

G.11   M.S., Review in English of Franz Hubmann, *Dream of Empire: The World of Germany in Original Photographs 1840–1914*, ed. by J. M. Wheatcroft (London: Routledge and Kegan Paul, 1973), *JES*, 3.3 (September 1973), 286

G.12   W.G.S., Review in English of Reinhard Urbach, *Die Wiener Komödie und ihr Publikum: Stranitzky und die Folgen* (Vienna: Jugend und Volk, 1973), *JES*, 3.3 (September 1973), 287–88

G.13   W.G.S., Review in English of Hans-Albert Walter, *Deutsche Exilliteratur 1933–1950*, 2 vols, I: *Bedrohung und Verfolgung bis 1933*, II: *Asylpraxis und Lebensbedingungen in Europa* (Darmstadt: Luchterhand, 1972), and *Die deutsche Exilliteratur 1933–1945*, ed. by Manfred Durzak (Stuttgart: Reclam, 1973), *JES*, 3.3 (September 1973), 289–90

G.14   W.G.S., Review in English of Helmut Dinse, *Die Entwicklung des jiddischen Schrifttums im deutschen Sprachgebiet* (Stuttgart: J. B. Metzlersche Verlagsbuchhandlung, 1974), *JES*, 4.3 (September 1974), 304

G.15   W.G.S., Review in English of Alexander Herzen, *My Past and Thoughts*, trans. by Constance Garnett, rev. by Humphrey Higgens, abridged by Dwight MacDonald (London: Chatto and Windus, 1974), *JES*, 5.1 (March 1975), 84

G.16   W.G.S., Review in English of Wolfgang Reif, *Zivilisationsflucht und literarische*

Wunschträume: Der exotische Roman im ersten Viertel des 20. Jahrhunderts (Stuttgart: J. B. Metzlersche Verlagsbuchhandlung, 1975), *JES*, 5.3 (September 1975), 285

G.17   W. G. Sebald, Review in English of Michael Butler, *The Novels of Max Frisch* (London: Oswald Wolff, 1976), *JES*, 8.2 (June 1978), 143–44

G.18   W. G. Sebald, Review in German of Hans Walther, *Franz Kafka: Die Forderung der Transzendenz* (*Abhandlungen zur Kunst-, Musik- und Literaturwissenschaft* 212) (Bonn: Bouvier, 1977), *Literatur und Kritik*, 13, 128 (September 1978), 506

G.19   M. Sebald, Review in English of Peter Hutchinson, *Literary Presentations of Divided Germany: The Development of a Central Theme in East German Fiction 1945–1970* (Cambridge: Cambridge University Press, 1977), *JES*, 9.4 (September 1979), 287–88

1981–1990

G.20   W. G. Sebald, Review in German of Friedbert Aspetsberger, *Literarisches Leben im Austrofaschismus: Der Staatspreis* (*Literatur in der Geschichte, Geschichte in der Literatur* 2) (Königstein i.Ts.: Anton Hain Meisenheim, 1980), *Literatur und Kritik*, 17, 157–58 (August–September 1981), 483–84

G.21   W. G. Sebald, Review in German of Gerhard Kurz, *Traum-Schrecken: Kafkas literarische Existenzanalyse* (Stuttgart: J. B. Metzlersche Verlagsbuchhandlung, 1980), *Literatur und Kritik*, 17, 161–62 (February–March 1982), 98–100

G.22   W. G. Sebald, Review in English of *Irish Studies in Modern Austrian Literature*, ed. by G. J. Carr and Eda Sagarra [five of the nine papers read at the first Irish Symposium in Austrian Studies, 19–20 February 1982] (Dublin: Trinity College, 1982), *MLR*, 80.1 (January 1985), 224–25

G.23   W. G. Sebald, Review in English of Günter Blamberger, *Versuch über den deutschen Gegenwartsroman: Krisenbewußtsein und Neubegründung im Zeichen der Melancholie* (Stuttgart: J. B. Metzlersche Verlagsbuchhandlung, 1985), *MLR*, 82.4 (October 1987), 1042–43

G.24   W. G. Sebald, Review in English of Endre Kiss, *Der Tod der k.u.k. Weltordnung in Wien: Ideengeschichte Österreichs um die Jahrhundertwende* (*Forschungen zur Geschichte des Donauraums* 8) (Vienna: Böhlau, 1986), *MLR*, 83.3 (July 1988), 788–89

G.25   W. G. Sebald, Review in English of Elizabeth Boa, *The Sexual Circus: Wedekind's Theatre of Subversion* (Oxford: Basil Blackwell, 1987), *British Journal of Aesthetics*, 28.4 (Autumn 1988), 399–400

G.26   W. G. Sebald, Review in English of Georg Reuchlein, *Bürgerliche Gesellschaft, Psychiatrie und Literatur: Zur Entwicklung der Wahnsinnsthematik in der deutschen Literatur des späten 18. und frühen 19. Jahrhunderts* (*Münchner Germanistische Beiträge* 35) (Munich: Wilhelm Fink, 1986), *MLR*, 83.4 (October 1988), 1031

G.27   W. G. Sebald, Review in English of *Deutsche Gegenwartsdramatik*, ed. by Lothar Pikulik, Hajo Kurzenberger, and Georg Guntermann, with a select bibliography by Christiane Helios, 2 vols (*Kleine Vandenhoeck-Reihe*, 1520–21) (Göttingen: Vandenhoeck und Ruprecht, 1986), *MLR*, 84.1 (January 1989), 266–67

G.28   W. G. Sebald, Review in English of Armin A. Wallas, *Texte des Expressionismus: Der Beitrag jüdischer Autoren zur österreichischen Avantgarde* (Linz: Edition neue texte, 1988), *JES*, 19.4 (December 1989), 343

G.29   W. G. Sebald, Review in English of Claudio Magris, *Donau: Biographie eines Flusses*, trans. from the Italian by Heinz-Georg Held (Munich: Hanser, 1988), *Austrian Studies*, 1 (1990), 183–84

G.30   W. G. Sebald, Review in English of Joseph McVeigh, *Kontinuität und Vergangenheitsbewältigung in der österreichischen Literatur nach 1945* (*Untersuchungen zur österreichischen Literatur des 20. Jahrhunderts* 10) (Vienna: Braumüller, 1988), *MLR*, 85.3 (July 1990), 531

1991–1996

G.31   W. G. Sebald, 'Kafka im Kino', Review in German of Hanns Zischler, *Kafka geht ins Kino* (Reinbek bei Hamburg: Rowohlt, 1996), *Zeit und Bild: Frankfurter Rundschau am Wochenende*, 15, 18 January 1997, p. ZB3; **G.31(a)** as '"Liebste, Bilder sind schön und nicht zu entbehren, aber eine Qual sind sie auch"', *Die Weltwoche* (Zurich), 26, 26 June 1997, pp. 54–55; **G.31(b)** as 'Kafka im Kino', in B.D.2, pp. 193–209; **G.31(c)** as 'Kafka im Kino', in B.D.2(a), pp. 193–209

G.31(b).1   As 'Kafka Goes to the Movies', in B.D.2.1, pp. 151–67; **G.31(b).1(a)** as B.D.2.1(a), pp. 156–73.

G.31(b).2   As 'Kafka Goes to the Movies', in B.D.2.2, pp. 156–73; **G.31(b).2(a)** as B.D.2.2(a), pp. 156–73

G.31(b).3   As 'Kafka en el cine', in B.D.2.3, pp. 173–87; **G.31(b).3(a)** in B.D.2.3(a), pp. 173–87

G.31(b).4   As 'Kafka no cinema', in B.D.2.4, pp. 195–210

G.31(b).5   As 'Kafka no cinema', in B.D.2.5, pp. 166–79

G.31(b).6   As 'Kafka v kině' [Czech version], trans. by Radovan Charvát, in 'W. G. Sebald a Inge Müllerová: Letecká válka a paměť literatury' ['Air War and the Memory of Literature'], *Revolver Revue* (Prague), 72 (4 September 2008), 209–44 (pp. 225–32); translation of B.D.2/2(a), pp. 193–209

G.31(b).7   As 'Kafka au cinéma', in B.D.2.6, pp. 187–202

G.31(b).8   As 'Kafka in de bioscoop', in B.D.2.7, pp. 198–214

H. Juvenilia (Prose and Poetry) (1961–1965)

H.A. School (1961–1963)

H.A.1   Wise [pseud.], 'die situation', *Der Wecker* (Schülerzeitschrift der Oberstdorfer Oberrealschule), [1].1 (November 1961), 8–10

H.A.2   Wise [pseud.], 'der böse Brecht', *Der Wecker*, [1].1 (November 1961), 22

H.A.3   Wiese [pseud.], 'Der Plunder des Malachias' [review of Bernhard Wicki's film *Das Wunder des braven Malachias* (1961)], *Der Wecker*, [1].1 (November 1961), 23–24

H.A.4   W. SEB., 'heiß', *Der Wecker*, [1].2 [Spring 1962], 10–11

H.A.5   [W. G. Sebald], 'Michaïl Sostschenko: Ein Portrait', *Der Wecker*, [1].2 [Spring 1962], 17–19

H.A.6   Wise [pseud.], 'L'Algérie: eine Betrachtung', *Der Wecker*, [1].4 [*c*. June 1962], 9–10; **H.A.6(a)** included in B.C.6 as a facsimile

H.A.7   Wise [pseud.], 'Camus', *Der Wecker*, [1].4 [*c*. June 1962], 26–29; **H.A.7(a)** included in B.C.6 as a facsimile

H.A.8   Wise [pseud.], 'An einem Sommertag' [sketch], *Der Wecker*, [1].4 [*c*. June 1962], 35–37; **H.A.8(a)** included in C.B.6 as a facsimile

H.A.9   [unsigned, untitled essay on the work of Truman Capote], *Der Wecker*, 2.1 [Autumn 1962], unpaginated

H.A.10   [W. G. Sebald], 'Aus einer Urkunde des Jahres 1293 p. Chr. n.', *sancta stupiditas* [*Abiturzeitung*, co-edited and largely written by Sebald], [July 1963], unpaginated

H.A.11   [W. G. Sebald] 'descriptio personarum', *sancta stupiditas* [July 1963], unpaginated

H.A.12   [W. G. Sebald], 'Die Breissen', *sancta stupiditas* [July 1963], unpaginated

H.B. University of Freiburg (1963–1965)

H.B.1   Winfried Sebald, 'Gottes Rosenöl-Baum' [review of Georg Lukács, *Skizze einer Geschichte der neueren deutschen Literatur* (1953)], *Freiburger Studenten-Zeitung*, 14.6 (November 1964), 21

H.B.2   Winfried Sebald, 'Jeden Abend...' [prose piece], *Freiburger Studenten-Zeitung*, 14.7 (December 1964), 26

H.B.3   Winfried Sebald, ['Four Poems'], *Freiburger Studenten-Zeitung*, 14.7 (December 1964), 26; **H.B.3(a)** in B.D.3, pp. 7–10

H.B.3(i)   ['Schwer zu verstehen...']; **H.B.3(i)(a)** in B.D.3, p. 7.

H.B.3(i)(a).1   ['Tungt å forstå ...'] [Norwegian version], trans. by Geir Pollen, *Vinduet. Gyldendals Tidsskrift for Litteratur*, 64.1 ([29 March] 2010), [87]

H.B.3(ii)   ['Schrebergartenkolonie...']; **H.B.3(ii)(a)** in B.D.3, p. 8.

H.B.3.(ii)(a).1   ['Hagekoloni ...'] [Norwegian version], trans. by Geir Pollen, *Vinduet. Gyldendals Tidsskrift for Litteratur*, 64.1 ([29 March] 2010), [88]

H.B.3(iii)   ['Nicht mehr bewegen ...']; **H.B.3(iii)(a)** in B.D.3, p. 9; **H.B.3(iii)(b)** in *Allmende: Zeitschrift für Literatur*, 29, no. 83 (June 2009), 121

H.B.3.(iii)(a).1   ['Bevege seg mer ...'] [Norwegian version], trans. by Geir Pollen, *Vinduet. Gyldendals Tidsskrift for Litteratur*, 64.1 ([29 March] 2010), [90]

H.B.3(iv)   ['Versiegelt die Absicht ...']; **H.B.3(iv)(a)** in B.D.3, p.10.

H.B.3(iv)(a).1   ['Forseglet de bevarte ...'] [Norwegian version], trans. by Geir Pollen, *Vinduet. Gyldendals Tidsskrift for Litteratur*, 64.1 ([29 March] 2010), [89]

H.B.4   'Nymphenburg', *Freiburger Studenten-Zeitung*, 14.7 (December 1964), 26; **H.B.4(a)** in B.D.3, p. 11

H.B.5   Winfried Sebald, ['Two Poems'], *Freiburger Studenten-Zeitung*, 15.1 (January 1965), 25; **H.B.5(a)** in B.D.3, pp. 12–13

H.B.5(i)   'Epitaph'; **H.B.5(i)(a)** in B.D.3, p. 12

H.B.5(ii)   'Schattwald im Tirol'; **H.B.5(ii)(a)** in B.D.3, p. 13

H.B.6   Winfried Sebald, 'Über den Regen: Notizen eines Frustrierten' [prose piece], *Freiburger Studenten-Zeitung*, 15.4 (June 1965), 16

H.B.7   Winfried Sebald, 'Teegeschichte' [prose piece], *Freiburger Studenten-Zeitung*, 15.4 (June 1965), 24

H.B.8   Winfried Sebald, 'Erinnertes Triptychon einer Reise aus Brüssel' [long poem in nine stanzas], *Freiburger Studenten-Zeitung*, 15.5 (July 1965), 26; **H.B.8(a)** in B.D.3, pp. 14–17

H.B.9   Winfried Sebald, 'Erinnern' [prose piece], *Freiburger Studenten-Zeitung*, 15.7 (December 1965), 24

H.B.10   Winfried Sebald, ['Four Poems'], *Freiburger Studenten-Zeitung*, 15.7 (December 1965), 25

H.B.10(i)   'Schön ist das Leben'; **H.B.10(i)(a)** in B.D.3, p. 18

H.B.10(ii)   'Morgenandacht für G.'; **H.B.10(ii)(a)** in B.D.3, p. 19

H.B.10(iii)   'Wintergedicht'; **H.B.10(iii)(a)** in B.D.3, p. 20

H.B.10(iv)   'Albumvers'; **H.B.10(iv)(a)** in B.D.3, p. 21

I. Letters (listed in order of publication)

See also Chapters 5, 7, and 11 in the present volume, which include quotations from unpublished letters by WGS.

I.1   W. G. Sebald, letter to the editor of *Das Nashorn* (see F.A.5) of 26 February 1995 (Poringland), *Das Nashorn*, 11, 36 (July 1995), unpaginated, 99 copies

I.2   W. G. Sebald, *Briefe an Wolfgang Schlüter* [32 letters and postcards from 24 April 1993 to 29 August 2001], in a limited, privately printed edition of six copies, ed. by Wolfgang Schlüter (Vienna: [n. pub.], 2002), unpaginated

I.3   Reinbert Tabbert, 'Tanti saluti cordiali. Max', *Literaturen*, 2004.5 (May 2004), 46–49; includes letters to Tabbert of 1 August 1968 (Manchester), 4 October 1973 (Poringland), and 14 May 1974 (Poringland); **I.3(a)** also published with a further letter dated 8 May 1968 on the following website: <http://www.wgsebald.de/schwindelbriefe.html/> [accessed 6 February 2011] (cf. I.4(a))

I.4   Reinbert Tabbert, 'Max in Manchester: Außen- und Innenansicht eines jungen Autors', *Akzente*, 50.1 (February 2003), 21–30; includes a letter to Tabbert of 7 April 1970 (Manchester) (p. 29); **I.4(a)** also published on the following website: <http://www. wgsebald.de/schwindelbriefe.html/> [accessed 6 February 2011] (cf. I.5(a))

I.5   Karl Gogl, 'Gedenkkonzert anlässlich des 60. Geburtstags von W. G. Sebald', *Oberallgäuer Meisterkonzerte Sonthofen: Programm 2004* (Sonthofen: [n. pub.], 2004), pp. 37–44; includes quotations from letters to Gogl of January 2001 and 16 March 2001 (p. 44)

I.6   W. G. Sebald, two letters to Theodor Adorno of 24 April 1967 (Manchester) and 14 December 1968 (St Gallen), together with a reply from Adorno of 28 April 1967, in *Sebald. Lektüren.*, ed. by Marcel Atze and Franz Loquai (Eggingen: Isele, 2005), pp. 12–16, with a commentary by Sven Meyer, pp. 17–28

I.7   Angelika Maass, 'Versuche der Vergegenwärtigung: Die Lichtschreibkunst des Photographen Christian Scholz' [review of Christian Scholz, *Portfolio W. G. Sebald* (2004)], *Librarium: Zeitschrift der Schweizerischen Bibliophilen Gesellschaft*, 48.2–3 (Autumn 2005), 142–43; includes a facsimile of a letter to Scholz of 13 January 1998

I.8   Patrick Charbonneau, 'Correspondance(s): Le Traducteur et son auteur', in *W. G. Sebald: Mémoire. Transferts. Images / Erinnerung. Übertragungen. Bilder*, ed. by Ruth Vogel-Klein (= *Recherches Germaniques*, special issue 2 ([late] 2005)) [proceedings of a conference in Paris, 15–16 October 2004], pp. 193–210; includes extensive quotations from Sebald's letters to his French translator Charbonneau, 1997–98

I.9   Torleiv Andersson, '"Det siste har jeg funnet på selv": noen betraktninger løst forbundet med et brev fra W. G. Sebald', *Vinduet: Gyldendals Tidsskrift for Litteratur*, 64.1 ([29 March] 2010), 76–79; includes facsimile of letter from WGS to Andersson of 21 February 2001 (p. 79)

J. Interviews, listed in the order in which they were given (as far as this can be ascertained)

Where known, the date of the interview is given in square brackets after the title.
See the Audio-Visual Bibliography for details of radio and television interviews
which are still to be published.

1971–1995

J.1   'Carl Sternheim: Versuch eines Porträts', [transcribed discussion], ed. by Marcel Atze, between Jakob Knauss, Hellmuth Karasek, Peter von Matt, and W. G. Sebald, first broadcast on 17 February 1971 on Schweizer Rundfunk's DRS II at 9.30 p.m., in *Sebald. Lektüren.*, ed. by Atze and Loquai, pp. 39–55 (cf. Audio-Visual Bibliography)

J.2   'Stille Katastrophen', edited interview with Renate Just, *Süddeutsche Zeitung (Magazin)* (Munich), 40, 5 October 1990, pp. 27–29; **J.2(a)** in *W. G. Sebald*, ed. by Loquai (1997), pp. 25–30

J.3   'See you again', edited interview with Burkhard Baltzer, *Schwäbisches Tagblatt* (Tübingen) (Lokale Kultur), 264, 15 November 1990, unpaginated

J.4   'Echo's van vroeger: Voortgang is verlies. De Oostenrijkse schrijver Sebald luistert naar de echo's die de tijd even opheffen', interview with Piet de Moor, *Knack* (Brussels),

22, 18, 6 May 1992, pp. 128–29 and 132; **J.4(a)** as an untitled section of Piet de Moor, *Schemerland: Stemmen uit Midden-Europa* (Amsterdam: van Gennep, [May] 2005), pp. 308–15; 2nd printing March 2006; 3rd printing July 2006. J.4(a) is an adapted and slightly shorter version of J.4

J.4.1   As 'Echoes from the Past', interview with Piet de Moor [English version], trans. by Reinier van Straten; see Part II of the present volume, p. 350–54

J.5   'Ein langwieriger Prozeß', interview with Sven Boedeker, *Nürnberger Nachrichten* (Feuilleton), 48, 27-28 February 1993, p. 26; **J.5(a)** 'Mit dem Vokabular im Gepäck', heavily edited interview with Sven Boedeker, *Der Tagespiegel* (Berlin), 14,494, 11 March 1993, p. 21 (J.5(a) is an abridged version in reported speech of J.5/J.5(b) and probably based on the same interview); **J.5(b)** 'Menschen auf der anderen Seite', interview with Sven Boedeker, *Rheinische Post* (*Rheinische Post am Wochenende*) (Geist und Leben) (Düsseldorf), 236, 9 October 1993, unpag. (J.5(b) is an expanded version of J.5)

J.6   'Bei den armen Seelen', interview with Burkhard Baltzer, *Saarbrücker Zeitung* (Feuilleton), 63, 16 March 1993, p. 10

J.7   '"Wildes Denken"', interview with Sigrid Löffler [probably 9 February 1993], *Profil* (Vienna), 24, 16, 19 April 1993, p. 106; **J.7(a)** in *W. G. Sebald*, ed. by Loquai, pp. 135–37

J.8   'Wie kriegen die Deutschen das auf die Reihe?', interview with Marco Poltronieri, *Wochenpost* (Zurich), 25, 17 June 1993, pp. 28–29; **J.8(a)** in *Far From Home: W. G. Sebald*, ed. by Franz Loquai (*Fußnoten zur Literatur* 31) (Bamberg: Universität Bamberg, 1995), pp. 35–40; **J.8(b)** in *W. G. Sebald*, ed. by Loquai, pp. 138–44

J.9   'W. G. Sebald over joden, Duitsers en migranten. Het fascisme heeft me gemaakt', heavily edited interview with Anneriek de Jong, *NRC Handelsblad*, 1176 (Cultureel Supplement, 230) (Rotterdam), 2 July 1993, p. 6

J.10   'Kopfreisen in die Ferne', edited interview with Sigrid Löffler, *Süddeutsche Zeitung* (Munich), 29, 4–5 February 1995, p. iii; **J.10(a)** in *Far From Home*, ed. by Loquai, pp. 17–21; **J.10(b)** in *W. G. Sebald*, ed. by Loquai, pp. 32–36

J.11   'Im Zeichen des Saturn: Ein Besuch bei W. G. Sebald', edited interview with Renate Just and Marc Volk (photos), *Die Zeit* (*Magazin*) (Hamburg), 42, 13 October 1995, pp. 26–27 and 30; **J.11(a)** in *W. G. Sebald*, ed. by Loquai, pp. 37–42

1996–2000

J.12   'Horter des Weggeworfenen', edited interview with Frank Dietschreit, *Der Tagesspiegel* (Berlin), 15,539, 16 February 1996, p. 21

J.13   'Die schwere Leichtigkeit', interview with Sven Siedenberg, *Süddeutsche Zeitung* (Munich), 75, 29 March 1996, p. 15; **J.13(a)** as 'Zeitreise eines Melancholikers', *Rheinische Post* (*Rheinische Post am Wochenende*) (Geist und Leben) (Düsseldorf), 87, 13 April 1996, unpaginated; **J.13(b)** as 'Anatomie der Schwermut', *Rheinischer Merkur* (Bonn), 16, 19 April 1996, p. 23; **J.13(c)** in *W. G. Sebald*, ed. by Loquai, pp. 146–48. J.13(c) is a reprint of J.13(b); J.13(a) is a slightly longer version of the other three interviews.

J.14   'Who is W. G. Sebald?', interview with Carole Angier, *Jewish Quarterly* (London), 43.4 (Winter 1996–97), 10–14; **J.14(a)** in *The Emergence of Memory: Conversations with W. G. Sebald*, ed. by Lynne Sharon Schwartz (New York: Seven Stories Press, [October] 2007), pp. 63–75

J.14(a).1   'Qui est W. G. Sebald? Entretien avec Carole Angier' [French version], trans. by Patrick Charbonneau and Delphine Chartier, in *L'Archéologue de la mémoire: Conversations avec W. G. Sebald*, ed. by Lynne Sharon Schwartz [French edition] (Arles: Actes Sud, [February] 2009), pp. 65–79. [The French edition omits Michael Hofmann, 'A Chilly Extravagance' (pp. 87–91).]

J.14.1   Carole Angier, 'Wer ist W. G. Sebald? Ein Besuch beim Autor der *Ausgewanderten*' [German version], in *W. G. Sebald*, ed. by Loquai, pp. 43–50

J.15 'Die Weltsicht ist verhangen', telephone interview with Martin Oehlen, *Kölner Stadt-Anzeiger*, 134, 13 June 1997, p. 8

J.16 'An Interview with W. G. Sebald', interview with James Wood [10 July 1997], *Brick: A Literary Journal* (Toronto), no. 59 (Spring 1998), 23–29; **J.16(a)** in *Brick*, no. 69 (Spring 2002), 83–95

J.17 'Ghost Hunter', interview with Eleanor Wachtel on *The Emigrants* [16 October 1997], first broadcast on 18 April 1998 in CBC Radio's *Writers & Company*. A synthesis of the original recording and the final broadcast version is published in *The Emergence of Memory*, ed. by Schwartz, pp. 37–61 (cf. Audio-Visual Bibliography)

J.17.1 'Chasseur de fantômes, entretien avec Eleanor Wachtel' [French version], trans. by Patrick Charbonneau and Delphine Chartier, in *L'Archéologue de la mémoire*, pp. 39–64

J.18 '"Aber das Geschriebene ist ja kein Dokument"', edited interview with Christian Scholz [14 November 1997] (*c.* 90% of an interview that took place in Zurich: transcript in DLA; see also Audio-Visual Bibliography), *Neue Zürcher Zeitung* (Schweizer Ausgabe) (Literatur und Kunst), 48, 26–27 February 2000, pp. 77–78; **J.18(a)** *Neue Zürcher Zeitung* (Internationale Ausgabe) (Literatur und Kunst), 48, 26–27 February 2000, pp. 51–52

J.18.1 As '"L'esistenza nomade delle fotografie"' [Italian version], trans. by Stefania Carretti, in *La cenere delle immagini: spazi della memoria, luoghi della perdita*, ed. by Riccardo Panatoni [catalogue of a photographic exhibition] (Genoa and Milan: Editore Marietti 1820, 2006), pp. 104–33

J.18.2 As '"Photography's Nomadic Existence"' [English version], trans. from the Italian by Giovanna Di Gioia, in *La cenere delle immagini*, ed. by Panatoni, pp. 105–33

J.18.3 As '"But the Written Word is Not a True Document": A Conversation with W. G. Sebald on Literature and Photography: Christian Scholz' [American version], trans. and adapted by Markus Zisselsberger, in *Searching for Sebald: Photography after W. G. Sebald*, ed. by Lise Patt with Christel Dillbohner (Los Angeles: Institute of Cultural Inquiry, 2007), pp. 104–09

J.19 'Katastrophe mit Zuschauer', interview with Andrea Köhler, *Neue Zürcher Zeitung* (Schweizer Ausgabe) (Literatur und Kunst), 272, 22–23 November 1997, p. 68; **J.19(a)** *Neue Zürcher Zeitung* (Internationale Ausgabe) (Literatur und Kunst), 272, 22–23 November 1997, p. 52 (see also D.65/D.65(a) and D.65bis)

J.20 'Alles schrumpft', edited interview with Jochen Wittmann, *Stuttgarter Zeitung*, 274, 27 November 1997, p. 33

J.21 'Leid und Scham und Schweigen und das Loch in der Literatur', interview with Denis Scheck on *Luftkrieg und Literatur*, *Basler Zeitung* (Das Feuilleton), 31, 6 February 1998, p. 37

J.22 'W. G. Sebald: A Profile', heavily edited interview with James Atlas [6–7 February 1998], *Paris Review*, 41, 151 (Summer 1999), 278–95

J.23 'Swimming the Seas of Silence', edited interview with Boyd Tonkin [literary editor of *The Independent*] on *Die Ringe des Saturn* [18 February 1998], *W: The Waterstone's Magazine*, 13 (Spring 1998), 90–99

J.24 'An Interview with W. G. Sebald', interview with Sarah Kafatou [17 May 1998], *Harvard Review*, 15 (Fall 1998), 31–35

J.25 'Characters, plot, dialogue? That's not really my style ...', Books Interview with Robert McCrum, *Observer*, Review section (London), 7 June 1998, p. 17

J.26 [No title], interview with Michaël Zeeman in Amsterdam [23 June 1998], first broadcast on 12 July 1998 in *Kamer met Uitzicht* (Netherlands TV, VPRO), transcribed by Gordon Turner, in *W. G. Sebald: History–Memory–Trauma*, ed. by Scott Denham and Mark McCulloh (*Interdisciplinary German Cultural Studies* 1) (Berlin and New York: Walter de Gruyter, 2006), pp. 21–29 (cf. Audio-Visual Bibliography)

J.27 'Living among the English', edited interview with Peter Morgan [10 July 1998],

Planet: The Welsh Internationalist (Aberystwyth), 158 (April–May 2003), 13–18 (cf. Audio-Visual Bibliography)

J.28   'Qu'est devenu Ernest?', edited interview with Claire Devarrieux, *Libération* (Paris) (Livres [Book Section]), 5486, 7 January 1999, p. 3; **J.28(a)** in *W. G. Sebald 2009*, ed. by Martina Wachendorff [publisher's catalogue] (Arles: Actes Sud, [February] 2009), pp. 19–21

J.29   'Le passé repoussé de l'Allemagne', heavily edited interview with Gérard de Cortanze, mainly on the French translation of *Die Ausgewanderten*, *Le Figaro Littéraire* (Littérature Étrangère) (Paris), 16,917, 14 January 1999, p. 5

J.30   'Lost in Translation?', interview with Jon Cook, Centre for the Creative and Performing Arts, UEA [9 February 1999]; see Part II of the present volume, p. 356–63

J.31   'The Questionable Business of Writing', interview with Toby Green, www.amazon.co.uk [recorded late 1999 prior to the publication of *Vertigo*, it first appeared on the Amazon website when *Vertigo* was published in December 1999, then again after the publication of *Austerlitz* in autumn 2001], [6 pp.] <http://www.amazon.co.uk/gp/feature.html?ie=UTF8&docId=21586> [accessed 9 April 2010]

J.32   [No title], interview with Volker Hage [22 February 2000], mainly on *Luftkrieg und Literatur*, *Akzente* (Munich), 50.1 (February 2003), 35–50; **J.32(a)** as 'Hitlers pyromanische Phantasien', in *Zeugen der Zerstörung: Die Literaten und der Luftkrieg: Essays und Gespräche*, ed. by Volker Hage (Frankfurt a.M.: Fischer, 2003), pp. 259–79

J.33   'The Permanent Exile of W. G. Sebald', interview with Jens Mühling [April 2000] [mainly on teaching creative writing *Pretext*], 7 (Spring–Summer 2003), pp. 15–26; **J.33(a)** in three parts under the heading 'Jens Mühling' on Terry Pitts's *Vertigo* website <http://sebald.wordpress.com/>

J.33.1   As 'W. G. Sebalds permanente eksil' [Norwegian version], trans. by Thomas J. R. Marthinsen, *Vinduet: Gyldendals Tidsskrift for Litteratur*, 64.1 ([29 March] 2010), 62–66

2001

J.34   'In Conversation with W. G. Sebald', interview with Christopher Bigsby [12 January 2001], in *Writers in Conversation with Christopher Bigsby*, ed. by Christopher Bigsby, 2 vols (Norwich: EAS Publishing / Pen&Inc., 2001), II, 139–65

J.35   'Der Spurensucher', heavily edited interview with Julia Kospach [12 February 2001], *Profil* (Kultur) (Vienna), 8, 19 February 2001, pp. 122–25

J.36   '"Ich fürchte das Melodramatische"', interview with Martin Doerry and Volker Hage [27 February 2001], mainly on *Austerlitz*, *Der Spiegel* (Hamburg), 11, 12 March 2001, pp. 228, 230 and 232–34

J.37   'The Meaning of Coincidence', interview with [Joseph] Joe Cuomo [13 March 2001] as part of the Queens College Reading Evenings in New York, first broadcast on 3 September 2001 in New York on Metro TV's *The Unblinking Eye* series, originally published in *The New Yorker on Line*; **J.37(a)** as 'A Conversation with W. G. Sebald', in *The Emergence of Memory*, ed. by Schwartz, pp. 93–117. J.37(a) is a more complete version of J.37.

J.37(a).1   'Conversation avec W. G. Sebald, entretien avec Joseph Cuomo' [French version], trans. by Patrick Charbonneau and Delphine Chartier, in *L'Archéologue de la mémoire*, ed. by Schwartz, pp. 93–113

J.38   'Die Melancholie des Widerstands', edited interview with Hans-Peter Kunisch, *Süddeutsche Zeitung* (Literatur) (Munich), 80, 5 April 2001, p. 20

J.39   '"Wir zahlen einen ungeheuren Preis"', interview with Hannes Hintermeier, *Münchner Abendzeitung*, 113, 17 May 2001, p. 22

J.40   'El Escritor Errante. W. G. Sebald: "Crecí en una familia posfascista alemana"', edited interview with Ciro Krauthausen, *El País*, 8817 (Babelia [literary supplement]), 503, 14 July 2001, pp. 2–4

J.41   '"Zoals een hond een lepel vergeet": Een gesprek met W. G. Sebald over *Austerlitz*'
[interview on *Austerlitz* with Jean-Pierre Rondas (22 May 2001); first broadcast (in part) as
'Sebald schrijft Breendonk' in *Rondas* on Radio Klara (Belgium) on 2 September 2001 (cf.
Audio-Visual Bibliography)], in *Dietsche Warande en Belfort*, 150.1 (February 2005), 77–89.

J.41.1   '"So wie ein Hund, der den Löffel vergißt": Ein Gespräch mit W. G. Sebald über
Austerlitz' [German version], in *Literatur im Krebsgang: Totenbeschwörung und memoria in der
deutschsprachigen Literatur nach 1989*, ed. by Arne De Winde and Anke Gilleir (*Amsterdamer
Beiträge zur neueren Germanistik*, 64) (Amsterdam and New York: Rodopi, 2008), pp. 351–63

J.42   'Mit einem kleinen Strandspaten Abschied von Deutschland nehmen', interview
with Uwe Pralle [August 2001], *Süddeutsche Zeitung* (Literatur) (Munich), 295, 22–23
December 2001, p. 16

J.43   'The Significant Mr. Sebald', edited interview with Maria Alvarez [15 August 2001],
Telegraph Magazine (London), 22 September 2001, pp. 55, 57, and 59; J.43(a) as 'Woe is
him', *Sydney Morning Herald* (*Good Weekend* magazine), 24 November 2001, pp. 44–45.

J.44   'Preoccupied with Death, but Still Funny', edited interview in Norwich with Arthur
Lubow [19–20 August 2001], *New York Times* (late edition), 51,964, 11 December 2001,
pp. E1–E2; J.44(a) [no title], significantly extended version of J.44, in 'A Symposium
on W. G. Sebald', *Threepenny Review* (Berkeley, CA), 23.1, 89 (Spring 2002), 18–21 (pp.
20–21); J.44(b) as 'Crossing Boundaries', in *The Emergence of Memory*, ed. by Schwartz,
pp. 159–73. J.44(b) is a reorganized, somewhat expanded, and heavily edited version of
J.44(a); see also the entry for T. J. Clark in Section 8 of the Secondary Bibliography for
the online version of the *Threepenny Review*.

J.44(b).1   'Franchir des frontières, entretien avec Arthur Lubow' [French version], trans.
by Patrick Charbonneau and Delphine Chartier, in *L'Archéologue de la mémoire*, ed. by
Schwartz, pp. 161–76

J.45   'Recovered Memories', interview with Maya Jaggi [13 September 2001], *Guardian*
(Saturday Review Section) (London), 48,221, 22 September 2001, pp. 6–7

J.46   'The Last Word', edited conversation with Maya Jaggi in the Queen Elizabeth Hall,
London, on the occasion of the St Jerome Lecture 2001 [24 September 2001], *Guardian*
(Section G2) (London), 48,298, 21 December 2001, pp. 4–5; J.46(a) as 'St Jerome Lecture
2001: W. G. Sebald in Conversation with Maya Jaggi and Anthea Bell', *In Other Words:
The Journal for Literary Translators*, no. 21 (Summer 2003), 5–18. J.46(a) is the unabridged
version of J.46 and contains additional material, as well as contributions by Anthea Bell
and questions by members of the audience.

J.47   'Sebastian Shakespeare Talks to W. G. Sebald', *Literary Review* (London), 280
(October 2001), 50

J.48   'Up against Historical Amnesia', interview with Kenneth Baker, *San Francisco
Chronicle* (Final Edition, Sunday Review Section), 235, 7 October 2001, p. R2

J.49   '"In This Distant Place": ALOUD at Central Library', conversation with Steve
Wasserman [17 October 2001]; see Part II of the present volume, pp. 364–75

J.50   'A Poem of an Invisible Subject', interview with Michael Silverblatt [*c.* 17–18 October
2001], first broadcast on 6 December 2001 in Santa Monica, CA, on KCRW's *Bookworm*,
in *The Emergence of Memory*, ed. by Schwartz, pp. 77–86 (cf. Audio-Visual Bibliography)

J.50.1   'Une poésie de l'invisible, entretien avec Michael Silverblatt' [French version],
trans. by Patrick Charbonneau and Delphine Chartier, in *L'Archéologue de la mémoire*, ed.
by Schwartz, pp. 81–91

J.51   'A Writer Who Challenges Traditional Storytelling', edited interview with Susan
Salter Reynolds [*c.* 17–18 October 2001], *Los Angeles Times* (Home Edition) (Southern
California Living), 325, 24 October 2001, p. E.1; J.51(a) 'Sifting through Shards of
Memory', *Sunday Star-Ledger* (Perspective) (Newark, NJ), 11 November 2001, p. 4; J.51(a)
is a significantly shortened version of J.51 and omits the subheadings and the following

five passages: 'Why? Well, it's ... bead on him."'; 'He thinks for a ... hairpieces."'; 'most of which he ... subject matter"'; 'One has the ... on a cruise?"'; '"A lot happens ... steep gradient."'

J.52 'Books: Outside the Box', edited interview with Malcolm Jones [*c.* 21 October 2001], *Newsweek*, no further details; see <http://www.newsweek.com/2001/10/24/books-outside-the-box.print.html>

J.53 'Talking with W. G. Sebald: Europe Unplugged', edited interview with Dan Cryer, *Newsday* (Currents and Books Section) (New York), 56, 28 October 2001, p. B11

J.54 'Past Imperfect: Although W. G. Sebald is Loved by Literary Critics ...', edited interview with Simon Houpt, *Globe & Mail* (Globe Books) (Toronto), 17 November 2001, p. D.3

K. Collected *obiter dicta*

K.1 'W. G. Sebald: The Collected "Maxims"', collected by David Lambert and Robert McGill [compiled from notes taken by the participants in an MA class on creative writing taught by Sebald at UEA in Autumn Semester, 2001], *Five Dials* [on-line literary periodical published by Hamish Hamilton, London], 5 (13 February 2009), 8–9 <http://fivedials.com/fivedials/> [accessed 3 April 2009]. See also Chapter 4 of the present volume, where Luke Williams draws on these notes as well as on his own.

L. Recorded Texts (in chronological order of release)

See the Audio-Visual Bibliography for details of radio adaptations.

L.1 W. G. Sebald, *Max Ferber*, recording of B.B.2, pp. 217–355, *Die Andere Bibliothek im Ohr* (Frankfurt a.M: Eichborn, 2000), two CDs read by the author. Following the English version, the name Max Aurach has been changed to Max Ferber.

L.2 W. G. Sebald, *Aus 'Logis in einem Landhaus'*; recording of an extract from A.6 read by the author and given as one of the Marbacher Autorenlesungen on 12 April 2000 in the DLA (one privately produced audiotape; catalogue number TTS ER 166)

L.3 W. G. Sebald, *Austerlitz* (Books on Tape 5871); recording of B.B.6.1, five 90-minute cassettes read by Richard Matthews (Newport Beach: Books on Tape Inc., 2002)

L.4 W. G. Sebald, *Campo Santo*, recording of B.D.2, pp. 5–53; recording of E.B.30, E.B.31, E.B.32, and E.B.33; two CDs read by Charles Brauer lasting 150 minutes (Hamburg: HörbucHHamburg, [16 September] 2005)

L.5 W. G. Sebald, 'Die Spuren, die Robert Walser hinterlassen hat' [short extract from A.6, pp. 127f./D.68(a)], in *Robert Walser: Eine Hommage in Wort und Klang* [CD read by Hans-Rudolf Twerenbold and Peter Fricke, with music by Marius Ungureanu lasting 73 minutes] (Reichertshausen: Faszination-Hören: Wort & Musik Hörbücher, [November] 2006)

L.6 W. G. Sebald, *Die Ausgewanderten. Vier lange Erzählungen* [recording of B.B.2; seven CDs read by Paul Herwig lasting 442 minutes] (Munich: Winter + Winter, 2007)

M. Translations by W. G. Sebald

M.A. Poetry (in chronological order of publication)

M.A.1 [McGough, Roger, four poems, trans. by W. G. Sebald], *ZET: Das Zeichenheft für Literatur und Graphik*, 3.12 (December 1975), 6–8; **M.A.1(a)** *Vorzugsausgabe*; identical with M.A.1 except for the inclusion of a loose print

M.A.1(i)   'Zauberers Balladen', pp. 6–7 [German version of 'Warlock Poems', in Roger McGough, *gig* (London: Jonathan Cape, 1973), pp. 40–42]

M.A.1(ii)   'Exsomnia', p. 8 [German version of 'exsomnia', in McGough, *gig*, p. 47]

M.A.1(iii)   'Tigerträume', p. 8 [German version of 'tigerdreams', in McGough, *gig*, p. 44]

M.A.1(iv)   'Auf dem Seil', p. 8 [German version of 'tightrope', in McGough, *gig*, p. 45]

M.A.2   Hulse, Michael, 'Michael Hulse: [Zwei] Gedichte', trans. by W. G. Sebald, *Sprache im technischen Zeitalter*, 33, 134 (June 1995), 161–64; **M.A.2(a)** see the present volume, p. 336–37

M.A.2(i)   'An Botho Strauss in Berlin', p. 162 [German version of 'To Botho Strauss in Berlin', in Michael Hulse, *Eating Strawberries in the Necropolis* (London: Harvill, 1991), p. 50]; **M.A.2(i)(a)** see the present volume, p. 336.

M.A.2(ii)   'Raffles Hotel Singapur', pp. 163–64 [German version of 'Raffles Hotel (Singapore)', in Hulse, *Eating Strawberries in the Necropolis*, pp. 11–12]; **M.A.2(ii)(a)** see the present volume, pp. 336–37.

M.B. Prose

M.B.1   Evans, Richard J., *Sozialdemokratie und Frauenemanzipation im deutschen Kaiserreich*, trans. by W. G. Sebald (Berlin: J. H. W. Dietz Nachfolger, 1979); 2nd printing 1984

M.B.2   Sheppard, Richard, ed., 'Nachwort des Herausgebers', trans. by W. G. Sebald, in *Die Schriften des Neuen Clubs 1908–1914*, ed. by Richard Sheppard, 2 vols (Hildesheim: Gerstenberg, 1980–83), II, pp. 419–577

N. Parodies of Sebald's Work

N.1   [Craig Brown], 'Diary: W. G. Sebald', *Private Eye*, 958, 4 September 1998, p. 25; parody of B.B.3.2

Postscript

When this Bibliography was concluded, the editors were aware of the following (re-) translations of Sebald's works planned or in preparation:

Nach der Natur (Portuguese: Telma Costa), (Swedish: Ulrika Wallenström)

Schwindel. Gefühle. (Hebrew: Tali Konas)

Die Ausgewanderten (Russian: Marina Koreneva), (Castilian: Miguel Sáenz), (Lithuanian: Ruta Jonynaite)

Die Ringe des Saturn (Czech [*Saturnovy prstence*]: Radovan Charvát), (Castilian: Miguel Sáenz)

Die Beschreibung des Unglücks / Unheimliche Heimat (English [*Silent Catastrophes*]: Jo Catling)

Logis in einem Landhaus (Swedish: Ulrika Wallenström)

Campo Santo (Greek: Iannis Kalifatidis), (Hebrew: Tali Konas), (Italian: Ada Vigliani), (Japanese: Hitoko Suzuki), (Swedish: Ulrika Wallenström)

The Emergence of Memory, ed. by Schwartz (Greek: Vassilis Douvitsas)

2
Secondary Bibliography

Compiled by Jo Catling, Richard Hibbitt, and Lynn Wolff

NOTE

This bibliography aims to show, as comprehensively as possible, the breadth and depth of secondary literature on W. G. Sebald published up to and including 2010. We would like to express our gratitude to all the Sebald scholars and readers who have alerted us to items for the bibliography and provided us with missing details, as well as to earlier compilers of Sebald bibliographies, especially Marcel Atze and Franz Loquai. We have, however, not included 'print on demand' items found in online catalogues.

Details of interviews with W. G. Sebald can be found in Section J of the Primary Bibliography. Reviews of Sebald's works and audio-visual material are collected in the separate bibliographies which follow this one.

CONTENTS

(1) Monographs
(2) Edited Books
(3) Special Journal Editions
(4) Comparative Studies
(5) Other Books and Journals Containing Material on WGS
(6) Articles and Book Chapters
(7) Entries in Reference Works
(8) Obituaries and Tributes
(9) Poems Written in Tribute to WGS
(10) Poems and Prose Featuring WGS
(11) MA and PhD Theses on WGS
(12) Art Works, Exhibitions, and Performances Inspired by WGS
(13) Online Resources
(14) Forthcoming Publications

(1) Monographs

Agazzi, Elena, *La grammatica del silenzio di W. G. Sebald* (Rome: Artemide, 2007)

Baumgärtel, Patrick, *Mythos und Utopie: Zum Begriff der 'Naturgeschichte der Zerstörung' im Werk W. G. Sebalds* (Frankfurt a.M.: Lang, 2010)

Blackler, Deane, *Reading W. G. Sebald: Adventure and Disobedience* (Rochester, NY: Camden House, 2007)

Carré, Martine, *W. G. Sebald: Le Retour de l'auteur* (Lyons: Presses universitaires de Lyon, 2008)

Covindassamy, Mandana, *W. G. Sebald: Cartographie d'une écriture en déplacement* (Paris: Presses universitaires de Paris Sorbonne, 2010)

Distler, Anton, *Kein Verstehen ohne fundamentale Ontologie: Eine philosophische Analyse des Werks von W. G. Sebald aufgrund der 'existentiellen Psychoanalyse' Jean-Paul Sartres* (Würzburg: Königshausen & Neumann, 2008)

Fuchs, Anne, *Die Schmerzensspuren der Geschichte: Zur Poetik der Erinnerung in W. G. Sebalds Prosa* (Cologne: Böhlau, 2004)

Hutchinson, Ben, *W. G. Sebald: Die dialektische Imagination* (Berlin: de Gruyter, 2009)

Long, J. J., *W. G. Sebald: Image, Archive, Modernity* (Edinburgh: Edinburgh University Press, 2007)

McCulloh, Mark R., *Understanding W. G. Sebald* (Columbia, SC: University of South Carolina Press, 2003)

Mosbach, Bettina, *Figurationen der Katastrophe: Ästhetische Verfahren in W. G. Sebalds Die Ringe des Saturn und Austerlitz* (Bielefeld: Aisthesis, 2008)

Öhlschläger, Claudia, *Beschädigtes Leben, Erzählte Risse: W. G. Sebalds poetische Ordnung des Unglücks* (Freiburg: Rombach, 2006)

Pic, Muriel, *W. G. Sebald: L'Image papillon, suivi de W. G. Sebald: L'Art de voler* (Paris: Les Presses du Réel, 2009)

Schedel, Susanne, *Wer weiß, wie es vor Zeiten wirklich gewesen ist? Textbeziehungen als Mittel der Geschichtsdarstellung bei W. G. Sebald* (Würzburg: Königshausen & Neumann, 2004)

Seitz, Stephan, *Geschichte als bricolage — W. G. Sebald und die Poetik des Bastelns* (Göttingen: Vandenhoeck & Ruprecht unipress, 2010)

(2) Edited Books

The individual chapters contained in the volumes below are listed in Section 6 of the bibliography.

Atze, Marcel, and Franz Loquai, eds, *Sebald. Lektüren.* (Eggingen: Isele, 2005)

Bülow, Ulrich von, Heike Gfrereis, and Ellen Strittmatter, eds, *Wandernde Schatten: W. G. Sebalds Unterwelt*, marbacherkatalog 62 (Marbach am Neckar: Deutsche Schillergesellschaft, 2008) [catalogue of the exhibition held in the Literaturmuseum der Moderne, Marbach am Neckar, 26 September 2008–1 February 2009]

Denham, Scott, and Mark McCulloh, eds, *W. G. Sebald: History–Memory–Trauma*, Interdisciplinary German Cultural Studies, 1 (Berlin: de Gruyter, 2006), Amsterdamer Beiträge zur neueren Germanistik, 72

Fischer, Gerhard, ed., *W. G. Sebald: Schreiben ex patria / Expatriate Writing* (Amsterdam: Rodopi, 2009)

Fuchs, Anne, and J. J. Long, eds, *W. G. Sebald and the Writing of History* (Würzburg: Königshausen & Neumann, 2007)

Görner, Rüdiger, ed., *The Anatomist of Melancholy: Essays in Memory of W. G. Sebald* (Munich: iudicium, 2003)

Heidelberger-Leonard, Irène, and Mireille Tabah, eds, *W. G. Sebald: Intertextualität und Topographie* (Berlin: LIT Verlag, 2008)

Köpf, Gerhard, ed., *Mitteilungen über Max: Marginalien zu W. G. Sebald*, Autoren im Kontext: Duisburger Studienbögen, 1 (Oberhausen: Laufen, 1998)

Long, J. J., and Anne Whitehead, eds, *W. G. Sebald: A Critical Companion* (Edinburgh: Edinburgh University Press, 2004)

Loquai, Franz, ed., *Far From Home: W. G. Sebald*, Fußnoten zur Literatur, 31 (Bamberg: Universität Bamberg, 1995) [see note on next entry]

——, ed., *W. G. Sebald*, Porträt, 7 (Eggingen: Isele, 1997) [This book can be seen as a significantly expanded version of *Far From Home: W. G. Sebald*; it contains nearly all the contents of the earlier work as well as a number of further pieces.]

Martin, Sigurd, and Ingo Wintermeyer, eds, *Verschiebebahnhöfe der Erinnerung: Zum Werk W. G. Sebalds* (Würzburg: Königshausen & Neumann, 2007)

Niehaus, Michael, and Claudia Öhlschläger, eds, *W. G. Sebald: Politische Archäologie und melancholische Bastelei* (Berlin: Schmidt, 2006)

Patt, Lise, ed., with Christel Dillbohner, *Searching for Sebald: Photography after W. G. Sebald* (Los Angeles: Institute of Cultural Inquiry, 2007)

Schwartz, Lynne Sharon, ed., *The Emergence of Memory: Conversations with W. G. Sebald* (New York: Seven Stories Press, 2007) [for contents see Primary Bibliography, Interviews (Section J)]

——, ed., *L'Archéologue de la mémoire: Conversations avec W. G. Sebald*, trans. by Patrick Charbonneau and Delphine Chartier (Arles: Actes Sud, 2009) [French translation of above]

Zisselsberger, Markus, ed., *The Undiscover'd Country: W. G. Sebald and the Poetics of Travel* (Rochester, NY: Camden House, 2010)

(3) Special Journal Editions

The individual articles contained in the volumes below are listed in Sections 6, 8, and 9 of the bibliography.

Anderson, Mark, ed., *Germanic Review*, 79.3 (Summer 2004)

Arnold, Heinz Ludwig, ed., *W. G. Sebald* (= *Text + Kritik: Zeitschrift für Literatur*, no. 158 (April 2003))

Bel, Jacqueline, and others, eds, *Geheugenteksten: W. G. Sebald en de poëtica van de herinnering* (= *Armada: Tijdschrift voor wereldliteratuur*, no. 40 (October 2005)) [in Dutch]

Busch, Walter, ed., *W. G. Sebald: Storia della distruzione e memoria letteraria* (= *Cultura Tedesca*, no. 29 (July–December 2005)) [in Italian]

Bush, Peter, ed., 'W. G. Sebald: Memorial Issue', *In Other Words: The Journal for Literary Translators*, no. 21 (2003)

Ceuppens, Jan, and Bart Philipsen, eds, *W. G. Sebald: Kaddisj voor een literair archeoloog* (= *DWB (Dietsche Warande en Belfort)*, 150.1 (2005)) [in Dutch]

Horstkotte, Silke, and Nancy Pedri, eds, *Poetics Today: International Journal for Theory and Analysis of Literature and Communication*, 29.1 (2008)

Krüger, Michael, ed., *W. G. Sebald zum Gedächtnis* (= *Akzente*, 50.1 (2003))

Lützeler, Paul Michael, and Stephan K. Schindler, eds, *Schwerpunkt: W. G. Sebald* (= *Gegenwartsliteratur: Ein Germanistisches Jahrbuch*, 6 (2007))

Villa, Luisa, and others, eds, 'Materiali su W. G. Sebald', *Nuova corrente*, 57, 146 (2010) [in Italian]

Vinger, Audun, ed., *Vinduet: Gyldendals tidsskrift for litteratur*, 64.1 (March 2010) [in Norwegian]

Vogel-Klein, Ruth, ed., *W. G. Sebald: Mémoire. Transferts. Images / Erinnerung. Übertragungen. Bilder* (= *Recherches Germaniques*, special issue 2 (2005)) [in French and German]

Zisselsberger, Markus, ed., *Stories of Heimat and Calamity: W. G. Sebald and Austrian Literature* (= *Modern Austrian Literature*, special issue, 40.4 (December 2007))

See also:

Anon., *W. G. Sebald: Een hommage aan een unieke auteur* (Amsterdam: De Bezige Bij, 2008) [illustrated publisher's promotional brochure with short critical pieces and summaries of works by WGS; in Dutch]

(4) Comparative Studies

Where appropriate, the articles or chapters contained in the sources below are also listed in Section 6 of the bibliography.

Agazzi, Elena, *Erinnerte und rekonstruierte Geschichte: Drei Generationen deutscher Schriftsteller und Fragen der Vergangenheit*, trans. from the Italian by Gunnhild Schneider and Holm Steinert (Göttingen: Vandenhoeck & Ruprecht, 2005) [on WGS, Treichel, Kleeberg, Langer, Sparschuh, Kuckart, Beyer, and Dückers]

Battiston, Régine, *Lectures de l'identité narrative: Max Frisch, Ingeborg Bachmann, Marlen Haushofer, W. G. Sebald* (Paris: Éditions Orizons, 2009)

Bruzelius, Margaret, *Romancing the Novel: Adventure from Scott to Sebald* (Lewisburg, PA: Bucknell University Press, 2007)

Calzoni, Raul, *Walter Kempowski, W. G. Sebald e i tabù della memoria collettiva tedesca* (Pasian di Prato: Campanotto, 2005)

Carrión, Jorge, *Viaje contra espacio: Juan Goytisolo y W. G. Sebald* (Madrid: Iberoamericana, 2009)

Ferguson, Jessie, *The Archimedean Author: Roberto Bolaño, W. G. Sebald, and Narrative After Borges* (San Francisco: San Francisco State University, 2007)

Johannsen, Anja K., *Kisten, Krypten, Labyrinthe: Raumfigurationen in der Gegenwartsliteratur: W. G. Sebald, Anne Duden, Herta Müller* (Bielefeld: transcript, 2008) [see also Maier, Anja K.]

Medin, Daniel, *Three Sons: Franz Kafka and the Fiction of J. M. Coetzee, Philip Roth and W. G. Sebald* (Evanston, IL: Northwestern University Press, 2010)

Polster, Heike, *The Aesthetics of Passage: The Imag(in)ed Experience of Time in Thomas Lehr, W. G. Sebald and Peter Handke* (Würzburg: Königshausen & Neumann, 2008)

Ritte, Jürgen, *Endspiele: Geschichte und Erinnerung bei Dieter Forte, Walter Kempowski und W. G. Sebald* (Berlin: Matthes & Seitz, 2009)

Santner, Eric L., *On Creaturely Life: Rilke, Benjamin, Sebald* (Chicago: University of Chicago Press, 2006)

Sareika, Rüdiger, ed., *Im Krebsgang: Strategien des Erinnerns in den Werken von Günter Grass und W. G. Sebald* (Iserlohn: Institut für Kirche und Gesellschaft, 2006)

Steinaecker, Thomas von, *Literarische Foto-Texte: Zur Funktion der Fotografien in den Texten Rolf Dieter Brinkmanns, Alexander Kluges und W. G. Sebalds* (Bielefeld: transcript, 2007)

Tennstedt, Antje, *Annäherungen an die Vergangenheit bei Claude Simon und W. G. Sebald: Am Beispiel von Le Jardin des plantes, Die Ausgewanderten und Austerlitz* (Freiburg: Rombach, 2007)

Vangi, Michele, *Letteratura e fotografia: Roland Barthes, Rolf Dieter Brinkmann, Julio Cortázar, W. G. Sebald* (Pasian di Prato: Campanotto, 2005) [see Section 11 for details of doctoral thesis written in German]

Wohlleben, Doren, *Schwindel und Wahrheit: Ethik und Ästhetik der Lüge in Poetik-Vorlesungen und Romanen der Gegenwart: Ingeborg Bachmann, Reinhart Baumgart, Peter Bichsel, Sten Nadolny, Christoph Ransmayr, W. G. Sebald, Hans-Ulrich Treichel* (Freiburg: Rombach, 2005)

(5) Other Books and Journals Containing Material on WGS

Where appropriate, the articles or chapters contained in the sources below are also listed in Section 6 of the bibliography.

BIGSBY, CHRISTOPHER, *Remembering and Imagining the Holocaust: The Chain of Memory* (Cambridge: Cambridge University Press, 2006)

CADUFF, CORINA, and ULRIKE VEDDER, eds, *Chiffre 2000: Neue Paradigmen der Gegenwartsliteratur* (Munich: Fink, 2005)

COHEN-PFISTER, LAUREL, and DAGMAR WIENRÖDER-SKINNER, eds, *Victims and Perpetrators: 1933–1945: (Re)Presenting the Past in Post-Unification Culture*, Interdisciplinary German Cultural Studies, 2 (Berlin: de Gruyter, 2006)

CROWNSHAW, RICHARD, *The Afterlife of Holocaust Memory in Contemporary Literature and Culture* (Houndmills: Palgrave Macmillan, 2010)

FAVRET, MARY A., *War at a Distance: Romanticism and the Making of Modern Wartime* (Princeton, NJ: Princeton University Press, 2010)

FORTE, DIETER, *Schweigen oder Sprechen*, ed. by Volker Hage (Frankfurt a.M.: Fischer, 2002) [of relevance to *Luftkrieg und Literatur*]

GORRA, MICHAEL, *The Bells in their Silence: Travels through Germany* (Princeton, NJ: Princeton University Press, 2004)

HAGE, VOLKER, *Zeugen der Zerstörung: Die Literaten und der Luftkrieg: Essays und Gespräche* (Frankfurt a.M.: Fischer, 2003)

HILL, SUSAN, *Howard's End is on the Landing: A Year of Reading From Home* (London: Profile, 2009) [refers to *The Rings of Saturn*]

HORSTKOTTE, SILKE, *Nachbilder: Fotografie und Gedächtnis in der deutschen Gegenwartsliteratur* (Cologne: Böhlau, 2009)

DE MOOR, PIET, *Schemerland: Stemmen uit Midden-Europa* (Amsterdam: Van Gennep, 2005) [in Dutch; contains sections of de Moor's interview with WGS (see Primary Bibliography, J.4 and the present volume, pp. 350-54) plus further commentary on his works, especially on *Luftkrieg und Literatur*]

NEWTON, ADAM ZACHARY, *The Elsewhere: On Belonging at a Near Distance* (Madison, WI: University of Wisconsin Press, 2005)

SILL, OLIVER, *Der Kreis des Lesens: Eine Wanderung durch die europäische Moderne* (Bielefeld: Aisthesis, 2001)

STONARD, JOHN-PAUL, *Fault Lines: Art in Germany 1945–1955* (London: Ridinghouse, 2007) [draws on *Luftkrieg und Literatur*]

TABERNER, STUART, *German Literature of the 1990s and Beyond: Normalization and the Berlin Republic* (Rochester, NY: Camden House, 2005) [references to the *Luftkrieg* debate and to the representation of Jews]

TAYLOR, CRAIG, ed., *Five Dials* (online magazine available in pdf format), no. 5 (2009) <http://fivedials.com/fivedials/> [accessed 3 September 2009]

VEES-GULANI, SUSANNE, *Trauma and Guilt: Literature of Wartime Bombing in Germany* (Berlin: de Gruyter, 2003)

WERTHEIMER, JÜRGEN, *Sisyphos und Bumerang: Zwischenberichte* (Tübingen: Klöpfer and Meyer, 2006) [pieces on WGS, Bernhard, Celan, Härtling, Heine, Herta Müller, and others]

(6) Articles and Book Chapters

ABBOTT, THEA, '"Where no friends are buried nor Pathways stopt up"', *Spiked: The Magazine for Ideas, Literature and the Arts for Norfolk*, no. 3 (1999), 16–17

Adams, Jeff, 'The Pedagogy of the Image Text: Nakazawa, Sebald and Spiegelman Recount Social Traumas', *Discourse: Studies in the Cultural Politics of Education*, 29.1 (2008), 35–49

Agazzi, Elena, 'Immagini d'Italia e d'Oltralpe in *Vertigini* di W. G. Sebald', *Il Veltro: Rivista della Civiltà Italiana*, 49.4–6 (2005), 232–43 [with German summary]

——'Riti antichi e persistenza del passato: Il percorso interrotto nell'opera-testamento *Campo Santo* di W. G. Sebald', in Busch, op. cit. (Section 3), pp. 145–61

——'Spuren von Johann Peter Hebel und Ernst Bloch: W. G. Sebalds *Logis in einem Landhaus*', in Lützeler and Schindler, op. cit. (Section 3), pp. 91–117

Agnew, Vanessa, 'Epilogue: Genealogies of Space in Colonial and Postcolonial Re-enactment', in *Settler and Creole Re-Enactment*, ed. by Vanessa Agnew and Jonathan Lamb (Houndmills: Palgrave Macmillan, 2009), pp. 294–317

Albes, Claudia, 'Die Erkundung der Leere: Anmerkungen zu W. G. Sebalds "englischer Wallfahrt" *Die Ringe des Saturn*', *Jahrbuch der Deutschen Schillergesellschaft*, 46 (2002), 279–305

——'Porträt ohne Modell: Bildbeschreibung und autobiographische Reflexion in W. G. Sebalds "Elementargedicht" *Nach der Natur*', in Niehaus and Öhlschläger, op. cit. (Section 2), pp. 47–75

Aliaga-Buchenau, Ana-Isabel, ' "A Time He Could Not Bear to Say Any More About": Presence and Absence of the Narrator in W. G. Sebald's *The Emigrants*', in Denham and McCulloh, op. cit. (Section 2), pp. 141–55

Anderson, Mark M., ' "Loin, mais loin d'où?": Sur W. G. Sebald', *Critique: Revue générale des publications françaises et étrangères*, 58, 659 (2002), 252–62

——'The Edge of Darkness: On W. G. Sebald', *October*, no. 106 (2003), 102–21

——'Fino allo scioglimento delle cose: La fotografia nell'opera di W. G. Sebald', in *Le muse inquiete: Sinergie artistiche nel Novecento tedesco*, ed. by Grazia Pulvirenti and others (Florence: Olschki, 2003), pp. 141–54

——'Introduction', in Anderson, op. cit. (Section 3), pp. 155–62

——'Wo die Schrecken der Kindheit verborgen sind: W. G. Sebalds Dilemma der zwei Väter' (translated from English), *Literaturen*, 2006.7–8, 32–39 [preceded by 'Porträt: W. G. Sebald: Das Leben hinter dem Werk', pp. 30–31]

——'Fathers and Son: W. G. Sebald', *BookForum: The Review for Art, Fiction, & Culture*, 13.4 (2007), 28–31

——'Vaders en zoon: W. G. Sebald', trans. by Raymond Noë, in *W. G. Sebald: Een hommage aan een unieke auteur* [no editor] (Amsterdam: De Bezige Bij, 2008), pp. 4–19 [Dutch translation of above]

——'Documents, Photography, Postmemory: Alexander Kluge, W. G. Sebald and the German Family', in Horstkotte and Pedri, op. cit. (Section 3), pp. 129–53

——'Tristes Tropes: W. G. Sebald und die Melancholie der deutsch-jüdischen Vergangenheit', in *Gedächtnis und Identität: Die deutsche Literatur nach der Vereinigung*, ed. by Fabrizio Cambi (Würzburg: Königshausen und Neumann, 2008), pp. 231–42

——'Melancholie is een vorm van verzet: W. G. Sebald en de Duits-joodse herinnering', trans. by Ria van Hengel, *Nexus*, 46 (2008), 109–20 [Dutch translation of above]

Andersson, Torleiv, ' "Det siste har jeg funnet på selv": Noen betraktinger løst forbundet med et brev fra W. G. Sebald', in Vinger, op. cit. (Section 3), pp. 76–79

Arnds, Peter O., ' "Wandering in the Field of Lethe": A Heideggerian Reading of W. G. Sebald's *Austerlitz*', in Lützeler and Schindler, op. cit. (Section 3), pp. 185–211 [title given incorrectly in the contents as 'Dans la Salle des Pas Perdus: Wandering, Dwelling and Myth in W. G. Sebald's *Austerlitz*']

——'Memory, Myth and the Migrant Experience in W. G. Sebald's *Austerlitz*, Günter Grass's *The Tin Drum*, and Salman Rushdie's *Midnight's Children*', in *Changing the Nation: Günter Grass in International Perspective*, ed. by Rebecca Braun and Frank Brunssen (Würzburg: Königshausen & Neumann, 2008), pp. 67–80

——'While the Hidden Horrors of History are Briefly Illuminated: The Poetics of Wandering in *Austerlitz* and *Die Ringe des Saturn*', in Zisselsberger, op. cit. (Section 3), pp. 322–44

ARNOLD, HEINZ LUDWIG, 'Mit intuitiver Kraft Umrisse farbig gemacht: Ein Porträt des Schriftstellers and Literaturwissenschaftlers Winfried Georg Sebald', *Schweizer Monatshefte fur Politik, Wirtschaft, Kultur*, 79.7–8 (1999), 63–65

ARNOLD-DE SIMINE, SILKE, 'Erinnerungspoetik als Naturgeschichte der Zerstörung? Die Rezeption von W. G. Sebalds *Luftkrieg und Literatur* (1999) in Deutschland und Grossbritannien', in *Wende des Erinnerns? Geschichtskonstruktionen in der deutschen Literatur nach 1989*, ed. by Barbara Beßlich, Katharina Grätz and Olaf Hildebrand (Berlin: Schmidt, 2006), pp. 115–32

——'Memory Cultures: The Imperial War Museum North and W. G. Sebald's *Natural History of Destruction*', in *Bombs Away! Representing the Air War over Europe and Japan*, ed. by Wilfried Wilms and William Rasch (Amsterdam: Rodopi, 2006), pp. 295–311

——'Remembering the Future: Utopian and Dystopian Aspects of Glass and Iron Architecture in Walter Benjamin, Paul Scheerbarth, and W. G. Sebald', in *Imagining the City*, ed. by Christian Emden, Catherine Keen, and David Midgley, 2 vols (Oxford: Lang, 2006), II: *The Politics of Urban Space*, pp. 149–69

ATZE, MARCEL, 'Bibliotheca Sebaldiana: W. G. Sebald: Ein Bibliophile? Eine Spekulation', in Loquai, *W. G. Sebald*, op. cit. (Section 2), pp. 228–43

——'Koinzidenz und Intertextualität: Der Einsatz von Prätexten in W. G. Sebalds Erzahlung *All'estero*', in Loquai, *W. G. Sebald*, op. cit. (Section 2), pp. 151–75

——'Die Reise findet statt, um brennende Fragen zu lösen: Zur Neuauflage von H. G. Adlers Roman *Eine Reise* nebst einer Anmerkung zu W. G. Sebalds *Luftkrieg und Literatur*', *literaturkritik.de*, 1 (1999), 49–56

——'"Wie Adler berichtet": Das Werk H. G. Adlers als Gedächtnisspeicher für Literatur (Heimrad Backer, Robert Schindel, W. G. Sebald)', *Text + Kritik*, no. 163 (July 2004), 17–30

——'"... und wer spricht über Dresden?" Der Luftkrieg als öffentliches und literarisches Thema in der Zeit des ersten Frankfurter Auschwitz-Prozesses 1963–1965', in Atze and Loquai, op. cit. (Section 2), pp. 105–15; repr. in Niehaus and Öhlschläger, op. cit. (Section 2), pp. 205–17

——'Die Gesetze von der Wiederkunft der Vergangenheit: W. G. Sebalds Lektüre des Gedächtnistheoretikers Maurice Halbwachs', in Atze and Loquai, op. cit. (Section 2), pp. 195–211

——'Casanova von der Schwarzen Wand: Ein Beispiel intertextueller Repräsentanz des Holocaust in W. G. Sebalds *Austerlitz*', in Atze and Loquai, op. cit. (Section 2), pp. 228–43

——'W. G. Sebald und H. G. Adler: Eine Begegnung in Texten', in Vogel-Klein, op. cit. (Section 3), pp. 87–97

ATZE, MARCEL, and SVEN MEYER, '"Unsere Korrespondenz": Zum Briefwechsel zwischen W. G. Sebald und Theodor W. Adorno', in Atze and Loquai, op. cit. (Section 2), pp. 17–38

AYREN, ARMIN, 'Sebald über Canetti', in Köpf, op. cit. (Section 2), pp. 9–20

BAIER, LOTHAR, 'Literaturpfaffen: Tote Dichter vor dem moralischen Exekutionskommando', *Freibeuter*, no. 57 (1993), 42–70 (pp. 56–65 on Sebald and Andersch)

BALES, RICHARD, 'The Loneliness of the Long-distance Narrator: The Inscription of Travel in Proust and W. G. Sebald', in *Cross-Cultural Travel: Papers from the Royal Irish Academy Symposium on Literature and Travel*, ed. by Jane Conroy (New York: Lang, 2003), pp. 507–12

——'"L'édifice immense du souvenir": Mémoire et écriture chez Proust et Sebald', in Vogel-Klein, op. cit. (Section 3), pp. 129–37

——'Homeland and Displacement: The Status of the Text in Sebald and Proust', in Fischer, op. cit. (Section 2), pp. 461–74

Ballis, Anja, 'Mit W. G. Sebald auf der Suche nach Heimat: Topographie des Erzählens in "Paul Bereyter"', in *Literatur im Unterricht: Texte der Moderne und Postmoderne in der Schule*, 6.3 (2005), 177–86

Baron, Ulrich, 'Triffst Du nur das Zauberwort: W. G. Sebalds *Die Ringe des Saturn* (1995)', in *Der deutsche Roman der Gegenwart*, ed. by Wieland Freund and Winfried Freund (Munich: Fink, 2001), pp. 56–61

Barzilai, Maya, 'Facing the Past and the Female Spectre in W. G. Sebald's *The Emigrants*', in Long and Whitehead, op. cit. (Section 2), pp. 203–16

——'On Exposure: Photography and Uncanny Memory in W. G. Sebald's *Die Ausgewanderten* and *Austerlitz*', in Denham and McCulloh, op. cit. (Section 2), pp. 205–18

——'Melancholia as World History: W. G. Sebald's Rewriting of Hegel in *Die Ringe des Saturn*', in Fuchs and Long, op. cit. (Section 2), pp. 73–89

Battafarano, Italo Michele, 'Zwischen Kitsch und Selbstsucht: und auch noch Spuren von Antisemitismus? Marginalia zu Alfred Andersch: Eine Forschungskontroverse Sebald, Heidelberger-Leonard und Weigel betreffend', *Morgen-Glantz*, 4 (1994), 241–57

Battiston, Régine, 'Identité et confidence de soi: Le Roman *Austerlitz* de W. G. Sebald', in *Questions de communication* [Université de Metz] (2006), 237–50

——'W. G. Sebald: Conflit et relecture de la littérature allemande d'après-guerre', in *Akten des XI. Internationalen Germanistenkongresses Paris 2005: Germanistik im Konflikt der Kulturen*, vi: *Migrations-, Emigrations- und Remigrationskulturen: Multikulturalität in der zeitgenössischen deutschsprachigen Literatur* (Berne: Lang, 2007), pp. 117–21

——'L'Indicible Espace de l'exil dans l'œuvre de Winfried Georg Sebald', in *Entre tensions et passions: (Dé)constructions de l'espace littéraire européen*, ed. by Eric Lysøe (Strasbourg: Presses Universitaires de Strasbourg, 2009), pp. 299–312

——'La Rupture comme seuil: Autour de W. G. Sebald', in *Seuils culturels et rites de passage: Littérature et culture*, ed. by Peter Schnyder (Paris: Éditions Orizons, 2009), pp. 193–205

——'"Le Monde d'Hier" de Winfried Georg Sebald', in Régine Battiston, *Lectures de l'identité narrative: Max Frisch, Ingeborg Bachmann, Marlen Haushofer, W. G. Sebald* (Paris: Éditions Orizons, 2009), pp. 159–213

——'Perte du foyer et de l'identité: Le déracinement dans *Austerlitz* de W. G. Sebald', in *Signes de feu*, ed. by Eric Lysøe (Paris: Éditions Orizons, 2009), pp. 173–82

Bauer, Karin, 'The Dystopian Entwinement of Histories and Identities in W. G. Sebald's *Austerlitz*', in Denham and McCulloh, op. cit. (Section 2), pp. 233–50

Baumgarten, Murray, '"Not Knowing What I Should Think": The Landscape of Post-memory in W. G. Sebald's *The Emigrants*', *Partial Answers: Journal of Literature and the History of Ideas*, 5 (2007), 267–87

Beck, John, 'Reading Room: Erosion and Sedimentation in Sebald's Suffolk', in Long and Whitehead, op. cit. (Section 2), pp. 75–88

Beer, Gillian, 'Revenants and Migrants: Hardy, Butler, Woolf and Sebald', *Proceedings of the British Academy*, 125 (2004), 163–82

Bell, Anthea, 'Translating W. G. Sebald's *Austerlitz*', *The Linguist*, 41.6 (2002), 162–63

——'From Creation to Recreation', in Bush, op. cit. (Section 3), pp. 37–41

——'On Translating W. G. Sebald', in Görner, op. cit. (Section 2), pp. 11–18

——'Translation as Illusion', *EnterText (Supplement): Selected Papers From the 'Shelving Translation' Conference Held at Oxford University in April 2004*, ed. by Rebecca Beard and Brenda Garvey, 4.3 (2004–05), 11–18 <http://www.brunel.ac.uk/about/acad/sa/artresearch/entertext/issues/entertext43sup> [accessed 17 June 2009]

Bell, Fraser, 'The Better Germany', *Queen's Quarterly*, 110 (2003), 295–304

Ben-Horin, Michal, 'Musik einer Erinnerungspoetik: Fallstudie über deutschsprachige und hebräische Literatur nach 1945', *Weimarer Beiträge: Zeitschrift für Literaturwissenschaft, Ästhetik und Kulturwissenschaften*, 50.3 (2004), 404–26

BERBERICH, CHRISTINE, '"England? Whose England?": (Re)Constructing England in Julian Barnes's *England England* and W. G. Sebald's *The Rings of Saturn*', *National Identities*, 10.2 (2008), 167–84

BERE, CAROL, 'The Book of Memory: W. G. Sebald's *The Emigrants* and *Austerlitz*', *Literary Review: An International Journal of Contemporary Writing*, 46.1 (Fall 2002), 184–92

BERNSTEIN, J. M., 'Mad Raccoon, Demented Quail, and the Herring Holocaust: Notes for a Reading of W. G. Sebald', *Qui parle* (Spring–Summer 2009), 31–58

BERTENS, HANS, 'Zelfs de ringen van Saturnus hadden hun oorsprong in een ramp', in Bel and others, op. cit. (Section 3), pp. 41–49

BIGSBY, CHRISTOPHER, 'W. G. Sebald: An Act of Restitution', in *Remembering and Imagining the Holocaust: The Chain of Memory* (Cambridge: Cambridge University Press, 2006), pp. 25–114

BLACKLER, DEANE, 'Sebald's Strange Cinematic Prose: Stasis and Kinesis', in Fischer, op. cit. (Section 2), pp. 369–88

BLUHM, LOTHAR, 'Herkunft, Identität, Realität: Erinnerungsarbeit in der zeitgenössischen deutschen Literatur', in *Grenzen der Identität und der Fiktionalität*, ed. by Ulrich Breuer and Beatrice Sandberg, Autobiographisches Schreiben in der deutschsprachigen Gegenwartsliteratur, 1 (Munich: iudicium, 2006), pp. 69–80 [on WGS and Monika Maron]

BOEHNCKE, HEINER, 'Clair obscur: W. G. Sebalds Bilder', in Arnold, op. cit. (Section 3), pp. 43–62

BOND, GREG, 'On the Misery of Nature and the Nature of Misery: W. G. Sebald's Landscapes', in Long and Whitehead, op. cit. (Section 2), pp. 31–44

BONGERS, WOLFGANG, 'Anatomisches denken: Sebald, Rembrandt, Hierro', in *Epochen-Krankheiten: Konstellationen von Literatur und Pathologie*, ed. by Frank Degler and Christian Kohlroß (St Ingbert: Röhrig, 2006), pp. 57–76

BONIFAZIO, MASSIMO, '"Zerstöret das Letzte, die Erinnerung nicht": Naive Geschichten und schlaues Erzählen im Werk W. G. Sebalds', in *Text und Welt: Beiträge auf der 11. Internationalen Tagung Germanistische Forschungen zum literarischen Text* (SAXA Sonderband 8), ed. by Christoph Parry (Vaasa/ Germersheim: SAXA, 2002), pp. 108–15

BONN, KLAUS, 'Homoerotik, Hasard, Hysterie unter anderem: Zur Figuration der Männlichkeit bei W. G. Sebald', *Forum Homosexualität und Literatur*, 49 (2007), 5–40

——'W. G. Sebalds laufende Bilder: der Film und die Worte', *Arcadia: Internationale Zeitschrift für Literaturwissenschaft*, 42.1 (2007),166–84

BORGMAN, ERIK, 'De altijd-al vallende ster: Max Sebald over J. P. Hebel en de onmogelijkheid van het heimwee', in Ceuppens and Philipsen, op. cit. (Section 3), pp. 57–64

——, LAURENS TEN KATE and BART PHILIPSEN, 'Desperate Affirmation: On the Aporetic Performativity of *Memoria* and Testimony, in the Light of W. G. Sebald's Story "Max Ferber": With a Theological Response', *Literature and Theology*, 19.3 (2005), 200–20

BOTTON, ALAIN DE, 'Artists of the Year: W. G. Sebald', *City Pages*, December 22 1999 <http://www.citypages.com/1999–12–22/news/artists-of-the-year/6/> [accessed 22 August 2008]

BOUJU, EMMANUEL, 'Boucle épigraphique et téléologie romanesque chez Claude Simon, W. G. Sebald et Graham Swift', in *Le début et la fin du récit. Une relation critique*, ed. by Andrea Del Lungo (Paris: Garnier, 2010), pp. 93–102

BOYERS, ROBERT, 'Rubble and Ice: W. G. Sebald', in *The Dictator's Dictation: The Politics of Novels and Novelists* (New York: Columbia University Press, 2005), pp. 199–216

BRAESE, STEPHAN, 'Bombenkrieg und literarische Gegenwart: Zu W. G. Sebald und Dieter Forte', *Mittelweg 36*, 11.1 (2002), 4–24

——'Im Schatten der "gebrannten Kinder": Zur poetischen Reflexion der Vernichtungs-Verbrechen in der deutschsprachigen Literatur der neunziger Jahre', in *Chiffre 2000: Neue Paradigmen der Gegenwartsliteratur*, ed. by Corina Caduff and Ulrike Vedder (Munich: Fink, 2005), pp. 82–106 (pp. 90–97 on WGS)

Briegleb, Klaus, 'Preisrede auf W. G. Sebald anläßlich der Verleihung des Lyrikpreises "Fedor Malchow" am 17.12.1991 im Hamburger Literaturhaus', *Hamburger Ziegel*, 1 (1992), 473–83

Brockmann, Stephen, 'W. G. Sebald and German Wartime Suffering', in *Germans as Victims in the Literary Fiction of the Berlin Republic*, ed. by Stuart Taberner and Karina Berger (Rochester, NY: Camden House, 2009), pp. 15–28

Brockmeier, Jens, 'Austerlitz's Memory', *Partial Answers: Journal of Literature and the History of Ideas*, 6.2 (2008), 347–67

Brunner, Maria E., 'Gesteigerte Formen der Wahrnehmung in *Schwindel. Gefühle.*', in Fischer, op. cit. (Section 2), pp. 475–92 [on Kafka reception]

Brunse, Niels, 'Erindringens digter', *Politiken*, 8 November 2003, Buch-Beilage section, p. 7 [in Danish]

——'Den skabende melankoli', *Standart*, no. 4, (December 2007), *StandIn* section, pp. 32–33 [in Danish]

Bruzelius, Margaret, 'Adventure, Imprisonment and Melancholy: Conrad and W. G. Sebald', in *Romancing the Novel: Adventure from Scott to Sebald* (Lewisburg, PA: Bucknell University Press, 2007), 182–213

——'Adventure, Imprisonment, and Melancholy: Heart of Darkness and *Die Ringe des Saturn*', in Zisselsberger, op. cit. (Section 2), pp. 247–73

Buch, Robert, 'Schlachtgemälde und Schlachtbeschreibung bei W. G. Sebald und Claude Simon', *Weimarer Beiträge: Zeitschrift für Literaturwissenschaft, Ästhetik und Kulturwissenschaften*, 56.1 (2010), 30–46

Bülow, Ulrich von, 'Sebalds Korsika-Projekt', in von Bülow, Gfrereis, and Strittmatter, op. cit. (Section 2), pp. 211–24

Busch, Stefan, 'Anmerkungen zu W. G. Sebalds *Luftkrieg und Literatur*', *Glossen: Eine internationale zweisprachige Publikation zu Literatur, Film, und Kunst in den deutschsprachigen Ländern nach 1945*, 17 (2003), unpaginated

Busch, Walter, 'La saggistica di W. G. Sebald: Una biografia intellettuale', in Busch, op. cit. (Section 3), pp. 7–32

Byatt, A. S. 'Vanishing Acts', *BookForum: The Review for Art, Fiction, & Culture*, 13.4 (2007), 29

Calzoni, Raul, '"Nemo profeta in patria": La fortuna di W. G. Sebald in Inghilterra e negli Stati Uniti', in Busch, op. cit. (Section 3), pp. 163–79

——'W. G. Sebald: Profilo biografico, nota bibliografica e appendice di letteratura secondaria', in Busch, op. cit. (Section 3), pp. 181–95

——'Chasms of Silence: The *Luftkrieg* in German Literature from a Reunification Perspective', in *Memories and Representations of War: The Case of World War I and World War II*, ed. by Vita Fortunati and Elena Lamberti, Textxet Studies in Comparative Literature (Amsterdam: Rodopi, 2009), pp. 255–72

Cardi, Maria Virginia, 'Für eine Ethik der Ruine', in *Die zerstörte Stadt: Mediale Repräsentationen urbaner Räume von Troja bis SimCity*, ed. by Andreas Böhn and Christine Mielke (Bielefeld: transcript, 2007), pp. 83–99

Carré, Martine, 'Du soliloque au rébus ou les avatars des discours impérialistes des XIXe et XXe siècles dans les *Anneaux de Saturne* de W. G. Sebald', in *Dialogues: Études réunies par Jean-Charles Margotton en hommage au Professeur René Girard* (= *Cahiers d'Études Germaniques*, 47 (2004)), pp. 159–70

——'Appuyez sur le bouton, le texte fera le reste: Ou de la photographie et du texte dans *Die Ausgewanderten–Les émigrants* et *Schwindel. Gefühle.–Vertiges* de W. G. Sebald', in *Images, mythes et sons: Des figures de l'art dans la littérature allemande: Für einen Augen- und Ohrenmenschen: Études en l'honneur de Jean-Charles Margotton*, ed. by Fabrice Malkani et Marie-Hélène Pérennec (Lyons: Centre de recherche Langues et Cultures Européennes, 2005), pp. 107–21

——'Le Roman d'énigme et ses liens avec le roman de la mémoire dans *Austerlitz* de W. G. Sebald', *Études Germaniques*, 64 (2009), 587–602

——'Saint Georges combattant le dragon: le mythe personnel de W. G. Sebald', in *'Au nom de Goethe!' Hommage à Gerald Stieg*, ed. by Marc Lacheny and Jean-François Laplénie (Paris: L'Harmattan, 2009), pp. 257–66

CARROLL, VICTOR H., 'Reliquaries of Memory: Photographs and Other Images in the Writings of W. G. Sebald', *Spiked: The Magazine for Ideas, Literature and the Arts for Norfolk*, no. 9 (2001), 24–26

CASTRO, BRIAN, '"Through a Glass Darkly": Thomas Bernhard and W. G. Sebald', *HEAT*, 7 (2004), 71–91

CASTRO, VIRGINA, 'Volver a narrar la Shoah: imágenes de la posmemoria en W. G. Sebald', *Anuario Argentino de Germanística*, 3 (2007), 317–24 [in Spanish]

CATLING, JO, 'Gratwanderungen bis an den Rand der Natur: W. G. Sebald's Landscapes of Memory', in Görner, op. cit. (Section 2), pp. 19–50

——'W. G. Sebald: Ein "England-Deutscher"? Identität–Topographie–Intertextualität', in Heidelberger-Leonard and Tabah, op. cit. (Section 2), pp. 25–53

——'Europäische Flânerien: W. G. Sebalds intertextuelle Wanderungen zwischen Melancholie und Ironie', in *Gedächtnis und Widerstand: Festschrift für Irène Heidelberger-Leonard*, ed. by Mireille Tabah with Sylvia Weiler and Christian Poetini (Tübingen: Stauffenberg, 2009), pp. 139–54

CATREIN, SUSANNE, and CHRISTOF HAMANN, 'Warschauer Lapidarium', in Sareika, op. cit. (Section 4), pp. 129–32

CERIANI, ROBERTA, 'Il tramonto della narrazione: Oralità e trauma in *Die Ausgewanderten* di W. G. Sebald', in Busch, op. cit. (Section 3), pp. 91–107

CEUPPENS, JAN, 'Im zerschundenen Papier herumgeisternde Gesichter: Fragen der Repräsentation in W. G. Sebalds *Die Ausgewanderten*', *Germanistische Mitteilungen*, 55 (2002), 79–96 <http://www.bgdv.be/gm55/ceuppens.pdf>

——'Seeing Things: Spectres and Angels in W. G. Sebald's Prose Fiction', in Long and Whitehead, op. cit. (Section 2), pp. 190–202

——'Janua Linguarum', in Ceuppens and Philipsen, op. cit. (Section 3), pp. 21–27 [on 'La Cour de l'ancienne école'; illustration by Quint Buchholz]

——'Transcripts: An Ethics of Representation in *The Emigrants*', in Denham and McCulloh, op. cit. (Section 2), pp. 251–63

——'Realia: Konstellationen bei Benjamin, Barthes, Lacan — und Sebald', in Niehaus and Öhlschläger, op. cit. (Section 2), pp. 241–58

——'W. G. Sebald', in *Duitstalige literatuur na 1945*, ed. by Anke Gilleir and Bart Philipsen, 2 vols (Louvain: Peeters, 2006), II: *Duitsland na 1989, Oostenrijk en Zwitserland*, pp. 87–106

——'Tracing the Witness in W. G. Sebald', in Fuchs and Long, op. cit. (Section 2), pp. 59–72

——'Das belgische Grabmal: Sebalds 19. Jahrhundert', in Heidelberger-Leonard and Tabah, op. cit. (Section 2), pp. 93–109

——'Falsche Geschichten: Recherchen bei Sebald und Gstrein', in *Literatur im Krebsgang: Totenbeschwörung und Memoria in der deutschsprachigen Literatur nach 1989*, ed. by Arne de Winde and Anke Gilleir (Amsterdam: Rodopi, 2008), pp. 229–317

——'Die Unlesbarkeit des Untergangs: "Postkatastrophale" Diskurse bei Sebald und Hölderlin', *Germanistische Mitteilungen*, 67 (2008), 195–212

CHANDLER, JAMES, 'About Loss: W. G. Sebald's Romantic Art of Memory', *South Atlantic Quarterly*, 102 (2003), 235–62

CHAPLIN, ELIZABETH, 'The Convention of Captioning: W. G. Sebald and the Release of the Captive Image', *Visual Studies*, 21.1 (2006), 42–53

CHARBONNEAU, PATRICK, 'Correspondance(s): Le traducteur et son auteur', in Vogel-Klein, op. cit. (Section 3), pp. 193–210

Clingman, Stephen, 'Transfiction: W. G. Sebald', in *The Grammar of Identity: Transnational Fiction and the Nature of the Boundary* (Oxford: Oxford University Press, 2009), pp. 167–204

Cooke, Simon, 'Cultural Memory on the Move in Contemporary Travel Writing: W. G. Sebald's *The Rings of Saturn*', in *Mediation, Remediation, and the Dynamics of Cultural Memory*, ed. by Astrid Erll and others (Berlin: de Gruyter, 2009), pp. 15–30

Corkhill, Alan, 'Angles of Vision in Sebald's *Nach der Natur* and *Unerzählt*', in Fischer, op. cit. (Section 2), pp. 347–68

Corless-Smith, Martin, 'That Purple Piece of Silk between Sebald and Browne, Or How We Spin our Literary Shrouds', *Denver Quarterly*, 40.1 (2005), 27–39

Cornet, Pascal, 'Schitterende geschiedenis: Aspecten van een vernieuwde romantische historiografie', *Vlaamse Gids*, 81.2 (1997), 30-33 [in Dutch]

Corngold, Stanley, 'Sebald's Tragedy', in *Rethinking Tragedy*, ed. by Rita Felski (Baltimore: Johns Hopkins University Press, 2008), pp. 218–40

Cornille, Jean-Louis, 'Vestiges et Vertiges: Perec sous Sebald', in *Plagiat et Créativité (Treize enquêtes sur l'auteur et son autre)* (Amsterdam: Rodopi, 2008), pp. 197-217

Cosentino, Christine, '"Der Krieg, ein Kinderspiel": Romane mit Kinderperspektive im Kontext der Luftkriegsdebatte', *Neophilologus*, 91 (2007), 687–99

Cosgrove, Mary, 'The Anxiety of German Influence: Affiliation, Rejection, and Jewish Identity in W. G. Sebald's Work', in *German Memory Contests: The Quest for Identity in Literature, Film, and Discourse since 1990*, ed. by Mary Cosgrove, Anne Fuchs, and Georg Grote (Rochester, NY: Camden House: 2006), pp. 229–52

——'Melancholy Competitions: W. G. Sebald Reads Günter Grass and Wolfgang Hildesheimer', *German Life and Letters*, 59.2 (2006), 217–32

——'Sebald for our Time: The Politics of Melancholy and the Critique of Capitalism in his Work', in Fuchs and Long, op. cit. (Section 2), pp. 91–110

——'Erinnerungsethik und "Dürer-Diskurs" im Werk W. G. Sebalds, Peter Weiss, Günter Grass und Jean Améry', in Heidelberger-Leonard and Tabah, op. cit. (Section 2), pp. 153–68

——'Narrating German Suffering in the Shadow of Holocaust Victimology: W. G. Sebald, Contemporary Trauma Theory, and Dieter Forte's Air Raids Epic', in *Germans as Victims in the Literary Fiction of the Berlin Republic*, ed. by Stuart Taberner and Karina Berger (Rochester, NY: Camden House, 2009), pp. 162–76

Covindassamy, Mandana, '"Trois anneaux de Saturne: Chateaubriand, Borges et Thomas Browne." Itération des références littéraires et production du sens', in Vogel-Klein, op. cit. (Section 3), pp. 157–72

——'Littérature et intermédialité: Plurilinguisme et multimédialité dans l'œuvre de W. G. Sebald', *Études Germaniques*, 62 (2007), 251–63

——'Présences brutes de l'instantané: W. G. Sebald lecteur d'Alexander Kluge et Klaus Theweleit', *Genèses de Textes*, 4 (2011, forthcoming)

Cowan, James L., 'Sebald's Austerlitz and the Great Library: A Documentary Study', in Fischer, op. cit. (Section 2), pp. 193–212; earlier online version of this piece posted at the Davidson Sebald Symposium in 2004 <http://www.davidson.edu/academic/german/denham/cowan.htm> [accessed 22 June 2010]

——'W. G. Sebald's *Austerlitz* and the Great Library: History, Fiction, Memory, Part I', *Monatshefte*, 102.1 (2010), 51–81

——'W. G. Sebald's *Austerlitz* and the Great Library: History, Fiction, Memory, Part II', *Monatshefte*, 102.2 (2010), 192–207

Craven, Peter, 'W. G. Sebald: Anatomy of Faction', *HEAT*, 13 (1999), 212–24

Crawshaw, Robert H., 'Lieux de mémoire, monuments et monumentalisme: la portée symbolique de l'architecture et de l'archive dans l'*Austerlitz* de W. G. Sebald', in *Les monuments du passé: traces et représentations d'une histoire dans la littérature*, ed. by Fiona McIntosh-Varjabédan et Joëlle Prugnaud (Villeneuve d'Ascq: Collection Université Charles-de-Gaulle Lille 3 travaux et recherches, 2008), pp. 169–83

CROWNSHAW, RICHARD, 'Reconsidering Postmemory: Photography, the Archive, and Post-Holocaust Memory in W. G. Sebald's *Austerlitz*', in *The Photograph* (= *Mosaic: A Journal for the Interdisciplinary Study of Literature*, 37.4 (December 2004)), 215–36

—— 'German Suffering or "Narrative Fetishism"? W. G. Sebald's *Air War and Literature: Zürich Lectures*', in Patt, op. cit. (Section 2), pp. 558–83

—— 'The Limits of Transference: Theories of Memory and Photography in W. G. Sebald's *Austerlitz*', in *Mediation, Remediation, and the Dynamics of Cultural Memory*, ed. by Astrid Erll and Ann Rigney (Berlin: de Gruyter, 2009), pp. 67–90

CUNNINGHAM, DAVID, 'After Adorno: The Narrator of the Contemporary European Novel', in *Adorno and Literature*, ed. by David Cunningham and Nigel Mapp (London: Continuum, 2006), pp. 188–200

CURTIN, ADRIAN, and MAXIM D. SHRAYER, 'Netting the Butterfly Man: The Significance of Vladimir Nabokov in W. G. Sebald's *The Emigrants*', *Religion and the Arts*, 9.3–4 (2005), 258–83

DARBY, DAVID, 'Landscape and Memory: Sebald's Redemption of History', in Denham and McCulloh, op. cit. (Section 2), pp. 265–77

DAUB, ADRIAN, '"Donner à voir": The Logics of the Caption in W. G. Sebald's *Rings of Saturn* and Alexander Kluge's *Devil's Blind Spot*', in Patt, op. cit. (Section 2), pp. 306–29

DEAKIN, ROGER, 'The Fearless Digressions of W. G. Sebald', *Five Dials*, 5 (2009), 14 <http://fivedials.com/fivedials/> [accessed 3 April 2009]

DEAN, TACITA, 'W. G. Sebald', *October*, no. 106 (Fall 2003), 122–36

—— 'W. G. Sebald', in *Selected Writings 12 Oct 2002–21 Dec 2002* (Paris: Paris Musées; Göttingen: Steidl, 2003) [Book III in a set of 7]

DECKERT, RENATUS, 'Auf eine im Feuer versunkene Stadt: Heinz Czechowski und die Debatte über den Luftkrieg', *Merkur*, 58 (2004), 255–59

DE LA DURANTAYE, LELAND, 'The Facts of Fiction, or the Figure of Vladimir Nabokov in W. G. Sebald', *Comparative Literature Studies*, 45 (2008), 425–45

DENHAM, SCOTT D., 'Die englischsprachige Sebald-Rezeption', in Niehaus and Öhlschläger, op. cit. (Section 2), pp. 259–68

—— 'Foreword: The Sebald Phenomenon', in Denham and McCulloh, op. cit. (Section 2), pp. 1–6

DENNELER, IRIS, '"Das Andenken ist ja im Grunde nichts anderes als ein Zitat": Zu Formel und Gedächtnis am Beispiel von W. G. Sebalds *Die Ausgewanderten*', in *Die Formel and des Unverwechselbare: Interdisziplinare Beiträge zur Topik, Rhetorik and Individualität*, ed. by Iris Denneler (Frankfurt a.M.: Lang, 1999), pp. 160–76

—— 'Das Gedächtnis der Namen: Zu W. G. Sebalds *Die Ausgewanderten*', in *Von Namen und Dingen: Erkundungen zur Rolle des Ich in der Literatur am Beispiel von Ingeborg Bachmann, Peter Bichsel, Max Frisch, Gottfried Keller, Heinrich von Kleist, Arthur Schnitzler, Franz Wedekind, Vladimir Nabokov und W. G. Sebald* (Würzburg: Königshausen & Neumann, 2001), pp. 133–58

—— 'Dichtkunst–Bildkunst: Zu einem Aspekt der ästhetischen Verfahrensweise W. G. Sebalds am Beispiel der *Ausgewanderten*, der *Ringe des Saturn* und *Austerlitz*', *Literatur für Leser*, 27.4 (2004), 227–46

—— 'Am Anfang A: Spuren von Familienähnlichkeiten in W. G. Sebalds Werk', in Vogel-Klein, op. cit. (Section 3), pp. 139–56

DETERING, HEINRICH, 'Schnee and Asche, Flut und Feuer: Über den Elementardichter W. G. Sebald', *Neue Rundschau*, 109.2 (1998), 147–58

DICKEY, COLIN, 'On Passports: W. G. Sebald and the Menace of Travel', *Image & Narrative: Online Magazine of the Visual Narrative*, 19 (2007): *Autofiction and/in Image / Autofiction visuelle* <http://www.imageandnarrative.be/autofiction/dickey.htm> [accessed March 2008]

DIEDRICH, LISA, 'Gathering Evidence of Ghosts: W. G. Sebald's Practices of Witnessing', in Patt, op. cit. (Section 2), pp. 256–79

DILLON, BRIAN, 'Photosensitive: On W. G. Sebald's Use of Language', *Frieze*, no. 70 (October 2002) <http://www.frieze.com/issue/article/photosensitive> [accessed 5 April 2010]

——'Fotosensible: Las imagenes en la obra de W. G. Sebald', *Revista de Occidente*, nos. 266–67 (2003), 200–04 [translation of above]

DITTBERNER, HUGO, 'Der Ausführlichste oder: ein starker Hauch Patina: W. G. Sebalds Schreiben', in Arnold, op. cit. (Section 3), pp. 6–14

DOCTOROW, E. L., 'W. G. Sebald', in *Creationists: Selected Essays 1993–2006* (New York: Random House, 2006), pp. 143–49 (first publ. as 'The Modern Novel's Master Strategist', *Los Angeles Times Book Review*, 23 March 2003) <http://articles.latimes.com/2003/mar/23/books/bk-doctorow23>

DOMINI, JOHN, 'Rings, Planets, Poles, Inferno, Paradise: A Poetics for W. G. Sebald', *Southwest Review*, 90.1 (2005), 96–107

DÖRING, JÖRG and ROLF SEUBERT, 'Alfred Andersch: Behält der Literaturpfaffe doch das letzte Wort?', *Frankfurter Allgemeine Zeitung*, 19 August 2008 <http://www.faz.net/> [accessed 7 April 2010] [refers to Sebald's essay on Andersch]

——'"Entlassen aus der Wehrmacht: 12.03.1941: Grund: 'Jüdischer Mischling' — laut Verfügung": Ein unbekanntes Dokument im Kontext der Andersch-Sebald-Debatte', *LiLi*, no. 151 (2008), 171–84

DOW ADAMS, TIMOTHY, 'Photographs on the Walls of the House of Fiction', in Horstkotte and Pedri, op. cit. (Section 3), pp. 175–95

DOWNING, ERIC, 'Epilogue (Nachbildung): Bildung, Archaeology, and Photography in W. G. Sebald', in *After Images: Photography, Archaeology, and Psychoanalysis and the Tradition of Bildung* (Detroit: Wayne State University Press, 2006), pp. 271–309

DREXLER, PETER, 'Erinnerung und Photographie: Zu W. G. Sebalds *Austerlitz*', in *Ikono-Philo-Logie: Wechselspiele von Texten und Bildern*, Potsdamer Beiträge zur Kultur- und Sozialgeschichte, 2, ed. by Renate Brosch (Berlin: trafo, 2004), pp. 279–302

DUBOW, JESSICA, 'Case Interrupted: Benjamin, Sebald and the Dialectical Image', *Critical Inquiry*, 33.4 (2007), 820–36

DUNKER, AXEL, '"Phantomschmerzen": Metonymische Diskurse in W. G. Sebalds *Die Ausgewanderten*', in *Flucht und Vertreibung in der deutschen Literatur*, ed. by Sascha Feuchert (Frankfurt a.M.: Lang, 2001), pp. 299–316

——'Metonymische Diskurse: W. G. Sebalds "Max Aurach"', in *Die anwesende Abwesenheit: Literatur im Schatten von Auschwitz* (Munich: Fink, 2003), pp. 111–39

——'Das fiktionale Gedächtnis der Dinge: Zu W. G. Sebalds *Austerlitz*', in *Literatur ohne Kompromisse: Ein Buch für Jörg Drews*, ed. by Sabine Kyora, Axel Dunker, and Dirk Sangmeister (Bielefeld: Aisthesis, 2005), pp. 455–68

DUNTHORNE, JOE, 'Austerlitz', *Five Dials*, 5 (2009), 7 <http://fivedials.com/fivedials> [accessed 3 April 2009]

DURZAK, MANFRED, 'Sebald, der unduldsame Kritiker: Zu seinen literarischen Polemiken gegen Sternheim und Andersch', in Fischer, op. cit. (Section 2), pp. 435–46

DUTTLINGER, CAROLIN, 'Traumatic Photographs: Remembrance and the Technical Media in W. G. Sebald's *Austerlitz*', in Long and Whitehead, op. cit. (Section 2), pp. 190–202

——'A Lineage of Destruction? Rethinking Photography in *Luftkrieg und Literatur*', in Fuchs and Long, op. cit. (Section 2), pp. 163–77

——'W. G. Sebald: The Pleasure and Pain of Beauty', *German Life and Letters*, 62.2 (2009), 327–42

——'"A Wrong Turn of the Wheel": Sebald's Journeys of (In)Attention', in Zisselsberger, op. cit. (Section 2), pp. 92–120

——'Sebald, *Austerlitz*', in *Landmarks in the German Novel*, II, ed. by Peter Hutchinson and Michael Minden, British and Irish Studies in German Language and Literature, 47 (Oxford: Lang, 2010), pp. 111–27

DYER, GEOFF, 'Sebald, Bernhard, and Bombing', *Brick*, no. 76 (Winter 2005), 92–96; repr. in *Working the Room: Essays* (Edinburgh: Canongate, 2010), pp. 231–38 [an earlier version of this piece appeared in *Pretext*, no. 9 (2004), 91–97]

ECKART, GABRIELE, 'Against "Cartesian Rigidity": W. G. Sebald's Reception of Borges', in Fischer, op. cit. (Section 2), pp. 509–22

ECKER, GISELA, '"Heimat" oder die Grenzen der Bastelei', in Niehaus and Öhlschläger, op. cit. (Section 2), pp. 77–88

ELCOTT, NOAM M., 'Tattered Snapshots and Castaway Tongues: An Essay at Layout and Translation with W. G. Sebald', in Anderson, op. cit. (Section 3), pp. 203–23

ELDRIDGE, RICHARD, 'Literature as Material Figuration: Benjamin, Sebald, and Human Life in Time', in *Visions of Value and Truth: Understanding Philosophy and Literature*, ed. by Floora Ruokonen and Laura Werner, *Acta Philosophica Fennica*, 79 (2006), 13–29

ELM, THEO, 'Kult der Langsamkeit: Peter Handke, Hermann Lenz, W. G. Sebald, Sten Nadolny', in *Kultbücher*, ed. by Rudolf Freiburg (Würzburg: Königshausen & Neumann, 2004), pp. 117–26

ELSAGHE, YAHYA, 'Das Kreuzworträtsel der Penelope: Zu W. G. Sebalds *Austerlitz*', in Lützeler and Schindler, op. cit. (Section 3), pp. 164–84

——'W. G. Sebalds *Austerlitz* als Beitrag zum deutsch-jüdischen Kulturdialog', in *Akten des XI. Internationalen Germanistenkongresses, Paris 2005*, Jahrbuch für Internationale Germanistik, series A: Kongressberichte, 88, ed. by Jean-Marie Valentin with Jean-François Candoni (Berne: Lang, 2007), pp. 245–50

——'Die unvollendete Geschichte: W. G. Sebalds Ecriture Cruciverbiste im Roman *Austerlitz*', *Neue Zürcher Zeitung*, 10–11 March 2007, p. 29

ENZENSBERGER, HANS MAGNUS (in conversation with David Constantine), 'The Peregrinations of Poetry (Sebald Lecture 2006)', transcribed by Yasmin Keyani, *In Other Words: The Journal for Literary Translators*, no. 29 (2007), 39–52

——'Publishing Sebald', *BookForum: The Review for Art, Fiction, & Culture*, 13.4 (2007), 30

——'Het publiceren van de werken van Sebald', trans. by Raymond Noë, in *W. G. Sebald: Een hommage aan een unieke auteur* [no editor] (Amsterdam: De Bezige Bij, 2008), pp. 21–23 [Dutch translation of above]

ESHEL, AMIR, 'Against the Power of Time: The Poetics of Suspension in W. G. Sebald's *Austerlitz*', *New German Critique*, 88.4 (2003), 71–96

FAMBRINI, ALESSANDRO, '"Ein Gefühl der Beklemmung": W. G. Sebald und die gescheiterte Utopie', in *Gedächtnis und Identität: Die deutsche Literatur nach der Vereinigung*, ed. by Fabrizio Cambi (Würzburg: Königshausen & Neumann, 2008), pp. 243–53

FEEHILY, CLAIRE, '"The Surest Engagement with Memory Lies in its Perpetual Irresolution": The Work of W. G. Sebald as Counter-Monument', in Fischer, op. cit. (Section 2), pp. 177–92

FEIEREISEN, FLORENCE and DANIEL POPE, 'True Fictions and Fictional Truths: The Enigmatic in Sebald's Use of Images in *The Emigrants*', in Patt, op. cit. (Section 2), pp. 162–87

FINCH, HELEN, '"Die irdische Erfüllung": Peter Handke's Poetic Landscapes and W. G. Sebald's Metaphysics of History', in Fuchs and Long, op. cit. (Section 2), pp. 179–97

FINKE, SUSANNE, 'W. G. Sebald: Der fünfte Ausgewanderte', in Loquai, *Far From Home*, op. cit. (Section 2), pp. 22–34; repr. in Loquai, *W. G. Sebald*, op. cit. (Section 2), pp. 214–27

FINKELDE, DOMINIK, 'Wunderkammer und Apokalypse: Zu W. G. Sebald's Poetik des Sammelns zwischen Barock und Moderne', *German Life and Letters*, 60.4 (2007), 554–68

FISCHER, GERHARD, 'W. G. Sebald's Expatriate Experience and his Literary Beginnings' (Introduction), in Fischer, op. cit. (Section 2), pp. 15–26

——'Schreiben *ex patria*: W. G. Sebald und die Konstruktion einer literarischen Identität', in Fischer, op. cit. (Section 2), pp. 27–44

——'Writing *ex patria*: W. G. Sebald and the Construction of a Literary Identity', in *Literature for Europe?*, ed. by Theo D'Haen and Iannis Goerlandt, Textxet Studies in Comparative Literature (Amsterdam: Rodopi, 2009), pp. 259–78 [translation of above]

——'W. G. Sebald (1944–2001)', in *Praktizierte Intermedialität: Deutsch-französische Porträts von Schiller bis Goscinny/Uderzo*, ed. by Fernand Hörner, Harald Neumeyer, and Bernd Stiegler (Bielefeld: transcript, 2010), pp. 265–89

Forster, Kurt W., 'Bausteine 1: Bilder geistern durch Sebalds Erzählungen, Geister bewohnen ihre Zeilen', in von Bülow, Gfrereis, and Strittmatter, op. cit. (Section 2), pp. 87–99

Franke, Konrad, 'Laudatio auf den Preisträger W. G. Sebald', in *Verleihung des Bremer Literaturpreises 2002: W. G. Sebald, Juli Zeh: Laudationes und Reden* (Bremen: Rudolf-Alexander-Schroder-Stiftung, 2002), pp. 13–18

Franklin, Ruth, 'Sebald's Amateurs', in Denham and McCulloh, op. cit. (Section 2), pp. 127–38

——'Rings of Smoke', *New Republic*, 23 September 2002, pp. 32–39; repr. in *The Emergence of Memory*, ed. by Schwartz, pp. 119–43 (cf. Reviews of *After Nature* and *On the Natural History of Destruction*)

Frey, Mattias, 'Theorizing Cinema in Sebald and Sebald with Cinema', in Patt, op. cit. (Section 2), pp. 226–41

Friedrichsmeyer, Sara, 'Sebald's Elective and Other Affinities', in Denham and McCulloh, op. cit. (Section 2), pp. 77–89

——'Sebalds Heringe und Seidenwürmer', trans. by Erhard Friedrichsmeyer, in Martin and Wintermeyer, op. cit. (Section 2), pp. 11–26

Fritzsche, Peter, 'The Archive', *History & Memory*, 17.1–2 (2005), 15–44

——'W. G. Sebald's Twentieth-Century Histories', in Denham and McCulloh, op. cit. (Section 2), pp. 291–99

Fuchs, Anne, '"Phantomspuren": Zu W. G. Sebalds Poetik Der Erinnerung in Austerlitz', *German Life and Letters*, 56 (2003), 281–98

——'Zur Ästhetik der Vernetzung in W. G. Sebalds Austerlitz', in Hartmut Böhme, Jürgen Barkhoff, and Jeanne Riou, eds, *Netzwerke: Ästhetiken und Techniken der Vernetzung 1800–1900–2000* (Cologne: Böhlau, 2004), pp. 261–78

——'W. G. Sebald's Painters: The Function of Fine Art in W. G. Sebald's Prose Works', *Modern Language Review*, 101.1 (2006), 167–83

——'A Heimat in Ruins and the Ruins as Heimat: W. G. Sebald's *Luftkrieg und Literatur*', in *German Memory Contests: The Quest for Identity in Literature, Film, and Discourse since 1990*, ed. by Mary Cosgrove, Anne Fuchs, and Georg Grote (Rochester, NY: Camden House, 2006), pp. 287–302

——'"Ein auffallend geschichtsblindes und traditionsloses Volk": Heimatdiskurs und Ruinenästhetik in W. G. Sebalds Prosa', in Niehaus and Öhlschläger, op. cit. (Section 2), pp. 89–110

——'Between Pathography and Ethnography: Sebald as a Diagnostic Reader', in Zisselsberger, op. cit. (Section 3), pp. 109–24

——'"Ein Hauptkapitel der Geschichte der Unterwerfung": Representations of Nature in W. G. Sebald's *Die Ringe des Saturn*', in Fuchs and Long, op. cit. (Section 2), pp. 121–38

——'Von Orten und Nicht-Orten: Fremderfahrung und dunkler Tourismus in Sebalds Prosa', in Heidelberger-Leonard and Tabah, op. cit. (Section 2), pp. 55–71

Fulda, Daniel, '"Selective History": Why and How "History" Depends on Readerly Narrativization, and the *Wehrmacht* Exhibition as an Example', in *Narratology Beyond Literary Criticism: Mediality, Disciplinarity*, ed. by Jan Christoph Meister; in collaboration with Tom Kindt and Wilhelm Schernus (Berlin: Walter de Gruyter, 2005), pp. 173–94

——'Wem gehört der Holocaust? Zur Aneignung der Judenvernichtung im kollektiven Gedächtnis des "Tätervolkes" und in drei autobiographischen Erzählungen der 1990er

Jahre', in *Interkulturalität und Nationalkultur in der deutschsprachigen Literatur*, ed. by Maja Razbojnikova-Frateva (Dresden: Thelem, 2006), pp. 221–47

FURLANI, ANDRE, 'Davenport and Sebald's Arts of Excursus', *Literary Imagination: The Review of the Association of Literary Scholars and Critics*, 8 (2006), 319–30

FURST, LILIAN R., 'Realism, Photography, and Degrees of Uncertainty', in Denham and McCulloh, op. cit. (Section 2), pp. 219–29

——'Memory's Fragile Power in Kazuo Ishiguro's *Remains of the Day* and W. G. Sebald's "Max Ferber"', *Contemporary Literature*, 48.4 (2007), 530–53

GABURRO, MONICA, 'Immagini proiettate nel solco malinconico de *Gli anelli di Saturno*', in Busch, op. cit. (Section 3), pp. 109–19

GALBRAITH, IAIN, 'Michael Hamburger's "Chandos Moment"? Reflections on the "Niemandsland-Variationen"', in *From Charlottenburg to Middleton: Michael Hamburger (1924–2007): Poet, Translator, Critic*, ed. by Joyce Crick, Martin Liebscher, and Martin Swales (Munich: iudicium, 2010), pp. 70–88 [includes reference to Hamburger's friendship with WGS]

GARLOFF, KATJA, 'The Emigrant as Witness: W. G. Sebald's *Die Ausgewanderten*', *German Quarterly*, 77.1 (2004), 76–93

——'The Task of the Narrator: Moments of Symbolic Investiture in W. G. Sebald's *Austerlitz*', in Denham and McCulloh, op. cit. (Section 2), pp. 157–69

——'Kafka's Crypt: W. G. Sebald and the Melancholy of Modern German Jewish Culture', *Germanic Review*, 82.2 (2007), 123–40

GASSELEDER, KLAUS, 'Erkundungen zum Prätext der Luisa-Lanzberg-Geschichte aus W. G. Sebalds *Die Ausgewanderten*: Ein Bericht', in Atze and Loquai, op. cit. (Section 2), pp. 157–75

GFREREIS, HEIKE, 'Sebald aus dem Nachlass gelesen', in von Bülow, Gfrereis, and Strittmatter, op. cit. (Section 2), pp. 227–34

——and ELLEN STRITTMATTER, 'Introduction', in von Bülow, Gfrereis, and Strittmatter, op. cit. (Section 2), pp. 7–9

GIL, ISABEL CAPELOA, '"La destruction fut ma Béatrice ...": W. G. Sebalds Poetik der Zerstörung als konstruktives Gedächtnis', in *Kulturelles Gedächtnis und interkulturelle Rezeption im europäischen Kontext*, ed. by Eva Dewes and Sandra Duhem (Berlin: Akademie Verlag, 2008), pp. 311–32

GILLETT, ROBERT, 'Terrorangriff und Terminologie: W. G. Sebald–Volker Hage–Hubert Fichte', *Kultur & Gespenster*, 1 (2006), 84–97

GNAM, ANDREA, '"Ich bin auch Mediziner, und ich bin es nicht im Nebenberuf"', *Neue Zürcher Zeitung*, 14–15 October 2006, Literatur und Kunst section, p. 31 [on WGS and Alfred Döblin]

——'Fotografie und Film in W. G. Sebalds Erzählung *Ambros Adelwarth* und seinem Roman *Austerlitz*', in Martin and Wintermeyer, op. cit. (Section 2), pp. 27–47

——'Erinnern und Vergessen: Alfred Döblin und W. G. Sebald', *Jahrbuch zur Kultur und Literatur der Weimarer Republik*, 11: *2007*, ed. by Sabina Becker with Eckhard Faul and Reiner Marx (Munich: Text + Kritik, 2008), pp. 131–39

GÓMEZ GARCÍA, CARMEN, 'La Canonización de W. G. Sebald en España', *Cuadernos Hispanoamericanos*, nos. 661–62 (July–August 2005), 139–47

——'"Ruinen der Gerechtigkeit": Zur Rezeption W. G. Sebalds in Spanien', in Atze and Loquai, op. cit. (Section 2), pp. 122–32

——'Sebald übersetzen, eine Stilfrage', *Komparatistik-Online: Tendenzen der europäischen Gegenwartsliteratur und -kultur*, 1 (2006) <http://komparatistik-online.de/> [accessed 1 August 2008]

GÖRNER, RÜDIGER, 'After Words: On W. G. Sebald's Poetry', in Görner, op. cit. (Section 2), pp. 75–80

——'Begehungen in drei Satzen', in Krüger, op. cit. (Section 3), 31–34

——'Im Allgäu, Grafschaft Norfolk: Über W. G. Sebald in England', in Arnold, op. cit. (Section 3), pp. 23–29

——'"Leere Koffer und gedächtnislose Gegenwart": W. G. Sebalds Topographieren im Korsika-Projekt', in Heidelberger-Leonard and Tabah, op. cit. (Section 2), pp. 111–23

GOUDINOUX, VÉRONIQUE, 'Tacita Dean, Thomas Sipp. Une proximité nommée Sebald', in L'Art qui manifeste, ed. by Anne Larue (Paris: L'Harmattan, 2008), pp. 113-19

GRADL, KARLHEINZ, 'Sehnsucht nach vollkommener Stille: W. G. Sebald und die Wiederentdeckung des romantischen Heimatbegriffs', Scheidewege, 35 (2005–06), 268–74

GRAY, RICHARD T., 'Sebald's Segues: Performing Narrative Contingency in The Rings of Saturn', Germanic Review, 84.1 (2009), 26–58

——'From Grids to Vanishing Points: Sebald's Critique of Visual-Representational Orders in Die Ringe des Saturn', German Studies Review, 32.3 (2009), 495–526

——'W. G. Sebald's Pre-Texts: "Dr. Henry Selwyn" and its Textual Predecessor', Seminar: A Journal of Germanic Studies, 45.4 (2009), 387–406

——'Writing at the Roche Limit: Order and Entropy in W. G. Sebald's Die Ringe des Saturn', German Quarterly, 83.1 (2010), 38–57

GREGORY-GUIDER, CHRISTOPHER C., 'The "Sixth Emigrant"? Traveling Places in the Works of W. G. Sebald', Contemporary Literature, 46.3 (2005), 422–49

——'Memorial Sights / Sites: Sebald, Photography, and the Art of Autobiogeography in The Emigrants', in Patt, op. cit. (Section 2), pp. 516–41

GRIFFITHS, CHRIS, 'W. G. Sebald', Book and Magazine Collector, no. 303 (January 2009), 92–101

GROES, BAS, 'Lost heimwee: Zoeken naar Sebald in The Rings of Saturn', in Ceuppens and Philipsen, op. cit. (Section 3), pp. 46–56

GUNTHER, STEFAN, 'The Holocaust as the Still Point of the World in W. G. Sebald's The Emigrants', in Denham and McCulloh, op. cit. (Section 2), pp. 279–90

HAAGENSEN, OLAF, 'W. G. Sebalds liv og verk: en skisse for nye lesere', in Vinger, op. cit. (Section 3), pp. 56–61

HAGE, VOLKER, 'Überblick and Debatte', in Deutsche Literatur 1998: Jahresüberblick, ed. by Volker Hage, Rainer Moritz and Hubert Winkels (Stuttgart: Reclam, 1999), pp. 249–90 [on Luftkrieg and Literatur]

HAHN, HANS JOACHIM, 'Leerstellen in der deutschen Gedenkkultur. Die Streitschriften von W. G. Sebald and Klaus Briegleb', German Life and Letters, 57.4 (2004), 357–71

HALL, KATHARINA, 'Jewish Memory in Exile: The Relation of W. G. Sebald's Die Ausgewanderten to the Tradition of the Yizkor Books', in Jews in German Literature since 1945: German-Jewish Literature?, ed. by Pól Ó Dochartaigh, German Monitor, 53 (Amsterdam: Rodopi, 2000), pp. 153–64

HAMBURGER, MICHAEL, 'Translator's Note on After Nature (1999)', Irish Pages, 1.1 (Spring 2002) (Inaugural Issue: Belfast in Europe), 108–09

——'Translator's Note on "Marienbad Elegy"', Irish Pages, 1.2 (Autumn-Winter 2002-03), 130–32

——'Translator's Note', in W. G. Sebald, Unrecounted, trans. by Michael Hamburger (London: Hamish Hamilton, 2004), pp. 1–9

——'W. G. Sebald als Dichter: Drei Annäherungen', in Pro Domo: Selbstauskünfte, Rückblicke und andere Prosa, ed. by Iain Galbraith (Vienna: Folio, 2007), pp. 109–23 [contains sections on Nach der Natur, 'Marienbader Elegie', and Unerzählt]

HARRIS, STEFANIE, 'The Return of the Dead: Memory and Photography in W. G. Sebald's Die Ausgewanderten', German Quarterly, 74.4 (2000–01), 379–91

HAWKINS, GAY, 'History in Things: Sebald and Benjamin on Transience and Detritus', in Fischer, op. cit. (Section 2), pp. 161–76

HEIDELBERGER-LEONARD, IRÈNE, 'Melancholie als Widerstand: Laudatio', in Verleihung *des Heine-Preises der Landeshauptstadt Düsseldorf an W. G. Sebald* (Düsseldorf: Kulturamt der Landeshauptstadt Düsseldorf, 2000), pp. 5–16; repr. in Krüger, op. cit. (Section 3), 122–30

——'Jean Amérys Werk: Urtext zu W. G. Sebalds "Austerlitz"?', in Vogel-Klein, op. cit. (Section 3), pp. 117–28

——'Zwischen Aneignung und Restitution: *Die Beschreibung des Unglücks* von W. G. Sebald: Versuch einer Annäherung', in Heidelberger-Leonard and Tabah, op. cit. (Section 2), pp. 9–23

HEIDT, TODD, 'Image and Text, Fact and Fiction: Narrating W. G. Sebald's *The Emigrants* in the First Person, *Image [&] Narrative*, 22 (2008) <http://www.imageandnarrative.be/autofiction2/heidt.html> [accessed 28 February 2010]

HELL, JULIA, 'The Angel's Enigmatic Eyes, or The Gothic Beauty of Catastrophic History in W. G. Sebald's *Air War and Literature*', *Criticism*, 46 (2004), 361–92

——'Eyes Wide Shut: German Post-Holocaust Authorship', *New German Critique*, 88 (2003), 9–36

——AND JOHANNES VON MOLTKE, 'Unification Effects: Imaginary Landscapes of the Berlin Republic', *Germanic Review*, 80 (2005), 74–95

HELLWEG, PATRICIA, 'Lokaltermin Wertach: Noch ein eigenartiger Novembergast', in Köpf, op. cit. (Section 2), pp. 21–31

HERZOG, DAGMAR, 'The German War', in *The Cambridge Companion to the Literature of World War II*, ed. by Marina Mackay (Cambridge: Cambridge University Press, 2009), pp. 98–110

HIRSCH, MARIANNE, 'The Generation of Postmemory', in Horstkotte and Pedri, op. cit. (Section 3), pp. 103–28

HITCHENS, CHRISTOPHER, 'Die Deutschen und der Krieg: W. G. Sebald schrieb über die Qual, zu einem Volk zu gehören, das, in Thomas Manns Worten, "sich nicht sehen lassen kann"', *Neue Rundschau*, 114.1 (2003), 116–26

HOFFMANN, TORSTEN, 'Das Interview als Kunstwerk: Plädoyer für die Analyse von Schriftstellerinterviews am Beispiel W. G. Sebalds', *Weimarer Beiträge: Zeitschrift für Literaturwissenschaft, Ästhetik und Kulturwissenschaften*, 55 (2009), 276–92

——AND UWE ROSE, '"Quasi jenseits der Zeit": Zur Poetik der Fotografie bei W. G. Sebald', *Zeitschrift für deutsche Philologie*, 125 (2006), 580–608

HOLDENRIED, MICHAELA, 'Zeugen–Spuren–Erinnerung: Zum intertextuellen Resonanzraum von Grenzerfahrungen in der Literatur jüdischer Überlebender, Jean Améry und W. G. Sebald', in *Grenzen der Fiktionalität und der Erinnerung*, ed. by Christoph Parry and Edgar Platen, Autobiographisches Schreiben in der deutschsprachigen Gegenwartsliteratur, 2 (Munich: iudicium, 2007), pp. 74–85

HÖLLER, HANS, 'Der "Widerstand der Ästhetik" und Die Fabel von der Rettung der Kunstwerke', in *Alfred Andersch: Perspektiven zu Leben and Werk*, ed. by Irène Heidelberger-Leonard (Opladen: Westdeutscher Verlag, 1994), pp. 142–51

HOMANN, ANDREA, 'Darstellungsmöglichkeiten von Geschichte: *Austerlitz* von W. G. Sebald und *Die Hochzeit von Auschwitz* von Erich Hackl', *Estudios Filológicos Alemanes*, 8 (2005), 205–12

HOORN, TANJA VAN, 'Erinnerungs-Poetiken der Gegenwart: Christoph Ransmayr, Reinhard Jirgl, W. G. Sebald', *Der Deutschunterricht: Beiträge zu seiner Praxis und wissenschaftlichen Grundlegung*, 57.6 (2005), 54–62

——'Auch eine Dialektik der Aufklärung: Wie W. G. Sebald Georg Wilhelm Steller zwischen Kabbala und magischer Medizin verortet (*Nach der Natur*)', *Zeitschrift für Germanistik*, 19.1 (2009), 108–20

HORSTKOTTE, SILKE, 'Pictorial and Verbal Discourse in W. G. Sebald's *The Emigrants*', *Iowa Journal of Cultural Studies*, 2 (2002), 33–50; available online <http://www.uiowa.edu/~ijcs/mediation/horstkotte.htm> [accessed 29 March 2010]

———'Fantastic Gaps: Photography Inserted into Narrative in W. G. Sebald's *Austerlitz*', in *Science, Technology and the German Cultural Imagination*, ed. by Christian Emden and David Midgley (Oxford: Lang, 2005), pp. 269–86

———'The Double Dynamics of Focalization in W. G. Sebald's *The Rings of Saturn*', in *Narratology Beyond Literary Criticism: Mediality, Disciplinarity*, ed. by Jan-Christoph Meister (Berlin: de Gruyter, 2005), pp. 25–44

———'Transgenerationelle Blicke: Fotografie als Medium von Gedächtnisradierung in *Die Ausgewanderten*, in Vogel-Klein, op. cit. (Section 3), pp. 47–64

———'Visual Memory and Ekphrasis in W. G. Sebald's *The Rings of Saturn*', *English Language Notes*, 44.2 (2006), 117–30

———'Photo-Text Topographies: Photography and the Representation of Space in W. G. Sebald and Monika Maron', in Horstkotte and Pedri, op. cit. (Section 3), pp. 49–78

———'Spectral Topographies: Locating Auschwitz in W. G. Sebald's Austerlitz and Stephan Wackwitz's An Invisible Country', in *Trajectories of Memory: Intergenerational Representations of the Holocaust in History and the Arts*, ed. by Christina Guenther and Beth Griech-Polelle (Newcastle upon Tyne: Cambridge Scholars Press, 2008), pp. 225–48

HUI, BARBARA, 'Mapping Historical Networks in *Die Ringe des Saturn*', in Zisselsberger, op. cit. (Section 2), pp. 277–98

HÜNSCHE, CHRISTINA, '"Die unbestreitbaren Vorteile einer fiktiven Vergangenheit": W. G. Sebald's *Die Ringe des Saturn* 1995 zwischen Geschichten erzählen und Geschichte schreiben', in Sareika, op. cit. (Section 4), pp. 35–54

HUTCHINSON, BEN, '"Egg boxes stacked in a crate": Narrative Status and its Implications', in Denham and McCulloh, op. cit. (Section 2), pp. 171–82

———'Die Leichtigkeit der Schwermut: W. G. Sebalds "Kunst der Levitation"', *Jahrbuch der Deutschen Schillergesellschaft*, 50 (2006), 457–77

———'"Umgekehrt wird man leicht selbst zum Verfolgten": The Structure of the Doublebind in W. G. Sebald', *Revista de Filología Alemana*, 14 (2006), 101–11

———'"Der Erzähler als Schutzengel": W. G. Sebald's Reading of Giorgio Bassani', in Lützeler and Schindler, op. cit. (Section 3), pp. 69–90

———'Bausteine 2: Sprachen', in von Bülow, Gfrereis, and Strittmatter, op. cit. (Section 2), pp. 115–27

———'"Ein Penelopewerk des Vergessens"? W. G. Sebald's Nietzschean Poetics of Forgetting', *Forum for Modern Language Studies*, 45 (2009), 325–36

———'"Seemann" oder "Ackermann"? Einige Überlegungen zu Sebalds Lektüre von Walter Benjamins Essay "Der Erzähler"', in Fischer, op. cit. (Section 2), pp. 277–96

HUYSSEN, ANDREAS, 'Air War Legacies: From Dresden to Baghdad', *New German Critique*, 90 (2003), 163–76

———'On Rewritings and New Beginnings: W. G. Sebald and the Literature about the "Luftkrieg"', *LiLi*, no. 31 (2001), 72–90

———'Rewritings and New Beginnings: W. G. Sebald and the Literature on the Air War', in *Present Pasts: Urban Palimpsests and the Politics of Memory* (Stanford, CA: Stanford University Press, 2003), pp. 138–57

ILSEMANN, MARK, 'Going Astray: Melancholy, Natural History, and the Image of Exile in W. G. Sebald's *Austerlitz*', in Denham and McCulloh, op. cit. (Section 2), pp. 301–14

ISENSCHMID, ANDREAS, 'Der Sebald-Satz', *Neue Zürcher Zeitung* (Internationale Ausgabe), 179, 5 August 1994, p. 30; *Neue Zürcher Zeitung* (Schweizer Ausgabe), 6–7 August 1994, Literatur und Kunst section, p. 55; repr. in Loquai, *W. G. Sebald*, op. cit. (Section 2), pp. 247–49

———'W. G. Sebald', in *Der Berliner Literaturpreis 1994*, ed. by Katharina Giebel, Ute Bredemeyer and Christa Müller on behalf of the Stiftung Preussische Seehandlung (Berlin: Volk & Welt, 1996), pp. 71–95 [cf. Primary bibliography E.B. 22]

ITKIN, ALAN, '"Eine Art Eingang zur Unterwelt": Katabasis in Austerlitz', in Zisselsberger, op. cit. (Section 2), pp. 161–85

JACKMAN, GRAHAM, 'Introduction', *German Life and Letters*, 57.4 (2004), 343–53

——'Gebranntes Kind? W. G. Sebald's Metaphysik der Geschichte', *German Life and Letters*, 57 (2004), 456–71

JACKSON, MARK, 'The Ethical Space of Historiography', *Journal of Historical Sociology*, 14 (2001), 467–80

JACOBS, CAROL, 'What Does it Mean to Count? W. G. Sebald's *The Emigrants*', *Modern Language Notes*, 119 (2004), 905–29

——'Was heißt Zählen? W. G. Sebalds *Die Ausgewanderten*', trans. by Peter Rehberg, in *Literatur als Philosophie — Philosophie als Literatur*, ed. by Eva Horn, Bettina Menke and Christoph Menke (Munich: Fink, 2006), pp. 173–91; repr. in Martin and Wintermeyer, op. cit. (Section 2), pp. 49–67 [translation of above]

JACOBS, KAREN, 'Optical Miniatures in Text and Image: Detail and Totality in Nabokov's *Speak Memory* and Sebald's *The Emigrants*', *Etudes Britanniques Contemporaines: Revue de la Société d'Etudes Anglaises Contemporaines*, 31 (2006), 105–15

JAMES, CLIVE, 'Canetti, Man of Mystery', in *The Revolt of the Pendulum: Essays 2005–2008* (London: Picador, 2010), pp. 49–55 [refers briefly to *Austerlitz*]; <http://www.clivejames.com/articles/clive/elias-canetti> [accessed 3 February 2011]

JARAY, TESS, 'A Mystery and a Confession', *Irish Pages: A Journal of Contemporary Writing*, 1.2 (2002–03), 137–39

JEFFERSON, MARGO, 'Writing in the Shadows', *The New York Times on the Web*, 18 March 2001 <http://www.nytimes.com/2001/03/18/books/on-writers-and-writing-writing-in-the-shadows.html>

JEUTTER, RALF, 'Am Rande der Finsternis: The Jewish Experience in the Context of W. G. Sebald's Poetics', in *Jews in German Literature since 1945: German-Jewish Literature?*, ed. by Pól Ó Dochartaigh, German Monitor, 53 (Amsterdam: Rodopi, 2000), pp. 165–79

JEZIORKOWSKI, KLAUS, 'Wiederholte Beschriftung: Beobachtungen zu Text- und Bildnis-Strukturen bei W. G. Sebald und zum Schreiben in mehreren Etagen', in *Palimpseste: Zur Erinnerung an Norbert Altenhofer*, ed. by Joachim Jacob and Pascal Nicklas (Heidelberg: Winter, 2004), pp. 221–32

——'Les phénomènes prismatiques: Quelques remarques sur l'optique de la conscience chez W. G. Sebald', in *Ecrire après Auschwitz: Mémoires croisées France–Allemagne*, ed. by Karsten Garscha, Bruno Gelas, and Jean-Pierre Martin (Lyons: Presses Universitaires de Lyon, 2006), pp. 221–34

——'Peripherie als Mitte: Zur Ästhetik von Zivilität: W. G. Sebald und sein Roman *Austerlitz*', in Martin and Wintermeyer, op. cit. (Section 2), pp. 69–80

JOCH, MARKUS, 'Streitkultur Germanistik: Die Andersch-Sebald-Debatte als Beispiel', in *Germanistik in und für Europa: Faszination–Wissen: Texte des Münchener Germanistentages 2004*, ed. by Konrad Ehlich (Bielefeld: Aisthesis, 2006), pp. 263–75

JOHNSON, AMY, 'Anatomy of an Exhibition: W. G. Sebald's *Rings of Saturn*', in *Curious Collectors, Collected Curiosities: An Interdisciplinary Study*, ed. by Janelle A. Schwartz and Nhora Lucia Serrano (Newcastle-on-Tyne: Cambridge Scholars Press, 2010), pp. 102–20

JORDHEIM, HELGE, 'Stil og historienmetafysikk: Sebald og tysk litteratur', in Vinger, op. cit. (Section 3), pp. 72–75

JUERS, EVELYN, 'W', *HEAT*, 3 (2002), 111–18

JUHL, EVA, 'Die Wahrheit über das Unglück: Zu W. G. Sebald, *Die Ausgewanderten*', in *Reisen im Diskurs: Modelle der literarischen Fremderfahrung von den Pilgerberichten bis zur Postmoderne: Tagungsakten des internationalen Symposions zur Reiseliteratur University College Dublin vom 10.–12. März 1994*, ed. by Anne Fuchs and Theo Harden with Eva Juhl (Heidelberg: Winter, 1995), pp. 640–59

Jurgensen, Manfred, 'Creative Reflection: W. G. Sebald's Critical Essays and Literary Fiction', in Fischer, op. cit. (Section 2), pp. 413–34

Kahn, Robert, '"Ce labyrinthe, une coupe transversale de mon cerveau": Fiction et réalité dans *Les Anneaux de Saturne* de W. G. Sebald', in *Fictions biographiques XIXe–XXIe siècles*, ed. by Anne-Marie Monluçon, Agathe Salha, and Brigitte Ferrato-Combe (= Cribles: Théories de la Littérature) (Toulouse: Presses Universitaires du Mirail, 2007), pp. 317–27

—— 'Les Lambeaux de la mémoire: *Dora Bruder* de Patrick Modiano et *Austerlitz* de W. G. Sebald', in *Culture et mémoire: Représentations contemporaines de la mémoire dans les espaces mémoriels, les arts du visuel, la littérature et le théâtre*, ed. by Carola Hähnel-Mesnard, Marie Liénard-Yeterian, and Cristina Marinas (Paris: École Polytechnique, 2008), pp. 401–08

Kasper, Judith, 'Intertextualitäten als Gedächtniskonstellationen im Zeichen der Vernichtung: Überlegungen zu W. G. Sebalds *Die Ausgewanderten*', in *Wende des Erinnerns? Geschichtskonstruktionen in der deutschen Literatur nach 1989*, ed. by Barbara Beßlich, Katharina Graetz and Olaf Hildebrand (Berlin: Schmidt, 2006), pp. 87–98

—— '"Il fuoco delle immagini"', in *La cenere delle immagini: spazi della memoria, luoghi della perdita*, ed. by Riccardo Panattoni (Genoa: Marietti 1820, 2006), pp. 58–103

Kastura, Thomas, 'Geheimnisvolle Fähigkeit zur Transmigration: W. G. Sebalds interkulturelle Wallfahrten in die Leere', *Arcadia: Internationale Zeitschrift für Literaturwissenschaft*, 31.1–2 (1996), 197–216

Kaufmann, David, 'Angels Visit the Scene of Disgrace: Melancholy and Trauma from Sebald to Benjamin and Back', *Cultural Critique*, 70.2 (2008), 94–119

Kellner, Hans, 'Emigrant Narratives and their Devices in Spiegelman, Foer, and Sebald', in *Trajectories of Memory: Intergenerational Representations of the Holocaust in History and the Arts*, ed. by Christina Guenther and Beth Griech-Polelle (Newcastle upon Tyne: Cambridge Scholars Press, 2008), pp. 175–90

Kempinski, Avi, 'Quel roman! Sebald, Barthes, and the Pursuit of the Mother-Image', in Patt, op. cit. (Section 2), pp. 456–71

Kerkhoven, Marianne van, 'Trauerarbeit: Een theaterbewerking van *De Emigrés* van W. G. Sebald', in Ceuppens and Philipsen, op. cit. (Section 3), pp. 39–45

Kilbourn, Russell J. A., 'Architecture and Cinema: The Representation of Memory in W. G. Sebald's *Austerlitz*', in Long and Whitehead, op. cit. (Section 2), pp. 140–54

—— 'Kafka, Nabokov ... Sebald: Intertextuality and Narratives of Redemption in *Vertigo* and *The Emigrants*', in Denham and McCulloh, op. cit. (Section 2), pp. 33–63

—— '"Catastrophe with Spectator": Subjectivity, Intertextuality and the Representation of History in *Die Ringe des Saturn*', in Fuchs and Long, op. cit. (Section 2), pp. 139–62

King, Nicola, 'Structures of Autobiographical Narrative: Lisa Appignanesi, Dan Jacobson, W. G. Sebald', *Comparative Critical Studies*, 1 (2004), 265–77

Kinross, Robin, 'Judging a Book by its Material Embodiment: A German–English Example', in *Unjustified Texts* (London: Hyphen Press, 2002), pp. 186–99 [on the German and English editions of *Die Ringe des Saturn*]

Kirchmann, Kay, 'Blicke auf Trümmer: Anmerkungen zur filmischen Wahrnehmungsorganisation der Ruinenlandschaften nach 1945', in *Die zerstörte Stadt: Mediale Repräsentationen urbaner Räume von Troja bis SimCity*, ed. by Andreas Böhn and Christine Mielke (Bielefeld: transcript Verlag, 2007), pp. 273–87

Kitchen, Judith, 'W. G. Sebald (1944–2001)', in *British Writers: Supplement VIII*, ed. by Jay Parini (New York: Scribner's, 2003), pp. 295–309

Klebes, Martin, 'Infinite Journey: From Kafka to Sebald', in Long and Whitehead, op. cit. (Section 2), pp. 123–39

—— 'W. G. Sebald: Family Resemblances and the Blurred Images of History', in *Wittgenstein's Novels* (London: Routledge, 2006), pp. 87–130

——'Sebald's Pathographies', in Denham and McCulloh, op. cit. (Section 2), pp. 65–75

——'No Exile: Crossing the Border with Sebald and Améry', in Fischer, op. cit. (Section 2), pp. 73–90

——'If You Come to a Spa: Displacing the Cure in *Schwindel. Gefühle.* and *Austerlitz*', in Zisselsberger, op. cit. (Section 2), pp. 123–41

KLEIN, JULIA M., 'Germans as Victims of World War II', *Chronicle of Higher Education*, 49.32 (2003), B16–17

KLING, VINCENT, 'The Prophetic Voice: W. G. Sebald and *On the Natural History of Destruction*', *Southern Humanities Review*, 38 (2004), 347–81

KLÜGER, RUTH, 'Wanderer zwischen falschen Leben: Über W. G. Sebald', in Arnold, op. cit. (Section 3), pp. 95–102

KNAAP, EWERT VAN DER, 'Vuurproef der literatuur: Sebald en de literaire herinnering aan de bombardementen', in Bel and others, op. cit. (Section 3), pp. 50–57

KOCHHAR-LINDGREN, GRAY, 'Charcoal: The Phantom Traces of W. G. Sebald's Novel-Memoirs', *Monatshefte*, 94.3 (2002), 368–80

KÖHLER, ANDREA, 'Gespräch mit Toten: W. G. Sebalds Wanderungen durch die Jahrhunderte', *Neue Zürcher Zeitung* (Internationale Ausgabe) (Literatur und Kunst section), 23–24 September 2000, pp. 49–50: repr. in W. G. Sebald, *W. G. Sebald: Gespräch mit Lebenden and Toten* (= Bogen 48) (Munich: Hanser, 2000), unpaginated pamphlet (cf. Primary Bibliography B.C.2)

——'Die Durchdringung des Dunkels: W. G. Sebald und Jan Peter Tripp: Ein letzter Blickwechsel', *Neue Zürcher Zeitung*, 14–15 December 2002, Literatur and Kunst section, pp. 49–50; repr. in W. G. Sebald, *Unerzählt* (Munich: Hanser, 2003), pp. 72–78

——'Penetrating the Dark', in W. G. Sebald, *Unerzählt*, trans. by Michael Hamburger (London: Hamish Hamilton, 2004), pp. 95–103 [translation of above]

——'W. G. Sebalds Gesichter', in Krüger, op. cit. (Section 3), pp. 15–20

——'Verabredung in der Vergangenheit: Das Archivierungswerk des Schriftstellers W. G. Sebald', *Merkur*, 59 (2005), 343–49

KÖPF, GERHARD, 'Message for Max', in Loquai, *Far From Home*, op. cit. (Section 2), pp. 91–93

——'Das Wertacher Sommerloch', in Köpf, op. cit. (Section 2), pp. 32–48

KORFF, SIGRID, 'Die Treue zum Detail: W. G. Sebald's *Die Ausgewanderten*', in *In der Sprache der Täter*, ed. by Stephan Braese (Opladen: Westdeutscher Verlag, 1998), pp. 167–97

KÖRTE, MONA, 'Armband, Handtuch, Taschenuhr: Objekte des letzten Augenblicks in Erinnerung and Erzählung', in *Die Kindertransporte 1938/39: Rettung and Integration*, ed. by Wolfgang Benz, Claudia Curio and Andrea Hammel (Frankfurt a.M.: Fischer, 2003), pp. 171–85 [reference to *Austerlitz*]

——, and TOBY AXELROD, 'Bracelet, Hand Towel, Pocket Watch: Objects of the Last Moment in Memory and Narration', *Shofar: An Interdisciplinary Journal of Jewish Studies*, 23 (2004), 109–20 [reference to *Austerlitz*; English version of above]

——'"Un petit sac": W. G. Sebalds Figuren zwischen Sammeln und Vernichten', in Atze and Loquai, op. cit. (Section 2), pp. 176–94

KOSLER, HANS CHRISTIAN, and FRANZ LOQUAI, 'Zu *Unheimliche Heimat*', in Loquai, *W. G. Sebald*, op. cit. (Section 2), pp. 75–78

KOUVAROS, GEORGE, 'Images That Remember Us: Photography and Memory in *Austerlitz*', *Textual Practice*, 19 (2005), 173–93; repr. with minor additions in Fischer, op. cit. (Section 2), pp. 389–412

KOVÁCS, EDIT, 'Halbdunkel: Zum Beschriften und Lesen von Fotografien in W. G. Sebalds Roman *Austerlitz*', *Jahrbuch der ungarischen Germanistik* (2005), 87–96

KRAENZLE, CHRISTINA, 'Picturing Place: Travel, Photography and Imaginative Geography in W. G. Sebald's *Die Ringe des Saturn*', in Patt, op. cit. (Section 2), pp. 126–45

Krauss, Andrea, '"Rohformen des Erzählens": Repräsentationskritik in W. G. Sebalds *Luftkrieg und Literatur*', *Weimarer Beiträge: Zeitschrift für Literaturwissenschaft, Ästhetik und Kulturwissenschaften*, 53 (2007), 503–18

Krejberg, Kasper Green, 'En slags feststemning: Apokryfe historier og kultiverede excesser: om W. G. Sebalds humor', in Vinger, op. cit. (Section 3), pp. 102–07

——'Literary Memories of a Forgotten War: How German Literature Keeps Breaking the Air War Taboo', in *ACT 20: Filologia, Memória e Esquecimento*, ed. by Fernanda Mota Alves, Sofia Tavares, Ricardo Gil Soeiro, and Daniela Di Pasquale (Apartado: Edições Húmus, 2010), pp. 97-114

Kreuzer, Helmut, 'Drei kurze Versuche: Achternbusch, Bense, Sebald', in *'Was in den alten Büchern steht...': Neue Interpretationen von der Aufklärung zur Moderne: Festschrift für Reinhold Grimm*, ed. by Karl-Heinz Schoeps and Christopher J. Wickham, Forschungen zur Literatur- and Kulturgeschichte, 32 (Frankfurt a.M.: Lang, 1991), pp. 179–83

Krüger, Brigitte, 'Erzählen im Gestus des Beglaubigens: Beobachtungen zu einer Erzählstrategie in W. G. Sebalds Roman *Austerlitz*', in *Genre of the Novel in Contemporary World Literature: A Leap or a Standstill?*, Interlitteraria, 9 (Tartu: Tartu Ülikooli Kirjastus, 2004), pp. 182–205

Kuhn, Irène, '"Noch sind sie um, die Toten...": W. G. Sebalds Thesen zu *Luftkrieg und Literatur*', *Revue d'Allemagne et des pays de langue allemande*, 37 (2005), 233–44

——, and Sibylle Muller, 'Traducteur-bricoleur. W. G. Sebald à Strasbourg: La Question de la traduction', in Vogel-Klein, op. cit. (Section 3), pp. 187–91

Lachmann, Tobias, 'Archäologie oder Restauration? Zur narrativen Re/konstruktion von Gewesenem in W. G. Sebalds *Die Ausgewanderten*', in Sareika, op. cit. (Section 4), pp. 71–94

Lamb, Jonathan, 'Sterne, Sebald, and Siege Architecture', *Eighteenth-Century Fiction*, 19.1–2 (2006), 21–41

Lambert, David, and Robert McGill, 'Writing Tips: The Collected "Maxims" of W. G. Sebald', *Five Dials*, 5 (2009), 8–9 <http://fivedials.com/fivedials> [accessed 3 April 2009]

Langston, Richard, 'Affective Affinities: Sebald and Kluge on Feeling History', in Lützeler and Schindler, op. cit. (Section 3), pp. 44–68

Lau, Jorg, 'Literatur: Eine Kolumne: Letzte Welten, umgrenztes Ich', *Merkur*, 50.5 (1996), 427–31 [on *Die Ringe des Saturn*, pp. 430–31]

Laurans, Jacques, 'Le Voyage d'hiver de W. G. Sebald', *Nouvelle Revue Française*, no. 574 (2005), 250–59

Lawson, Colette, 'The Natural History of Destruction: W. G. Sebald, Gert Ledig, and the Allied Bombings', in *Germans as Victims in the Literary Fiction of the Berlin Republic*, ed. by Stuart Taberner and Karina Berger (Rochester, NY: Camden House, 2009), pp. 29–41

Lemke, Anja, 'Das photographische Portrait zwischen Identität und Identifikation bei Walter Benjamin und W. G. Sebald', in *Bild und Eigensinn: Über Modalitäten der Anverwandlung von Bildern*, ed. by Petra Leutner and Hans-Peter Niebuhr (Bielefeld: transcript, 2006), pp. 160–78

——'Figurationen der Melancholie: Spuren Walter Benjamins in W. G. Sebalds *Die Ringe des Saturn*', *Zeitschrift für deutsche Philologie*, 127.2 (2008), 239–67

Lending, Mari, 'Historisk røntgen: Arkitekturfremstilling i W. G. Sebalds *Austerlitz*', in Vinger, op. cit. (Section 3), pp. 93–101

Lennon, Patrick, 'The Referential Potential of Fiction: W. G. Sebald's *The Rings of Saturn*', *Bell*, 1 (2003), 145–53

——'In the Weavers' Web: An Intertextual Approach to Sebald and Laurence Sterne', in Denham and McCulloh, op. cit. (Section 2), pp. 91–104

——'Depiction and Destruction: W. G. Sebald's Realism', in *Images and Imagery: Frames, Borders, Limits: Interdisciplinary Perspectives*, ed. by Leslie Boldt-Irons, Corrado Federici and Ernesto Virgulti, New York Studies on Themes and Motifs in Literature, 74 (New York: Lang, 2005), pp. 255–65

LEONE, MASSIMO, 'Literature, Travel and Vertigo', in *Cross-Cultural Travel: Papers from The Royal Irish Academy Symposium on Literature and Travel*, ed. by Jane Conroy (New York: Lang, 2003), pp. 513–22

——'Textual Wanderings: A Vertiginous Reading of W. G. Sebald', in Long and Whitehead, op. cit. (Section 2), pp. 89–101

LERM HAYES, CHRISTA-MARIA, 'Post-War Germany and "Objective Chance": W. G. Sebald, Joseph Beuys and Tacita Dean', in Patt, op. cit. (Section 2), pp. 412–39 [also publ. in an extended version as a separate book, containing five extra pages, extra illustrations, and a German version (Göttingen: Steidl, 2008)]

LETHEN, HELMUT, 'Sebalds Raster: Überlegungen zur ontologischen Unruhe in Sebalds *Die Ringe des Saturn*', in Niehaus and Öhlschläger, op. cit. (Section 2), pp. 13–30

LEWIS, BRIAN, 'The Queer Life and Afterlife of Roger Casement', *Journal of the History of Sexuality*, 14.4 (2005), 363–82

LEWIS, TESS, 'W. G. Sebald: The Past is Another Country', *New Criterion*, 20.4 (December 2001), 85–90

LJUNGBERG, CHRISTINA, 'Photographs in Narrative', in *Outside-In–Inside-Out*, ed. by Costantino Maeder, Olga Fischer, and William J. Herlofsky, Iconicity in Language and Literature, 4 (Amsterdam: Benjamins, 2005), pp. 133–49

LOBSIEN, VERENA OLEJNICZAK, 'Herkunft ohne Ankunft: Der Chronotopos der Heimatlosigkeit bei W. G. Sebald', in *Herkünfte: Historisch, Ästhetisch, Kulturell: Beiträge zu einer Tagung aus Anlaß des 60. Geburtstags von Bernhard Greiner*, ed. by Barbara Thums, Volker Mergenthaler, Nicola Kaminski and Doerte Bischoff, Beiträge zur Neueren Literaturgeschichte, 203 (Heidelberg: Winter, 2004), pp. 223–48

LOCHER, ELMAR, '"The Time is Out of Joint": Gli spettri di W. G. Sebald', in Busch, op. cit. (Section 3), pp. 67–89

LOCKWOOD, ALAN, 'Beylisms in W. G. Sebald's *Vertigo*', *The Brooklyn Rail*, 38 (2000) <http://www.thebrooklynrail.org/archives/index.html> [no longer available online]

LÖFFLER, SIGRID, 'W. G. Sebald, der Ausgewanderte', in *Kritiken, Portraits, Glossen* (Vienna: Deuticke, 1995), pp. 72–78

——'Laudatio auf W. G. Sebald', in *Mörike-Preis der Stadt Fellbach 1991-2000. Ein Lesebuch* (Fellbach: Stadt Fellbach, 2000), pp. 125-34

——'"Melancholie ist eine Form des Widerstands": Über das Saturnische bei W. G. Sebald und seine Aufhebung in der Schrift', in Arnold, op. cit. (Section 3), pp. 103–11

——, MARCO POLTRONIERI, and SVEN SIEDENBERG, 'Drei Gespräche', in Loquai, *W. G. Sebald*, op. cit. (Section 2), pp. 135–48

LONG, J. J., 'History, Narrative, and Photography in W. G. Sebald's *Die Ausgewanderten*', *Modern Language Review*, 98.1 (2003), 117–37

——'Intercultural Identities in W. G. Sebald's *The Emigrants* and Norbert Gstrein's *Die englischen Jahre*', *Journal of Multilingual and Multicultural Development*, 25.5–6 (2004), 512–28

——'Disziplin und Geständnis: Ansätze zu einer Foucaultschen Sebald-Lektüre', in Niehaus and Öhlschläger, op. cit. (Section 2), pp. 219–39

——'W. G. Sebald: A Bibliographical Essay on Current Reseach', in Fuchs and Long, op. cit. (Section 2), pp. 11–29

——'W. G. Sebald's Miniature Histories', in Fuchs and Long, op. cit. (Section 2), pp. 111–20

——'W. G. Sebald: The Ambulatory Narrative and the Poetics of Digression', in Fischer, op. cit. (Section 2), pp. 61–72

——'W. G. Sebald: The Anti-Tourist', in Zisselsberger, op. cit. (Section 2), pp. 63–91

——'The Sense of Sebald's Endings and Beginnings', in *Digressions in European Literature: From Cervantes to Sebald*, ed. by Alexis Grohmann and Caragh Wells (Basingstoke: Palgrave, 2011), pp. 193–204

——, and Anne Whitehead, 'Introduction', in Long and Whitehead, op. cit. (Section 2), pp. 3–15

Lothe, Jacob, 'Eksil, forteljesituasjon og sivilisasjonssamanbrot: W. G. Sebald og Joseph Conrad', in Vinger, op. cit. (Section 3), pp. 116–19

Loquai, Franz, 'Gehen gegen den Geschwindigkeitsrausch: Schriftsteller entdecken die Langsamkeit', *Foglio*, no. 3 (June–July 1996), 14–15

——'Erinnerungskünstler im Beinhaus der Geschichte: Gedankenbrosamen zur Poetik W. G. Sebalds', in Loquai, *W. G. Sebald*, op. cit. (Section 2), pp. 257–65

——'Max und Marcel: Eine Betrachtung über die Erinnerungskünstler Sebald und Proust', in Atze and Loquai, op. cit. (Section 2), pp. 212–27

——'Vom Beinhaus der Geschichte ins wiedergefundene Paradies: Zu Werk und Poetik W. G. Sebalds', in Atze and Loquai, op. cit. (Section 2), pp. 244–56

Louvel, Liliane, 'Photography as Critical Idiom and Intermedial Criticism', in Horstkotte and Pedri, op. cit. (Section 3), 31–48

Lubrich, Oliver, 'Bombed and Silenced: Foreign Witnesses of the Air War in Germany', *German Life and Letters*, 62 (2009), 415–29

Luchsinger, Martin, '"Lange war es mir nicht mehr so wohl gewesen": W. G. Sebald: *Schwindel. Gefühle.*', in *Mythos Italien: Denkbilder des Fremden in der deutschsprachigen Gegenwartsliteratur* (Cologne: Böhlau, 1996), pp. 137–49 [This is a section of Part II, Chapter 2, entitled 'Italienreisen in Gegenwartstexten'.]

Luckhurst, Roger, 'W. G. Sebald: The Last Traumatophile?', in *The Trauma Question* (London: Routledge, 2008), pp. 111–16 [This is a section of Chapter 2 of *The Trauma Question*, entitled 'Trauma in Narrative Fiction'.]

McChesney, Anita, 'On the Repeating History of Destruction: Media and the Observer in Sebald and Ransmayr', *Modern Language Notes*, 121.3 (2006), 699–719

McCulloh, Mark, 'Stylistics of Stasis: Paradoxical Effects in W. G. Sebald', *Style*, 38.1 (2004), 38–49

——'Destruction and Transcendence in W. G. Sebald', *Philosophy and Literature*, 30 (2006), 395–409

——'Introduction: Two Languages, Two Audiences: The Tandem Literary Œuvres of W. G. Sebald', in Denham and McCulloh, op. cit. (Section 2), pp. 7–20

McIsaac, Peter M., 'Autorschaft und Autorität bei W. G. Sebald', in *Deutschsprachige Gegenwartsliteratur seit 1989: Zwischenbilanzen–Analysen–Vermittlungsperspektiven*, ed. by Clemens Kammler and Torsten Pflugmacher (Heidelberg: Synchron, 2004), pp. 139–51

——'Inventoried Consciousness Today: Durs Grünbein and W. G. Sebald', in *Museums of the Mind: German Modernity and the Dynamics of Collecting* (University Park, PA: Penn State University Press, 2007), pp. 29–51

McKinney, Ronald H., 'W. G. Sebald and "the Questionable Business" of Post-Holocaust Writing', *Philosophy Today*, 49.2 (2005), 115–26

Mack, Michael, 'Between Elias Canetti and Jacques Derrida: Satire and the Role of Fortifications in the Work of W. G. Sebald', in Fischer, op. cit. (Section 2), pp. 233–56

Madden, Patrick, 'W. G. Sebald: Where Essay Meets Fiction', *Fourth Genre: Explorations in Nonfiction*, 10.2 (2008), 169–75

Maier, Anja K., '"Der panische Halsknick": Organisches und Anorganisches in W. G. Sebalds Prosa', in Niehaus and Öhlschläger, op. cit. (Section 2), pp. 111–26 [see also Johannsen, Anja K.]

——'Schmerzästhetik und Zeugenschaft bei W. G. Sebald und Anne Duden', in *Schmerz-differenzen: Physisches Leid und Gender in kultur- und literaturwissenschaftlicher Perspektive*, ed. by Iris Hermann and Anne-Rose Meyer (Königstein im Taunus: Helmer, 2006) pp. 115–39

Mair, Kimberly, 'Arrivals and Departures in the Sensual City: W. G. Sebald's Itineraries of the Senses in *Austerlitz*', *Senses & Society*, 2.2 (2007), 233–46

MALKMUS, BERNHARD, '"All of them Signs and Characters from the Type-Case of Forgotten Things": Intermedia Configurations of History in W. G. Sebald', in *Memory Traces: 1989 and the Question of Cultural Identity*, ed. by Silke Arnold-de Simine (Oxford: Lang, 2005), pp. 211–44

MARKS, JOHN, 'W. G. Sebald: Invisible and Intangible Forces', *New Formations*, 55 (2005), 89–103

MARTIN, JAMES P., '"Die bezaubernde Anmut eines chemischen Prozesses"': Photography in the Works of Gerhard Roth and W. G. Sebald', in Zisselsberger, op. cit. (Section 3), pp. 42–57

——'Melancholic Wanderings: W. G. Sebald's *Die Ringe des Saturn*', in Lützeler and Schindler, op. cit. (Section 3), pp. 118–40

——'*Campi Deserti*: Polar Landscapes and the Limits of Knowledge in Sebald and Ransmayr', in Zisselsberger, op. cit. (Section 2), pp. 142–60

MARTIN, NICHOLAS, 'Rocking the Boat? Victims, Perpetrators and Günter Grass', *Forum for Modern Language Studies*, 41.2 (2005), 187–99

MARTIN, SIGURD, 'Lehren vom Ähnlichen: Mimesis und Entstellung als Werkzeuge der Erinnerung im Werk W. G. Sebalds', in Martin and Wintermeyer, op. cit. (Section 2), pp. 81–103

MARTIN, STEWART, 'W. G. Sebald and the Modern Art of Memory', in *Photography and Literature in the Twentieth Century*, ed. by David Cunningham, Andrew Fisher and Sas Mays (Newcastle upon Tyne: Cambridge Scholars Press, 2005), pp. 180–99 [shorter version of this piece available online in *Radical Philosophy*, no. 132 (July–August 2005) <http://www.radicalphilosophy.com/default.asp?channel_id=2188&editorial_id=183>] [accessed 24 March 2010]

MASSCHELEIN, ANNELEEN, 'Hand in Glove: Negative Indexicality in André Breton's *Nadja* and W. G. Sebald's *Austerlitz*', in Patt, op. cit. (Section 2), pp. 360–87 [a slightly revised version of the German piece below]

——'Negative Hände: Die Darstellung der Negativität in Bretons *Nadja* und Sebalds *Austerlitz*', in *Literatur im Krebsgang: Totenbeschwörung und Memoria in der deutschsprachigen Literatur nach 1989*, ed. by Arne de Winde and Anke Gilleir (Amsterdam: Rodopi, 2008), pp. 319–50

MATHEWS, TIMOTHY, 'Reading W. G. Sebald with Alberto Giacometti', in *Stories and Portraits of the Self*, ed. by Helena Carvalhão Buescu and João Ferreira Duarte (Amsterdam: Rodopi, 2007), pp. 237–51

MEDICUS, THOMAS, 'Katastrophensammeln auf der Geisterinsel: Hat der Schriftsteller W. G. Sebald "Holocaust-Literatur" geschrieben? Anmerkungen zu einem Mißverständnis', *Mittelweg 36*, 18.5 (2008), 63–74

MEDIN, DANIEL L., 'Simply Made Up? Franz Kafka in W. G. Sebald's *Dr Ks Badereise nach Riva*', in *Über Gegenwartsliteratur: Interpretationen und Interventionen: Festschrift für Paul Michael Lützeler zum 65. Geburtstag von ehemaligen StudentInnen*, ed. by Mark W. Rectanus (Bielefeld: Aisthesis, 2008), pp. 245–60

MELBERG, ARNE, 'Bortom fiktionen: Sebald, Solstad med flera resenärer i landet prosa', *Norsk Litteraturvitenskapelig Tidsskrift*, 7.2 (2004), 98-108 [in Norwegian]

——'Romanen som fiktion, romanen som prosa: Sebald och Solstad', *Tidskrift för Litteraturvetenskap*, 33.2 (2004), 120-30 [in Norwegian]

——'Sebalds prosa', *Artes*, 2 (2005), 7–22 [in Norwegian]

——'Sebalds svindel', *Morgenbladet*, 15.5 (2005), unpaginated [in Norwegian]

——'Exile and the Modernist Writing of the Self: Anaïs Nin, Gombrowicz, Canetti, Sebald', in *Grenzen der Fiktionalität und der Erinnerung*, ed. by Christoph Parry and Edgar Platen, Autobiographisches Schreiben in der deutschsprachigen Gegenwartsliteratur, 2 (Munich: iudicium, 2007), pp. 86–97

—— 'Sebald's Photographic Prose', in *Aesthetics of Prose* (Oslo: Unipub, 2008), pp. 159–67

—— *Självskrivet* (Stockholm: Atlantis, 2008), pp. 104–18 [chapter in Swedish on WGS and life writing]

—— 'Den längsta meningen: W. G. Sebald låter meningen växa i takt med ämnets känslighet', in Vinger, op. cit. (Section 3), pp. 80–83

Mendieta, Eduardo, 'The Literature of Urbicide: Friedrich, Nossack, Sebald, and Vonnegut', *Theory & Event*, 10.2 (2007) (electronic journal) <http://muse.jhu.edu/journals/theory_and_event/toc/tae10.2.html> [accessed 15 October 2009]

Menke, Timm, 'W. G. Sebalds *Luftkrieg und Literatur* und die Folgen: Eine kritische Bestandsaufnahme', in *Bombs Away! Representing the Air War over Europe and Japan*, ed. by Wilfried Wilms and William Rasch (Amsterdam: Rodopi, 2006), pp. 149–63

Meyer, Anne-Rose, 'Ästhetische und ethische Dimensionen der Täter-Opfer-Problematik in W. G. Sebalds *Luftkrieg und Literatur*', in *Täter als Opfer? Deutschsprachige Literatur zu Krieg und Vertreibung im 20. Jahrhundert. [Poetica* 100], ed. by Stefan Hermes and Amir Muhić (Hamburg: Kovač, 2007), pp. 13–39

Meyer, Sven, 'Das Fähnlein auf der Brücke', in Krüger, op. cit. (Section 3), pp. 51–55

—— 'Fragmente zu Mementos: Imaginierte Konjekturen bei W. G. Sebald', in Arnold, op. cit. (Section 3), pp. 75–81

—— 'Der Kopf, der auftaucht: Zu W. G. Sebalds *Nach der Natur*', in Atze and Loquai, op. cit. (Section 2), pp. 67–77

—— 'Im Medium der Prosa: Essay und Erzählung bei W. G. Sebald', in Vogel-Klein, op. cit. (Section 3), pp. 173–85

Michel, Andreas, 'Heroes and Taboos: The Expansion of Memory in Contemporary Germany', *War, Literature, and the Arts: An International Journal of the Humanities*, 17.1–2 (2005), 58–73

Mielke, Christine, 'Geisterstädte: Literarische Texte und Bilddokumentationen zur Städtebombardierung des Zweiten Weltkriegs und die Personifizierung des Urbanen', in *Die zerstörte Stadt: Mediale Repräsentationen urbaner Räume von Troja bis SimCity*, ed. by Andreas Böhn and Christine Mielke (Bielefeld: transcript, 2007), pp. 125–80

Mitchelmore, Stephen, 'W. G. Sebald: *Austerlitz*: Looking and Looking Away', *Spike Magazine* <http://www.spikemagazine.com/1104sebald.php> [accessed 12 April 2010] [also discusses Sebald's other works]

Moeller, Robert G., 'Germans as Victims? Thoughts on a Post-Cold War History of World War II's Legacies', *History & Memory*, 17.1–2 (2005), 147–94

Molloy, Diane, 'Blurring the Boundaries: History, Memory and Imagination in the Works of W. G. Sebald', *Colloquy: Text Theory Critique*, 15 (2008), 163–76

Morgan, Peter, 'The Sign of Saturn: Melancholy, Homelessness and Apocalypse in W. G. Sebald's Prose Narratives', *German Life and Letters*, 58.1 (2005), 75–92

—— 'Literature and National Redemption in W. G. Sebald's *On the Natural History of Destruction*', in Fischer, op. cit. (Section 2), pp. 213–32

—— '"Your Story is now My Story": The Ethics of Narration in Grass and Sebald', *Monatshefte*, 101.2 (2009), 186–206

Morris, Leslie, 'How Jewish is it? W. G. Sebald and the Question of "Jewish" Writing in Germany Today', in *The New German Jewry and the European Context: The Return of the European Jewish Diaspora*, ed. by Y. Michal Bodemann (Houndmills: Palgrave Macmillan, 2008), pp. 111–28

Mosbach, Bettina, 'Schauer der ungewohnten Berührung: Zur Tieranalogie bei W. G. Sebald', in *Texte, Tiere, Spuren*, ed. by Norbert Otto Eke (= *Zeitschrift für deutsche Philologie*, 126 special issue (2007)), pp. 82–97

—— 'Superimposition as a Narrative Strategy in *Austerlitz*', in Patt, op. cit. (Section 2), pp. 390–411

——'Blinder Fleck: Zur Reflexion der Gewalt der Darstellung bei W. G. Sebald', in Fischer, op. cit. (Section 2), pp. 109–32

——and NICOLAS PETHES, 'Zugzwänge des Erzählens: Zur Relation von Oral History und Literatur am Beispiel W. G. Sebalds Roman *Austerlitz*', *Bios: Zeitschrift für Biographie-forschung und Oral History*, 21.1 (2008), 49–69

MOSER, CHRISTIAN, 'Peripatetic Investigations into Liminal Spaces: Sebald and the European Tradition of the Literary Walk', in Zisselsberger, op. cit. (Section 2), pp. 37–62

MÜCKE, DOROTHEA VON, 'Autorschaft und Autobiographie, Bild und Gedächtnis in W. G. Sebalds *Nach der Natur*', in *Automedialität: Subjektkonstitution in Schrift, Bild und neuen Medien*, ed. by Jörg Dünne and Christian Moser (Munich: Fink, 2008), pp. 143–60

MÜLDER-BACH, INKA, 'Der große Zug des Details: W. G. Sebald: *Die Ringe des Saturn*', in *Was aus dem Bild fällt: Figuren des Details in Kunst und Literatur (Festschrift Friedrich Teja Bach)*, ed. by Edith Futscher and others (Munich: Fink, 2007), pp. 283–309

MÜNCHBERG, KATHARINA, 'Glückhafte Vergegenwärtigung, unheimliche Wiederkehr: Zwei Formen der Erinnerung bei Proust und W. G. Sebald', in *Transgressions, défis, provocations: Transferts culturels franco-allemands (Actes du colloque international du 28 au 30 octobre 2004 à Aix-en-Provence)*, ed. by Thomas Keller (Aix-en-Provence: Université de Provence, Institut d'Études Germaniques, 2005), pp. 159–72

——'Der erfindungslose Dichter: W. G. Sebald', *Paragrana*, supplement 2 (2006), 201–15

NAAIJKENS, TON, 'Als een rog in de diepte van de zee: Een inleiding', in Bel and others, op. cit. (Section 3), pp. 3–9

——'Naar de natuur: Het begin van een oeuvre', in Bel and others, op. cit. (Section 3), pp. 58–73

NAYHAUSS, HANS-CHRISTOPH, GRAF VON, 'Adler und Sebald, Lichtenstein und Grass: Vom Umgang mit Dokumentationen bei der literarischen Produktion', in Fischer, op. cit. (Section 2), pp. 447–60

NEUMANN, GERHARD, '"lange bis zum Zerspringen festgehaltene Augenblicke": W. G. Sebald liest aus seinem Buch *Die Ringe des Saturn*', *Jahrbuch der Bayerischen Akademie der Schönen Künste*, 13 (1999), 553–67

NEUNER, THOMAS, 'Der Leser als Wanderer: W. G. Sebald, *Die Ringe des Saturn: Eine englische Wallfahrt*', *Medienobservationen*, 2006 <http://www.medienobservationen.lmu.de/artikel/literatur/neuner_sebald.html> [accessed 28 February 2010]

NEWTON, ADAM ZACHARY, 'Not Quite Holocaust Fiction: A. B. Yehoshua's Mr. Mani and W. G. Sebald's *The Emigrants*', in *Teaching the Representation of the Holocaust: Options for Teaching*, ed. by Marianne Hirsch and Irene Kacandes (New York: Modern Language Association of America, 2004), pp. 422–30

——'Place from Place, and Place from Flight: W. G. Sebald's *The Emigrants* and Aharon Appelfeld's *The Iron Tracks*', in *The Elsewhere: On Belonging at a Near Distance* (Madison, WI: University of Wisconsin Press, 2005), pp. 41–95

NIEHAUS, MICHAEL, 'No Foothold: Institutions and Buildings in W. G. Sebald's Prose', in Denham and McCulloh, op. cit. (Section 2), pp. 315–33

——'Ikonotext, Bastelei: *Schwindel. Gefühle.* von W. G. Sebald', in *Lesen ist wie Sehen: Intermediale Zitate in Bild und Text*, ed. by Silke Horstkotte and Karin Leonhard (Cologne: Böhlau, 2006), pp. 155–75

——'W. G. Sebalds sentimentalische Dichtung', in Niehaus and Öhlschläger, op. cit. (Section 2), pp. 173–87

——'Sebald's Scourges', translated by J. J. Long, in Fuchs and Long, op. cit. (Section 2), pp. 45–57

——'Bausteine 2: Figurieren: Geschichten und Geschichte', in von Bülow, Gfrereis, and Strittmatter, op. cit. (Section 2), pp. 101–13

——and CLAUDIA ÖHLSCHLÄGER, 'Vorwort', in Niehaus and Öhlschläger, op. cit. (Section 2), pp. 7–11

Nieraad, Jürgen, 'In und an den Grenzen der Erinnerungsgemeinschaft: B. Schlinks *Der Vorleser* und W. G. Sebalds *Die Ausgewanderten*', in *Deutsch 2000: Fremdwörter–NS-Sprache–Deutschunterricht*, ed. by Gabi Erlberg, Rainer Frank, and Rudolf Steffens (Aachen: Shaker, 2000), pp. 148–59

Nölp, Markus, 'W. G. Sebalds *Ringe des Saturn* im Kontext photobebilderter Literatur', in *Literaturtheorie am Ende? Fünfzig Jahre Wolfgang Kaysers 'Sprachliches Kunstwerk'*, ed. by Orlando Grossegesse and Erwin Koller (Tübingen: Francke, 2001), pp. 129–41

Nordmann, Alfred, 'Abgrund des Unverständnisses: W. G. Sebalds *Austerlitz*', in *Philosophie im Spiegel der Literatur*, ed. by Gerhard Gamm (= *Zeitschrift für Ästhetik und allgemeine Kunstwissenschaft*, special issue 9 (2007)), pp. 165–83

Öhlschläger, Claudia, 'Archäologie der Zerstörung: W. G. Sebalds kombinatorische Gedächtniskunst', *Einsichten*, 2 (2003), 38–41

——'"Die Bahn des korsischen Kometen." Zur Dimension "Napoleon" in W. G. Sebalds literarischem Netzwerk', in *Topographien der Literatur: Deutsche Literatur im transnationalen Kontext*, ed. by Hartmut Böhme and others (DFG-Symposium 2004) (Stuttgart: Metzler, 2005), pp. 536–58

——'"Cristallisation, c'est l'opération de l'esprit": Stendhals Theorie der Liebe und ihre Bedeutung für W. G. Sebalds Poetik der Einbildung', ed. by Peter Freese, Paderborner Universitätsreden, 98 (Paderborn: Universität Paderborn, 2005) [booklet, 36 pages]

——'Unschärfe: Schwindel. Gefühle.: W. G. Sebalds intermediale und intertextuelle Gedächtniskunst', in Vogel-Klein, op. cit. (Section 3), pp. 11–23

——'W. G. Sebald–Matthias Grünewald', in *Kunst im Text*, ed. by Konstanze Fliedl (Basle: Stroemfeld, 2005), pp. 259–79

——'*Die Ringe des Saturn*: Ein kosmologisches Strukturmodell für W. G. Sebalds Lektüre zivilisatorischer Abirrungen', in *Gestirn und Literatur im 20. Jahrhundert*, ed. by Maximilian Bergengruen, Davide Giuriato, and Sandro Zanetti (Frankfurt a.M.: Fischer, 2006), pp. 312–25

——'Der Saturnring oder Etwas vom Eisenbau: W. G. Sebalds poetische Zivilisationskritik', in Niehaus and Öhlschläger, op. cit. (Section 2), pp. 189–204

——'"Wieviel Heimat braucht der Mensch?" W. G. Sebald und Jean Améry', in *Benjamin und das Exil*, ed. by Bernd Witte (Würzburg: Königshausen & Neumann, 2006), pp. 99–110

——'"Effet du réel": Strategie di costruzione dell'illusione in W. G. Sebald', in *Scritture dell'immagine*, ed. by Antonella d'Amelia, Flora de Giovanni, and Lucia Perrone Capano (Naples: Liguori, 2007), pp. 347–61

——'Kristallisation als kulturelle Transformation: Stendhal, W. G. Sebald und das Problem der Wirklichkeitstreue', in Martin and Wintermeyer, op. cit. (Section 2), pp. 105–18

——'Medialität und Poetik des trompe-l'oeil: W. G. Sebald und Jan-Peter Tripp', in Lützeler and Schindler, op. cit. (Section 3), pp. 21–43

——'Unabschließbare Rahmen: Wege des Erzählens bei W. G. Sebald', in Heidelberger-Leonard and Tabah, op. cit. (Section 2), pp. 169–86

Osborne, Dora, 'Blind Spots: Viewing Trauma in W. G. Sebald's *Austerlitz*', *Seminar: A Journal of Germanic Studies*, 43 (2007), 517–33

——'Projecting the Heterotopia in W. G. Sebald's *Austerlitz*', in *The Politics of Place in Post-War Germany: Essays in Literary Criticism*, ed. by David Clarke and Renate Rechtien (Lampeter: Edwin Mellen Press, 2009), pp. 47–65

——'Topographical Anxiety and Dysfunctional Systems: *Die Ausgewanderten* and Freud's *Little Hans*', in Zisselsberger, op. cit. (Section 2), pp. 299–321

Pages, Neil Christian, 'No Place but Home: W. G. Sebald on the Air War and Other Stories', *Crossings: A Counter-Disciplinary Journal*, 7 (2004–05), 91–135

——'Crossing Borders: Sebald, Handke and the Pathological Vision', in Zisselsberger, op. cit. (Section 2), pp. 61–92

——'Tripping: On Sebald's "Stifter"', in Zisselsberger, op. cit. (Section 2), pp. 213–46

PAKENDORF, GUNTHER, 'Geschichte(n) nach Auschwitz: W. G. Sebald und die Stadt der Toten', *Acta Germanica*, 36 (2008), 75–89

——'Als Deutscher in der Fremde: Heimat, Geschichte und Natur bei W. G. Sebald', in Fischer, op. cit. (Section 2), pp. 91–108

PANE, SAMUEL, 'Trauma Obscura: Photographic Media in W. G. Sebald's *Austerlitz*', *Mosaic: A Journal for the Interdisciplinary Study of Literature*, 38.1 (March 2005), 37–54

PARRY, ANN, 'Idioms for the Unrepresentable: Post-War Fiction and the Shoah', *Journal of European Studies*, 27.4 (1997), 417–32; repr. in *The Holocaust and the Text: Speaking the Unspeakable*, ed. by Andrew Leak and George Paizis (Basingstoke: Macmillan, 2000), pp. 109–24

PARRY, CHRISTOPH, 'Die zwei Leben des Herrn Austerlitz: Biographisches Schreiben als nicht-lineare Historiographie bei W. G. Sebald', in *Grenzen, Grenzüberschreitungen, Grenzauflösungen: Zur Darstellung von Zeitgeschichte in deutschsprachiger Gegenwartsliteratur III*, ed. by Edgar Platen and Martin Todtenhaupt (Munich: iudicium, 2004), pp. 113–30

——'Die Rechtfertigung der Erinnerung vor der Last der Geschichte: Autobiographische Strategien bei Timm, Treichel, Walser und Sebald', in *Grenzen der Fiktionalität und der Erinnerung*, ed. by Christoph Parry and Edgar Platen, Autobiographisches Schreiben in der deutschsprachigen Gegenwartsliteratur, 2 (Munich: iudicium, 2007), pp. 98–110

——'Constructing European Identity in Fiction: Three Strategies', in *Literature for Europe?*, ed. by Theo D'Haen and Iannis Goerlandt, Textxet Studies in Comparative Literature (Amsterdam: Rodopi, 2009), pp. 279–98

PARK, ED, 'The Precognitions', *Village Voice (Literary Supplement)* (Fall 2002), 74–75

PATT, LISE, 'Searching for Sebald: What I Know for Sure' (Introduction), in Patt, op. cit. (Section 2), pp. 16–97

PAULSEN, WOLFGANG, 'Carl Sternheim and die Komödie des Expressionismus', in *Die deutsche Komödie im zwanzigsten Jahrhundert: Sechstes Amherster Kolloquium zur modernen deutschen Literatur 1972*, ed. by Wolfgang Paulsen, Poesie und Wissenschaft, 37 (Heidelberg: Stiehm, 1976), pp. 70–106 (pp. 93–95 on WGS)

PEARSON, ANN, '"Remembrance ... Is Nothing Other Than a Quotation": The Intertextual Fictions of W. G. Sebald', *Comparative Literature*, 60.3 (2008), 261–78

PEITSCH, HELMUT, 'Exilschriftsteller jüdischer Herkunft in W. G. Sebalds germanistischer Rezeption', *Gegenwartsliteratur: Ein Germanistisches Jahrbuch*, 9 (2010), 142–64

PELIKAN STRAUS, NINA, 'Sebald, Wittgenstein, and the Ethics of Memory', *Comparative Literature*, 61.1 (2009), 43–53

PESNEL, STÉPHANE, '"Der Schauder der Heimatlosigkeit, der über das Feld des Exils weht." W. G. Sebald lecteur de Joseph Roth: affinités littéraires et intégration créatrice de la référence rothienne', in Vogel-Klein, op. cit. (Section 3), pp. 65–86

PETHES, NICOLAS, 'Metalepse der Erinnerung: Zur Funktion von Fiktion bei der Restitution kollektiver Gedächtniskrisen: Am Beispiel von W. G. Sebalds *Austerlitz*', *Limbus: Australisches Jahrbuch für germanistische Literatur- und Kulturwissenschaft*, 1 (2008), 13–33

PFEIFFER, PETER C., 'Korrespondenz und Wahlverwandtschaft: W. G. Sebalds *Die Ringe des Saturn*', *Gegenwartsliteratur*, 2 (2003), 226–44

PFLAUMBAUM, CHRISTOPH, 'Die Ausrichtung der Blicke: Aspekte des Schauens und Angeschaut-Werdens im Werk W. G. Sebalds', *Weimarer Beiträge: Zeitschrift für Literaturwissenschaft, Ästhetik und Kulturwissenschaften*, 56.1 (2010), 47–68

PHILIPSEN, BART, 'Kaddisj voor een literair archeoloog: Over W. G. Sebald (1944–2001)', in Ceuppens and Philipsen, op. cit. (Section 3), pp. 15–18

PHILLIPS, ADAM, 'Celebrating Sebald', in *On Balance* (London: Penguin, 2010), pp. 226–52

PIC, MURIEL, 'Archive and Atmosphere: The "pas perdus" of Memory in W. G. Sebald', trans. by Laura Winn, *Atopia*, 5 (2004) <http://www.atopia.tk/index.php/fr/anamnesis5/> [accessed 7 September 2009]

———'Sebald's Anatomy Lesson: About Three Images-Documents from *On the Natural History of Destruction, The Rings of Saturn* and *Austerlitz*', *Colloquy, Text, Theory, Critique*, 9 (2005), 6–15; online <http://www.colloquy.monash.edu.au/issue009/> [accessed 7 September 2009]

———'Les Yeux écarquillés: W. G. Sebald face à la polémique du souvenir', *Critique*, no. 312 (December 2005), 938–50

———'Le Document et ses fictions: Le Montage littéraire chez W. G. Sebald', in *La Mémoire historique: Interroger, construire, transmettre*, ed. by Roselyne Mogin-Martin and others (Angers: Presses de l'Université d'Angers, 2006), pp. 29–36

———'Image-papillon et ralenti: W. G. Sebald ou Le Regard capturé', *Infra-Mince*, 2 (2006), 90–104

PICHLER, GEORG, 'Zu Fuß: Literarische Wanderungen (Johann Gottfried Seume, W. G. Sebald)', in *1945–1989–2000: Momentos de lengua, literaturas y culturas alemanas: Actas de la X Semana de Estudios Germánicos* (Madrid: Universidad Complutense, 2003), pp. 219–29

PIEGER, ANNA, 'Melancholie als Reise- und Schreibbewegung: Zu W. G. Sebalds *Die Ringe des Saturn*', *Castrvm peregrini*, no. 278 (2007), 46–64

PINTER, JOSEPH S., 'On the Convergence of Innis's International Political Economy and Sebald's Novels', *CLCWeb: Comparative Literature and Culture*, 10.1 (2008) <http://docs.lib.purdue.edu/cgi/viewcontent.cgi?article=1326&context=clcweb> [accessed 18 October 2010]

PLUMB, STEVE, 'Art and the Air Campaigns of 1940/41 and 1945: Visual Representation of the London and Dresden Bombing Raids', in *Bombs Away! Representing the Air War over Europe and Japan*, ed. by Wilfried Wilms and William Rasch (Amsterdam: Rodopi, 2006), pp. 281–94

POETINI, CHRISTIAN, 'Auf den Spuren Jean Amérys im Werk von W. G. Sebald', in Heidelberger-Leonard and Tabah, op. cit. (Section 2), pp. 141–52

POL, BARBER VAN DE, 'Een vorm van stereometrie: Over Austerlitz', in Bel and others, op. cit. (Section 3), pp. 28–35

POLLEN, GEIR, '"De mest vidløftige setninger": Noen ord omkring mine Sebald-oversettelser', in Vinger, op. cit. (Section 3), p. 114

PORRO, SIMONA, 'Visual Representations of Postmemory in *Maus* by A. Spiegelman and *Die Ausgewanderten* by W. G. Sebald', in *ACT 20: Filologia, Memória e Esquecimento*, ed. by Fernanda Mota Alves, Sofia Tavares, Ricardo Gil Soeiro, and Daniela Di Pasquale (Apartado: Edições Húmus, 2010), pp. 191–205

PRAGER, BRAD, 'A Collection of Damages: Critiquing the Violence of the Air War', *Forum for Modern Language Studies*, 41.3 (2005), 309–19

———'The Good German as Narrator: On W. G. Sebald and the Risks of Holocaust Writing', *New German Critique*, 96 (2005), 75–102

———'Sebald's Kafka', in Denham and McCulloh, op. cit. (Section 2), pp. 105–25

———'On the Liberation of Perpetrator Photographs in Holocaust Narratives', in *Visualizing the Holocaust: Documents, Aesthetics, Memory*, ed. by David Bathrick, Brad Prager, and Michael David Richardson (Rochester, NY: Camden House, 2008), pp. 19–37

———'Convergence Insufficiency: On Seeing Passages between Sebald and the "Travel Writer" Bruce Chatwin', in Zisselsberger, op. cit. (Section 2), pp. 189–212

PREECE, JULIAN, 'Günter Grass, his Jews and their Critics: From Klüger and Gilman to Sebald and Prawer', in *Jews in German Literature since 1945: German-Jewish Literature?*, ed. by Pól Ó Dochartaigh, German Monitor, 53 (Amsterdam: Rodopi, 2000), pp. 609–24

PRESNER, TODD SAMUEL, '"What a Synoptic and Artificial View Reveals": Extreme History and the Modernism of W. G. Sebald's Realism', *Criticism*, 46.3 (2004), 341–60

———'Vienna, Rome, Prague, Antwerp, Paris: The Railway Ruins of Modernity: Freud and Sebald on the Narration of German/Jewish Remains', in *Mobile Modernity: Germans, Jews, Trains* (New York: Columbia University Press, 2007), pp. 233–83

——'Hegel's Philosophy of World History via Sebald's Imaginary of Ruins. A Contrapuntal Critique of the "New Space" of Modernity', in *Ruins of Modernity*, ed. by Julia Hell and Andreas Schönle (Durham, NC: Duke University Press, 2010), pp. 193-211

PREUSSER, HEINZ-PETER, 'Regarding and Imagining: Contrived Immediacy of the Allied Bombing Campaign in Photography, Novel, and Historiography', in *A Nation of Victims? Representations of German Wartime Suffering from 1945 to the Present*, ed. by Helmut Schmitz, German Monitor, 67 (Amsterdam: Rodopi, 2007), pp. 141-59

PREVIŠIĆ, BORIS, 'Poetik der Marginalität: *Balkan Turn* gefällig?', in *Von der nationalen zur internationalen Literatur: Transkulturelle deutschsprachige Literatur und Kultur im Zeitalter globaler Migration*, ed. by Helmut Schmitz (Amsterdam: Rodopi, 2009), pp. 189-204 [brief reference to the representation of the Balkans in *Die Ringe des Saturn*]

PROSSER, SIMON, 'Compendium: An A to Z of W. G. Sebald', *Five Dials*, 5 (2009), 10-13 <http://fivedials.com/fivedials/> [accessed 3 April 2009]

PUNTÍ, JORDI, 'Lunáticos, suicidas y otras personas normales', *El Pais* (Babelia), 14 July 2001, p. 4 [in Spanish]

RADVAN, FLORIAN, 'Vom Sodiumglanz fremder Städte: W. G. Sebalds literarische Erinnerungen an *Die Ausgewanderten*', in Sareika, op. cit. (Section 4), pp. 55-70

——'W. G. Sebald, Schriftsteller und Scholar: Erinnerungen an einen Grenzgänger zwischen Literatur und Wissenschaft', *Kritische Ausgabe*, 18 (2010), 56-59

RAU, PETRA, 'The War in Contemporary Fiction', in *The Cambridge Companion to the Literature of World War II*, ed. by Marina Mackay (Cambridge: Cambridge University Press, 2009), pp. 207-19 (pp. 215-17 on *Austerlitz*)

REICHENSBERGER, RICHARD, 'Kreisende Prozesse der Erinnerung. "Zufall" und "Konstruktion" in W. G. Sebalds Roman *Austerlitz*', *Der Standard*, 28 March 2001

REINHARDT, STEPHAN, 'Zu Alfred Andersch: Erwiderung auf W. G. Sebalds Essay in LI 20', *Lettre International*, 11.21 (1993), 94

REINICKE, ANGELA, 'Authenticity, Truth and the Other in B. Wilkormirski's *Bruchstücke* and W. G. Sebald's *Die Ausgewanderten*', in *Cultural Memory: Essays on European Literature and History*, ed. by Edric Caldicott and Anne Fuchs (Oxford: Lang, 2003), pp. 85-97 (pp. 93-97 on WGS)

REMMLER, KAREN, '*On the Natural History of Destruction* and Cultural Memory: W. G. Sebald', *German Politics and Society*, 23.3 (2005), 42-64

——'The Shape of Remembering: W. G. Sebald's *Die Ringe des Saturn* and *Austerlitz*', in Lützeler and Schindler, op. cit. (Section 3), pp. 141-63

——'Traversing Home Territory: Cultures of Memory in W. G. Sebald's and Ingeborg Bachmann's Writing', in *Über Gegenwartsliteratur: Interpretationen und Interventionen: Festschrift für Paul Michael Lützeler zum 65. Geburtstag von ehemaligen StudentInnen*, ed. by Mark W. Rectanus (Bielefeld: Aisthesis, 2008), pp. 261-78

——'Against the Integration of Atrocity into Disaster: W. G. Sebald's Work of Memory', in Fischer, op. cit. (Section 2), pp. 133-60

RENNER, ROLF G., 'Intermediale Identitätskonstruktion: Zu W. G. Sebalds Austerlitz', in Fischer, op. cit. (Section 2), pp. 333-46

RENNER, URSULA, 'Fundstücke: Zu W. G. Sebald's *Austerlitz*', *Der Deutschunterricht: Beiträge zu seiner Praxis und wissenschaftlichen Grundlegung*, 4 (2005), 14-24

RESTUCCIA, FRANCES L., 'Sebald's Punctum: Awakening to Holocaust Trauma in *Austerlitz*', *European Journal of English Studies*, 9.3 (2005), 301-22

RIBÓ, IGNASI, 'The One-Winged Angel: History and Memory in the Literary Discourse of W. G. Sebald', *Orbis litterarum*, 64.3 (2009), 222-62

RIEDL, PETER PHILIPP, 'Über das Unsagbare in der Literatur: Zur Poetik von W. G. Sebald und Günter Grass', *Zeitschrift für deutsche Philologie*, 124.2 (2005), 261-84

RIORDAN, COLIN, 'Ecocentrism in Sebald's *After Nature*', in Long and Whitehead, op. cit. (Section 2), pp. 45-57

Rittau, Andreas, 'Intermédialité franco-allemande à deux voix: W. G. Sebald et Michel Butor face à un double silence, historique et écologique', *Germanisch-romanische Monatsschrift*, 58.2 (2008), 223–29

Ritter, Alexander, 'Eine Skandalinszenierung ohne Skandalfolge. Zur Kontroverse um Alfred Andersch in den neunziger Jahren', in *Literatur als Skandal: Fälle — Funktionen — Folgen*, ed. by Johann Holzer and Stefan Neuhaus (Göttingen: Vandenhoeck & Ruprecht, 2009), pp. 469–79

Robbins, Bruce, 'Comparative National Blaming: W. G. Sebald on the Bombing of Germany', in *Forgiveness, Mercy, and Clemency*, ed. by Austin Sarat and Nassar Hussain (Stanford, CA: Stanford University Press, 2007), pp. 138–55

Roder, J. H. de, 'De valse identiteit van W. G. Sebald? Enkele bedenkingen bij een heiligverklaring', in Bel and others, op. cit. (Section 3), 74–83

Römhild, Juliane, ' "Back in Sebaldland" ': Zur Rezeption von W. G. Sebald in der britischen Tagespresse', *Zeitschrift für Germanistik*, 15 (2005), 393–99

Rosenfeld, Natania, 'Enthrallments', *Hotel Amerika*, 3.1 (2004), 19–23

——'Turning Back: Retracing Twentieth-Century Trauma in Virginia Woolf, Martin Amis and W. G. Sebald', *Partial Answers: Journal of Literature and the History of Ideas*, 2.2 (2004), 109–37

——'Less Light: The End(s) of Aestheticism in Pater, Ondaatje, and Sebald', *Modernism/Modernity*, 13.2 (2006), 349–366

Rovagnati, Gabriella, 'Approdi negati: Destini di ebrei nella prosa di W. G. Sebald', in *Juden*, ed. by Roberta Ascarelli, *Cultura tedesca*, 23 (2001), 187–203

——' "Auswanderung, Adoption, Aufnahme": Bei der Übersetzung der Bücher von W. G. Sebald', *Sprache im technischen Zeitalter*, 39 (2001), 266–72

——'Canetti, Sebald und die Quellen des Feuers: Zum apokalyptischen Schluß von W. G. Sebalds Erzählung "Il ritorno in patria" ', in Atze and Loquai, op. cit. (Section 2), pp. 116–21

——'Das unrettbare Venedig des W. G. Sebald', in Atze and Loquai, op. cit. (Section 2), pp. 143–56

——'Il viaggio in Italia di W. G. Sebald', in Busch, op. cit. (Section 3), pp. 49–66

Rübel, Dietmar, 'Die Fotografie (Un)Erträglich Machen: Gerhard Richter gesehen mit W. G. Sebald', in *Sechs Vorträge über Gerhard Richter, Februar 2007, Residenzschloss Dresden*, ed. by Dietmar Elgar and Jürgen Müller (Dresden: Gerhard Richter Archiv; Cologne: König, 2007), pp. 47–69

Rubercy, Eryck de, 'Voyager avec W. G. Sebald', *Revue des deux mondes*, no. 3708 (July–August 2009), 67–78

Ruprecht, Lucia, 'Pleasure and Affinity in W. G. Sebald and Robert Walser', *German Life and Letters*, 62.2 (2009), 311–26

——'Virtuoso Servitude and (De)Mobilization in Robert Walser, W. G. Sebald and the Brothers Quay', *German Quarterly*, 83.1 (2010), 58–76

Ryan, Judith, 'Kolonialismus in W. G. Sebalds Roman *Austerlitz*', in *(Post-) Kolonialismus und Deutsche Literatur: Impulse der angloamerikanischen Literatur- und Kulturtheorie*, ed. by Axel Dunker (Bielefeld: Aisthesis, 2005), pp. 267–82

——'Fulgurations: Sebald and Surrealism', *Germanic Review*, 82.3 (2007), 227–49

——'The Long German Poem in the Long Twentieth Century', *German Life and Letters*, 60.3 (2007), 348–64 [discusses *After Nature*]

——' "Lines of Flight": History and Territory in *The Rings of Saturn*', in Fischer, op. cit. (Section 2), pp. 45–60

Sareika, Rüdiger, ' "Im Krebsgang": Strategien des Erinnerns in den Werken von Günter Grass und W. G. Sebald', in Sareika, op. cit. (Section 4), pp. 7–11

Schäfer, Burkhard, 'Zur Einführung: W. G. Sebald oder Die Verdrängung des Magischen Realismus und die Wiederkehr der unterdrückten Arten', in *Unberühmter Ort: Die*

Ruderalfläche im Magischen Realismus und in der Trümmerliteratur (Frankfurt a.M.: Lang, 2001), pp. 215–20

SCHALK, AXEL, 'Image and Text: W. G. Sebald's Montage Technique', in *New German Literature: Life-Writing and Dialogue with the Arts*, ed. by Frank Finlay, Julian Preece, and Ruth J. Owen, Leeds–Swansea Colloquia on Contemporary German Literature (Oxford: Lang, 2007), pp. 37–49

SCHERPE, KLAUS R., 'Auszeit des Erzählens: W. G. Sebalds Poetik der Beschreibung', *Weimarer Beiträge: Zeitschrift für Literaturwissenschaft, Ästhetik und Kulturwissenschaften*, 53.4 (2007), 485–502

——'Auszeit des Erzählens: W. G. Sebalds Poetik der Beschreibung', in Fischer, op. cit. (Section 2), pp. 297–316

SCHIFERLI, VICTOR, 'W. G. Sebald: Een korte introductie', in *W. G. Sebald: Een hommage aan een unieke auteur* [no editor] (Amsterdam: De Bezige Bij, 2008), pp. 2–3 [in Dutch]

SCHIFFERMÜLLER, ISOLDE, '*Austerlitz* o l'esigenza dei morti: sull'ultimo opera di W. G. Sebald', in Busch, op. cit. (Section 3), pp. 121–44

SCHLANT, ERNESTINE, 'Post-Unification: Bernhard Schlink, Peter Schneider, W. G. Sebald', in *The Language of Silence: West German Literature and the Holocaust* (New York: Routledge, 1999), pp. 209–34 (pp. 224–34 on WGS)

——'Nach der Wiedervereinigung: Bernhard Schlink, Peter Schneider, W. G. Sebald', in *Sprache des Schweigens: Die deutsche Literatur and der Holocaust* (Munich: Beck, 2001), pp. 278–90 [translation of above]

SCHLESINGER, PHILIP, 'On the Irrelevance of the Cold War: Some Reflections on the Work of W. G. Sebald', in *Post-Cold War Europe, Post-Cold War America*, ed. by Ruud Janssens and Rob Kroes, European Contributions to American Studies, 55 (Amsterdam: VU University Press, 2004), pp. 108-18

——'W. G. Sebald and the Condition of Exile', *Theory, Culture & Society*, 21.2 (April 2004), 43–67

SCHLICHT, CORINNA, 'Einblicke in österreichische Literatur: W. G. Sebalds Essays über Spezifika einer Literatur in Österreich', in *Mitteilungen über Max: Marginalien zu W. G. Sebald*, ed. by Gerhard Köpf (Oberhausen: Laufen, 1998), pp. 49–57

SCHLODDER, HOLGER, 'Die Schrecken der Überlebenden: Dialog-Collage über *Die Ausgewanderten* und *Die Ringe des Saturn*', in *W. G. Sebald*, ed. by Franz Loquai (Eggingen: Isele, 1997), pp. 176–82 (cf. Audio-Visual Bibliography)

SCHMIDT, GARY, 'Sublime Melancholy: The Function of the Homoerotic in Sebald's *Die Ausgewanderten*', in *Über Gegenwartsliteratur: Interpretationen und Interventionen: Festschrift für Paul Michael Lützeler zum 65. Geburtstag von ehemaligen StudentInnen*, ed. by Mark W. Rectanus (Bielefeld: Aisthesis, 2008), pp. 297–314

SCHMIDT-HANNISA, HANS-WALTER, 'Aberration of a Species: On the Relationship between Man and Beast in W. G. Sebald's Work', trans. by Linda Short, in Fuchs and Long, op. cit. (Section 2), pp. 31–43

SCHMITZ, HELMUT, '"... only signs everywhere of the annihilation": W. G. Sebald's *Austerlitz*', in *On their Own Terms: The Legacy of National Socialism in Post-1990 German Fiction* (Birmingham: Birmingham University Press, 2004), pp. 291–321

——'Introduction: The Return of Wartime Suffering in Contemporary German Memory Culture, Literature, and Film', in *A Nation of Victims? Representations of German Wartime Suffering from 1945 to the Present*, ed. by Helmut Schmitz, German Monitor, 67 (Amsterdam: Rodopi, 2007), pp. 1–30

——'Zweierlei Allegorie: W. G. Sebalds *Austerlitz* und Stephan Wackwitz's *Ein unsichtbares Land*', in Fischer, op. cit. (Section 2), pp. 257–76

——'Catastrophic History, Trauma and Mourning in W. G. Sebald and Jörg Friedrich', in *Beyond Political Correctness: Remapping German Sensibilities in the 21st Century*, ed. by

Christine Anton and Frank Pilipp, German Monitor, 72 (Amsterdam: Rodopi, 2010), pp. 27-50

SCHMITZ-EMANS, MONIKA, 'Sebalds Landschaften', *Colloquium Helveticum: Cahiers Suisses de Littérature Générale et Comparée*, 38 (2007), 241–70

SCHMUCKER, PETER, 'Zeit, Geschichte, Saturn: Geschichtsphilosophische Positionen bei Walter Benjamin und W. G. Sebald', part 1: *FOCUS MUL*, 22.3 (2005), 151-58; part 2: FOCUS MUL, 22.4 (2005), 221-32 (published by the University of Lübeck)

SCHNEIDER, THOMAS F., 'Documentary Warfare: Strukturen und Zielsetzungen in W. G. Sebalds, Volker Hages und Jörg Friedrichs Publikationen zur Repräsentation der alliierten Luftangriffe im Zweiten Weltkrieg', in *Information Warfare: Die Rolle der Medien (Literatur, Kunst, Photographie, Film, Fernsehen, Theater, Presse, Korrespondenz) bei der Kriegsdarstellung und -deutung*, ed. by Claudia Glunz, Artur Pelka, and Thomas F. Schneider (Göttingen: Universitätsverlag Osnabrück bei Vandenhoeck & Ruprecht Unipress, 2007), pp. 563–75

SCHOLZ, CHRISTIAN, 'Photographie and Erinnerung: W. G. Sebald im Porträt', in Krüger, op. cit. (Section 3), pp. 73–80

——'Pictures Remain and Live: Remembering W. G. Sebald', trans. by Markus Zisselsberger, in Patt, op. cit. (Section 2), pp. 542–49 [translation of above]

SCHULTE, CHRISTIAN, 'Die Naturgeschichte der Zerstörung: W. G. Sebalds Thesen zu *Luftkrieg and Literatur*', in Arnold, op. cit. (Section 3), pp. 82–94

SCHUMACHER, HEINZ, 'Aufklärung, Auschwitz, Auslöschung: Eine Annäherungen an *Paul Bereyter*', in Köpf, op. cit. (Section 2), pp. 58–84

SCHÜTTE, UWE, 'Ein Lehrer: In memoriam W. G. Sebald', in Krüger, op. cit. (Section 3), 56–62

——'Der Hüter der Metaphysik: W. G. Sebalds Essays über die österreichische Literatur', *Manuskripte*, 155 (2002), 124–28

——'"In einer wildfremden Gegend": W. G. Sebalds Essays über die österreichische Literatur', in Görner, op. cit. (Section 2), pp. 63–74

——'Für eine "mindere" Literaturwissenschaft: W. G. Sebald und die "kleine" Literatur aus der österreichischen Peripherie, und von anderswo', in Zisselsberger, op. cit. (Section 3), pp. 93–107

——'Ein Portrait des Germanisten als junger Mann: Zu W. G. Sebalds dissidenter Haltung gegenüber der Literaturwissenschaft in seinen akademischen Rezensionen', *Sprachkunst: Beiträge zur Literaturwissenschaft*, 39.2 (2008), 309–32

——'Weil nicht sein kann, was nicht sein darf: Anmerkungen zu W. G. Sebalds Essay über Jurek Beckers Romane', *Sinn und Form*, 62.2 (2010), 235–42 [This text follows as a commentary to the essay by WGS on Jurek Becker; cf. Primary Bibliography D.53.]

SCHUTTER, DIRK DE, 'A zwart', in Ceuppens and Philipsen, op. cit. (Section 3), 73–76 [on *Austerlitz* and *Logis in einem Landhaus*]

SCHWAB, GABRIELE, 'Writing Against Memory and Forgetting', *Literature and Medicine*, 25.1 (2006), 95–121

SCOTT, JOANNA, 'Sebald Crawling', *Salmagundi*, nos. 135–36 (2002), 243–54

SCURRY, AMELIA, 'Melancholy and History in W. G. Sebald's *The Rings of Saturn*', in *Remaking Literary History*, ed. by Helen Groth and Paul Sheehan (Newcastle-upon-Tyne: Cambridge Scholars Publishing, 2010), pp. 14-24

SEARS, JOHN, 'Photographs, Images and the Space of Literature in Sebald's Prose', in Patt, op. cit. (Section 2), pp. 204–25

SEIDEL ARPACI, ANNETTE, 'Lost in Translations? The Discourse of "German Suffering" and W. G. Sebald's *Luftkrieg und Literatur*', in *A Nation of Victims? Representations of German Wartime Suffering from 1945 to the Present*, ed. by Helmut Schmitz (Amsterdam: Rodopi, 2007), pp. 161–79

SELF, WILL, 'In the Footsteps of W. G. Sebald', *Guardian*, 7 February 2009, Review section, pp. 2–4

——'Absent Jews and Invisible Executioners: W. G. Sebald and the Holocaust', *In Other Words: The Journal for Literary Translators*, no. 35 (2010), 60–76 [transcript of the 2010 Sebald Lecture] [See also Audio-Visual Bibliography for link to recording on the BCLT website. An edited version of this piece was published under the title 'The Good German' in *Times Literary Supplement*, 22 January 2010, pp. 13–15; see the Editor's comment, 'This Week', ibid., p. 2. See also Gina Thomas, 'Der gute Deutsche', in the Reviews Bibliography (p. 579).]

SHAFFER, ELINOR, 'W. G. Sebald's Photographic Narrative', in Görner, op. cit. (Section 2), pp. 51–62

SHAHAR, GALILI, 'Figurations of *Unheimlichkeit*: Homelessness and the Identity of "Jews" in Sebald, Maron, and Honigmann', *Gegenwartsliteratur: Ein Germanistisches Jahrbuch*, 3 (2004), 28–45

SHEPPARD, RICHARD, 'Dexter — Sinister: Some Observations on Decrypting the Mors Code in the Work of W. G. Sebald', *Journal of European Studies*, 35 (2005), 419–63 [review article]

——'"Woods, Trees and the Spaces in between": A Report on Work Published on W. G. Sebald 2005–08', *Journal of European Studies*, 39 (2009), 79–128 [review article]

——'W. G. Sebald's Reception of Alfred Döblin', in *Alfred Döblin: Beyond the Alexanderplatz*, ed. by Steffan Davies and Ernest Schonfield (Berlin: de Gruyter, 2009), pp. 350–76

SHIELDS, ANDREW, 'Neun Sätze aus Austerlitz', in Krüger, op. cit. (Section 3), pp. 63–72

SIBLEWSKI, KLAUS, 'Vom Erzählen nach der Katastrophe: Über W. G. Sebald', *Sinn und Form*, 55.1 (2003), 117–28

SILL, OLIVER, '"Aus dem Jäger ist ein Schmetterling geworden": Textbeziehungen zwischen Werken von W. G. Sebald, Franz Kafka and Vladimir Nabokov', *Poetica*, 29 (1997), 596–623

——'Migration als Gegenstand der Literatur: W. G. Sebalds *Die Ausgewanderten* (1992)', in *Nation, Ethnie, Minderheit: Beiträge zur Aktualität ethnischer Konflikte*, ed. by Armin Nassehi (Cologne: Böhlau, 1997), pp. 309–30

——'Spiel: Wolfgang Hildesheimer, *Marbot: Eine Biographie* (1981); W. G. Sebald, *Die Ausgewanderten* (1993)', in *Der Kreis des Lesens: Eine Wanderung durch die europäische Moderne* (Bielefeld: Aisthesis, 2001), pp. 214–37 (pp. 226–37 on WGS)

——'Verwandlung: W. G. Sebald, *Schwindel. Gefühle.* (1990), *Die Ausgewanderten* (1993); Franz Kafka, "Der Jäger Gracchus" (vor 1917); Vladimir Nabokov, *Speak, Memory* (1966)', in *Der Kreis des Lesens: Eine Wanderung durch die europäische Moderne* (Bielefeld: Aisthesis, 2001), pp. 15–47

SIMIC, CHARLES, 'Conspiracy of Silence', *New York Review of Books*, 27 February 2003, pp. 8–9; repr. in *The Emergence of Memory*, ed. by Schwartz, pp. 145–58 (cf. reviews of *On the Natural History of Destruction*)

——'Verschwörung des Schweigens', in *Die Wahrnehmung des Dichters: Über Poesie und Wirklichkeit*, trans. by Thomas Poiss (Munich: Hanser, 2007), pp. 218–32 [translation of above]

SIMON, ULRICH, 'Der Provokateur als Literaturhistoriker: Anmerkungen zu Literaturbegriff und Argumentationsverfahren in W. G. Sebalds essayistischen Schriften', in Atze and Loquai, op. cit. (Section 2), pp. 78–104

SMITH, DUNCAN, 'Sebald's Beetles, Bombs, and the Unfulfilled Tasks of Literature', in *Patentlösung oder Zankapfel? 'German Studies' für den internationalen Bereich als Alternative zur Germanistik-Beispiele aus Amerika*, ed. by Peter Pabisch, Jahrbuch für Internationale Germanistik, series A: Kongressberichte, 72 (Berne: Lang, 2005), pp. 129–41

SOLHEIM, BIRGER, 'Die Wende als Möglichkeit eines neuen Blicks auf die Vergangenheit: Zeit- und Raumkonzepte zwischen Realität und Fiktion bei W. G. Sebald und Jürgen

Becker', in *Grenzen der Identität und der Fiktionalität*, ed. by Ulrich Breuer and Beatrice Sandberg, Autobiographisches Schreiben in der deutschsprachigen Gegenwartsliteratur, 1 (Munich: iudicium, 2006), pp. 318–31

SONTAG, SUSAN, 'A Mind in Mourning', in *Where the Stress Falls: Essays* (New York: Farrar, Straus and Giroux, 2001), pp. 41–48 (first publ. in *Times Literary Supplement*, 25 February 2000, pp. 3–4) (cf. Reviews of *Vertigo*)

—— 'Ein trauender Geist', trans. by Sabine Hübner, in W. G. Sebald, *W. G. Sebald: Gespräch mit Lebenden and Toten* (= Bogen 48) (Munich: Hanser, 2000), unpaginated pamphlet (cf. Primary Bibliography B.C.2); repr. in Krüger, op. cit. (Section 3), pp. 88–95 [translation of above]

SORNIG, DAVID, 'Picturing the Story: Image and Narrative in Brian Castro and W. G. Sebald', *Text*, 8.1 (2004) <http://www.textjournal.com.au/april04/sornig.htm/> [accessed 5 September 2009]

SPARRE, SULAMITH, 'W. G. Sebald über Erinnern und Heimweh: *Die Ausgewanderten*: Eine Dokumentation erfundener Lebensläufe', in Loquai, *W. G. Sebald*, op. cit. (Section 2), pp. 198–207

SPRECHER, CATHERINE, 'W. G. Sebald's *The Emigrants* and Franz Rosenzweig's Concept of Neighborly Love: On the Writing of History', in *Inventing the Past: Memory Work in Culture and History*, ed. by Otto Heim and Caroline Wiedmer (Basle: Schwabe, 2005) pp. 139–58

SPRINGER, BERND F., 'Geschichten statt Geschichte: Dieter Fortes erzählerische Aufarbeitung des Bombenkriegs im Kontext der Sebald-Debatte', *Revista de Filología Alemana*, 16 (2008), 189–210

STEINAECKER, THOMAS VON, 'Zwischen schwarzem Tod und weißer Ewigkeit: Zum Grau auf den Abbildungen W. G. Sebalds', in Martin and Wintermeyer, op. cit. (Section 2), pp. 119–35

STEINFELD, THOMAS, 'W. G. Sebald', in Krüger, op. cit. (Section 3), pp. 81–87

STEINLECHNER, GISELA, 'Strahlende Fundstücke: W. G. Sebalds fotografische Poetik', *Fotogeschichte*, 25 (2005), 43–49

STEINMANN, HOLGER, 'Zitatruinen unterm Hundsstern: W. G. Sebalds Ansichten von der Nachtseite der Philologie', in Niehaus and Öhlschläger, op. cit. (Section 2), pp. 145–56

STISTRUP-JENSEN, MERETE, 'Le Spectre des mots: *Austerlitz* de W. G. Sebald', in *Citer la langue de l'autre: Mots étrangers dans le roman, de Proust à W. G. Sebald*, ed. by Danielle Perrot-Corpet and Christine Queffélec (Lyons: Presses Universitaires de Lyon, 2007), pp. 203–16

STODDARD, ROGER ELIOT, 'W. G. Sebald: Some Uncollected Authors LXX', *Book Collector*, 58 (2009), 517–42

STONE, WILL, 'Location Location: At Risk of Internment: W. G. Sebald in Terezin and Breedonk', *Vertigo Magazine*, 4.3 (2009) 66–70 [with original photographs]

—— 'Reflections on W. G. Sebald', *Irish Pages: A Journal of Contemporary Writing*, 5.1 (2009), 89–99

STRASSER, PETRA, 'Blick zurück in die Zukunft: Erinnerung unter dem Aspekt der "Nachträglichkeit"; *Austerlitz*, W. G. Sebalds Erinnerung durch Raum und Zeit', in *Erinnern*, ed. by Wolfram Mauser and Joachim Pfeiffer, Freiburger literaturpsychologische Gespräche: Jahrbuch für Literatur und Psychoanalyse, 23 (Würzburg: Königshausen & Neumann, 2004), pp. 137–49

STRATHAUSEN, CARSTEN, 'Going Nowhere: Sebald's Rhizomatic Travels', in Patt, op. cit. (Section 2), pp. 472–91

STREIM, GREGOR, 'Der Bombenkrieg als Sensation und als Dokumentation. Gert Ledigs Roman *Vergeltung* und die Debatte um W. G. Sebalds *Luftkrieg und Literatur*', in *Krieg in den Medien*, ed. by Hans-Peter Preußer, Amsterdamer Beiträge zur neueren Germanistik, 57 (Amsterdam: Rodopi, 2005), pp. 293-312

SUMMERS-BREMNER, ELUNED, 'Reading, Walking, Mourning: W. G. Sebald's Peripatetic Fictions', *Journal of Narrative Theory*, 34.3 (2004), 304–34

——'Depressing Books: W. G. Sebald and the Narratives of History', in *Depression and Narrative: Telling the Dark*, ed. by Hilary Clark (Albany, NY: SUNY Press, 2008), pp. 229–42

SUNDE, OLE ROBERT, 'Sebald og silkeormen', in Vinger, op. cit. (Section 3), pp. 120–25

SWALES, MARTIN, 'Intertextuality, Authenticity, Metonymy? On Reading W. G. Sebald', in Görner, op. cit. (Section 2), pp. 81–88

——'Theoretical Reflections on the Work of W. G. Sebald', in Long and Whitehead, op. cit. (Section 2), pp. 23–28

SZENTIVANYI, CHRISTINA M. E., 'W. G. Sebald and Structures of Testimony and Trauma: There are Spots of Mist that No Eye Can Dispel', in Denham and McCulloh, op. cit. (Section 2), pp. 351–63

TABAH, MIREILLE, 'Erinnerung als Performanz: W. G. Sebalds *Austerlitz* versus Thomas Bernhards *Auslöschung*', in Heidelberger-Leonard and Tabah, op. cit. (Section 2), pp. 125–39

TABBERT, REINBERT, 'Max in Manchester: Außen- und Innenansicht eines jungen Autors', in Krüger, op. cit. (Section 3), pp. 21–30

——'Tanti saluti cordiali. Max: W. G. Sebald ... drei bislang unveröffentlichte Briefe an einen Studienfreund', *Literaturen*, 2004.5, 46–49 (cf. Primary Bibliography I.3)

——'Früher Schulweg im Allgäu: Zwei Kindheitserinnerungen des Schriftstellers W. G. Sebald', *Literatur in Bayern: Vierteljahresschrift für Literatur, Literaturkritik und Literaturwissenschaft*, 25, no. 97 (2009), 28–30

TABERNER, STUART, 'German Nostalgia? Remembering German-Jewish Life in W. G. Sebald's *Die Ausgewanderten* and *Austerlitz*', in Anderson, op. cit. (Section 3), pp. 181–202

TAGG, JOHN, 'The Violence of Meaning', *Crossings: A Counter-Disciplinary Journal*, 3 (1999) 187–122

TENNSTEDT, ANTJE, 'L'Illusion d'une communication orale dans *Die Ausgewanderten* et *Austerlitz* de W. G. Sebald', in *Dialogues: Études [...] en hommage au Professeur René Girard*, ed. by Jean-Charles Margotton (= *Cahiers d'Études germaniques*, 47 (2004)), pp. 33–43

TEUTSCH, ANNELIESE, 'W. G. Sebald: Erzählen wider das Vergessen', *Der Schwabenspiegel*, 4–5 (2004), 269–90

THEISEN, BIANCA, 'Prose of the World: W. G. Sebald's Literary Travels', *Germanic Review*, 79.3 (2004), 163–79

——'A Natural History of Destruction: W. G. Sebald's *The Rings of Saturn*', *Modern Language Notes*, 121.3 (2006), 563–81

THIRLWELL, ADAM, 'Kitsch and W. G. Sebald', *Areté: The Arts Tri-Quarterly*, no. 12 (2003), 27–54

TISCHEL, ALEXANDRA, 'Aus der Dunkelkammer der Geschichte: Zum Zusammenhang von Photographie und Erinnerung in W. G. Sebalds *Austerlitz*', in Niehaus and Öhlschläger, op. cit. (Section 2), pp. 31–45

TONNARD, ELISABETH, 'Eeuwig struikelen: Een wandeling met Sebald', *De gids*, 169.4 (2006), 311–21 [in Dutch]

TORGOVNICK, MARIANNA, '"They are ever returning to us, the dead": The Novels of W. G. Sebald', in *The War Complex: World War II in our Time* (Chicago: University of Chicago Press, 2005), pp. 115–30

URITESCU-LOMBARD, RAMONA, '"Heimat", Migration and Melancholy in W. G. Sebald's *Die Ausgewanderten*', in *Imaginäre Topografien: Migration und Verortung*, ed. by Klaus Müller-Richter and Ramona M. Uritescu-Lombard (Bielefeld: transcript, 2007), pp. 49–68

VÁSQUEZ, JUAN GABRIEL, 'La memoria de los dos Sebald', *Cuadernos Hispanoamericanos*, no. 648 (2004), 87–91

VEDDER, ULRIKE, 'Luftkrieg und Vertreibung: Zu ihrer Übertragung und Literarisierung in der Gegenwartsliteratur', in *Chiffre 2000: Neue Paradigmen der Gegenwartsliteratur*, ed. by Corina Caduff and Ulrike Vedder (Munich: Fink, 2005), pp. 59–79

VEES-GULANI, SUSANNE, 'Troubled Memories: Posttraumatic Stress, German Writers, and the Bombings of World War Two', *War, Literature, and the Arts*, 17.1–2 (2005), 175–94

——'The Experience of Destruction: W. G. Sebald, the Airwar, and Literature', in Denham and McCulloh, op. cit. (Section 2), pp. 335–49

VERAGUTH, HANNES, 'W. G. Sebald and die alte Schule: *Schwindel. Gefühle.*, *Die Ausgewanderten*, *Die Ringe des Saturn* and *Austerlitz*: Erinnerungskunst in vier Büchern, die so tun, als ob sie wahr seien (Zur Vergabe des Berliner Literaturpreises)', in Arnold, op. cit. (Section 3), pp. 30–42

VERSCHAFFEL, TOM, 'Alles is altijd anders: Bij Sebalds *Melancholische dwaalwegen*', in Ceuppens and Philipsen, op. cit. (Section 3), 28–38 [on *Schwindel. Gefühle.*]

VIGDERMAN, PATRICIA, 'Sebald in Starbucks', *Iowa Review*, 34.1 (2004), 93–96

VIGLIANI, ADA, 'Fra malinconia e ricordo: Vagabondaggi e divagazioni letterarie nell'opera di W. G. Sebald', in Busch, op. cit. (Section 3), pp. 33–48

VOGEL-KLEIN, RUTH, 'Mémoire, traces et silences: La Shoah en RFA: Les exemples de Peter Weiss et de W. G. Sebald', in *La Mémoire* (Actes du colloque de l'AGES), ed. by Jean-Charles Margotton and Hélène Perennec (Lyons: Presses Universitaires de Lyon, 2003), pp. 61–80

——'Détours de la mémoire: La Représentation de la Shoah dans la nouvelle *Max Aurach* de W. G. Sebald', in *L'Indicible dans l'espace franco-germanique an XXe siècle*, ed. by Françoise Retif, Les Mondes germaniques (Paris: L'Harmattan, 2004) pp. 154–74

——'W. G. Sebald, la guerre aérienne et la littérature', *Allemagne d'aujourd'hui*, no. 167 (January–March 2004), 141–51

——'"Stendhal nach Auschwitz": Zur Rezeption W. G. Sebalds in Frankreich', in Atze and Loquai, op. cit. (Section 2), pp. 133–42

——'Rückkehr und Gegen-Zeitigkeit: Totengedenken bei W. G. Sebald', in Vogel-Klein, op. cit. (Section 3), pp. 99–115

——'"Ein Fleckerlteppich": Interview with Gertrud Th. Aebischer-Sebald (March 2005)', in Vogel-Klein, op. cit. (Section 3), pp. 211–20

——'Les Traces de Kafka dans *Vertiges* de W. G. Sebald', in *Sillages de Kafka*, ed. by Philippe Zard (Paris: Editions Le Manuscrit, 2007), pp. 435–51

——'Französische Intertexte in W. G. Sebalds *Austerlitz*', in Heidelberger-Leonard and Tabah, op. cit. (Section 2), pp. 73–92

WACHENDORFF, MARTINA, 'Introduction to the 2009 Actes Sud brochure' <www.actes-sud. fr/sites/default/files/brochure_sebald_0.pdf>, p. 1 [on accompanying WGS to the Bibliothèque nationale in Paris in 1999; in French]

WAGNER, CHRISTIAN, 'Eine Voraberinnerung: Als die Anarchie baden ging oder: Die kurzen Sommer der Anarchie', in Köpf, op. cit. (Section 2), pp. 85–96

WAGNER, HANS-ULRICH, 'Audioarchäologe auf den Spuren eines archäologischen Erzählers: Ulrich Gerhardts Hörspiele nach W. G. Sebalds *Die Ausgewanderten*: Eine Hörspielkritik in vier Kapiteln', in Loquai, *W. G. Sebald*, op. cit. (Section 2), pp. 198–207 [review essay on Ulrich Gerhardt's radio play based on *The Emigrants*; cf. Audio-Visual Bibliography]

WALDER, DENNIS, 'Recalling the Hidden Ends of Empire: W. G. Sebald', in *Postcolonial Nostalgias: Writing, Representation and Memory* (London: Routledge, 2010), pp. 94–115

WALKOWITZ, REBECCA L., 'Sebald's *Vertigo*', in *Cosmopolitan Style: Modernism Beyond the Nation* (New York: Columbia University Press, 2006), pp. 153–70

WARD, DAVID C., 'Ghost Worlds of the Ordinary: W. G. Sebald and Gerhard Richter', *PN-Review*, 29.6 (2003), 32–36

WARD, SIMON, 'Ruins and the Imagination of Cultural Tradition after 1945', in *German Literature, History and the Nation: Papers from the Conference 'The Fragile Tradition', Cambridge 2002*, II, ed. by Christian Emden and David Midgley, Cultural History and Literary Imagination, 2 (Oxford: Lang, 2004), pp. 329–53

——'Ruins and Poetics in the Works of W. G. Sebald', in Long and Whitehead, op. cit. (Section 2), pp. 58–71

——'Responsible Ruins? W. G. Sebald and the Responsibility of the German Writer', *Forum for Modern Language Studies*, 42.2 (2006), 183–99

WARNER, MARINA, 'The Lost Life of Things', *Times Literary Supplement*, 11 July 2008, pp. 13–15 [edited version of the Sebald Lecture given in London, 2007; longer version published as 'Stranger Magic: True Stories and Translated Selves', *In Other Words: The Journal for Literary Translators*, no. 31 (Summer 2008), 26–41; cf. the correspondence from Daniel Waissbain in the *TLS*, 31 August and 13 August 2008]

WEBER, MARKUS R., 'Phantomschmerz Heimweh: Denkfiguren der Erinnerung im literarischen Werk W. G. Sebalds', in *Neue Generation — Neues Erzählen: Deutsche Prosa-Literatur der achtziger Jahre*, ed. by Walter Delabar and others (Opladen: Westdeutscher Verlag, 1993), pp. 57–67

——'Sechzehn Wege zu Austerlitz: W. G. Sebalds neues Prosabuch', *Neue deutsche Literatur*, 49.5 (2001), 100–08

——'Die fantastische befragt die pedantische Genauigkeit: Zu den Abbildungen in W. G. Sebalds Werken', in Arnold, op. cit. (Section 3), pp. 63–74

——'Chor der Toten: Das Friedhofsgefühl in W. G. Sebalds Nachlaß *Campo Santo*', *Neue Deutsche Literatur*, 52.1 (2004), 159–62

——'Bilder erzählen den Erzähler: Zur Bedeutung der Abbildungen für die Herausbildung von Erzählerrollen in den Werken W. G. Sebalds', in Vogel-Klein, op. cit. (Section 3), pp. 25–45

WEIHE, RICHARD, 'Wittgensteins Augen: W. G. Sebalds Film-Szenario "Leben Ws"', *fair: Zeitung für Kunst und Ästhetik*, 7.4 (2009), 11–12

WELLER, CHRISTIANE, 'Die Melancholie des Ortes: Stadt, Gewalt und Erinnerung', in Fischer, op. cit. (Section 2), pp. 493–508

WHITEHEAD, ANNE, 'The Butterfly Man: Trauma and Repetition in the Writing of W. G. Sebald', in *Trauma Fiction* (Edinburgh: Edinburgh University Press, 2004), pp. 117–39

WIECZOREK, STEFAN, 'De tot springens toe vastgehouden aanblik: Verstrengelingen van intermedialiteit en intertekstualiteit aan de hand van W. G. Sebalds verhaal 'Dr Henry Selwyn', trans. by Monique de Waal, in Bel and others, op. cit. (Section 3), pp. 10–20

WILLER, STEFAN, 'Being Translated: Exile, Childhood, and Multilingualism in G.-A. Goldschmidt and W. G. Sebald', in *German Memory Contests: The Quest for Identity in Literature, Film, and Discourse since 1990*, ed. by Mary Cosgrove, Anne Fuchs, and Georg Grote (Rochester, NY: Camden House: 2006), pp. 87–105

WILLIAMS, ARTHUR, 'The Elusive First-Person Plural: Real Absences in Reiner Kunze, Bernd-Dieter Huge and W. G. Sebald', in *'Whose Story?' Continuities in Contemporary German-Language Literature*, ed. by Arthur Williams, Stuart Parkes, and Julian Preece (Frankfurt a.M.: Lang, 1998), pp. 85–113 (pp. 98–100 on *Die Ausgewanderten*)

——'W. G. Sebald: A Holistic Approach to Borders, Texts and Perspectives', in *German Language-Literature Today: International and Popular?*, ed. by Arthur Williams, Stuart Parkes, and Julian Preece (Frankfurt a.M.: Lang, 2000), pp. 99–118

——'"Das korsakowsche Syndrom": Remembrance and Responsibility in W. G. Sebald', in *German Culture and the Uncomfortable Past: Representations of National Socialism in Contemporary Germanic Literature*, ed. by Helmut Schmitz (Aldershot: Ashgate, 2001), pp. 65–86

——'W. G. Sebald: Weit ausholende Annäherungen an ein problematisches Vaterland', in *Deutschsprachige Erzählprosa seit 1990 im europäischen Kontext: Interpretationen, Intertextualität, Rezeption*, ed. by Volker Wehdeking and Anne-Marie Corbin (Trier: Wissenschaftlicher Verlag, 2003), pp. 179–97

——'"immer weiter ostwärts und immer weiter zurück in der Zeit": Exploring the Extended Kith and Kin of W. G. Sebald's *Austerlitz*', in *Neighbours and Strangers: Literary and Cultural Relations in Germany, Austria and Central Europe since 1989*, ed. by Ian Foster and Juliet Wigmore (Amsterdam: Rodopi, 2004), pp. 121–41

——'W. G. Sebald: Probing the Outer Edges of Nature', in *Cityscapes and Countryside in Contemporary German Literature*, ed. by Julian Preece and Osman Durrani (Oxford: Lang, 2004), pp. 179–96

——'Modes of Restitution: Schreber as Countermodel for Sebald', in *The Worlds of Elias Canetti: Centenary Essays*, edited by William Collins Donahue and Julian Preece (Newcastle upon Tyne: Cambridge Scholars Publishing, 2007), pp. 225–46

——'Some Thoughts on W. G. Sebald, Drawing, Painting, and Music', in *New German Literature: Life-Writing and Dialogue with the Arts*, ed. by Julian Preece, Frank Finlay, and Ruth J. Owen, Leeds–Swansea Colloquia on Contemporary German Literature (Oxford: Lang, 2007), pp. 51–74

Wilms, Wilfried, 'Taboo and Repression in W. G. Sebald's *On the Natural History of Destruction*', in Long and Whitehead, op. cit. (Section 2), pp. 175–89

——'Speak No Evil, Write No Evil: In Search of a Usable Language of Destruction', in Denham and McCulloh, op. cit. (Section 2), pp. 183–204

Wils, Jean-Pierre, '"Mit reinster Traumklarheit"': Über Schönheit und Melancholie im Werk von W. G. Sebald', in *Versuche über Ethik* (Fribourg: Academic Press Fribourg; Freiburg: Herder, 2004), pp. 176–91

Wintermeyer, Ingo, '"... kaum eine Schmerzensspur hinterlassen ..."? Luftkrieg, Literatur und der "cordon sanitaire"', in Martin and Wintermeyer, op. cit. (Section 2), pp. 137–61

Wirtz, Thomas, 'Schwarze Zuckerwatte: Anmerkungen zu W. G. Sebald', *Merkur*, 55.6 (2001), 530–34

Witthaus, Jan-Henrik, 'Fehlleistung und Fiktion: Sebaldsche Gedächtnismodelle zwischen Freud und Borges', in Niehaus and Öhlschläger, op. cit. (Section 2), pp. 157–72

Wohlfahrt, Irving, 'Anachronie: Interferenzen zwischen Walter Benjamin und W. G. Sebald', *Internationales Archiv für Sozialgeschichte der deutschen Literatur: IASL*, 33.2 (2008), 184–242

Wohlleben, Doren, 'Poetik des Schwindels and Verschwindens bei Hartmut Lange, W. G. Sebald and Horst Stern', in *Differenzerfahrung and Selbst: Bewusstsein and Wahrnehmung in Literatur and Geschichte des 20. Jahrhunderts*, ed. by Bettina von Jagow and Florian Steger (Heidelberg: Winter, 2003), pp. 333–53

——'Effet de flou: Unschärfe als literarisches Mittel der Bewahrheitung in W. G. Sebalds *Schwindel. Gefühle*', in Niehaus and Öhlschläger, op. cit. (Section 2), pp. 127–43

——'Über die Photographie hinaus: Zur paraliterarischen Funktion der Photographien in W. G. Sebalds *Austerlitz*', in *Transmedialität: Zur Ästhetik paraliterarischer Verfahren*, ed. by Urs Meyer, Roberto Simanowski, and Christoph Zeller (Göttingen: Wallstein, 2006), pp. 185–202

——'Maske–Gesicht–Antlitz: Porträts bei W. G. Sebald in Bild and Text', in Lützeler and Schindler, op. cit. (Section 3), pp. 1–20

Wolff, Lynn, '"Das metaphysische Unterfutter der Realität": Recent Publications and Trends in W. G. Sebald Research', *Monatshefte*, 99.1 (2007), 78–101 [review article]

——'Literary Historiography: W. G. Sebald's Fiction', in Fischer, op. cit. (Section 2), pp. 317–32

——'W. G. Sebald: The Discursive Hybridity of a 20th-/21st-Century "Grenzgänger"', DAAD Conference: 'Deutschland und Europa: Grenzen und Grenzgänge(r)', Berlin, May 2010 <http://www.daad.de/imperia/md/content/de/zentren/wolff_l.pdf>

Wood, James, 'W. G. Sebald's Uncertainty', in *The Broken Estate: Essays on Literature and Belief* (London: Jonathan Cape, 1999), pp. 273–84

Wrobel, Dieter, '"Katastrophengeschichte" and "Trauerseide"', in *Postmodernes Chaos*, *chaotische Postmoderne: Eine Studie zu Analogien zwischen Chaostheorie und deutschsprachiger Prosa der Postmoderne* (Bielefeld: Aisthesis, 1997), pp. 304–45 [on *The Rings of Saturn*]

WUCHERPFENNIG, WOLF, 'W. G. Sebalds Roman *Austerlitz*: Persönliche und gesellschaftliche Erinnerungsarbeit', in *Erinnern,* ed. by Wolfram Mauser and Joachim Pfeiffer, Freiburger literaturpsychologische Gespräche: Jahrbuch für Literatur und Psychoanalyse, 23 (Würzburg: Königshausen & Neumann, 2004), pp. 151–63

WYLIE, JOHN, 'The Spectral Geographies of W. G. Sebald', *Cultural Geographies*, 14 (2007), 171–88

ZASLOVE, JERRY, 'W. G. Sebald and Exilic Memory: His Photographic Images of the Cosmogony of Exile and Restitution', *Journal of the Interdisciplinary Crossroads*, 3.1 (April 2006), online [no active link available]

ZELECHOW, BERNHARD, 'Identity and Erasure: W. G. Sebald's Fictions', in *European Culture in a Changing World: Between Nationalism and Globalism*, ed. by Daniel Meyer-Dinkgräfe (London: Cambridge Scholars Press, 2004), 164–71

ZILCOSKY, JOHN, 'Sebald's Uncanny Travels: The Impossibility of Getting Lost', in Long and Whitehead, op. cit. (Section 2), pp. 102–20

——'The Writer as Nomad? The Art of Getting Lost', *interventions*, 6.2 (2004), 229–41

——'Lost and Found: Disorientation, Nostalgia, and Holocaust Melodrama in Sebald's *Austerlitz*', *Modern Language Notes*, 121.3 (2006), 679–98

——'Verirrt und wieder zurechtgefunden: Orientierungslosigkeit und Nostalgie in Sebalds *Austerlitz*', in *Literatur und Migration*, ed. by Heinz-Ludwig Arnold (= *Text + Kritik*, special issue (2006)), pp. 120–30

ZINFERT, MARIA, 'Grauzonen. Das Schreiben von W. G. Sebald: Versuchsanordnung mit schwarzweißen Fotografieren', in *'Ein in der Phantasie durchgeführtes Experiment': Literatur und Wissenschaft nach Neunzehnhundert*, ed. by Raul Calzoni and Massimo Salgaro (Göttingen: Vandenhoeck & Ruprecht unipress, 2010), pp. 321–36

ZISSELSBERGER, MARKUS, 'Melancholy Longings: Sebald, Benjamin, and the Image of Kafka', in Patt, op. cit. (Section 2), pp. 280–301

——'Stories of *Heimat* and Calamity: W. G. Sebald and Austrian Literature', in Zisselsberger, op. cit. (Section 3), 1–27

——'Towards an Extension of Memory: W. G. Sebald reads Jean Améry', in *Trajectories of Memory: Intergenerational Representations of the Holocaust in History and the Arts*, ed. by Christina Guenther and Beth Griech-Polelle (Newcastle upon Tyne: Cambridge Scholars Press, 2008), pp. 191–224

——'A Persistent Fascination: Recent Publications on the Work of W. G. Sebald', *Monatshefte*, 101.1 (2009), 88–105 [review article]

——'The Afterlife of Literature: Sebald, Blanchot, and Kafka's "Hunter Gracchus"', *Journal of the Kafka Society of America*, 31/32.1–2 (2010), 112–29

——'Introduction: Fluchtträume/Traumfluchten: Journeys to the Undiscover'd Country', in Zisselsberger, op. cit. (Section 2), pp. 1–29

ZUCCHI, MATTHIAS, 'Linguistische Anmerkungen zum Sprachstil W. G. Sebalds', *Sinn und Form*, 56.6 (2004), 841–50

——'Zur Kunstsprache W. G. Sebalds', in Martin and Wintermeyer, op. cit. (Section 2), pp. 163–81

ZWART, JANE, 'The Faithful Trace of Misgiving in W. G. Sebald's *The Emigrants*', *Critique: Studies in Contemporary Fiction*, 47.3 (2006), 243–60

(7) Entries in Reference Works

BROWN, SHARON, '*Austerlitz*', in *Reference Guide to Holocaust Literature*, ed. by Thomas Riggs (Detroit: St James Press, 2002), pp. 370–71

Gunther, Stefan, 'W. G. Sebald' and 'The Emigrants', in Reference Guide to Holocaust Literature, ed. by Thomas Riggs (Detroit: St James Press, 2002), pp. 283–85; pp. 422–23

Huyssen, Andreas, 'Gray Zones of Remembrance', in A New History of German Literature (Cambridge, MA: Belknap Press / Harvard University Press, 2004), pp. 970–75, ed. by David Welbery, Judith Ryan and Hans-Ulrich Gumprecht

Neuhaus, Stefan, 'W[infried] G[eorg] Sebald: Die Ausgewanderten', Kindlers Neues Literatur Lexikon, 22, Supplement L–Z (Munich: Kindler 1998), pp. 458–59

Powers, Elizabeth, 'W. G. (Winfried Georg) Sebald: 1944–2001', in Multicultural Writers since 1945: An A-to-Z Guide, ed. by Alba Amoia and Bettina L. Knapp. (Westport, CT: Greenwood, 2004), pp. 458–62

Robinson, Michael 'Sebald, Winfried Georg Maximilian [Max] (1944–2001)', Oxford Dictionary of National Biography, online edn (Oxford University Press, Jan 2009) <http://www.oxforddnb.com/view/article/76593/> [accessed 25 April 2009]

Schalk, Axel, 'Winfried Georg Sebald', in Reclams Romanlexikon: Deutschsprachige erzählende Literatur vom Mittelalter bis zur Gegenwart, ed. by Frank Rainer Max and Christine Ruhrberg, 5 vols (Stuttgart: Reclam, 1998–2000), v: 20. Jahrhundert, pp. 437–39

Smith, Duncan, 'W. G. Sebald', in Encyclopedia of German Literature, ed. by Matthias Konzett (Chicago: Fitzroy Dearborn, 2000), pp. 890–91

Weber, Markus R., 'W. G. Sebald', in Kritisches Lexikon zur deutschsprachigen Gegenwartsliteratur, 8 (June 2002), unpaginated

Weidermann, Volker, 'Wahre Größe kommt von außen: W. G. Sebald', in Lichtjahre: Eine kurze Geschichte der deutschen Literatur von 1945 bis heute (Cologne: Kiepenheuer & Witsch, 2006), pp. 182–85

(8) Obituaries and Tributes

Anon., 'W. G. Sebald: Writer and Scholar Whose Imaginative Books Were like Journeys without a Map', The Times, 17 December 2001, p. 17

Anon. (tk), 'Sieger und Verlierer: Namen und Ereignisse, die in den zurückliegenden Monaten das literarische Leben bestimmten', Die Welt, 29 December 2001, p. 6

Anon. (nma), 'W. G. Sebald: Die Ausgewanderten, 1992: Im Labyrinth verschollener Erinnerungen', Frankfurter Allgemeine Sonntagszeitung, 17 March 2002, p. 31

Abbott, Thea, 'W. G. Sebald: Literature's Loss', Spiked: The Magazine for Ideas, Literature and the Arts for Norfolk, no. 10 (2002), 4

Arnold, Heinz Ludwig, 'W. G. Sebald 1944–2001', in Arnold, op. cit. (Section 3), pp. 3–5

Bahners, Patrick, 'Wanderers Nachtmarsch. Im Gedenkblätterwald: Zum Tode von W. G. Sebald', Frankfurter Allgemeine Zeitung, 17 December 2001, p. 43

Baker, Kenneth, 'Appreciation: Masterful Weaving of Historical Fact, Invention was W. G. Sebald's Legacy', San Francisco Chronicle, p. RV-4, 23 December 2001 <http://sfgate.com/cgi-bin/article.cgi?f=/c/a/2001/12/23/RV120788.DTL> [accessed 12 July 2008]

Bonifazio, Massimo, 'Qui sta l'altrove di uno scrittore della malinconia', Il Manifesto, 18 December 2001 <http://www.ilmanifesto.it/oggi/art47/htm> [accessed 19 January 2011]

Baron, Ulrich, 'Verborgene Mitteilungen in eigener Sache: Auf W. G. Sebald lastete der Fluch des Melancholikers', Die Weltwoche, 20 December 2001 <http://www.weltwoche.ch/weiche/artikel-fuer-abonnenten.html?hidID=531744>

Battersby, Eileen, 'On the Moral Right to Publish: A Rare Moral Grandeur', Irish Pages, 1.1 (Spring 2002), 228-31

Botsford, Keith, 'W. G. "Max" Sebald: 1944–2001', The Republic of Letters, no. 11 (December 2001) <http://www.bu.edu/trl/11/> [accessed 20 November 2010]

Blythe, Ronald, 'Word from Wormingford', Church Times (early January 2002), unpaginated

BREUER, THEO, 'W. G. Sebald 1944–2001', *Muschelhaufen*, 43 (2003), 168–69

BUSH, PETER, 'Editorial', in Bush, op. cit. (Section 3), 1–2

CASTRO, BRIAN, 'Blue Max: W. G. Sebald: A Tribute', *HEAT*, 3 (2002), 119–29

CATLING, JO, 'Silent Catastrophe: In memoriam W. G. (Max) Sebald 1944–2001', *New Books in German* (Spring 2002), unpaginated <http://www.new-books-in-german.com/featur27.htm> [accessed 5 April 2010]

CLARK, T. J., and OTHERS, 'A Symposium on W. G. Sebald', *Threepenny Review*, ed. by Wendy Lesser, 89 (Spring 2002) <http://www.threepennyreview.com/samples/sebaldsympos_sp02.html> [accessed 17 June 2008]

COZARINSKY, EDGARDO, 'Las heridas de la memoria: W. G. Sebald', *La Nación* (Buenos Aires), 30 December 2001, Suplemento Cultura, p. 8

CZERNIAWSKI, ADAM, '*In memoriam* W. G. Sebald 1944–2001', *Metre*, 16 (Autumn 2004), 136–38; repr. in *The Invention of Poetry* (Cambridge: Salt, 2005), pp. 110–13

DANIELI, ENRICO, 'Präparieren, Präparat, Präparationen: In memoriam W. G. Sebald', *Entwürfe: Zeitschrift für Literatur*, no. 32 (2002), 31–34

DULTZ, SABINE, 'Die Erinnerung spricht Deutsch: Zum Tod des Autors W. G. Sebald', *Münchner Merkur*, 17 December 2001, p. 16

DYER, GEOFF, 'W. G. Sebald (1944–2001)', *Guardian*, 2 January 2010, Review section, p. 5 [part of the feature 'Words and Memories']

HAMBURGER, MICHAEL, 'W. G. Sebald', *Europäische Ideen*, 124 (2002), 37

——'W. G. Sebald', in Arnold, op. cit. (Section 3), pp. 15–16

——'W. G. Sebald', *Decision*, 15 (2002), 28–29; repr. in Görner, op. cit. (Section 2), pp. 9–10; also as 'On the Death of W. G. Sebald', *Irish Pages*, 1.1 (Spring 2002), 109-10

HOARE, PHILIP, 'W. G. Sebald', *Independent*, 20 December 2001 [also refers to correspondence and meeting with WGS, and his interest in Hoare's book]

HOMBERGER, ERIC, 'W. G. Sebald: German Writer Shaped by the Forgetfulness of his Fellow Countrymen after the Second World War', *Guardian*, 17 December 2001, p. 20

JAGGI, MAYA, 'The Last Word', *Guardian*, 21 December 2001, section G2, p. 4 (cf. interview in Primary Bibliography J.46)

JONAS, SIR PETER, '"Wir alle sind doch Emigranten"', *Abendzeitung* (Kultur), (Munich), 28 January 2002, p. 17

KÖHLER, ANDREA, 'Verabredungen in der Vergangenheit. Zum Tod des Schriftstellers W. G. Sebald', *Neue Zürcher Zeitung*, 17 December 2001

KRÜGER, MICHAEL, 'Der Wanderer: Zum Tod von W. G. Sebald', *Süddeutsche Zeitung*, 17 December 2001, p. 16; repr. in *Verleihung des Bremer Literaturpreises 2002: W. G. Sebald, Juli Zeh: Laudationes und Reden* (Bremen: Rudolf-Alexander-Schroder-Stiftung, 2002), p. 19

——'Nichts, nicht das Geringste darf verloren gehen: Erinnerungen an den Schriftsteller W. G. Sebald und dessen Werk: Ein Besuch an seinen Grab in Großbritannien', *Stuttgarter Zeitung* (Wochenendbeilage), 220, 21 September 2002, p. 51

——, ed., *W. G. Sebald zum Gedächtnis* (= *Akzente*, 50.1 (2003)) [special memorial issue; see Section 6 for individual contributions by Rüdiger Görner, Andrea Köhler, Sven Meyer, Christian Scholz, Uwe Schütte, Andrew Shields, Susan Sontag, Thomas Steinfeld, and Reinbert Tabbert]

LANE, ANTHONY, 'Postscript: W. G. Sebald', *New Yorker*, 7 January 2002, p. 22

LOCKWOOD, ALAN, 'With Us, Without Us: In Memoriam W. G. Sebald', *The Brooklyn Rail* (March–April 2002) <http://www.brooklynrail.org/2002/03/books/with-us-without-us-in-memoriam-wg-sebald/> [accessed 5 September 2009]

LOQUAI, FRANZ, 'Abschied von Max: Zur Erinnerung an W. G. Sebald', *literaturkritik.de*, 4.1 (2002), 32–35 <http://www.literaturkritik.de/public/rezension.php?rez_id=4519&ausgabe=200201> [accessed 6 April 2010]

McCRUM, ROBERT, 'Untimely Death Robs Writer of Recognition He Deserved', *Observer*, 16 December 2001 <http://www.observer.co.uk/uk_news/story/0,6903,619/10,00.html> [accessed 16 December 2001]

MEDICUS, THOMAS, 'Leichtfüßiger Schwerarbeiter der Erinnerung', *Frankfurter Rundschau*, 17 December 2001

MÖLLER, ELISABETH, 'Ein Allgäuer Gewächs', *Allgäuer Anzeigeblatt*, 18 December 2001 <http://www.allgaeuer-anzeigeblatt.de/index.shtml?2001&press=0000003153> [accessed 3 February 2011]

MORFORD, MARK, 'W. G. Sebald: In Memoriam. On the Sudden, Tragic Death of a Quietly Radiant Author You've Probably Never Heard of', *San Francisco Chronicle*, 18 December 2001 <http://www.sfgate.com/cgi-bin/article.cgi?f=/g/a/2001/12/19/notes121901.DTL> [accessed 12 July 2008]

MOTION, ANDREW, 'W. G. Sebald', *Independent on Sunday*, 16 December 2001, p. 2

OEHLEN, MARTIN, 'W. G. Sebald kam bei einem Autounfall ums Leben', *Kölner Stadtanzeiger*, 17 December 2001

PLATH, JÖRG, 'Sänger der Verheerungen. Zum Tod des Schriftstellers und Literaturwissenschaftlers W. G. Sebald', *Der Tagesspiegel* [December 2001?]

REISSINGER, MARIANNE, 'Blick zurück nach Haus', *Abendzeitung* (Munich), 17 December 2001, p. 18

ROBINSON, MICHAEL, 'W. G. Sebald', *Independent*, 17 December 2001, Monday Review Section, p. 6; cf. *Broadview* [University of East Anglia staff magazine] (January 2002), 3

RÖSSLE, ALEX, 'Der Schriftsteller und Schüler am Gymnasium Oberstdorf Winfried G. Sebald' <http://fuehrer.oberstdorf-online.de/personen/sebald/> [accessed 22 August 2008]

SALTER REYNOLDS, SUSAN, 'The Literary Journey of a Wandering Soul: An Appreciation', *Los Angeles Times*, 18 December 2001 <http://articles.latimes.com/2001/dec/18/news/lv-sebald18>

SCHENKER, UELI, 'Ein unbestechlicher Zeuge: W. G. Sebald', *Orte*, no. 125 (2002), 58–59

SCHÜTTE, UWE, 'Vertrauen auf das Unmögliche. In Memoriam W. G. Sebald', *Wiener Zeitung*, 4-5 January 2002

—— 'Obituary. W. G. Sebald (1944-2001)', *Austrian Studies*, 11.1 (2003), 246-49

SCOTT, CLIVE, 'Remembering Max Remembering', *Spiked: The Magazine for Ideas, Literature and the Arts for Norfolk*, no. 10 (2002), 34

SMITH, ALI, 'In Memory of W. G. Sebald', *Critical Quarterly*, 44.2 (2002), 59–61

SMITH, CHRISTOPHER, *'Max': W. G. Sebald As I Saw Him* (Norwich: Solen Press, 2007) [privately published pamphlet in a limited edition of 60 numbered copies]

SONTAG, SUSAN, 'The World as India: In memoriam W. G. Sebald', in Bush, op. cit. (Section 3), pp. 19–36 [transcript of the St Jerome Lecture 2002]

STEINFELD, THOMAS, 'Das kosmopolitische Waisenkind: Zum Tod von W. G. Sebald', *Süddeutsche Zeitung*, 17 December 2001, p. 13; repr. in *Jahrbuch der Deutschen Akademie für Sprache und Dichtung 2001* (Göttingen: Wallstein, 2002), pp. 205–07

TABBERT, REINBERT, '"Weil du immer noch das ganze Alpenvorland mit dir rumträgst": Erinnerung an W. G. Sebald, einen Ausgewanderten aus dem Allgäu', *Literaturblatt für Baden und Württemberg*, no. 9.6 (2002), 10-11

THORPE, VANESSA, 'Cult Novelist Killed in Car Accident', *Observer*, 16 December 2001, p. 3

THURBER, JOHN, 'W. G. Sebald, 57: Author Challenged Norms', *Los Angeles Times*, 15 December 2001 <http://articles.latimes.com/2001/dec/15/local/me-15188>

TRIPP, JAN PETER, 'Im Schattenreich', in Vogel-Klein, op. cit. (Section 3), pp. 3–10

VOLLMANN, ROLF, 'Schwarzes Segel der Schwermut. Zum Tod des Schriftstellers W. G. Sebald', *Die Zeit*, 52, 19 December 2001, Feuilleton section, p. 36

WEH, STEFANIE, 'Lire et relire', *Decision: Zeitschrift für deutsche und französische Literatur*, 15 (2002) 28–34

WINIGER, DANIEL, 'In memoriam Winfried G. M. Sebald', *Der Schwabenspiegel*, 3 (2002), 107–09

(9) Poems Written in Tribute to WGS

AGEE, CHRIS, 'Sebald (1944-2001)', in *Next to Nothing* (Cambridge: Salt, 2008), p. 10

BERESFORD, ANNE, 'For Max', in *Collected Poems 1967–2006* (London: Katabasis, 2006), p. 323; also in *Decision: Zeitschrift für deutsche und französische Literatur*, 15 (2002), 24 (reprinted in present volume)

ENZENSBERGER, HANS MAGNUS, 'Ein Abschied von Max Sebald', *Neue Zürcher Zeitung*, 14–15 December 2002; repr. in W. G. Sebald, *Unerzählt* (Munich: Hanser, 2003), p. 5; also repr. as 'Für Max Sebald' in Hans Magnus Enzensberger, *Die Geschichte der Wolken: 99 Meditationen* (Frankfurt a.M.: Suhrkamp, 2003), pp. 34–35

——'A Parting from Max Sebald', trans. by Michael Hamburger, in W. G. Sebald, *Unrecounted*, trans. by Michael Hamburger (London: Hamish Hamilton, 2004), p. 10 [translation of above]; repr. in *Irish Pages*, 1.2 (2002/03), 136 and in *World Literature Today*, 79.1 (2005), 38–39 (cf. Primary Bibliography E.A.13)

——'For Max Sebald', trans. by David Constantine, in 'The Peregrinations of Poetry' (= Sebald Lecture 2006), *In Other Words: The Journal for Literary Translators*, no. 29 (2007), 29–52 (p. 48) [new translation of above]

HAMBURGER, MICHAEL, 'Redundant Epitaphs (for Friends not Named)', *Irish Pages*, 1.2 (Autumn–Winter 2002-03), 133-35; repr. in Arnold, op. cit. (Section 3), 17–19; repr. in Michael Hamburger, *Wild and Wounded: Shorter Poems 2000–2003* (London: Anvil, 2004), pp. 11–14 (reprinted in present volume)

——'W. G. Sebald: Überflüssige Grabschriften: Für ungenannte Freunde', trans. by Joachim Kalka, in Arnold, op. cit. (Section 3), pp. 20–22 [translation of above]

HULSE, MICHAEL, 'Il ritorno in patria', in *The Secret History* (Todmorden: Arc Publications, 2009), p. 63 (reprinted in present volume)

MOTION, ANDREW, 'After Nature and So On', in *Public Property* (London: Faber and Faber, 2002), p. 87

STONE, WILL, 'To Max (W. G. Sebald)', *Decision: Zeitschrift für deutsche und französische Literatur*, 15 (2002), 26–27; repr. in Görner, op. cit. (Section 2), pp. 89–90

SZIRTES, GEORGE, 'Meeting Austerlitz', in Long and Whitehead, op. cit. (Section 2), pp. 16–22; repr. in George Szirtes, *Reel* (Tarsett: Bloodaxe, 2004), pp. 17–24

WATTS, STEPHEN, 'For my Friend, Max Sebald', in Stephen Watts, *Gramsci & Caruso*, trans. by Petr Mikeš (Olomouc: Periplum, 2003), pp. 102–06 [poems in Czech translation with English originals] (reprinted in present volume)

——'Twee gedichten', trans. by Ton Naaijkens, in Bel and others, op. cit. (Section 3), pp. 36–40 [Dutch translation of above and of 'Fragments']

——'Al mio amico Max Sebald', trans. by Cristina Viti, *L'Immaginazione*, no. 243 (Lecce: Manni Editori, 2008) [Italian translation of above]

(10) Poems and Prose Featuring WGS

BECKER, CLAUDIA, 'Heimatlos: W. G. Sebald gewidmet', in *Die unverschämte Gegenwart: Jahrbuch für Literatur*, 15, ed. by Sigfrid Gauch and Verena Mahlow (Frankfurt a.M.: Brandes & Aspel, 2009) p. 123

BÜRGER, PETER, '"Nirgends ein Mensch zu sehen": Ein Spaziergang mit W. G. Sebald', *Akzente: Zeitschrift für Literatur*, 53.2 (2006), 182–91

KRYNICKI, RYSZARD, 'Erwachen (4. Mai 2004)', trans. from the Polish by Renate Schmidgall; Polish original published in *Kamien, szron.* (Kraków: Wyd. a5, 2005), p. 53

Motion, Andrew, 'Traffic', *Guardian*, 2 January 2010, Review section, p. 15

Rose, Martin, 'Amnesia orange' [Berliner Autorenwerkstatt 2008], *Sprache im technischen Zeitalter*, no. 189 (2009), 61–70

Stone, Will, 'After Shingle Street', in *Decision: Zeitschrift für deutsche und französische Literatur*, 18 (2005), 70

———'SS Fort Breedonk: In Memory of W. G. Sebald', in *Glaciation* (London: Salt Publishing, 2007), pp. 50–51

Szirtes, George, 'Backwaters: Norfolk Fields (for W. G. Sebald)', in *An English Apocalypse* (Tarset: Bloodaxe, 2001), pp. 103–08

Zuiderent, Ad, 'De uitgereisden: Commedia sebaldiana', in Bel and others, op. cit. (Section 3), pp. 21–27

(11) MA and PhD Theses on WGS

★ = *also published in book form*

Bloom, Edward George, 'Unfinished Stories: Exile, Conversation, and Jewish Identity in W. G. Sebald's *Austerlitz*' (MA, University of California at Santa Cruz, 2005)

Churchyard, Tom, '"Is this the End of Time?": W. G. Sebald's Challenge to the "Inexorable Advance of Progress"' (MPhil, University of Cambridge, 2010)

★Covindassamy, Mandana, 'A l'épreuve du dépaysement: W. G. Sebald: Cartographie d'une écriture en déplacement' (PhD, Université Paris Sorbonne–Paris IV, 2007)

★Distler, Anton, 'Kein Verstehen ohne fundamentale Ontologie: Eine philosophische Analyse des Werks von Winfried Georg Sebald aufgrund der "existentiellen Psychoanalyse" Jean-Paul Sartres' (PhD, University of Zurich, 2007)

Gelinek, Janika, 'Eine Art privater Wissenschaft. Schnittstellen von Literatur und Literaturwissenschaft im Werk von W. G. Sebald (MA, Humboldt-Universität Berlin, 2006)

Gregory-Guider, Christopher C., 'Autobiogeography and the Art of Peripatetic Memorialization in Works by W. G. Sebald, Patrick Modiano, Iain Sinclair, Jonathan Raban, and William Least Heat-Moon' (PhD, University of Sussex, 2005)

Grossman, Joan, 'Blackout: On Memory & Catastrophe' (PhD, European Graduate School, 2003)

Gunther, Stefan, 'From Remembering Accurately Towards a Hermeneutics of Memory: Representations of the Holocaust in Contemporary Fiction (Walter Abish, Art Spiegelman, W. G. Sebald, D. M. Thomas, Joseph Skibell)' (PhD, Brandeis University, 2000)

Hirsch, Susan, 'Art, Allegory, and Angles of Vision in W. G. Sebald's *Austerlitz*' (MA, Sonoma State University, CA, 2007)

Jones, Susanne Lenne, 'What's in a Frame? Photography, Memory, and History in Contemporary German Literature' (PhD, University of Cincinnati, 2005) [on Monika Maron, W. G. Sebald, and Irina Liebmann]

Kempinski, Avi, 'The Muted I: Locating a Narrator in the Works of W. G. Sebald' (PhD, University of Michigan, 2006)

★Klebes, Martin, 'Remembering Failure: Philosophy and the Form of the Novel' [on Winfried Georg Sebald, Ernst Wilhelm Haendler, Jacques Roubaud] (PhD, Northwestern University, 2003)

Knittel, Susanne Christine, 'Spaces of Memory in Giorgio Bassani, Ruth Klüger and W. G. Sebald' (MA, Universität Konstanz, 2004)

★Lash, Daniel James, 'Translation and Repetition: An Architectural Translation of W. G. Sebald's *The Rings of Saturn*' (MA, University of Cincinnati, 2004)

McGonagill, Doris, 'Warburg, Sebald, Richter: Toward a Visual Memory Archive' (PhD, Harvard University, 2006)

MARTIN, JAMES P., 'The Crisis of Cultural Knowledge in Michael Köhlmeier's *Telemach*, Christoph Ransmayr's *Morbus Kitahara* and W. G. Sebald's *Die Ringe des Saturn*' (PhD, Georgetown University, 2004)

★MEDIN, DANIEL L., 'Three Sons: Franz Kafka and the Fiction of J. M. Coetzee, Philip Roth, and W. G. Sebald' (PhD, Washington University, 2005)

MEYER, SVEN, 'Narrative Verfahren in W. G. Sebalds erzählender Prosa' (MA, Universität Kiel, 1999)

ORR, JEFFREY, 'Visuality, Genre, and Translation in Selected Works of Michael Ondaatje and W. G. Sebald' (PhD, University of Leeds, 2006)

★POLSTER, HEIKE, 'The Aesthetics of Passage: The Imag(in)ed Experience of Time in Thomas Lehr, W. G. Sebald and Peter Handke' (PhD, University of Washington in St Louis, 2007)

RECHTMAN, AMALIA, 'Child Survivors of the Holocaust: Literature, Trauma, Memory' (PhD, City University of New York, 2005)

REITANO, NATALIE, 'Against Redemption: Interrupting the Future in the Fiction of Vladimir Nabokov, Kazuo Ishiguro and W. G. Sebald' (PhD, City University of New York, 2006)

STAMOVA, DARINA, 'Melancholia in W. G. Sebald's *The Rings of Saturn* (MA, University of Delaware, 2008)

STEINER, MELANIE, '"Die auf keinen Begriff mehr zu bringende Welt." Identität und Erinnerung bei W. G. Sebald und Anselm Kiefer' (MA, University of Missouri, 2003)

TAYLOR, JANE ELIZABETH, 'Walking at Low Tide' (PhD, University of East Anglia, 2005)

★VANGI, MICHELE, 'Rezeption der Fotografie im literarischen Diskurs' (PhD, Universität Münster, 2006) [on WGS, Barthes, Brinkmann and Cortázar]

VASILAKIS, APOSTOLOS, 'Mnemotechnologies in Late-Twentieth-Century Philosophy and Literature' (PhD, Emory University, 2004)

★VEES-GULANI, SUSANNE HEIKE, 'Memory and Destruction: A Psychiatric Approach to Understanding Literary Depictions of Air Raids in World War II' (PhD, University of Illinois at Urbana-Champaign, 2001)

WARD, LEWIS, 'Holocaust Memory in Contemporary Narratives: Towards a Theory of Transgenerational Empathy' (PhD, University of Exeter, 2008)

WATTS, ANDREW, '"Fragments of a Former Moon" (novel) and "Metonymy and Trauma: Re-presenting Death in the Literature of W. G. Sebald"' (PhD, University of New South Wales, 2006)

★WOHLLEBEN, DOREN, 'Schwindel und Wahrheit: Ethik und Ästhetik der Lüge in Poetik-Vorlesungen und Romanen der Gegenwart: Ingeborg Bachmann, Reinhart Baumgart, Peter Bichsel, Sten Nadolny, Christoph Ransmayr, W. G. Sebald, Hans-Ulrich Treichel' (PhD, Universität Regensburg, 2004)

WOLFF, LYNN, 'A Hybrid Poetics for a Contentious Past: W. G. Sebald's Literary Historio-graphy' (PhD, University of Wisconsin, Madison, 2010)

ZISSELSBERGER, MARKUS, 'Fragments of One's Own Existence: The Reader W. G. Sebald' (PhD, Binghamton University, SUNY, 2008)

(12) Art Works, Exhibitions, and Performances Inspired by WGS

ANON. [THE INSTITUTE OF CULTURAL INQUIRY RESEARCH TEAM], 'A Truth That Lies Elsewhere', in Patt, op. cit. (Section 2), pp. 492–509

ANDREWS, KERRY JOHN, 'Shadow Rounds', Spitalfields Public Art Projects Commission, London, sound installation, 2007–09 [incorporated sections from *Austerlitz*] <http://www.spitalfields.co.uk/about_art.php> [accessed 7 May 2010]

BENNETT, CATHERINE, PAUL DAVIES, PHILIP RALPH and FERN SMITH, 'i-witness', stage adaptation of *The Rings of Saturn*, performed by the Volcano Theatre Company (Swansea), toured UK 2008–09 <http://www.volcanotheatre.co.uk/iwitness.htm> [accessed 7 May 2010]

Böll, Victor, 'Vom Fädenspinnen', commentary on the exhibition 'Schriftbilder: Entwürfe und Manuskripte: 9 Manuskriptseiten from *Die Ringe des Saturn*', 30 April–6 June 2001, Erdrand, Weweler, Belgium <http://www.erdrand.com/neu/v_sebald/ exposition/sebald_exposition_06.htm> [accessed 7 May 2010] [This web page has links to the images used and to Böll's commentary.]

Claydon, Stephen, Nathalie Djurberg, Saul Fletcher, Thomas Helbig, Dorota Jurczak, David Noonan, David Wojnarowicz, and Thomas Zipp, 'Rings of Saturn', exhibition, Tate Modern, London, 30 September-3 December 2006 <https://www.tate. org.uk/modern/exhibitions/theringsofsaturn> [accessed 7 May 2010]

Coates, Marcus, Tacita Dean, Alec Finlay and Guy Moreton, Alexander and Susan Maris, and Simon Pope, 'Waterlog', travelling group exhibition, Norwich and Lincoln, 2007 <http://waterlog.fvu.co.uk/> [accessed 7 May 2010]; see also *Waterlog: Journeys Round an Exhibition* (London: Film and Video Umbrella, 2007), publication to accompany the exhibition, with texts by Steven Bode, Brian Dillon, Matthew Hollis, Robert Macfarlane, Jeremy Millar, and George Szirtes

Cross, Dorothy, 'Antartica', in Patt, op. cit. (Section 2), pp. 550–57

Cullen, Deborah, 'Felix Gonzalez-Torres: The Jigsaw Puzzles', in Patt, op. cit. (Section 2), pp. 350–59

Dillbohner, Christel, 'Itinerary for a Walking Tour through East Anglia', in Patt, op. cit. (Section 2), pp. 388–89

Flannery, Anne, 'Sebald's Invisible Cities', in Patt, op. cit. (Section 2), pp. 302–05

Forrester, Axel, 'Max', in Patt, op. cit. (Section 2), pp. 512–13

Gaida, Klaus G., 'W. G. Sebald 1995' (2001), in *Gaida malt*, ed. by Wolfgang Urban (Rottenburg: Diözesanmuseum Rottenburg, 2002), p. 71

Geer, Suvan, 'Trying to Remember my Mother's Face', in Patt, op. cit. (Section 2), pp. 584–87

Helguera, Pablo, 'How to Understand the Light on a Landscape', in Patt, op. cit. (Section 2), pp. 110–19

Henneman, Inge, 'Bij W. G. Sebald: Uit de verzameling FotoMuseum Provincie Antwerpen', in Ceuppens and Philipsen, op. cit. (Section 3), 65–72

Hui, Barbara, 'Litmap: *The Rings of Saturn: An English Pilgrimage*', <http://barbarahui.net/ litmap/> [accessed 7 May 2010]

Isenberg, Noah, 'Dresden Mon Amour', *Artforum*, 12.2 (2005), 4

Jaray, Tess, 'From *The Rings of Saturn* and *Vertigo*', Purdy Hicks Gallery, London, 2001 (exhibition brochure) [some works subsequently displayed at the University of East Anglia]

LaFarge, Antoinette, 'All that Is Beyond Hearing: A Life of Arturo Ott', in Patt, op. cit. (Section 2), pp. 330–47

Lash, Daniel, 'Translation and Repetition: An Architectural Translation of W. G. Sebald's *The Rings of Saturn*', in Patt, op. cit. (Section 2), pp. 440–55

Marco, Matthew T., 'The Minimalls of Downey, California (excerpt)', in Patt, op. cit. (Section 2), pp. 242–47

Millar, Jeremy, 'A Firework for W. G. Sebald (2005–06)', in Patt, op. cit. (Section 2), pp. 592–99

Mirra, Helen, 'Excerpt from *Gray Index*', in Patt, op. cit. (Section 2), pp. 198–201

Moody, Rick, 'A Short Walk Through The Rings of Saturn', *The Believer*, 5.4 (May 2007), 3–15

Rochelle, Chris, 'Birdland', in Patt, op. cit. (Section 2), pp. 188–96

Scholz, Christian, 'Pictures Remain and Live: Remembering W. G. Sebald: W. G. Sebald in Portrait (Photo Portfolio)', trans. by Markus Zisselsberger, in Patt, op. cit. (Section 2), pp. 542–49

SKÚTA, 'The Colorful Auras Discovered in Old Black-and-White Negative Glass Plates of One Family Photographed at the Same Location', in Patt, op. cit. (Section 2), pp. 120–25

THEUMER, SUSANNE, 'Zerstöret das Letzte die Erinnerung nicht (W. G. Sebald): Radierungen zu Textauszügen aus dem Roman *Die Ausgewanderten*', exhibition (with publication) of drawings and engravings inspired by 'Dr Henry Selwyn': 2009, Halle an der Saale <http://www.interartshop.de/index.php> [accessed 7 May 2010]

VONNA-MICHELL, TRIS, 'Who is Reinhold Hahn', in Patt, op. cit. (Section 2), pp. 146–61

WAFFEL, CLAIRE, 'W. G. Sebald: La Voix Retrouvée', 270 Polaroids and Sound, 8.5 × 10.5 cm, 2004–07 <http://www.clairewaffel.com/projects/sebald/sebald.html> [accessed 7 May 2010]

WRIGHT, TIM, 'Sebald's Tree: The Development of a 90% True Digital Story', in Patt, op. cit. (Section 2), pp. 248–55

(13) Online Resources

PITTS, TERRY, 'Vertigo: Collecting and Reading W. G. Sebald' <http://sebald.wordpress.com/>

WIRTH, CHRISTIAN, 'W. G. Sebald' <http://www.wgsebald.de/>

(14) Forthcoming Publications

At the time of writing, the editors are aware of the following publications currently in preparation:

BAXTER, JEANNETTE, VALERIE HENITIUK, and BEN HUTCHINSON, eds, *A Literature of Restitution: Critical Essays on W. G. Sebald* (Manchester: Manchester University Press, 2011)

EGGERS, CHRISTOPH, *Das Dunkel durchdringen, das uns umgibt: Die Fotografie im Werk von W. G. Sebald* (Frankfurt a.M.: Lang, 2011)

SCHÜTTE, UWE, *W. G. Sebald* (Göttingen: Vandenhoeck & Ruprecht, 2011)

SHEPPARD, RICHARD, ed., *Journal of European Studies*, 41.3-4 (December 2011), special double issue on WGS

3

Reviews of Works by W. G. Sebald

Compiled by Jo Catling and Richard Hibbitt

NOTE

This list of reviews of W. G. Sebald's works is by no means exhaustive. In those cases where we have been unable to find full details for the items included, we hope that the name and date of publication will be sufficient information for any reader wishing to locate the review. Often, printed reviews are also available online; links are given where known, but readers are encouraged to search online for these and other sources. Where the review has no title except for that of the book, we simply give publication details. Where possible we have signalled if the same review is published in several different regional German newspapers, often under different titles. This list also registers subsequent newspaper articles on specific books which are not reviews as such, but contribute to the reception. Audio-visual reviews are listed in the separate Audio-Visual Bibliography that follows.

We would like to express our thanks to the staff of the Stadt- und Landes-Bibliothek in Dortmund and of the Deutsches Literaturarchiv Marbach, and to all the Sebald readers, scholars, and translators who provided information about the reviews, especially Ria van Hengel and Richard Sheppard. Please send any information about missing reviews or details to <j.catling@uea.ac.uk> or <r.hibbitt@leeds.ac.uk>. This information will be included in an online version of the bibliography.

Reviews are ordered chronologically by publication date (shown in parentheses after the title) of the item reviewed, using a simplified form of the classification system employed in the Primary Bibliography: Critical Works, Literary Works, and Later Works. For reasons of space the translations reviewed here are limited to Dutch, English, and French. Reviews of other translations will be published in the online version of the bibliography.

CONTENTS

Critical Works

A.1   *Carl Sternheim: Kritiker und Opfer der Wilhelmischen Ära* (1969)
A.2   *Der Mythus der Zerstörung im Werk Döblins* (1980)
A.3   *Die Beschreibung des Unglücks: Zur österreichischen Literatur von Stifter bis Handke* (1985)
A.4   *A Radical Stage: Theatre in Germany in the 1970s and 1980s* (1988, edited by WGS)

A.5   *Unheimliche Heimat: Essays zur österreichischen Literatur* (1991)
A.6   *Logis in einem Landhaus: Über Gottfried Keller, Johann Peter Hebel, Robert Walser und andere* (1998)
A.7   *Luftkrieg und Literatur* (1999) (*On the Natural History of Destruction*)

Literary Works

B.A.1 *Nach der Natur* (1988) (*After Nature*)
B.B.1 *Schwindel. Gefühle.* (1990) (*Vertigo*)
B.B.2 *Die Ausgewanderten* (1992) (*The Emigrants*)
B.B.3 *Die Ringe des Saturn* (1995) (*The Rings of Saturn*)
B.B.4 *Austerlitz* (2001)
B.A.2 *For Years Now* (with Tess Jaray) (2001)
B.A.3 *Unerzählt* (mit Jan Peter Tripp) (2003) (*Unrecounted*)

Later Works

B.D.2 *Campo Santo* (2003)
B.D.3 *Über das Land und das Wasser* (2008)
D.53 'Ich möchte zu ihnen hinabsteigen und finde den Weg nicht: Zu den Romanen Jurek Beckers' (2010)

Varia

On readings given by WGS
On prizes awarded to WGS
On exhibitions, conferences, lectures
Other reports

Critical Works

A.1. Carl Sternheim: Kritiker und Opfer der Wilhelminischen Ära (1969)

BERNHARDI, EUGENIO, 'Notizie sul caso Sternheim', *Annali di Ca'Foscari*, 9.1 (1970), 1–13
DAVIAU, DONALD G., 'W. G. Sebald: *Carl Sternheim*', *Germanic Review*, 47 (1972), 234–36
HILLACH, ANSGAR, *Germanistik*, 11 (1970), 402–03
KESTING, MARIANNE, 'Zweifel an Carl Sternheim: Das unveröffentlichte Frühwerk und eine Untersuchung', in Marianne Kesting, *Auf der Suche nach der Realität: Kritische Schriften zur modernen Literatur* (Munich: Piper, 1972), pp. 97–201
KONRAD, GUSTAV, *Welt und Wort*, 25.2 (1970), 55
OSBORNE, JOHN, 'W. G. Sebald: *Carl Sternheim*', *Modern Language Review*, 67 (1972), 471–72
PAULSEN, WOLFGANG, 'Carl Sternheim und die Komödie des Expressionismus', in *Die deutsche Komödie im zwanzigsten Jahrhundert: Sechstes Amherster Kolloquium zur modernen deutschen Literatur 1972*, ed. by Wolfgang Paulsen, Poesie und Wissenschaft, 37 (Heidelberg: Stiehm, 1976), pp. 70–106 (pp. 93–95 on WGS)
POLYUDOV, VALERY, 'Eins mit seinen Gegnern? Sebalds Sternheim-Polemik', *Die Zeit*, 14 August 1970, Literatur section, p. 15; repr. in *Sebald. Lektüren.*, ed. by Marcel Atze and Franz Loquai (Eggingen: Isele, 2005), pp. 56–58
——'Brief an die Redaktion', *Literatur und Kritik*, 51.6 (1971), 41–43
——'Sovremennaya chudožhestvennaya literatura za rubežhom: Informacionnyj', *Sbornik*, 88.3 (1971), 112–14 [in Russian]
SCHREY, GISELA, 'Carl Sternheim: "Kritiker and Opfer" seiner Zeit', *Frankfurter Hefte*, 26 (1971), 775–79
STAHL, K. H., 'W. G. Sebald: *Carl Sternheim*', *Wissenschaftlicher Literaturanzeiger*, 14 April 1970, p. 41

A.2. Der Mythus der Zerstörung im Werk Döblins (1980)

Drijard, A., *Études Germaniques*, 36 (1981), 100–01

Fries, Marilyn Sibley, *German Quarterly*, 56 (1983), 341–43

Müller-Salget, Klaus, 'Neuere Tendenzen in der Döblin-Forschung', *Zeitschrift für deutsche Philologie*, 103 (1984), 263–77

A.3. Die Beschreibung des Unglücks: Zur österreichischen Literatur von Stifter bis Handke (1985)

Anon. (a.Bn.), 'Die Beschreibung des Unglücks', *Neue Zürcher Zeitung* (Fernausgabe), 14–15 August 1994, p. 28

Heine-Schröder, Brigitte, 'Schwermut und Schreiben als Widerstand', *Der Literat*, 3 (1988), 384–85

Melzer, Gerhard, 'Österreichische Literatur in Einzelansichten: W. G. Sebalds Essaysammlung *Die Beschreibung des Unglücks*', *Neue Zürcher Zeitung*, 28–29 June 1986, Literatur und Kunst section, p. 68; repr. in *Far From Home: W. G. Sebald*, ed. by Franz Loquai, Fußnoten zur Literatur, 31 (Bamberg: Universität Bamberg, 1995), pp. 42–45, and *W. G. Sebald*, ed. by Franz Loquai, Porträt, 7 (Eggingen: Isele, 1997), pp. 55–57

Meyer-Gosau, Frauke, 'Von ungustiösen Mahlzeiten und Schriftdarstellern', *Freitag*, 13 January 1995, p. 12

Nehring, Wolfgang, 'W. G. Sebald: *Die Beschreibung des Unglücks*', *German Quarterly*, 60 (1987), 135–37

Nürnberger, Helmuth, *Germanistik*, 28 (1987), 912

Swales, Martin, 'W. G. Sebald: *Die Beschreibung des Unglücks*', *Modern Language Review*, 82 (1987), 248–50

Weinzierl, Ulrich, 'Die Angst der Dichter bei Frauen: Aufsätze zur österreichischen Literatur von W. G. Sebald', *Frankfurter Allgemeine Zeitung*, 23 November 1985; repr. in Loquai, *Far From Home*, pp. 41–42, and Loquai, *W. G. Sebald*, pp. 53–54

Wilflinger, Klara, *Zeit im Buch*, 40.3 (1986), 148–49

A.4. A Radical Stage: Theatre in Germany in the 1970s and 1980s (1988)

Rothschild, Thomas, 'W. G. Sebald: *A Radical Stage*', *Medienwissenschaft: Rezensionen, Reviews*, 7.1–2 (1990), 83

Rundell, Richard J., *Theatre Journal*, 43 (1991), 263–64

A.5. Unheimliche Heimat: Essays zur österreichischen Literatur (1991)

Herzog, Andreas, 'Der hoffnungslos sehnsüchtige Traum von Österreich', *Berliner Zeitung*, 3 July 1991, p. 19

Kosler, Hans Christian, 'Der Strohhalm der Illusion: W. G. Sebalds Essays zur österreichischen Literatur', *Süddeutsche Zeitung*, 19–20 October 1991, SZ am Wochenende section, p. iv; repr. in Loquai, *Far From Home*, pp. 64–66, and in Loquai, *W. G. Sebald*, pp. 75–76

Kubaczek, Martin, 'In der Fremde die Heimat suchen: Essays zur österreichischen Literatur', *Die Presse*, 13 July 1991, Literaricum section, p. viii

Lengauer, Hubert, 'W. G. Sebald: *Unheimliche Heimat*', *Wespennest*, no. 84 (September 1991), 73–75

Loquai, Franz, 'Von Gesinnungsbrüdern und Geistesverwandten: W. G. Sebalds Essays *Unheimliche Heimat*', *Mittelbayerische Zeitung*, 23–24 May 1992; repr. in Loquai, *Far From Home*, pp. 66–67, and in Loquai, *W. G. Sebald*, pp. 77–78

REITER, ANDREA, 'W. G. Sebald: *Unheimliche Heimat*', *Modern Language Review*, 88 (1993), 803–05

ROSENFELD, SIDNEY, *World Literature Today*, 66.1 (Winter 1992), 127–28

SCHÜPPEN, FRANZ, *Zeitschrift für deutsche Philologie*, 112 (1993), 634–37

WEINZIERL, ULRICH, 'Schon hört man die Holzwürmer', *Frankfurter Allgemeine Zeitung*, 11 July 1991, Literatur section, p. 26

A.6. Logis in einem Landhaus: Über Gottfried Keller, Johann Peter Hebel, Robert Walser und andere (1998)

ANON., *Rheinische Post*, 24 November 2000, Journal section, p. 4

ANON. (SAS), 'Auf den Spuren der Dichter', *Die Presse*, 24 October 1998, Journal: Der Bücher Pick section, p. 50

ARNOLD, HEINZ-LUDWIG, 'Wanderer in der Schwebe', *Deutsches Allgemeines Sonntagsblatt*, 22 January 1999, Literatur section, p. 31

AYREN, ARMIN, 'Folgenloses Wohlgefühl', *Stuttgarter Zeitung*, 24 March 1999, p. 34

BUGMANN, URS, 'W. G. Sebald: *Logis in einem Landhaus*: Lauter am Denken erkrankte Subjekte', *Neue Luzerner Zeitung*, 23 October 1998, Kultur section, p. 51

BUTLER, MICHAEL, 'The Human Cost of Exile', *Times Literary Supplement*, 2 October 1998, p. 10

FLASCH, KURT, 'Landhaus mit Wasseradern: W. G. Sebalds Wanderungen zu verstörten Brüdern', *Neue Zürcher Zeitung* (Internationale Ausgabe), 6 October 1998, Neue Literatur section, p. B5

JONG, ANNERIEK DE, 'Gecultiveerd heimwee', *NRC Handelsblad*, 13 November 1998, Boeken section, p. 4

KIEFER, SEBASTIAN, *Deutsche Bücher*, 36.4 (1999), 108–12

KRAUSE, TILMAN, 'Versenkung in Dichtung als geistige Sommerfrische', *Die Welt*, 7 October 1998, p. G3

MÖNNINGER, MICHAEL, 'Schwärmerischer Sachwalter der Nützlichkeit', *Berliner Zeitung*, 24–25 December 1998, Literatur section, p. v

OESTERLE, KURT, 'Habe die Ehre', *Süddeutsche Zeitung*, 13–14 February 1999, p. iv

OSTERKAMP, ERNST, 'Tribute an die Tiefe', *Frankfurter Allgemeine Zeitung*, 6 October 1998, Literatur section, p. L17

PFOHLMANN, OLIVER, 'Ausblicke von Schönheit und Intensität: W. G. Sebalds *Logis in einem Landhaus*', *literaturkritik.de*, 1 (1999), 97–98 <http://www.literaturkritik.de/public/rezension.php?rez_id=36> [accessed 6 April 2010]

——'Ist Bücherschreiben eine Verhaltensstörung?', *Saarbrücker Zeitung*, 6 January 1999, Kulturleben section, p. 18

SCHECK, DENIS, 'Lautlose Reise durch die Luft', *Frankfurter Rundschau*, 7 October 1998, Literatur Rundschau, Messebeilage, p. 2

SCHLÖSSER, HERMANN, *Wiener Zeitung*, 11 November 2002, Bücherservice section (also refers to *Luftkrieg und Literatur*); repr. in Hermann Schlösser, *Lesarten der Wirklichkeit: Literatur, Wissenschaft und Philosophie im Spiegel journalistischer Rezensionen*, ed. by Jost W. Kramer and Robert Schediwy (Bremen: Europäischer Hochschulverlag, 2010), pp. 136-44

SCHÜBLER, WALTER, 'Über die Neigung, sich zu "verdünnisieren"', *Die Presse*, 27 February 1999, Spectrum section, p. ii

SCHWARZ, ROBERT, *World Literature Today*, 73.3 (Summer 1999), 521

TREICHEL, HANS-ULRICH, 'Melancholie des Schreibens', *die tageszeitung*, 7 October 1998, Literataz section, p. vi

VOLLMANN, ROLF, 'Das andere Auge', *Die Zeit*, 28 January 1999, Literatur section, p. 41

French translation

A.6.1. Séjours à la campagne: Suivi de Au Royaume des ombres par Jan Peter Tripp, trans. by Patrick Charbonneau (2005)

Margantin, Laurent, 'La Terrible Opiniâtreté des hommes de lettres', *La Quinzaine Littéraire*, 16–31 December 2005, p. 31

Mercier, Christophe, 'Voix de traverse', *Le Figaro*, 27 October 2005, p. 5

Merckx, Ingrid, *Politis*; quoted in the 2009 Actes Sud brochure <http://www.actes-sud. fr/sites/default/files/brochure_sebald_0.pdf>, p. 25

Sangars, Romaric, *Chronic'Art*; quoted in the 2009 Actes Sud brochure <http://www. actes-sud.fr/sites/default/files/brochure_sebald_0.pdf>, p. 25

Schiltknecht, Wilfred, *Le Temps*; quoted in the 2009 Actes Sud brochure <http://www. actes-sud.fr/sites/default/files/brochure_sebald_0.pdf>, p. 25

Valentini, Ruth, *Nouvel Observateur*, 1 December 2005

A.7. Luftkrieg und Literatur (1999)

Many of the reviews listed here are predominantly about the general debate on the air war (*Luftkriegdebatte*), but they all touch on WGS. A number of pieces are reprinted in *Deutsche Literatur 1998: Jahresüberblick*, ed. by Volker Hage, Rainer Moritz, and Hubert Winkels (Stuttgart: Reclam, 1999), in the section 'Überblick und Debatte', pp. 249–90. These are indicated below where appropriate.

Anon. (SM), 'Volker Hage über den literarischen Luftkrieg', *Frankfurter Rundschau*, 9 October 2003, p. 19

Arend, Ingo, 'Stufen der Angst', *Freitag*, 9 April 1999, Literatur section, p. 16

Atze, Marcel, 'Die Reise findet statt, um brennende Fragen zu lösen: Zur Neuauflage von H. G. Adlers Roman *Eine Reise* nebst einer Anmerkung zu W. G. Sebald's *Luftkrieg and Literatur*', *literaturkritik.de*, 1.6 (1999), 49–56

Baron, Ulrich, 'Im Schatten zweier künstlicher Sonnen', *Rheinischer Merkur*, 6 February 1998; repr. in Hage, Moritz, and Winkels, pp. 275–78

Baumgart, Reinhard, 'Das Luftkriegstrauma der Literatur', *Die Zeit*, 29 April 1999, Literatur section, p. 55

Biller, Maxim, 'Unschuld mit Grünspan: Wie die Lüge in die deutsche Literatur kam', *Frankfurter Allgemeine Zeitung*, 13 February 1998; repr. in Hage, Moritz, and Winkels, pp. 278–83

Braun, Michael, 'Deutsche Apokalypse', *Listen*, 15 (1999), 6–7

Deggerich, Georg, 'Krieg der Wörter', *Am Erker*, 37 (1999), 116–17

Forte, Dieter, 'Menschen werden zu Herdentieren', *Der Spiegel*, 5 April 1999, pp. 220–23

Fühner, Ruth, 'Das Schweigen der Dichter', *Badische Zeitung*, 12 May 1999, Bücher section, p. 17

Gesing, Fritz, *Freiburger literaturpsychologische Gespräche*, 19 (2000), 230-37

Güntner, Joachim, 'Der Luftkrieg fand im Osten statt: Anmerkungen zu einer fehllaufenden Literaturdebatte', *Neue Zürcher Zeitung*, 24 January 1998; repr. in Hage, Moritz, and Winkels, pp. 271–75

——'Der Bombenkrieg findet zur Sprache: Zur Debatte um Jörg Friedrichs Buch *Der Brand*', *Neue Zürcher Zeitung* (Internationale Ausgabe), 7–8 December 2002, Feuilleton, p. 33

Hage, Volker, 'Feuer vom Himmel', *Der Spiegel*, 12 January 1998, pp. 138–41; repr. in Hage, Moritz, and Winkels, pp. 253–62; repr. in English as 'Can Germans be Victims?', *The European*, 19–25 January 1998

Harpprecht, Klaus, 'Stille, schicksallose: Warum die Nachkriegsliteratur von vielem geschwiegen hat', *Frankfurter Allgemeine Zeitung*, 20 January 1998; repr. in Hage, Moritz, and Winkels, pp. 267–69

ISENSCHMID, ANDREAS, 'Deutschlands schandbares Familiengeheimnis', *Tages-Anzeiger*, 14 December 1997; repr. in Hage, Moritz, and Winkels, pp. 250–53

KASTBERGER, KLAUS, 'Brandbomben auf Hamburg', *Falter*, 14 April 1999, p. 71

KRAUSE, TILMAN, 'Entwirklichung und Enthistorisierung', *Die Welt*, 19 April 1999, p. 13

KÜBLER, GUNHILD, 'Luftkrieg und Literatur: In seinen Zürcher Vorlesungen fasste W. G. Sebald ein heisses Eisen an', *Die Weltwoche*, 11 December 1997

LAU, JÖRG, 'Wo steht die Flak?', *Die Zeit*, 25 March 1999, p. 53

LUCHSINGER, MARTIN, 'Luftkrieg und Literatur: W. G. Sebalds "pyromanische" Poetikvorlesungen in Zürich', *Frankfurter Rundschau*, 25 November 1997, p. 10

NOLTE, JOST, 'Sebald oder Neues über Untergänge', *Die Welt*, 24 January 1998; repr. in Hage, Moritz, and Winkels, pp. 269–71

OESTERLE, KURT, 'Nachgetragene Vorwürfe', *Süddeutsche Zeitung*, 11 May 1999, p. 19

PFOHLMANN, OLIVER, 'Verdrängtes Grauen: W. G. Sebald zum Kapitel "Luftkrieg und Literatur"', *Augsburger Zeitung*, 19 May 1999

PREISENDÖRFER, BRUNO, 'Der steinerne Blick: "Zeugen der Zerstörung": Volker Hages Essay- und Gesprächsband zur Debatte über den Luftkrieg im Spiegel der Literatur', *Der Tagesspiegel*, 17 August 2003, p. 23

RITTER, HENNING, 'Aschereste: Luftkrieg und W. G. Sebald', *Frankfurter Allgemeine Zeitung*, 16 July 2003, p. N3

ROSENBERGER, NICOLE, 'Kinderleiche im Koffer', *Die Weltwoche*, 5 August 1999, p. 37

SAUDER, GERHARD, 'Die Sprachlosigkeit der Ruinierten. Besprechung von W. G. Sebald: *Luftkrieg und Literatur. Mit einem Essay zu Alfred Andersch*', *Studia Niemcoznawcze*, 21 (2001), 802–05

SCHALLIÉ, CHARLOTTE, *Focus on German Studies*, 9 (2002), 230–33

SCHAUB, MARTIN, '"Und setzet ihr nicht das Leben ein..."', *Tages-Anzeiger*, 10 February 1998, Kultur section, p. 55

SCHIRRMACHER, FRANK, 'Luftkrieg: Beginnt morgen die deutsche Nachkriegsliteratur?', *Frankfurter Allgemeine Zeitung*, 15 January 1998; repr. in Hage, Moritz, and Winkels, pp. 263–67

SCHLÖSSER, HERMANN, *Wiener Zeitung*, 11 November 2002, Bücherservice section (also refers to *Logis in einem Landhaus*); repr. in Hermann Schlösser, *Lesarten der Wirklichkeit: Literatur, Wissenschaft und Philosophie im Spiegel journalistischer Rezensionen*, ed. by Jost W. Kramer and Robert Schediwy (Bremen: Europäischer Hochschulverlag, 2010), pp. 136–44

SCHNEIDER, THOMAS E., *Deutsche Bücher*, 31 (2001), 332–34

SCHRÖDER, LOTHAR, 'Darf es bei den Tätern Opfer gegeben haben?', *Rheinische Post*, 10 December 2002, unpaginated (reviewed with Gert Ledig, *Vergeltung*)

SCHÜBLER, WALTER, 'Jamben und Bomben', *Die Presse*, 24 April 1999, Spectrum section: Das neue Buch, p. v

——'Jeder Ton falsch?', *Die Presse*, 2 August 2003, Spectrum section: Literatur, p. v (on the *Luftkriegdebatte*)

SCHÜTT, JULIAN, 'Der Verlust der "Schmerzensspur"', *Die Weltwoche*, 12 December 2002, p. 84

SCHÜTTE, WOLFRAM, 'Unterlassene Zeugenschaft', *Frankfurter Rundschau*, 27 March 1999, Feuilleton, p. ZB3

SCHÜTZ, ERHARD, 'Kollektive Verstocktheiten', *Die Tageszeitung*, 31 March 1999, Kultur section, p. 15

SEIBT, GUSTAV, 'Sprachlos im Feuersturm: Luftkriegs-Literatur, Holocaust-Mahnmal: Was können Kunst und Dichtung zur historischen Erinnerung beitragen?', *Berliner Zeitung*, 14–15 February 1998; repr. in Hage, Moritz, and Winkels, pp. 283–90

WIRTH, MICHAEL, 'Ein Defizit der deutschen Literatur? W. G. Sebalds "Luftkrieg"-Essay geht nicht auf', *Schweizer Monatshefte für Politik, Wirtschaft, Kultur*, 79.7–8 (1999), 62–63

English translation

A.7.1, A.7.2, A.7.3. On the Natural History of Destruction, trans. by Anthea Bell (2003)

BAKER, KENNETH, 'The Glossed-over Horrors of Air War', *San Francisco Chronicle* <http://www.sfgate.com/cgi-bin/article.cgi?f=/chronicle/archive/2003/02/23/RV190311.DTL> [accessed 6 April 2010]

BANVILLE, JOHN, 'Lest We Forget', *Guardian*, 22 February 2003, Saturday Review section <http://www.guardian.co.uk/books/2003/feb/22/highereducation.history> [accessed 6 April 2010]

BEEVOR, ANTHONY, 'A Nation that Was Bombed into Silence', *The Times*, 12 February 2003 <http://entertainment.timesonline.co.uk/tol/arts_and_entertainment/books/article873754.ece> [accessed 6 April 2010]

CONRADI, PETER J., *Independent*, 22 February 2003 <http://www.independent.co.uk/arts-entertainment/books/reviews> [accessed 6 April 2010]

COSTABILE-HEMING, CAROL ANNE, *H-Net: Humanities and Social Sciences Online* <http://www.h-net.org/reviews/showrev.php?id=8368> [accessed 11 February 2011]

CZARNY, NORBERT, 'The Weight of Silence', *Queen's Quarterly*, 111.1 (2004), 113

DYER, GEOFF, 'Terrible Rain', *LA Weekly*, 6 February 2003 <http://www.laweekly.com/2003-02-06/art-books/terrible-rain> [accessed 6 April 2010]

EDER, RICHARD, *The New York Times*, 5 February 2003 <http://www.nytimes.com/2003/02/05/books/books-of-the-times-giving-voice-to-an-awkward-silence-in-germany.html> [accessed 6 April 2010]

FRANKLIN, RUTH, 'Rings of Smoke', *New Republic*, 23 September 2002, pp. 32–39; repr. in *The Emergence of Memory*, ed. by Schwartz, pp. 119–43 (also on *After Nature*)

GIMSON, ANDREW, 'Looking—and Looking Away', *Spectator*, 15 February 2003, pp. 37–38

GLOVER, MICHAEL, 'The Nation that Learnt to Forget in Order to Survive', *Independent on Sunday*, 23 February 2003, Arts section, p. 15

HASTINGS, MAX, 'Explosions that Led to Silence', *Sunday Telegraph*, 23 February 2003, Review section, p. 12

HITCHENS, CHRISTOPHER, 'The Wartime Toll on Germany', *Atlantic Monthly* (January–February 2003), 182–89

JOHNSON, DANIEL, 'Breaking the Silence', *Times Literary Supplement*, 25 April 2003, pp. 7–8

LEONARD, JOHN, 'New Books', *Harper's Magazine* (March 2003), 75–76 <http://www.harpers.org/subjects/WinfriedGeorgSebald> [accessed 6 April 2010]

LINFIELD, SUSIE, 'Memory's Lair', *Boston Review* (Summer 2003) <http://bostonreview.net/BR28.3/linfield.html> [accessed 6 April 2010]

LINKER, DAMON, 'The Wrong Target?', *First Things: A Monthly Journal of Religion and Public Life* (May 2003), 55

MARSHALL, ALAN, 'Red Sky and Mourning', *Daily Telegraph*, 22 February 2003 <http://www.telegraph.co.uk/culture/4729942/Red-sky-and-mourning.html> [accessed 6 April 2010]

MERKIN, DAPHNE, 'Cordoning off the Past', *New York Times Book Review*, 6 April 2003 <http://www.nytimes.com/2003/04/06/books/cordoning-off-the-past.html> [accessed 6 April 2010]

PHILLIPS, ADAM, 'The Truth, the Whole Truth', *Observer*, 23 February 2003, Review section: Books, p. 17

RIEMER, ANDREW, 'Exile's Visions of Atrophy', *Sydney Morning Herald*, April 12-13 2003

SCHÜTZE, CHRISTIAN, 'On That Terrible Night...', *London Review of Books*, 21 August 2003, pp. 28–29

SIMIC, CHARLES, 'Conspiracy of Silence', *New York Review of Books*, 27 February 2003, pp. 8–9; repr. in *The Emergence of Memory*, ed. by Schwartz, pp. 145–58

UPCHURCH, MICHAEL, 'The Last Word from a Silenced Child of the War', *Sunday Seattle Times and Post-Intelligencer* (Fourth Edition), 9 March 2003, Arts and Entertainment section, p. K9

VIVIS, ANTHONY, '*Austerlitz* and *On the Natural History of Destruction*', *In Other Words: The Journal for Literary Translators*, no. 21 (2003) (W. G. Sebald memorial issue, ed. by Peter Bush), pp. 64–66

VOLLMANN, WILLIAM T., 'And Suppress the Unpleasant Things', *The Believer* (May 2003) <http://www.believermag.com/issues/200305/?read=article_vollmann> [accessed 6 April 2010]

WINDER, ROBERT, *New Statesman*, 24 February 2003 <http://www.newstatesman.com/200302240039> [accessed 6 April 2010]

Dutch translation

A.7.5. De natuurlijke historie van de verwoesting, trans. by Ria van Hengel (2004)

GELDER, ROELOF VAN, 'De vuurzee op papier', *NRC Handelsblad*, 7 May 2004

GRAAF, BEATRICE DE, 'W. G. Sebald over de Duitse oorlogsroman', *Trouw*, 24 April 2004

GROENEVELD, GERARD, 'Ook Duitsers hebben geleden', *De Volkskrant*, 30 April 2004

HAKKERT, THEO, 'Steden stierven in één nacht', *Tubantia*, 1 January 2005

PEARCE, JOSEPH, 'Leven op een puinhoop', *De Morgen*, 26 May 2004, Boeken section

ROZEMA, HILBRAND, 'De Duitse pijn komt naar buiten', *Nederlands Dagblad*, 7 May 2004

SCHAEVERS, MARK, 'Om zeker íéts te vernietigen, moesten we álles vernietigen', *Humo*, 11 May 2004, pp. 162–70

VERBIJ, ANTOINE, 'Rampenboeken', *Vrij Nederland*, 12 June 2004, De Republiek der Letteren section, 48–50

VOGELAAR, JACQ, 'Literaire luchtaanval', *De Groene Amsterdammer*, 15 May 2004

French translation

A.7.7. De la déstruction comme élément de l'histoire naturelle, trans. by Patrick Charbonneau (2004)

AMINE, PATRICK, *Artpress*; quoted in the 2009 Actes Sud brochure <http://www.actes-sud.fr/sites/default/files/brochure_sebald_0.pdf>, p. 27

CLUNY, CLAUDE MICHEL, 'L'Histoire schizophrène', *Le Figaro Littéraire*, 26 February 2004, Critiques section: Littérature étrangère, p. 5

CROM, NATHALIE, *La Croix*; quoted in the 2009 Actes Sud brochure <http://www.actes-sud.fr/sites/default/files/brochure_sebald_0.pdf>, p. 27

CZARNY, NORBERT, 'Le Poids du silence', *La Quinzaine Littéraire*, 16–31 January 2004, p. 12

HEURÉ, GILLES, *Télérama*; quoted in the 2009 Actes Sud brochure <http://www.actes-sud.fr/sites/default/files/brochure_sebald_0.pdf>, p. 27

RÉROLLE, RAPHAËLLE, 'La Bombe de W. G. Sebald', *Le Monde*, 6 February 2004, Le Monde des Livres section, p. iii

SEMO, MARC, 'Les Décombres sortent de l'ombre', *Libération*, 8 January 2004, Livres section, p. vii

VERNET, DANIEL, 'Un sujet de moins en moins tabou en Allemagne', *Le Monde*, 6 February 2004, Le Monde des Livres section, p. iii

Literary Works

B.A.1. Nach der Natur (1988)

Anz, Thomas, 'Feuer, Wasser, Steine, Licht: W. G. Sebalds eindrucksvoller Versuch *Nach der Natur*', *Frankfurter Allgemeine Zeitung*, 11 February 1989; repr. in Loquai, *Far From Home*, pp. 46–47, and in Loquai, *W. G. Sebald*, pp. 58–60

Kübler, Gunhild, 'Von der Schönheit einer weissen, leeren Welt: W. G. Sebald: *Nach der Natur*', *Neue Zürcher Zeitung*, 2 March 1989, Feuilleton, p. 47; repr. in Loquai, *Far From Home*, pp. 48–50, and in Loquai, *W. G. Sebald*, pp. 60–63

Wallmann, Hermann, 'Was alles hat Platz in einem langen Gedicht?', *Basler Zeitung*, 14 October 1988

English translation

B.A.1.1, B.A.1.2, B.A.1.3. After Nature, trans. by Michael Hamburger (2002)

Agee, Chris, 'In Dwindling Light', *Irish Times*, 3 August 2002, Weekend section

Baker, Kenneth, *San Francisco Chronicle*, 29 September 2002 <http://www.sfgate.com/cgi-bin/article.cgi?f=/c/a/2002/09/29/RV1810755.DTL&hw=sebald&sn=004&sc=527> [accessed 6 April 2010]

Beckerman Davis, Barbara, *Antioch Review*, 62.1 (Winter 2004), 171

Clanchy, Kate, *Waterstone's Books Quarterly*, [autumn?] (2002), 81

Coetzee, J. M., 'Heir of a Dark History', *New York Review of Books*, 24 October 2002, pp. 25–26; repr. as 'W. G. Sebald, *After Nature*' in *Inner Workings: Literary Essays 2002–2005* (London: Harvill Secker, 2007), pp. 145–54

——'Erbe einer düsteren Geschichte', trans. by Reinhild Böhnke, *Neue Rundschau*, 114.1 (2003), 127–35 (translation of above)

Faber, Michael, 'The Angel Sebald's Memories of Things to Come', *Scotland on Sunday*, 7 July 2002, Books section, p. 5

Franklin, Ruth, 'Rings of Smoke', *New Republic*, 23 September 2002, pp. 32–39; repr. in *The Emergence of Memory*, ed. by Schwartz, pp. 119–43 (also on A.7.1/2)

Farr, Sheila, 'Sebald's Poems are a Wistful Pleasure', *Sunday Seattle Times and Post-Intelligencer* (Fourth Edition), 24 November 2002, Arts and Entertainment Section, p. K11

Glover, Michael, 'Encounters Freighted With Meaning', *Financial Times*, 27 July 2002

Greening, John, 'Unforgotten Forests', *Times Literary Supplement*, 2 August 2002

Harman, Claire, 'Glimpse of a True Poet at Work', *Evening Standard*, 29 July 2002

Hoffman, Eva, 'Curiosity and Catastrophe', *New York Times Book Review*, 22 September 2002 <http://www.nytimes.com/2002/09/22/books/curiosity-and-catastrophe.html> [accessed 6 April 2010] (also published as '*After Nature*: Sebald's Early Work in Verse Engages Typical Themes')

Kinsella, John, 'Silences that Speak a Thousand Words', *Observer*, 7 July 2002

Marsden, Philip, 'The Quiet German', *Sunday Times*, 7 July 2002, p. 41

Pettingell, Phoebe, 'Old Masters of Suffering', *New Leader*, 85.4 (July–August 2002), 33–35

Romer, Stephen, 'Beyond Strangeways', *Guardian*, 6 July 2002, Saturday Review section, p. 25

Seddon, Nicholas, 'A World of Artifice', *The Tablet*, 24 August 2002

Shakespeare, Sebastian, 'An Exquisite Optician', *Literary Review*, June 2002, pp. 28–29

Smith, Ali, 'Blind Witness', *The Scotsman*, 3 August 2002

Sontag, Susan, 'Books of the Year', *Times Literary Supplement*, 6 December 2002

Szirtes, George, 'Panoramic Vision Through the Eye of a Needle', *Times*, 10 July 2002, Books section, p. 18

Thwaite, Anthony, 'Prosaic, in the Best Sense', *Sunday Telegraph*, 14 July 2002

Dutch translation

B.A.1.5. Naar de natuur, trans. by Ria van Hengel (2006)

JONG, ANNERIEK DE, 'Achter de fuchsia', *NRC Handelsblad*, 30 June 2006, Boeken section
VOGELAAR, JACQ, 'Afstand tot de wereld', *De Groene Amsterdammer*, 19 May 2006

French translation

B.A.1.6. D'après nature: Poème élémentaire, trans. by Patrick Charbonneau and Sibylle Müller (2007)

BAILLY, JEAN-CHRISTOPHE, 'Les Lignes brisées de l'explorateur Sebald', *Libération*, 8 November 2007, Livres section, p. v
KÉCHICHIEN, PATRICK, *'D'après nature* de W. G. Sebald', *Le Monde*, 8 February 2008, Le Monde des Livres section
SCHILTKNECHT, WILFRED, *Le Temps*; quoted in the 2009 Actes Sud brochure <www.actes-sud.fr/sites/default/files/brochure_sebald_0.pdf>, p. 13

B.B.1. Schwindel. Gefühle. (1990)

ANON., *Fachdienst Germanistik*, 8.10 (October 1990), 15–16
ANON. (hob), 'Ein morbider Trickspezialist der Literatur', *Reutlinger General-Anzeiger*, 14 December 1990, p. 8
ANON. (lu), 'Formenspiel um Faktenhaltiges', *Reutlinger Nachrichten*, 15 December 1990, p. 14
APPELT, HEDWIG, 'Auf der schaukelnden Barke', *Stuttgarter Zeitung*, 3 August 1990, p. 26
BENDER, RUTH, 'Die reale Welt zerrinnt zur Vision', *Kieler Nachrichten*, 20 December 1991, Kultur section, p. 22 (cf. On readings given by WGS)
BRAUN, MICHAEL, 'Protokoll einer Seelenlähmung', *die tageszeitung*, 6 August 1990, p. 17
DREWS, JÖRG, 'Meisterhaft suggerierte Angstzustände: *Schwindel. Gefühle.* von W. G. Sebald: Zitate, Echos, Bedeutsamkeiten', *Die Weltwoche*, 21 June 1990, p. 67; repr. in Loquai, *Far From Home*, pp. 54–56, and in Loquai, *W. G. Sebald*, pp. 67–69
FIAN, ANTONIO, 'Ein paar Vorurteile: Angewandt auf W. G. Sebalds *Schwindel. Gefühle.*', *Wespennest*, no. 83 (June 1991), 76–78; repr. in Antonio Fian, *Hölle, verlorenes Paradies* (Graz: Droschl, 1996), pp. 107–13
HARTL, EDWIN, 'Fahrten und Erfahrungen: Dichtender Dozent', *Die Presse*, 30 June–1 July 1990, Spectrum section: Das neue Buch, p. viii
HINTERMEIER, HANNES, *Münchner Abendzeitung*, 9 June 1990
ISENSCHMID, ANDREAS, 'Melencolia: Prosa zwischen Protokoll, Zitat und Traum: W. G. Sebalds *Schwindel. Gefühle.*', *Die Zeit*, 21 September 1990, Literatur section, p. 75; repr. in Loquai, *Far From Home*, pp. 57–61, and in Loquai, *W. G. Sebald*, pp. 70–74
JUST, RENATE, and CLAUS PFEIFFER (photography), 'Stille Katastrophen', *Süddeutsche Zeitung*, 5 October 1990, Magazin section, pp. 27–30; repr. in Loquai, *W. G. Sebald*, pp. 25–30 (cf. Interviews, Primary Bibliography J.2)
KREUZER, HELMUT, 'Netz-Werk: W. G. Sebalds Prosastücke *Schwindel. Gefühle.*: Über Stendhal, Kafka und ihn selbst', *Frankfurter Rundschau*, 15 October 1990, p. 15
LOQUAI, FRANZ, 'Ein betörend schönes, verstörend melancholisches Buch', *Mittelbayerische Zeitung*, 27–28 April 1991; repr. in Loquai, *Far From Home*, pp. 61–63
MEYER, MARTIN, 'Memoria: Zu W. G. Sebalds Buch *Schwindel. Gefühle.*', *Neue Zürcher Zeitung* (Fernausgabe), 10 May 1990, p. 45; repr. in Loquai, *Far From Home*, pp. 51–54, and in Loquai, *W. G. Sebald*, pp. 64–67
MORLANG, WERNER, 'Drei empfindsame Italienreisen. Zu W. G. Sebalds bestrickendes Prosabuch *Schwindel. Gefühle.*', *Tages-Anzeiger* (Zurich), 24 September 1990

PATZE, CHRISTINE, 'W. G. Sebald: *Schwindel. Gefühle.*', *Neue Deutsche Hefte*, 36 (1989–90), 729–31

PRASCHL, PETER, 'Nichts ist gewiß', *Stern*, 19 July 1990, p. 99

RUDLE, DITTA, 'Wahnwanderer: Vom Schwindel der Melancholie und anderer Gefühle', *Wochenpresse*, no. 15, 13 April 1990

SCHMID, ULRICH, 'Heimkehr ins Allgäu', *Allgäuer Zeitung*, 30 May 1990, Kultur section, p. 7

WEINZIERL, ULRICH, '*Schwindel. Gefühle.*: Der Prosaist W. G. Sebald', *Frankfurter Allgemeine Zeitung*, 30 June 1990

Dutch translations

B.B.1.1. Melancholische dwaalwegen: roman, trans. by Jos Valkengoed (1990)

ZEEMAN, MICHAËL, 'Op zoek naar een houding', *De Volkskrant*, 6 December 1991

B.B.1.2. Duizelingen, trans. by Ria van Hengel (new Dutch translation 2008)

SCHIFERLI, VICTOR, 'In het spoor van Casanova, Kafka en Stendhal', *Het Parool*, 10 September 2008, Boeken section

ZEEMAN, MICHAËL, 'De creatieve kracht van verbijstering', *De Volkskrant*, 10 October 2008

English translation

B.B.1.4, B.B.1.5. Vertigo, trans. by Michael Hulse (1999)

ANON., 'London Best Sellers', *Evening Standard* (London), 13 December 1999

ANON., 'Books of the Moment', *Daily Telegraph*, January 2000

ANON., 'Fall Guy', *Economist*, 15 July 2000

ANON. (EP), *The Times*, 23 September 2000

ANON., 'Paperbacks', *Observer*, 1 October 2000

ANON. (TL), *Sunday Times*, 1 October 2000

ALLARDICE, LISA, *Independent on Sunday*, 1 October 2000

BATTERSBY, EILEEN, 'Man from the Margins', *Irish Times*, 27 November 1999

——*Irish Times*, 23 September 2000

BISWELL, ANDREW, 'Topographies of the Self', *Stand*, n.s. 2.2 (June 2000)

BOTTON, ALAIN DE, 'A Compelling Paranoia', *Sunday Telegraph*, 12 December 1999

BROOKNER, ANITA, 'Pursued across Europe by Ghosts and Unease', *Spectator*, 25 December 1999

BYATT, A. S., 'Dizzying Memories', *Sunday Times*, 12 December 1999, Culture Section, p. 42

COUSINS, SALLY, 'Paperbacks', *Sunday Telegraph*, 22 October 2000

DILLON, MILLICENT, 'Putting the Past in Front of Him', *San Francisco Chronicle*, 16 July 2000 <http://www.sfgate.com/cgi-bin/article.cgi?f=/c/a/2000/07/16/RV75346.DTL&hw=sebald&sn=002&sc=584> [accessed 6 April 2010]

DI PIERO, W. S., 'Another Country', *New York Times Book Review*, 11 June 2000, p. 20; see also *New York Times Book Review*, 6 November 2000; also quoted in the 2001 Eichborn edition of *Schwindel. Gefühle.*, p. 298

DIRDA, MICHAEL, *Washington Post*, 25 June 2000, Book World section

DISKI, JENNY, 'I Thought I Saw Dante in Gonzagagasse', *London Review of Books*, 3 February 2000, p. 31

DYER, GEOFF, 'A Dizzying World of Whimsical Memory', *Independent*, 17 December 1999

EDER, RICHARD, 'Exploring a Present that Is Invaded by the Past', *New York Times*, 22 May 2000; quoted in the 2001 Eichborn edition of *Schwindel. Gefühle.*, p. 298

FIGES, EVA, 'Early Beauty', *Hampstead & Highgate Express*, 17 December 1999

FREEMAN, JOHN, 'Punch the Hourglass', *City Pages* (Minneapolis), 5 July 2000

HACKETT, JOYCE, *Boston Review*, Summer 2000 <http://bostonreview.net/BR25.3/hackett. html> [accessed 10 August 2009]

HARMAN, CLAIRE, 'Mr Sebald's Sinister Scrapbook', *Evening Standard* (London), 10 January 2000

IYER, PICO, 'Dead Man Writing: The Strange, Haunted World of W. G. Sebald', *Harper's Magazine*, 10 (October 2000), 86–90 <http://www.harpers.org/subjects/ WinfriedGeorgSebald> [accessed 6 April 2010]; repr. in *Sun After Dark: Flights into the Foreign* (London: Bloomsbury, 2005), pp. 65–75

JEFFRIES, STUART, 'Atlas of the Soul', *Guardian*, 18 December 1999

KIRSCH, ADAM, 'The Truth of Inventions', *Newsday*, 23 July 2000

KRAUSS, NICOLE, 'Arabesques of Journey', *Partisan Review*, 68 (2001), 646–50 <http://www. bu.edu/partisanreview/archive/2001/4/krauss.html> [accessed 19 June 2009]

KUNKEL, BENJAMIN, 'Germanic Depressive', *Voice Literary Supplement* (Summer 2000)

LANDON, PHILIP, *Review of Contemporary Fiction*, 20.3 (Fall 2000), 137

LANE, ANTHONY, 'Higher Ground: Adventures in Fact and Fiction from W. G. Sebald', *The New Yorker*, 29 May 2000, pp. 128–36 (also refers to other works); edited version in the 2001 Eichborn edition of *Schwindel. Gefühle.*, pp. 306–16

LEZARD, NICHOLAS, 'Don't Look Down', *Guardian*, 14 October 2000

MCCRUM, ROBERT, 'The World of Books', *Observer*, 12 December 1999

MALEY, WILLY, 'Fact and Fiction Combine to Make a High-Class Piece of Literature', *Sunday Herald* (Glasgow), 12 December 1999

NICOLL, RUARIDH, 'Dizzy with the Weight of Memories', *Herald* (Glasgow), 9 December 1999

O'BRIEN, EDNA, 'A Little Night Reading', *Sunday Times*, 23 July 2000

PARKS, TIM, 'The Hunter', *New York Review of Books*, 15 June 2000, pp. 52–56; repr. in *The Emergence of Memory*, ed. by Schwartz, pp. 23-36

PRICE, STUART, 'Going Out: Books', *Independent*, 27 November 1999

SHAKESPEARE, SEBASTIAN, 'Optical Illusions', *Literary Review* (London) (December–January 1999–2000)

———*Evening Standard* (London), 8 September 2000

SONTAG, SUSAN, 'A Mind in Mourning', *Times Literary Supplement*, 25 February 2000, pp. 3–4; edited version in the 2001 Eichborn edition of *Schwindel. Gefühle.*, pp. 299–306; repr. in *Die Welt* (Atlantic Daily edn), 4 April 2000, p. 36 (see also Secondary Bibliography for translation into German and various reprints)

SUTCLIFFE, WILLIAM, 'The Loneliness of the Emigrant', *Independent on Sunday*, 5 December 1999

TOYTON, EVELYN, 'Elegiac Disgust', *Threepenny Review* (Winter 2001)

WAGNER, ERICA, 'The Novelist on High', *The Times*, 2 December 1999, p. 46

French translation

B.B.1.6. Vertiges, trans. by Patrick Charbonneau (2001)

ANON. (S.B.), 'Sebald s'épanche', *Libération*, 11 January 2001, Livres section, p. viii

CASANOVA, NICOLE, ' "L'ange d'airain qui tue les voyageurs..." ', *La Quinzaine Littéraire*, 1–15 February 2001, pp. 10–11

CORTANZE, GÉRARD DE, 'Une étrange autobiographie', *Le Figaro Littéraire*, 1 February 2001, p. 5

CROM, NATHALIE, 'W. G. Sebald, l'inconsolable', *La Croix*, 11 January 2001, p. 17

DESHUSSES, PIERRE, 'Vertiges', *Le Monde*, 16 March 2001, Le Monde des Livres section, p. x

———'Sebald et la mélancolie', *Le Monde*, 20 June 2003, Le Monde des Livres section, p. vi

GABRIEL, FABRICE, 'Le Migrateur', *Les Inrockuptibles*, 16–22 January 2001, pp. 52–53

VALENTINI, RUTH, 'Les Raisons d'un succès Vertigineux: W. G. Sebald retrouve Stendhal et Kafka sur les bords du lac de Garde...', *Nouvel Observateur*, 1 February 2001

B.B.2. Die Ausgewanderten (1992)

ANON., *Fachdienst Germanistik*, 11.2 (February 1993), 15–16

ANON. (Ron), 'Schicksale', *Rheinischer Merkur*, 25 November 1994, p. 22

ANON., 'Ein Häufchen Knochen', *Der Spiegel*, 4 January 1993, pp. 129–31

ANON. (jae), 'Das Deutsch, das aus der Ferne kommt', *Berliner Zeitung*, 21 October 1992, p. 13

ANON. (T.M.), 'Dampfkesselfabrik', *Der Tagesspiegel*, 26 January 1993

BALTZER, BURKHARD, 'Das sind Bücher, auf die wir gewartet haben', *Saarbrücker Zeitung*, 27 November 1992, Feuilleton, p. 14

BARON, ULRICH, 'Dem Mäusevolk gilt heute meine Hoffnung', *Rheinischer Merkur*, 15 January 1993, Literatur section, p. 20; repr. in Loquai, *Far From Home*, pp. 84–87, and in Loquai, *W. G. Sebald*, pp. 96–99

BERNHARD, RENATE, 'Die entlarvte Realität: W. G. Sebald las bei Müller & Tillmanns', *Rheinische Post*, 3 May 1993, unpaginated (cf. On readings given by WGS)

BOEDECKER, SVEN, 'W. G. Sebalds neuer Erzählband: Verfall, nichts als Verfall und Leere', *Die Welt*, 13 March 1993, p. 5

—— 'Nabokov und andere Ausgewanderte', *Rhein-Neckar-Zeitung*, 6–7 March 1993, p. 47

—— 'Als würden die Toten ins Leben zurückkehren', *Berliner Zeitung*, 12 March 1993, Bücher section, p. 27

BOND, GREG, 'Ferne Heimat', *Freitag*, 4 December 1992, p. 12

BRAUN, MICHAEL, 'Aus dem Totenhaus der Seele', *Frankfurter Rundschau*, 30 September 1992, p. B2

CRAMER, SIBYLLE, 'Zartbitterstes: Ist es versuchte Nähe, ist es "Abwehrzauber"? Warum nur lieben alle den Kitsch W. G. Sebalds?', *die tageszeitung*, 9 July 1993, Kultur section, p. 16

DETERING, HEINRICH, 'Große Literatur für kleine Zeiten', *Frankfurter Allgemeine Zeitung*, 17 November 1992, Literatur section, p. L2; repr. in Loquai, *Far From Home*, pp. 71–75, and in Loquai, *W. G. Sebald*, pp. 82–87

DIECKS, THOMAS, *Deutsche Bücher*, 23 (1993), 117–19

DREWS, JÖRG, 'Wie eines jener bösen deutschen Märchen', *Süddeutsche Zeitung*, 2–4 October 1992, Beilage: SZ am Wochenende section, p. x; repr. in Jörg Drews, *Luftgeister and Erdenschwere: Rezensionen zur deutschen Literatur von 1967 bis 1999* (Frankfurt a.M.: Suhrkamp, 1999), pp. 185–89; also repr. in Loquai, *Far From Home*, pp. 68–71, and in Loquai, *W. G. Sebald*, pp. 79–82

—— 'Aus dem bis in den letzten Winkel aufgeräumten deutschen Land', *Badische Zeitung*, 31 October 1992, Lese-Lust section, p. 4

FALCKE, EBERHARD, 'Aus der Mordgeschichte dieses Jahrhunderts', *Die Zeit*, 27 November 1992, Literatur section, p. 69; repr. as 'Mords-Erinnerungen: W. G. Sebalds Erzählungen *Die Ausgewanderten*', in *Deutsche Literatur 1992: Jahresüberblick*, ed. by Franz Josef Görtz, Volker Hage, and Uwe Wittstock (Stuttgart: Reclam, 1993), pp. 263–67; also repr. in Loquai, *Far From Home*, pp. 76–79, and in Loquai, *W. G. Sebald*, pp. 87–90

GÖRNER, RÜDIGER, 'Los der Ausgewanderten: Literarische Untersuchungen der Exil-problematik', *Neue Zürcher Zeitung*, 29 January 1994, p. 38 (on *Die Ausgewanderten* and Goethe's *Unterhaltungen deutscher Ausgewanderten*)

HINTERMEIER, HANNES, 'Verstörende Erinnerungsarbeit', *Konturen: Magazin für Sprache, Literatur und Landschaft*, 1 (1993), 69–70

LODRON, HERBERT, 'Fremdsein hoch zwei', *Die Presse*, 7 November 1992, Spectrum section, p. viii

LÖFFLER, SIGRID, 'Dienst unter dem Schlot: Ein Schriftsteller wird entdeckt', *Profil*, 19 April 1993, pp. 104–05 (cf. Interviews, Primary Bibliography J.7)

LOQUAI, FRANZ, 'Der Archivar verwehter Spuren', *Deutsches Allgemeines Sonntagsblatt*, 12 February 1993, p. 26; repr. in Loquai, *Far From Home*, pp. 87–89

MATT, BEATRICE VON, 'Die ausgelagerten Paradiese', *Neue Zürcher Zeitung* (Fernausgabe), 12–13 December 1992, Literatur und Kunst section, p. 43; repr. in Loquai, *Far From Home*, pp. 79–84, and in Loquai, *W. G. Sebald*, pp. 91–95

NÜCHTERN, KLAUS, 'Nach Amerikum', *Falter*, 5–11 February 1993, Literatur section, p. 51

REINACHER, PIA, 'Was vergessen wird und sinkt, kehrt wieder', *Basler Zeitung*, 30 September 1992, Part V, p. 8

SONTAG, SUSAN, 'W. G. Sebalds Requiems', trans. by Wigand Lange, *Frankfurter Rundschau*, 10 December 1996, Literarische Rundschau section, p. 5

SPARRE, SULAMITH, 'W. G. Sebald über Erinnern und Heimweh', *Nürnberger Zeitung*, 16 January 1993; repr. in Loquai, *W. G. Sebald*, pp. 99–101

VETTER, HARALD, 'Verschollene', *Die Furche*, 12 November 1992, p. 18

WALLMANN, HERRMANN, 'Verlorenes Land', *Hannoversche Allgemeine Zeitung*, 27 March 1993, unpaginated

The following reviews are of a radio adaptation of *Die Ausgewanderten*; see Audio-Visual Bibliography, p. 584, for details.

GELDNER, WILFRIED, 'Eine Reise in die Vergangenheit: Ursendung eines Hörspiels über "Max Aurach"', *Süddeutsche Zeitung*, 20 May 1994, p. 22

WAGNER, HANS-ULRICH, 'Textarchäologie: W. G. Sebald: Max Aurach: Aurachs Mutter', *FUNK-Korrespondenz*, 17 February 1995, p. 30; repr. in Loquai, *W. G. Sebald*, pp. 198–207

Dutch translation

B.B.2.1. De emigrés: Vier geïllustreerde verhalen, trans. by Ria van Hengel (1992)

HAVENAAR, RONALD, 'Razende zielen', *NRC Handelsblad*, 15 July 2005, Boeken section, pp. 12–15

HERTMANS, STEFAN, 'Vernis: Een schare witte kippen', *De Groene Amsterdammer*, 30 June 1993, p. 21

JACOBS, HERMAN, 'Het gat in het zwijgen', *DSLETTEREN*, 22 July 2005

JANSEN, PETER, 'Zo keren ze dus terug, de doden', *Limburgs Dagblad*, 26 May 2005, p. 25

JONG, ANNERIEK DE, 'Het fascisme heeft me gemaakt', *NRC Handelsblad*, 2 July 1993, Cultureel Supplement, p. 6 (with interview; see Primary Bibliography J.9)

OVERSTIJNS, JEROEN, 'Kleine verhalen in de schaduw van een grote oorlog', *De Tijd*, 25 June 2005

PEARCE, JOSEPH, 'Ontwaakt, mijn volk', *De Morgen*, 3 August 2005, Boeken section, pp. 6–7

ROULEAUX, WIL, 'De ontoelaatbaarheid van het gevoel', *Vrij Nederland*, 8 May 1993, pp. 93–96

ROZEMA, HILBRAND, 'Griezelliteratuur op een hoog moreel niveau', *Nederlands Dagblad*, 10 June 2005, p. 18

SCHAEVERS, MARK, 'Het lot Europeaan te zijn', *Vrij Nederland*, 28 May 2005, pp. 56–59

WOLFF, MELCHIOR DE, 'Het Duitsland van herkomst', *De Volkskrant*, 30 October 1992, Kunst & Cultuur section, p. 4

The following reviews are of 'De Emigrés', Rudi Meulemans's theatre adaptation of *Die Ausgewanderten*, which was performed by the theatre group De Parade in Brussels and several Flemish cities in April and May 2005. The reviews also concern the book itself.

BELLON, MICHAËL, 'Op zoek naar verloren levens', *De Standaard*, 11 April 2005

——'Zoeken naar herinnering', *Brussel Deze Week*, 8 April 2005

LAUWAERT, GUIDO, 'Minieme gebaren, sacrale toon', *De Tijd*, 13 April 2005
SMET, JAN DE, 'Een vertraagde estafette', *De Morgen*, 12 April 2005

English translation

B.B.2.3, B.B.2.4. The Emigrants, trans. by Michael Hulse (1996)

[VARIOUS], 'Our Choice of the Christmas Crackers', *The Times*, 30 November 1996, Directory section,
[VARIOUS], 'The Cream of the Crop', *The Times*, 7 December 1996
ANON., 'Under Review', *Guardian*, 5 December 1996
ACIMAN, ANDRÉ, 'In the Crevasse', *Commentary*, 103.6 (1997), 61–64
ALI, TARIQ, *The Times*, 30 November 1996, Directory section
ANGIER, CAROLE, *Independent*, 30 November 1996, Weekend section
ANNAN, GABRIELE, 'Ghosts', *New York Review of Books*, 25 September 1997, pp. 29–30
ASCHERSON, NEAL, 'Butterfly Memories', *Independent on Sunday*, 14 July 1996
BAILEY, PAUL, A. S. BYATT, and OTHERS, 'Books of the Year', *Daily Telegraph*, 30 November 1996
BELL, PEARL K., 'Fiction Chronicle', *Committee on Intellectual Correspondence*, no. 3 (Winter 1998–99), 8–10
BRADY, PHILIP, 'Ghosts of the Present', *Times Literary Supplement*, 12 July 1996, p. 22
BROOKNER, ANITA, and OTHERS, 'Books of the Year', *Spectator*, 16 November 1996
BYATT, A. S., SUSAN SONTAG, and OTHERS, 'International Books of the Year', *Times Literary Supplement*, 29 November 1996
CHALMERS, MARTIN, 'Angels of History', *New Statesman & Society*, 12 July 1996, pp. 1–2
COE, JONATHAN, 'Tact', *London Review of Books*, 20 March 1997, pp. 24–25
——'Takt', trans. by Franz Loquai, in Loquai, *W. G. Sebald*, pp. 250–56 (translation of above)
COHEN, LISA, 'Books Review: Prose', *Boston Review* (February–March 1997), p. 45
DRABELLE, DENNIS, 'What They Left Behind', *Washington Post*, 15 December 1996
EDER, RICHARD, 'Death in Survival', *Newsday*, 27 October 1996
——'Taken Over by Dead Men's Ghosts', *Los Angeles Times*, 27 October 1996 <http://articles.latimes.com/1996-10-27/books/bk-8129_1_dead-men-s-ghosts> [accessed 6 April 2010]
FRASE, BRIGITTE, 'Yearning toward Each Other', *Hungry Mind Review* (Winter 1996–97)
GRANT, LINDA, *Guardian*, 28 November 1996
JOSIPOVICI, GABRIEL, 'The Forces of Memory', *Jewish Quarterly*, 43.4 (Winter 1996–97), 59–60
KELLAWAY, KATE, 'Frames of Reference', *Observer*, 9 June 1994, p. 76
LAPPIN, ELENA, 'German Tragedy', *Jerusalem Report (The Jewish Quarterly)*, 9 January 1997
McGONIGLE, THOMAS, 'Heeding the Past', *Chicago Tribune*, 20 October 1996
NEUBERGER, JULIA, 'Unbearable Jewish Loss', *The Times*, 21 June 1997
OZICK, CYNTHIA, 'The Posthumous Sublime', *New Republic*, 16 December 1996, pp. 33–38
——'Das Sublime, posthum: *Die Ausgewanderten* von W. G. Sebald', trans. by Franz Loquai, in Loquai, *W. G. Sebald*, pp. 183–97 (translation of above)
PATERSON, HARRIET, 'Ghostly Scrapbook of Departed Lives', *Independent*, 13 July 1996
PORLOCK, HARVEY, 'Poll of Polls', *Sunday Times*, 8 December 1996
SHORT, ROBERT, 'An Enormous Talent', *Broadview* (UEA staff magazine), 15 November 1996, p. 4
SONTAG, SUSAN, *Times Literary Supplement*, 29 November 1996
STARTLE, WILLIAM, 'Review of Books of the Year', *Sunday Telegraph*, 8 December 1996
TONKIN, BOYD, 'Reading in the Dark is an Amazing Debut', *Independent*, 29 November 1996, Christmas Book Section

VOURVOULIAS, BILL, 'The Loss World', *Village Voice*, 14 January 1997, pp. 51–53

——'Welt des Verlusts: W. G. Sebalds *Die Ausgewanderten*', trans. by Franz Loquai, in Loquai, *W. G. Sebald*, pp. 208–13 (translation of above)

WOLFF, LARRY, 'When Memory Speaks', *New York Times Review of Books*, 30 March 1997, p. 19

French translation

B.B.2.7. *Les Émigrants: quatre récits illustrés, trans. by Patrick Charbonneau (1999)*

BOULOUQUE, CLÉMENCE, 'L'Étrangeté familière de W. G. Sebald', *Le Figaro*, 17 April 2003, p. 7

CORTANZE, GÉRARD DE, 'W. G. Sebald: Le Passé repoussé de l'Allemagne', *Le Figaro Littéraire*, 14 January 1999, Critiques section: Littérature étrangère, p. 5 (cf. Interviews, Primary Bibliography J.29)

DESHUSSES, PIERRE, 'Mémoire en miroir', *Le Monde*, 22 January 1999, Littérature section, p. v

DEVARRIEUX, CLAIRE, 'Sebald, objectif hier', *Libération*, 7 January 1999, pp. 1–2

GOLDSCHMIDT, GEORGES-ARTHUR, 'Un voyage au cœur du souvenir', *La Quinzaine Littéraire*, 1–15 February 1999, pp. 6–7

LAPAQUE, SÉBASTIEN, *Le Figaro magazine*; quoted in the 2009 Actes Sud brochure <http://www.actes-sud.fr/sites/default/files/brochure_sebald_0.pdf>, p. 17

MAVRIER, RENAUD, *Télérama*; quoted in the 2009 Actes Sud brochure <http://www.actes-sud.fr/sites/default/files/brochure_sebald_0.pdf>, p. 17

POLAC, MICHEL, *Charlie Hebdo*; quoted in the 2009 Actes Sud brochure <http://www.actes-sud.fr/sites/default/files/brochure_sebald_0.pdf>, p. 17

ROLLIN, ANDRÉ, *Le Canard enchaîné*; quoted in the 2009 Actes Sud brochure <http://www.actes-sud.fr/sites/default/files/brochure_sebald_0.pdf>, p. 17

SEMPRUN, JORGE, 'Une mémoire européenne: En creux, sur le mode du manque, *Les Emigrants* de W. G. Sebald', *Journal du Dimanche*, 3 January 1999

VALENTINI, RUTH, 'Exilés, vos papiers', *Nouvel Observateur*, 21–27 January 1999, pp. 64–65

B.B.3. *Die Ringe des Saturn: Eine englische Wallfahrt (1995)*

ANON., *Fachdienst Germanistik*, 14.3 (March 1996), 16–17

ANON. (mw), 'Gefühle des Herings: Sanfter Tourismus mit W. G. Sebald', *Handelsblatt*, 19–20 January 1996, p. 97

ANON. (jae), 'Das Deutsch, das aus der Ferne kommt', *Berliner Zeitung*, 21 October 2002, p. 13

ANON. (seg), 'Schönheit der Schatten', *Frankfurter Rundschau*, 3 November 1995, p. 24

BAHNERS, PATRICK, 'Kaltes Herz', *Frankfurter Allgemeine Zeitung*, 9 December 1995, Bilder und Zeiten section, p. B5; repr. in Loquai, *W. G. Sebald*, pp. 126–31

BARON, ULRICH, 'Exzentrische Bahnen', *Rheinischer Merkur*, 13 October 1995, Merkur Extra section, p. i; repr. in Loquai, *W. G. Sebald*, pp. 120–23

BOEDECKER, SVEN, 'Mit der Schnauze am Boden', *Berliner Zeitung*, 13–14 January 1996, p. 38; also in *Stuttgarter Zeitung*, 5 January 1996, Feuilleton, p. 40

BRANG, GABRIELE, 'Was die Welt nicht nur im Innersten zusammenhält', *Berliner Lese-Zeichen*, 6 (1996), 84-85

BRAUN, MICHAEL, 'Unter dem Gestirn der Melancholie', *Freitag*, 27 October 1995, p. 12

——and HERMANN WALLMANN, 'Bilder einer langsam sich zermahlenden Erde: Ein Briefwechsel über W. G. Sebalds *Die Ringe des Saturn*', *Basler Zeitung*, 11 October 1995; repr. in Loquai, *W. G. Sebald*, pp. 112–20

Drews, Jörg, 'Gang über Leichenfelder', *Süddeutsche Zeitung*, 11 October 1995, Literatur section, p. L16; repr. in Jörg Drews, *Luftgeister and Erdenschwere: Rezensionen zur deutschen Literatur von 1967 bis 1999* (Frankfurt a.M: Suhrkamp, 1999), pp. 229–32; also repr. in Loquai, *W. G. Sebald*, pp. 108–11

——'Wallfahrt zu Exzentrikern', *Badische Zeitung*, 28 October 1995, Magazin section, p. 4

Fetz, Bernhard, 'Blick vom Totenberg', *Die Presse*, 3 February 1996, Spectrum section, p. vii

Fritz-Vannahme, Joachim, 'Promeneur im Proseminar', *Die Zeit*, 13 October 1995, Literatur section, p. 2

Hansen, W., 'De blauwe duivel in de rugzak', *De Volkskrant*, 20 October 1995

Isenschmid, Andreas, 'Melancholische Merkwürdigkeiten', *Die Weltwoche*, 9 November 1995, Kultur Bücher section, p. 69; repr. in Loquai, *W. G. Sebald*, pp. 124–26; also repr. in the 2001 Eichborn edition of *Die Ringe des Saturn*, pp. 373–76

Just, Renate, and Marc Volk (photographs), 'Im Zeichen des Saturn: Ein Besuch bei W. G. Sebald', *Die Zeit*, 13 October 1995, Magazin section, pp. 26–30; repr. in Loquai, *W. G. Sebald*, pp. 37–42 (cf. Interviews, Primary Bibliography J.11)

Kastura, Thomas, 'Stern des literarischen Herbstes', *RezenSöhnchen*, 17 (1995), 36–38

Loquai, Franz, 'Im ruhigen Rhythmus der Beharrlichkeit', *Mittelbayerische Zeitung*, 30 December 1995

——'In den Beinhäusern der Geschichte', *Das Sonntagsblatt*, 2 February 1996, Roman II section, p. 38

——'Wanderer auf der Schädelstätte der Geschichte', *Die Furche*, 21 December 1995, p. 26

Matt, Beatrice von, 'Archäologie einer Landschaft', *Neue Zürcher Zeitung* (Internationale Ausgabe), 30 September–1 October 1995, p. 49; repr. in Loquai, *W. G. Sebald*, pp. 102–08

Nolte, Jost, 'Sebald oder Neues über Untergänge', *Die Welt*, 24 January 1998, p. J5

Oberembt, Gert, 'Raupentrost und Trauerseide', *Der Tagesspiegel*, 2 December 1995, p. B3; repr. in *Die Horen*, 41 (1996), 183–85

Reinacher, Pia, 'Todessehnsucht, in Gold gefasst', *Tages-Anzeiger*, 8 January 1996

Rojan, Norbert, *Listen*, 40 (1995), 11

Rothfuss, Uli, 'Es liest: W. G. Sebald', *Der Literat*, 7 August 1996, p. 14 (cf. On readings given by WGS)

Schütte, Wolfram, 'Der Seidenspinner', *Frankfurter Rundschau*, 20 January 1996, Zeit und Bild section, p. ZB4

Wackwitz, Stephan, 'Langes Verglühen', *die tageszeitung*, 11–12 November 1995, Literataz section, p. 19

Dutch translation

B.B.3.1. De ringen van Saturnus: Een Engelse pelgrimage, trans. by Ria van Hengel (1996)

Moonen, Erik, 'Mooi maar somber', *De Morgen*, 20 February 1997, Café des Arts section, p. 24

Mulder, Reinjan, 'Een belachelijk landje', *NRC Handelsblad*, 19 January 1996, CS Literair section, p. 3

Verplancke, Marnix, 'Het verleden vanuit een vals perspectief', *De Morgen*, 26 September 2007, pp. 6–7

Vogelaar, Jacq, 'Melancholieke dwaalwegen', *De Groene Amsterdammer*, 16 November 2007, p. 45

English translation

B.B.3.2, B.B.3.3. The Rings of Saturn, trans. by Michael Hulse (1998)

ANON., *The New Yorker*, 7 September 1998, p. 382

ACIMAN, ANDRÉ, 'Out of Novemberland', *New York Review of Books*, 3 December 1998, pp. 44–47

ANGIER, CAROLE, 'In the Killing Fields: W. G. Sebald is England's — and East Anglia's — Great German Writer', *Independent*, 23 May 1998, Saturday Magazine section, p. 9

BAILEY, PAUL, 'Old Order Overthrown', *Daily Telegraph*, 6 June 1998, Arts and Books section, p. A6

CELYN JONES, RUSSELL, 'Long View from Southwold', *The Times*, 4 June 1998, p. 41

EDER, RICHARD, 'The Anatomy of Melancholy', *Los Angeles Times*, 28 June 1998 <http://articles.latimes.com/1998/jun/28/books/bk-64187> [accessed 6 April 2010]

ENRIGHT, D. J., 'The German Ocean', *London Review of Books*, 17 September 1998, p. 27

FERGUSON, JANE, 'The Rings of Saturn' (Paperback of the Week), *Observer*, 16 May 1999, Review section, p. 14

HOWELL-JONES, GARETH, 'A Doubting Pilgrim's Happy Progress', *Spectator*, 30 May 1998, pp. 34-35

MCCANN, CHRIS, 'Like a Punch in the Face', *The Stranger* (Seattle), 5–11 October 2006, p. 40 (review of Laird Hunt's novel *Like a Punch in the Face*, which acknowledges its debt to *Die Ringe des Saturn*)

MCCRUM, ROBERT, 'McCrum on Sebald', *Observer*, 7 June 1998, p. 15 (cf. Interviews, Primary Bibliography J.25)

MARTIN, BRIAN, 'Conversations on the Way', *Financial Times* [June 1998?]

MASON, WYATT, 'Mapping a Life', *American Book Review*, 20.4 (1999), 19–20

MORRISON, BLAKE, 'Suffolk through Death-Tinted Specs', *New Statesman*, 5 June 1998, p. 45

ROBERSON, MATTHEW, *Review of Contemporary Fiction*, 18.3 (Fall 1998), 241-42

SILMAN, ROBERTA, 'In the Company of Ghosts', *New York Times Book Review*, 26 July 1998, p. 5; repr. in the 2001 Eichborn edition of *Die Ringe des Saturn*, pp. 387–95

STOW, RANDOLPH, 'The Plangency of Ruins', *Times Literary Supplement*, 31 July 1998, p. 11

TATE, TRUDI, 'The Writer Among the Ruins', *Quadrant*, 42.11 (November 1998), 76-78

TONKIN, BOYD, 'Swimming the Seas of Silence', *W: The Waterstone's Magazine*, no. 13 (Spring 1998), 90–99 (cf. Interviews, Primary Bibliography J.23)

WOOD, JAMES, 'A Death Artist Writes', *Guardian*, 30 May 1998, Saturday Review section, p. 8

——'The Right Thread', *New Republic*, 6 July 1998 (edited version of this piece repr. in the 2001 Eichborn edition of *Die Ringe des Saturn*, pp. 387–95)

Note: The 2001 Eichborn edition of *Die Ringe des Saturn* also quotes the following sources in English on WGS, although the dates suggest that these are not so much reviews as references in the annual overviews of books published that year: Richard Eder, *Los Angeles Times*, 13 December 1998; Penelope Lively, *Daily Telegraph*, 21 November 1998; Javier Marías, *Times Literary Supplement*, 4 December 1998; Michael Ondaatje, *Daily Telegraph*, 21 November 1998; Jonathan Raban, *Times Literary Supplement*, 4 December 1998.

French translation

B.B.3.6. W. G. Sebald, Les Anneaux de Saturne, trans. by Bernard Kreiss (1999)

BOUQUET, STÉPHANE, 'Sebald tragique', *Libération*, 2 December 1999, Littérature section, p. iv

CROM, NATHALIE, 'W. G. Sebald, ou l'exercice de la mélancolie', *La Croix*, 9 September 1999, p. 17

DESHUSSES, PIERRE, 'En marchant en écrivant', *Le Monde des Livres*, 22 October 1999, Littérature section, p. iii

FABRYCY, ISABELLE, *Le Matin*; quoted in the 2009 Actes Sud brochure <www.actes-sud.fr/sites/default/files/brochure_sebald_0.pdf>, p. 23

GABRIEL, FABRICE, 'Reflets d'outre-monde', *Les Inrockuptibles*, 18 August 1999, p. 56

GOLDSCHMIDT, GEORGES-ARTHUR, 'Les Anneaux qui entourent le monde', *La Quinzaine Littéraire*, 1–15 October 1999, p. 8

GRISOLIA, MICHEL, 'Succès: Initiation au voyage intérieur', *L'Express*, 4 November 1999, Livres section, p. 57

PAGNARD, ROSE-MARIE, 'W. G. Sebald: Une leçon d'anatomie poétique', *Le Temps*, Livres section; an extract from this can be found in the 2009 Actes Sud brochure <http://www.actes-sud.fr/sites/default/files/brochure_sebald_0.pdf>, p. 23

VALENTINI, RUTH, 'Un Bavarois en Angleterre: Le promeneur solitaire', *Nouvel Observateur*, 14–20 October 1999, p. 58

B.B.4. *Austerlitz (2001)*

ANON., *Fachdienst Germanistik*, 19.5 (May 2001), 15–16

ANON. (G.B.), 'Die wahre Geschichte von W. G. Sebalds Roman *Austerlitz*', *Die Welt*, 9 July 2002, p. 27 (on Susi Bechhöfer)

ALTENBURG, MATTHIAS, 'Makellos gestelzt', *Die Woche*, 9 February 2001, Literatur und Buch section, p. 41

BERG, DETLEF, 'Lange Reise zurück zu sich selbst', *Hamburger Abendblatt*, 3 April 2001

CANTIENI, MONICA, '"Voilà le soleil d'Austerlitz!" Bestechende Prosa: W. G. Sebalds jüngstes Werk *Austerlitz*', *Aargauer Zeitung*, 18 April 2001

DEGGERICH, GEORG, 'Schmerzspur des Daseins', *Am Erker*, 41 (2001), 95

DETERING, HEINRICH, 'Von den irdischen Gütern retten, soviel man kann', *Literaturen*, 2001.3–4, 50–51

DREWS, JÖRG, 'Leben und sein unausdenkbares Gegenteil', *Süddeutsche Zeitung*, 24–25 February 2001, Literatur section, p. iv

——'Ein Leben um ein Nichts herum', *Badische Zeitung*, 3 March 2001, p. iv

DUNKER, AXEL, *Deutsche Bücher*, 32.1 (2002), 51–56

ELSAGHE, YAHYA, 'Die unvollendete Geschichte: W. G. Sebalds Ecriture Cruciverbiste im Roman *Austerlitz*', *Neue Zürcher Zeitung*, 10–11 March 2007, Literatur und Kunst section, p. 29

FREUND, WIELAND, 'Literaturforum: Tschechows Ring an Sebalds Finger', *Neue Gesellschaft, Frankfurter Hefte*, 48 (2001), 248–49

——'Belgische Begegnungen', *Rheinischer Merkur*, 23 March 2001, p. 1

GÖPFERT, REBEKKA, 'Susi Bechhöfer fragt zurück: W. G. Sebald lieh sich für *Austerlitz* ihre Biographie', *Frankfurter Rundschau*, 15 March 2003, p. T10

GREINER, ULRICH, 'Zum Spaß: Ein paar Unterschiede zwischen Kunst und Handwerk', *Die Zeit*, 26 April 2001, Literatur section, p. 53 (comparison with *Barbar Rosa* by Georg Klein)

ISENSCHMID, ANDREAS, 'Durch einen Seidenschleier sehen', *Tages-Anzeiger* (Zurich), 17 February 2001, Kultur section, pp. 49–50

JONG, ANNERIEK DE, 'Het kind herkent zichzelf niet meer', *NRC Handelsblad*, 13 April 2001, Boeken section, p. 6

KÖHLER, ANDREA, 'Der Staub der Toten, die Asche der Zeit', *Neue Zürcher Zeitung* (Internationale Ausgabe), 24–25 February 2001, Literatur and Kunst section, p. 49

KOSPACH, JULIA, 'Der Spurensucher', *Profil*, 19 February 2001, pp. 122–24 (cf. Interviews, Primary Bibliography J.35)

KRAUSE, TILMAN, 'Im Saal der verhallenden Schritte', *Die Welt*, 10 February 2001, Die literarische Welt: Buch der Woche section, p. 3

KÜBLER, GUNHILD, 'Dem Freund erzählen, was nicht zum Aushalten ist', *Die Weltwoche*, 15 February 2001, Kultur section, p. 41

KUNISCH, HANS-PETER, 'Die Melancholie des Widerstands', *Süddeutsche Zeitung*, 5 March 2001, p. 20

KURZ, PAUL KONRAD, 'Gegen den Verlust des Erinnerns', *Stimmen der Zeit*, 219.6 (2001), 426-28

LERNOUT, GEERT, 'Te veel vragen zonder antwoorden', *De Morgen*, 18 April 2001, pp. 15, 19

LESZCZYNSKA, ANNA, *Psyche*, 56.12 (2002), 1273-74

LOQUAI, FRANZ, 'Labyrinthische Spurensuche', *literaturkritik.de*, 3.7 (2001), pp. 135–38

MORITZ, RAINER, 'Aus dem Setzkasten der vergessenen Dinge', *Schweizer Monatshefte*, 81.7-8 (2001), 60-61

NICKEL, ECKHART, 'Verabredung mit Gestern', *Financial Times Deutschland*, 30 March 2001, Bücher section, p. v

NÜCHTERN, KLAUS, 'Nachts sind alle Tauben grau', *Falter*, 23 February–1 March 2001, Kultur section, p. 62

PETSCHNER, RAIMUND, 'Zeitgeistfern, zeitwahrheitsnah', *Neues Deutschland*, 20 July 2001, p. 12

PFOHLMANN, OLIVER, 'Verabredungen in der Vergangenheit: Poetologisches Programm formuliert: W. G. Sebalds neues Meisterwerk *Austerlitz*', *Fränkischer Tag*, 14 July 2001

PICHLER, GEORG, 'Die blinden Stellen', *Die Presse*, 17 March 2001, Literatur Spectrum section, p. vii

PLATH, JÖRG, 'Fremd bin ich eingezogen', *Der Tagesspiegel*, 18 March 2001, p. W4

RADISCH, IRIS, 'Der Waschbär der falschen Welt', *Die Zeit*, 5 April 2001, Literatur section, pp. 55–56

REICHENSBERGER, RICHARD, 'Kreisende Prozesse der Erinnerung: "Zufall" und Konstruktion" in W. G. Sebalds Roman *Austerlitz*', *Der Standard*, 28 March 2001

REILING, JESKO, 'Überblenden und Grenzen überschreiten', *Berner Zeitung*, 11 April 2001

RUTSCHKY, MICHAEL, 'Das geschenkte Vergessen', *Frankfurter Rundschau*, 21 March 2001, Literatur Rundschau section, p. 1

SCHELLER, WOLF, 'Getragen von außerordentlicher Erinnerungswut: Der Hanser-Verlag präsentiert den Roman *Austerlitz* von W. G. Sebald', *Der Bund*, 21 April 2001, Der kleine Bund section, p. 7

——'Gnadenloses Endspiel', *Nürnberger Nachrichten*, 12–13 April 2001 (shorter version of above)

SCHLODDER, HOLGER, 'Die Wiedergewinnung der verlorenen Zeit', *Darmstädter Echo*, 14 April 2001

SCHREINER, CHRISTOPH, 'Erlesenes Herzweh', *Saarbrücker Zeitung*, 14–16 April 2001, Literatur section, p. L12

SCHRÖDER, ALLARD, 'Deze echte herinneringen zijn vals', *Vrij Nederland*, 30 June 2001, p. 82

SCHRÖDER, JULIA, 'Das Dunkel erzählend durchdringen', *Stuttgarter Zeitung*, 21 March 2001, Section 2, p. i

SCHRÖDER, LOTHAR, 'Wahrheit im Abseits', *Rheinische Post*, 4 May 2001, Journal section, p. 4

SPEICHER, STEPHAN, 'Aus dem Reich der Toten', *Berliner Zeitung*, 7–8 July 2001, p. 6

STEINFELD, THOMAS, 'Die Wünschelrute in der Tasche eines Nibelungen', *Frankfurter Allgemeine*, 20 March 2001, Literatur section, p. L18

——'Europas Schrecken und Schönheit', *Süddeutsche Zeitung*, 9 February 2008, p. 13 (on the reissue of *Austerlitz* in the Süddeutsche Zeitung Bibliothek (B.B.4.(c)))

TÜRK, JOHANNES, 'Lektüre-Rausch ohne Erlösung', *Märkische Allgemeine* (Ostern), 15 April 2001

WACKWITZ, STEPHAN, 'Architekt der Erinnerung. Eine literarische Identitätssuche: W. G. Sebalds grandiose Erzählung *Austerlitz*', *A-Z München*, 10-11 February 2001

ZEEMAN, MICHAËL, 'De dingen hebben een geheim, net als de mensen', *De Volkskrant*, 11 May 2001

English translation

B.B.4.1, B.B.4.2, B.B.4.3. Austerlitz, trans. by Anthea Bell (2001)

ANON., *Daily Telegraph*, 3 August 2002

ANON., 'Novel of the Week', *The Week*, 13 October 2001, Arts section, p. 21

ANON., 'Strange but True', *Economist*, 22 October 2001, Books and Arts section, p. 69

ALVAREZ, MARIA, 'The Significant Mr Sebald', *Daily Telegraph*, 22 September 2001, Magazine section, pp. 54–59 (cf. Interviews, Primary Bibliography J.43)

ANNAN, GABRIELE, 'Ghost Story', *New York Review of Books*, 1 November 2001, pp. 26–27

BAKER, KENNETH, 'Remembering to Forget', *San Francisco Chronicle*, 7 October 2001 (cf. Interviews, Primary Bibliography J.48)

BANVILLE, JOHN, 'The Rubble Artist', *New Republic*, 26 November 2001, pp. 35–38 <http://www.powells.com/review/2001_12_06> [accessed 6 April 2010]

BARNES, STEVE, 'Bookmarks', *Wall Street Journal*, 12 October 2001

BECHHÖFER, SUSI, 'Stripped of my Tragic Past by a Bestselling Author', *Sunday Times*, 30 June 2002 (not a review but of interest to the reception)

BECKETT, ANDY, 'Long and Winding River', *Guardian*, 29 September 2001, Saturday Review section, p. 12

BELL, ANTHEA, 'The Will to Forget', *Daily Telegraph*, 6 October 2001

BERNSTEIN, MICHAEL ANDRÉ, 'Melancholy Baby', *Los Angeles Times*, 14 October 2001, Book Review section

BROOKNER, ANITA, 'A Journey without Maps', *Spectator*, 6 October 2001, pp. 64–65

BROWN, CRAIG, '415 Pages and One Photograph ... What a Book!', *Mail on Sunday*, 30 September 2001, p. 63

BYATT, A. S., 'Only Connect', *New Statesman*, 15 October 2001, pp. 52–53

CAMERON, PETER, 'Keeping Time', *Observer* (Raleigh, NC), 28 October 2001

CELYN JONES, RUSSELL, 'History Never Quite Lost, Never Quite Forgotten', *The Times*, 3 October 2001

CRYER, DAN, 'Talking with W. G. Sebald: Europe Unplugged', *Newsday* (New York), 28 October 2001, p. B11 (cf. Interviews, Primary Bibliography J.53)

CUSK, RACHEL, 'A Witness to our Hidden Ghosts', *Evening Standard* (London), 1 October 2001

DIRDA, MICHAEL, *Washington Post*, 14 October 2001, Book World section, p. 15

DYER, GEOFF, 'Do Lettuces Dream at Night?', *Independent on Sunday*, 17 October 2001, Arts etc. section, p. 15

EDER, RICHARD, 'Excavating a Life', *New York Times Book Review*, 28 October 2001, p. 10

GORRA, MICHAEL, *Atlantic Monthly* (Boston), November 2001, p. 146

HARRIS, ROGER, 'In Search of his own History', *The Sunday Star-Ledger* (Newark, NJ), 11 November 2001, section 10: Books, p. 4

HOFMANN, MICHAEL, 'Sebald's Fog', *Prospect*, October 2001, Arts & Books section, pp. 60–61 <http://www.prospectmagazine.co.uk/2001/10/sebaldsfog/> [accessed 30 March 2010]; repr. as 'A Chilly Extravagance', in *The Emergence of Memory*, ed. by Schwartz, pp. 87–91

HUGHES-HALLETT, LUCY, 'No Place to Go', *Sunday Times*, 6 October 2001

JAGGI, MAYA, 'Recovered Memories', *Guardian*, 22 September 2001, Saturday Review section, pp. 6–7 (cf. Interviews, Primary Bibliography J.45)

JONES, MALCOLM, 'The Big One Not Over Yet', *Newsweek*, 20 October 2001, p. 10

——'Books: Outside the Box', *Newsweek*, 25 October 2001 <http://www.msnbc.com/news/647743.asp> [accessed 30 March 2010] (cf. Interviews, Primary Bibliography J.52)

KAKUTANI, MICHIKO, 'In a No Man's Land of Memories and Loss', *New York Times*, 26 October 2001

KIRSCH, ADAM, 'Fated Memory', *Bookforum* (New York) (Oct–Dec 2001), p. 28

LANCHESTER, JOHN, 'The Will to Forget', *Daily Telegraph*, 6 October 2001

LAWSON, ANTHEA, 'Identity Crisis', *The Times*, 6–12 October 2001, Books section

LEHMANN, CHRIS, 'Recovered Memories', *Newsday*, 7 October 2001, pp. B12–B14

LEZARD, NICHOLAS, 'The Mystery of W. G. Sebald', *Guardian*, 13 July 2002, Review section, p. 31

McGOWN, ED, 'Paperback of the Week', *Observer*, 14 July 2002, Books section, p. 18

MARKOVITS, BENJAMIN, 'What Was it that So Darkened our World?', *London Review of Books*, 18 October 2002, pp. 23–24

MENDELSOHN, DANIEL, 'Foreign Correspondents', *New York*, 8 October 2001, pp. 70–72 (compares *Austerlitz* with Bernhard Schlink's *Flights of Love*)

MITCHELMORE, STEPHEN, 'W. G. Sebald: *Austerlitz*', *SpikeMagazine* (online), November 2001 <http://www.spikemagazine.com/1201sebald.php> [accessed 10 August 2009]

MURRAY, JOHN, 'Looking for his Parents', *Literary Review* (London) (October 2001), p. 51

OATES, JOYCE CAROL, 'Lest we Forget', *New York Review of Books*, 19 July 2007, pp. 47–50

O'BRIEN, MURRAGH, 'Even Railway Stations Can Have their Spiritual Side', *Independent on Sunday*, 21 July 2002, Books, Arts etc. section, p. 17

PRODGER, MICHAEL, 'The 20 Best Books of the Decade', *Sunday Telegraph*, 24 January 2010, Books Life section, pp. D6–D7

RIEMER, ANDREW, 'Journey of Memories and Forgetting', *Sydney Morning Herald*, 1 December 2001

RONCEVIC, MIRELA, *Library Journal*, 15 October 2001, p. 110

SAUMAREZ SMITH, CHARLES, 'Another Time, Another Place', *Observer*, 30 September 2001, Review section, p. 15

SHAKESPEARE, SEBASTIAN, 'Sebastian Shakespeare Talks to W. G. Sebald', *Literary Review* (London) (October 2001), p. 50 (cf. Interviews, Primary Bibliography J.47)

SINCLAIR, CLIVE, 'Breathing Brilliant Life into Memories and Ghosts', *Jewish Chronicle*, 2 November 2001, Books section, p. 32

SLAVITT, DAVID R., 'A Narrative of Memory, Trauma', *Sunday Boston Globe*, 28 October 2001

STRAUSS, MONICA, 'The Panoramic View Bred of Exile', *Aufbau*, 67.16 (2001), 1 and 14

TINDALL, GILLIAN, 'The Fortress of the Heart', *Times Literary Supplement*, 19 October 2001, p. 21

TONKIN, BOYD, 'Ghostly Trains of Thought', *Independent*, 24 October 2001, Weekend Review section

——'Goodbye, Cruel World: Hello Fantasy, Fame and Foodies', *Independent*, 28 December 2001, p. 17

——'The Gentle Ghosts of a Tragic History', *Independent*, 13 April 2002, Weekend Review section, p. 11

UPCHURCH, MICHAEL, '*Austerlitz* Unfolds a Hidden Life', *Sunday Seattle Times and Seattle Post-Intelligencer* (Fourth Edition), 7 October 2001, Northwest Life Section, p. J10

VIVIS, ANTHONY, '*Austerlitz* and *On the Natural History of Destruction*', *In Other Words: The Journal for Literary Translators*, no. 21 (2003) (W. G. Sebald memorial issue, ed. by Peter Bush), 64–66

WALDEN, GEORGE, 'The Force of Impersonality', *Sunday Telegraph*, 30 September 2001, Review section, p. 14

Walters, Colin, 'Walking the Dark Side of Memory', *Sunday Times* (Washington DC), 7 October 2001

Warner, Marina, 'Sebald: *Austerlitz*', 11 April 2002, text available online <http://courses. essex.ac.uk/lt/lt909/SebaldAusterlitz.rtf> [accessed 23 March 2010] (cf. On prizes awarded to WGS)

French translation

B.B.4.7. Austerlitz, trans. by Patrick Charbonneau (2002)

Azambuja, Miguel de, *Le Journal des psychologues*; quoted in the 2009 Actes Sud brochure <http://www.actes-sud.fr/sites/default/files/brochure_sebald_0.pdf>, p. 25

Crom, Nathalie, *La Croix*; quoted in the 2009 Actes Sud brochure <http://www.actes-sud.fr/sites/default/files/brochure_sebald_0.pdf>, p. 29

Cusset, Catherine, *Frenchmorning*; quoted in the 2009 Actes Sud brochure <http://www. actes-sud.fr/sites/default/files/brochure_sebald_0.pdf>, p. 29

Czarny, Norbert, 'Matière du souvenir', *La Quinzaine Littéraire*, 1–15 December 2002, pp. 13–14

Naulleau, Eric, *Le Matricule des Anges*; quoted in the 2009 Actes Sud brochure <http:// www.actes-sud.fr/pro/presse/brochures/brochure_sebald.pdf>, p. 29

Zékian, Stéphane, *La Nouvelle Revue Française*, no. 566 (2003), 317-22

Dutch translation

B.B.4.8. Austerlitz, trans. by Ria van Hengel (2003)

Belder, Hein de, 'Vergeten maar toch willen weten', *Tertio*, 10 September 2003

Hakkert, Theo, 'Achter de deuren van de kindertijd', *Veluws Dagblad*, 1 February 2003, p. 69

Jansen, Odile, 'Het trauma van de verdwenen Heimat', *Trouw*, 24 March 2001

Jansen-de Graaf, B. A., 'Weemoed met een kartelrandje', *Reformatorisch Dagblad*, 28 January 2004

Kamminga, Rudi, 'De onbedoelde zwanenzang van W. G. Sebald', *Dagblad van het Noorden*, 4 April 2003

Pol, Barber van de, 'Geen leven of dood, maar eeuwigheid', *De Volkskrant*, 14 March 2003

Rouleaux, Wil, 'Ontmoeting in Antwerpen', *Standaard der Letteren*, 13 March 2003

Rovers, Daniël, '*Austerlitz*: W. G. Sebald', *De Groene Amsterdammer*, 4 March 2010, p. 57

Rozema, Hilbrand, 'Sebald zocht achter piepende deuren', *Nederlands Dagblad*, 14 March 2003

Veldhuisen, Peter, 'De afgrond van het verleden', *Het Parool*, 11 April 2003

Vogelaar, Jack, 'Een compenserend geheugen', *De Groene Amsterdammer*, 5 July 2003, p. 39

B.A.2. For Years Now (with Tess Jaray) (2001)

Thwaite, Anthony, 'One Man's World', *Sunday Telegraph*, 30 December 2001, Review section, p. 12

B.A.3. Unerzählt (mit Jan Peter Tripp) (2003)

Anon., 'Unerzählt / Neues von und über W. G. Sebald', *Fachdienst Germanistik*, 21.5 (May 2003), 16–17

Anon. (TK), 'Warum die tiefen Blicke?', *Die Welt*, 23 August 2003, p. 4

Anon., *Der Tagesspiegel*, 19 March 2003, Kultur section, pp. 25–29 (an announcement rather than a review, printing several of the images over five pages)

ATZE, MARCEL, 'Die Geschichte der zugewandten Gesichter', *literaturkritik.de*, 5.7 (2003), 127–29

BARTMANN, CHRISTOPH, 'Aus einem Jenseits in ein anderes', *Süddeutsche Zeitung*, 22 July 2003, p. 14; also in *Kulturchronik*, 5 (2003), 10–11 (with cover illustration; in French, German, Spanish, and Russian versions)

JÄGER, LORENZ, 'Moralität, Natur und Geheimnis: W. G. Sebald und Jan Peter Tripp tauschen Blicke', *Frankfurter Allgemeine Zeitung*, 18 March 2003, Literatur section, p. L10

KÖHLER, ANDREA, 'Die Durchdringung des Dunkels: W. G. Sebald und Jan Peter Tripp: Ein letzter Blickwechsel', *Neue Zürcher Zeitung*, 14–15 December 2002, Literatur and Kunst section, pp. 49–50; repr. in W. G. Sebald, *Unerzählt* (Munich: Hanser, 2003), pp. 72–78; translation by Michael Hamburger included in B.A.3.1(2)

KOSPACH, JULIA, 'Augenpaare', *Profil*, 24 March 2003, p. 147

MEDIN, DANIEL, *Gegenwartsliteratur*, 2 (2003), 354–55

NEUBAUER, HANS-JOACHIM, 'Abgewandte Gesichter', *Rheinischer Merkur*, 20 March 2003, p. 22

PFOHLMANN, OLIVER, 'Denkbilder und Erinnerungsblitze oder: Wahrheiten am Rand', *Saarbrücker Zeitung*, 8 May 2003, p. C5; also published as 'Melancholischer Blick: "Unerzählte" Miniaturen aus dem Nachlass W. G. Sebalds und Radierungen Jan Peter Tripps', in *Augsburger Zeitung*, 30 April 2003, *Fränkischer Tag*, 5 July 2003, and online in *Oberpfalznetz* (2003) <http://www.oberpfalznetz.de/zeitung/111118-101,1,0.html> [accessed 6 April 2010]

SCHRÖDER, JULIA, 'Des Siebenschläfers Schatten ist der Tod', *Stuttgarter Zeitung*, 4 April 2003, Das Buch section, p. 34

English translation

B.A.3.1, B.A.3.2. Unrecounted, trans. by Michael Hamburger (2004)

ADAMS, TIM, 'The Eyes Have It', *Observer*, 19 September 2004, Review section: Literature, p. 8 <http://www.guardian.co.uk/books/2004/sep/19/fiction.wgsebald> [accessed 24 April 2010]

KAVENNA, JOANNA, *Sunday Telegraph*, 22 August 2004

SIMIC, CHARLES, 'The Solitary Notetaker', *New York Review of Books*, 11 August 2005, pp. 30–32 (also on *Campo Santo*)

STOSUY, BRANDON, 'After Sebald', *Village Voice* (New York), 18–24 May 2005, p. 42 (also on *Campo Santo* and on Hans Erich Nossack)

Later Works

B.D.2 Campo Santo, ed. by Sven Meyer (2003)

ADRIAN, MICHAEL, 'Das kleine, weiße Nichts', *Der Tagesspiegel*, 2 May 2004, p. 32

ATZE, MARCEL, 'Nachlaß-Boom?', *literaturkritik.de*, 6.4 (2004), 17–20

BRAUN, MICHAEL, 'Wo Lebende und Tote sich begegnen', *Frankfurter Rundschau*, 10 December 2003, p. 19

DEGGERICH, GEORG, 'Aus dem Nachlass', *Am Erker*, 46 (2003–04), 100–01

FUEST, LEONHARD, 'Unter dem Stern der Melancholie', *Financial Times Deutschland*, 29 August 2003, p. 23

HUBER, FLORIAN, 'Begriffe in Geschichten', *Wespennest*, no. 135 (June 2004), 107

ISENSCHMID, ANDREAS, 'Gruppenbild mit Ahnen', *Die Zeit*, 13 November 2003 <http://www.zeit.de/2003/47/L-Sebald> [accessed 6 April 2010]

JONG, ANNERIEK DE, 'Een brug van nu naar eeuwig', *NRC Handelsblad*, 20 February 2004, Boeken section

KÖHLER, ANDREA, 'Die Welt im Auge des Kranichs: W. G. Sebalds nachgelassene Prosa und verstreute Essays', *Neue Zürcher Zeitung*, 7 October 2003

KÜBLER, GUNHILD, 'Die Phantasie aufs Rad flechten', *Neue Zürcher Zeitung am Sonntag*, 14 September 2003, Kultur section, p. 69

LÖFFLER, SIGRID, 'Weltende auf Korsika', *Literaturen*, 2003.9, 44–46

MÜLLER, BURKHARD, 'Tücke der Toten', *Süddeutsche Zeitung*, 11–12 October 2003, p. 16

NEUBAUER, HANS-JOACHIM, 'Das heilige Feld', *Rheinischer Merkur*, 18 December 2003, Literatur section, p. 22

PFOHLMANN, OLIVER, 'Bis an den Rand der Selbstauflösung', *die tageszeitung*, 14 October 2003, p. 17

SCHRÖDER, JULIA, '"Wie stark der Wunsch nach Versöhnung in uns ist"', *Stuttgarter Zeitung*, 7 October 2003, Literatur section, p. vii

STRASSEGGER, REGINA, 'Was ich lese', *Die Presse*, 13 December 2003, unpaginated

WEBER, MARKUS R., 'Chor der Toten: Das Friedhofsgefühl in W. G. Sebalds Nachlaß *Campo Santo*', *Neue Deutsche Literatur*, 52.1 (2004), 159–62

English translation

B.D.2.1, B.D.2.2. Campo Santo, trans. by Anthea Bell (2005)

ANGIER, CAROLE, 'Signal from the Isle of the Dead', *Independent*, 11 February 2005, p. 24

ATHILL, DIANA, 'A Lost Voice', *Literary Review* (London) (April 2005), 29

COWLEY, JASON, 'Notes from a Time Traveller', *Observer*, 27 February 2005, Review section, p. 16

DIRDA, MICHAEL, *Washington Post*, 13 March 2005 <http://www.washingtonpost.com/wp-dyn/articles/A25577–2005Mar10.html> [accessed 6 April 2010]

EDER, RICHARD, 'Doomed to Repeat it Nonetheless', *Los Angeles Times*, 20 March 2005 <http://articles.latimes.com/2005/mar/20/books/bk-eder20> [accessed 6 April 2010]

FRANKLIN, RUTH, 'Speak, Memory, What Kind of Reader was W. G. Sebald?', *Slate Magazine*, 14 March 2005

HELLMAN, DAVID, 'Holy Ground of Collected Memories', *San Francisco Chronicle*, 20 March 2005 <http://www.sfgate.com/cgi-bin/article.cgi?f=/c/a/2005/03/20/RVGTVBNS2I1.DTL> [accessed 6 April 2010]

HUTCHINSON, BEN, 'W. G. Sebald: *Campo Santo*', *Focus on German Studies*, 11 (2004), 269–72

MACFARLANE, ROBERT, 'Life after Death', *Sunday Times*, 6 February 2005, Culture Section, p. 53

MOUNT, FERDINAND, 'A Master Shrouded by Mist', *Spectator*, 26 February 2005, pp. 40–42

POOLE, STEVEN, *Guardian*, 9 April 2005, Saturday Review section <http://www.guardian.co.uk/books/2005/apr/09/featuresreviews.guardianreview19/print> [accessed 6 April 2010]

SCHUESSLER, JENNIFER, 'Hanging out with Kafka', *New York Times*, 3 April 2005, Arts section <http://query.nytimes.com/gst/fullpage.html?res=9A01E5DF143FF930A35757C0A9639C8B63> [accessed 6 April 2010]

SILET, CHARLES L. P., *Magill's Literary Annual 2006*, ed. by John D. Wilson and Steven G. Kellman, 2 vols (Pasadena, CA: Salem Press, 2006), pp. 107–10

SIMIC, CHARLES, 'The Solitary Notetaker', *New York Review of Books*, 11 August 2005, pp. 30–32 (also on *Unrecounted*)

STOSUY, BRANDON, 'After Sebald', *Village Voice* (New York), 18–24 May 2005, p. 42 (also on *Unrecounted* and on Hans Erich Nossack)

THOMSON, IAN, *Daily Telegraph*, 21 February 2005

WILLIAMSON, GEORDIE, 'Notes from a Wounded Universe', *Evening Standard* (London), 28 February 2005

Dutch translation

B.D.2.7 Campo Santo, trans. by Ria van Hengel (2010)

PETERS, ARJAN, 'De kerkhoven van Corsica', *De Volkskrant*, 11 December 2010, Boeken section, p. 3

B.D.3. *Über das Land und das Wasser, ed. by Sven Meyer (2008)*

ANON., *Fachdienst Germanistik*, 26.12 (December 2008), 5–7 (p. 7)

BONNÉ, MIRKO, 'Woher ich komme, weiß ich nicht: Die berückend schönen Gedichte W. G. Sebalds', *Frankfurter Allgemeine Zeitung*, 17 January 2009, p. Z5

DOTZAUER, GREGOR, 'Längst sind die Spätheimkehrer aus den Gassen verschwunden', *Der Tagesspiegel*, 30 September 2008, p. 24

HANUSCHEK, SVEN, 'In den Treibhäusern lauern die Gurken', *Frankfurter Rundschau*, 13 September 2008, pp. 36–37

HUTCHINSON, BEN, *Times Literary Supplement*, 14 November 2008, p. 32

ISENSCHMID, ANDREAS, 'Der Strahl eines anderen Lichts', *Die Zeit*, 6 November 2008, p. 63 <http://www.zeit.de/2008/46/L-Sebald_neu> [accessed 7 April 2010]

KÖHLER, ANDREA, 'Der Wind im Zeichen des Widders: W. G. Sebalds nachgelassene Gedichte', *Neue Zürcher Zeitung* (Internationale Ausgabe), 13 October 2008, Sonderbeilage: Bücher Herbst 2008, p. SB5

LEHMKUHL, TOBIAS, 'Aus dem Leben eines Geistesjägers', *Süddeutsche Zeitung*, 26 September 2008, p. 18

OPITZ, MICHAEL, 'Prosa, die klingt wie Musik', *Deutschlandradio Kultur*, 30 January 2009, Feuilleton <http://www.dradio.de/dkultur/sendungen/kritik/911935/> [accessed 25 April 2010]

SCHMIDT-BERGMANN, HANSGEORG, *Allmende: Zeitschrift für Literatur*, 29 June 2009, 121

SCHRÖDER, JULIA, *Stuttgarter Zeitung*, 26 September 2008, p. 37

D.53 *'Ich möchte zu ihnen hinabsteigen und finde den Weg nicht: Zu den Romanen Jurek Beckers', ed. by Uwe Schütte (2010)*

ANON., 'Postume Polemik', *Der Spiegel*, 22 March 2010, p. 136

BUCHELI, ROMAN, 'Scheitern und Gelingen: Jurek Beckers *Jakob der Lügner* ein Melodrama? Eine nachgelassene Polemik von W. G. Sebald', *Neue Zürcher Zeitung*, 6 April 2010, *Neue Zürcher Zeitung* Online <http://www.nzz.ch/nachrichten/kultur/aktuell/scheitern_ und_gelingen_1.5380064.html> [accessed 6 April 2010]

KILB, ANDREAS, 'Finale im Dichterduell Sebald gegen Becker', *Frankfurter Allgemeine Zeitung*, 20 May 2010

SOBOCZYNSKI, ADAM, 'Die Empörung: Großer Nachlass-Fund: Wie W. G. Sebald Jurek Becker angriff', *Die Zeit*, 25 March 2010

STEINFELD, THOMAS, 'Massenelend und Melodram: Aus dem Nachlass: W. G. Sebalds vernichtende Kritik an Jurek Becker', *Süddeutsche Zeitung*, 23 March 2010, p. 14

See also Audio-Visual Bibliography, p. 586, for details of a recorded discussion on Deutschlandradio Kultur.

Varia

On readings given by WGS (see the Chronology for details of readings and book tours)

1991

Bender, Ruth, 'Die reale Welt zerrinnt zur Vision', *Kieler Nachrichten*, 20 December 1991, Kultur section, p. 22

1993

Anon., 'W. G. Sebald liest in der Stadtbibliothek', *Schwetzinger Zeitung*, 23-24 January 1993

Anon., 'Autoren treffen sich: Das 7. Freiburger Literaturgespräch vom 11.–13. November', *Südkurier*, 23 October 1993

Anon. (alt), 'Geschichte von ideologischen Irrsinn', *Wiesbadener Tagblatt*, 17 March 1993, Feuilleton, p. 7

Anon., 'W. G. Sebald las: Von der Flucht vor Deutschland: Die Verschwörung des Schweigens', *Münsterische Zeitung*, 20 March 1993, Kultur/Roman section, unpaginated

Anon., 'W. G. Sebald las: Es bohrt etwas', *Kieler Nachrichten*, 30 April 1993, Kultur section, p. 26

Anon., '"Die Vergangenheit der Zukunft": Freiburger Literaturgespräch mit europäischer Spitzenbesetzung', *StadtNachrichten* (Freiburg im Breisgau), 29 October 1993

Anon., 'Lesen in der Vergangenheit der Zukunft: Siebtes Freiburger Literaturgespräch mit zwölf Autoren aus sechs Ländern', *Schwarzwalder Bote*, 27 October 1993

Bernhard, Renate, 'Die entlarvte Realität: W. G. Sebald las bei Müller & Tillmanns', *Rheinische Post*, 3 May 1993, unpaginated

Broos, Susanne, 'Gespenster der Kindheit: Heute abend liest W. G. Sebald im Frankfurter Literaturhaus', *Frankfurter Rundschau*, 28 January 1993, p. 26

Ebel, Martin, 'Das siebte Freiburger Literaturgespräch — diesmal unerwartet lebhaft: Streifzüge in den Ruinen von gestern', *Badische Zeitung* (Freiburg), 15 November 1993, Kultur section

Fink, Philipp, 'Anschreiben gegen das Vergessen: "Freiburger Literaturgespräch" zum Thema "Die Vergangenheit der Zukunft"', *Südkurier*, 16 November 1993

Fuest, Leonard, 'W. G. Sebald: Geradezu opulente Prosa — meisterhaft erzählt', *Westfälische Nachrichten* (Münster), 20–21 March 1993, Münsterisches Feuilleton, unpaginated

Halter, Martin, 'Variationen über kein Thema: Zum siebten Freiburger Literaturgespräch', *Zürcher Tages-Anzeiger*, 16 November 1993

Heidenreich, Wolfgang, '7. Freiburger Literaturgespräche: Sie haben endlich alle entlarvt', *Badische Zeitung*, 26 November 1993

Höhn, Heidi, 'Auswanderer-Schicksal sensibel erzählt: "Bücher verbreche ich so nebenbei": W. G. Sebald in der Buchhandlung Riemann', *Neue Presse* (Coburg), 29 April 1993, Feuilleton, p. 13

Köhler, Andrea, 'Zukunftsentwürfe der Phantasie: Das 7. Freiburger Literaturgespräch', *Neue Zürcher Zeitung* (Fernausgabe), 18 November 1993, Feuilleton, p. 33

Rössler, Jürgen, 'Schicksal von vier Ausgewanderten: W. G. Sebald stellte sein neues vor/ Transparente Sprache', *Schwetzinger Zeitung*, 1 February 1993

Scherer-Frank, Jutta, 'Mit Sprachkraft gegen Vergessen angeschrieben', *Schwetzinger Woche*, 4 February 1993, Kultur section, p. 7

Schulte, Bettina, '7. Freiburger Literaturgespräch: "Die Vergangenheit der Zukunft": Von vielen höflichen und ein paar unhöflichen Stimmen', *Basler Zeitung*, 16 November 1993

Stitz, Sandra, 'Vielleicht heiße ich Wotan: W. G. Sebald stellte seinen Erzählband *Die Ausgewanderten* in Coburg vor', *Coburger Tageblatt*, 29 April 1993, Feuilleton, p. 6

1995

ANON., 'W. G. Sebald liest aus *Die Ringe des Saturn*', *Schwetzinger Zeitung*, 28-29 October 1995

J.R. [JÜRGEN RÖSSLER], 'Wallfahrt zum Untergang: W. G. Sebald stellte sein Buch *Die Ringe des Saturn* vor', *Schwetzinger Zeitung*, 7 November 1995

1996

ROTHFUSS, ULI, 'Es liest: W. G. Sebald', *Der Literat*, 7 August 1996, p. 14

1997

F.F. [FRANK FÜLLGRABE], 'Lesung im Heine-Haus: W. G. Sebald führt durch die englische Provinz: Was am Rande geschah', *Der Ilmenauer: Landeszeitung für die Lüneburger Heide*, 28 November 1997, p. 13

1998

ANON. (RP), 'Schlendernde Sätze: W. G. Sebald liest am Mittwoch bei Müller', *Rheinische Post*, 27 October 1998, unpaginated

ANON. (sy), 'Morgen zu W. G. Sebald ins Literaturhaus', *Frankfurter Rundschau*, 29 October 1998, p. 28

ANON. (prbs), 'Auf der Insel, für die Insel: W. G. Sebalds Lesung im Literaturhaus', *Frankfurter Rundschau*, 3 November 1998, p. 21

NOLL, WULF, 'Ein Mitreisender Monsieur Rousseaus: W. G. Sebald las in der Buchhandlung Müller', *Rheinische Post*, 30 October 1998, unpaginated

SCHRÖDER, JULIA, 'Das Verschwundene aufheben: W. G. Sebald zu Gast in Niedlichs Literarischem Salon in Stuttgart', *Stuttgarter Zeitung*, 7 April 1998, p. 27

SCHUBERT, MATTHIAS, 'Eine fast schon verlassene Welt. Literaturtage: W. G. Sebald las aus *Die Ringe des Saturn*', *Rhein-Neckar-Zeitung*, 2 June 1998

THOMAS, PETER, 'In der Falle der Literatur: W. G. Sebald liest in Darmstadt', *Darmstadter Echo*, Feuilleton, Ostern [1–13 April] 1998, p. 8

2000

OEHLEN, MARTIN, 'Dominant', *Kölner Stadtanzeiger*, 13 December 2000

2001

ALTMANN, ALEXANDER, 'Eine vertraute und gespenstische Welt: W. G. Sebald liest aus seinem neuen Roman *Austerlitz*', *Tageszeitung* (Munich), 4 April 2001

GRETHER, URS, 'Ein grosser Erzaehler', *BZ (Basellandschaftliche Zeitung)*, 7 June 2001

JANDL, PAUL, 'Spurensuche im Net-Dorf: Die 31. Rauriser Literaturtage zwischen Ordnung und Wahn', *Neue Zürcher Zeitung* (Schweizer Ausgabe), 2 April 2001, Feuilleton, p. 28

KUNISCH, HANS-PETER, 'Die Melancholie des Widerstands', *Süddeutsche Zeitung*, 5 March 2001, p. 20

LEHMGRÜBNER, ANJA, 'Ein Wanderer zwischen den Reisenden', *Kölner Stadt-Anzeiger*, 30 March–5 April 2001, p. 25; also in *TICKET* (Cologne), 30 March–5 April 2001

OEHLEN, MARTIN, 'Die Staubteilchen der Erinnerung: Der Autor liest in Köln aus seinem bewegenden Roman *Austerlitz*', *Kölner Stadt-Anzeiger*, 2 April 2001, p. 8

REISSINGER, MARIANNE, 'Zither-Laendler gegen Paranoia: Schriftsteller W. G. Sebald erzählt im Cuvilliés-Theater von schillernden "Moments musicaux"', *Abendzeitung* (Munich), 2 July 2001, p. 15

ROTH-HUNKELER, THERES, 'Der Bahnhof als Kathedrale: Lesung von W. G. Sebald in der Klubschule', *St Galler Tagblatt*, 9 April 2001, Kultur-Teil, p. 44

THUSWALDNER, ANTON, 'Die Fantasie als Fluchtpunkt des Lebens', *Salzburger Nachrichten*,

2 April 2001, Kultur section, p. 11 (on a reading at the Rauriser Literaturtage near Salzburg)

Tornau, Joachim F., 'Wanderungen heimatloser Melancholiker', *Göttinger Tageblatt*, 6 April 2001, Magazin (Kulturteil), p. 17

Wohlthat, Martina, 'W. G. Sebald im Literaturhaus: Tiefen des Vergessens', *Basler Zeitung*, 7 June 2001

On prizes awarded to W. G. Sebald

Fedor-Malchow-Lyrikpreis (1991)

Anon., *Börsenblatt*, 13 December 1991, p. 4268 [*sic*]

Panić, Ira, 'Der Denker wurde Dichter. Germanist W. G. Sebald bekam den erstmals vergebenen Fedor-Malchow-Lyrikpreis', *Hamburger Morgenpost*, 295/51, 19 December 1991, Kultur, p. 37

Berliner Literaturpreis (Bobrowski-Medaille) (1994)

Böttiger, Helmut, 'Laßt Autoren Autoren sein! Niedere Instinkte und kein Werkstattgespräch: W. G. Sebald und Erica Pedretti tragen im Vorlesewettbewerb des Berliner Literaturpreises den Sieg davon,' *Frankfurter Rundschau*, 20 June 1994, p. 7

Plath, Jörg, 'Medaillen ans Mittelfeld: Die Berliner Literaturpreise gingen diesmal an Erica Pedretti und W. G. Sebald', *die tageszeitung*, 21 June 1994, p. 13

Literatour Nord (1994)

Anon., '*Die Ausgewanderten*: Literatour Nord ehrt W. G. Sebald', *Frankfurter Allgemeine Zeitung*, 28 October 1994, p. 43

Mörike-Preis (Fellbach) (1997)

Schröder, Julia, 'Geehrte Ausgewanderte: Zur Verleihung des Mörike-Preises an W. G. Sebald in Fellbach', *Stuttgarter Zeitung*, 24 April 1997, p. 25

Heinrich-Böll-Preis (Cologne) (1997)

Anon., 'Kosmosformer: Kölner Böll-Preis an W. G. Sebald', *Frankfurter Allgemeine Zeitung*, 14 June 1997, p. 33

Oehlen, Martin, 'Erschaffung eines eigenen Kosmos: Sebald erhält Kölner Literaturpreis in November', *Kölner Stadt-Anzeiger*, 13 June 1997, Kulturteil, p. 8 (also announced in main part of the paper)

——'"Aus Feuer und Rauch": Der Kölner Heinrich-Böll-Preis wurde an W. G. Sebald verliehen', *Kölner Stadt-Anzeiger*, 29–30 November 1997, p. 37

Joseph-Breitbach-Preis (2000)

Köhler, Andrea, 'Gespräch mit Toten: W. G. Sebalds Wanderungen durch die Jahrhunderte', *Neue Zürcher Zeitung* (Internationale Ausgabe), 23–24 September 2000, Literatur und Kunst section, pp. 49–50; repr. in W. G. Sebald, *W. G. Sebald: Gespräch mit Lebenden and Toten* (= Bogen 48) (Munich: Hanser, 2000) (unpaginated pamplet containing text of Köhler's Laudatio)

Heinrich-Heine-Preis (Düsseldorf) (2000)

Anon., 'Arbeit an der Erinnerung: Heinrich-Heine-Preis für W. G. Sebald', *Neue Zürcher Zeitung* (Internationale Ausgabe), 11 July 2000, p. 36

ANON., 'Der Ausgewanderte: Düsseldorfer Heine-Preis an W. G. Sebald', *Frankfurter Allgemeine Zeitung*, 11 July 2000, p. 49

ANON., 'Europäisches Ereignis mit "Reisebild": Heine-Preisträger W. G. "Max" Sebald geehrt / Festakt im alten Düsseldorfer Rathaus', *Düsseldorfer Amtsblatt*, 23 December 2000, p. 1

ANON., 'Heine-Preis vergeben: In England lebender W. G. Sebald erhält renommierte Auszeichnung', *Westfälische Rundschau*, 14 December 2000

ANON., 'Melancholie als Widerstand: Laudatio von Professorin Irene Heidelberger-Leonard auf den Preisträger W. G. "Max" Sebald', *Düsseldorfer Amtsblatt*, 23 December 2000, pp. 4–5

ANON., 'Wie Heine ist er ein Meister des "Reisebildes": Ansprache von Oberbürgermeister Joachim Erwin', *Düsseldorfer Amtsblatt*, 23 December 2000, p. 4

SCHRÖDER, LOTHAR, 'Heine trifft', *Rheinische Post*, 11 July 2000, unpaginated

——'Aus der Zeit gefallen', *Rheinische Post*, 14 December 2000, unpaginated

——'Mitteilungen von Max', *Rheinische Post*, 13 December 2000, unpaginated

VOGT, ANDREA, 'Bilder vom Fliegen (W. G. Sebald las im Palais Wittgenstein)', *Rheinische Post*, 15 December 2000, unpaginated

WALLMANN, HERMANN, 'Kreuz- und Querlektüre', *Frankfurter Rundschau*, 20 December 2000, p. 18

Prix Laure-Bataillon (Nantes) (2000)

THOMAS, NICOLAS, 'Le prix L-Bataillon à W. G. Sebald', *Ouest-France* (Nantes), 16,844, 27 March 2000, p. 12

National Book Critics Circle Award (2001)

ANON., '*Austerlitz* Wins Book Critics Award for Fiction', *Seattle Post-Intelligencer*, 13 March 2002, Life and Arts Section, p. E5

VILLALON, OSCAR, 'Posthumous Book Award for British [*sic*] Author: W. G. Sebald's *Austerlitz* wins Top Honor for Fiction by National Book Critics Circle', *San Francisco Chronicle*, 12 March 2002, p. A-2

Bremer Literaturpreis (2001)

ANON., 'W. G. Sebald erhält Bremer Literaturpreis', *Frankfurter Rundschau*, 28 November 2001, p. 20

Independent Foreign Fiction Prize (2002)

ANON., 'Literaturpreis postum an Sebald', *Rheinische Post* (Düsseldorf), 29 January 2002, Feuilleton, unpaginated

SCHILLING-STRACK, ULRICH, 'Ein "Meisterwerk" außerordentlicher Klasse', *General-Anzeiger*, 15 April 2002, p. 14

TONKIN, BOYD, 'Winner's Rise to Fame Cut Short by Tragedy', *Independent*, 12 April 2002, p. 5 (contains extract from *Austerlitz*; see also Editorial on p. 18 of the same issue: 'The Best of Foreign Fiction Is Driven by Cultural Mixing')

WARNER, MARINA, 'Sebald: *Austerlitz*', 11 April 2002 (text of Laudatio) <http://courses.essex.ac.uk/lt/lt909/SebaldAusterlitz.rtf> [accessed 23 March 2010]

On exhibitions, conferences, lectures

'Waterlog', Norwich Castle Museum & Art Gallery, 3 February–15 April 2007 and Sainsbury Centre for Visual Arts, UEA, 30 January–24 June 2007; The Collection, Lincoln, 15 September 2007–13 January 2008 (exhibition of work by seven artists inspired by the east of England, with particular reference to *Die Ringe des Saturn*)

MIANO, SARAH EMILY, 'The Traveller', *Guardian*, 10 February 2007, Saturday Review section, p. 14

'W. G. Sebald: Zerstreute Reminiszenzen', Literaturhaus Stuttgart, 23 September–18 December 2008 (exhibition on WGS; opening event with Mark Anderson and Daniel Kehlmann on 22 September 2008; see Primary Bibliography B.C.6 for details of the accompanying book)

ANON., *Fachdienst Germanistik*, 26.12 (December 2008), 5–7 (pp. 5–6)
FRIEDL, ARMIN, 'Die in uns wuselnden Gedanken', *Stuttgarter Nachrichten*, 19 September 2008
LEHMKUHL, TOBIAS, 'Aus dem Leben eines Geistesjägers', *Süddeutsche Zeitung*, 26 September 2008, p. 18
PLATTHAUS, ANDREAS, 'Er ahndete nicht, er ahnte nur', *Frankfurter Allgemeine Zeitung*, 24 September 2008, p. 35
SCHLEIDER, TIM, 'Vom Glänzen der Heringe, vom Zucken der Leiber', *Stuttgarter Zeitung*, 24 September 2008
ZICK, MARTINA, 'Erinnerungen öffnen immer neue Gedankenfenster', *Stuttgarter Zeitung*, 18 September 2008

'Wandernde Schatten: W. G. Sebalds Unterwelt': Literaturmuseum der Moderne, Marbach, 26 September 2008–1 February 2009 (exhibition on WGS; for accompanying catalogue edited by Ulrich von Bülow, Heike Gfrereis, and Ellen Strittmatter; see Secondary Bibliography, Section 2)

ANON., *Fachdienst Germanistik*, 26.12 (December 2008), 5–7 (pp. 6–7)
ANON., *tageszeitung*, 25 September 2008, p. 17
BAHNERS, PATRICK, 'Man sieht viel in einer langen Mondnacht', *Frankfurter Allgemeine Zeitung*, 5 January 2009, p. 25
BÖHM, ROLAND, 'Der rätselhafte Autor', *Straubinger Tagblatt*, 25 September 2008 (piece written for the dpa (German Press Agency) and syndicated to various newspapers)
BUCHELI, ROMAN, 'In der Sehschule des Poeten', *Neue Zürcher Zeitung* (Internationale Ausgabe), 4–5 October 2008, p. 26
FRIEDL, ARMIN, 'Die in uns wuselnden Gedanken', *Stuttgarter Nachrichten*, 19 September 2008
——'Mit Eselohren und Büroklammern', *Stuttgarter Nachrichten*, 25 September 2008
GAMPERT, CHRISTIAN, 'Schwindelige Gefühle', transcript of broadcast on Deutschlandfunk, 25 September 2008, available online <http://www.dradio.de/dlf/sendungen/kulturheute/852219/> [accessed 8 August 2009]
GROSSER, UWE, 'Das Private ist Inspiration fürs Werk', *Heilbronner Stimme*, 25 September 2008
JONES, RICK, 'Out of the Twilight Zone', *Standpoint* (November 2008), pp. 46–47
KÖHLER, MONIKA, 'Annäherung an einen Unnahbaren', *Südkurier*, 25 September 2008
LEHMKUHL, TOBIAS, 'Aus dem Leben eines Geistesjägers', *Süddeutsche Zeitung*, 26 September 2008, p. 18
——'Zwischen Maulbeerbaum und Birke', interview with Heike Gfrereis, broadcast by Westdeutscher Rundfunk, 7 October 2008 (transcript available in DLA Marbach; cf. Audio-Visual Bibliography)
MANN, REINHOLD, 'Erzählen, Erfinden, Erinnern', *Schwäbische Zeitung* (Ulm), 25 November 2008 (emphasis on *Luftkrieg*; reference to Alexander Kluge and the bombing of Halberstadt)
MILZ, THOMAS, 'Mit präziser Melancholie', *Reutlinger General-Anzeiger*, 1 October 2008
RAPP, PATRICIA, 'Auch in seinem Nachlass bleibt der Autor rätselhaft', *Ludwigsburger Kreiszeitung*, 25 September 2008
RÜDENAUER, ULRICH, 'Kreisen um ein katastrophisches Zentrum', *Frankfurter Rundschau*, 30 September 2008, p. 39

——'Kreisen um die Katastrophe', *Kölner Stadt-Anzeiger*, 30 September 2008 (same piece as above)

——'Die Gegenwart der Toten', *Mannheimer Morgen*, 1 October 2008 (shorter version of the above)

SCHNEIDER, FRANZ, 'Die Eule und der Rucksack', *Rhein-Neckar-Zeitung* (Heidelberg), 11 October 2008

SPINNLER, ROLF, 'Ausgewandert aus dem eigenen Ich', *Stuttgarter Zeitung*, 26 September 2008, p. 37

——'Der Ich-Auswanderer', *Der Tagesspiegel*, 30 September 2008, p. 24 (almost identical to the above)

STÖCKMANN, JOCHEN, 'Melancholiker und Seelenfischer', transcript of broadcast on Deutschlandradio Kultur, 24 September 2008, available online <http://www.dradio.de/dkultur/sendungen/Frankfurter Allgemeine Zeitung it/851487/> [accessed 8 August 2009]

THEWES, DOMINIK, 'Marbach sonnt sich in Sebalds Glanz', *Marbacher Zeitung*, 25 September 2008

WESNER, RUDOLF, 'Ein rätselhafter Schriftsteller', *Südwest Presse* (Ulm), 25 September 2008

WITTSTOCK, UWE, 'Vom Geist zwischen den Vitrinen', *Die Welt*, 27 September 2008, p. 29

ZERWECK, DIETHOLF, 'Zwischen Spiegelwänden', *Esslinger Zeitung*, 27 September 2008

Other reports

On the Sebald Nachlass (archive) in Marbach (DLA)

ANON., 'Sebald-Nachlass geht ins Marbacher Archiv', *Stuttgarter Zeitung*, 21 September 2005, p. 29

BIENERT, MICHAEL, 'Einfallstore ins Unsichtbare', *Stuttgarter Zeitung*, 6 April 2006, p. 31

On the 2007 film W. G. Sebald: Der Ausgewanderte by Thomas Honickel

HINTERMEIER, HANS, 'Wenn nicht diese Weltschmerzanfälle wären', *Frankfurter Allgemeine Zeitung*, 2 November 2007, p. 38

MAIDT-ZINKE, KRISTINA, 'Melancholie in Suffolk: Ein Filmporträt nähert sich dem Literaten W. G. Sebald', *Süddeutsche Zeitung*, 4 November 2007, p. 21

On the conference held at UEA, 5–7 September 2008

BAHNERS, PATRICK, 'Magisch zieht des Dichters Grab Gedenkartikel an', *Frankfurter Allgemeine Zeitung*, 26 September 2008, p. 44

On the Sebald Lecture given by Will Self (London, January 2010)

ANON., 'Sebald and the Holocaust: Writer and Broadcaster Will Self Analysed the Work of Author W. G. Sebald during a Special Anniversary Lecture in London Last Month', *Broadview* (UEA staff magazine) (February 2010), p. 8

KUNDNANI, HANS, 'Sebald and the Holocaust', online response to Will Self's lecture <http://hanskundnani.com/2010/01/12/sebald-and-the-holocaust> [accessed 7 May 2010]

THOMAS, GINA, 'Der gute Deutsche', *Frankfurter Allgemeine Zeitung*, 25 January 2010, p. 28

TONKIN, BOYD, 'The Emigrant Who Haunts our Literature', *Independent*, 8 January 2010, Arts & Books section, p. 22

On the conference 'Alfred Andersch "Revisited": Die Sebald-Debatte und ihre Folgen'
(Frankfurt am Main, 19 November 2010)

HAHN, HANS-JOACHIM, 'Anderschs Leben und Werk als Gegenstand der Philologie', *literaturkritik.de*, no. 12 (December 2010) <http://www.literaturkritik.de/public/rezension. php?rez_id=15056&ausgabe=201012> [accessed 15 March 2011]

Hildebrand, Kathleen, 'Die Identitätsräuber', *Frankfurter Allgemeine Zeitung*, 24 November 2010 <http://www.faz.net/> [accessed 15 March 2011]

Miscellaneous

Anon., 'NESTA's best', *Broadview* (UEA staff magazine) (June 2000), p. 7 (on the NESTA award)

Anon. (J.S.), 'Glücksgefühle: Bruno Ganz liest W. G. Sebald', *Frankfurter Rundschau*, 18 October 2001, p. 32 (on a reading of *Il Ritorno in Patria* by Bruno Ganz in the Mozartsaal, Alte Oper, Frankfurt)

Bahners, Patrick, 'Kühner Kenner aller Kniffe: David Levine wird achtzig', *Frankfurter Allgemeine Zeitung*, 20 December 2006, Feuilleton, p. 32 (on Levine's portrait of WGS)

Evans, Julian, 'Platform', *New Statesman*, 21 April 2003, p. 54 (general piece on WGS)

Groot, Ger, 'Hervonden herinnering', *De Groene Amsterdammer*, 5 August 2005

Halter, Martin, 'Stilleben zu Lebzeiten: Jan Peter Tripp erinnert in der Bonndorfer Ausstellung "Die weiße Zeit" an W. G. Sebald', *Stuttgarter Zeitung*, 12 August 2004, p. 32

Howald, Stefan, 'Es hilft, dass W. G. Sebald in England lebt', *Tages-Anzeiger*, 11 July 1998, Kultur section <http://www.tagesanzeiger.ch/archiv/>

Johnson, Ken, 'Sometimes the Darkest Visions Boast the Blackest Humor', *New York Times*, 19 July 2008, The Arts section, pp. A17 and A21 (review of *After Nature*, an exhibition inspired by WGS, in the New Museum, New York, 19 July–21 September 2008)

Macfarlane, Robert, '1000 Novels Everyone Should Read', *Guardian*, 23 January 2009 (on *Austerlitz* and *Die Ringe des Saturn*) <http://caughtbytheriver.net/2009/01/wg-sebald-by-robert-macfarlane/> [accessed 29 March 2010]

Pfohlmann, Oliver, 'Der Schreck des Hirschkäfers: Notoristicher Unruhestifter: Neue Fundstücke zu W. G. Sebald', *Frankfurter Allgemeine Zeitung*, 10 February 2006, Feuilleton, p. 42 (piece drawing on *Sebald. Lektüren.*, ed. by Atze and Loquai)

Schlaffer, Hannelore, 'Schwanenhals und Sklaverei, Pro und Contra: Rolf Vollmann und W. G. Sebald über Charles Sealsfield', *Süddeutsche Zeitung*, 5 December 2006, Literatur section, p. 14

Steinfeld, Thomas, 'Der Eingewanderte: Literarische Größe: W. G. Sebald und Angelsachsen', *Frankfurter Allgemeine Zeitung*, 2 March 2000, p. 49 (on WGS and Susan Sontag among others)

4
Audio-Visual Bibliography

Compiled by Gordon Turner

The following audio-visual bibliography is composed largely of material collected and transcribed by Gordon Turner for the Sebald Sound Archive in Norwich (SSA) and material collected by the Deutsches Literaturarchiv Marbach (DLA). It encompasses readings, interviews, documentaries, discussion programmes, reviews, and adaptations. The physical sources include cassettes, copies of radio broadcasts, commercially available CDs, podcasts, video recordings, copies of television broadcasts, and films.

The bibliography is divided into audio and visual material and set out chronologically. It is subdivided into items featuring W. G. Sebald (WGS) in person, and items about his life and work. Wherever possible it gives the title of the recording or a short description, the medium, the date and place of first broadcast, the length, and the holding archive or library (if relevant). In most cases this is the SSA, the DLA, or the UEA library, but some sources may be available in the archives of the respective radio and television broadcasters, especially the ORF (Österreichischer Rundfunk) in Vienna.

In some cases a transcript of the recording is extant rather than the recording itself. These items are marked 'Transcript only'. In several cases we are unaware of the existence of an extant recording or a transcript of a radio or television broadcast, but have still listed the item. Details of publication or cross-references to the Primary and Secondary Bibliographies are given where appropriate (not all transcripts have been published). The reader is also recommended to consult the Chronology at the end of the book for further details of particular recordings.

Readers who have further details or information about recordings that are not listed here are asked to contact Gordon Turner at the following address: <gt21@talktalk.net>

CONTENTS

Audio Material
 Audio material featuring WGS
 Audio material about or based on WGS
Visual Material
 Visual material featuring WGS
 Visual material about or based on WGS
Varia

Audio Material

Audio material featuring WGS

1971   'Carl Sternheim: Versuch eines Porträts'
Discussion between Hellmuth Karasek, Jakob Knauss, Peter von Matt, and WGS
Schweizer Rundfunk, DRS II (Zurich), 17 February; 53 minutes 40 seconds
Transcribed with a commentary by Marcel Atze (see Primary Bibliography J.1)

1979   Interview with Professor Christian Graf von Krockow by WGS
Discussion of post-war Germany and economic success of West Germany
Mono sound recording, UEA Norwich, 25 minutes
Cassette (SSA)

1986   WGS contributes to a radio broadcast ('Radioessay') on Adalbert Stifter
ORF (Vienna), 27 August

1989   (1)   WGS contributes to a discussion programme on Joseph Roth with H.
Parschalk
ORF (Vienna), 4 April
(2)   WGS discusses *Nach der Natur* on the programme *Ex libris*
ORF (Vienna), 16 April

1990   (1)   WGS reading 'Ein Kaddisch für Österreich: Über Joseph Roth'
Sender Freies Berlin, March
(2)   WGS interviewed (with reading from *Schwindel. Gefühle.*)
Radio DRS (Zurich), 22 May
(3)   WGS interviewed (with reading from *Schwindel. Gefühle.*)
ORF (Vienna), 2 August

1992   *Literaturnacht*: WGS in discussion with three other authors
Bayerischer Rundfunk (Munich), 30 October, 2 hours

1993   (1)   WGS interviewed by WDR (Cologne), 24 January
(2)   WGS interviewed and reading from *Die Ausgewanderten*
Radio DRS (Zurich), 30 January
(3)   WGS interviewed and reading from *Die Ausgewanderten*
Saarländischer Rundfunk (Saarbrücken), 16 March
(4)   WGS interviewed and reading from *Die Ausgewanderten*
NDR (Münster), 18 March
(5)   *Literaturclub*: Discussion of plans for *Die Ringe des Saturn*
WGS in discussion with Daniel Cohn-Bendit, Peter Hamm, Andreas Isen-
schmid, and Cora Stephan
Radio DRS (Zurich), 14 June
(6)   WGS interviewed by Ralph Schock and reading from *Schwindel. Gefühle.*
Saarländischer Rundfunk (Saarbrücken), 16 July
(7)   Reading by WGS as part of the 'Videoopernwerkstatt' at the Bregenzer
Festspiele; Kuppelsaal, Vorarlberger Landesbibliothek, Bregenz, 18 July
Sound recording of the reading and workshop (cf. Visual Material, 1993:3)
Radio- und Videoarchiv, Vorarlberger Landesbibliothek, Bregenz (Austria) /
ORF (Vienna)

1994   (1)   'Die Wiederholung': discussion of Peter Handke (WGS with Peter von Matt)
Radio DRS (Zurich), 17 September
(2)   WGS reading from *Die Ringe des Saturn*
NDR (Hanover), 9 November

1996   (1)   'Zwischentöne': interview with WGS
        Deutschlandfunk, 28 November, 1 hour

1997   (1)   'Writers and Company': Eleanor Wachtel, interview with WGS
        CBC Radio (live Toronto–Boston link-up), 16 October, CD
        Transcribed from unedited and edited versions by Gordon Turner (SSA)
        Transcript published as 'Ghost Hunter'; see Primary Bibliography J.17
        (2)   'Der Schriftsteller W. G. Sebald': interview with WGS (with Heinrich
        Detering, Denis Scheck, and Gustav Seibt); probably recorded on 24 November,
        Deutschlandfunk (Berlin), 2 hrs, 26 November

1999   (1)   Jon Cook, Discussion with WGS (with WGS reading from *The Emigrants*)
        University of East Anglia, Norwich, 9 February
        Sound recording (UEA Library, SSA)
        Transcribed by Gordon Turner; see Part II of the present volume, pp. 356–63
        (2)   Christian Scholz, 'Der Schriftsteller und die Photographie'
        Radio essay and interview with WGS
        WDR (Cologne), 16 February
        (DLA) Transcript only; for publication (in the original German and in English and
        Italian translations), see Primary Bibliography J.18
        (3)   'Lecture-rencontre avec W. G. Sebald': WGS reading from *Die Ringe des
        Saturn* and discussing his work as part of the series *Lettres allemandes*
        Maison des Écrivains, Paris, 8 December
        Cassette and transcript (SSA); these can also be consulted in the Maison des
        Écrivains on request

2000   (1)   WGS reading from *Die Ausgewanderten* ('Max Ferber')
        2 CDs: 76 minutes, 75 minutes, with booklet
        Die andere Bibliothek im Ohr (record company)
        <http://www.hoergold.de/audiobooks/listings/> [accessed 26 March 2010]
        Also SSA; see Primary Bibliography L.1
        (2)   WGS reading from *Logis in einem Landhaus*, Marbach
        Marbacher Autorenlesungen, 12 April
        Cassette (DAT), 63 minutes, mono
        DLA ('Die Stimme des Autors'); see Primary Bibliography L.2

2001   (1)   Christopher Bigsby, Conversation with WGS
        Audio Visual Centre, UEA, 12 January
        2 minidiscs
        Transcribed from the original recording by Gordon Turner (SSA)
        Transcript also published; see Primary Bibliography J.34
        (2)   Doris Stoisser, 'Im Gespräch': interview with WGS
        Recorded at the Literaturtage, Rauris (Austria), March 2001
        Broadcast by ORF, Radio Burgenland, summer 2002
        Cassette, transcript by Gordon Turner (SSA)
        (3)   Sigried Wesener, '*Austerlitz*: Europäische Landschaften und Lebensspuren
        von W. G. Sebald': WGS reading from *Austerlitz* and in conversation
        Deutschlandradio (Berlin), 8 May
        (DLA) Transcript only. The transcript contains only the passages from *Austerlitz*
        and not the conversation.
        (4)   Jean-Pierre Rondas, '"So wie ein Hund, der den Löffel vergisst": Ein
        Gespräch mit W.G. Sebald über *Austerlitz*'
        Interview recorded in Norwich, 22 May, and broadcast as 'Sebald schrijft
        Breendonk', 2 September, *Rondas*, Radio Klara (Netherlands)
        (DLA) Transcript only; for publication see Primary Bibliography J.41

(5)   Interview with WGS featuring reading from *Austerlitz* (in English)
Saturday Review, BBC Radio 4, 29 September
(6)   Maya Jaggi, Conversation with WGS and Anthea Bell
St Jerome Lecture 2001, Queen Elizabeth Hall, London, 24 September
Archive recording, 2 CDs (SSA)
Full transcript by Gordon Turner (SSA); see Primary Bibliography J.46 for publication of edited and full transcript
(7)   Paul Allen, Interview with WGS
Night Waves, BBC Radio 3 (London), 5 October (with reading from *Austerlitz*)
Cassette (SSA)
(8)   Steve Wasserman, 'ALOUD at Central Library', Conversation with WGS, Los Angeles, 17 October 2001 (with reading from *Austerlitz*)
CD (SSA); see Primary Bibliography J.49
Transcribed by Richard and Carolyn Sheppard and Steve Wasserman; see Part II of the present volume, pp. 364–75
(9)   Michael Silverblatt, Interview with WGS, 18 October 2001
Broadcast on *Bookworm*, KCRW Santa Monica, 6 December 2001
2 CDs, transcribed from the original unedited and edited recording by Gordon Turner (SSA); transcript published as 'A Poem of an Invisible Subject' (see Primary Bibliography J.50)
Broadcast also available online <http://www.kcrw.com/etc/programs/bw/bw011206w_g_sebald> [accessed 6 April 2010]

Audio material about or based on WGS

1990   (1)   Frank Dietschreit, 'W. G. Sebald: *Schwindel. Gefühle.*' (review)
Buchzeit, Sender Freies Berlin, 9 July, 10 minutes
(2)   Michael Braun, 'W. G. Sebald: *Schwindel. Gefühle.*' (review)
Büchermarkt: Aus dem literarischen Leben, Deutschlandfunk (Berlin), 16 July 1990, 20 mins

1992   Frank Dietschreit, 'W. G. Sebald: *Die Ausgewanderten*' (review)
Buchzeit, Sender Freies Berlin, 4 September, 10 minutes

1994–1995
Ulrich Gerhardt / W. G. Sebald, 'Max Aurach' and 'Aurachs Mutter' / 'Ferbers Mutter'
Two radio plays adapted and directed by Ulrich Gerhardt for Bayerischer Rundfunk
'Max Aurach' first broadcast 20 May 1994, 63 minutes
'Aurachs Mutter' first broadcast 10 February 1995, 57 minutes
Bayerischer Rundfunk Schallarchiv; 2 cassettes (SSA)
See also Primary Bibliography C.1 and C.2 and the essay by Hans-Ulrich Wagner in the Secondary Bibliography, Section 6

1996   Frank Dietschreit, 'Strandgut in der Hosentasche oder Das Berühigende der Katastrophe: Über den Schriftsteller W. G. Sebald'
Buch am Sonntag, Sender Freies Berlin, 11 February, 25 minutes
See also a printed interview with WGS by Dietschreit, Primary Bibliography J.12

1998   Holger Schlodder, *Logis in einem Landhaus* (review)
NDR 3 (Landesfunkhaus Niedersachsen, Hanover), 25 September
(DLA) Transcript only

1999   (1)   Uwe Pralle, *Luftkrieg und Literatur* (review)
Kranich: Journal für Literatur, 15/19, RB2 (Bremen), 18 April 1999
(DLA) Transcript only

(2)   Gerhard Sauder, 'Die Sprachlosigkeit der Ruinierten', review of *Luftkrieg und Literatur*
SR2 (Saarbrücken), 9 October
(DLA) Transcript only
(3)   Walter Schübler, *Logis in einem Landhaus* (review)
Ex libris, ORF Vienna, 17 January 1999
(DLA) Transcript only

2001   (1)   'The Emigrants: Ambrose Adelwarth', adapted and directed by Edward Kemp, narrated by John Wood, *Sunday Play*, BBC Radio 3 (London)
Cassette, 85 minutes; rebroadcast 14 July 2002 (UEA Library, SSA); see Primary Bibliography C.3
(2)   Sabine Grimkowski, *Austerlitz* (Review)
NDR (Landesfunkhaus Niedersachsen, Hanover), 7 May
(DLA) Transcript only
(3)   Michael Braun, 'Was hat unsere Welt so sehr verfinstert? *Austerlitz*: Die poetische Geschichtsschreibung des Schriftstellers W. G. Sebald' (review)
12 May
(DLA) Transcript only
(4)   Paul Allen, Obituary
Night Waves, BBC Radio 3 (London), 17 December
Cassette (SSA)

2002   (1)   Richard Coles, Discussion of *After Nature* with Rüdiger Görner and Lavinia Greenlaw
Night Waves, BBC Radio 3 (London), 27 June 2002
Cassette (SSA)
(2)   Uwe Pralle, 'Zeitreisen durch die Gegenwart: Der europäische Schriftsteller W. G. Sebald'
NDR3 / ORB (Landesfunkhaus Niedersachsen, Hanover), 17 September
(DLA) Transcript only
(3) Reading of 'the Somerleyton section' from Part II of *The Rings of Saturn*, trans. by Michael Hulse
Twenty Minutes, BBC Radio 3 (London), 18 November
(4)   W. G. Sebald, *Austerlitz*, trans. by Anthea Bell, read by Richard Matthews
5 cassettes, 450 minutes, Books on Tape Inc., Newport Beach
See Primary Bibliography L.3

2003   (1)   Sarah Emily Miano, 'Max Sebald'
The Verb, BBC Radio 4 (London), 22 February
(2)   Holger Schlodder, *Unerzählt* (review)
NDR (Landesfunkhaus Niedersachsen, Hanover), 11 June
(DLA) Transcript only
(3)   Markus R. Weber, *Campo Santo* (review)
SR 2 (Saarbrücken), 20 September
(DLA) Transcript only
(4)   Holger Schlodder, *Campo Santo* (review)
NDR (Landesfunkhaus Niedersachsen, Hanover), 12 December
(DLA) Transcript only

2004   Andrea Köhler, 'Verabredungen in der Vergangenheit: Über W. G. Sebald': radio documentary directed by Stefan Hilsbecher
SWR, 20 January
(DLA) Transcript only

2005   (1)   W. G. Sebald, *Campo Santo*, read by Charles Brauer
2 CDs, 150 minutes, HörbucHHamburg, Hamburg
Contains the four 'Corsica' pieces; see Primary Bibliography L.4
(2)   Gabriele Fogg, 'Es geschah in der "Salle des pas perdus…". Geschichte von
den Identitätssuchern Jacques Austerlitz und Grace Elizabeth Mann'
Bayerisches Feuilleton, Bayerischer Rundfunk 2 (Munich), 55 mins, 3 December

2006   (1)   'Robert Walser: Eine Hommage in Wort und Klang', spoken by Hans
Rudolf Twerenbold and Peter Fricke, music by Marius Ungureanu
1 CD, 73 minutes, and 1 booklet, Faszination Hören, Reichertshausen
Contains a short extract entitled 'Die Spuren, daß Robert Walser hinterlassen hat'
from Sebald's essay on Walser; see Primary Bibliography A.6 and L.5
(2)   'W. G. Sebald: Surpris par la nuit': documentary in two parts
Radio France Culture, 21 and 22 June 2006:
(*a*)   'A la rencontre de Winfried Georg Sebald', introduced by Jean Thibaudeau,
directed by Ghislaine David, with Jean-Louis Baudry, Patrick Charbonneau, and
Jan Peter Tripp
(*b*)   'W. G. Sebald', by Thomas Sipp, directed by Pierre Willer, with Anthea Bell,
Anne Beresford, Ralf Jeutter, Ria Loohuizen, Gordon Turner, and 'la participation
exceptionnelle' of Michael Hamburger
Commentary and voice-over in French of interviews given in English
2 CDs: 79 minutes (SSA)
Both programmes are available to download <http://avantderniereschoses.
blogspot.com/2007/07/wg-sebald-france-culture-surpris-par-la.html> [accessed 9
April 2010]

2007   *Die Ausgewanderten: Vier lange Erzählungen*, read by Paul Herwig
7 CDs, 442 minutes, Winter & Winter, Munich
See Primary Bibliography L.6

2008   (1)   'European Voices: W. G. Sebald'
Aengus Woods and George Szirtes discuss the works of WGS
The Arts Show, RTE Radio 1 (Dublin), 6 July, 18 minutes 44 seconds <http://
www.rte.ie/arts/2008/0603/theartsshow_av.html?2382958,null,209> [accessed 25
April 2010]
(2)   Jochen Stöckmann, 'Melancholiker und Seelenfischer', review of Marbach
exhibition
Deutschlandradio Kultur, 24 September <http://www.dradio.de/dkultur/
sendungen/FrankfurterAllgemeineZeitungit/851487/> [accessed 8 August 2009]
(3)   Christian Gampert, 'Schwindelige Gefühle', review of Marbach exhibition
Deutschlandfunk, 25 September <http://www.dradio.de/dlf/sendungenkultur
heute/852219/> [accessed 8 August 2009]
(4)   'Wandernde Schatten: W. G. Sebalds Unterwelt'
Lecture given to mark the opening of the exhibition in Marbach, with Kurt W.
Forster and Ulrich Raulff, 26 September
Recording, mono, 44 minutes (DLA)
(5)   Tobias Lehmkuhl, 'Zwischen Maulbeerbaum und Birke: "Wandernde
Schatten": Die große Sebald-Ausstellung in Marbach' (review of the exhibition in
Marbach)
WDR 3 (Cologne), 7 October
(DLA) Transcript only
(6)   Hermann Wallmann, 'W. G. Sebald: *Über das Land und das Wasser*' (review)
WDR 3 (Cologne), 19 November
(DLA) Transcript only

2009   (1)   Julika Griem, 'Ist Sebald ein deutscher Autor?'
Discussion with Wolfgang Matz, Ellen Strittmatter, and Liliane Weissberg
Marbach, 9 January
Recording, mono, 93 minutes (DLA)
(2)   Michael Opitz, 'Prosa, die klingt wie Musik', review of *Über das Land und das Wasser*
Deutschlandradio Kultur, *Feuilleton*, 30 January <http://www.dradio.de/dkultur/sendungen/kritik/911935/> [accessed 25 April 2010]

2010   (1)   Will Self, 'Absent Jews and Invisible Executioners: W. G. Sebald and the Holocaust': recording of the Sebald Lecture 2010, London
<http://www.bclt.org.uk/index.php/events/sebald/> [accessed 24 March 2010]
(2)   Matthias Weichelt, discussion of W. G. Sebald's essay on Jurek Becker
Deutschlandradio Kultur, March, *c.* 5 minutes <http://ondemand-mp3.dradio.de/file/dradio/2010/03/24/drk_20100324_1009_6754e0aa.mp3> [accessed 26 March 2010]
(3)   Lynn Wolff, 'W. G. Sebald und H. G. Adler', lecture given at the conference 'H. G. Adler: Dichter - Gelehrter – Zeuge', 2 July
Electronic recording, 47 mins (DLA)

Visual Material

Visual material featuring WGS

1975   'Reiner Kunze spricht mit Max Sebald'
Video recording, UEA Norwich, 1 VHS cassette, 30 minutes, b&w
(UEA Library)

1977   'Max Sebald spricht mit Franz Reichert'
Video recording, UEA Norwich, 1 VHS cassette, b&w
(UEA Library)

1985   'Österreichische Porträts: Wer Österreich ist' (discussion of Austrian identity)
Café Central: Literary Discussion (WGS on panel with Friedrich Achleitner, Ursula Adam, Hannes Androsch, Erhard Busek, Herta Firnberg, Heinz Fischer, Rudolf Haller, Fritz Thorn, and Jochen Jung)
ORF (Vienna), 17 October
VHS cassette, 2 hours (SSA), ORF (Vienna)

1989   (1)   'Joseph Roth: Der Autor und seine Zeit' (featuring interview with WGS)
ORF (Vienna), 27 May
(2)   'States of the Nation: Germany in Transition'
Julian Hilton with Max Sebald and Joachim Fiebach, UEA, December
VHS cassette (UEA library)

1990   (1)   WGS interviewed by ZDF, 30 or 31 May
(2)   Ingeborg-Bachmann-Preis: readings and discussion by short-listed candidates including WGS, with Eleonore Fredy, Andreas Isenschmid, and Hellmuth Karasek
ORF (Vienna), 27 June
3 VHS colour cassettes (SSA), ORF (Vienna)
(3)   WGS discussing *Schwindel. Gefühle.*
3-sat, 6 August
(4)   *Aspekte*: WGS discussing *Schwindel. Gefühle.*
ZDF, 28 November
(5)   *Schaufenster*: 'Aspekte: Literaturpreis '90'
Discussion of *Schwindel. Gefühle.*, including readings by WGS

3-sat, 11 December, 10 minutes
VHS colour cassette (SSA)

1993   (1)   WGS interviewed by ZDF (with reading) in Wiesbaden, 15 March
(2)   *Bücherjournal*: Review of *Die Ausgewanderten* and interview with WGS by Karin Reiss
NDR (Münster), 18 March
VHS colour cassette, 22 minutes (SSA)
(3)   'Nabucco: Heimat and Fremde. Eine TV-Collage'
Film by Peter Dusek and Martin Polasek, featuring a reading by WGS as part of the 'Videoopernwerkstatt' at the Bregenzer Festspiele; Kuppelsaal, Vorarlberger Landesbibliothek, Bregenz, 18 July
Video recording of the reading and workshop (cf. Audio Sources)
Radio- und Videoarchiv, Vorarlberger Landesbibliothek, Bregenz (Austria) / ORF (Vienna)

1995   (1)   WGS interviewed by Niels Brunse, his Danish translator
Bogforum (book fair), Copenhagen, 17-21 November
Filmed by DR-TV but not broadcast
(2)   *Bücherjournal*: Interview with WGS and review of *Die Ringe des Saturn*; reading of extracts
NDR, 7 December
VHS colour cassette, 55 minutes (SSA)

1998   (1)   'Kamer met Uitzicht' (Room with a View): Arts and Literary Review
Interview with WGS by Michaël Zeeman
VPRO (Netherlands), 23 June, 23 minutes
VHS colour cassette (SSA)
Transcribed by Gordon Turner; see Primary Bibliography J.26
(2)   'The English' (part of the daily five-minute series on 'Britishness' broadcast immediately after Channel 4 News)
Audio excerpts and two video clips from the full interview with WGS by Peter Morgan
ITN (UK), 10 July
VHS colour cassette, 5 minutes (UEA Library, SSA)
Transcribed by Peter Morgan; see Primary Bibliography J.27

2000   'Tabu: Vergeltung: Die Literaten und der Luftkrieg'
Interviews with German writers including WGS
ZDF, 28 March
VHS colour cassette (SSA)

2001   (1)   Joseph Cuomo, Conversation with WGS (plus reading)
Queens College Evening Readings, New York, 13 March
Reading and interview broadcast as part of the series *The Unblinking Eye* on Metro TV (New York) on 3 September and the transcript published; see Primary Bibliography J.37 and *The Emergence of Memory*, ed. by Schwartz, pp. 93-117

(2)   *Treffpunkt Kultur*: 'W. G. Sebald, "Rauriser Literaturtage"'
WGS reading from *Austerlitz* and in discussion with Wolfgang Beyer, Andrea Hackl, Ulli Halmschlager, and Hella Pick; with further material on the *Kindertransport*
ORF, 2 April
ORF (Vienna)

(3)   *Literatur im Foyer*: 'Die Stars der Saison: Georg Klein und W. G. Sebald und die deutsche Literaturkritik'

Includes readings by WGS from *Austerlitz*, an interview, and a discussion; introduced by Andrea Köhler, with Ulrich Greiner, Stephan Speicher, and Hubert Spiegel; presented by Martin Lüdke
SWR, 6 June; 3-sat, 17 June
Video recording, VHS colour cassette, 60 minutes (DLA, SSA)

Visual material about or based on WGS

1991   'Das ungedruckte Buch', TV programme on *Schwindel. Gefühle.*
ZDF, October, 30 minutes

1992   *Literaturclub*: Discussion of *Die Ausgewanderten*
With Andreas Isenschmid, Gunhild Kübner, Jürg Laederach, and Hugo Loetscher
DRS (Zurich), 17 November
VHS colour cassette (SSA)

1993   *Literarisches Quartett*: Discussion and review of *Die Ausgewanderten*
Introduced by Marcel Reich-Ranicki, with Hellmuth Karasek, Sigrid Löffler, and Barbara Sichtermann
ZDF, 14 January
VHS colour cassette (SSA)

1996   *Buchhandlung*: Contains a short review of *Die Ringe des Saturn*
Deutsche Welle, February
VHS colour cassette, 3 minutes (SSA)

2001   (1)   *Bestenliste: Das Literaturmagazin*: 'W. G. Sebald: *Austerlitz*'
Report by Anne Bertheau; readings and discussion with Christoph Bauer, Peter Engel, Eberhard Falcke, Andrea Köhler, and Hubert Winkels
SWR (Baden-Baden), 11 March
VHS colour cassette, 60 minutes (DLA)
(2)   *Der Literaturexpress: Eine Reise mit Büchern*: 'W. G. Sebald: *Austerlitz*'
Report by Klaus Hensel, with Wilhelm Genazino, Robert Gernhardt, Annette Pehnt, and Wilfried F. Schoeller
Frankfurt, 2001
Video recording (DLA)

2003   *Literaturclub*: 'W. G. Sebald, *Campo Santo*' (review and discussion)
With Daniel Cohn-Bendit, Andreas Isenschmid, Gunhild Kübler, and Christina Weiss
Switzerland, 18 November
Video recording (DLA)

2004   *Literaturclub*: 'W. G. Sebald, *Austerlitz*' (review and discussion)
With Gabriele von Arnim, Daniel Cohn-Bendit, Hardy Ruoss, and Tilman Spengler
Switzerland, 24 April
Video recording (DLA)

2007   (1)   Thomas Honickel, 'W. G. Sebald: Der Ausgewanderte'
Film written and directed by Thomas Honickel
Contains contributions by Gertrud Aebischer, Hans Magnus Enzensberger, Günter Herburger, Michael Krüger, Sigrid Löffler, Peter von Matt, Wolfgang Schlüter, Richard Sheppard, Jan Peter Tripp, and Gordon Turner
Broadcast by BR3, 4 November
DVD, colour, 45 minutes (DLA, SSA)

(2)   Thomas Honickel, 'W. G. Sebald: The Emigrant'
Version of above with English subtitles (SSA)
(3)   Thomas Honickel, 'Sebald. Orte'
A film written and directed by Thomas Honickel
Collage of quotations and locations featured in Sebald's works
DVD, colour, German language, 60 minutes (SSA)
(4)   Thomas Honickel, 'Sebald. Places'
Version of the above with English subtitles (SSA)

2011   Grant Gee, 'Patience (After Sebald)', essay film, world premiere in Aldeburgh, 28-30 January; London premiere 21 February (see Chronology for details of related events)

Varia

The items below are based on information about the involvement of WGS in particular projects. To the best of our knowledge no recordings are extant.

1976   WGS acts as Literary Adviser for a 90-minute television programme on Carl Sternheim, produced by Jan Franksen and broadcast by the Third Programme of the station RIAS (Berlin) in November 1976. The film included a long interview with WGS by Jan Franksen.

1980   WGS contributes to a Swiss television film on the artistic and literary achievements of patients at Leo Navratil's Zentrum für Kunst und Psychotherapie, Gugging, near Vienna (October 1980).

1983   WGS drafts a script for a television film on the life of Immanuel Kant entitled 'Jetztund kömpt die Nacht herbey: Ansichten aus dem Leben und Sterben des Immanuel Kant'. The manuscripts (three different versions) are in the DLA. The film was commissioned by RIAS Berlin in 1982 but was never produced (see Chronology). WGS subsequently referred to the piece as 'Alter und Tod des Immanuel Kant'.

1989   WGS publishes his 'sketch for a possible screenplay for an unmade film' about Ludwig Wittgenstein: 'Leben Ws: Skizze einer möglichen Szenenreihe für einen nichtrealisierten Film'. See Primary Bibliography F.C.4. (This piece is reprinted in Part II of the present volume, pp. 324–33.)

1999   WGS contacted by APT Film and Television to approve a four-page treatment of *The Rings of Saturn* (entitled 'To the Dark Shore'), 12 March 1999 (DLA).

FIG. III.3. View of The Old Rectory from the garden,
shortly before the house was sold (summer 2006). © Jo Catling

5

An Index to
Interviews with W. G. Sebald

Compiled by Richard Sheppard

'Weil ich hungern muß, ich kann nicht anders,' sagte der Hungerkünstler.
'Da sieh mal einer,' sagte der Aufseher, 'warum kannst du denn nicht anders?'
'Weil ich,' sagte der Hungerkünstler [...] 'nicht die Speise finden konnte, die
mir schmeckt. Hätte ich sie gefunden, glaube mir, ich hätte kein Aufsehen
gemacht und mich vollgefressen wie du und alle.'

['Because I have to fast, I can't help it,' said the fasting-artist. 'Whatever next,'
said the overseer, 'and why can't you help it?' 'Because,' said the fasting-artist
[...] 'because I could never find the nourishment I liked. Had I found it, believe
me, I would never have caused any stir, and would have eaten my fill just like
you and everyone else.']

FRANZ KAFKA, 'Ein Hungerkünstler' (1924) ('A Fasting-Artist')[1]

NOTE

The classification used here corresponds to the system used for the Primary Bibliography. References are to names, topics, or titles mentioned, raised, or discussed by WGS himself, with or without prompting by the interviewer. Names, topics, or titles raised only by the interviewer have, with one or two exceptions, not been noted. Where an interview occupies only one page of print, the pagination is not provided. While, in every case, the longest available version of the interview has been used to make the index, this was not always the first version of the interview to be published.

Cross-references to items within the same section of the index are shown in the form '*see also* novels' and precede those to items in a different section, which give the section title as well as that of the entry (e.g. '*see also* Psychology: suicide').

The interviews are listed below chronologically with title, name of interviewer, and date of interview where known; otherwise the date refers to the month of first broadcast or publication. Full details are given in Section J of the Primary Bibliography. Interviews are in German unless otherwise indicated.

---

[1]   Frank Kafka, 'Ein Hungerkünstler', *Die Erzählungen* (Frankfurt a.M.: Fischer, 1961); 'A Fasting-Artist', trans. by Malcolm Pasley, in *Metamorphosis and Other Stories* (London: Penguin, 1992), pp. 210–19 (pp. 218–19).

Contents

References to Persons, Literary Movements, and Literary Institutions
References to Own Works (in chronological order)
Topics Addressed by WGS

> *(Auto-)biographical matters*
> *Germany and the NS-Zeit (Third Reich)*
> *The human condition, history, philosophy, religion*
> *Nature and the environment*
> *Places (apart from Germany)*
> *Psychology*
> *Writing, films, the arts*

Key

J.1	'Carl Sternheim', discussion, February 1971
J.2	'Stille Katastrophen' (Just), October 1990
J.3	'See You Again' (Baltzer), November 1990
J.4.1	'Echoes of the Past' (de Moor), May 1992 (English, trans. from Dutch)
J.5(b)	'Menschen auf der anderen Seite' (Boedecker), March 1993 (pub. October 1993)
J.6	'Bei den armen Seelen' (Baltzer), March 1993
J.7	'"Wildes Denken"' (Löffler), [9?] February 1993
J.8	'Wie kriegen die Deutschen das auf die Reihe?' (Poltronieri), June 1993
J.9	'W.G.S. over joden, Duitsers en migranten' (de Jong), July 1993 (Dutch)
J.10	'Kopfreisen in die Ferne' (Löffler), February 1995
J.11	'Im Zeichen des Saturn' (Just), October 1995
J.12	'Horter des Weggeworfenen' (Dietschreit), February 1996
J.13(a)	'Die schwere Leichtigkeit' (Siedenberg), March 1996
J.14	'Who is W. G. Sebald?' (Angier), winter 1996–97 (English)
J.15	'Die Weltsicht ist verhangen' (Oehlen), June 1997
J.16	'An Interview with W. G. Sebald' (Wood), 10 July 1997 (English)
J.17	'Ghost Hunter' (Wachtel), 16 October 1997 (English)
J.18(a)	'"Aber das Geschriebene ist ja kein Dokument"' (Scholz), 14 November 1997
J.19(a)	'Katastrophe mit Zuschauer' (Köhler), November 1997
J.20	'Alles schrumpft' (Wittmann), November 1997
J.21	'Leid und Scham und Schweigen' (Scheck), February 1998
J.22	'W. G. Sebald: A Profile' (Atlas), 6–7 February 1998 (English)
J.23	'Swimming the Seas of Silence' (Tonkin), 18 February 1998 (English)
J.24	'An Interview with W. G. Sebald' (Kafatou), 17 May 1998 (English)
J.25	'Characters, Plot, Dialogue?' (McCrum), June 1998 (English)
J.26	[*Kamer met Uitzicht*] (Zeeman), 23 June 1998 (English)
J.27	'Living among the English' (Morgan), 10 July 1998 (English)
J.28	'Qu'est devenu Ernest?' (Devarrieux), January 1999 (French)
J.29	'Le Passé repoussé de l'Allemagne' (de Cortanze), January 1999 (French)
J.30	'Lost in Translation?' (Cook), February 1999 (English)
J.31	'The Questionable Business of Writing' (Green), late 1999 (English)
J.32	[on *Luftkrieg*] (Hage), 22 February 2000
J.33	'The Permanent Exile of W. G. Sebald' (Mühling), [n.d.] April 2000 (English)
J.34	'In Conversation with W. G. Sebald' (Bigsby), 12 January 2001 (English)
J.35	'Der Spurensucher' (Kospach), 12 February 2001
J.36	'"Ich fürchte das Melodramatische"' (Doerry and Hage), 27 February 2001

J.37(a)   'The Meaning of Coincidence' (Cuomo), 13 March 2001 (English)
J.38   'Die Melancholie des Widerstands' (Kunisch), April 2001
J.39   '"Wir zahlen einen ungeheuren Preis"' (Hintermeier), May 2001
J.40   'El Escritor Errante: W. G. Sebald' (Krauthausen), July 2001 (Spanish)
J.41.1   '"So wie ein Hund, der den Löffel vergißt"' (Rondas), 22 May 2001
J.42   'Mit einem kleinen Strandspaten' (Pralle), [n.d.] August 2001
J.43   'The Significant Mr. Sebald' (Alvarez), 15 August 2001 (English)
J.44(b)   'Preoccupied with Death, but Still Funny' (Lubow), 19–20 August 2001 (English)
J.45   'Recovered Memories' (Jaggi), 13 September 2001 (English)
J.46(a)   [St Jerome lecture] 'The Last Word' (Jaggi / Bell), 24 September 2001 (English)
J.47   'Sebastian Shakespeare Talks to W. G. Sebald' (Shakespeare), October 2001 (English)
J.48   'Up against Historical Amnesia' (Baker), October 2001 (English)
J.49   'ALOUD at Central Library' ('In This Distant Place') (Wasserman), 17 October 2001 (English)
J.50   'A Poem of an Invisible Subject' (Silverblatt), 17–18 October 2001 (English)
J.51   'A Writer Who Challenges Traditional Storytelling' (Reynolds), c. 17–18 October 2001 (English)
J.52   'Books: Outside the Box' (Jones), c. 21 October 2001 (English)
J.53   'Talking with W. G. Sebald: Europe Unplugged' (Cryer), October 2001 (English)
J.54   'Past Imperfect' (Houpt), November 2001 (English)

References to Persons, Literary Movements, and Literary Institutions

17th- and 18th-century English prose writers:
    admiration for their 'miraculous achievements': J.24, 33; J.25; J.43, 59
19th-century German prose fiction:
    influence of its language/prosodic rhythms: J.49, 369; J.50, 77–78
    relative unimportance of plot: J.50, 77–78
Achternbusch, Herbert: J.7
Adler, H. G. (survivor of Theresienstadt, poet and author):
    Theresienstadt 1941–45 as a source for Austerlitz: J.45, 6
Adorno, Theodor: J.26, 26; J.38
    critique of German Idealism: J.42
    Dialektik der Aufklärung, influence on: J.8, 28; J.20; J.31
    Negative Dialektik, turgidity of: J.31
Aichinger, Ilse: J.32, 39
Améry, Jean: J.5(b); J.8, 29; J.14, 13; J.17, 38; J.24, 34; J.30, 357; J.36, 232; J.42; J.50, 86
    link with Die Ausgewanderten: J.14, 13; J.17, 38; J.24, 33–34; J.30, 357; J.45, 6
    reading Améry a turning point: J.36, 232
Andersch, Alfred: J.7; J.36, 232; J.42; J.45, 6
    Efraim: J.36, 232
Aubrey, John: J.47
    Brief Lives, admiration for: J.25
Austen, Jane: J.16, 27
    world of certainties: J.16, 27
Bachmann, Ingeborg: J.32, 39
Baroque theatre: J.1, 45
Barthes, Roland:
    La Chambre claire: J.18(a), 51; J.28; J.48
    importance of Barthes's ideas on old photos: J.5(b); J.18(a), 51; J.48
Bassani, Giorgio (see also Italian writing, modern): J.47

Bayer, Konrad (avant-garde Austrian writer who committed suicide aged 32):
    Der Kopf Vitus Berings: stimulus for *Nach der Natur*: J.31; J.37(a), 99; J.38
Bechhöfer, Susi (author of *Rosa's Child* (1998)):
    model for Jacques Austerlitz: J.36, 228; J.37(a), 111; J.45, 6, 7; J.46(a), 6; J.49, 372 and
        375, n. 4
Beckett, Samuel: J.30, 363
Begley, Louis (American novelist):
    Wartime Lies: J.36, 232
Bell, Anthea: J.46(a), 10
Benjamin, Walter: J.23, 93; J.31; J.36, 234; J.40, 2; J.50, 86
Berger, John: J.48
Bernhard, Thomas: J.11, 30; J.16, 28; J.36, 233; J.44(b), 170; J.46(a), 14–15; J.47; J.50, 82–84
    absolute moral position: J.50, 83
    influence of Bernhard's monologues: J.44(b), 170; J.50, 84
    'periscopic writing': J.5(b); J.16, 28; J.17, 37; J.36, 233; J.44(b), 170; J.50, 83
    Die Verstörung (Gargoyles): J.50, 84
Bettelheim, Bruno: J.5(b)
Bienek, Horst: J.32, 37
Blumenberg, Hans:
    Schiffbruch mit Zuschauer, J.19(a)
Böll, Heinrich: J.3; J.7; J.9; J.16, 29; J.30, 360; J.32, 40; J.42; J.45, 6; J.53
    Das Brot der frühen Jahre, J.32, 40
    self-pity: J.53
Bonaparte, Napoleon: *see* The human condition: Napoleonic era
Borges, Jorge Luis: J.40, 4
    importance of the fantastic and eccentric, J.40, 4
    importance of the 'recovery of memory', J.40, 4
Borowski, Tadeusz (Polish writer who survived Dachau and Auschwitz but later committed
    suicide):
    link with *Die Ausgewanderten*: J.17, 38
Brandt, Willy: J.23, 97
Broch, Hermann: J.29
Browne, Sir Thomas: J.25; J.34, 159; J.47
    admiration for: J.25; J.43, 59
    begins reading his work *c*. 1985: J.34, 159
    Browne as metaphysician: J.34, 159
Brueghel, Pieter:
    Landscape with the Fall of Icarus (a postcard of which was pinned to the noticeboard
        outside his office at UEA for a time in the late 1990s): J.23, 92
Calvino, Italo: J.51
Canetti, Elias: J.16, 29; J.17, 51
    Die Blendung (Auto-da-fé): J.4.1, 351, 376 n.2
    Die gerettete Zunge (autobiography): J.16, 29
Casanova, Danielle (Communist in the French Resistance, murdered in Auschwitz): J.37(a),
    97–98
Casanova de Seingalt, Giacomo Girolamo: J.3
Celan, Paul: J.36, 232; J.42
    link with *Die Ausgewanderten*: J.17, 38
Chateaubriand, François-René de: J.4.1, 351; J.31; J.44(b), 167
    Itinéraire de Paris à Jérusalem: J.2, 29; J.16, 28
    Mémoires d'outre-tombe: J.27, 18

Chekhov, Anton:
  Three Sisters: J.1, 43
Coleridge, Samuel Taylor: J.16, 29; J.24, 33
Conrad, Joseph: J.34, 148; J.46(a), 15
Cowper, William: J.47
Dante Alighieri: J.17, 55
De Winter, Leon (Dutch Jewish writer): J.36, 232
Dickens, Charles: J.41.1, 354; J.53
  Bleak House: J.50, 82
Döblin, Alfred: J.14, 11; J.29
  cities as slaughterhouses (reference to *Berlin Alexanderplatz*): J.4.1, 351, 354 n. 2
  Sebald's PhD on: J.37(a), 94
  troubled relationship with his Jewishness: J.14, 11
documentary literature (1960s): J.25; J.32, 39; J.36, 230
  criticized for focussing too narrowly on the Shoah: J.21
Donne, John: J.47
Dostoyevsky, Fyodor: J.37(a), 115
Duden, Anne (contemporary German writer): J.30, 361
Dürrenmatt, Friedrich: J.33, 23
Enzensberger, Hans Magnus: J.5(b); J.8, 28; J.11, 26; J.42
  on the *Wirtschaftswunder*: J.19(a)
Expressionism:
  dislikes: J.3; J.33, 24
  mistrust of *Pathos*: J.9
Fichte, Hubert:
  Detlevs Imitationen 'Grünspan' as a prototype: J.21
Flaubert, Gustave: J.22, 292; J.34, 158; J.40, 3
  writing scruples: J.37(a), 109; J.40, 3
Fontane, Theodor: J.25
  Effi Briest: Sebald uses the phrase 'aber das ist ein weites Feld' (reference to Fontane's
    novel *Effi Briest* (1894–95) where, towards the end, Effi's father forestalls any
    further discussion of his daughter's tragic death by saying to his wife: 'Ach, Luise,
    laß ... das ist ein *zu* weites Feld' [Oh Luise, leave it ... that is *far* too big a subject].
    Ein weites Feld is also the title of a novel (1995) by Günter Grass that deals with the
    reunification of Germany): J.47
Ford, Henry: J.41.1, 361
Forte, Dieter (critic): J.32, 45–46
Friedländer, Saul: J.49, 372, 375 n. 5
  When Memory Comes: J.49, 372–73
Frisch, Max: J.33, 23
Genet, Jean: J.33, 25
Genscher, Hans-Dietrich (West German politician (FDP), Foreign Minister 1974–92): J.8, 28
Goethe, Johann Wolfgang von:
  Stella: J.1, 45
Grass, Günter (*see also* Fontane, Theodor): J.16, 29; J.30, 360
Greene, Graham: J.34, 153
Grünewald, Matthias: J.17, 42; J.44(b), 168
Gruppe 47: J.32, 39–40; J.37(a), 99
  masculinism: J.32, 39–40
Hamburger, Michael: J.11, 27; J.13(a); J.28
Handke, Peter: J.4.1, 352; J.8, 28; J.13(a); J.16, 29; J.30, 360; J.33, 22
  willingness to experience extreme situations: J.13(a)

Hebel, Johann Peter: J.5(b); J.20; J.47
    effect of his prose: J.24, 33
    Schatzkästlein des Rheinischen Hausfreundes: J.24, 33
Hegel, Georg Wilhelm Friedrich: J.31; J.42
Hemingway, Ernest: J.49, 370
Herbeck, Ernst: J.22, 291
Herbert, Zbigniew:
    Still Life with a Bridle: J.49, 372
Hildesheimer, Wolfgang: J.14, 11
Hitler, Adolf: J.32, 47; J.42; J.48
Hochhuth, Rolf: J.9
Hoffmann, E. T. A.: J.17, 48
    Der Sandmann: J.4.1, 352
Hofmannsthal, Hugo von: J.29
Hulse, Michael (poet and WGS's first translator): J.30, 360–61
    how he was chosen: J.30, 360–61
    their working relationship: J.30, 360
Humboldt, Alexander von: J.50, 81
Ibsen, Henrik: J.1, 47
Italian writing, modern (*see also* Bassani, Giorgio):
    admiration for: J.43, 59
Jacobean drama: J.24, 33
Jarry, Alfred: J.1, 44
Jean Paul (Jean Paul Friedrich Richter): J.44(b), 166; J.47
Jonas, Sir Peter: J.39
Jung, Carl Gustav:
    rejects Jungian teaching: J.37(a), 96–97
Jünger, Ernst:
    aestheticization of catastrophe impermissible: J.19(a)
    Strahlungen: J.19(a)
Kafka, Franz: J.3; J.4.1, *passim*; J.12; J.18(a), 51–52; J.31; J.36, 230; J.37(a), 115–17; J.51; J.54
    appears in *Schwindel. Gefühle.*: J.37(a), 116–17; J.51
    Forschungen eines Hundes: J.37(a), 115–16
    Der Jäger Gracchus: J.31
    photographs (of Kafka): J.18(a), 51–52
    Der Proceß, references to in *Schwindel. Gefühle.*: J.3
Keller, Gottfried: J.5(b); J.20; J.24, 33; J.44(b), 166; J.47; J.49, 369–70; J.50, 77
Kempowski, Walter: J.41.1, 357
    Das Echolot (multi-volume collage of documents, letters and reports by eyewitnesses of
        World War II): J.32, 39
Kermode, Frank:
    The Sense of an Ending: J.34, 156
Kleist, Heinrich von: J.2, 29; J.20; J.44(b), 166
Kluge, Alexander: J.10; J.32, 38–39; J.36, 230; J.42
    cleverest post-war writer: J.32, 43; J.42
    excepts him from his criticism of post-war German writers: J.21
    Der Luftangriff auf Halberstadt am 8. April 1945: J.19(a); J.32, 38
    (non-)impact of his use of photos: J.7; J.18(a), 51
    social pessimism: J.32, 43
Kohl, Helmut: J.23, 97
Krüger, Michael (Sebald's publisher at Hanser): J.32, 49

Lanzmann, Claude: J.45, 7
    director of *Shoah* (1985): J.17, 53
Ledig, Gert (one of the few post-war German novelists to deal with an air raid):
    Vergeltung: J.32, 38
Lessing, Gotthold Ephraim:
    Lessing as a Jewish name: J.17, 47
Levi, Primo: J.5(b); J.8, 29; J.16, 24; J.22, 291; J.24, 34; J.30, 357; J.43, 57
    link with *Die Ausgewanderten*: J.17, 38; J.24, 33–34; J.30, 357
Leviné-Meyer, Rosa (wife of Eugen Leviné, the Communist leader of the 2nd Munich
    Soviet in 1919 who was executed for high treason 4 June 1919): J.40, 3
Levinson (Leverton), Bertha (editor of books on the *Kindertransporte*) (see also *Writing, films,
    the arts: films*): J.49, 373
Lévi-Strauss, Claude: J.10; J.17, 38
    bricolage: J.7
Lichtenberg, Christoph (18th-century German aphorist): J.26, 29
Maeterlinck, Maurice: J.1, 48
Manheim, Ralph (American translator): J.16, 29; J.30, 360
Mann, Thomas: J.16, 25; J.32, 39; J.34, 153
    Doktor Faustus: J.32, 39; J.39
Marlowe, Christopher: J.24, 33
Melville, Herman:
    Billy Budd: J.53
Montaigne, Michel Eyquem de:
    Journal de voyage (1580–81): J.11, 30
Murnau, F. W. (silent-film director): J.51
Musil, Robert: J.33, 19
Nabokov, Vladimir: J.5(b); J.12; J.14, 13–14; J.17, 51; J.30, 363; J.31; J.34, 148; J.46(a), 16; J.49,
    369, 371
    ability to write in English: J.17, 51; J.30, 363; J.34, 148; J.46(a), 16
    admires the first 100 pages of *Speak, Memory*, dealing with Nabokov's childhood in St
        Petersburg: J.5(b)
    influence of *Speak, Memory* on *Die Ausgewanderten*: J.14, 13–14; J.17, 52–53
    learnt from him the importance of detail: J.49, 369
    Lolita: J.49, 371
    Pnin: J.49, 369
Nestroy, Johann: J.36, 234
Newton, Sir Isaac: J.31
Nossack, Hans Erich: J.32, 45
    Der Untergang (book on Operation Gomorrah, the week of fire-storm raids on
        Hamburg in 1943): J.32, 45
Onians, Ernest (*c.* 1905–95: Suffolk pig-swill millionaire and reclusive art collector):
    amusement at: J.23, 99
Papon, Maurice (French civil servant and Prefect of Police in Paris who was tried (1995–98)
    for crimes against humanity during and after the Occupation, in France and elsewhere):
    J.17, 45
Pascal, Blaise: J.51
Pepys, Samuel: J.47
    Diaries: J.2, 29
Poussin, Nicolas:
    Et in Arcadia ego: J.23, 99
    The Destruction and Sack of Jerusalem: J.23, 99

Ransmayr, Christoph (20th-century Austrian writer): J.5(b)

Ranwell, Beryl (German Sector secretary at UEA): J.30, 359

Realism (19th-century literary movement) (*see also* Writing, films, the arts: Realism as a literary mode)
    admiration for 19th-century Realists: J.5(b); J.7; J.12; J.17, 41
    their solution to the basic moral problem of writing: J.36, 232
    what distinguishes him from 19th-century Realists: J.45, 6

Reich-Ranicki, Marcel (the doyen of German literary journalism who criticized Sebald's use of illustrations):
    Sebald's opinion of: J.5(b)

Richter, Hans Werner: J.32, 39

Richter, Jean Paul Friedrich, *see* Jean Paul

Roth, Joseph: J.18(a), 51; J.36, 228; J.47

Rousseau, Jean-Jacques: J.24, 32; J.50, 81
    Île Saint-Pierre (St Petersinsel) in Lake Biel/Bienne: J.44(b), 167–68
    output as a writer: J.36, 234; J.37(a), 109

St Sebaldus of Nuremberg: J.24, 32

Schiller, Friedrich von:
    Schiller as a Jewish name: J.17, 47

Schmidt, Arno: J.33, 24; J.42

Shakespeare, William: J.24, 33; J.34, 159

Sheldrake, Rupert (controversial 20th-century British plant physiologist who writes on parapsychology): J.50, 81

Simon, Claude:
    Le Jardin des Plantes: J.32, 41

Sontag, Susan: J.10; J.47
    effect of her positive comments: J.39
    on photography: J.48

Steller, Georg Wilhelm (18th-century German botanist and zoologist; cf. *Nach der Natur*): J.37(a), 99; J.44(b), 168

Stendhal (Marie-Henri Beyle): J.3; J.4.1, 350; J.12; J.34, 157; J.37(a), 97
    autobiography: J.34, 157
    La Chartreuse de Parme: J.16, 27
    De l'amour: J.4.1, 350
    La Vie d'Henri Brulard: J.16, 24, 27; J.45, 6

Sterne, Laurence: J.47

Sternheim, Carl: J.1, 40–54; J.14, 11
    1913: J.1, 50
    ambivalence towards bourgeoisie: J.1, 40–49
    Ein bürgerliches Heldenleben: J.1, 40
    Bürger Schippel: J.1, 53–54
    characters, woodenness of: J.1, 42, 47, 48
    contradiction between dramatic form and intentions: J.1, 42–44
    conventionality: J.1, 51–54
    dramatic language: J.1, 50–54
    satire, weakness of: J.1, 47
    social criticism: J.1, 39–47
    stageability of plays: J.1, 45
    Tabula rasa, J.1, 53
    troubled relationship with own Jewishness: J.14, 11

Stifter, Adalbert: J.24, 33; J.44(b), 166; J.47; J.49, 369; J.50, 77

Strauß, Johann:
  Die Fledermaus: J.41.1, 361
Theweleit, Klaus: J.10
  impact of his use of pictures: J.7
Tolstoy, Leo: J.19(a)
Trümmerliteratur: J.21
Turner, J. M. W.:
  appears in Sebald's works: J.41.1, 363
  resemblance between his painting and Sebald's writing: J.41.1, 363
Updike, John: J.47
Vauban, Marshal (designer of fortresses): J.41.1, 354
Voltaire (François-Marie Arouet): J.37(a), 109
Waldheim, Kurt: J.24, 32
Walser, Martin:
Walser–Bubis Debate (October–December 1998): J.41.1, 358–59; J.42; J.43, 57, 59
Walser, Robert: J.3; J.4.1, 353; J.20; J.24, 32; J.47
  appears in *Schwindel. Gefühle.*: J.3
  story of his death transposed to Sebald's publisher: J.44(b), 171
Weiss, Peter: J.4.1, 353; J.14, 11; J.32, 40; J.36, 230, 232; J.45, 6
  Abschied von den Eltern: J.42
  archaeology: J.42
  Die Ästhetik des Widerstands: J.13(a)
  authenticity of his voice: J.32, 40; J.42; J.45, 6
  bridge to Améry and Celan: J.42
  effect on Weiss of his German-Jewish background: J.42
  Die Ermittlung: J.42
  Fluchtpunkt: J.42
  the question of guilt: J.42
  reception of: J.42
Wiles, Sir Andrew (mathematician who proved Fermat's Last Theorem in 1995; Sebald erroneously refers to him as Andrew Giles): J.34, 160
Wilkomirski, Binjamin (pseudonym of Bruno Grosjean / Bruno Dössekke, who claimed to be a Holocaust survivor and published his fictional memoirs (*Bruchstücke* (*Fragments*)) in the 1990s): J.41.1, 362–63
Wittgenstein, Ludwig: J.14, 14; J.16, 29; J.17, 46; J.29; J.31; J.34, 148, 155; J.48
  echoes in *Die Ausgewanderten*: J.14, 14; J.17, 46; J.34, 155; J.48
  model for Jacques Austerlitz: J.48
  Sebald's film script about Wittgenstein ('Leben Ws'; see the present volume, pp. 324–33): J.16, 29
Wolff, Kurt: J.3
  publishing house (the German publishing house which specialized in Expressionist texts): J.1, 51
Woolf, Virginia: J.47; J.50, 80–81
Zuckerman, Solly (Lord Zuckerman) (scientific adviser to Churchill during World War II who opposed area bombing): J.21

References to Own Works (listed in chronological order)

Nach der Natur: J.2, 29; J.5(b); J.11, 27; J.17, 42; J.25; J.37(a), 98–99; J.44(b), 168
  origins: J.5(b)
Schwindel. Gefühle.: J.3; J.4.1, *passim*; J.8, 29; J.10; J.18(a), 51; J.24, 32; J.25; J.31; J.34, 141, 143, 145, 149; J.37(a), 97, 103–04; J.40, 3

coincidence: J.37(a), 96
easy to write: J.37(a), 112
as a homage to Kafka, Walser and Weiss: J.4.1, 353
hybridity: J.25; J.34, 156
and *Jäger Gracchus*: J.31; J.37(a), 103–04
loss of title's meaning in translation: J.34, 157
mixture of realism and non-realism: J.4.1, 353–54
origins of: J.4.1, *passim*; J.14, 13
personal perspective of: J.8, 29
reception in the Allgäu: J.14, 12; J.34, 153
as self-exploration: J.3; J.4.1, 352; J.37(a), 103; J.40, 3
significance of the wasps' nest in the attic: J.24, 32
structure: J.4.1, 350; J.37(a), 104
W and S as imaginary places: J.34, 141
Die Ausgewanderten: J.5(b); J.6; J.7; J.8, 28–29; J.10; J.14, 12–14; J.16, 24–25, 27; J.17, *passim*;
   J.18(a), 51; J.20; J.24, 31–34; J.28; J.30, 357–60; J.34, 155; J.35, 125; J.37(a), 104–05; J.39;
   J.40, 3
Ambros Adelwarth's relationship with Cosmo Solomon: J.9; J.17, 55; J.30, 358
Armin Mueller as teacher: J.9
its characters related to himself: J.8, 29; J.35, 125
factual basis/origins of the stories: J.5(b); J.14, 13; J.16, 25; J.17, 38–39, 43–45, 52; J.24,
   34; J.28; J.34, 155; J.35, 125; J.37(a), 106; J.46(a), 6
falsification of Ambros Adelwarth's diary and visiting card: J.14, 13–14; J.46(a), 14
falsification of the photo of the Normandy hotel: J.46(a), 14
falsification of the *Residenzplatz* photograph: J.16, 27; J.44(b), 163
French translation of: J.30, 359
influence of Chateaubriand's *Itinéraire de Paris à Jérusalem*: J.16, 27
influence of Nabokov's *Speak, Memory*: J.14, 14; J.17, 52–53
mental anguish of his characters: J.9; J.17, 55–56
Paul Bereyter as a victim of the Shoah: J.8, 29
Paul Bereyter's mixed (German-Jewish) background as a double bind: J.8, 29; J.17, 44–47
photo of Jewish family in Bavarian costume: J.34, 154; J.46(a), 13; J.48
reasons for the book's success: J.8, 28
why Max Aurach was changed to Max Ferber: J.45, 7
Die Ringe des Saturn: J.10; J.12; J.13(a); J.16, 24; J.19(a); J.20; J.22, 279–81, 285–86, 291–95;
   J.23, 94–99; J.24, 32; J.26, 27–28; J.30, 359; J.31; J.37(a), 94–96; J.40, 3; J.41.1, 354; J.42;
   J.44(b), 163; J.49, 374
Alec Garrard and his model: J.24, 34
background and origins: J.11, 27–30; J.13(a); J.27, 14; J.34, 158–59, 162; J.37(a), 94; J.49, 370
chance: J.49, 374
complex temporal sequences: J.13(a)
as a fictional construct: J.23, 94
spiral movement downwards: J.26, 27
symbolism of the rings: J.42
time it took to translate: J.30, 359
Luftkrieg und Literatur: J.19(a); J.21; J.25; J.32, *passim*; J.34, 150–51; J.36, 234; J.46(a), 7; J.48
Dieter Forte's criticism: J.32, 45–46
fear that it would appeal to the wrong people: J.32, 37, 49
origins of his interest (1970s): J.21; J.32, 49
public response: J.32, 49–50; J.46(a), 7
stimulated by meeting Lord Zuckerman (28 September 1981): J.21

Logis in einem Landhaus: J.25

Austerlitz: J.34, 162–63; J.35, 125; J.37(a), 102; J.38; J.40, 2; J.41.1, 355–56; J.42; J.43, 57; J.46(a),
    6; J.48; J.49, *passim*; J.50, 79, 86
    50% of the photos taken specially: J.36, 234
    Breendonk: J.41.1, 354–55, 359; J.50, 86
    difficulty of writing it: J.34, 148; J.37(a), 108–09, 112
    elegy: J.37(a), 103
    its language as a pastiche: J.49, 371
    long-term spiritual effects of political persecution: J.46(a), 6; J.49, 368, 372
    models for Jacques Austerlitz: J.35, 125; J.36, 228; J.37(a), 110–11; J.41.1, 356; J.43, 57; J.45,
        6; J.46(a), 6; J.47; J.49, 372
    narrative relationships: J.36, 233; J.49, 371
    nocturama: J.50, 79
    non-autobiographical: J.34, 158
    photo on front cover: J.36, 228
    its realism: J.41.1, 356; J.44(b), 164; J.47; J.49, 372
    research involved: J.36, 230
    resonance of the name Austerlitz: J.36, 230
    sequel to *Die Ausgewanderten*: J.34, 162; J.47
    Theresienstadt, visit to: J.41.1, 358; J.45, 6
    visits to Belgium: J.34, 146
    works by association: J.50, 79

Topics Addressed by WGS

(Auto-)biographical matters

1968: *see* politics and student revolts
Auschwitz trials (1963–65): J.17, 48
    impact on when a student: J.17, 48; J.28; J.34, 147; J.37(a), 104–06; J.45, 6
exile/emigration, experience of: J.6; J.7; J.8, 28; J.16, 29; J.17, 48–50; J.22, 286; J.23, 97; J.24,
    34; J.26, 22–23; J.40, 2; J.41.1, 357; J.49, 372–73
    affinity with displaced persons: J.44(b), 167; J.49, 373
    by his family: J.9; J.43, 59
    has sharpened his perceptions of Germany: J.42
    positive effect of exile on German writers: J.32, 40
family background and childhood (Allgäu): J.2, 29; J.4.1, 350; J.8, 28; J.9; J.17, 39–40, 43–44;
    J.26, 22; J.29; J.34, 140–42; J.37(a), 100–01; J.40, 2; J.43, 57; J.44(b), 159; J.45, 6; J.46(a),
    11–12; J.49, 367–70; J.51; J.52
    bombing of Sonthofen in 1945: J.32, 42; J.52
    early awareness of catastrophe and death: J.10; J.17, 39; J.45, 6
    family background: J.9; J.14, 11; J.16, 27–28; J.18(a), 51; J.22, 289; J.23, 92–93; J.28, 33;
        J.28; J.29; J.34, 140–43; J.42; J.43, 59; J.49, 367, 370
    father: J.4.1, 354; J.9; J.14, 11; J.22, 289; J.28; J.29; J.32, 35–36; J.34, 142–43; J.36, 234; J.38;
        J.43, 57, 59; J.44(b), 161, 170–71; J.45, 6; J.46(a), 11; J.49, 367; J.50, 84–85; J.53
    formative power of years 1944–50: J.19(a); J.25, 22–23; J.32, 35–36; J.36, 234; J.46(a), 17
    grandfather: J.17, 50; J.24, 33; J.28; J.34, 142; J.35, 123; J.36, 232; J.43, 59; J.44(b), 170–71;
        J.45, 6; J.46(a), 11
    grandfather's influence on his sensitivity to language: J.35, 123
    idyllic: J.8, 28; J.29; J.34, 144; J.43, 57
    nostalgia for Alpine environment: J.12

parents passively implicated in the *NS*-regime: J.45, 6

photograph albums, gaps in: J.9; J.29; J.49, 367

pre-modern nature of Allgäu in the post-war years: J.8, 28; J.17, 39–40; J.34, 140–42; J.40, 2; J.49, 370

revisits Wertach (1987): J.8, 28; J.34, 145

the silence: J.34, 140; J.37(a), 101

greatest wish: to live outside time: J.47

names (Winfried Georg): his preference for Max, and dislike of his two given names: J.4.1, 354; J.9; J.11, 26; J.12; J.34, 163–64; J.35, 124; J.38; J.43, 55

noise/peace and quiet: J.31; J.34, 140

aversion to noise: J.11, 30; J.34, 140

desire for peace and quiet: J.11, 30; J.17, 61; J.47

effect on our senses: J.31

personal life, refusal to talk about: J.46(a), 6

politics and student revolts:

anarchist streak: J.34, 150; J.37(a), 107

apocalyptic view of politics: J.8, 28–29

denies being a '1968er': J.38

move away from politics: J.38

student revolts: J.46(a), 6

terrorist groups of the 1970s: J.46(a), 6

provocativeness:

as a teaching strategy; J.3

in public situations: J.3

refuges and idylls (*see also* Places: East Anglia (etc.)): J.2, 29

the Aareinsel, near Thun: J.2, 29

Crown Hotel, Southwold: J.11, 27; J.22, 291

darkroom: J.51

dust-covered rooms: J.17, 58–59

England as an idyll spoilt by Thatcherism: J.12

Fribourg: J.34, 149

from memory: J.41.1, 362

ideal refuge possibly a Swiss hotel (cf. Nabokov's biography): J.45, 7

Île Saint Pierre (St Petersinsel) in Lake Biel/Bienne: J.44(b), 167–68

nature: J.8, 29

the past: J.26, 23; J.31; J.49, 370

the 'potting shed' of writing: J.5(b); J.15; J.16, 24; J.17, 61; J.20; J.25; J.34, 152, 165; J.35, 123; J.37(a), 98–99; J.38; J.53

Sailors' Reading Room, Southwold: J.11, 27; J.22, 292; J.27, 15

small houses: J.48

Suffolk: J.11, 26, 27

Victoria Hotel, Holkham: J.2, 29–30

success, its downside: J.5(b); J.34, 164–65

surgery, fear of: J.4.1, 351

Thatcherism (*see also* universities): J.12

tourism and travel: J.4.1, 353; J.15; J.17, 43; J.44(b), 167

dislikes tourism: J.44(b), 167

importance to him of travel: J.2, 29; J.15; J.18(a), 51; J.36, 230; J.51

spiritual and psychological effects of tourism: J.4.1, 353

Treblinka trials (1963–64):

impact on him as a student: J.17, 48

universities (*see also* Thatcherism): J.34, 150
    bureaucracy of English universities: J.2, 29
    criticisms of Freiburg (1963–65): J.14, 11; J.16, 29; J.17, 48; J.22, 289–90; J.23, 93; J.31; J.34, 146–47; J.37(a), 106–07
    disappearance of eccentricity from English universities: J.27, 16
    effect on English universities of the 'Stalinist' reforms of the 1980s and 1990s: J.25; J.27, 16; J.43, 59; J.45, 6
    ideological pluralism in English universities after 1968: J.37(a), 107; J.38
    in England: J.2, 29; J.5(b); J.25; J.27, 16; J.37(a), 107
    in Germany: J.9; J.12; J.14, 11; J.16, 29; J.17, 48; J.22, 289–90; J.27, 16; J.28; J.31; J.34, 146–47, 150; J.37(a), 106–07
    lack of hierarchies in English universities in the 1960s: J.34, 150; J.45, 6
    his life as a university teacher and writer: J.15
    new mood and ethos in English universities: J.27, 16; J.31; J.34, 150; J.43, 59
    rejection of the German *Wissenschaftsideal*: J.42
    student literacy, decline in: J.43, 59
work in progress, retirement: J.36, 234; J.38; J.41.1, 356, 360; J.42; J.43, 55, 59; J.44(b), 163–65, 168

Germany and the NS-Zeit (Third Reich)

air raids: *see* Germany, aerial devastation of:
Auschwitz-Birkenau (KZ): J.5(b); J.41.1, 355
    dislike of 'Auschwitz-Industry': J.5(b); J.24, 34; J.34, 146; J.41.1, 355
    Auschwitz trials (1963–65): *see* (Auto-)biographical matters:
Bergen-Belsen (KZ): J.23, 97
    film of liberation, shown in his school (*c.* 1961): J.6; J.7; J.14, 10–11; J.23, 93; J.28; J.32, 36; J.37(a), 105; J.45, 6; J.46(a), 11–12
    impact of: J.7
concentration camps (*Konzentrationslager* (KZ)) (*see also* Auschwitz-Birkenau; Bergen-Belsen; Dachau; Handke, Peter; Horrific, the; Shoah, the; Theresienstadt; Treblinka):
    impossibility of writing about: J.50, 80
    unwillingness to visit: J.34, 146; J.41.1, 355
Dachau (KZ): J.41.1, 355
éducation sentimentale of his parents' generation by the Nazis: J.36, 234
fascism (see also *Writing, films, the arts*: gigantism):
    and haircuts: J.4.1, 354
German language: J.5(b)
    alienation from German due to his stay in England: J.25; J.26, 28–29; J.39; J.46(a), 17; J.49, 371
    becoming a minority language: J.16, 29
    dangers of a mismatch of language and subject matter: J.5(b)
    dislikes modern German/*Neudeutsch*: J.35, 123; J.39; J.44(b), 166
    the even tone and rhythmic nature of his prose: J.30, 359–60, 363
    fascist jargon: J.1, 50; J.45, 6; J.46(a), 10; J.47
    grew up speaking dialect: J.5(b); J.42
    Hochdeutsch virtually a second language: J.42
    homogenization/decay of language: J.24, 33; J.36, 234
    'labyrinthine' sentences: J.24, 33
    lack of paragraphs: J.34, 155–56; J.46(a), 15
    the language of his prose fiction: J.5(b); J.19(a); J.24, 33; J.30, 359–60, 363; J.38; J.39; J.42; J.50, 78

linguistic borderlines: J.22, 286

as a raft: J.42

tension between his prose style and subject matter: J.5(b); J.12; J.16, 28; J.19(a)

why he writes in German, not English: J.14, 13; J.17, 51; J.25; J.26, 28–29; J.30, 363; J.34, 147–48; J.40, 2; J.46(a), 16–17; J.47; J.48; J.49, 371

German literature and novels, post-war: J.5(b); J.46(a), 8

the direction in which contemporary literature should go: J.21

dislike of, scepticism about: J.4.1, 354; J.15

failure of contemporary writers to do research: J.18(a), 51; J.32, 39, 40–41

failure to address the aerial destruction of Germany: J.19(a); J.21; J.32, 37, 41, 47–48; J.42; J.49, 368; J.52

failure to deal adequately/tactfully/compassionately with the *NS-Zeit* and the Shoah: J.7; J.8, 29; J.5(b); J.12; J.17, 44, 48; J.21; J.22, 290; J.23, 93; J.27, 14; J.28; J.32, 35–37; J.34, 142–45, 161; J.37(a), 105; J.39; J.42; J.45, 6; J.46(a),8; J.49, 367–68; J.53

massive gap between first post-war generation of German writers and Jean Améry and Peter Weiss: J.45, 6

morally compromised: J.50, 83

moral presumption: J.45, 6

provincialism of contemporary German literature: J.39

roots of its shortcomings: J.32, 40

German literature, pre-modern:

liking for: J.15; J.43, 59; J.49, 369–70; J.50, 77

Germans, Germany (*see also* German literature and novels, post-war; (Auto-)biographical matters: universities):

alienation from/dislike of contemporary Germany: J.7; J.8, 29; J.10; J.13(a); J.22, 284–85; J.23, 93; J.42; J.43, 57; J.44(b), 166–67; J.51; J.54

ambivalence towards: J.8, 29; J.12; J.14, 12; J.22, 292–93; J.29; J.42; J.43, 57; J.45, 7; J.49, 373; J.51

atrocity in Tulle (1944): J.51

collective derangement of: J.51

conformism: J.27, 15

directness: J.33, 20

dislike of German 'national character': J.22, 284–85; J.45, 7

dislike of official culture of *Vergangenheitsbewältigung* and memorialization: J.8, 29; J.13(a); J.41.1, 358; J.42; J.45, 6

'economic miracle': J.19(a)

fled its authoritarianism (1965): J.12

German and English society compared: J.33, 24–25

Germany's apparent absence from his work: J.42

Germany's history as the 'dark centre' of his work: J.26, 27–28; J.41.1, 358

Germany's history since 1870: J.17, 51; J.32, 44

Germany's lack of (a sense of) history: J.52

Germany's post-1945 elimination of/silence about the past: J.7; J.8, 29; J.9; J.12; J.17, 44, 48; J.19(a); J.21; J.22, 290; J.23, 93; J.27, 14; J.28; J.32, 35–36; J.34, 142–45; J.35, 124; J.37(a), 105; J.42; J.43, 57; J.44(b), 161–62; J.45, 6; J.46(a), 11; J.48; J.49, 367–68; J.50, 84–85

Germany's rapid collapse 1941–43: J.32, 44–45

haunted by spectres when he visits: J.29; J.45, 7

impoverishment by persecution of minority groups: J.45, 7

initiators of aerial warfare against civilians/area bombing: J.32, 46–47

lack of a real resistance movement in Nazi Germany: J.8, 29; J.14, 11

    might consider returning to work there: J.12; J.22, 292, 294
    '*Minimülltonnen auf dem Tisch*' as an image of everything he dislikes: J.12
    moral duplicity and wilful blindness of Germans: J.41.1, 358
    nostalgia for an Alpine environment/the Allgäu: J.12; J.14, 12; J.43, 57
    passive resistance = passive collaboration: J.14, 11; J.21
    racism and xenophobia, contemporary: J.8, 29
    reunification, negative comments on: J.8, 29
    revisits frequently: J.29; J.49, 373
    unfamiliarity with most of Germany: J.17, 50–51
    unreadability as a literary virtue in Germany: J.33, 24
    winter oppressiveness of Alpine environments: J.15
    'world champions' at guilt/lack of interest in the past: J.40, 2
Germany, aerial devastation of: J.48
    affinity with a devastated Germany: J.36, 234; J.46(a), 17
    bombing of Sonthofen in 1945: J.32, 42
    breach of the Geneva Convention: J.19(a)
    its controversial nature in England: J.32, 42–43
    the 'economic miracle' as sublimation of the experience of destruction: J.8, 29; J.19(a);
        J.42; J.51
    Hamburg firestorm raids: J.32, 43
    as 'just punishment' for war guilt?: J.19(a); J.32, 45
    its military effectiveness uncertain: J.19(a); J.32, 42
    its morality: J.32, 46
    Munich (1947): J.32, 35–36; J.44(b), 160; J.51
    as a natural history of destruction: J.19(a)
    origins of his interest in: J.32, 49
    the raids surpass description, even by eyewitnesses: J.19(a); J.52
    as revenge: J.32, 46–47
    as unstoppable process/destruction for its own sake: J.19(a)
    why so few writers have tried to deal with it: J.19(a); J.21
Germany, reunification of: J.8, 29
    addressed by Peter Weiss: J.42
    guilt, responsibility, and shame, the burden of: J.32, 47
    guilt as such less important than reflection on the past: J.29
    omnipresence/inescapability of: J.31
    rejects notion of inherited guilt: J.45, 6
    Sebald's sense of: J.17, 51; J.20; J.26, 28; J.34, 144–45; J.43, 59; J.42; J.43, 59; J.51
    the shame of German history since the Thirty Years War: J.32, 44
historical amnesia: (*see also* Germans, Germany; German literature and novels, post-war;
    guilt, responsibility, and shame, the burden of):
Holocaust: *see* Shoah, the
Jews: J.4.1, 354
    assimilation of by German society: J.4.1, 354; J.17, 47; J.34, 154, 163: J.46(a), 13; J.48
    avoids the problem of contemporary Israel: J.45, 7
    interest in Jewish cultural history: J.17, 47; J.34, 160–62; J.44(b), 167
Munich:
    experience of bombed-out Munich (1947): J.32, 35; J.34, 142; J.44(b), 161; J.51; J.52
    his six months in (1976): J.17, 50
Shoah, the (*see also* Germans, Germany; German literature and novels, post-war): J.34,
    161–62; J.36, 232–33; J.39
    Claude Lanzmann's nine-hour film (1985): J.17, 53; J.45, 7

compared to the Head of Medusa: cannot be looked at directly: J.45, 7; J.46(a), 8; J.50, 80

connection with war and environmental disasters: J.26, 28; J.42

continuing destructiveness of the Shoah: J.6; J.8, 29; J.17, 38; J.41.1, 359–60; J.45, 6; J.50, 81

detests the term 'Holocaust literature': J.45, 7

dissociates himself from the 'Holocaust industry': J.39; J.41.1, 355

in documentary literature of the 1960s: J.21

does not want to be considered a Holocaust specialist: J.39

gypsies: J.34, 145

local links with the Shoah in Germany: J.7; J.9; J.39; J.41.1, 355

need to continue investigating the Shoah: J.41.1, 358–59; J.42; J.43, 57, 59; J.47

not a unique event: J.42

pogrom in Guenzenhausen (Franconia): J.9

problems facing a German gentile writing about the Shoah: J.36, 232; J.45, 7; J.46(a), 8

Theresienstadt (KZ): J.40, 2; J.41.1, 358; J.45, 6

Treblinka (KZ): J.41.1, 355

Wehrmachtsausstellung (travelling exhibition 1995–99 which was seen by an estimated 1.2 million visitors and which proved that the Army (*Wehrmacht*) was more deeply implicated than had been conventionally believed in the planning and implementation of a war of annihilation against Jews, prisoners of war, and civilians): J.42

The human condition, history, philosophy, religion

9/11: J.48; J.51; J.52

agnosticism, Sebald's: J.20

anthropocentric view of the world, loss of: J.4.1, 351

catastrophe (see also *Germany and the NZ-Zeit*: Germany, aerial devastation of; history): J.10; J.11, 26; J.16, 25; J.19(a); J.32, 35–36, 43; J.41.1, 358

catastrophe remembered in *Die Ausgewanderten*: J.16, 25

dangers of studying catastrophe: J.32, 43

early sense of being part of a silent catastrophe: J.10

fascination with since childhood: J.19(a)

fear of environmental catastrophe: J.20

intimations of: J.8, 28–29

limitations of eyewitness accounts: J.19(a)

moral questionability of fascination: J.19(a)

mythologization of catastrophe no longer permissible: J.19(a)

narrators' helplessness in the face of: J.19(a)

narrow line between successful and unsuccessful description or narration of: J.19(a)

colonialism and imperialism: J.23, 96, 99; J.31; J.42

death and decay, consciousness of: J.17, 39–40; J.30, 361–62; J.44(b), 171–72; J.45, 6

depression (see also *Psychology*: suicide): J.5(b); J.17, 54–56; J.36, 234

despair (see also *modernity*): J.26, 25

its causes: J.17, 56

enantiodromia, the dialectic of: J.25

good intentions: J.20

libraries: J.41.1, 356

machines: J.31

his own writing: J.24, 32; J.35, 123; J.43, 55

project of the Enlightenment: J.41.1, 354; J.42

social fluidity: J.8, 28

Enlightenment, the:
 critical of 19th-century view of man/autonomous individual: J.4.1, 351–52; J.8, 28;
  J.37(a), 117
 self-defeating nature of the project of the Enlightenment: J.41.1, 354; J.42
food: J.2, 29; J.39
history (*see also* catastrophe; *Germany and the NS-Zeit*: Germany, aerial devastation of): J.11,
 26; J.17, 57–58; J.42; J.53; J.54
 ambivalence towards the past: J.49, 370
 as apocalypse or catastrophe: J.4.1, 350–51; J.11, 27; J.12; J.19(a); J.42
 attitude towards historical apologies: J.23, 96–97
 and chaos theory: J.54
 as determinant of persons: J.26, 23
 English and German attitudes to the past contrasted: J.23, 96, 99
 as enigma: J.54
 explains why he is not a historian: J.7; J.44(b), 162
 our failure to learn from history: J.52
 finds it hard to have opinions about historical events like 9/11: J.52
 and literature: J.54
 our loss of a sense of: J.4.1, 351; J.13(a); J.31; J.41.1, 360–61
 as meaningless or chaotic: J.17, 58; J.32, 43
 need to know about the past: J.26, 23–24; J.29
 nostalgia for the past: J.49, 370
 past as a criterion for judging the present: J.26, 24
 pessimism about the future: J.17, 57; J.20; J.26, 23; J.44(b), 161
 preference for the past: J.17, 57; J.26, 23
 sense of living towards the end of a civilization: J.25
 silent history of things: J.41.1, 357
 tempting illusion of the past: J.17, 57; J.31
 as tragedy: J.17, 57–58
 vertigo of the past: J.17, 57
 Western history as an aberration with occasional 'saving graces': J.26, 28
Holocaust: *see Germany and the NS-Zeit*: Shoah, the
homogenization:
 adverse effect on writing: J.33, 25
 of cultures: J.41.1, 360
 of Europe: J.23, 98
 of Germany: J.7; J.8, 29; J.27, 14, 16; J.34, 141; J.45, 7; J.52
 of landscapes: J.49, 370
 of language: J.31; J.39
 of time: J.34, 141
 of work: J.31
humour (*see also* irony): J.2, 29; J.11, 30; J.22, 292; J.23, 93–94; J.26, 25; J.44(b), 170; J.45, 7
 parodied in *Private Eye* (see Primary Bibliography, N.1): J.45, 7
 political power of: J.27, 17
irony (*see also* humour)
 as the complement or reverse of melancholy: J.26, 25
 English irony: J.27, 16
 historical irony: J.8, 29
 importance of irony: J.26, 25
 the irony of his pictures: J.34, 154
large is bad (*see also Writing, films, the arts*: gigantism): J.4.1, 352; J.31; J.44(b), 166; J.48; J.54

inherent connection of large size with fascism: J.4.1, 352
life (*see also* mortality): J.3; J.18(a), 51; J.30, 357
    fragility of: J.18(a), 51
    futility of as his central theme: J.20
    senselessness of: J.37(a), 97
    unbearability of: J.3
    uncontrollability of: J.37(a), 117
loss: J.30, 357, 362
    of our ability to see the dead: J.24, 33
    of authentic language: J.31
    of childhood: J.43, 57
    of extended family: J.43, 59
    of fear of the dead: J.41.1, 362
    of freedom in English universities: J.43, 59
    of home/*Heimat*: J.41.1, 59; J.49, 370, 373–74
    life as continual loss: J.20
    of linguistic biodiversity: J.31
    as a major cause of melancholy: J.4.1, 351
    of ontological security: J.4.1, 351; J.31
    of organic nature: J.20; J.31; J.37(a), 102–03; J.41.1, 361
    of power of our senses: J.31
    of reality of money: J.31
    of our roots in nature: J.8, 29; J.17, 56; J.31
    of self-knowledge: J.31
    of sense of detail and specificity: J.31
    of sense of history/memory: J.4.1, 351; J.13(a); J.31; J.41.1, 360–61
    of sense of transcendence: J.4.1, 352
machines
    our domination by: J.31; J.37(a), 101–02
memory and the act of remembering: *see* Psychology
metaphysics: J.4.1, 352; J.34, 159; J.37(a), 115–16; J.44(b), 165
modernity (*see also* despair; *Writing, films, the arts*: gigantism): J.8, 28
    ambivalence towards: J.49, 370
    deleterious effects of the speeding up of modern life: J.30, 359
    disquiet about: J.52
    excepts the wireless and the motor car from his critique: J.44(b), 166
    fears its fluidity and mobility: J.8, 28
    negative about: J.8, 28
    ontological insecurity: J.4.1, 351; J.16, 27; J.17, 54–56; J.31
    pain caused by: J.8, 28; J.17, 55–56; J.27, 16–17; J.31
    repelled by: J.44(b), 165–66
    technology, dislikes: J.44(b), 166; J.46(a), 18
mortality, ageing, illness (*see also* life): J.4.1, 351; J.18(a), 51; J.22, 295
    omnipresence of illness: J.22, 295
outrage at ageing: J.18(a), 51
Napoleonic era:
    as a development of the Enlightenment ideal: J.42
    frequency of references to in his work: J.36, 230
    prefigures the *NS-Zeit*: J.36, 230; J.42
painkillers and other nostrums (*see also* despair; modernity; *Writing, films, the arts*: gigantism):
    J.8, 28; J.11, 27; J.17, 55–56; J.24, 34

posthistory: J.32, 48
postmodern/ism/ity:
    rare use of the term: J.22, 286
Roman Catholicism: J.27, 17
    dislike of rituals, religious and secular: J.27, 17
small is good (see also *The human condition*: large is bad): J.4.1, 352; J.31; J.44(b), 167–68;
    J.48; J.54
Uncanny, the: J.4.1, 352, 354; J.5(b)
    and old photos: J.5(b); J.16, 27; J.17, 39–40, 53; J.18(a), 51; J.23, 95; J.26, 24; J.27, 18; J.31;
        J.49, 366; J.51
    premonitions: J.4.1, 353
'View of life?': J.30, 361

Nature and the environment

animals:
    exploitation by man: J.4.1, 351
    likes and respects: J.4.1, 351; J.17, 56; J.41.1, 357
    mass graves of: J.42
    slaughter on the roads: J.11, 26
butterflies and moths: J.50, 80–81
    fascinated by their death: J. 24, 34–35
nature
    alienation from: J.8, 29; J.17, 56; J.31
    connects environmental disasters with war and the Shoah: J.26, 28; J.42
    disappearance of organic nature: J.20; J.31; J.37(a), 102–03; J.41.1, 361
    exploitation of in the name of material progress: J.39
    rejection of organic imagery: J.1, 51–52
scientists:
    prefers their books to novels: J.50, 81
storms (October 1987): J.10

Places (apart from Germany)

America (see also *The human condition*: 9/11):
    contemporary America: J.51
    visits to: J.14, 13; J.16, 28
    youthful idealization of: J.17, 48–49; J.28
Belgium:
    Breendonk as place and symbol: J.41.1, 354–55, 359
    familiarity with since the 1960s: J.41.1, 353–54
    a paradigm for Europe: J.41.1, 354
cemeteries
    their attraction for him: J.40, 4
cities (*see also* Manchester): J.22, 284–85
    degeneration of: J.4.1, 351
Corsica: J.17, 40; J.37(a), 97–98, 102–03; J.44(b), 160
    failure to complete his project on: J.21
    pre-modern aspects of its culture: J.17, 40
East Anglia, University of; Norfolk; Suffolk (see also *(Auto-)biographical matters*: refuges and
    idylls): J.11, 27; J.12; J.15; J.23, 94, 99; J.27, 15–16; J.31
    apocalyptic vision of Suffolk: J.11, 26–27; J.12; J.23, 96; J.27, 15

desolate airfields: J.32, 48
dryness: J.12; J.13(a)
open skies: J.15
presence of history: J.27, 14
pristine nature: J.22, 292
UEA, positive response to: J.34, 149–51
England, the English, Englishness (*see also* East Anglia (etc.); Manchester): J.8, 29; J.11, 27;
    J.12; J.15; J.27, *passim*; J.42
attitudes to the imperial past: J.45, 7
attitudes to World War II: J.32, 42; J.34, 150–51
changed for the worse: J.47
confused relationship with England: J.54
enduring class system: J.45, 6
feels increasingly less at home in: J.42; J.43, 59; J.44(b), 166; J.45, 7
in the late 1960s (last phase of Empire): J.12
more likely than Germany to produce good literature: J.33, 24–25
negative about contemporary England: J.8, 29; J.27, 16–17
Parliament's (in)ability to cope with things: J.8, 29
positive comments on English diplomacy, generosity, hospitality, humour (concealing
    seriousness), politeness, respect for privacy, and tolerance of eccentricity: J.16, 29;
    J.27, 16; J.33, 20; J.34, 150, 160; J.42
prefers English readers to German ones: J.45, 7
Royal Family, the, and its rituals: J.27, 17
slow collapse of Empire: J.27, 14–15
Manchester (1966–70): J.6; J.10; J.17, 49, 58; J.27, 14; J.34, 149; J.35, 124; J.37(a), 105; J.40, 2;
    J.42; J.45, 6
colourful colleagues at Manchester University: J.27, 16
(first) encounters with Jewish individuals and a Jewish community: J.6; J.5(b); J.14, 11;
    J.34, 161; J.37(a), 105–06; J.38; J.42; J.46(a), 12; J.50, 84
(first, traumatic) encounter with a (moribund) industrial city: J.10; J.16, 29; J.34, 149;
    J.42
St Gallen, his year in, as a teaching assistant (1968–69): J.17, 49
Suffolk: *see* East Anglia (etc.)
Switzerland: J.33, 25; J.34, 147; J.44(b), 167–68
the Aareinsel, near Thun: J.2, 29
Fribourg: J.34, 149; J.38
Île Saint-Pierre (St Petersinsel) in Lake Biel/Bienne: J.44(b), 167–68
reservations about: J.17, 49–50
Vienna and the surrounding riverscapes: J.49, 370

Psychology

aggression, human: J.51; J.52
dreams: J.34, 149
melancholy/saturnine temperament (see also *The human condition*: loss): J.4.1, 351; J.8, 29;
    J.9, J.10; J.13(a); J.15; J.20; J.22, 292; J.26, 25; J.29; J.30, 361; J.34, 159–60; J.35, 125; J.36,
    234; J.40, 2; J.43, 57; J.44(b), 170
as an attitude of resistance that sharpens the mind: J.38
basic condition of creative work: J.40, 2
caused by loss: J.4.1, 351
cerebral, not emotional state: J.40, 2

dislikes psychological explanations for: J.11, 30
distinguishes between melancholy, depression, and resignation: J.36, 234
ignorance of its origins: J.15
possible connection with his departure from the Allgäu (1963): J.15
memory and the act of remembering: J.4.1, 353; J.9; J.17, 54; J.34, 144
  in *Austerlitz*: J.34, 163
  complex relationship with the act of forgetting: J.49, 368
  as destructive: J.6; J.8, 29; J.9; J.16, 25; J.17, 54–56; J.24, 32; J.29; J.32, 48; J.41.1, 359–60;
    J.46(a), 7
  intensity of his own memory: J.9
memory and myth-making: J.34, 144
  as the moral backbone of literature: J.46(a), 7
  places have memory: J.45, 6
  unreliability of: J.34, 144, 157
mental asylums: J.17, 54–56
psychoanalysis and psychotherapy:
  dangers of: J.17, 60; J.41.1, 359–60; J.49, 368
  lack of faith in: J.2, 29; J.24, 32
  telling stories can be therapeutic: J.49, 368
  return of the repressed (*see also* suicide; *Germany and the NS-Zeit*: Shoah, the; *The
    human condition*: depression): J.8, 29; J.9; J.16, 25; J.34, 163; J.41.1, 359–60, 362; J.45,
    6; J.46(a), 7; J.49, 367–68
self-destructiveness: J.4.1, 351
  in himself: J.2, 29
  in humanity in general: J.11, 30
  writing as a self-destructive process: J.3
suicide (*see also* survivor's syndrome; *The human condition*: depression): J.5(b); J.6; J.16, 25;
  J.17, 38, 54–56; J.24, 33–34
survivor's syndrome (*see also* suicide; *The human condition*: depression): J.5(b); J.17, 38, 52;
  J.24, 34; J.30, 357
unconscious, the
  its role in 'disorderly research': J.33, 18; J.37(a), 96

Writing, films, the arts

architecture, buildings (*see also* gigantism; *The human condition*: large is bad)
  lifelong preoccupation with architecture: J.52
art, works of (*see also* bricolage; chance (etc.); writing)
  comforting function: J.4.1, 352
  the 'sublime': J.31
  timeless/ability to stop time: J.4.1, 352–53; J.17, 41–42; J.51
bricolage (*see also* art, works of; chance (etc.); writing): J.22, 282; J.34, 141
  defined: J.7; J.10
  in his childhood: J.34, 141; J.44(b), 159
chance, coincidence, and the unexpected (*see also* art, works of; *bricolage*; writing; *Psychology*:
  unconscious, the): J.4.1, 352–53; J.5(b); J.7; J.11, 27, 30; J.14, 14; J.26, 25–26; J.28; J.37(a),
  96–97; J.41.1, 356–57; J.44(b), 162; J.45, 6; J.49, 374
  old photos and chance: J.16, 27; J.18(a), 51; J.26, 24; J.27, 18; J.46(a), 13
  its place in research: J.33, 18–19; J.37(a), 94–96; J.41.1, 357; J.44(b), 162
  privileged moments when writing: J.5(b); J.36, 234; J.39
  randomness of his thinking: J.34, 148

creative writing
    teaching it: J.33, 17–24
    usefulness of workshops: J.33, 19–20
dead, the: J.4.1, 354
    their ability to speak through old photos: J.49, 366
    more interested in the dead than the living: J.4.1, 354; J.17, 39–40
    their presence or proximity: J.24, 33; J.44(b), 160; J.45, 6; J.47
detective fiction: J.3; J.4.1, 353; J.26, 26; J.34, 155; J.37(a), 103
diaries/memoirs/letters, preference for: J.2, 29; J.25; J.27, 17–18
epiphanic moments while writing: J.5(b); J.36, 234; J.39; J.50, 85–86
films:
    Accident (Joseph Losey): J.2, 28
    Blow Up (Michelangelo Antonioni): J.49, 367
    Into the Arms of Strangers (film about the *Kindertransporte* (2000) based on work edited by
        Bertha Levinson (Leverton)): J.36, 233; J.49, 373, 375 n. 6
    F. W. Murnau (likes the work of): J.51
    Schindler's List (Steven Spielberg) (very critical of): J.36, 233; J.41.1, 355; J.45, 7
    Shoah (Claude Lanzmann's nine-hour film (1985)): J.17, 53
gigantism: J.44(b), 166; J.48
    links between fascism and certain kinds of architecture: J.4.1, 352; J.45, 7
horrific, the, and terror ('Das Grauen[hafte]'): J.13(a); J.18(a), 51; J.19(a); J.21; J.36, 233; J.52
    critical of 'gratuitous invention of horror': J.52
    its move to the centre of literary concerns *c.* 1900: J.19(a)
    need for writers to approach it circumspectly or obliquely: J.8, 29; J.14, 14; J.16, 28; J.21;
        J.34, 146; J.36, 233; J.41.1, 358
    its (non-)representability: J.21; J.32, 38; J.34, 146; J.45, 7; J.46(a), 8; J.50, 80, 86; J.52
hybridity of his work: J.34, 156
illustrations: *see* photos, pictures, postcards
imagery, his:
    backpack: J.17, 51; J.20
    butterfly net: J.17, 51–53
    dream imagery: J.34, 149
    dust/ash: J.17, 58–59; J.24, 32; J.50, 82
    'echoes from another world': J.4.1, 353
    fire: J.4.1, 351; J.11, 27
    fortresses: J.41.1, 359
    mist or fog: J.41.1, 363; J.50, 82
    oblique use of symbols: J.17, 53
    railways: J.17, 54
    Saturn and its rings: J.11, 27; J.42
    wasps' nest as an image of an ideal structure: J.24, 32
    weaving: J.44(b), 163
impossibility of categorizing his texts: J.10; J.17, 37; J.22, 282; J.25; J.27, 17; J.34, 152; J.52;
    J.54
intertextuality:
    as homage: J.4.1, 353
language: *see Germany and the NS-Zeit*: German language: homogenization
literary criticism:
    failure of *Literaturwissenschaft*: J.32, 40
    frustration with the limitations of *Literaturwissenschaft*: J.15; J.34, 151–52
    has given up writing academic articles and book-reviewing: J.33, 22; J.48

inadequacy of 'textimmanent criticism': J.17, 48
low status of biographical research among German Germanisten: J.32, 40–41
preference for essayistic exploration: J.34, 152
rejection of the 'Wissenschaftsideal': J.42
his unsystematic research methods: J.37(a), 94
loners/lost souls/outsiders/solitude/stragglers, his preference for (see also (Auto-)biographical
matters: exile/emigration, experience of): J.11, 30; J.25; J.33, 22; J.34, 160; J.35, 124);
J.44(b), 167; J.50, 84;
madness:
proximity to creativity: J.8, 29; J.22, 290–91; J.37(a), 114
margins: see peripheries
melodrama:
dislikes/fears: J.7; J.23, 96; J.36, 233; J.45, 7
epitomized by Schindler's List: J.36, 233
music: J.24, 33; J.39
narrative relationships and stance (see also novels; 'prose fiction'; third-person narration;
writing): J.3; J.5(b); J.8, 29; J.16, 25–26; J.30, 362
desire to create a sense of narrative uncertainty: J.16, 25–26
distinguishes sharply between himself as person, author, narrator, and his characters:
J.36, 233; J.44(b), 169; J.49, 374–75
explains why his characters sound like their narrator: J.30, 362; J.44(b), 169–70
multiple levels of narration in his work: J.30, 362
narrators are distinct from but related to himself: J.8, 29; J.30, 362; J. 43, 55–57; J.45,
6; J.48
narrators attempt to stay outside the characters: J.6; J.30, 362
narrators of autobiographical works in general: J.3; J.6
narrators' dispassionate neutrality in the face of catastrophe: J.19(a); J.32, 45–46; J.41.1,
358
narrators as explorers: J.30, 362
narrators' helplessness in the face of catastrophe: J.19(a)
narrators in his own work: J.5(b); J.8, 29; J.16, 25–26; J.30, 362; J.32, 41–42; J.34, 158;
J.40, 2
narrators as witnesses: J.30, 362
need for narrative discretion/sensitivity/tact, meticulousness, obliqueness, and distance:
J.8, 29; J.14, 14; J.16, 28; J.21; J.34, 146; J.36, 233; J.41.1, 358; J.45, 7; J.46(a), 8; J.50,
80
paradoxical relationship between himself as author and his narrators: J.30, 362
novels (see also narrative relationships and stance; novels; 'prose fiction'; third-person
narration; writing)
defines himself and his work against the conventions of 'standard fiction' / the novel:
J.3; J.5(b); J.7; J.16, 27; J.17, 37; J.20; J.22, 282; J.25; J.28; J.36, 230; J.44(b), 169; J.47;
J.48; J.49, 374–75; J.51; J.52; J.53; J.54
exhaustion/limitations of the novel form: J.27, 17–18; J.43, 55; J.44(b), 169; J.54
inability to create complex plots: J.3; J.30, 362
inability to write dialogue: J.20; J.25
inability to write 'a proper novel': J.30, 362
insists that his books are not novels: J.52
need for books with a historical consciousness: J.54
novels' inability to deal with the aerial destruction of Germany: J.32, 41
parochiality of modern English novel: J.45, 6
preference for a more open form on moral grounds: J.43, 55
reads almost no contemporary fiction: J.48; J.50, 81; J.53

relative unimportance of plots in 19th-century German prose fiction: J.49, 369; J.50, 77–78

omniscience: *see* third-person narration

open-endedness:
    negative about: J.1, 47
    positive about: J.52

painting:
    fascination with the painter's craft: J.4.1, 352–53

paragraphs, lack of: *see Germany and the NS-Zeit*: German language

peripheries, concern with/preference for: J.11, 27; J.17, 50
    creativity and: J.47
    elimination of Germany's peripheral zones: J.7; J.10
    focus on Germany's peripheries: J.42; J.49, 370; J.50, 77
    interest in lesser-known writers: J.25
    interest in the peripheral aspects of pictures: J.18(a), 51
    marginal position of his narrators: J.19(a)
    peripherality of the Allgäu and Wales: J.34, 144; J.41.1, 360; J.42
    his peripheral status in England: J.54
    peripheral vision: J.34, 146
    preference for peripheral genres (e.g. diaries, letters, memoirs): J.25; J.27, 18; J.34, 147

photos, pictures, postcards (*see also* chance (etc.); *The human condition*: uncanny, the): J.2, 29; J.5(b); J.7; J.10; J.14, 14; J.15; J.16, 27; J.18(a), 51–52; J.25; J.31; J.34, 154; J.46(a), 13–14; J.49, 366–67
    5–10% of those used in his fiction are not genuine or have been altered: J.16, 25; J.46(a), 14; J.49, 366
    ability to stimulate narratives: J.14, 13; J.16, 24; J.18(a), 51; J.26, 24–25; J.27, 18; J.28; J.48; J.53
    ability to stop time: J.17, 41–42; J.48; J.49, 352–53; J.51
    ambivalent use of (they legitimate/authenticate/document and alienate/disturb/provoke questions): J.7; J.10; J.14, 14; J.17, 41; J.27, 18; J.33, 15; J.49, 366–67; J.51; J.53
    as documents of an absence or an unknowable past: J.31; J.46(a), 6
    early memory of a photo of a dead soldier: J.44(b), 171
    ghostly/uncanny quality/intimations of a parallel world of the dead: J.5(b); J.16, 27; J.17, 39–40, 53; J.18(a), 51; J.23, 95; J.26, 24; J.27, 18; J.31; J.49, 366
    ironic use of: J.34, 154
    link with chance: J.16, 27; J.18(a), 51; J.26, 24; J.27, 18; J.46(a), 13
    long-standing interest in old photos: J.18(a), 51; J.25; J.26, 27; J.31; J.44(b), 162; J.46(a), 13
    as a means of documenting the improbable: J.18(a), 51; J.26, 27; J.27, 18
    as a means of negotiating his desire to efface himself and yet be heard: J.31
    not interested in producing quality photos: J.18(a), 51
    photo albums and social history: J.18(a), 51; J.34, 154; J.44(b), 172; J.46(a), 13; J.49, 367
    photography as research: J.18(a), 51; J.36, 234
    prefers black-and-white photos as the intersection place of life and death: J.18(a), 51–52; J.27, 18; J.31
    prefers photos to portraits: J.18(a), 51
    as reified memory: J.16, 27
    tension with the verbal text: J.38; J.53
    unreliability: J.14, 13–14; J.16, 27; J.26, 27; J.31; J.44(b), 163; J.46(a), 14
    unforgettability of some photos: J.18(a), 52; J.48; J.49, 366
    as a way into an exotic or unreal world: J.18(a), 51

press clippings in his work: J.26, 26–27
   some are forgeries: J.26, 27
'prose fiction' (*see also* novels; third-person narration; writing; References to persons (etc.):
   Bernhard, Thomas): J.17, 37; J.34, 156; J.44(b), 168–69; J.52; J.53
   defines his use of the term: J.45, 6; J.47
   'periscopic fiction': J.5(b); J.16, 28; J.17, 37; J.44(b), 170; J.48; J.50, 83
   what propels 'prose fiction' forward: J.53; J.54
realism as a literary mode (*see also References to persons (etc.)*: Realism (19th-century literary
   movement)):
   adjusts the historical where necessary: J.52
   the fictional nature of his work: J.38
   makes deliberate mistakes: J.52
   his prose as 'an adjusted realism': J.20; J.25; J.29; J.46(a), 6–7; J.52
   the realism of his prose fiction: J.4.1, 353; J.5(b); J.7; J.17, 41; J.22, 282; J.23, 94; J.25; J.34,
      141, 153; J.41.1, 356; J.45, 7
research, writers must engage in (like reporters): J.5(b); J.18(a), 51; J.21; J.32, 39; J.36, 228;
   J.38; J.41.1, 356
   increasing fascination with: J.41.1, 356
   need to rescue historical evidence: J.46, 368
   photography as research: J.18(a), 51; J.36, 234
   rejection of the '*Wissenschaftsideal*': J.42
   his unsystematic research: J.37(a), 94; J.41.1, 356–57; J.44(b), 162
   walking as research: J.34, 160; J.42; J.50, 81
self-consciousness:
   as a 19th-century phenomenon: 18th-century authors less self-conscious: J.40, 3
style: *see Germany and the NS-Zeit*: German language
third-person narration (*see also* narrative relationships and stance; novels; 'prose fiction';
   writing): J.16, 26–27
   necessity of providing sources: J.44(b), 170; J.49, 374–75
   'periscopic writing' as the antithesis: J.16, 28; J.17, 37; J.44(b), 170; J.48; J.50, 83
   rejects the omniscient narrator: J.12; J.16, 26; J.31; J.44(b), 169; J.48; J.49, 374–75; J.50,
      83; J.51
   wants his characters to speak for themselves: J.30, 362; J.45, 6
transition from critical to creative writing: J.34, 152; J.37(a), 99
translation, translations, translators: J.16, 29; J.30, 358–62; J.46(a), 10–11, 16; J.47
   difficulties involved in: J.30, 358–61; J.49, 371
   his interventions in: J.23, 94; J.34, 164–65; J.42; J.45, 7; J.46(a), 16; J.48; J.49, 372
unclassifiability of his texts: *see* hybridity of his work
walking: *see* research
writers, literary culture, the literature industry: J.2, 29; J.4.1, 354; J.33, 22–23
   denies that he is a *littérateur*: J.4.1, 350
   dislike of the commodification of literature: J.31
   dislike of writers' egoism and grandiloquence: J.2, 29; J.54
   dislike of writers, literary culture, the literary machine, the 'culture–literature industry':
      J.2, 29; J.4.1, 354; J.22, 294; J.23, 93; J.33, 22–23; J.34, 152; J.51
   ironic attitude to 'Dichter': J.15
   misfortune of being a writer: J.23, 98
   moral failings of writers: J.2, 29; J.17, 59–60; J.31
   as quest for a home: J.49, 373
   has no writer friends: J.17, 61
   the writer as con man or impostor: J.6; J.16, 28; J.31; J.34, 157; J.37(a), 108

writing (*see also* art, works of; *bricolage*; chance (etc.); narrative relationships and stance; novels; 'prose fiction'; third-person narration)

    aesthetics and morality: the truth value of fiction: J.1, 54; J.17, 60–61; J.31; J.34, 157; J.36, 233; J.37(a), 108–09; J.45, 7; J.50, 83

    ambivalence of: J.26, 25–26

    as an act of remembering (what people prefer to forget): J.4.1, 352; J.23, 97; J.29; J.46(a), 7

    as archaeology: J.10; J.32, 40; J.42; J.44(b), 163

    as an attempt to bring order into chaos: J.4.1, 352

    as an attempt to create 'pools of timelessness': J.4.1, 352–53

    as an attempt to deal with reality: J.10

    as an attempt to deal with terror: J.13(a)

    as an attempt to deal with the unbearability of life: J.3; J.6

    as an attempt to lighten the weight of heavy things: J.13(a); J.24, 33

    as an attempt to rescue something from the stream of history: J.26, 24

    as auto-therapy: J.34, 145; J.51

    basic problem in the 20th century defined: J.13(a)

    as bearer of metaphysical meaning: J.48

    as *bricolage*: J.7; J.51

    as a cage: J.25; J.35, 123; J.43, 55

    as a cerebral, not a bodily activity: J.40, 2

    as collecting: J.11, 27, 30; J.12; J.41.1, 357

    as conmanship: J.6; J.16, 28; J.31; J.34, 157; J.37(a), 108

    as conversations with the dead: J.6

    darker sides of: J.17, 60; J.31

    desirability of distance between experience and 'Literarisierung': J.21

    as a drive towards the extreme: J.16, 28

    as a forensic activity: J.4.1, 353

    German history as the 'dark centre' of his work: J.26, 27–28

    in general: J.2, 29

    as ghost-hunting: J.17, 42, 53

    increasing difficulty of: J.5(b); J.20; J.23, 97–98; J.37(a), 109; J.45, 7; J.48; J.51

    as lying: J.45, 7; J.51

    as a means of authentication: J.17, 40

    as a means of making readers question authority: J.45, 6

    as a means of preserving/vitrifying the past: J.13(a); J.24, 32; J.26, 24

    as a means of provocation: J.16, 26; J.45, 6

    moral questionability of: J.14, 14; J.17, 59–60; J.19(a); J.31; J.34, 153; J.36, 232–33; J.37(a), 107–08; J.45, 7; J.47; J.53

    moral responsibility of: J.9

    the need to be concrete: J.33, 19

    as obsessive or neurotic behaviour: J.17, 60; J.31; J.34, 160; J.37(a), 114; J.44(b), 169; J.51

    own confused or mixed motives for writing: J.6; J.11, 30; J.17, 60; J.31

    own growing frustration with critical writing: J.15

    own study in Poringland: J.11, 30

    own way of working, work regime: J.6; J.9; J.20; J.22, 278; J.24, 33; J.30, 360; J.34, 162; J.36, 234; J.37(a), 109; J.38; J.41.1, 356; J.43, 55; J.44(b), 162, 163; J.48; J.51

    own youthful attempts at: J.4.1, 350; J.17, 61; J.51

    prefers prose to poetry: J.15; J.45, 6; J.50, 77

    privileged moments when writing: J.5(b); J.36, 234; J.39

    as a quest for identity: J.4.1, 350; J.29

as a quest for integrity or truth: J.6; J.34, 158
as a reaction against the objectivity of the 'Wissenschaftsideal': J.42
reasons for his late start as a creative writer: J.5(b); J.16, 24; J.25; J.38
as a refuge from the educational reforms of the 1980s and 1990s: J.45, 6
as a refuge from the frustrations of his professional life (a 'potting shed'): J.5(b); J.15; J.16,
    24; J.17, 61; J.20; J.25; J.34, 152, 165; J.37(a), 98–99; J.38; J.53
as a self-conscious process: J.5(b); J.25
as a self-destructive process: J.3
as (self-)exploration: J.3; J.4.1, 350; J.6; J.22, 291; J.29
should be a part-time activity: J.33, 21
wasps' nest as an image of a work of literature: J.24, 32
as a way of exploring the night side of life: J.6
why writers panic: J.40, 2
writing and restlessness: J.31

6
W. G. Sebald: A Chronology

Compiled by Richard Sheppard
(additional information by Jo Catling)

Sebald is a quite obscure saint and almost all that we know about him is legendary.
W. G. SEBALD, interview with Sarah Kafatou (1998) (J.24), p. 32

Sebald-Weg: Betreten auf eigene Gefahr
[Sebald Trail: Enter at own risk]
Warning notice in the forest between the
Zollhaus Oberjoch and Wertach im Allgäu

The following chronology has been compiled using sources too numerous to list in full here, chief among which are the papers in the Sebald *Nachlass* in the Deutsches Literaturarchiv Marbach (DLA); W. G. Sebald's personal file at the University of East Anglia (UEA); newspaper reports and information kindly provided by relatives, colleagues and friends. Nevertheless, it remains very much 'work in progress', and many of the dates must be considered provisional pending better information. Anyone who wishes to correct or improve an entry, or to add new information, is asked to contact the Editors and the compiler of this chronology.

Dates of events in Sebald's personal and professional life are shown in bold type; passages in his works of prose fiction which parallel those events are contained in square brackets. Historical events — in world history, in the lives of poets, other literary figures, or persons connected with UEA — are designated by italic type.

Abbreviations of Sebald's works
(for editions see the Primary Bibliography)

A	*Austerlitz*
BU	*Die Beschreibung des Unglücks*
CS	*Campo Santo*
DA	*Die Ausgewanderten (The Emigrants)*
LiL	*Logis in einem Landhaus (A Place in the Country)*
LuL	*Luftkrieg und Literatur (On the Natural History of Destruction)*
NN	*Nach der Natur (After Nature)*
RS	*Die Ringe des Saturn (The Rings of Saturn)*
SG	*Schwindel. Gefühle. (Vertigo)*
U	*Unerzählt (Unrecounted)*
UH	*Unheimliche Heimat*

FIG. III.4. The memorial plaque on the house in Wertach where WGS was born
(cf. FIGS. 1.3, 1.4) © Jo Catling

Other abbreviations

BA	British Academy
BCLT	British Centre for Literary Translation (at UEA)
CUTG	Conference of University Teachers of German in Great Britain (now ATG)
DAAD	Deutscher Akademischer Austausch Dienst
DLA	Deutsches Literaturarchiv Marbach
EAS	School of English and American Studies (at UEA)
EUR	School of Modern Languages and European Studies (at UEA)
GI	Goethe-Institut
KZ	*Konzentrationslager* (concentration camp)
MLA	Modern Language Association
NESTA	National Endowment for Science, Technology and the Arts
NSDAP	National Socialist Party
ORF	Österreichischer Rundfunk
SRF	Schweizer Rundfunk
SS	summer semester
UEA	University of East Anglia, Norwich
WS	winter semester

1943

24 July–3 August: Operation Gomorrah (the British fire-storm raids on Hamburg which destroyed the city and killed c. 40,000 people)

*28–29 August: first of several Allied air raids on Nuremberg [cf. NN: **B.A.1**, pp. 73–74]*

> [autumn 1943: Max Aurach/Ferber comes to Manchester for the first time as an 18-year-old art student; *DA*: **B.B.2**, p. 247]

1 November: the two warehouses belonging to the Magasins Généraux at 43 Quai du Gare, Paris 13ème, that are used to hold the looted possessions of French Jews, officially become Lager Austerlitz. It is staffed by the inmates of KZ Drancy who process the possessions and dispatch them by train to Germany.

18 May 1944–autumn 1963:
lives in the Allgäu (Bavaria: Wertach and Sonthofen)

18 May 1944: born in Grüntenseestraße 3, Wertach, Bavaria

6 June 1944: D-Day: the invasion of Normandy by the Western Allies

*9 June 1944: massacre of 99 French civilians in Tulle by members of the SS-Panzer Division Das Reich (cf. **D.76**); on the following day members of the same Division destroy Oradour-sur-Glane, about 50 miles to the north, and massacre 642 men, women, and children*

At about the same time, the father of a French friend of WGS who was in the Resistance is brutally murdered by the SS in the same area (**J.44(b)**, pp. 164–65)

12 August 1944: evacuation of the Lager Austerlitz

26 August 1944: the German occupying forces blow up the Lager Austerlitz, reducing it to rubble

27 January 1945: liberation of KZ Auschwitz-Birkenau by the Red Army

31 January 1945: WGS's father Georg (1911–99), a serving officer with a transport unit of the *Wehrmacht*, is taken prisoner in France not far from Tulle

13 February 1945: first Allied fire-storm raid on Dresden

22 February and 29 April 1945: Sonthofen damaged by tactical bombing (the USAAF was possibly trying to hit, inter alia, the Aerodynamics Institute, part of which had been evacuated from Aachen in 1944)

13 April 1945: liberation of KZ Bergen-Belsen (where Jean Améry is a prisoner) by the British

29 April 1945: liberation of KZ Dachau by the Americans

8 May 1945: VE-Day; 15 August 1945: VJ-Day

January/February 1947: Sebald's family moves to Grüntenseestraße 9, Wertach (Weinstube Steinlehner) after the return of Georg Sebald from a French POW camp on the Haut Plateau de Larzac

mid-March 1947: Georg Sebald is cleared of all involvement with the NSDAP and begins work as a civilian official with the police in Sonthofen

1947: en route to Franconia with his father and older sister, WGS experiences devastated Munich (**J.44(b)**, p. 161)

2 June 1949: death of his maternal grandmother Theresia Egelhofer (née Harzenetter; b. 1880 as the daughter of Genoveva Adelwarth; buried in Wertach churchyard)

c. 1950: sees a photo of a car-crash victim that his father had taken in the *Wehrmacht* (J.44(b), p. 171)

> [summer 1951: according to the narrator of *DA*, the relatives who had emigrated to the USA in the late 1920s come and visit them in Wertach for several weeks. This is the only time that the narrator remembers meeting great-uncle Adelwarth; **B.B.2**, pp. 97 and 108] (cf. Fig. I.15)

WS 1950/51: Martin Heidegger reinstated to his teaching position at the University of Freiburg

16 December 1952: the Sebald family and WGS's widowed maternal grandfather, Josef Egelhofer (1872–1956), move from Wertach to nearby Sonthofen (Am alten Bahnhof 3a; his parents later move to the larger Am alten Bahnhof 8a)

January 1953–summer 1954: attends the *Volksschule* in Sonthofen

autumn 1954–summer 1956: attends the Catholic (Franciscan) *Gymnasium* Sankt Maria Stern, Immenstadt (just to the north of Sonthofen)

16 March 1956: Georg Sebald becomes an officer (Major) in the *Bundeswehr* (established 12 November 1955)

14 April 1956: death of Josef Egelhofer; buried in Wertach churchyard 17 April

autumn 1956–July 1963: attends the *Oberrealschule* in Oberstdorf (to the south of Sonthofen, near the Austro-Bavarian border)

> [[autumn] 1956: Austerlitz begins to study Architectural History at the Courtauld Institute; visits Paris in early October 1957; *A*: **B.B.4**, pp. 157–58]

25 December 1956: death of Robert Walser

13 August 1961: building work starts on the Berlin Wall

November 1961–July 1963: co-edits and contributes to a school magazine, *Der Wecker* (**H.A.1–H.A.12**), which wins a state prize in February 1963

April 1962: the film about the liberation of Bergen-Belsen is shown at the school

10–11 April 1962: plays the second guard in a school production of Anouilh's *Antigone* (Fig. 2.15)

31 May 1962: execution of Adolf Eichmann in Jerusalem

11 October 1962–8 December 1965: Second Vatican Council

1962/63: visits his elder sister Gertrud who is working as an *au pair* in Hampstead (London)

15 July 1963: awarded his *Zeugnis der Reife* (*Abitur* or school-leaving certificate)

autumn 1963–summer 1965: studies at the Albert-Ludwigs-Universität, Freiburg im Breisgau

autumn 1963: UEA admits its first students

WS 1963/64: attends 'English Pronunciation (Elementary)' (Ms P. Wylde Brown); 'Deutsch-Englische Übersetzung'; 'Interpretation amerikanischer Dramen' (Lutz)

December 1963: begins to buy books by Walter Benjamin and members of the Frankfurt School

23 December 1963–19 August 1965: Auschwitz trials in Frankfurt am Main

29 January–5 February 1964: plays Cocky in Eugene O'Neill's *In the Zone* (Fig. 2.16)

SS 1964–SS 1965: lives in the *Studentenheim* at Maximilianstraße 15 (the 'Max-Heim', Figs. 2.6, 2.7)

SS 1964: attends 'Einführung in das Studium der neueren deutschen Literaturgeschichte (romantisches Märchen, Dichtung)' (Prof. Erich Ruprecht, Dr Horst Meixner); 'Englische Intonation' (Bellinghausen); 'Einführung in das Altenglische'; 'Einführung in das Mittelhochdeutsche'; 'Essay-Writing'

1–2 July 1964: plays Snug the Joiner / Lion in *A Midsummer Night's Dream*

WS 1964/65: attends 'The Lost Generation: American Literature Following World War I' (Prof. Darriel Abel); 'Deutsche Lustspiele' (Prof. Wolfram Mauser); 'Neidhart von Renenthal'

21 November 1964: founding member of the 'Gruppe 64' (cf. Fig. 2.8), which plays an increasingly important part in the production of the *Freiburger Studenten-Zeitung* 1964–65 (17 items published by WGS between November 1964 and December 1965: **H.B.1–H.B.10**)

December 1964: probable first visit to Brussels

> [December 1964: the narrator of *RS* pays his first visit to Brussels; **B.B.3**, p. 155]

SS 1965: attends 'Das Drama in den neunziger Jahren' (Prof. Ronald Peacock); 'Henry David Thoreau' (Prof. Darriel Abel)

9 and 12 July 1965: directs first German production of J. P. Donleavy's *Fairy Tales of New York* in the Studio-Bühne Freiburg

summer 1965: visits Brussels (cf. **H.B.8**); brief holiday in Italy with Albrecht Rasche

4 October 1965–summer 1966: studies at the University of Fribourg (Switzerland); living in sister's flat at 11, rue de Lausanne

WS 1965/66: probably attends 'Shakespeare's *Cymbeline*' (Prof. James Smith); 'The History of Post-Expressionist German Literature' (Prof. Ernst Alker; also SS 1966); 'The Comedies of Hofmannsthal with special reference to *Der Schwierige*' (Prof. Ernst Alker)

3 March 1966: presents a *mémoire de licence* on Carl Sternheim

17 March 1966: appointed as *Lektor* at the University of Manchester (1966–67)

> [early summer 1966: Austerlitz goes on his last walk with Gerald (through the vineyards above Lake Geneva); **B.B.4**, p. 159]

SS 1966: probably attends 'Deutsche Wortbildung' (Prof. Eduard Studer); 'Some Aspects of Jacobean Tragedy' (Prof. James Smith); '*Coriolanus*' (Prof. James Smith); 'Selected Chapters from *Felix Krull*' (Prof. Ernst Alker)

July 1966: receives his *licence ès lettres* (*summa cum laude*)

summer 1966: begins to call himself 'Max'

autumn 1966–summer 1968: *Lektor* at the University of Manchester

> [autumn 1966: the narrator of *DA* moves to Manchester, claiming that he has never before been more than five to six hours away by train from home; **B.B.2**, p. 219]

> [*c.* autumn 1966: the narrator of *A* first meets Austerlitz; **B.B.4**, p. 14]

13 September 1966: registers with the Manchester police

September 1966: lives for a few weeks at 12 Ferndene Road, Withington, then moves to 25 Stockton Road, Chorlton-cum-Hardy (Figs. 2.24, 2.25)

October 1966: begins thinking about doing the *Dozentenausbildung*, the training course that prepares candidates to work for the Goethe-Institut as language teachers, with the GI in Munich

14 January 1967: moves, together with another *Lektor*, Reinbert Tabbert, to a ground-floor flat at 26 Kingston Road, Didsbury (Figs. 2.28–31)

[spring 1967: the narrator of *DA* is living in a house looking out on canals and an industrial landscape; **B.B.2**, p. 234]

16 March 1967: completes the (untitled and unpublished) *roman à clef* about his time in Freiburg begun the previous autumn (DLA)

24 April 1967: first letter to Theodor W. Adorno

25 May 1967: reappointed *Lektor* (1967–68)

[June 1967: the narrator of *A* visits Breendonk; **B.B.4**, pp. 36 and 40]

[summer 1967: the narrator of *DA* goes for a walk with Max Aurach; **B.B.2**, p. 244]

July 1967: Tabbert returns to Germany

2 June 1967: the student revolt begins in Berlin when the police shoot Benno Ohnesorg during a visit by the Shah of Iran

1 September 1967: marriage in Sonthofen; WGS and his wife move to the upper-floor flat at 26 Kingston Road; (Sir) Peter Jonas, who was studying music in Manchester, has a room in the same house

19 November 1967: contacts the GI in Munich

6 December 1967: applies to the GI in Munich to do the *Dozentenausbildung*

March 1968: presents his MA thesis on Carl Sternheim at the University of Manchester (awarded a distinction on 11 July): begins turning it into a book shortly afterwards

5–6 March 1968: directs Büchner's *Leonce und Lena* in the University Theatre, Manchester (Fig. 2.36)

5 July 1968: visits the GI in Munich

summer 1968: holiday in Yugoslavia

autumn 1968–summer 1969: teacher of English and German in the *Oberstufe* of the Institut auf dem Rosenberg (an international boarding school), St Gallen (Switzerland); the Sebalds live at Metzgergasse 14; WGS develops an interest in Alfred Döblin

[late November 1968: Austerlitz and Marie de Verneuil visit Salle church in Norfolk; **B.B.4**, pp. 194–95]

29 October 1968: the MS of his book on Carl Sternheim (**A.1**) reaches the Kohlhammer Verlag

December 1968: applies (unsuccessfully) for a Junior Research Fellowship at Sidney Sussex College, Cambridge, having asked Adorno to act as a referee

6 February 1969: Kohlhammer accepts the Sternheim book for publication (contract 21 March 1969)

31 March 1969: Georg Sebald retires from the *Bundeswehr* as a Lieutenant-Colonel

14–16 April 1969: in Munich to discuss textual queries with the Kohlhammer Verlag

22 May 1969: reappointed *Lektor* (1969–70) at University of Manchester

27 July 1969: withdraws application to the GI in Munich

late July: returns proofs of Sternheim book to the Kohlhammer Verlag

3 October 1969: publication of Sternheim book based on MA thesis (*Carl Sternheim: Kritiker und Opfer der Wilhelminischen Ära*: **A.1**) (see Chapter 2 in the present volume)

autumn 1969–summer 1970: *Lektor* at the University of Manchester

mid-October 1969: registers at Manchester as a part-time PhD student working on Alfred Döblin

1970: interest in Kafka is awakened by meeting Miguel Kafka in Klosterneuburg

spring 1970: turns down a post in the Drama Department of the University of Bangor

21 March 1970: applies for the post of Assistant Lecturer in German Language and Literature in the then EUR at UEA (Norwich)

20 April 1970: suicide in Paris of Paul Celan

26 May 1970: interviewed for the post in Earlham Hall, UEA; offered the job on 28 May; accepts it 1 June

20 June 1970: start of a three-month holiday in France (Pont-Aven, Finistère); also visits house in Bordeaux where Hölderlin was a tutor in early 1802

summer 1970: reads Jurek Becker's *Jakob der Lügner* but dislikes it and fails to finish it

early September 1970: Switzerland

1 October 1970–December 1975; July 1976–14 December 2001: UEA

[late September–early October: the narrator of *DA* and Clara rent a flat at 'Prior's Gate, Hingham'; **B.B.2**, pp. 7 and 14]

October 1970–c. April 1971: the Sebalds rent a flat in Vicar Street, Wymondham, Norfolk

9 October 1970: registers at UEA as a PhD student working on Döblin's novels (supervisor: Professor James W. McFarlane)

29 October 1970: invited by Schweizer Rundfunk (SRF) to take part in radio discussion on Sternheim

November 1970: probably meets Elias Canetti on a flight from Zurich (Kloten airport) to London (**D.59/59(c)**)

1971

[5 February: the narrator of *A* claims to have been in Zurich, during a short visit to Switzerland, when a fire broke out at Lucerne station; **B.B.4**, pp. 14–16]

17 February: first radio broadcast (SRF); discussion on Sternheim with Hellmuth Karasek and Peter von Matt (**J.1**)

March: beginning of UEA's 'revolutionary period' when students occupy the Arts Block (see Fig. 2.40)

c. **April**: the Sebalds acquire their own house at 38 Orchard Way, Wymondham. While living there, WGS writes a collection of poems entitled *Schullatein* (some published in **B.D.3**).

[mid-May: the narrator of *DA* and Clara move out of Prior's Gate to their own house; **B.B.2**, p. 29]

September: first review (**G.1**) appears in the *Journal of European Studies* (founded in spring 1971 by three older colleagues in EUR)

1972

summer: an essay on Döblin is accepted by *Die neue Rundschau* but is never published

[late August: Austerlitz accompanies Marie de Verneuil on a visit to Marienbad; **B.B.4**, pp. 294-309]

1973

20 March: UEA's Higher Degree Committee grants permission for WGS to submit his doctoral thesis within three years rather than the normal four

18 June: sends the MS of his doctoral thesis for consideration by the J. B. Metzlerische Verlagsbuchhandlung

August: submits doctoral thesis

1 October: promoted Lecturer

autumn term: on study leave to research 'some of the problems Jewish writers encountered as protagonists on the German literary scene' (application of 26 November 1972); works in Landesbibliothek Coburg, University Libraries of Erlangen and Munich, the Germanisches Museum (Nuremberg), and the Schweizerische Landesbibliothek (Berne) (report of 10 January 1974)

22 October: visits the GI in Munich to explore the possibility of doing a *Dozentenausbildung*

1974

mid-April: PhD viva, with external examiners Dr Gilbert W. McKay (St Peter's College, Oxford) and Prof. H. M. Waidson (Swansea); doctorate awarded 5 July 1974

April–June: attempts to interest numerous publishing houses in publishing his PhD thesis as a book

7–10 July: gives a paper on *Das Schloß* at the Kafka conference at UEA to mark the 50th anniversary of the author's death (cf. **D.8/D.8(a)**)

autumn term: on study leave to research 'the relationship between German culture and its Jewish representatives' (application of 11 February); works at the Parkes Library (University of Southampton), and Jews' College, London; drafts an essay on 'the Ambiguity of Tolerance' (**D.28**); begins to discuss the possibility of a book on 'the specific problems and achievements of German-Jewish writers over the last two centuries' with Metzler; writes an essay on Handke's *Kaspar* (**D.9**) (report of 2 October 1975); probably reads the German translation of Foucault's *Folie et déraison* at about the same time

8 November: tries to interest Kohlhammer Verlag in publishing his PhD thesis

1975

2 February: applies to the GI in Munich to do the year-long *Dozentenausbildung* in 1976

6 February: submits a detailed proposal for a book on the history of Jewish assimilation in German literature to the J. B. Metzlerische Verlagsbuchhandlung

16–20 June: attends the GI's introductory and selection conference at Leoni, south-west of Munich

25 June: accepted by the GI to train as a *Dozent*

June: applies to UEA for unpaid leave of absence for the calendar year 1976

summer: sale of the Wymondham house; the family, including Jodok, their vegetarian labrador, move back to his in-laws' house near Coburg; during the autumn term WGS stays with Gordon Turner and his family in Norwich

autumn term: begins to offer 'Literature and Politics in C20th Germany' as a (co-taught) special subject option (until summer term 1981)

27 October: signs training contract with the GI for the calendar year 1976

November: plans to make a television documentary on Sternheim for the Third Programme of Sender Freies Berlin (RIAS) and spends the second week of December working on the project in Berlin. The project is put on hold when the producer, Jan Franksen, is injured in an accident.

11–12 December: in Munich

> [late 1975: the narrator of *A* returns to Munich with the intention of settling there after an absence of nine years; **B.B.4**, p. 49]

1976

1 January–30 September: trains as a teacher of German language at the Goethe-Institut, Munich; returns to UEA for the autumn term

January–late June: in Munich, where he lives in the *Olympiadorf* (Olympic village, built 1972)

May: visits Jan Peter Tripp in Stuttgart (their first contact since school)

28 June–16 September: sent on teaching practice to Schwäbisch-Hall but is dissatisfied with the conditions there and withdraws from the GI course on 20 August

Whitsun: the Sebalds buy the dilapidated Old Rectory, Poringland, to the south-west of Norwich, and spend years renovating it (WGS lives there until his death); to help finance the repairs, he translates Richard Evans's *Sozialdemokratie und Frauenemanzipation* (**M.B.1**) in 1977–78

autumn term: Film Studies begins at UEA with the (initially three-year) appointment of Charles Barr; Richard Evans becomes a Lecturer in European History in EUR

November: participates in the 90-minute documentary on Sternheim that was planned a year previously. It is broadcast in the Third Programme of RIAS Berlin and involves a long interview with Jan Franksen.

late: rumours begin to circulate that UEA may be closed along with other newly founded universities such as Stirling and Essex

1977

autumn term: becomes a member of the University Drama Committee (until summer term 1981); also EUR Admissions Officer (until summer term 1981); plays a major role in persuading EUR to restyle itself as the School of Modern Languages and European History (1 August 1978) and diversify its courses (applications rise accordingly); *ex officio* member of UEA Admissions Committee (which he attends punctiliously) and EUR's Planning Committee for the same, four-year period

1978

29 April 1978: Cinema City opens in Norwich with a showing of Joseph Losey's 'Mr. Klein' (1976)

summer term: on study leave to write an extended essay on 'Prostitution and Morals in the works of Schnitzler and v[on] Horváth' (application of 23 January 1978) after discussing the subject with his colleague, Richard Evans, whose related article, 'Prostitution, State and Society in Imperial Germany', had appeared in *Past and Present* in February 1976 (cf. **D.22**); begins to turn his (English) doctoral thesis into a 'substantially revised and completely rewritten' book (in German) 'incorporating considerable quantities of new material' (report of 12 April 1979)

May: lectures on Döblin at the University of Klagenfurt (Austria), where Dr Franz Kuna (1933–2010), his former UEA colleague, is now Professor

17 October: suicide of Jean Améry

1979

mid-January: German MS of Döblin book ready (**A.2**: *Der Mythus der Zerstörung im Werk Döblins*)

May: writes foreword to Döblin book

early May: → Stuttgart → Vienna

3 May: Margaret Thatcher leads the Conservative Party to an overwhelming victory in the General Election; major cuts in university expenditure loom and continue for the next decade; UEA particularly badly hit

autumn term: member of EUR–LAW (School of Law) Joint Committee (until 1986)

late November: corrects the proofs of the Döblin book

1980

9–10 January: Dr Ray Furness comes to UEA as an external examiner

spring term: begins to teach a joint seminar with Dr Thomas Elsaesser entitled 'German Cinema / Weimar Culture'

21 January: signs contract with Klett Verlag for book on Döblin; it appears on 21 March and remains in print until 12 March 1990

*16/17 February: death in Manchester of Stanley Sephton Kerry [**B.B.3**, pp. 185–87] (cf. Fig. 2.35)*

*21 February: death of Alfred Andersch (see **D.57**)*

22–24 September: gives a paper entitled 'Anarchy and Satire: Some Notes on Thomas Bernhard' at the CUTG conference at the University of Sussex (cf. **D.16**)

autumn term: on study leave to research 'problems of literature and psychopathology' (application of [?] January 1980) with a grant of £490 from the British Academy (BA)

16 October: Norwich → Coburg (arrives 17 October)

19 October → Freising [?]

20 October → Vienna

21–22 October → Klosterneuburg

23–28 October: spends time with the schizophrenic poet Ernst Herbeck / Alexander Herbrich at Leo Navratil's Zentrum für Kunst und Psychotherapie, part of the Niederösterreichische Landesanstalt für Psychiatrie und Neurologie, Gugging, near Klosterneuburg, outside Vienna; contributes 'to a [Swiss] television film on the artistic and literary achievements of the clinic's patients' (report of 10 January 1981)

29 October → Venice (until 31 October)

1–3 November → Sonthofen

3 November → Innsbruck

4–5 November → Zurich

6–7 November → Sonthofen

8–9 November → Wertach

10–11 November → Sonthofen

12 November → Zurich

> [October: the narrator of *SG* travels to Vienna (**B.B.1**, p. 41);
> → Klosterneuburg for a day, p. 47
> → Venice (31 October–3 November), pp. 59, 72–73, and 79
> → Verona (3–5 November), pp. 83, 91, and 94
> → Innsbruck (6 November–?), p. 95]

November: probably starts writing a six-part collection of poetry entitled *Über das Land und das Wasser* (some of it is collected posthumously in **B.D.3**); he probably continues working on this until late 1983–early/mid-1984 since it includes **E.A.1** (i.e. **B.A.1**, pp. 36–68)

November/December: writes a paper on Herbeck (**D.17**) (report of 10 January 1981), a copy of which he sends to Navratil

1981

> [2 January: the narrator of *DA* claims to have flown to Newark, NJ, to visit Tante Fini and Onkel Kasimir; **B.B.2**, p. 103]

spring term: probably teaches the seminar on film with Elsaesser for the second time

mid-April: gives paper on 'Die Ästhetik des Bastlers (Herbeck)' at a conference of the Schweizerische Verband für Psychiatrie on 'Schizophrenie und Sprache' at the Psychiatrische Kantonsspital at Waldau, near Berne → Venice → Klagenfurt (*c.* 1–20 April)

28 September: interviews Lord (Solly) Zuckerman at UEA on the World War II area bombing campaign (to which Zuckerman had been opposed); cf. **D.18** and **D.66** (see p. 340 in the present volume and Fig. 8.1 on p. 212).

October: Vice-Chairman of UEA Admissions Committee (until summer term 1982)

27 October: tries to interest the Klaus Wagenbach Verlag in a book of essays on 20th-century Austrian literature

18 November: lectures on Döblin at the Goethe Institut London

28 December: arrives in New York; attends the International (MLA) Alfred Döblin-Colloquium in late December and gives a paper (**D.19**); makes contact with members of his mother's family in New Jersey who had emigrated to the USA in the mid-1920s and sees the photo of his Uncle Ambros dressed in Arab costume [cf. *DA*: **B.B.2**, p. 137] → London (3 January 1982)

1982

spring/summer term: begins to teach an independent course on Weimar film

12–18 April: attends Britisch-Deutsches Germanistentreffen in Berlin and gives a paper on Achternbusch (**D.20**); meets Jan Franksen (13 April)

10 May: death of Peter Weiss

autumn term: Chairman of German Sector (EUR) (until summer term 1983); publication of **D.18** in which, for the first time, he addresses the literary representation of the area bombing of Germany in World War II

1983

January: origins of his essay on 'Kafkas Evolutionsgeschichten' (**D.36**)

spring: works on the second (G. W. Steller) section of *NN*, 'Und blieb ich am äußersten Meer' (**E.A.1**)

spring–November: works on a film script of the life of Immanuel Kant for Sender Freies Berlin (RIAS), called 'Jetzund kömpt die Nacht herbey', three versions of which are extant in his papers in DLA. It is never broadcast, and over the next year he attempts, unsuccessfully, to place it with a range of magazines and even some small theatres.

29 March: sends a first version of 'Konstruktionen der Trauer' to *Deutsche Vierteljahresschrift* (politely refused) and then, in April, to *Der Deutschunterricht* (**D.24**)

5 May: in London

summer term: on study leave to research Modern German and Austrian literature with a grant of £650 from the BA; spends two weeks at the Adalbert Stifter-Archiv (Linz); visits Gerhard Roth near Graz; visits Peter Handke near Graz (probably between 14 and 16 June); lectures on Gerhard Roth and Gert Jonke at the Forum Stadtpark, Graz (report of 26 September 1983)

6–7 June: Aachen: lectures on Stifter and Handke at the TU (Techische Universität) (**D.26**)

8 June: → Mittelbergheim to see Jan Peter Tripp

9–10 June: → Freiburg i.Br.; delivers a provocative paper at the international Döblin conference (**D.21**)

10–12 June: → Zurich

13 June: → Innsbruck; lectures at the University on Stifter and Handke (D.26)

14–16 June: → Salzburg; meets Jochen Jung of Residenz Verlag

17 June: → Munich

c. 20 June: → Norwich

29 July: → Alsace; visits Jan Peter Tripp in Mittelbergheim

1 August: → Zurich

2 August: → Fribourg (Switzerland); lectures at the University there on Robert Walser →
Sonthofen (leaves 20 August)

21 August: → England

autumn term: becomes a member of UEA Senate (until summer term 1986) and attends
meetings regularly

*1983–86: During this period UEA is in serious financial deficit and subject to the continuing erosion of
its governmental income (1985–86). The Thatcher government, with Sir Keith Joseph (1918–94) as its
Secretary of State for Education and Science (1981–86), undertakes a major appraisal of the university
system, especially the role played by research, and starts to introduce the system of performance indicators
that would become known as the RAE (1985). The University Grants Commission issues its crucial
letters on funding in May 1986; and various universities, including UEA, are severely criticized
for their low completion rates for higher degrees and their alleged failure to guarantee the right of
speech to right-wing speakers (e.g. John Carlisle MP (b. 1942), who visited UEA on 24 April 1986).
Dr Richard Evans becomes Professor of European History in EUR having been turned down there
for a Readership the year before.*

30 December: suicide of his primary school teacher Armin Müller (the news reaches him
in January 1984)

   [This is what the narrator in *DA* also says; **B.B.2**, p. 41]

1984

3 January: Jochen Jung invites WGS to contribute an essay on Stifter to *Österreichische
Porträts* (writes it by 3 May (**D.27(a)**))

early: sends the second (G. W. Steller) section of *NN*, 'Und blieb ich am äußersten Meer',
to the Deutsche Verlags-Anstalt, Stuttgart, and then, on 25 July, to edition herodot,
Göttingen

28 March: → London (Austrian Institute)

   [early summer: the narrator of *DA* claims to have visited Ithaca, NY; **B.B.2**, p. 153]

11 June: in Denmark

October: completed parts of *NN* begin to appear in *Manuskripte* (**E.A.1–E.A.3**)

1985

28 February–2 March: attends Second Irish Symposium on Austrian Studies at Trinity
College, Dublin; lectures on Hofmannsthal's *Andreas* (**D.30**) → Norwich, 3 March

21 March: 'Grünewald slides' (entry in appointment diary)

10 May: Jochen Jung accepts *Die Beschreibung des Unglücks* (**A.3**) for publication in the
Residenz Verlag

19 May: → Zurich: lectures at the American School, 20 May, and the Collège Leman, 21 May

22 May: → Lausanne: lectures on 'Die Beschreibung des Unglücks: Zum Melancholie-problem in der österreichischen Literatur' in the Section Allemande of the Faculté des Lettres at the University

23 May: → Zurich

c. **24 May:** → Norwich

23 July: → Harwich

24 July: → Strasbourg

25–28 July: → Mittelbergheim (Alsace), to visit Jan Peter Tripp

28 July: → Stuttgart

29–30 July: → Salzburg

31 July–1 August: → Munich

2 August: → Norwich

8 August: applies to the University of Hamburg for leave to submit a *Habilitation* (second doctorate, which qualifies the holder for a chair in a German university). All documentation relating to this application has been lost, probably destroyed during internal relocation of departments.

1 September: publication of *Die Beschreibung des Unglücks* (**A.3**); sends a dedicated copy to Elias Canetti

autumn term: on study leave to research West German literature, with a grant of £1099 from the BA; probably gets to know the work of Jean Améry and writes 'Mit den Augen des Nachtvogels' (cf. **D.32** and **D.33**); begins 'Die Zerknirschung des Herzens' (**D.34**)

11 September: enters *Die Beschreibung des Unglücks* (**A.3**) as his *Habilitationsschrift* (his appointed examiners are Prof. Schwanitz, Prof. Schönert, Prof. Böhme, Prof. Schnuller, and Prof. Croplay)

September: reads from 'Wie der Schnee auf den Alpen' (**E.A.2**), later the first section of *NN*, at the Literarisches Colloquium, Am Sandwerder 5, Berlin

1 October: promoted to Senior Lecturer

17 October: participates, with Jochen Jung, Herta Firnberg, Heinz Fischer, Friedrich Achleitner, Hannes Androsch, and others in a two-hour TV panel discussion entitled 'Wer ist Österreich?' for *Café Central*, ORF's weekly programme on cultural and political matters, on the occasion of the publication of *Österreichische Porträts* (**D.27(a)**)

18 October: → Munich

November: contacts the Staatsarchiv in Munich with a query about the life and origins of Rudolf Eg[e]lhofer (1896-1919), the leader of the Red Army in Munich during the Munich Soviet of 1919 (executed 3 May 1919)

1986

early: completes 'Die Zerknirschung des Herzens' (**D.34**)

[?]: lectures on 'Hermann Broch zwischen Heimat und Exil' (cf. **D.37**) at the University of Lausanne

26 February: in Hamburg to attend the Colloquium in respect of his *Habilitation*

March: applies to the DAAD for a grant to spend the period 17 July–30 August in Germany (see below)

16 April: *Habilitation* at the University of Hamburg

6 May: *Études Germaniques* accepts his article on Jean Améry (**D.33(a)**)

17 July–30 August: in Germany working on two projects: (1) essays on post-1945 German literature (with special reference to Jean Améry); (2) preparatory work and conversations re the conference on contemporary German drama due to take place at UEA 30 March–1 April 1987 (see Appendix 6.1, pp. 184–86)

27 August: broadcasts a radio essay on Adalbert Stifter on ORF

21–30 September: in West Germany

25 September: Würzburg: 27 September, lectures on 'Jean Améry's Stellung in der deutschen Nachkriegsliteratur' at the University of Würzburg

28 September: → Frankfurt a.M.

30 September: → Norwich

autumn term: becomes member of EUR Promotions Committee and Planning Committee; also Chairman of the Working Party on Teaching Rationalization

25 November: writes the report for the DAAD on his six-week stay in West Germany (17 July–30 August)

1987

8 January: Jochen Jung invites him to contribute to *Träume* (c.f. **F.C.3**)

30 March–1 April: chairs a conference on Contemporary German Drama at UEA (see Appendix 6.1) and contributes a paper on Herbert Achternbusch (**D.38**)

11 April: death of Primo Levi (probable suicide)

23 July: → Munich: research trip (with a grant of £1021 from the BA) to research 'Heimat and Exil: Austrian literature of the 19th and 20th centuries'

24–25 July: → Salzburg

26 July–1 August: → Vienna

4 August: → Venice → Milan, where a new passport is issued by the German Consulate

5 August: → Verona

6 August: → Riva

7 August: → Innsbruck

8–10 August: → Sonthofen

11–12 August: → Munich (Staatsarchiv); reads the file on Rudolf Eg[e]lhofer [Pol. Dir. München 10040])

[summer (late July): the narrator of *SG* travels back to Vienna
→ Venice; **B.B.1**, pp. 97 and 99
→ Verona → Desenzano (1 August), pp. 101–02
→ Limone sul Garda by bus (1–3 August), pp. 101 and 121
→ Desenzano by bus → Milan by train (3–4 August), pp. 121–27
→ Verona (4–6 August), pp. 136–37 and 158
stays on the Continent for the rest of the year, p. 295]

28 August: broadcast on Adalbert Stifter (ORF, Vienna)

autumn term: Chairman of German Sector (EUR)

1 October: promoted to Reader

night of 15–16 October: a hurricane hits southern England and does great damage, bringing down many trees in WGS's garden [cf. **B.B.3**, pp. 329–33] (see also Fig. II.2 and D.67)

late autumn: sends the MS of *NN* to the Greno Verlag; Franz Greno reads it, consults with Hans Magnus Enzensberger and decides to publish it

[October: the narrator of *SG* spends the month in Bruneck]

[November: → W. (by bus), **B.B.1**, p. 195, via Innsbruck, Reutte, Weißbach, Haller, Tannheim, Schattwald, and Oberjoch, p. 201
→ W. (on foot) for the first time in *c.* 30 years, p. 210
early December: returns home via the Hook of Holland, pp. 286–87
→ London, pp. 292–95]

2 December: makes the case (successfully) for Michael Hamburger to be awarded an Honorary DLitt at UEA Congregation on 30 June 1988 (see Part II of the present volume, p. 346–47)

1988

10–11 January: → Munich; meets Hans Magnus Enzensberger and works in the Staatsbibliothek

12 January: → Passau; lectures at the University on Jean Améry and Austria (D.42)

13 January: → Munich

14 January: → Norwich

spring term: on study leave to 'complete a further section of a book on C19th and C20th Austrian literature, one examining the foundering of the "new world" dreams shared by Sealsfield, Lenau and Kurnberger' (letter of confirmation to WGS, 24 February 1987); spends it in Norwich and Vienna

18 February: lectures at Magdalen College, Oxford, on post-1945 German Literature at the invitation of Dr Richard Sheppard, who left UEA in September 1987 to become Fellow and Tutor in German at Magdalen College

March: first part of *SG* appears in *Manuskripte* (E.B.1)

4 April: → Straelen: 5 April, visits the Europäisches Übersetzer-Kollegium (EÜK), Kuhstraße 15–17 (founded 10 January 1978), probably in connection with his plans for the BCLT at UEA

6 April: → Düsseldorf

8 April: → Nördlingen; visits Greno Verlag and signs a contract re *NN* dated 5 April

9 April: → Norwich

June: first part of *DA* appears in *Manuskripte* (**E.B.12**)

summer: publication of *Nach der Natur* (**B.A.1**)

23 September: together with A. S. Byatt, speaks at an event organized by the Arts Council in London in connection with the setting up of the BCLT at UEA

1 October: promoted to Professor of European Literature (UEA)

October: sends a copy of *NN* to Elias Canetti

early December: attends a conference devoted to Jean Améry organized by Irène Heidelberger-Leonard at the Université Libre de Bruxelles and gives a paper on Améry and Primo Levi (**D.43**)

1989

Sets up the BCLT at UEA and becomes its first Director (to 1995): George Hyde is Deputy Director and Adam Czerniawski first Translator in Residence; Czerniawski later becomes Associate Director; Anthony Vivis becomes Translator in Residence (1992–93)

5 January: attends Arts Council meeting about BCLT

27–28 January: in Brussels

*12 February: death of Thomas Bernhard (cf. **D.48**)*

1 March: makes an application for Arts Council funding for the BCLT

3 April: → Vienna

4 April: takes part in a broadcast radio discussion on Joseph Roth with H. Parschalk for the ORF

5 April: takes part in a symposium on Joseph Roth (cf. **D.47**) organized by the Österreichische Gesellschaft für Literatur, Palais Wilczek, Herrengasse 5

7 April: → Salzburg

13 April: → London

16 April: presents *NN* in *Ex Libris* on ORF

4–6 May: chairs conference on contemporary German drama at UEA

27 May: interviewed for a TV programme entitled 'Joseph Roth: Der Autor und seine Zeit' on ORF

3 September: in Berlin [?], taking part in a conference organised by the DAAD on contemporary German literature, where he meets Professor Manfred Durzak

12 September: → Strasbourg (probably to visit Jan Peter Tripp at Mittelbergheim)

14 September: → Passau

15–19 September: → Wertach

19–21 September: → Sonthofen → Norwich

autumn term: Richard Evans becomes Professor of History at Birkbeck College in the University of London

September–October: the Greno Verlag sells its imprint Die Andere Bibliothek to Eichborn Verlag; the rights of *NN* revert to WGS in 1991

18–19 October: → London

20 October: → Zurich

21 October: → Lucerne

22 October: → Zurich → Norwich

9 November: fall of the Berlin Wall

mid-November: *SG* under active consideration by the Eichborn Verlag

15–17 December: in Stuttgart

29 December: in London

1990

22 February: reads from *SG* to an audience of six in the Taylor Institution, Oxford, at the invitation of Dr Richard Sheppard → London (23 February)

March: publication of *Schwindel. Gefühle.* (**B.B.1**)

March: reads 'Ein Kaddisch für Österreich: Über Joseph Roth' (**D.47**) in Sender Freies Berlin (RIAS)

13 March: suicide of the psychologist Bruno Bettelheim (referred to in several early interviews)

17 March: → Munich

18–20 March: → Vienna

20–22 March: → Sonthofen

23 March: → Norwich

12 April: MS of 'Das vorvergangene Jahr' ready for publication in *Der Komet* (**F.A.3**)

4–6 May: Zurich

22 May: interviewed on and reads from *SG* for DRS (Swiss radio), Studio Zürich

30/31 May: interviewed by ZDF

summer term: on study leave intending at first to write a book on post-war German literature with particular reference to Alfred Andersch. Instead, he finishes work on *UH* and produces a research paper on contemporary Austrian writing (probably **D.51**) with a grant of £1154 from the BA (report of 13 May 1991)

26 June: → Klagenfurt (Hotel Moser Verdino, Domgasse 2); competes for the Ingeborg Bachmann-Prize there (2 July): awarded to Birgit Vanderbeke

27 June: participates in various ORF programmes dealing with the prize competition

summer: possible first visit to Corsica (cf. **J.37**, p. 97) [or 1991 (RWS)]

2 August: interviewed on and reads from *SG* for ORF

6 August: presents *SG* on 3-sat

18 September: → Wuppertal; reading in Buchhandlung Schöningh, Friedrich-Ebert-Straße 17

20–21 September: → Straelen to visit the Europäisches Übersetzer-Kollegium

19 September: Dutch translation rights of *SG* sold to Van Gennep

18 October: in Cambridge

19 October: gives paper entitled 'Die Errettung der Heimat durch den bösen Blick: Ein Kapitel aus der neuesten österreichischen Literatur' at a symposium in honour of Irma Frowen, 'Heimat in Wort', at the Institute of Germanic Studies (London) (**D.51(a)**)

24–25 October: in Graz

26–27 October: → Vienna

autumn: beginning of the seminar series at UEA 'Writing in the Shadow of the Shoah': organized by WGS, it involves a wide range of speakers and continues until autumn 1992 (see Appendix 6.2, pp. 187–88)

autumn: first meeting with Michael Hulse when Hulse is a guest lecturer at the BCLT

7 November: in the Allgäu in connection with filming for ZDF's *Aspekte-Literaturpreis*

9 November: Tübingen: reads from *SG* in Reinhard Schulte's Buchhandlung, Gartenstraße 32

10 November: → Sonthofen

11 November: → Norwich

28 November: presents *SG* in TV programme *Aspekte* (ZDF)

December: proposed for ZDF's *Aspekte-Literaturpreis* (awarded to Ulrich Woelk for *Freigang*)

10 December: reading tour to promote *SG* → Frankfurt a.M. (Theater am Turm, Bleichstraße 57; interviewed for ZDF)

11 December: → Schwäbisch-Gmünd (Buchhandlung Schmidt, Ledergasse 2)

12 December: → Reutlingen (Jacob-Fetzer Buchhandlung)

13 December: → Essen

14 December: → Cologne (Buchhandlung Klaus Bittner, Albertusstraße 6)

15–16 December: → Gütersloh area

17 December: → Paderborn

c. 18 December: → Norwich

16 December: Pan Books decline to commission an English translation of *SG*

1991

18 February: sends a polemical essay on Jurek Becker to Irène Heidelberger-Leonard for a book she is editing on Becker, which she decides not to include (copy in DLA; recently published by Uwe Schütte (**D.53**); see also Chapter 6 in the present volume)

1 March: publication of *Unheimliche Heimat* (**A.5**)

19 March: Weidenfeld and Nicolson decline to commission English translation of *SG*

25–27 March: lectures on peripherality as a stimulus to creativity at a conference on contemporary Austrian writing at Sheffield University

12 April: → Prague

7 May: applies for scholarship from the *Deutscher Literaturfonds* for January–July 1992 in order to work on *DA*

29 May: Victor Gollancz declines to commision English translation of *SG*

> [end June: the narrator of *DA* visits Bad Kissingen (25 June) and Steinach travelling via Amsterdam, Cologne, Frankfurt a.M., Aschaffenburg and Gemünden; **B.B.2**, pp. 327 and 330]

2–8 July: → Sonthofen

11 September: death of Ernst Herbeck (cf. **D.56***)*

> [mid-September 1991: the narrator of *DA* visits Deauville; **B.B.2**, p. 171]

October: an early version of part of Part v of *RS* appears in *Neue Zürcher Zeitung (Folio)* as 'Postkarte: Waterloo' (**F.C.5**) (see Part II of the present volume, pp. 334–35)

27 November: addresses the Translators Association at the Society of Authors (on the need for more literary translation in English)

29 November: DTV (Munich) expresses an interest in producing a paperback edition of *BU* and *UH*

17 December: receives the Fedor-Malchow-Lyrikpreis (awarded by the Hamburgische Kultur-Stiftung) in the Literaturhaus, Hamburg, Schwanenwik 38

18 December: → Kiel; reads from *SG* in the Kulturviertel im Sophienhof, Sophienblatt 30

1992

early January: applies to the DAAD for a grant to spend the period May–June in Germany working on two projects: (1) essays on Jurek Becker (**D.53**) and Alfred Andersch (**D.57**); (2) consultations with colleagues in Düsseldorf and Munich on other areas of academic work — e.g. literary translation — currently being undertaken at UEA

15 January: spends the day working on 'der Tübinger Arbeit über Europa' (**D.55**)

3 February: → Frankfurt a.M. → Tübingen

4 February: gives a paper at the two-day 1. Tübinger Literaturforum, organized by Prof. Jürgen Wertheimer of the Deutsches Seminar, Wilhelmstraße 50, on 'Europäische Kultur: Chimäre oder Wirklichkeit' (**D.55**)

5 February: → Frankfurt a.M. → Norwich

7 February: finishes work on 'Ambros Adelwarth' (produces typescript 7–8 March)

10 February: meeting with Michael Hulse

c. **5 March**: awarded a grant by the DAAD, partly to work on Andersch and Becker

28 March: → Germany → Langenau, to read in the Pflegehofsaal, Kirchgasse 9

1 April: → Ulm

3 April: → Strasbourg

4–5 April: → Mittelbergheim, to visit Jan Peter Tripp

6 April: → Frankfurt a.M. → Norwich

9 April: → Arts Council meeting in London

20 April: declines (by phone) to take part in a seminar entitled 'Widerstände: Formen und Fiktionen' being organized by the Forum Stadtpark Graz for 22–24 October

24 April: in London to look at paintings by Mantegna at the Royal Academy exhibition

May: interview with Piet de Moor (**J.4**; see the present volume, pp. 350–54)

summer term: on study leave 'to complete a book on Jewish / German exiles'; probably writes his controversial essay on Alfred Andersch (**D.57**)

August: writes the report for the **DAAD** on his nine-week stay in West Germany Easter– early August

[summer: Austerlitz has a breakdown; **B.B.4**, p. 202]

[*c.* 9 August: the narrator of *RS* begins his walk through the Suffolk near the end of the 'dog days' (*c.* 9 July–11 August) and exactly a year before his hospitalization (**B.B.3**, p. 9), starting with a trip to Somerleyton and Lowestoft, pp. 41–62]

As a matter of meteorological fact, August 1992 was the wettest August in England and Wales since 1956 and the coldest August there since 1988.

September: publication of *DA*

autumn: after completing the Andersch essay, the success of *DA*, and the start of work on *RS*, probably gives up his long-standing idea of publishing a book on German post-war literature with particular reference to exiled Jews

30 October: → Munich

1–2 November: → Sonthofen

3–4 November: → Munich (reads from *DA* in Autorenbuchhandlung, Wilhelmstraße 41)

5–8 November: → Frankfurt a.M.

9 November: → London

16 November: Arts Council, London

4–5 December: 'European Writers' Forum' at UEA, under the auspices of the BCLT with funding from the Arts Council; including a reading by Hans-Magnus Enzensberger (see Appendix 6.3, pp. 189–90)

1993

1 January: visits Lowestoft [cf. **B.B.3**, pp. 55–62]

14 January: *DA* discussed by Hellmuth Karasek, Sigrid Löffler, and Barbara Sichtermann in Marcel Reich-Ranicki's *Das Literarische Quartett* (ZDF)

23–31 January: reading tour in Germany and Switzerland to promote *DA* → Bremen (Literaturtage)

24 January: → Cologne

25 January: interviewed for WDR; Buchhandlung Klaus Bittner, Albertusstraße 6

26 January: → Schwetzingen (Stadtbibliothek, Kronenstraße 1)

27 January: → Langenau (Pflegehofsaal, Kirchgasse 9; Buchhandlung Mahr, Lange Straße 8)

28 January → Frankfurt a.M. (Literaturhaus, Schöne Aussicht 2)

29 January → Freiburg i.Br. (Buchhandlung Herder, Kaiser-Joseph-Straße 180)

30 January: → Zurich: Swiss radio (SR DRS); Schauspielhaus-Keller, Rämisstraße 34

31 January: → Amsterdam → Norwich

9 February: probably interviewed by Sigrid Löffler (**J.7**)

21 February: visits Somerleyton [cf. **B.B.3**, pp. 41–55]

late February (?): interviewed by Sven Boedecker (**J.5**)

3–5 March: in Hamburg [?] being interviewed on *DA* by Karin Reiss for NDR TV (probably shown on 18 March)

11–c. 19 March: reading tour to promote *DA*

12 March: → Amsterdam → Berlin (Literaturhaus, Fasanenstraße 23)

15 March: → Wiesbaden (3rd Wiesbadener Büchertage): interview with ZDF and reading in the Pariser Hoftheater, Spiegelgasse 9, in conjunction with the Buchhandlung 'Vaternahm'

16 March: → Saarbrücken: Schloßkeller, Schloßplatz, in the context of a Forum organized by the *Volkshochschule* entitled 'Neue Literatur'

17 March: Bill Swainson (Harvill) sends *DA* (recommended by Adam Czerniawski) to Michael Hulse to read

17 March: → Hanover (Georgsbuchhandlung, Georgstraße 52)

18 March: → Münster (Pumpenhaus, Gartenstraße 123); interviewed for *NDR*

21 March: interview with Martin Chalmers of *New Statesman*

27–31 March: takes part in a seminar organized by Bertelsmann

[March 1993: the narrator of *RS* is in Berlin; **B.B.3**, pp. 275–76]

spring: publishes highly polemical and controversial essay on Alfred Andersch (**D.57**), probably as a result of reading Stephan Reinhardt's biography (1990); Reinhardt's rejoinder exists in the DLA *Nachlass*

c. 25 April–2 May: reading tour to promote *DA* → Amsterdam → Frankfurt a.M.

27 April: → Coburg (Buchhandlung Riemann, Markt 9) → Frankfurt a.M.

28 April: → Kiel (Buchhandlung Stöberecke, Blücherplatz 20)

29 April: → Hamburg (Literaturhaus, Schwanenwik 38)

30 April: → Düsseldorf: Buchhandlung 'Literatur bei Rudolf Müller', Neustraße 38, Düsseldorf Altstadt (reads from 'Max Aurach')

1 May: → Amsterdam → Norwich

early May: nominated by Hans Magnus Enzensberger as one of three German authors for the European Prize for Literature, awarded in December to the Dutch writer Cees Nooteboom

14 June: interviewed on Swiss radio for *Literaturclub* (DRS) on his plans for *RS*, during the writing of which he avidly reads the work of Sir Thomas Browne (which he may have first encountered as early as 1985 (**J.34**, p. 159))

16 June: meets Arthur Williams (EUR external examiner for German, 1993–96) at UEA

late June / early July: interviewed by Anneriek de Jong in Amsterdam (**J.9**)

16 July: interview with Ralph Schock, Saarländischer Rundfunk, preceded by reading from *SG*

17–24 July: → Switzerland

17 July: → Zurich

18–19 July: → Bregenz; 18 July: 4th Videoopernwerkstatt der Bregenzer Festspiele: reads from *DA* in the Kuppelsaal, Landesbibliothek, Fluherstraße 4; broadcast on ORF, on 31 July in the context of a discussion on 'Heimat und Fremde'

9–30 August: Norfolk and Norwich Hospital (Ingham Ward, Room 21) for a back operation (25 August). In J.34 (pp. 158–59), this is attributed to the effects of his peregrination along the Suffolk coast.

> [*c.* 9 August: the narrator of *RS* is admitted to hospital in Norwich and begins *RS*; **B.B.3**, pp. 9–10. (The date is also that of the death of Janine Dakyns in 1994.)]

13 September: Arts Council Literary Panel (BCLT?)

14 September: Niels Brunse asked to translate *DA* into Danish

autumn semester 1993–94: on sick leave following his back operation

UEA begins its new MA course in Literary Translation in EUR, with input from BCLT

1 October: → Wuppertal → Aachen → Detmold (2 October)

5 November: → Amsterdam → The Hague

6 November: → Frankfurt a.M.→ Oldenburg

7 November: competes for the Preis der LiteraTour Nord by reading from *DA* in Oldenburg and Bremen

8 November: → Hamburg

9 November: → Hanover

11–13 November: → Freiburg i.Br. to take part in the 7. Freiburger Literaturgespräch ('Die Vergangenheit der Zukunft'), in the Neuer Ratssaal of the Rathaus alongside 11 other writers (including Ruth Klüger, who gives the first reading)

12 November: reads from *DA*, probably 'Ambros Adelwarth'

15 November: Michael Hulse commissioned to translate *DA* into English

10 December: → H[eidel]berg [?] → England (*c.* 17 December)

1994

spring semester: on study leave 'to continue research on post-war and contemporary German literature' (letter of confirmation to WGS, 4 June 1993); instead he continues to research and write *RS* (completed early 1995) (report of 14 February 1996)

early February: awarded the Berliner Literaturpreis (Stiftung Preußische Seehandlung) together with Jürgen Becker, Hugo Dittberner, Norbert Gstrein, Brigitte Kronauer, Reinhard Lettau, and Erica Pedretti

11 April: death of Michael Parkinson (EUR) [cf. **B.B.3**, pp. 12–13]

26 April: George Steiner gives the inaugural (BCLT) St Jerome Lecture ('An Exact Art') in the Sainsbury Centre for the Visual Arts, UEA

spring: Michael Hulse begins to translate *DA* into English

16–18 June: competes for the Johannes Bobrowski-Medaille zum Berliner Literaturpreis with the other six prizewinners during a two-day long read-in at the Literarisches Colloquium, Am Sandwerder 5, Berlin; awarded to WGS and Erica Pedretti (18

June). After the ceremony, takes the medal to the place on the Wannsee where Kleist committed suicide and throws it in ('I didn't know what else to do with that bloody great chunk of metal': WGS to RWS) — the medal is not in the *Nachlass*. (See also Chapter 3 in the present volume, p. 121)

1 August: the School of Modern Languages and European History (EUR) is reconfigured as the School of Modern Languages and European Studies (EUR) following the establishment of a separate School of History

9 August: death of Janine Dakyns (EUR) [cf. **B.B.3**, pp. 13–17]

6 **November**: awarded the Preis der LiteraTour Nord in the DG-Bank, Berliner Allee 5, Hanover

1995

1 **January**: acquires a reader's ticket for the Public Record Office in Kew, London (now the National Archives): valid for three years but never renewed; probably reads files relating to the liberation of KZ Belsen

3 **March**: takes part in a meeting at the London GI (organized by the BCLT) to discuss recognition of literary translation at the next research assessment (RAE)

29 **March**: sends a letter 'to those who attended the meeting in London, to those who have already expressed their support, and to names likely to be sympathetic to our request' asking for expressions of support for a document that could be sent to the Chairs of the RAE assessment panels

[13 April (Maundy Thursday): the narrator of *RS* has completed writing up his notes and states that Clara's father — i.e. his father-in-law — has died on the same day; **B.B.3**, pp. 364–66. The date is also that beneath the alleged signature of Roger Casement from 1916 in *RS* (**B.B.3**, p. 168), one day before the actual death of Sebald's maternal grandfather in 1956, and two days after the actual death of Michael Parkinson in 1994.]

27–30 **April**: in Wolfenbüttel at the first of a series of annual literary colloquia convened by the Stiftung Niedersachsen and chaired by Heinz Ludwig Arnold (together with Marcel Beyer, Iain Galbraith, Michael Hamburger, Sarah Kirsch, Sten Nadolny, and Austrian poet Peter Waterhouse)

28 **April**: 'Hommage für Michael Hamburger': public reading evening in the Augusteerhalle (Herzog-August-Bibliothek), where Hamburger reads passages from two longer poems ('Travelling' and 'In Suffolk') and Waterhouse reads his German translations. WGS gives his first public reading of his description of a visit to Hamburger's house from the MS of *RS*.

12–14 **May**: Amsterdam → Frankfurt a.M. → Würzburg → Bamberg

13 **May**: reading at a Handke conference at Bamberg University during the 'Frühjahrs-buchwochen'

June: finishes writing *RS*

3–17 **September**: visits Corsica to research a (never-completed) book, some parts of which appeared in *CS* and some parts of which have appeared in *Wandernde Schatten: W. G. Sebalds Unterwelt*, the catalogue accompanying the exhibition in Marbach's Literatur-museum der Moderne in 2008–2009 (**B.D.2**, pp. 7–52, and **F.D.2**, pp. 129–209)

October: visits his colleague Dr Stephen Wilson, the author of *Feuding, Conflict and Banditry in Nineteenth-Century Corsica* (1988), at home in Norwich, and mentions his visit to Corsica on leaving; later acknowledges Dr Wilson's book as a major source of his own knowledge about Corsica

October: publication of *Die Ringe des Saturn* (*RS*)

27 October–4 November: reading tour to launch *RS*:

28 October: Amsterdam → Hanover

29 October: Schieder-Schwalenberg (near Detmold), 'IV. Literaturbegegnung Schwalenberg' (**E.B.21**)

30 October → Cologne (Lengfeld'sche Buchhandlung, Kolpingplatz 1)

31 October → Aachen

1 November → Frankfurt a.M. (Huss'sche Universitäts-Buchhandlung, Kiesstraße 41)

2 November → Schwetzingen (Stadtbibliothek, Kronenstraße 1)

3 November → Freiburg i.Br. (Buchhandlung Rombach, Bertoldstraße 10)

4 November[?] → Basle → Amsterdam

17–21 November: attends the annual book fair (*Bogforum*) in Copenhagen to promote the Danish edition of *DA*. The major Danish TV station DR-TV records an interview with WGS by Niels Brunse in its temporary studio at the *Bogforum*, but the interview is never broadcast.

19 November: Michael Hulse sends final typescript of his translation of *DA* (*The Emigrants*) to Harvill

1996

8–13 January: Hamburg → Oldenburg → Flensburg → Kiel → Lübeck (interviews and readings)

22–30 March: Munich, Sonthofen, Lindau (interviews)

25 March: reads from *RS* in the hall of his old school in Oberstdorf

May: in Bamberg [?] (cf. **F.A.6**)

20–29 June: Frankfurt a.M. → Speyer (reading) → Freiburg i.Br. → Biel/Bienne → Zug (reading) → Zurich (25 June; reading at ETH) → Winterthur (reading) → Wangen im Allgäu (27 June; reading and seminar, Öffentliche Bücherei, Kornhaus); ferry to Romanshorn → Zurich → England

June–September: publication of *The Emigrants* (first book by WGS to appear in English translation)

1–8 September: Corsica

12 October: elected as a corresponding member of the Deutsche Akademie für Sprache und Dichtung (speech of acceptance given on 24 October 1997 in the Orangerie, Bessunger Straße 44, Darmstadt (**D.64**), followed by a speech by H. C. Artmann, 1997 winner of the Büchner-Prize)

November: work starts on the English translation of *RS* (completed September 1997)

28 November: possibly interviewed for *Zwischentöne*, Deutschlandfunk

29 November: Susan Sontag reviews the English translation of *DA* very favourably in *TLS*; her positive recommendation of the book prior to publication probably draws WGS to the attention of the Wylie Agency

[December: the narrator of *A* meets Austerlitz after a gap of two decades when he goes to seek specialist medical help in London after nearly losing the sight of his right eye; **B.B.4**, p. 50]

late 1996 / early 1997: Michael Hulse begins to translate *RS* into English

mid-December: gives up working on the Corsica project

17 December: opening of the Bibliothèque François Mitterand, France's new Bibliothèque nationale, on the site of Lager Austerlitz

1997

Invited to move to the University of Hamburg in order to found and run an institute for creative writing: considers the offer for nine months before turning it down, deciding that he cannot go back to Germany to live

24 January: Alexander Smoltczyk publishes 'Die Türme des Schweigens', an illustrated article on the redevelopment of the site of the Lager Austerlitz, in *Zeitmagazin*, 5, pp. 10–17

13 March (Jewish Book Week): → London to receive the *Jewish Quarterly* / Wingate Prize for Literature (1996) for *The Emigrants*; see *Jewish Quarterly*, 44.2 (Summer 1997), 56

14 March: death of Jurek Becker

[19 March: the narrator of *A* meets Austerlitz in his house in Alderney Street, London; **B.B.4**, pp. 169–70 and 236]

21 April: → Konstanz → Fellbach, near Stuttgart (22–24 April)

22 April: receives the Mörike-Preis in the Fellbach Rathaus, Großer Saal; reads from *DA* and nominates Wolfgang Schlüter for the *Förderpreis* (**D.62/D.62(a)**) (see Fig. 7.4)

23 April: Fellbach Stadtbücherei, 'Lebens-Entwürfe: Reading and Conversation with Wolfgang Schlüter'

25 April: returns to England via Konstanz

May: in Bamberg [?] (cf. **F.A.6**)

20 May: reading in Münster (Westfälisches Landesmuseum, Domplatz 10)

June: nominated for the Heinrich-Böll-Preis; receives it in Cologne on 27 November

21 June: reading in Braunschweig (Volkshochschule, Alte Waage 15), in a series entitled 'Poeta doctus' organized by the city's Literaturbüro

10 July: interview with James Wood at the PEN American Centre, 588 Broadway, New York (**J.16**)

autumn semester: on study leave 'to complete a book on Jewish / German exiles and to work on a translation of *Die Ringe des Saturn*' (letter of confirmation to WGS of 19 March 1996); drops the first part of the plan, completes the second, and works on *LiL* (**A.6**) (report of 3 March 1998)

3–9 September: in Sonthofen

mid-September: English translation of *RS* complete

[September: the narrator of *A* is invited to visit Austerlitz in Paris; **B.B.4**, p. 358]

4–18 October: reading tour in the USA to promote *The Emigrants* (organized by the Goethe-Institut)

4 October: → Amsterdam

5–7 October: → New York

6–7 October: stays at Gramercy Park Hotel, 2 Lexington Avenue, New York; reads at Goethe-Institut (6 October) and PEN (7 October); meets publishers at New Directions; meeting with Andrew Wylie

8–10 October: → Chicago

11–17 October: → Boston and elsewhere in New England

14 October: reads in the Goethe-Institut, 170 Beacon Street, where he is introduced to Saul Bellow and Keith Botsford, editor of *The Republic of Letters*, by Michael Hulse (cf. **E.B.4**, **E.B.23** and **E.B.39**)

15 October: reads at Holy Cross College, Worcester, MA

16 October: interviewed by Eleanor Wachtel (**J.17**) and reads at Brown University, Providence, RI

17 October: reads at Yale University, New Haven, CT

18 October: → Amsterdam → Norwich

23–26 October: in Frankfurt (discussions with Michael Krüger) → Darmstadt for the autumn meeting of the Deutsche Akademie für Sprache und Dichtung, to which he is elected on 24 October; reads out **D.64**

30 October: → Zurich: first of three *Poetikvorlesungen* arranged by the Deutsches Seminar of the University of Zurich. The lectures take place in the Zürcher Puppentheater, Stadelhoferstrasse 12, at 8.15 p.m. on 30 October, 13 November, and 4 December; a version of the lectures appears as 'Operation Gomorrah' in the *Neue Zürcher Zeitung* on 22–23 November 1997 (**D.65bis**), and they also form the basis of *LuL* (**A.7**). Gives two four-hour seminars, on 31 October and 1 November

2 November: → Norwich

13 November: → Zurich; second *Poetikvorlesung*, plus two four-hour seminars, on 14 and 15 November

14 November: interview with Christian Scholz (**J.18/J.18(a)**)

16–*c*. 23 November: Norwich

c. 23–*c*. 28 November: in Germany

24 November: → Berlin; readings in the studio of the Literarisches Colloquium, Am Sandwerder 5, Berlin, and Deutschlandfunk, Haus des Rundfunks, Masurenallee 8–14; programme 'Der Schriftsteller W. G. Sebald' broadcast 26 November (?) on Deutschlandfunk, featuring interview with WGS by Heinrich Detering, Gustav Seibt and Denis Scheck

26 November: → Lüneburg; reads from *RS* in the Heine-Haus, Am Ochsenmarkt 2

27 November: → Cologne to receive the Heinrich Böll-Preis der Stadt Köln in the Historisches Rathaus, Portalsgasse: he reads out **D.66** (see Part Two of present volume, pp. 338-42)

28 November: reads from *RS* in the Zentralbibliothek, Josef-Haubrich-Hof

29 November: → Norwich

4 December: → Zurich

5–6 December: third *Poetikvorlesung*, plus two four-hour seminars; [*Weltwoche* interview?]

8 December: → Norwich

23 December: in Detmold

24 December: → Schieder-Schwalenberg [?]

late 1997 / early 1998: Actes Sud asks Patrick Charbonneau to translate *DA* into French

1998

3–4 January: in London (meets Stephen Watts, visits East End)

22–25 January: → Detmold (exhibition, Literaturverein) → Walberberg (between Cologne and Bonn), as a special guest of the British Council at its annual Walberberg Seminar in a Dominican monastery. Founded by Malcolm Bradbury in 1986, the Walberberg Seminar is the British Council's largest and oldest annual overseas literary seminar. The seminar topic for 1998 is 'Translation', chaired by A. S. Byatt: WGS attends on 24–25 January together with his translator Michael Hulse.

24 January: reads from his works in German; Hulse then reads the English translation; reading is followed by panel discussion on 'German Literature in Britain', chaired by German translator Melanie Walz and Scottish poet and translator Iain Galbraith. Other writers attending the seminar include Philip Hensher, John Fuller, A. L. Kennedy, Lawrence Norfolk, and Tibor Fischer. (See Chapter 7 in the present volume and Fig. 7.5.)

25 January: → Norwich

26 January: agreement with the Wylie Agency over the publication and promotion of *A*

6/7 February: interview with James Atlas (**J.22**)

8 February: interview with Boyd Tonkin (Literary Editor of *The Independent*) (**J.23**)

6–7 March: in Sheffield

22 March: writes the introduction to *LiL*

April: signs a contract with the Hanser Verlag

2–4 April: → Amsterdam → Antwerp (Breendonk)

5 April: → Stuttgart

6 April: reads from *RS* in the Buchhandlung, Wendelin Niedlich, Schmale Straße 14, Stuttgart

6–7 April: → Sonthofen

8 April: → Karlsruhe

9 April: → Darmstadt: reading in the Glückert-Haus, Alexandraweg 23

10 April: → Norwich

26–28 April: London → Manchester; meets Peter Jordan, Portico Library

11 May: elected a member of the Bayerische Akademie der schönen Künste

15 May: → Amsterdam → [Rotterdam (TV interview?)]

16 May: → Heidelberg (3rd Heidelberger Literaturtage, 14–17 May); reads from Part IX of *RS* in the 'Spiegelzelt' on the Universitätsplatz in the Heidelberg Altstadt

17 May: interviewed by Sarah Kafatou (**J.24**) in the Renaissance Hotel

c. 18 May: → Norwich

1 June: granted study leave for autumn semester 2000 'to complete a second volume of essays on post-war German writing to include Jean Améry, Peter Weiss, Primo Levi and Wolfgang Hildesheimer, and research in Germany leading to further Projects' (letter of confirmation to WGS of 1 June 1998)

2–4 June: in London

5 June: → Brighton

11–13 June: external examiner in Leeds

15 June: → Hanover

17 June: → Norwich

23 June: Amsterdam; interview with Michaël Zeeman (**J.26**), broadcast on VPRO (Netherlands), 12 July

10 July: 40-minute interview with Peter Morgan for Channel Four News (**J.27**) as part of a series on 'the precarious nature of Britishness' (edited down to five minutes and broadcast before end of July)

14 September: publication of *Logis in einem Landhaus* (*LiL*) (**A.6**)

October: Patrick Charbonneau completes the French translation of *DA*

24–31 October: reading tour to promote *LiL* (during which he reads up to five novels by Giorgio Bassani in German translation) → Amsterdam → Zurich

26 October: → Lucerne (Bücher-apéro im Hofgebäude, Raeber Bücher, Frankenstraße 7–9)

27 October: → Zurich (Buchhandlung Zum Elsässer, Limmatquai 18)

28 October: → Düsseldorf (Buchhandlung 'Literatur bei Rudolf Müller', Düsseldorf-Altstadt, Neustraße 38)

29 October: → Hamburg (Heine Buchhandlung, Schlüterstraße 1)

30 October: → Frankfurt a.M. (Literaturhaus, Schöne Aussicht 2) → Mainz (visits Gutenberg Museum); flies Frankfurt a.M. → Amsterdam

31 October: → Norwich

6 December: → Paris (7–8 December), probably in connection with the imminent publication of *Les Émigrants* (**B.B.2.7**); meets Charbonneau for the first time, together with Martina Wachendorff of Actes Sud, in a hotel in the Quartier Latin

1999

[?]: awarded the *Prix du Meilleur Livre Étranger* (category 'Essai')

9–14 January: → Zurich → Sonthofen

18 January: in London

9 February: reading from *DA* at UEA Drama Studio and conversation with Jon Cook,

as part of the Centre for the Creative and Performing Arts 'Visiting Writers' series (J.30) (see Part II of the present volume, pp. 356–63)

13–16 February: → Amsterdam → Frankfurt a.M. (Eichborn)

15 February: → Hanover; Literarischer Salon, Königsworther Platz 1; reading, probably from *LuL*, and discussion 'Erinnerung, Trauma und Gewalt' with the academic Reinhold Görling

16 February: → Norwich

5–8 March: → Vienna; 5 March, reading in Kunsthalle Wien im Museumsquartier, 'Abschied von der Utopie' (Monika Maron reads earlier on the same evening), in series 'Literatur im März: Abschiede', organized by Kunstverein Wien Alte Schmiede

11 March: publication of *Luftkrieg und Literatur* (*LuL*) (**A.7**)

12–18 April: → Prague and Terezín (KZ Theresienstadt): → Nuremberg

23 April: at the instigation of Steve Wasserman, awarded the *Los Angeles Times* Book Prize (fiction category) for *The Rings of Saturn* (published 29 May 1998) at that newspaper's annual Festival of Books (accepted by Barbara Epler of New Directions on his behalf)

26 April: → Munich → Erfurt by the afternoon of 30 April when he reads from *RS* to the spring meeting of the Deutsche Akademie für Sprache und Dichtung (29 April–1 May) in the Festsaal des Rathauses → Munich → Norwich

11–13 June: → Hamburg and Kiel

11 June: reads from *LuL* in the Literaturhaus, Schwanenwik 38 → Kiel (12 June) → England

14 June: together with Michael Hamburger reads from *After Nature* in the Aldeburgh Cinema at the 52nd Aldeburgh Festival; attends recital by Alfred Brendel in the evening

18 June: death of father, Georg Sebald

19–20 June: → Dublin (*Irish Times* interview [?])

21–25 June: → Munich to attend father's funeral in Sonthofen

13 July: in Cambridge

19 July–22 July: → Frankfurt a.M. → Munich (discussions with Eichborn and Hanser)

1 August: EUR is restructured and its name changed to the School of Language, Linguistics and Translation Studies; WGS and three EUR colleagues from Literature (plus one from Media Studies) are transferred to the School of English and American Studies (EAS); other EUR colleagues from Contemporary and Media Studies join the School of Social Studies

14 August: → Salzburg (attends part of Hans Magnus Enzensberger's 70th birthday celebrations; Salzburg Festival [?])

16–19 August: → Marienbad; 'Marienbader Elegie' (**F.A.8/F.A.8(a)**)

20 August: → Norwich

6–9 September: Paris, possibly in connection with the publication of *Les Anneaux de Saturne* (**B.B.3.6**)

9–11 October: Graz (Joanneum Museum)

18 October (a.m.): in conversation with Boyd Tonkin in the Town Hall, Cheltenham, during the Cheltenham Festival

12 November: in Belfast

late November / early December: interview with Toby Green (J.31)

December: Anthea Bell is asked to translate *LuL* and *A* (she receives the MS in summer 2000)

4 December: Cambridge, probably to see Richard Evans in connection with NESTA Fellowship

8–9 December: in Paris on the occasion of a colloquium on 'L'Extraterritorialité de la langue allemande' organized by the University of Paris X (Nanterre)

8 December: reads from *RS* at the Maison des Écrivains, 53, rue de Verneuil, Paris 7ème

9 December: publication of *Vertigo* (**B.B.1.5**)

2000

8 January: in London

14 January: Cambridge, probably to see Richard Evans in connection with NESTA application

spring term: begins to teach creative writing in EAS and, to his surprise, enjoys doing so (cf. **J.33** and **K.1**)

26 January: invited to apply for a NESTA Fellowship (NESTA was set up by the government in 1998 'to support outstanding creative talent and innovation in the arts and sciences')

February: Michael Hamburger begins translating *NN* for Hamish Hamilton

2 February: Arts Council, London

5–8 February: Munich (Literaturhaus)

18–23 February: → Amsterdam → Berlin

22 February: interview with Volker Hage of *Der Spiegel* (**J.32**) and a conversation with Florian Illies in the studio of the Literarisches Colloquium, Am Sandwerder 5 (co-production with Deutschlandfunk, Cologne)

25 February: Susan Sontag publishes review of *Vertigo*, 'A Mind in Mourning', in the *TLS* and *New York Review of Books*

21 March: takes part in a panel discussion in the Sainsbury Centre for the Visual Arts, UEA, with Dr Jane Beckett, Tess Jaray, and Katarzyna Murawska-Muthesius on the veteran Slovenian artist Zoran Mušič (1909–2005) on 'how we handle personal trauma as an artistic phenomenon', in the context of an exhibition of his work (Mušič was arrested by the Gestapo in 1943, tortured, and survived a year in Dachau where he secretly made drawings on scraps of paper: his post-war work includes paintings of what he saw in Dachau)

22 March: → Paris

23 March: → Nantes Town Hall with Patrick Charbonneau to receive the Prix Laure-Bataillon for *Les Émigrants*, awarded by MEET (Maison des Écrivains et des

Traducteurs, Nantes / Saint-Nazaire, for the best translation of the year) from the Deputy Mayors (Culture) of Nantes and Saint-Nazaire

24–25 March: → Paris (Bibliothèque nationale) → Norwich

28 March: interviewed (with other authors) on aerial warfare for ZDF

April: interview with Jens Mühling (UEA), mainly on teaching creative writing (**J.33**)

12 April: → Stuttgart; reads from *LiL* in Marbach am Neckar (DLA) (**L.2**)

13 April: → Berlin

14 April: reading in the American Academy, Am Sandwerder 17–19, Wannsee

15 April: → Stuttgart → Öhningen (opening of Jan Peter Tripp exhibition) → England

4–9 May: in St Malo

26–31 May: in Frankfurt a.M. (Hessischer Rundfunk recording[?]); Eichborn

4 June: Cambridge, probably to see Richard Evans in connection with NESTA application

9–18 June: in Bavaria and the Allgäu (Sonthofen, Rot a.d. Rot, Wertach, Kempten (symposium?)

7 July: invited to read at the *Kulturtage* in Lana, in the very north of the South Tirol (Italy); unable to attend owing to a missed plane connection

mid-July: nominated for the Heinrich-Heine-Preis; receives it in Düsseldorf in mid-December

mid-July: awarded the Joseph-Breitbach-Preis (Germany's most generously endowed literary prize), together with Ilse Aichinger and Markus Werner; receives it in the Mainzer Akademie der Wissenschaften

2 August: applies to spread NESTA Fellowship over four spring semesters (2001–2004) and to continue teaching at UEA for the four winter semesters. His original project involves writing a piece of 'semi-documentary prose fiction' on his family during the period 1900–1950 (cf. **J.44(b)**, pp. 163–65)

late August, early September: visits Dieppe, Saint-Quentin, Bienne, Fribourg

September [?]–8 October: Jan Peter Tripp's exhibition in the Galerie Brandstätter, An der Stalden 5, Öhningen am Bodensee, contributes **D.73** to exhibition catalogue

autumn term: on study leave; works through the English translations of *A*, *LuL*, and *NN*; research on his new writing project in Germany, France, and Switzerland

21–26 September: Paris → Mainz → Zurich; en route visits Jan Peter Tripp in Mittelbergheim; they make plans for *U* and visit Hartmannswillerkopf, the scene of fierce fighting throughout World War I

22 September: → Mainz (Akademie der Wissenschaften)

23–24 September: → Zurich

25 September: → Norwich

6–14 October: due to take part in the Poetry International Festival (Royal Festival Hall, London) but cancels

mid-October: awarded NESTA Fellowship and consults Richard Evans about a suitable 'appointed mentor': Evans offers his services

23–29 November: Strasbourg

23 November: meets novelists Robert Bober and Frederic Raphael at a soirée in the Librairie Strasbourgeoise

24–26 November: together with Bober and Charbonneau, takes part in a translation workshop organized by Irène Kuhn and Sibylle Muller entitled 'Exile, extraterritorialité et mémoire' in the Maison Rose, Wolxheim (25 km from Strasbourg); reads from *A*; Jan Peter Tripp is also present

8–14 December: Vienna (research in Josephinum) and Düsseldorf (Heinrich-Heine-Preis)

11 December: reads from *A* in the Österreichische Gesellschaft für Literatur, Palais Wilczek, Herrengasse 5, Vienna (moderated by Martin Esslin)

13 December: → Düsseldorf: receives Heine-Preis der Stadt Düsseldorf in the Palais Wittgenstein, Bilkerstraße 7–9, laudatio by Irène Heidelberger-Leonard; reads 'Die Alpen im Meer' (E.B.32) instead of giving a speech

2001

11 January: in Cambridge, to consult Richard Evans about NESTA project

12 January: interviewed by Professor Christopher Bigsby at UEA (J.34)

spring semester: on leave (NESTA Fellowship)

17 January: → Paris

18–19 January: launch of *Vertiges* (B.B.1.6)

20–22 January: → Rouen

23–24 January: → Paris

25 January: → England

27 January: first National Holocaust Memorial Day: invited to participate in evening event in the Institute of Contemporary History and the Wiener Library, but in the end declines invitation

1–5 February: Norwich → Amsterdam → Berlin to participate in a conference in the studio of the Literarisches Colloquium, Am Sandwerder, entitled 'Übersetzen als geistige Kunst' (2–3 February)

2 February (evening): takes part in a conversation with Gabriella Rovagnati entitled 'Übersetzen als Kunst'

4 February: → Amsterdam

5 February: publication of *Austerlitz* (B.B.4)

10 February: attends memorial service for Sir Malcolm Bradbury in Norwich Cathedral

12 February: interviewed in a Norwich hotel by Julia Kospach for *Profil* (J.35)

15 February, late afternoon: reads from *A* to the German Studies Group at Gonville and Caius College, Cambridge (reading organized by Richard Evans, a Fellow of that College)

27 February: *Spiegel* interview with Martin Doerry and Volker Hage (J.36)

8–14 March: in New York

13 March: interview with Joseph Cuomo as part of the Queens College Evening Readings [subsequently broadcast] (J.37)

13 March: Niels Brunse asked to translate *A* into Danish

14 March: reads at Barnes and Noble, Union Square

16 March: back in Norwich

29 March–8 April: reading tour to promote *A*

29 March–1 April: → Salzburg region; takes part in the Rauriser Literaturtage (29 March–1 April)

2 April: discusses *A* in 'Treffpunkt Kultur' on ORF → Cologne (Theater im Bauturm, Aachener Straße 24)

3 April: → Schwetzingen (Stadtbibliothek, Kronenstraße 1)

4 April: → Göttingen (Literarisches Zentrum, Düstere Straße 20)

5 April: → Munich (Autorenbuchhandlung, Wilhelmstraße 8)

6 April: → St Gallen (Musiksaal, Klubschule Migros, Bahnhofplatz 2)

7 April: → Zurich → Amsterdam

8 April: → Norwich

10 April: invited to read from *A* as President's Guest at the annual CUTG meeting (St John's College, Oxford); cancels at the last minute owing to illness

25 April: → London

26 April: attends the opening of the Tess Jaray exhibition 'From the Rings of Saturn and Vertigo' at the Purdy Hicks Gallery, London

27–29 April: → Antwerp

29 April: → Liège

30 April: → Weweler, probably for opening of 'Erdrand' exhibition

30 April–6 June: 'Schriftbilder: Entwürfe und Manuskripte', photographic exhibition of manuscript pages from *RS* organized by Klaus G. Gaida (Weweler, Belgium) under the heading 'Erdrand'

3 May: → England

8 May: Deutschlandradio, Berlin: broadcast of *'Austerlitz*: Europäische Landschaften und Lebensspuren von W. G. Sebald', programme presented by Sigried Wesener, featuring WGS reading from *Austerlitz* and in conversation

22 May: interview in Norwich on *A* with Jean-Pierre Rondas (J.41) (broadcast on 2 September as 'Sebald schrijft Breendonk')

26 May: trip to Bremen

28 May–11 June: research trip to Munich; reading tour; visit to Sonthofen

31 May → Munich: first and only visit to the Kriegsarchiv, Leonrodstraße 57, where he orders and copies a large number of documents relating to the history of the 1. Bayrisches Infanterieregiment in World War I

5 June: → Basle (Literaturhaus, Barfüssergasse 3)

6 June: → Mainz: takes part in SWR programme 'Literatur im Foyer: Die Stars der Saison:

Georg Klein und W. G. Sebald und die deutsche Literaturkritik', includes readings by WGS from *A*, interview and discussion; broadcast on 6 June (SWR) and 17 June (3-sat) (see Audio-Visual Bibliography)

7 June: → meets Jan Peter Tripp

8–11 June: → Sonthofen

May / June: Eichborn publishes the *Jubiläumsausgabe* of *NN*, *SG*, *DA*, and *RS* (**B.D.1**)

21–26 June: London

7 July: in Munich at the invitation of his friend from Manchester days, Sir Peter Jonas, *Intendant* of the Staatsoper, Munich (1993–2006); reads 'Moments musicaux' (**D.75**) in the Cuvilliéstheater (Altes Residenztheater), Residenzstraße 1, as a prelude to the first performance of Bellini's *I Puritani* in the 2001 Opernfestspiele (24 June–31 July)

12 July: consultation in Cambridge with Richard Evans

22–30 July: → Paris → Saint-Quentin → Rouen

August: interview with Uwe Pralle (**J.42**); visits mother and friends in Sonthofen

15 August: interview with Maria Alvarez (**J.43**)

19–20 August: interview with Arthur Lubow in Norwich for the *New York Times* (**J.44**)

3–10 September: → Geneva → Fribourg

c. **9 September**: → Ependes (near Fribourg) for a friends and family meeting at the house of his niece

11 September: 19 al-Qaeda terrorists crash four aircraft into targets in North America, killing themselves and 2974 people from over 90 countries

13 September: interview with Maya Jaggi (**J.45**)

24 September: conversation with Maya Jaggi and Anthea Bell in the Royal Festival Hall, London, on the occasion of the St Jerome Lecture (**J.46(a)**)

29/30 September: interviewed on *Saturday Review*, BBC Radio 4, and then reads from *A* in English

early October: phone interview with Kenneth Baker (**J.48**)

5 October: interviewed on *Night Waves*, BBC Radio 3, and reads from *A* in English

autumn semester: teaches an MA course on creative writing at UEA (see **K.1** and Chapter 4 in the present volume)

14–*c.* 23 October: reading tour in North America to promote *A*

15 October: → New York; Kaufmann Concert Hall, 92nd Street Y Unterberg Poetry Center, 1395 Lexington Avenue, reading evening with Susan Sontag

16 October: → Philadelphia; Blauvelt Theatre, Friends Select School, 1651 Benjamin Franklin Parkway (organized by the proprietor of the Joseph Fox Bookstore, 1724 Sansom Street); a member of the audience recalls that most of the subsequent questions concerned his use of photography and unique blending of fiction and non-fiction

17 October: → Los Angeles (Mark Taper Auditorium, LA Public Library, 630 West 5th Street); public conversation with Steve Wasserman — then the Editor of *The LA*

Times Book Review — as part of the ALOUD literary series, curated by Louise Steinman and presented by the Library Foundation of LA (**J.49**) (see Part II of the present volume, pp. 364–75); reads **B.4.2**, pp. 109–17

17–18 October: interviews with Michael Silverblatt (**J.50**; broadcast 6 December) and Susan Salter Reynolds (**J.51**)

19 October: → San Francisco (Black Oak Bookstore, 1491 Shattuck Avenue, Berkeley)

20 October: → Seattle (Elliott Bay Book Co., 101 South Main Street)

→ New York (**J.53**) and Toronto (**J.54**)

late October: in Sonthofen to visit mother and friends

7 November: telephone interview

16–19 November: in Stuttgart

17 November: speaks in the Alte Reithalle (Hotel Maritim), Seidenstraße 34, Stuttgart, at the opening of the adjacent Literaturhaus, Breitscheidstraße 4 (**D.76**)

18 November: reading from *A* in the Literaturhaus (session moderated by Sigrid Löffler)

November/December: nominated for the Fiction Prize of the National Book Critics Circle of the USA for *A* (awarded posthumously in the Tishman Auditorium of New York University's Law School, 11 March 2002; accepted on his behalf by Andrew Wylie (The Wylie Agency) and Scott Moyers (Random House)

26 November: in London to have lunch with Rick Hall at NESTA

late November: nominated (together with Juli Zeh) for the Bremer Literaturpreis der Rudolf Alexander Schröder-Stiftung (awarded posthumously 26 January 2002)

3 December: attends the launch of *For Years Now* (**B.A.2**) in London

c. **4 December**: last phone conversation with Charbonneau who has, by now, translated *c.* 100 pages of *A*

14 December: dies while driving near Norwich: buried in St Andrew's churchyard, Framingham Earl, Norfolk, early January 2002

Postscript: 2002–2011

(including posthumous awards, conferences dedicated to,
and exhibitions inspired by, the works of WGS)

26 January 2002: Bremer Literaturpreis der Rudolf Alexander Schröder-Stiftung awarded posthumously in the Altes Rathaus, Bremen

29 January 2002: Sir Peter Jonas, Michael Krüger (Hanser Verlag), and Sigrid Löffler discuss WGS and read from his work at a memorial evening in the Literaturhaus, Salvatorplatz 1, Munich

5 February 2002: death of mother, Rosa Genoveva (b. 1914); buried with her husband in Sonthofen cemetery; WGS's name is also on the grave even though he is not buried there

11 March 2002: Fiction Prize of the National Book Critics Circle awarded posthumously in New York

7 and 21 March 2002: Dr Hermann Weizmann reads from WGS's work in the Kultur-Werkstatt, Altstädter Straße 7, Sonthofen

9 April 2002: 'W. G. Sebald (1944–2001)', readings and discussion with Andreas Isen-schmid, Norbert Miller, and Wolfgang Schlüter, Literarisches Colloquium Berlin (organized in conjunction with Literaturhaus Berlin and the Stiftung Preußische Seehandlung)

11 April 2002: *Austerlitz* wins the *Independent* Foreign Fiction Prize

18 May 2002: Bruno Ganz reads from *SG* in Gut Böckel, Bieren (Westphalia) at the opening of the 2002 'Wege durch das Land' literature and music festival in Ostwestfalen-Lippe

3 June 2002: Anthea Bell wins Helen and Kurt Wolff Prize for her translation of *Austerlitz*

17 June 2002: Michael Hamburger reads from *After Nature* in The Pumphouse, Aldeburgh

August 2002: publication of UK edition of *After Nature* (**B.A.1.2**)

September–1 November 2002: Schloss Fachsenfeld: exhibition of work by Jan Peter Tripp, including *U*; Bruno Ganz reads at opening

23 September 2002: Anthea Bell awarded Schlegel-Tieck Prize for translation of *Austerlitz* (Queen Elizabeth Hall, London South Bank)

6 November 2002: 'Erinnerung und Gedächtnis bei W. G. Sebald', lecture by Sigrid Löffler and reading by Elmar Roloff as part of the Literaturtage Fellbach (23 October–23 November 2002)

16 November 2002: first anniversary of the opening of the Literaturhaus Stuttgart: Panel discussion on WGS (Jan Peter Tripp, Michael Krüger, Patrick Charbonneau, moderated by Florian Höllerer), accompanying exhibition of *U* (to 28 February 2003)

31 January 2003: 'The Anatomist of Melancholy: W. G. Sebald Memorial Day' at the Institute of Germanic Studies, University of London; Michael Krüger reads from *CS* and shows plates from *U*)

8 March 2003: publication of *Campo Santo* (**B.D.2**)

10 March 2003: publication of *Unerzählt* (**B.A.3**)

13–16 March 2003: The third Davidson occasional symposium on German Studies takes place at Davidson College, near Charlotte, NC: this is the first major international conference to be devoted to WGS's life and work

17 June 2003: Patrick Charbonneau receives the Prix Gérard de Nerval (awarded by the Société des Gens de Lettres) in the Hotel de Massa, Paris 14ème (the seat of the Société) for his translations of works by WGS

14 October 2003: Dr Hermann Weizmann reads from WGS's work in the Hotel Hirsch, Marktstraße 21, Wertach

25 November–19 December 2003: 'für Sebald', exhibition of drawings and sculptures by Wolfgang Mayer, *kunst ug*, Obere Wank 12, Nesselwang (Allgäu)

January 2004: WGS's papers (*Nachlass*) and the first part of his annotated library are deposited in the DLA, followed in summer 2006 by the second part of the library and in 2008 by a few other items in time for the exhibition 'Wandernde Schatten'

1–4 March 2004: symposium 'W. G. Sebald' at Carl Friedrich von Siemens Stiftung, Munich

7 March 2004: memorial concert in the Allgäu-Stern-Hotel, Buchfinken Weg 2, Sonthofen (Professor Michael Enders and Wolf Euba read from WGS's work)

27 March 2004: 'Approaching W. G. Sebald', 15th Yale Graduate Student Conference

20 June–5 September 2004: 'Jan Peter Tripp — Die weiße Zeit', exhibition ('Hommage an W. G. Sebald') in Schloß Bonndorf (Waldshut), including Tripp's portraits of WGS (reading from WGS' work by Bruno Ganz on 20 June)

8–24 July 2004: 'W. G. Sebald 1944–2001: Lebensstationen eines Autors', an exhibition organized by Professor Reinbert Tabbert to mark what would have been WGS's 60th birthday, takes place in the Stadtbibliothek, Spendhausstraße 2, Reutlingen

15–16 October 2004: 'W. G. Sebald: Mémoire. Transferts. Images', symposium at École Normale Supérieure and Maison Heine, Paris (with Jan Peter Tripp)

26–28 November 2004: 'Kanalrunde W. G. Sebald', seminar at Nordkolleg Rendsburg

10 December 2004: 'The Natural History of Destruction: W. G. Sebald's View of History', symposium at Humanities Institute of Ireland (Dublin)

30 January–13 March 2005: exhibition 'Jan Peter Tripp: Bilder, Objekte, Radierungen', Kunstverein Schallstadt, Am Käppele 2, Schallstadt (13 March 2005: Finissage 'Im Schattenreich', Jan Peter Tripp on WGS and WGS on Jan Peter Tripp (read by Etta Schwanitz)

21 February–31 March 2005: Professor Tabbert's exhibition, now entitled 'W. G. Sebald 1944–2001: Lebensstationen eines Autors aus dem Allgäu', shown in the Foyer of the *Rathaus*, Sonthofen

10 March–3 June 2005: the Sonthofen exhibition, under its original title, transfers to Ansgar Weber's Buchhandlung Seitenblick, Goetzstraße 2, Leipzig

8–13 April 2005: De Parade, a Flemish theatre group directed by Rudi Meulemans, stage *De Emigrés*, an adaptation of *DA*, at the Kaaitheaterstudio, 81, rue Notre-Dame du Soleil, Brussels

1 June 2005: Niels Brunse receives the Übersetzerpreis der Kunststiftung Nordrhein-Westfalen for his work as a translator, including his translations of works by WGS into Danish

17 June 2005: 'Memory and Displacement: A Seminar on W. G. Sebald', at the Wiener Library, Goldsmiths College, University of London

1–3 July 2005: 'W. G. Sebald's Use of Images', international, multidisciplinary conference at University College Cork (Ireland)

13 November 2005: Inauguration of the 'Sebald-Weg', a marked path tracing the descent by the narrator of 'Il ritorno in patria' in *SG*, in Wertach

20–23 July 2006: 'W. G. Sebald and Expatriate Writing', Sydney German Studies Symposium in the Goethe-Institut, Sydney, New South Wales (Australia)

August 2006: sale of The Old Rectory, Poringland

30 September–3 December 2006: 'Rings of Saturn' exhibition, Level 2 Gallery, Tate Modern, London; inspired by *RS*, eight artists 'explore the nature of history [...] and its critical moments of transition, energy and change' <http://www.tate.org.uk/modern/exhibitions/theringsofsaturn/>

6 October 2006: Hans Magnus Enzensberger, in conversation with David Constantine, gives the annual BCLT NESTA Sebald lecture (formerly known as St Jerome lecture) at UEA with the title 'The Peregrinations of Poetry'

January 2007: Terry Pitts sets up website *Vertigo: Collecting and Reading W. G. Sebald* <http://sebald.wordpress.com/>. More than 263,000 hits by October 2010

3 February–24 June 2007: *Waterlog* exhibition at Norwich Castle Museum and Art Gallery (3 February–15 April) and the Sainsbury Centre for Visual Arts, UEA (30 January–24 June). It later moves to Lincoln. The exhibition comprises a series of specially commissioned visual works by seven artists (Marcus Coates, Tacita Dean, Alec Finlay, Guy Moreton, Alexander and Susan Maris, Simon Pope), 'invoking the digressive literary journeys of the writer W. G. Sebald' through East Anglia

7 June 2007: death of Michael Hamburger

14–15 June 2007: first academic event on WGS at UEA: 'W. G. Sebald and the European Tradition', international symposium at UEA, Norwich, supported by the British Academy (organized by the editors of the present volume)

29 September 2007: 'The Printed Path: Landscape, Walking and Recollection'. Symposium at Tate Britain, London, curated by Jeremy Millar and Steven Bode, with contributions from Marina Warner and Iain Sinclair, and interventions from artists Tacita Dean, Alec Finlay and Simon Pope

2 November 2007: Ria van Hengel, WGS's Dutch translator, receives the 2007 Martinus Nijhoff Prijs, the most important prize for literary translators in the Netherlands

6 November 2007: Iannis Kalifatidis awarded the 2006 Greek National Prize for literary translation for his Greek translations of works by WGS

30 November–1 December 2007: 'W. G. Sebald: Intertextualität und Topographie', international colloquium at the Université Libre de Bruxelles, Belgium

18 July–21 September 2008: 'After Nature', an exhibition of visual work inspired by WGS, takes place in the New Museum, 235 Bowery, Lower East Side, New York

5–7 September 2008: 'W. G. Sebald: An International and Interdisciplinary Conference', UEA (School of Literature and Creative Writing in collaboration with BCLT)

25 September–26 October 2008: 'Il ritorno in patria', exhibition of engravings by Jan Peter Tripp and poems by WGS from *U* in Kunsthaus Villa Jauss, Oberstdorf, with a 'Festakt' (1 October) with readings and talks by Mark Anderson, Hans Magnus Enzensberger, Jürgen Kaeser, and Jan Peter Tripp to mark the permanent loan of the last luxury edition of *U* (**B.A.3(c)**) to their former school, now the Gertrud-von-le-Fort Gymnasium in Oberstdorf

22 and 26 September 2008: two exhibitions on WGS open in Germany: 'Wandernde Schatten' (cf. **F.D.2**) at the Literaturmuseum der Moderne, DLA Marbach (until end January 2009) and 'Zerstreute Reminiszenzen' (**B.C.6**), Literaturhaus Stuttgart (23 September–17 December 2008 then → Passa Porta, International House of Literature, A. Dansaertstraat 46, Brussels, 5 February–1 March 2009)

12 October 2008: Schloß Bonndorf (Waldshut): Frank Arnold reading from WGS's work as part of the 'baden-württembergischer Literatursommer'

19 May–26 June 2009: 'W. G. Sebald: Photographies, documents, manuscrit original du roman *Austerlitz*', using documentary material from DLA, in Goethe-Institut, 17, rue d'Iéna, Paris 16ème (finissage, including a reading with Patrick Charbonneau)

February 2009: engravings by Jan Peter Tripp and poems by WGS from *U* acquired by the 'Initiative Villa Jauss' go on display in their former school, the Gertrud-von-le-Fort Gymnasium in Oberstdorf

3 September 2009: '"Ein ungeheuerer Appell": In memoriam W. G. Sebald', part of *Kulturtage Lana 09: Kultur und Gedächtnis* (Ansitz Schaller in der Vill, Lana, Südtirol, Italy), with Walter Busch, Iain Galbraith, Elmar Locher, and Raoul Schrott

5 February 2010: 'Traces, Memory and the Holocaust in W. G. Sebald's Writing: An Interdisciplinary Seminar', Centre for Jewish Studies, University of Manchester

January 2010: sale of Marsh Acres (Michael Hamburger's Suffolk home)

1 January 2010: Anthea Bell awarded the OBE in Britain's New Year's Honours list

18 May 2010: 'W. G. Sebalds nachgelassener Essay über Jurek Becker', reading and discussion with Uwe Schütte, Olaf Kutzmutz, and Gernot Krämer, Berlin, Literaturhaus (Fasanenstraße), organized by *Sinn und Form* (see **D.53**)

15 July 2010: Anthea Bell receives Honorary DLitt at UEA Congregation 2010

September 2010: The inaugural PEN / W. G. Sebald Award for a Fiction Writer in Mid-Career is given to Susan Choi, author of the books *The Foreign Student, American Woman*, and *A Person of Interest*. The award 'honours an author who has published at least three significant works of literary fiction, either novels or short story collections, with the promise of more to come. The $10,000 prize was established by an anonymous donor to recognize a writer in his or her prime whose powerful and courageous writing honours the legacy of W. G. Sebald. <http://www.pen.org/page.php/prmID/2061> [accessed 2 January 2011]

12 November 2010: Death of Alec Garrard (b. 1930) in Norwich [see **B.B.3**, Part IX]

19 October 2010: 'Alfred Andersch "revisited": Die Sebald-Debatte und ihre Folgen', Literaturhaus Frankfurt. Symposium on Alfred Andersch and WGS's critique of him (see **D.53**)

15 December 2010: Ada Vigliani is awarded the Premio Nini Agosti Castellani, the annual prize for the best translation into Italian, for *Gli anelli di Saturno*, her translation of *RS*

28-30 January 2011: 'After Sebald — Place & Re-Enchantment: A Weekend Exploration', Snape Maltings, Aldeburgh, comprising 'Towards Re-Enchantment: a Symposium on Place and Its Meanings' with Alexandra Harris, Rachel Lichtenstein, Richard Mabey, and Robert Macfarlane, bracketed by the world premiere of Grant Gee's film *Patience (After Sebald)*, recreating the walk from *RS* (28 January), and a concert by Patti Smith, *Max. A Tribute*, featuring her eponymous unpublished poem and readings / performance from *AN*

3 March-17 April 2011: 'On The Line', exhibition organized by LACE in Los Angeles, including works by Sarah Seager based on *A*

26 March 2011: 'Memory Destroys – Photographs in the Work of W. G. Sebald', opening of exhibition at 2P Contemporary Art Gallery, Hong Kong

2 April–25 June 2011: 'Sebald — Photography Collage Installation', Düsseldorf <http://www.flickr.com/photos/zigs1/> [accessed 11 April 2011]

Fig. III.5. The inscription on the memorial bench (see Fig. III.6).
The text is the penultimate poem in *Unerzählt* (*Unrecounted*);
the translation by Michael Hamburger reads as follows:

Unrecounted
always it will remain
the story of the averted
faces

Photograph © Richard Hibbitt (2007)

*The Editors and Richard Sheppard would like to express their grateful thanks
to the following for their generous sponsorship of this volume*

Richard Bateman
Theresa Bateman
Sarah Cameron
Dr Cath Catt
Ann Clark
Dr Mike Clark
DAAD London Office
Anne Fitzpatrick
Dr Christa Gaug
Revd Mieke Gaynor
Professor Steve Giles
Mike Gill
John Goldthorpe
Ruth Guy
Michelle Jaffé
Marci King

Mike Kwan
Petra Leseberg
Les Myford
Anne Mylan
Alison Ravnkilde
Belinda Rhodes
Professor Brian Rowley
Clare Savory
Rachel Savory
Fiona Traynor
Liz Walsh
Andy Webb
Rebecca Whittingham-Booth
Wendy Widmer
Caroline Winter-Jones

FIG. III.6. The memorial bench in the grounds of UEA, between the main site and the Broad
© Richard Sheppard (2005)

INDEX OF WORKS BY W. G. SEBALD

❖

Die Ausgewanderten (*The Emigrants*) 1, 3, 6, 10, 18, 27, 29, 33, 35, 36, 38 fig., 64, 84 fig., 103 n. 94, 121, 131, 177, 195, 196, 197, 198, 218, 222 fig., 223 fig., 248, 249, 279, 280, 284, 285, 342, 354, 358, 601, 621–26, 629–31, 635, 638–44, 646–48, 653, 656
  editions /extracts 453–55, 477–78, 496
  reviews 560–63
  'Ambros Adelwarth' 8, 27, 29, 35, 248, 358, 460, 621, 629, 638, 641
  'Dr Henry Selwyn' 33, 284, 445 fig., 477
  'Max Aurach / Max Ferber' 8, 64, 65 fig., 100 n. 67, 222, 249, 285, 460, 478, 561, 594, 621, 624, 640
  'Paul Bereyter' 10, 38 fig., 477–78
Austerlitz 1, 2, 7, 9, 10, 11, 64, 70, 100 n. 51, 144, 145, 146, 156, 158, 209, 210, 211, 212, 213, 214, 219, 223, 226 fig., 227 fig., 241 n. 8, 242 n. 20, 245 n. 82, 250, 255, 257, 275, 291, 293 n. 16, 296 n. 63, 301, 302, 303, 304, 306, 332, 342, 349, 602, 623–25, 644, 646, 649, 650–55, 658
  editions /extracts 457–58, 459, 481
  reviews 555, 556–70, 575, 577, 580
  Andromeda Lodge 212, 257, 263 n. 25, 296 n. 63, 338
  Ashman, Gerald / Fitzpatrick, Gerald 10, 257, 342 n. *see also* Works by W. G. Sebald, 'Feuer und Rauch'
  Austerlitz, Jacques (character) 8, 209, 250, 306, 365, 369, 372
'Ausgrabung der Vergangenheit' 10, 296 n. 69, 344–45, 346, 472
Die Beschreibung des Unglücks 1, 161, 165, 168, 180 n. 19, 279, 284, 449, 496, 550, 631, 632
Campo Santo (*see also* 'Corsica project') 1, 7, 211, 214, 257, 459–60, 465, 479–81, 496, 571–73, 585, 586, 589, 655
Carl Sternheim: Kritiker und Opfer der Wilhelminischen Ära 83, 449, 481, 549
'Feuer und Rauch' 10, 338–42, 471–72
  Aylmer, Gerald 263 n. 25, 338–40, 342 n.
For Years Now 1, 451, 475, 570, 654
'Die hölzernen Engel von East Anglia' ('The Carved Wooden Angels of East Anglia') 4, 9, 92, 94, 319–23, 485
'Ich möchte zu ihnen hinabsteigen...' [on Jurek Becker] 164, 179 n. 15, 468, 573, 637, 638

'Leben Ws' 9, 324–33, 485, 590, 600 *see also* Wittgenstein, Ludwig
Logis in einem Landhaus (*A Place in the Country*) 1, 34, 60, 165, 230, 269, 275, 295 n. 43, 449, 495, 496, 551–52, 583, 584, 585, 602, 647
Luftkrieg und Literatur (*On the Natural History of Destruction*) 1, 7, 10, 164, 209, 210, 211, 255, 450, 471, 482, 493, 552–55, 584, 585, 593, 601, 648
Der Mythus der Zerstörung im Werk Döblins 164, 175, 345 n., 449, 550, 628
Nach der Natur (*After Nature*) 1, 3, 9, 18, 56, 68, 84 fig., 92, 121, 166, 248, 255, 268, 279, 284, 300, 320, 323, 348, 451, 474–75, 496, 556–57, 600, 635
Die Ringe des Saturn (*The Rings of Saturn*) 1, 6, 8, 9, 10, 11, 51, 73, 74 fig., 75, 92, 119 fig., 125 fig., 131, 199, 200, 202 fig., 203 fig., 206 fig., 209, 224, 249, 252, 253 fig., 254 fig., 256 fig., 266, 267, 268, 273, 275, 284, 286, 323, 335, 342, 345 fig., 346, 545–46, 601, 623, 639, 640, 641, 642, 643, 644, 645, 646, 647, 648, 649, 652, 653, 657, 658
  editions and extracts 455–57, 478–79, 496
  reviews 563–66, 575, 577, 580
Schwindel. Gefühle. (*Vertigo*) 1, 3, 11, 18, 24 fig., 32, 60, 103 n. 100, 156, 166, 167, 176, 181 n. 27, 207, 209, 248, 267, 275, 278, 279, 285, 293 n. 16, 294 n. 21, 305, 350, 354, 361, 600–01, 634, 636, 637, 638, 640, 649, 656, 657
  editions and extracts 452–53, 476–77, 496
  reviews 557–59
  'All'estero' 275, 279, 280, 281
  'Il ritorno in patria' 32, 248, 272, 275, 276, 277, 656, 657
Über das Land und das Wasser (*Across the Land and the Water*) 1, 323, 573, 629
Unerzählt (*Unrecounted*) 1, 230, 240, 245 n. 82, 332 n., 348, 570–71, 585, 655, 659 fig.
Unheimliche Heimat 1, 161, 166, 279, 284, 291, 550–51, 637
'Waterloo' 9, 334–35, 485, 638
Uncompleted projects:
  'Corsica project' (*see also Campo Santo*) 1, 7, 8, 10, 211, 214, 257–58, 258 fig., 260 fig., 262 n. 23 & 24, 342, 485, 586, 642, 644
    Ashman, James Mallord 257
  'W[orld] W[ar]' 8, 257, 259–60 *see also* World War I

GENERAL INDEX

Aachen 340

Achleitner, Friedrich 587

Achternbusch, Herbert 6, 94, 165, 168–69, 171, 183, 186, 381, 463, 466, 594, 630, 633

Acle, Norfolk 320

Adam, Ursula 587

Adler, H. G. 187, 381, 587, 594

Adnams (brewery) 94, 320

Adorno, Theodor W. 6, 53, 62, 63, 75, 76, 77, 78, 82, 87, 96 nn. 15–17, 102 n. 94, 148, 155, 163, 270, 286, 287, 420, 490, 594, 624

   The Authoritarian Personality 76, 103 n. 96

   Dialektik der Aufklärung 76, 287 *see also* Horkheimer, Max

   Jargon der Eigentlichkeit 62, 78

   Kierkegaard: Konstruktion des Ästhetischen 76

   Minima Moralia 53, 75, 76, 96 nn. 16 & 17, 163

   Noten zur Literatur 62, 75, 76, 78, 96 n. 17, 103 n. 96

   Versuch über Wagner 75

Aebischer-Sebald, Gertrud 17 fig., 19 fig., 29 fig., 30 figs, 31, 32, 36, 37 n. 17, 40, 56, 57, 61, 295 n. 48, 589, 622

Aenderl, Barbette 39 fig., 44 fig.

'air war' *see Luftkrieg*; World War II

Albertian window, the 234

Albert-Ludwigs-Universität, Freiburg im Breisgau *see* University of Freiburg

Albinoni, Tomaso, 'Adagio in G minor' 80

Aldborough, Norfolk 321

Alde, River (Suffolk) 319

Aldeburgh, Suffolk 319, 323, 655, 658

Aldeburgh Festival 648

Alderney Road Cemetery, London 301

Alemannic literature, writers 1, 20, 161, 165, 166

alienation effect, the 80, 81

Alker, Ernst 56, 99 n. 35, 180 n. 19, 623

Allen, Paul 584, 585

Allgäu 3, 12, 17, 18, 20, 22 fig., 25, 26, 29, 34, 35, 36, 64, 70, 157, 165, 174, 558, 621, 637, 643, 650, 656

Allgäuer Anzeigeblatt 97

Alps, the 9, 17, 18, 165, 300, 304, 305, 306, 370

Altenberg, Peter 161, 279, 381–82, 467

Alvarez, Maria 494, 594, 653

America *see* United States of America

American Dream, the 51

Améry, Jean [Hans Mayer] 34, 35, 135, 161, 188, 211, 213, 214, 357, 382, 450, 464–65, 467, 594, 621, 628, 632, 633, 634, 635, 647

Amsterdam 151, 319, 638, 640, 641, 642, 643, 645, 647, 648, 649, 651, 652

Andersch, Alfred 135, 164, 175, 209, 213, 214, 382, 450, 469, 579, 594, 628, 636, 638, 639, 640, 658

   Efraim 214

Anderson, Mark 577, 657

Androsch, Hannes 587, 632

'Angel of History' 50 fig., 75, 97 n. 18 *see also* Benjamin, Walter, *Angelus Novus*

Angier, Carole 489

Anouilh, Jean 51, 622

   Antigone 51, 52 figs, 95 n. 13, 622

Antelme, Robert 188, 408

Antonioni, Michelangelo, *Blow Up* 367

Antwerp 219, 240, 646, 652 *see also* Breendonk

Appelfeld, Aharon 187

architecture 158, 352, 434, 612

Ardennes Forest, the 365

area bombing *see Luftkrieg*; World War II

Aristotle 249

Arnhem, Battle of 119 fig.

Arnhem Oosterbeek Military Cemetery 119 fig.

Arnim, Gabriele von 589

Arosa Hotel, Manchester 65 fig., 66 *see also* Manchester

Artmann, H. C. 643

Aspekte-Literaturpreis *see* Sebald, W. G., awards, prizes and distinctions

Atlas, James 97, 492, 593, 646

Atze, Marcel 13 n. 3, 100 n. 67, 102 n. 94, 105 n. 124, 265, 270, 272, 273, 275, 582

Aubrey, John, *Brief Lives* 264, 403

Auerbach, Frank 198

Augsburg 20

Auschwitz 34, 148, 157, 621

Auschwitz trials 54, 622

Auslandsgermanistik 154

Austerlitz, Battle of 18

Austerlitz, Gare d' (Paris) 257

Austerlitz (Lager Austerlitz, Paris) 293 n. 16, 621, 644

   see also Bibliothèque nationale de France

Austerlitz, Quai d' (Paris) 257, 621

Australia 208, 373, 656

Austria 18, 20, 33, 60, 121, 161, 162, 165, 328, 634

Austrian Institute 180 n. 19, 272, 631

Austrian literature 3, 35, 60, 161, 162, 165, 166, 168, 170, 174, 180 n. 19, 282, 284, 300, 304, 630, 633, 634

Austro-Hungarian Empire 60, 281

'autobiographical pact' 249
Aylsham, Norfolk 283, 320, 321

Babel, Isaac 150
Bachmann, Ingeborg 275, 295 n. 44, 382
    Ingeborg-Bachmann-Preis *see* Sebald, W. G., awards,
        prizes and distinctions
Bacon, Francis (Lord Verulam) 286, 403
Baconsthorpe, Norfolk 321
Baden-Württemberg 18, 159, 658
Bader, Thomas (Buchhandlung zum Wetzstein,
        Freiburg i. Br.) 264
Baez, Joan 41, 95
Baines, Jocelyn 199, 201
Baker, Kenneth 494
Bakhtinian carnival 230
Bakunin, Mikhail Aleksandrovich 276, 277
Baltzer, Burkhard 489
Balzac, Honoré de 241 n. 8, 285, 408, 658, 659, 660
    Le Colonel Chabert 241 n. 8
Bamberg 17, 483, 642, 643, 644
Baqué, Dominique 217
Barcklow, Bob 53 fig.
Barker, Francis 286
    The Tremulous Private Body 286
Barker, Jonathan 194 fig.
Barthes, Roland 7, 217, 220, 223, 224, 225, 229, 234,
        239, 240, 241 n. 8, 286, 408
    Camera Lucida 7, 217, 220, 223, 224, 234, 239, 240,
        242 n. 19
Basle 370, 652
Bassani, Giorgio 264, 285, 411, 594, 647
    Brille mit Goldrand 264
Baudelaire, Charles 66, 224, 346
    L'Invitation au voyage 224
    La Vie antérieure 224
Baudry, Jean-Louis 586
Bauer, Christoph 589
Bavaria 18, 20, 42, 60, 357, 621, 650
Bavarian accent 33, 36, 110, 111, 145
Bavarian 'Gemütlichkeit' 23
Bayerische Akademie der schönen Künste *see* Sebald,
        W. G., awards, prizes and distinctions
BCLT (British Centre for Literary Translation) 9,
        10, 191 fig., 192 fig., 193 fig., 195, 210, 255, 299,
        301, 348, 634, 635, 637, 639, 641, 642, 657 *see also*
        University of East Anglia
Bebel, Ferdinand August 276, 277
Bechhöfer, Susi, *Rosa's Child* 372, 375 n. 2
Becker, Jurek 164, 468, 573, 587, 625, 637, 638, 644, 658
    Jakob der Lügner 625
    see also Works by W. G. Sebald, 'Ich möchte zu
        ihnen hinabsteigen...'
Beckett, Samuel 133, 138, 363
Bedford College, University of London 55
Belgium 70, 197, 610, 624, 646, 652, 657 *see also*
        Antwerp, Brussels, Waterloo

Bell, Anthea 5, 6–7, 145, 208, 209–15, 291, 297 n. 86,
        586, 649, 653, 655, 658 *see also* translation prizes
belle époque 358
Bellow, Saul 207, 645
Benjamin, Walter 7, 8, 12, 50, 53, 54, 60, 62, 63, 66,
        75, 76, 77, 84, 85, 94, 96 n. 17, 97 n. 18, 163, 217,
        218, 220, 235, 236, 265, 270, 273, 286, 287, 290,
        303, 356, 364, 376 fig., 377, 382–83, 559, 595, 622
    Angelus Novus 12, 96 n. 17, 97 n. 18
    Einbahnstraße / One-Way Street and Other Writings
        62, 96 n. 17, 235
    Illuminationen 62, 77, 96 n. 17, 287
    Ursprung des deutschen Trauerspiels 84
Benn, Gottfried, 'Untergrundbahn' 56
Beresford, Anne 25, 284, 586
Berger, John 7, 217, 220, 229, 235, 238, 264, 286, 432
    About Looking 7, 217, 238
    Preface to Timothy O' Grady and Steve Pyke, *I
        Could Read the Sky* 220
    *A Seventh Man: The Story of a Migrant Worker in
        Europe* 229
    Ways of Seeing 264
Bergson, Henri 221, 229
Berlin 105 n. 121, 121, 198, 217, 327, 328, 346, 363,
        369, 622, 624, 627, 630, 635, 636, 640, 645, 649,
        650, 651, 655
Berne 626, 629
Bernhard, Thomas 20, 35, 136, 138, 161, 264,
        294 n. 34, 383–84, 462, 468, 628, 635
    Wittgensteins Neffe 264
Bertheau, Anne 589
Beßler, Eduard 42, 43 fig.
Bettelheim, Bruno 595, 636
Beyer, Wolfgang 588
Beyle, Marie-Henri *see* Stendhal
Bibliothèque nationale de France, Paris 70, 241 n. 8,
        644, 650
Biedermeier 33
Biel / Bienne 34, 643 *see also* Lake Biel / Bienne
Bigsby, Christopher 64, 181 n. 52, 493, 583, 651
Bildungsroman 77
Bilz, Rudolf 168
Binnroth (Swabia) 19
'biographism' 175
Black Forest, Germany 20, 35
Blakeney, Norfolk 321
Blamires, David 66, 71 fig., 72 fig.
Blank, Herbert (Wissenschaftliches Antiquariat,
        Stuttgart) 272, 282, 378
Bleston 297 n. 85, 484 *see also* Butor, Michel
Blickling Hall, Norfolk 321
Bloch, Ernst 53, 75, 76, 84, 96 nn. 15 & 17, 421
    Durch die Wüste: Frühe Aufsätze 84
Blut und Boden-Literatur 60
Blythburgh, Suffolk 323
Boa, Elizabeth 167
Bober, Robert 408, 651

Boedecker, Sven 491, 593
Böll, Heinrich 118, 135, 136, 341, 360, 384, 595
    Der Engel schwieg 341
    Heinrich-Böll-Preis *see* Sebald, W. G., awards, prizes
        and distinctions
bombing of Germany in World War II *see Luftkrieg*
Bordeaux 338, 625
Borges, Jorge Luis 8, 83, 265, 266–67, 275, 285, 413,
    595
    'Tlön, Uqbar, Orbis Tertius', 266–67
Börner, Holger 50 fig.
Botsford, Keith 207, 645
Boxford, Suffolk 322
Bradbury, Malcolm 156, 360, 361, 646, 651
Brahms, Johannes 326
Brandon Creek, Norfolk 321
Braun, Lily 276, 277
Braun, Michael 584, 585
Brauneck (mountain), Bavaria 222 fig.
Braunmüller, Werner 49 fig., 50 fig.
Brecht, Bertolt 45, 46, 71, 80, 104 n. 106, 134, 384–85,
    488
Bregenz 582, 588, 641
bricolage 168, 257, 263 n. 30
British Council *see* Walberberg
Britten, Benjamin 319
Broch, Hermann 60, 376 fig., 385, 466, 595, 633
Brod, Max 251, 284
Brooke-Rose, Christine 347 fig.
Browne, (Sir) Thomas 8, 199, 200, 249, 266–67, 275,
    286, 293 n. 7, 355 fig., 356, 377, 404, 479, 595, 640
Brunse, Niels 588, 641, 643, 652, 656 *see also* translation
    prizes
Brussels 56, 623, 635, 656
    'Hotel Kongo' 335
    Maison du Cygne 334
Büchner, Georg, *Leonce und Lena* (production directed
    by WGS) 79, 79 fig., 80, 96 n. 14, 624
    Lenz 137
    Büchner-Preis 643
Budapest 370
Budberg, Baron von 217, 218 fig.
Bundeswehr 98 n. 29, 622, 625
Bunk, Helmut 44 fig., 49 fig.
Bunyan, John, *Pilgrim's Progress* 51
Burnham Overy, Norfolk 321
Bury St Edmunds, Suffolk 321, 323
    Angel Corner House 321
    Angel Hotel 321
Busek, Erhard 587
Butley, Suffolk 319
Butor, Michel 66, 100 n. 59, 265, 275, 285, 290,
    297 n. 85, 408
    L'Emploi du temps 66, 100 n. 59, 285, 297 n. 85
butterflies 12, 213, 282, 291 *see also* moths
Byatt, A. S. 194 fig., 635, 646
Byatt, Antonia 191 fig.

Caister-on-Sea, Norfolk 320
Calvino, Italo 285, 412, 595
Cambridge, England 82, 92, 120, 321, 324, 325, 326,
    327, 329, 330, 331, 332, 624, 637, 648, 649, 650,
    651, 653
Campo Santo, Pisa 158
Camus, Albert 488
Canetti, Elias 6, 72, 101 n. 73, 139, 161, 172–73, 236,
    354 n. 3, 385, 461, 462, 470, 625, 632, 635
    Die Blendung (Auto-da-fé) 101 n. 73, 354 n. 3
Capote, Truman 488
Carey, Peter 148
Carver, Raymond 147
Casanova (de Seingalt), Giacomo Girolomo 280, 285
Casement, Roger 200, 642
Castle Acre, Norfolk 321
Castle Rising, Norfolk 321
Catholicism 59, 60, 242
Catling, Jo 127 n. 3, 131
Cayrol, Jean 187
Celan, Paul 187, 385–86, 595
'Chandos letter' / 'Ein Brief' *see* Hofmannsthal, Hugo
    von
Charbonneau, Patrick 586, 646, 647, 650, 651, 654,
    655, 658 *see also* translation prizes
Chateaubriand, François Auguste René, Vicomte de
    262 n. 5, 285, 351, 409, 595
    Itinéraire de Paris à Jérusalem 262 n. 5
Chatwin, Bruce 214, 404, 473
Chekhov, Anton 55, 140, 404, 596
Chorlton-cum-Hardy, Manchester 66, 66 fig.,
    297 n. 85, 624
Clare, Suffolk 322
Clare College, Cambridge 326
Coetzee, J. M., *Disgrace* 149
Cohn-Bendit, Daniel 582, 589
coincidence, 'coincidences' 3, 9, 31, 34, 35, 37 n. 11, 48
    fig., 76, 81, 145, 156, 176, 177, 220, 237, 250, 259,
    275, 278, 279, 348, 352, 357, 493, 612
Colchester, Essex 92, 199
Coles, Richard 585
Cologne 196, 207, 211, 340, 342, 637, 638, 639, 643,
    644, 646, 652
Communism 60
Comparative Literature 71, 88, 109, 131, 154
Conrad, Joseph 6, 199, 200, 201, 202 fig., 203 fig.,
    204, 205, 206 fig., 404, 596
    Heart of Darkness 199, 204
Constable, John 94
contingency 217, 220
Cook, Jon 11, 189, 363, 493, 583, 648
Cornell University 331
Corsica 1, 8, 214, 257, 305, 437, 610, 636, 642, 643
'Corsica project' *see* Works by W. G. Sebald, *Campo
    Santo* and Uncompleted projects
de Cortanze, Gérard 493, 593
Crace, Jim, *Being Dead* 147

Cross, Tony 91

Cryer, Dan 495, 594

Cuomo, Joseph 493, 588, 594, 652

Czechoslovakia 250, 365, 437–38 *see also* Marienbad; Prague

Czerniawski, Adam 190, 191 fig., 195, 296 n. 69, 635, 640

DAAD (Deutscher Akademischer Austausch Dienst) 64, 633, 635, 638, 639

Dante Alighieri 285, 412, 558

Danube, River 167, 176, 370

David, Ghislaine 586

Dakyns, Janine 125 fig., 273, 477, 641, 642

Dean, Barbara 79 fig.

death, preoccupation with 24, 25, 37 n. 11, 83, 92, 102 n. 92, 104 n. 118, 155, 178, 226, 241 n. 8, 250, 305, 324, 341, 353, 354, 370 *see also Nachlass*
  'bodies in woodshed' 25, 305, 370
  of grandfather 34, 36, 176 *see also* Egelhofer, Josef
  photography's connection with 225, 226, 235, 239, 241 n. 8

Delbo, Charlotte 188, 409

Deleuze, Gilles 168

DeLillo, Don, *Underworld* 147

Denbigh, Wales 365

Denham, Scott 13 n. 3

Dennington, Suffolk 320

Der Wecker (school magazine) 44 fig., 622

Detering, Heinrich 583, 645

Deutsch, Mr and Mrs 101 fig.

Deutsche Akademie für Sprache und Dichtung 643, 645, 648 *see* Sebald, W. G., awards, prizes and distinctions

Deutsches Literaturarchiv, Marbach (DLA) 8, 11, 105 n. 28, 179 n. 15, 180 n. 27, 240 n. 2 & 30, 247–63, 265, 270, 377, 581, 619, 650, 656, 657 *see also* Literaturmuseum der Moderne; Sebald, W. G., *Nachlass*; *Nachlassbibliothek*

Devarrieux, Claire 493

dialect 20, 31, 36, 99 n. 48, 604
  Alemannic 20
  Allgäu 29

Dickens, Charles 283, 404

Diderot, Denis 280

Didsbury, Manchester 65 fig., 69, 70, 72, 72 fig., 73, 73 fig., 624

Die Brücke (stage ensemble) 81, 107

Die Tageszeitung (taz) 86

Die Zeit 4, 9, 85, 92, 291, 318

Dietschreit, Frank 491, 584, 593

Disraeli, Benjamin 68

Dittberner, Hugo 167, 265, 641

DLA *see* Deutsches Literaturarchiv, Marbach

Döblin, Alfred 1, 120, 161, 164, 175, 354 n. 2, 386, 449, 461, 462, 463, 486, 624, 625, 626, 628, 630 *see also* Works by W. G. Sebald, *Der Mythus der*

Zerstörung im Werk Döblins
  Berge, Meere, Giganten 83
  Berlin Alexanderplatz 113, 354

Doderer, Heimito von 60, 161, 386

Doerry, Martin 493, 593, 651

Donleavy, J. P. *Fairy Tales of New York* (production directed by WGS) 51, 80, 623

Donne, John 286, 404

Dresden 85, 621

Dryden, John 59

Dubois, Philippe 217

Duden, Anne 187, 361

Dumontin, Louis 335

Dunwich Heath, Suffolk 268, 284, 478

Durrell, Martin 73

Durzak, Manfred 105 n. 121, 167, 635

Dusek, Peter 587

Dylan, Bob 41

Earl of Bristol, the (4th), Bishop of Derry *see* Ickworth Hall, Suffolk

EAS (School of English and American Studies, UEA) 122, 131, 648, 649

East Anglia 9, 10, 59, 92, 94, 250, 319–23, 357, 437, 603, 657

East Bergholt, Suffolk 319

East End (London) 9, 301, 302, 330, 646

Eberhard, Kurt 42, 44 fig., 45 fig., 95, 95 n. 4

Ebert-Schifferer, Sybille 234

Eco, Umberto 266

éducation sentimentale 18, 99 n. 49, 257

Egelhofer, Annie 27, 35, 64

Egelhofer, Fanny 28 fig., 29, 64

Egelhofer, Josef 31, 32, 33, 34, 176, 622

Egelhofer, Rosa Genoveva 17, 29, 655

Egelhofer, Rudolf 34, 257

Egelhofer, Theresia (*née* Harzenetter) 621

Eich, Günter 106 n. 137, 386, 461

Eichborn Verlag 636

Eisner, Kurt 276, 277

ekphrasis 7, 218, 219, 220, 235

Eliot, T. S. 12, 302
  The Waste Land 302

Elsaesser, Thomas 88, 130, 628, 629

Ely, Cambridgeshire 321, 322, 323

Empson, William, *Seven Types of Ambiguity* 99 n. 47

Emrich, Wilhelm 61

Engel, Peter 589

England 5, 6, 18, 36, 55, 64, 75, 112, 154, 155, 157, 174, 191 fig., 198, 211, 284, 304, 320, 339, 356, 360, 365, 368, 369, 372, 373, 577, 580, 611, 631, 641, 644, 648, 650, 651, 652

Enlightenment tradition 176

Enzensberger, Hans Magnus 136, 189, 190, 191 fig., 340, 341, 386, 589, 634, 639, 640, 657

Erlangen 64, 626

Eschweiler, Gerhard 40 fig., 44 fig.

EUR (School of European Studies/ School of Modern
   Languages and European History, UEA) 87, 88,
   89, 91, 94, 109, 117, 122, 162, 625, 626, 627, 628,
   630, 633, 634, 640, 641, 642, 648
European literature 109, 282 *see also* Sebald, W. G.,
   teaching
   modern European drama 120
'European Writers' Forum', UEA 183, 189–90, 191
   fig., 639 *see also* BCLT
Evans, Richard 496, 627, 628, 631, 635, 649, 650, 651,
   653
exile 36, 60, 68, 87, 95 n. 11, 121, 122, 151, 162, 164,
   178, 332, 356, 357, 369, 602, 633
Expressionism 56, 61, 62, 63
Eye, Suffolk 320

Fakenham, Norfolk 320, 321
Falcke, Eberhard 589
Fasching 40 figs, 124
Fascism 354 *see also* National Socialism, NSDAP
Fellini, Federico, *Roma* 456
Fiebach, Joachim 587
Firnberg, Herta 587, 632
First World War *see* World War I
Fischer, Heinz 587, 632
Fischer, Tibor 194 fig., 646
Fitzgerald, Edward 96 n. 14, 319, 405
Flamingo Hotel, Antwerp 219, 219 fig. *see also* Antwerp
Flanner, Janet 340
Flasch, Kurt 175
Flaubert, Gustave 140, 264, 285
   Trois contes 264
Flower, John 91
Fontane, Theodor 91, 137, 140, 387, 596
forgetting 11, 221, 238, 368, 612
Forster, Kurt W. 586
Foucault, Michel 626
Fourier, (François-Marie) Charles 276, 277
Fowler, Roger 155
Framingham Earl, Norfolk 310, 311, 654
   St Andrews church 311 fig., 654
Framlingham, Suffolk 319
France 86, 149, 259, 369, 372, 621, 625, 650
Frankfurt am Main 622
Frankfurt School, the 3, 53, 54, 62, 76, 96 nn. 15 &
   16, 97 n. 18, 163, 270, 287, 622
Frankfurter Allgemeine Zeitung 54, 374
Frankfurter Rundschau 9, 86, 211, 332, 342
Frank-G[ebhardt], Thea 100 n. 67, 249
Franksen, Jan 590, 627, 630
Fredy, Eleonore 587
Freiburg im Breisgau 3, 20, 41 fig., 45, 46 fig., 47 fig.,
   86, 272, 622 *see also* 'Gruppe 64'; 'Max-Heim';
   University of Freiburg
Freiburger Studenten-Zeitung 48, 51, 55, 623
Freikorps 34, 257
Fressingfield, Suffolk 320

Freud, Sigmund 103 n. 97, 167–68, 364, 422
   Freudian psychoanalysis 167–68
   Mourning and Melancholia 364
   see also das Unheimliche / the Uncanny
Freund, Gisèle 217
Freytag, Gustav 162
Fribourg, Switzerland 58 fig., 59 fig., 60, 61, 64, 79,
   109, 110, 304, 623, 631, 650, 653 *see also* University
   of Fribourg
Friedländer, Saul, *When Memory Comes* 372, 375 n. 3
Fritton, Norfolk 320
Fuks, Ladislav 187
Fuller, John 194 fig., 646
Furness, Ray 72 fig., 82, 180 n. 19, 628

Galaske, Rainer 41 fig., 44
Galbraith, Iain 194, 642, 646, 658
Garonne, River 338
Gascar, Pierre 188
Gasseleder, Klaus 249
Gatenby, Greg 198, 207
GDR literature 167
Gebhardt, Thea *see* Frank-G[ebhart], Thea; Lanzberg,
   Luise
'Gedächtnisbild' (memory image) 222, 232 *see also*
   Kracauer, Siegfried
Gee, Grant 589, 658
Genazino, Wilhelm 589
Generaloberst-Beck-Kaserne, Sonthofen 52 fig., 98 fig.
Geneva 653
Gerhardt, Ulrich 584
German Idealism 53
German cinema of the 1920s 4, 130, 131, 134, 282, 628
   see also Thomas Elsaesser; Sebald, W. G.: teaching,
   Weimar Republic
German literature 4, 59, 60, 61, 63, 71, 83, 89,
   97 n. 19, 121, 131, 154, 161, 164, 197, 280, 286,
   346, 627, 632, 633, 635, 636, 641
   German novel, the 59
   modern German theatre 80, 300
   post-1945 German literature 63, 83, 123, 164, 633,
      636 *see also* Sebald, W. G., teaching
   post-war/contemporary German theatre 5, 81, 158,
      183, 184–86, 466
   post-Expressionist German literature 59
German Romantics 54
German Social Democracy 89
Germanistik 5, 45, 161, 162, 163, 164, 173, 174, 176, 286
   see also Auslandsgermanistik
Germany 1, 3, 6, 18, 20, 25, 27, 32, 36, 51, 56, 61 fig.,
   63, 73, 85, 87, 92, 110, 112, 114, 116, 119, 151, 154,
   157, 161, 162, 163, 165, 204, 207, 304, 346, 356,
   358, 359, 360, 361, 366, 367, 368, 369, 373, 624,
   633, 638, 639, 644, 645, 647, 650, 654
   during the 1920s 27
Gernhardt, Robert 589
Glasgow 71

Goethe, Johann Wolfgang von 8, 20, 74, 91, 94 n., 161, 280, 281, 283, 287, 288 fig., 346, 387–88, 596
    Faust 269, 288 fig.
    Italienische Reise 281, 281 fig., 296 nn. 60 & 61
    Novelle 137
    Unterhaltungen deutscher Ausgewanderten 280
    Wilhelm Meisters Lehrjahre 94
Goethe-Institut
    London 207, 272, 630
    Manchester 79
    Munich 81, 82, 92, 116, 627
    New York 645
    Paris 658
    Sydney 656
Gogl, Karl 490
Good, Colin 85, 112, 156
Görner, Rüdiger 585
Gotthelf, Jeremias (Albert Bitzius) 282
Graham, Robert Bontine Cunninghame 200
Grass, Günter 135, 148, 214, 360, 388, 596, 463
    Aus dem Tagebuch einer Schnecke 136, 138, 139, 214
    Die Blechtrommel 70
Graz 170, 279, 468, 630, 637, 638, 649
    see also Manuskripte
Great War *see* World War I
Greece 68
Green, Toby 262 n. 19, 493, 593, 649
Greene, Graham 212, 596
Greenlaw, Lavinia 585
Greiner, Ulrich 588
Grenzgänger 5, 156
Griem, Julika 586
Grillparzer, Franz 161, 280, 418, 486
Grimkowski, Sabine 585
Grollandschule, Bremen ('Nashornschule') 483
Grossman, David 187
Grünten (mountain), Allgäu 20
'Gruppe 64' 47 fig., 48, 48 fig., 97 n. 20, 623 *see also* 'Max-Heim', University of Freiburg
Gugging psychiatric hospital 167, 168, 180 n. 27, 590, 629 *see also* Klosterneuburg *and* Navratil, Leo
Guttsman, Willi 89, 90 fig., 106 n. 134
Guys Hospital 329

Habsburg Empire 60 *see also* Austro-Hungarian Empire
Hackl, Andrea 588
Hage, Volker 482, 493, 593, 649 *see also Luftkrieg*
Haller, Albrecht von 300
Haller, Rudolf 587
Halmschlager, Ulli 588
Hamann, J. G. 477
Hamburger, Michael 6, 9, 10–11, 100 n. 62, 190, 224, 230, 265, 268, 269, 284, 289, 290, 292, 294 n. 23, 296 n. 69, 300, 312–13, 343 fig., 344–48, 347 fig., 405, 472, 474, 475, 483, 586, 596, 634, 642, 648, 649, 655, 657, 658, 659
    'Afterlives' 11, 345 n. 2

translations of Hölderlin, *see* Hölderlin, Johann Christian Friedrich
Hamish Hamilton 210, 213
Handke, Peter 6, 119, 131, 161, 170, 173–74, 449, 461–62, 463, 464, 582, 630
    Die Angst des Tormanns beim Elfmeter 136, 463
    Kaspar 133, 461–62
    Langsame Heimkehr 173
    Die Wiederholung 173, 174
    Wunschloses Unglück 174
Harley Street, London 304
Harris, Sir Arthur 85
Harris, Stefanie 232
Hartmannswillerkopf, Alsace 650
Harvill Press 6, 195–96, 197, 199, 208, 209, 210, 359, 361, 640, 643
Harwich 319, 322, 323
Hauptmann, Gerhard 55
Haverhill, Suffolk 322
Hebbel, Friedrich 278
Hebel, Johann Peter 3, 20, 31, 33, 35, 53, 96 n. 15, 137, 165, 264, 389, 449, 472, 597
    Kalendergeschichten 96 n. 15, 264
Hegel, Georg Wilhelm Friedrich 167
Heidegger, Martin 344, 422, 622 *see also* University of Freiburg
Heidelberger-Leonard, Irène 214, 335, 468, 577, 635, 637
Heimat 10, 165, 166, 170, 177, 178, 291, 324, 331, 332, 588, 633, 637, 641
'Heimat-/Anti-Heimatliteratur' 166
Heine, Heinrich 285, 645
    Heine-Preis *see* Sebald, W. G., awards, prizes and distinctions
Hemingway, Ernest 370
Henry Simon Chair of German, University of Manchester 55, 71
Hensher, Philip 194 fig., 646
Hensel, Klaus 589
Heraclitus 229, 230, 315
Herbeck, Ernst / Alexander Herbrich 1, 3, 6, 34, 167–68, 169, 171, 176, 180 n. 27, 264, 279, 301, 304, 390, 462, 469, 476, 629, 638
    Alexander 264
Herbert, Zbigniew, *Still Life with a Bridle* 372, 375 n. 1
Herburger, Günter 296 n. 69, 390, 589
Herzen, Alexander 414, 486
Herzl, Theodor 277
Hesse, Hermann 72
Heveningham, Suffolk 320
Hildebrandslied, the 162
Hildesheimer, Wolfgang 83, 214, 390, 463, 597, 647
    Tynset 83, 135, 463
Hill, David Octavius 221
Hilsbecher, Stefan 585
Hilton, Julian 587
Hine, Lewis 224, 224 fig.
Hingham, Norfolk 106 n. 140, 625

Hintermeier, Hannes 493, 594
Hirsch, Marianne 241 n. 13
Hitler, Adolf 63
Hochland (Catholic journal) 60
Hochreith (mountain), Austria 327, 328, 332
Hoffmann, E. T. A. 51, 96 n. 14, 352
    Der goldene Topf 51, 96 n. 14
    Der Sandmann 137, 140, 352
Hofmannsthal, Hugo von 35, 55, 59, 60, 63, 72,
    100 n. 51, 161, 268–69, 289, 290, 292, 391, 462,
    464, 481, 623, 631
    'Chandos letter' / 'Ein Brief' 63–64, 268–69
    Der Schwierige 59, 623
Hölderlin, Johann Christian Friedrich 8, 9, 20, 34, 35,
    68, 268, 284–85, 300, 344, 346, 348, 391, 477, 625
    'Brod und Wein' 284
    'Elegie' 477
    'Der Main' 68
    'Patmos' 9, 284, 300
    translations by Michael Hamburger 268, 284, 300
Holeczek, Bernhard 48
Holkham, Norfolk 94, 321, 484
    Victoria Hotel 321, 484, 603
Holocaust, the *see* Shoah, the
Holt, Norfolk 321
Holy Land, the 358
Honickel, Thomas 579, 589
Horkheimer, Max 53, 75, 76, 78, 84, 85, 163, 422
    Dialektik der Aufklärung 76, 287 *see also* Adorno,
        Theodor
    Kritische Theorie 84
Horringer, Suffolk 322
Horváth, Ödon von 151, 391, 463, 628
Houpt, Simon 495, 594
Hrabal, Bohumil, *Schöntrauer-Trilogie* 264
Hubmann, Franz, *Dream of Empire: The World of
    Germany in Original Photographs 1840–1914* 218, 486
Huizingen, Belgium 334
Hulse, Michael, 6, 9, 10, 11, 13 n. 12, 194, 195–208,
    209, 256 fig., 266, 285, 315, 336–37, 358, 360, 637,
    638, 640, 641, 642, 643, 644, 645, 646
    'An Botho Strauss in Berlin' (trans. by WGS) 10,
        336
    'Raffles Hotel in Singapur' (trans. by WGS) 10,
        336–37
Hunt, Hugh 79
Hütteldorf Monastery, Austria 325
Hyde, George 195, 635

Ibsen, Henrik 89
Ickworth Hall, Suffolk 322
Iken, Suffolk 319
Industrial Revolution 92
Innerhofer, Franz 170
Inter-Nationes 272
Ipswich, Suffolk 199
Irving, David 85

Isenschmid, Andreas 582, 587, 588, 589, 655
Italy 18, 56, 281 fig., 305, 350, 353, 623
    Altipiano, the 305
    Lakes 18 *see also* Lake Garda
Ithaca, New York 18, 198, 358, 631

Jacobean Tragedy 59, 623
Jaggi, Maya 145, 152 n. 3, 494, 584, 594, 653
Jahnn, Hans Henry, *Perrudja* 75, 83
Japan 358
Jaray, Tess 1, 570, 649, 652
Jarman, Derek, *Wittgenstein* 332
Jean Paul (Johann Paul Friedrich Richter) 391, 477,
    597
Jerusalem 18, 68, 148, 248, 622
Jeutter, Ralf 192 fig., 586
Jewish culture, names 31, 196, 354, 606
Jewish emigrants from Nazi Germany 35, 639
Jewish nineteenth-century writers 170
Jewish thinkers of the Frankfurt School 53
Jonas, Peter 82, 624, 653, 655
Jones, Malcolm, 495, 594
de Jong, Anneriek 491, 593, 640
Jordan, Peter and Dorothy 69, 100 n. 67, 647
Journal of European Studies 13 n. 16, 91, 162, 179 n. 2,
    322, 626
Joyce, James 269
Jung, Jochen 631, 632, 633
Jünger, Ernst 118, 259
Just, Renate 490, 491

Kaeser, Jürgen 44 fig., 49 fig., 50 fig., 657
Kafatou, Sarah 446, 492, 593, 619, 647
Kafka, Franz 1, 6, 60, 71, 78, 113, 118, 120, 130, 131,
    132, 141,145, 147, 155, 161, 167, 171–72, 180 n. 19
    & 27, 211, 214, 251, 262 n. 19, 278, 279–80, 282,
    290, 300, 350, 351, 352, 353, 392–94, 461, 466,
    470, 486, 487, 488, 592, 597, 625, 626, 630
    'Ein Bericht für eine Akademie' 132, 155, 171–72
    'Der Jäger Gracchus' 35
    Der Proceß 55, 78, 132, 141
    Das Schloß 113, 132, 141, 461, 626
Kafka, Miguel 625
Kalhammer, Walter 44 fig., 49 fig., 50 fig.
Kant, Immanuel 12, 590, 630
Kantor, Tadeusz 187
Karasek, Hellmuth 85, 86, 582, 587, 589, 625, 639
Kasack, Hermann 135, 462
Karl, Frederick 199
Keller, Gottfried 20, 33, 34, 60, 137, 165, 177, 274, 370,
    394, 449, 472, 597
Keller, Ruedi 64, 71, 71 fig., 72, 73, 79, 87
Kemp, Edward 585
Kempten, Allgäu 31, 650
Kempter Calender 31
Kennedy, A. L. 194 fig., 646
Kermode, Frank, *The Sense of an Ending* 286

Kerry, Stanley Sephton 73, 74 fig., 628
Kersey, Suffolk 322
Kew, London 327, 642
Keynes, John Maynard 325
Kierkegaard, Søren 76, 152
Kindermann, Gottfried-Karl 162
Kindertransport 375
King's Lynn, Norfolk 321, 323
Kiš, Danilo 187
Klagenfurt 121, 628, 629, 636
Klein, Georg 588, 653
Kleist, Heinrich von 177, 178, 264, 274, 394, 587, 642
    'Die Marquise von O.', 137, 140, 264
KLG (*Kritisches Lexikon zur deutschsprachigen
    Gegenwartsliteratur*) 282
Klosterneuburg 168, 180 n. 27, 279, 329, 332, 625, 629
Klosterwald 29
Kluge, Alexander 136, 165, 394, 462, 597
Klüger, Ruth 175, 641
Knack magazine (Brussels) 11, 350–54
Knauss, Jakob 582
Köhler, Andrea 492, 585, 588, 589, 593
Könemann, Ludwig 196
Korzeniowski, Apollo 201, 204, 205
Kosler, Hans Christian 166
Kosovo 209, 210
Kospach, Julia 493, 593
Kouvaros, George 232
Kracauer, Siegfried 7, 134, 217, 230, 232, 233
    'Die Photographie' 232
    Theory of Film: The Redemption of Physical Reality 233
Krantz, Judith 364
Kraus, Karl 60, 395
Krauss, Rosalind 217
Krauthausen, Ciro 493, 594
Kreutzer, Leo 162
Kriegsarchiv, Munich 259, 652
Krockow, Christian Graf von 582
Krüger, Michael 589, 645, 655
Kübler, Gunhild 589
Kuna, Franz 91, 180 n. 19, 461, 628
Kunisch, Hans-Peter 493, 594
Kunze, Reiner 587
Küsters, Lotte *see* Liebsch, Ursula

Lake Constance (Bodensee) 325, 357, 370, 650
Lake Garda 281, 477, 634
Lake Geneva 275, 623
Lambert, David 152 n. 8, 495
Lana (Südtirol), Italy 650, 658
Landauer, Gustav 276, 277
Langer [?] [Austrian Germanist] 162
Lanzberg, Luisa 249 *see also* Frank-G[ebhardt, Thea]
    and Works by W. G. Sebald, *Die Ausgewanderten*
Larkin, Philip 242 n. 23
Lasker-Schüler, Else 187
Lavenham, Suffolk 94, 322

Lebensphilosophie (vitalism) 78
Lehmkuhl, Tobias 586
Lejeune, Philippe *see* 'autobiographical pact'
Leningrad 327
Lessing, Gotthold Ephraim 4, 9, 81, 107, 161, 396
    Minna von Barnhelm 4, 9, 81, 107, 460
Leverton, Bertha [Levinson, Bertha] 373, 375 n. 4
    I Came Alone: The Stories of the Kindertransports 375 n. 4
    Into the Arms of Strangers: Stories of the Kindertransport
        (film version directed by Mark Jonathan Harris)
        375 n. 4
Levi, Primo 139, 187, 285, 305, 357, 412, 467, 598, 633,
    635, 647
Lévi-Strauss, Claude 168, 257, 263 n. 30, 286, 422 *see
    also* bricolage
    La Pensée sauvage 168, 263 n. 30
Liebsch, Ursula (*née* Küsters, Lotte) 49 fig., 50 fig.
Limon, Daniel 115 fig.
Lindau, Lake Constance 357, 643
Liston's Music Hall, Manchester 84 fig.
Literaturhaus *see* Stuttgart
Literaturmuseum der Moderne, Marbach [LiMo] 270,
    271 fig., 297 n. 89, 643, 657 *see also* Deutsches
    Literaturarchiv
    'Wandernde Schatten', exhibition on W. G. Sebald
        270, 271 figs., 296 n. 63, 297 n. 88, 578–79,
        586, 642, 657
littérature mineure (Deleuze and Guattari) 168
Liverpool Street Station, London 145, 152, 301, 302
Lobsien, Verena Olejniczak 98 n. 33, 295 n. 44
Loddon, Norfolk 320
Łódź ghetto 164
Löffler, Sigrid 193 fig., 459, 491, 589, 593, 639, 640,
    654, 655
London 5, 9, 64, 74, 92, 144, 145, 152 n. 7, 198, 212,
    300, 301, 302, 303, 304, 306, 319, 327, 329, 330,
    361, 365, 372, 622, 625, 626, 630, 631, 634, 635,
    636, 638, 639, 642, 644, 646, 647, 648, 649, 652,
    653, 654 *see also* Alderney Road Cemetery, East
    End, Liverpool Street Station, Tower Hamlets,
    Whitechapel
Long Island *see* New York
Long, J. J. 13 n. 3, 100 n. 51
Long Melford, Suffolk 322
    Melford Hall 321
Loohuizen, Ria 586
Loquai, Franz 13 n. 3, 287
Lorenz, Konrad 168
Los Angeles 11, 375
Los Angeles Times 364, 375
Lubow, Arthur 494, 594
Ludham, Norfolk 320
Lüdke, Martin 588
Ludwig II, King of Bavaria 18
Luftkrieg 85, 164, 212, 339, 340, 552, 553, 554, 578, 588,
    629, 630 *see also* Works by W. G. Sebald, *Luftkrieg
    und Literatur*

Lustig, Arnost 187
Luik, Viivi 195
Lukács, Georg 55, 62, 63, 64, 75, 76, 77, 102 n. 92, 422, 489

MacLehose, Christopher 198 see also Harvill Press
Maisky, Ivan 327
Malcolm, Norman 331
Manchester 3, 4, 64, 65 fig., 66 fig., 67 fig., 68, 69 fig., 72, 73, 74, 81, 82, 83, 85, 92, 100 n. 67, 101 fig., 104 n. 116, 116, 165, 177, 196, 198, 232 fig., 274, 304, 324, 332, 484, 621, 628, 637, 653 see also University of Manchester, University of Manchester Theatre
Manea, Norman 188
Manheim, Ralph 214, 360
Mann, Thomas 20, 71, 74, 118, 131, 161, 217, 397, 598
    Der Tod in Venedig / Death in Venice 217
    Doktor Faustus 282
    Felix Krull 59, 78–79, 103 n. 95, 623
Mannheim, Karl 75, 84
    Ideologie und Utopie 84
Manningtree, Essex 319
Manuskripte (journal) 279, 631
Marat, Jean-Paul 334
Marbach am Neckar 9, 10, 61, 255, 270, 274, 583, 650 see also Deutsches Literaturarchiv, Marbach; Literaturmuseum der Moderne
Märchen 113, 172, 623
Marcuse, Herbert 53, 75, 76, 78, 108 n. 92, 103 n. 99, 163
    Kultur und Gesellschaft 76
Marienbad 438, 483, 626, 648
Maron, Monica 648
Marxism 62, 85
Matt, Peter von 86, 582, 589, 625
Matz, Wolfgang 262 n. 21, 586
'Max-Heim' (Studentenheim, Maximilianstraße, Freiburg im Breisgau) 46, 46 fig., 47 fig., 48, 51, 53, 71, 623 see also 'Gruppe 64', University of Freiburg
May, Karl 341
McCrum, Robert 492, 593
McCullin, Don 238
McEwan, Ian 149
McFarlane, James Walter 89, 90 fig., 189, 191 fig., 625
McGough, Roger 10, 495–96
McGill, Robert 152 n. 8, 495
McVeigh, Joseph 162, 487
Meier, Franz 39 figs.
Meixner, Horst 96 n. 14, 623
melancholy 6, 7, 55, 68, 70, 83, 92, 121, 154, 171, 174, 210, 214, 220, 235, 236, 241 n. 8, 243 n. 36, 301, 350, 351, 354, 361, 364, 611–12
Melbourne Literature Festival 208
Melchinger, Siegfried, Geschichte des politischen Theaters 156

Melzer, Gerhard 165
Memmingen, Allgäu 26
memory 154, 158, 159, 164, 176, 217, 218, 220–23, 225–26, 228–30, 232, 235, 237, 238–39, 285, 293 n. 16, 302–03, 353, 364, 365, 367, 368, 369, 373, 612 see also post-memory
Merleau-Ponty, Maurice 230
Messerschmidt, Daniel 248
metaphysics, metaphysical 42, 166, 173–74, 181 n. 52, 234, 241 n. 8, 242 n. 19, 352, 609
    German metaphysics 92
Miano, Sarah Emily 585
Middleton (Marsh Acres), Suffolk see also Hamburger, Michael 348, 478, 658
Modernism 92, 143, 144
modernity 46, 64
Mohr, Jean 229
Moor, Piet de, 'Echoes from the Past' 11, 354, 491, 593, 639
Moravia 306
Morgan, Peter 492, 588, 593, 647
Mörike, Eduard 33, 91, 165, 397, 470–71
    Mörike-Preis see Sebald, W. G., awards, prizes and distinctions
Morris, Jan 117, 128
Mosse, Werner 89, 90 fig.
moths 7, 12, 212, 213, 291, 296 n. 63 see also butterflies
Moyers, Scott 291, 654
Mueller, Armin 38 fig.
Mühling, Jens 493, 593, 650
Munich 20, 34, 36, 39 fig., 100 n. 67, 165, 169, 259, 291, 300, 372, 621, 624, 625, 626, 627, 631, 632, 633, 634, 636, 638, 639, 643, 648, 649, 652, 653, 655, 656
Munich Soviet (1919) 257, 632
Mušič, Zoran 649
Musil, Robert 45, 60, 161, 398, 598

Nabokov, Vladimir 12, 35, 139, 197, 198, 214, 264, 291, 305, 363, 369, 371, 406, 470, 598
    Lolita 371
    Pnin 369
    Speak, Memory 122, 198, 264
Nachlass 7, 8, 247–63, 270, 273, 333, 571, 573, 578, 579, 619, 640, 642, 656 see also Sebald, W. G., Nachlass
Nachlassbibliothek see Sebald, W. G., library
Nadar (Gaspard Félix Tournachon) 238
Nadler, Josef 162
Naegeli, Johannes 33, 234, 243 n. 52 see also Works by W. G. Sebald, Die Ausgewanderten
Naples 351
Napoleon 18, 63, 78
Napoleonic period 53
narration 82, 150, 156, 234 see also plot
narrators 33, 143, 149, 248, 260, 265, 267, 270, 275, 278, 362

National Socialism   3, 35, 54, 55, 59, 60, 63, 86, 101, 151, 157, 162, 213, 236 *see also* NSDAP, SS, Third Reich
 anti-Nazi Germanists 60
 Nazi Germany 35, 54, 61 fig., 101
 Nazi press 60
nationalism 34, 60
NATO 209, 210
Naturalism 45
Navratil, Leo 180 n. 27, 433, 629
Navratil, Michel Marcel 286
Nazis, Nazism *see* National Socialism
necrophilia 220
neo-Nazism 86
NESTA (National Endowment for Science, Technology, and the Arts) *see* Sebald, W. G., awards, prizes, and distinctions
Nestroy, Johann Nepomuk 103 n. 105, 398, 486
Neue Zürcher Zeitung 10, 335, 350, 638, 645
Neuschwanstein (castle), Bavaria 18
New Criticism 53, 99 n. 47 *see also werkimmanente Kritik*
New York 18, 35, 51, 64, 328, 330, 358, 630, 644, 645, 652, 654 *see also* Ithaca
 Long Island 358
New York Times 291, 653
New Zealand 373
Newcastle-upon-Tyne 329
Nietzsche, Friedrich 54, 62, 120, 241 n. 8, 423
Nobel Prize 148
Norfolk 9, 85, 127, 243 n. 27, 304, 310 fig., 319, 320–21, 625
Norfolk Broads, the 320
Norfolk, Lawrence 194 fig., 646
North Creake, Norfolk 321
Northamptonshire 339
Northey, Anthony 280
Norwich 5, 81, 92, 106 n. 140, 112 fig., 144, 145, 156, 165, 191 fig., 198, 199, 249, 257, 266, 273, 301, 304, 320, 322, 323, 355 fig., 625–29, 631–38, 640, 643, 645–48, 650–54, 657, 658
Nossack, Hans Erich 135, 462, 598
NSDAP (Nationalsozialistische Deutsche Arbeiterpartei) 54, 328, 621
Nuremberg 621, 626, 648

O'Grady, Timothy, *I Could Read The Sky* 220 *see also* Berger, John and Pyke, Steve
O'Neill, Eugene, *In the Zone* 51, 53 fig., 622
Oberjoch 30 fig., 619, 634
Oberstdorf 36, 39 fig., 40 fig., 43 fig., 45 fig., 49 fig., 52 fig., 97 n. 19, 233, 643, 657, 658
 Nebelhorn Hotel 40 fig.
 Oberrealschule Oberstdorf (now the Gertrud-von-le-Fort Gymnasium) 41 fig., 42, 43 fig., 622
Oedipus complex 78, 103 n. 97

Oehlen, Martin 492, 593
Ohain, Belgium 335
Ohnesorg, Benno 105 n. 121, 624
Omar Kayyam [*sic*] 319 *see also* Fitzgerald
'Operation Gomorrah' 339–40, 471, 482, 598, 621, 645 *see also Luftkrieg*
Orbis Litterarum 211
Ordensburg, Sonthofen 98 fig., 259
Ore, River (Suffolk) 319
Orford, Suffolk 319
Orford Ness 95
Ottertal 330, 331
'*outre-tombe*' 251
Oxburgh Hall, Oxborough, Norfolk 321
Oxford 71, 74, 257, 346, 365, 634, 636, 652
Oxford Union 117

Paris 9, 70, 143, 151, 238, 257, 293 n. 16, 359, 363, 365, 583, 621, 622, 625, 645, 647, 649, 650, 651, 653, 656
Parkinson, Michael Henry 119 fig., 477, 641, 642
Parry, Idris 71 fig., 72, 75, 180 n. 19
Parschalk, H. 582, 635
Pascal, Fanja 326, 329
Passannanti, Erminia 192 fig.
Peacock, Ronald 55, 64, 71, 73, 87, 88, 623, 628
Pehnt, Annette 589
Pennines, the 332
Pepys, Samuel 286
Perec, Georges 143, 147, 187, 264, 285, 410
 Life A User's Manual 147
 W ou le souvenir de l'enfance 139, 264, 285
peripheries 106 n. 140
Pessoa, Fernando 8, 143, 285, 297 n. 75, 413
 Odes of Ricardo Reis 285, 297 n. 75
Philadelphia 366, 653
photographs 7, 8, 9, 11, 12, 81, 105 n. 128, 176, 213, 218, 220, 221–26, 228–34, 236, 237, 238, 239, 241 n. 8, 250, 252, 255, 239, 283, 305, 322, 333, 365, 366, 367
photography 7, 8, 217–45, 250, 332, 365, 653
Pick, Hella 588
Pietragrua, Angela 240
pigeons 212, 291, 297 n. 86, 339, 342
Pisanello [Vittore Pisano [?]] 476
plot 61, 145, 151, 259, 362 *see also* narrative
Poland 82
Polasek, Martin 587
Polish campaign, the 259
Poljudow, Valerij 85, 86
Polstead, Suffolk 322
post-war German literature *see* German literature; *see also* Sebald, W. G., teaching
post-memory 221, 237
post-war generation, 114
post-war years (in Germany) 61 fig., 257, 305, 367, 370
Prague 9, 211, 228, 250, 306, 365, 368, 369, 372, 637, 648

Pralle, Uwe 494, 584, 585, 594, 653
Prinzhorn, Hans 168
Proust, Marcel 7, 78, 106 n. 141, 228, 270, 285, 287, 410, 475
Proustian notion of involuntary memory 7, 228
Prudhoe, John 80, 81
psychoanalysis 168
punctum 223, 224, 224 fig., 241 n. 8, 242 n. 23 *see also* Barthes, Roland
Pyke, Steve, *I Could Read the Sky*, 220, *see also* Berger, John and O'Grady, Timothy

Qualtinger, Helmut 82

racism 60
Raimund, Ferdinand 398, 463
Ramsey, Frank Plumpton 325
Ramsey, Lettice 325
Random House 210, 291, 654
Ranwell, Beryl 189, 192 fig., 255, 256, 282, 348, 359
Ranworth, Norfolk 320
Raphael, Frederic 651
Rasche, Albrecht 46 fig., 47 fig., 48, 51, 54, 56, 73, 103 n. 97, 623
Raulff, Ulrich 586
Rawicz, Piotr 187
Realism / Realist writing 33, 143, 145, 149, 150
    'UEA realist aesthetic' 149 *see also* Sebald W. G., teaching; creative writing
Red Army 257, 621, 632
Reedham, Norfolk 320
Reepham, Norfolk 320
Rehm, Walter 45, 54, 55
Reich, Friedemann 50 fig.
Reichert, Franz 587
Reich-Ranicki, Marcel 589, 639
Reichswehr 98 fig.
Reinhardt, Stephan 175, 640
Reiss, Karin 587, 640
Rendlesham, Suffolk 319
Reuterwanne (mountain), Allgäu 61 fig.
Reutlingen 60, 637, 656
Rhine, River 370
Richards, Ben 330
Rilke, Rainer Maria 60, 72, 195, 399
Riva, Italy 280, 281, 633 *see also* Lake Garda
Robbe-Grillet, Alain 143, 144
    Jealousy 138, 144
Rockland St Mary, Norfolk 320
Romanticism 34, 45, 54, 80, 96 n. 14, 113
Rondas, Jean-Pierre 275, 278, 279, 282, 494, 583, 652
Rosset, Clément 239
Rot an der Rot (Swabia) 26, 650
Roth, Gerhard 161, 173, 176, 399, 464, 630
    Landläufiger Tod 173, 176, 464
Roth, Joseph 60, 270, 467, 399, 582, 587, 599, 635, 636

Rousseau, Jean-Jacques 205, 275, 285, 295 n. 43, 410, 472, 599
Rowley, Brian 89, 91 fig.
Rowohlt *Bildmonographien* 87, 283, 283 fig., 284 fig., 286, 286 fig., 287, 290
Royal Air Force 365
Rudnicki, Adolf 188
Rugby School 339
rugby 226 fig., 228
Ruoss, Hardy 589
Ruprecht, Erich 54, 96 n. 14, 623
Rushdie, Salman 143, 144
    Midnight's Children 144
Russell, Bertrand Arthur William 325
Russian exile community 371

Sagarra, Albert 73 fig.
Sagarra, Eda 71, 73 fig., 180 n. 19
Sailors' Reading Room, Southwold 275
Saint-Exupéry, Antoine-Marie-Roger de 285
Salle, Norfolk 320, 624
Salter Reynolds, Susan 279, 494, 594, 654
Sander, August 238
Sandringham, Norfolk 94, 321
Santorini, Greece 56
Sarraute, Nathalie 143, 138, 285
Sauder, Gerhard 585
Schäfer, Walter Erich 158–59
Scheck, Denis 492, 583, 593, 645
Scherer, Bruno Stephan 59–60
Schiel, Friedrich 82
Schiller, Friedrich, 20, 59, 73, 127 n. 4, 195, 277–78, 295 n. 48
    Die Verschwörung des Fiescos zu Genua 127 n. 4
Schilling, Klaus 50 fig.
Schlodder, Holger 584, 585
Schlüter, Wolfgang 193 fig., 296 n. 69, 400, 471, 490, 589, 644, 655
Schmidt, Adalbert 162, 179 n. 5
Schmidt, Arno 135, 265
Schmidt, K. H. 50 fig.
Schneider, [?], *Schulleiter*, Volkschule Sonthofen 38 fig.
Schnitzler, Arthur 60, 400, 463, 464, 628
Schoeller, Wilfried F. 589
Scholl, Hans and Sophie 97 n. 19
Scholz, Christian 490, 492, 583, 593, 645
Schübler, Walter 585
Schulte-Sasse, Jochen 163
Schulze, Ingo 147, 152 n. 9
Schütte, Uwe 34, 91, 106 n. 140, 179 n. 15, 468, 637, 658
Schwaben *see* Swabia
Schwäbisch Hall *see* Sebald, W. G.
Schwanitz, Dietrich 46, 47 fig., 48, 51, 73, 95 n. 11, 97 nn. 20 & 21, 632
    Der Campus 46, 95 n. 11

Schwanitz, Etta (*née* Uphoff)   47 fig., 51, 53, 54, 55, 70, 94, 95 n. 11, 101 n. 69, 656

Schwartz, Lynne Sharon   11

Sciascia, Leonardo   285

Scott, Clive   7, 115 fig., 127 n. 3, 217, 223, 225–30, 233, 240 n. 2, 242 n. 23, 243 nn. 36 & 38, 290, 452

The Spoken Image   7, 217, 223, 225–30, 233, 240 n. 2, 242 n. 23, 243 nn. 36 & 38

Sealsfield, Charles   161, 401, 467, 634

Sebald, Beate   31

Sebald, Georg   17, 32, 621, 622, 625, 648

Sebald, W. G. [Winfried Georg]:

awards, prizes and distinctions:

Aspekte-Literaturpreis   587, 637

Bayerische Akademie der schonen Künste (elected 1998)   525, 646

Berliner Literaturpreis (Johannes-Bobrowski-Medaille) (1994)   121, 356, 478, 516, 536, 576, 641–42

Ingeborg-Bachmann-Preis   121, 477, 587, 636

Heinrich-Böll-Preis (1997)   10, 207, 263 n. 25, 342, 471, 644, 645 (*see also* Works by W. G. Sebald, 'Feuer und Rauch')

Joseph-Breitbach-Preis (2000)   576, 650

Bremer Literaturpreis (2001)   512, 541, 577, 654, 655

Deutsche Akademie fur Sprache und Dichtung (elected 1997)   471, 643, 645, 648

European Prize for Literature   640

Fiction Prize of the National Book Critics Circle of the USA (2001)   577, 654, 655

Heinrich-Heine-Preis (2000)   480, 514–15, 576–77, 650, 651

Independent Foreign Fiction Prize (2002)   577, 655

Jewish Quarterly / Wingate Prize for Literature (1996)   644

Prix Laure-Bataillon (2000)   577, 649–50

Literatour Nord (1994)   459, 576, 641, 642

Los Angeles Times Book Prize (fiction) (1999)   648, 653

Fedor-Malchow-Lyrikpreis (1991)   506, 576, 638

Mörike-Preis der Stadt Fellbach (1997)   193 figs, 470–71, 477, 521, 576, 644

NESTA award (National Endowment for Science, Technology, and the Arts)   12 n. 1, 46, 99 n. 49, 257, 259, 273, 580, 649, 650, 651, 654, 657

see also translation prizes

birth, birthplace   17, 19 fig., 20 fig., 226

date of birth   103 n. 94, 226

childhood and family   16–37, 61 fig. 260 fig. *see also* Allgäu, Aebischer-Sebald, Egelhofer, Oberstdorf, Sebald, school, Sonthofen, Wertach

grandfather *see* Egelhofer, Josef

death (and reactions to)   37 n. 11, 110, 124–26, 152, 155–56, 213–14, 251, 257, 299, 303

obituaries and tributes   309–15, 540–43

drama productions (school and university)   51, 52 fig., 53 fig., 79–81, 127 n. 4

educational qualifications:

Abitur (school-leaving certificate)   42, 43 fig., 44 fig., 48, 99

licence (BA degree) (Université de Fribourg)   3, 56, 79, 161, 304

MA (University of Manchester) *see* Sternheim, Carl

PhD *see* University of East Anglia; Döblin, Alfred

Habilitation (University of Hamburg)   95 n. 11, 165, 632, 633

Freiburg im Breisgau   41 fig., 45–48, 51, 53–56, 71 *see also* 'Max-Heim', University of Freiburg

Fribourg   56–64 *see also* University of Fribourg

Goethe-Institut, Munich   82, 92, 116

interviews   350–75, 490–95, 592–618 *see also names of individual interviewers*

library   2, 11, 265–97, 377–441

Manchester   3, 4, 64–81, 82–83, 100 nn. 57 & 59, 101 fig., 107, 109, 119, 165, 180 n. 19, 232 fig., 297 n. 85, 304, 611, 646, 653 *see also* Chorlton-cum-Hardy, Didsbury, Withington, University of Manchester

Nachlass (archive)   247–63, 270, 273, 333, 573, 579 *see also* Deutsches Literaturarchiv, Marbach; W. G. Sebald, library

names, given, dislike of / using name 'Max'   94, 97–98 n. 29, 354, 623

Norwich   5, 88, 92, 106 n. 140, 112 fig., 145, 156, 165, 191 fig., 198, 199, 270, 301, 304, 355 fig., 625–54; *see also* University of East Anglia

Old Rectory, Poringland   93 figs, 155, 270, 273, 274 fig., 276 fig., 280 fig., 282, 284 fig., 345 fig., 377, 591 fig.

school:

Gymnasium Sankt Maria Stern, Immenstadt   95 n. 2, 622

Oberrealschule Oberstdorf   39 fig., 40 fig., 42–45, 49 fig., 50 fig., 52 fig., 53 fig., *see also* Starzlach

Volkschule Sonthofen   38 fig.

Schwäbisch Hall   116, 627 *see also* Goethe-Institut

St Gallen   3, 4, 81–82, 104 n. 112, 304, 624, 652

Institut auf dem Rosenberg (Rosenberg-Schule)   81, 624

University of East Anglia (UEA)   3, 55, 79, 81, 83, 86–92, 94, 97 nn. 18 & 27, 100 n. 49, 101 n. 73, 105 n. 124, 105 n. 128, 109–54, 153 fig., 162, 165, 171 n. 2, 179 n. 5, 180 n. 19, 181 n. 33, 183–90, 191 fig., 192 fig., 255, 272, 273, 282, 284, 290, 294 n. 34, 296 n. 65, 299, 301, 303, 333, 346, 348, 356, 376 figs., 377, 449, 466, 477, 493, 495, 583, 587, 622, 625–53, 657, 658, 660 *see also* BCLT, EAS, EUR

teaching:

Creative Writing   122, 131, 143–52, 284, 493, 495, 613, 649, 650, 653

European literature 87, 109, 130, 133, 138, 139, 140, 165, 179 n. 2, 282

German language 109, 115–17, 123–24, 127 n., 128–29, 130, 131 *see also* Goethe-Institut; University of Manchester

German literature 4, 83, 109, 111, 113–14, 118–20, 123, 127, 130–32, 135–37, 141–42

Wymondham 92, 94, 106 n. 140, 127, 497 fig.

Seckford Hall, Suffolk 319

Seckford, Thomas 319

Second Vatican Council 59, 622

Second World War *see* World War II

Seelos, Mathild 276 *see also* Works by W. G. Sebald, *Schwindel. Gefühle.*

Seething airfield, Norfolk 263 n. 25, 338, 339

Seibt, Gustav 583, 645

Self, Will 586

Seume, Johann Gottfried, *Spaziergang nach Syrakus* 205

Shaffer, Elinor 231, 348 n.

Shakespeare, Sebastian 494, 594

Shakespeare, William 42, 46, 51, 59, 96 n. 14, 104 n. 107, 277–78, 283, 284 fig., 286, 286 fig., 287, 290, 295 nn. 44 & 48, 406–07, 623

As You Like It 96 n. 14

Coriolanus 59, 623

Cymbeline 59

Hamlet 80, 104 n. 107, 287

King Lear 268, 284

A Midsummer Night's Dream 51, 287

The Winter's Tale 295 n. 44

Shaw, Fiona 302

Shaw, George Bernard, *Man and Superman* 55, 97 n. 27

Sheppard, Richard, 13 nn. 3 & 16, 92, 127 n. 1, 179 n. 1, 348, 589, 634, 636

Shingle Street, Suffolk 319

Shoah, the 34, 148, 164, 183, 219, 553, 579, 586, 637, 651, 658

'Writing in the Shadow of the Shoah', research seminar series at UEA 186–87, 637

Short, Robert 88

Sichtermann, Barbara 598, 639

Sidney Sussex College, Cambridge 82, 104 n. 115, 624

Siedenberg, Sven 491, 593

Silverblatt, Michael 494, 584, 594, 654

Simon, Claude 138, 264, 285, 292, 298 fig.

Le Jardin des Plantes 264, 292

Le Tramway 292, 298 fig.

Simon, Ulrich 163

Sipp, Thomas 586

Skinner, Francis 326

Skrine, Peter 71 fig.

Smith, James 56, 99 n. 34, 623

Smith, Patti 658

Society of Authors (Translators Association) 638

Solothurn 56

Solothurner Literaturtage 344 n. 10

Somerleyton Hall and maze, Suffolk 8, 249–50, 267–68, 294 n. 20, 478, 585, 639, 640

Sontag, Susan 7, 8, 217, 218, 235–38, 239, 241 n. 12, 245 n. 87, 280, 364, 585, 639, 640, 664, 649, 653

'A Mind in Mourning' 245 n. 87

On Photography 7, 217, 218, 235–38, 239, 241 n. 12

Regarding the Pain of Others 236

Under the Sign of Saturn 236

Sonthofen 20 fig., 25, 25 fig., 26, 28 fig., 31, 36, 38 fig., 39 fig., 40 fig., 41 fig., 44 fig., 48, 50 fig., 52 fig., 86, 95 n. 2, 97 n. 19, 98 fig., 98 n. 29, 103 n. 100, 259, 295 n. 48, 496 fig., 621, 622, 624, 629, 631, 633, 635, 636, 637, 638, 639, 643, 645, 646, 647, 648, 650, 653, 654, 655, 656

Soulages, François 239

Southery, Norfolk 321

Southwold, Suffolk 275, 320, 323

Soviet Union 86

Soviet University of Perm 85

SPD (German Social Democratic Party) 95 n. 14

Speicher, Stephan 588

Spengler, Tilman 589

Spiegel, Hubert 588

Sprache im technischen Zeitalter 10, 197

Sraffa, Piero 325

SS (*Schutzstaffel*) 34, 621

St George 22 fig., 24, 24 fig., 361

St Jerome Lecture 152 n. 3, 306, 641, 653, 657 *see also* BCLT

St Peter Mancroft Church, Norwich 355 fig.

St Gallen *see* Sebald, W. G.

Stalingrad, Battle of 98 n. 29, 305

Stalinism 55, 91

Starobinski, Jean 286

Starzlach, River, Allgäu 20

Starzlachkamm, Winkel, Allgäu 50 fig.

Steiner, George 187

Steinman, Louise 375, 654

Steller, G[eorg] W[ilhelm] 248

Stendhal (Marie-Henri Beyle) 1, 240, 279, 280, 281, 285, 293 n. 16, 296 n. 65, 335, 350, 352, 411, 599

De l'amour 350

Fabrizio del Dongo (*La Chartreuse de Parme*) 335

Stern, Mario Rigoni 305

Sternheim, Carl 1, 3, 4, 56, 60–64, 75–79, 83–86, 88, 99 nn. 47 & 48, 103 nn. 94, 95 & 98, 104 n. 106, 105 nn. 121, 124, 125 & 126, 119, 120, 161, 163, 164, 175, 178, 179 n. 1, 449, 460, 481, 549, 582, 590, 623, 624, 625, 627

Die Kassette 103 n. 95

Die Schule von Uznach oder Neue Sachlichkeit 62

Stevenson, Robert Louis 283, 408

Stifter, Adalbert 20, 33, 34, 35, 60, 137, 140, 161, 179 n. 5, 180 n. 19, 264, 369, 401, 449, 464, 582, 599, 630, 631, 633, 634

Aus der Mappe meines Urgroßvaters 264

Stoisser, Doris 583
Stoke-by-Nayland, Suffolk 322
Storck, Joachim W. 55
Strand, Paul 238
Straus, Roger 371
Strittmatter, Ellen 296 n. 61, 586
Stryjkowski, Julian 188
Studer, Eduard 56–59, 623
studium 223, 231, 232 *see also* Barthes, Roland
Stuttgart 156, 159, 193 fig., 233, 272, 627, 628, 631, 632, 636, 644, 646, 650, 654, 656
    Literaturhaus 159, 160 fig., 459, 473, 577, 654, 655, 656
'Stuttgarter Ballettwunder' 158
Süddeutsche Zeitung 157
Sudek, Josef 306
Sudermann, Hermann 277–78
Suffolk 9, 10, 121, 243 n. 27, 268, 319–20, 322–23, 346, 639, 641, 642, 658
Surabaya 156
surgery, fear of 351, 603
Surlingham, Norfolk 320
Surrealism 88
survivor syndrome 187, 357, 612
Sutton Hoo, Suffolk 319
Swabia 18, 19, 20, 26, 31, 33, 165
Swaby, Stephen 79 fig., 80, 81, 103 n. 105
Swaffham, Norfolk 321
Swainson, Bill 195, 197, 208 n. 8, 640
Swales, Martin 166, 220
Switzerland 3, 4, 10, 18, 20, 33, 35, 36, 56, 58 fig., 70, 81, 104 n. 116, 165, 304, 344, 357, 624, 625, 631, 639, 641, 650
    French-speaking 3, 35, 56
Syberberg, Hans Jürgen 236
Szirtes, George 586

Tabbert, Reinbert 9, 64, 68, 69, 69 fig., 70, 72, 73, 81–82, 83, 94 n., 97 n. 18, 99 n. 48, 100 n. 65, 101 n. 81, 102 nn. 90 & 92, 103 n. 102, 104 nn. 103 & 107, 216 fig., 322 n., 490, 624, 656
Tennyson, Alfred [Lord] 319
Text+Kritik 197
The Times 83
Theresienstadt 7, 213, 648
Theweleit, Klaus 286, 431
Thibaudeau, Jean 586
Third Reich 18, 54, 113, 164, 207 *see also* National Socialism
Thistlethwaite, Frank 90 fig.
Thorn, Fritz 587
Tiffauges, Abel 225
timelessness 11, 353
Tolstoy, Leo 150, 600
Tonkin, Boyd 492, 593, 646, 649
tourism 92, 235, 294 n. 20, 321, 353

Tournier, Michel, *The Erl-King* 225
Tower Hamlets, London 301, 302
Trakl, Georg 71
translation 10, 11, 87, 109, 116–17, 120, 122, 128, 131, 157, 183, 191–215, 255, 267, 290, 345 n. 2, 358–61, 362, 371–72, 638, 641, 642, 646, 648, 651
    translation prizes (where known) (*see also* Sebald, W. G., awards, prizes, and distinctions)
        Greek National Prize for literary translation (Iannis Kalifatadis) 657
        Helen and Curt Wolff Prize (Anthea Bell) 655
        Independent Foreign Fiction Prize (Anthea Bell) 655
        Prix Laure-Bataillon (Patrick Charbonneau) 649
        Lessing Prize for translators (Hitoko Suzuki) 458
        Prix Gérard de Nerval (Patrick Charbonneau) 656
        Martinus Nijhoff Prijs (Ria van Hengel) 657
        Premio Nini Agosti Castellani (Ada Vigliani) 658
        Schlegel-Tieck Prize (Anthea Bell)
        Übersetzerpreis der Kunststiftung Nordrhein-Westfalen (Niels Brunse) 656
Trattenbach, Austria 326, 328
Trauerarbeit (work of mourning) 364
Trauerlaufbahn (career in mourning) 177
trauma, traumatic experience 164, 199, 223, 231, 242 n. 20, 329, 357, 363, 368, 371, 649
Tripp, Jan Peter 1, 7, 214, 217, 230, 233–35, 236 fig., 245 n. 82, 246 fig., 433, 449, 451–52, 469, 472, 475, 483, 570–71, 586, 589, 627, 630, 631, 632, 635, 638, 650, 651, 653, 655, 656, 657, 658
trompe l'œil 233–35
Turner, Gordon 568, 589, 627
twinning / *dédoublement* 218
Tyrol 18, 36, 165

UEA *see* University of East Anglia
unconscious, the 158
das Unheimliche / the Uncanny 81, 224, 303, 306, 366
United States of America 27, 28 fig., 29, 35, 155, 199, 210, 291, 346, 356, 363, 373, 364–65, 369, 630, 645, 653–54
University of Bangor 87, 625
University of East Anglia 4–5, 11, 81, 85, 87–92, 89 fig., 90 fig., 91 fig., 106 nn. 134 & 135, 109–54, 179 nn. 2 & 5, 180 n. 19, 183–90, 192 fig., 212 fig., 269, 272, 290, 294 n. 40, 301, 303, 346–47, 348, 356, 363, 376 figs., 461, 493, 583, 587, 622, 625, 627–28, 631, 641, 657, 658, 660 *see also* BCLT, EAS, EUR; *see also* Sebald, W. G., University of East Anglia
    Creative Writing programmes 4, 122, 131, 144, 284 *see also* Sebald, W. G., teaching
    Centre for Creative and Performing Arts 363
University of Essex 92
University of Freiburg im Breisgau 3, 20, 41 fig., 42, 45–48, 46 fig., 47 fig., 51, 54–56, 60, 61, 64, 70–71, 73, 79, 80, 86, 91, 95 nn. 5, 6, 11 & 19, 96

nn. 14, 16 & 17, 97 n. 27, 103 n. 97, 110, 344, 489, 622–23
University of Fribourg 3, 35, 56, 57 fig., 61, 64, 79, 98 n. 30, 99 nn. 43 & 44, 109, 180 n. 19, 623, 631
University of Hamburg 46, 165, 632, 633, 644
University of Manchester 3, 55, 64–66, 65 fig., 71–75, 71 fig., 72 fig., 73 fig., 74 fig., 79–81, 79 fig., 82–83, 87–88, 94 n., 101 n. 71, 97 n. 18, 102 n. 90, 107 n. 119, 180 n. 19, 623–24, 625, 658 see also Sebald, W. G.
University of Manchester Theatre 79, 81, 107, 107 fig., 634 see also Büchner, Georg, Leonce und Lena
Untermeitingen 19
Uphoff, Etta see Schwanitz, Etta
Urals 86
US Air Force 339
USA see United States of America

Valéry, Paul 269
Venice 228, 285, 629, 633, 634
Verne, Jules 102 n. 91
Verona 9, 275, 281, 294 n. 21, 353, 629, 633, 634
    Biblioteca Civica 275
    Giardini Giusti 281, 296 n. 60
Victoria Hotel, Holkham see Holkham
Vienna 332 n., 370, 581, 590, 628, 629, 633, 634, 635, 636, 637, 648, 651
Viennese-Jewish world 35
Vilnius 306
Vinaver, Eugène 71
Vivis, Anthony 131, 183, 635
Vogel-Klein, Ruth 37 n. 17, 263 n. 31
Vologda 200, 201, 204
Vorarlberg, the 370

Wachtel, Eleanor 37 n. 4, 305, 492, 583, 593, 645
Wagenbach, Klaus 280, 630
Wagner, Richard 54, 72, 98 n. 29
Walberberg seminar 194 fig., 207, 646
Wales 365, 437, 438
Wallbank-Turner, Rosemary 74
Wallmann, Hermann 586
Walser, Robert 3, 6, 8, 20, 34, 35, 37 n. 11, 165, 175–78, 205, 264, 269, 272, 275, 296 n. 69, 301, 304, 344, 353, 402, 449, 459, 472, 482, 495, 586, 600, 622, 631
    Aus dem Bleistiftgebiet 264
    Kleist in Thun 177
    Der Räuber 177
Walsingham, Norfolk 321
Wandering Jew 35 see also Kafka, Franz, 'Der Jäger Gracchus'
Wannsee, Berlin 121, 177–78, 642, 650
Ward, Simon 239
Wasserman, Steve 11, 375, 494, 584, 594, 648, 653–54
Waterhouse, Peter 642
Waterloo, Battle of 334–35 see also Works by W. G. Sebald, 'Waterloo'

Watts, Stephen 9, 284, 646
    'Lord in Dream' 9, 300–01
    'Fragment...' 303
Weber, Markus 444, 585
Weber, Max 76
Wedekind, Frank 55, 167, 295 n. 40
Wehrmacht 17, 98 n. 29, 621, 622
Weichelt, Matthias 586
Weihe, Richard 183, 333
Weil, Jiří 187
Weill, Grete 187
Weimar Republic 97 n. 19, 130, 158, 628, 630
Weiss, Christina 589
Weiss, Peter 5, 136, 157–58, 165, 167, 170, 188, 211, 213, 214, 353, 402, 450, 465, 600, 630, 647
    Abschied von den Eltern 139, 157–58
    Die Ermittlung 135, 157
    Fluchtpunkt 157
    Marat/Sade 133, 167
Weissberg, Liliane 586
Wellington, Duke of 335
Wells-next-the-sea, Norfolk 321, 323
Werfel, Franz 60
werkimmanente Kritik 53, 62, 85, 91, 92, 96 n. 16 see also New Criticism
Wertach 3, 9, 17, 17 fig., 18, 19 fig., 20, 20 fig., 21 fig., 22 fig., 23, 24 fig., 25, 26, 26 fig., 27, 28 fig., 29, 29 fig., 30 fig., 32 fig., 34, 61 fig., 95 n. 2, 103 n. 100, 306, 476, 619, 620 fig., 621, 622, 629, 635, 650, 656 see also Works by W. G. Sebald, Schwindel. Gefühle.
    church of St Ulrich 20 fig., 22 fig.
    Weinstube Steinlehner 28 fig., 621
Wesener, Sigried 583, 652
Westdeutscher Rundfunk 105 n. 124
Whitechapel, London 301, 310 see also East End
Wicklow, Ireland 331
Wilde, Oscar 55
Wilhelmine era in Germany, the 62, 83, 85, 86, 130 see also Sternheim, Carl
    Wilhelmine bourgeoisie 84
    Wilhelminian ideology 62, 86
Wilkinson, Elizabeth 73
Willer, Pierre 586
Williams, Cedric 127, 127 n. 2
Wilton's Music Hall, London 302
Winkels, Hubert 589
Winkler, Josef 170, 181 n. 38
Winterton, Norfolk 320
Wirth, Christian 294 n. 32
Withington, Manchester 65 fig., 66, 100 n. 57, 624
Wittgenstein (film dir. by Derek Jarman) 332 n.
Wittgenstein, Kurt 327
Wittgenstein, Ludwig 9–10, 180 n. 27, 198, 270, 303, 309, 324–33, 376 fig., 423–24, 485, 590, 600
    Tractatus [Logico-Philosophicus] 303, 329
Wittgenstein, Margarete 325

Wittgenstein, Mining 330
Wittgenstein, Paul 327, 328
Wittmann, Jochen 492, 593
Wolff, Lynn 13 n. 3, 587
Wölfli, Adolf 181 n. 33
Wood, James 144, 492, 593, 644
Woodbridge, Suffolk 319
Woods, Aengus 586
World War I 23, 27 fig., 29, 33, 34, 259, 291, 306, 358,
    364, 623, 650, 652
World War II 1, 23, 113, 122, 164, 207, 209, 211, 212
    fig., 259, 346, 365, 629, 630
Wright, Georg Henrik von 331
Wylie, Andrew 208, 644, 645, 646, 654
Wymondham, Norfolk see Sebald. W. G.
Wymondham Abbey 94, 323

Yanovska, Sofya 327

Yare, River (Norfolk) 320
Yiddish literature 162
Yugoslavia 81, 82, 624

Zeeman, Michaël 492, 588, 593, 647
ZET (Zeichenheft für Literatur und Graphik) 10, 480
Zilcosky, John 280
Zischler, Hanns 211, 394, 488
Zoshchenko, Mikhail 488
Zuckerman, [Lord] Solly 10, 211, 212 fig., 340, 629
Zurich 86, 625, 629, 630, 631, 632, 636, 640, 641, 643,
    645, 646, 647, 650, 652
Zurich lectures 1, 10, 164, 209, 342 n., 450, 471, 482,
    645, 646 see also Works by W. G. Sebald, Luftkrieg
    und Literatur
Zweig, Arnold 462
Zweig, Stefan 35

Made in the USA
Middletown, DE
21 March 2021